# Representative American Speeches 1937–1997

## Also from The H.W. Wilson Company

### Print

Greek and Latin Authors 800 B.C.–A.D. 1000
European Authors 1000–1900
British Authors Before 1800
British Authors of the Nineteenth Century
American Authors 1600–1900
World Authors 1900–1950: Volumes I-IV
World Authors 1950–1970
World Authors 1970–1975
World Authors 1975–1980
World Authors 1980–1985
World Authors 1985–1990
Spanish American Authors: The Twentieth Century

The Junior Authors Series: Volumes I-VII

Great Composers: 1300–1900
Composers Since 1900
Composers Since 1900: First Supplement
Musicians Since 1900
American Songwriters

American Reformers

World Artists 1950–1980
World Artists 1980–1990

Facts About the Presidents
Facts About the British Prime Ministers
Facts About the Supreme Court
Facts About the Congress

Nobel Prize Winners
Nobel Prize Winners 1987-1991 Supplement
Nobel Prize Winners 1992–1996 Supplement

World Film Directors: Volumes I, II

### Electronic formats

World Authors: 800 B.C.–Present
World Authors: 1900–Present
World Authors: 1950–Present
Current Biography: 1940–Present
Current Biography: 1983–Present
Wilson Biographies

# Representative American Speeches 1937–1997


Editor
**Calvin McLeod Logue**

Contributing Editors
A. Craig Baird
Lester Thonssen
Waldo W. Braden
Owen Peterson

The H.W. Wilson Company
New York ◆ Dublin
1997

**Library of Congress Cataloging-in-Publication Data**
Representative American speeches, 1937–1997 / Calvin McLeod Logue.
general editor.
p. cm.
Includes index.
ISBN 0-8242-0931-1
1. Speeches, addresses, etc., American. I. Logue, Calvin M. (Cal McLeod), 1935– ,
PS661.R46 1997
815'.5408—dc21 97–34361
CIP



Printed in the United States of America

06 05 04 03 02 01 00 99 98 97 19 9 8 7 6 5 3 2 1

The H.W. Wilson Company
950 University Avenue
Bronx, NY 10452

http://www.hwwilson.com

# Contents

# Preface

Since 1937, The H. W. Wilson Company has published an annual compilation entitled *Representative American Speeches.* Professor A. Craig Baird began the series, in his own words, to make available to students addresses of "different types" that "are representative of the kind and quality done" during a particular time period. Professor Baird edited the *Representative American Speeches* series from 1937 to 1959. Professor Lester Thonssen edited the series from 1959 to 1970; Professor Waldo W. Braden, from 1970 to 1980; Professor Owen Peterson, from 1980 to 1995; and Professor Jean DeHart and I have edited the annual compilations from 1995 to the present. In recognition of Professors Baird's, Thonssen's, Braden's, and Peterson's editorship of the *Representative American Speeches* series, the National Communication Association presented them with the 1992 Winans-Wichelns award for distinguished scholarship.

My criterion for selecting the more than 150 speeches contained in this compilation, from the some 1,250 previously published in *Representative American Speeches,* was that the speeches address themes which are relevant to both today's citizenry and, potentially, to people of the twenty-first century. In recasting the brief introductions to each speech, I followed closely the information presented by the editors of the original *Representative American Speeches* volumes.

I would like to thank Michael P. Schulze, director of The H. W. Wilson Company's General Reference department, who envisioned this anthology. I am also appreciative of the support and advice provided by Hilary Claggett, senior editor, and Joseph Sora, managing editor. I am also grateful for the information researched by Daniel Davis and Wendy Eudy, for assistance provided by John Campbell and others at the University of Georgia Library, and for support made available by Don Rubin and the Speech Communication Department at the University of Georgia. I dedicate this anthology to little Jeffrey, Jordan, and their contemporaries who, in the twenty-first century, will likely encounter many of the issues addressed in these speeches.

*—Calvin M. Logue*

# Introduction

Free expression is the lifeblood of democracy. The character of communication in society gauges democracy's well-being. Responsible public discourse raises the quality of choices that democracy provides. Informed public address, made by citizens of diverse voices and convictions, contributes vitally to society's progress, as it makes democracy a dynamic, experienced part of the overall culture. Responsible communication is therefore a continuing process of societal education which brings the citizenry in close contact with the tenets and goals of the democratic state. In the August 4, 1945 edition of the *Atlanta Constitution*, columnist Channing Cope envisioned the ideal, deliberative "country store" of democracy. He wrote: "A potbellied stove occupied the center of the store. . . .About it gathered the wise and the foolish, the noisy and the silent, each giving expression by one means or another to their views, or lack of them, on all important matters of the moment." While this image is an apt description of American public discourse, it omits the challenge of establishing a seat at the "fire" for those historically denied participation in an equitable communal dialogue. As the speeches contained in this compilation provide a glimpse into the breadth and depth of American public discourse, they stand as an answer to that challenge, and as a testament to the presence of democratic principles and ideals within the American framework.

To monitor the strength of democratic processes, citizens should preserve, study, and evaluate public oratory. Freely given speeches reflect something of the character, motivations, values, and goals of both the speakers and the culture which chooses to preserve that speech. In the more than 150 speeches contained in this anthology, we observe Americans deliberating over a sixty-year period about 16 significant and interconnected themes: political community; the nature and function of government; civil liberties; international affairs; war; human rights; civil rights; media; education; the arts; religion; business, industry, and labor; science, technology, and space; the environment; urban issues; and crime and terrorism. By examining these texts, and others along with them, one gains a better understanding of the complex relationship that exists between our past concerns, our present values, and those issues which may dominate our future.

*Political Community.* The first chapter in this anthology contains speeches which discuss American political life. In these addresses, American leaders from all walks of life recall various threats to democracy, which range from totalitarianism to uncontrolled vilification. To counter such threats, Mildred McAfee Horton, former president of Wellesley College, advised paying more attention to the "implications" of familiar, notably "American" symbols. She counseled that instead of merely mimicking "catch words" like "liberty, individuality, [and] free enterprise," the nation should embody, and practice, "more communicable and demonstrable convictions."

*Nature and Function of Government.* Confronted with complex social, political, and economic problems over the last sixty years, national leaders have often differed in their opinions on the kind of government that would best balance the interest of individuals with the interests of the population as a whole. Essentially, this debate centers on the extent to which the executive, legislative, and judicial branches should govern and provide for the general welfare of the citizenry. The poles of this debate are seen in speeches by Franklin Delano Roosevelt and Ronald Reagan. Having been granted wider powers to deal with a devastating economic depression in 1937, President Franklin D. Roosevelt envisioned a government that could "solve for the individual the ever-rising problems of a complex civilization." In contrast, President Reagan, in 1981, promised to return the "power and resources" of the nation to the people.

*Civil Liberties.* Throughout the twentieth century, many questioned whether restrictions should be placed upon public expression. In 1950, Eleanor Roosevelt defended the right to publicly assert individual interest without impingement. When "it is hard to get a hearing for certain causes," she maintained, "democracy is in danger." In 1961, Rabbi Julius J. Nodel prescribed tempering freedom of expression with "controlled power" and diplomacy. In 1967, as college students and others crowded the streets in opposition to the Vietnam War, Dr. Daniel J. Boorstin, professor of history at the University of Chicago, distinguished between "disagreement" that "produces debate," and "dissent" that leads mainly to "dissension." Concerned that many Americans watch too much television, John E. Frohnmayer, a lawyer specializing in First Amendment rights, declared that television restricts our right to free speech because it has replaced "town meetings or activities where the people of this country assemble to discuss the issues of the day." If we are to maintain the civil liberties upon which the country is founded, Frohnmayer concluded we need "vigorous and honest debate to redefine the truth and the values that define us."

*International Affairs.* In the past 60 years, the United States has consistently increased the extent to which it is involved with countries outside of its borders. In effect, America has departed from the isolationism of the 1920s to become a world power. This transition has not been seamless, or without its conflicts and disagreements. A variety of philosophies and outlooks, often formed in response to particular events, have shaped our policy toward other nations. In 1943, as the United States, alongside the other Allied nations, battled the Axis powers, freshman representative James W. Fulbright envisioned an organization of nations committed to world peace. In 1958, Secretary of State John Foster Dulles supported a display of "retaliatory power and the will to use it" as the best Cold War strategy. By 1976, Secretary of State Henry A. Kissinger expressed his determination to "prevent Soviet military power from being used for political expansion." Keenly aware of the nation's difficulties in Vietnam, Kissinger admitted that "we cannot escalate every political dispute into a central crisis." Given the reality of nuclear warfare, Kissinger's prudence echoes a recurring theme that has tempered the initiatives of leaders throughout the Cold War and into the present day.

*War.* From 1937 to 1997, leaders attempted to convince citizens that personal and monetary sacrifices for war were often justifed. Thanks in part to a massive propaganda effort, citizens, during World War II, were in fact more inclined to donate their time and money to the overall war effort. With the Korean War ending in a prolonged "truce," and the Vietnam War in defeat, this kinship between citizen and leader diminished. International policy decisions were often met with harsh, and sometimes violent, criticisms. As leaders decided when and where to send American soldiers, they were placed increasingly on the defensive. As early as 1965, in opposition to the Vietnam War, Senator Wayne Morse asked the question increasingly on the minds of many Americans: "Why are we fighting?" By 1967, President Lyndon B. Johnson was hard-pressed to justify the 47,000 Americans killed and 300,000 wounded in the Vietnam War. President George Bush, because of the United States' failure in Vietnam, was careful to pledge that the 1990 United Nations–backed attack upon Iraq would be swift and definitive, as he declared, "We will not fail!"

*Human Rights.* Human rights achieved a greater priority in legislative agendas during the twentieth century. Leaders resolved not to forget the millions of Jews murdered by Hitler's Nazis, nor the multitude of women and ethnic groups that have been denied equal protection and opportunity under the law. In 1942, Wendell L. Willkie, a successful lawyer and one-time Republican nominee for president, told of the Nazis "in boots and brown shorts" who murdered nearly the entire population of Lidice, Czechoslovakia. In 1943, Attorney General Francis Beverly Biddle pointed out that the rights of many had been overlooked by the very democracy America professes to espouse. In 1945, Eric A. Johnston, then president of the United States Chamber of Commerce, promoted the "sacred dignity of the human being, regardless of race or class or place of birth." In a similar vein, Ralph J. Bunche, former chair of the Department of Political Science at Harvard University, criticized the "bigotries and intolerances" that "everywhere prevail." In 1978, President Jimmy Carter sought "to rekindle the beacon of human rights in American foreign policy," while Representative Shirley Chisholm criticized the United States government for continuing to prevent full "political participation" by women and particular ethnic groups. Academia was also affected by the quest to afford human rights for all, as acclaimed professor Henry Louis Gates, Jr. asked that American educators adopt a multicultural perspective and provide students with a brand of knowledge that transcends Western tradition and understanding.

*Civil Rights.* After World War II, many mobilized on behalf of their own rights. In response to this cry for equality, civil-rights laws were passed in 1964. These laws were meant to guarantee equal rights regardless of race, religion, gender, or age. Effecting this pledge produced mixed results, however, and the quest to obtain civil rights for all was by no means brought to an end. Dr. Martin Luther

King, Jr. continued to urge that we reconcile our differences so that we can become one country under God. Wendell Chino, president of the Mescalero Apache Tribe, announced that he was "sick" of "political platitudes," as he demanded that funding be provided for Native-American tribes. Chino desired that his people become educated so that they could better prepare themselves for life in the New World. Others fought to retain their native culture. For example, Bayard Rustin advised African Americans to "develop black institutions and a black image." Whatever their strategy, all of these speakers hoped to gain an equality for their people that "platitudes" alone could not achieve.

*Media.* The way in which people communicated changed dramatically between 1937 and 1997. Simple communication now involves a variety of technology, including computers, satellites, and microscopic wiring. As early as 1937, Carl W. Ackerman, dean of the Columbia Graduate School of Journalism, noted that "through the press and the radio, ideas are traveling with the speed and force of lightning." Such technology, because it enables media to reach incredibly large audiences, has brought the role and responsibility of the journalist into a new importance. In 1961, Newton N. Minow, then chair of the Federal Communications Commission (FCC), told broadcasters that they have a duty to the American people which must be performed "with intelligence and with leadership." In 1988, questioning media's role in society, Anthony Lewis, columnist for the *New York Times*, criticized "the established press" for abandoning its once adversarial role with the nation's leaders. Such antagonism between press and government allowed the media to fulfill their role as watchdog, according to Lewis. Many have argued that the emergence of television as a fundamental aspect of mainstream America is one of the most significant developments to occur in the twentieth century. In 1980, Anne Rawley Saldich warned that "television has openly usurped certain functions that are traditionally governmental." She asserted that while "television has been a great asset to democracy," the medium, and those who shape its form and content, have a potential to achieve a "tyranny" over the American citizenry. George Gerbner echoed Saldich's assessment of the impact of television on American life when he declared that "television . . . has become the functional equivalent of a new religion."

*Education.* The role of education within the fabric of American society also underwent profound changes during the last 60 years. A series of court decisions, beginning with *Brown* vs. *Board of Education* (1954), ended racially segregated schools. Similarly, many colleges and universities changed their curricula to reflect the increased presence of women and various ethnic groups. It follows that education, in general, took a step away from the academic "ivory tower," as it became more firmly connected to its social context. Dr. Matina S. Horner, then president of Radcliffe College, remarked that schools must become environments devoted to preparing "young women and men to meet the demanding academic and social pressures which change has brought." Education's relationship with surrounding social issues and pressures was more tangibly seen as schools were asked to assist in coping with the problems of drug abuse, violence, and domestic strife. In 1987, William J. Bennett, then secretary of education, insisted that schools, in addition to parents and guardians, must "offer explicit moral guidance." In light of a rapidly changing student body, and an outside world whose temptations are all too present, education has been asked to expand its reach beyond mere instruction and provide genuine guidance for students.

*The Arts.* The role, function, and propriety of art within society continued to be an object of debate. Many criticized certain works of art as fundamentally inappropriate, while others upheld art's vital role in society's well-being. In 1965, Dr. Esther M. Jackson, professor of speech and theatre at Adelphi University, maintained that, unlike the sciences, religion, medicine, and public education, "the arts in general have seemed least prepared to cope with the major social, political, and cultural changes of the sixties." In 1988, Arthur M. Schlesinger, Jr., professor of humanities at the City University of New York, reminded his audience that civilization itself relies on creative productions that may not "meet the box-office test." For Schlesinger, there must be another end for art than financial gain. Representative Barbara Jordan described this end, remarking that the arts can "reinvigorate our national spirit." We need art, according to Jordan, because it shows us who we are and who we can become.

*Religion.* Religious leaders often found themselves challenged by the dramatic changes in day-to-day life that occurred throughout the last 60 years. At times, debates on technology's ethical and moral implications lagged behind the actual implementation of that technology. Keenly aware of an atomic bomb's destructive potential, Dr. Reinhold Niebuhr, in 1947, described a "despair" that he believed the "optimism of modern culture" could not cure. "The defense of a civilization," he insisted, "also requires political and moral strategy," and not simply the ability to destroy an enemy. In a similar vein, Rabbi Charles E. Shulman recommended that Americans recall how to place greater importance on "the things of the spirit that have been so greatly neglected in recent years." For Shulman, the modern age, while it has provided much in the way of physical convenience, has overlooked the need for spiritual nourishment. The strategies adopted by many religious leaders, particularly during the 1980s, were also subject to criticism. As religion, particularly evangelism, became more closely allied with the political Right, many believed that a dangerous polarization was occurring in American society. Patricia Roberts Harris, then secretary of Health and Human Services, spoke against what she called a "religious absolutism" that she believed irrevokably divided opinion.

*Business, Industry, and Labor.* Issues that most directly affected the American labor force between 1937 and 1997 included automation, economic depression, government involvement in unions, profiteering, health care, "downsizing," and job exportation. In 1939, Matthew Woll, then vice president of the American Federation of Labor, declared that "man is not an automaton, a commodity or article of commerce, [or] an economic abstraction." "Democracy," he reminded, "rests upon. . . the worth of the individual." Dr. Ruth Alexander, a popular newspaper columnist and radio debater, urged industrialists to "speak up for themselves," because it is their individual workers and not the state that create goods and provide jobs. Meanwhile, labor leaders had to contend with the flood of automation that displaced many workers. In 1963, John I. Snyder, Jr., a manufacturer of automation machinery, candidly declared that "automation is here to stay," as it is necessary if we hope to remain competitive in the world markets. The fundamental change wrought by the introduction of technology into the workplace was summarized by Senator Bill Bradley, who explained how "for centuries, the determinants of national wealth have been capital, natural resources, and an abundance of labor. Today none of them is as important as knowledge." Economic security for the worker is no longer dependent on the simple desire and will to work, but rather the knowledge to master those systems and technologies which are an unmistakable part of the workplace.

*Science, Technology, and Space.* Between 1937 and 1997, scientific innovations influenced the lives of individuals, society, and culture like no other force of the twentieth century. Computers, cellular phones, the Internet, satellites, etc., all combined to expand our reach into the world. The ramifications of such sweeping changes were the focus of much public discourse. As early as 1939, Dr. Arthur H. Compton, professor of physics at the University of Chicago, observed that technology's "great new powers" can be used either for great benefit or terrible harm. It follows that with technological progress comes responsibility, and the need to question the range of potential effects that come with each step forward. Dr. Harrison S. Brown underscored this assessment, as he noted that humanity too often accepts "science and technology as its benefactors, seldom questioning where it. . .lead[s]." Many, however, had great praise for the advances made by science. John H. Glenn, Jr., the first American to orbit Earth in a space capsule, argued that dollars invested in space research would bring "dividends" for all. The range of innovations that are a direct result of our advance into space tend to support Senator Glenn's understanding.

*Environment.* Increasingly from 1937 to 1997, our relationship to the environment was at the center of public discourse. America and other industrialized nations discussed how to best enjoy and profit from innovations in transportation and manufacturing without threatening the land, water, and air that sustain all life. In 1962, August Heckscher, special White House consultant on the arts, called for maintaining "beauty and fitness in the environment," because they are the values which "make a civilization." Many condemned the rapid pace of progress, asserting that in our quest to advance we have overlooked the consequences of such advancement. In 1962, Dr. Barry Commoner, professor of plant physiology at Washington University in St. Louis, warned that as we create new technology "we have been massively intervening in the natural world, without being aware of many of the biological consequences." In a similar vein, Gus Speth, president of the World Resources Institute, maintained that "pollution is occurring on a vast and unprecedented scale around the globe." Dr. Margaret Mead, the acclaimed anthropologist, declared that we must change our "present way of life" if we hope to have a habitable environment in the twenty-first century. In contrast, others asserted that environmental concerns were approaching fanaticism. In 1996, Representative Helen Chenoweth criticized Secretary of the Interior Bruce Babbitt's espousal of an "environmental religion," which, according to Chenoweth, depicts environmental concerns as a "moral philosophy." Chenoweth believed that this has the potential to "make villains of hard-working, productive citizens."

*Urban Issues.* Speakers often attempted to reconcile the many services that urban governments provide for their constituencies with the economic and social problems that are often a part of American cities. David Dinkins, former mayor of New York City, listed the advantages of urban life, which include cultural venues, universities, and public transportation. To maintain these benefits, he argued that the federal government must fund child care, mass transit, public education, and drug enforcement. Whitney M. Young, Jr., executive director of the National Urban League, also asserted that unless the government is willing to support urban centers, life there will "collapse."

*Crime and Terrorism.* Violence and crime have been an unmistakable part of the American landscape throughout the twentieth century. In 1971, Judge George Edwards related how "fear of criminal attack and homicide. . .may indeed be the most destructive single force in the deterioration of the American city." Undertaking an argument that has recently received much attention, Edwards advocated prohibiting the possession of all concealable handguns. Mark W. Cannon, administrative assistant to the chief justice of the United States, also discussed a means by which he believed crime could be reduced. Cannon emphasized the need to "transmit positive values, norms, and attachments from one generation to another." Through such generational reinforcement, Cannon believed, we can gradually eliminate those inclinations which lead one to a life of crime. In addition to crimes committed against individuals, speakers also condemned acts of terrorism. In 1976, Clarence M. Kelley, then director of the Federal Bureau of Investigation, defined terrorism as "the ultimate evil in our society." Clearly, the recent past has seen more than its fair share of terrorist acts, including the 1993 bombing of the World Trade Center and the 1995 bombing of the Alfred P. Murrah Federal Building in Oklahoma City. In response to both these acts, the Reverend F. Forrester Church IV declared such terrorism to be the consequence "when thoughtful people do not work hard to temper their prejudices."

# I. Political Community

## Editor's introduction

How does the United States actually *work*? In other words, what are the qualities of the overall "conversation" that occurs between leaders of government; between government and citizenry; and within the citizenry itself? The successes and failings of this conversation, or interaction, are the focus of this chapter. Here, educators, judges, politicians, public officials, clergy, and social activists discuss what is required to maintain beneficial and open discussion so that the country can move forward. Implicit in all of the speeches contained in this chapter is that without orderly, open communication, and a genuine concern for the "whole," the well-being of the United States inevitably suffers.

Regrettably, discussion between the federal government and the American citizenry has, at times, been less than harmonious. African Americans, Native Americans, women, and other citizens fiercely challenged the social conventions and laws that historically denied them equal opportunity. The government's reaction to this challenge was not always receptive, and many believe this contributed to the great civil unrest of the 1960s and 1970s. Communication was also hampered when demagogic scare tactics used by Joseph McCarthy in the 1940s and 1950s led to Communist "witch hunts" which destroyed many careers. Outright protest of government involvement in military actions has also detracted from beneficial communication within the overall community. Wars, and other American military endeavors, were often rationalized by leaders as being in the best interest of America, much to the confusion, if not anger, of many Americans.

According to the *New York Times*, "There is a fine line between the decline of civil discourse and the rise of critical energy" (April 16, 1995). As civil discourse decays, vehement and unchecked criticism arises in its place. This process is accelerated by self-centeredness, unanchored individualism, bigotry, suspicion, vilification and a shortage of responsible leadership. The addresses in this chapter offer suggestions for maintaining positive interaction within the community at large. Collectively, these speeches provide a vision of the ideal political community, which includes a respect for the dignity of the individual, as well as of one's neighbors; equal justice under the law; a sharing in the responsibility for upholding the common good; and a restoration of faith in the American citizenry.

Robert Maynard Hutchins counseled that the ideal community can be attained only when actions are for the "good of the community" and not the good of the individual. For Barbara Jordan, citizens can best serve their country when they first believe in their own abilities, and then strive to "uphold . . . the common good." Mildred McAfee Horton advised acquiring a far deeper awareness of those principles, being "liberty, individuality, [and] free enterprise," upon which America is founded. In all of the speeches that follow, speakers urged their audiences to transcend individual concern and embody an honest and genuine belief in the surrounding community.

# A Philosophy of Life[1]

Robert Maynard Hutchins

*Born January 17, 1899, Brooklyn, NY; died May 14, 1977; A.B., Yale University, 1921; J.D., Yale Law School, 1925; dean, Yale Law School, 1927-29; president, 1929-45, chancellor, 1945-51, University of Chicago; director, Ford Foundation, 1951-54; president, 1954-69, chairman, 1969-74, Fund for the Republic; founder, chairman, 1959-74, president, 1975-77, Center for the Study of Democratic Institutions; author,* No Friendly Voice *(1936),* Education for Freedom *(1943),* St. Thomas and the World State *(1949),* The Conflict in Education in a Democratic Society *(1953),* The University of Utopia *(1953).*

## Editor's introduction

As president of the University of Chicago, Robert Maynard Hutchins gave this national commencement address over NBC radio, in which he advised students to live proportioned and orderly lives, and to make moral choices for the good of their communities. For it is the community, and not the individual, that represents the higher good, according to Hutchins. Hutchins also asserted that the modern state must adhere to this ethic by creating laws and devising educational systems which foster and maintain the health and well-being of the community at large. For Hutchins, such laws and educational systems are signs of a leadership whose ends lay within the community—a leadership he urged graduates to espouse.

---

I hope that you will never have a "philosophy of life." As I understand this phrase it means that one who says he has a philosophy of life has got himself adjusted to his environment. He is now prepared to compromise on any issue at any time. Injustice is all right. Brutality is all right. Fraud, corruption, dishonesty are all right. The only thing that is not all right is something that endangers the security of the individual in question, or that threatens his income, or damages his reputation. Peace in a vegetable sense and prosperity in a material sense are the aims of one who talks about his philosophy of life.

It is obvious that those who have the effrontery to call this attitude a philosophy of life are confused about what is good. They think that goods outside a person are those which determine his success. And since those goods can apparently be best obtained and retained by adjustment to the environment, that adjustment is usually rapid and complete. They forget that there are some things in every environment to which no honest man should ever adjust himself.

Since you are about to proceed into direct and remorseless contact with the environment, we should try to determine on this occasion the kind of adjustment you should make to it. This means that we must decide what goods you should strive for. Clearly we should try to find some for you if we can that are stable, that are within your own powers, and that are higher goods to which lower ones are ordered. We should try, in short, to work out a human philosophy of life, valid for all men, something more than a set of dodges and devices developed by an individual to shirk the pain of thinking and of moral choice. The problem, then, is what are the goods that man should seek, not what should you think of to cheer yourself up when the baby is sick, or to appease your conscience when you have cheated a client or customer, or to reconcile yourself to the murder or starvation of helpless people in Spain or elsewhere.

We see at once that the goods that man should seek cannot be some of those to which men have been willing to devote their lives.

[1]Broadcast as a national commencement address, from the University of Chicago, in Chicago, Illinois, on June 18, 1937.

They cannot be money, fame, or power. These goods are goods of fortune. Hence they cannot be achieved by your own efforts. If you want them it is probably wise for you to work as hard as possible and to be as intelligent as possible. But any man who has attained them must admit occasionally and to himself that his success has resulted largely from chance. The accidents of friendship, location, education, and birth have led as many men to wealth and glory as the practice of puritanism. Even if you have all the virtues and the highest kind of I.Q., you cannot be sure that society will give you your reward. On the contrary, there is some justification for the saying that society either corrupts its best men or kills them.

As goods of fortune external goods are, of course, goods of the moment. We have reason to know that men may see their money vanish without warning and through no fault of their own. We can hardly blame those who lost their property or their jobs in the last depression. Yet assets painfully accumulated through years and even generations were swept away overnight. In our own time we have seen great political and military reputations explode with a frequency, rapidity, and spontaneity which must be discouraging to those who have set their hearts on similar reputations for themselves.

We know that there must be proportion in whatever goods there are. All men want all good things. But any reasonably mature infant knows that there is such a thing as too much food. The delights of domesticity do not blind us to the fact that it is possible to have too large a family, too many houses, and too much furniture in each room. We are clear that there must be proportion in regard to most external goods. The one we are most confused about is the one we have created ourselves, namely, money. There is no limit to its goodness; it is always good, and the more of it the better. Yet the question that was asked 2,500 years ago is still unanswerable, "How can that be wealth of which a man may have a great abundance and yet perish with hunger, like Midas in the fable, whose insatiable prayer turned everything that was set before him into gold?"

As there is a proportion of goods, so also is there an order of them. As work is for the sake of leisure, and war, if there is any excuse for it, is for the sake of peace; as the body is trained for the sake of healthy appetites, and healthy appetites for the sake of the mind, so external goods are for the sake of something else. That they are good no one can deny. But they are not good in themselves and there are other goods beyond them. They are means and not ends. Most people will admit this, but when they say, "I have to earn a living first. When I am able to live then I will think about higher things." This doctrine of one thing at a time, this theory of successive justification is gross confusion of means and ends. Our way of life is distorted from the first unless we see the end from the first. In classical and mediaeval language the end of human action is the first principle of human action. We must know the end to understand the beginning we should make.

The modern state suffers from the same confusion about the role of external goods and about means and ends that afflict its citizens.

The true state is not organized for economic purposes, or for military purposes, or for the purpose of multiplying the population. It is not organized to achieve influence or empire. Least of all is it organized as an end in itself. It is organized to obtain for all its citizens, in the measure that they can partake of them, the goods we are seeking for you.

I hasten to add that these goods may be achieved only in a political society. The completely isolated individual is, in the ancient phrase, either a beast or a god; he is not a man. The good of the community, moreover, is higher than the good of the citizen, so that it is in the nature of things that he should surrender his temporal good and even his life for the welfare of the community, and that social life should impose upon him many restraints and sacrifices. Still the state exists for man, not man for the state. The totalitarian state is a perversion and a monstrosity. The state which demands that its people think what it tells them to think, the state which holds that the person is a part of the state and nothing else has no claim to the name. It is an organization of force.

The methods by which a political society tries to preserve its character are in general two: the laws and the educational system. If, for example, a country has adopted an imperialistic policy, the laws will tend to promote it, and there will be a lot of talk in the schools about manifest destiny and the white man's burden. So the state anxious for wealth or glory or the elevation of the national character will adapt its laws and educational system to the end it has in view.

The state can be no better than the citizens who compose it. But the citizens are made better or worse by the laws and education of the state. Thus the character of the citizens both forms and is formed by the character of the state. Here we come to understand the role of leadership. Even in bad states good men may arise. In the course of history some countries have grown better rather than worse, and none has ever stayed the same over any considerable period of time. The changes that have taken place in them are not wholly fortuitous. They have resulted in part at least from the deliberate activities of people. The improvement of the American educational system, of the national character, and of the government of this country must depend in some degree on our ability to find leaders who understand what the good for man and hence for the state may be.

The college and university graduates of the United States are a minute fraction of the population. They have enjoyed, and not wholly at their own expense, opportunities far beyond their contemporaries. We cannot suppose that the community has provided the vast funds consumed by this enterprise in order to give students an agreeable vacation from their families and pleasant postponement of the task of earning a living. No, the community has had a childlike faith that from institutions of learning some leadership might emerge. The results to date have hardly justified the ecstatic hopes of Thomas Jefferson and others a century and a half ago. You may have heard that your generation is the hope of America. Perhaps it is; mine used to be. But if your generation makes no better use of its education than mine has there is little hope that the millennium will soon arrive, or if it does that education will have been responsible for its coming. Taking the country over there is little evidence that its college and university graduates as such have ever done, said, or even thought anything which suggested that they could be singled out to lead the way in improving the education, government, or character of our people. Since they are, we must suppose, our best men, and since we know that few of them have been killed, we must assume that they have been corrupted. They must have developed a philosophy of life.

The goods which are stable, which are within your power, the goods to which external and bodily goods are ordered, are the goods of the character and the mind. They are the main constituent of any abiding happiness. They are the insignia as well of the true state. The true state seeks the common good. It tries to secure happiness for all to the degree to which they can participate in it. Since the main constituent of happiness is intellectual and moral excellence, only a state which promotes intellectual and moral excellence can promote the common good and be a true state. It is the duty of the citizen to lead the good life. The state exists for the sake of this life.

The object of your education has been to help you form moral and intellectual habits of the sort that lead to excellence. But you have been practicing them in relatively sheltered surroundings. As habits are formed by acting in a certain way, so they are lost by ceasing to act in that way.

If you stop thinking when you receive your diploma, you will at length lose the capacity to think. If you begin to compromise, if your courage oozes when it costs something to fight, if you say, "Leave well enough alone," or "Don't rock the boat," or "I have a philosophy of life," then you will be lost to yourselves and to your country.

This country is endowed with material advantages beyond all others in the world. The genius of its people, the extent of its resources, and its impregnable position combine to suggest that it is equipped to be the ideal state for which antiquity yearned, that state which added to such advantages the noblest gifts of the intellect and character and the will to live for their exercise in every relation of life, and whose education, institutions, and laws developed those gifts and called them into full play. Is it too much to hope that the United States may yet achieve this ideal? Perhaps it may do so if you and your successors can see and hold fast that which is good. If you can, you will earn the blessings of your Alma Mater and at the last the gratitude of your country.

# The Function of Democracy[2]

## William O. Douglas

*Born October 16, 1898, Maine, MN; died January 19, 1980; A.B., Whitman College, 1920; LL.B., Columbia University, 1925; faculty, Columbia Law School, 1925-28; faculty, Yale Law School, 1928-39; chairman, Securities and Exchange Commission, 1937-39; associate justice of the United States Supreme Court, 1939-75.*

### Editor's introduction

As Hitler raged through Europe, Supreme Court Associate Justice William O. Douglas gave this speech, in which he described Hitler's actions in Europe as a fundamental challenge to the tenets of democracy. On this occasion, Douglas illustrated to his audience "the function of democracy." He also recalled our role within, and obligation to, that democratic system. In addition, Douglas encouraged his audience to find "the desire for service," so that they would be better prepared to protect democracy if the need arose.

---

There probably have been but few generations which have felt as poignantly as ours the challenge in the poet's dictum that—

"Each age is a dream that is dying
Or one that is coming to birth."

We know that we are more than mere spectators on a world revolutionary scene. We know that those revolutionary forces are infections in the world blood stream and that we shall be profoundly affected even though that disease will not ultimately triumph.

For these reasons we are all thinking deeply and profoundly about our responsibilities in this present world crisis.

Not so long ago I heard a professional group cheer the boast of a speaker that he had not mentioned once in his address the word "democracy."

Democracy, however, is no empty word, no mere shibboleth. It is a word to fill the heart with pride.

It reflects the faith of nations in the common sense of the common man.

It carries the precious cargo of equal justice under the law, the right freely to speak and write and to worship God, the right of free assembly, and equality of political and social opportunity.

It is the way of life which respects the dignity of man, which recognizes no special class of citizenship based on wealth or poverty, or color, race, or creed.

These are commonplaces to us. We are inclined to take them for granted as we are the sun, and moon, and stars. But in these days of world upheaval unguarded assumption of the permanency of any institution is hazardous.

For these reasons, now is the time for open avowal of our faith, not for silence. Now is the time to utilize vigorously our constitutional rights so as to preach and practice incessantly the truths of democracy.

As Francis Hackett has put it, "We, the democrats, have not supposed that we must assert ourselves aggressively. Our faith has been sapped because of that" (*I Chose Denmark*, 1940). Aggressive assertion of an unbounded devotion to this way of life not only replenishes the people's faith—it helps create the alertness in thought and action necessary to transform that faith into a work-a-day creed.

With the world on fire we know it is not enough for us to vote and pay taxes and earn a living. Fifty years ago the thought was current that the nation could afford the luxury of having little skill in government because it required the use of its best brains and talents in the de-

[2]Delivered to the Commonwealth Club of San Francisco, in San Francisco, California, on June 20, 1941.

velopment of the country. But we know that we can ill afford any such diversions from active participation in this current campaign.

The needs of democracy cannot be filled merely by service within the normal orbit of our daily lives. Those needs must also be satisfied through civic, municipal, county, state, and national activities. And, somehow or other, our contributions must be made through those channels by devoting at least a part of our reserves of energy to public enterprises.

We have it in our power, by giving only a part of our lives, to provide a leadership in thought and action which will create a genuine—a spiritual—renaissance of the democratic faith. Those millions of Americans who have a real appreciation of the blood and sweat and sacrifice which through the centuries have ingrained into our present society the noblest ideals of mankind are the strongest sort of bulwark against those forces which would dislodge society from its moorings.

1. We must make sure that our citizens retain their old tradition of participating in the important decisions which affect their lives, their property, their ideals. The gap between local democracy and national representative government must not be allowed to widen. The people must remain part of an integrated national system, so that they feel an intimate contact with their government, so that it does not become a thing apart—removed and remote from them. One of the ways of maintaining that bridge is through the many articulate but unofficial groups concerned with some aspect of our social, economic, or governmental problems. Through them many a citizen can become an active participant in the body politic and actually share in the decisions which affect his own welfare. Such groups help make democratic government the imperishable possession of each citizen. Hence they are strong underpinning for an aroused and alert democracy. May the leaders of community thought, devoted to democratic ideals, assume responsibility for making them effective agencies through which the people may undertake active daily roles of citizenship.

2. The function of democracy, unlike totalitarian governments, is to train men—little men as well as big men—not for subjugation but for independence. We know that therein lies the great strength of democracy. We know that only in that way can the great spiritual values of a whole people be cultivated and preserved. Yet we also know that that requires great skills in view of the complexities of a technological age. It means that every citizen must have a stake in his country adequate to justify in his eyes the sacrifices which any contingency may entail. It means that some way or other big men and little men must work as partners in our national endeavors. It means that powerful men and weak men must be joint venturers in preserving America in its own image. It means that government must serve a whole people—regardless of lines of wealth or poverty, strength, or weakness. And our endeavor must be not the detection of motes in each other's eyes but an objective, united assault on common problems.

To integrate the energies of little men and big men, share and share alike, into all local, state, and national undertakings is a task which requires continuous statesmanship. But success in that effort is a permanent achievement. It means that no caste system takes root. It means that equality and fraternity are given practical recognition. It means that men from all walks of life will find common adventure and thrills in serving jointly a great cause. It means that the eyes of men will be lifted from mean objectives to lofty ideals.

The sense of fraternity, the desire for service, the adventurous instinct are deep in the soul of America. They have been successfully appealed to before by offer of far less noble causes than the democracies now tender.

3. There must not grow up in this country any second or third or fourth class of citizenship.

There is only one class of citizenship in this nation. There is no room for any inferior grade. Where one has been allowed, the result has been the downward spiral of disunity. Then hate and intolerance have been incorporated. Under those conditions the enemies of democracy invariably have risen to power. Under those conditions there is an insistence on a conformity which is the beginning of a disintegrating process.

Every nonconformist who is beaten, every practitioner of the right of free speech who is jailed, every unpopular exponent of a religious faith who is deprived of his constitutional rights bring every free man a step closer to incarceration or punishment, or discreet and frightened conformity. Infraction of the Bill of Rights knows no terminal points. We know from the experience of other peoples that what starts as suppression of an unpopular minority swings as easily to persecutions on the right or on the left, until few can afford to be nonconformists. Those who started as instigators of oppression of a minority often turned out to be the next victims. We know that the concentration camps of Europe are not operated on racial, economic, social, or intellectual lines.

We should ever be mindful that all the battles for freedom are not won in the courts. "Only a persistent, positive translation of the liberal faith into the thoughts and acts of the community is the real reliance against the unabated temptation to straitjacket the human mind" (Frankfurter, *Law and Politics*). Vigilant patrol of the domestic scene against infraction of these fundamental constitutional rights will guarantee that the American sense of fair play will carry the day.

4. A contemporary observer has said that as a result of the incredible sophistries and the brutal and ruthless attacks by totalitarian leaders on the democratic processes, "The Declaration of Independence may now be referred to without apology, and even policemen on the beat are becoming dimly aware that there is such a thing as the Bill of Rights."

Certainly, those assaults have made us all realize more keenly than ever before that there is only one liberty, and that is liberty within the law. Without that cementing element there can never be confidence in order—the real basis of all security. And without a common sense of security there can be no effective compact among men based on conceptions of equality and fraternity. That entails, as a practical necessity, a constant recognition of the responsibilities as well as the rights of citizenship. There will be some who will be willing to exploit the Bill of Rights in order to destroy or mutilate the system which makes the Bill of Rights possible. But the defense against them is vigorous assertion by millions of Americans of their constitutional rights so as to preserve our basic freedoms, not to defile them. It is to be found in an alert and aroused citizenry intent on making the democratic processes function in any and all crises and resolved not to permit the forces of discord, fear, hesitation, or inaction to paralyze the operations of government.

Those who appreciate the human sacrifices which have made our free institutions possible know that rights are accompanied by responsibilities. They know that recognition of those responsibilities is the certain method of preserving and nurturing those rights. When rights and responsibilities go hand in hand, there is the strongest guaranty possible that liberty within the law is not mere temporary luxury but a permanent necessity for a free people. When the energies of the people are absorbed in that common endeavor the whisperers of hate and intolerance loom no more important than the occupants of psychiatric wards.

Whatever may be the specific ways and means, whatever the effort, the pole star will always be the ingredients of the democratic faith. These have recently been stated by an eminent American, Carl Becker, as follows:

"To have faith in the dignity and worth of the individual man as an end in himself, to believe that it is better to be governed by persuasion than by coercion, to believe that fraternal good will is more worthy than a selfish and contentious spirit, to believe that in the long run all values are inseparable from the love of truth and the disinterested search for it, to believe that knowledge and the power it confers should be used to promote the welfare and happiness of all men rather than to serve the interests of those individuals and classes whom fortune and intelligence endow with temporary advantage—these are the values which are affirmed by the traditional democratic ideology."

In final analysis our individual and joint efforts must have as their end product the way of life which underwrites those eternal truths.

In 1775, when this nation was uniting against the tyranny of that age, a great patriot said, "We are not weak if we make a proper use of those means which the god of nature hath placed in our power."

Today those words ring as true as they did then.

The means which God has placed in our power embrace not only material resources but also great inner spiritual strength, an abiding sense of fair play, an abundance of common sense, a deep sense of fraternity, a great reserve of ingenuity, a desire for service. To evoke these qualities from all the people in times of peace as well as war will mean that our rich heritage of freedom will remain imperishable. Utilization of those tremendous reserves of strength will guarantee that this age is not a dream that is dying but one that is coming to glorious birth.

# American Education and the World's Needs[3]

Mildred McAfee Horton

*Born May 12, 1900, Parkville, MO; died September 2, 1994; A.B., Vassar College, 1920; M.A., University of Chicago, 1928; instructor, Monticello Seminary, 1920-22; professor, Tusculum College, 1923-27; dean, Oberlin College, 1927-32; president, Wellesley College, 1936-42, 1946-1949; director, Women Appointed for Voluntary Emergency Service (WAVES), 1942-45.*

## Editor's introduction

At the time of this address, Mildred McAfee Horton, then president of Wellesley College, had been recently discharged from the military, where she had served during World War II as director of the Women Appointed for Voluntary Emergency Service (WAVES) division. Her time as director of WAVES prompted her to insist that Americans look beyond their borders and "live in relation to a world instead of in relation to one region or continent of it." Given recent advances in communications technology, and the subsequent creation of a "global village," Horton's remarks are both poignant and prophetic. Yet, as Horton points out, our foray into the world community cannot begin until we express the truth of our "national philosophy." According to Horton, without a knowledge of the basis for our own community, we can hardly attempt to define that community to those who live outside it.

---

Mr. Chairman, Distinguished Guests, and Friends of Cleveland: For the last thirty-six hours my sentiment about this forum has been: "Having a wonderful time." As I now face this cozy audience, half of which could leave without my knowledge, I am tempted to add the rest: "Wish you were here."

One of the very great satisfactions of getting out of uniform is that as a civilian I can now differ in public with superior officers.

Last night, General Bradley, who definitely ranks me, simply ruined my speech. He said America in its international relations has achieved maturity, and the whole point of my speech is that I think we are quite adolescent.

I suppose this reflects the difference in opinion of two people, each of whom loves his country, and one deals with veterans, and the other with college students.

I submit that the very fact of having a forum like this reminds me of the title of William Carleton's article in the current *American Scholar*, "Are We Politically Adolescent?" The serious contemplation of the part one plays in the life of his own family is a normal activity of adolescence. But I submit that mature adults, well integrated in their life, don't spend much time wondering what their role in that life is.

But Americans in the family of nations do seem to me to have many of the features of Henry Aldrich, who is entirely willing to accept the destiny of the world or of his own family as his chief responsibility. And what would Judy do in those hours of the radio when she isn't getting dates, if she weren't saving the family?

I do recognize this forum, of course, as a symptom of the fact that America too wants to grow up. We have, indeed, got past the stage through which so many youngsters go of looking at their parents and wondering how they could have such intelligent children.

In the twenties all the world knew that we were blood brothers, sons, and daughters of Europe and the Orient, but we made every effort to deny it, as rapidly growing, somewhat poorly adjusted children often do. But we are over that now. In the forties it is more characteristic of us to admit that we are part of the family of nations, not perhaps by choice, but by obvious relationship. By this time we have grown to full

[3]Delivered at the 21st Annual Institute on World Affairs, in Cleveland, Ohio, on January 9, 1947.

physical strength and we have periods of keen adult insight. I shall call this forum one of those periods. But we have blank spots of juvenile self-righteousness. We love our relatives in the family of nations, when they take us seriously, give us hard jobs to do, which are fitted to our strength, and commend us for doing them better than they could have done them. But we distrust our relatives when, having performed our active, ingenious, technical task we blunderingly volunteer to take on the management of the entire family and find the other members of the family a little hesitant about turning it over to us.

All this is natural with adolescence but means that neither we nor the other members of the family of nations will be at ease until we get over this phase and finish this well-started process of growing up.

One difference between adolescence and maturity is the difference in the size of the world in which the adolescent lives from that of the adult. A mature person—as I would choose to describe maturity—has moved out of self-centeredness into a recognized relationship with a large group. He assumes responsibility because it is inherent in his relationship with people who expect certain things of him. He is not self-conscious in his participation in communal activities. He is identified with them so that he is not doing something *for* his neighbors in their common effort; but he is doing something *with* them for their joint satisfaction.

My favorite WAVE story, and I might say there were many of them, is of the fresh-caught recruit who was enjoying a new-found maturity. She was asked by a former teacher how she endured Navy regimentation. And she replied: "Endure it? I like it. Everybody knows what is expected of her and what will happen if she doesn't do it, but it is all impersonal. And while there is a lot of discipline, none of it is for my own good."

I submit that even partial adults like to have attention directed at something bigger than their own self-interest.

Now, one of the newly strong trends in American education is the recognition of the fact that Americans must learn to live in relation to a world instead of in relation to one section or one region or one continent of it. And that is a fairly new point of view.

Some forty years ago or thereabouts, I spent a few months in England at an age which I choose to consider tender. It was very hard on a little patriot to discover that the point of view of my English schoolmates was that the only reason America was there and an independent nation was that the British were too busy about important matters in the 18th century to bother with our Revolutionary War.

For such heresy in those days, my only retaliation was to join an equally uninformed and patriotic sister in singing as loudly and as rudely as possible, and with no premonition of my later relationship to Britannia's subjects:

"Rule, Britannia, Britannia rules the waves,

"And Britons ever, ever, ever, shall be slaves."

But it is out of just such juvenile behavior that international friendships must be merged when teaching on either side of the Atlantic or Pacific is so provincial—and you know we really are provincial. How often have you heard the statement made that American children don't really need to learn foreign languages? Anything worth reading will be translated, and anywhere you go there will be people who can speak English. And so what? Who but an adolescent would expect all the rest of the family to adapt its ways to his?

Do you recall that stage of personal growth at which you learned a new fact at school and were simply amazed to find your adult relatives had known it for a long time? As war-awakened Americans I wonder if we seem a bit like that to some of the peoples of whom we have become conscious since our armies and navies were stationed in various parts of the world. We discovered the Burma Road, West China, Siam, India, the Balkans, North Africa, the islands of the Pacific. Our sudden interest has been keen and I hope intelligent. But, in all, a few people—Christian missionaries, business men, explorers—have known for quite a long time that the world was full of interesting places and interesting people, and other lands have dealt for some centuries with problems about which we have just become aware.

I hope we will spare ourselves the embarrassment of claiming priority of discovery just because we only now hit upon the facts.

Now a mature person, as compared with an immature adolescent, has a self-control which makes him effective in accomplishing his purposes. He knows what his purposes are and he knows how to accomplish them.

Americans are not distinguished for the clarity of their convictions; for their strength, yes; for their clarity, no. By and large, we have not done much thinking about the things which matter most to us as Americans. We have many catch words which we like to use—freedom, liberty, individuality, free enterprise, the American way—but we have not done much to study the implications of these words. One reason for this is probably that our form of government is now one of the oldest in the modern world. Our Civil War which tested "whether that nation, or any nation so conceived and so dedicated, can long endure" was eighty-three years ago, and all of us have grown up in a society whose basic tenets could be taken for granted. They have been challenged in two world wars but we have been far enough away from the impact of that challenge that we could and did rise in self-defense without having to do much analytical thinking about what we were defending.

One of the things we used to deplore about German youth was the fact that it was so well indoctrinated in Nazi theory that it was invulnerable to argument. Young Communists, I am told, are apparently trained now not only to know what they believe and why they believe it, but what other people don't believe about it and what the answer is as to what the other person does not believe.

American educators are loath to indoctrinate young Americans, but in our zeal to avoid indoctrination I sometimes think we have deprived young citizens of a foundation for the faith that is in them. They believe in democracy enough to die for it, but they don't always recognize it when they see it nor distinguish it from its enemies when it is attacked.

A great many American young people have had almost no experience in thinking out their personal or national philosophy. Meanwhile, our fellow citizens in the world community are very articulate, explicit, and definite in their plan of action. We don't like the way they have achieved that definiteness by indoctrination from the top of a totalitarian government, but we owe it to our fellow citizens and to our convictions to use our free method of education to accomplish a result which can match the well, though dictatorially, formulated opposition. If we really have the truth we ought to be able to express it.

To the extent that other philosophies threaten to endanger the world, we need to be able to deal with them. That means understanding them so that we can know what there is to fear and not waste fear on what is merely strange. That is the main reason for my honest hope that Russian young people will be permitted soon to come to study in the United States, and that American youth may have the chance to see Russians live behind that curtain that we talk about so much.

I had occasion to look up the word "iron" in the dictionary recently. It can mean "hard, rude, or unyielding," but, you know, another definition is that it is "the most important of the metallic elements; very tenacious but malleable, ductile, and strongly magnetic." To Americans that mysterious iron curtain is "strongly magnetic."

As we try to understand philosophies different from our own, we certainly need to know our own and to understand it so that we can defend it as to the crucial points and modify the unimportant points. No amount of ranting against communism, fascism, naziism, totalitarianism or Bilboism will cure the advocate of those theories. The only cure for bigotry or falsehood is potent truth, and truth is not potent when it is fuzzy, poorly formulated, and diffuse. Nor is truth potent when it is concerned only with words and not with deeds. The adolescent has a high standard for himself and an exorbitant one for his relatives. He insists that they should do what he *says* and not what he *does*. The mature man judges himself on the basis of his own ideals and knows that his actions speak louder than his words.

The December *Harper's* magazine carries a translation of Ilya Ehrenburg's report on his trip to America as prepared for Russian readers. It ought to be required reading for those of us who share with the rest of mankind the difficulty of seeing ourselves as others see us. To the visitor the facts of racial segregation, deprivation of voting privileges, economic inequalities are as significant and characteristic of American life as our magnificent technology. I hope I shall not be accused of being a victim of Russian propaganda if I quote an observation which seems to me important. Mr. Ehrenburg said:

"It would seem that in this country of diverse races united by patriotism, national equality would prevail. However, America, which never knew feudalism, has established a racial hierarchy. The aristocracy are the English, Scotch, and Irish.

"At the bottom of the scale are the Negroes.

"In the war against Hitlerism America played a prominent part; yet racialism here has a legal standing . . . . I met a lawyer in Nashville who spent a long time trying to persuade me that there are "inferior and superior races." He reiterated the theories of Rosenberg and other ideologists of the Third Reich. Then he showed me the portrait of his brother, who was killed on the Rhine; he was proud of his brother, who had perished in the struggle against racialists."

I wish a visitor from a country we need to know had not had the experiences which would lead Ehrenburg to write this:

"When an American friend asked me what should be done to improve our mutual relations, I replied: 'Set up a single standard.' . . . Too frequently I saw two standards here: one for the virtuous Anglo-Saxons and another for the dishonorable 'Reds.'"

Americans need communicable and demonstrable convictions, and a plea for convictions instead of prejudices is really a plea for intellectual discipline. A young and growing nation can substitute vigor and strength for trained minds and is still impressed in its accomplishment, but we can't do that as we approach maturity.

America has a phenomenal educational system. We have cultivated individuality, ingenuity, and versatility but, you know, we have been less successful in cultivating trained minds. I suppose brains are not too popular in any society. Here we nominally like brains but actually no brainy people are very popular. We are observing widespread popular support for scientists because they are so practical. Thinkers aren't so popular. It is really no wonder there is a dearth of teachers because teachers represent intellectual activity. The minute that we really want disciplined minds for ourselves and our children we will begin to pay teachers money and prestige to provide those disciplined minds.

Of course, there are always a few enthusiasts who would rather teach than eat. Those are the ones who are living on their salaries.

But, as a matter of fact, we really are growing into a very much more mature status than we used to have. We are trying to learn to recognize the interests of other adult citizens of our own world. The extent to which we know our neighbors is limited, but it is so much more than we ever used to know that it is encouraging. Witness this Council. Witness the kind of mature statesmanship demonstrated by the speakers this evening in the persons of Secretary Byrnes and Senator Vandenberg.

Witness the reestablishment of study arrangements for students in foreign lands, the flow of students from all around the world who are welcomed with genuine enthusiasm on every campus of this country. Witness the Fulbright Bill to finance study of Americans abroad. Witness the zealous participation of the United States in UNESCO, in the World Council of Churches, in the International Federation of University Women, in the World Student Christian Movement, the International Student Congress, International Labor Organization, the YMCA, the YWCA, the United Service to the Near East and China, and all those other projects for which you raise money and for which you wish I would put in a plug.

We are moving now into a world-wide relationship which we do find fascinating.

Our distinguished guests from overseas have done us the honor to come to this gathering to discuss what the world expects of us. May I ask of them the patience to give us the time to grow up to that responsibility which we genuinely do want to assume.

We have the strength of a privileged population. There are those among us who fear that our standard can be maintained only at the cost of a lower standard for the rest of the world. Many of us know that in the long run the whole family must rise or fall together. We offer our people to the world relationship with their growing sense of their responsibility for it.

We have the vigor of a wealthy country. There are some of us who think that those who have must keep that which they have in order to have it in the future. There are many more of us who know that shared wealth is infinitely more productive than hoarded wealth, and we offer our material assets as our part in the world community.

We have within limits the adventurous spirit of a relatively secure country. We dare to experiment, to run risks, to "try anything once." We are bold to undertake the solution of anybody's problem. Now, that may make us a menace or a boon in our world relationships. But we urge you, our foreign friends, to take advantage of our inexperience to let us try some things which need doing but which are impractical. Youth is always impractical but if age dampens its zeal too zealously we lose some dramatic accomplishments.

America can be counted upon to provide plans, personnel. The way in which students would like to go anywhere in the world to be of help is stimulating and a little appalling for those to whom they would go.

But we can provide plans, personnel, equipment, money, all the necessary enthusiasm for a conglomerate mass of experiments. That is wasteful and confusing and perhaps unnecessary, undoubtedly adolescent, but it is the way that we will learn; and we need the understanding of the Old World as we struggle into our mature partnership.

As a people we have some articles of faith which, although they need clarification, amplification, and implementation, are values we are eager to share with the world.

We believe in people; we believe in truth; we believe in justice; we believe in mercy; we believe in kindness; we believe in the power of love and the essential weakness of hate. We don't always practice what we believe. We vary widely in our reasons for believing it, but we believe that such belief is a contribution to a world—and a world in which we want to belong fully and freely and acceptably.

No adolescent grows to maturity expeditiously through his own unaided efforts. We, too, hope for help in achieving mature status, however much we seem to repudiate it, once you believe that we basically welcome it from our older friends. If they are scared of us we will probably take an adolescent's pleasure in making them jump.

If they are angered by us, we will probably resent their wrath and do little to avoid it. If they are sentimental about us, pampering and indulging us fatuously, we will hold them in contempt. But if they believe in us surely we will respond to that belief.

I thank you.

# Political Conscience[4]

## Margaret Chase Smith

*Born December 14, 1897, Skowhegan, ME; died May 29, 1995; office executive,* Skowhegan Independent Reporter, *1919-28; treasurer, New England Process Co., 1928-30; representative (R) from Maine, 1940-48; senator (R) from Maine, 1948-72.*

### Editor's introduction

In this speech, Senator Margaret Chase Smith attacked Senator Joseph McCarthy's "know nothing, suspect everything" search for alleged Communists. Smith asserted that the American political community is based not upon "hate and character assassination sheltered by the shield of congressional immunity," but rather upon "the right to criticize; the right to hold unpopular beliefs; the right to protest; the right of independent thought." She ended her speech by giving a signed "Statement of Seven Republican Senators" to the Senate. The statement demanded that members of the Senate think patriotically rather than politically.

---

Mr. President: I would like to speak briefly and simply about a serious national condition. It is a national feeling of fear and frustration that could result in national suicide and the end of everything that we Americans hold dear. It is a condition that comes from the lack of effective leadership in either the legislative branch or the executive branch of our government. That leadership is so lacking that serious and responsible proposals are being made that national advisory commissions be appointed to provide such critically needed leadership.

I speak as briefly as possible because too much harm has already been done with irresponsible words of bitterness and selfish political opportunism. I speak as simply as possible because the issue is too great to be obscured by eloquence. I speak simply and briefly in the hope that my words will be taken to heart. I speak as a Republican. I speak as a woman. I speak as a United States Senator. I speak as an American.

The United States Senate has long enjoyed world-wide respect as the greatest deliberative body in the world. But recently that deliberative character has too often been debased to the level of a forum of hate and character assassination sheltered by the shield of congressional immunity.

It is ironical that we Senators can in debate in the Senate directly or indirectly, by any form of words impute to any American, who is not a senator, any conduct or motive unworthy or unbecoming an American—and without that non-senator American having any legal redress against us—yet if we say the same thing in the Senate about our colleagues we can be stopped on the grounds of being out of order.

It is strange that we can verbally attack anyone else without restraint and with full protection and yet we hold ourselves above the same type of criticism here on the Senate floor. Surely the United States Senate is big enough to take self-criticism and self-appraisal. Surely we should be able to take the same kind of character attacks that we "dish out" to outsiders.

I think that it is high time for the United States Senate and its members to do some soul searching—for us to weigh our consciences—on the manner in which we are performing our duty to the people of America—on the manner in which we are using or abusing our individual powers and privileges.

I think that it is high time that we remembered that we have sworn to uphold and defend the Constitution. I think that it is high time that we remembered that the Constitution, as amended, speaks not only of the freedom of

[4]Delivered to the United States Senate, in Washington, D.C., on June 1, 1950.

speech but also of trial by jury instead of trial by accusation. Whether it be a criminal prosecution in court or a character prosecution in the Senate, there is little practical distinction when the life of a person has been ruined.

Those of us who shout loudest about Americanism in making character assassinations are all too frequently those who, by our own words and acts, ignore some of the basic principles of Americanism—the right to criticize; the right to hold unpopular beliefs; the right to protest; the right of independent thought.

The exercise of these rights should not cost one single American citizen his reputation or his right to a livelihood, nor should he be in danger of losing his reputation or livelihood merely because he happens to know someone who holds unpopular beliefs. Who of us doesn't? Otherwise none of us could call our souls our own. Otherwise thought control would have set in.

The American people are sick and tired of being afraid to speak their minds lest they be politically smeared as "Communists" or "Fascists" by their opponents. Freedom of speech is not what it used to be in America. It has been so abused by some that it is not exercised by others. The American people are sick and tired of seeing innocent people smeared and guilty people whitewashed. But there have been enough proved cases to cause nation-wide distrust and strong suspicion that there may be something to the unproved, sensational accusations.

As a Republican, I say to my colleagues on this side of the aisle that the Republican Party faces a challenge today that is not unlike the challenge that it faced back in Lincoln's day. The Republican Party so successfully met that challenge that it emerged from the Civil War—as the champion of a united nation—in addition to being a party that unrelentingly fought loose spending and loose programs.

Today our country is being psychologically divided by the confusion and the suspicions that are bred in the United States Senate to spread like cancerous tentacles of "know nothing, suspect everything" attitudes. Today we have a Democratic Administration that has developed a mania for loose spending and loose programs. History is repeating itself—and the Republican Party again has the opportunity to emerge as the champion of unity and prudence.

The record of the present Democratic Administration has provided us with sufficient campaign issues without the necessity of resorting to political smears. America is rapidly losing its position as leader of the world simply because the Democratic Administration has pitifully failed to provide effective leadership.

The Democratic Administration has completely confused the American people by its daily contradictory grave warnings and optimistic assurances—that show the people that our Democratic Administration has no idea of where it is going. The Democratic Administration has greatly lost the confidence of the American people by its complacency to the threat of communism here at home and the leak of vital secrets to Russia through key officials of the Democratic Administration. There are enough proved cases to make this point without diluting our criticism with unproved charges.

Surely these are sufficient reasons to make it clear to the American people that it is time for a change and that a Republican victory is necessary to the security of this country. Surely it is clear that this nation will continue to suffer as long as it is governed by the present ineffective Democratic Administration.

Yet to displace it with a Republican regime embracing a philosophy that lacks political integrity or intellectual honesty would prove equally disastrous to this nation. The nation sorely needs a Republican victory. But I don't want to see the Republican Party ride to political victory on the Four Horsemen of Calumny—Fear, Ignorance, Bigotry and Smear. I doubt if the Republican Party could—simply because I don't believe the American people will uphold any political party that puts political exploitation above national interest. Surely we Republicans aren't that desperate for victory.

I don't want to see the Republican Party win that way. While it might be a fleeting victory for the Republican Party, it would be a more lasting defeat for the American people. Surely it would ultimately be suicide for the Republican Party and the two-party system that has protected our American liberties from the dictatorship of a one-party system.

As members of the minority party, we do not have the primary authority to formulate the policy of our government. But we do have the responsibility of rendering constructive criticism, of clarifying issues, of allaying fears by acting as responsible citizens.

As a woman, I wonder how the mothers, wives, sisters and daughters feel about the way in which members of their families have been politically mangled in Senate debate—and I use the word "debate" advisedly.

As a United States Senator, I am not proud of the way in which the Senate has been made a publicity platform for irresponsible sensationalism. I am not proud of the reckless abandon in which unproved charges have been hurled from this side of the aisle. I am not proud of the obviously staged, undignified countercharges that have been attempted in retaliation from the other side of the aisle.

I don't like the way the Senate has been made a rendezvous for vilification, for selfish political gain at the sacrifice of individual reputations and national unity. I am not proud of the way we smear outsiders from the floor of the Senate and hide behind the cloak of congressional immunity and still place ourselves beyond criticism on the floor of the Senate.

As an American, I am shocked at the way Republicans and Democrats alike are playing directly into the Communist design of "confuse, divide and conquer." As an American, I don't want a Democratic Administration "whitewash" or "cover up" any more than I want a Republican smear or witch hunt.

As an American, I condemn a Republican "Fascist" just as much as I condemn a Democrat "Communist." I condemn a Democrat "Fascist" just as much as I condemn a Republican "Communist." They are equally dangerous to you and me and to our country. As an American, I want to see our nation recapture the strength and unity it once had when we fought the enemy instead of ourselves.

It is with these thoughts that I have drafted what I call a "Declaration of Conscience." I am gratified that Senator Tobey, Senator Aiken, Senator Morse, Senator Ives, Senator Thye and Senator Hendrickson, have concurred in that declaration and have authorized me to announce their concurrence.

STATEMENT OF SEVEN REPUBLICAN SENATORS

1. We are Republicans. But we are Americans first. It is as Americans we express our concern with the growing confusion that threatens the security and stability of our country. Democrats and Republicans alike have contributed to that confusion.

2. The Democratic Administration has initially created the confusion by its lack of effective leadership, by its contradictory grave warnings and optimistic assurances, by its complacency to the threat of communism here at home, by its oversensitiveness to rightful criticism, by its petty bitterness against its critics.

3. Certain elements of the Republican Party have materially added to this confusion in the hopes of riding the Republican Party to victory through the selfish political exploitation of fear, bigotry, ignorance and intolerance. There are enough mistakes of the Democrats for Republicans to criticize constructively without resorting to political smears.

4. To this extent, Democrats and Republicans alike have unwittingly, but undeniably, played directly into the Communist design of "confuse, divide and conquer."

5. It is high time that we stopped thinking politically as Republicans and Democrats about elections and started thinking patriotically as Americans about national security based on individual freedom. It is high time that we all stopped being tools and victims of totalitarian techniques—techniques that, if continued here unchecked, will surely end what we have come to cherish as the American way of life.

Margaret Chase Smith, Maine
Charles W. Tobey, New Hampshire
George D. Aiken, Vermont
Wayne L. Morse, Oregon
Irving M. Ives, New York
Edward J. Thye, Minnesota
Robert C. Hendrickson, New Jersey

# The Preparation of Citizens for Their Political Duties[5]

Learned Hand

*Born January 27, 1872, Albany, NY; died August 18, 1961; A.B., 1893, A.M., 1894, Harvard University; LL.B., Harvard Law School, 1896; LL.D, Columbia, 1930; lawyer, private practice, 1897-1909; judge, District Court for Southern New York, 1909-24; judge, U.S. Court of Appeals, 1924-51.*

## Editor's introduction

Announcing the theme of this speech as education, Judge Learned Hand discussed the proper "preparation of citizens for [both] their political duties," and their service to the overall political community. According to Hand, such preparation stems from an education in the humanities—history, literature, philosophy, and the arts. These disciplines, Hand stated, are "essential to political wisdom" because they classify and arrange those eternal themes and challenges which each generation must encounter anew. Hand remarked that "no generation can safely start at scratch." A foundation in the humanities insures a familiarity with the "slow, hesitant, wayward course of human life," and therefore functions as a preparation for the realities endured by the community.

---

Chancellor Myers, Regents of the University, Ladies and Gentlemen:

The honor which the University of the State confers upon me today is doubly grateful: It is one that all would crave, and in my own case it has an especial personal value; for I was born in a house only a few roads from the building in which we now are, and I lived there for over thirty years. I can remember how, as a little boy, in the early morning I used to hear all the chisels begin together to chip the stones that were to be used in building the Capitol and how it seemed to me that that sound and the construction of that building were part of the permanent order of things and would always go on. Now, will you forgive me, if towards the close of a long life I lapse into a sentimental mood, as I reflect that an old man has been called back to the same spot where he took his first breath to be told that he has deserved well of his state during the intervening years. My father was born in New York, my grandfather lived in it all his professional life; they were loyal citizens of their state, and I like to fancy that their shades would join in my satisfaction at this evidence of your approval.

The theme today is education, as to which you, the Regents of the University, have an overarching superintendence. What I have to say will be directed towards one aspect of your responsibility: the preparation of citizens for their political duties. I shall argue that the "humanities," instead of being regarded only as a solace, a refuge, and an enrichment of the individual—as indeed they are—are also an essential factor in training him to perform his duties in a democratic society, as important even as acquaintance with the persons and the current events on which he is called upon to pass. The gifted men who contrived that great compromise, the Constitution of the United States, and secured its ratification by a society which might very probably have repudiated it upon a referendum, were well aware of the dangers which surrounded a totalitarian government, as well when power was lodged in the people at large, as when it rested in one man, or in an aristocracy. Indeed, some of the ablest of them, Hamil-

[5]Delivered to the 86th convocation of the State University of New York Board of Regents, in Albany, New York, on October 24, 1952.

ton for example, did not believe that any society could endure in which the voters had uncontrolled authority, even though the suffrage was as limited as it then was; and the experience of France in the next ten years seemed to them a demonstration that they had been right. The compunctions that all felt, including the people at large, were the reason why so many of the states made the first ten amendments practically a condition upon ratification, and they were all at once added, as you know. It is not important here whether it was from the outset inevitable that the word of the Supreme Court should be final as to what the Amendments meant; but it is important that they, and in particular the First and Fifth, contained hallowed phrases which thoughtful people at the end of the eighteenth century usually believed to embody mandates that either were of divine origin, or could be deduced from the inherent nature of man in society. Against these mandates no statute should prevail, and the Amendments, so far as they embodied them, were, strictly speaking, redundant. Moreover, it would not be true to say that this belief is not still widely held; indeed, one of the striking political agitations of the present is the recrudescence of the notion of "Natural Law" after its general repudiation by English-speaking lawyers in the nineteenth century. We are even assured that those who do not share it are "materialists" and amoral upholders of the doctrine that might makes right.

Most parts of the Constitution are specific enough to be treated like other legal commands; when we have to decide their meaning, we can proceed just as in the case of a dispute over the meaning of a statute; we look to their history and their setting with confidence that these will disclose their purpose. And that also applies to a large part of the Amendments themselves. For instance, no general cultural background is needed to reach a right opinion as to whether a statute has infringed the provision that the accused must be tried in the district where the crime was committed, or that he must be "confronted" by "the witnesses against him." But the situation is quite different when we are dealing with the broad clauses on which the conduct of a free society must in the end depend. What is "freedom of speech and of the press"; what is the "establishment of religion and the free exercise thereof"; what are "unreasonable searches," "due process of law," and "equal protection of the law": all these are left wholly undefined and cannot be effectively determined without some acquaintance with what men in the past have thought and felt to be their most precious interests. Indeed, these fundamental canons are not jural concepts at all, in the ordinary sense; and in application they turn out to be no more than admonitions of moderation, as appears from the varying and contradictory interpretations that the judges themselves find it necessary to put upon them. Nor can we leave to courts the responsibility of construing and so of enforcing them, for the powers of courts are too limited to reach the more controversial questions that arise under them. For, as you know, courts will not intervene—or at least they constantly avow that they should not—unless the action challenged infringes the Constitution beyond any fair dispute. While there are any plausible arguments in support of a measure, they must abstain; and so it results that in much the larger part of such controversies it is the voters, speaking through their delegates, who have the final word and the final responsibility; and that in the end it is they and they alone, who can and will preserve our liberties, if preserved they are to be. For their guidance there are no vade mecums, no handbooks, no manuals; they must depend upon such enlightenment as they can muster from within, and upon their conscience, so far as they have one. That enlightenment and that conscience they may indeed find in divine revelation; but when they do, they tap sources that I am not qualified to discuss; not any better qualified than I am to discuss what doctrines are inherent in the nature of man in society. I know of none of either sort, nor can I find direction from those who profess to know. It is because I am shorn of such resort that, to me at any rate, there appears to be no escape in each situation from balancing the conflicting interests at stake with as detached a temper as we can achieve.

A constitution, a statute, a regulation, a rule—in short, a "law" of any kind—is at once a prophecy and a choice. It is a prophecy, because it attempts to forecast what will be its effects: whom it will benefit and in what ways; on whom its impact will prove a burden; how much friction and discontent will arise from the adjustments that conformity to it will require; how completely it can be enforced; what enforcement will cost; how far it will interfere with other projects or existing activities; and in general, the whole manifold of its indirect consequences. A thoroughgoing and dependable knowledge of these is obviously impossible. For example, although we can anticipate with some degree of assurance who will pay a steeply graded income tax and in what amounts, there is no way to tell what its indirect effects will be: what activities of the taxpayers in the higher brackets it will depress; if they do not work so hard, in what way they will occupy their newly acquired leisure; how any new activities they may substitute will affect others; whether this will be offset by a loss of the mellowed maturity and the wisdom of those who withdraw. Such prophecies infest law of every sort, the more deeply as it is far reaching; and it is an illusion to suppose that there are formulas or statistics that will help in making them. They can rest upon no more than enlightened guesses; but these are likely to be successful as they are made by those whose horizons have been widened, and whose outlook has been clarified, by knowledge of what men have striven to do, and how far their hopes and fears have been realized. There is no substitute for an open mind, enriched by reading and the arts.

So much for what I have called the element of prophecy; refractory as it is, at least it depends only upon facts, however inaccessible. There remains the much more difficult element of choice. In such inquiries, as I have said, I see no escape from a calculus of, and balance between, the group interests—that is, the desires and values—whose conflict the measure under consideration is an attempt to adjust. But desires and values are not quantitatively measurable, for they seldom have any common constituents, and without these they cannot be objectively compared. On the other hand, an individual has the necessary means in his own case, for, although his personal desires and values are absolute, irreducible and undeducible, and have just that authority which he feels them to have, he has as authoritative a competence to compare them and to prefer one to another, as he has to appraise them separately. Thus, although such preferences are themselves as final as the desires and values, it would be easy to choose between the desires and values of conflicting social groups, if we could safely impute to them our own preferences. But by what right can we do so; and, if we cannot, what other means of vicarious choice have we? I submit that we have none except in so far as we can imaginatively project ourselves into the position of the groups between which we must choose. Surely I need not dilate upon how hard it is to do that. Even in our own affairs how often have we tried to anticipate how we shall feel on a future occasion, only to be surprised by the unexpected difference, when it comes to pass. And if it is hard to foreshadow our own feelings, how much harder is it to do so for others? It is not enough to be personally detached, although that is of course a condition; we must also acquire a capacity for an informed sympathy with and understanding of, the desires and the values of others; and that, I submit, only those have any chance of attaining whose experience is supplemented by some acquaintance, the wider the better, with what others have thought and felt in circumstances as near as possible to those of the groups in question.

I dare hope that it may now begin to be clearer why I am arguing that an education which includes the "humanities" is essential to political wisdom. By "humanities" I especially mean history; but close beside history and of almost, if not quite, equal importance are letters, poetry, philosophy, the plastic arts and music. Most of the issues that mankind sets out to settle, it never does settle. They are not solved, because, as I have just tried to say, they are incapable of solution properly speaking, being concerned with incommensurables. At any rate, even if that be not always true, the opposing parties seldom do agree upon a solution; and the dispute fades into the past unsolved, though perhaps it may be renewed as history and fought over again. It disappears because it is replaced by some compromise that, although not wholly acceptable to either side, offers a tolerable substitute for victory; and he who would find the substitute needs an endowment as rich as possible in experience, an experience which makes the heart generous and provides his mind with an understanding of the hearts of others. The great moderates of history were more often than not men of that sort, steeped, like Montaigne and Erasmus, in knowledge of the past. Let me quote from one of these, our own Franklin. After long, and at times bitter, controversy the final draft of the Constitution was accepted on Saturday, September 12, and was sent to be engrossed over the weekend. Nevertheless, there was still doubt about what might happen on Monday when the delegates were to sign. On Sunday Franklin wrote out a statement which Wilson read for him the next day. It is too long to quote *in extenso*, but I cannot forbear a sentence or two, so appropriate is it to what I am trying to say.

"I agree to this constitution with all its faults, if they are such, because I think a general government necessary for us and there is no form of government but what may be a blessing to the people if well administered, and believe further that this is likely to be well administered for a course of years, and can only end in despotism, as other forms have done before it, when the people shall have become so corrupted as to need despotic government, being incapable of any other. I doubt too whether any other convention we can obtain may be able to make a better constitution. For when you assemble a number of men to have the advantage of their joint wisdom, you inevitably assemble with those men all their prejudices, their passions, their errors of opinion, their local interests and their selfish views. From such an assembly can a perfect production be expected? . . . Thus, I consent Sir, to this constitution because I expect no better, and because I am not sure it is not the best."

Out of such a temper alone can come any political success which will not leave behind rancor and vindictiveness that is likely so deeply to infect its benefits as to make victory not worth while; and it is a temper best bred in those who have at least what I like to call a bowing acquaintance with the "humanities." For these are fitted to admonish us how tentative and provisional are our attainments, intellectual and moral; and how often the deepest convictions of one generation are the rejects of the next. That does not indeed deny the possibility that, as time goes on, we shall accumulate some body of valid conclusions; but it does mean that these we can achieve only by accumulation; that wisdom is to be gained only as we stand upon the shoulders of those who have gone before. Just as in science we cannot advance except as we take over what we inherit, so in statecraft no generation can safely start at scratch. The subject matter of science is recorded observation of the external world; the subject matter of the statecraft is the soul of man, and of that too there are records—the records I am talking about today. The imagination can be purged and the judgment ripened only by an awareness of the slow, hesitant, wayward course of human life, its failures, its successes, but its indomitable will to endure.

I cannot but think that we of this generation are politically in especial need of such education. Our nation is embarked upon a venture, as yet unproved; we have set our hopes upon a community in which men shall be given unchecked control of their own lives. That community is in peril; it is invaded from within, it is threatened from without; it faces a test which it may fail to pass. The choice is ours whether, when we hear the pipes of Pan, we shall stampede like a frightened flock, forgetting all those professions on which we have claimed to rest our polity. God knows, there is risk in refusing to act till the facts are all in; but is there not greater risk in abandoning the conditions of all rational inquiry? Risk for risk, for myself I had rather take my chance that some traitors will escape detection than spread abroad a spirit of general suspicion and distrust, which accepts rumor and gossip in place of undismayed and unintimidated inquiry. I believe that that community is already in process of dissolution where each man begins to eye his neighbor as a possible enemy, where nonconformity with the accepted creed, political as well as religious, is a mark of disaffection; where denunciation, without specification or backing, takes the place of evidence; where orthodoxy chokes freedom of dissent; where faith in the eventual supremacy of reason has become so timid that we dare not enter our convictions in the open lists to win or lose. Such fears as these are a solvent which can eat out the cement that binds the stones together; they may in the end subject us to a despotism as evil as any that we dread; and they can be allayed only in so far as we refuse to proceed on suspicion, and trust one another until we have tangible ground for misgiving. The mutual confidence on which all else depends can be maintained only by an open mind and a brave reliance upon free discussion. I do not say that these will suffice; who knows but we may be on a slope which leads down to aboriginal savagery. But of this I am sure: If we are to escape, we must not yield a foot upon demanding a fair field, and an honest race, to all ideas. "Blame not before thou hast examined; understand first and then rebuke. Answer not before thou hast heard; interrupt not in the midst of speech." Those words were written nearly two thousand years ago; they came out of an experience already long, and refined in the fires of passion and conflict; they are the product of a wisdom, bought by ages of bitter trial; and by that wisdom alone shall we be saved, we, who boast ourselves to be the apostles of a faith in the eventual triumph of wisdom. Listen also to these as ancient words that tell of the excellence of wisdom. "There is in her a spirit quick of understanding, holy, alone in kind, manifold, subtile, freely moving, clear in utterance, unpolluted, distinct, unharmed, loving what is good, keen, unhindered, beneficent, loving toward man, steadfast, sure, free from care, all-powerful, all-surveying, and penetrating through all spirits that are quick of understanding, pure, most subtile . . . . And if a man longeth even for much experience, he knoweth the things of old, and divineth the things to come; he understandeth subtilities of speeches and interpretations of dark sayings; he forseeth signs and wonders, and the issues of seasons and times. I determined therefore to take her unto me to live with me, knowing that she is one who would give me good thoughts for counsel, and encourage me in cares and griefs . . . . For she knoweth all things and hath understanding thereof; and in my doing she shall guide me in the ways of soberness, and she shall guard me in her glory. And so shall my works be acceptable, and I shall judge the people righteously, and shall be worthy of my Father's throne."

# Converting Liabilities into Assets[6]

Louis L. Mann

*Born 1890, in Louisville, KY; died February 2, 1966; B.A., 1910, M.A., 1912, University of Cincinnati; B.L.H., Hebrew Union College, 1911; ordained rabbi, 1914; Ph.D., Yale University, 1920; D.D., Hebrew Union College, 1944; rabbi, Chicago Sinai Congregation, 1923-66; lecturer, University of Chicago, 1924-53.*

## Editor's introduction

On May 31, 1953, Louis L. Mann spoke to the Sunday Evening Club, a Chicago-based organization that sponsored speeches by the nation's leading preachers. Mann related, almost entirely in anecdotes, how liabilities, handicaps, and frustrations can lead to success, service, and benefit for the community at large. Liabilities, according to Mann, provide for us an obstacle to overcome, and in the act of overcoming, we transform that which hinders us into that which propels us forward.

---

I have chosen as my subject tonight, "Converting Liabilities into Assets." I think I could state my theme in the form of a paradox. *The greatest asset is to have a liability.* The greatest liability is to have no liability. A very interesting book appeared some time ago written by eleven psychiatrists who had locked themselves up together in a hotel for about a week to discuss a very important problem, "Why Men Fail." They came out with a dozen conclusions—some four or five of which I'll share with you this evening. The first is, that the *majority* of people who succeed in life are not more gifted than those who fail. Second: the majority of those who fail in life are not less gifted than those who succeed. Third: the majority of people go all through life using less than 40 percent of their God-given abilities. That's like an eight-cylinder car chugging and jerking along on three cylinders. Four: the majority of people who have handicaps, liabilities and frustrations, who are crippled or blind or deaf, who have every reason to fail—now mark you—the majority who have every reason to fail—fail to fail. They make good.

The *one* greatest cause for human failure is an alibi. An alibi is "personal enemy number one." An alibi is not a mere excuse for failure, but a rationalization which means a ready excuse, a plausible excuse, a well sounding excuse, which one hugs so tightly that one will not let it go and hence will find occasion to use it.

I can illustrate what I have in mind by referring to some very familiar biographies. I choose familiar ones because I believe they will drive my point home so much the better. During the last war I happened to have done some psychological reconditioning for the government at Gardner Hospital in Chicago. I dealt with young men and young women who had come home from struggle crippled and maimed as well as with mental problems of various kinds. I came across two people—strangely enough how things will happen—near whom one and the same shrapnel burst and amputated the right arm of each of these men. One of them said to me as I was making my rounds, "I'll sit back and take it easy and get $107 a month as long as I live; I can sit on the cracker barrel and be a philosopher." The other man heard him and he shook his left arm at me and he said, "Nothing will stop me. I'm going right ahead as if nothing had happened." This leads me to the conclusion which is part of my theme this evening: *what happens to us is less significant than what happens within us.*

I'm going to divide what I have to say in four parts; the first, I'm going to call Frustrations. I take my first example from the Bible. There was a prophet whose name was Hosea. He had a great liability; his wife went wrong. She was unfaithful and as happened in ancient times, she

[6]Delivered to the Sunday Evening Club, in Chicago, Illinois, on May 31, 1953.

was taken down to the market place to be sold at auction to the highest bidder. Hosea wanted to be a thousand miles from that place that day, but somehow or other when the time for the auction came and people went to the market place; he found himself in the procession and then in the front row and strangely enough he became the highest bidder. She was his, not for a wife, but to take her back home to save her from greater degradation and shame. During the weeks and months that intervened, there came over him little by little a sense of forgiveness, and overwhelming pity seized his heart and a spiritual love emanated from his whole being; then it dawned upon him if a mere humble creature, like himself could so forgive and so love, how much greater must be the love of God for all of his unfortunate creatures. So, 740 years before Jesus, Hosea converted a liability into an imperishable asset and taught the world its greatest idea—*God is Love.*

Some years ago I visited Westminster Abbey where lie buried the immortals of the British empire. I walked around and saw some of the little slabs in the walls not more than nine inches wide. I recognized many of my book friends and as I passed one of those slabs, the shivers ran up and down my spine. Did that ever happen to you? It brought a story to my mind. He was a man whom I sympathetically called one of nature's stepchildren. He was born a hunchback and lame; he was a cripple, deformed and could hardly stand on his feet. He knew that nature had enslaved him. As he thought his problem through, an idea came to him: there are slaves whom nature has not enslaved, but whom man's inhumanity to man had enslaved. So he gave his whole life to freeing the enslaved. Once he was to make a speech; nobody could see him; they picked him up off the floor and put him upon the desk so that he could be seen. That night Boswell, the biographer of Johnson, was in the audience. When he left he said, "I saw them put a little shrimp on the table, but before he got through, he was a whale." Who was the "little shrimp" they put on the table and got to be "a whale"? It made my spine tingle. William Wilberforce. More than any one man in the entire British empire in its entire history he had freed the black man from bondage. On that little slab, were these imperishable words: "William Wilberforce, the attorney general for the unprotected and the friendless." The *attorney general for the unprotected and the friendless.* Frustrations!

What about the handicaps? I am thinking for the moment of a man named Whistler. The great ambition of his life was to be a soldier. He got an appointment and he went to West Point. At the end of the first year, to use the language of the streets, he "flunked" his chemistry. He was allowed to come back and the next year, he flunked his chemistry again and they had to drop him. He went back home. Some people go on a drunk when such things happen to them. They lose their courage in life, they feel they are no good, they are "washed out," they're done. He began scratching in the sand and he found that he could draw things. Then he began taking up colors and found out that he could mix colors and paint. I needn't tell you that Whistler became one of the great artists of all times. Now some of you are going to tell me he achieved fame *in spite* of his handicap and I say to you, *because* of his handicap. Later on in life when they were feasting him for his greatness and genius he said rather whimsically and wistfully, "If Silicon had been a gas, I would have been a major general." Silicon wasn't a gas.

Take an oyster. From an evolutionary point of view, it is a mollusk; it is way down in the evolutionary scale by millions of years. When a grain of sand gets into an oyster, it has a liability and it wiggles attempting to expel the liability. An oyster has a brain one millionth as big as a pin head. Instinct causes it to wiggle out the grain of sand. It usually succeeds. But when it fails to get rid of a liability like a grain of sand, it clamps down, closes up and converts that liability into a precious pearl. Converting liabilities into assets! Handicaps.

I am thinking now of obstacles. A long way back there was a man named Demosthenes. You remember him? Demosthenes couldn't speak. When he dreamed, he dreamed of a mighty audience in front of him, and in his dream felt that by the sheer inflection of his voice, he could make strong men cry one moment and laugh the next. Then he awakened and found that it was not a dream but a nightmare—he couldn't talk. It was before the day of apartment houses and yet the neighbors found fault with the noises that he made when he tried to speak. So Demosthenes went down to the seashore where there were no people. He saw pebbles lying on the shore and the strange idea came to him—he didn't have enough liabilities! He felt that if he just filled up his mouth with pebbles and, if he could talk just as well with a mouth full of pebbles—he couldn't talk worse—maybe by removing one of the pebbles each week, he would learn how to speak. Need I tell you that Demosthenes became not one of the greatest, but in all likelihood, the greatest orator of all time? You wouldn't say to me, "*In spite* of his handicap?" Nay, *because* of his handicap!

Think for a moment of John Bunyan. He lived two hundred years ago in England. His religious and theological views were unconventional and because of the moral climate of the day he was thrust into prison. He was a tinker, a mender of pots and pans, and he left behind a wife and four daughters, one of whom was stone blind. They put him in Bedford jail for seven years where he had only dry bread for food, dirty water for drink and a stone for a pillow. He certainly had enough alibis if he wanted an alibi. But something happened to him, the humble tinker, became a great thinker and in the alchemy of his spirit it was transformed and transfused and transfigured into spiritual assets. He wrote *The Pilgrims' Progress*, one of the great religious classics of all times. *In spite* of his difficulties? Nay, *because* of his difficulties.

Think for a moment of Epictetus, a slave who fell into the hands of another slave. A former slave in the nature of things, becomes a vindictive master. That explains the Bible's insight, "Remember the stranger for ye were strangers in the land of Egypt." The master twisted his leg and as Epictetus was a Stoic, he did not wince. He twisted it just a little more and Epictetus said rather calmly, "If you twist it just a little more than that, it will break." And he gave it another jerk and there it broke! He lay there uncared for, week after week, month after month and year after year. During that time he composed what he called his "discourses," a great book on human ethics, the best antidote in the world to worry. He tells us himself in that book that sometimes he felt that his breast would split wide open and his heart leap out in ecstatic joy, because even though his body was in chains, his soul was free. *In spite* of his hardships? Nay, *because* of his hardships!

Some years ago I was asked to give a commencement address at one of the great western universities. I gave about sixteen that year and I could see diplomas walking in by themselves. The president of the university and I stood and watched the graduates as they marched in. As we stood there the president said to me: "Oh, if you could only have been here two years ago. What a great commencement we had."

I said, "Did you have a *good* speaker that year?"

He said, "Oh, something happened, I wish you could have witnessed it; I could hardly believe what I saw."

And I asked, "Just what was it?"

Said he, "Four years earlier a little clump of flesh that called himself a student came to us; we didn't know whether to take him or not. The first week the professor of English said, 'When I call your name, rise, and after that I'll know you by name.' A name was called and no one rose; it was called a second time and still no one arose. The professor became just a bit indignant and said, 'Didn't I ask you to rise?' A voice chirped back, 'I'm sorry, sir, I haven't stood on my feet since I am two years old.' The four years passed and that little clump of flesh had won every honor that the university had ever bestowed. When the football captain had got his diploma, people applauded; when the baseball captain got his diploma, people applauded; when the Phi Beta Kappas got their diplomas, nobody applauded; then a name was called, and the football captain and the baseball captain made a basket out of their arms and they took this little clump of humanity and carried him across the stage." Then the president said to me, "The applause was so deafening that the walls began to tremble and the chandeliers began to swing. Dr. Mann, I have never witnessed anything like that in all my life."

It isn't what happens *to us*, it's what happens *within us* that really counts.

Some of you may remember my "friend" Socrates. He had a great liability. He had "matrimonial indigestion." Do you know what that is? His wife didn't agree with him. She nagged and nagged and nagged, till she got tired nagging and then she scolded till she got tired scolding and then she started to nag all over again. Some men go out and get drunk and others jump into the river under such conditions. Socrates went out on the street. He couldn't even get a "thin" word in "edgewise" at home and so he talked to everybody on the street. When a man said, "Socrates, it's a nice day," he asked, "What do you mean by a 'nice day'? If it were this way every day, we'd all starve to death. The umbrella man would go broke." Then he would go to another man and finally they accused him of being the brightest man in the whole community and he said, "I plead guilty. I'm the brightest man that ever lived. I *know* that I know nothing and I've met no one that knows that much." Converting liabilities into assets!

Abraham Lincoln came from down in Kentucky where I come from. No books and no libraries and no schools! His father, though authors have tried to smooth it over, was just an old drunk. His mother was a remarkable woman. She died when he was nine years old. He always called her his "angel mother." He went into business and spent seventeen years to pay off the debts of a worthless partner for which he was not legally responsible, but took on the moral responsibility. He fell in love with a beautiful girl and became engaged to her. She died. He ran for the legislature and was defeated. He tried for the land office and didn't get it; he ran for the United States Senate and was defeated. One defeat after another but in the alchemy of the spirit that man grew and grew until he became what I truly believe to have been the greatest American of all time. Converting liabilities into assets!

I close with this illustration. A little boy lived in Edinburgh. He had trouble with his leg, so he went to the doctor. The doctor said he couldn't help him but that there was only one doctor who could and he lived in London. It was before the days of the "rule of thumb"—hitch-hiking. So he rode on the train part of the way, he tried to walk on his poor leg part of the way, and in the last stretch he crawled on his stomach like a worm. The doctor saw him and said that one of the legs would have to be amputated immediately, but that he would try to save the other. He lay on a bed week after week and month after month without a smile from anyone save from those angels in white, sometimes called "nurses." Then a great day came, there was to be an international meeting of great physicians. Twelve world specialists were brought in to examine him, to see if they could save that other leg. While they were out in consultation, he reached over to one of the beds and got a stub of a pencil and then reached out to another bed and got a piece of wrapping paper and there wrote these lines. The moment I begin them, you will know that I am talking of the "Invictus" by William Ernest Henley:

Out of the night that covers me, Black as the pit from pole to pole,

I thank whatever gods may be For my unconquerable soul.

In the fell clutch of circumstance I have not winced nor cried aloud,

Under the bludgeonings of chance My head is bloody, but unbowed.

Beyond this place of wrath and tears Looms but the Horror of the shade,

And yet the menace of the years Finds and shall find me unafraid.

It matters not how strait the gate, How charged with punishments the scroll,

I am the master of my fate; I am the captain of my soul.

"Invictus." Unconquerable, insuperable, indomitable. Not what happens *to us*, but in the divine alchemy of the spirit transfused, transformed, transfigured, what happens *within us*. Invictus—unconquerable!

# The Eroding Authority[7]

Lewis F. Powell, Jr.

*Born September 19, 1907, Suffolk, VA; B.S., 1929, LL.B., 1931, Washington and Lee University; LL.M., Harvard Law School, 1932; partner, Hunton, Williams, Gay, Powell and Gibson, 1938-71; U.S. Army Air Force, 1942-46; chair, Richmond Public School Board, 1959-61; president, American Bar Association, 1964-65; associate justice of the United States Supreme Court, 1972-87.*

## Editor's introduction

In this speech, Supreme Court Associate Justice Lewis F. Powell, Jr., addressed the absence of "those values the individual once gained from respect for authority and from responsible participation in a larger community life." The focus of his speech is the gap that had arisen between many, particularly the young, and those in authority. Powell attributed this gap to an overriding concern with "highly individualized self-interest" that is not merely an aspect of youth, but of society in general. In lieu of communal values, Powell believed that we have a tendency to uphold singular or individual values and, consequently, to criticize, or even condemn, those external institutions, such as bodies of government and law enforcement, which unite us as a community.

---

When President Jaworski invited me to give the "lay sermon," my initial reaction was negative. I have never addressed a religious gathering larger than a small teenage Sunday School class. Even the latter made me uneasy, as I have no competency to sermonize to others.

Your President assured me, however, that you would be a tolerant audience—expecting little and hoping only for brevity.

Lawyers and judges are most at home when they are talking about "rights." I was tempted to select a subject in this area, as safeguarding the values protected by the Bill of Rights remains the highest responsibility of our profession.

But there is reason for concern as to other values, once held high in our civilization. I will talk briefly about some of these—without attempting to say anything original or profound. At most, in the meditative atmosphere of a Prayer Breakfast, I will ask you to think with me about some of the relationships and concepts that tend to be denigrated in modern society.

In general, I have in mind those values the individual once gained from respect for authority and from responsible participation in a larger community life. Today, we are being cut adrift from the type of humanizing authority which in the past shaped the character of our people.

I am thinking, not of governmental authority, but rather the more personal forms we have known in the home, church, school and community. These personal authorities once gave direction to our lives; they were our reference points, the institutions and relationships which molded our characters.

We respected and grew to maturity with teachers, parents, neighbors, ministers and employers—each imparting their values to us. These relationships were something larger than ourselves, but never so large as to be remote, impersonal or indifferent. We gained from them an inner strength, a sense of belonging as well as of responsibility to others.

This sense of belonging was portrayed nostalgically in the film *Fiddler on the Roof.* Those who saw it will remember the village of Anatevka in the last faint traces of sunset on Sabbath eve. There was the picture of Tevye, the father, blessing his family, close together around their

[7]Delivered at the annual convention of the American Bar Association, in San Francisco, California, on August 13, 1972. Reprinted with permission of Lewis F. Powell, Jr.

wooden dining room table. They sang what must have been ancient Hebrew hymns, transmitted from family to family through untold generations. The feeling of individual serenity in the common bond of family life was complete.

Sadly, this is not the portrait of contemporary American life. The refuge we once found in family and other community relationships is a fading concept. We are all familiar with the causes, though we may differ in evaluating their influence. The shape and style of our lives have been revolutionized by changes beyond our control: by advances of science and technology, by mass communications, mass transportation and the bewildering problems of an urbanized society. Whatever the causes, many of the old ethics and values seem threatened by new ones.

A nationally syndicated columnist, Joseph Kraft, recently described the reorientation of values as a "nearly universal war on authority." He referred to many young people who

" . . . assert their values in ways that are not benign. They undermine the chief restraint on Western society—the restraint of conformity, which is another way of saying respect for other people and their values. They are subversive of parental and school authority. And as their protests gain attention and concessions, other groups are encouraged to follow suit." [*Washington Post*, May 21, 1972]

One need not be this pessimistic to recognize a considerable truth in what Joe Kraft says. The overriding concern—not merely of youth but of large segments of our people—often seems to be a highly individualized self-interest. In the familiar phrase, everyone wants "to do his own thing." Or putting it differently, self assertion seems to be the modern aspiration: to be independent of—if not indeed to reject—the familiar disciplines of home, school, church and community.

The work ethic, in many ways the cornerstone of a viable society, is also scorned by many—by some who simply think society owes them a living, and by others who equate dedication to work with a materialism which they wish to repudiate.

Perhaps the primary belief of the New Ethic is that the individual owes little loyalty or obligation to the types of authority I have mentioned, or to their traditional values. Rather, one's chief allegiance is to his own conscience and his own desires.

We see manifestations of this unanchored individualism in the new mores of our time. We see it, for example, not merely in hostile attitudes toward existing institutions but in excessively tolerant views toward personal conduct: sexual morality, use of drugs, and disobedience of laws believed by the individual to be unjust. Even the concept of honor is now widely questioned.

This is no occasion for a parade of horrors. I will, however, cite two recent stories in the national press.

The first described the flourishing new business of producing college theses and term papers, available for sale to the thousands of students who practice cheating. The University of Wisconsin is reported to have withheld grades from some six hundred students suspected of submitting, as their own work, papers they had bought from commercial firms. Many colleges and schools have been forced to abandon any pretense of maintaining honor systems.

Another recent front-page story was headlined "Sex at Home for Young." It described the "changing concept of sexual morality," and addressed the question: "What happens when the liberated young return [home] for the weekend, with a friend of the opposite sex and expect to share the same bedroom?"

I do not pretend to know whether immorality today is more widespread than in some of the other more notably boisterous ages of the past. It is certainly more visible and openly tolerated. But whatever the facts may be, the greater concern must be with the impact upon the home. The relationships clustered around the home, between husband and wife and parents and children, are the most sacred of all human relationships.

Leaving random examples, and returning to the broader causes of the alienation of so many young people, I wonder if persistent and often destructive self-criticism is not a cause. It has become increasingly fashionable to question and attack the most basic elements of our society. It is said that religion is irrelevant, our democracy is a sham, the free enterprise system has failed, and that somehow America has become a wholly selfish, materialistic, racist society—with unworthy goals and warped priorities.

It is also persistently said—and this is directed to lawyers and judges—that our system of criminal justice is repressive. If these criticisms are accepted, there is little wonder that our institutions and inherited values are no longer respected.

We have always been prone to self-criticism. Certainly no thoughtful person would wish to mute the type of debate and dissent which have strengthened our democracy. No traditions are more firmly rooted, nor more essential to the ultimate preservation of our liberties, than the rights of speech, press and assembly protected by the First Amendment.

One might wish, however, for a somewhat better balance and for a higher level of responsibility in the criticism. America, its institutions, and the values of our people deserve a better billing than they often receive.

It may be that—in our concern with the present and our serious social problems—we are losing a proper perspective of history. History enables one to understand the importance of evolution; it balances the frustration of "how-far-we-have-to-go" with the satisfaction of "how-far-we-have-come." It teaches us tolerance for the human shortcomings and imperfections which are not uniquely of our generation, but of all time. Indeed, it immortalizes all of us in the sense that we are not seen solely as the product of the present day, but as links in an ageless chain of human struggle and progress.

We, as a people, are entitled to recall that the history of America is a proud and decent one. However slow and painful progress at times may seem, the consistent American vision is of a society in which all men—without regard to race, creed, belief or origin—can live in self-respect and pursue responsibly their own aspirations.

It is of course true that we have witnessed racial injustice in the past, as has every other country with significant racial diversity. But no one can fairly question the present national commitment to full equality and justice. Racial discrimination, by state action, is now proscribed by laws and court decisions which protect civil liberties perhaps more broadly than in any other country. But laws alone are not enough. Racial prejudice in the hearts of men cannot be legislated out of existence; it will pass only in time, and as human beings of all races learn in humility to respect each other—a process not furthered by recrimination or undue self-accusation.

The frequently made charge that criminal justice is unfair and repressive is another example of exaggerated self-criticism. Whatever may be said as to the past, the present dedication to fairness in criminal trials—in courts throughout America—cannot be doubted. Former California Chief Justice Roger J. Traynor, whose name will rank among the great American jurists of all time, has said: "It is irresponsible to echo such demagogic nonsense as the proposition that one group or another in this country cannot get a fair trial . . . . No country in the world has done more to insure fair trials."

It would be irrational to say that all of the criticisms of America and its institutions are unfounded. Yet, excessive self-flagellation can weaken—or even destroy—the ties that bind a people together. This, it seems to me, has been happening in this country. The time has come when thoughtful judgments as to our institutions, and our role in history, should be tempered by the wisdom and perspective of history. In the long view, America has been a remarkably responsible member of the society of nations. Our system of government and our institutions have forged a country which in many respects has been the envy of the world.

I have referred to our history because it is inseparable from the traditional values of our people. The revisionist concept of this history contributes to the eroding of these values and to the weakening of the authority of the institutions which sustain them—the home, church, school and community. I believe these institutions are irreplaceable.

And as to values, I was taught—and still believe—that a sense of *honor* is necessary to personal self-respect; that *duty*, recognizing an individual subordination to community welfare, is as important as rights; that *loyalty*, which is based on the trustworthiness of honorable men, is still a virtue; and that *work and self-discipline* are as essential to individual happiness as they are to a viable society. Indeed, I still believe in *patriotism*—not if it is limited to parades and flag-waving, but because worthy national goals and aspirations can be realized only through love of country and a desire to be a responsible citizen.

Finally, on this Sunday morning, I affirm my belief in the *worthiness of religion*, and of its indispensable role in the development of the human spirit.

And speaking of the spirit, I am afraid that this talk—which I will now end—has done little to uplift our spirits. Perhaps lay sermons are meant to be this way. In the brief time available

I have accented negative rather than positive aspects of contemporary America. There is much that is positive and cause for optimism. The idealism, and genuine concern, of so many of the young afford real hope for the future.

And we must always remember that the values and institutions, which now seem endangered, have survived other periods of doubt and challenge. In the ebb and flow of history, I am confident that their intrinsic merit will again be reaffirmed.

# A New Beginning: A New Dedication[8]

Barbara Jordan

*Born February 21, 1936, Houston, TX; died January 17, 1996; B.A., Texas Southern University, 1956; LL.B., Boston University, 1959; lawyer, private practice, 1959-66; member, Texas State Senate, 1967-72; representative (D) from Texas, 1973-79; lecturer, University of Texas, 1979-96.*

## Editor's introduction

In this rousing 10-minute speech, Representative Barbara Jordan noted that Americans "are a people in search of a national community." She further asserted that Americans are part of "a society in which all of us are equal." If such a community is not realized and fully understood, Jordan believed that America would become "a collection of interest groups . . . each seeking to satisfy private wants." Heroically condemning this personal or private interest, Jordan brought the convention attendees to their feet as she upheld the "American ideal" of democracy, and the common realization of its benefits.

---

One hundred and forty-four years ago, members of the Democratic party first met in convention to select a presidential candidate. Since that time, Democrats have continued to convene once every four years and draft a party platform and nominate a presidential candidate. And our meeting this week is a continuation of that tradition.

But there is something different about tonight. There is something special about tonight. What is different? What is special? I, Barbara Jordan, am a keynote speaker.

A lot of years passed since 1832, and during that time it would have been most unusual for any national political party to ask that a Barbara Jordan deliver a keynote address . . . but tonight here I am. And I feel that notwithstanding the past that my presence here is one additional bit of evidence that the American Dream need not forever be deferred.

Now that I have this grand distinction what in the world am I supposed to say?

I could easily spend this time praising the accomplishments of this party and attacking the Republicans but I don't choose to do that.

I could list the many problems which Americans have. I could list the problems which cause people to feel cynical, angry, frustrated: problems which include lack of integrity in government; the feeling that the individual no longer counts; the reality of material and spiritual poverty; the feeling that the grand American experiment is failing or has failed. I could recite these problems and then I could sit down and offer no solutions. But I don't choose to do that either.

The citizens of America expect more. They deserve and they want more than a recital of problems.

We are a people in a quandary about the present. We are a people in search of our future. We are a people in search of a national community.

We are a people trying not only to solve the problems of the present: unemployment, inflation . . . but we are attempting on a larger scale to fulfill the promise of America. We are attempting to fulfill our national purpose; to create and sustain a society in which all of us are equal.

Throughout our history, when people have looked for new ways to solve their problems, and to uphold the principles of this nation, many times they have turned to political parties. They have often turned to the Democratic party.

What is it, what is it about the Democratic party that makes it the instrument that people

[8]Delivered at the Democratic National Convention, in New York, New York, on July 12, 1976.

use when they search for ways to shape their future? Well I believe the answer to that question lies in our concept of governing. Our concept of governing is derived from our view of people. It is a concept deeply rooted in a set of beliefs firmly etched in the national conscience, of all of us.

Now what are these beliefs?

First, we believe in equality for all and privileges for none. This is a belief that each American regardless of background has equal standing in the public forum, all of us. Because we believe this idea so firmly, we are an inclusive rather than an exclusive party. Let everybody come.

I think it no accident that most of those emigrating to America in the nineteenth century identified with the Democratic party. We are a heterogeneous party made up of Americans of diverse backgrounds.

We believe that the people are the source of all governmental power; that the authority of the people is to be extended, not restricted. This can be accomplished only by providing each citizen with every opportunity to participate in the management of the government. They must have that.

We believe that the government which represents the authority of all the people, not just one interest group, but all the people, has an obligation to actively underscore, actively seek to remove those obstacles which would block individual achievement . . . obstacles emanating from race, sex, economic condition. The government must seek to remove them.

We are a party of innovation. We do not reject our traditions, but we are willing to adapt to changing circumstances, when change we must. We are willing to suffer the discomfort of change in order to achieve a better future.

We have a positive vision of the future founded on the belief that the gap between the promise and reality of America can one day be finally closed. We believe that.

This, my friends, is the bedrock of our concept of governing. This is a part of the reason why Americans have turned to the Democratic party. These are the foundations upon which a national community can be built.

Let's all understand that these guiding principles cannot be discarded for short-term political gains. They represent what this country is all about. They are indigenous to the American idea. And these are principles which are not negotiable.

In other times, I could stand here and give this kind of exposition on the beliefs of the Democratic party and that would be enough. But today that is not enough. People want more. That is not sufficient reason for the majority of the people of this country to vote Democratic. We have made mistakes. In our haste to do all things for all people, we did not foresee the full consequences of our actions. And when the people raised their voices, we didn't hear. But our deafness was only a temporary condition, and not an irreversible condition.

Even as I stand here and admit that we have made mistakes I still believe that as the people of America sit in judgment on each party, they will recognize that our mistakes were mistakes of the heart. They'll recognize that.

And now we must look to the future. Let us heed the voice of the people and recognize their common sense. If we do not, we not only blaspheme our political heritage, we ignore the common ties that bind all Americans.

Many fear the future. Many are distrustful of their leaders, and believe that their voices are never heard. Many seek only to satisfy their private work wants. To satisfy private interests.

But this is the great danger America faces. That we will cease to be one nation and become instead a collection of interest groups; city against suburb, region against region, individual against individual. Each seeking to satisfy private wants.

If that happens, who then will speak for America?

Who then will speak for the common good?

This is the question which must be answered in 1976.

Are we to be one people bound together by common spirit sharing in a common endeavor or will we become a divided nation?

For all of its uncertainty, we cannot flee the future. We must not become the new puritans and reject our society. We must address and master the future together. It can be done if we restore the belief that we share a sense of national community, that we share a common national endeavor. It can be done.

There is no executive order; there is no law that can require the American people to form a national community. This we must do as individuals and if we do it as individuals, there is no President of the United States who can veto that decision.

As a first step, we must restore our belief in ourselves. We are a generous people so why can't we be generous with each other? We need to take to heart the words spoken by Thomas Jefferson; "Let us restore to social intercourse that harmony and that affection without which liberty and even life are but dreary things."

A nation is formed by the willingness of each of us to share in the responsibility for upholding the common good.

A government is invigorated when each of us is willing to participate in shaping the future of this nation.

In this election year we must define the common good and begin again to shape a common good and begin again to shape a common future. Let each person do his or her part. If one citizen is unwilling to participate, all of us are going to suffer. For the American idea, though it is shared by all of us, is realized in each one of us.

And now, what are those of us who are elected public officials supposed to do? We call ourselves public servants but I'll tell you this: we as public servants must set an example for the rest of the nation. It is hypocritical for the public official to admonish and exhort the people to uphold the common good if we are derelict in upholding the common good. More is required of public officials than slogans and handshakes and press releases. More is required. We must hold ourselves strictly accountable. We must provide the people with a vision of the future.

If we promise as public officials, we must deliver. If we as public officials propose, we must produce. If we say to the American people it is time for you to be sacrificial; sacrifice. If the public official says that, we (public officials) must be the first to give. We must be. And again, if we make mistakes, we must be willing to admit them. We have to do that. What we have to do is strike a balance between the idea that government should do everything and the idea, the belief, that government ought to do nothing. Strike a balance.

Let there be no illusions about the difficulty of forming this kind of a national community. It's tough, difficult, not easy. But a spirit of harmony will survive in America only if each of us remembers that we share a common destiny. If each of us remembers when self-interest and bitterness seem to prevail, that we share a common destiny.

I have confidence that we can form this kind of national community.

I have confidence that the Democratic party can lead the way. I have that confidence. We cannot improve on the system of government handed down to us by the founders of the Republic, there is no way to improve upon that. But what we can do is to find new ways to implement that system and realize our destiny.

Now, I began this speech by commenting to you on the uniqueness of a Barbara Jordan making the keynote address. Well I am going to close my speech by quoting a Republican President and I ask you that as you listen to these words of Abraham Lincoln, relate them to the concept of a national community in which every last one of us participates: "As I would not be a slave, so I would not be a master."

This expresses my idea of Democracy. Whatever differs from this, to the extent of the difference is no democracy.

# The Lessons of Life[9]

## Marian Wright Edelman

*Born June 6, 1939, Bennettsville, SC; B.A., Spelman College, 1960; LL.B., 1963, LL.D., 1969, Yale University; staff attorney, 1963-64, director, 1964-68, National Association for the Advancement of Colored People Legal Defense and Education Foundation; partner, Southern Center for Public Policy, 1968-73; director, Harvard University Center for Law and Education, 1971-73; founder, president, Children's Defense Fund, 1973–.*

### Editor's introduction

Marian Wright Edelman, president of the Children's Defense Fund, spoke to a crowd of 10,000 and told them of the importance of community service. Recalling her experiences as an African-American child in a segregated community, Edelman noted that "Caring black adults were buffers against the segregated prison of the outside world that told black children we weren't important." For Edelman, these adults stand as an embodiment of service to the community. It is the attitude of these adults, and their belief in a "common good," that Edelman hoped to impart upon the graduates before her.

---

It is a great honor to share this day of accomplishment, celebration, and transition with the graduates of 1990 and your families. I am pleased that more than 80 of you applied to and 40 of you are going to participate in Teach for America which sends graduates to serve in teacher-shortage areas. I hope many more of you will wander off the beaten career path and help redefine what success is in the America of the 1990s.

When I was growing up, service was as essential a part of my upbringing as eating and sleeping and going to school. Caring black adults were buffers against the segregated prison of the outside world that told black children we weren't important. But we didn't believe it because our parents said it wasn't so. Our teachers said it wasn't so. And our preachers said it wasn't so. The childhood message I internalized was that as God's child, no man or woman could look down on me and I could look down on no man or woman.

We couldn't play in segregated public playgrounds or sit at drugstore lunch counters so my daddy, a Baptist minister, built a playground and canteen behind the church. Whenever he saw a need, he tried to respond. There were no Black homes for the aged so my parents began one across the street and our whole family helped out. I didn't like it a lot at the time, but that's how I learned it was my responsibility to take care of elderly family members and neighbors and that everyone was my neighbor.

I went everywhere with my parents and members of the congregation and community were my watchful extended parents. They reported on me when I did wrong and applauded when I did well. Doing well meant being considerate towards others, achieving in school, and reading. The only time my daddy wouldn't give me a chore was when I was reading. So I read a lot!

Children were taught that nothing was too lowly to do and that the work of our heads and hands were both valuable. As a young child I was sent with an older brother to help clean the bed and bed sores of a poor, sick woman and learned just how much even the smallest helping hands can mean to a lonely person in need.

Black adults in our families, churches, and community made children feel valued and important. They spent time with us and struggled

[9]Delivered at the Yale University Class Day exercises, in New Haven, Connecticut, on May 27, 1990. Reprinted with permission of Marian Wright Edelman. 

to keep us busy. And while life was often hard and resources scarce, we always knew who we were and that the measure of our worth was inside our heads and hearts and not outside in material possessions or personal ambition. Like Walker Percy, my elders knew instinctively that you could get all A's and still flunk life.

I was taught that the world had a lot of problems; that Black people had an extra lot of problems, but that I should face up to and was obligated to struggle and change them; that extra intellectual and material gifts brought with them the privilege and responsibility of sharing with others less fortunate; and that service is the rent each of us pays for living, the very purpose of life and not something you do in your spare time or after you have reached your personal goals.

I'm grateful for these childhood legacies: a living faith reflected in daily service; the discipline of hard work and stick-to-it-ness; and a capacity to struggle in the face of adversity. Giving up was not part of my elders' lexicon: You got up every morning and did what you had to do and you got up every time you fell down and tried as many times as you had to until you got it done right. They had grit. They valued family life and family rituals, and tried to be and expose us to good role models. And role models were those who achieved in the outside world, like my namesake Marian Anderson, and those who lacked formal education or money but who taught us by the special grace of their lives Christ's and Gandhi's and Heschel's message that the kingdom of God is within. And every day I still try to be half as good as those ordinary people of grace who were kind and patient with children and who shared whatever they had with others.

I was 14 years old the night my daddy died. He had holes in his shoes but two children out of college, one in college, another in divinity school, and a vision he was able to convey to me dying in an ambulance that I, a young black girl, could be and do anything, that race and gender are shadows, and that character, self-discipline, determination, attitude, and service are the substance of life.

I want to convey that same vision to you today as you graduate into an ethically polluted nation where instant sex without responsibility, instant gratification without effort, instant solutions without sacrifice, getting rather than giving, and hoarding rather than sharing are the too-frequent signals of our mass media, popular culture, and political life.

The standard for success for too many Americans has become personal greed rather than common good. The standard for striving and achievement has become getting by rather than making an extra effort or service to others. Truth telling and moral example have become devalued commodities. Nowhere is the paralysis of public or private conscience more evident than in the neglect and abandonment of millions of children of all races and classes whose futures we adults hold in trust. Their futures will shape the ability of our nation to compete morally and economically as much as yours as children of privilege.

Yet:

Every 8 seconds of the school day, an American child drops out (500,000 a year);

Every 26 seconds of the day, an American child runs away from home (1.2 million a year);

Every 47 seconds, an American child is abused or neglected (675,000 a year);

Every 67 seconds, an American teenager has a baby (472,000 a year);

Every 7 minutes, an American child is arrested for a drug offense;

Every 30 minutes an American child is arrested for drunken driving;

Every 53 minutes an American child dies from poverty in the wealthiest nation on earth (9,855 a year);

The 1990s will be an era of struggle for the American conscience and future. The battles will not be as dramatic as Gettysburg or Vietnam, but they will shape our place in the twenty-first century world. The bombs poised to blow up the American dream and shred America's social fabric emanate from no enemies without. They are ticking away within ourselves, our families, our neighborhoods, and cities, and in our loss of national purpose and direction.

We have lost our sense of what is important as a people. And too many young people, white, black, brown, rich, and poor, are growing up unable to handle life in hard places, without hope, and without steady compasses to navigate the morally polluted seas they must face in adulthood.

Since I believe it is the responsibility of every adult—parent, teacher, preacher, and professional—to make sure that children and young people hear what we have learned from the lessons of life, hear what we think matters, hear over and over that we love you, that you are never alone, and that you should never believe that life is not worth living or cheap, your own or anybody else's, at home or abroad, I want to share a few lessons with you today to take along as you leave Yale. You can take them or leave them, but you can't say you were never told. Too many of us who are parents have been so busy today making sure our children had all the things we didn't that we may not have shared the things we did have that enabled us to survive and succeed.

At Yale, you got your lessons from your teachers first and then got examined on how well you learned them. In life the test and consequences come before the lessons. And in an era of AIDS and potentially lethal drugs, the consequences can be fatal.

*Lesson one:* Don't feel entitled to anything you don't sweat and struggle for. And help our nation understand that it is not entitled to world leadership based on the past or on what we say rather than how well we perform and meet changing world needs. For those black and other racial minority graduates among you, I want you to remember that you can never take anything for granted in America, even with a Yale degree and even if too many whites still feel "entitled" solely by the accident of birth. And you had better not start now as racial intolerance resurges all over our land. It may be wrapped up in new euphemisms and better etiquette, but as Frederick Douglass warned us earlier, it's the same old snake.

Douglass also reminded all of us that "men may not get all they pay for in this world, but they must certainly pay for all they get."

So I hope you will struggle to achieve. Don't think for a moment that you've got it made with your Yale degree and are entitled to move up the career ladder. It may get you in the door, but it won't get you to the top or keep you there. You've got to work your way up, hard and continuously. Don't be lazy. Do your homework. Pay attention to detail. Take care and pride in your work. Few of us are gifted enough to get by on first drafts. People who are sloppy in little things tend to be sloppy in big things. Be reliable. Take the initiative in creating your own opportunity and don't wait around for other people to discover you or do you a favor. Don't assume a door is closed; push on it. Don't assume if it was closed yesterday, it's closed today. And don't any of you ever stop learning and improving your mind and spirit. If you do, you and America are going to be left behind.

You have come of age in a political era when too many political leaders and voters are looking for a free lunch. As a people we seem unable or unwilling to juggle difficult competing demands or to make hard choices and sacrifices to rebuild family and community for the good of the nation. Many whites favor racial justice as long as things remain the same. Many voters hate Congress, but love their own Congressman as long as s/he takes care of their special interests. Many husbands are happier to share their wives' added income than the housework and child care. Many Americans decry the growing gap between the rich and the poor and middle class and escalating child suffering as long as somebody else's taxes are raised and somebody else's program is cut. We have got to grow beyond our national adolescence!

*Lesson two:* Set goals and work quietly and systematically toward them. Too many of us talk big and act small. So often we get *bogged* down in our ego needs and lose sight of broader community and national goals. It's alright to want to feel important as long as it is not at the expense of *doing* important deeds, even if we don't get the credit. You can get a lot achieved in life if you don't mind doing the work and letting other people get the credit. You know what you do and the Lord knows what you do and that's all that matters.

*Lesson three:* Assign yourself. My daddy used to ask us whether the teacher gave us any homework. If we said no, he'd say "well assign yourself." Don't wait around for your boss or your friend or your spouse to direct you to do what you are able to figure out and do for yourself. Don't do just as little as you can to get by as so many Americans are doing today in our political and economic life. If you see a need, don't ask why doesn't somebody do something, ask why don't I do something. Don't wait around to be told what to do. There is nothing more wearing than people who have to be asked or reminded to do things repeatedly. Hard work, initiative, and persistence are still the non-magic carpets to success for most of us. Help teach the rest of the country how to achieve again by your example.

*Lesson four:* Use your political and economic power for the community. Vote and hold those you vote for accountable. Less than half the young people under 25 registered and only 36 percent voted in the 1988 election. Run for political office and enter government service. And don't think that you or your reelection or job are the only point once you do: strengthening families and communities and protecting American ideals are the point of gaining power. Don't confuse social and political charm with decency or sound policy. It's wonderful to go to the White House or Congress for a chat or a meal but words and sociability alone will not meet children's or the nation's needs. Political leadership and different budget priorities will. Speak truth to power. And put your own money and leadership behind rhetoric about concern for families and children in your own homes, in your own law firms, and corporations and in whatever areas you decide to pursue.

*Lesson five:* Never work just for money. Money alone won't save your soul or build a decent family or help you sleep at night. We are the richest nation on earth with one of the highest incarceration, drug addiction, and child poverty rates in the world. Don't confuse wealth or fame with character. And don't tolerate or condone moral corruption whether it's found in high places or low places or is white, brown or black. It is not okay to push or use drugs even if every person in America is doing it. It is not okay to cheat or lie even if every Milken, Boesky, North, Secord, or public official does. Be honest. And demand that those who represent you be honest. Don't confuse morality with legality. Dr. King noted that everything Hitler did in Nazi Germany was legal. Don't give anyone the proxy for your conscience. And don't spend every dollar you earn. Save a dime and share a dime.

*Lesson six:* Don't be afraid of taking risks or of being criticized. If you don't want to be criticized then don't say anything, do anything, or be anything. Don't be afraid of failing. It's the way you learn to do things right. It doesn't matter how many times you fall down. All that matters is how many times you keep getting up. "It's not failure," former Morehouse College president Dr. Benjamin Mays said, it's "a sin," it's "low aim." And don't wait for everybody to come along to get something done. It's always a few people who get things done and keep things going. This country needs more shepherds and fewer sheep.

*Lesson seven:* Take parenting and family life seriously. And insist that those you work for and who represent you do so. As a nation, we mouth family values we do not practice. Seventy nations provide medical care and financial assistance to all pregnant women; we are not one of them. Seventeen industrialized nations have paid maternity/paternity leave programs: we are not one of them and our Yalie President of the United States is threatening to veto an unpaid parental leave bill. Today, over half of mothers of infants are in the labor force and 62 percent of the net growth in the 1990s labor force will be women. We still don't have a safe, affordable, quality child care system. And the men in Congress are still bickering rather than completing action on child care bills passed by both Houses and the White House, despite President Bush's frequent photo opportunities and promises at child care centers during the 1988 presidential campaign, threatens still another veto.

It is time for the mothers of this nation to tell the men of this nation to get with it and stop the political hypocrisy so that parents can have a real choice about whether to remain at home or choose to work outside the home without worrying about the well-being of their children.

What a dilemma parents, especially women face today in a society that supports neither the option to care for children at home without falling into poverty or of going into the labor force with adequate, affordable child care. On the twentieth anniversary of the admission of women to Yale, I fear these critical issues will not be given the priority they demand until more women are in decision-making roles. Abigail Adams gave the charge in 1779 when she wrote John Adams to:

"Remember all Men would be tyrants if they could. If perticuliar care and attention is not paid to the Ladies we are determined to foment a Rebellion, and will not hold ourselves bound by any laws in which we have no voice, or Representation."

I hope your generation will raise your sons to be fair to other people's daughters and to *share*, not just help with, parenting and family responsibilities. I hope you will help strengthen the American tradition of family by stressing family rituals: prayers if you are religious, and if not, regular family meals and gatherings. Be moral examples for your children. If you cut corners, they will too. If you lie, they will too.

If you spend all your money on yourself and tithe no portion of it for our colleges, churches, synagogues, and civic causes, they won't either. And if you snicker at racial and gender jokes, another generation will pass on the poison my generation still did not have the will to snuff out.

*Lesson eight:* Remember and help America remember that the fellowship of human beings is more important than the fellowship of race and class and gender in a decent, democratic society. Be decent and fair and insist that others be so in your presence. Don't tell, laugh, smile at or acquiesce in racial, ethnic, religious or gender jokes, or any practices intended to demean rather than enhance another human being. Stare them down. Walk away from them. Make them unacceptable in your homes, religious congregations, and clubs. Counter through daily moral consciousness the proliferating voices of racial and ethnic and religious division which are gaining respectability over the land, including college campuses. Let's face up to rather than ignore our ongoing racial problems which are both America's historic and future Achilles heel. White folks did not create black folks. Men did not create women. Christians did not create Jews. So who gives anybody the right to feel entitled to diminish another?

How many more potential Martin Kings, Colin Powells, Frederick Gregorys, Sally Rides, and Barbara McClintocks is our nation going to waste before it wakes up and recognizes that its ability to compete in the new century is as inextricably intertwined with its poor and minority children as with its white and privileged ones, with its girls as well as its boys?

Let's not spend more time, whites or blacks, pinning and denying blame rather than remedying the problem. Rabbi Abraham Heschel put it aptly: "we are not all equally guilty but we are all equally responsible" for building a decent and just America.

*Lesson nine:* Listen for the sound of the genuine within yourself. "Small," Einstein said, "is the number of them that see with their own eyes and feel with their own hearts." Try to be one of them. The black theologian Howard Thurman, told the young ladies of my alma mater Spelman College, that there is "something in every one of you that waits and listens for the sound of the genuine in yourself which is the only true guide you'll ever have. And if you cannot hear it, you will all of your life spend your days on the ends of strings that somebody else pulls." There are so many noises and pulls in our lives, so many competing demands and signals that many of us never find out who we are. Learn to be quiet enough to hear the sound of the genuine within yourself so that you might then hear it in other people.

*Lesson ten:* Be confident that you can make a difference. Don't get overwhelmed. Sometimes I get frantic about all I have to do and spin my wheels. I then recall Carlyle's words that: "Our main business is not to see what lies dimly at a distance, but to do what lies closely at hand." Try to take each day and each task as they come, breaking them down into manageable pieces for action while struggling to see the whole. And don't think you have to "win" immediately or even at all to make a difference. Sometimes it's important to lose for things that matter.

I frequently end speeches with the words of Sojourner Truth, an illiterate slave woman, who could neither read nor write but was full of moral energy against slavery and second class treatment of women. One day during an anti-slavery speech she was heckled by an old white man. "Old woman, do you think that your talk about slavery does any good? Why I don't care any more for your talk than I do for the bite of a flea." "Perhaps not, but the Lord willing, I'll keep you scratching," she replied.

A lot of people think they have to be big dogs to make a difference. That's not true. You just need to be a flea for justice bent on building a decent America. Enough fleas biting strategically can make even the biggest dog uncomfortable and transform even the biggest nation. Bite so that we can transform America together in the 1990s.

Nathan Hale, facing the firing squad in 1776, said: "I regret that I have only one life to give to my country." You have only one life to live for your country. Live it creatively and well, and ensure that America's ideals are strengthened because you held them high for generations to come.

# Participating in the Process[10]

Janet Reno

*Born July 21, 1938, Miami, FL; A.B., Cornell University, 1960; LL.B., Harvard University, 1963; partner, Lewis and Reno, 1967; staff director, Florida House of Representatives judiciary committee, 1971; lawyer, Steel, Hector & Davis, 1976-78; attorney general, Dade County, FL, 1978-93; U.S. attorney general, 1993–.*

## Editor's introduction

On April 19, 1995, a terrorist bombing of the Alfred P. Murrah Federal Building in Oklahoma City left 167 dead and injured 467. Several weeks after, U.S. Attorney General Janet Reno spoke to the Santa Clara University Law School graduating class of 1995. In the speech, Reno asked the graduates to use their skills of persuasion to "speak out against violence and hatred." Reno also noted that a career in public service would afford these graduates with ample opportunity to effect genuine change in the community at large.

---

Thank you Father, thank you Dean Player, and, to the graduates, to the faculty, to the family and friends who helped the graduates get here, thank you for this high honor, for this degree from a great law school and a great university.

From this law school, from this great land of the west with its rich and wonderfully old heritage, but a land that is also taking us into the twenty-first century, from the family and friends that surround you today, you will draw strength and courage and wisdom for the rest of your life.

It has been a little over two years ago that I came to Washington to face one of the greatest challenges that any lawyer could undertake. I came alone but, in so many respects, I was not alone. Memories and spirit and people came with me; their spirit was with me. My law school dean was with me, the man who admitted women to Harvard Law School and encouraged us to continue our efforts, a man who over these 30 years until he died last year made it a point of seeking me out at bar meetings to keep me encouraged and supported every step of the way.

It was my American history teacher in high school who got me to thinking that I really could be a lawyer; it was my college roommate who gave me coffee at 2:00 a.m. in the morning as I was trying to prepare for my Constitutional Law course; it was the brother who teased me unmercifully as I was growing up, and even to this day calls me to tease me when he thinks I'm getting too big headed; there was my baby sitter who called from all the way across the nation to tell me how proud he was of me.

All of these people, and so many more, have been with me every step of the way. And the lessons that I have learned along the way have been with me.

The Dean made reference to a house. When I came to Washington, I suddenly found—and I guess I knew it but it hits you with a grim reality that you're responsible for the FBI, the DEA, the Bureau of Prisons, Immigration and Naturalization, and most of the government's lawyers—and you say, where do I begin?

I was reminded of the afternoon my mother picked us up at school. We had lived in a small, little wooden house that was too big for the children who were growing fast. My father didn't have enough money to hire a contractor to build the house and my mother announced that she was going to build the house. And we said, "What do you know about building a house?" She said, "I'm going to learn."

[10]Delivered at the Santa Clara University Law School commencement exercises, in Santa Clara, California, on May 20, 1995.

And she went to the brick mason, to the electrician, to the plumber and she talked to them about how to build a house; and she built the house. She dug the foundation with a pick and shovel, she laid the block, she put in the wiring and the plumbing; and my father would help her with the heavy beams when he came home from work at night.

She and I lived in that house till just before she died, before I came to Washington when she died. And every time I came down the driveway and saw that house standing there, as a prosecutor, as a lawyer having a difficult problem to solve, that house was a symbol to me that you can do anything you really want to if it's the right thing to do and you put your mind to it.

But that house taught me a more important lesson on August the 24th, 1992, when hurricane Andrew hit the area and devastated it. About 3:00 in the morning, my mother got up as the winds began to howl. She was old and frail and dying, but she was totally unafraid. She went over and sat down in her chair, folded her hands and, as the winds crashed trees around the house, she just sat there, for she knew how she had built that house; she had not cut corners, she put in good materials, she'd done it the right way.

When we came out in the early dawn, it looked like a World War I battlefield, but the house had only lost one shingle and some screens. That's the lesson that I carried with me to Washington in trying to figure out how to begin to administer the Department of Justice.

And so, draw strength and understanding and wisdom from those who have touched your lives, from the lessons that you've learned and will learn along the way, and go forth to use the law, its principles and its processes, to help others. Go forth and be yourself. Be known for who you are, not for the law firm you're with, not for the house that you live in, not for the money you make, but be known for who you are, what you stand for, and what you do for others.

The law has been a marvelous instrument for me; I have loved it, I have loved what it can do for people. And there are challenges that all of us, the new graduates, the Attorney General, the seasoned practitioner, all of us face. First, we have watched this nation racked by a terrible violence in this past month but we saw this nation come together in a remarkable way. We saw the people of this nation speak out against the hatred and the violence that had spawned that blast. We saw the people of America reach out and hold the victims and the survivors and help them begin to heal.

Yesterday, I was in Oklahoma City and talked to survivors, talked to people who had been injured, talked to people who had lost loved ones, and they said the feeling that had come from across America is something that kept them going.

I have watched America reach out and support law enforcement in every step of the way in holding the people accountable for this terrible evil, in cooperating in every way possible. I have seen America speak out to ensure that we protect the freedoms and the rights that we hold so dear and that we honor the rule of law as we bring these people to justice. I have seen America reach out and defend this nation.

We criticize government, but there is no other government in the history of the world that has ever afforded its people such freedoms and such opportunities. We must continue to speak out against the hatred and the violence that would undermine it.

Lawyers sometimes tend to get stuck in their little rut, they focus just on their case, their billable hours, their clients, and they don't look beyond. And too many professions are as focused. Look beyond and remember what we stand for. We must, as a nation, continue to speak out against violence, against hatred. And there's nobody more persuasive than a good lawyer; let us put those skills to work.

You can do it in simple and small ways. For example, in Billings, Montana, in November of 1993, bricks were thrown into the homes of two Jewish families in the community. The *Billings Gazette* responded immediately by publishing a full-page menorah. The non-Jewish community throughout Billings started putting the menorah up in their windows; thousands of windows appeared with menorahs. As the Jewish community worshipped at the Hanukkah service, non-Jewish people stood outside to make sure that nothing happened and those responsible faded away.

We have seen another example this past week of a profile of someone speaking out. We're not Republicans and Democrats in this process, we're Americans as we speak out. And I applaud George Bush for his actions and for his eloquence when he resigned his membership with the NRA. It is a true test of leadership when you're able to tell your friends they're wrong. Demonizing the men and women of law enforcement who put their lives on the line each day in defense of our freedoms is just plain wrong.

Everyone in public life, every lawyer, every American, can learn from the powerful example of President Bush that there are times when you have to tell your friends they've done the wrong thing.

And we must think in other contexts. I will always remember my father who came as a twelve-year-old to Racine, Wisconsin. He spoke not a word of English. He never forgot that people teased him about his funny language and his funny clothes and he tried to be kind to people for the rest of his life. Four years later, he was the editor of a high school newspaper; and, for 43 years, he wrote beautiful English for the *Miami Herald.*

We must remember where we came from and speak out against bigotry, speak out against those who would be intolerant.

Secondly, get involved, don't sit on the sidelines; use the remarkable skills that you've developed here either as a negotiator, litigator, or just a person who thinks with the common sense and applies it to the law.

Public service is a wonderful opportunity. When I graduated from Harvard Law School in 1963 and couldn't get the job that I wanted, I was envious of those lawyers going on to Wall Street and to silk-stocking firms across the country. Now, as I meet them, they are envious of my opportunity and my career for public service.

You don't have to do just one or the other; but public service along the way is an experience and an opportunity that you will never forget.

Think broadly. I swore I would never be a prosecutor; I thought prosecutors were more interested in securing convictions than seeking justice. My predecessor suggested that I might become the State Attorney and do something about that concept. But, if you become a prosecutor, think beyond. This is a great nation but it's a nation that can be improved on; and let's work to do it.

The prosecutor who convicts that person and sends him to jail and doesn't make sure that we have enough jail cells, doesn't make sure we have good treatment in the jails to solve the problem that caused him to go there in the first place, is not the prosecutor doing his or her job.

Public defenders are so important. It is something I will never forget: about ten years ago, a young man came up to me and said, "You defended me when I was a juvenile. I was charged with a delinquent act. You got me off on the right foot. And I'm married, I've got a job; everything's been okay ever since."

But the prosecutor or the public defender who ends the job in the court room isn't doing the job. That public defender who watches somebody walk out of the court room free on a motion to dismiss, knowing they have a crack addiction, who doesn't try to do something about it, either in changing attitudes in the legislature, changing attitudes in Congress or trying to find a treatment program that will provide that help, isn't doing his or her best to help the client.

But, if you don't want public service, just think about what you can do as a lawyer participating in the process. Too many lawyers get into it from a narrow self-interest. Somebody is trying to rezone property next to them, they get upset with city hall, they get into the zoning battle, they learn about it, and some of them just turn away after they've won their battle and go back to what they were doing. But more and more and more, lawyers are getting involved in the processes of government as lay people working from the outside to improve government and to make it more real for all people. Don't sit on the sidelines.

I invite all of you to come to the Department of Justice one day, to the Attorney General's conference room, and look at the two great murals that were put on those walls in 1937. One is a mural of justice granted, a hopeful scene of people progressing with great industry, with art and music, towards a better future; the other is justice denied, a wasteland of brown-shirted thugs taking people out in chains to prisons, of brown-shirted thugs breaking violins and taking pens and paper. Those murals were put on the wall of the Department of Justice in 1937, four years before we went into World War II, four years before we really spoke out against tyranny. We cannot sit on the sidelines.

And, in one area, all of us must focus attention; we have sat on the sidelines, been indifferent, and ignored the future of America for too long. Our children are our most precious possession; but our children are being killed on the streets of America, our children are not getting the education they need, our children are not getting the development and the opportunity and the positive structure they need to grow to be strong, constructive human beings. And too many lawyers along the way have focused on a personal injury law suit or a large corporate transaction and forgotten what our future is all about.

Unless we invest in our children today and legal principles and process and structure that can give them a strong and positive future, we are not going to have a work force with the skills that can fill the jobs that can maintain this nation as a first-rate nation.

I love lawyers because they can be so creative, so innovative, so bold; let us take the creativity, the energy, the intellect that abounds across the campuses of the great universities of this nation here today and put it to work as an investment in our future, not in smokestacks, not in technology, but in what counts most, our people. And to do that, we have to concentrate on a third issue; we've got to make the law real for all Americans.

The American Bar Association has done a study in which they found that about half of those households of 3,000 low- and moderate-income households have at least one legal need. The most prominent was for personal finances, consumer issues, housing and real property, personal and economic injury, wills and estates, and family law. The sad conclusion of that survey is that 71 percent of low-income and 61 percent of moderate-income legal needs are not being addressed by the civil justice system in America today. What that means is that, for far too many Americans, the law is worth little more than the paper it's written on.

Too many Americans feel disenfranchised and that they can't get their problems solved. Too many Americans have confronted lawyers who get them a judgment then don't follow through. Too many Americans have gotten lawyers who don't listen to them and are more interested in the processes of the court that don't go to solving the person's problem.

On the east wall of the building of the Department of Justice in Washington is a statement chiseled into the stone. It says, "The common law is derived from the will of mankind issuing from the people, framed by mutual confidence, and sanctioned by the light of reason." If people do not have access to the law, if they do not feel part of the law, they become disenfranchised and opposed. All of us, as lawyers, have a special responsibility to make the law real for all Americans.

We can begin to start speaking in small, old words and get rid of, once and for all, the legalese that has dominated this profession for too long. We can start speaking in terms that people can understand rather than Roman numerals and alphabets and titles that they don't understand. We can go to legislatures, we can go to court processes and rules and start framing issues in ways that people can understand. The average person is real smart until lawyers start confusing the issues sometimes.

But most of all, we have got to remember that the law is people. It is not a motion to dismiss, it is not a Federal Rule of Civil Procedure, it is not a judgment that is the goal. What we are trying to do is solve people's problems and protect their freedoms and protect their interests. And, to solve people's problems, we have to listen to them and look at them as if they are the most important people around, not as if we're trying to see our next appointment or are more interested in our billable hours. We have got to figure out how to solve people's problems.

Some are concerned about lawyer-bashing in this country; I think the greatest single thing we can do about that attitude is to solve people's problems, do it in a cost-effective way, do it in a caring way, and make a difference.

But the most important thing I urge you to consider as you start this great adventure is remember the most precious possession you have and will have, your family and your friends.

I remember that lady who built the house. She worked in the home when she wasn't building the house; she taught us to play baseball, to bake sponge cakes, to appreciate Beethoven's symphonies. She taught us her favorite poets, she taught us to play fair, she loved us with all her heart. And there is no childcare in the world that will ever be a substitute for what that lady was in our life.

I look at the young lawyers in America today trying to raise families; getting breakfast on the table and the children off to school; coming home after trial after they've prepped their witnesses for the next day; getting through the last vestiges of rush hour; putting dinner on the table; getting the children bathed, their homework done. Saturdays, they run errands; Sundays, they start preparing for trial again. And suddenly, the six-year-olds will be 16 and 26 before they know it.

Bringing up a child is the single most difficult thing I have ever done in my life. A little over ten years ago a friend died leaving me as the legal guardian for her 15-year-old twins, a boy and a girl. The girl was in love; and I've learned an awful lot about raising children in the last ten years.

I've learned it takes intelligence, hard work, luck, and an awful lot of love; but I have also learned that it is one of the most rewarding experiences that you can have, to send a young lady off to college and then see her graduate cum laude in three years and, on those occasions, have her throw her arms around my neck and say, "Thank you, I couldn't have done it without you."

All I ask of you as you go out in this wonderful new career is remember your family, remember the children that you will have. If we can send a man to the moon, surely, surely, surely; we can achieve professional fulfillment while at the same time putting our children and our family first.

When you go to that law firm, when you go to that Department of Justice, the public defender's office, the prosecutor's office, ask them about flex time and telecommuting for both parents, not just for one.

And then, as you remember all the people that have touched your life, as you remember this place, go forth, build a strong family, develop a practice that helps others truly, and go out and let us find peace in this world.

God bless you all.

# II. Nature and Function of Government

## Editor's introduction

The nature, function, and role of the American government within American society have been the focus of debate throughout the twentieth-century. This debate springs from several tensions, which include: conservative ideology versus liberal ideology; the rights of the group versus the rights of the individual; and personal responsibility versus enforced responsibility. Given that as recently as 1995 only 26 percent of the population believed the federal government to be serious about solving the nation's problems, recalling those speeches which best articulate the government's role in the United States seems particularly poignant.

Indeed, there has been a "clash of cultures" over what extent government should be involved in the lives of the citizenry. Buoyed by leading the nation out of the Great Depression, Franklin D. Roosevelt claimed that the government could "solve for the individual the ever-rising problems of a complex civilization," even those "once considered unsolvable." While recognizing that Roosevelt had to exercise assertive leadership during the nation's social and economic crises, journalist Walter Lippmann feared that such leadership would initiate the "decline of democracy and the rise of personal government." This "road to hell," as Lippmann depicted it, is paved with "unlimited powers . . . hitherto reserved to the states."

Dorothy Thompson envisioned a government of bureaucrats more concerned with serving their own interests than the American people. In contrast, John F. Kennedy did not see this fracture between the people and their government, as he described a "New Frontier" of "unknown opportunities and perils," in which citizen and state would be challenged as one. With the nation reeling from Watergate, Archibald Cox asked law to provide the "spirit of cooperation that used to run deep in the American people." For Cox, government was a force which must necessarily provide laws that create an internal harmony among the American people. The belief that government, and the laws created by it, are subject to the American people was echoed by Ronald Reagan. Concerned about citizens' loss of "faith in their governmental process," Reagan promised to return power and resources to the people. Newt L. Gingrich, in his "Contract with America," affirmed the relationship between government and citizenry, noting that one of the challenges of government is to create an "opportunity society," in which hard work is properly gratified.

# Second Inaugural Address[1]

## Franklin Delano Roosevelt

*Born January 30, 1882, Hyde Park, NY; died April 12, 1945; A.B., Harvard University, 1904; state senator, New York State Assembly, 1910-13; assistant secretary of the Navy, 1913-20; governor of New York, 1929-33; president of the United States, 1933-45.*

### Editor's introduction

On a rainswept day, Franklin Delano Roosevelt gave his second presidential inaugural address. To a large extent, the nation had recovered from the Great Depression, and Roosevelt took this occasion to praise the new federalism which he believed responsible for that recovery. Roosevelt's federalism called for a strong, centralized government to function as "the instrument of our united purpose to solve for the individual the ever-rising problems of a complex civilization." Roosevelt saw government as a force necessary "to solve problems utterly beyond individual or local solution." This speech highlights Roosevelt's basis for this belief, as well as his desire to maintain the effectiveness of the United States government.

---

When four years ago we met to inaugurate a President, the Republic, single-minded in anxiety, stood in spirit here. We dedicated ourselves to the fulfillment of a vision—to speed the time when there would be for all the people that security and peace essential to the pursuit of happiness. We of the Republic pledged ourselves to drive from the temple of our ancient faith those who had profaned it; to end by action, tireless and unafraid, the stagnation and despair of that day.

We did those first things first.

Our covenant with ourselves did not stop there. Instinctively we recognized a deeper need—the need to find thru government the instrument of our united purpose to solve for the individual the ever-rising problems of a complex civilization. Repeated attempts at their solution without the aid of government had left us baffled and bewildered. For without that aid we had been unable to create those moral controls over the services of science which are necessary to make science a useful servant instead of a ruthless master of mankind. To do this we knew that we must find practical controls over blind economic forces and blindly selfish men.

We of the republic sensed the truth that democratic government has innate capacity to protect its people against disasters once considered inevitable—to solve problems once considered unsolvable. We would not admit that we could not find a way to master economic epidemics just as, after centuries of fatalistic suffering, we had found a way to master epidemics of disease. We refused to leave the problems of our common welfare to be solved by the winds of chance and the hurricanes of disaster.

In this we Americans were discovering no wholly new truth; we were writing a new chapter in our book of self government.

This year marks the one hundred and fiftieth anniversary of the constitutional convention which made us a nation. At that convention our forefathers found the way out of the chaos which followed the revolutionary war; they created a strong government with powers of united action sufficient then and now to solve problems utterly beyond individual or local solution. A century and a half ago they established the Federal government in order to promote the general welfare and secure the blessings of liberty to the American people.

Today we invoke those same powers of government to achieve the same objectives.

Four years of new experience have not belied our historic instinct. They hold out the

[1]Delivered at the inauguration of the president of the United States, in Washington, D.C., on January 20, 1937.

clear hope that government within communities, government within the separate States, and government of the United States can do the things the times require, without yielding its democracy. Our task in the last four years did not force democracy to take a holiday.

Nearly all of us recognize that as intricacies of human relationships increase, so power to govern them also must increase—power to stop evil; power to do good. The essential democracy of our nation and the safety of our people depend not upon the absence of power, but upon lodging it with those whom the people can change or continue at stated intervals thru an honest and free system of elections. The Constitution of 1787 did not make our democracy impotent.

In fact, in these last four years, we have made the exercise of all power more democratic; for we have begun to bring private autocratic powers into their proper subordination to the public's government. The legend that they were invincible—above and beyond the processes of a democracy—has been shattered. They have been challenged and beaten.

Our progress out of the depression is obvious.

But that is not all that you and I mean by the new order of things. Our pledge was not merely to do a patch-work job with second-hand materials. By using the new materials of social justice we have undertaken to erect on the old foundations a more enduring structure for the better use of future generations.

In that purpose we have been helped by achievements of mind and spirit. Old truths have been relearned; untruths have been unlearned. We have always known that heedless self-interest was bad morals; we know now that it is bad economics. Out of the collapse of a prosperity whose builders boasted their practicality has come the conviction that in the long run economic morality pays. We are beginning to wipe out the line that divides the practical from the ideal, and in so doing we are fashioning an instrument of unimagined power for the establishment of a morally better world.

This new understanding undermines the old admiration of worldly success as such. We are beginning to abandon our tolerance of the abuse of power by those who betray for profit the elementary decencies of life.

In this process evil things formerly accepted will not be so easily condoned. Hard-headedness will not so easily excuse hard-heartedness. We are moving toward an era of good feeling. But we realize that there can be no era of good feeling save among men of good will.

For these reasons I am justified in believing that the greatest change we have witnessed has been the change in the moral climate of America.

Among men of good will, science and democracy together offer an ever-richer life and ever-larger satisfaction to the individual. With this change in our moral climate and our rediscovered ability to improve our economic order we have set our feet upon the road of enduring progress.

Shall we pause now and turn our back upon the road that lies ahead? Shall we call this the promised land? Or shall we continue on our way? For "each age is a dream that is dying, or one that is coming to birth."

Many voices are heard as we face a great decision. Comfort says, "Tarry a while." Opportunism says, "This is a good spot." Timidity asks, "How difficult is the road ahead?"

True, we have come far from the days of stagnation and despair. Vitality has been preserved. Courage and confidence have been restored. Mental and moral horizons have been extended.

But our present gains were won under the pressure of more than ordinary circumstance. Advance became imperative under the goad of fear and suffering. The times were on the side of progress.

To hold to progress today, however, is more difficult. Dulled conscience, irresponsibility, and ruthless self-interest already reappear. Such symptoms of prosperity may become portents of disaster. Prosperity already tests the persistence of our progressive purpose.

Let us ask again: Have we reached the goal of our vision of that 4th day of March, 1933? Have we found our happy valley?

I see a great nation, upon a great continent, blessed with a great wealth of natural resources. Its hundred and thirty million people are at peace among themselves; they are making their country a good neighbor among the nations. I see a United States which can demonstrate that, under democratic methods of government, national wealth can be translated into a spreading volume of human comforts hitherto unknown—and the lowest standard of living can be raised far above the level of mere subsistence.

But here is the challenge to our democracy: In this nation I see tens of millions of its citizens—a substantial part of its whole population—who at this very moment are denied the greater part of what the very lowest standards of today call the necessities of life.

I see millions of families trying to live on incomes so meager that the pall of family disaster hangs over them day by day.

I see millions whose daily lives in city and on farm continue under conditions labeled indecent by a so-called polite society half a century ago.

I see millions denied education, recreation, and the opportunity to better their lot and the lot of their children.

I see millions lacking the means to buy the products of farm and factory and by their poverty denying work and productiveness to many other millions.

I see one-third of a nation ill-housed, ill-clad, ill-nourished.

It is not in despair that I paint you that picture. I paint it for you in hope—because the nation, seeing and understanding the injustice in it, proposes to paint it out. We are determined to make every American citizen the subject of this country's interest and concern, and we will never regard any faithful, law-abiding group within our borders as superfluous. The test of our progress is not whether we add more to the abundance of those who have much; it is whether we provide enough for those who have too little.

If I know aught of the spirit and purpose of our nation we will not listen to comfort, opportunism, and timidity. We will carry on.

Overwhelmingly we of the Republic are men and women of good will—men and women who have cool heads and willing hands of practical purpose as well. They will insist that every agency of popular government use effective instruments to carry out their will.

Government is competent when all who compose it work as trustees for the whole people. It can make constant progress when it keeps abreast of all the facts. It can obtain justified support and legitimate criticism when the people receive true information of all that government does.

If I know aught of the will of our people they will demand that these conditions of effective government shall be created and maintained. They will demand a nation uncorrupted by cancers of injustice and, therefore, strong among the nations in its example of the will of peace.

Today we reconsecrate our country to long-cherished ideals in a suddenly-changed civilization. In every land there are always at work forces that drive men apart and forces that draw men together. In our personal ambitions we are individualists. But in our seeking for economic and political progress as a nation, we all go up, or else we all go down, as one people.

To maintain a democracy of effort requires a vast amount of patience in dealing with differing methods, a vast amount of humility. But out of the confusion of many voices rises an understanding of dominant public need. Then political leadership can voice common ideals, and aid in their realization.

In taking again the oath of office as President of the United States, I assume the solemn obligation of leading the American people forward along the road over which they have chosen to advance.

While this duty rests upon me I shall do my utmost to speak their purpose and to do their will, seeking Divine guidance to help us each and every one to give light to them that sit in darkness and to guide our feet into the way of peace.

# Rise of Personal Government in the United States[2]

Walter Lippmann

*Born September 23, 1889, New York, NY; died December 14, 1974; A.B., Harvard University, 1910; associate editor,* The New Republic, *1914-17, 1919; editor,* New York World, *1921-31; writer,* New York Herald Tribune, *1931-74; author,* Drift and Mastery: An Attempt to Diagnose the Current Unrest *(1914),* The Stakes of Diplomacy *(1915),* Public Opinion *(1922),* The Phantom Public *(1925),* Men of Destiny *(1927),* A Preface to Morals *(1929),* The Method of Freedom *(1934),* The New Imperative *(1935),* An Inquiry into the Principles of the Good Society *(1937),* U.S. War Aims *(1944),* The Communist World and Ours *(1959),* The Coming Tests with Russia *(1961),* Western Unity and the Common Market *(1962).*

## Editor's introduction

Considered one of the most prominent journalists and thinkers of the twentieth century, Walter Lippmann gave this speech in analysis and protest of Roosevelt's New Deal legislation. Lippmann opposed President Franklin D. Roosevelt's claim that the federal government could "solve for the individual the ever-rising problems of a complex civilization." Essentially, Roosevelt and Lippmann disagreed on the role of government in American society. Lippmann branded the expanded powers procured by Roosevelt to combat the Great Depression a type of "personal government" which, while appropriate "on the ground of emergency," should not become a permanent element of America's political system. It follows that Lippmann advocated less federal presence and greater state authority.

---

My subject this evening is the rise of personal government in the United States. I shall attempt to define the magnitude of this phenomenon, to diagnose its causes, and to indicate the remedies. But by way of introduction I wish to make it clear that I am not concerned with the character or with the purpose of the individual who happens to be the personal embodiment of this radically new form of government in America. I have known him for twenty years and I do not impute to him any sinister ambition whatsoever. His partisans in this audience may not believe that now, but before I have finished, I hope to persuade even them that I say this in all sincerity. For I believe it can be shown that the phenomenon we are witnessing has its roots in conditions that preceded by a long time the election of Mr. Roosevelt, and that democratic government had become too devitalized by its own failings to deal with the great social crisis of 1929-35. My thesis is that while Mr. Roosevelt had to assume extraordinary personal powers to deal with that emergency, there is the grave possibility that he is now engaged in perpetuating these extraordinary personal powers and in habituating the American people to the practice of personal government. I do not believe, and I do not in any way mean to insinuate that Mr. Roosevelt seeks to perpetuate his own personal power beyond the four-year term to which he is elected. But I do believe that, if in these four years the habits of constitutionalism are destroyed, it may be very difficult to revive them.

In order to make clear the magnitude of the change we are witnessing, I shall recall to your minds the powers which the President has asked for in the last four years. Though he has

[2]Delivered at Johns Hopkins University, in Baltimore, Maryland, on April 21, 1937.

not yet obtained all these powers, he has asked for all of them. I should like you to consider them, not separately, but as a whole. So far as I know he regards them all as the necessary and desirable powers of the President of the United States. They are a measure, therefore, of the scope and of the degree to which the President himself, the dominant party, and a very large part of the population, now approve the conception of personal government as an alternative to the traditional checks and balances of constitutional federalism.

It should be noted that though most of these powers were asked and were granted originally for a limited period of one or two years on the ground of emergency, they are now treated as permanent elements of the personal political program of the President. All the powers I shall name are additional powers over and above those which by law and usage had previously belonged to the President.

He has asked Congress to delegate to him the power to frame laws, enforceable by penal and civil penalties, governing wages, hours, prices, the control of production, the use of new inventions, the legal right to do business, and the commercial practice of all industries, trades and services in the United States. This power was granted by Congress for a period of from one to two years. The power to license was, I think, voluntarily renounced at the end of one year. But all the other powers, in substance, the power to bring all industry under Federal laws enacted by the President, have never been renounced.

I am not talking, mind you, about whether the objectives of N.R.A. were good or bad. I am talking about the fact that the National Industrial Recovery act called for a delegation of personal power by which the President, or his agents, could enact Federal laws affecting manufacturing, trade, the service industries, and to some degree even the arts and professions. Taken in conjunction with the powers granted in the Agricultural Adjustment act as they affected the processors of farm products, it may be said that the power to legislate for the whole economic organization of the United States was from 1933 to 1935 vested in the President of the United States. This power has been struck down by the Supreme Court. But the President has never deleted the demand for this power from his personal political program.

He has asked and obtained from Congress the delegation of its constitutional power to regulate the value of money, and that power is today exercised not by an independent monetary authority, but by his personal appointees. Now I have no doubt that Congress is unable to exercise directly its constitutional power to regulate the value of money, that a popular assembly is incapable of determining the correct price of gold or the proper volume of credit, or the desirable rate of interest, and that this power has to be delegated. All I am concerned with here is to point out that this crucial power over the incomes of every person has been delegated, not to an independent authority such as the Federal Reserve Board was designed to be, but to the Treasury and the Federal Reserve Board, as in effect, agents of the President.

He has asked and obtained the blanket power to distribute funds through what is in effect a special Presidential budget equal to the total budget of the government when he was inaugurated, and under legal powers which are virtually undefined, and when defined have in important respects been circumvented or ignored. By his own personal discretion the President allocates to states, municipalities, government bureaus and to individuals several billions of dollars. He has used it to dig canals and to produce plays and to publish books and to finance political propaganda and even to strengthen the Army and the Navy. Some of these projects have been excellent. I am glad the Army and Navy have been strengthened in these troubled times. But I am concerned to point out that the historic rule that the representative assembly shall control the expenditure of public money, has been suspended in respect to about half the Federal budget.

He has asked, though he has not yet been granted, the authority to reorganize and to redistribute the powers of the executive branch of the government. Considered on its merits, as a proposal made under the normal condition of effective checks and balances in the government, this seems to me in principle desirable. But in view of all the other powers which Mr. Roosevelt seeks to vest in the Presidency, it has a cumulative significance which cannot be ignored. It substitutes for the statutory organization of the executive branch of the government the personal organization of the President.

He has asked, though he has not yet been granted, the authority to bring the quasi-judicial independent commissions within the administrative orbit of his own personally appointed Cabinet officers. While the intention to control the judicial functions of these commissions is denied, it is admitted that their administrative and executive functions are to be brought under the direction of the President.

He has asked, but has been denied by the Supreme Court, the power to dismiss members of these independent commissions whose views do not run with his own.

Thus he has asked Congress to delegate to him the legislative power over economic affairs, the legislative power of appropriation in respect to half the budget, the legislative power to define the statutory functions of the executive branch of the government, the administrative control of the independent quasi-judicial commissions, and he has asked the Supreme Court, in the Humphrey case, to consent to his control over the personnel and over the opinions of the independent commissions.

In so far as Congress has consented to this colossal delegation of personal power, it was moved originally by a patriotic conviction that extraordinary measures were necessary to deal with an emergency and its scruples were satisfied by the assurance that these powers were for a limited period of time and for use in the emergency.

But since the summer of 1935, when the emergency had clearly been overcome, a new situation has arisen. By creating the most powerful political machine that has ever existed in the history of this country, the immense powers granted to the President for the emergency have been employed to perpetuate those powers. That machine is equipped with funds, with patronage, with the power to give and to withhold privileges in every community, down to the smallest hamlet in the land. In practically every state in the union it exercises the power of political life and death over governors, mayors, county officials, Senators and Representatives, and it controls by means of direct subsidies or favor of one kind and another large compact organized minorities in almost every constituency.

The Mayor of the City of New York, for example, is dependent directly upon Washington for the success of his own political career: without the grants, loans, and doles which come from Washington, he would be compelled either to practice a most unpopular economy or to impose most unpopular taxes. The same is true of the Governor of the State of New York, and I have no doubt it is true of most governors and most mayors. The net effect is that the local political organizations throughout the country have become subordinate branches of the President's personal political organization, and it is an exceptionally bold politician indeed who can stand out against it.

Thus the extraordinary powers delegated by Congress to the President have been used and are being used to pack the Congress with men who would not dare, and in fact would not wish, to restore the normal balance of power between Congress and the President. To such a degree are we now living under a personally packed Congress that the chairman of the Judiciary Committee of the Senate has publicly announced, as if it were very funny, that he has no convictions on any public question, and that he changes his deepest convictions when he is ordered to change them. To such a point has the personal domination of Congress been carried that the President actually attached to his message on the judiciary the text of the bill he requires Congress to pass.

That bill was introduced by a Congressman who never read it, and it now bears his name, and Senators who have dared to call their souls their own by opposing the bill have seen their own states invaded by the manager of the Presidential machine, and have had notice served on their local supporters, that the bill is a party measure and that opposition is disloyalty to the party.

Yet this party measure, which a Democrat can oppose only at the risk of his political life, is a direct violation of the platform adopted by the Democratic party last June. This party measure was decided on by the President personally after an election in which his spokesmen expressly denied that he intended to make such a proposal. It was adopted as a party measure without consulting the Cabinet or the party leaders in Congress, and though it would unquestionably be defeated if the Senators were free to vote their convictions, the attempt is being made to drive it thru by the overwhelming pressure of the Presidential machine. Thus the personal decision of one man has become superior to the pledges adopted by the representative assembly of his own party, and Senators who remain true to the pledges of their own party are treated as rebels who are to be punished.

The avowed objective of this measure is the domination of the only remaining independent branch of the government. The judiciary bill is not a proposal to amend the Constitution. It is not a proposal to restrict or to regulate the power of judicial review. It is not a proposal to provide for the regular retirement of justices and the regular infusion of younger judges. It is a proposal to vest in this President the power to make six personal appointments. Under this bill if Mr. Roosevelt appointed six men no older than Mr. Justice Story, who ascended the bench at the age of thirty-two, the majority of the court would represent the personal philosophy of one man for nearly forty years.

And what is the personal philosophy of that one man? What is to be the constitutional philosophy of the six new judges? It is to be, as we learned in Mr. Roosevelt's fireside chat, that the general welfare clause of the Constitution should give the Federal government authority to do whatever it deems desirable for the general welfare. Thus we are confronted with a proposal to make a new Supreme Court which will be dominated by judges who believe that the Federal government has power to do anything which Congress considers conducive to the general welfare. This is no proposal to liberalize the court. For no liberal justice has ever believed that the general welfare clause means what Mr. Roosevelt says it means, that it is a blanket grant of power. This is a proposal to suspend the very essence of constitutional government. For anyone can read anything he likes into the phrase "general welfare," and so in place of a Federal government of limited powers, we are asked to consent to a government in which the ruling majority of Congress, as directed by the President, is sovereign without limitations in American affairs.

I ask you to consider this program as a whole and to ask yourselves soberly and searchingly whether it must not be described as the decline of democracy and the rise of personal government. I know that the President and his partisans say that they have a mandate from the people, that they carried forty-six states and polled 27 million votes. But I say that they have no mandate from the people for this program, that they never disclosed it to the people, that they were careful not to submit it to the people, and that this can be proved by the record. They were asked during the campaign whether they intended to revive the N. R. A. When the President's son was reported as saying that they intended to do this, the reports were denied. They were asked whether they intended to seize control of the Supreme Court. The chairman of the Senate Judiciary Committee indignantly denied it. When they went before the people from June to November they gave the voters to understand that the emergency was virtually passed, and that the reforms of the second Administration would be carried out under the normal checks and balances of the American political system. It is only since the election that we have learned that the whole collection of emergency powers are to be revived and perpetuated by overthrowing the resistance of the Supreme Court. And we are told that this epoch-making change in the basic character of the government is to be carried out by a margin of eight or ten votes obtained from Senators who do not dare to vote as they believe. That, ladies and gentlemen, is not American democracy as we have known it. It is a bloodless, deviously legalized *coup d'état.*

The implications of this change are as yet understood only by a minority of the American people, and I have no doubt that the President's supporters are right when they tell us that a sizeable majority of the voters are quite content with it. That does not seem to me a sufficient excuse. I do not think that the popularity of the man is a good enough reason for changing the fundamental character of a government. For I hold it to be the duty of public men to guard the institutions of their country, and not to induce the people to consent, unwittingly and without full consideration, to deep and fundamental changes in their national life.

To vest virtually unlimited powers, hitherto reserved to the states, in the Federal government, to delegate those powers to the President and to nullify judicial review is, in fact, a radical change in the inner substance of the American government. While this change may be popular for a time, the day is bound to come when the people will need the protection of their institutions, only to find to their dismay that those institutions no longer exist.

Suppose it were true that Mr. Roosevelt is capable of exercising the personal supremacy which his program calls for. What of it? Do we have any assurance that all his successors will be as benevolent as he is? If such power is to be concentrated in the President—the power of the states, the legislative power of Congress, the power of the purse, and the judicial power, is there any doubt that to possess such transcendent power must become the fierce and intransigent and dominating ambition of our whole political existence? For such great power as that, men, factions, parties, regions and classes will fight to the bitter end. This is the road to hell, and while there is no doubt that it is paved from one end to the other with good intentions, Americans have always had the political wisdom jealously to refuse to concentrate supreme power in any man or in any branch of government.

I said at the outset that I do not regard this swift and far-reaching development of personal government as something deliberately conceived by sinister ambition. Though I think it is shocking that the Administration does not see the dangers and change its course, I am entirely convinced that the moving cause is not personal ambition and that there is no taint of conspiracy in it. I ascribe the development to a sincere progressivism in men who have lost their constitutional bearings during a great social crisis, and have now become so enchanted with the end that they no longer consider the means.

The question we must ask ourselves is why the American political system proved to be so inadequate in the crisis that sincere and loyal men feel that they have to consent to this profoundly un-American kind of personal government. The answer to that, I think, is that all the organs of American government had become seriously devitalized and impaired before the crisis broke, and that is why we have fallen into personal government.

We may begin with the Executive. Over a generation, but particularly since the war, the function of the Executive has been greatly enlarged and greatly complicated. These new functions called for a trained and unpolitical Civil Service under a policy-making cabinet. But though we enlarged the function of government, we failed to develop the necessary Civil Service. The result of that has been that the department heads who make up the Cabinet have been so preoccupied with administration that they are unable to act collectively as makers of policy. The effect has been to concentrate in the President the whole burden of deciding policy. And since policy is inseparable from administration, the President has become personally responsible for the whole vast executive function. He does not really have colleagues. He has only subordinates, and the lines of authority all run loosely but directly to him personally. This is more personal power than any man can exercise. But the worst effect of it is to persuade the people, the politicians, and the President himself, that they must look to him for personal decisions on all important matters.

President Wilson, who was a deep student of government, did manage to delegate and fix responsibility outside himself. But President Hoover never understood that the executive power cannot be exercised by one man, and President Roosevelt has not understood it either. Mr. Hoover delegated almost nothing of importance, and he was overwhelmed by his responsibilities. Mr. Roosevelt does delegate. But rarely does he delegate to responsible officials. The policy-making function is exercised by informal advisers who are accountable only to the President personally. So far has this been carried that the only members of the Cabinet who can be said to exercise real responsibility are the Secretary of State and the Secretary of Agriculture. The policy of economic appeasement through the lowering of tariff barriers is Secretary Hull's policy, and Secretary Wallace is, I believe, in fact the prime mover in agricultural policy. But for the rest the President does not have any recognized responsible advisers on high questions of public policy. His advisers are those whom he personally chooses to consult, those who happen from time to time to enjoy his personal sympathy. Thus no one thinks of the Secretary of the Treasury as the responsible adviser in fiscal policy, or of the Secretary of Commerce as the responsible advisor on policy toward business, or of the Attorney-General on matters of law. Above all, no one thinks of the Cabinet as having any collective responsibility. The advisers of the President are not the Cabinet, they are not even the responsible heads of the departments. They are individuals who have no responsibility except to the President personally.

Both because this system aggrandizes the individual who happens to be President, because it isolates him on an impossible eminence, and because it is so disorderly that only arbitrary decisions can untangle it, this method of governing prepares the rise of personal government. The remedy is the creation of a Civil Service presided over by a responsible cabinet which is the collective adviser of the President. The Executive is one of the coordinate branches of the government. But owing to the fact that the Civil Service is undeveloped and that the Cabinet has withered away, the executive power has become concentrated in the White House, and it is now regarded as the personal enterprise of the man who happens to be President.

The vitality of Congress has also been profoundly impaired, chiefly, I believe, because Congress has been intellectually corrupted by a false conception of the function of a representative assembly. This false conception goes back to the beginning. Congress has thought of itself as the initiator of laws, particularly of laws appropriating money and bestowing privileges, such as tariff rates and public works. But that is not the true function of a representative assembly. Its function, particularly in regard to money—and most legislation involves money—is to control expenditure, to grant, or to refuse to grant, the funds and the powers which the Executive asks. The principle was established more than two hundred years ago in the English parliament. We have just begun to adopt it under the name of an executive budget.

An executive budget means that Congress can refuse or reduce the appropriations the Executive asks for, but that it cannot increase them, and that it cannot initiate new expenditures without imposing new taxes to cover them. Only under this system can an elected representative cease to be a broker between his constituents who want favors and those who have the power to dispense favors.

Until recent years the power to dispense favors has resided in Congress itself, and the standing of a representative with the politicians at home, and with organized self-seeking minorities, has depended upon his ability to wangle and logroll material favors out of Congress itself. This task occupied so much of his energy that little was left for statesmanlike deliberation on public questions. It called for so many compromises of his convictions that he had ceased to be free to deliberate. The result was that statesmen could rarely hope to be nominated, and (if they devoted themselves to public matters) could rarely hope to be re-elected. By the law of the survival of the fittest, those who survived were those who served the pressure groups rather than the public interest.

In the crisis of 1932-33 the demoralization of Congress by pressure groups had reached a point where their discordant clamor had made Congress incapable of acting decisively in the national interest. Representative government was paralyzed and impotent, and since the emergency had to be dealt with, it became necessary to suspend the deliberative functions of Congress and to place Congress under the strict discipline of the President.

This had to be done because the preoccupation of individual Congressmen with patronage and privilege and subsidies had overwhelmed their function as members of representative assembly. In the midst of a crisis they had become incapable of acting as a coordinate branch of the government, and under the spur of grim necessity they had to be made subordinate in order that they would cease to obstruct.

The restoration of the vitality of Congress can come only through a purge which will remove patronage and pork from Congressional control. That means a real Civil Service and a true executive budget. When Congressmen can no longer obtain patronage and pork, the kind of Congressman who is an expert in obtaining patronage and pork, but is otherwise uninterested in public questions, will no longer be the politician who survives most successfully.

Finally, we must recognize that in the past fifty years the vitality of the states, as organs of a Federal system, has been deeply impaired. Their authority to regulate business and to provide social services has been so severely restricted by a line of decisions of the Supreme Court, that at last only the Federal government has seemed capable of exercising the police power. These decisions, generally under the due process clause of the Fourteenth Amendment, were inspired, I suppose, by a nationalist sentiment following the Civil war that the progress of the national economy must not be interfered with by local sovereignties. Since the Civil war the reaction against states' rights was extreme among the Republican judges, among the judges whose convictions had been formed in the struggle against slavery and disunion.

The balance of powers in a federal system is always a delicate one. In the reaction which followed the Civil war that balance was dangerously upset, and the Republicans who now proclaim the virtues of states' rights need to be reminded that they are responsible for the impairment of the majority of the states. Not until the dissenting justices, beginning with the great Holmes, began to speak, has the pendulum begun to swing back. It has been swinging back during the past ten years. Only now can it be said that the dissenters have become a bare and uncertain majority of the court. That task of reconstruction is, however, just begun, and if we are to escape the centralization of all powers in Washington, we cannot too quickly or resolutely restore the powers of the states. In the meantime the dominant party in the United States is led by men who no longer believe that it is possible or desirable to restore the federal character of the government. The present Democratic leadership is as scornful of states' rights as were the radical Republicans in the generation after the Civil war, and once again the unhappy ghost of Thaddeus Stevens walks in the land. It must be admitted that the radical Republicanism of the post-Civil war period was provoked by the application of states' rights to the point where it disunited the nation. It must also be admitted that the radical Democracy of the New Dealers has been provoked by the cumulative frustration of the police power of the states.

Now it is easy enough to understand why progressive men who have been frustrated in their attempts at regulation and reform in the states should have lost patience with the federal system itself, and should be demanding what is in effect the abolition of federalism. But I hold that it is the duty of the President and of Congress not to let provocation determine their policy, and that the true remedy is the restoration of federalism, not its abolition. Thus, though I am irreconcilably opposed to the proposed plan for reorganizing the federal judiciary, I am perfectly clear in my own mind that the court must overrule its own decisions where they rob the states of their police power.

For I am satisfied that the growing complexity of American economic life makes more necessary, not less necessary a vitally efficient federal form of government. Just because the economy requires more regulation than it did a hundred years ago, it is impracticable and dangerous to concentrate the regulative power in one centralized government. For there remain, in spite of all the big national business corporations decisive local differences in the standards of life, in the productivity of labor, in the efficiency of capital. It is impossible to fix one price or one wage rate or one rule about hours of labor for the whole United States. It is impossible to provide identical social services or to impose standardized education requirements, or to insist upon the same commercial practice throughout this continental domain. And while it is undoubtedly true that more of our affairs require national legislation than formerly, and that very many of them require more nearly uniform legislation, it is certain that if we did not have a federal system, we should have to reinvent it. Our real task is to restore it.

My conviction that federalism is not the obsolete doctrine from a horse-and-buggy age but is, on the contrary, a vital political principle for the future, is confirmed by what we see of the development of constitutionalism in Britain. In the horse-and-buggy age the government at Westminster was sovereign throughout the British Empire. Today in the age of the radio and electricity and the airplane, there are three autonomous parliaments in the British Isles, there is an autonomous federal system in Canada and another in Australia, there is an autonomous parliament in South Africa and in New Zealand, not to mention Egypt and India. So when I hear that federalism has been rendered obsolete by modern inventions and the evolution of big business, I am unconvinced. For what I see is that the latest constitutional developments of the freest people in the world is not away from but toward that very federal principle which we have inherited.

Not long ago, in fact just before the President's plan for reorganizing the Supreme Court was disclosed, Senator Borah made an eloquent speech saying that what the American people needed was to be rebaptized in the principles of constitutional liberty. To that I have tried to contribute this evening, first by recalling the degree in which constitutionalism has given away to personal government, and then by seeking to indicate the vital points at which the constitutional vitality of the Executive, of Congress, and of the separate states has been impaired.

It is not necessary, I think, to exhort this audience gathered in the Maryland Free State about how necessary constitutionalism is to the preservation of human dignity. You understand, and need not be told, that men can live with dignity and security only under a constitutional government, and that personal government, however benevolent in intention, is in the end always arbitrary, capricious, corrupt, and impermanent. You have come to realize, I believe as I have, reluctantly, skeptically, but at last clearly, that we are faced—now—with the choice between the restoration of constitutional government and a rapid descent into personal government. And that now, before it is too late, we have to make our stand and fight for the fundamental liberties of the American people.

# Stopping Propaganda[3]

## Dorothy Thompson

*Born July 9, 1894, Lancaster, NY; died January 30, 1961; speaker, New York Woman Suffrage campaign, 1915-17; foreign correspondent,* Philadelphia Public Ledger *and* New York Evening Post, *1920-28; writer,* On the Record *syndicated newspaper column, 1941-58; author,* The Courage to Be Happy *(1957).*

### Editor's introduction

On May 9, 1939, Dorothy Thompson, women's suffrage advocate, foreign press correspondent, and radio commentator, broadcast this address, over radio, to the American Federation of Women's Clubs. Concerned that departments of government were spending taxpayers' dollars merely to perpetuate their own existence, Thompson insisted they return to the more defensible function of providing services to America's public.

---

We are certainly more governed by propaganda than we have ever been in our lifetimes. The propaganda departments of governments are at least as important as their foreign offices and, if reports are to be credited, cost hundreds of millions.

The idea that governments should use the money of the taxpayers to sell themselves to their own people is now so generally accepted that nobody seems to get wrought up about it, even when those governments are democratic governments, like our own. Before the war, the Counsel on Public Relations—which is just a flossy name for a press agent—was unknown in our own government. Today Washington is full of ex-newspaper men attached to every conceivable government agency, whose job it is to prepare hand-outs for the press—little pamphlets, brochures, and even quite handsome books, at the government's expense to tell the people who did or didn't elect them to do a job, just how well they are doing it.

Our Department of Agriculture used once to confine its printed matter entirely to telling farmers how to deal with hoof and mouth disease, how to grow chickens and make them pay, what sort of fertilizer to put on acid soil and what kind would reduce alkalinity and a thousand other sorts of education useful to the farmer.

But now part of its effort is expended to "sell" the Department's policy. We used to think that the voters were capable of judging an administration by its fruits, but that is very old-fashioned indeed. Even the Relief Administration has press agents attached to all its various branches throughout the country, although you would think that if there was anything that didn't require advertising it was Santa Claus.

It has always seemed to me that it was the business of a political party to advertise its program, and, if that party is in power, to advertise the results of that program, out of its own party funds, and not to use the money of the taxpayers, who may belong to the opposite party, to "sell" themselves to the voters. Because, obviously, if an administration can draw on the tax funds for promotion purposes, it has an enormous advantage over its opponents.

In any country where there is a free press, the use of the tax funds for the promotion of an administration is necessarily limited in its scope. But in the dictatorships, where they not only control the biggest advertising budgets ever heard of in history but the press and radio as well, the propaganda department becomes second in importance only to the police. The two most important individuals in Germany, for instance, are Himmler and Goebbels. Herr Himmler is in charge of the Gestapo, the fa-

[3]Broadcast to the American Federation of Women's Clubs, on May 9, 1939.

mous secret police which terrorizes the people into obedience, and Mr. Goebbels is in charge of talking them into obedience. Under the dictatorships government propaganda is just as important in controlling the things that are *not* said, as the things that *are* said. Just now, all of Europe is engaged in a gigantic struggle which in its immediate phase takes the form of a war of nerves. The business of the propaganda department is not only to keep the populace enthusiastic about the government, but to keep it from knowing any unpleasant facts, such as what the national debt and deficit is, and what the external dangers are. Because if the people knew in any general way in what a really bad way they are, heaven knows what might happen to the government.

All dictatorships know that their greatest menace is a free press and free discussion. You have probably noticed that in his last two speeches Hitler has raved against the world press and even accused it of trying to start a world war. The reason for his rage is that no country can be completely severed from the world. Very few Germans can read English or French, but some can; and some English and French publications get into Germany, and so do foreign broadcasts. And what happens is that the people, who are sick and tired of government propaganda, listen to anything that comes from outside with considerably more credulousness than they do to what comes from their own government. On the other hand, nations which *have* free discussion are subjected to a much greater nervous strain, perhaps, than nations which know nothing, or nearly nothing. The democracies have the jitters because they are aware of the dangers. The dictatorships argue that what the people don't know won't hurt them, and that ignorance is bliss.

But this, also, is only true up to a point. When the people begin to see all about them the evidences of collapse, and at the same time to realize that they are being kept in complete ignorance of the facts, they begin to have an awful feeling of impotent rage and despair. There is nothing more demoralizing than sudden, overwhelming disillusionment. That is why it is always wiser for governments to tell the people the exact truth, even if that truth be painful, than to lead them on in a doped condition, until, at last, the truth is realized all at once.

Some of you may remember that we once had a great boom in this country—in the years 1924 to 1929. There were plenty of people then who knew that the boom was very artificial; that we were actually in a happy delirium of inflation, and some of those people wanted the government to warn the country. But most people in the government thought that telling the truth would be bad for business and would create demoralization. So they kept on spreading optimism, and when the crash came it was all the worse because people had not been expecting it at all.

I admit that to tell the truth is not popular. In the world as it is at present, the truth is not at all pleasant. It happens to be our fate to live in one of those titanic periods of history which are really revolutionary, when the whole structure of society is undergoing profound change; one of those periods when a great many things come to a head—mistakes and crimes and accumulated discontent, whenever the results of man's genius—his science and invention—add a disturbing element.

Everyone naturally wants peace and quiet and the prospect of a nice comfortable life, and anyone who tells him that he is not in the least likely to get it in his lifetime, and that, on the contrary, he must plan to live with the greatest intelligence and self-sacrifice and not expect very much for himself but must try to make a decent world for his grandchildren—anyone who tells him that is likely to be called a calamity howler or a Cassandra. However, in my experience, the people who have the courage to face facts are those who achieve the greatest inner peace.

One can never stop all propaganda, because in one sense all ideas are propaganda. The other day I listened to a discussion of whether propaganda had any place in art, and one man said that freedom from propaganda was the test of art. But I think that is nonsense. The greatest poets who ever lived wrote propaganda—they wrote to further a way of life or a philosophy of life in which they believed. St. Paul was a propagandist, but that doesn't dismiss the thirteenth chapter of first Corinthians. Shakespeare was the greatest of all propagandists for the aristocratic spirit. Walt Whitman was a great poet and a great propagandist for democracy.

All propagators of ideas are propagandists, and in this sense we are all, constantly, subjected to propaganda. What we need most is to be able to distinguish between kinds of propaganda. And, above all, we ought to be able to trace the sources of propaganda.

Just now, for instance, we are being subjected to an enormous amount of propaganda from foreign countries. That propaganda is concentrated, in the first place, upon influencing our foreign policy. Some of it is very subtle and some of it is very crude; some of it is quite open, and some of it is hidden. But what we ought to bear in mind is that our foreign policy is bound to be in harmony with some portion of this propaganda. Let me give you an illustration: One part of our own population want us to make a common front with Great Britain and France in resisting aggression. In case of war they want us to refuse to sell arms and even essential raw materials to aggressors and to aid the nations which are defending themselves. Inasmuch as Great Britain and France and some of the small countries of Central Europe have no intention of starting a war, but are very much afraid that they will be warred upon, these nations are making propaganda for this policy. But that does not mean that all the people who are advocating the policy are victims of British propaganda.

In the same way, the Germans and Italians and others of the so-called dynamic nations who intend to expand on this earth by fair means or foul, are extremely anxious that the United States should be neutral in *their* sense of the word—that we should give no aid or comfort of any kind to any nation defending itself. So the Germans are making an enormous propaganda in this country in favor of isolation. But that does not mean that all the people who are isolationists are the victims of German propaganda.

Mr. Stimson believes in collective security and in the first policy, so some stupid people are saying he is pro-British. Professor Beard believes in the second, so some stupid people are saying he is pro-German. Both are honest men, making up their minds according to the best of their knowledge, quite regardless of whether one or another foreign government has the same idea.

There is, of course, another kind of foreign propaganda which is very vicious. It is the foreign propaganda which conceals its source altogether. For instance, at this moment the German government is flooding this country with anti-Semitic literature designed to work up popular feeling against the Jews. The reason that they are doing it is to divide and confuse public opinion here. They never indicate on all the little leaflets that are sent out where they come from. And hiding themselves under anonymity or with fake names of petty organizations that they have captured or set up for their own purposes, they are spreading maliciously untrue statements. People are being told that this country is being flooded with refugees. Actually, this is pure and simple malicious propaganda and not in the least in harmony with the facts. The facts are that the American immigration quotas have not been extended at all, while the conditions under which one can get a quota number have been made more rigorous. Only 42,685 persons entered the United States last year from all the countries of the world, although 153,774 were entitled to come under the quota laws; and in the six years from 1932 to 1938, 4,487 more aliens left this country than were admitted under the immigration laws.

Whenever we get a pamphlet or leaflet designed to influence our opinions, we ought to ask: "Who is responsible for this information?" If it is anonymous, we ought to throw it into the wastebasket right away. If it is not, we ought to ask: "What is this organization? Who is in it? Is he reputable?" And if one cannot find the answer to *that* question, we ought to throw it into the wastebasket. And, finally, we must always ask two more questions: "What is the purpose of this propaganda? And: Are the facts in it true?"

I happen to believe with Lincoln that you can fool some of the people all of the time and all of the people some of the time, but not all of the people all of the time.

In the long run, even the dictatorships will learn that—to their own awful undoing. For there is nothing that so arouses the resentment of people as the realization that they have been lied to and fooled. The first business of any democracy is to protect the Truth—for the protection of the Truth is the protection of itself.

# The New Frontier[4]

## John F. Kennedy

*Born May 29, 1917, Brookline, MA; died November 22, 1963; B.S., Harvard University, 1940; U.S. Navy, 1941-45; representative (D) from Massachusetts, 1946-52; senator (D) from Massachusetts, 1953-60; president of the United States, 1960-63; author,* Why England Slept *(1940),* Profiles in Courage *(1956),* A Nation of Immigrants *(1959),* America, the Beautiful *(1964).*

### Editor's introduction

With this speech, John F. Kennedy accepted the Democratic Party's nomination for the presidency of the United States, having received 806 votes to Lyndon Johnson's 409. In this acceptance speech, Kennedy envisioned government as walking hand in hand with the American people towards "unknown opportunities and perils." In effect, he challenged the American people to face this frontier of change and revolution under the leadership of their government, and in the face of a growing Communist presence.

---

With a deep sense of duty and high resolve, I accept your nomination.

I accept it with a full and grateful heart—without reservation—and with only one obligation—the obligation to devote every effort of body, mind and spirit to lead our party back to victory and our nation back to greatness.

I am grateful, too, that you have provided me with such an eloquent statement of our party's platform. Pledges which are made so eloquently are made to be kept. "The Rights of Man"—the civil and economic rights essential to the human dignity of all men—are indeed our goal and our first principles. This is a platform on which I can run with enthusiasm and conviction.

And I am grateful, finally, that I can rely in the coming months on so many others—on a distinguished running-mate who brings unity to our ticket and strength to our platform, Lyndon Johnson—on one of the most articulate statesmen of our time, Adlai Stevenson—on a great spokesman for our needs as a nation and a people, Stuart Symington—and on that fighting campaigner whose support I welcome, President Harry S. Truman.

I feel a lot safer now that they are on my side again. And I am proud of the contrast with our Republican competitors. For their ranks are apparently so thin that not one challenger has come forth with both the competence and the courage to make theirs an open convention.

I am fully aware of the fact that the Democratic party, by nominating someone of my faith, has taken on what many regard as a new and hazardous risk—new, at least, since 1928. But I look at it this way: the Democratic party has once again placed its confidence in the American people, and in their ability to render a free, fair judgment. And you have, at the same time, placed your confidence in me, and in my ability to render a free, fair judgment—to uphold the Constitution and my oath of office—and to reject any kind of religious pressure or obligation that might directly or indirectly interfere with my conduct of the presidency in the national interest. My record of fourteen years supporting public education—supporting complete separation of church and state—and resisting pressure from any source on any issue should be clear by now to everyone.

I hope that no American, considering the really critical issues facing this country, will waste his franchise by voting either for me or against me solely on account of my religious affiliation. It is not relevant, I want to stress, what some

[4]Delivered in acceptance of the Democratic nomination for the presidency of the United States, at the Democratic National Convention, in Los Angeles, California, on July 15, 1960.

other political or religious leader may have said on this subject. It is not relevant what abuses may have existed in other countries or in other times. It is not relevant what pressures, if any, might conceivably be brought to bear on me. I am telling you now what you are entitled to know: that my decisions on every public policy will be my own—as an American, a Democrat and a free man.

Under any circumstances, however, the victory we seek in November will not be easy. We all know that in our hearts. We recognize the power of the forces that will be aligned against us. We know they will invoke the name of Abraham Lincoln on behalf of their candidate—despite the fact that his political career has often seemed to show charity toward none and malice for all.

We know that it will not be easy to campaign against a man who has spoken or voted on every known side of every known issue. Mr. Nixon may feel it is his turn now, after the New Deal and the Fair Deal—but before he deals, someone had better cut the cards.

That "someone" may be the millions of Americans who voted for President Eisenhower but balk at his would-be, self-appointed successor. For just as historians tell us that Richard I was not fit to fill the shoes of bold Henry II—and that Richard Cromwell was not fit to wear the mantle of his uncle—they might add in future years that Richard Nixon did not measure to the footsteps of Dwight D. Eisenhower.

Perhaps he could carry on the party policies—the policies of Nixon, Benson, Dirksen and Goldwater. But this nation cannot afford such a luxury. Perhaps we could afford a Coolidge following Harding. And perhaps we could afford a Pierce following Fillmore. But after Buchanan, this nation needed a Lincoln—after Taft we needed a Wilson—after Hoover we needed Franklin Roosevelt . . . . And after eight years of drugged and fitful sleep, this nation needs strong, creative Democratic leadership in the White House.

But we are not merely running against Mr. Nixon. Our task is not merely one of itemizing Republican failures. Nor is that wholly necessary. For the families forced from the farm will know how to vote without our telling them. The unemployed miners and textile workers will know how to vote. The old people without medical care—the families without a decent home—the parents of children without adequate food or schools—they all know that it's time for a change.

But I think the American people expect more from us than cries of indignation and attack. The times are too grave, the challenge too urgent, and the stakes too high—to permit the customary passions of political debate. We are not here to curse the darkness, but to light the candle that can guide us through that darkness to a safe and sane future. As Winston Churchill said on taking office some twenty years ago: if we open a quarrel between the present and the past, we shall be in danger of losing the future.

Today our concern must be with that future. For the world is changing. The old era is ending. The old ways will not do.

Abroad, the balance of power is shifting. There are new and more terrible weapons—new and uncertain nations—new pressures of population and deprivation. One third of the world, it has been said, may be free—but one third is the victim of cruel repression—and the other one third is rocked by the pangs of poverty, hunger and envy. More energy is released by the awakening of these new nations than by the fission of the atom itself.

Meanwhile, Communist influence has penetrated further into Asia, stood astride the Middle East and now festers some ninety miles off the coast of Florida. Friends have slipped into neutrality—and neutrals into hostility. As our keynoter reminded us, the President who began his career by going to Korea ends it by staying away from Japan.

The world has been close to war before—but now man, who has survived all previous threats to his existence, has taken into his mortal hands the power to exterminate the entire species some seven times over.

Here at home, the changing face of the future is equally revolutionary. The New Deal and the Fair Deal were bold measures for their generations—but this is a new generation.

A technological revolution on the farm has led to an output explosion—but we have not yet learned to harness that explosion usefully, while protecting our farmers' right to full parity income.

An urban population revolution has overcrowded our schools, cluttered up our suburbs, and increased the squalor of our slums.

A peaceful revolution for human rights—demanding an end to racial discrimination in all parts of our community life—has strained at the leashes imposed by timid executive leadership.

A medical revolution has extended the life of our elder citizens without providing the dignity and security those later years deserve. And a revolution of automation finds machines replacing men in the mines and mills of America, without replacing their income or their training or their need to pay the family doctor, grocer and landlord.

There has also been a change—a slippage—in our intellectual and moral strength. Seven lean years of drouth and famine have withered the field of ideas. Blight has descended on our regulatory agencies—and a dry rot, beginning in Washington, is seeping into every corner of America—in the payola mentality, the expense account way of life, the confusion between what is legal and what is right. Too many Americans have lost their way, their will and their sense of historic purpose.

It is time, in short, for a new generation of leadership—new men to cope with new problems and new opportunities.

All over the world, particularly in the newer nations, young men are coming to power—men who are not bound by the traditions of the past—men who are not blinded by the old fears and hates and rivalries—young men who can cast off the old slogans and delusions and suspicions.

The Republican nominee-to-be, of course, is also a young man. But his approach is as old as McKinley. His party is the party of the past. His speeches are generalities from *Poor Richard's Almanac.* Their platform, made up of left-over Democratic planks, has the courage of our old convictions. Their pledge is a pledge to the status quo—and today there can be no status quo.

For I stand tonight facing West on what was once the last frontier. From the lands that stretch three thousand miles behind me, the pioneers of old gave up their safety, their comfort and sometimes their lives to build a new world here in the West. They were not the captives of their own doubts, the prisoners of their own price tags. Their motto was not "every man for himself"—but "all for the common cause." They were determined to make that new world strong and free, to overcome its hazards and its hardships, to conquer the enemies that threatened from without and within.

Today some would say that those struggles are all over—that all the horizons have been explored—that all the battles have been won—that there is no longer an American frontier.

But I trust that no one in this vast assemblage will agree with those sentiments. For the problems are not all solved and the battles are not all won—and we stand today on the edge of a New Frontier—the frontier of the 1960's—a frontier of unknown opportunities and perils—a frontier of unfulfilled hopes and threats.

Woodrow Wilson's New Freedom promised our nation a new political and economic framework. Franklin Roosevelt's New Deal promised security and succor to those in need. But the New Frontier of which I speak is not a set of promises—it is a set of challenges. It sums up not what I intend to *offer* the American people, but what I intend to *ask* of them. It appeals to their pride, not their pocketbook—it holds out the promise of more sacrifice instead of more security.

But I tell you the New Frontier is here, whether we seek it or not. Beyond that frontier are uncharted areas of science and space, unsolved problems of peace and war, unconquered pockets of ignorance and prejudice, unanswered questions of poverty and surplus. It would be easier to shrink back from that frontier, to look to the safe mediocrity of the past, to be lulled by good intentions and high rhetoric—and those who prefer that course should not cast their votes for me, regardless of party.

But I believe the times demand invention, innovation, imagination, decision. I am asking each of you to be new pioneers on that New Frontier. My call is to the young in heart, regardless of age—to the stout in spirit, regardless of party—to all who respond to the Scriptural call: "Be strong and of good courage; be not afraid, neither be thou dismayed."

For courage—not complacency, is our need today—leadership—not salesmanship. And the only valid test of leadership is the ability to lead, and lead vigorously. A tired nation, said David Lloyd George, is a Tory nation—and the United States today cannot afford to be either tired or Tory.

There may be those who wish to hear more—more promises to this group or that—more harsh rhetoric about the men in the Kremlin—more assurances of a golden future, where taxes are always low and subsidies ever high. But my promises are in the platform you have adopted—our ends will not be won by rhetoric and we can have faith in the future only if we have faith in ourselves.

For the harsh facts of the matter are that we stand on this frontier at a turning-point in history. We must prove all over again whether this nation—or any nation so conceived—can long endure—whether our society—with its freedom of choice, its breadth of opportunity, its range of alternatives—can compete with the single-minded advance of the Communist system.

Can a nation organized and governed such as ours endure? That is the real question. Have we the nerve and the will? Can we carry through in an age where we will witness not only new breakthroughs in weapons of destruction—but also a race for mastery of the sky and the rain, the ocean and the tides, the far side of space and the inside of men's minds?

Are we up to the task—are we equal to the challenge? Are we willing to match the Russian sacrifice of the present for the future—or must we sacrifice our future in order to enjoy the present?

That is the question of the New Frontier. That is the choice our nation must make—a choice that lies not merely between two men or two parties, but between the public interest and private comfort—between national greatness and national decline—between the fresh air of progress and the stale, dank atmosphere of "normalcy"—between determined dedication and creeping mediocrity.

All mankind waits upon our decision. A whole world looks to see what we will do. We cannot fail their trust, we cannot fail to try.

It has been a long road from that first snowy day in New Hampshire to this crowded convention city. Now begins another long journey, taking me into your cities and homes all over America. Give me your help, your hand, your voice, your vote. Recall with me the words of Isaiah: "They that wait upon the Lord shall renew their strength; they shall mount up with wings as eagles; they shall run, and not be weary."

As we face the coming challenge, we too, shall wait upon the Lord, and ask that He renew our strength. Then shall we be equal to the test. Then we shall not be weary. And then we shall prevail.

# Presidential Campaign Speech[5]

## Barry Goldwater

*Born January 1, 1909, Phoenix, AZ; president, 1937-53, chairman of the board, Goldwater, Inc., 1953–; U.S. Army Air Force, 1941-45; chief of staff, Arizona National Guard, 1945-52; councilman, Phoenix city council, 1949-52; senator (R) from Arizona, 1953-64, 1969-87; republican candidate for president, 1964; author,* Why Not Victory *(1962),* The Conscience of the Majority *(1970),* Delightful Journey *(1970),* The Coming Breakpoint *(1976),* With No Apologies *(1979).*

### Editor's introduction

During the last days of his campaign for the presidency of the United States, Barry Goldwater gave this speech as his climax address of the campaign. Here, he defined the kind of government he would install if elected. Like Walter Lippmann before him, Goldwater, a noted conservative, opposed a federal government he saw as becoming ever "more powerful." In place of an expanded federal presence, Goldwater called for "free enterprise and individual liberty." For Goldwater, federal power meant the sacrifice of "daily freedom"—a sacrifice he described as contradicting the principles "on which this nation was founded."

---

I can't help wondering, sometimes, if you've asked yourselves why my campaign is what it is.

I wonder, my fellow Americans, if you think I don't know what views would be most popular. Do you think I don't know what labor wants to hear, what management wants to hear, what housewives and diplomats and white collar workers want to hear?

Do you honestly think, after all these years in politics, that I don't know the easy ways to get votes? The promises to make? The subjects to talk about—and the ones to avoid?

Well, I do!

Let me tell you—it's impossible to live in Washington these days and not learn these things.

Well, then, you ask why don't I take the easy way?

There are a couple of reasons. First of all, if I just went around telling people what they wanted to hear, I'd sound like Lyndon Baines Johnson. And I still think the American people are entitled to a choice.

But more important, if I had to cater to every special interest in the country to get elected, I wouldn't want the job.

If you ever hear me quoted in this campaign, saying soothing and comforting words about how wonderful everything is in the world and how secure the peace is and how strongly and firmly we stand as the leaders of Freedom—look again because somebody is kidding you!

If you ever hear me quoted as wildly and irresponsibly promising that wages will go up and prices down, that taxes will go down and spending up, that more and more power in the Federal Government means more and more freedom for the people—look again because somebody is kidding you!

If you ever hear me quoted as promising to make you free by forcibly bussing your children from your chosen neighborhood school to some other one just to meet an arbitrary racial quota—look again because somebody is kidding you!

Now let's get down to some basics.

I want to see an American nation and people that are healthy, sound, prosperous, free, se-

[5]Delivered during the 1964 campaign for the presidency of the United States, in New York, New York, on October 26, 1964.

cure, and progressive. I would hope that the interim President feels the same way.

The difference between us is that I say these things are best attained and furthered through the free enterprise and individual liberty upon which this nation was founded—the free enterprise and individual liberty that account for our growth to greatness.

I have a deep faith in the manhood of American men—and in American women.

There was a time when references to the principles that guided our founding fathers were considered the very essence of Americanism—when the style of freedom that Americans have fought and died for was considered the hope of the world.

If this is no longer true, then perhaps it is time for government by decree. Perhaps it is time to mold public opinion rather than ask for it. Perhaps it is time for the people to come straggling back inside the protective walls and settle down to squabbling over their shares of the public dole. As long as they're fed three times a day, they can always be reminded that they enjoy "freedom" from hunger.

You know, once before a great and self-governing people gave up their liberty—a liberty far less than ours. They put themselves in the hands of their leader, asking only to be fed and entertained. They traded their votes for "bread and circuses." They traded their Senate for an Emperor.

We call them Romans. They lost their nation when they traded away their freedom.

Let me refresh your memory about freedom. For thirty years your own government has been changing the meaning of the word. They began by telling us it meant freedom from want and fear. They have now begun to suggest that it means freedom from poverty and unemployment. Soon, no doubt, it will mean freedom from work, from responsibility—even from worry.

My friends, these are the rewards of freedom, not freedom itself. Never forget, there was only one freedom—only one freedom—on which this nation was founded. That was freedom from government—from too much, oppressive government.

Those now in power would like us to forget that the right guaranteed us all was not happiness, but the pursuit of happiness.

I ask you tonight, what is happening to us? Sometimes I think we should pity them because I'm not sure they know what they're doing. But it is a fact that Lyndon Johnson and his curious crew seem to believe that progress in this country is best served simply and directly through the ever-expanding gift power of the everlastingly growing Federal Government.

One thing we all know—and I assure you I do: that's a much easier way to get votes than my way. It always has been. It's political Daddyism and it's as old as demagogues and despotism.

You want something for nothing? The Federal Government will give it to you.

You want to avoid responsibility for bringing up your children and educating them? The Federal Government will take over.

You want to duck the job of facing your local problems and solving them? The Federal Government will do it for you.

Never mind the fact that the power and the money to do these things has to be taken from you before the Federal Government can do them for you. Every step in this direction is a loss of freedom for you!

Relax. Don't worry. The Federal Government will do for you all those things you find unpleasant to do for yourselves. And daily that government will grow more powerful. Daily it will enter new businesses and practices, new areas of private enterprise, where it has no place.

And daily its leaders will expand their power to buy your votes and elect their own successors. Yes, expand their power over you, the people, far beyond anything ever dreamed of by the framers of our Constitution. And daily freedom goes down the drain.

And always, they are driving and confusing you with the basic dishonesty that permeates so much political campaigning.

I speak of peace. Your interim President tells you I want to start a war—which is ridiculous, and you know it.

I speak of strengthening the Social Security system. Your interim President tells you I want to destroy it—which is ridiculous, and you know it.

I refer to the fundamental principles on which our great country was founded. My opposition tells you I am living in the past—which is ridiculous, and you know it.

When I demand a more discriminating and practical foreign aid policy, the word is that Barry Goldwater is an isolationist—which I'm not, and you know it. You know we need a more discriminating and practical foreign aid policy.

Well, my friends, a man—an intelligent man—can carry on this silly political double talk just so long. And it seems to me the voters can listen to just so much of it. And I think you're reaching the end of your rope.

I am determined to penetrate the smokescreen that's been placed between you and me the only way I know how—by continuing to stand straight and talk straight.

I do recognize that there is a natural, human wish in the hearts of some people to find relief from worry, from fear, from the responsibilities of being people.

It is this very wish that makes them surrender their initiative and their independence in return for empty promises.

Empty promises are cheap—and cheaper by the dozen.

I, for one, am an ordinary mortal who cannot bring himself to make these unkeepable promises. I believe that the things we must do can only be done by truly free people, governing themselves.

I want to see us do it that way. I'm not ready for the Federal Government to take over those things which we haven't yet done, or even tried. I am not yet prepared to say that our inner needs—the needs to be looked after and protected and shielded and mothered—are going to force us, as they have other peoples, to give to our central government in Washington the same kind of power from which we bravely revolted in the first place.

I believe in the great American Dream. I say we can be a people led but not driven—governed, but not ruled—organized, but not regimented—taxed, but not bled.

I believe we were right when we decided that freedom meant being free—and that freedom is an endowment—a gift from God—when we founded not a government, but a more perfect union.

I believe that the hope of the world rests not with the American Government—but with the American people.

And now, perhaps you'd like to have me do a little political forecasting for you. Everyone else has been doing it.

Let me begin by telling you about some of the votes I'm not going to get.

The Nazi and Fascist types—the bigots—are not going to vote for me because my grandfather was a Polish Jew. But do we want these votes?

The Communists and radical left-wingers are not going to vote for me because I don't believe we should let the Communists frighten us out of our freedom. But do we want these votes?

The lazy, dole-happy people who want to feed on the fruits of somebody else's labor won't vote for me. But do we want these votes?

The Socialist, ADA-type followers of Hubert Horatio Humphrey are not going to vote for me. The ones who don't care if the Social Security system goes bankrupt as long as it keeps making more and more unkeepable promises—the ones who are willing to believe that communism can be "accommodated." None of them will vote for me. But do we want these votes?

Now, may I tell you who, I believe, will vote for me?

People who take the trouble to reread, thoughtfully, the Declaration of Independence and the Constitution of the United States will vote for me. They're the people who realize that too much government, no matter how juicy the promises sound, is against their best interest.

People who have learned to be suspicious of never-ending promises of "something for nothing"—they will vote for me.

People who have the courage and the intelligence to listen to the truth, and think about it. People whose votes can't be bought. They'll vote for me.

People who are sick to death of politicians coming out in favor of happiness and declaring war on misery. People who are fed up with so-called leaders of government promising to legislate worry out of existence. People who will listen for a little while to such transparent, vote-grabbing demagoguery and say—"Baloney."

They'll vote for me.

But most of all, it will be the people who know that something must be done.

When our Central Intelligence Agency reports our international prestige is already below the peril point, something must be done. Johnson is stalling because elections are coming.

Consider that dragged-out disarmament conference, laboring under the grave danger of commitments without adequate safeguards of compliance. Something must be done.

Johnson has adjourned the conference until after the election.

Americans are dying in Vietnam. He sits tight and silent until after the election.

Critical questions face the General Assembly of the United Nations. Will Russia be made to pay her debts to the UN or will they be forgiven. Johnson has postponed the opening session until after the election.

Think of Bobby Baker, Matt McCloskey, Billie Sol Estes—the 150 quickie security clearances and other lax security practices disclosed by the Otepka Hearings. But Lyndon Johnson clamps on the lid until after the election.

The Defense Department, the State Department, the White House itself—they all might as well wear large signs saying "Closed Till after Election."

Not that they aren't busy. The Department of Defense has been busy announcing the success of some missile and radar projects begun under President Eisenhower's Administration. The State Department has been busy avoiding issues and postponing critical business. And the White House goes night and day, directing the strategy and making excuses—claiming credit for all that's good and pleading ignorance of all that's evil.

Our Government is in a state of moratorium until "after the election." And the office of President is being occupied, on a part-time basis, by the interim President, who's busy sweeping the business of his office under the rug with Bobby Baker, Billie Sol Estes, Matt McCloskey, and goodness knows what else, until after election.

What kind of a private club are these people running? Whose government is it anyway? I say it's yours, not theirs.

People who know that the White House goes begging for a full-time tenant, who know that it must be occupied by a President of the people, not by a wheeler-dealer—people who know that giveaway promises can't cover up a policy of drift, deception and defeat—these people are going to do something about it.

That means you.

One last question:

—If I said to you tonight that the Federal Government will tell you what business you can be in—what profits you can make—where you can be in business;

—If I tell you that the Federal Government will make decisions about schools and whether or not your child can pray in them; or if your child will attend a particular school to satisfy a slide rule quota;

—If I say to you that the Federal Government will make vital decisions about your children when they're young and your parents when they're old;

—If I tell you that the Federal Government will tell you how much to pay those you hire and what to charge for the things you sell;

—If I told you tonight that the Federal Government will deny you the other side of every right—such as the right not to associate, as well as the right to associate;

—If I told you all those things, what country would you think I was talking about?

Well, I'm talking about America! Today!

With God's blessing, let's get it back!

# Creativity in Law and Government[6]

Archibald Cox

*Born May 17, 1912, Plainfield, NJ; B.A., Harvard University, 1934; LL.B., Harvard Law School, 1937; lawyer, Ropes, Gray, Best, Coolidge & Rugg, 1938-41; attorney, Department of Justice, 1941-43; associate solicitor, Department of Labor, 1943-45; professor, Harvard Law School, 1946-65; solicitor general, Department of Justice, 1961-65; special Watergate prosecutor, 1973.*

## Editor's introduction

On October 29, 1973, because Archibald Cox defied President Nixon and insisted upon direct access to the Watergate tapes, Nixon arranged for Cox's dismissal from the job of special Watergate prosecutor. On January 22, 1974, in the speech reprinted below, Cox gave his much anticipated reaction to his dismissal. In doing so, Cox also provided what he believed to be the government's role and function in American society. Cox asserted that the government, and the laws which emanate from it, must counter the American people's "slide into general cynicism" by creating laws and "prescribing the procedures and forms of organization by which men and women may live and work together." Approaching the question of government's role as an academic, and not a politician, Cox envisioned the ideal function of government and law as a force committed to civility, employing "minimum force and [a] maximum of reason and respect for human personality."

---

At a time when World War II and the reconstruction of Europe were challenging the finest minds in the Western world Jean Paul Monnet, the great French economist and statesman, asked an American friend:

"Will you please explain to me why the men whom I regard as the most effective—the most fruitful, the most creative—are lawyers."

Not all agree. Sir Thomas More wrote that in Utopia

"They have no lawyers among them, for they consider [lawyers] as a sort of person whose profession it is to disguise matters, and to wrest the laws."

Utopia achieved there would indeed be no need for lawyers, nor for doctors—and perhaps not for butchers, bakers or candlestick makers. But until then lawyers are surely required, and I take enough pride in the best men of my profession to think that Jean Paul Monnet's observation upon the creativity of lawyers, stripped of invidious comparisons, was perceptive and correct. My plan this evening is to try to describe the creativity of lawyers, to carry the ideas over into government, and then to speculate about the sources of creativity in both areas but chiefly in government.

Of course the creativity of the lawyer is not that of the artist, the poet, the musician, or even the novelist, although one of the lawyer's tools, like the novelist's, is words. The challenging sphere of the men of law is formulating the rules and prescribing the procedures and forms of organization by which men and women may live and work together. Every practicing lawyer, whether he deals in constitutional issues, advice to corporations, collective labor agreements or wills and family relations is concerned with the concepts, the institutions, the rules and forms of organization that channel human endeavor. Lawyers are undoubtedly wordsmiths, for words are the tools for expressing intellectual concepts—concepts not emotions—with the degree of exactness and consistency necessary to rules by which persons can guide their activities in relation to each other and which, in appropriate cases, society can enforce.

[6]Delivered at Amherst College, in Amherst, Massachusetts, on January 22, 1974. Reprinted with permission of Archibald Cox.

I do not mean to leave the impression that the intellectual side of the law—the side that many students view as nit-picking and logic-chopping—is the whole story. The words and concepts the skilled lawyer finds so delightful as tools, must never become the master. The law's concern is men and women, their daily lives, their joys and sorrows, their fears and aspirations, their mean pursuits and high adventures. Without sympathetic understanding of life, perhaps without understanding the persons with whom he deals better than they understand themselves, a lawyer is not worthy of the name. But in the end he must work in intellectual terms, with reasoned analysis, concepts and words, because he deals chiefly in rules written either for private individuals seeking to order their future relations or by government in the form of law. Others understand human lives and activities as well as and often better than lawyers. The lawyer's uniquely professional contribution comes on the intellectual side in developing and articulating the forms of organization, procedures and other rules necessary to bring some degree of ordered cooperation, and therefore opportunity, to the affairs of men.

A few examples may illustrate my meaning.

The economic base of our society is mass production and transportation of goods and mass consumption. The development of both depended upon lawyers' ingenuity. Mass production and mass transportation depend upon the aggregation of the individual assets of many people, upon pooled and borrowed capital, and the pooling and borrowing require convenient rules covering the terms of the loan, the relations between borrowers and lenders or joint venturers, and the multitude of future contingencies. Today we know the necessary rules, institutions and concepts by the names of corporation, stock, bond, trust indenture, equipment trust certificate, etc. But these legal instruments did not exist two hundred years ago; some lawyer had to conceive them. Sometimes true imagination on a large scale was necessary, sometimes only a small refinement; but in either case the corporate and financial instruments are not the products of natural evolution like tigers, mice and men, but of human creativity. Take the conditional sales contract or its British version the hire-purchase agreement as an example. The arrangement is now as familiar as the wheel, and familiarity has made it as hard as it is in the case of the wheel to understand the true inventiveness required for the conception. But in the beginning the conditional sale was some lawyer's exceedingly bright idea and, despite many abuses requiring reform, it or something like it was and probably still is essential to the material base of our civilization.

For a second example consider industrial relations. Surely one of the great areas of human progress in the last half century has been in the lot of the industrial wage earner, through labor unions and collective bargaining. Through the unions' countervailing power real wages have been protected or increased, job insecurity has been minimized, and a large measure of industrial justice for individual workers has been brought into the mine, mill and factory. The basic needs were recognized without lawyers. No legal skill or training was required for the idea that workers should band together and require the employer to deal with them as a group. Lawyers did play major roles, although perhaps they were unnecessary, when it came time to give government protection to a right to form, join and assist labor unions, to put employers under a legal duty to bargain collectively, and to borrow the principle of majority rule from the political sphere. But these general ideas need both corollary rules to give them substance and procedures and institutions for carrying them out. Collective bargaining agreements had to be written to which individual workers would look as a source and definition of rights; grievance procedures and a system of arbitration had to be developed to administer the agreement in the case of disputes; and the industrial law of the plant had to be integrated with the courts and conventional legal system. In these areas constructive and imaginative lawyers were extraordinarily useful if not indispensable.

Turning from what the legal profession calls private law to government, we should probably all agree that the most creative acts in our political history were done at the Philadelphia Convention in 1787 and under Chief Justice Marshall during the first third of the nineteenth century. The Convention created a new and unique form of federal union in which both state and Federal governments deal directly with the same citizens in the same geographical area, each with its own taxes, courts and administrators, each assigned a functional jurisdiction sometimes overlapping the other's. Apart from the steadying influence of Washington and

Franklin, the leading figures at the Convention were all lawyers. I do not know whether they fully understood the complex federal system they originated or simply provided the seed idea which others rationalized and nurtured. Either way theirs was an extraordinarily creative legal and political idea, not only in the sense that it was markedly original but also in its generative power. John Marshall's notion of judicial review of both Federal and state legislation had legal antecedents, but it was a marked advance and provided another uniquely American institution of government which is enormously useful in protecting the individual against government and probably indispensable to the operation of the federal system.

For my final example I turn to the inquiry of the Judiciary Committee of the House of Representatives into the proposed impeachment of President Nixon, looking ahead to possible impeachment by the House and possible trial and conviction in the Senate. Here the lawyers particularly but also the men in government and other forms of public life, indeed all of us, face novel and unusually difficult challenges to our creativity. We write upon an almost-clean slate. Little law or political precedent is available to guide the hard decisions. Yet, regardless of the outcome, the value of the proceeding will depend upon whether the process is so conducted that the country perceives it as a fair and legitimate measure for restoring integrity to government. If President Nixon should be impeached and convicted, the question of legitimacy will be paramount. If President Nixon is acquitted, the country will still need assurance about the integrity of that conclusion. Whatever the event, we may fairly ask that the leadership build better for the future than their predecessors at the impeachment of Andrew Johnson.

The central challenge is to formulate the principles—the general standards of conduct—by which a President is to be judged in a proceeding that vacates, without direct expression of the popular will, a choice made by the people—in this case overwhelmingly made by the people—in the regular election only a few years before. Too much discussion, both public and private, has been concerned either with loose generalities about the ultimate question of impeachment *vel non*, or with the excitement and speculation stirred by particular disclosures. Too little hard debate has focused upon what should be impeachable offenses—upon why some wrongdoing should be grounds for impeachment while other misconduct is left to popular judgment at the polls. I am convinced that the legitimacy of the final conclusion in the view of the American people will depend upon the success of counsel and other public men in formulating general standards of conduct fairly applicable to any President and in educating the public upon their meaning and legal and moral base. For Democratic Senators and Representatives to keep silent upon the ground that impeachment is a Republican problem and for Republicans to keep silent while they test the political winds is to deny the country the debate necessary to educated self-government and the development of governmental institutions.

*A priori* we might give any one of three polar meanings to the "high crimes and misdemeanours" for which a President, a judge or any other civil officer may be impeached.

(1) William Giles, President Jefferson's majority leader in the Senate, advised his colleagues during the proceedings against Supreme Court Justice Samuel Chase that "impeachment is nothing more than an enquiry, by the two houses of Congress, whether the office of any public man might not be better filled by another." Justice Chase was acquitted. The view of impeachment expressed by Giles never again had serious support (unless one counts as "serious" the speech of Congressman Gerald Ford a few years ago advocating the impeachment of Justice Douglas).

(2) The strictest view of the constitutional phrase "high crimes and misdemeanors" holds that impeachable offenses are confined to violations of the criminal law and to "high," i.e., very serious crimes, whether felonies or misdemeanors. This reading has better standing than the first, but the weight of the argument is against it.

The English parliamentary precedents, which were familiar to the Founding Fathers, included instances of noncriminal conduct and, although the Founding Fathers desired to cut back on the precedents, the constitutional phrasing makes it unlikely that they chose technical criminality as the line of demarcation. In the late eighteenth century "misdemeanor" was often used as a synonym for any misbehavior, rather than to describe a criminal offense not punishable as a felony. Since the Constitution speaks first of "crimes," giving "misdemeanors" its technical meaning in the criminal law renders it merely redundant, unless the aim is to authorize impeachment not only for "high crimes" but also for "petty misdemeanors," such as making excessive noise in a public place, racing an automobile or blasphemy. This seems unlikely. The recorded debates at the Philadelphia Convention and the subsequent expositions of the framers also make it pretty clear that impeachment was intended to be a vehicle for dealing with officials whose wrongs require removal from office even though not technically criminal. Refusal to perform the functions of an office while clinging to the status and perquisites seems a good illustration.

(3) We are left with a third view; i.e., that "high crimes and misdemeanors" covers some but surely not all "political," in the sense of governmental, offenses.

Reaching this conclusion moves us along, but it is only the beginning of the challenge. What are the wrongs against the people, the body politic, for which a President may properly be impeached?

It would be easier if history provided a list of legitimate grounds for impeachment, but the only precedents are scattered pretty far afield from current issues. Working with a clean slate, perhaps we can best begin by asking what deep-seated needs any rule we formulate must satisfy.

The Gallup Poll and like measures of public opinion report that a very large majority believe that President Nixon is guilty of covering up wrongdoing, but of those expressing an opinion, a majority oppose removal by impeachment. The difference, in my opinion, is attributable to a fear of impeachment not unlike the fear of regicide and the horror of the regicide once accomplished during the time of Cromwell and King Charles I. Of course, impeachment cannot be wholly illegitimate—the Constitution provides for it—but I think that the country has a deep, intuitive understanding that impeachment is extraordinary, radical surgery, legitimate only upon some equally fundamental wrong, doing such grave injury to the nation as to make any incumbent's further continuance in office unacceptable even though his previous entitlement was based upon popular election.

Surely any wrong so fundamental as to require setting aside the results of one election without holding another must be one that can be stated in general terms plainly applicable to any President at any time. The need is to quiet the fear that impeachment may be or become a partisan substitute for a premature election. Political opposition, emotion, dislike, distrust, and lack of public confidence (which may be temporary even when mixed with suspicion of some kind of wrongdoing) are not enough.

Equally surely, in my opinion, any general standard of political conduct the violation of which would support impeachment must have a broad and generally accepted moral base, understood by the country, so that again the same rule would apply to any President, so that we should not be resolving questions of public policy by impeachment nor should we be making up new rules of conduct as we go along.

Of course, it is unnecessary to draw up a complete code of presidential conduct. Mixing pragmatism with principle is one source of much of the creativity in Anglo-American law and government. We work eclectically up to a point, passing judgment upon particular sets of facts, but we also test our judgment by asking whether it rests upon reasons that we can articulate and apply to other situations having the same essential elements, with enough generality both in scope and continuity, to give guarantees against caprice, prejudice, self-interest or unreasoned emotion.

So here, the articulation of minimum acceptable standards of conduct for any President or high executive officer can begin with facts proved or assumed. It is fair to say that evidence may be available to show that President Nixon's lawyers and accountants, without deliberate misrepresentation, zealously sought every loophole and cut every corner in an effort to avoid or minimize the payment of taxes; to show that others acting on his behalf likewise stretched every possible point to add to the convenience and comfort of Key Biscayne and San Clemente at public expense; and, finally, to show that in some cases they claimed more than the law allows. Bad taste? Surely. Avaricious? Yes. Bad leadership? Again, surely. Morally shabby? I think so, even though the same shabbiness infects thousands of tax returns and expense accounts. Grounds for impeachment? I wonder. We are hardly prepared to say that any officer of the United States who, without concealing or misrepresenting material facts, claims a tax deduction not due should be removed from office. If not, does my phrasing omit some essential element in President Nixon's situation? What makes the omitted element decisive?

Let us try again. Is it tolerable or a high offense against the liberty and security of a whole people for a President to approve in principle electronic surveillance, mail covers and burglaries for the purpose of gathering domestic intelligence, over the objection of the established agencies to set in motion a small force of his own irregulars—the Caulfields, Ulasewiczes, Liddys and Hunts—who will operate from the executive offices outside all the regularizing rules and procedures of the established agencies in order to effectuate Administration policy and political objectives, and to hamper inquiry into their activities?

Move to a third area. The President's duty is to see that the laws are faithfully executed. Is it an impeachable violation of this responsibility for him to refrain for months from any form of personal intervention when there is first suspicion and later at least some evidence that his highest personal aides and party officials are obstructing justice by covering up criminal misconduct, for him to withhold disclosure and refuse evidence when investigation leads to papers taken into his files, and for his aides, apparently with his approval, to cooperate with those seeking to avoid indictment and conviction?

I do not imply answers to these questions, nor do I suggest that my factual predicates represent the actual facts. The evidence may show more or less. The point I wish to emphasize is that it is past time for all those deeply concerned with our government to bend some of their time and effort away from the fun of factual disclosures to the very arduous task of formulating and thus creating a substantive law of impeachment where now there is none. Whether the present proceedings help to rebuild confidence in our system of government or push us further down the slope to cynicism and despair will depend upon the ability of the House Judiciary Committee to sense the as-yet-unstated moral intuition of the country and articulate it in operative principles by which President Nixon's conduct can be judged.

The task is one for the theorists and practitioners of political science as well as lawyers; it is also typical of the lawyer's creative art.

Some may wonder whether I mean to portray the lawyer and even the government man as so heavily a technician and, if I do, whether the truly creative man is not the dreamer who perceives the broad ills of society, outlines the remedies, and inspires the mere technicians. I stress the intellectual nuts and bolts for several reasons:

(1) This is the most distinctive side of the law. Lawyers can dream as well as other men and sometimes better, but the reforming dreams are not confined to lawyers.

(2) The nuts and bolts, the nitty-gritty, is essential to the creation of meaningful new social, economic or political institutions. The artistic dreamer may see cathedrals in the clouds or in the flames of a hearth fire but he cannot build cathedrals without knowing the laws of mechanics, of stresses and strains and the capacities of stone and steel and bricks and mortar. For the Gothic cathedral one needed the spirit reaching towards God but also the flying buttress. The lawyer and government men are the architects of social, economic and political organization.

(3) Although others may be dreamers, the lawyer with great professional skill seems to be uniquely placed for creativity. Familiarity with the technical concepts, rules and institutions, public and private, that may order the affairs of men encourages new ideas not only because it gives an appreciation of the flow of invention but also because it carries the sense of power and capacity that is one of the sources of creativity in any field.

The last point is easily pressed too far. The lawyer too caught up in the present law is often an obstacle to change, and existing institutions, I think, are themselves impediments to new arrangements in both law and government. To illustrate, we shall always need a strong presidency but surely there is also need for new mechanisms securing greater responsiveness and responsibility to the people's other representatives and much freer flow of information. If we could sweep the chessmen off the board and start afresh, perhaps some form of parliamentary government would be preferable, but all the forces suggested by words like habit, tradition, expectations and continuity work so strongly against the acceptability of such a change as almost surely to prevent it. Those forces, even as we resist them, press for meeting the need by successive smaller, separately interstitial measures that may revolutionize even though each alone seems not too inconsistent with the basic structure. Similarly, the reform of the government of metropolitan areas would be vastly easier without the incubus of existing city, country and state boundaries. Not even a violent revolution can wholly wipe out the restrictions of the past. The expert in the existing rules has perhaps the best chance to perceive how they can be changed.

But when these things are said, I must confess that the law itself contains few of the ultimate forces generating creativity. The British legal philosopher, Lord Radcliffe observed:

"The law needs a compass to guide it. What drives us [lawyers] back from time to time to search further, to question outright what are our purposes is the insistence of the layman, the man who is not versed in law, that it shall stand for something more, for some vindication of a sense of right and wrong that is not merely provisional or just the product of historical forces."

I would answer that the law has one generative commitment—the goal of civility, the commitment to ordering the affairs of men with a minimum of force and maximum of reason and respect for human personality. The commitment is vastly important but, except for this, Lord Radcliffe is right. To return to my metaphor, the spirit that made Gothic cathedrals reach towards God, the forces that set the goals of a society, the ultimate sources of creativity lie outside the law and even government, even though they may infuse political leaders and the legal profession.

What can we say of those sources and therefore of the chance of renewed creativity in law and government? I can offer only a few random observations.

Surely one of the springs of creativity in the government of any free society is the spirit of cooperation that used to run deep in the American people. Alfred North Whitehead observed that no other people in the history of mankind had ever shown such innate qualities of toleration and cooperation. The will to cooperate flows chiefly, I think, from mutual trust and confidence in the importance of what I can only call the goals of the joint adventure in which we are all engaged. In a free society confidence in the goals of the enterprise is confidence in mankind—and ourselves.

Do these qualities survive in the realm of government? Confidence in the institutions of government and mutual trust between the elected governors and the governed had begun to erode long before Watergate, but surely the danger of a long slide into general cynicism, distrust and despair has been intensified by the evidence giving reason to believe that power, position and the very processes of government were criminally perverted at or near the very highest level of executive office for the sake of building or perpetuating personal and political power. The first essential in reversing the trend is restoration of confidence in the integrity of government.

The process will be slow and hard. Some steps are but the fair administration of justice: the continued vigorous investigation of the Watergate affair, the successful prosecution of offenders, the careful and impartial, but unrelenting, pursuit of the question of impeachment. Other steps must be legislative: for example the quick substitution of public financing for private contributions in political campaigns.

Still other steps can be only described as moral. Above all else we need to restore to government a stronger appreciation of the line separating fundamental judgments of right and wrong in the conduct of government and political life, on the one side, from mere political loyalties and political opinions on the other side. Too many of us grew up in an atmosphere of positivism and relativism in which the assertion of moral imperatives was taken as proof of ignorance and naiveté, at least among those wishing to be supposed persons of experience and sophistication. Others took the imperatives for granted, supposing that the fundamentals would look out for themselves. The cynics found justification in Leo Durocher's "Nice guys finish last," or in presidential aide Charles Colson's "It's only hard-nosed politics." One way or the other, success in gaining power took precedence and personal or party loyalty became a justification for silently going along if not actually participating in wrongdoing. It is time for a change.

The question remains whether, in a broader sense, we retain the innate spirit of cooperation of which Whitehead wrote and the belief in the goals of the enterprise on which I think it depends.

It is harder to have such confidence today because we have learned so much about ourselves. The quick conquest of a continent and the Horatio Alger story bred a folklore of endless resources and easy success. For all but the unfortunate, technology and industrial organization poured out a seemingly endless flow of material comforts. American might in two wars led us to suppose that our power extended to the farthest reaches of the globe. Recent decades dispelled these illusions. Our cities became unlivable. The succession of new cars, new television sets and new refrigerators proved a wasteland. Our power in the world is limited. We have lost our innocence and learned our capacity for evil; witness the bombs dropped on Southeast Asia and the gap that still exists between our pretenses and practices in the treatment of blacks, Chicanos and native Americans.

It takes honesty and courage to face these facts, but those whose realism leads them to despair suffer their own form of illusion. The men and women who sought freedom across the seas, who crossed the prairies and the great plains to conquer the mountains and build gardens in the desert, knew the costs, the struggle, the defeats and disappointments. They knew their fallibility and capacity for evil. But our forebears also had the greater insight for a vision of the ultimate perfectibility of man and the greater courage to pursue their vision even when they knew that neither they nor their children nor their children's children would wholly achieve it. Edward Everett Hale voiced the true spirit of those who pursued the American dream—

"I am only one,
But still I am one.
I cannot do everything,
But I can do something . . .
What I can do I ought to do . . .
And what I ought to do by the grace of God I will do.

If you will forgive an even more personal thought, I add this final word!"

Watergate can be made a turning point and therefore a blessing. It has shocked out of lethargy the conscience of the nation. Possibly my view is too self-centered and too much influenced by the moving letters I still receive, but it seems to me that the "fire storm"—to borrow a phrase from General Haig—which exploded over the weekend of October 21-22 had its source in the longing of countless simple, direct and moral people for a new measure of candor, simplicity and rectitude in the conduct of government—and for a confidence in them that would bespeak our confidence in ourselves. The turn of events was extraordinary. On a Friday and Saturday the President announced that he was discharging the special prosecutor, terminating independent investigation of the Watergate affair and related offenses, and refusing to produce relevant tapes and documents in accordance with the order of a court. The public outcry forced an immediate 180-degree turnabout. Within days, the court was assured that the tapes and documents would be produced. Within weeks, the independence of the Watergate special prosecution force was restored, the staff was retained unimpaired, and a vigorous and independent special prosecutor was appointed. This sequence of events demonstrates better than any other occurrence within memory the extent of this country's dedication to the principle that ours is a government of laws and not of men. It gave proof of the people's determination and ability to compel their highest officials to meet their obligations under the law as fully and faithfully as others. On this occasion, as so often in our history when fundamental questions were at stake, the people had a far better sense of the goals of the enterprise and needs of the nation than those claiming wider experience and greater sophistication.

The spirit is there. The power is there. The question is whether those who seek to be political leaders have the wit and will to evoke that spirit, articulate it, and take measures restoring confidence in the integrity of the government.

# A New Federalism: State of the Union Address[7]

Ronald Reagan

*Born Feburary 6, 1911, Tampico, IL; B.A., Eureka College, 1932; sports announcer, 1933-37; motion picture and television actor, 1937-1966; U.S. Army, 1942-55; president, Screen Actors Guild, 1947-52, 1959-60; program supervisor, General Electric Theater, 1952-62; governor of California, 1967-74; president of the United States, 1981-88.*

## Editor's introduction

Ronald Reagan's first State of the Union address was particularly anticipated because of the highly controversial changes in the role of the federal government he proposed. In essence, Reagan adopted a notably conservative view of the government's role, declaring that "After 50 years of taking power away from the hands of the people in their states and local communities, we have started returning power and resources to them." In addition, Reagan announced his administration had already "cut the growth of . . . new federal regulations in half."

---

Mr. Speaker, Mr. President, distinguished Members of the Congress, honored guests, and fellow citizens:

Today marks my first State of the Union address to you, a constitutional duty as old as our Republic itself.

President Washington began this tradition in 1790 after reminding the nation that the destiny of self-government and the "preservation of the sacred fire of liberty" is "finally staked on the experiment entrusted to the hands of the American people." For our friends in the press, who place a high premium on accuracy, let me say: I did not actually hear George Washington say that. But it is a matter of historic record.

But from this podium, Winston Churchill asked the free world to stand together against the onslaught of aggression. Franklin Delano Roosevelt spoke of a day of infamy and summoned a nation to arms. Douglas MacArthur made an unforgettable farewell to a country he loved and served so well. Dwight Eisenhower reminded us that peace was purchased only at the price of strength. And John F. Kennedy spoke of the burden and glory that is freedom.

When I visited this chamber last year as a newcomer to Washington, critical of past policies which I believed had failed, I proposed a new spirit of partnership between this Congress and this administration and between Washington and our state and local governments. In forging this new partnership for America, we could achieve the oldest hopes of our Republic—prosperity for our nation, peace for the world, and the blessings of individual liberty for our children and, something for all of humanity.

It's my duty to report to you tonight on the progress that we have made in our relations with other nations, on the foundation we've carefully laid for our economic recovery, and finally, on a bold and spirited initiative that I believe can change the face of American government and make it again the servant of the people.

Seldom have the stakes been higher for America. What we do and say here will make all the difference to autoworkers in Detroit, lumberjacks in the Northwest, steelworkers in Steubenville who are in the unemployment lines; to black teenagers in Newark and Chicago; to hard-pressed farmers and small businessmen; and to millions of everyday Americans who harbor the simple wish of a safe and financially secure future for their children. To understand the state of the Union, we must look not only at where we are and where we're going but where we've been. The situation at this time last year was truly ominous.

[7]Delivered to a joint session of Congress, in Washington, D.C., on January 26, 1981.

The last decade has seen a series of recessions. There was a recession in 1970, in 1974, and again in the spring of 1980. Each time, unemployment increased and inflation soon turned up again. We coined the word "stagflation" to describe this.

Government's response to these recessions was to pump up the money supply and increase spending. In the last 6 months of 1980, as an example, the money supply increased at the fastest rate in postwar history—13 percent. Inflation remained in double digits, and government spending increased at an annual rate of 17 percent. Interest rates reached a staggering 21.5 percent. There were 8 million unemployed.

Late in 1981 we sank into the present recession, largely because continued high interest rates hurt the auto industry and construction. And there was a drop in productivity, and the already high unemployment increased.

This time, however, things are different. We have an economic program in place, completely different from the artificial quick-fixes of the past. It calls for a reduction of the rate of increase in government spending, and already that rate has been cut nearly in half. But reduced spending alone isn't enough. We've just implemented the first and smallest phase of a 3-year tax-rate reduction designed to stimulate the economy and create jobs. Already interest rates are down to 15.75 percent, but they must still go lower. Inflation is down from 12.4 percent to 8.9, and for the month of December it was running at an annualized rate of 5.2 percent. If we had not acted as we did, things would be far worse for all Americans than they are today. Inflation, taxes, and interest rates would all be higher.

A year ago, Americans' faith in their governmental process was steadily declining. Six out of 10 Americans were saying they were pessimistic about their future. A new kind of defeatism was heard. Some said our domestic problems were uncontrollable, that we had to learn to live with this seemingly endless cycle of high inflation and high unemployment.

There were also pessimistic predictions about the relationship between our administration and this Congress. It was said we could never work together. Well, those predictions were wrong. The record is clear, and I believe that history will remember this as an era of American renewal, remember this administration as an administration of change, and remember this Congress as a Congress of destiny.

Together, we not only cut the increase in government spending nearly in half, we brought about the largest tax reductions and the most sweeping changes in our tax structure since the beginning of this century. And because we indexed future taxes to the rate of inflation, we took away government's built-in profit on inflation and its hidden incentive to grow larger at the expense of American workers.

Together, after 50 years of taking power away from the hands of the people in their states and local communities, we have started returning power and resources to them.

Together, we have cut the growth of the new federal regulations nearly in half. In 1981 there were 23,000 fewer pages in the *Federal Register* which lists new regulations, than there were in 1980. By deregulating oil we've come closer to achieving energy independence and helped bring down the cost of gasoline and heating fuel.

Together, we have created an effective federal strike force to combat waste and fraud in government. In just 6 months it has saved the taxpayers more than $2 billion, and it's only getting started.

Togther we've begun to mobilize the private sector, not to duplicate wasteful and discredited programs, but to bring thousands of Americans into a volunteer effort to help solve many of America's social problems.

Together we've begun to restore that margin of military safety that ensures peace. Our country's uniform is being worn once again with pride.

Together we have made a New Beginning, but we have only begun.

No one pretends that the way ahead will be easy. In my Inaugural Address last year, I warned that the "ills we suffer have come upon us over several decades. They will not go away in days, weeks, or months, but they will go away . . . because we as Americans have the capacity now, as we've had it in the past, to do whatever needs to be done to preserve this last and greatest bastion of freedom."

The economy will face difficult moments in the months ahead. But the program for economic recovery that is in place will pull the economy out of its slump and put us on the road to prosperity and stable growth by the latter half of this year. And that is why I can report to you tonight that in the near future the state of the Union and the economy will be better—much better—if we summon the strength to continue on the course that we've charted.

And so, the question: If the fundamentals are in place, what now? Well, two things. First, we must understand what's happening at the moment to the economy. Our current problems are not the product of the recovery program that's only just now getting underway, as some would have you believe; they are the inheritance of decades of tax and tax and spend and spend.

Second, because our economic problems are deeply rooted and will not respond to quick political fixes, we must stick to our carefully integrated plan for recovery. That plan is based on four commonsense fundamentals: continued reduction of the growth in federal spending; preserving the individual and business tax reductions that will stimulate saving and investment; removing unnecessary federal regulations to spark productivity; and maintaining a healthy dollar and a stable monetary policy, the latter a responsibility of the Federal Reserve System.

The only alternative being offered to this economic program is a return to the policies that gave us a trillion-dollar debt, runaway inflation, runaway interest rates and unemployment. The doubters would have us turn back the clock with tax increases that would offset the personal tax-rate reductions already passed by this Congress. Raise present taxes to cut future deficits, they tell us. Well, I don't believe we should buy that argument.

There are too many imponderables for any one to predict deficits or surpluses several years ahead with any degree of accuracy. The budget in place, when I took office, had been projected as balanced. It turned out to have one of the biggest deficits in history. Another example of the imponderables that can make deficit projections highly questionable—a change of only one percentage point in unemployment can alter a deficit up or down by some $25 billion.

As it now stands, our forecast, which we're required by law to make, will show major deficits starting at less than a hundred billion dollars and declining, but still too high. More important, we're making progress with the three keys to reducing deficits: economic growth, lower interest rates, and spending control. The policies we have in place will reduce the deficit steadily, surely, and in time, completely.

Higher taxes would not mean lower deficits. If they did, how would we explain that tax revenues more than doubled just since 1976; yet in that same 6-year period we ran the largest series of deficits in our history. In 1980 tax revenues increased by $54 billion and in 1980 we had one of our all-time biggest deficits. Raising taxes won't balance the budget; it will encourage more government spending and less private investment. Raising taxes will slow economic growth, reduce production, and destroy future jobs, making it more difficult for those without jobs to find them and more likely that those who now have jobs could lose them. So, I will not ask you to try to balance the budget on the backs of the American taxpayers.

I will seek no tax increases this year, and I have no intention of retreating from our basic program of tax relief. I promise to bring the American people—to bring their tax rates down and to keep them down, to provide them incentives to rebuild our economy, to save, to invest in America's future. I will stand by my word. Tonight I'm urging the American people: Seize these new opportunities to produce, to save, to invest, and together we'll make this economy a mighty engine of freedom, hope, and prosperity again.

Now, the budget deficit this year will exceed our earlier expectations. The recession did that. It lowered revenues and increased costs. To some extent, we're also victims of our own success. We've brought inflation down faster than we thought we could, and in doing this, we've deprived government of those hidden revenues that occur when inflation pushes people into higher income tax brackets. And the continued high interest rates last year cost the government about $5 billion more than anticipated.

We must cut out more nonessential government spending and root out more waste, and we will continue our efforts to reduce the number of employees in the Federal work force by 75,000.

The budget plan I submit to you on February 8th will realize major savings by dismantling the Departments of Energy and Education and by eliminating ineffective subsidies for business. We'll continue to redirect our resources to our two highest budget priorities—a strong national defense to keep America free and at peace and a reliable safety net of social programs for those who have contributed and those who are in need.

Contrary to some of the wild charges you may have heard, this administration has not and will not turn its back on America's elderly or America's poor. Under the new budget, funding for social insurance programs will be more than double the amount spent only 6 years ago. But it would be foolish to pretend that these or any programs cannot be made more efficient and economical.

The entitlement programs that make up our safety net for the truly needy have worthy goals and many deserving recipients. We will protect them. But there's only one way to see to it that these programs really help those whom they were designed to help. And that is to bring their spiraling costs under control.

Today we face the absurd situation of a federal budget with three-quarters of its expenditures routinely referred to as "uncontrollable." And a large part of this goes to entitlement programs.

Committee after committee of this Congress has heard witness after witness describe many of these programs as poorly administered and rife with waste and fraud. Virtually every American who shops in a local supermarket is aware of the daily abuses that take place in the food stamp program, which has grown by 16,000 percent in the last 15 years. Another example is Medicare and Medicaid—programs with worthy goals but whose costs have increased from 11.2 billion to almost 60 billion, more than 5 times as much, in just 10 years.

Waste and fraud are serious problems. Back in 1980, federal investigators testified before one of your committees that "corruption has permeated virtually every area of the Medicare and Medicaid health care industry." One official said many of the people who are cheating the system were "very confident that nothing was going to happen to them." Well, something is going to happen. Not only the taxpayers are defrauded; the people with real dependency on these programs are deprived of what they need, because available resources are going not to the needy, but to the greedy.

The time has come to control the uncontrollable. In August we made a start. I signed a bill to reduce the growth of these programs by $44 billion over the next 3 years while at the same time preserving essential services for the truly needy. Shortly you will receive from me a message on further reforms we intend to install—some new, but others long recommended by your own congressional committees. I ask you to help make these savings for the American taxpayer.

The savings we propose in entitlement programs will total some $63 billion over 4 years and will, without affecting social security, go a long way toward bringing federal spending under control.

But don't be fooled by those who proclaim that spending cuts will deprive the elderly, the needy, and the helpless. The federal government will still subsidize 95 million meals every day. That's one out of seven of all the meals served in America. Head Start, senior nutrition programs, and child welfare programs will not be cut from the levels we proposed last year. More than one-half billion dollars has been proposed for minority business assistance. And research at the National Institute of Health will be increased by over $100 million. While meeting all these needs, we intend to plug unwarranted tax loopholes and strengthen the law which requires all large corporations to pay a minimum tax.

I am confident the economic program we've put into operation will protect the needy while it triggers a recovery that will benefit all Americans. It will stimulate the economy, result in increased savings and provide capital for expansion, mortgages for homebuilding, and jobs for the unemployed.

Now that the essentials of that program are in place, our next major undertaking must be a program—just as bold, just as innovative—to make government again accountable to the people, to make our system of federalism work again.

Our citizens feel they've lost control of even the most basic decisions made about the essential services of government, such as schools, welfare, roads, and even garbage collection. And they're right. A maze of interlocking jurisdictions and levels of government confronts average citizens in trying to solve even the simplest of problems. They don't know where to turn for answers, who to hold accountable, who to praise, who to blame, who to vote for or against. The main reason for this is the overpowering growth of federal grants-in-aid programs during the past few decades.

In 1960 the federal government had 132 categorical grant programs, costing $7 billion. When I took office, there were approximately 500, costing nearly a hundred billion dollars—13 programs for energy, 36 for pollution control, 66 for social services, 90 for education. And here in the Congress, it takes at least 166 committees just to try to keep track of them.

You know and I know that neither the President nor the Congress can properly oversee this jungle of grants-in-aid; indeed, the growth of these grants has led to the distortion in the vital functions of government. As one Democratic governor put it recently: The national government should be worrying about "arms control; not potholes."

The growth in these federal programs has—in the words of one intergovernmental commission—made the federal government "more pervasive, more intrusive, more unmanageable, more ineffective and costly, and above all, more (un)accountable." Let's solve this problem with a single, bold stroke: the return of some $47 billion in federal programs to State and local government, together with the means to finance them and a transition period of nearly 10 years to avoid unnecessary disruption.

I will shortly send this Congress a message describing this program. I want to emphasize, however, that its full details will have been worked out only after close consultation with congressional, state, and local officials.

Starting in fiscal 1984, the federal government will assume full responsibility for the cost of the rapidly growing Medicaid program to go along with its existing responsibility for Medicare. As part of a financially equal swap, the states will simultaneously take full responsibility for Aid to Families with Dependent Children and food stamps. This will make welfare less costly and more responsive to genuine need, because it'll be designed and administered closer to the grassroots and the people it serves.

In 1984 the federal government will apply the full proceeds from certain excise taxes to a grassroots trust fund that will belong in fair shares to the 50 states. The total amount flowing into this fund will be $28 billion a year. Over the next 4 years the states can use this money in either of two ways. If they want to continue receiving federal grants in such areas as transportation, education, and social services, they can use their trust fund money to pay for the grants. Or to the extent they choose to forego the federal grant programs, they can use their trust fund money on their own for those or other purposes. There will be a mandatory pass-through of part of these funds to local governments.

By 1988 the states will be in complete control of over 40 federal grant programs. The trust fund will start to phase out, eventually to disappear, and the excise taxes will be turned over to the states. They can then preserve, lower, or raise taxes on their own and fund and manage these programs as they see fit.

In a single stroke we will be accomplishing a realignment that will end cumbersome administration and spiraling costs at the federal level while we ensure these programs will be more responsive to both the people they're meant to help and the people who pay for them.

Hand-in-hand with this program to strengthen the discretion and flexibility of state and local governments, we're proposing legislation for an experimental effort to improve and develop our repressed urban areas in the 1980s and '90s. This legislation will permit states and localities to apply to the federal government for designation as urban enterprise zones. A broad range of special economic incentives in the zones will help attract new business, new jobs, new opportunity to America's inner cities and rural towns. Some will say our mission is to save free enterprise. Well, I say we must free enterprise so that together we can save America.

Some will also say our states and local communities are not up to the challenge of a new and creative partnership. Well, that might have been true 20 years ago before reforms like reapportionment and the Voting Rights Act, the 10-year extension of which I strongly support. It's no longer true today. This administration has faith in state and local governments and the constitutional balance envisioned by the Founding Fathers. We also believe in the integrity, decency, and sound, good sense of grassroots Americans.

Our faith in the American people is reflected in another major endeavor. Our Private Sector Initiatives Task Force is seeking out successful community models of school, church, business, union, foundation, and civic programs that help community needs. Such groups are almost invariably far more efficient than government in running social programs.

We're not asking them to replace discarded and often discredited government programs dollar for dollar, service for service. We just want to help them perform the good works they choose and help others to profit by their example. Three hundred and eighty-five thousand corporations and private organizations are already working on social programs ranging from drug rehabilitation to job training, and thousands more Americans have written us asking how they can help. The volunteer spirit is still alive and well in America.

Our nation's long journey towards civil rights for all our citizens—once a source of discord, now a source of pride—must continue with no backsliding or slowing down. We must and shall see that those basic laws that guarantee equal rights are preserved and, when necessary, strengthened.

Our concern for equal rights for women is firm and unshakable. We launched a new Task Force on Legal Equity for Women and a Fifty-States Project that will examine state laws for discriminatory language. And for the first time in our history, a woman sits on the highest court in the land.

So, too, the problem of crime—one as real and deadly serious as any in America today. It demands that we seek transformation of our legal system, which overly protects the rights of criminals while it leaves society and the innocent victims of crime without justice.

We look forward to the enactment of a responsible Clean Air Act to increase jobs while continuing to improve the quality of our air. We're encouraged by the bipartisan initiative of the House and are hopeful of further progress as the Senate continues its deliberations.

So far, I've concentrated largely, now, on domestic matters. To view the state of the Union in perspective, we must not ignore the rest of the world. There isn't time tonight for a lengthy treatment of social—or foreign policy, I should say, a subject I intend to address in detail in the near future. A few words, however, are in order on the progress we've made over the past year, reestablishing respect for our nation around the globe and some of the challenges and goals that we will approach in the year ahead.

At Ottawa and Cancún, I met with leaders of the major industrial powers and developing nations. Now, some of those I met with were a little surprised that I didn't apologize for America's wealth. Instead, I spoke of the strength of the free marketplace system and how that system could help them realize their aspirations for economic development and political freedom. I believe lasting friendships were made, and the foundation was laid for future cooperation.

In the vital region of the Caribbean Basin, we're developing a program of aid, trade, and investment incentives to promote self-sustaining growth and a better, more secure life for our neighbors to the south. Toward those who would export terrorism and subversion in the Caribbean and elsewhere, especially Cuba and Libya, we will act with firmness.

Our foreign policy is a policy of strength, fairness, and balance. By restoring America's military credibility, by pursuing peace at the negotiating table wherever both sides are willing to sit down in good faith, and by regaining the respect of America's allies and adversaries alike, we have strengthened our country's position as a force for peace and progress in the world.

When action is called for, we're taking it. Our sanctions against the military dictatorship that has attempted to crush human rights in Poland—and against the Soviet regime behind that military dictatorship—clearly demonstrated to the world that America will not conduct "business as usual" with the forces of oppression. If the events in Poland continue to deteriorate, further measures will follow.

Now, let me also note that private American groups have taken the lead in making January 30th a day of solidarity with the people of Poland. So, too, the European Parliament has called for March 21st to be an international day of support for Afghanistan. Well, I urge all peace-loving peoples to join together on those days, to raise their voices, to speak and pray for freedom.

Meanwhile, we're working for reduction of arms and military activities, as I announced in my address to the nation last November 18th. We have proposed to the Soviet Union a far-reaching agenda for mutual reduction of military forces and have already initiated negotiations with them in Geneva on intermediate-range nuclear forces. In those talks it is essential that we negotiate from a position of strength. There must be a real incentive for the Soviets to take these talks seriously. This requires that we rebuild our defenses.

In the last decade, while we sought the moderation of Soviet power through a process of restraint and accommodation, the Soviets engaged in an unrelenting buildup of their military forces. The protection of our national security has required that we undertake a substantial program to enhance our military forces.

We have not neglected to strengthen our traditional alliances in Europe and Asia, or to develop key relationships with our partners in the Middle East and other countries. Building a more peaceful world requires a sound strategy and the national resolve to back it up. When radical forces threaten our friends, when economic misfortune creates conditions of instability, when strategically vital parts of the world fall under the shadow of Soviet power, our response can make the difference between peaceful change or disorder and violence. That's why we've laid such stress not only on our own defense but on our vital foreign assistance program. Your recent passage of the Foreign Assistance Act sent a signal to the world that America will not shrink from making the investments necessary for both peace and security. Our foreign policy must be rooted in realism, not naivete or self-delusion.

A recognition of what the Soviet empire is about is the starting point. Winston Churchill, in negotiating with the Soviets, observed that they respect only strength and resolve in their dealings with other nations. That's why we've moved to reconstruct our national defenses. We intend to keep the peace. We will also keep our freedom.

We have made pledges of a new frankness in our public statements and worldwide broadcasts. In the face of a climate of falsehood and misinformation, we've promised the world a season of truth—the truth of our great civilized ideas: Individual liberty, representative government, the rule of law under God. We've never needed walls or minefields or barbed wire to keep our people in. Nor do we declare martial law to keep our people from voting for the kind of government they want.

Yes, we have our problems; yes, we're in a time of recession. And it's true, there's no quick fix, as I said, to instantly end the tragic pain of unemployment. But we will end it. The process has already begun and we'll see its effect as the year goes on.

We speak with pride and admiration of that little band of Americans who overcame insuperable odds to set this nation on course 200 years ago. But our glory didn't end with them. Americans ever since have emulated their deeds.

We don't have to turn to our history books for heroes. They're all around us. One who sits among you here tonight epitomized that heroism at the end of the longest imprisonment ever inflicted on men of our Armed Forces. Who will ever forget that night when we waited for television to bring us the scene of that first plane landing at Clark Field in the Philippines, bringing our POW's home? The plane door opened and Jeremiah Denton came slowly down the ramp. He caught sight of our flag, saluted it, said, "God bless America," and then thanked us for bringing him home.

Just 2 weeks ago, in the midst of a terrible tragedy on the Potomac, we saw again the spirit of American heroism at its finest—the heroism of dedicated rescue workers saving crash victims from icy waters. And we saw the heroism of one of our young government employees, Lenny Skutnik, who, when he saw a woman lose her grip on the helicopter line, dived into the water and dragged her to safety.

And then there are countless, quiet, everyday heroes of American life—parents who sacrifice long and hard so their children will know a better life than they've known: church and civic volunteers who help to feed, clothe, nurse, and teach the needy; millions who've made our nation and our nation's destiny so very special—unsung heroes who may not have realized their own dreams themselves but then who reinvest those dreams in their children. Don't let anyone tell you that America's best days are behind her, that the American spirit has been vanquished. We've seen it triumph too often in our lives to stop believing in it now.

A hundred and twenty years ago, the greatest of all our Presidents delivered his second State of the Union message in this chamber. "We cannot escape history," Abraham Lincoln warned. "We of this Congress and this administration will be remembered in spite of ourselves." The "trial through which we pass will light us down, in honor or dishonor, to the latest generation."

Well, that President and that Congress did not fail the American people. Together they weathered the storm and preserved the Union. Let it be said of us that we, too, did not fail; that we, too, worked together to bring America through difficult times. Let us so conduct ourselves that two centuries from now, another Congress and another President, meeting in this chamber as we are meeting, will speak of us with pride, saying that we met the test and preserved for them in their day the sacred flame of liberty—this last, best hope of man on Earth.

God bless you, and thank you.

# A Contract with America[8]

Newt L. Gingrich

*Born June 17, 1943, Harrisburg, PA; B.A., Emory University, 1965; M.A., 1968, Ph.D., 1971, Tulane University; professor, West Georgia College, 1970-78; representative (R) from Georgia, 1978–; Speaker of the House of Representatives, 1995–; author,* Window of Opportunity: A Blueprint for the Future *(1984),* To Renew America *(1995),* Contract with America *(1995),* 1945 *(1995).*

## Editor's introduction

The 1994 elections produced dramatic results, with the most notable being Republican-held majorities in both houses of Congress for the first time in 40 years. In the January 4, 1995 opening session of the House of Representatives, majority leader Newt L. Gingrich, later to become Speaker of the House, defined the Republican "Contract with America." Essentially, Gingrich declared that the creation of a partnership between Republicans and Democrats was necessary to circumvent tangled bureaucracy and government gridlock. Only in this way did Gingrich believe government would be able to effect genuine change. It follows that while the "Contract with America" doesn't necessarily articulate a philosophical or political basis for the role of government, it asserts that the value of government is directly related to the degree its actions are "felt in the neighborhoods, in the communities . . . by real people living real lives."

---

We are starting the 104th Congress. I do not know if you have ever thought about this, but for 208 years, we bring together the most diverse country in the history of the world. We send all sorts of people here. Each of us could find at least one Member we thought was weird. I will tell you, if you went around the room the person chosen to be weird would be different for virtually every one of us. Because we do allow and insist upon the right of a free people to send an extraordinary diversity of people here.

Brian Lamb of C-SPAN read to me Friday a phrase from de Tocqueville that was so central to the House. I have been reading Remini's biography of Henry Clay and Clay, as the first strong Speaker, always preferred the House. He preferred the House to the Senate although he served in both. He said the House is more vital, more active, more dynamic, and more common.

This is what de Tocqueville wrote:

"Often there is not a distinguished man in the whole number. Its members are almost all obscure individuals whose names bring no associations to mind. They are mostly village lawyers, men in trade, or even persons belonging to the lower classes of society."

If we include women, I do not know that we would change much. But the word "vulgar" in de Tocqueville's time had a very particular meaning. It is a meaning the world would do well to study in this room. You see, de Tocqueville was an aristocrat. He lived in a world of kings and princes. The folks who come here do so by the one single act that their citizens freely chose them. I do not care what your ethnic background is, or your ideology. I do not care if you are younger or older. I do not care if you are born in America or if you are a naturalized citizen. Every one of the 435 people have equal standing because their citizens freely sent them. Their voice should be heard and they should have a right to participate. It is the most marvelous act of a complex giant country trying to argue and talk. And, as Dick Gephardt said, to have a great debate, to reach great decisions, not through a civil war, not by bombing one of our regional capitals, not by killing a half mil-

[8]Delivered to the United States House of Representatives, in Washington, D.C., on January 4, 1995.

lion people, and not by having snipers. Let me say unequivocally, I condemn all acts of violence against the law by all people for all reasons. This is a society of law and a society of civil behavior.

Here we are as commoners together, to some extent Democrats and Republicans, to some extent liberals and conservatives, but Americans all. Steve Gunderson today gave me a copy of the "Portable Abraham Lincoln." He suggested there is much for me to learn about our party, but I would also say that it does not hurt to have a copy of the portable F.D.R.

This is a great country of great people. If there is any one factor or acts of my life that strikes me as I stand up here as the first Republican in 40 years to do so, is when I first became whip in 1989, Russia was beginning to change, the Soviet Union as it was then. Into my whip's office one day came eight Russians and a Lithuanian, members of the Communist Party, newspaper editors. They asked me, "What does a whip do?"

They said,

"In Russia we have never had a free parliament since 1917 and that was only for a few months, so what do you do?"

I tried to explain, as Dave Bonior or Tom DeLay might now. It is a little strange if you are from a dictatorship to explain you are called the whip but you do not really have a whip, you are elected by the people you are supposed to pressure—other members. If you pressure them too much they will not reelect you. On the other hand if you do not pressure them enough they will not reelect you. Democracy is hard. It is frustrating.

So our group came into the Chamber. The Lithuanian was a man in his late sixties, and I allowed him to come up here and sit and be Speaker, something many of us have done with constituents. Remember, this is the very beginning of perestroika and glasnost. When he came out of the chair, he was physically trembling. He was almost in tears. He said,

"Ever since World War II, I have remembered what the Americans did and I have never believed the propaganda. But I have to tell you, I did not think in my life that I would be able to sit at the center of freedom."

It was one of the most overwhelming, compelling moments of my life. It struck me that something I could not help but think of when we were here with President Mandela. I went over and saw Ron Dellums and thought of the great work Ron had done to extend freedom across the planet. You get that sense of emotion when you see something so totally different than you had expected. Here was a man who reminded me first of all that while presidents are important, they are in effect an elected kingship, that this and the other body across the way are where freedom has to be fought out. That is the tradition I hope that we will take with us as we go to work.

Today we had a bipartisan prayer service. Frank Wolf made some very important points. He said,

"We have to recognize that many of our most painful problems as a country are moral problems, problems of dealing with ourselves and with life."

He said character is the key to leadership and we have to deal with that. He preached a little bit. I do not think he thought he was preaching, but he was. It was about a spirit of reconciliation. He talked about caring about our spouses and our children and our families. If we are not prepared to model our own family life beyond just having them here for one day, if we are not prepared to care about our children and we are not prepared to care about our families, then by what arrogance do we think we will transcend our behavior to care about others? That is why with Congressman Gephardt's help we have established a bipartisan task force on the family. We have established the principle that we are going to set schedules we stick to so families can count on time to be together, built around school schedules so that families can get to know each other, and not just by seeing us on C-SPAN.

I will also say that means one of the strongest recommendations of the bipartisan committee, is that we have 17 minutes to vote. This is the bipartisan committee's recommendations, not just mine. They pointed out that if we take the time we spent in the last Congress where we waited for one more member, and one more, and one more, that we literally can shorten the business and get people home if we will be strict and firm. At one point this year we had a 45-minute vote. I hope all of my colleagues are paying attention because we are in fact going to work very hard to have 17 minute votes and it is over. So, leave on the first bell, not the second bell. Ok? This may seem particularly inappropriate to say on the first day because this will be the busiest day on opening day in congressional history.

I want to read just a part of the Contract With America. I don't mean this as a partisan act, but rather to remind all of us what we are about to go through and why. Those of us who ended up in the majority stood on these steps and signed a contract, and here is part of what it says:

"On the first day of the 104th Congress the new Republican majority will immediately pass the following reforms aimed at restoring the faith and trust of the American people in their government: First, require all laws that apply to the rest of the country also to apply equally to the Congress. Second, select a major, independent auditing firm to conduct a comprehensive audit of the Congress for waste, fraud or abuse. Third, cut the number of House committees and cut committee staffs by a third. Fourth, limit the terms of all committee chairs. Fifth, ban the casting of proxy votes in committees. Sixth, require committee meetings to be open to the public. Seven, require a three-fifths majority vote to pass a tax increase. Eight, guarantee an honest accounting of our federal budget by implementing zero baseline budgeting."

Now, I told Dick Gephardt last night that if I had to do it over again we would have pledged within 3 days that we will do these things, but that is not what we said. So we have ourselves in a little bit of a box here.

Then we go a step further. I carry the *T.V. Guide* version of the contract with me at all times.

We then say that within the first 100 days of the 104th Congress we shall bring to the House floor the following bills, each to be given full and open debate, each to be given a full and clear vote, and each to be immediately available for inspection. We made it available that day. We listed 10 items. A balanced budget amendment and line-item veto, a bill to stop violent criminals, emphasizing among other things an effective and enforceable death penalty. Third was welfare reform. Fourth, legislation protecting our kids. Fifth was to provide tax cuts for families. Sixth was a bill to strengthen our national defense. Seventh was a bill to raise the senior citizen's earning limit. Eighth was legislation rolling back Government regulations. Ninth was a commonsense legal reform bill, and tenth was congressional term limits legislation.

Our commitment on our side, and this is an absolute obligation, is first of all to work today until we are done. I know that is going to inconvenience people who have families and supporters. But we were hired to do a job, and we have to start today to prove we will do it. Second, I would say to our friends in the Democratic Party that we are going to work with you, and we are really laying out a schedule working with the minority leader to make sure that we can set dates certain to go home. That does mean that if 2 or 3 weeks out we are running short we will, frankly, have longer sessions on Tuesday, Wednesday, and Thursday. We will try to work this out on a bipartisan basis to, in a workmanlike way, get it done. It is going to mean the busiest early months since 1933.

Beyond the Contract I think there are two giant challenges. I know I am a partisan figure. But I really hope today that I can speak for a minute to my friends in the Democratic Party as well as my own colleagues, and speak to the country about these two challenges so that I hope we can have a real dialog. One challenge is to achieve a balanced budget by 2002. I think both Democratic and Republican governors will say we can do that but it is hard. I do not think we can do it in a year or two. I do not think we ought to lie to the American people. This is a huge, complicated job.

The second challenge is to find a way to truly replace the current welfare state with an opportunity society.

Let me talk very briefly about both challenges. First, on the balanced budget I think we can get it done. I think the baby boomers are now old enough that we can have an honest dialog about priorities, about resources, about what works, and what does not work. Let me say I have already told Vice President Gore that we are going to invite him to address a Republican conference. We would have invited him in December but he had to go to Moscow. I believe there are grounds for us to talk together and to work together, to have hearings together, and to have task forces together. If we set priorities, if we apply the principles of Edward Deming and of Peter Drucker we can build on the Vice President's reinventing government effort and we can focus on transforming, not just cutting. The choice becomes not just do you want more or do you want less, but are there ways to do it better? Can we learn from the private sector, can we learn from Ford,

IBM, from Microsoft, from what General Motors has had to go through? I think on a bipartisan basis we owe it to our children and grandchildren to get this government in order and to be able to actually pay our way. I think 2002 is a reasonable timeframe. I would hope that together we could open a dialog with the American people.

I have said that I think Social Security ought to be off limits, at least for the first 4 to 6 years of the process, because I think it will just destroy us if we try to bring it into the game. But let me say about everything else, whether it is Medicare, or it is agricultural subsidies, or it is defense or anything that I think the greatest Democratic President of the 20th century, and in my judgment the greatest President of the 20th century, said it right. On March 4, 1933, he stood in braces as a man who had polio at a time when nobody who had that kind of disability could be anything in public life. He was President of the United States, and he stood in front of this Capitol on a rainy March day and he said,

"We have nothing to fear but fear itself."

I want every one of us to reach out in that spirit and pledge to live up to that spirit, and I think frankly on a bipartisan basis. I would say to members of the Black and Hispanic Caucuses that I would hope we could arrange by late spring to genuinely share districts. You could have a Republican who frankly may not know a thing about your district agree to come for a long weekend with you, and you will agree to go for a long weekend with them. We begin a dialog and an openness that is totally different than people are used to seeing in politics in America. I believe if we do that we can then create a dialog that can lead to a balanced budget.

But I think we have a greater challenge. I do want to pick up directly on what Dick Gephardt said, because he said it right. No Republican here should kid themselves about it. The greatest leaders in fighting for an integrated America in the 20th century were in the Democratic Party. The fact is, it was the liberal wing of the Democratic Party that ended segregation. The fact is that it was Franklin Delano Roosevelt who gave hope to a Nation that was in distress and could have slid into dictatorship. Every Republican has much to learn from studying what the Democrats did right.

But I would say to my friends in the Democratic Party that there is much to what Ronald Reagan was trying to get done. There is much to what is being done today by Republicans like Bill Weld, and John Engler, and Tommy Thompson, and George Allen, and Christy Whitman, and Pete Wilson. There is much we can share with each other.

We must replace the welfare state with an opportunity society. The balanced budget is the right thing to do. But it does not in my mind have the moral urgency of coming to grips with what is happening to the poorest Americans.

I commend to all Marvin Olasky's "The Tragedy of American Compassion." Olasky goes back for 300 years and looked at what has worked in America, how we have helped people rise beyond poverty, and how we have reached out to save people. He may not have the answers, but he has the right sense of where we have to go as Americans.

I do not believe that there is a single American who can see a news report of a 4-year-old thrown off of a public housing project in Chicago by other children and killed and not feel that a part of your heart went, too. I think of my nephew in the back, Kevin, and how all of us feel about our children. How can any American read about an 11-year-old buried with his teddy bear because he killed a 14-year-old, and then another 14-year-old killed him, and not have some sense of "My God, where has this country gone?" How can we not decide that this is a moral crisis equal to segregation, equal to slavery? How can we not insist that every day we take steps to do something?

I have seldom been more shaken than I was after the election when I had breakfast with two members of the Black Caucus. One of them said to me,

"Can you imagine what it is like to visit a first-grade class and realize that every fourth or fifth young boy in that class may be dead or in jail within 15 years? And they are your constituents and you are helpless to change it?"

For some reason, I do not know why, maybe because I visit a lot of schools, that got through. I mean, that personalized it. That made it real, not just statistics, but real people.

Then I tried to explain part of my thoughts by talking about the need for alternatives to the bureaucracy, and we got into what I think frankly has been a pretty distorted and cheap debate over orphanages.

Let me say, first of all, my father, who is here today, was a foster child. He was adopted as a teenager. I am adopted. We have relatives who were adopted. We are not talking out of some vague impersonal Dickens "Bleak House" middle-class intellectual model. We have lived the alternatives.

I believe when we are told that children are so lost in the city bureaucracies that there are children who end up in dumpsters, when we are told that there are children doomed to go to schools where 70 or 80 percent of them will not graduate, when we are told of public housing projects that are so dangerous that if any private sector ran them they would be put in jail, and the only solution we are given is, "Well, we will study it, we will get around to it," my only point is that this is unacceptable. We can find ways immediately to do things better, to reach out, break through the bureaucracy and give every young American child a better chance.

Let me suggest to you Morris Schectman's new book. I do not agree with all of it, but it is fascinating. It is entitled "Working Without a Net." It is an effort to argue that in the 21st century we have to create our own safety nets. He draws a distinction between caring and caretaking. It is worth every American reading.

He said caretaking is when you bother me a little bit, and I do enough, I feel better because I think I took care of you. That is not any good to you at all. You may be in fact an alcoholic and I just gave you the money to buy the bottle that kills you, but I feel better and go home. He said caring is actually stopping and dealing with the human being, trying to understand enough about them to genuinely make sure you improve their life, even if you have to start with a conversation like, "If you will quit drinking, I will help you get a job." This is a lot harder conversation than, "I feel better. I gave him a buck or 5 bucks."

I want to commend every member on both sides to look carefully. I say to those Republicans who believe in total privatization, you cannot believe in the Good Samaritan and explain that as long as business is making money we can walk by a fellow American who is hurt and not do something. I would say to my friends on the left who believe there has never been a government program that was not worth keeping, you cannot look at some of the results we now have and not want to reach out to the humans and forget the bureaucracies.

If we could build that attitude on both sides of this aisle, we would be an amazingly different place, and the country would begin to be a different place.

We have to create a partnership. We have to reach out to the American people. We are going to do a lot of important things. Thanks to the House Information System and Congressman Vern Ehlers, as of today we are going to be on line for the whole country, every amendment, every conference report. We are working with C-SPAN and others, and Congressman Gephardt has agreed to help on a bipartisan basis to make the building more open to television, more accessible to the American people. We have talk radio hosts here today for the first time. I hope to have a bipartisan effort to make the place accessible for all talk radio hosts of all backgrounds, no matter their ideology. The House Historian's office is going to be more aggressively run on a bipartisan basis to reach out to Close Up, and to other groups to teach what the legislative struggle is about. I think over time we can and will this Spring rethink campaign reform and lobbying reform and review all ethics, including the gift rule.

But that isn't enough. Our challenge shouldn't be just to balance the budget or to pass the Contract. Our challenge should not be anything that is just legislative. We are supposed to, each one of us, be leaders. I think our challenge has to be to set as our goal, and maybe we are not going to get there in 2 years. This ought to be the goal that we go home and we tell people we believe in: that there will be a Monday morning when for the entire weekend not a single child was killed anywhere in America; that there will be a Monday morning when every child in the country went to a school that they and their parents thought prepared them as citizens and prepared them to compete in the world market; that there will be a Monday morning where it was easy to find a job or create a job, and your own government did not punish you if you tried.

We should not be happy just with the language of politicians and the language of legislation. We should insist that our success for America is felt in the neighborhoods, in the communities, is felt by real people living real lives who can say, "Yes we are safer, we are healthier, we are better educated, America succeeds."

This morning's closing hymn at the prayer service was the "Battle Hymn of the Republic." It is hard to be in this building, look down past Grant to the Lincoln Memorial and not realize how painful and how difficult that battle hymn is. The key phrase is, "As he died to make men holy, let us live to make men free."

It is not just political freedom, although I agree with everything Congressman Gephardt said earlier. If you cannot afford to leave the public housing project, you are not free. If you do not know how to find a job and do not know how to create a job, you are not free. If you cannot find a place that will educate you, you are not free. If you are afraid to walk to the store because you could get killed, you are not free.

So as all of us over the coming months sing that song, "As he died to make men holy, let us live to make men free," I want us to dedicate ourselves to reach out in a genuinely nonpartisan way to be honest with each other. I promise each of you that without regard to party my door is going to be open. I will listen to each of you. I will try to work with each of you. I will put in long hours, and I will guarantee that I will listen to you first. I will let you get it all out before I give you my version, because you have been patient with me today, and you have given me a chance to set the stage.

But I want to close by reminding all of us of how much bigger this is than us. Because beyond talking with the American people, beyond working together, I think we can only be successful if we start with our limits. I was very struck this morning with something Bill Emerson used, a very famous quote of Benjamin Franklin, at the point where the Constitutional Convention was deadlocked. People were tired, and there was a real possibility that the Convention was going to break up. Franklin, who was quite old and had been relatively quiet for the entire Convention, suddenly stood up and was angry, and he said:

"I have lived, sir, a long time, and the longer I live the more convincing proofs I see of this truth, that God governs in the affairs of men, and if a sparrow cannot fall to the ground without His notice, is it possible that an empire can rise without His aid?"

At that point the Constitutional Convention stopped. They took a day off for fasting and prayer.

Then, having stopped and come together, they went back, and they solved the great question of large and small States. They wrote the Constitution, and the United States was created. All I can do is pledge to you that, if each of us will reach out prayerfully and try to genuinely understand each other, if we will recognize that in this building we symbolize America, and that we have an obligation to talk with each other, then I think a year from now we can look on the 104th Congress as a truly amazing institution without regard to party, without regard to ideology. We can say, "Here, America comes to work, and here we are preparing for those children a better future."

Thank you. Good luck and God bless you.

# A Government That Helps People Help Themselves[9]

Bill Clinton

*Born August 19, 1946, Hope, AR; B.S., Georgetown University, 1968; Rhodes Scholar, Oxford University, 1968-70; J.D., Yale University Law School, 1973; faculty, University of Arkansas School of Law, 1973-76; attorney general, Arkansas, 1976-77; governor, Arkansas, 1979-81, 1983-92; president of the United States, 1992–.*

## Editor's introduction

In response to the bombing of the federal building in Oklahoma City, President Bill Clinton insisted that "personal freedom" carries the requisite of self-discipline. When that is not the case, the results, as illustrated by the bombing, are often disastrous. In this speech, Clinton extended the notions of freedom tempered by self-discipline and the role of the government within American society. Clinton remarked that in place of creating bureaucracy, "the government ought to . . . reward responsibility with more opportunity [and] empower people to make the most of their own lives." Government is therefore understood as a facilitator, or a means by which virtues such as hard work and discipline are gratified with all that is embodied by the "American Dream."

---

Thank you very much, Mr. President, Mr. Speaker, Governor Branstad, Mr. Chief Justice, and members of the Supreme Court, distinguished Iowa state officials. And former Congressman Neil Smith, my good friend, and Mrs. Smith, thank you for being here. To all of you who are members of the Iowa legislature, House and Senate, Republican and Democrat, it is a great honor for me to be here today.

I feel that I'm back home again. When I met the legislative leadership on the way in and we shared a few words and then they left to come in here, and I was standing around with my crowd, I said, you know, I really miss state government. I'll say more about why in a moment.

I'd like to, if I might, recognize one of your members to thank him for agreeing to join my team—Representative Running will now be the Secretary of Labor's representative. Would you stand up, please. Thank you.

Representative Running is going to be the representative of the Secretary of Labor for region 7—Iowa, Nebraska, Missouri and Kansas. And if you will finish your business here pretty soon, he can actually go to Kansas City and get to work—which I would appreciate.

I'm delighted to be back in Iowa. I had a wonderful day here, and it was good to be here when it was dry—although a little rain doesn't do any harm.

We had a wonderful meeting today at Iowa State University with which I'm sure all of you are familiar, this National Rural Conference we had, designed to lay the groundwork for a strategy for rural America to include not only the farm bill, but also a rural development strategy and a strategy generally to deal with the problems of rural America—with the income disparities with the rest of America, the age disparities with the rest of America, and the problems of getting services and maintaining the quality of life in rural America.

I want to thank Governor Branstad for his outstanding presentation and the information he gave us about the efforts being made in Iowa in developing your fiber optic network and developing the health care reform initiatives for rural Iowans and many other areas. I want to

[9]Delivered to the Iowa State Legislature, in Des Moines, Iowa, on April 25, 1995.

thank Senator Harkin for his presentation, particularly involving the development of alternative agricultural products as a way to boost income in rural America. And I want to say a special word of thanks to the people at Iowa State. They did a magnificent job there, and I know you are all very proud of that institution, and you would have been very, very proud of them today, the way they performed.

I'm also just glad to be back here in the setting of state government. You know, Governor Branstad and I were once the youngest governors in America, but time took care of it. And now that he's been reelected, he will actually serve more years than I did. I ran for a fifth term as governor. We used to have two-year terms, and then we switched to four-year terms. And only one person in the history of our state had ever served more than eight years, and only one person had ever served more than—two people had served more than two terms, but those were two-year terms—in the whole history of the state. So I was—I had served 10 years. I'd served three two-year terms and one four-year term, and I was . . . attempting to be reelected. And I had a high job approval rating, but people were reluctant to vote for me, because in my state people are very suspicious of too much political power, you know. And I thought I was still pretty young and healthy, but half of them wanted to give me a gold watch, you know, and send me home.

And I never will forget one day when I was running for my fifth term, I was out at the State Fair doing governor's day at the State Fair, which I always did, and I would just sit there and anybody that wanted to talk to me could up and say whatever was on their mind, which was, for me a hazardous undertaking from time to time—since they invariably would do exactly that. And I stayed there all day long, and I talked about everything under the moon and sun with the people who came up and, long about the end of the day, this elderly fellow in overalls came up to me and he said, Bill, you going to run for governor, again? And I hadn't announced yet. I said, I don't know. If I do, will you vote for me? He said, yes, I always have. I guess I will again. And I said, well, aren't you sick of me after all these years? He said, no, but everybody else I know is.

But he went on to say—and that's the point I want to make about state government—he said, people get tired of it because all you do is nag us. You nag us to modernize the economy, you nag us to improve the schools, you just nag, nag, nag. But he said, I think it's beginning to work. And what I have seen in state after state after state over the last 15 years as we have gone through these wrenching economic and social changes in America and as we face challenge after challenge after challenge, is people able consistently to come together to overcome their differences, to focus on what it will take to build a state and to move forward. And we need more of that in America.

In Iowa, you do embody our best values. People are independent, but committed to one another. They work hard and play by the rules, but they work together. Those of us who come from small towns understand that everybody counts. We don't have a person to waste. And the fact that Iowa has done such a good job in developing all of your people is one of the reasons that you are so strong in every single national indicator of success that I know of. And you should be very, very proud of what, together, you have done.

I saw some of that American spirit in a very painful way in Oklahoma City this week, and all of you saw it as well. I know you share the grief of the people there. But you must also share the pride of all Americans in seeing the enormity of the effort which is being exerted there, by firemen and police officers, and nurses, by rescue workers, by people who have come from all over America and given up their lives to try to help Oklahoma City and the people there who have suffered so much loss rebuild.

I want to say again what I have tried to say for the last three days to the American people. On this National Day of Service, there is a service we can do to ensure that we build on, and learn from, this experience.

We must always fight for the freedom of speech. The first Amendment, with its freedom of speech, freedom of assembly and freedom of worship, is the essence of what it means to be an American. And I dare say every elected official in this room would give his or her life to preserve that right for our children and our grandchildren down to the end of time.

But we have to remember that that freedom has endured in our nation for over 200 years because we practiced it with such responsibility; because we had discipline; because we understood from the Founding Fathers forward that you could not have very, very wide latitude in personal freedom until you also had, or unless you also had, great discipline in the exercise of that freedom.

So while I would defend to the death anyone's right to the broadest freedom of speech, I think we should all remember that words have consequences. And freedom should be exercised with responsibility. And when we think that others are exercising their freedom in an irresponsible way, it is our job to stand up and say that is wrong. We disagree. This is not a matter of partisan politics. It is not a matter of political philosophy. If we see the freedom of expression and speech abused in this country, whether it comes from the right or the left, from the media or from people just speaking on their own, we should stand up and say no, we don't believe in preaching violence; we don't believe in preaching hatred; we don't believe in preaching discord. Words have consequences.

If words did not have consequences, we wouldn't be here today. We're here today because Patrick Henry's words had consequences, because Thomas Jefferson's words had consequences, because Abraham Lincoln's words had consequences. And these words we hear today have consequences—the good ones and the bad ones, the ones that bring us together, and the ones that drive a wedge through our heart.

We never know in this society today who is out there dealing with all kinds of inner turmoil, vulnerable to being pushed over the edge if all they hear is a relentless clamor of hatred and division. So let us preserve free speech, but let those of us who want to fight to preserve free speech forever in America say, we must be responsible and we will be.

My fellow Americans, I come here tonight, as I went recently to the state legislature in Florida, to discuss the condition of our country, where we're going in the future, and your role in that. We know we are in a new and different world—the end of the Cold War, a new and less organized world we're living in, but one still not free of threats. We know we have come to the end of an industrial age and we're in an information age, which is less bureaucratic, more open, more dependent on technology, more full of opportunity but still full of its own problems, than the age that most of us were raised in.

We know that we no longer need the same sort of bureaucratic, top-down, service-delivering, rule-making, centralized government in Washington that served us so well during the industrial age, because times have changed. We know that with all the problems we have and all the opportunities we have, we have to think anew about what the responsibilities of our government in Washington should be, what your responsibility should be here at the state level, and through you to the local level, and what should be done more by private citizens on their own with no involvement from the government.

We know now what the central challenge of this time is, and you can see it in Iowa. You could see it today with the testimony we heard at the Rural Conference. We are at a 25-year low in the combined rates of unemployment and inflation. Our economy has produced over 6 million new jobs. But paradoxically, even in Iowa where the unemployment rate has dropped under 3.5 percent, most Americans are working harder today for the same or lower incomes than they were making 10 years ago. And many Americans feel less job security even as the recovery continues.

That is largely a function of the global economic competition, the fact that technology raises productivity at an almost unbelievable rate so fewer and fewer people can do more and more work, and that depresses wages. The fact that unless we raise it in Washington next year, the minimum wage will reach a 40-year low.

There are a lot of these things that are related one to the other. But it is perfectly clear that the economics are changing the face of American society. You can see it in the difference in income in rural America and urban America. You can see it in the difference—the aging process in rural America as compared with urban America. And if we want to preserve the American Dream, we have got to find a way to solve this riddle.

I was born in the year after World War II at the dawn of the greatest explosion of opportunity in American history and in world history. For 30 years after that, the American people, without regard to their income or region, grew and grew together. That is, each income group over the next 30 years roughly doubled their income, except the poorest 20 percent of us that had an almost 2.5 times increase in their income. So we were growing and growing together.

For about the last 15 or 20 years, half of us have been stuck so that our country is growing, but we are growing apart even within the middle class. When you put that beside the fact that we have more and more poor people who are not elderly—which was the case when I was little, but now are largely young women and their little children, often where there was either no marriage or the marriage is broken up so there is not a stable home and there is not an adequate level of education to ensure an income—you have increasing poverty and increasing splits within the middle class. That is the fundamental cause, I believe, of a lot of the problems that we face in America and a lot of the anxiety and frustration we see in this country.

Every rich country faces this problem. But in the United States, it is a particular problem—both because the inequality is greater and because it violates the American Dream. I mean, this is a country where if you work hard and you play by the rules, you obey the law, you raise your children, you do your best to do everything you're supposed to do, you ought to have an opportunity for the free enterprise system to work for you.

And so we face this challenge. I have to tell you that I believe two things: One, the future is far more hopeful than worrisome. If you look at the resources of this country, the assets of this country, and you compare them with any other country in the world, and you image what the world will be like 20 or 30 years from now, you'd have to be strongly bullish on America. You have to believe in our promise.

Secondly, I am convinced we cannot get there unless we develop a new way of talking about these issues, a new political discourse. Unless we move beyond the labeling that so often characterizes, and in fact mischaracterizes, the debate in Washington, D.C.

Now we are having this debate in ways that affect you, so you have to be a part of it, because one of the biggest parts of the debate is, how are we going to keep the American Dream alive? How are we going to keep America, the world's strongest force for freedom and democracy, into the next century, and change the way the government works?

There is broad consensus that the government in Washington should be less bureaucratic, less oriented toward rule-making, smaller, more flexible, that more decisions should be devolved to the state and local government level, and where possible, more decisions should be given to private citizens themselves. There is a broad agreement on that.

The question is, what are the details? What does that mean? What should we do? What should you do? That's what I want to talk to you about. There are clearly some national responsibilities, clearly some that would be better served here at your level.

The main reason I ran for President is, it seemed to me that we were seeing a national government in bipartisan gridlock, where we'd had 12 years in which we exploded the deficit, reduced our investment in people, and undermined our ability to compete and win in the world. And I wanted very badly to end the kind of gridlock we'd had and to see some real concrete action taken to go forward, because of my experience doing what you're doing now.

My basic belief is that the government ought to do more to help people help themselves, to reward responsibility with more opportunity, and not to give anybody opportunity without demanding responsibility. That's basically what I think our job is.

I think we can be less bureaucratic. We have to enhance security at home and abroad. But the most important thing we have to do is to empower people to make the most of their own lives.

Now, we have made a good beginning at that. As I said, we've been able to get the deficit down. You know here in Iowa, because you're a farming state, that we've had the biggest expansion of trade in the last two years we've seen in a generation. We now have a $20 billion surplus in agricultural products for the first time ever—this means more to me than you—but we're selling rice to the Japanese, something that my farmers never thought that we'd ever do. We're selling apples in Asia. We are doing our best in Washington—some of us are— to get the ethanol program up and going. This administration is for it, and I hope you will help us with that.

And we're making modest efforts which ought to be increased to work with the private sector to develop alternative agricultural products. Today I saw corn-based windshield wiper fluid, and something that I think is important, biodegradable, agriculturally-rooted golf tees. And a lot of other things that I think will be the hallmark of our future. We have only scratched the surface of what we can do to produce products from the land, from our food and fiber, and we must do more.

In education we are beginning to see the outlines of what I hope will be a genuine bipartisan national partnership in education. In the last two years we increased Head Start, we reduced the rules and regulations the federal government imposes on local school systems, but gave them more funds and flexibility to meet national standards of education. We helped states all over the country to develop comprehensive systems of apprenticeships for young people who get out of high school and don't want to go to college, but don't want to be in dead-end jobs.

We are doing more to try to make our job training programs relevant. And we have made literally millions of Americans eligible for lower cost, better repayment college loans under our direct loan program, including over 350,000 students and former students in Iowa—including all those who are at Iowa State University. Now, if you borrow money under that program, you get it quicker with less paperwork at lower cost, and you can pay it back in one of four different ways based on the income you're going to earn when you get out of college. Believe it or not, it lowers costs to the taxpayers.

And we have demanded responsibility. We've taken the loan default costs to the taxpayers from $2.8 billion a year down to $1 billion a year. That is the direction we ought to be going in.

We've worked hard to increase our security at home and abroad. The crime bill, which was passed last year by the Congress after six years of endless debate, provides for 100,000 more police officers on our street. We have already—over the next five years—we've already awarded over 17,000 police officers to over half the police departments in America, including 158 communities here in Iowa. It strengthens punishment under federal law.

The three strikes and you're out law in the crime bill is now the law of the land. The first person to be prosecuted under this law was a convicted murderer accused of an armed robbery in Waterloo last November. If he's convicted, he will go to jail for the rest of his life.

The capital punishment provisions of the crime bill will cover the incident in Oklahoma City—something that is terribly important, in my view, not only to bring justice in this case, but to send a clear signal that the United States does not intend to be dominated and paralyzed by terrorists from at home or abroad—not now, not ever. We cannot ever tolerate that.

We are also more secure from beyond our borders. For the first time since the dawn of the nuclear age, there are no Russian missiles pointed at America's children. And those nuclear weapons are being destroyed every day.

We have reduced the size of the federal government by more than 100,000. We are taking it down by more than a quarter of a million. We have eliminated or reduced 300 programs. And I have asked Congress to eliminate or consolidate 400 more. We have tried to give more flexibility to states—several states have gotten broad freedom from federal rules to implement health care reform. And we have now freed 27 states from cumbersome federal rules to try to help them end welfare as we know it.

In the almost two years since Iowa received only the second welfare waiver our administration issued, the number of welfare recipients in Iowa who hold jobs is almost doubled from 18 to 33 percent. You are doing it without punishing children for the mistakes of their parents—and I want to say more on that later—but you are doing it. And that is clear evidence that we should give the states the right to pursue welfare reform. They know how to get the job done better than the federal government has done in the past. We should give you all more responsibility for moving people from welfare to work.

Now, here's where you come in, because I want to talk in very short order, one right after the other, about the decisions we still have to make in Washington. Do we still have to cut the federal deficit more? Yes, we do. We've taken it down by $600 billion. The budget, in fact, would be balanced today if it weren't for the interest we have to pay on the debt run up between 1981 and 1992.

But it's still a problem and you need to understand why it's a problem. It's a problem because a lot of people who used to give us money to finance our government deficit and our trade deficit, need their money at home now. That's really what's happening in Japan. They need their money at home now.

We must continue—we must say to the world, to the financial markets—we will not cut taxes except in the context of reducing the deficit. America is committed. Both parties are committed. Americans are committed to getting rid of this terrible burden on our future. We must continue to do it.

Now, the question is, how are we going to do that? Should we cut unnecessary spending? Of course, we should. How do you define it? Should there be more power to state and local governments and to the private sector? You bet. But what are the details?

In other words, what we've got to do in Washington now is what you do all the time. We've got to move beyond our rhetoric to reality. And I think it would be helpful for you because we need your voice to be heard. And at least my experience in the Governors Association was, or working in my own legislature was, that on these issues we could get Republicans and Democrats together. So let me go through what we've done, and what's still to be done.

First of all, I agree with this new Congress on three issues that were in the Republican Contract—and two of them are already law. Number one, Congress should apply to itself all the laws it puts on the private sector. We should know when we make laws in Washington what we're doing to other people by experiencing it ourself. That was a good thing.

Number two, I signed the unfunded mandates legislation to make it harder, but not impossible when it [is] important, but much harder, for Congress to put on you and your taxpayers unfunded mandates from the federal government where we make you pay for something that we in Washington want to do. I strongly support that, and I think all of you do, as well.

The third thing we are doing that we have not finished yet, although both Houses have approved a version of it, is the line-item veto. Almost every governor has it. I don't want to embarrass anybody here, but I don't know how many times I had a legislature say, now, Governor, I'm going to slip this in this bill because I've got to do it, and then you can scratch it out for me. And it was fine. We did it. Now if they slip it in a bill, I have to decide what to do or not. I have to decide.

When the farmers in Iowa desperately needed the restoration of the tax deduction for health insurance, the 25 percent tax deduction that self-employed farmers and others get for health insurance, there was a provision of that bill I didn't like very much. I had to decide, am I going to give this back to 3.3 million self-employed Americans and their families, to lower the cost of health care by tax day, or not? But when we have the line-item veto, it won't be that way. And we need it.

Here are the hard ones. Number one, the farm bill. Should [w]e reduce farm supports? Yes, we should, as required by GATT. I worked hard to get the Europeans to the table in agriculture in this trade agreement. A lot of you understand that. The deal was, they would reduce their subsidies more than we would reduce ours, so we would at least move toward some parity, so that our farmers would get a fair break for a change. Now some say, let's just get rid of all these farm support programs.

Well, if we do it now, we give our competitors the advantage we worked for eight years to take away. We put family farms more at risk. Now if anybody's got better ideas about what should be in the Farm Bill, that's fine. If anybody's got a better idea about how to save the family farmers, let's do it. If anybody has new ideas about what should be put in for rural development, fine. But let us do no harm. Let us not labor under the illusion that having fought so hard to have a competitive agricultural playing field throughout the world, having achieved a $20 billion surplus in agriculture, we can turn and walk away from the farmers of the country in the name of cutting spending. That is not the way to cut the federal deficit.

I'll give you another example. Some believe that we should flat fund the school lunch program. And then there's a big argument in Washington, is it a cut or not. Let me tell you something, all these block grants are designed not only to give you more flexibility, but to save the federal government money. Now it may be a good deal, or it may not. You have to decide. But when we wanted to cut the Agriculture Department budget—we're closing nearly 1,200 offices, we're reducing employment by 13,000, we eliminated 14 divisions in the Department of Agriculture—my own view is, that is better than putting an arbitrary cap on the school lunch program, which will be terribly unfair to the number—to the numerous school districts in this country that have increasing burdens from low income children. There are a lot of kids in this country—a lot of kids—the only decent meal they get every day is the meal they get at school. This program works. If it's not broke, we shouldn't fix it. So I don't agree with that. But you have to decide.

Welfare reform. I've already said, we have now given more welfare reform waivers to states to get out from under the federal government than were given in the last 12 years put together. In two years, we've given more than 12 years. I am for you figuring out how you want to run you[r] welfare system and move people from welfare to work. I am for that.

But here are the questions. Number one, should we have cumbersome federal rules that say you have to penalize teenage girls who give birth to children and cut them off? I don't think so. We should never punish children for the mistakes of their parents. And these children who become parents prematurely, we should say, you made a mistake, you shouldn't do that—no child should do that. But what we're going to do is to impose responsibilities on you for the future, to make you a responsible parent, a responsible student, a responsible worker. That's what your program does. Why should the federal government tell you that you have to punish children, when what you really want to do is move people from welfare to work so that more people are good parents and good workers. You should decide that. We do not need to be giving you lectures about how you have to punish the kids of this country. We need a welfare bill that is tough on work and compassionate toward children—not a welfare bill that is weak on work and tough on children. I feel that that should be a bipartisan principle that all of us should be able to embrace.

Now, the second issue in welfare reform is whether we should give you a block grant. Instead of having the welfare being an individual entitlement to every poor person on welfare, should we just give you whatever money we gave you last year or over the last three years and let you spend it however you want? There are two issues here that I ask you to think about, not only from your perspective, but from the perspective of every other state.

In Florida, the Republicans in legislature I spoke with were not for this. And here's why. The whole purpose of the block grant is twofold. One is, we give you more flexibility. The second is, we say in return for more flexibility, you ought to be able to do the job for less money, so we won't increase the money you're getting over the next five years, which means we'll get to save money and lower the deficit. If it works for everybody concerned it's a good deal.

But what are the states—there are two problems with a block grant in this area, and I want you to help me work through it, because I am for more flexibility for the states. I would give every state every waiver that I have given to any state. I want you to decide what to do with this. I want you to be out there creating innovative ways to break the cycle of welfare dependency.

But there are two problems with this. Number one, if you have a state with a very large number of children eligible for public assistance and they're growing rapidly, it's very hard to devise any formula that keeps you from getting hurt in the block grants over a five-year period. And some states have rapidly growing populations—Florida, Texas, probably California.

Number two, a total block grant relieves the state of any responsibility to put up the match that is now required for you to participate in the program. Now, you may say, well, we would do that anyway. We have a tradition in Iowa of taking care of our own. But what if you lived in a state with a booming population growth, with wildly competing demands for dollars? And what about when the next recession comes? Keep in mind, we're making all these decisions today in the second year in which every state economy is growing. That has not happened in a very long time.

Will that really be fair? How do you know that there won't be insurmountable pressure in some states just to say, well, we can't take care of these children anymore; we've got to give the money to our school teachers; we've got to give the money to our road program; we've got to give the money to economic development; we've got environmental problems. So I ask you to think about those things. We can find a way to let you control the welfare system and move people from welfare to work, but there are two substantive problems with the block grant program that I want to see overcome before I sign off on it, because there is a national responsibility to care for the children of the country, to make sure a minimal standard of care is given. Thank you.

In the crime bill, there is a proposal to take what we did last time, which was to divide the money between police, prisons and prevention, and basically give you a block grant in prevention, and instead create two separate block grants, one for prisons and one for police and prevention, in which you would reduce the amount of money for police and prevention and increase the amount of money for prisons, but you could only get it if you decided—a mandate, but a funded one—if you decided to make all people who committed serious crimes serve 85 percent of their sentences.

So Washington is telling you how you have to sentence people but offering you money to build prisons. The practical impact means that a lot of that money won't be taken care of, and we will reduce the amount of money we're spending for police and for prevention programs. I think that's a mistake.

I'm more than happy for you to have block grants for prevention programs. You know more about what keeps kids out of jail and off the streets and from committing crime in Des Moines or Cedar Rapids or Ames or any place else than I would ever know. But we do know that the violent crime rate has tripled in the last 30 years, and the number of police on our streets has only gone up by 10 percent. And we know there is city, after city, after city in America where the crime rate has gone down a lot, a lot when police have been put on the street in community policing roles.

So I say, let's keep the 100,000 police program. It is totally nonbureaucratic. Small towns in Iowa can get it by filling out a one-page, eight-question form. There is no hassle. And we should do this because we know it works. There is a national interest in safer streets, and it's all paid for by reducing the federal bureaucracy. So my view is, keep the 100,000 police, give the states flexibility on prevention. And I hope that you will agree with that. That, at any rate, is my strong feeling.

Lastly, let me say on education, I simply don't believe that we should be cutting education to reduce the deficit or pay for tax cuts. I don't believe that. I just don't believe that.

So my view—my view on this is that the way to save money is to give every university in the country and every college in the country the right to do what Iowa State has done—go to the direct loan program, cut out the middle man, lower the cost of loans, save the taxpayer money.

I am strongly opposed to charging the students interest on their student loans while they're in college. That will add 18 to 20 percent to the cost of education for a lot of our young people. We'll have fewer people going to school. We want more people going to school. I think that is a mistake.

I believe if we're going to have a tax cut, it should be targeted to middle class people and to educational needs. I believe strongly we should do two things more than anything else. Number one, give more people the advantage of an IRA, which they can put money into and save and then withdraw to pay for education or health care costs, purchase of a first-time home, or care of an elderly parent tax-free. Number two, allow the deduction of the cost of education after high school to all American middle-class families. Now, that, I think, will make a difference.

This is very important for you because, remember, we have a smaller total tax cut, if we target it to the middle class, we can have deficit reduction without cutting education. We can have deficit reduction without having severe cuts in Medicare. Governor Branstad said today, one of our biggest problems is the unfairness of the distribution of Medicare funds. You are right. It's not fair to rural America. But there's a lot more coming, and more than you need to have if we have an excessive tax cut that is not targeted to education and to the middle class.

So that, in brief, is the laundry list of the new federalism—the things you need to decide on. I do not believe these issues I have spoken with you about have a partisan tinge in Des Moines. They need not have one in Washington.

But I invite you, go back home—this is being televised tonight—go back home and talk to the people you represent, and ask them what they want you to say to your members of Congress about what we do in Washington; what you do in Des Moines; what we do in our private lives; what should be spent to reduce the deficit; what should be spent on a tax cut; what should be in a block grant; and where should we stand up and say we've got to protect the children of the country. These are great and exciting issues.

Believe me, if we make the right decisions—if we make the right decisions, the 21st century will still be the American century.

Thank you all, and God bless you.

# Four Points of the Compass: Restoring America's Sense of Direction[10]

Balint Vazsonyi

*Born 1936, Budapest, Hungary; Artist Diploma, Liszi Academy, 1956; M.M., Florida State University, 1960; Ph.D., University of Budapest, 1982; professor, Indiana University, 1978-84; dean of music, New World School of the Arts, 1993-95; director, Center for the American Founding, 1995–.*

## Editor's introduction

In this speech, Balint Vazsonyi, artist and director of the Center for the American Founding, attacks the "group rights and arbitrary privileges" that he asserts have made "a mockery of the constitutional rights of the individual." For Vazsonyi, American government has departed from a concern for the individual. To counter this "erosion of America's founding principles," Vazsonyi, with the Center for the American Founding, proposes the "Four Points of the Compass"—"rule of law, individual rights, the sanctity of property, and the sense of national identity."

---

Although the press appears not to have noticed, President Clinton, in his Second Inaugural Address, called for a new Constitution. He borrowed language from the Declaration of Independence, where in 1776 Thomas Jefferson presented the argument for a new government. On January 20, 1997, Mr. Clinton proclaimed, "We need a new government for a new century." He proceeded set forth all the things this new government would *give* the American people.

Today, I come before you to argue that we need just the opposite. We, at the Center for the American Founding, believe that a tool is necessary to guide us back to the path of our existing Constitution. We offer this tool to the decision makers, legislators, and judges of America and ask all of you to help us develop it to its full potential. Because it points the way, we think of it as a compass.

What kind of country will exert its best efforts for the benefit of all mankinds? Or engage in war without expectation of gain? What kind of country makes it possible that a person who did not grow up in it feel sufficiently at home to step forward with a major initiative? What kind of country has long-time professionals coming together to hear a relative novice with a foreign accent speak on national issues? What kind of country? A country that is one of a kind.

**A Unique Nation**

As we contemplate the future, it is essential that we keep in mind that America, indeed, is one of a kind. Some believe with all their hearts that people, and their aspirations, are the same everywhere. This may be so. But the *nation* established here more than 200 years ago has neither precedent nor a parallel in the known history of this planet. Not its capacity for success; not its capacity for strength; not its capacity for goodness. It is one of a kind.

One of a kind. A big term. You hear it and think of Shakespeare. Or Beethoven. Or George Washington. We look at their work and try to understand what makes it so. It is a hopeless endeavor. But with America, there are definite ingredients we can identify quite easily: the rule of law, individual rights, guaranteed property, and so forth. A funny thing, ingredients. We acknowledge their importance in all sorts of scenarios, yet ignore them when it comes to matters of life and death. If we eat something mem-

[10]Delivered to the Heritage Foundation, in Washington, D.C., on February 13, 1997. Reprinted with permission of The Heritage Foundation.

orable, we want the recipe. With food, we know without the shadow of a doubt that the ingredients make the thing.

Chocolate ice cream, for example, takes chocolate, cream, and sugar. If, instead, you use ground beef, mustard, and A-1 Steak Sauce, you don't expect chocolate ice cream to come out of the process. Whatever else is the end creation, chocolate ice cream it will not be. Ice cream comes in many varieties. America is one of a kind. Do we honestly expect it to remain America if the ingredients are changed?

Over the past decades, rule of law has been displaced by something called "social justice." Group rights and arbitrary privileges make a mockery of the constitutional rights of the individual. Where not so long ago all Americans could feel secure in their right to acquire and hold property, government today is no longer discussing whether—only how *much* of it—to confiscate, and how to redistribute it. As you see, the ingredients have already undergone drastic change. Is it reasonable to hope that America will nevertheless remain America?

And the greatest variety of assaults is launched against something I have come to refer to as "national identity." Now, I realize that some people might have a reaction to that phrase because the term has been used by others as a wedge. I use it as a magnet. As such, it is a necessity. Something needs to bind people together, especially when they have converged, and continue to converge, upon a place from every corner of the globe.

Identity is about being similar or being different. Since our differences have been amply provided for by nature, we have to agree about those aspects of our lives that will make us similar. For the shared history that other nations have, Americans have successfully substituted a shared belief in, and adherence to, certain principles. A common language took the place of a shared culture. No state religion was established, but a Bible-based morality is taken for granted. Add to this a certain work ethic, an expectation of competence in your field of work (whether you split the atom or sweep the floors), a spirit of voluntary cooperation, insistence on choice, a fierce sense of independence—and you have the ingredients of the American identity. And, if you prefer to call it American character or, as George Washington did, "national character," it will serve our purpose so long as we remain agreed about the ingredients. For it is these ingredients that have distinguished us from other societies, and enabled those who sweep the floors today to split the atom tomorrow.

**The Founders' Compass**

Today, our nation's leaders are engaged in choosing a path to pursue. Yet, all along, we have had a path to *follow*. It is clearly pointed in the Declaration of Independence, and our Founding Fathers complemented it with a superb road map they called the Constitution of the United States. Add to this the glossary we know as the *Federalist Papers* and it is hard to see why and how we could have lost our sense of direction. But lost it we have. That is why we need a compass—the compass in the title of these remarks.

Between 1776 and 1791, our compass was calibrated to keep us on the path of betterment—as individuals and as a nation. We even had a kind of "North Star," a magnetic North, in what we call the rule of law. But instead, we now have rule by the law*maker*. Every member of the executive branch, every member of the judiciary has become a potential lawmaker, and, in most cases, they use its potential to the hilt.

Yet the rule of law stands for the exact opposite. As its basic property, it places the fundamental tenets beyond the reach of politics and politicians. Whereas it confers legitimacy upon subsequent laws that spring from its eternal well, it denies legitimacy to all legislative maneuvers that corrupt its purpose. It holds the makers, executors, and adjudicators of the law accountable at all times. Above all, it demands equal application to every man, woman, and child. Within its own framework, a prescribed majority may amend the law. But as the law stands at any given moment, it must be applied equally. If accomplished, nothing in the history of human societies can match the significance and magnificence of equality before the law.

The aspiration for equality before the law began with the Magna Carta or even earlier, in King Arthur's court, where knights sat at a *round* table. But it took Thomas Jefferson to etch the concept in the minds of freedom-loving people everywhere, more permanently than posterity could have etched the words in the marble of the Jefferson Memorial. And even then, after those immortal words of the Declaration of Independence had been written, it took most of two centuries before America, land of the many miracles, almost made it a reality for the first time ever.

**Attack on Rule of Law, Individual Rights**

But it was not to be. The rule of law, our only alternative to the law of the jungle, came under attack just as it was about to triumph. The attacker displayed the irresistible charm of the temptress, the armament of the enraged avenger, dressed itself in intoxicating clichés, and wore the insignia of the highest institutions of learning. It called itself "social justice."

Let me make it clear: I do not speak of social conscience. *That* is a frame of mind, a noble sentiment, a measure of civilization. Precisely for that reason, while it has everything to do with our conduct, it has nothing whatsoever to do with laws. "Social justice," on the other hand, aims at the heart of our legal system by setting an unattainable goal, by fueling discontent, by insinuating a permanent state of hopelessness.

But above all, social justice is unacceptable as the basis for a stable society because, unlike the law, it is what anyone says it is on any given day. We need only to move back a few years, or travel a few thousand miles, and one is certain to find an entirely different definition of social justice. At the end of the day, it is nothing more than an empty slogan, to be filled by power-hungry political activists so as to enlist the participation of well-intentioned people.

The rule of law and a world according to "social justice" are mutually exclusive. One cannot have it both ways.

What have the rule of law and the pursuit of "social justice" respectively spawned over time? The rule of law gave birth to a series of individual rights. In other words, rights vested solely in individuals. Only individuals are capable of having rights, just as only individuals can be free. We say a society is free if the individuals who make up that society are free. For individuals to be free, they must have certain unalienable rights, and others upon which they had agreed with one another.

Social justice has spawned an aberration called "group rights." Group rights are the negation of individual rights. Group rights in effect say, "You cannot and do not have rights as an individual—only as a member of a certain group." The rule of law knows nothing about groups; therefore, it could not provide for, or legitimize rights of, groups. Groups have no standing in the eyes of the law. And, since their so-called rights are invariably created and conferred by persons of temporary authority, they are "subject to change without notice," as the saying goes, just like the definition of social justice itself.

Individual rights recognize and promote similarity. Group rights promote differences and stereotypes. Individual rights and group rights are mutually exclusive. One cannot have it both ways.

Among our individual rights, the right to acquire and hold property has a special place. If ever a concept came to be developed to protect the weak against the strong, to balance inborn gifts with the fruits of sheer diligence and industry, *property inviolate* is its name. But who am I to speak, after John Locke, Thomas Jefferson, and James Madison have pronounced on this topic. They held that civilized society is predicated upon the sanctity of private property, and that to guarantee it is government's primary function. Without absolute property there is no incentive. Without absolute property there is no security. Without absolute property there is no liberty. The freedom to enter into contract, the freedom to keep what is mine, and the freedom to dispose of what is mine underlies all our liberties.

Neither the search for "social justice" nor so-called group rights recognize, or respect, private property. They look upon flesh-and-blood individuals as faceless members of a multitude who, together, create a certain amount of goods. These goods belong to what they call the "Community." Then certain people decide who needs what and, being privy to some higher wisdom, distribute—actually *re*distribute—the goods. Redistribution is pursuant to group rights expressed in something called *entitlement.* Entitlements are based neither upon law nor upon accomplishment. Entitlements are based on membership in a certain group, and we have seen that groups are designated by persons of temporary authority, rather than the law.

The right to property and entitlements through redistribution are mutually exclusive. One cannot have it both ways.

Multicultural Identity

We have been ordered by the prophets of social justice to replace our national identity with something they call "multiculturalism." I will confess that some time in the past, I might have shared the allergic reaction some of you experience in the face of "national" and "identity." But then I noticed the enormous importance the social justice crowd attaches to the destruction of the American identity. Just think:

bilingual education and multilingual ballots. Removal of the founding documents from our schools. Anti-American history standards. Exiling the Ten Commandments. Replacing American competence with generic "self-esteem." Replacing voluntarism with coercion. Encouraging vast numbers of new immigrants to ignore the very reasons that brought them here in the first place. The list goes on, and sooner or later it will affect national defense, if it hasn't already.

And for those who would point to Yugoslavia as proof of the tragedy nationalism can cause, let me say that a healthy national identity is utterly distinct from nationalism. Like the United States, Yugoslavia was created. But unlike in the case of the United States, ingredients for a national identity were not provided, and Yugoslavia imploded at the first opportunity precisely for that reason. Had it not done so, it would have succumbed to the first external attack, for no Croat would lay down his life for the good of Serbs or Bosnians. Will Americans lay down their lives if America is nothing but a patchwork of countless group identities?

Will the armed forces of the United States fight to uphold, defend, and advance the cause of multiculturalism?

This is not a frivolous question.

The questions before us are serious, and legion. We are virtually drowning in what we call "issues," and they are becoming increasingly difficult to sort out. How do we find our position? And, once we find our position, how do we argue its merit? Above all, how do we avoid the plague of every issue coming at us like an octopus and, just as we figure out how to tackle each arm, turning into a turtle inside its impenetrable shell?

Re-Calibrating the Compass

We asked you to hear me today, because the Center for the American Founding has a proposal to submit. We call it "Four Points of the Compass" because these points provide direction, because, in a manner of speaking, they constitute a re-calibration of our compass, which the events of the past 30 years have distorted. They are the rule of law, individual rights, the sanctity of property, and the sense of national identity. As you have seen, they are interconnected; they literally flow from one another, just as the false compass points that have come to displace them—social justice, group rights, redistribution and multiculturalism—are interconnected and flow from one another. What is multiculturalism, if not a redistribution of cultural "goods?" What is redistribution if not a group right? What is a group right if not the implementation of some political activist's version of "social justice?"

For 30 years, we have acquiesced in a steady erosion of America's founding principles. The time has come to reverse the movement. Rather than contending with countless individual issues, all we need to do is take the debate down a few notches, closer to the core. We submit that all future policy and legislative initiatives be tested against the four points of the compass. Does the proposed bill negate the rule of law? Does it violate individual rights? Does it interfere with the sanctity of property? Does it constitute an assault on national identity? The proposal could proceed only if the answer is "no" in each case. In other words: Only if the answers are "no" is the bill a "go."

A few items need tidying up. How do we know what the rule of law can accommodate, and how far do we take individual rights? The answer, in both cases, comes from Article VI of the Constitution. "This Constitution, and the laws of the United States which shall be made in Pursuance thereof . . . shall be the supreme Law of the Land; and the Judges in every State shall be bound thereby." It is as uncomplicated as that.

In the coming months, we intend to approach the citizens of this great nation and their representatives at all levels with a call to consider adopting this approach. We will hold panel discussions and town meetings so as to invite, engage, and incorporate the wisdom and experience of Americans everywhere. There will be retreats and, by year's end, there will be a book with all the details. We do not underrate the magnitude of the step we are proposing, but we honestly believe it will make life a great deal easier. With a simple stroke, it will become clear that one cannot take an oath upon the Constitution and support group rights. One cannot take an oath upon the Constitution and support the confiscation of property without compensation. One cannot take an oath upon the Constitution and support measures that are clearly at odds with the mandate for national defense.

We cannot have it both ways. We have to choose our compass and remember the four points. They are, as we have seen, inseparable.

Therefore: Only if the answers are "no" is the bill a "go."

I do not believe that last November the people of this country voted for the lukewarm bath of bipartisanship. I believe the people of this country said: If you don't give us a real choice, we won't give you a real election. Yes, people probably have grown tired of the "issues," but they are, I am certain, eager to partake in an effort to choose either a return to our original path, or a clean and honest break with the past.

Those who feel that the time has come to change the supreme law of the land should come forward, say so, and engage in an open debate. But let us not continue a pattern of self-delusion. We are heirs to a remarkable group of men who, 200-plus years ago, had every reason to feel similarly overwhelmed by the number of decisions they had to make. Their response was to make very few laws, for they knew that the fewer the laws, the broader the agreement. They knew people find it hard to agree on everything. So they sought agreement on core principles they held to be non-negotiable.

Today, we propose the four that ought to be non-negotiable. They are, as we have seen, inseparable. We call them the four points of the compass. Together, they can and will restore America's sense of direction.

# III. Civil Liberties

## Editor's introduction

While the Constitution of the United States promises its citizens freedom to speak, write, and worship, the nature, extent, and reality of that promise have been the objects of debate throughout our history. As it has not always been assumed that such civil liberties apply to all Americans, it has been asked whether the needs and wants of the poor, or of those having certain ethnic backgrounds, achieve the voice that is granted the demands of the rich and powerful. In addition, the limit of the First Amendment, being the point when an individual's freedom of expression impinges upon the well-being of another, has been brought under scrutiny. Does such a limit exist? And, if so, who defines it? What limits, if any, should be placed upon the painter, sculptor, singer, filmmaker, or speaker? How are we to respond when, for example, an artistic expression is condemned as "pornographic and blasphemous" and subsequently banned? How do our laws account for book burnings, performed in the name of protecting children from supposedly harmful material? The means by which the press can obtain a story also fall into the arena of civil liberties, as the extent to which freedom of the press conflicts with rights of privacy or national security has been the focus of much scrutiny.

The speakers presented in this chapter have attempted to answer many of the questions posed above, while exploring various dimensions and implications of civil liberties in our democratic system. Often these speeches were given in reaction to an event, or series of events, such as the uncovering of the Watergate affair, or Patrick Buchanan's condemnation of the government-funded Robert Mapplethorpe exhibits. In 1974, Supreme Court Associate Justice Potter Stewart defended the press's right to uncover such scandals as the Watergate affair, while several years earlier, Daniel Boorstin condemned the media for feeding the social unrest of the 1960s by focusing on the discord between youth and establishment, and not the issues upon which that discord is based. As Boorstin pointed out, regardless of the consequence, the drama of social unrest often makes for a better story. In opposition to the banning and burning of books occurring in 1974, in Kanawha County, West Virginia, and East Baton Rouge, Louisiana, Judith F. Krug pointed out, quite insightfully, that the liberty of intellectual freedom depends on not only freedom of expression, but also the ability to witness that expression.

Not all of the speeches in this chapter are tied to a specific occurrence, and they should be understood as of a more theoretical nature. In 1940, Eleanor Roosevelt declared that, "In spite of our Constitution, many of us in this country do not enjoy real liberty." Certain causes, she contended, had difficulty being heard, a fact she saw as a threat to the democratic system upon which the country is founded. In a similar vein, Justice Felix Frankfurter envisioned the ideal, free society as being devoted to the dignity of every individual. Inevitably, such dignity is dependent upon the potential of any and all citizens to achieve a recognized voice when that dignity is threatened. Rabbi Julius J. Nodel observed that "many Americans confuse freedom with license." In contrast, "A free man," he said, "is a person with controlled power." In essence, Nodel asserted that civil liberties such as freedom of expression will achieve their maximum value to the community if spirited and open debate is melded with personal discipline.

# Civil Liberties—The Individual and the Community[1]

## Eleanor Roosevelt

*Born October 11, 1884, New York, NY; died November 7, 1962; co-founder, Val Kill Furniture Shop, 1924-33; owner, vice-principal, teacher, Todhunter School, 1927-33; first lady of the United States, 1933-45; writer, "My Day" syndicated newspaper column, 1936-39; assistant director, Office of Civilian Defense, 1941-45; representative to the United Nations, 1945, 1947-52, 1961; chair, United Nations Commission on Human Rights, 1946-51; author,* It's Up to the Women *(1933),* My Days *(1935),* This I Remember *(1950),* India and the Awakening East *(1953),* On My Own *(1959).*

### Editor's introduction

Having addressed the needs of the underprivileged in earlier speeches, First Lady Eleanor Roosevelt took this occasion to defend the right to assert the value of individual interest. For Roosevelt, civil liberty functions as a cornerstone of democracy, and she contended that when "it is hard to get a hearing for certain causes . . . democracy is in danger." As this speech indicated, Roosevelt upheld the notion that unless the civil liberties of all people, regardless of race or religion, are upheld, the democratic principles upon which America is founded will necessarily crumble.

---

Ladies and Gentlemen: I am glad you gave an award to the press tonight, because that gave them the opportunity to tell us just what they could do. Now we have come here tonight because of civil liberties. I imagine a great many of you could give my talk far better than I could, because you have had first-hand knowledge in the things you have had to do in Chicago over the years to preserve civil liberties. Perhaps, however, I am more conscious of the importance of civil liberties in this particular moment of our history than anyone else, because as I travel through the country and meet people and see things that have happened to little people, I realize what it means to democracy to preserve our civil liberties. All through the years we have had to fight for civil liberty, and we know that there are times when the light grows rather dim, and every time that happens democracy is in danger. Now largely because of the troubled state of the world as a whole civil liberties have disappeared in many other countries. It is impossible, of course, to be at war and to keep freedom of the press and freedom of speech and freedom of assembly. They disappear automatically. And so in many countries where ordinarily they were safe, today they have gone. In other countries, even before war came, not only freedom of the press and freedom of assembly and freedom of speech disappeared, but freedom of religion disappeared. And so we know that here in this country we have a grave responsibility. We are at peace. We have no reason for the fears which govern so many other peoples throughout the world; therefore, we have to guard the freedoms of democracy. *Civil liberties* emphasizes the liberty of the individual. In many other forms of governments the importance of the individual has disappeared. The individual lives for the state. Here in a democracy the government still exists for the individual, but that does not mean that we do not have to watch and that we do not have to examine ourselves to be sure that we preserve the civil liberties for all our people, which are the basis of our democracy. Now you

[1]Delivered to the Chicago Civil Liberties Union, in Chicago, Illinois, on March 14, 1940.

know if we are honest with ourselves, in spite of all we have said, in spite of our Constitution, many of us in this country do not enjoy real liberty. For that reason we know that everywhere in this country every person who believes in democracy has come to feel a real responsibility to work in his community and to know the people of his community, and to take the trouble to try to bring about the full observance for all our people of their civil liberties.

I think I will tell you a little story that brought home to me how important it was that in every community there should be someone to whom people could turn, who were in doubt as to what were their rights under the law, when they couldn't understand what was happening to them. I happen to go every now and then to a certain mining community and in that mining community there are a number of people who came to this country many years ago. They have been here so many years that they have no other country. This is their country. Their children have been born here. They work here. They have created great wealth for this country, but they came over at a time when there was not very much feeling of social responsibility about giving them the opportunity to learn the language of the country to which they had come, or telling them how to become citizens, or teaching about the government of this country. I had contact with a family where the man had been here over thirty-five years, and the first time I went to see him in his house it came about this way. I was standing with a group of people, and a young girl with arms full of packages came along the road. She stopped to look at me and said, "Why, you are Mrs. Roosevelt. My mama say, 'She is happy if you come to her house'." I said, "Where is her house?" "Up the run." So I walked with her and when I got to the house a Polish woman was sitting at the table. The girl walked in and said, "Mama, this is Mrs. Roosevelt," and the woman got up and threw both arms around me, and I was kissed on both cheeks. She told me she had been expecting me to come for a long time. She wanted me to come because she wanted me to see how really nice her house was, and we went through the four rooms and it was nice. She had made crochet pieces which decorated every table. The bedspreads were things of real beauty. We admired everything together. We came back to the kitchen and she said, "You eat with us?" and I said, "No, I just had breakfast." She wouldn't let me leave without eating something, so we had a piece of bread there together.

Six months later I came back and I went again to visit my friend. The minute I crossed the threshold I knew something had happened in that house. It was quite dark. In a few minutes the old man came through from the back room, and he said, "Mrs. Roosevelt, you have come. I have wanted to ask you something for a long time. The mine, it close down, no more work. I work on W.P.A. for a time and then they tell me I no citizen. Mrs. Roosevelt, I vote. I vote often. Why I no citizen?" There was nobody that stood out in the community that he dared trust, that he felt he could go to find out what his rights were, or what he should do. Well, of course, it was true he had never become a citizen. His children were born in this country; they were citizens, but he was not. And they had lived, those two people, by being allowed by the county to take in four old men who would have gone otherwise to the county poor house. Six people were living on the allowance for those four old men. The allowance was pitifully small. As I looked at the stove at what they were going to have for supper, I realized the woman wouldn't again say, "Sit down and eat." There wasn't enough for a stranger, and that was the breakdown of her morale. It hurt you. Something was wrong with the spirit of America that an injustice like that could happen to a man who, after all, worked hard and contributed to the wealth of the country. It should have been somebody's business, first of all, to see that he learned the English language well enough to find things out for himself. Secondly, when he was in trouble, to fight for his rights and to tell him how to go about to remedy what was wrong. I felt there was something wrong with any community where you had to wait many months for a stranger to come to listen to your story and help you straighten out what was a manifest injustice. He couldn't be on W.P.A. He could start out to become a citizen, and he could get relief and, at least, have the feeling that there was an interest on the part of some one in justice. I think that is, perhaps, one of the greatest things that the civil liberties committees do, and I wish we had one in every place throughout the country—one group of people who really care when things go wrong and do something when there is an infringement of the individual's rights.

There are many times when even with freedom of the press and freedom of speech, it is hard to get a hearing for certain causes. I often think that we, all of us, should think very much more carefully than we do about what we mean by freedom of speech, by freedom of the press, by freedom of assembly. I sometimes am much worried by the tendency that you find today in our country only to think that these are rights for the people who think as we do. Some people seem to think these rights are not for people who disagree with them. I believe that you must apply to all groups the right to all forms of thought, to all forms of expression. Otherwise, you practically refuse to trust people to choose for themselves what is wise and what is right, and in doing that you deny the possibility of a democratic form of government. You have to be willing to listen or to allow people to state any point of view they may have, to say anything they may believe, and trust that when everyone has had his say, when there has been free discussion and really free expression in an influenced press, in the end the majority of the people will have the wisdom to decide what is right. We have to have faith that even when the majority seems to decide as we think wrongly, we still believe the fundamental principles that we have laid down, and we wait for the day to come when the thing that we believe is right becomes the majority decision of the people.

Well, of course, that means that we have to have a real belief that people have sufficient intelligence to live in a democracy, and that is something which we are really testing out in this country today, because we are the only great democracy and we are the only great democracy that is at peace and that can go on and live in what we consider a normal and free way of living. It is only here that people don't have to tremble when they say what they think. I don't know how many of you have read a book that I have been reading, but I think it is a most vivid picture of the kind of fear that has gradually come to all the people of Europe. It is *Stricken Field* by Martha Gellhorn, a young woman who was a war correspondent. The story was put in novel form and is about the taking over of Czechoslovakia. Certain people in Czechoslovakia were considered dangerous to the new regime—and the whole description is horrible of what they call "going underground," living in hiding, afraid to speak to each other, afraid to recognize each other on the streets, for fear they would be tortured to death. Only great fear could bring people to treat other people like that, and I can only say that it seems to me that we should read as vivid a story as this now, just to make us realize how important it is that for no reason whatsoever we allow ourselves to be dominated by fears so that we curtail civil liberties. Let us see that everybody who is really in danger in our community has, at least, his or her day in court. Constituted authority has to work under the law. When the law becomes something below the surface, hidden from the people, something which is underground, so to speak, and over which the people no longer hold control, then all of us are in danger.

Never before was it so important that every individual should carry his share of responsibility and see that we do obey the laws, live up to the Constitution, and preserve everyone of those precious liberties which leave us free as individuals. One of the things that we have to be particularly alive to today is the growth of religious prejudice and race prejudice. Those are two things which are a great menace because we find that in countries where civil liberties have been lost, both religious and race prejudice have been rampant. I think it would be well for us, if we could define what we mean when we say that we believe in religious freedom. I sat at a desk in a political campaign once. I was running the office dealing with women for the National Democratic Committee. Over my desk came literature and material which I did not suppose any one would print in the United States, and much of it was written and published by people who belong to various religious denominations. It seems to me that the thing we must fix in our minds is that from the beginning this country was founded on the right of all people to worship God as they saw fit, and if they do not wish to worship they are not forced to worship. That is a fundamental liberty. When religion begins to take part in politics, we violate something which we have set up, which is a division between church and state.

As far as having respect for the religion of other people and leaving them to live their lives the way they wish, we should teach that to every child. Every child should know that his religion is his own and nobody else has the right to question it. In addition to that I think we should begin much earlier to teach all the children of our nation what a wonderful heritage they have for freedom. For freedom from prejudice, because they live in a nation which is made up of a great variety of other nations. They have before them and around them every day the proof that people can understand each other and can live together amicably, and that races can live on an equal basis, even though they may be very different in background, very different in culture. We have an opportunity to teach our children how much we have gained from the coming to this land of all kinds of races, how much it has served in the development of the land, and somehow I think we have failed in many ways in bringing it early enough to children how great is their obligation to the various strains that make up the people of the United States. Above all, there should never be race prejudice here; there should never be a feeling that one strain is better than another. Indians are the only real inhabitants of the country who have a right to say that they own this country! I think this is the reason that we should preserve freedom of mind on the things which are basic to civil liberties. And it should be easy for us to live up to our Constitution.

I am very much interested to find that in our younger generation, however, there is a greater consciousness of what civil liberties really mean, and I think that is one of the hopeful things in the world today, that youth is really taking a tremendous interest in the preservation of civil liberties. It is a very hard period in the world for youth because they are faced with new kinds of problems. We don't know the answers to many of the problems that face us today and neither do the young people, and the problems are very much more important to the young because they must start living. We have had our lives. The young people want to begin and they can't find a way to get started. Perhaps that has made them more conscious of civil liberties. Perhaps that is why when you get a group of them together you find them fighting against the prejudices which have grown up in our country, against the prejudices which have made it hard for the minority groups in our country. The other night someone sent up a question to me: "What do you think should be done about the social standing of the Negro race in this country?" Well now, of course, I think the social situation is one that has to be dealt with by individuals. The real question that we have to face in this country is what are we doing about the rights of a big minority group as citizens in our democracy. That we have to face. Any citizen in this country is entitled to equality before the law; to equality of education; to equality at earning a living, as far as his abilities have made it possible for him to do; to equality of participation in government so that he or she may register their opinion in just the way that any other citizens do. Now those things are basic rights, belonging to every citizen in every minority group, and we have an obligation, I think, to stand up and be counted when it comes to the question of whether any minority group does not have those rights as citizens in this country. The minute we deny any rights of this kind to any citizen we are preparing the way for the denial of those rights to someone else. We have to make up our minds what we really believe. We have to decide whether we believe in the Bill of Rights, in the Constitution of the United States, or whether we are going to modify it because of the fears that we may have at the moment.

Now I listened to the broadcast this afternoon with a great deal of interest. I almost forgot what a fight had been made to assure the rights of the working man. I know there was a time when hours were longer and wages lower, but I had forgotten just how long that fight for freedom, to bargain collectively, and to have freedom of assembly, had taken. Sometimes, until some particular thing comes to your notice, you think something has been won for every working man, and then you come across as I did the other day a case where someone had taken the law into his own hands and beaten up a labor organizer. I didn't think we did those things any more in this country, but it appears that we do. Therefore, someone must be always on the lookout to see that someone is ready to take up the cudgels to defend those who can't defend themselves. That is the only way we are going to keep this country a law-abiding country, where law is looked upon with respect and where it is not considered necessary for anybody to take the law into his own hands. The minute you allow that, then you have acknowledged that you are no longer able to trust in your courts and in your law-enforcing machinery, and civil liberties are not very well off when anything like that happens; so I think that after listening to the broadcast today, I would like to remind you that behind all those who fight for the Constitution as it was written, for the rights of the weak and for the preservation of civil liberties, we have a long line of courageous people, which is something to be proud of and something to hold on to. Its only value lies, however, in the fact that we profit by example and continue the tradition in the future. We must not let those people back of us down; we must have courage; we must not succumb to fears of any kind; and we must live up to the things that we believe in and see that justice is done to the people under the Constitution, whether they belong to minority groups or not. This country is a united country in which all people have the same rights as citizens. We are grateful that we can trust in the youth of the nation that they are going on to uphold the real principles of democracy and put them into action in this country. They are going to make us an even more truly democratic nation.

# Public Opinion and Democratic Government[2]

Felix Frankfurter

*Born November 15, 1882, Vienna, Austria; died February 22, 1965; B.A., College of the City of New York, 1902; LL.B., Harvard University Law School, 1906; assistant U.S. attorney, Southern District of New York, 1906-11; law officer, Department of War, 1911-14; professor, Harvard University Law School, 1914-39; special assistant to the Secretary of War, 1917-39; chair, War Labor Policies Board, 1918; co-founder, American Civil Liberties Union, 1920; associate justice of the United States Supreme Court, 1939-62.*

## Editor's introduction

To a crowd of writers, editors, and publishers, Supreme Court Associate Justice Felix Frankfurter provided a concise and refreshing interpretation of the political philosophy underlying the American form of government. Key to that system is the upholding of "the dignity of every individual." All else, including "votes and parties and platforms," are simply the "political machinery," or means by which the democratic system functions. It follows then that government, according to Frankfurter, is meant to preserve "the kind of civilization we cherish," being one in which the civil liberty, and therefore "the dignity of every individual," is the primary concern.

---

The unfolding of America's destiny may be said to fall thus far into five stages. There was the founding of our Nation. Washington's character was indispensable to keep the Thirteen Colonies together for achieving independence. After the military victory, his character was equally indispensable to fuse the thirteen independent states into a nation.

Jefferson gave the nation its democratic mission. His claims on posterity summarize the three indispensable aims in the unceasing effort to realize democracy: the Declaration of Independence symbolizes political freedom; the Virginia Statute for Religious Freedom sought to put an end to tyranny over the inner life of man; the founding of the University of Virginia expressed the realization that neither political nor religious freedom can long be enjoyed without the continuous systematic pursuit of truth through free inquiry.

Lincoln saw that freedom within a nation must be indivisible and his compassionate nature did not flinch even from the awfulness of war in order to establish that the republic cannot survive half free and half slave.

Fifty years later it became clear that the country's inner strength is not sufficient safeguard for our great democratic experiment—that we are part of the world and that the world must be safe for our democracy.

But even that turned out not to have been enough. And so, within less than another quarter century, war came again for millions of Americans scattered all over the globe, on land, in the air and on sea, because the nation had come to realize that totalitarian regimes imperiled our democracy. This does not mean, of course, that other nations must copy our form of government, or that there is no such thing as a long and painful historic process, or that overnight we can turn democratic formulas into a working civilization. It does mean that democratic aims must be pursued with passion and pertinacity.

Democracy is neither a mystical abstraction nor a mechanical gadget. It is the teaching of experience, and is vindicated by nature herself. Nature plants gifts and graces in ways that defy all the little artifices of man, and in the long course of human history democracy has proven

[2]Delivered at the Willkie Awards for Journalism dinner, at the National Press Club, in Washington, D.C., on February 28, 1947.

itself beyond any other form of social arrangement that which evokes these gifts in the largest measure. All the devices of political machinery—votes and parties and platforms—are merely instruments to enable men to live with one another under conditions which bring forth the maximum gifts of each for the fullest enjoyment of all. The kind of civilization we cherish is the society which was launched by the Declaration of Independence, which was to move within the spacious framework of the Constitution, which was rededicated by Lincoln at Gettysburg and in his second inaugural. It is a society in which the dignity of every individual is central, regardless of the accidents of antecedents; a society in which there is no unimportant people; a society in which institutions are progressively to be shaped so as to bring to maximum fruition the potentialities of men. One does not have to think too well of what our civilization has thus far achieved to refuse to destroy its good together with its evil in arrogant and humorless hope of writing in the future nothing but good on a clean slate. The answer to the defects of our society is not denial of the democratic faith. The answer is more loyal practice of that faith. If one faith can be said to unite a great people, surely the ideal which holds us together beyond any other is our belief in the moral worth of the individual, whatever his race, color or religion. And the glare of war revealed fissures in our spiritual structure, deeper ones than we had heretofore realized.

Until recently men did not talk much about these great simple themes. The pace of material development preoccupied the energies of men; it too often overawed their thoughts. The deficiencies of democracy became a favorite jibe of the worldly wise, and the promise of democracy was too romantically conceived. We are desperately in need not of new truths but of passionate devotion to old truths. Not so long ago we used to hear a great deal about a new plateau of commercial values, and almost imperceptibly it was assumed that we were also being elevated to a new plateau of moral values. The law of political and economic institutions is the law of change. But there are eternal verities—those conditions without which freedom is outraged and faith replaced by cynicism. Ultimately, there can be no freedom for self unless it is vouchsafed for others; there can be no security where there is fear; and a democratic society presupposes confidence and candor in the relations of men with one another and active collaboration for the common ends of life.

For we are enlisted in a common enterprise—the bold experiment of freedom. It involves the most exacting collaborative effort. It demands the exercise of reason on the largest scale and self-discipline of the highest order. For its ultimate reliance in achieving the common good is the responsibility of the individual. No office in our land is more important than that of being a citizen.

We are, in short, engaged in the most difficult of all arts—the art of living together in a gracious society. For this it is not enough to be literate; it is not even enough to be literary. While mankind is literate as never before, environment for reason is least congenial. Thus, while the conditions for a good life have not changed, they now operate in a much more complicated setting. We talk glibly about the annihilation of distance. Speed of communication has, of course, brought many gains, but these triumphs of science have brought in their train far-reaching and subtle problems which we have not solved because we have hardly begun to face them. The mobility of words too often brings in its train immobility of reflection.

In our jealous regard for freedom of the press we pay little heed to the vast change of circumstances in which that freedom operates. It touches uncritical sensibilities even to recognize the potential opportunities for arousing prejudices, confusing judgment, and regimenting opinion represented by chain newspapers, syndicated articles, headline exploitation, the movies, the radio and private polls. Moreover, we now know better than did the Eighteenth Century, in which the modern democratic faith was born, how slender a reed is reason—how recent its emergence in men, how deep the counterveiling instincts and passions, indeed how treacherous the whole rational process. Moreover the whole temper of our society is hurried; its atmosphere and appurtenances are hostile to reflection. Thus, while mankind is literate as never before, reason is asked to flourish when the conditions for it are least favorable. And yet democracy beyond any other form of society is dependent on reason.

Without respect for freedom of inquiry and freedom of opinion there is no democracy. But no less indispensable is the assurance of the means by which opinion really remains free.

Modern instruments of dissemination may unwittingly make the public the victims either of gullibility or of cynicism or of both. But only critically disciplined readers and listeners can generate that healthy public opinion which a democratic government expresses. Informed opinion and free activity cannot issue without an atmosphere in which free and informed thoughts are dominant.

# Freedom's Holy Light[3]

Julius J. Nodel

*Born 1915, Baltimore, MD; B.A., Washington University, MO, 1938; B.H.L., 1940, M.H.L., 1943, Hebrew Union College; assistant rabbi, Euclid Avenue Temple, 1943-44; U.S. Navy, 1944-46; assistant rabbi, The Temple, 1944-50; senior rabbi, Temple Beth Israel, 1950-59; vice president, West Coast Zionist Region, 1957-58; senior rabbi, Temple Shaare Emerth, 1959–.*

## Editor's introduction

Concerned that "many Americans confuse freedom with license," Rabbi Julius Nodel defined a free person as one "with controlled power." He argued that "unless we attach divinity to diplomacy; unless we give meaning to strength by bracing it with spirituality, we shall never know the true blessings of security and democracy and peace." Anarchistic freedom, or liberty without restraint, is, according to Nodel, an "empty existence," and we should understand that our civil liberties must be bridled by common sense, reason, and law. If our freedoms and liberties are not tempered in such a fashion, the "soul" of the United States, being the "inalienable rights of man," will perish at the hands of bigots, demagogues, and economic exploiters.

---

I hardly need tell you that I am profoundly honored to be here today; to be accorded the opportunity to participate in the opening session of this important national forum, and to have the privilege of sharing some of my thoughts with you.

Though the clergy is frequently under fire, those who would attempt to discredit individual churches have, in some cases, been successful; but any aim at the heart of religion has always missed its mark. The heart of religion is God. The first amendment of the Constitution assumes belief in God. The Declaration of Independence is based on the authority of God; and the words "liberty" and "in God we trust" do not appear by chance on every American coin.

When Moses, in the name of God, spoke to Pharaoh and said, "Let my people go that they may serve Me," he equated for the first time in human history freedom and religion. Only those people who serve God can be free. Where there is freedom of religion, there is freedom for the individual. Where there is individual freedom, there is national security. Where there is national security, there is truth, and decency, and honor, and progress, and peace.

Therefore, I feel that my position, at the opening of these sessions, to bring a message spiritual in character, is evidence of the fact that you consider, and rightly so, that your loyalty to America and your loyalty to God are of one piece, integrated and harmonious. You who are assembled here have been proud and eager to serve America in war and in peace. You have expressed your steadfast commitments to the ideals of religion. In both ways, you serve your country with the duty and the faith becoming to free men.

America has a great stake in freedom and the free world has a great stake in American freedom. For many people freedom is an abstraction. It becomes a reality for them only when it is denied them. Like other abstract concepts such as peace, justice, love, and mercy, freedom has no meaning except in terms of contrasted experience with its antonyms. The antonyms of freedom are slavery, imprisonment, personal restrictions, and sometimes death. Most Americans today do not know what it is to be a slave or to be imprisoned or to experience harassment or to wait for the sinister knock on the door of their house. They take American freedom for granted.

[3]Delivered to the Women's Forum on National Security, in Washington, D.C., on January 27, 1961.

Worse, many Americans confuse freedom with license. When license becomes the liberty for anybody to do anything at any time, then freedom from want becomes freedom from work; freedom of worship becomes freedom from worship; freedom of speech becomes freedom from truth; freedom from fear becomes freedom from duty. Such confused individuals become our greatest security risks because, in the final analysis, our national security depends on the mental and emotional health of each person within the nation. When a people becomes idle, irreverent, unreliable and irresponsible; when a people lacks vision, vitality and vigilance, the nation perishes. It is not enough to have many rights; it is more important to use intelligently a few privileges, just as it is not enough to possess great scientific know-how unless its discoveries are controlled by great moral know-why.

Freedom can either be used or abused. I can best explain what I mean by telling you at the risk of being misinterpreted, that I would be filled with dread for the safety of the world if the Soviet government would now grant its subject citizens the privileges of free speech, free press and free assembly. Unaccustomed to the procedures of a democratic nation under God; denied religious expression and opportunity for spiritual evaluation for almost a half century, the sudden release of the Russian people into a free society would result in a pandemonium of unbridled license, immorality, fratricide and who knows what great horrors perpetrated upon all mankind. People must be made ready for freedom; educated to the ways of freedom; trained for the uses of freedom. After bondage, a slave people must wander in the desert of moral and spiritual rehabilitation before it can enter into the promised land of freedom.

A people, any people, which has not been trained to use its freedom, may freely destroy itself. The greatest danger occurs when a people, unprepared for freedom, suddenly finds itself free with massive material and technical power at its disposal with which to menace the world, if it is unrestrained by absence of political or moral authority. The Russian people could become that menace if the Soviet government were overthrown now and if freedom without law supplanted Kremlin control, repugnant as the Kremlin police state is to us. The prospect of such a condition illustrates what I mean by the uses and abuses of freedom. Freedom within law promotes security. Freedom without law means tragic anarchy. My definition of a slave is a person without power who is controlled. A barbarian is a person with power and uncontrolled. A freeman is a person with controlled power.

The people of Soviet Russia are slaves. That is unfortunate. They could become barbarians if they were given their freedom now. That could be disastrous. They might have the potential of becoming freemen if somehow a religious faith in God could possess them. That would usher in a new era of hope for the world. For then, they would not, they could not, be Communists.

What I am trying to point out with these speculations of hope (but not probability, in our times, at least) is that, in our great concern with the problem of national security we sometimes talk out of both sides of our mouth when we speak in the same breath of building up nuclear stockpiles and peace; when with the same lips we speak of diplomatic strategy and democracy; when we try to make the words "strength" and "security" define each other. I am not a pacifist, though I love peace. Nor am I unaware of the fact that our civilization has not destroyed itself already only because our hands have been restrained by mutual terror. But, unless we add morality to science; unless we attach divinity to diplomacy; unless we give meaning to strength by bracing it with spirituality, we shall never know the true blessings of security and democracy and peace.

In one of our national anthems we sing, "Long may our land be bright, with freedom's holy light. Protect us by Thy might, great God our King." "Freedom's holy light," what a significant phrase this is! How important it is that we understand the holiness of freedom and the freedom of holiness. How important it is that we understand American freedom. How important it is that we understand America.

In 1492, Columbus, a foreigner, discovered America. In 1961 too many native Americans have not yet discovered America. Columbus discovered physical America. Our duty and spirit of divine venture should impel us to rediscover spiritual America—the America of Washington's hope and Jefferson's vision, Lincoln's promise and Whitman's dream; the America of Emerson's thinking and Wilson's world unity; the America God created, America capable of being and becoming. America will not be fulfilled until we all become American in the pristine sense of its meaning. Until we Americans find our own souls, America will remain an unknown potential, an undiscovered land—in physical proportions a giant, in spiritual capacity a pygmy, in future power, unlimited, but in positive moral strength, a mere child. There comes a time when material expansion and spiritual contraction create such enormous opposing stresses and tensions that only a mammoth upheaval followed by disintegration and disappearance becomes the inevitable catastrophe.

America is a conception to be created. We have not yet created that conception for ourselves or in the eyes of the world. If we go stumbling blindly on our way, then the reason is that freedom's holy light has not yet reached our eyes. We cannot interpret America to the world if we ourselves do not understand America, what she is, what we want her to be. But if we seek America we shall create America. If we discover America, we shall reveal her to ourselves and to the world.

Unfortunately, to the average American, America means material opportunity. Opportunity to make money as one likes and to spend it as one wills. To the average American, money is the currency of power, of success, of all that makes life worthwhile—an America worth living in. And the liberty to waste it is considered by some as the highest form of freedom. To the average American, America is a land of material superlatives. America is the richest, strongest, greatest country under the sun. That America is not the country richest in righteousness, strongest in spiritual idealism, greatest in moral power does not seem to seriously trouble the conscience of the average American. To the average American, America is a shop in which to make things that sell for money. America is pay dirt in which to dig until you strike oil, coal, iron, copper. America is a field of cotton, grain, timber to be turned into luxuries. And, thus, the average American has only discovered the soil of America. He has not yet discovered the soul of America.

Of course, this attitude may be understood but not condoned when we pause for a moment to realize that we are a very young nation; that our country is only 185 years old. We must wonder at our surprising youth, and when we compare our youth to the age of the chief nations of the world, we know that we are yet in our infancy; and when we observe the immense material development we have achieved and the millions of our population, the marvel is even greater.

However, there are two views of greatness. The common one is material in its content. Expanse of territory is usually the first element stressed. All of our days we have heard orators speak about the fact that our country extends "from Canada to the north to the Gulf of Mexico on the south; from the rock-ribbed coasts of Maine to the golden shores of California." Now we can add to that "the far frozen reaches of Alaska and the tropical beauties of Hawaii." The next element usually stressed is our natural resources; and then comes population and then production and then wealth and then military might. These form the basis of most of our pride and outward security. In a very true sense these are great and perhaps belong in any catalog of our national assets.

The element, however, which should concern us most and which I have chiefly in mind today is the spiritual, the ideal; not railroads and airlines, not missiles and spacecraft, not climate, not numbers, not wealth, not geographical area but character, conduct, service. The material things of life are mostly here when we arrive on earth, laid at our feet by Almighty God. For them we deserve no credit. Someone may ask, "How about production, invention, accumulation, wealth?" My answer is, "Who giveth thee the power to get wealth?"

If we leave this forum with the assurance that we can attain security by means of things, then we shall have failed. The more important field of exploration is within the question whether our country is truly great in courage, faith and good character. Are our spiritual assets great? Have we used up all the religious dividends and moral principal our forefathers bequeathed to us without building up a fund of our own for our progeny to inherit? Are we so aware only of what we are against that we forget what we are for? Are we so busy gazing out from the ramparts we defend that we lose sight of ourselves? Are we so preoccupied excoriating our enemies that we take no time out for appraising our own sins? Is national security limited only to defending our country from its enemies without and its un-American forces within? These are some of the essential questions we should answer, for by dealing with these questions we make confession, and confession is good for the soul.

America has a soul. That is what has to be defended. America is an idea. That is what has to be made secure. America is a dream; it is a vision of something spiritually majestic. America is a republic resting upon certain self-evident truths which have to do with inalienable rights of man. America is good will and brotherhood and understanding and mutual cooperation between men of all colors and creeds. To expend less interest and less vigilance in securing these ideas and values which give America its reason for existence is as unpatriotic a gesture as to ignore the foreign forces which might attack the mass of land called America.

Who are our worst security risks? Not only the subversive groups and front organizations for foreign "isms." The bigot who rides by night with a white robe and mask hiding his face from respectable humanity is a security risk. The fomenter of hatreds who sends scurrilous printed material through the mail defaming American citizens who happen not to be of his church is a security risk. Those who deliberately thwart the decisions of the highest judicial body in our land are security risks. The demagogues and the political witch hunters are security risks. Those who corrupt our free institutions for personal gain are security risks. Those who have lost their faith in democracy so that by panic or fear they would blindly destroy constitutional freedoms are security risks. Those who abuse our constitutional freedoms in the service of foreign dictators are security risks. The economic exploiter, the corrupt labor agitator or the fanatic church leader who tries to use the state for the promotion of his theology are all security risks. And why? Because they live in America but they do not understand the life of America; they profess their Americanism but betray its meaning, and its message to a frightened world.

The fears in the world today are created by the retreat from idealism rather than by the scarcity of bread and the abundance of bullets. When men's hopes for a better world and opportunity in the future for their children are shattered, then even the bread which they eat is tasteless and they recklessly face the bullets. But when their faith in their fellow man is renewed, they are willing to make any sacrifice in the midst of scarcity, and will offer up the last drop of their blood to defend their faith.

Because man's knowledge today is great, man's power also is great, and his potential is all but unlimited within the boundaries of his finite nature. His knowledge and his intelligence give him not only means of power, but can be used also to implement the ways he may choose to exert his power.

The United States along with all nations today is in a state of precarious balance, but the choice of our destiny, and of the destiny of everything bound up with us, belongs to us. Nothing stands still. The needs of today are not what they were yesterday nor will necessarily be the needs of tomorrow. Each passage of time means growth or decay. Growth is active and requires effort. Decay is passive and requires no effort. Growth and spirituality have a great deal in common. Unless we choose to bend every effort to advance in our national spirituality so that we can fulfill our national destiny, then, other things being equal, our spirituality grows weaker and our ideals become flabby and our destiny grows faint. We can forfend this "twilight of the gods" by recognizing the fact that materialism is always ready to profit in an area of spiritual weakness, and so still further to increase the weakness. We need only look upon our world scene to prove the operation of this law.

Despite the great advances we have made in prolonging human life through the discoveries of medical research; despite our success in eradicating hunger from great undernourished areas; despite our success in supporting national self-determination of former oppressed peoples; despite our invasions against illiteracy and superstition; despite our extension of lines of communication between peoples all over the globe; despite the advances we have made in providing greater welfare for the sick, the aged, the fatherless and the widow; yet, these material benefits have not evoked a corresponding sense of security in the hearts and minds of people living everywhere today. The pleasures of living are immense compared to what they were only fifty years ago, but they have not increased the happiness of life. Men are more disturbed and confused today than they ever were. Some important ingredient is missing.

Within our own nation, we have greater freedom than we have ever enjoyed. Through automation, we have freedom from the sheer physical toil that used to break the backs and shorten the lives of our fathers and grandfathers. We have greater space freedom, to move around more quickly and to travel further than the horse and buggy or the sailboat or covered wagon could ever take our forefathers. We have greater freedom from the hundred and one restrictions in dress and speech and social formalities which restrained a previous generation. Yet, with all our freedoms, we are not happier. Some important ingredient is missing. We have great freedom in this land of ours; more than any other people on earth—but, freedom for what? When you have no great cause for which to use your freedom, when you have no great faith to which you can dedicate your freedom, then you abuse your freedom by wasting your time, your energy, your resources.

Just to live in freedom is no great achievement in and of itself. That kind of freedom merely boils down to empty existence. That kind of freedom brings no personal satisfaction and does not contribute to national purpose or security. For if something should happen to the material things which have produced this kind of euphoric freedom, you have nothing more to live by or to live for. Only freedom plus a faith brings happiness. Not any faith. Communism is a faith, but I don't mean that. Fascism is a faith, and I don't mean that. Nor do I mean faith in science or faith in military prowess or faith in education or faith in the state. None of these will provide the happiness and the security that we need. None of these can provide nourishment for the soul for which we hunger. The faith of which I speak is a belief in that power which is on the earth but not of the earth—that power which we call God.

Our American freedom plus our religious faith will remove from us the timid serenity which permits the wrongs in our society to go on as they are and will transform us from a mood of tremulous security into a life of action buttressed by secure conviction. Materialist benefits will no longer be the only handmaiden of our freedom. The hopes of young people will be enlarged. Purpose will take the place of cynicism and indifference. Fear, which is endemic among people of all ages, will be dissolved. The rich with their allowances and expense accounts and the poor with their frustrations of envy and emulation will no longer be obsessed with the standard of living but with the quality of life. Crime and violence and juvenile delinquency will no longer grow apace with social indifference. Uses will be found for individual efforts and skills which are rapidly being supplanted by mechanical devices. And the immense total of decent, kindly actions and impulses, which will ensue from living in peace with ourselves and with our neighbors will testify to the untapped resources of democracy. Then will all mankind look to America. Men will turn away from those philosophies of despair, selfishness, indolence, greed, cruelty, callousness and tyranny and try to pattern themselves after an America which has learned how to enjoy its freedom with a faith in the things for which that freedom was fought for and established.

Let us return to our homes from the sessions of this forum armored with the resolve and the implements for eradicating the forces of materialism, of self-interest, of competitive divisiveness, of bigotry and faithlessness from our Government, our politics, our communities, our commerce, our schools, our families, and our churches, wherever and whenever we detect the pernicious influence of those forces.

While we are here in our nation's capital and before we return to our homes let us each, if we have not already done so, make a pilgrimage to Arlington Cemetery. Let us stand with contrite hearts before that marble monolith under which the Unknown of the battlefield rests; where a holy stillness seems to reign as one vast sob imprisoned in the heart of a world in shock. There, the good and the faithful, the pious and the proud, the ruthless and the indifferent, the gullible fools and the scorpion merchants and the workers of error, will realize that the world's sins of greed and hate and fear and treachery and despondency are not yet washed away by earth's red drops and heaven's tears which have moistened that soil. And our bloodguilt will not be atoned unless we who were born to freedom on American soil, and we who adopted America for our own, will securely and openly and proudly resolve to give no license to stiff stupidity, nor stature to vain, selfish, hollow minds; to strive for the growing sweets of freedom; for a deeper faith; for a broader knowledge; for sincere cooperation; for greater unity and universal love, adding happiness to man's earthly home.

# Dissent, Dissension, and the News[4]

Daniel J. Boorstin

*Born October 1, 1914, Atlanta, GA; B.A., Harvard University, 1934; B.A., 1936, B.C.L., 1937, Oxford University; professor, Harvard University, 1938-41; assistant professor, Swarthmore College, 1942-43; professor, University of Chicago, 1944-69; director, Library of Congress, 1975-87; author,* The Mysterious Science of the Law *(1941),* The Genius of American Politics *(1953),* The Americans *(1958-73),* America and the Image of Europe: Reflections on American Thought *(1960),* The Image: What Happened to the American Dream *(1962),* Landmark History of the American People *(1968-70),* The Sociology of the Absurd *(1970),* Democracy and Its Discontents *(1974),* The Republic of Technology *(1978),* The Fertile Verge *(1980),* A History of the United States *(1981),* The Discoverers *(1983),* Hidden History *(1987).*

## Editor's introduction

While demonstrations protested America's continued involvement in Vietnam, Professor Daniel Boorstin, in this highly lucid speech, sought to distinguish between dissent and disagreement as a means of disciplining our freedom of expression. The demonstrations, he theorized, reflect the "spirit of dissent stalk[ing] our land." Boorstin noted, "it is an easier job to make a news story of men who are fighting" than it is to describe them at peace. According to Boorstin, as dissent becomes the focus, it becomes the norm, and our freedom of expression, rather than creating a controlled debate with mutual concern for the issue, becomes a force of separation, and subsequently a cause of violence and further strife.

---

Gentlemen, it's a great pleasure and privilege to be allowed to take part in your meeting. It is especially a pleasure to come and have such a flattering introduction, the most flattering part of which was to be called a person who wrote like a newspaperman.

The historians, you know, sometimes try to return that compliment by saying that the best newspapermen write like historians but I'm not sure how many of the people present would consider that a compliment.

This afternoon I would like to talk briefly about the problems we share, we historians and newspapermen, and that we all share as Americans.

About sixty years ago Mark Twain, who was an expert on such matters, said there are only two forces that carry light to all corners of the globe, the sun in the heaven and the Associated Press. This is, of course, not the only view of your role. Another newspaperman once said it's the duty of a newspaper to comfort the afflicted and afflict the comfortable.

If there ever was a time when the light and the comfort which you can give us was needed, it's today. And I would like to focus on one problem.

It seems to me that dissent is the great problem of America today. It overshadows all others. It's a symptom, an expression, a consequence and a cause of all others.

I say dissent and not disagreement. And it is the distinction between dissent and disagreement which I really want to make. Disagreement produces debate but dissent produces dissension. Dissent, which comes from the Latin, means originally to feel apart from others.

People who disagree have an argument, but people who dissent have a quarrel. People may disagree but may both count themselves in the

[4]Delivered to the Associated Press Managing Editors' Association, in Chicago, Illinois, on October 18, 1967. Reprinted with permission of Daniel J. Boorstin. 

majority, but a person who dissents is by definition in a minority. A liberal society thrives on disagreement but is killed by dissension. Disagreement is the life blood of democracy, dissension is its cancer.

A debate is an orderly exploration of a common problem that presupposes that the debaters are worried by the same question. It brings to life new facts and new arguments which make possible a better solution. But dissension means discord. As the dictionary tells us, dissension is marked by a break in friendly relations. It is an expression not of a common concern but of hostile feelings. And this distinction is crucial.

Disagreement is specific and programmatic, dissent is formless and unfocused. Disagreement is concerned with policy, dissenters are concerned with identity, which usually means themselves. Disagreers ask, What about the war in Vietnam? Dissenters ask, What about me? Disagreers seek solutions to common problems, dissenters seek power for themselves.

The spirit of dissent stalks our land. It seeks the dignity and privilege of disagreement but it is entitled to neither. All over the country on more and more subjects we hear more and more people quarreling and fewer and fewer people debating. How has this happened? What can and should we do about it?

This is my question this afternoon. In the first place I would like to remind you of one feature of the situation which suggests it may not be as desperate as it seems. This is what I would call the law of the conspicuousness of dissent which is another way of saying there never is quite as much dissent as there seems.

I will start from an oddity of the historical record which other American historians can confirm for you.

When we try to learn, for example, about the history of religion in the United States we find that what is generally described as that subject is a history of religious controversies. It's very easy to learn about the Halfway Covenant problem, the Great Awakening, the Unitarian controversies, the Americanist controversies and so on. But if we want to learn about the current of daily belief of Americans in the past it's very difficult.

And this is the parable of the problem of history. If we want to learn about the history of divorce there are many excellent histories of divorce, but if we want to learn about the history of marriage we'll find there are practically none.

Similarly if we want to learn about eating and drinking habits there are some excellent histories of vegetarianism and food fads, some first-rate histories of prohibition but almost no good histories of eating and drinking.

Why is this the case?

It is simply because of what I would call the law of the conspicuousness of dissent. Controversies, quarrels, disagreements leave a historical debris of printed matter, not to mention broken heads and broken reputations. Carry Nation smashing up a bar makes much more interesting reading and is more likely to enter the record than the peaceable activity of the bartender mixing drinks. But this may lead us to a perverse emphasis. How have people lived and thought and felt and eaten and drunk and married in the past? Interests are focused on the cataracts, the eddies, the waterfalls and whirlpools. But what of the stream?

This is a natural bias of the record and it equally affects the reporting of news. It is obvious that a sermon is less newsworthy than a debate and a debate still less newsworthy than a riot. This is all obvious but it has serious consequences for the condition of our country today. The natural bias of the record tends to lead us to emphasize and inevitably overemphasize the extent of dissent.

Secondly, the rise and multiplication of media. The profession which you gentlemen represent together with the American standard of living leads us also towards the exaggeration of the importance of dissent in our society. Since dissent is more dramatic and more newsworthy than agreement, media inevitably multiply and emphasize dissent. It is an easier job to make a news story of men who are fighting with one another than it is to describe their peaceful living together.

All this has been reinforced by certain obvious developments in the history of the newspaper and the other media within the last half century or so—the increasingly frequent and repetitious news reporting. The movement from the weekly newspaper to the daily newspaper to several editions a day, the rise of radio reporting of news every hour on the hour with news breaks in between, all require that there be changes to report. There are increasingly voluminous spaces both of time and of print which have to be filled.

And all these reports become more and more inescapable from the attention of the average citizen. In the bar, on the beach, in the automobile, the transistor radio reminds us of the headaches of our society. Moreover, the increasing vividness of reports also tempts us to depict objects and people in motion, changing, disputing. The opportunity to show people in motion and to show them vividly had its beginning, of course, in the rise of photography and Mathew Brady's pioneer work in the Civil War and then more recently with the growth of the motion picture and television. All this tempts us to get a dramatic shot of a policeman striking a rioter or vice versa. We now have tape recorders on the scene on which people can express their complaints about anything.

Moreover, the rise of opinion is a new category. The growth of opinion polling has led to the very concept of "opinion" as something people can learn about. There was a time when information about the world was divided into the category of fact or the category of ideas. But more recently, especially with the growth of market research in this century, people now must have opinions. They are led to believe by the publication of opinion polls that their opinion—whether it be on the subject of miniskirts or marijuana or foreign policy—is something that separates them from others. Moreover, if they have no opinion, even that now puts them in a dissenting category.

Then there is the rise of what I call secondary news. News about the news. With an increasingly sophisticated readership and more and more media we have such questions as whether a news conference will be canceled; will someone refuse to make a statement; is the fact that Jackie Kennedy denied there was a supposed engagement between her and Lord Harlech itself a kind of admission. What is really news?

Moreover, the very character of American history has accentuated our tendency to dissent. We are an immigrant society. We are made up of many different groups who came here and who felt separate from one another, who were separated not so much by doctrine or belief as by the minutiae of daily life. By language, religious practices, cuisine and even manners. Until the 1930's and 40's, the predominant aim of those who were most concerned in this country with the problem of immigration was to restrict immigration or to assimilate those immigrants who were admitted. To "Americanize the immigrant"—this was the motto of those who were most concerned with this question.

But in the last few decades we have had a movement from "assimilation" to "integration." And this is an important distinction. In about the 1930's Louis Adamic began writing and in his book *A Nation of Nations* in 1945 he began an emphasis which has been often repeated. It was no longer the right of the immigrant to be Americanized, to be assimilated, it was now the right of the immigrant to remain different. The ideal ceased to be that of fitting into the total society and instead became the right to retain your differences. Symptoms of this were such phenomena in politics as the rise of the balanced ticket, a ticket which consists of outspoken and obvious representatives of different minorities. It brought with it the assumption that the only 100 per cent American is the person who is only partly American. It led General Eisenhower to make something of his German name and his German background which had not occurred to very many of us before. It encouraged John F. Kennedy to exploit his Irish background, the notion being that one was more fully American by being partly something else.

This sense of separateness and the power of minorities developed alongside two great movements. One, in the social sciences—the growth of literature, much of which stems from universities in this area, and especially from the University of Chicago—a literature of the social sciences which came to show minorities who they were, where they were, and what their power might be.

Gunnar Myrdal's book *American Dilemma*, which was quoted by the Supreme Court integration decision of 1954, was a very good illustration of this. The rise of opinion polling also led into this. People in small groups were reminded that they had a power and a locale which they had not known before. Stokely Carmichael himself has referred to this on several occasions—that he may represent a group which is not very numerous but he knows where they are. They're in crucial places where they can exercise power.

Alongside this change in our thinking and this extension of our knowledge came a change in technology which I would call the rise of "flow technology." Minimum speed forty miles an hour. This means that while formerly, in order to do damage to other people, it was necessary for you to set things in motion—to wave your arms or wield a club—now when the economy and the technology are in motion, if you want to cause damage you need only stop and the other people do the damage. This is a parable which was illustrated in the blackout in New York, the stall-ins and sit-ins. At a time when certain students seized the administration building at a neighboring university last year all they had to do was to hold that one building. All the salary checks flowed through the IBM machines in that building and they were able to throw a monkey wrench into the machinery.

This has the effect of developing what I would call a minority veto psychology. Small groups have more power than ever before. In small numbers there is strength. This results in the quest for minority identity. Whereas formerly people used to change their names to sound more American, to try to fit into the background, now the contrary seems to be occurring.

And we find symptoms of this in the intellectual world. Perhaps that is a misnomer—I should say rather in the world of those who consider themselves or call themselves intellectuals. I find in this world today, in this country, a growing belief in the intrinsic virtue of dissent. It's worth noting that some of the greatest American champions of the right to disagree and to express disagreement—Thomas Jefferson, Oliver Wendell Holmes, Jr., William James, John Dewey and others—were also great believers in the duty of the community to be peacefully governed by the will of the majority. But more recently dissent itself has been made into a virtue. Dissent for dissent's sake. We have a whole group of magazines these days dedicated not to this or that particular program or social reform nor this or that social philosophy but simply to dissent.

Professional dissenters do not and cannot seek to assimilate their program or ideals into American culture. Their main object is to preserve their separate identity as a dissenting minority. They're not interested in the freedom of anybody else. The motto of this group might be an emendation of the old maxim of Voltaire which I'm sure you've all heard. But nowadays people would say, "I do not agree with a word you say. And I will defend to the death *my* right to say so."

Once upon a time our intellectuals competed for their claim to be spokesmen of the community. Now the time has almost arrived when the easiest way to insult an intellectual is to tell him that you or most other people *agree* with him. The way to menace him is to put him in the majority for the majority must run things and must have a program and dissent needs no program.

Dissent, then, has tended to become the conformity of our most educated classes. In many circles to be an outspoken conformist, that is, to say that the prevailing ways of the community are *not* "evil," requires more courage than to run with the dissenting pack.

The conformity of nonconformity, the conformity of dissent produces little that is fruitful in its conclusions and very little effective discussion or internal debate. For the simple reason that it does not involve anybody in attacking or defending any program. Programs, after all, are the signs of "the Establishment."

The situation that I have described leads to certain temptations which afflict the historian as well as the newsman and among these temptations I would like to include the tendency to stimulate and accentuate dissent rather than disagreement. To push disagreement toward dissent so that we can have a more dramatic or reportable event. To push the statement of a program toward the expression of a feeling of separateness or isolation.

There is an increasing tendency also to confuse disagreement with dissent. For example, the homosexuals in our society who are a group who feel separate (and are from one point of view a classic example of what we mean by the dissenter) now articulate their views in declarations and statements. Nowadays they become disagreers, they have formed Mattachine societies, they issue programs and declarations. This, I would say, is good.

But on the other hand we find disagreers who are increasingly tempted to use the techniques of dissent. Students who disagree about the war in Vietnam use the techniques of dissent, of affirming their secession from society, and this is bad.

The expressions of disagreement may lead to better policy but dissent cannot.

The affirmations of differentness and feeling apart cannot hold a society together. In fact these tend to destroy the institutions which make fertile disagreement possible, and fertile institutions decent. A sniper's bullet is an eloquent expression of dissent, of feeling apart. It doesn't express disagreement. It is formless, inarticulate, unproductive. A society of disagreers is a free and fertile and productive society. A society of dissenters is a chaos leading only to dissension.

Now I would like in conclusion to suggest that we are led to a paradox. A paradox which must be solved. A free and literate society with a high standard of living and increasingly varied media, one that reaches more and more people more and more of the time—such a society finds it always easier to dramatize its dissent rather than disagreement. It finds it harder and harder to discover, much less to dramatize, its agreement on anything. This ends then in some questions which I will pose to you gentlemen to which I hope you may have answers. At least they seem to me to be crucial ones.

First, is it possible to produce interesting newspapers that will sell but which do not dramatize or capitalize on or catalyze dissent and dissension, the feeling of apartness in the community? Is it possible to produce interesting newspapers that will sell but which do not yield to the temptation to create and nourish new dissent by stirring people to feel apart in new ways?

Second, is it possible at the same time to find new ways of interesting people in disagreement in specific items and problems and programs and specific evils?

Finally, is it possible for our newspapers—without becoming Pollyannas or chauvinists or super patriots or Good Humor salesmen—to find new ways of expressing and affirming, dramatizing and illuminating, what people agree upon?

This is your challenge. The future of American society in no small measure depends on whether and how you answer it.

# Or of the Press[5]

Potter Stewart

*Born January 23, 1915, Jackson, MI; died December 7, 1985; B.A., Yale University, 1937; LL.B., Yale University Law School, 1941; lawyer, Debevoise, Stevenson, Plimpton & Page, 1942, 1945-50; U.S. Navy, 1942-45; partner, Dinsmore, Shohl, Sawyer & Dinsmore, 1947-51; vice mayor of Cincinnati, 1952-53; judge, U.S. Court of Appeals, 1954-58; associate justice of the United States Supreme Court, 1958-81.*

## Editor's introduction

As investigative reporting became a major force during the Vietnam War and the Watergate affair, the American press achieved unprecedented power and prominence. Consequently, antagonism towards the media grew and many assert that it has continued to the present day. As freedom of the press is one of our most basic civil liberties, Supreme Court Associate Justice Potter Stewart, who typically voted with the liberal wing of the Supreme Court in cases involving the First Amendment, contended that while many Americans believe that the organized press exercises "illegitimate power" in covering affairs of the nation, it "has performed precisely the function it was intended to perform by those who wrote the First Amendment of our Constitution." That function, according to Associate Justice Stewart, "is . . . to do battle against secrecy and deception in the government."

---

Mr. Justice White, President Brewster, Dean Goldstein, Mr. Ruebhausen, ladies and gentlemen:

It is a pleasure to be here today with my colleague Byron White, and I am very grateful to him for his generous words of introduction. And it is, of course, a pleasure to participate with him and with all of you in this convocation marking the commencement of the sesquicentennial year of the Yale Law School.

Just how it is that this *is* the law school's 150th anniversary is a subject that I am happy to leave for others to explain. All I know is that it is supposed to have something to do with a couple of young men who, in the year 1824, persuaded a friendly printer to give their proprietary law school a little free advertising space in the Yale College catalog.

But many great institutions have had humble beginnings. Even the Roman Empire, you will remember, traced its history back to no more than two hungry little boys and a friendly wolf.

Yet, however obscure the origins of this law school may have been, all of us know that by the early years of this century it was emerging as an important center for legal study. And by the time my classmates and I showed up here as first-year students in 1938, the Yale Law School had long since been universally recognized as one of a very few great national law schools in the Western world.

Just to speak the names of those, now gone, in whose classrooms I sat during my three years as a student here is to call the roll of some of the most notable legal scholars and law teachers in our country's history: Charles Clark, Arthur Corbin, Edwin Borchard, George Dession, Ashbel Gulliver, Walton Hamilton, Underhill Moore, Harry Shulman, Roscoe Steffens, Wesley Sturges.

And, although we hardly realized it then, the law school's student body during those three years was quite a remarkable collection of people as well. The membership of a single student eating club during that three-year period included, as it turned out, the two members of the

[5]Delivered at Sesquicentennial Convocation of the Yale University Law School, in New Haven, Connecticut, on November 2, 1974.

Supreme Court who are here today, a United States Senator, three members of the House of Representatives, two governors of Pennsylvania, two secretaries of the army, an under secretary of defense, a nominee for the vice presidency of the United States, a Vice President of the United States, and the incumbent President of the United States.

The Yale Law School of that era had already acquired a distinctive reputation for its leadership in the so-called realist movement. Yet it was a place then, as it is a place now, where, in the words of Dean Goldstein, "widely divergent theories of law and society were taught and debated, a school which cannot be described as representing an orthodoxy of left, center, or right." It was then, as it is now, an exciting place and a challenging place, where a teacher's reach sometimes exceeded a student's grasp and where, as a result, every student was invited to stretch himself, in intellect and understanding, to heights and breadths well beyond his previous experience. There was a tradition here then, as there is now, of free inquiry, of independent thought, and of skeptical examination of the very foundations of existing law.

It is in that tradition that I turn this morning to an inquiry into an aspect of constitutional law that has only recently begun to engage the attention of the Supreme Court. Specifically, I shall discuss the role of the organized press—of the daily newspapers and other established news media—in the system of government created by our Constitution.

It was less than a decade ago—during the Vietnam years—that the people of our country began to become aware of the twin phenomena on a national scale of so-called investigative reporting and an adversary press—that is, a press adversary to the executive branch of the federal government. And only in the two short years that culminated last summer in the resignation of a President did we fully realize the enormous power that an investigative and adversary press can exert.

The public opinion polls that I have seen indicate that some Americans firmly believe that the former Vice President and former President of the United States were hounded out of office by an arrogant and irresponsible press that had outrageously usurped dictatorial power. And it seems clear that many more Americans, while appreciating and even applauding the service performed by the press in exposing official wrongdoing at the highest levels of our national government, are nonetheless deeply disturbed by what they consider to be the illegitimate power of the organized press in the political structure of our society. It is my thesis this morning that, on the contrary, the established American press in the past ten years, and particularly in the past two years, has performed precisely the function it was intended to perform by those who wrote the First Amendment of our Constitution. I further submit that this thesis is supported by the relevant decisions of the Supreme Court.

Surprisingly, despite the importance of newspapers in the political and social life of our country, the Supreme Court has not until very recently been called upon to delineate their constitutional role in our structure of government.

Our history is filled with struggles over the rights and prerogatives of the press, but these disputes rarely found their way to the Supreme Court. The early years of the Republic witnessed controversy over the constitutional validity of the short-lived Alien and Sedition Act, but the controversy never reached the Court. In the next half-century there was nationwide turmoil over the right of the organized press to advocate the then subversive view that slavery should be abolished. In Illinois a publisher was killed for publishing abolitionist views. But none of this history made First Amendment law because the Court had earlier held that the Bill of Rights applied only against the federal government, not against the individual states.

With the passage of the Fourteenth Amendment, the constitutional framework was modified, and by the 1920s the Court had established that the protections of the First Amendment extend against all government—federal, state, and local.

The next fifty years witnessed a great outpouring of First Amendment litigation, all of which inspired books and articles beyond number. But, with few exceptions, neither these First Amendment cases nor their commentators squarely considered the Constitution's guarantee of a free press. Instead, the focus was on its guarantee of free speech. The Court's decisions dealt with the rights of isolated individuals, or of unpopular minority groups, to stand up against governmental power representing an angry or frightened majority. The cases that came to the Court during those years involved the rights of the soapbox orator, the nonconformist pamphleteer, the religious evangelist. The Court was seldom asked to define the rights and privileges, or the responsibilities, of the organized press.

In very recent years cases involving the established press finally have begun to reach the Supreme Court, and they have presented a variety of problems, sometimes arising in complicated factual settings.

In a series of cases, the Court has been called upon to consider the limits imposed by the free press guarantee upon a state's common or statutory law of libel. As a result of those cases, a public figure cannot successfully sue a publisher for libel unless he can show that the publisher maliciously printed a damaging untruth.

The Court has also been called upon to decide whether a newspaper reporter has a First Amendment privilege to refuse to disclose his confidential sources to a grand jury. By a divided vote, the Court found no such privilege to exist in the circumstances of the cases before it.

In another noteworthy case, the Court was asked by the Justice Department to restrain publication by the New York *Times* and other newspapers of the so-called Pentagon Papers. The Court declined to do so.

In yet another case, the question to be decided was whether political groups have a First Amendment or statutory right of access to the federally regulated broadcast channels of radio and television. The Court held there was no such right of access.

Last term the Court confronted a Florida statute that required newspapers to grant a "right of reply" to political candidates they had criticized. The Court unanimously held this statute to be inconsistent with the guarantees of a free press.

It seems to me that the Court's approach to all these cases has uniformly reflected its understanding that the free press guarantee is, in essence, a *structural* provision of the Constitution. Most of the other provisions in the Bill of Rights protect specific liberties or specific rights of individuals: freedom of speech, freedom of worship, the right to counsel, the privilege against compulsory self-incrimination, to name a few. In contrast, the free press clause extends protection to an institution. The publishing business is, in short, the only organized private business that is given explicit constitutional protection.

This basic understanding is essential, I think, to avoid an elementary error of constitutional law. It is tempting to suggest that freedom of the press means only that newspaper publishers are guaranteed freedom of expression. They *are* guaranteed that freedom, to be sure, but so are we all, because of the free speech clause. If the free press guarantee meant no more than freedom of expression, it would be a constitutional redundancy. Between 1776 and the drafting of our Constitution, many of the state constitutions contained clauses protecting freedom of the press while at the same time recognizing no general freedom of speech. By including both guarantees in the First Amendment, the founders quite clearly recognized the distinction between the two.

It is also a mistake to suppose that the only purpose of the constitutional guarantee of a free press is to insure that a newspaper will serve as a neutral forum for debate, a "marketplace for ideas," a kind of Hyde Park corner for the community. A related theory sees the press as a neutral conduit of information between the people and their elected leaders. These theories, in my view, again give insufficient weight to the institutional autonomy of the press that it was the purpose of the Constitution to guarantee.

In setting up the three branches of the federal government, the founders deliberately created an internally competitive system. As Mr. Justice Brandeis once wrote:

"The [founders'] purpose was, not to avoid friction, but, by means of the inevitable friction incident to the distribution of the governmental powers among three departments, to save the people from autocracy."

The primary purpose of the constitutional guarantee of a free press was a similar one: to create a fourth institution outside the government as an additional check on the three official branches. Consider the opening words of the free press clause of the Massachusetts Constitution, drafted by John Adams: "The liberty of the press is essential to the security of the state."

The relevant metaphor, I think, is the metaphor of the fourth estate. What Thomas Carlyle wrote about the British government a century ago has a curiously contemporary ring:

"Burke said there were three estates in Parliament; but, in the reporters' gallery yonder, there sat a fourth estate more important far than they all. It is not a figure of speech or witty saying; it is a literal fact—very momentous to us in these times."

For centuries before our revolution, the press in England had been licensed, censored, and bedeviled by prosecutions for seditious libel. The British Crown knew that a free press was not just a neutral vehicle for the balanced discussion of diverse ideas. Instead, the free press meant organized, expert scrutiny of government. The press was a conspiracy of the intellect, with the courage of numbers. This formidable check on official power was what the British Crown had feared—and what the American founders decided to risk.

It is this constitutional understanding, I think, that provides the unifying principle underlying the Supreme Court's recent decisions dealing with the organized press.

Consider first the libel cases. Officials within the three governmental branches are, for all practical purposes, immune from libel and slander suits for statements that they make in the line of duty. This immunity, which has both constitutional and common law origins, aims to insure bold and vigorous prosecution of the public's business. The same basic reasoning applies to the press. By contrast, the Court has never suggested that the constitutional right of free *speech* gives an *individual* any immunity from liability for either libel or slander.

In the cases involving the newspaper reporters' claims that they had a constitutional privilege not to disclose their confidential news sources to a grand jury, the Court rejected the claims by a vote of five to four, or, considering Mr. Justice Powell's concurring opinion, perhaps by a vote of four and a half to four and a half. But if freedom of the press means simply freedom of speech for reporters, this question of a reporter's asserted right to withhold information would have answered itself. None of us—as individuals—has a "free speech" right to refuse to tell a grand jury the identity of someone who has given us information relevant to the grand jury's legitimate inquiry. Only if a reporter is a representative of a protected *institution* does the question become a different one. The members of the Court disagreed in answering the question, but the question did not answer itself.

The cases involving the so-called right of access to the press raised the issue whether the First Amendment allows government, or indeed *requires* government, to regulate the press so as to make it a genuinely fair and open "marketplace for ideas." The Court's answer was no to both questions. If a newspaper wants to serve as a neutral marketplace for debate, that is an objective which it is free to choose. And, within limits, that choice is probably necessary to commercially successful journalism. But it is a choice that government cannot constitutionally impose.

Finally the Pentagon Papers case involved the line between secrecy and openness in the affairs of government. The question, or at least one question, was whether that line is drawn by the Constitution itself. The Justice Department asked the Court to find in the Constitution a basis for prohibiting the publication of allegedly stolen government documents. The Court could find no such prohibition. So far as the Constitution goes, the autonomous press may publish what it knows, and may seek to learn what it can.

But this autonomy cuts both ways. The press is free to do battle against secrecy and deception in government. But the press cannot expect from the Constitution any guarantee that it will succeed. There is no constitutional right to have access to particular government information, or to require openness from the bureaucracy. The public's interest in knowing about its government is protected by the guarantee of a free press, but the protection is indirect. The Constitution itself is neither a Freedom of Information Act nor an Official Secrets Act.

The Constitution, in other words, establishes the contest, not its resolution. Congress may provide a resolution, at least in some instances, through carefully drawn legislation. For the rest, we must rely, as so often in our system we must, on the tug and pull of the political forces in American society.

Newspapers, television networks, and magazines have sometimes been outrageously abusive, untruthful, arrogant, and hypocritical. But it hardly follows that elimination of a strong and independent press is the way to eliminate abusiveness, untruth, arrogance, or hypocrisy from government itself.

It is quite possible to conceive of the survival of our Republic without an autonomous press. For openness and honesty in government, for an adequate flow of information between the people and their representatives, for a sufficient check on autocracy and despotism, the traditional competition between the three branches of government, supplemented by vigorous political activity, might be enough.

The press could be relegated to the status of a public utility. The guarantee of free speech would presumably put some limitation on the regulation to which the press could be subjected. But if there were no guarantee of a free press, government could convert the communications media into a neutral "marketplace of ideas." Newspapers and television networks could then be required to promote contemporary government policy or current notions of social justice.

Such a constitution is possible; it might work reasonably well. But it is not the Constitution the founders wrote. It is not the Constitution that has carried us through nearly two centuries of national life. Perhaps our liberties might survive without an independent established press. But the founders doubted it, and, in the year 1974, I think we can all be thankful for their doubts.

Let me emphasize again what I tried to indicate at the beginning of this discussion. The First Amendment views that I have expressed are my own. I have not spoken for the Court, and particularly I have not spoken for Mr. Justice White. While he and I are in agreement about many things, we have also sometimes disagreed—from as long ago as 1939 to as recently as last Tuesday. And, whatever else we may have learned at this law school, I think each of us learned somewhere along the way that the person who disagrees with you is not necessarily wrong.

In my opening remarks I spoke of the law school that I knew as a student. But I am not here today in the role of an aging alumnus with wistful memories of the way things used to be. All of us are here not so much to commemorate a golden past as to celebrate the present, and to express our faith in a bright and solid future.

I spoke earlier of the distinguished members of the faculty who are gone. The fact is that many of the finest teachers of my day are still here, or only recently retired: Fleming James, Myres McDougal, J. W. Moore, Fred Rodell, Eugene Rostow. And the more important fact is that the law school through the years has been remarkably successful in its continuing program of faculty self-renewal—drawing here teachers and scholars of proven achievement or extraordinary promise. Of them all, I mention only the name of Alexander Bickel, not just because of his nationally recognized distinction, but because I am so sorry he cannot be with us today.

Among the students now here there are undoubtedly future judges and justices, perhaps future Senators and congressmen and governors and Cabinet officers, and maybe even a future President. But that is not what was really important about the Yale Law School of a generation ago, nor what is important now, nor what will be important in future years. The number of our graduates who have gone into government service is exceedingly high. But public service is surely not limited to government service. The real impact of the Yale Law School will always be most broadly felt through the leadership of its sons and daughters in countless other areas of professional and business activity.

Whatever place any of us may now occupy, all of us share one priceless experience in common. All of us have spent three of the most formative years of our lives in *this* place—challenged by the ideal of excellence, and prepared by that challenge to go forth from here with the will and the confidence to do our best with any task that life may bring.

The opportunity for that priceless experience at this great law school, for generations of young men and women yet to come, is surely worth preserving for *at least* another 150 years.

# In Defense of Liberty: Extremism and Other Vices[6]

Judith F. Krug

*Born March 15, 1940, Pittsburgh, PA; B.A., University of Pittsburgh, 1961; M.A., University of Chicago, 1964; assistant librarian, University of Chicago, 1961-62; reference librarian, John Crerar Library, Chicago, 1962-63; cataloger, Northwestern University Dental School, 1963-65; research analyst, American Library Association, 1965-67; director, Office for Intellectual Freedom, American Library Association, 1967–.*

## Editor's introduction

In 1974, in Kanawha County, West Virginia, citizens complained of school textbooks being "antireligious, communistic, and pornographic." Abandoning verbal protest, some turned to bombs and burnings while others went on strike. In the East Baton Rouge parish of Louisiana, parents similarly complained about their children's study materials. Within this context, Judith Krug, director of the American Library Association's Office for Intellectual Freedom, warned of "an oppressive blanket of pervasive anti-intellectualism." She further insisted that "intellectual freedom means not only the ability of creators to express themselves through whatever media they choose, but also access to their creations." For Krug, freedom of expression is not limited to the act itself, but includes the right to witness the results of that act.

---

"It shows what a poor job our schools have done in the past if so many people feel that the free exchange of opinion is communism and the total absence of debate is 'freedom.'" A teacher from Kanawha County, West Virginia, made that statement. And it seems to me to exemplify where we stand today in our battle to preserve the concept of intellectual freedom.

Since this essay is devoted to intellectual freedom, I should first define my use of the term. In its pure sense, the concept embodies the right of any person to believe what he wants on any subject, and to express his beliefs orally or graphically, publicly or privately, as he deems appropriate. The ability to express opinions, however, does not mean very much if there is not someone on the receiving end to hear what one is saying or read what one has written. And so intellectual freedom has a second part: total and complete freedom of access to all information and ideas, regardless of the media of communication used. This, in turn, gives each person the basis on which to form his own opinions and decisions. Once these are formed, he, too, is free to express his beliefs. Intellectual freedom, then, is a circle—a circle broken if either the ability to produce or access to the productions is stifled.

As I use the term, *intellectual freedom* means not only the ability of creators to express themselves through whatever media they choose, but also *access* to their creations—access by all persons, regardless of their age, race, sex, religion, national origin, or social or political points of view.

The concept derives from the First Amendment and is fundamental to our constitutional republican form of government. And because it is primary, the strong and sustained attack now being made on it—in the name of liberty and freedom—is all the more frightening.

[6]Delivered at Louisiana State University, in Baton Rouge, Louisiana, on April 17, 1975. Reprinted with permission of Judith F. Krug.

Where did it all start? How did our opinions and our beliefs, even our language, become so twisted? I can't answer those questions, of course. I might point out that the seeds of conservatism are an integral part of the fabric of American society, and that these seeds have played a great role in the development of our country and our society—more so than their number would seem to warrant. But as we approach our two hundredth birthday, the seeds seem to be flowering.

After a decade of nourishment composed of assassinations, riots, Vietnam, Watergate, a runaway economy, depression, unemployment, a general attack on authority, the flowers springing forth intertwine to form an oppressive blanket of pervasive anti-intellectualism. In my opinion, this anti-intellectualism presents to the concept of intellectual freedom its greatest challenge since the days of Joe McCarthy. Anti-intellectualism, as defined by Richard Hofstadter is "A resentment and suspicion of the life of the mind and of those who are considered to represent it; and a disposition constantly to minimize the value of that life."

Now, no matter how you turn it, intellectual freedom concerns itself with the life of the mind. Indeed, the concept—in its physical representations (materials)—provides the food from which the mind nourishes its life. And we need look only as far as Kanawha County, West Virginia, to see a manifestation of the resentment and suspicion to which Hofstadter refers.

The textbook controversy which spawned in that West Virginia community concerned the adoption of elementary language arts textbooks, involving more than three hundred separate materials from several publishers. The controversy is possibly the most violent outburst over textbooks that has ever occurred in the history of American education. And it is the extremes to which the elements in the controversy were carried that make it unique—not the elements, themselves, which composed it.

Many people have wondered just what horrendous things elementary "language arts" readers could have in them to have created so much havoc. It's rather hard to explain to these people that the books are merely collections of poems, essays, stories, and the like. They're not particularly special and even the fact that a few stories contain profanity—which a lot of the people objected to—did not make the books very different from what you find in almost any magazine on the newsstand today. In fact, the particular books could easily have been replaced by others.

Having participated as the American Library Association's representative in the National Education Association's inquiry into the Kanawha County textbook controversy, I have come to believe that the textbooks weren't really the reason for the fight in Charleston. They were, instead, the excuse. I say this because, during the course of its investigation, the panel questioned not only textbook supporters, but a large number of the protesters—and when we asked the average Kanawha County resident to what they objected in the books, they couldn't tell us. They did hand out mimeographed pages from a sex education handbook—but that handbook was not even in circulation in Charleston schools. In fact, one of the most nefarious pieces of propaganda circulated by the protesters contained quotes from a *high school* textbook that was not even on the list of the materials being protested against and the quotes were sandwiched between reproductions from a sex education manual, of which there was one copy in the entire county—in the public library!

The panel was told about stories supposedly contained in the books, but which subsequent research showed didn't even exist. There was one about "the man who chokes a girl to death." It turned out to be a story about a doctor who forces a frightened little girl to open her mouth so he can save her life.

Well, then, if the fight wasn't really over the textbooks—what was it all about? It was about fear, it was about frustration, it was about helplessness and powerlessness. It was about a county that physically covers 940 square miles, miles encompassing a sophisticated metropolitan area (Charleston) and the creeks and hollows of the southern end of what is known as Appalachia. It was about the powerbrokers residing in Charleston and the "hillbillies" who people the creeks and hollows. Yet, the hillbillies were not as you might see them in your stereotyped image. Excellent transportation and communication—good roads, television and telephone—have brought the twentieth century to this region. But while modern conveniences have brought the twentieth century in some aspects, it has not infringed upon the religion—which is fundamentalist. And so the controversy was also about "people who believe in books and people who believe in The Book."

The controversy was about the West Virginia education laws, laws that mandate that each county will have only one school district; laws that stipulate state adoption of books for the elementary grades; and laws that decree that the materials used as basic texts within the school districts be multicultural and multiethnic.

The controversy was also about the loss of parental control over the local schools, due to consolidation—or so the protesters believed. "Consolidation," which became a rallying point for the protesters, referred to the closing of the one- and two-room schoolhouses that were previously situated within the various local population groupings. Many children in the creeks and hollows are now bused as much as thirty miles each way each day. Removal of the site of education from within the community increased the parents' feelings of helplessness and isolation, for they no longer could easily check on what their kids were doing in school. They no longer could see who was teaching their children, and they no longer could easily voice their protests against what they considered blasphemous "Commie" ideas. Interestingly, the people spoke of consolidation as if it happened yesterday—when in truth it began approximately forty years ago, in 1935!

The controversy was about the parents' belief that their children are not learning: newer textbooks introduced into the Kanawha County classrooms are not only multicultural and multiethnic—but reflect modern, progressive theories of education. No longer are the three Rs set out at specific times of the day and as subjects within themselves. Rather, traditional subjects are contained as strands running throughout, in this case, the English curriculum.

Multiethnic, multicultural texts, however, are not unique to Kanawha County—nor indeed, to West Virginia. In fact, the reduction of cultural and rural isolation of American children have been objectives openly promulgated by the United States Congress and the United States Office of Education. Indeed, large amounts of federal funds are directly connected to the willingness of all the states and all the school districts to adopt materials which help to reduce such cultural isolation. In Kanawha County, however, the "new" textbooks, encompassing as they do a new philosophy of education and a new method of instruction, gave a dissatisfied people a handle on which to hang a protest. It is a protest that brought prolonged civil strife and uncivil conduct, pitting neighbor against neighbor, church against church, the school system against segments of the community, provoking discord among the teachers themselves, and doing violence to the education of students. The controversy raised questions about the basic nature, purpose, and changing methods of public education, and the rights of the various groups involved in it—parents, students, educators and school boards—to determine the content of educational programming.

The controversy also brought to the surface a latent, institutionalized racism and provided for certain extremist groups, a means by which to further their own programs. And finally, the Kanawha County textbook controversy provided the most visible example to date of the anti-intellectualism pervading the country.

This anti-intellectualism is one of Richard Nixon's legacies. That it is directed toward education and the educated is another. We cannot be surprised at such legacies—not from a man who dismissed the protections of the Bill of Rights as anachronistic, and confessed that he had no confidence in the virtue or in the intelligence of the American people, or, for that matter, in their representatives in Congress. It was because of this latter belief (or maybe the belief was the justification of the action) that he chose to conceal his own activities, foreign and domestic alike, in a fog of secrecy. And now that the fog is lifting, the gulf between our professed beliefs and reality is more than most Americans can assimilate.

The result is a dismay, a bewilderment, about what has happened to "America." Life is so complex today that most people have absolutely no hope of controlling what happens around them and to them—and even more important, most people can't even understand what's happening.

The people do know that there is a problem—and in the true American tradition, "if there's a problem, we'll solve it." We'll solve it even if it can't be identified or understood. And one obvious solution is to reform the schools and the libraries—those great big edifices that take so much of our tax money and to thank us, they plant revolutionary ideas in our kids' minds. Reform begins by reinstituting local control and after this is accomplished, it is easy to return to the teaching of "traditional" principles and values. To quote one of the dissidents from Kanawha County, "we must go back to those principles which made America great and kept it that way for two hundred years."

Unfortunately, going back to those traditional principles and values must, by the very nature of the protesters' demands, erase every civil and human right that has been won in the last twenty-five years: the right of racial and ethnic minority groups to be included in the textbooks; the right of all students to learn that in the world and in this society, white is not always right; that white, middle-class values are not the only, nor even always the best, values; and that the history of the United States is not one long, unblemished record of Christian benevolence and virtue.

Of course, there's no denying that going back to the "traditional" values of America not only makes life easier, but certainly more understandable. Those were the good old days when free enterprise held sway and the end justified any means—sweatshops, slave wages, child labor, stepping on anyone who got in your way as you progressed up the ladder to wealth and security; the days when George Washington didn't tell a lie at all, and when he was sleeping around—by golly, he really was sleeping.

In this movement backward—in the drive to return to a less complex, more understandable era—much help, unfortunately, is available. It's unfortunate because the "help" is exacerbating the anti-intellectualism. In the last few months, the demands have been growing to remove materials from classrooms and school libraries that first, do not meet "community standards" and second, that undermine the family as the basic societal unit.

The first demand can be traced directly to a *mis*interpretation of the Supreme Court's First Amendment decisions of June 1973 and June 1974; a misinterpretation promulgated, particularly, by Citizens for Decency Through Law. CDL, which contends that it is not an organization devoted to censorship, but rather one which is anxious to help the citizens uphold the law of the land, appears wherever the forces of darkness seem to be faltering—before state legislatures considering new legislation affecting the right to read, at rallies protesting textbooks and library materials, before church groups anxious to find means by which to regain their wandering flocks. CDL's national spokesman was in Kanawha County, West Virginia, for seven weeks. When I asked this man if his presence in Kanawha County meant that CDL was against the textbooks, he said, "No, we are not." The next logical question—and my next question—was, "Well, then, what were you doing there?" He did not respond—but one of the Kanawha County protesters did. I was informed that "Bob" was there advising them on the kinds of activities they could undertake and statements they could make in order to reach their goal of removing all of the protested books from the Kanawha County school system. After all, I was told, the Supreme Court said that each local community could determine what kind of materials they wanted.

That, of course, was not exactly what the Supreme Court had said. Indeed, in overturning the decisions of the lower courts in the *Carnal Knowledge* case, the Supreme Court specifically said that local standards did not permit the particular community "unbridled discretion" in determining what could be banned.

And yet, censorship is an easy solution to complex—if not insoluble—problems. There are people who believe that if children are not permitted to read books related to drugs, books like *Go Ask Alice*, the drug problem will disappear. There are people who believe that reading Eldridge Cleaver's *Soul on Ice* results in "rape, illegitimacy, abortion, sex perversion, and venereal disease" (Concerned Citizens Committee of Greenwich, Connecticut). There are people who believe that banning *Boss* by Mike Royko will simultaneously ban machine politics; others who believe that *Catcher in the Rye* is responsible for children's disrespect for their parents, if not all adults. And there are actually people who believe that textbook content flows linearly and uninterruptedly from the printed page into the student's mind, causing an immediate change in behavior; that textbook content is always absorbed, and never forgotten; that the teacher agrees with everything in the textbook and teaches it literally; that children in school learn in isolation, never influenced by their peers and never testing what the textbook says against their own experience; and finally, that textbooks and learning are synonymous.

And to all these people censorship by community standards is the solution. It's a simplistic solution, but it's easily attainable and very real to those who will accept it.

Thanks to the misinterpretation of the Supreme Court guidelines, a school administrator in Hartford, Michigan, during a recent controversy over *Each Other's Victims*, by Milton Travers, could recommend a community referendum as the means to preclude future problems. What he meant was that every book that was adopted for the school curriculum—and every book that was selected for the school libraries—should be placed before the community for its vote. The majority, in every case, would carry the day.

And it's not only school administrators who see community standards as the final solution. Recently, the mayor of Covina, California, suggested that residents should be allowed to vote in their own communities "to determine if we want to consider some people legitimate businessmen." What raised his ire was a bookstore which was not X-rated but carried materials he considered salacious. The mayor went on to say that "there is no way the county can succeed unless we can protect the rights of the majority." If I remember correctly, however, the Bill of Rights guarantees the rights of the minority. For if minority rights are lost, if the First Amendment founders, we have indeed lost the matrix of our freedoms.

Utilizing "community standards" to determine the availability of materials is only one part of the attack. The second part can be traced to the dismay and bewilderment—even fear—of the citizenry in general; it is a fear around which many extremist groups are focusing programs. One example is the new Conservative Caucus, which includes in its platform, a plank entitled The Right to Educational Freedom. As an explanation, the Conservative Caucus states:

"The right of parents to define the conditions and content of their children's education must outweigh the power of government to interfere in the selection of textbooks or teachers, or to use the schools to advance the political, cultural and social objectives of government officials. There must be *no forced busing*."

Another relatively new group is the Heritage Foundation, which "pledges itself to the pursuit and dissemination of truth as it is embodied in the Constitution of the United States and the free market economic principles on which the Constitution is predicated."

A final example is the John Birch Society's Project of the Month, for February 1975. The Birch project urged all members to do their part to reestablish the family as the basic societal unit and to reassert parental authority, by undertaking, among other activities, a careful review of the materials that children are "forced" to use in the classroom and the school library.

Ironically, it was a Kanawha County resident who brought the Birch project to our attention. She had called the Office for Intellectual Freedom seeking help to counter an attack on school libraries by the same Board of Education member who gained notoriety in the textbook controversy. The books targeted for immediate removal included *The Naked Ape, Soul on Ice*, and *The Cheerleader* by Ruth Doan McDougal. Having removed the offending books, the next step in the project was to develop guidelines. These guidelines would rid libraries of those materials that undermine "traditional principles and values" and would also ensure that such revolutionary ideas never again found their way into the libraries of the Kanawha County school system.

Guidelines are not new to Kanawha County, for in November 1974 the Board adopted a set of guidelines for textbook selection. Among these guidelines is one that states: "Textbooks for use in the classrooms of Kanawha County shall recognize the sanctity of the home and emphasize its importance as the basic unit of American society." Another guideline states: "Textbooks must not intrude into the privacy of students' homes by asking personal questions about the inner feelings or behavior of themselves or their parents by direct question, statement or inference." As envisioned by the promulgator of these guidelines, they mean that a teacher may no longer ask a student, "How do you feel about that," or "What do you think about this?" Another guideline directs: "Textbooks shall teach the true history and heritage of the United States . . . ." And to that I must ask—just who is to determine the *true* history and heritage?

I should point out that just as the guidelines are not unique to Kanawha County, neither was that telephone call an isolated incident. You need only look at recent issues of the ALA's *Newsletter on Intellectual Freedom* to see how very much the pressures have escalated in just the past eight months.

Who loses in these incidents? Certainly, the children. But just as importantly, every such incident, every project, every misinterpretation erodes—however slightly—the bedrock of the constitutional republic. Censorship is anathema to the United States of America. And censorship occurs when just one human being is precluded from making known his ideas to another human being. The situation has reached crisis proportions when a school district in the United States mandates the selection of textbooks that contain the truth and by virtue of the mandate indicate that those who have passed it, indeed, know the truth. It is incredible to me that we have not learned over the past two hundred years—and particularly the last two years—that the First Amendment is indivisible, that it is indeed the matrix of all our freedoms and the bedrock of the constitutional republic. What the protesters in Kanawha County—and all would-be censors throughout the United States—seem to have forgotten is that the constitutional republican form of government is only as effective as its electorate is enlightened. If we are going to have government by the people, for the people, and of the people—the people must have information available to them on which to form their decisions, their opinions, and their actions.

Sadly, the threats facing the concept of intellectual freedom today are not the kind of threats to which we've become accustomed. We are not currently dealing with well-meaning individuals—but rather with highly sophisticated, well-financed, and extremely arrogant groups. These groups are manipulating the citizenry by playing on the fears that a complex and uncontrollable society have raised. And they are focusing on the soft underbelly of the republic, for they are attacking the school system and through the school system our children to whom the torch of liberty must eventually pass. And if the children are not permitted to develop their abilities to think, to discern truth from falsehood, to perceive right from wrong while they are growing up—then the quest for a quality education is meaningless and the constitutional republic must fail.

And yet I do not believe that the republic must fail, for once recognizing that there is a problem, we can formulate the issues and seek means to combat them. Indeed, we might look on the current situation as a golden opportunity. We may finally have reached the time where the outlook for intellectual freedom is so bad that it couldn't be better. Perhaps our time has come—for the library remains the only public institution in the United States where materials representing all points of view are available. The library does not require attendance, nor any particular point of view, nor required reading, nor even acceptance. It does provide a pool of information covering the spectrum of social and political thought from which each individual, according to his own needs, wants, and intellectual development, can choose what he wishes. The library is still the one and only place where the dictates of the First Amendment can be fulfilled.

Article III of the *Library Bill of Rights* says, "Censorship should be challenged by libraries in the maintenance of their responsibility to provide public information and enlightenment." While our record is respectable, even the library profession has not challenged every instance of censorship. And of those we have challenged, we surely have not been uniformly successful. Yet, winning or losing seems to me to be less important than continuing to bring censorship, in all its guises and disguises, to the public's attention.

And as we strive to fulfill our responsibilities, we can take heart and draw sustenance from the words of James Madison, which still ring true 150 years after they were written:

"A popular government, without popular information, or the means of acquiring it, is but a prologue to a farce or a tragedy; or perhaps both. Knowledge will forever govern ignorance; and a people who mean to be their own governors, must arm themselves with the power which knowledge gives."

# Free Expression and Human Rights[7]

John E. Frohnmayer

*Born June 1, 1942, Medford, OR; B.A., Stanford University, 1964; U.S. Navy, 1966-69; M.A., University of Chicago, 1969; J.D., University of Oregon, 1972; lawyer, Johnson, Harrang and Mercer, 1972-75; lawyer, Tonkon, Torp, Galen, Marmaduke and Booth, 1975–; chair, Oregon Arts Commission, 1980-84; chair, National Endowment for the Arts, 1989-92; author,* Leaving Town Alive: Confessions of an Arts Warrior *(1993).*

## Editor's introduction

Less than a month before this speech was given, John E. Frohnmayer resigned the chair of the National Endowment for the Arts in a furor of controversy aroused by Patrick Buchanan, who had berated the Bush administration for "wasting our tax dollars on pornographic and blasphemous art." The artworks in question were by the late Robert Mapplethorpe, photographs which were being shown in NEA-supported touring exhibitions. President Bush responded to Buchanan by asking for Frohnmayer's resignation. In this speech, Frohnmayer isolated three tensions surrounding the First Amendment and asserted that they must be solved through "vigorous and honest debate" if we are "to redefine the truth and the values that define us." According to Frohnmayer, only in this fashion will the sanctity of future artistic expression be guaranteed.

---

Thank you very much. I am here with the important people: my wife, my lawyer, my rowing companion Susan, down there, and of course those of you from the press who have been my constant companions over the last three years.

One caveat at the start of my remarks. They are mine; I am not speaking on behalf of the administration.

And one other preliminary, please. And that is that this speech was conceived as a part of the symposium that Sandy Unger and the people at American University have put together with the press club with foreign journalists about freedom of expression and its fate and condition around the world.

As a consequence, I am going to be talking about the First Amendment and some of the problems that we have had with it here in the United States over the last three years.

But I specifically direct my remarks to those foreign journalists because I believe that First Amendment is our dearest liberty, and one which we should be constantly attempting to export and promote in the rest of the world.

Democracy is constantly in the process of becoming. It is never fixed, it is never secure, and it's never comfortable. To protect and renew and maintain our democracy, we have the First Amendment. And one of the very nice things about the freedom of expression calendar, which I have back on my desk, is that everyday one can re-read the First Amendment, and so let me re-read it for you: "Congress shall make no law respecting an establishment of religion, or prohibiting the free exercise thereof, or abridging the freedom of speech or of the press or of the right of the people peaceably to assemble and to petition the government for a redress of grievances."

Each generation must re-enfranchise both our democracy and the First Amendment. And because of three tensions in our society, we as a generation are having more difficulty than most:

What we are really involved here with, in my view, and the arts are the focal point of this, is a redefinition of the social contract for our generation.

[7]Delivered at the National Press Club, in Washington, D.C., on March 23, 1992. Reprinted with permission of John E. Frohnmayer.

I will return to these three tensions in just a moment. But first, the First Amendment tells us that religion, ideas, associations, and the right to criticize the government, belong to the people. Since all art deals with expression—with ideas—all art is speech, and therefore, all art is protected by the First Amendment from government interference except in three very clearly defined areas, which are well known to all of you. Those are: criminal behavior—perjury, fraud, bribery, forgery, that sort of thing; physical dangerous behavior—this is the line of cases following *Chaplinsky v. New Hampshire*, the fighting-words doctrine, or the famous saw that all of you know, crying "Fire" in a crowded theater; and, finally, obscenity.

And obscenity has a very clear definition. It's the three-part definition from *Miller v. California*. And unfortunately, in the discourse that I have been so much a part of over the last three years, the attackers of the National Endowment have paid very little attention to the legal definition of obscenity.

They have rather used it to mean whatever it is they don't happen to like. That's not what the word means.

But the rub comes when we, as the government, support individual free expression under the general welfare provision of the Constitution. All civilized governments have done that, and all civilized governments, including our own, should do that. But when the government does support free expression, it must do so with a level playing field, no blacklists, and no ideological preconceptions.

When the artist or speaker expresses what some deem to be dangerous or radical or blasphemous or crude ideas, we encounter the kind of free-for-all that we have seen over the last three years. Congress has gotten more mail on this issue, much of it generated by right-wing fundamentalist groups, than Congress has gotten on the savings and loan crisis. And just to put that into perspective, the savings and loan crisis will cost each of us over $2,000. The National Endowment for the Arts costs each of you 68 cents per year.

So, how do we deal with it? First, a little history. For every great age of art, there has been a great age of repression. And one of my favorites of this is Mannheim, Germany, in 1853, when the statue of Venus de Milo was put on trial for nudity and obscenity. This was the statue herself, sitting up there without arms, and draped as you know.

The account does not tell us whether she was read her rights, asked to testify, or even, if she'd been struck with a fit of modesty, how without arms she would have been able to clothe herself.

Another notable example, in the United States in the 1920's, the jazz age, there was an anti-jazz movement. To censor this form of American music, a professor proved that women, pregnant women, who listened to jazz had deformed babies. Jazz was described by its critics as decadent and the devil's music composed of jungle rhythms. Even serious critics had problems with the art, stating that since jazz was improvised, it was contrary to discipline.

And critics had their way in some instances. In Chicago a law was passed that made it illegal to play a trumpet or a saxophone after dark. And a ship, an ocean liner, got partway out into the Atlantic, and turned around and summarily dumped the band on the dock for having the temerity to play jazz.

Closer to home, and more immediate, the endowment funded a film called "Poison," which depicts allegorically the AIDS epidemic, societal violence, homosexual relations. It is an award-winning film, picked by a panel of award-winning directors and film experts.

Congress received thousands of protest letters, most of which came from people who hadn't seen it.

Similarly, the Endowment has funded a publication called the *portable lower east side*, which contained a graphic and disturbing poem depicting the thoughts of a 13-year-old black child involved in a brutal rape and near killing of a female jogger on Central Park.

Six lines were taken out of context and mailed to members of Congress by the Rev. Donald Wildmon from Tupelo, Mississippi, and I am told that my defense of the literary merit of that poem was the precipitating event of my firing.

Much of the poem was later printed in the *Washington Post*, which allowed citizens an opportunity to judge for themselves whether it had artistic value.

Artists, often without varnish and sometimes without much civility, tell us the truth as they see it. And sometimes they're right, and sometimes they're not. Sometimes they're profound. We hope that everything we fund is, but we know that this . . . is research into the life of our minds and hearts, and that research does not always produce results.

And sometimes the artists tell us unkind truths about ourselves, truths which are difficult to hear, which make us uncomfortable. But as a famous artist put it, artistic growth is a refining of the sense of truthfulness. The stupid believe that to be truthful is easy. Only the artist, the great artist, knows how difficult it is.

Similarly, several works have been attacked by religious groups claiming sacrilege, or blasphemy, specifically the work of Andres Serrano entitled "Piss Christ" and the work of David Wojnarowicz depicting Christ with a crown of thorns and a needle in his arm.

Neither of these works, unfortunately, in my view, have provoked theological debate about Christ taking on the sins of the world or the cross as a symbol of man's inhumanity to the son of God. Rather they have been widely depicted, and I think accepted by most, as blasphemous, without any inquiry, really, of what the artist intended by making these pieces.

This is another issue that is entirely driven by fundamentalist religious groups, and I regret to tell you that mainline religion has not entered the field of this debate, and I think that is a great loss, both to us and to them.

So that sets the stage, and now let me return to the tensions that I mentioned earlier. You remember I said that there were three of them, and the first is the tension between the First Amendment and its premise that we solve our problems through the vigorous clash of ideas, and pervasive strain of anti-intellectualism as the unwillingness to use thought, facts, and critical discourse to solve our problems. And we once had a political party which is well known to all of you called the Know-Nothings, whose agenda was against Negroes, foreigners, and Catholics. And Abraham Lincoln said that if the Know-Nothings gained control, he would prefer "emigrating to some country where they make no pretense of loving liberty, where despotism can be taken pure and without the base alloy of hypocrisy."

Recently, the utter unimportance of facts in the attacks have come from alleged religious leaders. But I would tell you that the most shameless of those attacks was that mounted recently by would-be presidential candidate, Patrick Buchanan.

The second tension is between the clause prohibiting the establishment of religion in the First Amendment, and the sense of closeness that is so pervasive in American political discourse. Take out a nickel. It says, "In God we trust." When we say the Pledge of Allegiance, we pledge relating to one nation under God.

Political leaders feel comfortable telling God to bless us, and there is a sense that one must exercise religion, no matter what it is, to succeed in politics.

Couple political use of religious trappings and the theological reductionism that underlies both fundamentalism and anti-intellectualism, and we see why people are calling for laws against blasphemy. And, of course, you know that the reason that we don't have laws against blasphemy is that both the establishment and the free-exercise clause of the First Amendment prohibit it absolutely.

The third tension is between the right of assembly and the electronic isolation that our technology has brought us. T. S. Eliot said television is a medium of entertainment which permits millions of people to listen to the same joke at the same time and remain lonesome.

And with the exception of an occasional school board meeting, in my experience there are precious few town meetings or activities where the people of this country assemble to discuss the issues of the day.

The lobbing of electronic bombs by print or airwaves seldom allows an issue to be squarely confronted, let alone debated.

I would say parenthetically that it doesn't have to be that way, and I would suggest one remedy would be unfettered political debates on television where there are no rules other than the give-and-take under the control of a moderator.

But Thomas Mann said—and he said this at the time that he was fighting the repression of Hitler's Germany in the 1930s—"speech is civilization itself." The word, even the most controversial word, preserves contact. It is silence which isolates.

And in front of our television sets, we are both silent and isolated. So how do we in this generation reenfranchise the First Amendment and deal with these three tensions that we just described?

It will take in my view a commitment to build a new social understanding, a vigorous and honest debate to redefine the truth and the values that define us.

We hear a lot these days about family values, but I don't see many people defining that term. Truths in this generation and in this time are not self-evident. And unless we take advantage of the permission the First Amendment gives us to duke it out intellectually, our diverse society will become increasingly brittle until the point that it breaks.

We must address calmly and honestly at least these following issues: racial and ethnic differences; tolerance; equality of economic opportunity; education; individual responsibility.

The answer to none of these issues is clear, so we must be prepared to live with the ambiguity, with frustration, with failure, with false starts. To do so will require a generosity of spirit that can be borne only of a commitment not to let our noble experiment in democracy die.

I have some suggestions as to how this discourse might be promoted, and not surprisingly, they involve the arts. The National Endowment for the Arts has a mandate, and I quote to you from our enabling legislation.

The world leadership which has come to the United States cannot rest solely upon superior power, wealth, and technology, but must be solidly founded on worldwide respect and admiration for the nation's high qualities as a leader in the realm of ideas and of the spirit.

Art helps define the American spirit, that mix of practicality and spirituality that we must nurture and encourage and defend. Passionate idealists founded this country, and the Constitution reflects that spirit which liberates and guarantees the ascendancy of ideas.

We must educate our children, their hearts and their minds and their bodies, and if we are to remain a world leader, a nation of real community, we must teach those children the necessary habits of the mind: mental toughness, and love of knowledge.

The arts teach that creativity. They challenge students to think broadly, and to attempt anew, and to risk failure. The arts free young people to see and to hear as well as to read and write, to make order out of chaos, to view the world's challenges and problems through multiple perspectives.

The arts help children to dare new expression, try various approaches to problem solving, use intuition as well as reason, and develop the discipline required for success in any area of life.

But the arts are also fundamental to a democratic system, because they demand involvement. Every child who has honestly written a poem or performed a song or dance has been forever changed. That child has made a covenant of honesty and of risk, of communication and of commitment to a community.

That child has laid vulnerable a part of the self, and has placed faith in the community to respond. In short, that child has become a citizen.

Second, the second way in which the arts can help this discourse which will save us as a country: the arts give us the opportunity to help rebuild community. In this increasing attack oriented society, we must find some way to begin the dialogue that helps to rebuild the social consensus.

The arts often through nonverbal means give us that opportunity. Look at music, how jazz and salsa and Eastern traditions have influenced Western composition and performance. And the same is true in dance.

Students in grade school, in a class for example in Los Angeles, who have had a week-long session of artists in the schools teaching them Latino or Hispanic music and dance, and visual arts, are far less likely to go out after school and bash the Latino and Hispanic kids in that class.

T. S. Eliot wrote, poetry can communicate before it is understood.

Third, intellectual research. We spend billions of dollars on scientific research. But how much do we spend on development of our humanism? We have cleaved our brains in half, and have left off development of our creative side. That ephemeral ability to make connections between seemingly unrelated ideas or theorems so essential to the growth of mankind's knowledge, is the stock and trade of the arts.

Japan and Germany know this, and art education, art support, and reverence for the arts is central to their societies. Perhaps we will remember it too, and perhaps it will not be too late.

And that leads me to the fourth point, which is intensely practical and which assumes that economic well-being is necessary to a healthy society.

Our second most positive balance of trade item, after the export of jet planes, is the export of copyrightable materials: movies, television, literature, software. The National Endowment for the Arts has been the farm club for this industry for the last 27 years. The insignificant sum of 68 cents has helped fuel this economic engine of incredible value and wealth to this society.

And on a purely economic analysis, it would be foolhardy to cripple the National Endowment for the Arts.

Upon my abrupt departure, there's been lots of talk about what to do with the Endowment. Rich Bond, the head of the Republican Party, is reported to have said that he might suggest to the President simply to abolish the agency. How cowardly. How ignorant.

What a craven example to the rest of the world.

I fervently hope that the President, if that suggestion is made, will reject such rubbish. Leadership is confronting and wrestling with our problems, not surrendering to what is easiest. Others, Leonard Garment among them, counsel funding only safe art, the work of dead white European males.

We are a diverse country. We have diverse voices. It's our greatest strength, and our greatest challenge. To retreat to such a fortress mentality is to abdicate leadership, to admit governmental impotence, and to deprive the next generation of its opportunity to struggle with new work, new ideas, new challenges.

That's not the America that I love.

And some have counseled that Congress simply needs cover. We have to give them some palliative so that they can claim to have stood tall against obscenity when Senator Helms or others introduce their next obscenity amendment, every year, every month, maybe every day.

The decency language that was inserted in 1990 is such a palliative. Decency, of course, is in the mind of the hearer, the receiver of information. The First Amendment, as we remember, protects the speaker.

To me the most damning sound bite is not, "My opponent voted for obscenity." It is, rather, "My opponent jettisoned our precious right of free expression to cover his fanny." All of us in government are sworn to defend the Constitution against all enemies, foreign and domestic. And for two-thirds of both Houses of Congress to have voted for the latest Helms language, which is unconstitutional under every test I know, in my view, violates the oath.

The answer of how to save the arts Endowment is very simple, my friends. It is to reaffirm that we, as a country, want to be a leader in the realm of ideas and of the spirit.

It is to read and to believe and to embrace the First Amendment, which allows us to be that leader. To kill the Endowment because of a few disturbing lines or images poses a far greater threat to this nation than anything the Endowment has ever funded.

It would be a craven admission that we are not strong enough to let all voices be heard.

You and I don't have to like everything that the Endowment supports, because your government is not the sponsor of those ideas. The government is merely an enabler. It's like the box that the British provide for speakers to stand on in the Hyde Park's Speaker's Corner. The government provides the box, the speaker provides the ideas.

And those ideas belong to our diverse and sometimes brilliant group of artists, patriots who are bold enough to tell the truth as they see it.

And to those of you from other lands where speaking the truth has cost you the lives of loved ones, personal imprisonment, and hardships of the soul that we in America cannot imagine, I dedicate these words of the poet, Sam Hazzo:

"I wish you what I wish myself, hard questions, and the nights to answer them. And grace if disappointed. And a right to seem the fool for justice. That's enough. Cowards might ask for more. Heroes have died for less."

# IV. International Affairs

## Editor's introduction

From the United States' 1941 declaration of war on Japan to the recently proposed expansion of NATO into Eastern Europe, America's international involvement has been both active and dramatic. The rapid advance of both communications and weapons technology has presented new challenges to our diplomacy, as well as new means of meeting those challenges. Throughout it all, impassioned debate has raged on issues of national security, a reliable peace, and the American obligation to the rest of the world. We questioned our response to Hitler's advances through Europe. We watched and waited as opposing warships in the Caribbean pushed the possibility of nuclear annihilation to near reality. We expressed our solidarity with those trapped behind the Berlin Wall, and we argued over the best ways to constructively interact with the Soviet Union and the Eastern bloc after the Berlin Wall fell. The speeches in this chapter provide a sampling of opinions and beliefs on all these events, as well as a summary of the leadership which guided us through this very volatile period of American history.

As the Cold War began to take root in the fears and anxieties of American citizens, and Communism became a word capable of ruining careers and increasing arms, Secretary of State Dean G. Acheson described relations between the Soviet Union and the United States as a tension between good and evil. These Cold War enemies, insisted Acheson, could only negotiate if the Soviet Union would meet the conditions set by his administration and outlined in the speech contained herein. A similar condemnation of Communism came from John Foster Dulles in 1958. He prescribed "having retaliatory power, and the will to use it," and believed that formal recognition of the People's Republic of China would be a fatal blow to those non-Communist governments struggling to survive in the Far East. Nearly 20 years later, Henry A. Kissinger echoed the deep American resistance to Communism as he insisted that the United States was unquestionably resolved to obstruct the Soviet military from "political expansion" into non-Communist countries. Yet, even in Kissinger's martial argument the seeds of change in America's posture toward the Soviet Union and her Communist ideology crept in: "But at the same time," he qualified, "we cannot escalate every political dispute into a central crisis." As Kissinger notes, the lessons of the Vietnam War are a powerful reminder of the consequences of rigid political mandates.

Vigilance and fear were not the only characteristics of twentieth-century American international policy. Perusing oratory of the day, one finds a minority of voices calling for conciliation and negotiation. In 1943, J. William Fulbright strove to find a way to circumvent the carnage and bloodshed of war. With such a goal in mind, the freshman representative from Arkansas introduced a resolution that the Congress favor "the creation of appropriate international machinery with power adequate to establish and to maintain a just and lasting peace among the nations of the world." The American step into the global community had commenced. It was continued in dramatic and historic fashion in 1947 by George C. Marshall, who called for nations to assist in Europe's recovery from the devastation of World War II. Rather than provide Europe with a temporary alleviation, Marshall believed that the United States "should provide a cure." Similarly expressing deep concern for the state of the world, Albert Einstein warned that the assumption "of achieving security through national armament is . . . a disastrous illusion." He saw the rapid arms buildup of the Cold War as an exercise in idiocy which could lead only to holocaust. "It is impossible to achieve peace," this famed scientist concluded, "as long as every single action is taken with a possible future conflict in view." The initial fear of Communism, so evident in Dean Acheson's speech, had abated somewhat by 1964 when J. William Fulbright asserted that the assumed "evil" inherent to the Communist state was the stuff of myth and not reality.

# America and Internationalism[1]

## J. William Fulbright

*Born April 9, 1905, Sumner, MO; died February 9, 1995; A.B., University of Arkansas, 1925; B.A., 1928, M.A., 1931, Oxford University; LL.B., George Washington University, 1934; attorney, Department of Justice, 1934-35; instructor, George Washington University, 1935-36; instructor, 1936-39, president, 1939-41, University of Arkansas; representative (D) from Arkansas, 1943-45; senator (D) from Arkansas, 1945-74.*

### Editor's introduction

As a newly elected representative, J. William Fulbright gave this speech to defend his resolution to create "appropriate international machinery with power adequate enough to establish and to maintain a just and lasting peace among the nations of the world." In essence, Fulbright called for a renewed American involvement in international affairs, while he refuted the attitudes of those who were decrying international commitments as leading America to a loss of national independence. Anticipating the "global community" that so dominates our current political and economic thinking, Fulbright declared that "the lesson of history is that the unit of government will in time proceed to the international level." Given such agreements as the North American Free Trade Agreement (NAFTA) and the European Union (EU), Fulbright's statements were clearly prophetic.

---

I deem it an honor and a great privilege to be invited to address this distinguished gathering of the leaders of the American Bar. I cannot deny that it was with considerable trepidation that I accepted the invitation to come here today, realizing as I do that I am exposing to you and to the world how very limited is the knowledge and the wisdom of a freshman Congressman.

Your president requested in his invitation that I present to you this morning some of my thoughts concerning the proper relations of this nation with the other nations of the world. I do not have the temerity to express these thoughts as being those of an experienced international lawyer. I thought, however, that coming from a Representative of an agricultural district, of which there are many in Congress, they might be of interest to you as an indication of what the common citizens of this country are thinking about the war and what we should do about it.

Many of us feel in our bones, so to speak, if not in our heads, that if we are to survive in this world as a republic of free men, we must do something about recurrent total wars. We feel that we are sacrificing our finest boys and expending our material wealth and resources for something we do not quite understand. We know that we must do it, yet we want so very much to understand why we must do it, and what is to be gained by our sacrifices, and how we may avoid in the future the necessity of such senseless destruction and suffering.

The obvious answer to why we must fight now is that we were attacked and must defend ourselves. But why were we attacked at this particular time? Many abstruse and learned volumes have been written on the causes of the war, but if any single circumstance can be said to have caused this war, I think that Hitler's belief that his opponents would follow the "one by one" road to destruction would head the list. In spite of all the alleged social, ideological or economic causes of war, I think the decisive cause is the conviction of the aggressor that he can win. The principal consideration in the German mind in arriving at this conviction in 1939 was, I am sure, the each-for-himself, the one-by-one, isolationist philosophy of the United States and the other non-Axis countries. These

[1]Delivered to the American Bar Association, in Chicago, Illinois, on August 26, 1943.

sovereign nations attempted to deny the essential interdependence of nations. Hitler, relying upon our Neutrality Act and a pact with Russia, sought to apply the old principle that "ten men can overcome a thousand if each of the thousand says: 'I will fight for myself alone; I will not cooperate with the others,'" in which case the ten do not face a thousand, but face only one—one at a time. It makes one shudder to think how close to complete success Hitler came after the fall of France. From such a demonstration surely we now recognize that individual defense is in the long run a physical impossibility and, therefore, that our only hope for security is in collective action.

If it is true that the decisive cause of this war was Hitler's belief that the United Nations would not unite as they have done, but would go down to defeat one by one, then the answer to "What we may gain from this war" should be clear. We shall have acquired the experience and knowledge by which we may prevent, or at least make less frequent, the recurrence of these appalling tragedies. The immediate fruit of our victory will be the prevention of our enslavement by the Nazis and the Japs, a vastly important, but somewhat negative benefit. Since, however, we do not desire the conquest of large territories, the only great and positive good that we can hope to achieve from our victory is the assurance of a peaceful world in which man's energy and genius may be devoted to creative and beneficial, rather than to destructive and savage, enterprises.

I believe that our recent experiences and the history of government over the centuries, which is largely the chronicle of man's efforts to achieve freedom by the control of arbitrary force, indicate that only by the collective action of a dominant group can security be attained. It was in this belief that I introduced House Concurrent Resolution 25 which is, as a matter of fact, the real reason why I am here today. Before I read the resolution, may I say that perhaps the most significant thing about it is the fact that it originated in the House of Representatives and is, at the moment, a nonpartisan measure. Both are important. Our foreign policy must be consistent, and must not be a partisan affair shifting with every election. Further, since the House of Representatives is at all times more nearly reflective of the will of the people than any other body, it should play a part in the formation of fundamental policy. Only with Congressional sanction can the other nations of the world rely with assurance upon commitments of our executive. The adoption of this resolution by the House and the Senate will create a precedent for the further participation by the House of Representatives in the matter of foreign policy, and give that policy stability and force.

This resolution reads as follows: "Resolved by the House of Representatives (the Senate concurring), that the Congress hereby expresses itself as favoring the creation of appropriate international machinery with power adequate to establish and to maintain a just and lasting peace among the nations of the world, and as favoring the participation by the United States therein."

This simple statement is, I believe, the first step in the development of a foreign policy which should enable us to achieve a greater degree of security than we have hitherto had. It tells the world that the United States recognizes that any organization for peace must be based upon power adequate to enforce peace, and that the United States will share both in supplying that power and in the responsibility for the exercise of that power. One may say that this is a commitment that this nation undertakes to participate with the other nations of the world in a genuine and bona fide effort to find some reasonable means to solve the international disputes by methods other than by war.

Much has been said about a provision for the use of force. The words "power adequate to establish and to maintain a just and lasting peace" not only envisage the use of some kind of force, but may also include the power, if necessary, to control the productive capacity of instruments of aggressive warfare. The traditional "police force" which disturbs so many people may not be nearly so important as control of strategic materials and productive capacity.

This commitment to participate is, of course, only the first small step in the process of creating a system of international relations that makes sense. Some people have been misled by the false impression that our own Constitution was suddenly, as if by magic, produced from the minds of our founding fathers. Nothing could be further from the truth. Rather than being a document of original principles or ideas, it was more in the nature of a codification of principles and institutions of human freedom which had been evolving through countless centuries.

Millions of brave men and women, of many lands, had sacrificed their fortunes and their lives in the struggle for human freedom which that instrument so beautifully and so perfectly described and established in this great continent. It is important to remember that institutions and principles for the government of men, whether they be of morals, economics or politics, do not spring full blown from the minds of mortals. They evolve, and all too slowly, but in the evolutionary process they acquire validity and stability. With this in mind, it seems to me that, in venturing into the uncharted realm of international controls, it would be a mistake to attempt a complete blueprint which, I am confident, would sooner or later prove too restrictive and perhaps fatally so. The first step, therefore, should be the adoption of broad and basic principles. After that step is taken, then may we consider the succeeding moves to be made.

It might be more helpful to our purpose to discuss some of the things this resolution does not contemplate. Many opponents of collective security seek to confuse the issues by proclaiming at length that we do not want an international WPA. The question of relief and rehabilitation has little to do with the formulation of a foreign policy or the creation of machinery to keep the peace. It may be that relief in the form of food or other goods has a place in military operations in occupied countries or in the settlement of this particular war. But this war is but a tragic and horrible episode which one of these days must end. A proper foreign policy, together with the machinery to keep the peace, is continuing in its nature; it does not consist of sporadic instances of emotional altruism or niggardly selfishness. To be successful it will require the assiduous daily attention of the best brains of our country. It is brains and leadership that we must supply and not gifts of bread and milk and money and oil. It is not contemplated that we, the people of the United States, are to give our goods to others, that we are to raise the standards of living of the peoples of the world, or even to give them all a free and democratic government. If we can contribute leadership and our fair share of the force found necessary to make an international system of control effective, that is all the world can or should expect. As a matter of fact, if these total wars can be prevented for a reasonable length of time, most of the peoples of the world probably can work out their own economic and political salvation.

Participation by this nation in a system designed to prevent war is inspired and justified primarily by the desire to preserve that integrity and freedom of the individual which is the great distinction of our nation. It is, of course, true that in saving our own freedom we will inevitably benefit other peoples of the world. But surely we will not refuse to save ourselves simply because in doing so we may help save others.

Another shrewd, but no less false and emotional, flank attack on the proposal for collective security is the cry that we must never sacrifice our sovereignty. The professional patriots beat their breasts and wave the flag and shout "sovereignty," hoping thereby to frighten us, like sheep, back into the corral of isolationism. In the minds of many the word "sovereignty" has some mystical connotation in some way associated with divinity. In days gone by when men were slaves, their masters imposed their will by an appeal to the divine right of kings. "Your sovereign by appointment from the all highest" was the doctrine. By some peculiar quirk, today in this republic men talk as if the federal government, even if it is made of bureaucrats, is a sovereign body, above and apart from the people. Of course it is not. If sovereignty means anything and resides anywhere, it means control over our own affairs and resides in the people. The people, according to our republican principles, are sovereign. They may delegate all, or any part, of the power to manage their affairs to any agency they please. So far they have delegated part to their city government, part to the county, part to the state, and part to the federal government. We may recall that, under the Articles of Confederation, in 1781, our people delegated certain limited powers to the central government. When these powers proved inadequate, for the purpose of preserving order and tranquillity, further powers were delegated under the Constitution in 1787. Does it make sense to say that in creating the Constitution and establishing order our people sacrificed their sovereignty? On the contrary, they acquired through that delegation the means of preserving order and their individual freedom.

Certainly, it cannot be denied that twice within twenty-five years we have been forced, against our will, into wars which have seriously threatened our free existence. To this extent the supreme control over our affairs, over our destiny, is at present incomplete. Our sovereignty is imperfect. Therefore, if we can remedy this defect, by a delegation of limited power to an agency designed to prevent war, in which we participate fully and equally with others, how can this be called a sacrifice, a giving up of anything? Rather, I should say, it is the acquisition of something infinitely precious to civilized man.

I realize, of course, that international lawyers and professional diplomats may be shocked by this unorthodox and perhaps rustic conception of sovereignty. I know that the textbooks, and the authorities say that a nation must be legally free to determine its relations with other countries to be sovereign and independent. But these academic concepts have lost much of their force in the light of present circumstances. France, Poland, Belgium, and Holland, according to the books, were, and still may be, sovereign nations, but I wonder how much comfort that is to the starving citizens of those nations. To argue about, or to insist upon the preservation of sovereignty in its strict legalistic sense is reminiscent of the medieval treatises of the monks on how many angels can sit upon the point of a needle. Bitter experience has shown us that traditional national sovereignty as a foundation for international relations is a death trap. Nations, as well as men, in this modern world of swift transportation and instantaneous communication, are interdependent; their fate is inextricably interwoven whether we like it or not. Until we recognize this basic fact of the modern world, we can make no progress toward the prevention of war, the greatest affliction of our civilization.

In an appeal to prejudice and emotion, the devotees of the status quo attempt to scare us by saying we would be turning over the control of our country to the Communists, or as some would say, to those clever British. This is, of course, rank nonsense. We will have our own representatives who can be relied upon to safeguard our interests. It may have been excusable, during the youth of our country, to assume that these "furriners," as Gene Talmadge might say, would outsmart us. But surely today, having proved our capacity in so many ways, we are not going to insist that we are too stupid to participate with the other civilized peoples of the earth in a common undertaking. It is true, of course, that since this nation has outgrown its swaddling clothes and must now play a man's part in the world, it should find the means to induce its men of wisdom and understanding into its public service. For too long, already, have we looked upon public service as a place for the unscrupulous or the incompetent. The rewards of wealth, power, and especially honor, have been reserved for our successful industrialists, scientists, movie actors and entertainers. How many times have we all heard our best citizens say, "I simply cannot afford to give up my practice, or my business, to run for Congress, or to go to Washington in a department at eight to ten thousand a year"? The plain fact is that we can no longer afford not to have our wisest men in, for all of us, the most important business in the world. Not even the Germans, with all their ingenuity in developing ersatz food, clothing, and fuel, have been able to find a substitute for brains and judgment. I think it is safe to say that it is this shortage that will account for the destruction of that country.

Many of our people, both in and out of Congress, have a natural fear of the unfamiliar. Having had little to do with the other peoples of the world, they cannot believe that most of them, especially those of the United Nations, are quite like us in their instincts, their desires, their hopes, and their fears. We have built up, through the years of our isolation from the world, a suspicion and distrust of practically all the peoples of Europe and Asia; and we cannot believe that those peoples want peace and security as much as we do.

It is natural, therefore, that, before accepting even a simple declaration of policy, such as this resolution embodies, our people insist upon asking, "Where do we go from here?" They want to know exactly what is to be done, what kind of organization we are to have, how the power is to be distributed, how much it will cost us, what all the risks are. In a few words, they want a blueprint of the whole thing before making any commitment at all.

Upon reflection it is clear that this cannot be done. This is not a unilateral undertaking for us alone to plan. In its essence it is cooperative, and no man or nation alone can say exactly what shall be done. To describe how or where we go after we decide to assume our share of the responsibility for the solution of international problems should not and cannot be the specification of plans and blueprints. It is rather the description of a course of action, a continuing, day to day process of working with other peoples—peoples, it is true, who differ from us superficially, and who may compete with us for the goods of this earth, but who, basically, do not desire war any more than we do. No man can say at this time what can or what cannot be done in cooperation with other nations because we have never tried it. On the other hand, we do know, only too well, the cost of noncooperation.

In the absence of a definite Congressional declaration, it is probably premature and unwise to attempt a further description of where we go from here or of the process of building a peace. Nevertheless, I shall venture a few suggestions.

The creation of machinery to maintain order should not be burdened with the difficult, controversial problems arising from this war. In other words, the peace treaty concluding this war should not undertake to provide for the development of cooperative security. The failure of the Versailles treaty is a case in point. We should not permit such questions as the Russian-Polish border, or the fate of Latvia, of Tripoli, to endanger the primary and essential goal, which is the prevention of war in the future by collective action. I think, therefore, that, as soon as we accept the principle of participation, immediately we should proceed to participate by direct negotiations with our principal allies in an effort to find a basis and method of permanent united action. As soon as any methods or procedures are tentatively agreed upon, they should then be submitted to the Congress for approval. It is probable that a series of agreements will evolve in the course of the development of a workable system. The scope of these agreements should not be restricted by an inflexible blueprint hastily adopted at the peace table.

As a matter of fact, where we go from here depends upon how intelligent we are, and how successful we are in getting wise men to lead us. Our leaders must have vigor and they must have confidence in our power and in the fundamental rightness of our democratic principles. For ten years—yes, for twenty-five years—we have been timid, cautious, compromising, and undecided in our attitude toward the rest of the world. We have not stood for anything positively and affirmatively. We have had a negative fearfulness that we might become involved in a struggle in which our very freedom was at stake, and for years we shrank from lending a hand. We can thank the Japs for making the decision for us; otherwise, even yet, we might be hesitating while freedom and the dignity of man were eliminated from this earth.

We must have a policy, and we must have leaders who make decisions according to principles in which we believe and not according to volatile and transitory emotions or nearsighted expediency. One of the principal values of a clear-cut policy is that it enables us to distinguish our friends from our enemies, to determine which course of action is for our own self-interest, and to avoid the indecision which led many of our people to believe that we could do business with Hitler, or that we could exist as a free people in a Nazi dominated world. Charity, prejudice, sympathy or expediency should not be the basis of a foreign policy. It must be built upon a profound evaluation of self-interest, of economics, of physical power, of geographic relations, and of fundamental human desires. These matters cannot be blueprinted, but surely men exist who understand their significance.

Such men are the principal contribution we can, and must, make to the future welfare of this nation. Such men, I believe, are to be found in this body of trained lawyers. You who understand the evolutionary process of democratic constitutional government, you must help this nation assume its proper role in the world and you must lend your talents so that this process may be fruitful. You men who understand the art of government and appreciate the psychology of human relations must take the lead in building the peace. I have heard the analogy of an architect, of an engineer used with regard to the building of a peace. But lawyers know that in dealing with human relations that analogy is not applicable. Men are not stones or brick or steel to be handled with precision and finality. We cannot build a peace like we do an Empire State building and go off and admire it, sure that it will be there on the morrow. Political institutions, like human beings or growing plants, must be constantly cultivated or they will wither and die. They are living organisms, not structures of steel and stone.

We read much about the danger of socialism and communism in this country. But why should we be so frightened? Have we no faith in the inherent merit of our republican, capitalistic system? I think our system can hold its own with any in its ability to bring the greatest good to the greatest number, which is the final justification for any government. But no system is automatic. It can be no better in the long run than the men who direct it. Too often do we criticize it and too seldom are we willing to participate in it. While I have little faith in blueprints, I do have great faith in the ability of our people to rise to great emergencies. The fundamental superiority of democracy is that it is fluid, that great men can in a crisis rise to the top, that from the lower strata a revivifying surge of new and virile blood can, like cream in a separator, flow out the top when the body is sufficiently agitated.

In spite of the numerous objections to participation by this country in a system of mutual security, I believe that our chances of success now are excellent. The very fact that our failure to participate in 1919 has resulted in this present war is in itself reason to hope that we may be wiser this time. Having tried and found wanting the policy of isolation during these last twenty-five years, I cannot believe that our people will make the same mistake a second time.

Further, I think we may find cause for hope in the long-time history of man's effort to bring order into his turbulent life. The history of government tells us that through the centuries there has been a gradual growth in the size of the unit of government. From the early family and tribal units we have progressed through the various stages of cities, states and nations. Probably the most compelling reason for this development was the desire of the peoples to substitute law and order for the physical strife that so often occurred among these groups. This development has decreased the number of disputes and battles but, on the other hand, has vastly increased the intensity and destruction of the wars. With the tremendous increase in power and mobility resulting from modern science, we have created a force that threatens to destroy us. The art of government has not kept pace with the physical sciences. But the lesson of history is that the unit of government will in time proceed to the international level. The question is: Do we have the intelligence to do it now or must we wait one hundred or five hundred years to achieve that goal?

In conclusion, I think this war has definitely demonstrated the futility of Maginot Lines and defensive armaments, as well as neutrality acts and isolation as methods of discouraging aggression. With modern weapons of warfare, the advantage is always with the aggressor who has the initiative in the first instance. This being true, the only alternative I can think of as a means to physical security is concerted or cooperative action by a dominant group. We recognized centuries ago that an individual can have no security of person no matter how heavily armed he might be and, therefore, we created a government with power to give us cooperative protection. Nations, as well as individuals, are inescapably interdependent for security, as well as for many of the other values which constitute a civilized way of life. The rapid progress of the war toward victory presses us for a decision. Already we have shown indecision in our political strategy in Africa and Italy, and Russia within the week gives evidence of dissatisfaction. I can think of nothing that would do more to strengthen the determination of our allies and insure the fruits of our victory than a positive declaration by the United States and by all the United Nations that this time we intend to work together, in peace as well as in war, to destroy the ruthless and savage forces of aggression.

In 1919 honorable but misguided men, jealous of their personal prerogatives and distrustful of a new idea, defeated our first opportunity to create order in the world. It is obvious that similar men will oppose our efforts now; not directly, but just as they did in 1919, by indirection and pretense, by reservations and restrictions, but largely by an appeal to the emotions and prejudices which all too often overcome our intelligence. Nevertheless, I am confident that we now have a Senate and a House of Representatives of intelligence and understanding, determined to rise above personal or party interests in their consideration of this vital question. In this, our second opportunity, may God grant us wisdom.

# The Marshall Plan[2]

## George C. Marshall

*Born December 31, 1880, Uniontown, PA; died October 16, 1959; A.B., Virginia Military Institute, 1901; U.S. Army, 1902-59; instructor, Army Staff College, 1906-8; instructor, Massachusetts National Guard, 1911-12; chief of operations, First Army, 1918-19; chief of staff, Eighth Army Corps., 1919; instructor, Army War College, 1927-32; Army Chief of Staff, 1939; General of the Army, 1944-59; U.S. secretary of state, 1947-49; U.S. secretary of defense, 1950-51; winner of the Nobel Peace Prize, 1953.*

### Editor's introduction

At the time it was given, this speech was described as "routine" by the Harvard University news office. Yet it would become the foundation statement of U.S. aid policy in postwar Europe. In this speech, George C. Marshall provided the basis for what later developed into the European Recovery Program, the goal of which was the "revival of a working economy in the world so as to permit the emergence of political and social conditions in which free institutions can exist." He called upon those countries affected by the fighting of World War II to provide the United States with a program of economic reconstruction. In July of 1947, 16 European nations (the Soviet Union and most of eastern Europe boycotted the convention) met at the Paris Economic Conference and concluded that they would require $22,440,000,000 in aid. Despite concerns about its role in the eventual Cold War division of Europe, the Marshall Plan is considered one of America's finest examples of global leadership and enlightened self-interest.

---

I need not tell you gentlemen that the world situation is very serious. That must be apparent to all intelligent people. I think one difficulty is that the problem is one of such enormous complexity that the very mass of facts presented to the public by press and radio make it exceedingly difficult for the man in the street to reach a clear appraisement of the situation. Furthermore, the people of this country are distant from the troubled areas of the earth and it is hard for them to comprehend the plight and consequent reactions of the long-suffering peoples, and the effect of those reactions on their governments in connection with our efforts to promote peace in the world.

In considering the requirements for the rehabilitation of Europe, the physical loss of life, the visible destruction of cities, factories, mines, and railroads was correctly estimated, but it has become obvious during recent months that this visible destruction was probably less serious than the dislocation of the entire fabric of European economy. For the past 10 years conditions have been highly abnormal. The feverish preparation for war and the more feverish maintenance of the war effort engulfed all aspects of national economies. Machinery has fallen into disrepair or is entirely obsolete. Under the arbitrary and destructive Nazi rule, virtually every possible enterprise was geared into the German war machine. Long-standing commercial ties, private institutions, banks, insurance companies and shipping companies disappeared, through loss of capital, absorption through nationalization or by simple destruction. In many countries, confidence in the local currency has been severely shaken. The breakdown of the business structure of Europe during the war was complete. Recovery has been seriously retarded by the fact that 2 years after the close of hostilities a peace settlement with Germany and Austria has not been agreed upon. But even given a more prompt solution of these difficult problems, the rehabilitation of the economic struc-

[2]Delivered at the Harvard University commencement exercises, in Cambridge, Massachusetts, on June 5, 1947.

ture of Europe quite evidently will require a much longer time and greater effort than had been foreseen.

There is a phase of this matter which is both interesting and serious. The farmer has always produced the foodstuffs to exchange with the city dweller for the other necessities of life. This division of labor is the basis of modern civilization. At the present time it is threatened with breakdown. The town and city industries are not producing adequate goods to exchange with the food-producing farmer. Raw materials and fuel are in short supply. Machinery is lacking or worn out. The farmer or the peasant cannot find the goods for sale which he desires to purchase. So the sale of his farm produce for money which he cannot use seems to him an unprofitable transaction. He, therefore, has withdrawn many fields from crop cultivation and is using them for grazing. He feeds more grain to stock and finds for himself and his family an ample supply of food, however short he may be on clothing and the other ordinary gadgets of civilization. Meanwhile people in the cities are short of food and fuel. So the governments are forced to use their foreign money and credits to procure these necessities abroad. This process exhausts funds which are urgently needed for reconstruction. Thus a very serious situation is rapidly developing which bodes no good for the world. The modern system of the division of labor upon which the exchange of products is based is in danger of breaking down.

The truth of the matter is that Europe's requirements for the next 3 or 4 years of foreign food and other essential products—principally from America—are so much greater than her present ability to pay that she must have substantial additional help, or face economic, social, and political deterioration of a very grave character.

The remedy lies in breaking the vicious circle and restoring the confidence of the European people in the economic future of their own countries and of Europe as a whole. The manufacturer and the farmer throughout wide areas must be able and willing to exchange their products for currencies the continuing value of which is not open to question.

Aside from the demoralizing effect on the world at large and the possibilities of disturbances arising as a result of the desperation of the people concerned, the consequences to the economy of the United States should be apparent to all. It is logical that the United States should do whatever it is able to do to assist in the return of normal economic health in the world, without which there can be no political stability and no assured peace. Our policy is directed not against any country or doctrine but against hunger, poverty, desperation, and chaos. Its purpose should be the revival of a working economy in the world so as to permit the emergence of political and social conditions in which free institutions can exist. Such assistance, I am convinced, must not be on a piecemeal basis as various crises develop. Any assistance that this Government may render in the future should provide a cure rather than a mere palliative. Any government that is willing to assist in the task of recovery will find full cooperation, I am sure, on the part of the United States Government. Any government which maneuvers to block the recovery of other countries cannot expect help from us. Furthermore, governments, political parties, or groups which seek to perpetuate human misery in order to profit therefrom politically or otherwise will encounter the opposition of the United States.

It is already evident that, before the United States Government can proceed much further in its efforts to alleviate the situation and help start the European world on its way to recovery, there must be some agreement among the countries of Europe as to the requirements of the situation and the part those countries themselves will take in order to give proper effect to whatever action might be undertaken by this Government. It would be neither fitting nor efficacious for this Government to undertake to draw up unilaterally a program designed to place Europe on its feet economically. This is the business of the Europeans. The initiative, I think, must come from Europe. The role of this country should consist of friendly aid in the drafting of a European program and of later support of such a program so far as it may be practical for us to do so. The program should be a joint one, agreed to by a number, if not all European nations.

An essential part of any successful action on the part of the United States is an understanding on the part of the people of America of the character of the problem and the remedies to be applied. Political passion and prejudice should have no part. With foresight, and a willingness on the part of our people to face up to the vast responsibility which history has clearly placed upon our country, the difficulties I have outlined can and will be overcome.

# Peace in the Atomic Era[3]

Albert Einstein

*Born March 14, 1879, Ulm, Germany; died April 18, 1955; Ph.D., University of Zurich, 1905; teacher, Winterthur Technical School, 1901; patent examiner, Swiss Patent Office, 1902-9; professor, University of Zurich, 1909-12; professor, University of Leyden, 1912-28; director, Kaiser Wilhelm Institute, 1913-28; winner of Nobel Prize in physics, 1921; scientist, Princeton University Institute for Advanced Study, 1933-55; author,* The Special Theory of Relativity *(1905),* The Meaning of Relativity *(1923),* Builders of the Universe *(1932),* On the Method of Theoretical Physics *(1933),* The World as I See It *(1934),* Out of My Later Years *(1950).*

## Editor's introduction

In September 1939, physicist Albert Einstein wrote a historic letter to President Franklin Delano Roosevelt advising him on the possibilities of atomic warfare. This speech, Einstein's first public statement since the U.S. decided to proceed with production of the hydrogen bomb, is really a continuation of his concern regarding the potential dangers of a nuclear world. Einstein did not believe that a nation's security could be assured through "national armament." Indeed, a nuclear buildup, or arms race, would only lead to intimidation and "mutual fear and distrust." Einstein gave these remarks for broadcast on a television program conducted by Eleanor Roosevelt. Also participating in the thirty-minute program were Senator Brien McMahon, chair of the Congressional Committee on Atomic Energy, and Dr. J. Robert Oppenheimer, former director of the atomic energy research project, in Los Alamos, New Mexico, where the first atomic bomb was developed.

---

I am grateful to you for the opportunity to express my conviction in this most important political question.

The idea of achieving security through national armament is, at the present state of military technique, a disastrous illusion. On the part of the U.S.A. this illusion has been particularly fostered by the fact that this country succeeded first in producing an atomic bomb. The belief seemed to prevail that in the end it were possible to achieve decisive military superiority. In this way, any potential opponent would be intimidated, and security, so ardently desired by all of us, brought to us and all of humanity. The maxim which we have been following during these last five years has been, in short: Security through superior military power, whatever the cost.

This mechanistic, technical-military psychological attitude had inevitable consequences. Every single act in foreign policy is governed exclusively by one view point. How do we have to act in order to achieve utmost superiority over the opponent in case of war? Establishing military bases at all possible strategically important points on the globe. Arming and economic strengthening of potential allies. Within the country! Concentration of tremendous financial power in the hands of the military, militarization of the youth, close supervision of the loyalty of the citizens, in particular, of the civil servants by a police force growing more conspicuous every day. Intimidation of people of independent political thinking. Indoctrination of the public by radio, press, school. Growing restriction of the range of public information under the pressure of military secrecy.

The armament race between the U.S.A. and the U.S.S.R., originally supposed to be a preventive measure, assumes hysterical character. On both sides, the means to mass destruction

[3]Broadcast from New York, New York, on February 12, 1950. Reprinted with permission of the Jewish National and University Library, Hebrew University of Jerusalem.

are perfected with feverish haste—behind the respective walls of secrecy. The H-Bomb appears on the public horizon as a probably attainable goal. Its accelerated development has been solemnly proclaimed by the President. If successful, radioactive poisoning of the atmosphere and hence annihilation of any life on earth has been brought within the range of technical possibilities. The ghostlike character of this development lies in its apparently compulsory trend. Every step appears as the unavoidable consequence of the preceding one. In the end, there beckons more and more clearly general annihilation.

Is there any way out of this impasse created by man himself? All of us, and particularly those who are responsible for the attitude of the U.S. and the U.S.S.R., should realize that we may have vanquished an external enemy, but have been incapable of getting rid of the mentality created by the war. It is impossible to achieve peace as long as every single action is taken with a possible future conflict in view. The leading point of view of all political action should therefore be: What can we do to bring about a peaceful coexistence and even loyal cooperation of the nations. The first problem is to do away with mutual fear and distrust. Solemn renunciation of violence (not only with respect to means of mass destruction) is undoubtedly necessary. Such renunciation, however, can only be effective if at the same time a supranational judicial and executive body is set up empowered to decide questions of immediate concern to the security of the nations. Even a declaration of the nations to collaborate loyally in the realization of such a "restricted world government" would considerably reduce the imminent danger of war.

In the last analysis, every kind of peaceful cooperation among men is primarily based on mutual trust and only secondly on institutions such as courts of justice and police. This holds for nations as well as for individuals. And the basis of trust is loyal give and take.

What about international control? Well, it may be of secondary use as a police measure. But it may be wise not to overestimate its importance. The times of Prohibition come to mind and give one pause.

# A Basis for Russian-American Peace[4]

Dean G. Acheson

*Born April 11, 1893, Middleton, CT; died October 12, 1971; B.A., Yale University, 1915; LL.B., Harvard University, 1918; secretary to Associate Justice Louis D. Brandeis, 1919-21; lawyer, Covington, Burling and Rublee, 1921-33; under secretary of U.S. treasury, 1933; lawyer, Covington, Burling, Rublee, Acheson and Schorb, 1934-41; U.S. assistant secretary of state, 1941-45; U.S. under secretary of state, 1945-47; U.S. secretary of state, 1949-53; winner of Pulitzer Prize in non-fiction, 1970; author,* Present at the Creation: My Years in the State Department *(1970).*

## Editor's introduction

At the time this speech was given, the Cold War between the Soviet Union and the United States was accelerating, as was their mutual military armament buildup. In this address, Dean Acheson, adopting an age-old philosophical argument, insisted that the United States "welcomes diversity" and "values the individual as an end in himself." In contrast, he maintained, the Soviet Union practiced the "devil's" policy, being "the end justifies the means." The two countries, Acheson argued, could only "exist concurrently" if certain issues were agreed upon, including a shared definition of peacetime terms, a withdrawal of Soviet forces from the "Satellite area"; a cessation of Soviet obstruction in the United Nations, and a renewed control of atomic power.

---

I wish to make a report to you about the tensions between the United States and the Soviet Union.

Now, the right and obligation of the Secretary of State to speak to his fellow citizens, or to the representatives of other nations, about our foreign relations is not derived from any claim on his part to special knowledge or wisdom which makes him right and other people wrong. It is derived from the fact that our forefathers by free choice worked out and approved a Constitution. This Constitution, with the amendments and interpretations which have made it a living and growing thing, has survived to this day as an expression of the will of the entire people. A President is duly elected under this Constitution with a heavy and solemn responsibility to direct the foreign relations of the American people. The President has, in accordance with law and with the advice and consent of the Senate, appointed a man to serve as Secretary of State to assist him in the conduct of our foreign affairs. This right to speak on your behalf results directly from the constitutional processes by which the American people provide a government for themselves in an orderly, clear and democratic manner.

A little over thirty years ago there came into power in one of the great countries of the world a group of people who also claim the right to speak on your behalf. That claim was based not on any Constitutional procedure, or on any expression of the will of those whose representatives they professed to be. It was based on a claim which those men made to a monopoly of the knowledge of what was right and what was wrong for human beings. They further profess that their claim is based on a body of thought taken over in large part from the writings of a mid-nineteenth century German economist and theorist, Karl Marx.

I have no desire to debate here the errors of one version or another of what is today called "Marxism." But I think it must be recognized in the light of the experience of the last hundred years that many of the premises on which Marx based his thought have been belied by the known facts of what has actually happened in

[4]Delivered to the conference on International Cooperation for World Economic Development, in Berkeley, California, on March 16, 1950.

the decades since Marx made his studies. Marx's law of capitalist accumulation, his law as to the rate of profit, his prediction of the numerical decline of the middle classes, and of the increase of the class struggle: none of these calculations has been borne out by the experience of the societies of the West. Marx did not foresee the possibility of democratic solutions.

Furthermore, the body of doctrine now professed by the Moscow-controlled Communists is only tenuously identified with Marx's writings and is largely overlaid with Russian imperialism. We certainly cannot accept the thesis that such a doctrine can serve as the justification for the right of a small group of individuals to speak for the great masses of human beings who have never selected them as their spokesmen and whose own opinions they have never consulted.

Now for three decades this group of people, or their successors, has carried on as the rulers of that same great country. They have always, at the same time, maintained the pretense that they are the interpreters of the aspirations of peoples far beyond their borders. In the light of that professed philosophy they have conducted, as masters of the Russian state, a foreign policy which now is the center of the most difficult and troublesome problems of international affairs, problems designed to keep the peoples of the world in a state of deepest apprehension and doubt. In addition to this, they have operated within the limits of the Soviet state on the basis of a domestic policy founded, they say, on the same philosophy.

There are many points in this philosophy, and particularly in the way in which it has already been applied in practice in the Soviet Union and elsewhere, which are not only deeply repugnant to us, but raise questions involving the most basic conceptions of good and evil—questions involving the ultimate moral nature of man. There is no use in attempting to ignore or gloss over the profundity of this conflict of view.

The free society values the individual as an end in himself. It requires of him only that self-discipline and self-restraint which make the rights of each individual compatible with the rights of every other individual. Individual freedom, therefore, implies individual responsibility not to exercise freedom in ways inconsistent with the freedom of other individuals, and responsibility positively to make constructive use of freedom in the building of a just society.

In relations between nations, the prime reliance of the free society is on the strength and appeal of its principles, and it feels no compulsion sooner or later to bring all societies into conformity with it.

It does not fear, rather it welcomes, diversity and derives its strength from freedom of inquiry and tolerance even of antipathetic ideas.

We can see no moral compromise with the contrary theses of international communism: that the end justifies the means, that any and all methods are therefore permissible, and that the dignity of the human individual is of no importance as against the interest of the state.

To our minds, these principles mean, in their practical application, the arrogation to individual human leaders, with all their inevitable frailties and limitations, of powers and pretenses which most of us would be willing to concede only to the infinite wisdom and compassion of a Divine Being. They mean the police state, with all that that implies; a regimentation of the worker which is hardly distinguishable from slave labor; a loss to society of those things which appear to us to make life worth living; a denial of the fundamental truths embodied in all the great religions of the world.

Here is a moral issue of the clearest nature. It cannot be evaded. Let us make no mistake about it.

Yet it does not follow from this that the two systems, theirs and ours, cannot exist concurrently in this world. Good and evil can and do exist concurrently in the whole great realm of human life. They exist within every individual, within every nation, and within every human group. The struggle between good and evil cannot be confined to governments. That struggle will go on, as it always has, in the wider theater of the human spirit itself.

But it also does not follow from this coexistence of good and evil that the two systems, theirs and ours, will necessarily be able to exist concurrently. That will depend largely on them, for we ourselves do not find impossibility in the prospect of coexistence with the Soviet system.

However much we may sympathize with the Soviet citizens who for reasons bedded deep in history are obliged to live under it, we are not attempting to change the governmental or social structure of the Soviet Union. The Soviet regime, however, has devoted a major portion of its energies and resources to the attempt to impose its system on other peoples. In this attempt it has shown itself prepared to resort to any method or stratagem including subversion, threats and even military force.

Therefore, if the two systems are to coexist, some acceptable means must be found to free the world from the destructive tensions and anxieties of which it has been the victim in these past years and the continuance of which can hardly be in the interests of any people.

I wish, therefore, to speak to you about those points of greatest difference which must be identified and sooner or later reconciled if the two systems are to live together, if not with mutual respect, at least in reasonable security. What is it which the leaders of international communism could do to make such coexistence more tolerable to everyone?

There are a number of things they could do, which, while leaving much yet to do, would give the world new confidence in the possibility of peaceful change, in the principle and processes of peaceful settlement as an effective means of finding workable solutions in areas of disagreement.

Let us look first at the points where we and they are perhaps most closely in contact, and where the establishment of peace in its narrowest, most limited sense is dangerously impeded by the absence of common ground.

One: *Definition of Terms of Peace.*

It is now nearly five years since the end of hostilities, and the victorious allies have been unable to define the terms of peace with the defeated countries. This is a grave, a deeply disturbing fact. For our part, we do not intend nor wish, in fact we do not know how, to create satellites. Nor can we accept a settlement which would make Germany, Japan, or liberated Austria satellites of the Soviet Union. The experience in Hungary, Rumania, and Bulgaria has been one of bitter disappointment and shocking betrayal of the solemn pledges by the wartime allies. The Soviet leaders joined in the pledge at Tehran that they looked forward "with confidence to the day when all peoples of the world may live free lives, untouched by tyranny, and according to their varying desires and their own consciences." We can accept treaties of peace which would give reality to this pledge and to the interests of all in security.

With regard to Germany, unification under a government chosen in free elections under international observation is a basic element in an acceptable settlement. With that need recognized and with a will to define the terms of peace, a German treaty could be formulated which, while not pretending to solve all of the complex and bitter problems of the German situation, would, nevertheless, go far toward a relaxation of a set of major tensions.

With regard to Austria, that unhappy country is still under occupation because the Soviet leaders do not want a treaty. The political and economic independence of Austria is being sabotaged by the determination of the Soviets, camouflaged in technicalities, to maintain their forces and special interests in Eastern Austria.

With regard to Japan, we feel that the Soviet leaders could recognize the interest which nations other than the members of the Council of Foreign Ministers have in a Japanese peace treaty and could refrain from taking positions and insisting on procedures which block progress toward a treaty.

In the Far East generally, there are many points where the Soviet leaders could, if they chose, relax tensions. They could, for example, permit the United Nations' Commission in Korea to carry out its duties by allowing the Commission's entry into North Korea and by accepting its report as the basis for a peaceful settlement of that liberated country's problems. They could repatriate Japanese prisoners of war from Siberian camps. They could refrain from subverting the efforts of the newly independent states of Asia and their native leaders to solve their problems in their own way.

Two: *Use of Force.*

With regard to the whole group of countries which we are accustomed to think of as the Satellite area, the Soviet leaders could withdraw their military and police force and refrain from using the shadow of that force to keep in power persons or regimes which do not command the confidence of the respective peoples, freely expressed through orderly representative processes. In other words, they could elect to observe, in practice, the declaration to which they set their signatures at Yalta concerning liberated Europe.

In this connection we do not insist that these governments have any particular political or social complexion. What concerns us is that they should be truly independent national regimes, with a will of their own and with a decent foundation in popular feeling. We would like to feel, when we deal with these governments, that we are dealing with something representative of the national identity of the peoples in question. We cannot believe that such a situation would be really incompatible with the security of the Soviet Union.

This is a question of elementary good faith, and it is vital to a spirit of confidence that other treaties and other agreements will be honored. Nothing would so alter the international climate as the holding of elections in the satellite states in which the true will of the people could be expressed.

Three: *Obstruction in the United Nations.*

The Soviet leaders could drop their policy of obstruction in the United Nations and could instead act as if they believe the United Nations is, as Stalin himself has recently called it, a serious instrumentality for the maintenance of international peace and security. They are simply not acting that way now.

Their policy of walk-out and boycott is a policy that undermines the concept of majority decision. Indeed, they seem deliberately to entrench themselves in a minority position in the United Nations. This was illustrated last fall when they voted against the Essentials of Peace Resolution which solemnly restated and reaffirmed the principles and purposes of the United Nations Charter and which pointed to practical steps which members should take to support the peace.

A respect for the expressed will of the majority is as fundamental to international organization as it is to democracy. We know that a majority of the General Assembly has generally not agreed with the Soviet Union, whereas we ourselves have generally been on the majority side. There is nothing artificial about this situation. It has not been the result of any sleight of hand or pressures on our part. We do not have any satellites whose votes we control. The significant fact is that proposals which have commended themselves to a majority of the members of the United Nations have also commended themselves to us.

Let the Soviet Union put forward in the United Nations genuine proposals conducive to the work of peace, respectful of the real independence of other governments, and appreciative of the role which the United Nations could and should play in the preservation of world stability and the cooperation of nations. They will then doubtless have a majority with them. We will rejoice to see them in such a majority. We will be pleased to be a member of it ourselves.

Four: *Effective Control of Atomic Energy.*

The Soviet leaders could join us in seeking realistic and effective arrangements for the control of atomic weapons and the limitation of armaments in general. We know that it is not easy for them under their system to contemplate the functioning on their territory of an authority in which people would participate who are not of their political persuasion.

If we have not hesitated to urge that they as well as we accept this requirement it is because we believe that a spirit of genuine responsibility to mankind is widely present in this world. Many able administrators and scientists could be found to operate such an authority who would be only too happy, regardless of political complexion, to take an elevated and enlightened view of the immense responsibility which would rest upon them. There are men who would scorn to use their powers for the negative purpose of intrigue and destruction. We believe that an authority could be established which would not be controlled or subject to control by either ourselves or the Soviet Union.

Five: *Attempts at Undermining Established Governments.*

The Kremlin could refrain from using the Communist apparatus controlled by it throughout the world to attempt to overthrow, by subversive means, established governments with which the Soviet Government stands in an outward state of friendship and respect. In general, it could desist from, and could cooperate in efforts to prevent, indirect aggression across national frontiers—a mode of conduct which is inconsistent with the spirit and the letter of the United Nations Charter.

Six: *Proper Treatment of Diplomatic Representatives.*

The Soviet leaders could cooperate with us to the end that the official representatives of all countries are treated everywhere with decency and respect and that an atmosphere is created in which these representatives could function in a normal and helpful manner, conforming to the accepted codes of diplomacy.

The standards of conduct of our own representatives are known from more than a century and a half of American diplomatic experience. These standards are such that all countries which have accepted our representatives in a spirit of respect and confidence over periods of many decades have certainly remained none the worse for it. The independence of those countries has not been undermined; their peoples have not been corrupted; their economies have not been scathed by sabotage.

When we now find our representatives treated as criminals, when we see great official propaganda machines reiterating that they are sinister people and that contact with them is pregnant with danger—we cannot believe that such insinuations are advanced in good faith, and we cannot be blind to the obvious implications of such an attitude.

Seven: *Distortion of Motives of Others.*

In general, the Soviet leaders could refrain, I think, from systematically distorting to their own peoples the picture of the world outside their borders, and of our country, in particular.

We are not suggesting that they become propagandists for any country or system other than their own. But the Soviet leaders know, and the world knows with what genuine disappointment and concern the people of this country were brought to the realization that the wartime collaboration between the major allies was not to be the beginning of a happier and freer era in the association between the peoples of the Soviet Union and other peoples.

What are we now to conclude from the morbid fancies which their propaganda exudes of a capitalist encirclement, of a United States craftily and systematically plotting another world war? They know, and the world knows, how foreign is the concept of aggressive war to our philosophy and our political system. They know that we are not asking to be objects of any insincere and effusive demonstrations of sentimental friendship. But we feel that the Soviet leaders could at least permit access to the Soviet Union of persons and ideas from other countries so that other views might be presented to the Russian people.

These are some of the things which we feel that the Soviet leaders could do, which would permit the rational and peaceful development of the coexistence of their system and ours. They are not things that go to the depths of the moral conflict. They are not things that promise the Kingdom of Heaven. They have been formulated by us, not as moralists but as servants of government, anxious to get on with the practical problems that lie before us, and to get on with them in a manner consistent with mankind's deep longing for a respite from fear and uncertainty.

Nor have they been formulated as a one-sided bargain. A will to achieve binding, peaceful settlements would be required of all participants. All would have to produce unmistakable evidence of their good faith. All would have to accept agreements in the observance of which all nations could have real confidence.

The United States is ready, as it has been and always will be, to cooperate in genuine efforts to find peaceful settlements. Our attitude is not inflexible, our opinions are not frozen, our positions are not and will not be obstacles to peace. But it takes more than one to cooperate. If the Soviet Union could join in doing these things I have outlined, we could all face the future with greater security. We could look forward to more than the eventual reduction of some of the present tensions. We could anticipate a return to a more normal and relaxed diplomatic atmosphere, and to progress in the transaction of some of the international business which needs so urgently to be done.

I fear, however, that I must warn you not to raise your hopes. No one who has lived through these postwar years can be sanguine about reaching agreements in which reliance can be placed and which will be observed by the Soviet leaders in good faith. We must not, in our yearning for peace, allow ourselves to be betrayed by vague generalities or beguiling proffers of peace which are unsubstantiated by good faith solidly demonstrated in daily behavior. We are always ready to discuss, to negotiate, to agree, but we are understandably loath to play the role of international sucker. We will take the initiative in the future as we have in the past in seeking agreement whenever there is any indication that this course would be a fruitful one. What is required is genuine evidence in conduct, not just in words, of an intention to solve the immediate problems and remove the tensions which divide us. I see no evidence that the Soviet leaders will change their conduct until the progress of the free world convinces them that they cannot profit from a continuation of these tensions.

So our course of action in the world of hard reality which faces us is not one that is easily charted. It is not one which this nation can adopt without consideration of the needs and views of other free nations. It is one which requires all the devotion and resolve and wisdom that can be summoned up. We have had and continue to have the assistance and advice of distinguished leaders in all walks of life. We have the benefit of the great public discussion which has been proceeding in the democratic way, by free inquiry and free expression.

It is my purpose in talking with you to point a direction and to define the choices which confront us. We need to stand before the world with our own purpose and position clear.

We want peace, but not at any price. We are ready to negotiate, but not at the expense of rousing false hopes which would be dashed by new failures. We are equally determined to support all real efforts for peaceful settlements and to resist aggression.

The times call for a total diplomacy equal to the task of defense against Soviet expansion and to the task of building the kind of world in which our way of life can flourish. We must continue to press ahead with the building of a free world which is strong in its faith and in its material progress. The alternative is to allow the free nations to succumb one by one to the erosive and encroaching processes of Soviet expansion.

We must not slacken, rather we must reinvigorate, the kind of democratic efforts which are represented by the European Recovery Program, the North Atlantic and Rio Pacts, the Mutual Defense Assistance Program, the Point IV Program for developing the world's new workshops and assistance in creating the conditions necessary to a growing, many-sided exchange of the world's products.

We must champion an international order based on the United Nations and on the abiding principles of freedom and justice, or accept an international society increasingly torn by destructive rivalries.

We must recognize that our ability to achieve our purposes cannot rest alone on a desire for peace, but that it must be supported by the strength to meet whatever tasks Providence may have in store for us.

We must not make the mistake, in other words, of using Soviet conduct as a standard for our own. Our efforts cannot be merely reactions to the latest moves by the Kremlin. The bipartisan line of American foreign policy has been and must continue to be the constructive task of building, in cooperation with others, the kind of world in which freedom and justice can flourish. We must not be turned aside from this task by the diversionary thrusts of the Soviet Union. And if it is necessary, as it sometimes is, to deal with such a thrust or the threat of one, the effort should be understood as one which, though essential, is outside the main stream of our policy.

Progress is to be gained in the doing of the constructive tasks which give practical affirmation to the principles by which we live.

The success of our efforts rests finally on our faith in ourselves and in the values for which this Republic stands. We will need courage and steadfastness and the cool heads and steady nerves of a citizenry which has always faced the future "with malice toward none; with charity toward all; with firmness in the right, as God gives us to see the right."

# Policy for the Far East[5]

John Foster Dulles

*Born February 25, 1888, Washington, D.C.; died May 24, 1959; B.A., Princeton University, 1908; LL.D., Sorbonne, 1909; LL.B., George Washington University Law School, 1911; U.S. Army, 1918; lawyer, 1911-19, partner, 1919-49, Sullivan & Cromwell; representative, United Nations General Assembly, 1946; consultant, Department of State, 1950; U.S. secretary of state, 1953-59; author,* War, Peace and Change *(1939),* War or Peace *(1950).*

## Editor's introduction

Following a long and distinguished career in government service, U.S. Secretary of State John Foster Dulles made this speech which summarized America's watch on Communist aggression and American policy towards the Far East. With regard to American policy in Asia, Dulles noted the great Communist presence there, and was defensive about the general American consensus that the United States should recognize Red China rather than Quemoy-Formosa (Taiwan). At the time this speech was given, technology was fast "shrinking" the world, and what affected one nation was felt by many. The need to operate under this understanding was underscored by Dulles's observation that Communist leaders acted globally, rarely thinking in terms of just their own nation or region.

---

I always consider that United States foreign policy is designed to serve one of the basic purposes of our Constitution, to "secure the Blessings of Liberty to ourselves and our Posterity." There was a time when foreign policy played a relatively minor role in that great task. Today its role is major.

The world has been so shrunk by the developments of science and technology that events anywhere impinge on men everywhere. Furthermore, international communism, seeking its "one world," operates against us on a global basis.

Its leaders have always considered that the United States was the hardest nut for them to crack. They hope, however, to do so by first getting control of the rest of the world, leaving the United States so encircled and isolated and subject to such economic strangulation that, as Stalin put it, we will recognize that continuing struggle is hopeless and will "voluntarily" accept the Communist concept.

During the period preceding and following the Second World War international communism made immense gains in Europe and in Asia. Now it rules about 900 million people.

In recent years that expanding process has been checked. That has been the result of overall policies that I shall briefly recall before turning more particularly to the Pacific scene.

*Retaliatory Power*

It is our policy to check the Communist use or threat of force by having retaliatory power, and the will to use it, so that the Communist use of force would obviously be unprofitable to them.

I emphasize both the power and the will. One without the other is useless. Also, that will must be made sufficiently manifest that potential aggressors, when they make their calculations, will calculate that they could not aggress without disaster to themselves.

It is not pleasant to have to plan in these terms. But in the world as it is, there is no other way to peace and security for ourselves and for other parts of the endangered free world.

*Forces-in-Being*

It is, however, not enough merely to have great retaliatory striking power. It is necessary to have forces-in-being at endangered points. Nations which are in close proximity to powerful aggressive forces need the reassurance of

[5]Delivered to the California Chamber of Commerce, in San Francisco, California, on December 4, 1958.

some visible force within their own territory. They are not content to be wholly dependent upon forces and decisions elsewhere.

Furthermore, vast retaliatory power should not be, and will not be, invoked lightly. There must be an ability to oppose what may be limited probings in ways less drastic than general nuclear war.

A capacity quickly to help Lebanon; such power as was rapidly deployed in the Taiwan area; the presence of United States forces in such areas as Berlin, West Germany, and Korea—all contribute essentially to the peace and security of our own country.

Most of the "limited war" forces are contributed by our allies. For example, they contribute 80 per cent of the ground forces. We help to maintain and support these forces by supplying, where needed, military weapons and occasionally some financial support.

This is truly a system of "collective" security. It provides security both for the United States and for our allies.

*Coping with Political and Economic Subversion*

We also have policies to cope with the Communist tactics of political and economic subversion.

The former colonial areas have long been marked out as special prey for communism. Lenin taught that international communism should stimulate "nationalism" to the point of breaking, totally, political, economic, and cultural ties between the so-called "colonial and dependent areas" and the Western powers. Then, it was calculated, the new countries would become so dependent upon the Communist nations that the former colonial peoples could, as Lenin put it, be "amalgamated" into the Communist bloc.

That strategy is being actively pursued today, taking advantage of the liberating policies of the colonial powers.

During the postwar period twenty-one new nations have been granted political independence, and others are on the threshold of independence. International communism is striving to gain control of these new countries. Its efforts are reinforced by the rapid economic development going on within the existing Sino-Soviet orbit. There harsh discipline and extreme austerity extract rapid economic growth out of the people. The newly independent and the less developed countries see this growth and are told that with Communist help and guidance they could make the same progress. International communism is now in a position to supply many technicians and considerable amounts of economic aid to support its subversive program.

That means that these free nations which possess accumulated capital need to assist the less developed countries to carry out, in freedom, development programs. The peoples of the less developed countries must feel that they live in an environment that is made dynamic by forces that will lift them out of what, for most, has been a stagnant morass of poverty.

This task is, primarily, one for private capital and normal trade. But government must effectively supplement private efforts. When it does so, it is demonstrably acting to secure for us and our posterity the blessings of liberty.

If these new countries, representing much of Asia and Africa, fall to communism and if the same lure operates in Latin America, then international communism would have gone far to having the United States within the cruel clutch of its encirclement.

*Demonstrating What Free Men Can Do*

It is never sufficient to be defensive. Freedom must be a positive force that will penetrate.

Only individuals and free enterprise can impart that quality. In a struggle where individual freedom is the issue, government cannot carry all the responsibility. Governments of the free can do much. But the essential exponents of freedom are free people.

Our nation was founded as a great experiment in freedom. Our people were endowed with a sense of mission. As put in the opening paragraph of *The Federalist* papers, we hoped by our "conduct and example" to demonstrate to all the world the advantages of a free and self-governing society. And, in fact, we did just that.

When our nation was formed, the tide of despotism was high. We contributed largely to rolling it back. What we did became known as the "Great American Experiment," and it caught the imagination of men everywhere.

We must be imbued with that spirit and set that example.

Freedom is still a magnet that attracts. Let me recall these facts:

Of the Chinese Communist prisoners taken in Korea, two thirds rejected repatriation.

From Communist China the people flee to Hong Kong and Macao.

In Korea about 2 million have gone from the Communist north to the south.

In Vietnam nearly 1 million went from the Communist north to the south.

During the Hungarian rebellion, 200,000 escaped to freedom.

In Germany over 3 million have gone from east to west.

Indeed, the evidence suggests a "law" of popular gravitation to democratic freedom.

Within the past five years there have been violent outbreaks in East Berlin, East Germany, Poland, Hungary, and Communist China.

Today the Soviet rulers threaten West Berlin. Why? It is because they are put on the defensive by the inspiring demonstration there of what free men can do.

Communist rulers have shown a formidable capacity to impose their rule. But, if free men will show the good fruits of freedom, the enslavers will always be on the defensive and will face the ultimate collapse of their system.

*The Pacific and the Far East*

Let me now turn to the Pacific and the Far East. I first mention certain aspects of the situation that are distinctive.

1. In Asia international communism now controls a great population and land mass represented by the China mainland, Tibet, North Korea, and North Vietnam.

2. The non-Communist countries are scattered about the rim of this great mass. For the most part they constitute separated insular or peninsular positions. Historically, they lack common ties; there is little sense of regional unity. As between some of the free Asian countries, there is antagonism.

3. The Communist regime in Peiping, closely leagued with Moscow, is bearing down hard on the free Asian countries with its massive weight of numbers, its rising military power, and its infiltration among overseas Chinese. They constitute a large and influential element in most of the free Asian countries. It penetrates labor unions, student groups, and left-wing political parties. It has an elaborate underground apparatus and extensive propaganda facilities.

4. Internally, Red China is feverishly imposing a communization program designed quickly to transform the Chinese nation into a great military and industrial power. The program involves human slavery and cruelty on a scale unprecedented in all world history. But it is producing material results.

5. The communization program inevitably creates widespread discontent. The dictators of that program, in order to divert hostility from themselves, pretend that their program is needed because the United States threatens to attack. They have launched a virulent "Hate America" campaign.

6. Of the eleven free Far Eastern countries, eight have gained their independence only since 1945. They inevitably lack experience in public administration. They are in an early stage of economic development. Their industries remain to be created. Their standards of living are low.

These conditions of the Far East are quite different from those of Western Europe, for example. There the free countries are contiguous; they have a similar culture; they are well developed economically.

Despite the differing circumstances that must always be taken into account, the basic principles which I have outlined are nevertheless applicable in the Far East and can preserve freedom there.

*Collective Security Arrangements*

We have developed collective security arrangements in the Far East to the maximum extent so far practical. Of these security arrangements the most significant is that created by the Southeast Asia Collective Defense Treaty. In addition, the United States has bilateral security arrangements with the Republics of the Philippines, Korea, and China and with Japan. We have a trilateral treaty with Australia and New Zealand.

The United States, in support of these collective defense treaties, maintains large mobile power, air and sea, in the Pacific, and some ground forces, particularly in Korea. These are part of a free-world defense network in the Far East involving some 1,750,000 troops, most of them battle-experienced. These forces deter, and can resist, Communist armed aggression. They are backed up by the retaliatory striking power of the United States, if this is needed.

There have been no Communist territorial gains in the Far East since 1954 when SEATO was formed and these bilateral treaties made.

The recent Communist show of force in the Taiwan area was for the avowed purpose of liquidating the government of the Republic of China and expelling the United States from the Western Pacific. It was pushed to the point of ascertaining whether the United States had the will to fight if challenged. We showed that will and avoided a loss which would have been not merely Quemoy but, ultimately, the entire free-world position in the Western Pacific.

*U.S. Attitude Toward Chinese Communist Regime*

In addition to contributing to military security, the United States promotes the general economic and political health of the free nations of the Far East. This is in accord both with our tradition and with our interest. Also we thereby combat the Chinese Communist tactics of subversion.

In this connection I should like to mention our attitude toward Communist China. I spoke of this rather fully in a talk which I made here in San Francisco in June of last year. What I now say is designed to supplement and not to subtract from what I then said.

Developments make it ever more clear that, if we were to grant political recognition to the Chinese Communist regime, that would be a well-nigh mortal blow to the survival of the non-Communist governments in the Far East. Such recognition and the seating of the Chinese Communists in the United Nations would so increase their prestige and influence in the Far East, and so dishearten our allies there, that the Communist subversive efforts would almost surely succeed.

Contrary arguments come largely from two sources. There are those who argue that, since the Chinese Communist regime exists and has power on the mainland, we ought to accord it political recognition.

There is, however, no principle of international law to this effect. Recognition is a privilege which can be accorded or withheld. There are several *de facto* regimes in the world that we do not recognize. We act, in these matters, as our national interest dictates.

The Chinese Communist regime is bitterly hostile to the United States. It is dedicated to expelling all our influence from the Western Pacific. It is determined to take over the free peoples and resources of the area. It violates all established principles of international law and of civilized conduct.

Why should we give aid and comfort to such a regime and to such policies?

Some argue we should recognize the Chinese Communist regime in the hope that large and profitable trade would follow. That is an illusion. The mainland of China has never been a large customer of the United States, and its trade is even more closely regimented under Communist rule.

The United States today is exporting to the non-Communist countries of the Far East at the rate of over $2.5 billion a year. This figure excludes the value of military items exported under our mutual security programs.

It is certain that, if the Communists should take over these free nations of the Far East, our trade with them would drastically shrink, as has been the case with our trade with the Soviet Union and its European satellites. We must also recall that, because Communist nations look on trade primarily as a political instrument, citizens of free nations can rarely engage in such trade profitably or safely.

Should we, then, in the quest of a few millions of dollars of unreliable trade with Communist China jeopardize exports of $2.5 billion?

We deal with the Chinese Communist regime wherever that is expedient. We do not pretend that it does not exist. We have been in almost constant negotiations with it for particular purposes, at Panmunjom, at the Geneva conference on Indo-China, in bilateral negotiations at Geneva and now at Warsaw.

But it is certain that diplomatic recognition of the Chinese Communist regime would gravely jeopardize the political, the economic, and the security interests of the United States. The Pacific instead of being, as it is today, a friendly body of water would in great part be dominated by hostile forces and our own defenses there would be driven back to or about our continental frontiers.

*"Dumping" Practices*

There is developing a special threat to free-world trade in the Far East. That is the "dumping" practice of Communist China. The Chinese mainland people desperately need for themselves all that they are capable of producing. But they are denied, so that the rulers may prosecute their expansionist designs.

When millions of Chinese are dying of starvation, rice is exported for political purposes.

Goods manufactured in China are being dumped in Southeast Asia at prices that disrupt normal trade. These include textiles, bicycles, sewing machines, fountain pens, and the like. This is particularly a present threat to the trade of Japan in South and Southeast Asia.

This problem as it arises in the Far East is one phase of the economic offensive now being initiated by the Sino-Soviet bloc. Your Government is intensively studying this problem. We have asked business people—some from the group I am addressing—to study it. There is no doubt in my mind but what concrete measures will be needed to assure that in the face of this unfair competition free enterprise will continue to play its full role as a dynamic and expanding force in developing the economies of the free-world nations.

*Preserving Chinese Culture*

One essential sought by our Far Eastern policy is to assure that the Chinese Communists do not acquire, as an exclusive propaganda tool of their own, the prestige that attaches to Chinese culture. This prestige is great.

Chinese culture has ancient historic roots and is an influence today throughout the Far East. It derives from the family life, the veneration of the ancestor, and the training of youth to respect their parents. It comprehends the creation and admiration of what is beautiful in color, form, and arrangement. It stimulates and honors education in the broad humanitarian and philosophical sense of that word.

Today, on the mainland, not only Chinese culture but every aspect of human dignity is sought to be eradicated.

Under the Chinese Communist "commune" system, individuality and personality are brutally suppressed. The individual is valued, and allowed to survive, only as a laborer for the state. "All-purpose" workers, in blocs of tens of thousands, are herded into crude dormitories, with men and women largely segregated, and children placed in wholesale nurseries, so that the women can also be part of the slave labor force. The venerated graves of ancestors are everywhere being desecrated. The respected customs and beliefs of the people, the basic values of family life, education in the broad sense, the art of the beautiful are being obliterated in the name of the "great leap" decreed by Peiping.

It is important to all the world that Chinese culture be preserved. Fortunately there is a qualified custodian of that culture—the government of the Republic of China, with its present seat at Taipei.

A few weeks ago I went to Taipei to discuss the general situation with the President and other members of that government. Out of that consultation came a declaration which is, I think, noteworthy. Let me read these passages:

The government of the Republic of China declared its purpose to be a worthy representative of the Chinese people and to strive to preserve those qualities and characteristics which have enabled the Chinese to contribute so much of benefit to humanity."

And,

"The government of the Republic of China considers that the restoration of freedom to its people on the mainland is its sacred mission. It believes that the foundation of this mission resides in the minds and the hearts of the Chinese people and that the principal means of successfully achieving its mission is the implementation of Dr. Sun Yat-sen's three people's principles (nationalism, democracy and social well-being) and not the use of force."

These declarations have significance not just for China but for all the Far East and indeed for all the free world. They give welcome reassurances that the Republic of China will not by any rash act engulf the world in war. Also they assure that Chinese culture will live on as a symbol and inspiration to all the Chinese people and indeed to all of us.

*A Noble Strategy of Victory*

There are some who question whether the foreign policies we are following will succeed.

It can be affirmed with absolute confidence that our policies will succeed if they are steadfastly pursued.

Materialistic despotisms, with their iron discipline, their mechanistic performance, their hard and shiny exterior, always seem formidable. Democracies seem to stumble and falter; they advertise their differences and always seem vulnerable. But history has demonstrated again and again that democracies are almost always stronger than they seem and despotisms are always more vulnerable than they appear. For example: It is impossible for Communist nations to develop into modern industrial states without a large degree of education. But minds so educated also penetrate the fallacies of Marxism and increasingly resist conformity.

Also there are increasing demands on the part of the subject peoples for more consumer goods, for more of the fruits of their labor. These demands cannot be indefinitely repressed or satisfied merely with recurrent promises.

Such internal pressures are bound to alter the character of the Communist regimes, particularly if these regimes are denied the glamor and prestige of great external successes.

It may be recalled that when Khrushchev, in 1956, attacked the abuses of Stalin he explained that they could not have been corrected earlier because "many victories were gained during his lifetime."

To deny external successes to international communism is not merely a negative, defensive policy. It accelerates the evolution within the Sino-Soviet bloc of governmental policies which will increasingly seek the welfare of their own peoples rather than exploit these peoples in the interest of world conquest.

If the non-Communist nations hold fast to policies which deter armed aggression, if they prevent subversion through economic and revolutionary processes, and, above all, if they demonstrate the good fruits of freedom, then we can know that freedom will prevail.

President Eisenhower, speaking in Paris at the NATO meeting a year ago, outlined the policies of the free world. Concluding, he said, "There lies before the free nations a clear possibility of peaceful triumph. There is a noble strategy of victory—not victory over any peoples but victory for all peoples."

That is the strategy to which we are dedicated. Its price will be high, not only in terms of money but above all in terms of will, of perseverance, of faith. Given those qualities, victory is assured.

# Anti-Westernism: Cause and Cure[6]

Vera Micheles Dean

*Born March 29, 1903, St. Petersburg, Russia; died October 10, 1972; B.A., Radcliffe College, 1925; A.M., Yale University, 1926; Ph.D., Radcliffe College, 1928; research associate, 1928-33, editor, 1933-38, research director, 1938-61, Foreign Policy Association; visiting professor, Smith College, 1952-54; author,* New Governments in Europe *(1934);* Europe in Retreat *(1939);* Foreign Policy Without Fear *(1953).*

## Editor's introduction

In this speech, author and lecturer Dr. Vera Micheles Dean explained why non-Western countries, both Communist and non-Communist, were often hostile to Western civilization, particularly the United States. Dean believed that the cure for this hostility lay in a paradox, as she remarked that "the cure for anti-Westernism is Westernization," or allowing leaders of non-Western nations to choose those aspects of Western culture which will best serve their own people. In order for this to occur, Dean asserted that the West should resist the assumption that Western practices are inherently superior and representative of the "norm."

---

In Cuba, one of our Latin American neighbors, Fidel Castro denounces the United States. In Iraq, until 1958 an active member of the Baghdad pact, crowds jeer at an American diplomat, and a Communist-dominated regime comes to power. The mayor of Manila, speaking on Edward R. Murrow's *Small World* TV program, tells us why we are losing friends in Asia in terms so bitter as to befit a foe rather than a friend of the United States.

As these and other incidents are reported from around the globe, Americans ask themselves: Why are these non-Western peoples against the West—and particularly why are they against the United States? What is anti-Westernism? And how can it be cured?

So deeply is the West imbued with the sense of benefits it has conferred on the non-Western areas in the past, and is ready to confer in the future, that we find it difficult to believe anti-Westernism can exist and flourish without the help of communism. Yet, this is the harsh reality we must face in Asia, the Middle East, and Africa if we are not to fall prey to perilous illusions.

The Russians did not need to lift a finger, fire a gun, or spend a single ruble to foment anti-Westernism in Egypt or Saudi Arabia, in Indonesia or Jordan. It's in the air. It is deeply imbedded in the consciousness of peoples who have lived under the rule of Britain, France, or the Netherlands, not of Russia. True, the Russians capitalize with marked success on a sentiment against the West which corresponds to their own, but they did not in the first place create it. This sentiment can exist and has existed apart from communism—just as some plants need no soil or fertilizer to remain alive. In fact, anti-Westernism was a sturdy plant in Russia itself during the nineteenth century under the czars, long before the Bolsheviks came on the scene.

But, if these manifestations in Russia were not initially a product of communism, were they an exclusive product of Russia's historical development? Is the anti-Westernism we see today in other areas of the world just a carbon copy of that practiced in Russia? Would it vanish if the West could discover some magic formula for eliminating Russia or sealing it off from the rest of the world?

[6]Delivered at the Conference of the National Association of Women Deans and Counselors, in Cleveland, Ohio, on March 21, 1959.

The answer, disappointing as it is for the West, must be in the negative. From New Delhi to Cairo, from Jakarta to Karachi and Nairobi, men and women who have never read Marx, Lenin, or Stalin, and who often abhor what they know of Russia, are in the grip of the same emotions and ideas which fan the as yet unfinished controversy between Westernizers and Slavophiles in Russia. Their anti-Westernism, like that of the Russians, is an explosive mixture of contradictory reactions inspired by rising nationalism.

Non-Westerners admire our material achievements—the fruits of modern science and technology. They long to have their own peoples benefit by these fruits, to which they feel entitled by reason of living in the twentieth century; this is the essence of what has been well called the revolution of rising expectations. But they realize, with a poignancy which no Westerner, however sympathetic, can possibly understand—because like intense fear or joy it cannot be expressed in rational terms but must be experienced to be known—that their own countries are poor and retarded, ridden with disease and ignorance. The contrast between what they see around them, in Egypt or Indonesia, and what they painfully wish to achieve is so staggering as to fill them with a sense of hopelessness and frustration. Instead of trying to escape from this state of mind by tackling the nearest practical job, no matter how modest it may be, they are likely to vent their feelings of disappointment against the West, making it the scapegoat for all the ills from which they and their countrymen suffer.

The situation becomes all the more painful—for non-Western peoples and for the West—where the rulers, today or in the recent past, are or have been Westerners who may well have concentrated on their own interests such as the building of strategic facilities or the development of resources needed by Western industry, rather than on improvement of the economic, social, and political conditions in the areas under their control. Then the anti-Westernism which is found even in independent nations such as Japan becomes dangerously aggravated by anticolonialism and, since the foreign rulers are representatives of white nations, also by racialism. To all these feelings must be added the fear of some, who want to maintain ancient political and religious customs, that the impact of the West will destroy the fabric of the nation's traditional life. They want to oust all Westerners before this horrifying prospect has come to pass.

We, however, are particularly puzzled by the tendency of the non-Western nations to denounce Western colonialism yet say little or nothing about the colonialism of the USSR. Here again Russia's past experience is much closer to that which Asia, the Middle East, and Africa are now undergoing than is the experience of the Western nations. Russia itself was a relatively backward nation as late as the 1920's. It, too, both wanted to learn from the West yet feared its impact on institutions and on national security.

This does not mean, and should not be interpreted to mean, that the Asian and African countries accept Russia without criticisms or qualms. They are aware of the dangers of eventual pressure from Moscow. They are not enthusiastic about Russian dictatorship—although, being often accustomed to authoritarianism at home, they are less repelled by it abroad than the nations of the Atlantic community, where democracy is—more or less—an old story. Russia was not invited to the Afro-Asian conference at Bandung in 1955, presumably because it is a Eurasian, not an Asian or African, country. But Russia's experience in modernizing its economy and in making the difficult transition from ancient times to the nuclear age within a third of a century is of intense interest to all non-Western areas, which feel that they have more to learn, in a practical way, from a country far closer to their current problems and experiences than from such advanced nations as the U.S.A. and Britain. This sense of affinity with Russia—economic and social if not always political—on the part of non-Western peoples of diverse religious faiths, political traditions, and international aspirations constitutes our most difficult hurdle in our efforts to find a cure for anti-Westernism.

This cure cannot be found by denouncing communism, by demanding that the non-Western nations abandon all contacts with Russia and Communist China, or by threatening to cut off aid unless they agree to join our side. Such moves would merely reinforce their hostility to and suspicion of the West and cause them to strengthen rather than weaken their still tenuous bonds with Moscow.

As in the case of some other troubles, the most promising remedy is the hair of the dog.

The cure for anti-Westernism is Westernization, but it cannot be forced on peoples by military pressure or financial handouts. Nasser in Egypt or Nehru in India, like the Japanese after 1867 or the Russians after 1917, must be free to take the initiative in accepting or rejecting what the West has to offer. They must be free to pick and choose those features of our development they think best adapted to their own particular needs.

The essence of anti-Westernism, in Czarist Russia as in the USSR and other areas, is resistance to the assumption, which the West makes as a matter of course, that our civilization is superior to the civilizations of other regions and represents a norm which should be the ideal goal of Asians, Arabs, and Africans. When Glubb Pasha, upon reaching London after his expulsion from Jordan, was asked what it was the West had done wrong, he said that, while the West had committed mistakes, it had also done much good but that its main error is its "superciliousness" toward the non-West. If the West is to succeed, it must learn to restrain its natural feeling of pride in its own achievements—a feeling which, when transposed to non-Western lands, looks and sounds like arrogance—and display modesty in offering to improve the conditions of Egyptians or Indians.

We must, moreover, constantly bear in mind that, as a matter of historical fact, many of these today economically underdeveloped countries had achieved a high type of civilization and culture when our own ancestors were still relative savages. It is no wonder, then, that they think they have something to preserve.

Nor is it enough for us to point out that the Communist powers now practice the imperialism which the Western nations are in process of relinquishing. For Asia, Africa and the Middle East, colonialism and imperialism have been associated with the West, and symbolized by the unequal treatment accorded by whites to non-whites. What Russia does in Eastern Europe, repugnant as it may be to all non-Communists, is regarded as a conflict between white peoples. The situation changes, however, when non-whites try to subjugate and repress non-whites, as shown by the sharp reaction in Asia against Communist China's actions in Tibet.

What, then, can the United States do to counter Soviet influence? First, we must renew our efforts to facilitate orderly self-determination for those peoples who are still under colonial rule. This does not mean that all will benefit by achieving independence overnight but that we should show genuine concern for their desire to rule themselves in at least a limited form—perhaps, for a stated period of time, under the supervision of the United Nations.

Second, when we advocate independence, we must accept the fact that independence includes the right for a free nation to choose its own course in world affairs. We must stop criticizing those of the non-Western nations which, like India or Burma, choose neutralism in preference to membership in one or other of the military blocs that have emerged out of the cold war.

Third, we must look at foreign aid not merely as a weapon in the cold war. We must understand that it is in our national interest to give aid to the underdeveloped countries, even if communism did not exist, in order to improve economic and social conditions in the world community of which we are a part. Once we realize that the goal of foreign aid is not just to defeat communism but to advance the development of non-Western areas, then we should think of long-term aid of a more substantial character than we have undertaken in the past. Economists calculate that we could and should allocate $3 billion a year during two or three decades for economic, as distinguished from military, aid. This figure may seem large, but it is less than 1 per cent of our national income.

Fourth, we must realize that foreign aid cannot be considered apart from foreign trade. The non-Western nations have no desire to become permanent pensioners. They do not just want to receive handouts; they want to stand on their own feet and gain self-respect. But they can do this only if they can repay the long-term loans we may make to them. And this they can do only if they can sell their products in Western markets. This means that we and our allies must rethink the character of world trade.

And, finally, we must learn that relations with the non-Western nations, if they are to be successful, have to be a two-way street. We have much to offer in terms of democratic procedures and technological skills, but we can greatly enrich ourselves by sharing their contributions to the world's cultural heritage through religion, philosophy, art, literature, and music.

This five-point program may sound like a tall order. But no one who has faith in the American way of life can believe that we are unable to meet Russia's challenge for peacetime competition in the non-Western World. As the *New Yorker* said about the world domination dreams of the Nazis when Germany conquered France in 1941: "We, too, can dream dreams and see visions."

# Cuban Missile Crisis[7]

## John F. Kennedy

*Born May 29, 1917, Brookline, MA; died November 22, 1963; B.S., Harvard University, 1940; U.S. Navy, 1941-45; representative (D) from Massachusetts, 1946-52; senator (D) from Massachusetts, 1953-60; president of the United States, 1960-63; author,* Why England Slept *(1940),* Profiles in Courage *(1956),* A Nation of Immigrants *(1959),* America, the Beautiful *(1964).*

### Editor's introduction

Initiating the most direct confrontation between Soviet and American ships to date, President John F. Kennedy, in this speech, announced plans to block all Soviet shipments of missiles to Cuba. The blockade began at 10 a.m. the day after this speech was given, and with it, fear of global thermonuclear war swept the nation and the world. For three days following the American blockade, sharp disagreements erupted between American Ambassador Adlai E. Stevenson and Soviet Envoy Valerian A. Zorin. On Sunday, October 28, President Kennedy and Soviet Premier Khrushchev entered into an agreement by which the missiles would be dismantled and returned to the Soviet Union. Response to the speech was highly favorable, and it is considered by many to be one of the major documents of the twentieth-century.

---

This Government, as promised, has maintained the closest surveillance of the Soviet military build-up on the island of Cuba. Within the past week, unmistakable evidence has established the fact that a series of offensive missile sites is now in preparation on that imprisoned island. The purpose of these bases can be none other than to provide a nuclear capability against the Western Hemisphere.

Upon receiving the first preliminary hard information of this nature last Tuesday morning [October 16] at 9:00 A.M., I directed that our surveillance be stepped up. And having now confirmed and completed our evaluation of the evidence and our decision on a course of action, this Government feels obliged to report this new crisis to you in fullest detail.

The characteristics of these new missile sites indicate two distinct types of installations. Several of them include medium-range ballistic missiles, capable of carrying a nuclear warhead for a distance of more than one thousand nautical miles. Each of these missiles, in short, is capable of striking Washington, D.C., the Panama Canal, Cape Canaveral, Mexico City, or any other city in the southeastern part of the United States, in Central America, or in the Caribbean area.

Additional sites not yet completed appear to be designed for intermediate-range ballistic missiles—capable of traveling more than twice as far—and thus capable of striking most of the major cities in the Western Hemisphere, ranging as far north as Hudson's Bay, Canada, and as far south as Lima, Peru. In addition, jet bombers, capable of carrying nuclear weapons, are now being uncrated and assembled in Cuba, while the necessary air bases are being prepared.

This urgent transformation of Cuba into an important strategic base—by the presence of these large, long-range, and clearly offensive weapons of sudden mass destruction—constitutes an explicit threat to the peace and security of all the Americas, in flagrant and deliberate defiance of the Rio Pact of 1947, the traditions of this nation and hemisphere, the joint resolution of the 87th Congress, the Charter of the United Nations, and my own public warnings to the Soviets on September 4 and 13. This action also contradicts the repeated assurances of Soviet spokesmen, both publicly and

[7]Broadcast to the nation, from Washington, D.C., on October 22, 1962.

privately delivered, that the arms build-up in Cuba would retain its original defensive character, and that the Soviet Union had no need or desire to station strategic missiles on the territory of any other nation.

The size of this undertaking makes clear that it has been planned for some months. Yet only last month, after I had made clear the distinction between any introduction of ground-to-ground missiles and the existence of defensive antiaircraft missiles, the Soviet government publicly stated on September 11 that, and I quote, "the armaments and military equipment sent to Cuba are designed exclusively for defensive purposes," and, I quote the Soviet government, "there is no need for the Soviet government to shift its weapons for a retaliatory blow to any other country, for instance Cuba," and that, and I quote the government, "the Soviet Union has so powerful rockets to carry these nuclear warheads that there is no need to search for sites for them beyond the boundaries of the Soviet Union." That statement was false.

Only last Thursday, as evidence of this rapid offensive buildup was already in my hand, Soviet Foreign Minister Gromyko told me in my office that he was instructed to make it clear once again, as he said his government had already done, that Soviet assistance to Cuba, and I quote, "pursued solely the purpose of contributing to the defense capabilities of Cuba," that, and I quote him, "training by Soviet specialists of Cuban nationals in handling defensive armaments was by no means offensive," and that "if it were otherwise," Mr. Gromyko went on, "the Soviet government would never become involved in rendering such assistance." That statement also was false.

Neither the United States of America nor the world community of nations can tolerate deliberate deception and offensive threats on the part of any nation, large or small. We no longer live in a world where only the actual firing of weapons represents a sufficient challenge to a nation's security to constitute maximum peril. Nuclear weapons are so destructive and ballistic missiles are so swift, that any substantially increased possibility of their use or any sudden change in their deployment may well be regarded as a definite threat to peace.

For many years, both the Soviet Union and the United States, recognizing this fact, have deployed strategic nuclear weapons with great care, never upsetting the precarious status quo which insured that these weapons would not be used in the absence of some vital challenge. Our own strategic missiles have never been transferred to the territory of any other nation, under a cloak of secrecy and deception; and our history, unlike that of the Soviets since the end of World War II, demonstrates that we have no desire to dominate or conquer any other nation or impose our system upon its people. Nevertheless, American citizens have become adjusted to living daily on the bull's-eye of Soviet missiles located inside the U.S.S.R. or in submarines.

In that sense, missiles in Cuba add to an already clear and present danger—although it should be noted the nations of Latin America have never previously been subjected to a potential nuclear threat.

But this secret, swift, and extraordinary build-up of Communist missiles—in an area well known to have a special and historical relationship to the United States and the nations of the Western Hemisphere, in violation of Soviet assurances, and in defiance of American and hemispheric policy—this sudden, clandestine decision to station strategic weapons for the first time outside of Soviet soil—is a deliberately provocative and unjustified change in the status quo which cannot be accepted by this country, if our courage and our commitments are ever to be trusted again by either friend or foe.

The 1930's taught us a clear lesson: Aggressive conduct, if allowed to grow unchecked and unchallenged, ultimately leads to war. This nation is opposed to war. We are also true to our word. Our unswerving objective, therefore, must be to prevent the use of these missiles against this or any other country, and to secure their withdrawal or elimination from the Western Hemisphere.

Our policy has been one of patience and restraint, as befits a peaceful and powerful nation, which leads a world-wide alliance. We have been determined not to be diverted from our central concerns by mere irritants and fanatics. But now further action is required—and it is under way; and these actions may only be the beginning. We will not prematurely or unnecessarily risk the costs of world-wide nuclear war in which even the fruits of victory would be ashes in our mouth—but neither will we shrink from that risk at any time it must be faced.

Acting, therefore, in the defense of our own security and of the entire Western Hemisphere, and under the authority entrusted to me by the Constitution as endorsed by the Resolution of the Congress, I have directed that the following *initial* steps be taken immediately:

*First:* To halt this offensive build-up, a strict quarantine on all offensive military equipment under shipment to Cuba is being initiated. All ships of any kind bound for Cuba from whatever nation or port will, if found to contain cargoes of offensive weapons, be turned back. This quarantine will be extended, if needed, to other types of cargo and carriers. We are not at this time, however, denying the necessities of life as the Soviets attempted to do in their Berlin blockade of 1948.

*Second:* I have directed the continued and increased close surveillance of Cuba and its military build-up. The foreign ministers of the OAS [Organization of American States] in their communiqué of October 6, rejected secrecy on such matters in this hemisphere. Should these offensive military preparations continue, thus increasing the threat to the hemisphere, further action will be justified. I have directed the armed forces to prepare for any eventualities; and I trust that in the interest of both the Cuban people and the Soviet technicians at the sites, the hazards to all concerned of continuing this threat will be recognized.

*Third:* It shall be the policy of this nation to regard any nuclear missile launched from Cuba against any nation in the Western Hemisphere as an attack by the Soviet Union on the United States, requiring a full retaliatory response upon the Soviet Union.

*Fourth:* As a necessary military precaution, I have reinforced our base at Guantánamo, evacuated today the dependents of our personnel there, and ordered additional military units to be on a stand-by alert basis.

*Fifth:* We are calling tonight for an immediate meeting of the organ of consultation under the Organization of American States, to consider this threat to hemispheric security and to invoke Articles 6 and 8 of the Rio Treaty in support of all necessary action. The United Nations Charter allows for regional security arrangements—and the nations of this hemisphere decided long ago against the military presence of outside powers. Our other allies around the world have also been alerted.

*Sixth:* Under the Charter of the United Nations, we are asking tonight that an emergency meeting of the Security Council be convoked without delay to take action against this latest Soviet threat to world peace. Our resolution will call for the prompt dismantling and withdrawal of all offensive weapons in Cuba, under the supervision of UN observers, before the quarantine can be lifted.

*Seventh and finally:* I call upon Chairman Khrushchev to halt and eliminate this clandestine, reckless, and provocative threat to world peace and to stable relations between our two nations. I call upon him further to abandon this course of world domination, and to join in an historic effort to end the perilous arms race and transform the history of man. He has an opportunity now to move the world back from the abyss of destruction—by returning to his government's own words that it had no need to station missiles outside its own territory, and withdrawing these weapons from Cuba—by refraining from any action which will widen or deepen the present crisis—and then by participating in a search for peaceful and permanent solutions.

This nation is prepared to present its case against the Soviet threat to peace, and our own proposals for a peaceful world, at any time and in any forum—in the OAS, in the United Nations, or in any other meeting that could be useful—without limiting our freedom of action. We have in the past made strenuous efforts to limit the spread of nuclear weapons. We have proposed the elimination of all arms and military bases in a fair and effective disarmament treaty. We are prepared to discuss new proposals for the removal of tensions on both sides—including the possibilities of a genuinely independent Cuba, free to determine its own destiny. We have no wish to war with the Soviet Union—for we are a peaceful people who desire to live in peace with all other peoples.

But it is difficult to settle or even discuss these problems in an atmosphere of intimidation. That is why this latest Soviet threat—or any other threat which is made either independently or in response to our actions this week—must and will be met with determination. Any hostile move anywhere in the world against the safety and freedom of peoples to whom we are committed—including in particular the brave people of West Berlin—will be met by whatever action is needed.

Finally, I want to say a few words to the captive people of Cuba, to whom this speech is being directly carried by special radio facilities. I speak to you as a friend, as one who knows of your deep attachment to your fatherland, as one who shares your aspirations for liberty and justice for all. And I have watched and the American people have watched with deep sorrow how your nationalist revolution was betrayed—and how your fatherland fell under foreign domination. Now your leaders are no longer Cuban leaders inspired by Cuban ideals. They are puppets and agents of an international conspiracy which has turned Cuba against your friends and neighbors in the Americas—and turned it into the first Latin American country to become a target for nuclear war—the first Latin American country to have these weapons on its soil.

These new weapons are not in your interest. They contribute nothing to your peace and well-being. They can only undermine it. But this country has no wish to cause you to suffer or to impose any system upon you. We know that your lives and land are being used as pawns by those who deny you freedom.

Many times in the past, the Cuban people have risen to throw out tyrants who destroyed their liberty. And I have no doubt that most Cubans today look forward to the time when they will be truly free—free from foreign domination, free to choose their own leaders, free to select their own system, free to own their own land, free to speak, and write, and worship without fear or degradation. And then shall Cuba be welcomed back to the society of free nations and to the associations of this hemisphere.

My fellow citizens, let no one doubt that this is a difficult and dangerous effort on which we have set out. No one can foresee precisely what course it will take or what costs or casualties will be incurred. Many months of sacrifice and self-discipline lie ahead—months in which both our patience and our will will be tested—months in which many threats and denunciations will keep us aware of our dangers. But the greatest danger of all would be to do nothing.

The path we have chosen for the present is full of hazards, as all paths are—but it is the one most consistent with our character and courage as a nation and our commitments around the world. The cost of freedom is always high—but Americans have always paid it. And one path we shall never choose, and that is the path of surrender or submission.

Our goal is not the victory of might, but the vindication of right—not peace at the expense of freedom, but both peace *and* freedom, here in this hemisphere, and, we hope, around the world. God willing, that goal will be achieved.

# Ich Bin Ein Berliner[8]

## John F. Kennedy

*Born May 29, 1917, Brookline, MA; died November 22, 1963; B.S., Harvard University, 1940; U.S. Navy, 1941-45; representative (D) from Massachusetts, 1946-52; senator (D) from Massuchusetts, 1953-60; president of the United States, 1960-63; author,* Why England Slept *(1940),* Profiles in Courage *(1956),* A Nation of Immigrants *(1959),* America, the Beautiful *(1964).*

### Editor's introduction

Erected in August of 1961, the Berlin Wall was perhaps the greatest physical reminder of the fundamental division between Communism and Democracy. President John F. Kennedy toured West Berlin in June of 1963. Tens of thousands followed him and his entourage as he viewed the Wall. Angered by the East German veiling of the Wall's Brandenburg Gate in red cloth, Kennedy conveyed a message of solidarity with Germans, including those confined to East Germany. He declared that "Lasting peace in Europe can never be assured as long as one German out of four is denied the elementary right of free men." Needless to say, many thousands of West Berliners welcomed Kennedy in an excited, tumultuous throng, prompting him to later remark that if he had given the command "March to the Wall—tear it down!" the crowd would have done so.

---

I am proud to come to this city as the guest of your distinguished Mayor [Willy Brandt], who has symbolized throughout the world the fighting spirit of West Berlin. And I am proud to visit the Federal Republic with your distinguished Chancellor [Konrad Adenaur] who for so many years has committed Germany to democracy and freedom and progress, and to come here in the company of my fellow American, General [Lucius] Clay, who has been in this city during its great moments of crisis and will come again if ever needed.

Two thousand years ago the proudest boast was "civis Romanus sum." Today, in the world of freedom, the proudest boast is "Ich bin ein Berliner."

I appreciate my interpreter translating my German!

There are many people in the world who really don't understand, or say they don't, what is the great issue between the free world and the communist world. Let them come to Berlin. There are some who say that communism is the wave of the future. Let them come to Berlin. And there are some who say in Europe and elsewhere we can work with the communists. Let them come to Berlin. And there are even a few who say that it is true that communism is an evil system, but it permits us to make economic progress. Lass' sie nach Berlin kommen. Let them come to Berlin.

Freedom has many difficulties and democracy is not perfect, but we have never had to put a wall up to keep our people in, to prevent them from leaving us. I want to say, on behalf of my countrymen, who live many miles away on the other side of the Atlantic, who are far distant from you, that they take the greatest pride that they have been able to share with you, even from a distance, the story of the last 18 years. I know of no town, no city, that has been besieged for 18 years that still lives with the vitality and the force, and the hope and the determination of the city of West Berlin. While the wall is the most obvious and vivid demonstration of the failures of the communist system, for all the world to see, we take no satisfaction in it, for it is, as your Mayor has said, an offense not only against history but an offense against humanity, separating families, dividing husbands and wives and brothers and sisters, and dividing a people who wish to be joined together.

[8]Delivered at the Rudolph Wilde Platz, in West Berlin, Germany, on June 26, 1963.

What is true of this city is true of Germany—real, lasting peace in Europe can never be assured as long as one German out of four is denied the elementary right of free men, and that is to make a free choice. In 18 years of peace and good faith, this generation of Germans has earned the right to be free, including the right to unite their families and their nation in lasting peace, with good will to all people. You live in a defended island of freedom, but your life is part of the main. So let me ask you, as I close, to lift your eyes beyond the dangers of today, to the hopes of tomorrow, beyond the freedom merely of this city of Berlin, or your country of Germany, to the advance of freedom everywhere, beyond the wall to the day of peace with justice, beyond yourselves and ourselves to all mankind.

Freedom is indivisible, and when one man is enslaved, all are not free. When all are free, then we can look forward to that day when this city will be joined as one and this country and this great continent of Europe in a peaceful and hopeful globe. When that day finally comes, as it will, the people of West Berlin can take sober satisfaction in the fact that they were in the front lines for almost two decades.

All free men, wherever they may live, are citizens of Berlin, and, therefore, as a free man, I take pride in the words "Ich bin ein Berliner."

# Foreign Policy—Old Myths and New Realities[9]

J. William Fulbright

*Born April 9, 1905, Sumner, MO; died February 9, 1995; A.B., University of Arkansas, 1925; B.A., 1928, M.A., 1931, Oxford University; LL.B., George Washington University, 1934; attorney, Department of Justice, 1934-35; instructor, George Washington University, 1935-36; instructor, 1936-39, president, 1939-41, University of Arkansas; representative (D) from Arkansas, 1943-45; senator (D) from Arkansas, 1945-74.*

## Editor's introduction

On March 25, 1964, Senator J. William Fulbright addressed the U.S. Senate about the need for a new perspective on international affairs. This speech was perhaps the most talked about address of 1964, as it represented a turning point in the Cold War. According to Fulbright, there was far less reason for the gripping fear of Communism, so prevalent in the 1950s, and most notably manifest in Senator Joseph McCarthy's Communist witch hunt. Fulbright was the first to point this out. He suggested that "the character of the Cold War [had] been profoundly altered" since its commencement, and in response, we must rethink and retool our foreign policy. Fulbright's comments were based on the awareness that certain Communist countries, including Poland and Yugoslavia, were anything but "organized conspiracies" determined to "destroy the free world." At most, these countries were reluctant upholders of a Communist political system.

---

Mr. President, there is an inevitable divergence, attributable to the imperfections of the human mind, between the world as it is and the world as men perceive it. As long as our perceptions are reasonably close to objective reality, it is possible for us to act upon our problems in a rational and appropriate manner. But when our perceptions fail to keep pace with events, when we refuse to believe something because it displeases or frightens us, or because it is simply startlingly unfamiliar, then the gap between fact and perception becomes a chasm, and action becomes irrelevant and irrational.

There has always—and inevitably—been some divergence between the realities of foreign policy and our ideas about it. This divergence has in certain respects been growing, rather than narrowing; and we are handicapped, accordingly, by policies based on old myths, rather than current realities. This divergence is, in my opinion, dangerous and unnecessary—dangerous, because it can reduce foreign policy to a fraudulent game of imagery and appearances; unnecessary, because it can be overcome by the determination of men in high office to dispel prevailing misconceptions by the candid dissemination of unpleasant, but inescapable, facts.

Before commenting on some of the specific areas where I believe our policies are at least partially based on cherished myths, rather than objective facts, I should like to suggest two possible reasons for the growing divergence between the realities and our perceptions of current world politics. The first is the radical change in relations between and within the Communist and the free world; and the second is the tendency of too many of us to confuse means with ends and, accordingly, to adhere to prevailing practices with a fervor befitting immutable principles.

Although it is too soon to render a definitive judgment, there is mounting evidence that events of recent years have wrought profound changes in the character of East-West relations. In the Cuban missile crisis of October 1962, the United States proved to the Soviet Union that a policy of aggression and adventure involved

[9]Delivered to the United States Senate, in Washington, D.C., on March 25, 1964.

unacceptable risks. In the signing of the test-ban treaty, each side in effect assured the other that it was prepared to forgo, at least for the present, any bid for a decisive military or political breakthrough. These occurrences, it should be added, took place against the background of the clearly understood strategic superiority—but not supremacy—of the United States.

It seems reasonable, therefore, to suggest that the character of the cold war has, for the present, at least, been profoundly altered: by the drawing back of the Soviet Union from extremely aggressive policies; by the implicit repudiation by both sides of a policy of "total victory"; and by the establishment of an American strategic superiority which the Soviet Union appears to have tacitly accepted because it has been accompanied by assurances that it will be exercised by the United States with responsibility and restraint. These enormously important changes may come to be regarded by historians as the foremost achievements of the Kennedy Administration in the field of foreign policy. Their effect has been to commit us to a foreign policy which can accurately—though perhaps not prudently—be defined as one of "peaceful coexistence."

Another of the results of the lowering of tensions between East and West is that each is now free to enjoy the luxury of accelerated strife and squabbling within its own domain. The ideological thunderbolts between Washington and Moscow which until a few years ago seemed a permanent part of our daily lives have become a pale shadow of their former selves. Now instead the United States waits in fascinated apprehension for the Olympian pronouncements that issue from Paris at six-month intervals while the Russians respond to the crude epithets of Peiping with almost plaintive rejoinders about "those who want to start a war against everybody."

These astonishing changes in the configuration of the postwar world have had an unsettling effect on both public and official opinion in the United States. One reason for this, I believe, lies in the fact that we are a people used to looking at the world, and indeed at ourselves, in moralistic rather than empirical terms. We are predisposed to regard any conflict as a clash between conflicting interests. We are inclined to confuse freedom and democracy, which we regard as moral principles, with the way in which they are practiced in America—with capitalism, federalism, and the two-party system, which are not moral principles but simply the preferred and accepted practices of the American people. There is much cant in American moralism and not a little inconsistency. It resembles in some ways the religious faith of the many respectable people who, in Samuel Butler's words, "would be equally horrified to hear the Christian religion doubted or to see it practiced."

Our national vocabulary is full of "self-evident truths" not only about "life, liberty, and happiness," but about a vast number of personal and public issues, including the cold war. It has become one of the "self-evident truths" of the postwar era that just as the President resides in Washington and the Pope in Rome, the Devil resides immutably in Moscow. We have come to regard the Kremlin as the permanent seat of his power and we have grown almost comfortable with a menace which, though unspeakably evil, has had the redeeming virtues of constancy, predictability, and familiarity. Now the Devil has betrayed us by traveling abroad and, worse still, by dispersing himself, turning up now here, now there, and in many places at once, with a devilish disregard for the laboriously constructed frontiers of ideology.

We are confronted with a complex and fluid world situation and we are not adapting ourselves to it. We are clinging to old myths in the face of new realities and we are seeking to escape the contradictions by narrowing the permissible bounds of public discussion, by relegating an increasing number of ideas and viewpoints to a growing category of "unthinkable thoughts." I believe that this tendency can and should be reversed, that it is within our ability, and unquestionably in our interests, to cut loose from established myths and to start thinking some "unthinkable thoughts"—about the cold war and East-West relations, about the underdeveloped countries and particularly those in Latin America, about the changing nature of the Chinese Communist threat in Asia and about the festering war in Vietnam.

The master myth of the cold war is that the Communist bloc is a monolith composed of governments which are not really governments at all but organized conspiracies, divided among themselves perhaps in certain matters of tactics, but all equally resolute and implacable in their determination to destroy the free world.

I believe that the Communist world is indeed hostile to the free world in its general and long-term intentions but that the existence of this animosity in principle is far less important for our foreign policy than the great variations in its intensity and character both in time and among the individual members of the Communist bloc. Only if we recognize these variations, ranging from China, which poses immediate threats to the free world, to Poland and Yugoslavia, which pose none, can we hope to act effectively upon the bloc and to turn its internal differences to our own advantage and to the advantage of those bloc countries which wish to maximize their independence. It is the responsibility of our national leaders both in the executive branch and in Congress, to acknowledge and act upon these realities, even at the cost of saying things which will not win immediate widespread enthusiasm.

For a start, we can acknowledge the fact that the Soviet Union, though still a most formidable adversary, has ceased to be totally and implacably hostile to the West. It has shown a new willingness to enter mutually advantageous arrangements with the West and, thus far at least, to honor them. It has therefore become possible to divert some of our energies from the prosecution of the cold war to the relaxation of the cold war and to deal with the Soviet Union, for certain purposes, as a normal state, with normal and traditional interests.

If we are to do these things effectively, we must distinguish between communism as an ideology and the power and policy of the Soviet state. It is not communism as a doctrine, or communism as it is practiced within the Soviet Union or within any other country, that threatens us. How the Soviet Union organizes its internal life, the gods and doctrines that it worships, are matters for the Soviet Union to determine. It is not Communist dogma as espoused within Russia but Communist imperialism that threatens us and other peoples of the non-Communist world. Insofar as a great nation mobilizes its power and resources for aggressive purposes, that nation, regardless of ideology, makes itself our enemy. Insofar as a nation is content to practice its doctrines within its own frontiers, that nation, however repugnant its ideology, is one with which we have no proper quarrel. We must deal with the Soviet Union as a great power, quite apart from differences of ideology. To the extent that the Soviet leaders abandon the global ambitions of Marxist ideology, in fact if not in words, it becomes possible for us to engage in normal relations with them, relations which probably cannot be close or trusting for many years to come but which can be gradually freed of the terror and the tensions of the cold war.

In our relations with the Russians, and indeed in our relations with all nations, we would do well to remember, and to act upon, the words of Pope John in the great Encyclical, *Pacem in Terris:*

"It must be borne in mind that to proceed gradually is the law of life in all its expressions, therefore, in human institutions, too, it is not possible to renovate for the better except by working from within them, gradually. Violence has always achieved only destruction, not construction, the kindling of passions, not their pacification, the accumulation of hate and ruin, not the reconciliation of the contending parties. And it has reduced men and parties to the difficult task of rebuilding, after sad experience, on the ruins of discord."

Important opportunities have been created for Western policy by the development of "polycentrism" in the Communist bloc. The Communist nations, as George Kennan has pointed out, are, like the Western nations, currently caught up in a crisis of indecision about their relations with countries outside their own ideological bloc. The choices open to the satellite states are limited but by no means insignificant. They can adhere slavishly to Soviet preferences or they can strike out on their own, within limits, to enter into mutually advantageous relations with the West.

Whether they do so, and to what extent, is to some extent at least within the power of the West to determine. If we persist in the view that all Communist regimes are equally hostile and equally threatening to the West, and that we can have no policy toward the captive nations except the eventual overthrow of their Communist regimes, then the West may enforce upon the Communist bloc a degree of unity which the Soviet Union has shown itself to be quite incapable of imposing—just as Stalin in the early postwar years frightened the West into a degree of unity that it almost certainly could not have attained by its own unaided efforts. If, on the other hand, we are willing to reexamine the view that all Communist regimes are alike in the threat which they pose for the

West—a view which had a certain validity in Stalin's time—then we may be able to exert an important influence on the course of events within a divided Communist world.

We are to a great extent the victims, and the Soviets the beneficiaries, of our own ideological convictions, and of the curious contradictions which they involve. We consider it a form of subversion of the free world, for example, when the Russians enter trade relations or conclude a consular convention or establish airline connections with a free country in Asia, Africa, or Latin America—and to a certain extent we are right. On the other hand, when it is proposed that we adopt the same strategy in reverse—by extending commercial credits to Poland or Yugoslavia, or by exchanging ambassadors with a Hungarian regime which has changed considerably in character since the revolution of 1956—then the same patriots who are so alarmed by Soviet activities in the free world charge our policymakers with "giving aid and comfort to the enemy" and with innumerable other categories of idiocy and immorality.

It is time that we resolved this contradiction and separated myth from reality. The myth is that every Communist state is an unmitigated evil and a relentless enemy of the free world; the reality is that some Communist regimes pose a threat to the free world while others pose little or none, and that if we will recognize these distinctions, we ourselves will be able to influence events in the Communist bloc in a way favorable to the security of the free world.

"It could well be argued [writes George Kennan] . . . that if the major Western powers had full freedom of movement in devising their own policies, it would be within their power to determine whether the Chinese view, or the Soviet view, or perhaps a view more liberal than either would ultimately prevail within the Communist camp" ["Polycentrism and Western Policy," *Foreign Affairs*, January 1964].

There are numerous areas in which we can seek to reduce the tensions of the cold war and to bring a degree of normalcy into our relations with the Soviet Union and other Communist countries—once we have resolved that it is safe and wise to do so. We have already taken important steps in this direction: the Antarctic and Austrian treaties and the nuclear test-ban treaty, the broadening of East-West cultural and educational relations, and the expansion of trade.

On the basis of recent experience and present economic needs, there seems little likelihood of a spectacular increase in trade between Communist and Western countries, even if existing restrictions were to be relaxed. Free world trade with Communist countries has been increasing at a steady but unspectacular rate, and it seems unlikely to be greatly accelerated because of the limited ability of the Communist countries to pay for increased imports. A modest increase in East-West trade may nonetheless serve as a modest instrument of East-West détente—provided that we are able to overcome the myth that trade with Communist countries is a compact with the Devil and to recognize that, on the contrary, trade can serve as an effective and honorable means of advancing both peace and human welfare.

Whether we are able to make these philosophic adjustments or not, we cannot escape the fact that our efforts to devise a common Western trade policy are a palpable failure and that our allies are going to trade with the Communist bloc whether we like it or not. The world's major exporting nations are slowly but steadily increasing their trade with the Communist bloc and the bloc countries are showing themselves to be reliable customers. Since 1958 Western Europe has been increasing its exports to the East at the rate of about 7 per cent a year, which is nearly the same rate at which its over-all world sales have been increasing.

West Germany—one of our close friends—is by far the leading Western nation in trade with the Sino-Soviet bloc. West German exports to bloc countries in 1962 were valued at $749.9 million. Britain was in second place—although not a close second—with exports to Communist countries amounting to $393 million in 1962. France followed with exports worth $313.4 million, and the figure for the United States—consisting largely of surplus food sales to Poland under Public Law 480—stood far below at $125.1 million.

Our allies have made it plain that they propose to expand this trade, in nonstrategic goods, wherever possible. West Germany, in the last sixteen months, has exchanged or agreed to exchange trade missions with every country in Eastern Europe except Albania. Britain has indicated that she will soon extend long-term credits to Communist countries, breaching the five-year limit which the Western allies have hitherto observed. In the light of these facts, it is difficult to see what effect the tight American trade restrictions have other than to deny the United States a substantial share of a profitable market.

The inability of the United States to prevent its partners from trading extensively with the Communist bloc is one good reason for relaxing our own restrictions, but there is a better reason: the potential value of trade—a moderate volume of trade in nonstrategic items—as an instrument for reducing world tensions and strengthening the foundations of peace. I do not think that trade or the nuclear test ban, or any other prospective East-West accommodation, will lead to a grand reconciliation that will end the cold war and usher in the brotherhood of man. At the most, the cumulative effect of all the agreements that are likely to be attainable in the foreseeable future will be the alleviation of the extreme tensions and animosities that threaten the world with nuclear devastation and the gradual conversion of the struggle between communism and the free world into a safer and more tolerable international rivalry, one which may be with us for years and decades to come but which need not be so terrifying and so costly as to distract the nations of the world from the creative pursuits of civilized societies.

There is little in history to justify the expectation that we can either win the cold war or end it immediately and completely. These are favored myths, respectively, of the American right and of the American left. They are, I believe, equal in their unreality and in their disregard for the feasibilities of history. We must disabuse ourselves of them and come to terms, at last, with the realities of a world in which neither good nor evil is absolute and in which those who move events and make history are those who have understood not how much but how little it is within our power to change.

Mr. President, in an address on February 18 at Bad Godesburg, the United States Ambassador to Germany, Mr. George McGhee, spoke eloquently and wisely about the character and prospects of relations between the Communist and the free worlds. I ask unanimous consent that Ambassador McGhee's address, "East-West Relations Today," be inserted in the *Record* at the end of my remarks.

Latin America is one of the areas of the world in which American policy is weakened by a growing divergency between old myths and new realities.

The crisis over the Panama Canal has been unnecessarily protracted for reasons of domestic politics and national pride and sensitivity on both sides—for reasons, that is, of only marginal relevance to the merits of the dispute. I think the Panamanians have unquestionably been more emotional about the dispute than has the United States. I also think that there is less reason for emotionalism on the part of the United States than on the part of Panama. It is important for us to remember that the issue over the canal is only one of a great many in which the United States is involved, and by no means the most important. For Panama, on the other hand, a small nation with a weak economy and an unstable government, the canal is the pre-eminent factor in the nation's economy and in its foreign relations. Surely in a confrontation so unequal, it is not unreasonable to expect the United States to go a little farther than halfway in the search for a fair settlement.

We Americans would do well, for a start, to divest ourselves of the silly notion that the issue with Panama is a test of our courage and resolve. I believe that the Cuban missile crisis of 1962, involving a confrontation with nuclear weapons and inter-continental missiles, was indeed a test of our courage, and we acquitted ourselves extremely well in that instance. I am unable to understand how a controversy with a small and poor country, with virtually no military capacity, can possibly be regarded as a test of our bravery and will to defend our interests. It takes stubbornness but not courage to reject the entreaties of the weak. The real test in Panama is not of our valor but of our wisdom and judgment and common sense.

We would also do well to disabuse ourselves of the myth that there is something morally sacred about the treaty of 1903. The fact of the matter is that the treaty was concluded under circumstances that reflect little credit on the United States. It was made possible by Panama's separation from Colombia, which probably could not have occurred at that time without the dispatch of United States warships to prevent the landing of Colombian troops on the isthmus to put down the Panamanian rebellion. The United States not only intervened in Colombia's internal affairs but did so in violation of a treaty concluded in 1846 under which the United States had guaranteed Colombian sovereignty over the isthmus. President Theodore Roosevelt, as he boasted, "took Panama," and proceeded to negotiate the canal treaty with a compliant Panamanian regime. Panamanians contend that they were "shotgunned" into the treaty of 1903 as the price of United States protection against a possible effort by Colombia to recover the isthmus. The contention is not without substance.

It is not my purpose here to relate the events of sixty years ago but only to suggest that there is little basis for a posture of injured innocence and self-righteousness by either side and that we would do much better to resolve the issue on the basis of present realities rather than old myths.

The central reality is that the treaty of 1903 is in certain respects obsolete. The treaty has been revised only twice, in 1936 when the annual rental was raised from $250,000 to $430,000 and other modifications were made, and in 1955 when further changes were made, including an increase in the annual rental to $1.9 million, where it now stands. The canal, of course, contributes far more to the Panamanian economy in the form of wages paid to Panamanian workers and purchases made in Panama. The fact remains, nonetheless, that the annual rental of $1.9 million is a modest sum and should probably be increased. There are other issues, relating to hiring policies for Panamanian workers in the zone, the flying of flags, and other symbols of national pride and sovereignty. The basic problem about the treaty, however, is the exercise of American control over a part of the territory of Panama in this age of intense nationalist and anticolonialist feeling. Justly or not, the Panamanians feel that they are being treated as a colony, or a quasi-colony, of the United States, and this feeling is accentuated by the contrast between the standard of living of the Panamanians, with a per capita income of about $429 a year, and that of the Americans living in the Canal Zone—immediately adjacent to Panama, of course, and within it—with a per capita income of $4,228 a year. That is approximately ten times greater. It is the profound social and economic alienation between Panama and the Canal Zone, and its impact on the national feeling of the Panamanians, that underlies the current crisis.

Under these circumstances, it seems to me entirely proper and necessary for the United States to take the initiative in proposing new arrangements that would redress some of Panama's grievances against the treaty as it now stands. I see no reason—certainly no reason of "weakness" or "dishonor"—why the United States cannot put an end to the semantic debate over whether treaty revisions are to be "negotiated" or "discussed" by stating positively and clearly that it is prepared to negotiate revisions in the canal treaty and to submit such changes as are made to the Senate for its advice and consent.

I think it is necessary for the United States to do this even though a commitment to revise the treaty may be widely criticized at home. It is the responsibility of the President and his advisers, in situations of this sort, to exercise their own best judgment as to where the national interest lies even though this may necessitate unpopular decisions.

An agreement to "negotiate" revisions is not an agreement to negotiate any particular revision. It would leave us completely free to determine what revisions, and how many revisions, we would be willing to accept. If there is any doubt about this, one can find ample reassurance in the proceedings at Geneva, where several years of "negotiations" for "general and complete disarmament" still leave us with the greatest arsenal of weapons in the history of the world.

The problem of Cuba is more difficult than that of Panama, and far more heavily burdened with the deadweight of old myths and prohibitions against "unthinkable thoughts." I think the time is overdue for a candid reevaluation of our Cuban policy even though it may also lead to distasteful conclusions.

There are and have been three options open to the United States with respect to Cuba: first, the removal of the Castro regime by invading and occupying the island; second, an effort to weaken and ultimately bring down the regime by a policy of political and economic boycott; and finally, acceptance of the Communist regime as a disagreeable reality and annoyance but one which is not likely to be removed in the near future because of the unavailability of acceptable means of removing it.

The first option, invasion, has been tried in a halfhearted way and found wanting. It is generally acknowledged that the invasion and occupation of Cuba, besides violating our obligations as a member of the United Nations and of the Organization of American States, would have explosive consequences in Latin America and elsewhere and might precipitate a global nuclear war. I know of no responsible statesman who advocates this approach. It has been rejected by our Government and by public opinion and I think that, barring some grave provocation, it can be ruled out as a feasible policy for the United States.

The approach which we have adopted has been the second of those mentioned, an effort to weaken and eventually bring down the Castro regime by a policy of political and economic boycott. This policy has taken the form of extensive restrictions against trade with Cuba by United States citizens, of the exclusion of Cuba from the inter-American system and efforts to secure Latin American support in isolating Cuba politically and economically, and of diplomatic efforts, backed by certain trade and aid sanctions, to persuade other free world countries to maintain economic boycotts against Cuba.

This policy, it now seems clear, has been a failure, and there is no reason to believe that it will succeed in the future. Our efforts to persuade our allies to terminate their trade with Cuba have been generally rebuffed. The prevailing attitude was perhaps best expressed by a British manufacturer who, in response to American criticisms of the sale of British buses to Cuba, said: "If America has a surplus of wheat, we have a surplus of buses."

In cutting off military assistance to Great Britain, France, and Yugoslavia under the provisions of Section 620 of the Foreign Assistance Act of 1963, the United States has wielded a stuffed club. The amounts of aid involved are infinitesimal; the chances of gaining compliance with our boycott policy are nil; and the annoyance of the countries concerned may be considerable. What we terminated with respect to Britain and France, in fact, can hardly be called aid; it was more of a sales promotion program under which British and French military leaders were brought to the United States to see—and to buy—advanced American weapons. Terminating this program was in itself of little importance; Britain and France do not need our assistance. But terminating the program as a sanction against their trade with Cuba can have no real effect other than to create an illusory image of "toughness" for the benefit of our own people.

Free world exports to Cuba have, on the whole, been declining over recent years, but over-all imports have been rising since 1961.

Mr. President, I ask unanimous consent that there be inserted in the *Record* at the conclusion of my remarks two tables provided by the Department of State showing the trade of selected free world countries with Cuba from 1958 to 1963.

Mr. President, the figures shown in these tables provide little basis for expecting the early termination of free world trade with Cuba. The export table shows United States exports to Cuba in both 1962 and 1963 exceeding those of any other free world country. These American exports consisted almost entirely of ransom payments for the Bay of Pigs prisoners and should not be confused with normal trade.

There is an interesting feature to this table, which may not be well known. It is that the exports from Cuba to various allies of ours, particularly Japan, the United Kingdom, Morocco, and others have been going up, and have been very substantial. This reflects, I believe, the importation from Cuba of sugar to a great extent, and also accounts for the accumulation by Cuba of substantial foreign aid as a result of the dramatic increase in the price of sugar during the past couple of years.

The exports from the free world to Cuba have been going up in similar instances, in the case of Japan, but generally speaking they have not been increasing. Of course, since 1958, when we accounted for more than half of Cuba's exports, they have gone down rather dramatically. In any case, the tables will speak for themselves.

I should like to make it very clear that I am not arguing against the desirability of an economic boycott against the Castro regime but against its feasibility. The effort has been made and all the fulminations we can utter about sanctions and retaliation against free world countries that trade with Cuba cannot long conceal the fact that the boycott policy is a failure.

The boycott policy has not failed because of any "weakness" or "timidity" on the part of our Government. This charge, so frequently heard, is one of the most pernicious myths to have been inflicted on the American people. The boycott policy has failed because the United States is not omnipotent and cannot be. The basic reality to be faced is that it is simply not within our power to compel our allies to cut off their trade with Cuba, unless we are prepared to take drastic sanctions against them, such as closing our own markets to any foreign company that does business in Cuba, as proposed by Mr. Nixon. We can do this, of course, but if we do, we ought first to be very sure as apparently Mr. Nixon is, that the Cuban boycott is more important than good relations with our closest allies. In fact, even the most drastic sanctions are as likely to be rewarded with defiance as with compliance. For practical purposes, all we can do is to ask other countries to take the measures with respect to Cuba which we recommend. We have done so and in some areas have been successful. In other areas, notably that of the economic boycott, we have asked for the full cooperation of other free world countries and it has been largely denied. It remains for us to decide whether we will respond with a sustained outburst of hollow and ill-tempered threats, all the while comforting ourselves with the myth that we can get anything we want if we only try hard enough—or, in this case, shout loud enough—or we can acknowledge the failure of our efforts and proceed, coolly and rationally, to reexamine the policies which we now pursue in relation to the interests they are intended to serve.

The prospects of bringing down the Castro regime by political and economic boycott have never been very good. Even if a general free world boycott were successfully applied against Cuba, it is unlikely that the Russians would refuse to carry the extra financial burden and thereby permit the only Communist regime in the Western Hemisphere to collapse. We are thus compelled to recognize that there is probably no way of bringing down the Castro regime by means of economic pressures unless we are prepared to impose a blockade against nonmilitary shipments from the Soviet Union. Exactly such a policy has been recommended by some of our more reckless politicians, but the preponderance of informed opinion is that a blockade against Soviet shipments of nonmilitary supplies to Cuba would be extravagantly dangerous, carrying the strong possibility of a confrontation that could explode into nuclear war.

Having ruled out military invasion and blockade, and recognizing the failure of the boycott policy, we are compelled to consider the third of the three options open to us with respect to Cuba: the acceptance of the continued existence of the Castro regime as a distasteful nuisance but not an intolerable danger so long as the nations of the hemisphere are prepared to meet their obligations of collective defense under the Rio Treaty.

In recent years we have become transfixed with Cuba, making it far more important in both our foreign relations and in our domestic life than its size and influence warrant. We have flattered a noisy but minor demagogue by treating him as if he were a Napoleonic menace. Communist Cuba has been a disruptive and subversive influence in Venezuela and other countries of the hemisphere, and there is no doubt that both we and our Latin American partners would be better off if the Castro regime did not exist. But it is important to bear in mind that, despite their best efforts, the Cuban Communists have not succeeded in subverting the hemisphere and that in Venezuela, for example, where communism has made a major effort to gain power through terrorism, it has been repudiated by a people who in a free election have committed themselves to the course of liberal democracy. It is necessary to weigh the desirability of an objective against the feasibility of its attainment, and when we do this with respect to Cuba, I think we are bound to conclude that Castro is a nuisance but not a grave threat to the United States and that he cannot be gotten rid of except by means that are wholly disproportionate to the objective. Cuban communism does pose a grave threat to other Latin American countries, but this threat can be dealt with by prompt and vigorous use of the established procedures of the inter-American system against any act of aggression.

I think that we must abandon the myth that Cuban communism is a transitory menace that is going to collapse or disappear in the immediate future and face up to two basic realities about Cuba: first, that the Castro regime is not on the verge of collapse and is not likely to be overthrown by any policies which we are now pursuing or can reasonably undertake; and second, that the continued existence of the Castro regime, though inimical to our interests and policies, is not an insuperable obstacle to the attainment of our objectives, unless we make it so by permitting it to poison our politics at home and to divert us from more important tasks in the hemisphere.

The policy of the United States with respect to Latin America as a whole is predicated on the assumption that social revolution can be accomplished without violent upheaval. This is the guiding principle of the Alliance for Progress and it may in time be vindicated. We are entitled to hope so and it is wise and necessary for us to do all that we can to advance the prospects of peaceful and orderly reform.

At the same time, we must be under no illusions as to the extreme difficulty of uprooting long-established ruling oligarchies without disruptions involving lesser or greater degrees of violence. The historical odds are probably against the prospects of peaceful social revolution. There are places, of course, where it has occurred and others where it seems likely to occur. In Latin America, the chances for such basic change by peaceful means seem bright in Colombia and Venezuela and certain other countries; in Mexico, many basic changes have been made by peaceful means, but these came in the wake of a violent revolution. In other Latin American countries, the power of ruling oligarchies is so solidly established and their ignorance so great that there seems little prospect of accomplishing economic growth or social reform by means short of the forcible overthrow of established authorities.

I am not predicting violent revolutions in Latin America or elsewhere. Still less am I advocating them. I wish only to suggest that violent social revolutions are a possibility in countries where feudal oligarchies resist all meaningful change by peaceful means. We must not, in our preference for the democratic procedures envisioned by the Charter of Punta del Este, close our minds to the possibility that democratic procedures may fail in certain countries and that where democracy does fail violent social convulsions may occur.

We would do well, while continuing our efforts to promote peaceful change through the Alliance for Progress, to consider what our reactions might be in the event of the outbreak of genuine social revolution in one or more Latin American countries. Such a revolution did occur in Bolivia, and we accepted it calmly and sensibly. But what if a violent social revolution were to break out in one of the larger Latin American countries? Would we feel certain that it was Cuban- or Soviet-inspired? Would we wish to intervene on the side of established authority? Or would we be willing to tolerate or even support a revolution if it was seen to be not Communist but similar in nature to the Mexican revolution or the Nasser revolution in Egypt?

These are hypothetical questions and there is no readily available set of answers to them. But they are questions which we should be thinking about because they have to do with problems that could become real and urgent with great suddenness. We should be considering, for example, what groups in particular countries might conceivably lead revolutionary movements, and if we can identify them, we should be considering how we might communicate with them and influence them in such a way that their movements, if successful, will not pursue courses detrimental to our security and our interests.

The Far East is another area of the world in which American policy is handicapped by the divergence of old myths and new realities. Particularly with respect to China, an elaborate vocabulary of make-believe has become compulsory in both official and public discussion. We are committed, with respect to China and other areas in Asia, to inflexible policies of long standing from which we hesitate to depart because of the attribution to these policies of an aura of mystical sanctity. It may be that a thorough reevaluation of our Far Eastern policies would lead us to the conclusion that they are sound and wise, or at least that they represent the best available options. It may be, on the other hand, that reevaluation would point up the need for greater or lesser changes in our policies. The point is that, whatever the outcome of a rethinking of policy might be, we have been unwilling to undertake it because of the fear of many Government officials, undoubtedly well founded, that even the suggestion of new policies toward China or Vietnam would provoke a vehement public outcry.

I do not think the United States can, or should, recognize Communist China, or acquiesce in its admission to the United Nations under present circumstances. It would be unwise to do so, because there is nothing to be gained by it so long as the Peiping regime maintains its attitude of implacable hostility toward the United States. I do not believe, however, that this state of affairs is necessarily permanent. As we have seen in our relations with Germany and Japan, hostility can give way in an astonishingly short time to close friendship; and, as we have seen in our relations with China, the reverse can occur with equal speed. It is not impossible that in time our relations with China will change again—if not to friendship, then perhaps to "competitive coexistence." It would therefore be extremely useful if we could introduce an element of flexibility, or, more precisely, of the capacity to be flexible, into our relations with Communist China.

We would do well, as former Assistant Secretary Hilsman has recommended, to maintain an "open door" to the possibility of improved relations with Communist China in the future. For a start, we must jar open our minds to certain realities about China, of which the foremost is that there really are not "two Chinas," but only one—mainland China; and that it is ruled by Communists, and is likely to remain so for the indefinite future. Once we accept this fact, it becomes possible to reflect on the conditions under which it might be possible for us to enter into relatively normal relations with mainland China. One condition, of course, must be the abandonment by the Chinese Communists, tacitly, if not explicitly, of their intention to conquer and incorporate Taiwan. This seems unlikely now; but far more surprising changes have occurred in politics, and it is quite possible that a new generation of leaders in Peiping and Taipei may put a quiet end to the Chinese civil war, thus opening the possibility of entirely new patterns of international relations in the Far East.

Should such changes occur, they will open important opportunities for American policy; and it is to be hoped that we shall be able and willing to take advantage of them. It seems possible, for instance, that an atmosphere of reduced tensions in the Far East might make it possible to strengthen world peace by drawing mainland China into existing East-West agreements in such fields as disarmament, trade, and educational exchange.

These are long-range prospects, which may or may not materialize. In the immediate future, we are confronted with possible changes in the Far East resulting from recent French diplomacy.

French recognition of Communist China, although untimely and carried out in a way that can hardly be considered friendly to the United States, may nonetheless serve a constructive long-term purpose, by unfreezing a situation in which many countries, none more than the United States, are committed to inflexible policies by long-established commitments and the pressures of domestic public opinion. One way or another, the French initiative may help generate a new situation in which the United States, as well as other countries, will find it possible to reevaluate its basic policies in the Far East.

The situation in Vietnam poses a far more pressing need for a reevaluation of American policy. Other than withdrawal, which I do not think can be realistically considered under present circumstances, three options are open to us in Vietnam: First, continuation of the antiguerrilla war within South Vietnam, along with renewed American efforts to increase the military effectiveness of the South Vietnamese army and the political effectiveness of the South Vietnamese government; second, an attempt to end the war, through negotiations for the neutralization of South Vietnam, or of both North and South Vietnam; and, finally, the expansion of the scale of the war, either by the direct commitment of large numbers of American troops or by equipping the South Vietnamese army to attack North Vietnamese territory, possibly by means of commando-type operations from the sea or the air.

It is difficult to see how a negotiation, under present military circumstances, could lead to termination of the war under conditions that would preserve the freedom of South Vietnam. It is extremely difficult for a party to a negotiation to achieve by diplomacy objectives which it has conspicuously failed to win by warfare. The hard fact of the matter is that our bargaining position is at present a weak one; and until the equation of advantages between the two sides has been substantially altered in our favor, there can be little prospect of a negotiated settlement which would secure the independence of a non-Communist South Vietnam.

Recent initiatives by France, calling for the neutralization of Vietnam, have tended to confuse the situation, without altering it in any fundamental way. France could, perhaps, play a constructive mediating role if she were willing to consult and cooperate with the United States. For somewhat obscure reasons, however, France has chosen to take an independent initiative. This is puzzling to Americans, who recall that the United States contributed $1.2 billion to France's war in Indochina of a decade ago—which was 70 per cent of the total cost of the conflict. Whatever its motivation, the problem posed by French intervention in southeast Asia is that while France may set off an unforeseeable chain of events, she is neither a major military force nor a major economic force in the Far East, and is therefore unlikely to be able to control or greatly influence the events which her initiative may precipitate.

It seems clear that only two realistic options are open to us in Vietnam in the immediate future: the expansion of the conflict in one way or another, or a renewed effort to bolster the capacity of the South Vietnamese to prosecute the war successfully on its present scale. The matter calls for thorough examination by responsible officials in the executive branch; and until they have had an opportunity to evaluate the contingencies and feasibilities of the options open to us, it seems to me that we have no choice but to support the South Vietnamese government and army by the most effective means available. Whatever specific policy decisions are made, it should be clear to all concerned that the United States will continue to meet its obligations and fulfill its commitments with respect to Vietnam.

These, I believe, are some, although by no means all, of the issues of foreign policy in which it is essential to reevaluate long-standing ideas and commitments in the light of new and changing realities. In all the issues which I have discussed, American policy has to one degree or another been less effective than it might have been because of our national tendency to equate means with ends and therefore to attach a mythological sanctity to policies and practices which in themselves have no moral content or value except insofar as they contribute to the achievement of some valid national objective. I believe that we must try to overcome this excessive moralism, which binds us to old myths and blinds us to new realities and, worse still, leads us to regard new and unfamiliar ideas with fear and mistrust.

We must dare to think about "unthinkable" things. We must learn to explore all of the options and possibilities that confront us in a complex and rapidly changing world. We must learn to welcome rather than fear the voices of dissent and not to recoil in horror whenever some heretic suggests that Castro may survive or that Khrushchev is not as bad a fellow as Stalin was. We must overcome our susceptibility to "shock"—a word which I wish could be banned from our newspapers and magazines and especially from the *Congressional Record.*

If Congress and public opinion are unduly susceptible to "shock," the executive branch, and particularly the Department of State, is subject to the malady of chronic and excessive caution. An effective foreign policy is one which concerns itself more with innovation abroad than with conciliation at home. A creative foreign policy—as President Truman, for one, knew—is not necessarily one which wins immediate general approval. It is sometimes necessary for leaders to do unpleasant and unpopular things, because, as Burke pointed out, the duty of the democratic politician to his constituents is not to comply with their every wish and preference but to give them the benefit of, and to be held responsible for, the exercise of his own best judgment.

We must dare to think about "unthinkable things," because when things become "unthinkable," thinking stops and action becomes mindless. If we are to disabuse ourselves of old myths and to act wisely and creatively upon the new realities of our time, we must think and talk about our problems with perfect freedom, remembering, as Woodrow Wilson said, that "The greatest freedom of speech is the greatest safety because, if a man is a fool, the best thing to do is to encourage him to advertise the fact by speaking."

# America's Permanent Interests[10]

Henry A. Kissinger

*Born May 27, 1923, Füerth, Germany; U.S. Army, 1943-59; B.A., 1950, M.A., 1952, Ph.D., 1952, Harvard University; presidential consultant, 1955-69; professor, Harvard University, 1957-69; director, Harvard University Defense Studies Program, 1959-69; assistant to the president for national security affairs, 1969-1972; winner of Nobel Peace Prize, 1973; U.S. secretary of state, 1973-77; business consultant, 1977–; author,* A World Restored *(1973),* Nuclear Weapons and Foreign Policy *(1957),* The Necessity for Choice *(1961),* The Troubled Partnership *(1965),* White House Years *(1979),* Years of Upheaval *(1982),* American Foreign Policy *(1982),* Observations: Selected Speeches and Essays, 1982-1984 *(1985),* Diplomacy *(1994).*

## Editor's introduction

*Newsweek* called this speech "unusually acerbic," and *The Boston Globe* described it as more blunt and broad than any Kissinger had given in the past. Here, Henry Kissinger, then U.S. Secretary of State, responded to criticism from Ronald Reagan and Henry Jackson, a Democratic senator from Washington. Both politicians, particularly Ronald Reagan, made Kissinger's policies under President Ford campaign issues. The *National Observer* described the conflict between Reagan and Kissinger as "Reagan's old-fashioned, simplistic approach to world affairs" in opposition to Kissinger's "complex, devious pragmatism." In this speech, Kissinger reflected on past accomplishments, including bringing an end to the Vietnam War and renewing a relationship with the People's Republic of China, while he affirmed that a balance of power between the United States and the USSR was necessary if nuclear war was to be averted.

---

I deeply appreciate the honor you bestow upon me today not only because it is given me by old Massachusetts friends, but also for the name it bears. Throughout his long career as legislator, governor, and secretary of state, Christian Herter embodied the ideals of selfless public service and responsible patriotism which have always marked our nation's great leaders. Most of all Christian Herter was a man who had faith in his country and its goodness. He understood the decisive role this nation must play in the world for security and progress and justice.

In this election year, some ten years after Chris Herter's death, we would all do well to remember his wisdom. For America is still the great and good country he knew it was, and our participation in the international scene remains decisive if our era is to know peace and a better life for mankind. We must never forget that this nation has permanent interests and concerns that must be preserved through and beyond this election year.

This can be a time of national renewal—when Americans freely renegotiate their social compact. Or if the quest for short-term political gain prevails over all other considerations, it can be a period of misleading oversimplification, further divisiveness, and sterile recrimination.

This Administration has for many months been prepared to put its policies, its premises, and its design for the future before the American people. The President has often spoken about our concerns and hopes in the world. In the past 14 months alone, I have given 17 major speeches, some 20 major news conferences, and countless interviews across this country, and I have testified 39 times before congressional committees. Certainly there is room for differences on the policies to be pursued in a complex and dangerous world. But

[10]Delivered to the Boston World Affairs Council, in Boston, Massachusetts, on March 11, 1976.

those who challenge current policies have an obligation to go beyond criticisms, slogans, and abuse and set forth in detail their premises and alternatives, the likely costs, opportunities, and risks.

America has come through a difficult time—when our institutions have been under challenge, our purposes doubted, and our will questioned. The time has come, as Adlai Stevenson said, to " . . . talk sense to the American people." As a nation we face new dangers and opportunities; neither will wait for our decisions next November and both can be profoundly affected by what we say and do in the meantime. Complex realities cannot be dissolved or evaded by nostalgic simplicities.

Throughout the turmoil of this decade our foreign policy has pursued our fundamental national goals with energy and consistent purpose.

We are at peace for the first time in over a decade. No American fighting men are engaged in combat anywhere in the world.

Relations with our friends and allies in the Atlantic community and with Japan have never been stronger.

A new and durable relationship with the People's Republic of China has been opened and fostered.

Confrontation in the heart of Europe has been eased. A four-power agreement on Berlin has replaced a decade and a half of crisis and confrontation.

We negotiated an interim agreement limiting strategic arms with the Soviet Union, which forestalled the numerical expansion of Soviet strategic programs while permitting us to undertake needed programs of our own.

We are now negotiating a long-term agreement which, if successfully concluded, will—for the first time in history—set an upper limit on total numbers of strategic weapons, requiring the Soviet Union to dismantle some of its existing systems.

Significant progress toward a durable settlement in the Middle East has been made. Much work and many dangers remain, but the peace process is underway for the first time since the creation of the State of Israel.

There is a new maturity and impetus to our relations with Latin America reflecting changing realities in the hemisphere and the growing importance of these countries on the international scene.

The United States has taken the role of global leadership in putting forward a comprehensive agenda for a new and mutually beneficial relationship between the developed and developing nations.

We have defended human rights and dignity in all international bodies as well as in our bilateral relations.

This is a record of American accomplishment that transcends partisanship, for much of it was accomplished with the cooperation of both parties. It reflects the ideals of the American people. It portends for this nation a continuing role of moral and political leadership—if we have the understanding, the will, and the unity to seize the opportunity history has given us.

Thirty years ago this country began its first sustained peacetime involvement in foreign affairs. We achieved great things, and we can continue to do so as long as we are prepared to face the fact that we live in a more complex time.

Today the Soviet Union is a superpower. Nothing we could have done would have halted this evolution after the impetus that two generations of industrial and technological advance have given to Soviet military and economic growth. But together with others we must assure that Russian power and influence are not translated into an expansion of Soviet control and dominance beyond the USSR's borders. This is prerequisite to a more constructive relationship.

Today scores of new nations have come into being, creating new centers of influence. These nations make insistent claims on the global system, testing their new economic power and seeking a greater role and share in the world's prosperity.

Today the forces of democracy are called upon to show renewed creativity and vision. In a world of complexity—in a world of equilibrium and coexistence, of competition and interdependence—it is our democratic values that give meaning to our sacrifice and purpose to our exertions. Thus the cohesion of the industrial democracies has a moral as well as a political and economic significance.

Americans are a realistic people who have never considered the definition of a challenge as a prophecy of doom or a sign of pessimism. Instead we have seen it as a call to battle. " . . . the bravest," said Thucydides, "are surely those who have the clearest vision of what is before them, glory and danger alike, and yet notwithstanding go out to meet it." That has always been the test of democracy—and it has always been the strength of the American people.

Let me now deal with America's permanent interests: peace, progress, and justice.

Since the dawn of the nuclear age, the world's fears of catastrophe and its hopes for peace have hinged on the relationship between the United States and the Soviet Union.

In an era when two nations have the power to visit utter devastation on the world in a matter of hours, there can be no greater imperative than assuring that the relationship between the superpowers be managed effectively and rationally.

This is an unprecedented task. Historically a conflict of ideology and geopolitical interests, such as that which characterizes the current international scene, has almost invariably led to conflict. But in the age of thermonuclear weapons and strategic equality, humanity could not survive such a repetition of history. No amount of tough rhetoric can change these realities. The future of our nation and of mankind depends on how well we avoid confrontation without giving up vital interests and how well we establish a more hopeful and stable relationship without surrender of principle.

We, therefore, face the necessity of a dual policy: On the one hand we are determined to prevent Soviet military power from being used for political expansion; we will firmly discourage and resist adventurist policies. But at the same time we cannot escalate every political dispute into a central crisis; nor can we rest on identifying foreign policy with crisis management. We have an obligation to work for a more positive future. We must couple opposition to pressure and irresponsibility with concerned efforts to build a more cooperative world.

History can inform—or mislead—us in this quest.

For a generation after World War II statesmen and nations were traumatized by the experience of Munich; they believed that history had shown the folly of permitting an adversary to gain a preponderance of power. This was and remains a crucial lesson.

A later generation was chastened by the experience of Vietnam; it is determined that America shall never again overextend and exhaust itself by direct involvement in remote wars with no clear strategic significance. This too is a crucial lesson.

But equally important and too often neglected is the lesson learned by an earlier generation. Before the outbreak of the first World War, there was a virtual equilibrium of power. Through crisis after crisis nations moved to confrontation and then retreated to compromise. Stability was taken for granted until—without any conscious decision to overturn the international structure—a crisis much like any other went out of control. Nation after nation slid into a war whose causes they did not understand but from which they could not extricate themselves. The result was the death of tens of millions, the destruction of the global order, and domestic upheavals whose consequences still torment mankind.

If we are to learn from history, we cannot pick and choose the lessons from which we will draw inspiration. The history of this century tells us that:

An imbalance of power encourages aggression;

Overcommitment cannot be sustained domestically; and

An equilibrium based on constant confrontation will ultimately end in cataclysm.

But the lessons of history are never automatic; each generation must apply them to concrete circumstances.

There is no question that peace rests, in the first instance, on the maintenance of a balance of global stability. Without the ultimate sanction of power, conciliation soon becomes surrender. Moderation is a virtue only in those who are thought to have a choice.

No service is done to the nation by those who portray an exaggerated specter of Soviet power and of American weakness, by those who hesitate to resist when we are challenged, or by those who fail to see the opportunities we have to shape the US-Soviet relationship by our own confident action. Soviet strength is uneven; the weaknesses and frustrations of the Soviet system are glaring and have been clearly documented. Despite the inevitable increase in its power, the Soviet Union remains far behind us and our allies in any overall assessment of military, economic, and technological strength; it would be reckless in the extreme for the Soviet Union to challenge the industrial democracies. And Soviet society is no longer insulated from the influences and attractions of the outside world or impervious to the need for external contacts.

The great industrial democracies posses the means to counter Soviet expansion and to moderate Soviet behavior. We must not abdicate this responsibility by weakening ourselves either by failing to support our defenses or refusing to use our power in defense of our interest; we must, along with our allies, always do what is necessary to maintain our security.

It is true that we cannot be the world's policeman. Not all local wars and regional conflicts affect global stability or America's national interest. But if one superpower systematically exploits these conflicts for its own advantage—and tips the scales decisively by its intervention—gradually the overall balance will be affected. If adventurism is allowed to succeed in local crises, an ominous precedent of wider consequence is set. Other nations will adjust their policies to their perception of the dominant trend. Our ability to control future crises will diminish. And if this pattern is not broken, America will ultimately face harder choices, higher costs, and more severe crises.

But our obligation goes beyond the balance of power. An equilibrium is too precarious a foundation for our long-term future. There is no tranquillity in a balance of terror constantly contested. We must avoid the twin temptations of provocation and escapism. Our course must be steady and not reflect momentary fashions; it must be a policy that our adversaries respect, our allies support, and our people believe in and sustain.

Therefore we have sought with the Soviet Union to push back the shadow of nuclear catastrophe—by settling concrete problems, such as Berlin, so as to ease confrontations and negotiating on limitation of strategic arms to slow the arms race. And we have held out the prospect of cooperative relations in the economic and other fields if political conditions permit their implementation and further development.

It goes without saying that this process requires reciprocity. It cannot survive a constant attempt to seek unilateral advantage. It cannot, specifically, survive any more Angolas. If the Soviet Union is ready to face genuine coexistence, we are prepared to make every effort to shape a pattern of restraint and mutual interest which will give coexistence a more reliable and positive character making both sides conscious of what would be lost by confrontation and what can be gained by cooperation. And we are convinced that when a vigorous response to Soviet encroachment is called for, the President will have the support of the American people—and of our allies—to the extent that he can demonstrate that the crisis was imposed upon us; that it did not result from opportunities we missed to improve the prospects of peace.

No policy will soon, if ever, eliminate the competition and irreconcilable ideological differences between the United States and the Soviet Union. Nor will it make all interests compatible. We are engaged in a protracted process with inevitable ups and downs. But there is no alternative to the policy of penalties for adventurism and incentives for restraint. What do those who speak so glibly about one-way streets or preemptive concessions propose concretely that this country do? What precisely has been given up? What level of confrontation do they seek? What threats would they make? What risks would they run? What precise changes in our defense posture, what level of expenditure over what period of time, do they advocate? How concretely do they suggest managing the US-Soviet relationship in an era of strategic equality?

It is time we heard answers to these questions.

In short we must—and we shall—pursue the two strands of our policy toward the Soviet Union: firmness in the face of pressure and the vision to work for a better future. This is well within our capacities. We owe this to our people, to our future, to our allies, and to the rest of mankind.

The upheavals of this century have produced another task—the fundamental need of reshaping the structure of international relations. For the first time in history the international system has become truly global. Decolonization and the expansion of the world economy have given birth to scores of new nations and new centers of power and initiative. Our current world, numbering nearly 150 nations, can be the seedbed for growing economic warfare, political instability, and ideological confrontation—or it can become a community marked by unprecedented international collaboration. The interdependence of nations—the indivisibility of our security and our prosperity—can accelerate our common progress or our common decline.

Therefore just as we must seek to move beyond a balance of power in East-West relations so must we transcend tests of strength in North-

South relations and build a true world community.

We do so in our own self-interest for today's web of economic relationships links the destinies of all mankind. The price and supply of energy, the conditions of trade, the expansion of world food production, the technological bases for economic development, the protection of the world's environment, the rules of law that govern the world's oceans and outer space—these are concerns that affect all nations and that can be satisfactorily addressed only in a framework of international cooperation.

Here too we need to sustain a complex policy. We must resist tactics of confrontation; but our larger goal must be to shape new international relationships that will last over decades to come. We will not be stampeded by pressures or threats. But it is in our own interest to create an international economic system that all nations will regard as legitimate because they have a stake in it and because they consider it just.

As the world's strongest power, the United States could survive an era of economic warfare. But even we would be hurt, and no American true to the humane heritage of his country could find satisfaction in the world that confrontation would bring in its wake. The benefits of common effort are so apparent and the prospects of economic strife so damaging that there is no moral or practical alternative to a world of expanded collaboration.

Therefore at the World Food Conference in 1974, at the special session of the United Nations General Assembly last September, and in the Conference on International Economic Cooperation now underway in Paris the United States has taken the lead in offering programs of practical cooperation. We have presented—and are vigorously following through—on a wide range of proposals to safeguard export earnings, accelerate industrial and agricultural growth, better conditions of trade and investment in key commodities, and meet the plight of the poorest countries. In every area of concern we have proposed forms of collaboration among *all* nations, including the other industrial countries, the newly wealthy oil producers, and the developing countries themselves.

It is the West—and overwhelmingly this nation—that has the resources, the technology, the skills, the organizational ability, and the goodwill that attract and invite the cooperation of the developing nations. In the global dialogue among the industrial and developing worlds the Communist nations are conspicuous by their absence and, indeed, by their irrelevance.

Yet at the very moment when the industrial democracies are responding to the aspirations of the developing countries, many of the same countries attempt to extort what has, in fact, been freely offered. Lopsided voting, unworkable resolutions, and arbitrary procedures too often dominate the United Nations and other international bodies. Nations which originally chose nonalignment to shield themselves from the pressures of global coalitions have themselves formed a rigid, ideological, confrontationist coalition of their own. One of the most evident blocs in the world today is, ironically, the almost automatic alignment of the nonaligned.

The United States remains ready to respond responsibly and positively to countries which seriously seek justice and an equitable world economic system. But progress depends on a spirit of mutual respect, realism, and practical cooperation. Let there be no mistake about it: Extortion will not work and will not be supinely accepted. The stakes are too high for self-righteous rhetoric or adolescent posturing.

At issue is not simply the economic arrangements of the next quarter century but the legitimacy of the international order.

Technology and the realities of interdependence have given our generation the opportunity to determine the relationships between the developed and developing countries over the next quarter century. It is the quality of statesmanship to recognize that our necessity, our practical aspirations, and our moral purpose are linked. The United States is ready for that challenge.

Our efforts to build peace and progress reflect our deep-seated belief in freedom and in the hope of a better future for all mankind. These are values we share with our closest allies, the great industrial democracies.

The resilience of our countries in recovering from economic difficulty and in consolidating our cooperation has an importance far beyond our immediate well-being. For while foreign policy is unthinkable without an element of pragmatism, pragmatism without underlying moral purpose is like a rudderless ship.

Together the United States and our allies have maintained the global peace and sustained the world economy for more than thirty years. The spirit of innovation and progress in our societies has no match anywhere, certainly not in societies laying claim to being "revolutionary." Rarely in history have alliances survived—let alone flourished—as ours have in vastly changing global and geopolitical conditions. The ideals of the industrial democracies give purpose to our efforts to improve relations with the East, to the dialogue with the Third World, and to many other spheres of common endeavor.

Our ties with the great industrial democracies are, therefore, not alliances of convenience but a union of principle in defense of values and a way of life.

It is in this context that we must be concerned about the possibility of Communist parties coming to power—or sharing in power—in governments in NATO [North Atlantic Treaty Organization] countries. Ultimately the decision must, of course, be made by the voters of the countries concerned. But no one should expect that this question is not of concern to this government. Whether some of the Communist parties in Western Europe are, in fact, independent of Moscow cannot be determined when their electoral self-interest so overwhelmingly coincides with their claims. Their internal procedures—their Leninist principles and dogmas—remain the antithesis of democratic parties. And were they to gain power they would do so after having advocated for decades programs and values detrimental to our traditional ties.

By that record they would inevitably give low priority to security and Western defense efforts, which are essential not only to Europe's freedom but to maintaining the world balance of power. They would be tempted to orient their economies to a much greater extent toward the East. We would have to expect that Western European governments in which Communists play a dominant role would, at best, steer their countries' policies toward the positions of the nonaligned. The political solidarity and collective defense of the West—and thus NATO—would be inevitably weakened if not undermined. And in this country the commitment of the American people to maintain the balance of power in Europe—justified though it might be on pragmatic, geopolitical grounds—would lack the moral base on which it has stood for thirty years.

We consider the unity of the great industrial democracies crucial to all we do in the world. For this reason we have sought to expand our cooperation to areas beyond our mutual defense—in improved political consultation, in coordinating our approaches to negotiations with the East, in reinforcing our respective economic policies, in developing a common energy policy, and in fashioning common approaches for the increasingly important dialogue with the developing nations. We have made remarkable progress in all these areas. We are determined to continue. Our foreign policy has no higher priority.

This then is the design of our foreign policy:

We have the military and economic power together with our allies to prevent aggression.

We have the self-confidence and vision to go beyond confrontation to a reduction of tensions and ultimately a more cooperative world.

We have the resources, technology, and organizational genius to build a new relationship with the developing nations.

We have the moral courage to hold high, together with our allies, the banners of freedom in a turbulent and changing world.

The challenges before us are monumental. But it is not every generation that is given the opportunity to shape a new international order. If the opportunity is missed, we shall live in a world of chaos and danger. If it is realized we will have entered an era of peace and progress and justice.

But we can realize our hopes only as a united people. Our challenge—and its solution—lies in ourselves. Our greatest foreign policy problem is our divisions at home. Our greatest foreign policy need is national cohesion and a return to the awareness that in foreign policy we are all engaged in a common national endeavor.

The world watches with amazement—our adversaries with glee and our friends with growing dismay—how America seems bent on eroding its influence and destroying its achievements in world affairs through an orgy of recrimination.

They see our policies in Africa, the eastern Mediterranean, in Latin America, in East-West relations undermined by arbitrary congressional actions that may take decades to undo.

They see our intelligence system gravely damaged by unremitting, undiscriminating attack.

They see a country virtually incapable of behaving with the discretion that is indispensable for diplomacy.

They see revelations of malfeasance abroad on the part of American firms wreak grave damage on the political structures of friendly nations. Whatever wrongs were committed—reprehensible as they are—should be dealt with in a manner consistent with our own judicial procedures—and with the dignity of allied nations.

They see some critics suddenly pretending that the Soviets are ten feet tall and that America, despite all the evidence to the contrary, is becoming a second-rate nation. They know these erroneous and reckless allegations to be dangerous, because they may, if continued, persuade allies and adversaries of our weakness, tempting the one to accommodation and the other to adventurism.

They see this Administration—which has been condemned by one set of critics for its vigorous reaction to expansionism in Southeast Asia, in the Middle East, in Africa—simultaneously charged by another group of opponents with permitting unilateral Soviet gains.

They see that the Administration, whose defense budgets have been cut some $39 billion by the Congress in the past seven years, is simultaneously charged with neglecting American defenses.

The American people see all this, too, and wonder when it will end. They know that we cannot escape either our responsibilities or the geopolitical realities of the world around us. For a great nation that does not manage events will soon be overwhelmed by them.

If one group of critics undermines arms control negotiations and cuts off the prospect of more constructive ties with the Soviet Union while another group cuts away at our defense budgets and intelligence services and thwarts American resistance to Soviet adventurism, both combined will—whether they have intended it or not—end by wrecking the nation's ability to conduct a strong, creative, moderate, and prudent foreign policy. The result will be paralysis, no matter who wins in November. And if America cannot act, others will, and we and all the free peoples of the world will pay the price.

So our problem is at once more complex and simpler than in times past. The challenges are unprecedented but the remedies are in our own hands. This Administration has confidence in the strength, resilience, and vigor of America. If we summon the American spirit and restore our unity, we will have a decisive and positive impact on a world which, more than ever, affects our lives and cries out for our leadership.

Those who have faith in America will tell the American people the truth:

That we are strong and at peace;

That there are no easy or final answers to our problems;

That we must conduct a long-term and responsible foreign policy, without escape and without respite;

That what is attainable at any one moment will inevitably fall short of the ideal;

That the reach of our power and purpose has its limits;

That nevertheless we have the strength and determination to defend our interests and the conviction to uphold our values; and finally

That we have the opportunity to leave our children a more cooperative, more just, and more peaceful world than we found.

In this Bicentennial year we celebrate ideals which began to take shape around the shores of Massachusetts Bay some 350 years ago. We have accomplished great things as a united people; there is much yet to do. This country's work in the world is not a burden but a triumph—and the measure of greatness yet to come.

Americans have always made history rather than let history chart our course. We, the present generation of Americans, will do not less. So let this year mark the end of our divisions. Let it usher in an era of national reconciliation and rededication by all Americans to their common destiny. Let us have a clear vision of what is before us—glory and danger alike—and go forward together to meet it.

# Our China Policy in a Wider Context[11]

Zbigniew Brzezinski

*Born May 28, 1928, Warsaw, Poland; B.A., 1949, M.A., 1950, McGill University; Ph.D., Harvard University, 1953; assistant professor, Harvard University, 1953-60; professor, Columbia University, 1960-77, 1981-89; consultant, Department of State, 1966-68; national security adviser, 1977-81; author,* The Permanent Purge *(1956),* Ideology and Foreign Affairs *(1959),* Totalitarian Dictatorship and Autocracy *(1961),* Ideology and Power in Soviet Politics *(1962),* Alternative to Partition *(1965),* The Fragile Blossom *(1972),* Between Two Ages *(1972),* Game Plan *(1986),* In Quest of National Security *(1988),* The Grand Failure *(1989),* Out of Control *(1993).*

## Editor's introduction

Although Mao Zedong and the Chinese Communist party had formally established the People's Republic of China by 1950, the United States did not formally recognize it until 1979, opting instead to pledge support to Chian Kai-Shek's nationalist government, situated on the island of Taiwan. On January 1, 1979, the U.S. government opened formal diplomatic relations with the People's Republic of China. Many, including Senator Barry Goldwater, believed such a move to be a "stab . . . in the back [of] the nation of Taiwan." To both counter criticism and elucidate its meaning and basis, a briefing session for 500 American business leaders was held at the State Department. In this session, presidential security adviser Zbigniew Brzezinski defended the Carter administration's recognition of China, stating that the administration had "recognized reality" and the fact that China was "going to play an increasing role in world affairs." Concerns about China's Communism were therefore put aside, and acknowledgment of China's inevitable importance to the world economy was finally given primacy.

---

My purpose is to place our China policy in a wider context.

As I address you, a number of troubling developments dominate the headlines:

—The Shah of Iran . . . [left] for a rest, leaving behind him a new administration which will seek to return tranquility to an unsettled country in which the United States has an enormous stake.

—Vietnam has invaded its neighbor, Cambodia. Through an act of aggression, it has imposed a subservient regime upon a Cambodian people wearied of the inhumane, callous rule of Pol Pot.

—Among the first governments to recognize the new Vietnamese-installed regime in Phnom Penh was Afghanistan, a strategically important country which borders on Iran and Pakistan and in which Soviet influence has increased significantly in recent months.

—The situation in the Horn of Africa and South Yemen, Angola, and southern Africa remains uncertain, as Cuban troops continue to promote Soviet interests.

—Indeed, all the developing countries in the arc from northeast Asia to southern Africa continue to search for viable forms of government capable of managing the process of modernization. Their instability, uncertainty, and weakness can be exploited and intensified by outside powers.

Balanced against these unsettling developments, however, are a number of quieter yet more significant, positive developments:

—Progress has been made in bringing peace to the Middle East. The progress is slow and of-

[11]Delivered at the State Department, in Washington, D.C., on January 15, 1979. Reprinted with permission of Zbigniew Brzezinski.

ten painful. But through the persistent diplomacy of President Carter and Secretary Vance, we are, I believe, inexorably moving toward the realization of the Camp David accords. We are promoting reconciliation to one of the most volatile disputes in the world.

—In Latin America, United States policy has undergone significant change and our relations with most countries in the region are at or near all time highs. The ratification of the Panama Canal treaties was an historical milestone.

—We have significantly improved the nature of our relations with black African countries.

—Our relations with India have never been better; and we are retaining our ties of friendship with Pakistan.

—In East Asia, a delicate balance of power exists favorable to our interests. We have normalized relations with China, in part, to consolidate the balance.

—Such regional organizations as ASEAN [Association of Southeast Asian Nations] and OAU [Organization for African Unity] are playing an increasingly positive role in bringing stability to their regions.

—In recognition of the growing conventional military capability of the Soviet Union, we are increasing our military expenditures, as are our NATO allies, to make sure our European defenses remain strong.

—While we have not yet managed to establish a more stable world monetary and trading system, we have made progress in recent months in stabilizing the dollar and in creating a more orderly and growing world market through MTN.

—We will reach a SALT II agreement which will place a cap on the deployment of new and more missiles and which introduces a note of stability in the precarious strategic balance between the Soviet Union and the United States.

Added to these favorable developments are those of the spirit. After the debilitating decade of Vietnam and Watergate, our people are returning to their social moorings and exhibiting their traditional will and idealism. Worldwide, too, we have once again assumed the mantle of moral leadership, with the importance we attach to human rights, nuclear non-proliferation, and limitation of conventional arms sales. Certainly as much as and probably more than any other major power, the United States is addressing in a forthright manner the problems of our age. We remain an innovative society and a worldwide source of inspiration.

These positive developments are the result of the President's commitment—as he enunciated at Notre Dame more than a year ago—to a policy of constructive global engagement, a policy of trying to influence the changes of our era in directions that are compatible with our interests and values. Under that broad heading, we have crystallized seven fundamental objectives for our foreign policy:

*First*, to enhance our military security;

*Second*, to reinforce our ties with our key allies and promote a more cooperative world system;

*Third*, to respond in a positive way to the economic and moral challenge of the so-called North-South relationship;

*Fourth*, to improve relations between East and West;

*Fifth*, to help resolve the more threatening regional conflicts and tensions;

*Sixth*, to cope with such emerging global issues as nuclear proliferation and arms dissemination;

And *finally*, to reassert traditional American values—especially human rights.

At the outset, I should note that American foreign policy confronts a fundamental analytical question: Are the issues of the moment which I mentioned earlier—Iran, Indochina, the Horn, Afghanistan—indications of longer term trends? Do we respond to these issues not only with the sense of urgency which is obviously called for, but with a sense of historical despair as well? Or are the positive developments more indicative of our era? Should we continue on course?

In short, is an optimistic or pessimistic view of history justified? It seems to me that this issue underlies the emerging foreign policy debate in the United States.

Without being Pollyanna-ish, this administration is basically optimistic. We recognize the future is ours only with effort. Continued American vigilance, preparedness, and decisiveness are necessary to grasp the better future before us. But an optimistic view of history and of America's future lies at the heart of this administration's foreign policy and of our China policy.

I do not mean to downplay or belittle the seriousness of the current foreign policy challenges. Important, indeed vital, issues are at stake. But in each situation, we are developing responses appropriate to the challenges involved. The United States will suffer occasional setbacks, but we will continue to be able to offset our losses with gains elsewhere—such as those that have occurred in recent years in our relations with India, Egypt, Eastern Europe, Ghana, the Sudan, and East Asia.

What we emphatically reject are apocalyptic visions about the future ability of the United States to pursue and defend our interests abroad. The pessimism that one hears from many quarters conveys a sense of Armageddon and of the need to rush to the barricade at every challenge without forethought.

Today, we seek neither a world order based on a Pax Americana, nor an order based on a Soviet-American condominium. Neither order is possible or just.

Rather, we are in the process of creating a diverse and stable community of independent states. Working with our traditional allies, for we cannot do the job alone, we are beginning to create a framework for wide-ranging international cooperation involving the United States, Western Europe, Japan, and many of the emerging regional powers such as Mexico, Venezuela, Brazil, Nigeria, Saudi Arabia, India, and Indonesia. And with the establishment of full diplomatic relations with the People's Republic of China, we very significantly increase the scope of international cooperation.

We wish, of course, to include the Soviet Union in that framework of cooperation. Indeed, a fundamental choice the Soviet Union faces is whether to become a responsible partner in the creation of a global system of genuinely independent states or whether to exclude itself from global trends and derive its security exclusively from its military might and its domination of a few clients. We hope and encourage the Soviet Union to be cooperative, but, whichever path the Soviet Union chooses, we will continue our efforts to shape a framework for global cooperation based not on domination but on respect for diversity.

We recognize that the world is changing under the influence of forces no government can control. The world's population is experiencing a political awakening on a scale without precedent in its history. The global system is undergoing a significant redistribution of political and economic power.

The record of the past two years suggests, however, that the United States need not fear this change. To the contrary, the record shows that we can shape this change to our benefit and attain security in a world of diversity.

Not only does the record of the past two years suggest realistic optimism is warranted. Our own past and the quality of our people also encourage confidence. For, our national experience as a nation of diverse origins and of change speaks to the emerging global condition. Not just our wealth, not just our military might, but our history as a pluralistic people and our commitment to the values of freedom and independence which now stir all of mankind give us a naturally key role in shaping the trends of our time.

Given our assessment of history and the goals of the administration, these points should be made about our China policy:

—We see normalization as having long-term, historic significance. It comprises part of our effort to consolidate and improve our relations with all the emerging powers in the world. And none of these powers is more important than China, with its nearly billion people and third largest defense budget in the world.

—We did not normalize out of tactical or expedient considerations. Rather we recognized reality. The People's Republic of China is going to play an increasing role in world affairs, and it was important for us to have a continuing, broadened, and structured relationship with this government.

—We recognize that the PRC and we have different ideologies and economic and political systems. We recognize that to transcend the differences and to make our new relationship successful will require patience, wisdom, and understanding. We harbor neither the hope, nor the desire, that through extensive contacts with China we can remake that nation into the American image.

—Indeed, we accept our differences. Normalization is an important part of our global effort to create a stable community of diverse and independent nations. As President Carter stated in his cable to Premier Hua Kuo-feng on January 1, "The United States desires a world of diversity in which each nation is free to make a distinctive contribution . . . to the manifold aspirations . . . of mankind. We welcome the growing involvement of the People's Republic of China in world affairs."

—We consider China as a key force for global peace simply by being China: an independent and strong nation reaching for increased contact with the rest of the world while remaining basically self-reliant and resistant of any efforts by others to dominate it.

—As Vice President Mondale stated, "We feel bonds of friendship, but sentiment alone cannot bridge the gap between us. What has brought us together is an awareness of our parallel interests in creating a world of economic progress, stability, and peace."

The community of interest we share with China is particularly evident in Asia, where we both desire peace, stability, and nations free of outside domination.

East, Southeast, and South Asia is one of the most important regions of the world today. The economies of the area are booming; the people are dynamic. The United States has great economic and security interests around the rim of Asia: In Japan, South Korea, all the Pacific islands down to the Philippines, and in Southeast Asia as well.

To protect our interests, we retain a strong military presence in the region, we maintain appropriate weapon sales throughout the region, and we are prepared to act on our interests should the need arise.

Few actions will contribute more to the security and stability of our important positions around the rim of Asia, however, than a constructive involvement with China. As we improve our relations with Peking, China will also wish to keep us involved in the region and not, as in the past, seek to drive us away.

For the first time in decades, we can enjoy simultaneously good relations with both China and Japan. It is difficult to overstress the importance of this fact. Normalization consolidates a favorable balance of power in the Far East and enhances the security of our friends.

Now the Chinese are turning outward and extending their hand to the West. We are prepared to respond less in confidence that in the future their hand will remain extended than in the knowledge that without a reciprocal gesture, their hand would certainly be withdrawn. And by developing bonds of commerce and shared understanding, we reduce the chances of future animosity.

That is why we have completed the process of normalization begun by President Nixon, President Ford, and Secretary Kissinger.

Normalization therefore is an act rooted in historical optimism and political realism. This change in our China policy does not represent retreat or abandonment of our previous positions. Rather, it reflects our determination to be globally engaged, to welcome diversity, and to shape our future.

For a generation, we said "No" to the reality of East Asia. We refused to recognize reality, we sought to isolate China, and we lived by myths—with two wars and with incalculable cost to the region and to us.

Now, we say "Yes" to reality. We are confident that as an Asian and Pacific power with a positive relationship with Peking, we will significantly contribute to the peace and prosperity of the American people and of all peoples in the region.

# Thoughts on the 125th Anniversary of the Battle of Gettysburg[12]

Carl Sagan

*Born November 9, 1934, New York, New York; died December 20, 1996; B.A., 1954, B.S., 1955, M.S., 1956, Ph.D., 1960, University of Chicago; visiting assistant professor, Stanford University School of Medicine, 1962-63; staff member, Smithsonian Astrophysical Observatory, 1963-68; assistant professor, Harvard University, 1962-68; professor, Cornell University, 1968-96; director, Laboratory for Planetary Studies, Cornell University, 1968-96; host, creator,* Cosmos *television series, 1980; author,* The Cosmic Connection: An Extraterrestrial Perspective *(1973),* The Dragons of Eden: Speculations on the Evolution of Human Intelligence *(1977),* Broca's Brain: Reflections on the Romance of Science *(1979),* Cosmos *(1980),* Contact *(1985),* The Demon-Haunted World *(1996).*

## Editor's introduction

With the setting sun illuminating both the Eternal Light Peace Memorial and the land on which a total of 51,000 soldiers were killed or wounded during the Battle of Gettysburg, Professor Carl Sagan addressed both the threat of nuclear war and American-Soviet relations. Referring to the Civil War as the prototype of industrialized war, Sagan reminded the audience that since the Civil War, technology has "advanced the art of mass murder" to the point where the human species can now be rendered extinct. Given such a capability, Sagan urged that we escape our "deadly embrace with the Soviet Union" and terminate the Cold War. Sagan praised Mikhail Gorbachev in this speech, and he regarded peace with the Soviet Union to be a genuine possibility.

---

Thank you Judge Spicer. I'm moved and honored to join you in the commemoration of this doleful and instructive milestone in world history.

Fifty-one thousand human beings were killed or wounded here, ancestors of some of us, brothers of us all. This was the first full-fledged example of an industrialized war, with machine-made arms and railroad transport of men and materiel. This was the first hint of an age yet to come, our age; an intimation of what technology bent to the purposes of war might be capable. The new Spencer repeating rifle was used here. In May 1863, a reconnaissance balloon of the Army of the Potomac detected movement of Confederate troops across the Rappahannock River, the beginning of the campaign that led to the Battle of Gettysburg. That balloon was a precursor of air forces and strategic bombing and reconnaissance satellites.

A few hundred artillery pieces were deployed in the three-day battle of Gettysburg. What could they do? What was war like then? Here is an eyewitness account by Frank Haskel of Wisconsin, who fought on this battlefield for the Union Armies. It is from a letter to his brother:

"We could not often see the shell before it burst, but sometimes, as we faced towards the enemy and looked above our heads, the approach would be heralded by a prolonged hiss, which always seemed to me to be a line of something tangible terminating in a black globe distinct to the eye as the sound had been to the

[12]Delivered at the 125th celebration of the Battle of Gettysburg, in Gettysburg National Military Park, Gettysburg, Pennsylvania, on July 3, 1988. 

ear. The shell would seem to stop and hang suspended in the air an instant and then vanish in fire and smoke and noise . . . . Not ten yards away from us a shell burst among some bushes where sat three or four orderlies holding horses. Two of the men and one horse were killed."

It was a typical event from the Battle of Gettysburg. Something like it was repeated thousands of times. Those ballistic projectiles, launched from the cannons that you can see all over this Gettysburg Memorial, had a range, at best, of a few miles. The amount of explosive in the most formidable of them was some twenty pounds, roughly one-hundredth of a ton of TNT. It was enough to kill a few people.

But the most powerful chemical explosives used 80 years later, in World War II, were the blockbusters, so-called because they could destroy a city block. Dropped from aircraft, after a journey of hundreds of miles, each carried about ten tons of TNT, a thousand times more than the most powerful weapon at the Battle of Gettysburg. A blockbuster could kill a few dozen people.

At the very end of World War II, the United States used the first atomic bombs to annihilate two Japanese cities. Each of those weapons had the equivalent power of about ten thousand tons of TNT, enough to kill a few hundred thousand people. One bomb.

A few years later the United States and the Soviet Union developed the first thermonuclear weapons, the first hydrogen bombs. Some of them had an explosive yield equivalent to ten million tons of TNT; enough to kill a few million people. One bomb. Strategic nuclear weapons can now be launched to any place on the planet. Everywhere on Earth is a potential battlefield now.

Each of these technological triumphs advanced the art of mass murder by a factor of a thousand. From Gettysburg to the blockbuster, a thousand times more explosive energy; from the blockbuster to the atomic bomb, a thousand times more; and from the atomic bomb to the hydrogen bomb a thousand times still more. A thousand times a thousand, times a thousand is a billion; in less than one century, our most fearful weapon has become a billion times more deadly. But we have not become a billion times wiser in the generations that stretch from Gettysburg to us.

The souls that perished here would find the carnage of which we are now capable unspeakable. Today, the United States and the Soviet Union have booby-trapped our planet with almost 60,000 nuclear weapons. Sixty thousand nuclear weapons! Even a small fraction of the strategic arsenals could without question annihilate the two contending superpowers, probably destroy the global civilization, and possibly render the human species extinct. No nation, no man should have such power. We distribute these instruments of apocalypse all over our fragile world, and justify it on the grounds that it has made us safe. We have made a fool's bargain.

The 51,000 casualties here at Gettysburg represented one-third of the Confederate army, and one-quarter of the Union army. All those who died, with one or two exceptions, were soldiers. The best-known exception was a civilian in her own house who thought to bake a loaf of bread and, through two closed doors, was shot to death; her name was Jennie Wade. But in a global thermonuclear war, almost all the casualties will be civilians, men, women and children, including vast numbers of citizens of nations that had no part in the quarrel that led to the war, nations far removed from the northern mid-latitude "target zone." There will be billions of Jennie Wades. Everyone on Earth is now at risk.

In Washington there is a memorial to the Americans who died in the most recent major U.S. war, the one in Southeast Asia. Some 58,000 Americans perished, not a very different number from the casualties here at Gettysburg. (I ignore, as we too often do, the one or two million Vietnamese, Laotians, and Kampucheans who also died in that war.) Think of that dark, somber, beautiful, moving, touching memorial. Think of how long it is; actually, not much longer than a suburban street: 58,000 names. Imagine now that we are so foolish or inattentive as to permit a nuclear war to occur, and that, somehow, a similar memorial wall is built. How long would it have to be to contain the names of all those who will die in a major nuclear war? About a thousand miles long. It would stretch from here in Pennsylvania to Missouri. But of course, there would be no one to build it, and very few to read the roster of the fallen.

In 1945, at the close of World War II, the United States and the Soviet Union were virtually invulnerable. The United States, bounded east and west by vast and impassable oceans, north and south by weak and friendly neighbors, had the most effective armed forces, and the most powerful economy on the planet. We had nothing to fear. So we built nuclear weapons and their delivery systems. We initiated and vigorously pumped up an arms race with the Soviet Union. When we were done, everyone in the United States had handed their lives over to the leaders of the Soviet Union. Today, if Moscow decides we should die, twenty minutes later we're dead. In nearly perfect symmetry, the Soviet Union had the largest standing army in the world in 1945, and no significant military threats to worry about. It joined the United States in the nuclear arms race so that today everyone in the Soviet Union has handed their lives over to the leaders of the United States. If Washington decides they should die, twenty minutes later they're dead. The lives of every American and every Soviet citizen are now in the hands of a foreign power. I say we have made a fool's bargain. We—we Americans, we Soviets—have spent 43 years and vast national treasure in making ourselves exquisitely vulnerable to instant annihilation. We have done it in the name of patriotism and "national security," so no one is supposed to question it.

Two months before Gettysburg, on May 3, 1863, there was a Confederate triumph, the battle of Chancellorsville. On the moonlit evening following the victory, General Stonewall Jackson and his staff, returning to the Confederate lines, were mistaken for Union cavalry. Jackson was shot twice in error by his own men. He died of his wounds.

We make mistakes. We kill our own.

There are some who claim that since we have not yet had an accidental nuclear war, the precautions being taken to prevent one must be adequate. But not three years ago we witnessed the disasters of the Challenger space shuttle and the Chernobyl nuclear power plant, high technology systems, one American, one Soviet, into which enormous quantities of national prestige had been invested. There were compelling reasons to prevent these disasters. In the preceding year, confident assertions were made by officials of both nations that no accidents of that sort could happen. We were not to worry. The experts would not permit an accident to happen. We have since learned that such assurances do not amount to much.

We make mistakes. We kill our own.

This is the century of Hitler and Stalin, evidence—if any were needed—that madmen can seize the reins of power of modern industrial states. If we are content in a world with nearly 60,000 nuclear weapons, we are betting our lives on the proposition that no present or future leaders, military or civilian—of the United States, the Soviet Union, Britain, France, China, Israel, India, Pakistan, South Africa, and whatever other nuclear powers there will be—will ever stray from the strictest standards of prudence. We are gambling on their sanity and sobriety even in times of great personal and national crisis, all of them, for all times to come. I say this is asking too much of us. Because we make mistakes. We kill our own.

The nuclear arms race and the attendant Cold War cost something. They don't come free. Apart from the immense diversion of fiscal and intellectual resources away from the civilian economy, apart from the psychic cost of living out our lives under the Damoclean sword, what has been the price of the Cold War?

The American cost we can readily tabulate. (The Soviet cost is, very likely, about the same.) By the time the Reagan Administration leaves office in January, 1989, how much will the United States have spent on the Cold War? The answer, in current dollars, is about $10 trillion. That's the one with the big "T"; ten trillion dollars. Of this sum, more than a third has been spent by the Reagan Administration, which has added more to the national debt than all previous administrations combined, back to the presidency of George Washington.

How much could you buy for $10 trillion? The answer is: everything. You could buy everything in the United States, except the land. Everything. All the houses, airplanes, factories, skyscrapers, highways, railroads, stores, homes, food, clothing, medicine, furniture, toys, games, baby's diapers . . . . Everything in the United States but the land could be bought for what we have spent on the Cold War. A business that spent its capital so recklessly and with so little effect would have been bankrupt long ago. Executives who could not recognize so clear a failure of corporate policy would long before now have been dismissed by the stockholders.

What else could the United States have done with that money (not all of it, because prudent defense is, of course, necessary, but with some fraction of it; a third or a quarter, something like that)? We could have made major progress toward eliminating hunger, homelessness, infectious disease, illiteracy, ignorance, poverty, not just in the United States, but worldwide. We could have helped make the planet agriculturally self-sufficient and removed many of the causes of violence and war, and this could have been done with enormous benefit to the American economy. Think what prodigies of human inventiveness in art, architecture, medicine, science, and technology could have been supported for decades with the tiniest fraction of that money, and how they could have enriched our lives.

We have made a fool's bargain. We have been locked in a deadly embrace with the Soviet Union, each side always propelled by the abundant malefactions of the other; almost always looking to the short term—to the next congressional or presidential election, to the next Party Congress—and almost never seeing the big picture.

Dwight Eisenhower, who was closely associated with this Gettysburg community, said "The problem in defense spending is to figure out how far you should go without destroying from within what you are trying to defend from without." I say we have gone too far.

How do we get out of this mess? A Comprehensive Test Ban Treaty would stop all future nuclear weapons tests; they are the chief technological driver that propels, on both sides, the nuclear arms race. We need to abandon the ruinously expensive notion of Star Wars, which cannot protect the civilian population from nuclear war and subtracts from, not adds to, the national security of the United States. If we want to enhance deterrence, there are far better ways to do it. We need to make safe, massive, bilateral, intrusively inspected reductions in the strategic and tactical nuclear arsenals of the United States, the Soviet Union, and all other nations. (The INF Treaty represents a tiny step, but in the right direction.) That's what we should be doing.

Because nuclear weapons are comparatively cheap, the big ticket item has always been, and remains, conventional military forces. An extraordinary opportunity is now before us. Something no one had anticipated, something approaching a miracle has happened in the Soviet Union. There is somebody in charge there, somebody not just more reasonable than any Soviet leader in recent memory, somebody not just smart, but somebody with a long-term vision, with concern for precisely the same problems in his nation that we should be concerned for in ours. There is a clear commonality of purpose. Mr. Gorbachev has proposed massive conventional force reductions in Europe; he's willing, he says, to do it asymmetrically, in which the Soviets reduce their forces more than the Americans do. I say such conventional force reduction is in the interest of peace, and in the interest of a sane and healthy American economy. We ought to meet him halfway.

The world today spends $1 trillion a year on military preparations, most of it on conventional arms. The United States and the Soviet Union are the leading arms merchants. Much of that money is spent only because the nations of the world are unable to take the unbearable step of reconciliation with their adversaries. That trillion dollars a year takes food from the mouths of poor people. It cripples potentially effective economies. It is a scandalous waste, and we should not countenance it.

It is time to learn from those who fell here. And it is time to act.

In part the American Civil War was about freedom; about extending the benefits of the American Revolution to all Americans, to make valid for everyone that tragically unfulfilled promise of "liberty and justice for all." I'm concerned about a lack of historical pattern recognition. Today the fighters for freedom do not wear three-cornered hats and play the fife and drum. They come in other costumes. They may speak other languages. They may adhere to other religions. The color of their skin may be different. But the creed of liberty means nothing if it is only our own liberty that excites us. People elsewhere are crying, "No taxation without representation," and in Southern Africa, or the West Bank of the Jordan River, or Eastern Europe, or Central America they are shouting in increasing numbers, "Give me liberty or give me death." Why are we unable to hear most of them? We Americans have powerful nonviolent means of persuasion available to us. Why are we not using these means?

The Civil War was mainly about union; union in the face of differences. A million years ago, there were no nations on the planet. There were no tribes. The humans who were here were divided into small family groups of a few dozen people each. They wandered. That was the horizon of our identification, an itinerant family group. Since then, the horizons have expanded. From a handful of hunter-gatherers, to a tribe, to a horde, to a small city-state, to a nation, and today to immense nation-states. The average person on the Earth today owes his or her primary allegiance to a group of something like 100 million people. It seems very clear that if we do not destroy ourselves first, the unit of primary identification of most human beings will before long be the planet Earth and the human species. To my mind, this raises the key question: whether the fundamental unit of identification will expand to embrace the planet and the species, or whether we will destroy ourselves first. I'm afraid it's going to be very close.

The identification horizons were broadened in this place 125 years ago, and at great cost to North and South, to blacks and whites. But we recognize that expansion of identification horizons as just. Today there is an urgent, practical necessity to work together on arms control, on the world economy, on the global environment. It is clear that the nations of the world now can only rise and fall together. It is not a question of one nation winning at the expense of another. We must all help one another or all perish together.

On occasions like this it is customary to quote homilies; phrases by great men and women that we've all heard before. We hear, but we tend not to focus. Let me mention one, a phrase that was uttered not far from this spot by Abraham Lincoln: "With malice toward none, with charity for all . . . " *Think* of what that means. This is what is expected of us, not merely because our ethics command it, or because our religions preach it, but because it is necessary for human survival.

Here's another: "A house divided against itself cannot stand." Let me vary it a little: A species divided against itself cannot stand. A planet divided against itself cannot stand. And [to be] inscribed on this Eternal Light Peace Memorial, which is about to be rekindled and rededicated, is a stirring phrase: "A World United in the Search for Peace."

The real triumph of Gettysburg was not, I think, in 1863 but in 1913, when the surviving veterans, the remnants of the adversary forces, the Blue and the Gray, met in celebration and solemn memorial. It had been the war that set brother against brother, and when the time came to remember, on the fiftieth anniversary of the battle, the survivors fell, sobbing, into one another's arms. They could not help themselves.

It is time now for us to emulate them, NATO and the Warsaw Pact, Israelis and Palestinians, whites and blacks, Americans and Iranians, the developed and the underdeveloped worlds.

We need more than anniversary sentimentalism and holiday piety and patriotism. Where necessary, we must confront and challenge the conventional wisdom. It is time to learn from those who fell here. Our challenge is to reconcile, not *after* the carnage and the mass murder, but *instead* of the carnage and the mass murder.

It is time to act.

# The Eagle and the Bear: Can They Dance Together?[13]

Suzanne Massie

*Born January 8, 1931, New York, NY; A.B., Vassar College, 1951; researcher, reporter,* Time *magazine, 1952-53; managing editor,* Gourmet *magazine, 1953-67; freelance writer, 1967–; presidential consultant on Russian affairs, 1983-89; scholar, Harvard University Russian Research Center, 1986–; professor, General Theological Seminary, 1993–; author,* Journey *(1975),* Land of the Firebird: The Beauty of Old Russia *(1980),* Pavlovsk: The Life of a Russian Palace *(1990).*

## Editor's introduction

Organized by Colorado senator Tim Wirth, the Wirth Seminar strives to create a more open, understandable, and accessible notion of government by presenting a wide range of prominent speakers who attempt to elucidate various issues of the day. At the 1989 seminar, entitled "Future Perspectives on the Economy, Environment, Education, and U.S.–U.S.S.R. Relations," Professor Suzanne Massie spoke on sudden changes in Soviet-American relations. Prior to this speech, the Communist governments in Hungary, Poland, Romania, East Germany, Bulgaria, and Czechoslovakia had collapsed in rapid succession. Clearly, the notions of East vs. West and Democracy vs. Communism were about to crumble. Massie, who counseled President Ronald Reagan on Russian affairs and culture, took this occasion to remind listeners that at one time, and despite opposed government systems, America and Russia enjoyed healthy, amicable, and profitable relations. Given recent events, Massie stated that it was time to consider such relations as part of our mutual futures.

---

I deeply love my own country and people, and it has happened that I have come to know and love another country and people who we regarded as enemy. I began my work twenty-three years ago. Since then I have come to know hundreds of Russians from every walk of life. The Russian people and culture have enriched my life and have now become as familiar to me as my own. When I began it was not easy and sometimes even dangerous for us to be friends. It was definitely not a time of glasnost. Shadowy men who frowned on such contacts skulked in corners. We were often harassed and frightened, and passed through some very dark days. Yet somehow we managed to reach out, to trust each other and to maintain friendships, friendships made all the more precious because they were forced to survive barriers, long separations, enforced silence and distance. Many years have now gone by. Some of those who I first met when they were babies are now married and having children of their own. I am proud to have a godchild in the Soviet Union born on Christmas day two and a half years ago and six other children who call me aunt, one, who calls me "Aunt America," a name that particularly delights me.

Through these years I understood how fortunate I was to have the opportunity to go through the dark looking glass that separated our nations and I always hoped that our two peoples would one day have a chance to know each other as I had. I tried to make this happen in my own way by speaking out against what I thought was wrong and writing about what I found beautiful—and there was much of both. My efforts were not always regarded benignly by either side. The bureaucracy of both countries has at times regarded me as dangerous, curious, and a little mad.

[13]Delivered to the 15th annual Wirth Seminar, in Washington, D.C., on April 21, 1989.

Perhaps this is understandable, for as I am a writer and a historian I have a little different perspective, a worm's eye view if you like. I am interested first and foremost in people: their dreams, sorrows, aspirations, their past. My father was a very independent Swiss and from my earliest childhood I was taught to believe in the power of the individual. He instilled in me the belief that each of us can affect the world we live in for good or evil. For me, history is made by people, not by impersonal economic and political forces beyond our efforts to control, and we can all change and affect it.

Certainly one thing that one observes as a historian is that history has a funny way of doing flip flops: today's guerrilla fighter is tomorrow's patriot; yesterday's wartime enemies, today's treasured allies, and vice versa. Even national symbols are not sacrosanct. Teddy Roosevelt once proposed that the United States change its national symbol to the grizzly bear, a brave, independent animal, said he, much better than that "dandified vulture" we had adopted. In those days, Russia's symbol was the eagle: a double-headed one, that faced both East and West, a symbol still useful to remember today.

Since during the past fifty years, with the exception of a brief flirtation during World War II, the eagle and the bear have been glowering and rattling swords at each other, it has been difficult for Americans, who have very short memories, to recall that throughout history, with the exception of recent times, Russia and the United States enjoyed the most amicable relations. In the era of Imperial Russia, gestures between the land of the tsars and our young republic abounded and the United States considered Russia to be one of its firmest supporters in the international community. These friendly relations reached a peak in the 1860s and '70s during the reign of Tsar Liberator Alexander II. This emperor who instituted reforms, in addition to his crowning achievement—the liberation of the serfs in 1861, two years before Lincoln freed the slaves in the United States—was an object of respect and even veneration in the United States.

During those decades, Russian interest in the United States also increased greatly. Russians eagerly read the works of Edgar Allan Poe and James Fenimore Cooper, as well as those of Washington Irving, Hawthorne, Emerson, Longfellow, Whitman, Lowell, Holmes, and Bret Harte. Russians soaked up American adventure novels, and learned the names of our states, cities, and rivers. Young Russians dreamed of America as the land of excitement and romance. The great novelist Ivan Turgenev hailed Americans as "the greatest poets of our time—not the poetry of words—but of action."

In 1860, Alexander II wrote admiringly of the United States as "presenting a spectacle of prosperity without example in the annals of history" and the Tsar and his ministers were firm in the belief that the Union must be preserved. When the French urged the British and the Russians to join them in full recognition of the Confederacy, the Imperial Government refused. And when in 1863 at a critical moment in the Civil War a Russian frigate and two Russian corvettes steamed into New York harbor, the event caused as much joy in the United States as it did surprise and consternation in France and England. Mrs. Lincoln paid a visit to the frigate *Oslabyia*, the first time a First Lady had set foot on a foreign warship. Toasts were drunk to Tsar and President. In New York, the Russians were greeted by cheering crowds and ecstatic newspaper headlines which proclaimed "NEW ALLIANCE CEMENTED." At an elegant ball given at the Academy of Music, tables were decorated with huge figures of Peter the Great, Washington, Lincoln, and Alexander in sugar and cake. Russian officers, among them Rimsky-Korsakov, then eighteen years old and a naval cadet, whirled hoopskirted New York ladies who wore on their bodices buttons from the coats of Russian officers.

When the overland telegraph brought additional good news that another Russian fleet had arrived in San Francisco, jubilation reigned all over America. Years later one gentleman recalled that his mother had clasped him to her bosom exclaiming, "We're saved! The Russians have come!" Lincoln referred to the Russian visits in his Thanksgiving Proclamation was one of "God's bounties of so extraordinary a nature that they cannot fail to penetrate the heart."

The timely appearance of the Russian fleet caused the French and English to hesitate in giving support to the Confederacy. And, after the war, a grateful America did not forget. In 1866, after an assassination attempt on the life of Alexander II, President Andrew Johnson sent a formal message to the Emperor and the House and Senate passed a joint resolution congratulating the Russian people on his escape. This was a unique event in American history; never before had a message been sent to a foreign nation expressing personal feeling for its sovereign.

Assistant Secretary of the Navy Gustavus Fox personally delivered the message, crossing the Atlantic in a new Monitor class ship which anchored in St. Petersburg. He was nearly overwhelmed by the spontaneous outpouring of enthusiasm by the Russian people. The flag of the United States flew everywhere, people sang American songs and, in the city of Kostroma, people threw their coats on the road for the American visitors to walk on. Fox was made an honorary citizen of several Russian cities.

Alexander's letter to President Johnson thanking him for the resolution of Congress was suffused with warmth and I think bears repeating today:

"The two people find in their past no recollections of old grievances, but on the contrary, memorials only of amicable treatment . . . . These cordial relations which are as advantageous to their reciprocal interests as to those of civilization and humanity conform to the views of Divine Providence, whose final purpose is peace and concord among all nations. It is with a lively satisfaction that I see these bonds continually strengthening . . . . I pray you to express them to Congress and to the American people, of which that body is their organ. Tell them how much I—and with me all Russia—appreciate the testimonials of friendship which they have given me and how heartily I shall congratulate myself on seeing the American nation growing in power and prosperity by the Union and continued practice of the civic virtues which distinguish it.

Your good friend, Alexander"

It was in the glow of these good feelings that Russian-American negotiations for the sale of Alaska were completed in 1867. And because of that purchase we are today still only three miles distant from each other.

Today after many years of confrontation in the twentieth century it is perhaps time to consider the question: Could the eagle and the bear dance together again? Today we see a new liberalizing Russian leader who is extending many invitations. Over the past four years he has with quite astonishing speed moderated Soviet foreign policy, promoted economic reforms, courageously increased openness and self-criticism, allowed greater autonomy for the national republics within the Soviet Union, introduced a measure of democracy, and made significant moves in human rights and increasing religious freedom. But where is our Abe?

Over the past twenty-five years I have observed a curious phenomenon in American policy. Somehow we always seem to be one leader behind. We treated Khrushchev as if he were Stalin, Brezhnev as if he were Khrushchev and now Gorbachev as if he were Brezhnev. Because of this unfortunate predilection we have often missed opportunities in the past. I believe that this is the greatest opportunity we have had to try to forge a new relationship with the Soviet Union and it would be tragic if we were to muff this one now. We moan a lot about Gorbachev's successful "peace" offensives. What are we suggesting that is better? We have clung to our model of a Soviet foreign policy so entrenched that it could never evolve, while at the same time remaining convinced that we, because of our more flexible and responsive system, have a greater ability for change. Yet now, it is our leaders who seem curiously paralyzed. Perestroika (restructuring) and glasnost (openness) may be on the front pages of our newspapers and passed into our language, but not into our policy or our actions. Instead, we have responded with a bureaucratic sounding phrase "status quo plus" which sounds suspiciously like an American translation of "Brezhnevian stagnation."

Certainly there are many who have a large investment in old policies. Careerists are reluctant to link themselves to any Soviet leader by making definite pronouncements. After all, who knows what might happen between now and a future confirmation hearing? Careers in Washington are made by stressing one's "hawkishness," "vigilance," "prudence," not by going out on a limb and expressing the need for new approaches toward policies, some of which are now almost fifty years old.

By arguing that "we can't do much" or "America should act only in American interests" the establishment seems to be treating the whole issue as a spectator sport in which it need not play a role. There is an astonishing lack of creativity, initiative, and vision on our part. Bureaucratic equivocation seems to be our only answer to ferment and action on the part of the USSR. I was personally astonished to read a few weeks ago that after three months of the combined work of the NSC, the State Department, the CIA, and the Pentagon pronounced, and I quote, that "the hardest task is to probe Russian intentions and tactics"! The elephant seems to have labored only to bring forth a mouse. It is not such a mystery and there is no need to examine the entrails of a rooster to divine the facts. The picture is clear and spread out for all to see and read on the pages of Soviet newspapers. The Soviet Union is in the process of wrenching change—coping with deep and perilous troubles—physically, psychologically, ecologically, and economically. The outcome of all this ferment is as yet unknown, but I think we should no longer be talking so much about "intentions" but rather more realistically about the "possibilities" of the Soviet Union.

Now as they struggle to resolve their problems what should we do? Gloat? Bash them? Or reach out a hand? Many of Gorbachev's invitations to the dance have been rebuffed. A good example is Afghanistan, which the Soviet Union regarded as a turning point in its relations with the new administration.

It is clear that we made an incorrect assessment that the Communist regime would collapse as soon as the Soviet armies pulled out. It is now evident that we were mistaken. We could have concluded that we had not made a correct assessment and responded to Soviet initiatives. Two months ago, the Soviet Union was proposing a solution which looked very much like the status quo before the invasion, a coalition of all parties including the former king with strong United Nations participation. Instead, it was our reaction to push harder, thus escalating the conflict again. Because of our negative response, the Soviet Union has perhaps had to reassess their policy and we may not be able to get what we could have only a short time ago. Our mutual goal, after all, should be to see an end to a bloody conflict in which the principal victims are innocent civilians, not a continuation of a war through proxies.

Considering our actions, it has seemed to me a little ironic that we have been asking the Soviet Union as a test of its good intentions to help out in Central America. What are we doing to help them out in an area which is of vital concern to them?

Another kind of missed opportunity occurred recently. A week ago the *New York Times* reported that the Soviet Union, dipping into an emergency fund of foreign currency, had begun a major push to buy Western consumer goods—razor blades to soap powders, shoes, and pantyhose. These would have a retail value of 5 billion rubles, perhaps equivalent to 1 billion dollars. Most of these contracts, now already concluded, were signed with Japanese and European companies, not with the United States. This is perhaps not so much because of MFN but because of the generally negative political climate. In both of these very different cases, we missed the lead.

We all know that in order to dance one needs to hear the same tune and learn complementary steps. As citizens, we should all think about what these steps might look like; but, while we are retooling and studying our broad policy, there are some mutually beneficial tangible moves that we might consider that come to my mind:

1. We should, I believe, energetically propose a generous and comprehensive plan to join forces with the Soviet Union to combat the problems of environmental degradation which threaten our common planet. We are being told today by environmental experts that we have ten years to turn the situation around. In the Soviet Union the situation may be even worse; their experts are saying that for them it is now and perhaps even yesterday. In the course of a conversation I had last June with a high-ranking Soviet official he remembered that President Reagan once said that if our planet were to be suddenly threatened with danger by aliens from outer space, we would quickly join together to fight the common enemy. "I believe," said this Soviet official, "that the enemy is here—and it is the destruction of the environment."

2. We should more vigorously explore the possibility of joining forces to combat terrorism as was proposed recently at an international police conference.

3. We could perhaps be a little more sensitive to certain pressing regional concerns of the Soviet Union. As one speaker at a recent conference I attended asked, "How would you like to have Iran on your border?" The Soviet Union is the fourth largest Muslim country in the world and, along with the United States and Brazil, one of the three largest Christian countries. The double-headed eagle looking both toward East and West symbolized this concern.

4. The Soviet Union has enormous problems of health. According to Soviet statistics 38´of

Soviet children do not receive DPT shots. The Soviet Union has 140,000 cases of tuberculosis in children vs. our forty. The Soviet Union is fiftieth in infant mortality. There is no point in dwelling on the reasons for this; more importantly, I believe it is an area where we could perhaps reach out the hand of cooperation without the slightest fear of jeopardizing our national security. I myself am hoping to study the problems of handicapped children in the Soviet Union.

5. Although I am not an expert in the field of arms control, I hope that we could use the opportunity that is being presented now to pursue and conclude arms agreements. For one reason or another the Soviet Union seems ready to put a great deal on the table. Why linger incessantly to explore and test these overtures?

6. More cultural exchange: there are excellent films being made in the Soviet Union today—we see very few. The theater is vigorous and provocative yet the Taganka theater has never been to the United States, nor has Efreimov's Moscow Art Theater. We have no regular exchanges of television programs although there are now many interesting programs being made and shown in the Soviet Union.

7. The Soviet Union is eagerly looking for agricultural technology and know-how, among other things for cattle feed additives rather than grain purchases. Nothing much has been done by our side. We have demonstrated little flexibility and just don't seem to be listening.

8. It might also be helpful if we stopped talking about how long Gorbachev will "last." He has already lasted four years—the full term of an American President—and is now entering his second. Instead of worrying so much about what will happen to him and how long and who next (a fruitless exercise since no one can predict with certainty who our next President might be) we might perhaps better deal with what we have now. One has only to think how strange it would be to say that there was no certainty in dealing with President Bush since he might not last longer than four years. The old saying goes: the past is over, the future unknown; today is all we know for certain.

We all know it is hard to adjust to changing human relationships. In our own personal lives we know that when a partner—or an adversary—changes it is often easier for us to deny the change than it is to wrestle with the personal growth that a new adaptation demands.

Change in the Soviet Union has come faster than anyone could have possibly predicted a few years ago. Only two years ago I gave a speech on the surprising happenings of that year in the Soviet Union. These ranged from the serious to the frivolous; an Yves St. Laurent show in the Hermitage, Pizza Hut, and, could one believe it, even talk of a baseball team in Kiev. Everyone laughed. One man in the audience jovially declared "But we already have the Red Sox!" I ended my talk then by musing, "A baseball team in Kiev. If we are sensitive enough and imaginative enough to recognize change when we see it, we may one day be playing a new kind of World Series." Well, the baseball team from Kiev has just played Annapolis. "Peetchers" and "beizball bats" have now entered the Russian vocabulary along with "beezness" and "democratizatsiya." The Russians lost, but cheerfully said, "It's your game and we came here to learn." Which of their games are we trying to learn? It seems that we are dropping the ball, and if we are not careful it is we who may end up losing not only the chance to play with a new team, but the whole world series.

It might be useful for us to remember sometimes that we are not always at the center of their radar screen as we rather vainly like to believe, but sometimes only at the far corner. The Soviet Union is an empire of one hundred nations which covers eleven time zones. Russia is only one of fifteen republics. The empire's frontiers are loosening, and as they do Russia and the Soviet Union are not only faced with extraordinary problems, but will have to consider new relationships and directions.

We have another serious problem to consider. A Soviet diplomat once said to his counterpart at one of the arms talks, "We are about to do a terrible thing to you. We are about to deprive you of an enemy." We need to ask ourselves: Can we live without an enemy? Engagement seems to be easier for us than disengagement.

Now in Abe and Alex's time the United States and Russia got along fine and yet no two systems could have been more different than an ancient autocracy and a young republican democracy. So the difference in systems is not the problem. The problem has been a militant expansionist Marxist-Leninist ideology.

In over twenty years, even while Soviet newspapers and officials were reviling us almost daily, I have never heard an expression of hostility from any Russian man in the street. Curiosity, bewilderment—apprehension sometimes—but basically, the Russians really like us. I have been told, "Tell your countrymen we love you more than the Europeans do." The Russian people do admire us, and for the right reasons. They admire our energy, our spontaneity, our imagination, and our know-how.

Even the Soviet government and Soviet officials often pay us the compliment of trying to behave like us. They dress like our bureaucrats, talk like our bureaucrats, use incomprehensible acronyms just like ours.

The Russians are not our enemies. It has been the Soviet government that has called us enemy and today, even they are no longer doing so.

Russians today, as they were in Abe Lincoln's day, are still fascinated by America. The United States—not Europe, not Japan—remains the standard of all excellence, the standard by which they measure everything. Many Russians still look to us as a model. Gorbachev's new step of creating a Congress of People's Deputies is an attempt to separate the executive from the legislative branch of government. One of the recently elected delegates to this new congress is a man who happened to be here last summer. He watched the Bush-Dukakis debates in Peoria and took home a video tape, and his wife recently reported by phone that he used it to good effect in his successful campaign.

The word "democracy" is now on Russian lips everywhere used by officials, printed on posters, and in the pages of newspapers. Yet it obviously does not mean the same thing to them as it does to us. For however encouraging glasnost may be and the steps away from totalitarianism toward a greater pluralism it certainly is not and will not be our system, and if we are going to be satisfied only with a mirror image, we are bound to be disappointed, for Russia is different, has always been different, and her way will not be ours. And what do we expect? Primaries in Minsk? Psychologists say that only narcissists want mirror images. Perhaps we should explore the differences; we might learn something.

We are a country of impatience, they of patience. We are a country of rationality, they of emotion. They are comfortable with contradiction and mystery, we are not. We may not know it yet, but we need the strength of the Russian people, their profound spirituality, and the wisdom and perspective they have so dearly won through their suffering.

We might be as enriched by this contact in the future as we have been in the past. One has only to think how much Russia has given to our common Western cultural heritage; to name but a few of a long, long list: Dostoevsky, Tolstoy, the ballet, Diaghilev, Stanislavsky, Tchaikovsky, Gershwin, Stravinsky, Chagall, Balanchine.

It may be time for us to start dancing together again. A Hindu proverb says: "When two bulls fight, the grass gets crushed." We are both exhausted from our fighting and while we have been occupied with this expansive struggle, former adversaries are getting stronger at our mutual expense.

We Americans have a short history. It is hard for us to understand a country with a long history. And in Russia everything is long: their roads are long, their queues are long, their names, church services, novels, and their history is long. I think we need to take a little longer view. Seventy years is a drop in the historical bucket for a country that is over a thousand years old. Russia has seen many leaders, many have passed into the mist, but Russia is still there.

I believe that today we should be working with a new and changing Soviet Union to develop a mutually beneficial relationship, one which sees the gradual strengthening of forces which are friendly to the United States and the world: the growing freedom of the press, the broader political participation, the strengthening of universal ethical and religious values, and the law as the moral base of society.

In order to achieve this, we need patience and a little perestroika and self-criticism of our own. We must rigorously reexamine our old prejudices and stereotypes, and understand the complex forces and problems at work in the USSR. We need to bring a far more nuanced and compassionate approach to Russian national aspirations and concerns and not tar all of these as being extremist and retrograde as we have a tendency to do now. Perhaps most of all we must strive to get over our often provincial ignorance of some of the most basic facts of Russian history and the complexities of Soviet life and society. Only when we do this can we perhaps start looking down the road to a day when we will not be adversaries, but perhaps even partners—not enemies, but friends—as in other periods of history when we once were.

This may still sound Utopian today—although less than it did four years ago—yet it is possible, and perhaps looking at the problems which are coming at us from the rest of the world, even necessary for us both.

Before we too quickly dismiss such a possibility let us think for a moment about what has happened already. Who could have predicted, what odds would you have given two years ago that we would be playing baseball and eagerly scanning the front pages of the *New York Times* for the results of Soviet elections?

President Reagan's favorite Russian proverb was "Trust but verify." It is a good principle, but the first word is trust. Without that there is nothing to verify.

The bear has gotten up on its hind legs and has started to move quite friskily, even more insistently tapping out a rhythm that says in the words of Lewis Carroll "Will you, won't you, will you, won't you, will you join the dance?" It is time to think, for the eagle to stop sitting it out, to get up and lift its wings. The movements might look a bit awkward at first, but with the time and practice, the result might just be a creditable waltz.

In Russia, this week following Orthodox Easter which fell this past Sunday is known as "Bright Week" to symbolize the joy of hope returned after a dark season. We should rejoice that today the Russians and other peoples of the Soviet Union are seeking a new relationship between themselves, their government, and the rest of the world. In this Easter season of spring, which brings with it the promise of rebirth in both nature and man, it is possible to hope, and I do.

As for the future, I would like to leave you with a thought expressed to me by a Russian poet.

"Perhaps we are all witnesses in a gigantic trial whose outcome is determined and yet still hidden from us, but whose outline we can sometimes glimpse as we can sometimes, behind driving rain, glimpse the silhouettes of angels."

# Completing Marshall's Plan in Europe[14]

William J. Perry

*Born October 11, 1927, Vandergrift, PA; B.S., 1949, M.S., 1950, Stanford University; Ph.D., Pennsylvania State University, 1957; director of defense laboratories, GTE Sylvania Co., 1954-64; co-founder, president, ESL Inc., 1964-77; U.S. under secretary of defense, 1977-81; executive vice president, Harnbrecht & Quist, 1981-85; founder, president, Technology Strategies and Alliances, 1985-93; U.S. deputy secretary of defense, 1993-94; U.S. secretary of defense, 1994-97.*

## Editor's introduction

Because Russian leaders were concerned about NATO's plans to expand its membership to include Eastern European nations, Defense Secretary Perry attempted, unsuccessfully, to convince them that NATO "actually contributes to the security of Russia as well as to the security of its own members." Hoping to make George C. Marshall's vision of a Europe "united in peace, freedom, and democracy" a reality, Perry insisted that if Eastern European nations joined NATO, a zone of security would be created for Russia. Many others, however, feel that the expansion of NATO into Eastern Europe will only threaten Russian-American relations. A resolution remains to be seen.

---

Behind my desk at the Pentagon hangs a portrait of the great statesman George C. Marshall. Marshall, who was the third secretary of defense in the United States, is a role model of mine. He had a great vision for Europe—a Europe which from the Atlantic to the Urals was united in peace, freedom and democracy—and a strong trans-Atlantic partnership sustained by bipartisan political support in the United States.

Marshall not only had this vision, he also had a plan to make this vision a reality in post-war Europe. And in a famous speech at Harvard University in 1947, he outlined what came to be called the Marshall Plan.

A little known fact is that joining Marshall on the dais that day was the famous poet T.S. Eliot, who 10 years earlier had written:

*Footfalls echo in the memory*
*Down the passage we did not take*
*Towards the door we never opened.*

These words by T.S. Eliot foreshadowed the fate of Marshall's plan in Eastern and Central Europe, because on that day 50 years ago, as the footfalls of World War II still echoed across a shattered continent, the Marshall Plan offered Europe a new passage toward reconstruction and renewal. Half of Europe took this passage and opened the door to prosperity and freedom. Half of Europe was denied this passage when Joseph Stalin slammed the door on Marshall's offer. And for 50 years, the footfalls of what might have been echoed in our memories.

Today, as the Cold War becomes an echo in our memory, we have a second chance to make Marshall's vision a reality: To go down the passage we did not take 50 years ago, towards the door we never opened. Behind that door lies George Marshall's Europe. To open this door, we do not need a second Marshall Plan, but we do need to draw on Marshall's vision.

Marshall recognized that peace, democracy and prosperity were ultimately inseparable. And Marshall understood that if you identify what people desire most and provide them with a path to reach it, then they will do the hard work necessary to achieve their goals.

In the late 1940s, what Western European countries desired most was to rebuild their societies and economies. And the Marshall Plan provided a path for achieving this goal. By taking this passage, the nations of Western Europe built an economic powerhouse. And along the way, they built strong democracies and a strong security institution called NATO.

[14]Delivered at the Wehrkunde Conference on Security, in Munich, Germany, on February 4, 1996.

Today, countries in the other half of Europe are struggling to rebuild their societies and economies, and the one thing they all desire is greater security. NATO's challenge is to provide these Europeans a path for achieving their security goal. And along the way, we want them very much to develop strong democracies and strong economies.

This other half of Europe includes the nations of Central and Eastern Europe and the newly independent states. It includes Russia, and it includes the nations of the former Yugoslavia. Today, NATO is reaching out to all three areas and providing a path to Marshall's Europe.

The primary path NATO has provided is the Partnership for Peace. Just as the Marshall Plan worked because it was rooted firmly in the self-interest of both the United States and Europe, so too does the Partnership for Peace work because it is rooted firmly in the self-interest of both NATO and the partner nations.

PFP is bringing the newly free nations of Europe and the former Soviet Union into the security architecture of Europe as a whole. Our nations are working and training together in military joint exercises. But make no mistake, the Partnership for Peace is more than just joint exercises. Just as the Marshall Plan had an impact well beyond the economies of Western Europe, PFP is echoing beyond the security realm in Central and Eastern Europe, and into the political and economic realms as well.

Just as the Marshall Plan used economic revival as the catalyst for political stabilization—and ultimately the development of the modern Europe—the PFP uses security cooperation as a catalyst for political and economic reform.

PFP members are working to uphold democracy, tolerate diversity, respect the rights of minorities and respect freedom of expression. They are working to build market economies. They are working hard to develop democratic control of their military forces, to be good neighbors and respect the sovereign rights outside their borders. And they are working hard to make their military forces compatible with NATO.

For those partner countries that are embracing PFP as a passage to NATO membership, these actions are a key to opening that door. For many of these nations, aspiration to NATO membership has become the rock on which all major political parties base their platforms. It is providing the same overlapping consensus that NATO membership engenders in NATO countries, making compromise and reconciliation possible.

In Hungary, all six major political parties in the Parliament united to pass a resolution in support of IFOR [implementation force], the Bosnia peace implementation force, by a vote of 300 to 1. In Poland, the new president—a former member of the former communist party—reaffirmed Poland's NATO aspirations. In Slovakia, Hungary and Rumania, governments are quietly resolving border disputes and putting into place protection for ethnic minorities. For these countries, the Partnership for Peace is becoming a passage to democracy and market reform, as well as a passage to security cooperation with the West.

But even those countries that do not aspire to NATO membership are realizing many of the same political and social gains from active participation in the PFP. Moreover, PFP is providing them the tools and the opportunities to develop closer ties to NATO, and learn from NATO—even as they choose to remain outside the alliance. And PFP is building bonds among the partner nations—even outside the framework of cooperation with NATO.

That is why defense ministers from many partner nations have said to me that even if, or when, they eventually join NATO, they want to sustain their active participation in PFP. In short, by creating the Partnership for Peace, NATO is doing more than just building the basis for enlargement. It is, in fact, creating a new zone of security and stability throughout Europe.

That is why I believe that the creation of the Partnership for Peace has been one of the most significant events of the post-Cold War era. By forging networks of people and institutions working together to preserve freedom, promote democracy and build free markets, the PFP today is a catalyst for transforming Central and Eastern Europe, much as Marshall Plan transformed Western Europe in the '40s and '50s. It is the passage this half of Europe did not take in 1947; it is the door that we never opened.

To lock in the gains of reform, NATO must ensure that the ties we are creating in PFP continue to deepen and that we actually proceed with the gradual and deliberate, but steady, process of outreach and enlargement to the East. NATO enlargement is inevitable. And if

NATO enlargement is a carrot encouraging reforms, then we cannot keep that carrot continually out of reach. So it is critical that we implement the second phase of NATO enlargement agreed upon at the NAC (North Atlantic Council) Ministerial Meeting in December.

And even as some countries join NATO, it will be important to keep the door open for others down the road. We must make sure that PFP continues to provide a place in the security architecture of Europe so that we keep the door open to Marshall's Europe even for those nations that do not aspire to become NATO members.

For Marshall's vision to be truly fulfilled, one of the nations that must walk through this door is Russia. Russia has been a key player in Europe's security for over 300 years. It will remain a key player in the coming decades, for better or for worse. Our job is to make it for the better.

Unlike with the Marshall Plan 50 years ago, Russia today has chosen to participate in the Partnership for Peace. And in the spirit of Marshall, we welcome Russia's participation and hope that over time it will take on a leading role in PFP commensurate with its importance as a great power.

But for Russia to join us as a full and active partner in completing Marshall's vision, NATO and Russia need to build on our common ground, even when we don't agree with each other's conclusions. It is fair to say that most members of Russia's political establishment do not welcome or even accept NATO's plans for enlargement. Anybody that doubted that yesterday, if you heard Mr. [Andrey] Kokoshin's [first deputy minister of defense] speech, realized the extent of the opposition to NATO enlargement in Russia.

When I was in Russia last June, I had a number of conversations with Russian government leaders and Duma members about the future of European security. I offered them a series of postulates about that future. I told them if I were in Russia's shoes, I would want the future security picture in Europe to have the following characteristics:

First, I said, if I were a Russian leader, I would want the United States to be involved in the security of Europe. They agreed with that postulate.

Then, I said, if I were a Russian leader, I would want to see Germany an integrated part of the European security structure. And they agreed with that postulate.

And third, I said, if I were a Russian leader, I would want Russia to be in the security architecture of Europe, not isolated outside of it. They agreed with this postulate also.

Finally, I asked them how could a Russian leader best achieve these goals?

I concluded they could only be achieved through a healthy and vibrant NATO. That is, NATO, far from being a threat to Russia, actually contributes to the security of Russia as well as to the security of its own members.

When I reached that conclusion, most of the Russians I talked to fell off the cliff. They agreed with each of my premises, but they did not agree with my conclusion. But in the absence of NATO and its partnership arrangements, I do not see any way of achieving those goals—our shared goals—of a safe and peaceful Europe.

I have to tell you that I did not persuade my Russian colleagues with my argument. But I do believe that as Russia deepens its involvement with NATO, it will come to believe in the truth of my conclusion as well as my premises. And I believe that Russia will want to have a cooperative relation with NATO and a leading role in the Partnership for Peace and that Russia will come to understand that NATO enlargement means enlarging a zone of security and stability that is very much in Russia's interest, not a threat to Russia.

But the way for this new understanding to occur is for NATO to continue to reach out to Russia not only from the top down but from the bottom up. Last year at Wehrkunde, I proposed that NATO and Russia begin a separate plan of activities, outside the Partnership for Peace. Since then, we have all discussed and even agreed upon this proposal in principle, but we have not yet put it on paper. We must do so. We cannot let disagreements over the "theology" of building NATO-Russia relations get in the way of "here and now" opportunities to work together where our interests clearly overlap. Instead of letting theology dictate our practice, we should let our practice shape our theology.

One example of where the United States is already doing this is with our program of bilateral training exercises with Russia. We have held four such exercises in the last year, each a great success, and each conducted in a spirit of trust and good will. This summer, the United

States and Russia will move beyond the bilateral and jointly participate in a major regional Partnership for Peace exercise with forces from Ukraine, Russia, United States and other regional powers.

Our bilateral contact program with Russia is not confined to joint exercises or even to just the security field. Through the Gore-Chernomyrdin Commission, it extends to the fields of science and technology, space, defense conversion, business development, the environment, health care and agriculture.

Just this past week the commission met in Washington, and Mr. Kokoshin and I both participated in the defense conversion program of this commission. I urge all NATO nations to build on this model. These contacts provide important exchanges of information. They help break down years of distrust and suspicion. They weave the Russians into the kind of personal and professional networks that have long characterized relations among all of the allies. These are the kind of activities that will build trust between Russia and NATO. And these are the kind of activities that will keep Russia on the passage toward integration with Europe, to pass through that open door.

Mr. [Russian Defense Minister Army Gen. Pavel] Grachev and I attended the joint U.S.-Russia exercise in Kansas last October. And we met after the exercise with the American and the Russian soldiers conducting that exercise, and talked to them. He told the Russian soldiers what they were doing was very important, that they should extend their friendship and cooperation with the American soldiers and that this was the basis for creating a peaceful world for their children. The American soldiers were as much interested in what he was saying as the Russians were, I can assure you.

Ironically, the place where a distinct NATO-Russia relationship is occurring in practice is in Bosnia. Today, as we speak, a Russian brigade is serving in the American Multinational Division of IFOR. It took an enormous amount of work to make this happen. Minister Grachev and I met four times over a two-month period to iron out the details. Gens. [Army Gen. George] Joulwan and [Army Maj. Gen. William] Nash work closely every day with their counterparts, Gen. [Col. Gen. Leontiy] Shevtsov and Col. [Alexandr] Lentsov. NATO and Russia do have a special relationship today in Bosnia, and Russia is demonstrating its commitment to participating in the future security architecture of Europe.

The reason we are all working so hard to make this relationship successful is not just because of the additional troops Russia brings to Bosnia, but because Russia's participation in Bosnia casts a very long shadow that will have an impact on the security of Europe for years to come. When we deal with the most important security problem which Europe has faced since the Cold War was over, we want to have Russia inside the circle working with us, not outside the circle throwing rocks at us.

Indeed, the more you think about what NATO and Russia are doing together in Bosnia, the more amazing it becomes. I can only imagine what Gen. [Dwight D.] Eisenhower, the first SACEUR [supreme allied commander Europe], would think if he saw a general from Russia sitting with Gen. Joulwan, today's SACEUR, at the SHAPE [Supreme Headquarters Allied Powers Europe] compound reviewing a secret NATO OPLAN [operational plan]. We need to build on this model, to institutionalize it and expand it to cover the entire range of NATO and Russia's overlapping security interests. By so doing, NATO and Russia can move forward as full partners in completing Marshall's vision.

Just as the NATO-Russia relationship is being forged in Bosnia, so too is the future of NATO itself. I was in Bosnia several weeks ago. I was struck by the dedication and professionalism of every unit from every country that is participating. I was also struck by the stark contrast between the devastation and suffering I saw in Sarajevo, and the rebirth and renewal I have seen in the other capitals of Central and Eastern Europe.

Bosnia is what happens when newly independent nations focus on old hatreds instead of new challenges. Four years ago, some people in the former Yugoslavia chose not to join Marshall's Europe. And the death and bloodshed that resulted will long echo in our memory. But today, the door to Marshall's Europe is open again for them—and holding that door open are NATO, Russia and the newly free peoples of Central and Eastern Europe.

The success or failure of IFOR is crucial to whether or not we will complete Marshall's vision. It is in Bosnia where we are sending the message that NATO is the bedrock on which the future security and stability of Europe will be built. It is in Bosnia where NATO is first reaping the benefits of joint peacekeeping training with our new peace partners. It is in Bosnia where future NATO members are showing themselves ready and able to shoulder the burdens of membership. And it is in Bosnia where we are showing that we can work as partners with Russian forces. Bosnia is not a peacekeeping exercise. It is the real thing.

Bosnia is also teaching us important lessons about the kind of NATO that Marshall's Europe will require. Ever since the end of the Cold War, NATO has struggled to develop a mechanism for executing the new missions using NATO assets with the voluntary participation of NATO members.

In the conference room, we have so far failed to come up with an agreement on a combined joint task force, CJTF. But in the field, we have cut through these theological arguments and put together IFOR, which is a CJTF. As with the NATO-Russia relationship, we need to take the practical lessons learned in putting IFOR together and extrapolate back until we have a CJTF that works.

Bosnia also casts in sharp relief something we have suspected for some time: that it is time for NATO to adapt itself internally to deal with the new challenges of this new era. NATO was not well structured for the Bosnia mission. At a time when our political and geostrategic thinking has been completely reoriented, symbolized by our partnership in peacekeeping with former adversaries, and at a time when our individual military forces have streamlined and modernized for the battlefield of the future, NATO's command and decision-making structure is still geared for the challenges and the battlefields of the past. The time has come to streamline and modernize NATO, recognizing that our challenge is no longer simply to execute a known plan with already designated forces, as it was during the Cold War.

We must make NATO's command structure more responsive and more flexible, and streamline the planning and force preparation process, and simplify and speed up the entire decision-making process. And we must complete the task of giving NATO's European members a stronger identity within the alliance. These kinds of internal changes will ready NATO for enlargement and will allow us to better respond to the future challenges to European security and stability.

It is in this context that we welcome the French decision to participate more fully in NATO's military bodies. And we look forward to working with France as we transform the alliance and realize Marshall's vision of a Europe united in peace, freedom and democracy.

In 1947, Marshall told America that it must "face up to the responsibility which history has placed upon our country." Today, it is not only America, but also Russia; is not only NATO nations, but all of Europe—all of us must face up to the responsibility which history has placed upon us. This means reaching out to each other not only in the spirit of friendship, but also in the spirit of self-interest. This means working towards our goals not only from the top down, but also the ground up. And it means recognizing that when the outside world changes, we must look inside our institutions and see what changes are needed there.

If we do these things, then next year, when we commemorate the 50th anniversary of the Marshall Plan, we will be able to say that we made Marshall's vision our own; that Partnership for Peace is a strong, permanent pillar of Europe's security architecture; that NATO and Russia have a relationship where trust, understanding and cooperation are givens, not goals; that all the nations of the former Yugoslavia are adding, not detracting, from Europe's security; and that we have taken the passage to a new Europe and opened the door to a new era of peace, freedom and democracy.

Thank you very much.

# V. War

## Editor's introduction

Whether involved in declared wars or undeclared conflicts, the United States spent nearly one third of the years between 1937 and 1997 in battle with foreign powers. The most notable of these engagements were World War II, the Korean War, the Vietnam War, and the Gulf War. The cumulative effect of these wars upon American life is inestimable, as is the ethical and moral challenge all wars pose for our citizenry and our leaders. While the names of the wars have changed, and the weaponry and battle tactics evolved, the reality of war has not changed—nearly 375,000 Americans were killed in the aforementioned wars, and some 700,000 were injured. The following speeches detail both the angst faced by a country in the face of battle, and the strategies and methodologies adopted by our leaders and heroes of war.

Owing largely to his appeasement policy, which many believe enabled Adolph Hitler to annex both Austria and Czechoslovakia without protest from other world powers, Neville Chamberlain, prime minister of England from 1937 to 1940, has not been remembered as an effective leader. Yet Chamberlain's dilemma—how to react to Hitler's 1938 and 1939 advances into eastern Europe—was also felt by American leaders. In 1939, President Franklin D. Roosevelt, while pledging that the United States would remain neutral, knew that only a miracle would end Hitler's rampage through Europe. Roosevelt vowed to avoid involvement in the war that had overtaken Europe by 1939. However, on December 7, 1941, the Japanese attacked Pearl Harbor. In response, Roosevelt ordered "that all measures be taken for our defense" so that eventual victory over the Axis powers could be secured.

During World War II, much American discourse focused upon how best to sustain the morale of both the nation and her allies. Between August and September 1940, the German Air Force bombed Great Britain relentlessly. Dorothy Thompson, a well-known women's suffrage advocate and radio commentator, praised the courage and fortitude of Hitler's arch adversary, Winston Churchill. She declared that Churchill, thanks to his gift of oratory, had aroused his nation to defend "the sceptered isle" and preserve freedom.

One of the most dramatic and far-reaching effects of World War II was the rift created between America and the Soviet Union. This division, grounded in ideology and manifest in arms buildups and territorial expansion, persisted until 1989, and came to be known as the Cold War. At the end of World War II, Korea was divided along the 38th parallel. The northern section, in a Soviet zone of occupation, declared itself the People's Democratic Republic of Korea, and the southern section, in a U.S. zone of occupation, declared itself the Republic of Korea. On June 25, 1950, when North Korean troops, supported by the Soviet Union, marched across the 38th parallel and attempted to seize South Korea, President Harry S. Truman, in concert with the United Nations, resolved to resist the aggression and prevent any further spread of Communism. On December 15, 1950, President Truman defined for the American public what the nation must do to stop the North Korean advance on United Nations forces in Korea. The next day the President declared a state of emergency. While war was not inevitable, Truman remarked, in a reference to the pre-World War II appeasement of Adolph Hitler, "security cannot be bought by appeasement." To defeat the North Korean forces (and Soviet supported Chinese army), Truman increased the size of the military, built more military equipment, cut non-military expenditures, and raised taxes.

On July 26, 1953, President Dwight D. Eisenhower signed an armistice with North Korea. Little was accomplished by the confrontation, as the border between North and South Korea remained unchanged. Eisenhower contended that during the "Police Action" that has come to be known as the Korean War, only the "sacrifice" of brave soldiers kept "freedom alive." The adversaries, being Americans, North Koreans, and South Koreans, would move from the battlefield to the negotiating table, where the haggling has continued unto the present day.

While the Korean War ended in a military stalemate the Vietnam war ended in defeat for both American and United Nations soldiers. Like Korea, Vietnam was divided into northern and southern sections. Soon after that division was declared by the 1954 Geneva conference, tensions arose between the Communist leader of North Vietnam, Ho Chi Minh, and the president of South Vietnam, Ngo Dinh Diem. The North Vietnamese military, having mastered guerrilla tactics, provided serious opposition to the South Vietnamese government. To block North Vietnam's attempt to unite all of Vietnam under Communism, John Foster Dulles, then United States secretary of state, arranged to have economic and military aid provided for South Vietnam. By 1962, President John F. Kennedy had stationed 11,000 "military advisers" in South Vietnam. By 1966, there were 190,000 U.S. troops in Vietnam, and by 1969 that number had risen to 540,000.

In 1964, most Americans supported President Lyndon B. Johnson's initiatives against the North Vietnamese Communists. Four years later, because of mounting American sacrifices and few visible results, powerful sentiments against our presence in Vietnam arose. Public rhetoric polarized between an "establishment" that feared the spread of Communism and a society that no longer understood, or upheld, the war against Communism as a basis for continued international conflict. Criticism of the United States' sponsorship of the Vietnam War went from the halls of campuses to the streets. On April 23, 1965, Wayne Morse, in a speech included here, echoed the sentiments of many participating in sit-ins and teach-ins by publicly questioning our reasons for being in Vietnam.

In vain, the Johnson administration attempted to rationalize its policies and initiatives. On April 23, 1965, Secretary of State Dean Rusk, who was instrumental in planning Korean War policies, claimed that the goal of American foreign policy was the preservation of freedom in the face of an ever expanding Communist power. Drawing upon the citizenry's collective memory of Hitler appeasement policies, Johnson warned that "most of us remember the fearful cost of ignoring aggression." While "ready . . . for discussion" to end the Vietnam War, he said, "we shall stay the course," a calculation that drove him from the presidency.

On August 2, 1990, when Iraq invaded neighboring Kuwait, the Bush administration was forced to choose between verbal protest and military action. Because of the citizenry's memory of a costly, prolonged, and failed Vietnam policy, President Bush pledged that retaliation against Iraq would be swift, definitive, and successful. On August 5, 1990, Bush stated that Iraq's occupation of Kuwait "would not stand." Reminding Americans that the United States' decision was backed by 20 United Nations members, Bush issued a statement announcing that a military attack on Baghdad and Kuwait had begun. "Our objectives are clear," he said: "Saddam Hussein's forces will leave Kuwait." Bush's predictions were accurate. In a decisive victory, the United States, along with United Nations soldiers, drove the Iraqi military from Kuwait.

# This Nation Will Remain Neutral[1]

Franklin Delano Roosevelt

*Born January 30, 1882, Hyde Park, NY; died April 12, 1945; A.B., Harvard University, 1904; state senator, New York State Assembly, 1910-13; assistant secretary of the Navy, 1913-20; governor of New York, 1929-33; president of the United States, 1933-45.*

## Editor's introduction

On September 1, 1939, Hitler's armies invaded Poland. Britain and France, having pledged to defend Poland, declared war on Germany two days later. The night of that declaration, President Franklin D. Roosevelt spoke to "one of the largest and most diverse audiences ever addressed" at that time. He confronted the difficult question of what actions were in the best interest of the United States, and concluded that America "will remain a neutral nation." Yet, despite his claim of neutrality, Roosevelt was quite aware that Hitler's actions were deplorable, and he made no claims to neutral thought or neutral conscience. Americans welcomed Roosevelt's speech with open arms, and according to a *New York Times* poll, it sparked a five percent rise in Roosevelt's popularity.

---

Tonight my single duty is to speak to the whole of America.

Until four-thirty this morning I had hoped against hope that some miracle would prevent a devastating war in Europe and bring to an end the invasion of Poland by Germany.

For four long years a succession of actual wars and constant crises have shaken the entire world and have threatened in each case to bring on the gigantic conflict which is today unhappily a fact.

It is right that I should recall to your minds the consistent and at times successful efforts of your Government in these crises to throw the full weight of the United States into the cause of peace. In spite of spreading wars I think that we have every right and every reason to maintain as a national policy the fundamental moralities, the teachings of religion and the continuation of efforts to restore peace—for some day, though the time may be distant, we can be of even greater help to a crippled humanity.

It is right, too, to point out that the unfortunate events of these recent years have been based on the use of force or the threat of force. And it seems to me clear, even at the outbreak of this great war, that the influence of America should be consistent in seeking for humanity a final peace which will eliminate, as far as it is possible to do so, the continued use of force between nations.

It is, of course, impossible to predict the future. I have my constant stream of information from American representatives and other sources throughout the world. You, the people of this country, are receiving news through your radios and your newspapers at every hour of the day.

You are, I believe, the most enlightened and the best informed people in all the world at this moment. You are subjected to no censorship of news, and I want to add that your Government has no information which it has any thought of withholding from you.

At the same time, as I told my Press Conference on Friday, it is of the highest importance that the press and the radio use the utmost caution to discriminate between actual verified fact on the one hand, and mere rumor on the other.

I can add to that by saying that I hope the people of this country will also discriminate most carefully between news and rumor. Do not believe of necessity everything you hear or read. Check up on it first.

You must master at the outset a simple but unalterable fact in modern foreign relations.

[1] Broadcast throughout the Western Hemisphere, from Washington, D.C., on September 3, 1939.

When peace has been broken anywhere, peace of all countries everywhere is in danger.

It is easy for you and me to shrug our shoulders and say that conflicts taking place thousands of miles from the continental United States, and, indeed, the whole American Hemisphere, do not seriously affect the Americas—and that all the United States has to do is to ignore them and go about our own business. Passionately though we may desire detachment, we are forced to realize that every word that comes through the air, every ship that sails the sea, every battle that is fought does affect the American future.

Let no man or woman thoughtlessly or falsely talk of America sending its armies to European fields. At this moment there is being prepared a proclamation of American neutrality. This would have been done even if there had been no neutrality statute on the books, for this proclamation is in accordance with international law and with American policy.

This will be followed by a Proclamation required by the existing Neutrality Act. I trust that in the days to come our neutrality can be made a true neutrality.

It is of the utmost importance that the people of this country, with the best information in the world, think things through. The most dangerous enemies of American peace are those who, without well-rounded information on the whole broad subject of the past, the present and the future, undertake to speak with authority, to talk in terms of glittering generalities, to give to the nation assurances or prophecies which are of little present or future value.

I myself cannot and do not prophesy the course of events abroad—and the reason is that because I have of necessity such a complete picture of what is going on in every part of the world, I do not dare to do so. And the other reason is that I think it is honest for me to be honest with the people of the United States.

I cannot prophesy the immediate economic effect of this new war on our nation but I do say that no American has the moral right to profiteer at the expense either of his fellow citizens or of the men, women and children who are living and dying in the midst of war in Europe.

Some things we do know. Most of us in the United States believe in spiritual values. Most of us, regardless of what church we belong to, believe in the spirit of the New Testament—a great teaching which opposes itself to the use of force, of armed force, of marching armies and falling bombs. The overwhelming masses of our people seek peace—peace at home, and the kind of peace in other lands which will not jeopardize peace at home.

We have certain ideas and ideals of national safety and we must act to preserve that safety today and to preserve the safety of our children in future years.

That safety is and will be bound up with the safety of the Western Hemisphere and of the seas adjacent thereto. We seek to keep war from our firesides by keeping war from coming to the Americas. For that we have historic precedent that goes back to the days of the Administration of President George Washington. It is serious enough and tragic enough to every American family in every State in the Union to live in a world that is torn by wars on other continents. Today they affect every American home. It is our national duty to use every effort to keep them out of the Americas.

And at this time let me make the simple plea that partisanship and selfishness be adjourned; and that national unity be the thought that underlies all others.

This nation will remain a neutral nation, but I cannot ask that every American remain neutral in thought as well. Even a neutral has a right to take account of facts. Even a neutral cannot be asked to close his mind or his conscience.

I have said not once but many times that I have seen war and that I hate war. I say that again and again.

I hope the United States will keep out of this war. I believe that it will. And I give you assurances that every effort of your Government will be directed toward that end.

As long as it remains within my power to prevent, there will be no blackout of peace in the United States.

# Let's Face the Facts[2]

## Dorothy Thompson

*Born July 9, 1894, Lancaster, NY; died January 30, 1961; speaker, New York Women Suffrage campaign, 1915-17; foreign correspondent,* Philadelphia Public Ledger *and* New York Evening Post, *1920-28; writer,* On the Record *syndicated newspaper column, 1941-58; author,* The Courage to Be Happy *(1957).*

### Editor's introduction

Described as "lightning-like in speed and vitriolic in content," the speeches given during the week of July 19 to July 26, 1940, were a series of international, verbal assaults. President Theordore Roosevelt launched the attack during his reelection campaign for the presidency by contrasting the United States' "moral decency" with Germany's "firing squad" mentality. Several hours later, Adolph Hitler summarized the German victories since 1939 and attempted to demoralize the English by suggesting that it was not with the English people but with their leaders that he fought. To curtail Hitler's propaganda, Dorothy Thompson, radio commentator and foreign press correspondent, spoke to Canadians, who were under the British Commonwealth and therefore fighting alongside the British armies in Europe. Expelled from Germany because she ridiculed Adolph Hitler as incapable of providing leadership, Thompson likened World War II to a battle between the gallant Winston Churchill and the murderous Hitler.

---

Men and Women of Canada: In speaking to you this evening over the Canadian Broadcasting Corporation, I am exercising the prerogative that is still enjoyed by the citizens of free nations: the right to have an opinion of one's own, a view of affairs of one's own, and the right to express it. I am in the happy position of holding no public office, of speaking for nobody but myself. Yet what I think and feel is not unique. It is shared, as I well know, by many thousands of citizens of the United States.

This week we read of a peace offer that has been made by Hitler to Great Britain—made in his usual way of an open speech broadcast on the radios of the world, couched in now familiar terms, launched for purposes of international propaganda, and vague except for one thing.

It seems that Germany has no quarrel with Great Britain. Hitler's quarrel is exclusively with this particular British Government, and especially with its head, Mr. Churchill. If Mr. Churchill will only resign and a government come in which is acceptable to Mr. Hitler, he will be glad to make peace immediately. He has no desire to destroy the British Empire. The man standing in the way of peace is Churchill, and the so-called fifth columnists are "only honest men, seeking peace." That is Hitler's argument.

Now, of course, we have all become familiar with this. Mr. Hitler had no quarrel with Austria, only with Mr. Schuschnigg. So the moment Schuschnigg resigned he made peace with Austria by annexing it. He had no quarrel with Czechoslovakia, only with Mr. Beneš. So when Mr. Beneš resigned he made peace with Czechoslovakia by turning it into a Nazi Protectorate. He had no quarrel with any of the countries he has absorbed—only with those leaders who opposed the absorption. Mr. Hitler has no quarrel with traitors in any country on earth. They are his agents, and, as his agents, are honest men seeking peace. His quarrel is only with patriots.

I think we may expect that the whole force of the German propaganda in the immediate future will be concentrated on trying to break down Britain by removing her leadership. But

[2]Broadcast to the citizens of Canada, on July 21, 1940.

in this struggle, as in all great struggles, nations do become embodied in the persons of the men who lead them.

In a poetic sense, I might say in a Shakespearean sense, it really is Hitler who faces Churchill. For if Hitler has made himself the incorporation of Germany, Churchill really is the incorporation of Britain.

These two men are the very symbols of the struggle going on in the world.

If we can detach ourselves for a moment from all the pain of this struggle, and look at these two men, we see one of those heroic dramas which literature can never approximate. On the one side is the furious, unhappy, frustrated and fanatic figure who has climbed to unprecedented power on the piled-up bodies of millions of men, carried and pushed upward by revolutionary forces, supported by vast hordes of youth crying destruction to the whole past of civilized man. Their upward surge in Germany was accompanied by the wailing and the groans of those "honest men of peace" who once lived in Germany, but were seized in their homes or on the streets and hurled into concentration camps or the barracks of the gangs, there to be beaten insensible with steel rods, or forced upon their knees to kiss a hated hooked cross. That is what Germany did to pacifists long before the war began. Out of Germany poured hordes of refugees, "scattered like leaves from an enchanter fleeing pestilence-stricken multitudes." The followers of Hitler laid their hands upon British and American money loaned to Germany to help her rebuild after the last war and with it began grinding out guns and cannons and ships and tanks and airplanes, crying war, crying revenge, crying dominion. Only when others reluctantly turned their hands to the making of hated cannon, did they yell, peace, peace. They stood in armor plate from their heads to their feet, their belts full of hand grenades, their pockets full of bombs, crying across their borders to those who, seeing, took a rifle from the wall: warmonger, warmonger!

He who stood atop this pyramid of steel-clothed men, stretched out his right hand and grabbed a province, and his left, and snatched another. The pyramid grew higher and higher. It made a mountain of blood and steel from the top of which the furious and fanatic one could see all the kingdoms of the earth. How small is the world, he thought. How easy to conquer. Look down upon these rich democracies. They possess most of the earth. Their youth play cricket and baseball and go to movies. Their life is a dull round of buying and selling, of endless discussion in silly parliaments and congresses. They have lost the will to power and domination. They have been scrapping their battleships and arguing against budgets for armaments. And for a quarter of a century in all their schools and colleges they have been preaching to their youth peace, fellowship, reconciliation. And he laughed, a wild laugh of thirsty joy, crying down to the serried rows on rows of uniformed fanatic youth: strike, and the world will be yours!

He looked across at Britain, and was satisfied. Britain was ruled by business men and bureaucrats. They were cautious men. The business men thought in terms of good bargains; the bureaucrats thought in terms of conferences and negotiations. They were decorous and they were old. They were very sure of Britain. Nobody has ever beaten Britain, not for hundreds of years. Britain was safe. The Germans were annoying again. The Germans were perennially annoying. But Britain was not a tight little island. Britain was a world, a good world, a free world. As it had been, so it would remain—world without end. Amen. And so they closed their briefcases and went fishing or shooting on week-ends. Nobody wanted war. War was unthinkable, really.

Yes, but in England there was a man.

Winston Churchill was no longer young. He was in his sixties. Yet, there was something perennially youthful about him, as there is always something youthful about those who have done what they wanted to do, and have been happy. He had had a good life, the best life any man can have: a life of action and a life of intellect. His father was the son of the Duke of Marlborough. His ancestors had served England and fought her wars and led her peace for as far back as one could remember. But he was the younger son of a younger son and therefore and fortunately, poor. What does a young man of spirit do, with quick blood in his veins, no money and a great tradition behind him? He goes to his country's wars. Young Winston was a soldier of fortune, a fighter on two Continents, a war correspondent, his heart mettlesome, his eye keen, living in his times, living in them up to the hilt, preserving every impression on paper, and seeing everything against the colored tapestry of the great history of Britain. O, yes, he was in love with life. He had no complexes and no neuroses. Shakespeare has described his kind. He called them "this happy breed of men!"

And what did he stand for in the history of England? Light and generosity; Home Rule for Ireland; tolerance and equality for the defeated Boers, generosity to the defeated Germans—he was no lover of the Treaty of Versailles; social reform and the rights of labor, as President of the Board of Trade; Imperial preference for the Dominions, for Canada.

He was no ascetic. He loved good food, good wine, pretty and witty women, gifted men, action and pleasure, color and sound. He was the great life-affirmer. Life was not buying and selling; life was not this margin of profit here or that margin of loss there; life was not the accumulation of riches; life itself was riches—the lovely sight of ships—nothing more beautiful than a ship, nothing more English than a ship, the ships of explorers, of traders, of fighters. To be First Lord of the Admiralty was a job for a man who loves ships, and because he loves ships, loves both their harbors and the oceans of the world.

The lovely forms of landscapes! Home from war and out of responsible office, he took himself a palette and colors and began to paint—like you, Mr. Hitler—to paint the world he loved. He loved this world with the catholic appetite of the artist of life. For he was, and is, a soldier, a sailor, an artist and a poet. Is not a man rich if he is born with the English language in his mouth? What a language! A glorious and imperial mongrel, this great synthesis of the Teutonic and the French, the Latin and the Greek, this most hospitable of tongues, this raider of the world's ideas, full of words from the Arabic desert and the Roman forum and the lists of the Crusades. The English language fell from his tongue with that candid simplicity which is its genius, and with that grandeur which is its glory. But people said, "The trouble with Winston is he is too brilliant."

When a man is sixty, and has lived life to the fullest, when he has loved life and treated it gallantly, he has the right to retire, and be quiet, and cultivate his garden among his old friends. That is what civilized men have always done and always will do: "leave action and responsibility now to the young ones." That's what he thought.

Ah, but what was wrong with the young ones? The trained eye cannot be closed. The quick mind moves and thinks even if the body lies upon its back watching the clouds move lazily across an English sky. The poet sees what the commercial trader and the common politician do not. And suddenly the soldier-poet leaps to his feet. Something is about to happen! That which he loves more than food and wine and color and sound and action and rest and his garden; something that he loves more than life—that which is his life: his blood, his soul—that which is ancestry and friendship, family and friends, that which is the future—all the great past, all the stumbling present, all the future, the great future, of a language, of a race, is threatened. There is a cloud creeping over the landscape, the shadow of the growing pyramid grows higher. And the old passion for his greatest love wells up in the man's heart—the passion of his childhood, of his adolescence, of his youth, of his maturity, to which never for an instant was he fickle. For England! For Britain! For the Britain of the English soil and the far-flung Navy! For the Britain of the world language and the world commonwealth. For the Britain with her deathless attachment to law and to freedom.

What is this world, he thinks, if Britain falls? What will become of the ever expanding Commonwealth of Nations and the commonwealth of man?

It is too early to retire and cultivate one's garden. "If I forget thee, oh, Britain," he must have cried to himself, "let my right hand forget its cunning and my tongue cleave to the roof of my mouth."

So he puffed his way back to where the politicians were holding their conferences. Yes, he puffed his way. He was quite portly now, and not so young as he had been. But the tongue in his head was the old, great English tongue, and it had something to say.

Do you know what he said, Mr. Hitler? What Winston Churchill said? You once said something like that, too. You said, "Deutschland Erwache!" Germany Awaken! Churchill said, "England, Awaken!" You don't like Mr. Churchill, Herr Hitler. But you would have liked him, I think, if he had been a German.

But it was very hard to wake up England. Still, everybody listened to him—listened interestedly, admiringly, politely. You can't help listening to that tongue. Month in and month out he said, "Britain Awaken!" Month in and month out, with nothing but one seat in Parliament, and with words, he rediscovered for Britain what Britain in her greatest moments is: the parent of the world citizen; the home of the chivalrous; the defender of the faith. The defender of what faith? Of faith in God and in his common destiny, in his common right to citizenship on this planet.

Not in generations have such words of passionate love and measured indignation fallen from English lips as Churchill uttered in the series of speeches called "While England Slept."

And while he spoke to them, while he spoke mostly to unheeding ears, the shadow was lengthening and finally loomed so tall and menacing that all the world could see. And then, when it was over them with all the full darkness of its horror and destruction, the people of England, the common people of England, lifted Churchill on their hands, crying, "Speak and fight for us!"

It was very, very late, when Churchill took up his last fight for Britain. He inherited an unholy mess. Let us tell the truth. He inherited all that the men of little faith, the money-grubbers, the windy pacifists, the ten-to-five o'clock bureaucrats had left undone. But he said no word against them. He did not do what you, Hitler, have done to your predecessors—hold them up to ridicule and contempt. No word of complaint crossed his lips. He is half a generation older than Hitler, but he took up the fight for the sceptered isle, that precious stone, set in a silver sea; he took up the fight for the world-wide commonwealth of men, held together by the most slender thread of common language and a common way of life—and he fights his last fight, for the ways and the speech of men who have never known a master.

Why don't you take your hat off to Churchill, Mr. Hitler, you who claim to love the leadership principle? Why don't you take your hat off to a member of that race you profess to serve, the race of fair and brave and gallant northern men? By what irony of history have those who oppose you become those very men of the north, the Dutch and the Norwegians, Frenchmen, and those half-German, half-Norman folk who call themselves Britons?

Who is the friend of the white race? You, who have ganged up with Japan to drive the white race out of Asia, or Churchill who believes in the right of white men to live and work wherever they can hold their own on this planet?

You, who have waged war upon the white race, and attempted to divide it into superior white folks and inferior white folks, masters and slaves, or Churchill, who stands for the idea of commonwealth and equality?

Who is the prototype of the white man of the future, the world citizen, Churchill, or the world enemy? What do you hate in Churchill that you would not love in a German man? Do you despise him because he is a soldier, and a writer, and an artist? What has become of your charges of English money-grubbers in the face of this rosy old warrior-artist?

And who today is the plutocrat, who is the have nation, and who is the have-not nation?

The greatest have-not nation in the world today is the British Isles. Forty-two million people on an island assailed from the coasts of violated Norway, from the coasts of violated Holland, from the coasts of violated Belgium, and from defeated France, without resources of food or raw materials except as she can buy them or obtain them from her Allies across the oceans of the world. Does not the heroism of this embattled and impoverished Isle impress you, Hitler, you who praise heroism? Would you have more respect for some lickspittle or some cheap pocket imitation of yourself? Who is the plutocratic nation—Britain, in whose great house live today the children of the London slums, or Nazi Germany, the great *nouveau riche* kidnapper of provinces, collector of ransoms, stuffed with the delicatessen of the Danes and the Czechs and the Dutch, heavy hands spread out upon huge knees, with a gun like a gangster's diamond on every finger!

The plutocratic England you attack is today a socialist state—a socialist state created without class war, created out of love and led by an aristocrat for whom England builds no eagle's nests or palaces out of the taxes of her people, a man who cares nothing for money, or ever has, but only for Britain, and for the coming world that a free and socialist British society will surely help to build if ever it is built.

In your speech this week, Mr. Hitler, you said that it caused you pain to think that you should be chosen by destiny to deal the death blow to the British Empire. It may well cause you pain. This ancient structure, cemented with blood, is an incredibly delicate and exquisite mechanism, held together lightly now, by imponderable elements of credit and prestige, experience and skill, written and unwritten law, codes and habits. This remarkable and artistic thing, the British Empire, part Empire and part Commonwealth, is the only world-wide organization in existence, the world equalizer and equilibriator, the only world-wide stabilizing force for law and order on the planet, and if you bring it down the planet will rock with an earthquake such as it has never known. We in the United States will shake with that earthquake and so will Germany. And the Britons, the Canadians, the New Zealanders, the Australians, the South Africans, are hurling their bodies into the breach to dam the dykes against world chaos.

I think that often in your sleepless nights you realize this, Mr. Hitler, and sweat breaks over you, thinking for a moment, not of a Nazi defeat, but of a Nazi victory.

And the master of the dyke against world chaos is you, Churchill, you gallant, portly little warrior. I do not know what spirits surround Hitler. I do not hear the great harmonics of Beethoven, but only the music of Wagner, the music of chaos. I do not see the ghost of Goethe nor the ghost of Bismarck, the last great German who knew when to stop.

But around you, Winston Churchill, is a gallant company of ghosts. Elizabeth is there, and sweetest Shakespeare, the man who made the English Renaissance the world's renaissance. Drake is there, and Raleigh, and Wellington. Burke is there, and Walpole, and Pitt. Byron is there, and Wordsworth, and Shelley. Yes, and I think Washington is there, and Hamilton, two men of English blood, whom gallant Englishmen defended in your Parliament. And Jefferson is there, who died again, the other day, in France. All the makers of a world of freedom and of law are there, and among them is the Shropshire lad, to whom his ghostly author calls again: "Get ye the men your fathers got, and God will save the Queen."

And when you speak, Churchill, brave men's hearts everywhere rush out to you. There are no neutral hearts, Winston Churchill, except those that have stopped beating. There are no neutral prayers. Our hearts and our prayers say, "God give you strength, God bless you. May you live to cultivate your garden, in a free world, liberated from terror, and persecution, war, and fear."

# War Address[3]

## Franklin Delano Roosevelt

*Born January 30, 1882, Hyde Park, NY; died April 12, 1945; A.B., Harvard University, 1904; state senator, New York State Assembly, 1910-13; assistant secretary of the Navy, 1913-20; governor of New York, 1929-33; president of the United States, 1933-45.*

### Editor's introduction

Following negotiations between President Roosevelt, Secretary of State Cordell Hull, and the Japanese government, Japanese special envoy Sabuso Kurusu traveled to America to continue negotiating Japan's withdrawal from China. During this second round of negotiations, the Japanese naval and air forces attacked the Pearl Harbor military base in Hawaii, and it was generally assumed that discussions with Kurusu were a Japanese ploy to divert the U.S. military's attention from that Japanese attack. Following the surprise attack, President Franklin Delano Roosevelt asked Congress to declare war on Japan. He condemned Japan's offensive and promised "absolute victory." A six-minute ovation followed the address, ceasing only when Roosevelt left the House chamber. War was immediately declared in the Senate by a vote of 82 to 0, and in the House by a vote of 388 to 1.

---

To the Congress of the United States:

Yesterday, December 7, 1941—a date which will live in infamy—the United States of America was suddenly and deliberately attacked by naval and air forces of the Empire of Japan.

The United States was at peace with that nation and, at the solicitation of Japan, was still in conversation with its government and its emperor looking toward the maintenance of peace in the Pacific.

Indeed, one hour after Japanese air squadrons had commenced bombing in Oahu, the Japanese ambassador to the United States and his colleague delivered to the Secretary of State a formal reply to a recent American message.

While this reply stated that it seemed useless to continue the existing diplomatic negotiations, it contained no threat or hint of war or armed attack.

It will be recorded that the distance of Hawaii from Japan makes it obvious that the attack was deliberately planned many days or even weeks ago.

During the intervening time, the Japanese government has deliberately sought to deceive the United States by false statements and expressions of hope for continued peace.

The attack yesterday on the Hawaiian Islands has caused severe damage to American naval and military forces. Very many American lives have been lost.

In addition, American ships have been reported torpedoed on the high seas between San Francisco and Honolulu.

Yesterday the Japanese government also launched an attack against Malaya.

Last night Japanese forces attacked Hong Kong.

Last night Japanese forces attacked Guam.

Last night Japanese forces attacked the Philippine Islands.

Last night the Japanese attacked Wake Island.

This morning the Japanese attacked Midway Island.

Japan has, therefore, undertaken a surprise offensive extending throughout the Pacific area. The facts of yesterday speak for themselves. The people of the United States have already formed their opinions and well understand the implications to the very life and safety of our nation.

As commander in chief of the army and navy I have directed that all measures be taken for our defense.

[3]Delivered to a joint session of Congress, in Washington, D.C., on December 8, 1941.

Always will we remember the character of the onslaught against us.

No matter how long it may take us to overcome this premeditated invasion, the American people in their righteous might will win through to absolute victory.

I believe I interpret the will of the Congress and of the people when I assert that we will not only defend ourselves to the uttermost but will make very certain that this form of treachery shall never endanger us again.

Hostilities exist. There is no blinking at the fact that our people, our territory and our interests are in grave danger.

With confidence in our armed forces—with the unbounding determination of our people—we will gain the inevitable triumph—so help us, God.

I ask that the Congress declare that since the unprovoked and dastardly attack by Japan on Sunday, December 7, a state of war has existed between the United States and the Japanese Empire.

# Orchestrated Hell[4]

Edward R. Murrow

*Born April 25, 1908, Greensboro, NC; died April 27, 1965; B.A., Washington State University, 1930; president, National Student Federation of America, 1930-32; assistant director, Institute of International Education, 1932-35; director, Department of Talks and Special Events, CBS, 1935-37; director, CBS European Bureau, 1937-45; foreign correspondent, CBS, 1947-61; narrator, producer,* See It Now *television series, 1951-58; director, U.S. Information Agency, 1961-63; author,* So This Is London *(1941).*

## Editor's introduction

Considered to have set the standard for the television news industry, Edward R. Murrow gave this gripping broadcast in which he described a Royal Air Force (R.A.F.) bombing of Berlin. This speech is one of the best examples of a firsthand account, as it relates in dramatic yet factual detail an event which the typical civilian would not be privy to. On this particular raid, 41 R.A.F. bombers were shot down, and several reporters, who like Murrow had gone to observe the pilots, never returned.

---

This is London. Yesterday afternoon, the waiting was over; the weather was right; the target was to be the big city. The crew captains walked into the briefing room, looked at the maps and charts and sat down with their big celluloid pads on their knees. The atmosphere was that of a school and a church. The weather man gave us the weather. The pilots were reminded that Berlin is Germany's greatest center of war production. The intelligence officer told us how many heavy and light ack-ack guns, how many searchlights we might expect to encounter. Then, Jock, the Wing Commander, explained the system of markings, the kind of flare that would be used by the Pathfinders. He said that concentration was the secret of success in these raids and as long as the aircraft stayed well bunched, they would protect each other. The Captains of Aircraft walked out.

I noticed that the big Canadian with the slow, easy grin had printed "Berlin" at the top of his pad and then embellished it with a scroll. The red-headed English boy with the two-weeks-old moustache was the last to leave the room. Late in the afternoon, we went to the locker room to draw parachutes, Mae Wests, and all the rest. As we dressed, a couple of the Australians were whistling. Walking out to the bus that was to take us to the aircraft, I heard the station loud-speakers announcing that that evening all personnel would be able to see a film, "Star-Spangled Rhythm" free.

We went out and stood around the big, black, four-motored Lancaster—"D for Dog." A small station wagon delivered a thermos bottle of coffee, chewing gum, an orange and a bit of chocolate for each man. Up in that part of England, the air hums and throbs with the sound of aircraft motors all day. But for half an hour before take-off, the skies are dead, silent, and expectant. A lone hawk hovered over the air field, absolutely still as he faced into the wind. Jack, the tail gunner, said, "It would be nice if we could fly like that." Jock looked at his watch and moved toward the aircraft. Nothing was said. We all followed.

"D for Dog" eased around the perimeter track to the end of the runway. We sat there for a moment. The green light flashed and we were rolling—ten seconds ahead of schedule! The take-off was smooth as silk. The wheels came up and "D for Dog" started the climb. As we came up through the clouds, I looked right and left, and counted fourteen black Lancasters climbing for the place where men must burn oxygen to live. The sun was going down and its

[4]Broadcast over CBS World News radio, from London, England, on December 3, 1943.

red glow made rivers and lakes of fire on tops of the clouds. Down to the southward, the clouds piled up to form castles, battlements, and whole cities—all tinged with red.

Soon we were out over the North Sea. Dave, the navigator, asked Jock if he couldn't make a little more speed. We were nearly two minutes late. By this time, we were all using oxygen. The talk on the inter-com was brief and crisp. Everyone sounded relaxed. For a while, the eight of us in our little world in exile moved over the sea. There was a quarter moon on the starboard beam. Jock's quiet voice came through the inter-com, "That'll be flak ahead." We were approaching the enemy coast. The flak looked like a cigarette lighter in a dark room—one that won't light. Sparks but no flame. The sparks crackling just above the level of the cloud tops. We flew steady and straight, and soon the flak was directly below us.

"D-Dog" rocked a little from right to left but that wasn't caused by the flak. We were in the slip stream of other Lancasters ahead and we were over the enemy coast. And then a strange thing happened. The aircraft seemed to grow smaller. Jack in the rear turret, Wally—the mid-upper gunner, Titch—the wireless operator, all seemed somehow to draw closer to Jock in the cockpit. It was as though each man's shoulder was against the other's. The understanding was complete. The inter-com came to life and Jock said, "Two aircraft on the port beam." Jock in the tail said, "Okay, sir, they're Lancs." The whole crew was a unit and wasn't wasting words.

The cloud below was ten tenths. The blue-green jar of the exhausts licked back along the leading edge, and there were other aircraft all around us. The whole great aerial armada was hurtling towards Berlin. We flew so for twenty minutes, when Jock looked up at a vapor trail curling across above us, remarking in a conversational tone that from the look of it he thought there was a fighter up there. Occasionally the angry red of ack-ack burst through the clouds, but it was far away and we took only an academic interest. We were flying in the third wave, Jock asked Wally in the mid-upper turret, and Jack in the rear turret if they were cold. They said they were all right, and thanked him for asking. Even asked how I was and I said, "All right so far." The cloud was beginning to thin out. Up to the north we could see light, and the flak began to liven up ahead of it.

Boz, the bomb aimer, cracked through on the inter-com, "There's a battle going on on the starboard beam." We couldn't see the aircraft, but we could see the jets of Cod traces being exchanged. Suddenly there was a burst of yellow flame and Jock remarked, "That's a fighter going down—note the position." The whole thing was interesting, but remote. Dave, the navigator, who was sitting back with his maps, charts, and compasses, said, "The attack ought to begin in exactly two minutes." We were still over the clouds. But suddenly those dirty gray clouds turned white. We were over the outer searchlight defenses. The clouds below us were white and we were black. "D-Dog" seemed like a black bug on a white sheet. The flak began coming up, but none of it close. We were still a long way from Berlin. I didn't realize just how far.

Jack observed, "There's a kite on fire dead ahead." It was a great golden slow-moving meteor slanting towards the earth. By this time we were about thirty miles from our target area in Berlin. That thirty miles was the longest flight I have ever made. Dead on time, Boz, the bomb aimer, reported, "Target indicators going down." At the same moment the sky ahead was lit up by bright yellow flares. Off to starboard, another kite went down in flames. The flares were spouting all over the sky—red and green and yellow—and we were flying straight for the center of the fireworks. "D-Dog" seemed to be standing still, the four propellers thrashing the air. But we didn't seem to be closing in. The clouds had cleared, and off to the starboard a Lanc was caught by at least fourteen searchlight beams. We could see him twist and turn and finally break out. But still the whole thing had a quality of unreality about it. No one seemed to be shooting at us, but it was getting lighter all the time. Suddenly, a tremendous big blob of yellow light appeared dead ahead, another to the right, and another to the left. We were flying straight for them.

Jock pointed out to me the dummy fires and flares to the right and left. But we kept going in. Dead ahead there was a whole chain of red flares looking like stop lights. Another Lanc was coned on our starboard beam. The lights seemed to be supporting it. Again we could see those little bubbles of colored lead driving at it from two sides. The German fighters were at him. And then with no warning at all, "D-Dog" was filled with an unhealthy white light. I was standing just behind Jock and could see all the seams on the wings. His quiet Scots voice beat into my ears. "Steady, lads, we've been coned." His slender body lifted half out of his seat as he jammed the control column forward and to the left. We were going down.

Jock was wearing woolen gloves with the fingers cut off. I could see his fingernails turn white as he gripped the wheel. And then I was on my knees, flat on the deck, for he had whipped the "Dog" back into a climbing turn. The knees should have been strong enough to support me but they weren't and the stomach seemed in some danger of letting me down, too. I picked myself up and looked out again. It seemed that one big searchlight, instead of being 20,000 feet below, was mounted right on our wing tip. "D-Dog" was corkscrewing. As we rolled down on the other side, I began to see what was happening to Berlin.

The clouds were gone, and the sticks of incendiaries from the preceding waves made the place look like a badly laid out city with the street lights on. The small incendiaries were going down like a fistful of white rice thrown on a piece of black velvet. As Jock hauled the "Dog" up again, I was thrown to the other side of the cockpit and there below were more incendiaries, glowing white and then turning red. The cookies—the 4,000-pound high explosives—were bursting below like great sunflowers gone mad. And then, as we started down again, still held in the lights, I remembered that the "Dog" still had one of those cookies and a whole basket of incendiaries in his belly and the lights still held us. And I was frightened.

While Jock was flinging her about in the air, he suddenly flung over the inter-com, "Two aircraft on the port beam." I looked astern, and saw Wally, the mid-upper, whip his turret around to port, and then look up to see a single-engined fighter slide just above us. The other aircraft was one of ours. Finally, we were out of the cone, flying level. I looked down on the white fires, the white fires had turned red. They were beginning to merge and spread, just like butter does on a hot plate. Jock and Boz, the bomb aimer, began to discuss the target. The smoke was getting thick down below. Boz said he liked the two green flares on the ground almost dead ahead. He began calling his directions. And just then, a new bunch of big flares went down on the far side of the sea of flame and flare that seemed to be directly below us. He thought that would be a better aiming point. Jock agreed and we flew on. The bomb doors were open. Boz called his directions, "Five left, five left" and then there was a gentle, confident, upward thrust under my feet and Boz said, "Cookie gone." A few seconds later, the incendiaries went and "D-Dog" seemed lighter and easier to handle.

I thought I could make out the outline of streets below. But the bomb aimer didn't agree, and he ought to know. By this time, all those patches of white on black had turned yellow, and started to flow together. Another searchlight caught us but didn't hold us. Then through the inter-com came the word, "One can of incendiaries didn't clear; we're still carrying it." And Jock replied, "Is it a big one or a little one?" The word came back, "Little one, I think, but I'm not sure, I'll check." More of those yellow flares came down and hung about us. I haven't seen so much light since the war began. Finally, the inter-com announced that it was only a small container of incendiaries left, and Jock remarked, "Well, it's hardly worth going back and doing another run-up for that." If there had been a good fat bundle left, he would have gone back through the stuff and done it all over again.

I began to breathe and to reflect again—that all men would be brave if only they could leave their stomachs at home. Then there was a tremendous whoomp, an unintelligible shout from the tail gunner and "D-Dog" shivered and lost altitude. I looked at the port side and there was a Lancaster that seemed close enough to touch. It whipped straight under us, missed us by twenty-five, fifty feet, no one knew how much. The navigator sang out the new course and we were heading for home. Jock was doing what I had heard him tell his pilots to do so often—flying dead on course. He flew straight into a huge green searchlight, and as he rammed the throttles home, remarked, "We'll have a little trouble getting away from this one." And again, "D-Dog" dove, climbed and twisted and was finally free. We flew level then. I looked at the port beam, at the target area. There was a red, sullen, obscene glare. The fires seemed to have found each other—and we were heading home.

In a little more than half an hour, Berlin had received about three times the weight of bombs that had ever fallen on London in the course of a long winter night. For a little while, it was smooth sailing. We saw more battles. Then another plane in flames. But no one could tell whether it was ours or theirs. We were still near the target. Dave, the navigator, said, "Hold her steady, skipper, I want to get an astral site." And Jock held her steady. And the flak began coming up at us. It seemed to be very close. It was winking off both wings. But the "Dog" was steady. Finally, Dave said "Okay, skipper, thank you very much." And a great orange blob of flak smacked up straight in front of us. And Jock said, "I think they're shooting at us." I'd thought so for some time.

And he began to throw "D for Dog" up, around, and about again. And when we were clear of the barrage, I asked him how close the bursts were and he said, "Not very close. When they're really near, you can smell 'em." That proved nothing, for I'd been holding my breath. Jack sang out from the rear turret, said his oxygen was getting low, thought maybe the lead had frozen. Titch, the wireless operator, went scrambling back with a new mask and a bottle of oxygen. Dave, the navigator, said, "We're crossing the coast." My mind went back to the time I had crossed that coast in 1938, in a plane that had taken off from Prague. Just ahead of me sat two refugees from Vienna—an old man and his wife. The co-pilot came back and told them that we were outside German territory. The old man reached out and grasped his wife's hand.

The work that was done last night was a massive blow of retribution for all those who have fled from the sound of shots and blows on a stricken continent.

We began to lose height over the North Sea. We were over England's shore. The land was dark beneath us. Somewhere down there below, American boys were probably bombing-up Fortresses and Liberators, getting ready for the day's work. We were over the home field. We called the control tower and the calm clear voice of an English girl replied, "Greeting 'D-Dog'. You are diverted to Mule Bag." We swung round, contacted Mule Bag [code for an airfield], came in on the flare path, touched down very gently, ran along to the end of the runway and turned left. And Jock, the finest pilot in Bomber Command, said to the control tower, "D-Dog clear of runway."

When we went in for interrogation, I looked on the board and saw that the big slow-smiling Canadian and the red-headed English boy with the two-weeks-old moustache hadn't made it. They were missing. There were two reporter friends of mine on this operation who didn't come back either—Norman Stockton of Australian Associated Newspapers, and Lowell Bennett, an American representing International News Service. There is something of a tradition amongst reporters that those who are prevented by circumstances from filing their stories will be covered by their colleagues. This has been my effort to do so.

In the aircraft in which I flew, the men who flew and fought it, poured into my ears their comments on fighters, flak and flares in the same tone that they would have used in reporting a host of daffodils. I have no doubt that Bennett and Stockton would have given you a better report of last night's activities.

Berlin was a kind of orchestrated hell, a terrible symphony of light and flame. It isn't a pleasant kind of warfare—the men doing it speak of it as a job. Yesterday afternoon, when the tapes were stretched out on the big map all the way to Berlin and back again, a young pilot with old eyes said to me, "I see we're working again tonight." That's the frame of mind in which the job is being done. The job isn't pleasant; it's terribly tiring. Men die in the sky while others are roasted alive in their cellars. Berlin last night wasn't a pretty sight. In about thirty-five minutes, it was hit with about three times the amount of stuff that ever came down on London in a night-long blitz. This is a calculated, remorseless campaign of destruction. Right now, the mechanics are probably working on "D-Dog" getting him ready to fly again. I return you now to C.B.S., New York.

# National Emergency[5]

Harry S. Truman

*Born May 8, 1884, Lamar, MO; died December 26, 1972; farmer, 1901-13; National Guard, 1905-11; U.S. Army, 1918-19; proprietor, haberdashery shop, 1919-21; judge, Jackson County Court, 1922-24, 1927-35; senator (D) from Missouri, 1934-45; vice president of the United States, 1945; president of the United States, 1945-53.*

## Editor's introduction

As Chinese and North Korean armies threatened to push the United Nations forces into the Yellow Sea, President Harry S. Truman delivered this speech in which he defined for the American public what the nation must do to stop the further spread of Communism. The next day Truman declared a state of emergency, and what has become known as the Korean War began.

---

I am talking to you tonight about what our country is up against, and what we are going to do about it.

Our homes, our nation, all the things we believe in are in great danger. This danger has been created by the rulers of the Soviet Union.

For five years we have been working for peace and justice among nations. We have helped to bring the free nations of the world together in a great movement to establish a lasting peace.

Against this movement for peace, the rulers of the Soviet Union have been waging a relentless attack. They have tried to undermine or overwhelm the free nations, one by one. They have used threats and treachery and violence.

In June, the forces of Communist imperialism broke out into open warfare in Korea. The United Nations moved to put down this act of aggression, and, by October, had all but succeeded.

Then in November, the Communists threw their Chinese armies into the battle against the free nations.

By this act, they have shown that they are now willing to push the world to the brink of a general war to get what they want. This is the real meaning of the events that have been taking place in Korea.

That is why we are in such grave danger. The future of civilization depends on what we do—on what we do now, and in the months ahead.

We have the strength and we have the courage to overcome the danger that threatens our country. We must act calmly, wisely and resolutely.

Here are the things we will do:

First, we will continue to uphold, and if necessary to defend with arms, the principles of the United Nations, the principles of freedom and justice.

Second, we will continue to work with the other free nations to strengthen our combined defenses.

Third, we will build up our own army, navy and air force and make more weapons for ourselves and our allies.

Fourth, we will expand our economy and keep it on an even keel.

Now, I want to talk to you about each one of these things.

First, we will continue to uphold the principles of the United Nations. We have no aggressive purpose. We will not use our strength for aggression. We are a tolerant and a restrained people, deeply aware of our moral responsibilities and deeply aware of the horrors of war.

We believe in settling differences by peaceful means, and we have made honest efforts to bring about disarmament. We will continue those efforts, but we cannot yield to aggression.

[5]Broadcast nationwide, from Washington, D.C., on December 15, 1950.

Though the present situation is highly dangerous, we do not believe that war is inevitable. There is no conflict between the legitimate interests of the free world and those of the Soviet Union that cannot be settled by peaceful means. We will continue to take every honorable step we can to avoid general war.

But we will not engage in appeasement. The world learned from Munich that security cannot be bought by appeasement.

We are ready, as we have always been, to take part in efforts to reach a peaceful solution of the conflict in Korea. In fact, our representatives at Lake Success are taking part in just such efforts today.

We do not yet know whether the Chinese Communists are willing to enter into honest negotiations to settle the conflict in Korea. If negotiations are possible, we shall strive for a settlement that will make Korea a united, independent and democratic country. That is what the Korean people want, and that is what the United Nations has decided they are entitled to have.

Meanwhile our troops in Korea are continuing to do their best to uphold the United Nations. General [J. Lawton] Collins, Chief of Staff of the Army, who returned a few days ago from Korea, reported that our military forces there are well organized and well equipped. I am confident that our military forces, together with their comrades in arms from many nations, will continue to give a good account of themselves. They know they are fighting for the freedom and security of their own homes and families.

The danger we face exists not only in Korea. Therefore, the second thing we are going to do is to increase our efforts, with other free nations, to build up defenses against aggression on other parts of the world. In dealing with the Korean crisis, we are not going to ignore the danger of aggression elsewhere.

There is actual warfare in the Far East, but Europe and the rest of the world are also in great danger. The same menace—the menace of Communist aggression—threatens Europe as well as Asia.

To combat this menace, other free nations need our help, and we need theirs. We must work with a sense of real partnership and common purpose with these nations. We must stand firm with our allies, who have shown their courage and their love of freedom.

The United States, Canada and the ten nations of Western Europe who are united with us in the North Atlantic Treaty, have already begun to create combined military defenses. Secretary of State [Dean] Acheson is flying to Europe on Sunday. He and representatives of these nations will complete the arrangements for setting up a joint army, navy and air force to defend Europe. The defense of Europe is of the utmost importance to the security of the United States.

We will continue to provide assistance to European countries, and to other free countries in other parts of the world, because their defense is also important to our own defense.

The Communist rulers are trying their hardest to split the free nations apart. If they should succeed, they would do staggering damage to the cause of freedom. Unity with our allies is now, and must continue to be, the foundation of our effort.

Working together, the free nations can create military forces strong enough to convince the Communist rulers that they cannot gain by aggression.

Working together, the free nations can present the common front, backed by strength, which is necessary if we are to be in a position to negotiate successfully with the Kremlin for peaceful settlements. Working together, we hope we can prevent another world war. In order to succeed, we in our country have a big job ahead of us.

That is why the third thing we must do to meet the present danger is to step up our own defense program. We are expanding our armed forces very rapidly. We are speeding up the production of military equipment for our own armed forces and for our allies.

We have a large navy. We have a powerful air force. We have units around which a strong army can be built. But measured against the danger that confronts us, our forces are not adequate.

On June 25, when the Communists invaded the Republic of Korea, we had less than 1.5 million men and women in our army, navy and air force.

Today, our military strength has reached about 2.5 million. Our next step is to increase the number of men and women on active duty to nearly 3.5 million.

I have directed the armed forces to accomplish this as soon as possible. The army and the navy will be able to do this within a few months. It will take the air force somewhat longer. In addition to these men and women on active duty, we have about two million more in the National Guard and the Reserves who are subject to call.

As part of the process of achieving a speedier build-up, the number of men to be called up under the Selective Service System has been raised, and two additional National Guard divisions are being ordered to active duty in January.

At the same time we will have a very rapid speed-up in the production of military equipment. Within one year we will be turning out planes at five times the present rate of production. Within one year combat vehicles will be coming off the production line at four times today's rate. Within one year the rate of production of electronics equipment for defense will have multiplied four and a half times.

These will not be weapons for our own armed forces alone. They will constitute an arsenal for the defense of freedom. Out of this arsenal we will be able to send weapons to other free nations to add to what they can produce for their own defenses. And in this same arsenal we will provide a large reserve of weapons to equip additional units in our own armed forces whenever that may be necessary.

Furthermore, while we are working toward these immediate goals in manpower and equipment, we will also expand our training and production facilities so as to make possible a very rapid expansion to full mobilization if that becomes necessary.

We can handle this production program, but it will require hard work. It will require us to make a lot of changes in our ordinary ways of doing things.

And this brings me to our fourth big job. In order to build the military strength we need, we will have to expand our production greatly. We must also prevent inflation, and stabilize the cost of living.

If we are to make the weapons we need soon enough, we shall have to cut back on many lines of civilian production. But we can not build up and maintain our armed might, and the industrial strength underlying it, simply by cutting back civilian production. We must produce more—more steel, more copper, more aluminum, more electric power, more cotton, more of many other things.

We must set very high targets and be willing to make an all-out effort to reach them. Workers will be called upon to work more hours. More women, and more young people and older workers will be needed in our plants and factories. Farmers will have to set higher production goals. Business men will have to put all their know-how to work to increase production.

A defense effort of the size we must now undertake will inevitably push prices up, unless we take positive action to hold them down.

We have already taken a number of steps. We have put restrictions on credit buying. We have increased taxes. I hope that the Congress will enact an excess-profits tax at this session. Still further taxes will be needed.

We can not escape paying the cost of our military program. The more we pay by taxes now, the better we can hold prices down. I have directed that recommendations be prepared, for early submission to the Congress, to put the increased cost of defense as nearly as possible on a "pay-as-you-go" basis.

I have also instructed the Director of the Budget to reduce the nonmilitary expenditures in the new federal budget to the minimum required to give effective support to the defense effort.

The measures I have just mentioned—credit control, higher taxes and reduced nonmilitary expenditures—are essential. They are our primary defense against inflation, because they strike at the sources of inflation. But as we move into a greatly increased defense effort, we must also take direct measures to keep prices in line.

The government is starting at once to impose price controls upon a number of materials and products. These will be mainly items important to defense production and the cost of living.

In those fields where price control is imposed, the government will also undertake to stabilize wages, as the law requires.

In the immediate future, a series of control orders will be announced by the Economic Stabilization Agency.

In addition, the agency will announce fair standards for prices and wages in those cases where mandatory controls are not imposed. I ask everyone concerned not to set prices and wages higher than these standards will allow. If these standards are violated, it will speed-up the imposition of mandatory controls, including roll-backs where needed.

As we move ahead with this mobilization effort, there will be increased need for central control over the many government activities in this field. Accordingly, I am establishing an Office of Defense Mobilization. I am appointing Mr. Charles E. Wilson to be director of this office. Mr. Wilson is resigning as president of the General Electric Company to take this job.

In his new position, he will be responsible for directing all the mobilization activities of the government, including production, procurement, manpower, transportation and economic stabilization.

The government is also moving forward with preparations for civil defense. I have appointed former Governor Millard Caldwell of Florida to be Federal Civilian Defense Administrator.

In addition, I have recommended legislation to the Congress which will authorize the Federal Government to help states and cities in their civil defense preparations. I hope the Congress will enact this legislation soon, so that the civil defense work which has already started can be greatly speeded up.

These are our plans for making our country stronger.

As we go forward, we must keep clearly in mind the meaning of what we are doing. Our freedom is in danger. Sometimes we may forget just what freedom means to us. It is as close to us, as important to us, as the air we breathe. Freedom is in our homes, in our schools, in our churches. It is in our work and our government and the right to vote as we please. Those are the things that would be taken from us if communism should win.

Because our freedom is in danger we are united in its defense. Let no aggressor think we are divided. Our great strength is the loyalty and fellowship of a free people. We pull together when we are in trouble, and we do it by our own choice, not out of fear, but out of love for the great values of our American life, that we all have a share in.

In this great defense effort that we are undertaking, things may not always go as smoothly as we would wish, either in Washington or in your home town. But remember that we are building our defenses in the democratic way and not by the iron rule of dictatorship.

Those of us who work in the government will do our best. But the outcome depends, as it has always depended, on the spirit and energy of our people. The job of building a stronger America must be done on our farms, in our factories and in our homes. It must be done by every one of us, wherever we are, and whatever our jobs may be.

Our fighting men in Korea have set an example that should inspire us all. Attacked by superior numbers, and in the bitterest of winter weather, they were resolute, steady and determined. Their steadfast courage in the face of reverses is one of the most heroic stories in our country's history.

In the days ahead, each of us should measure his own efforts, his own sacrifices, by the standard of our heroic men in Korea.

Many of you who are young people will serve in the armed forces of your country. Nothing you will do later in life will be of greater benefit to your homes, your communities, or your friends.

Many others of you will have to work longer hours in factories or mines or mills. Think of this not as longer hours, but as more planes, more tanks, more ships, more of all the things that are needed for the defense of your homes and your way of life.

All of us will have to pay more taxes and do without things we like. Think of this, not as a sacrifice, but as an opportunity, an opportunity to defend the best kind of life that men have ever devised on this earth.

As I speak to you tonight, aggression has won a military advantage in Korea. We should not try to hide or explain away that fact.

By the same token, we should draw renewed courage and faith from the response of the free world to that aggression.

# American Policy in the Pacific[6]

## Douglas MacArthur

*Born January 26, 1880, Little Rock, AR; died April 5, 1964; graduate, U.S. Military Academy, 1903; 2nd lieutenant, Philippines and Japan, 1903-6; aide, President Theodore Roosevelt, 1906-7; chief of staff, 42nd Rainbow Division, 1918; superintendent, U.S. Military Academy, 1919-22; chief of general staff, 1930; military advisor, Commonwealth Government of Philippines, 1935; field marshall, Philippine Army, 1936-37; retired, 1937-41; supreme Allied commander, 1941-51; commander, occupational forces in Japan, 1945-51; commander, U.N. forces in Korea, 1950-51.*

### Editor's introduction

Having driven the North Korean forces over the 38th parallel, President Truman granted General Douglas MacArthur permission to continue the offensive and push the North Koreans back to the Chinese border. MacArthur's advance provoked the Chinese army, who responded with a counter-offensive which pushed the U.N. forces back across the 38th parallel. After fighting back up to the 38th parallel, MacArthur asked Truman for permission to bomb Chinese bases in Manchuria. Truman denied such permission, and MacArthur began to publicly criticize U.S. policy in Korea. In response, Truman, upon the recommendation of the Joint Chiefs of Staff, revoked MacArthur's command on April 11, 1951. One week later, MacArthur, now 71, addressed a joint session of Congress and, via broadcast, the American people. In his speech, MacArthur provided a philosophical and historical overview of Asia's recent history, as well as a very personal and emotional defense of his own career. The millions who watched and listened were undoubtedly moved by MacArthur's dramatic movements and rhythmic, emotion-filled voice.

---

Mr. President, Mr. Speaker, distinguished Members of the Congress, I stand on this rostrum with a sense of deep humility and great pride; humility in the wake of those great American architects of our history who have stood here before me; pride in the reflection that this forum of legislative debate represents human liberty in the purest form yet devised.

Here are centered the hopes, and aspirations, and faith of the entire human race.

I do not stand here as advocate for any partisan cause, for the issues are fundamental and reach quite beyond the realm of partisan consideration. They must be resolved on the highest plane of national interest if our course is to prove sound and our future protected. I trust, therefore, that you will do me the justice of receiving that which I have to say as solely expressing the considered viewpoint of a fellow American. I address you with neither rancor nor bitterness in the fading twilight of life with but one purpose in mind, to serve my country.

The issues are global and so interlocked that to consider the problems of one sector oblivious to those of another is but to court disaster for the whole.

While Asia is commonly referred to as the gateway to Europe, it is no less true that Europe is the gateway to Asia, and the broad influence of the one cannot fail to have its impact upon the other.

There are those who claim our strength is inadequate to protect on both fronts, that we cannot divide our effort. I can think of no greater expression of defeatism. If a potential enemy can divide his strength on two fronts, it is for us to counter his effort.

The Communist threat is a global one. Its successful advance in one sector threatens the destruction of every other sector. You cannot appease or otherwise surrender to communism

[6]Delivered to a joint session of Congress and broadcast nationwide, from Washington, D.C., on April 19, 1951.

in Asia without simultaneously undermining our efforts to halt its advance in Europe.

Beyond pointing out these general truisms, I shall confine my discussion to the general areas of Asia. Before one may objectively assess the situation now existing there, he must comprehend something of Asia's past and the revolutionary changes which have marked her course up to the present. Long exploited by the so-called colonial powers, with little opportunity to achieve any degree of social justice, individual dignity, or a higher standard of life such as guided our own noble administration of the Philippines, the peoples of Asia found their opportunity in the war just past to throw off the shackles of colonialism and now see the dawn of new opportunity and heretofore unfelt dignity and the self-respect of political freedom.

Mustering half of the earth's population and 60 per cent of its natural resources, these peoples are rapidly consolidating a new force, both moral and material, with which to raise the living standard and erect adaptations of the design of modern progress to their own distinct cultural environments. Whether one adheres to the concept of colonization or not, this is the direction of Asian progress and it may not be stopped. It is a corollary to the shift of the world economic frontiers, as the whole epicenter of world affairs rotates back toward the area whence it started. In this situation it becomes vital that our own country orient its policies in consonance with this basic evolutionary condition rather than pursue a course blind to the reality that the colonial era is now past and the Asian peoples covet the right to shape their own free destiny. What they seek now is friendly guidance, understanding, and support, not imperious direction; the dignity of equality, not the shame of subjugation. Their prewar standard of life, pitifully low, is infinitely lower now in the devastation left in war's wake. World ideologies play little part in Asian thinking and are little understood. What the peoples strive for is the opportunity for a little more food in their stomachs, a little better clothing on their backs, a little firmer roof over their heads, and the realization of a normal nationalist urge for political freedom. These political-social conditions have but an indirect bearing upon our own national security, but do form a backdrop to contemporary planning which must be thoughtfully considered if we are to avoid the pitfalls of unrealism.

Of more direct and immediate bearing upon our national security are the changes wrought in the strategic potential of the Pacific Ocean in the course of the past war. Prior thereto, the western strategic frontier of the United States lay on the littoral line of the Americas with an exposed island salient extending out through Hawaii, Midway, and Guam to the Philippines. That salient proved not an outpost of strength but an avenue of weakness along which the enemy could and did attack. The Pacific was a potential area of advance for any predatory force intent upon striking at the bordering land areas.

All this was changed by our Pacific victory. Our strategic frontier then shifted to embrace the entire Pacific Ocean which became a vast moat to protect us as long as we held it. Indeed, it acts as a protective shield for all of the Americas and all free lands of the Pacific Ocean area. We control it to the shores of Asia by a chain of islands extending in an arc from the Aleutians to the Marianas held by us and our free allies.

From this island chain we can dominate with sea and air power every Asiatic port from Vladivostok to Singapore and prevent any hostile movement into the Pacific. Any predatory attack from Asia must be an amphibious effort. No amphibious force can be successful without control of the sea lanes and the air over those lanes in its avenue of advance. With naval and air supremacy and modest ground elements to defend bases, any major attack from continental Asia toward us or our friends of the Pacific would be doomed to failure. Under such conditions the Pacific no longer represents menacing avenues of approach for a prospective invader—it assumes instead the friendly aspect of a peaceful lake. Our line of defense is a natural one and can be maintained with a minimum of military effort and expense. It envisions no attack against anyone nor does it provide the bastions essential for offensive operations, but properly maintained would be an invincible defense against aggression.

The holding of this littoral defense line in the western Pacific is entirely dependent upon holding all segments thereof, for any major breach of that line by an unfriendly power would render vulnerable to determined attack every other major segment. This is a military estimate as to which I have yet to find a military leader who will take exception.

For that reason I have strongly recommended in the past as a matter of military urgency that under no circumstances must Formosa fall under Communist control.

Such an eventuality would at once threaten the freedom of the Philippines and the loss of Japan, and might well force our western frontier back to the coasts of California, Oregon, and Washington.

To understand the changes which now appear upon the Chinese mainland, one must understand the changes in Chinese character and culture over the past fifty years. China up to fifty years ago was completely nonhomogeneous, being compartmented into groups divided against each other. The war-making tendency was almost nonexistent, as they still followed the tenets of the Confucian ideal of pacifist culture. At the turn of the century, under the regime of Chan So Lin, efforts toward greater homogeneity produced the start of a nationalist urge. This was further and more successfully developed under the leadership of Chiang Kai-shek, but has been brought to its greatest fruition under the present regime, to the point that it has now taken on the character of a united nationalism of increasingly dominant aggressive tendencies. Through these past fifty years, the Chinese people have thus become militarized in their concepts and in their ideals. They now constitute excellent soldiers with competent staffs and commanders. This has produced a new and dominant power in Asia which for its own purposes is allied with Soviet Russia, but which in its own concepts and methods has become aggressively imperialistic with a lust for expansion and increased power normal to this type of imperialism. There is little of the ideological concept either one way or another in the Chinese make-up. The standard of living is so low and the capital accumulation has been so thoroughly dissipated by war that the masses are desperate and avid to follow any leadership which seems to promise the alleviation of local stringencies. I have from the beginning believed that the Chinese Communists' support of the North Koreans was the dominant one. Their interests are at present parallel to those of the Soviet, but I believe that the aggressiveness recently displayed not only in Korea, but also in Indochina and Tibet and pointing potentially toward the south, reflects predominantly the same lust for the expansion of power which has animated every would-be conqueror since the beginning of time.

The Japanese people since the war have undergone the greatest reformation recorded in modern history. With a commendable will, eagerness to learn, and marked capacity to understand, they have, from the ashes left in wars' wake, erected in Japan an edifice dedicated to the primacy of individual liberty and personal dignity, and in the ensuing process there has been created a truly representative government, committed to the advance of political morality, freedom of economic enterprise and social justice. Politically, economically, and socially Japan is now abreast of many free nations of the earth and will not again fail the universal trust. That it may be counted upon to wield a profoundly beneficial influence over the course of events in Asia is attested by the magnificent manner in which the Japanese people have met the recent challenge of war, unrest, and confusion surrounding them from the outside, and checked communism within their own frontiers without the slightest slackening in their forward progress. I sent all four of our occupation divisions to the Korean battle front without the slightest qualms as to the effect of the resulting power vacuum upon Japan. The results fully justified my faith. I know of no nation more serene, orderly, and industrious—nor in which higher hopes can be entertained for future constructive service in the advance of the human race.

Of our former wards, the Philippines, we can look forward in confidence that the existing unrest will be corrected and a strong and healthy nation will grow in the longer aftermath of war's terrible destructiveness. We must be patient and understanding and never fail them, as in our hour of need they did not fail us. A Christian nation, the Philippines stand as a mighty bulwark of Christianity in the Far East, and its capacity for high moral leadership in Asia is unlimited.

On Formosa, the Government of the Republic of China has had the opportunity to refute by action much of the malicious gossip which so undermined the strength of its leadership on the Chinese mainland.

The Formosan people are receiving a just and enlightened administration with majority representation on the organs of government; and politically, economically, and socially appear to be advancing along sound and constructive lines.

With this brief insight into the surrounding areas I now turn to the Korean conflict. While I was not consulted prior to the President's decision to intervene in the support of the Republic of Korea, that decision from a military standpoint proved a sound one. As I say, a brief and sound one as we hurled back the invaders and decimated his forces. Our victory was complete and our objectives within reach when Red China intervened with numerically superior ground forces. This created a new war and an entirely new situation, a situation not contemplated when our forces were committed against the North Korean invaders, a situation which called for new decisions in the diplomatic sphere to permit the realistic adjustment of military strategy. Such decisions have not been forthcoming.

While no man in his right mind would advocate sending our ground forces into continental China—and such was never given a thought—the new situation did urgently demand a drastic revision of strategic planning if our political aim was to defeat this new enemy as we had defeated the old.

Apart from the military need as I saw it to neutralize sanctuary, protection given to the enemy north of the Yalu, I felt that military necessity in the conduct of the war made necessary:

First, the intensification of our economic blockade against China.

Second, the imposition of a naval blockade against the China coast.

Third, removal of restrictions on air reconnaissance of China's coastal areas and of Manchuria.

Fourth, removal of restrictions on the forces of the Republic of China on Formosa with logistical support to contribute to their effective operation against the Chinese mainland.

For entertaining these views all professionally designed to support our forces committed to Korea and bring hostilities to an end with the least possible delay and at a saving of countless American and Allied lives, I have been severely criticized in lay circles, principally abroad, despite my understanding that from a military standpoint the above views have been fully shared in past by practically every military leader concerned with the Korean campaign, including our own Joint Chief of Staff.

I called for reinforcements, but was informed that reinforcements were not available. I made clear that if not permitted to utilize the friendly Chinese force of some 600,000 men on Formosa; if not permitted to blockade the China coast to prevent the Chinese Reds from getting succor from without; and if there were to be no hope of major reinforcements, the position of the command from the military standpoint forbade victory. We could hold in Korea by constant maneuver and at an approximate area where our supply line advantages were in balance with the supply line disadvantages of the enemy, but we could hope at best for only an indecisive campaign, with its terrible and constant attrition upon our forces if the enemy utilized his full military potential. I have constantly called for the new political decisions essential to a solution. Efforts have been made to distort my position. It has been said in effect that I was a warmonger. Nothing could be further from the truth. I know war as few other men now living know it, and nothing to me is more revolting. I have long advocated its complete abolition as its very destructiveness on both friend and foe has rendered it useless as a means of settling international disputes. Indeed, on the 2d of September 1945, just following the surrender of the Japanese nation on the battleship *Missouri*, I formally cautioned as follows:

"Men since the beginning of time have sought peace. Various methods through the ages have been attempted to devise an international process to prevent or settle disputes between nations. From the very start, workable methods were found insofar as individual citizens were concerned, but the mechanics of an instrumentality of larger international scope have never been successful. Military alliances, balances of power, leagues of nations, all in turn failed, leaving the only path to be by way of the crucible of war. The utter destructiveness of war now blots out this alternative. We have had our last chance. If we will not devise some greater and more equitable system, Armageddon will be at our door. The problem basically is theological and involves a spiritual recrudescence and improvement of human character that will synchronize with our almost matchless advances in science, art, literature, and all material and cultural developments of the past two thousand years. It must be of the spirit if we are to save the flesh."

But once war is forced upon us, there is no other alternative than to apply every available means to bring it to a swift end. War's very object is victory—not prolonged indecision. In war, indeed, there can be no substitute for victory.

There are some who for varying reasons would appease Red China. They are blind to history's clear lesson. For history teaches with unmistakable emphasis that appeasement but begets new and bloodier war. It points to no single instance where the end has justified that means—where appeasement has led to more than a sham peace. Like blackmail, it lays the basis for new and successively greater demands, until, as in blackmail, violence becomes the only other alternative. Why, my soldiers asked of me, surrender military advantages to an enemy in the field? I could not answer. Some may say to avoid spread of the conflict into an all-out war with China; others, to avoid Soviet intervention. Neither explanation seems valid. For China is already engaging with the maximum power it can commit and the Soviet will not necessarily mesh its actions with our moves. Like a cobra, any new enemy will more likely strike whenever it feels that the relativity in military or other potential is in its favor on a world-wide basis.

The tragedy of Korea is further heightened by the fact that as military action is confined to its territorial limits, it condemns that nation, which it is our purpose to save, to suffer the devastating impact of full naval and air bombardment, while the enemy's sanctuaries are fully protected from such attack and devastation. Of the nations of the world, Korea alone, up to now, is the sole one which has risked its all against communism. The magnificence of the courage and fortitude of the Korean people defies description. They have chosen to risk death rather than slavery. Their last words to me were "Don't scuttle the Pacific."

I have just left your fighting sons in Korea. They have met all tests there and I can report to you without reservation they are splendid in every way. It was my constant effort to preserve them and end this savage conflict honorably and with the least loss of time and a minimum sacrifice of life. Its growing bloodshed has caused me the deepest anguish and anxiety. Those gallant men will remain often in my thoughts and in my prayers always.

I am closing my fifty-two years of military service. When I joined the Army even before the turn of the century, it was the fulfillment of all my boyish hopes and dreams. The world has turned over many times since I took the oath on the plain at West Point, and the hopes and dreams have long since vanished. But I still remember the refrain of one of the most popular barrack ballads of that day which proclaimed most proudly that "Old soldiers never die; they just fade away." And like the old soldier of that ballad, I now close my military career and just fade away—an old soldier who tried to do his duty as God gave him the light to see that duty.

Good-by.

# The Korean Armistice[7]

Dwight D. Eisenhower

*Born October 14, 1890, Denison, TX; died March 28, 1969; graduate, U.S. Military Academy, 1915; commanding officer, Camp Colt tank corps, 1917-19; assistant executive, office of the assistant secretary of war, 1929-33; aide, General Douglas MacArthur, 1935-40; chief of staff, Third Army, 1941; chief of operations, U.S. Army, 1942; commander, European theater of operations, 1942-45; chief of staff, U.S. Army, 1945-48; president, Columbia University, 1948-52; supreme Allied commander, Europe, 1950-52; president of the United States, 1953-61; author,* Crusade in Europe *(1948),* Mandate for Change *(1963),* Waging Peace *(1965),* At Ease *(1967),* In Review, Pictures I've Kept *(1969).*

## Editor's introduction

Approximately one hour after a truce was signed in Panmunjom, South Korea, President Dwight D. Eisenhower gave this address to inform Americans that peace in Korea had in fact been achieved. Such peace was reached only after Eisenhower threatened to use nuclear weapons. During the three-year war, an estimated 54,000 American soldiers were killed in combat, and over 103,000 were injured. Chinese and North Korean casualties were at least 10 times as high. While Eisenhower was pleased that the "carnage" had ceased, he was careful to point out that the Korean War had accomplished little in terms of unifying Korea or eliminating Communism.

---

My fellow citizens: tonight we greet, with prayers of Thanksgiving, the official news that an armistice was signed almost an hour ago in Korea. It will quickly bring to an end the fighting between the United Nations forces and the Communist armies. For this nation the cost of repelling aggression has been high. In thousands of homes it has been incalculable. It has been paid in terms of tragedy.

With special feelings of sorrow—and of solemn gratitude—we think of those who were called upon to lay down their lives in that far-off land to prove once again that only courage and sacrifice can keep freedom alive upon the earth. To the widows and orphans of this war, and to those veterans who bear disabling wounds, America renews tonight her pledge of lasting devotion and care.

Our thoughts turn also to those other Americans wearied by many months of imprisonment behind the enemy lines. The swift return of all of them will bring joy to thousands of families. It will be evidence of good faith on the part of those with whom we have signed this armistice.

Soldiers, sailors and airmen of sixteen different countries have stood as partners beside us throughout these long and bitter months. America's thanks go to each. In this struggle we have seen the United Nations meet the challenge of aggression—not with pathetic words of protest, but with deeds of decisive purpose. It is proper that we salute particularly the valorous armies of the Republic of Korea, for they have done even more than prove their right to freedom. Inspired by President Syngman Rhee, they have given an example of courage and patriotism which again demonstrates that men of the West and men of the East can fight and work and live together side by side in pursuit of a just and noble cause.

And so at long last the carnage of war is to cease and the negotiation of the conference table is to begin. On this Sabbath evening each of us devoutly prays that all nations may come to see the wisdom of composing differences in this fashion before, rather than after, there is resort to brutal and futile battle.

[7]Broadcast nationwide, from Washington, D.C., on July 26, 1953.

Now as we strive to bring about that wisdom, there is, in this moment of sober satisfaction, one thought that must discipline our emotions and steady our resolution. It is this: We have won an armistice on a single battleground—not peace in the world. We may not now relax our guard nor cease our quest.

Throughout the coming months, during the period of prisoner screening and exchange, and during the possibly longer period of the political conference which looks toward the unification of Korea, we and our United Nations Allies must be vigilant against the possibility of untoward developments.

And, as we do so, we shall fervently strive to insure that this armistice will, in fact, bring free peoples one step nearer to a goal of a world of peace.

My fellow citizens, almost ninety years ago, Abraham Lincoln, at the end of the war, delivered his second inaugural address. At the end of that speech he spoke some words that I think more nearly would express the true feelings of America tonight than would any other words ever spoken or written. You recall them:

"With malice toward none, with charity for all, with firmness in the right as God gives us to see the right, let us strive on to finish the work we are in . . . to do all which may achieve and cherish a just and lasting peace among ourselves and with all nations."

This is our resolve and our dedication.

# To What Purpose War in Asia?[8]

Wayne Morse

*Born October 20, 1900, Madison, WI; died July 22, 1974; Ph.B., 1923, M.A., 1924, University of Wisconsin; assistant professor, University of Minnesota, 1924-28; LL.B., University of Minnesota, 1928; J.D., Columbia University, 1932; professor, 1929-44, dean, 1931-44, University of Oregon School of Law; senator (R) from Oregon, 1945-52; senator (Ind.) from Oregon, 1953-55; senator (D) from Oregon, 1956-68; author,* The Administration of Criminal Justice in Oregon *(1932).*

## Editor's introduction

Throughout 1965, students and faculty organized sessions in which participants debated the morality and feasibility of the Vietnam War. Such events, which began at the University of Michigan, were known as "teach-ins" and were described by the *New York Times* as "catalysts not only for the conversion of ideas, but for the dispersion of ideas." Senator Wayne Morse, while serving on the Senate Committee on Foreign Relations, became one of the nation's most outspoken critics of American involvement in Vietnam. A lifelong devotee and practitioner of debate, Morse spoke with a cool, concise logic that is practically devoid of rhetorical excess. He asked the simple question that would continue to plague Americans: "Why are we fighting?" Morse concluded that fighting in Vietnam was illogical, as well as detrimental to our international relations.

---

It is with both pleasure and pride that I accepted your invitation to speak on behalf of the Faculty-Student Committee to Stop the War in Vietnam. I am proud not only to be here, but I am proud that the University of Oregon is part of a great swelling tide of opposition in this country to the war in Asia, and to the use of force which is rapidly becoming the monster that controls its maker instead of the other way around.

There is today a war in Asia that is as much the making of the United States as it is of any other country. And one cannot read the daily paper or listen to the presentations of Administration officials in the confines of the Senate Foreign Relations Committee without realizing that the only plans of the American Government are plans for making it steadily bigger.

The whys and wherefores of this war are but vaguely known to the American people and even to the Congress. The contingencies being planned for are not known at all. The ways in which the bombing of the North are supposed to produce peace remain in the realm of pure mysticism.

Yet this week, Secretary of Defense McNamara, Ambassador Taylor, General Wheeler, General Westmoreland, Admiral Sharp, and other military commanders met in Hawaii to plan the further military steps by the United States within South Vietnam against North Vietnam. They take the form of the familiar prescription the military establishment has dished up for Southeast Asia for the last five years—to increase the South Vietnamese forces from 575,000 to 735,000 men, to build-up American ground combat forces to several divisions, and to intensify the bombing of military targets and supply routes from the north into the south.

It is to the great peril of the United States and the American people that it is in a military conference of military men in Hawaii that the foreign policy of this country is being made, a foreign policy that is leading the American people into the jaws of both China and Russia, while at the same time stripping us of friends and allies in all parts of the world.

[8]Delivered to the Faculty-Student Committee to Stop the War in Vietnam, at the University of Oregon, in Eugene, Oregon, on April 23, 1965.

Five years ago we were concerned about a civil war in Vietnam. So we threw American money, weapons, and prestige into that war in an effort to turn the tide in favor of the faction we preferred. Today, more than 30,000 United States troops are in the war, hundreds of American aircraft are attacking North Vietnam, and more of the same is being planned. From a civil war in South Vietnam, the conflict has seen North Vietnam brought directly into the battle, the setting up of Soviet anti-aircraft missiles to ward off United States planes, and the preparation by China to send its armed forces into the fray.

All this has come about because the United States has preferred war to seeing itself proved wrong and mistaken in its support ten years ago of Ngo Dinh Diem.

The take-over by the military of American policy in Asia is producing not one advantage for the United States. It is not strengthening freedom in Vietnam, North or South. It is not gaining friends, admirers, or allies in Asia for the United States. Yet if it is not to strengthen freedom and maintain strong allies in Asia, what in the world is our policy in Asia?

Why are we fighting? Why do we insist that South Vietnam must remain non-Communist (one cannot say "free" because it is not free)? Why do our advocates of more war in Vietnam believe the United States must fight the Vietcong itself if it is not for the notion that by so doing we are going to establish and maintain some kind of anti-Communist ring around China and North Vietnam?

The whole object of the war effort is to contain China and to keep the other nations of Asia from falling into her sphere. But the use of military means to reach that end is destroying the very end itself.

It is destroying it by driving into opposition the countries we claim we are saving.

There are in Asia six nations that in terms of area, population, industrial capacity, and resources must be regarded as major powers. They are the Soviet Union, China, India, Pakistan, Japan, and Indonesia. Of these, we are driving headlong into direct military conflict with two: China and the Soviet Union. In fact, our expansion of the war by bombing North Vietnam made that result inevitable, for it compelled both those Communist countries to compete with each other in the race to come to the aid of North Vietnam.

So when the Soviet Union announced that many "volunteers" desired to go to North Vietnam, and offered its anti-aircraft missiles, with Russian technicians to man them, China upped the stakes by announcing its preparations to send the Chinese army into the fray, not as volunteers, but in defense of a country on its borders that was under attack.

Nearly all the assessments offered to date by our American spokesmen have sought to allay fears that the war in Vietnam would drive China and Russia back together. Time and again, questioning members of Congress have been told that such a result was not considered likely, because Russia is too anxious to concentrate her attention and resources on improving the living standards of her own people.

But what is at stake for Russia and China is the leadership of the Communist world. Neither can afford to allow a sister Communist state, especially a small one, to be shot up like a fish in a barrel by the United States without coming to her aid in one form or another.

It is not a question of whether China and Russia are going to become warm international bedfellows. But it is a question of whether they are going to put men and weapons into North Vietnam that will mean a major war with the United States, and that is exactly what both are preparing to do.

Where do we stand with the other great powers of Asia? How about Pakistan and India?

Because Pakistan has persistently criticized the United States war effort in Vietnam, and expressed a certain degree of sympathy and support for China in recent years, a planned visit to this country by its President Ayub was postponed at our request. And in order to even up things between Pakistan and her arch enemy, India, we asked Prime Minister Shastri to postpone his visit, too.

Mr. Shastri promptly announced he was canceling his visit to Washington, though he would come to Canada, and to Moscow. Next June we will witness the spectacle of a Prime Minister, on the receiving end of close to half a billion in American aid each year, visiting Canada, from where he receives next to nothing, but passing up the United States because our relations are too strained. That, incidentally, tells you a lot about our foreign-aid program, as well as our policy in Asia.

The reaction to Washington's postponement of the visits has not only been violent, but has served to strengthen both Pakistan and India in their objections to United States intervention in Asia. Mr. Shastri, for example, repeated his demand that the United States halt its air attacks on North Vietnam, a statement widely hailed in India as one that "stands up" to President Johnson and what Indian papers are calling his bullying diplomacy. For the first time in his career, Mr. Shastri has all political factions in India firmly united behind him in his response to the clumsy attempt to whip India into line along with Pakistan on the question of the war in Vietnam.

In Pakistan, we read that the toll of United States dead in Vietnam does not alter the image of the struggle there as one with racial overtones in which the United States is seen as insensitive to the military devastation of an Asian country. Memories of Hiroshima are being evoked, and the government-controlled Pakistani newspapers are pointedly asking whether the United States would be risking its present bombing strategy in any European country. A leading newspaper, *Dawn*, observes that it is "painful to see how little Americans know of the heart of Asia, where they want to act as perpetual policemen to 'protect' Asians against Asians. Should large-scale war flare up in Vietnam," it continues, "Asia will emerge in ruins and the very prospect which the West today dreads so much—the rise of communism—will then become a certainty."

A fifth leading nation of the area is Indonesia. In a recent television interview, President Sukarno responded to a question about Communist aggression in Vietnam with an insulting question of his own: "What Communist aggression?" On Wednesday we learn that Indonesia intends to be counted in on any Asian side against the United States, because that is the meaning of its announcement that thousands of "volunteers" are appearing at government offices to go to the defense of North Vietnam.

The only major Asian power that gives so much as lip service to the American war effort is Japan. Yet her people are so opposed to that war that the Japanese Prime Minister Sato sent his own personal representative to tour the area and to make his own assessment of the effectiveness and future of our policy. His report to Sato was all against us.

He found that probably 30 per cent of the Vietcong were Communists, that the Vietcong cannot be considered as controlled by either Hanoi or Peking, and that the United States was greatly mistaken in thinking that military force would solve matters. It may be some time before Japan officially changes its position but its repeated statements to China that Japan and China have no great conflicts between them is a hint of what is to come.

The war hawks and their newspaper mouthpieces will tell you that we must stop concerning ourselves with what other countries think, and do what *we* think is right in Asia. But everything they want us to do there is supposed to be for the benefit not of the United States, but of India, Pakistan, Japan, Indonesia, and the smaller countries of the area to save them from communism. Why is it, then, that they do not appreciate that we know better what is right for them than they do?

I suggest that the editorial I have quoted from *Dawn* tells our military leadership in the Pentagon something that they apparently will never figure out for themselves; namely, that the great advances made by communism have been made in the ruins of war. The destruction and desolation of military force can kill a lot of Communists. But it also makes Communists where none existed before. And it produces the disruption and breakdown of society which is the great opportunity that communism seizes.

There is nothing wrong with President Johnson's offer of April 7 to help develop the Mekong River Valley. But what is wrong with the speech he made on that occasion is that he revealed no plans for ending the war which is making development impossible anywhere in Southeast Asia. And within two weeks, his military high command was meeting in Hawaii to plan the next escalation of the action.

I ask you, as I have asked Administration officials as they have come before the Senate Foreign Relations Committee: Can you tell me how carrying the war to the north is going to bring an end to the war?

And the answer is the one we hear week after week from our Secretary of State, by way of his chant about making China and North Vietnam leave their neighbors alone. To go 8,000 miles away—alone—to make someone else leave their neighbors alone is perhaps the most hypocritical assumption of the role of international policeman that any nation ever claimed for itself.

It is not going to defeat the Vietcong. It is going to have no other result than to bring China and Russia, as well as the United States, into the war.

Why, indeed, should North Vietnam stop whatever it is that she is doing that Secretary Rusk cannot describe but what he assures us North Vietnam knows—when it has been our own position that we would not quit the war while we were losing? Do we think North Vietnam will cry "surrender" and ask for negotiations when we would not under the same circumstances? Do we think that North Vietnam will do as we say but not as we did, which was to escalate the war in order to put ourselves in a stronger bargaining position?

The returns are coming in on all these assumptions and they spell not peace on American terms but bigger and more terrible war.

I do not suggest that at any point has North Vietnam been innocent of illegal action under the Geneva Agreement. Nor do I doubt that in recent months and perhaps in recent years, the Vietcong movement has received considerable advice and support from North Vietnam. But violations by one side do not excuse violations by the other. Terrorist methods employed by one side have been matched by terrorism employed by the other. The United States had the clear duty and obligation under international law to petition the United Nations for redress of North Vietnam's violation of the Geneva Agreement. Why didn't we? History for generations to come will continue to ask the United States that question. It will also continue to find us as having been guilty of substituting the jungle law of military might for our often professed ideal of the rule of law through international agreement in cases of threats to the peace of the world. In Southeast Asia we have walked out on our ideals and joined the Communists in becoming a threat to the peace of the world.

Each escalation by the United States has resulted in a responding escalation within South Vietnam, and we are now at the point where the next escalation could well result in a direct response from Hanoi. Each violation and retaliation has served to worsen and not to improve the American position.

What I am saying is that our reliance upon wealth and military power to bring about a pro-Western government in South Vietnam has been a failure. It does not matter that our designs upon that country are not the same as were the French designs. Our methods are much the same, and they are failing every bit as surely as did the French methods.

If we do not seek traditional colonial objectives, we do seek in Vietnam the nationalist objective of American military security as we see it. We have already demonstrated that far from seeking the free political choice for the people of Vietnam we do not intend to let them choose anything contrary to American interests. We have let Vietnam and the entire world know that the United States considers South Vietnam as something to be "lost" or "held" by the United States, and we will kill as many of its people and destroy as much of its property as is necessary to "hold" it.

Our success with that objective is going to be all downhill, just as it has been downhill for ten years. We could not cope with rebellion within the south and now we cannot cope with assistance to it from the north. We have thrown our Seventh Fleet, hundreds of aircraft, and thousands of United States troops into the battle without success and we have not yet encountered the army of North Vietnam, much less that of China.

Our raids on North Vietnam have been illegal under the United Nations charter. And they have failed in their purpose of making the Vietcong give up. One thing they *have* done has been to alienate the major countries of Asia and to cause serious alarm among the countries of Western Europe.

Our real problem in Vietnam is that we cannot control the situation by the means we know best—money and military force. We cannot control it because we want the area to remain pro-Western and to serve as a bulwark against Chinese expansion. Those are not realistic nor realizable objectives in the middle of the twentieth century. We never will have peace in Asia on those terms.

But we can have a peace in Asia when control of Indochina is removed from the ideological conflict between this country and China. To do that will require international supervision and self-determination for Vietnam. To return to the Geneva Accord offers some hope for ending the war. But it would require a return to the Accord by the United States and South Vietnam, too. In the end I expect that we will settle for just that, but in the meantime we and the world may pass through a trial of bloodshed before we find out that American fortunes in Asia are no more achievable than were French, British, and Dutch fortunes before us.

Neither the United States nor North Vietnam now has much chance to settle this terrible war by bilateral negotiations. It has gone too far. It is going much further if a third force consisting of the nations of the world who are not now involved in the fighting is not brought to bear on this Asian crisis. That is why many of us who are urging a negotiated settlement with honor and security for all participants have recommended a formal presentation of the threat to world peace created by the war to the procedures of the United Nations.

Unless the nonparticipating nations come forward and live up to their clear obligations under international law, they are not likely to be nonparticipants much longer. Mankind can very well be on the brink of a Third World War. Procedures of international law created by existing treaties do provide for the convening of an international peace conference on the crisis. I ask Great Britain, Canada, Japan, France, Russia, Italy, Belgium, Australia, New Zealand—yes, I ask all nations who profess that they want world peace—when, oh when, are you going to keep your obligations solemnly assumed by your signatures to existing treaties which provide for peaceful procedures for settling threats to peace? Is it your answer that they may not work? Then what is your alternative? War? The time has come for 85, 90, 95 and more nations to say to the United States and South Vietnam on the one hand and the Communist nations on the other who are jointly threatening the peace of the world: "We beg you to cease your fire and come to an International Conference Table."

Oh, I know the specter of Munich is immediately raised, and we are reminded that we could not do business with Hitler and it is better to fight now than later. But in all these comparisons with the years that led up to World War II, I never yet have heard anyone argue that the United States should, in 1938, have acted alone to send troops to Czechoslovakia to fight Germany. What the "Munich" criers have in mind for Munich is not that the negotiation should never have been held, but that a concert of nations should have acted together to serve notice and to take steps to stop further aggression. And that is what I am urging that we do in Vietnam.

The United States can accomplish nothing on the mainland of Asia so long as we are acting alone and in isolation from the large free nations of the area. To do so can mean nothing but perpetual war. Our present policy is not saving Asia from war or from communism, either, yet it compels our friends to choose between one or the other. That is not an acceptable alternative to the people of Asia or of the United States, and I am satisfied that we have much more to offer by way of leadership if we apply President Johnson's admonition to "Come, and reason together."

# Speech to The American Society of International Law[9]

Dean Rusk

*Born February 9, 1909, Cherokee County, GA; died December 20, 1994; B.A., Davidson College, 1931; as Rhodes Scholar, B.S., 1933, M.A., 1934, Oxford University; professor, 1934-40, dean of faculty, 1938-40, Mills College; U.S. Army, 1940-46; assistant chief of international security affairs, 1946; director, office of special political affairs, 1947-48; director, office of United Nations affairs, 1948-49; assistant secretary of state, 1949-52; president, Rockefeller Foundation, 1952-60; U.S. secretary of state, 1960-69; professor, University of Georgia, 1969-84; author,* As I Saw It *(1990).*

## Editor's introduction

Having helped formulate the United States' military intervention in Korea, former Secretary of State Dean Rusk articulated the basis for the buildup of troops in Vietnam that occurred during the Kennedy and Johnson administrations. In sharp contrast to Senator Wayne Morse, Rusk defended the American presence in Vietnam as necessary to protecting national security. According to Rusk, abandoning involvement in Vietnam would permit a "Communist world revolution," which he believed to be a real possibility.

---

When this distinguished Society was founded fifty-nine years ago, the then Secretary of State Elihu Root became its first president. With the passage of time, the secretary of state has been elevated to a less demanding role, that of honorary president. Secretary Root himself not only established the precedent of becoming president while Secretary of State; he also superseded it by continuing to serve as your president for eighteen years. The *Proceedings* of the first meeting indicate that Secretary Root not only presided and delivered an address, but that he also selected the menu for the dinner.

The year 1907, when the first of the Society's annual meetings was held, today appears to have been one of those moments in American history when we were concentrating upon building our American society, essentially untroubled by what took place beyond our borders. But the founders of this Society realized that the United States could not remain aloof from the world. It is one of the achievements of this Society that, from its inception, it has spread the realization that the United States cannot opt out of the community of nations—that international affairs are part of our national affairs.

Questions of war and peace occupied the Society at its first meeting. Among the subjects discussed were the possibility of the immunity of private property from belligerent seizure upon the high seas and whether trade in contraband of war was unneutral. Limitations upon recourse to force then proposed were embryonic, as is illustrated by the fact one topic for discussion related to restrictions upon the use of armed force in the collection of contract obligations. The distance between those ideas and the restrictions upon recourse to armed force contained in the Charter of the United Nations is vast. It is to these Charter restrictions—and their place in the practice and malpractice of States—that I shall address much of my remarks this evening.

Current United States policy arouses the criticism that it is at once too legal and too tough. Time was when the criticism of American concern with the legal element in in-

[9]Delivered to the American Society of International Law, in Washington, D.C., on April 23, 1965.

ternational relations was that it led to softness—to a "legalistic-moralistic" approach to foreign affairs which conformed more to the ideal than to the real. Today, criticism of American attachment to the role of law is that it leads not to softness, but to severity. We are criticized not for sacrificing our national interests to international interests, but for endeavoring to impose the international interest upon other nations. We are criticized for acting as if the Charter of the United Nations means what it says. We are criticized for treating the statement of the law by the International Court of Justice as authoritative. We are criticized for taking collective security seriously.

This criticism is, I think, a sign of strength—of our strength, and of the strength of international law. It is a tribute to a blending of political purpose with legal ethic.

American foreign policy is at once principled and pragmatic. Its central objective is our national safety and well-being—to "secure the blessings of liberty to ourselves and our posterity." But we know we can no longer find security and well-being in defenses and policies which are confined to North America, or the Western Hemisphere, or the North Atlantic Community. This has become a very small planet. We have to be concerned with all of it—with all of its land, waters, atmosphere, and with surrounding space. We have a deep national interest in peace, the prevention of aggression, the faithful performance of agreements, the growth of international law. Our foreign policy is rooted in the profoundly practical realization that the Purposes and Principles of the United Nations Charter must animate the behavior of States, if mankind is to prosper or is even to survive. Or at least they must animate enough States with enough will and enough resources to see to it that others do not violate those rules with impunity.

The Preamble and Articles One and Two of the Charter set forth abiding purposes of American policy. This is not surprising, since we took the lead in drafting the Charter—at a time when the biggest war in history was still raging and we and others were thinking deeply about its frightful costs and the ghastly mistakes and miscalculations which led to it.

The kind of world we seek is the kind set forth in the opening sections of the Charter: a world community of independent states, each with the institutions of its own choice, but cooperating with one another to promote their mutual welfare . . . a world in which the use of force is effectively inhibited . . . a world of expanding human rights and well-being . . . a world of expanding international law . . . a world in which an agreement is a commitment and not just a tactic.

We believe that this is the sort of world a great majority of the governments of the world desire. We believe it is the sort of world man must achieve if he is not to perish. As I said on another occasion: "If once the rule of international law could be discussed with a certain condescension as a Utopian ideal, today it becomes an elementary practical necessity. *Pacta sunt servanda* now becomes the basis for survival."

Unhappily a minority of governments is committed to different ideas of the conduct and organization of human affairs. They are dedicated to the promotion of the Communist world revolution. And their doctrine justifies any technique, any ruse, any deceit, which contributes to that end. They may differ as to tactics from time to time. And the two principal Communist powers are competitors for the leadership of the world Communist movement. But both are committed to the eventual Communization of the entire world.

The overriding issue of our time is which concepts are to prevail: those set forth in the United Nations Charter or those proclaimed in the name of a world revolution.

The paramount commitment of the Charter is Article 2, paragraph 4, which reads: "All Members shall refrain in their international relations from the threat or use of force against the territorial integrity or political independence of any State, or in any other manner inconsistent with the Purposes of the United Nations."

This comprehensive limitation went beyond the Covenant of the League of Nations. This more sweeping commitment sought to apply a bitter lesson of the interwar period—that the threat or use of force, whether or not called "war," feeds on success. The indelible lesson of those years is that the time to stop aggression is at its very beginning.

The exceptions to the prohibitions on the use or threat of force were expressly set forth in the Charter. The use of force is legal:

" . . . as a collective measure by the United Nations, or

" . . . as action by regional agencies in accordance with Chapter VIII of the Charter, or

" . . . in individual or collective self-defense."

When Article 2, paragraph 4 was written it was widely regarded as general international law, governing both Members and non-Members of the United Nations. And on the universal reach of the principle embodied in Article 2, paragraph 4, wide agreement remains. Thus, last year, a United Nations Special Committee on Principles of International Law concerning Friendly Relations and Cooperation among States met in Mexico City. All shades of United Nations opinion were represented. The Committee's purpose was to study and possibly to elaborate certain of those principles. The Committee debated much and agreed on little. But on one point, it reached swift and unanimous agreement: that all States, and not only all Members of the United Nations, are bound to refrain in their international relations from the threat or use of force against the territorial integrity or political independence of any State. Nonrecognition of the statehood of a political entity was held not to affect the international application of this cardinal rule of general international law.

But at this same meeting in Mexico City, Czechoslovakia, with the warm support of the Soviet Union and some other Members, proposed formally another exemption from the limitations on use of force. Their proposal stated that: "The prohibition of the use of force shall not affect . . . self-defense of nations against colonial domination in the exercise of the right of self-determination."

The United States is all for self-defense. We are against colonial domination—we led the way in throwing it off. We have long favored self-determination, in practice as well as in words—indeed, we favor it for the entire world, including the peoples behind the Iron and Bamboo curtains. But we could not accept the Czech proposal. And we were pleased that the Special Committee found the Czech proposal unacceptable.

The primary reason why we opposed that attempt to rewrite the Charter—apart from the inadmissibility of rewriting the Charter at all by such means—was that we knew the meaning behind the words. We knew that like so many statements from such sources, it used upside-down language—that it would in effect authorize a State to wage war, to use force internationally, as long as it claimed it was doing so to "liberate" somebody from "colonial domination." In short, the Czech resolution proposed to give to so-called "wars of national liberation" the same exemption from the limitation on the use of force which the Charter accords to defense against aggression.

What is a "war of national liberation"? It is, in essence, any war which furthers the Communist world revolution—what, in broader terms, the Communists have long referred to as a "just" war. The term "war of national liberation" is used not only to denote armed insurrection by people still under colonial rule—there are not many of those left outside the Communist world. It is used to denote any effort led by Communists to overthrow by force any non-Communist government.

Thus the war in South Vietnam is called a "war of national liberation." And those who would overthrow various other non-Communist governments in Asia, Africa, and Latin America are called the "forces of national liberation."

Nobody in his right mind would deny that Venezuela is not only a truly independent nation but that it has a government chosen in a free election. But the leaders of the Communist insurgency in Venezuela are described as leaders of a fight for "national liberation"—not only by themselves and by Castro and the Chinese Communists, but by the Soviet Communists.

A recent editorial in *Pravda* spoke of the "peoples of Latin America . . . marching firmly along the path of struggle for their national independence" and said: "the upsurge of the national liberation movement in Latin American countries has been to a great extent a result of the activities of Communist parties." It added: "The Soviet people have regarded and still regard it as their sacred duty to give support to the peoples fighting for their independence. True to their international duty the Soviet people have been and will remain on the side of the Latin American patriots."

In Communist doctrine and practice, a non-Communist government may be labeled and denounced as "colonialist," "reactionary," or a "puppet," and any State so labeled by the Communists automatically becomes fair game . . . while Communist intervention by force in non-Communist states is justified as "self-defense" or part of the "struggle against colonial domination." "Self-determination" seems to mean that any Communist nation can determine by itself that any non-Communist state is a victim of colonialist domination and therefore a justifiable target for a war of "liberation."

As the risks of overt aggression, whether nuclear or with conventional forces, have become increasingly evident, the Communists have put increasing stress on the "war of national liberation." The Chinese Communists have been more militant in language and behavior than the Soviet Communists. But the Soviet Communist leadership also has consistently proclaimed its commitment in principle to support wars of national liberation. This commitment was reaffirmed as recently as Monday of this week by Mr. Kosygin.

International law does not restrict internal revolution within a state, or revolution against colonial authority. But international law does restrict what third powers may lawfully do in support of insurrection. It is these restrictions which are challenged by the doctrine, and violated by the practice, of "wars of liberation."

It is plain that acceptance of the doctrine of "wars of liberation" would amount to scuttling the modern international law of peace which the Charter prescribes. And acceptance of the practice of "wars of liberation," as defined by the Communists, would mean the breakdown of peace itself.

Vietnam presents a clear current case of the lawful versus the unlawful use of force. I would agree with General Giap and other Communists that it is a test case for "wars of national liberation." We intend to meet that test.

Were the insurgency in South Vietnam truly indigenous and self-sustained, international law would not be involved. But the fact is that it receives vital external support—in organization and direction, in training, in men, in weapons and other supplies. That external support is unlawful, for a double reason. First, it contravenes general international law, which the United Nations Charter here expresses. Second, it contravenes particular international law: The 1954 Geneva Accords on Vietnam, and the 1962 Geneva Agreements on Laos.

In resisting the aggression against it, the Republic of Vietnam is exercising its right of self-defense. It called upon us and other states for assistance. And in the exercise of the right of collective self-defense under the United Nations Charter, we and other nations are providing such assistance.

The American policy of assisting South Vietnam to maintain its freedom was inaugurated under President Eisenhower, and continued under Presidents Kennedy and Johnson. Our assistance has been increased because the aggression from the North has been augmented. Our assistance now encompasses the bombing of North Vietnam. The bombing is designed to interdict, as far as possible, and to inhibit, as far as may be necessary, continued aggression against the Republic of Vietnam.

When that aggression ceases, collective measures in defense against it will cease. As President Johnson has declared: " . . . if that aggression is stopped, the people and Government of South Vietnam will be free to settle their own future, and the need for supporting American military action there will end."

The fact that the demarcation line between North and South Vietnam was intended to be temporary does not make the assault on South Vietnam any less of an aggression. The demarcation lines between North and South Korea and between East and West Germany are temporary. But that did not make the North Korean invasion of South Korea a permissible use of force.

Let's not forget the salient features of the 1962 agreements on Laos. Laos was to be independent and neutral. All foreign troops, regular or irregular, and other military personnel were to be withdrawn within seventy-five days, except a limited number of French instructors as requested by the Laos government. No arms were to be introduced into Laos except at the request of that government. The signatories agreed to refrain "from all direct or indirect interference in the internal affairs" of Laos. They promised also not to use Lao territory to intervene in the internal affairs of other countries—a stipulation that plainly prohibited the passage of arms and men from North Vietnam to South Vietnam by way of Laos. An International Control Commission of three was to assure compliance with the Agreements. And all the signatories promised to support a coalition government under Prince Souvanna Phouma.

What happened? The non-Communist elements complied. The Communists did not. At no time since that agreement was signed have either the Pathet Lao or the North Vietnam authorities complied with it. The North Vietnamese left several thousand troops there—the backbone of almost every Pathet Lao battalion. Use of the corridor through Laos to South Vietnam continued. And the Communists barred the areas under their control both to the government of Laos and the International Control Commission.

To revert to Vietnam: I continue to hear and see nonsense about the nature of the struggle there. I sometimes wonder at the gullibility of educated men and the stubborn disregard of plain facts by men who are supposed to be helping our young to learn—especially to learn how to think.

Hanoi has never made a secret of its designs. It publicly proclaimed in 1960 a renewal of the assault on South Vietnam. Quite obviously its hopes of taking over South Vietnam from within had withered to close to zero—and the remarkable economic and social progress of South Vietnam contrasted, most disagreeably for the North Vietnamese Communists, with their own miserable economic performance.

The facts about the external involvement have been documented in White Papers and other publications of the Department of State. The International Control Commission has held that there is evidence "beyond reasonable doubt" of North Vietnamese intervention.

There is no evidence that the Vietcong has any significant popular following in South Vietnam. It relies heavily on terror. Most of its reinforcements in recent months have been North Vietnamese from the North Vietnamese Army.

Let us be clear about what is involved today in Southeast Asia. We are not involved with empty phrases or conceptions which ride upon the clouds. We are talking about the vital national interests of the United States in the peace of the Pacific. We are talking about the appetite for aggression—an appetite which grows upon feeding and which is proclaimed to be insatiable. We are talking about the safety of nations with whom we are allied—and the integrity of the American commitment to join in meeting attack. It is true that we also believe that every small state has a right to be unmolested by its neighbors even though it is within reach of a great power. It is true that we are committed to general principles of law and procedure which reject the idea that men and arms can be sent freely across frontiers to absorb a neighbor. But underlying the general principles is the harsh reality that our own security is threatened by those who would embark upon a course of aggression whose announced ultimate purpose is our own destruction. Once again we hear expressed the views which cost the men of my generation a terrible price in World War II. We are told that Southeast Asia is far away—but so were Manchuria and Ethiopia. We are told that if we insist that someone stop shooting that is asking them for unconditional surrender. We are told that perhaps the aggressor will be content with just one more bite. We are told that if we prove faithless on one commitment that perhaps others would believe us about other commitments in other places. We are told that if we stop resisting that perhaps the other side will have a change of heart. We were asked to stop hitting bridges and radar sites and ammunition depots without requiring that the other side stop its slaughter of thousands of civilians and its bombings of schools and hotels and hospitals and railways and buses.

Surely we have learned over the past three decades that the acceptance of aggression leads only to a sure catastrophe. Surely we have learned that the aggressor must face the consequences of his action and be saved from the frightful miscalculation that brings all to ruin. It is the purpose of law to guide men away from such events, to establish rules of conduct which are deeply rooted in the reality of experience.

Before closing, I should like to turn away from the immediate difficulties and dangers of the situation in Southeast Asia and remind you of the dramatic progress that shapes and is being shaped by expanding international law.

A "common law of mankind"—to use the happy phrase of your distinguished colleague, Wilfred Jenks—is growing as the world shrinks, and as the vistas of space expand. This year is, by proclamation of the General Assembly, International Cooperation Year, a year "to direct attention to the common interests of mankind and to accelerate the joint efforts being undertaken to further them." Those common interests are enormous and intricate, and the joint efforts which further them are developing fast, although perhaps not fast enough.

In the nineteenth century, the United States attended an average of one international conference a year. Now we attend nearly 600 a year. We are party to 4,300 treaties and other international agreements in force. Three fourths of these were signed in the last twenty-five years. Our interest in the observance of all of these treaties and agreements is profound, whether the issue is peace in Laos, or the payment of United Nations assessments, or the allocation of radio frequencies, or the application of airline safeguards, or the control of illicit traffic in narcotics, or any other issue which States have chosen to regulate through the lawmaking process. The writing of international cooperation into international law is meaningful only if the law is obeyed—and only if the international institutions which administer and develop the law function in accordance with agreed procedures, until the procedures are changed.

Everything suggests that the rate of growth in international law—like the rate of change in almost every other field these days—is rising at a very steep angle.

In recent years the law of the sea has been developed and codified—but it first evolved in a leisurely fashion over the centuries. International agreements to regulate aerial navigation had to be worked out within the period of a couple of decades. Now, within the first few years of man's adventures in outer space, we are deeply involved in the creation of international institutions, regulations, and law to govern this effort.

Already the United Nations has developed a set of legal principles to govern the use of outer space and declared celestial bodies free from national appropriation.

Already nations, including the United States and the Soviet Union, have agreed not to orbit weapons of mass destruction in outer space.

Already the Legal Subcommittee of the United Nations Committee on Outer Space is formulating international agreements on liability for damage caused by the reentry of objects launched into outer space and on rescue and return of astronauts and space objects.

Already the first international sounding rocket range has been established in India and is being offered for United Nations sponsorship.

To make orderly space exploration possible at this stage, the International Telecommunications Union had to allocate radio frequencies for the purpose.

To take advantage of weather reporting and forecasting potential of observation satellites, married to computer technology, the World Meteorological Organization is creating a vast system of data acquisition, analysis, and distribution which depends entirely on international agreement, regulation and standards.

And to start building a single global communications satellite system, we have created a novel international institution in which a private American corporation shares ownership with forty-five governments.

This is but part of the story of how the pace of discovery and invention forces us to reach out for international agreement, to build international institutions, to do things in accordance with an expanding international and transnational law.

Phenomenal as the growth of treaty obligations is, the true innovation of twentieth century international law lies more in the fact that we have nearly eighty international institutions which are capable of carrying out those obligations.

It is important that the processes and products of international cooperation be understood and appreciated; and it is important that their potential be much further developed. It is also important that the broader significance of the contributions of international cooperation to the solving of international problems of an economic, social, scientific and humanitarian character not be overestimated. For all the progress of peace could be incinerated in war.

Thus the control of force in international relations remains the paramount problem which confronts the diplomat and the lawyer—and the man in the street and the man in the rice field. Most of mankind is not in an immediate position to grapple very directly with that problem, but the problem is no less crucial. The responsibility of those, in your profession and mine, who do grapple with it is the greater. I am happy to acknowledge that this Society, in thinking and debating courageously and constructively about the conditions of peace, continues to make its unique contribution and to make it well.

# Address to a Joint Session of the Tennessee State Legislature[10]

## Lyndon B. Johnson

*Born August 27, 1908, Johnson City, Texas; died January 22, 1973; B.S., Texas State Teachers College, 1930; administrator, Texas National Youth Administration, 1935-36; representative (D) from Texas, 1937-61; commander, Naval Reserve, 1941-64; vice president of the United States, 1961-63; president of the United States, 1963-1968.*

### Editor's introduction

Only months before President Lyndon B. Johnson's Vietnam policy caused him to not seek a second term in office, Johnson attempted to convince the Tennessee State Legislature, and the nation, that the military situation in Vietnam had substantially improved. Hoping to arouse the collective memory of Hitler's unchecked advance through Europe, Johnson remarked that "most of us remember the fearful cost of ignoring aggression." Johnson urged that we "stay the course" and not only continue, but increase, our presence in Vietnam. The *New York Times* remarked that when he gave the speech, Johnson appeared "calmly determined, like a poker player who has made up his mind to raise the stakes."

---

It is always a very special privilege and pleasure for me to visit Tennessee.

For a Texan, it is like homecoming, because much of the courage and hard work that went into the building of the Southwest came from the hills and the fields of Tennessee. It strengthened the sinews of thousands of men—at the Alamo, at San Jacinto, and at the homes of our pioneer people.

This morning, I visited the Hermitage, the historic home of Andrew Jackson. Two centuries have passed since that most American of all Americans was born. The world has changed a great deal since his day. But the qualities which sustain men and nations in positions of leadership have not changed.

In our time, as in Andrew Jackson's, freedom has its price.

In our time, as in his, history conspires to test the American will.

In our time, as in Jackson's time, courage and vision, and the willingness to sacrifice, will sustain the cause of freedom.

This generation of Americans is making its imprint on history. It is making it in the fierce hills and the sweltering jungles of Vietnam. I think most of our citizens—after a very penetrating debate which is our democratic heritage—have reached a common understanding on the meaning and on the objectives of that struggle.

Before I discuss the specific questions that remain at issue, I should like to review the points of widespread agreement.

It was two years ago that we were forced to choose, forced to make a decision between major commitments in defense of South Vietnam or retreat—the evacuation of more than 25,000 of our troops, the collapse of the Republic of Vietnam in the face of subversion and external assault.

Andrew Jackson would never have been surprised at the choice we made.

We chose a course in keeping with American tradition, in keeping with the foreign policy of at least three administrations, with the expressed will of the Congress of the United

[10]Delivered to a joint session of the Tennessee State Legislature, in Nashville, Tennessee, on March 15, 1967.

States, with our solemn obligations under the Southeast Asian Treaty, and with the interest of 16 million South Vietnamese who had no wish to live under Communist domination.

As our commitment in Vietnam required more men and more equipment, some voices were raised in opposition. The Administration was urged to disengage, to find an excuse to abandon the effort.

These cries came despite growing evidence that the defense of Vietnam held the key to the political and economic future of free Asia. The stakes of the struggle grew correspondingly.

It became clear that if we were prepared to stay the course in Vietnam, we could help to lay the cornerstone for a diverse and independent Asia, full of promise and resolute in the cause of peaceful economic development for her long-suffering peoples.

But if we faltered, the forces of chaos would scent victory and decades of strife and aggression would stretch endlessly before us.

The choice was clear. We would stay the course. We shall stay the course.

I think most Americans support this fundamental decision. Most of us remember the fearful cost of ignoring aggression. Most of us have cast aside the illusion that we can live in an affluent fortress while the world slides into chaos.

I think we have all reached broad agreement on our basic objectives in Vietnam.

First, an honorable peace, that will leave the people of South Vietnam free to fashion their own political and economic institutions without fear of terror or intimidation from the North.

Second, a Southeast Asia in which all countries—including a peaceful North Vietnam—apply their scarce resources to the real problems of their people: combating hunger, ignorance, and diseases.

I have said many, many times, that nothing would give us greater pleasure than to invest our own resources in the constructive works of peace rather than in the futile destruction of war.

Third, a concrete demonstration that aggression across international frontiers or demarcation lines is no longer an acceptable means of political change.

There is, I think, a general agreement among Americans on the things that we do not want in Vietnam.

We do not want permanent bases. We will begin with the withdrawal of our troops on a reasonable schedule whenever reciprocal concessions are forthcoming from our adversary.

We do not seek to impose our political beliefs upon South Vietnam. Our republic rests upon a brisk commerce in ideas. We will be happy to see free competition in the intellectual marketplace whenever North Vietnam is willing to shift the conflict from the battlefield to the ballot box.

So, these are the broad principles on which most Americans agree.

On a less general level, however, the events and frustrations of these past few difficult weeks have inspired a number of questions about our Vietnam policy in the minds and hearts of a good many of our citizens. Today, here in this historical chamber, I want to deal with some of those questions that figure most prominently in the press and in some of the letters which reach a President's desk.

Many Americans are confused by the barrage of information about military engagements. They long for the capsule summary which has kept tabs on our previous wars, a line on the map that divides friend from foe.

Precisely what, they ask, is our military situation, and what are the prospects of victory?

The first answer is that Vietnam is aggression in a new guise, as far removed from trench warfare as the rifle from the longbow. This is a war of infiltration, of subversion, of ambush. Pitched battles are very rare, and even more rarely are they decisive.

Today, more than 1 million men from the Republic of Vietnam and its six allies are engaged in the order of battle.

Despite continuing increases in North Vietnam infiltration, this strengthening of allied forces in 1966 under the brilliant leadership of General Westmoreland, was instrumental in reversing the whole course of this war.

We estimate that 55,000 North Vietnamese and Vietcong were killed in 1966, compared with 35,000 the previous year. More were wounded, and more than 20,000 defected.

By contrast, 9,500 South Vietnamese, more than 5,000 Americans, and 600 from other allied forces were killed in action.

The Vietnamese Army achieved a 1966 average of two weapons captured from the Vietcong to every one lost, a dramatic turnaround from the previous two years.

Allied forces have made several successful sweeps through territories that were formerly considered Vietcong sanctuaries only a short time ago. These operations not only cost the enemy large numbers of men and weapons, but are very damaging to his morale.

What does all of this mean? Will the North Vietnamese change their tactics? Will there be less infiltration of main units? Will there be more of guerilla warfare?

The actual truth is we just don't know.

What we do know is that General Westmoreland's strategy is producing results, that our military situation has substantially improved, that our military success has permitted the groundwork to be laid for a pacification program which is the long-run key to an independent South Vietnam.

Since February, 1965, our military operations have included selective bombing of military targets in North Vietnam. Our purposes are three:

To back our fighting men by denying the enemy a sanctuary;

To exact a penalty against North Vietnam for her flagrant violations of the Geneva Accords of 1954 and 1962;

To limit the flow, or to substantially increase the cost of infiltration of men and material from North Vietnam.

Our intelligence confirms that we have been successful.

Yet, some of our people object strongly to this aspect of our policy. Must we bomb, many people will ask. Does it do any military good? Is it consistent with America's limited objectives? Is it an inhuman act that is aimed at civilians?

On the question of military utility, I can only report the firm belief of the Secretary of Defense, the Joint Chiefs of Staff, the Central Intelligence Agency, General Westmoreland and our commanders in the field, and all the sources of information and advice available to the Commander-in-Chief and that is that the bombing is causing serious disruption and is bringing about added burdens to the North Vietnamese infiltration effort.

We know, for example, that half a million people are kept busy just repairing damage to bridges, roads, railroads, and other strategic facilities, and in air and coastal defense and repair of power plants.

I also want to say categorically that it is not the position of the American Government that the bombing will be decisive in getting Hanoi to abandon aggression. It has, however, created very serious problems for them. The best indication of how substantial is the fact that they are working so hard every day with all their friends throughout the world to try to get us to stop.

The bombing is entirely consistent with America's limited objectives in South Vietnam. The strength of Communist main-force units in the South is clearly based on their infiltration from the North. I think it is simply unfair to our American soldiers, sailors, and marines and our Vietnamese allies to ask them to face increased enemy personnel and fire power without making an effort to try to reduce that infiltration.

As to bombing civilians, I would simply say that we are making an effort that is unprecedented in the history of warfare to be sure that we do not. It is our policy to bomb military targets only.

We have never deliberately bombed cities, nor attacked any target with the purpose of inflicting civilian casualties.

We hasten to add, however, that we recognize, and we regret, that some people, even after warning, are living and working in the vicinity of military targets and they have suffered.

We are also too aware that men and machines are not infallible, and that some mistakes do occur.

But our record on this account is, in my opinion, highly defensible.

Look for a moment at the record of the other side.

Any civilian casualties that result from our operations are inadvertent, in stark contrast to the calculated Vietcong policy of systematic terror.

Tens of thousands of innocent Vietnamese civilians have been killed, tortured, and kidnapped by the Vietcong. There is no doubt about the deliberate nature of the Vietcong program. One need only note the frequency with which Vietcong victims are village leaders, teachers, health workers, and others who are trying to carry out constructive programs for their people.

Yet, the deeds of the Vietcong go largely unnoted in the public debate. It is this moral double bookkeeping which makes us get sometimes very weary of our critics.

But there is another question that we should answer: Why don't we stop bombing to make it easier to begin negotiations?

The answer is a simple one:

We stopped for five days and twenty hours in May 1965. Representatives of Hanoi simply returned our message in a plain envelope.

We stopped bombing for thirty-six days and fifteen hours in December 1965 and January 1966. Hanoi only replied: "A political settlement of the Vietnam problem can be envisaged only when the United States Government has accepted the four-point stand of the Government of the Democratic Republic of Vietnam, has proved this by actual deeds, has stopped unconditionally and for good its air raids and all other acts of war against the Democratic Republic of Vietnam."

Only last month we stopped bombing for five days and eighteen hours, after many prior weeks in which we had communicated to them several possible routes to peace, any one of which America was prepared to take. Their response, as you know, delivered to His Holiness the Pope, was this: The United States "must put an end to their aggression in Vietnam, end unconditionally and definitively the bombing and all other acts of war against the Democratic Republic of Vietnam, withdraw from South Vietnam all American and satellite troops, recognize the South Vietnamese National Front for Liberation, and let the Vietnamese people settle themselves their own affairs."

That is where we stand today.

They have three times rejected a bombing pause as a means to open the way to ending the war, and go together to the negotiating table.

The tragedy of South Vietnam is not limited to casualty lists.

There is much tragedy in the story of a nation at war for nearly a generation. It is the story of economic stagnation. It is the story of a generation of young men—the flower of the labor force—pressed into military service by one side or the other.

No one denies that the survival of South Vietnam is heavily dependent upon early economic progress.

My most recent and my most hopeful report of progress in this area came from an old friend of Tennessee, of the Tennessee Valley Authority—David Lilienthal, who recently went as my representative to Vietnam to begin to work with the Vietnamese people on economic planning for that area.

He reported—and with some surprise, I might add—that he discovered an extraordinary air of confidence among the farmers, village leaders, trade unionists, and the industrialists. He concluded that their economic behavior suggests "that they think they know how all of this is going to come out."

Mr. Lilienthal also said that the South Vietnamese were among the hardest working people that he had seen in developing countries around the world, that "to have been through twenty years of war and still have this amount of 'zip' almost ensures their long-term economic development."

Mr. Lilienthal will be going with me to Guam Saturday night to talk with our new leaders about the plans he will try to institute there.

Our AID programs are supporting the drive toward this sound economy.

But none of these economic accomplishments will be decisive by itself. And no economic achievement can substitute for a strong and free political structure.

We cannot build such a structure—because only the Vietnamese can do that.

I think they are building it. As I am talking to you here, a freely elected constituent assembly in Saigon is now wrestling with the last details of a new constitution, one which will bring the Republic of Vietnam to full membership among the democratic nations of the world.

We expect that constitution to be completed this month.

In the midst of war, they have been building for peace and justice. That is a remarkable accomplishment in the annals of mankind.

Ambassador Henry Cabot Lodge, who has served us with such great distinction, is coming to the end of his second distinguished tour of duty in Saigon.

To replace him, I am drafting as our Ambassador to the Government of Vietnam, Mr. Ellsworth Bunker—able and devoted, full of wisdom and experience acquired on five continents over many years.

As his Deputy, I am nominating and recalling from Pakistan, Mr. Eugene Locke, our young and very vigorous Ambassador to Pakistan.

To drive forward with a sense of urgency the work in pacification in Vietnam, I am sending Presidential Assistant Robert Komer.

To strengthen General Westmoreland in the intensive operations that he will be conducting in the months ahead, I am assigning to him additional top-flight military personnel, the best that the country has been able to provide.

So you can be confident that in the months ahead we shall have at work in Saigon the ablest, the wisest, the most tenacious, and the most experienced team that the United States of America can mount.

In view of these decisions and in view of the meetings that will take place this weekend, I thought it wise to invite the leaders of South Vietnam to join us in Guam for a part of our discussions, if it were convenient for them. I am gratified to be informed that they have accepted our invitation.

I should also like for you to know that the representatives of all the countries that are contributing troops in Vietnam will be coming to Washington for April 20 and 21 meetings for a general appraisal of the situation that exists.

This brings me to my final point, the peaceful and just world that we all seek.

We have just lived through another flurry of rumors of "peace feelers."

Our years of dealing with this problem have taught us that peace will not come easily.

The problem is a very simple one: it takes two to negotiate at a peace table and Hanoi has just simply refused to consider coming to a peace table.

I don't believe that our own position on peace negotiations can be stated any more clearly than I have stated it many times in the past—or that the distinguished Secretary of State, Mr. Rusk, or Ambassador Goldberg, or any number of other officials have stated it in every forum that we could find.

I do want to repeat to you this afternoon—and through you to the people of America—the essentials now, lest there be any doubts.

United States representatives are ready at any time for discussions of the Vietnam problem or any related matter, with any government or governments, if there is any reason to believe that these discussions will in any way seriously advance the cause of peace.

We are prepared to go more than halfway and to use any avenue possible to encourage such discussions. And we have done that at every opportunity.

We believe that the Geneva Accords of 1954 and 1962 could serve as the central elements of a peaceful settlement. These accords provide, in essence, that both South and North Vietnam should be free from external interference, while at the same time they would be free independently to determine their positions on the question of reunification.

We also stand ready to advance toward a reduction of hostilities, without prior agreement. The road to peace could go from deeds to discussions, or it could start with discussions and go to deeds.

We are ready to take either route. We are ready to move on both of them.

Reciprocity must be the fundamental principle of any reduction in hostilities. The United States cannot and will not reduce its activities unless and until there is some reduction on the other side. To follow any other rule would be to violate the trust that we undertake when we ask a man to risk his life for his country.

We will negotiate a reduction of the bombing whenever the Government of North Vietnam is ready and there are almost innumerable avenues of communication by which the Government of North Vietnam can make their readiness known.

To this date and this hour, there has been no sign of that readiness.

Yet, we must—and we will—keep trying.

As I speak to you today, Secretary Rusk and our representatives throughout the world are on a constant alert. Hundreds and hundreds of quiet diplomatic conversations, free from the glare of front-page headlines, or of klieg lights, are being held and they will be held on the possibilities of bringing peace to Vietnam.

Governor Averell Harriman, with twenty-five years of experience of troubleshooting on the most difficult international problems that America has ever had, is carrying out my instructions that every possible lead, however slight it may first appear, from any source, public or private, shall be followed up.

Let me conclude by saying this: I so much wish that it were within my power to assure that all those in Hanoi could hear one simple message—America is committed to the defense of South Vietnam until an honorable peace can be negotiated.

If this one communication gets through and its rational implications are drawn, we should be at the table tomorrow. It would be none too soon for us. Then hundreds of thousands of Americans—as brave as any who ever took the field for their country—could come back home.

And the man who could lead them back is the man whom you trained and sent from here, our own beloved, brilliant General "Westy" Westmoreland. As these heroes came back to their homes, millions of Vietnamese could begin to make a decent life for themselves and their families without fear of terrorism, without fear of war, or without fear of Communist enslavement.

That is what we are working and fighting for. We must not—we shall not—and we will not—fail.

# A Memorial to American Vietnam War Veterans[11]

Albert Keller, Jr.

*Born 1915, Peoria, IL; U.S. Army Air Force, 1943-45; accountant, David Bradley Mfg. Co., 1945-50; office manager and accountant, Azzarelli Construction Co., 1955-59; chief deputy county clerk, Kankakee, Illinois, 1959-64; administrative assistant, 1964-82, alderman, 1969-73, Kankakee County, Illinois; accountant, American Red Cross, 1973-82; national commander of the American Legion, 1982–.*

## Editor's introduction

Before 200,000 people on a cold, rainy Saturday, Albert Keller, Jr., war hero and World War II prisoner of war, dedicated the Vietnam Veterans Memorial. In this brief address, Commander Keller both praised Vietnam veterans "who fought a lonely battle" and recalled the less than gracious spirit that greeted their return. He noted that many believed the Vietnam War to be a source of shame and humiliation, but asserted that, in reality, the war allowed Americans to rediscover their ability "to care, to give, and to honor."

---

Thank you, Jan. Today we dedicate a memorial to a generation of Americans who fought a lonely battle. We dedicate the Vietnam Veterans Memorial to those who died in that war, yes. But, more than that, we dedicate it to those countless thousands who survived that war, only to face a battle that honor bound them to.

In the jungles and the dusty deltas of Vietnam, our young soldiers stood together and cared for their wounded and dead. If no other characteristic distinguished the Vietnam veteran, it was his unfaltering devotion to his comrades. They let no wound go untended. They left no dead behind. And they came home expecting the nation to care about their comrades as they did.

But instead, they encountered indifference and a deep desire to have Vietnam, and those who fought there, left behind.

But this generation of veterans would not have it so. For years the wounded spirit festered. And for years the Vietnam veteran tended to himself and did what he would alone. And for years the wounded memory of his comrades cried out to be healed, waiting, hoping, crying out in a hundred tortured ways.

The Vietnam veterans yearned for a way to tend to this last wound of the war. And, finally, they decided, as they had learned in the war itself, that they would have to tend to one another alone.

But today, we know they were wrong. The American people, inspired by the undaunted determination of those men and women, responded in a historic conversion of compassion, caring and generosity. Standing at last before them was the opportunity to express the gratitude and the honor that they longed to give, but knew not how to grant.

There are those who say that the war in Vietnam brought shame on America. There are those who say this memorial would bring shame on those who fought the war. But there are those, like the men and women that I represent, who say, "Not so." There is no shame in answering the nation's call. There is no shame in serving with honor and courage in difficult times. And there is no shame in enshrining the names of fallen comrades in immutable stone for generations to recall.

There is a legacy left for us from the Vietnam experience, and it was left to the young who fought there to show it to us. And that is the rediscovery of our capacity to care, to give, and to honor. That is no small legacy for a nation to receive.

[11]Delivered at the dedication of the Vietnam Veterans Memorial, in Washington, D.C., on November 13, 1982.

This memorial symbolizes, not only the supreme gift of nearly 58,000 young Americans, but also the priceless gift of renewed awareness in our capacity as a people.

With this dedication, we come not to the end of America's commitment to Vietnam veterans, but the beginning of a new awareness of their unparalleled contribution to the nation.

Generations to come will walk before these gleaming walls and, like them, will reflect. They will consider the memories of those who died. They will consider the legacy of the living veterans left. And they will take from this Memorial a promise to be ever true to their American heritage.

My fellow veterans, families and friends, we are here today to honor, to remember and to consecrate forever this piece of America, to insure that coming generations understand how dearly we hold those who served our nation in Vietnam. How painfully we recognize that the debt we owe those listed here can never be paid. And how hopefully we stand together as a nation of peace.

There are some very special people here with us today. They symbolize America's future. They are the children of our nation's Vietnam veterans.

Let us salute this nation's Vietnam this afternoon by joining hands in a silent pledge that together we will care for their children, as we pray that Vietnam was America's war to end all wars.

# Operation Desert Storm[12]

George H. W. Bush

*Born June 12, 1924, Milton, MA; U.S. Navy, 1942-45; B.A., Yale University, 1948; founder, president, Bush-Overby Co., 1950-53; co-founder, Zapata Petroleum Corp., 1953-54; co-founder, president, Zapata Offshore Co., 1954-66; representative (R) from Texas, 1966-70; permanent representative to the United Nations, 1970-73; chairman, Republican National Committee, 1970-74; chief, U.S. Liaison Office in People's Republic of China, 1974-76; director, Central Intelligence Agency, 1976; vice president of the United States, 1981-88; president of the United States, 1989-92.*

## Editor's introduction

On August 2, 1990, Iraqi forces invaded Kuwait. On August 5, President George Bush stated that the occupation of Kuwait by Iraq "would not stand." Five months of United Nations diplomatic efforts, all aimed at getting Iraqi forces to withdraw from Kuwait, proved fruitless. With the support of 20 United Nations members, President Bush announced over national television that a military attack on Baghdad and Kuwait had begun. Watched by 79 percent of American households, Bush attempted to justify a military engagement with a country most Americans knew little about. As *Insight on the News* asked, "How do you frame the issue so the people are behind you?" Bush worded this address in a bold style, clearly reminiscent of Lyndon B. Johnson's attempt to vindicate the country's involvement in Vietnam.

---

Five months ago, Saddam Hussein started this cruel war against Kuwait; tonight the battle has been joined. This military action, taken in accord with United Nations resolutions and with the consent of the United States Congress, follows months of constant and virtually endless diplomatic activity on the part of the United Nations, the United States and many, many other countries.

Arab leaders sought what became known as an Arab solution, only to conclude that Saddam Hussein was unwilling to leave Kuwait. Others travelled to Baghdad in a variety of efforts to restore peace and justice. Our Secretary of State James Baker held an historic meeting in Geneva only to be totally rebuffed.

This past weekend, in a last ditch effort, the Secretary General of the United Nations went to the Middle East with peace in his heart, his second such mission, and he came back from Baghdad with no progress at all in getting Saddam Hussein to withdraw from Kuwait.

Now, the 28 countries with forces in the Gulf area have exhausted all reasonable efforts to reach a peaceful resolution, have no choice but to drive Saddam from Kuwait by force. We will not fail.

As I report to you, air attacks are under way against military targets in Iraq. We are determined to knock out Saddam Hussein's nuclear bomb potential. We will also destroy his chemical weapons facilities. Much of Saddam's artillery and tanks will be destroyed.

Our operations are designed to best protect the lives of all the coalition forces by targeting Saddam's vast military arsenal.

Initial reports from General Schwarzkopf are that our operations are proceeding according to plan.

Our objectives are clear. Saddam Hussein's forces will leave Kuwait. The legitimate government of Kuwait will be restored to its rightful place and Kuwait will once again be free.

Iraq will eventually comply with all relevant United Nations resolutions and then when peace is restored, it is our hope that Iraq will live as a peaceful and cooperative member of the family of nations, thus enhancing the security and stability of the Gulf.

[12]Broadcast nationwide, from Washington, D.C., on January 16, 1991.

Some may ask, "Why act now? Why not wait?" The answer is clear. The world could wait no longer.

Sanctions, though having some effect, showed no signs of accomplishing their objective. Sanctions were tried for well over five months and we and our allies concluded that sanctions alone would not force Saddam from Kuwait.

While the world waited, Saddam Hussein systematically raped, pillaged and plundered a tiny nation—no threat to his own. He subjected the people of Kuwait to unspeakable atrocities, and among those maimed and murdered—innocent children. While the world waited Saddam sought to add to the chemical weapons arsenal he now possesses an infinitely more dangerous weapon of mass destruction, a nuclear weapon.

And while the world waited, while the world talked peace and withdrawal, Saddam Hussein dug in and moved massive forces into Kuwait. While the world waited, while Saddam stalled, more damage was being done to the fragile economies of the Third World, the emerging democracies of Eastern Europe, to the entire world, including to our own economy.

The United States, together with the United Nations, exhausted every means at our disposal to bring this crisis to a peaceful end.

However, Saddam clearly felt that by stalling and threatening and defying the United Nations he could weaken the forces arrayed against him.

While the world waited Saddam Hussein met every overture of peace with open contempt. While the world prayed for peace Saddam prepared for war.

I had hoped that when the United States Congress, in historic debate, took its resolute action Saddam would realize he could not prevail and would move out of Kuwait in accord with the United Nations resolutions. He did not do that.

Instead, he remained intransigent, certain that time was on his side. Saddam was warned over and over again to comply with the will of the United Nations—leave Kuwait or be driven out. Saddam has arrogantly rejected all warnings. Instead, he tried to make this a dispute between Iraq and the United States of America.

Well, he failed. Tonight, 28 nations, countries from five continents—Europe and Asia, Africa and the Arab League—have forces in the Gulf area standing shoulder-to-shoulder against Saddam Hussein. These countries had hoped the use of force could be avoided. Regrettably, we now believe that only force will make him leave.

Prior to ordering our forces into battle, I instructed our military commanders to take every necessary step to prevail as quickly as possible and with the greatest degree of protection possible for American people before that this will not be another Vietnam.

And I repeat this here tonight. Our troops will have the best possible support in the entire world. And they will not be asked to fight with one hand tied behind their back.

I'm hopeful that this fighting will not go on for long and that casualties will be held to an absolute minimum. This is an historic moment. We have in this past year made great progress in ending the long era of conflict and Cold War. We have before us the opportunity to forge for ourselves and for future generations a new world order, a world where the rule of law, not the law of the jungle, governs the conduct of nations. When we are successful, and we will be, we have a real chance at this new world order, an order in which a credible United Nations can use its peacekeeping role to fulfill the promise and vision of the U.N.'s founders.

We have no argument with the people of Iraq. Indeed, for the innocents caught in this conflict, I pray for their safety. Our goal is not the conquest of Iraq. It is the liberation of Kuwait.

It is my hope that somehow the Iraqi people can even now convince their dictator that he must lay down his arms, leave Kuwait and let Iraq itself rejoin the family of peace-loving nations.

Thomas Paine wrote many years ago: "These are the times that try men's souls." Those well-known words are so very true today.

But even as planes of the multinational forces attack Iraq, I prefer to think of peace, not war. I am convinced not only that we will prevail, but that out of the horror of combat will come the recognition that no nation can stand against a world united, no nation will be permitted to brutally assault its neighbor.

No president can easily commit our sons and daughters to war.

They are the nation's finest. Ours is an all-volunteer force, magnificently trained, highly motivated. The troops know why they're there. And listen to what they say, for they've said it better than any president or prime minister ever could. Listen to Hollywood Huddleston, Marine lance corporal.

He says, "Let's free these people so we can go home and be free again." And he's right. The terrible crimes and tortures committed by Saddam's henchmen against the innocent people of Kuwait are an affront to mankind and a challenge to the freedom of all.

Listen to one of our great officers out there, Marine Lieutenant General Walter Boomer. He said, "There are things worth fighting for. A world in which brutality and lawlessness are allowed to go unchecked isn't the kind of world we're going to want to live in."

Listen to Master Sergeant J.K. Kendall of the 82nd Airborne. "We're here for more than just the price of a gallon of gas. What we're doing is going to chart the future of the world for the next 100 years. It's better to deal with this guy now than five years from now."

And finally, we should all sit up and listen to Jackie Jones, an Army lieutenant, when she says, "If we let him get away with this, who knows what's going to be next?" I've called upon Hollywood and Walter and J.P. and Jackie and all their courageous comrades in arms to do what must be done.

Tonight America and the world are deeply grateful to them and to their families.

And let me say to everyone listening or watching tonight: When the troops we've sent in finish their work, I'm determined to bring them home as soon as possible. Tonight, as our forces fight, they and their families are in our prayers.

May God bless each and every one of them and the coalition forces at our side in the Gulf, and may He continue to bless our nation, the United States of America.

# VI. Human Rights

## Editor's introduction

Human rights and civil rights (the next chapter is devoted to civil rights) address many of the same issues, however, discussions on human rights are usually of a more general nature, as they tend to assert the rights and privileges of all human beings, as opposed to those of a particular race or religion. In doing so, such speeches highlight various practices that are perceived as treating people unequally. While denials of human rights have undoubtedly occurred, passionate attempts to both understand and preserve those human rights have also been the focus of much debate and discussion. Eric A. Johnson, president of the United States Chamber of Commerce, has asserted that human rights, being the "sacred dignity of the human, regardless of race or class or place of birth," must be cherished if a band of individuals is to call itself a "civilization." In like fashion, former president Jimmy Carter heavily stressed the fundamental value of human rights. His administration repeatedly suspended or reduced American aid to nations that violated human rights, and he was outspoken in his criticism of Soviet and Czechoslovakian harassment of political protesters. Affirming government's obligation to preserve human rights, Carter once stated that "the first duty of a government is to protect its own citizens." As the speeches contained in this chapter will convey, Carter and Johnson are not alone in their belief in the elemental and basic necessity of human rights to both the American citizenry and humanity at large.

Adam Clayton Powell, Jr., owing to a loss of faith in the purpose and resolve of individual states, insisted that only federal legislation would remedy discriminatory hiring practices. As Powell accused American industry of not providing equal opportunity for all citizens, Representative Shirley Chisholm accused the United States government of failing to encourage women and minority groups to actively participate in the political process. Chisholm noted that failing to vote prevents voices from being heard, and human rights, in the form of equal political representation, from being achieved. Adopting a similar argument, Henry Louis Gates, Jr., then W. E. B. DuBois professor of literature at Cornell University, asked the academic community to look beyond their Western ethnocentricity and adopt a more reflective, multicultural perspective. Chisholm's belief that all people, regardless of gender or ethnic background, must have equal representation in the political process is echoed by Gates, who asserts that all people must be equally represented in the literature that is taught in our schools.

# Lidice[1]

## Wendell L. Willkie

*Born February 18, 1892, Elwood, IN; died October 8, 1944; B.A., 1913, LL.B., 1916, University of Indiana; lawyer, Firestone Co., 1918-24; lawyer, Mather and Newbitt, 1924-29; attorney, 1929-33, president, 1933-40, Commonwealth and Southern; Republican nominee for president, 1940.*

### Editor's introduction

Six weeks before this speech was given, General Reinhard Heydrich, SS chief and Adolph Hitler's governor of Czechoslovakia, was assassinated. In retaliation, Nazi soldiers murdered all the male citizens of Lidice, Czechoslovakia, forced the women into a concentration camp, and sent the children to "centers of education." They effectively eliminated Lidice from existence, completing their mission by burning the town to the ground. In memory of those Czechoslovakians, citizens of Stern Park Gardens gathered to rename their community "Lidice." Wendell L. Willkie, a very successful and politically influential lawyer, spoke on this moving occasion. With characteristic vigor, Willkie dramatized the tragedy and expounded on his philosophy of the unconquerable "free spirit," of which he believed Hitler was most afraid.

---

Fellow Citizens and all who love freedom everywhere:

Let me tell you a story. Ten miles west of Prague, in Czechoslovakia, there was a little village called Lidice, spelled L I D I C E. It was a mining village, a mile off the main highway, with some lovely old inns, a blacksmith or two, a shoemaker, a wheelwright, a tailor. The village had been there for over six hundred years.

Above the ninety roofs of the town rose the spire of St. Margaret's Church, built in 1736, the home of the faith of the community. This town was remote, peaceful, almost like a village in a fairy tale. But it was not a village in a fairy tale, for its people had tasted the bread and wine of freedom. In this village one of the main streets was named Wilson Street, after an American who had a vision and wanted to share it with the world. And the people of Lidice dreamed the same dream, saw the same vision.

But the Nazis came, and with them misery and hardship. The altar of St. Margaret's Church was no longer open to the people as it had been for over two hundred years. Men had to watch their words and in their actions they could no longer be free. But in their hearts, the hearts of the inn-keeper and the tailor and the farmer and the miner and the priest, was the stubborn independence of their fathers.

Not far from Lidice ran a winding road. On this road on May 27th, six weeks ago, at 10:30 in the morning, a motor car was passing carrying Hitler's governor of Czechoslovakia, Hangman Heydrich, for his cruelties the most hated man in all Europe. The car was held up by two unknown men. Bullets burrowed into the spine of Reinhard Heydrich. The two patriots disappeared, and one of them, it is said, is now safe in London.

I do not wish to speak of the reign of terror that thereupon swept over all Czechoslovakia. I wish to speak today only of Lidice, and I will give you only the facts. This is not my version of the facts. This is not a version of the facts issued by any of the United Nations as propaganda. These are the facts as officially attested by the German government. They are facts of which the Nazis are proud. They are facts they wish the world to know. They are facts they believe will frighten you and me, and turn our hearts and our knees to water, and make us cry "Truce!"

For Heydrich the Hangman died in agony, as he had caused thousands of innocent people

[1]Delivered on July 12, 1942, at the ceremonies renaming Stern Park Gardens, Illinois.

to die. No proof from that day to this has ever been adduced to show that any of the inhabitants of Lidice had anything to do with the assassination. But the Nazis made their own proof. They were afraid not to, for Heydrich was one of their great men. "One of the best Nazis," Hitler called him, and that, no doubt, is true.

On June 10th an official German statement was issued, not for domestic consumption, but for the world to hear. I quote from it:

"It is officially announced that in the course of the search for the murderers of General Heydrich, it has been ascertained that the population of the village of Lidice supported and assisted the perpetrators who came into question . . . . Because the inhabitants, by their support of the perpetrators have flagrantly violated the law, all men of the village have been shot. The women have been deported to a concentration camp and the children sent to appropriate centers of education. All buildings of the village were leveled to the ground and the name of the village was immediately abolished."

That is the official Nazi report.

They came in the night, men in boots and brown shirts, and they took from their homes the bewildered miners and farmers, the tailor and the priest, the boy of seventeen and the old man of seventy, more than two hundred in all, and they shot them, because they could think of no other way to avenge the death of Heydrich. Fifty-six women they took also and killed, and proudly listed their names. The rest of the women they drove into what they called concentration camps; and these women the world will never see again. They herded the pale, terror-stricken children into trucks and carried them off to correction schools where they would be taught that they must honor the murderers of their fathers and the brutalizers of their mothers. The ninety homes they burned to the ground, the church of St. Margaret they stamped into the earth. And the name of the little town of Lidice, through which ran the street called after a President of the United States, they rubbed out, they thought, from history.

Why did they do this deed, more terrible than anything that has happened since the Dark Ages, a deed not of passion, but of cold, premeditated, systematic murder and rapine? Why? They did it because they are afraid. They are afraid because the free spirit in men has refused to be conquered. Theirs is a system of force and terror and Lidice is the terrible symbol of that system.

But it is not the only one. Of the five hundred thousand men, women and children who have been shot in Europe by the Nazis, at least twenty-five thousand have perished in mass massacres. Poland, Norway, Belgium, Yugoslavia, all have their Lidices. But this one—a symbol of all—we have sworn to remember, if only because the Nazis themselves demand that we forget it. Once more, they have misjudged the human spirit.

Because a hangman was killed, Lidice lives. Because a hangman was killed, Wilson Street must once again be part of a little Bohemian town. Because the lanterns of Lidice have been blacked out, a flame has been lit which can never be extinguished. Each of the wounds of those two hundred men and fifty-six women is a mouth that cries out that other free men and free women must not suffer a like fate. Everywhere, but particularly in our own country, the wave of stubborn, stern resolve rises. Lidice lives. She lives again, thirty-five hundred miles from Wilson Street and St. Margaret's Church, in this little village in Illinois.

I look about me here, and I can see in the distance the black smoke of steel factories, swarming with American workers of all bloods and races. No contrast could be greater than the peaceful Lidice the Nazis thought they had destroyed, and this Illinois country, alive with factories in which the arms of victory are being forged. But I tell you that the two are related. For while such deeds as Lidice are done in another country, we cannot rest until we are sure that they will never be done in our own.

Let us here highly resolve that the memory of this little village of Bohemia, now resurrected by the people of a little village in Illinois, will fire us, now and until the battle is over, with the iron resolution that the madness of tyrants must perish from the earth, so that the earth may return to the people to whom it belongs, and be their village, their home, forever.

# Democracy and Racial Minorities[2]

Francis Beverly Biddle

*Born May 9, 1886, Paris, France; died October 4, 1968; B.A., 1909, LL.D., 1911, Harvard University; secretary to Associate Supreme Court Justice Oliver Wendell Holmes, 1912-17; partner, Barnes, Biddle, & Myers, 1917-39; chair, National Labor Relations Board, 1934-35; director, Federal Reserve Bank, 1938-39; judge, U.S. Court of Appeals, 1939-40; U.S. solicitor general, 1940-41; U.S. attorney general, 1941-45; author,* In Brief Authority *(1962).*

## Editor's introduction:

In this speech, former United States Attorney General Francis Beverly Biddle discussed the problems and difficulties which continue to plague race relations in America. While Biddle's talk was limited to Japanese, Jewish, and African-American groups, the themes upon which he touched are relevant to the plight of all groups hoping to achieve equality in the American societal structure. According to Biddle, the alleviation of racial tension will not occur through law enforcement, but rather by eliminating its true cause—public ignorance.

---

I propose to discuss tonight some of the broader aspects of presently existing minority problems in our American democracy, particularly as they concern three racial groups, whose relation to the greater body of our nation has been brought into sharp focus by two years of war. I refer to the Japanese, the Jews and the Negroes.

I note with interest that the Seminary is broadening the scope of its work to consider questions that touch not only the Jewish community, but its relationship to our national life. And the emphasis of my theme tonight is that the approach of all of us to these troublesome problems of minorities cannot any longer be local or provincial, or in the terms even of the difficulties facing any particular group, or for evolving the traditions or the tenets of any single race or any one religion. For the war has shown that at least certain of the more acute minority problems are national in their scope, and, what is even more important, national in their effect on our American integrity. Not any longer, then, can the difficulties of any particular minority be the sole concern of that minority. It is the very nature of our American democracy that it is made up of minorities—Catholic, and Jewish, Negro and Japanese, Quakers and Indians, organized labor and farmers. This is peculiarly true of us, because our American heritage draws strength from the fact that our shores have since the beginning held invitation and asylum to those minorities driven out from other countries by the oppressions of the majority—from the majority power of landlord, or religious sect, or government—and come here to find tolerance and acceptance. Is it not of our American essence and tradition that these dissenters against suppression have found that they could and did live side by side under the sky of a democracy that welcomed differences because it believed in the practice of freedom? Minorities are then inherent in our national life, more than in most of the older nations; and that here they could be *united* is our pride and the admiration of our friends. We have achieved union without insisting on uniformity.

I suggest to you that the problem of minorities is today of deep spiritual significance to your religion, for it stems from the religious tradition of the dignity of man as man. The importance of the human personality is a fundamental concern on their highest levels of both Jewish and Christian faith. It is profoundly a religious idea that is now gravely imperiled throughout the world. And our religious bodies can afford

[2]Delivered at the fifth anniversary of the Institute of Religious Studies, in New York, New York, on November 11, 1943.

the whole world a moral leadership in this conception, so close to the democratic faith—but only if that leadership is bravely exercised first here in our own country.

It is a curious paradox that although during this war certain civil liberties have suffered less than in the first World War, the tensions arising from the place of these three racial minorities in the national life have greatly increased. In the last war the right of alien enemies, particularly of course Germans who were living in our country, and of those radicals who opposed the war, and our entry into it, were little respected. National prejudice then ran against anyone of German ancestry, no matter how long he had lived here or how loyal he was to us. It ran, too, against anyone who showed opposition to the war. Freedom of speech was less tolerated, and more newspapers were suppressed on the ground that they were seditious. There were many more prosecutions, both state and federal, often on ill-considered and petty grounds. And the years that directly followed the war were characterized by mass raids that expressed a blind resentment against foreigners, who were too often classed in the popular mind as radical and therefore un-American.

These attacks have not recurred in this war or at least to a far less degree. The Italians and the Germans in the United States have not felt the brunt of popular hatred (I do not include our treatment of the Japanese, which I shall discuss later).

There are obvious explanations for this. National, state and local governments have acted more wisely, and have not permitted the war psychology to whip them into harsh and unnecessary measures of repression.

Actually there were far fewer Italians and Germans in 1941 than in 1917. There are no accurate census figures of the number of Germans and Italians in this country in 1917. But we have the 1920 figures, which give us a fairly accurate picture for purposes of comparison. In 1920, there were 458,388 German aliens in the United States. In 1940, when they were registered under the Federal law, there were 314,432. And under the alien certification program of 1942, the number had dropped to 270,556. In terms of percentage to population, the change of relation would of course be much more marked. With our quota limitation system we were rapidly absorbing the foreign-born. It may be also that in some ways the American public itself has changed, has grown more tolerant in this quarter century, is more unified, less unstable, more mature and less prone to treat the alien as a whipping boy.

On the other hand our treatment of Japanese American citizens hardly accords with these other signs of greater tolerance.

When in April of 1942, the United States Army decided to exclude the 110,000 persons of Japanese origin, citizens and non-citizens alike, from the West Coast as a military precaution to protect our Western Defense Command, the treacherous attack by the Japanese on Pearl Harbor was four months fresh, and there had been movements of airplanes and submarines which indicated the possibility of an attack. On June 3, 1942, Japanese planes raided Dutch Harbor in Alaska. The Japanese in the United States were concentrated in vital spots along the West Coast—in Portland, San Francisco and Los Angeles. It was not surprising that public opinion in those states where Japanese were concentrated in great numbers was deeply disturbed over the possibility of sabotage and reacted violently against all persons of Japanese origin, loyal and disloyal alike. The legal theory on which they were excluded was that anyone—citizen and alien alike—could be moved out of a war area for its protection. The theory was valid enough. But, like most theories, its ultimate test depended on the reasonableness of its exercise. To say that citizens could be moved out of a war might depend on the size of the area. If they could be moved away from the two coasts, away from possible points of attack, how far inland could they be taken? Could citizens be retained in any specified part of the country? Roughly two thirds of the persons moved were American citizens by reason of their birth in the United States, under the provisions of the American Constitution which protected them as effectively as it protected other citizens, irrespective of the color of their skins or the nationality of their ancestry. But in terms of public antipathy no distinction was drawn between citizens and aliens, between loyal and disloyal. In the eyes of the public, all persons of Japanese ancestry were Japs; and we had seen what the "Japs" had done to our soldiers.

The relocation centers were not designed as places of internment but as a refuge. In most instances local communities at first would not have them, at least in substantial numbers. Today the loyal Japanese who are American citizens are being gradually reestablished outside the centers in places where they may gain tolerance and acceptance. The Relocation Authority has no power to intern American citizens; and constitutionally it is hard to believe that any such authority could be granted to the government. The decision of the Supreme Court in the Hirabayashi case, decided last spring, indicates this conclusion. The Court sustained the validity of curfew orders applied by the military authorities prior to the evacuation of the Japanese on the West Coast. The validity of the evacuation orders was not even considered, let alone the far more difficult problem of detention. Even the curfew order was said by Mr. Justice Murphy in his concurring opinion to go "to the very brink of constitutional power."

I emphasize this particular problem—very special in its aspects—because it is far from solution; and public opinion, often hostile or indifferent, has made its solution infinitely more difficult.

We have too casually accepted, I think, this perhaps necessary but obviously temporary meeting of the problem. We have hardly recognized its serious consequences and the fact that it has never occurred before. Would anyone, before the war, have complacently accepted the proposition that the government could move 75,000 American citizens out of their homes, and hold them with enemy aliens for relocation?

I do not believe that among those of Japanese parentage born and bred in America, graduated from our public schools, many of them speaking nothing but English, there are not men and women and young people who are loyal to our country. Of course eighteen months in detention camps may have made some of them waver in their loyalty. But I am glad of the policy of the Relocation Authority which is directed towards sorting out the loyal citizens and returning them back into the community.

Last August a group of Japanese aliens in one of the internment camps operated by the Department of Justice at Crystal City, Texas, was repatriated. This was a "family" camp, so-called because wives and children of the interned alien enemies were allowed to live with them in family groups. Among them was a Japanese family whose two sons, American-born, had already been released on their stated desire to remain in the United States, even though their family was returning to Japan. The morning the repatriates were scheduled to leave, the two Japanese boys returned to the camp to say goodbye to their parents. Just at sunrise, as the American flag was being raised, and as the entire population of the camp gathered about the flagpole for a farewell ceremony, the two young Japanese-Americans stepped forward, saluted the flag and sang "God Bless America." They then left to join the American Army.

Recently a report from Fifth Army headquarters made special mention of Japanese Americans fighting side by side with other Americans in Italy. I am told that more than five thousand men of Japanese origin are today enrolled in our army. Neither Japan nor Germany can boast of American battalions in their ranks. The Fifth Army says of these Japanese-Americans: "They obviously believe in what they're doing, and look calmly secure because of it." Our sons are today fighting side by side with the sons of Italians, of Germans, and of Japanese. Is anything more needed to entitle the loyal Japanese Americans to recognition?

For this is the essence of our democracy in practice. The *Washington Evening Star* in a recent editorial, reporting the dispatch I have mentioned, made this admirable comment:

"All races, all colors, make us up. And when wars like the present one engulf us, all races and all colors take up arms for America. When we strike back at our enemies, the American kin of those enemies do the striking—Americans of Italian extraction, of German extraction, even of Japanese extraction. We are of almost every extraction conceivable, black, white and yellow, and so we are tied together not by any mystical philosophy of blood or common ethnic traits, but solely and simply by an idea—the idea of democracy, of individual freedom, of liberty under law, of a justice before which all of us stand equal."

What has rendered peculiarly acute any mistreatment of racial minorities—Japanese, Negro, Jewish—is our reiterated insistence on democratic equality of opportunity, irrespective of race, and the total nature of this war compared to the last. Far more now than then, every man, white or black, Jew or Gentile, is enlisted to fight or to work for the common cause. But how can every man believe that the cause is a common one including him as well as another, if he sees discrimination against him as a member of a race or of a religion; discrimination in the army in which he must fight, in industry, in the civil offices of the government? I do not believe that many will deny the discrimination, or its evil effects on our democratic ideals, except those whose prejudices, though honestly held, blind them to the tragic contradictions involved in such behavior.

I know that there are those who contend that any discussion of these tense and difficult relationships in the midst of a war is unwise. Why stir up trouble—so the argument runs—and give ammunition for propaganda and the appearance of disunity to our enemies? Why not put off an attempt at solution until the war is over? If those conditions were sporadic or local in their origin the argument would have more weight. But they are not. They involve many sections of our country, and are creating a national psychology of intolerance that makes them infinitely more difficult and serious. Moreover the appearance of national disunity on the outside, serious as it is, seems to me less evil than the actual disunity inside our ranks. It is not exact to say that the recent outbreaks of racial violence in America have been fostered by Axis propaganda. But it is certainly true to conclude that the effect of such violence serves well the enemies' purpose. Immediately after they occurred the Detroit race riots were reported and commented on from short-wave radios in Germany and Japan; and the news soon traveled into Africa and China and India.

But when all is said and done, I am less concerned about how the United States looks to her enemies. What I care about is what she looks like to her friends; to those who love and believe in her; to Americans in the field who fight and die for her; to Americans at home and abroad who want to be able to speak with pride and without any mental reservation when they say with Thomas Jefferson "this government, the best hope of man."

I am not seeking to fix responsibility in any group or in any class for these unhappy conditions. The blame is universal, for surely all Americans must share the responsibility for this so un-American condition in a country which is, I believe, on the whole, honestly dedicated to democratic living. And just as the blame must be shared by all alike, so it concerns us all—government, society, the churches, whose function here is indistinguishable from the democratic concept; labor, and the employers of labor, the press and the school and college.

Too often in the past the Negro problem has been thought of and talked about as if it were sectional, as if it existed in certain states in the South and was not a problem in the North. Whatever once was true, it is perfectly clear that the problem is now national in its scope and is not confined to any particular part of the country. The Los Angeles disorders, the Detroit riots, the New York disorders, all of recent months, show that racial clashes since the war started do not occur only in the South and do not spring only from the ancient prejudices and hatred and fears inherited from the Civil War, and from the outnumbering of the whites by Negroes in certain parts of the South, but are implicit in great industrial societies that have never known slavery or the inherited memories of a slave relationship.

War unifies a country, not merely by giving expression to a common effort, but by throwing together vast masses of young men who in their training at the camps exchange ideas and the points of view of other parts of the country. A large proportion of the camps, obviously for practical reasons, has been built in the South; and the Negro officers and soldiers trained there have without doubt been treated in many cases with discrimination, rudeness and even brutality by white civilians and white police officers. The result among the Negroes is bitter disillusionment and anguish, as anyone knows who has talked to colored troops or read the letters they have sent home. The Army has been alive to the serious effect of this treatment on morale, and has made efforts to improve it. An article in the August *Infantry Journal* deals frankly with this form of race prejudice. Let me quote from it:

"Sometimes the prejudice against the Negroes flares up in the Army. It is not a problem, however, in a camp where it is well understood that a soldier in the United States uniform is a soldier, not a white or a Negro, Christian or Jew, rich man or poor, but a soldier, and as such is worthy of respect."

We must realize then that the problem of the relation of the white to the Negro, in fact the problems of most racial minorities, are national in their scope. They concern all of us, for they go to the roots of our democratic standards. I have emphasized the Negro soldier, for mistreatment or disrespect of the Negro citizen in uniform, who fights to defend our flag, is disavowal of those things for which our flag is the symbol—a free nation under God. To this promise of American life we have two commitments which we cannot revoke, which we cannot disregard. Our national Constitution guarantees equality of treatment and opportunity to all. More recently we have assumed obligations of defending the democracy elsewhere in the world attacked by totalitarian aggression. These principles and promises must be fulfilled in the due course of the evolution of our democratic life. Nor can we assume the obligations of a defense of world democracy if our example of democracy at home, in this fundamental aspect, is neither consistent nor courageous. Race intolerance is no longer a matter merely of domestic concern. For it undermines our moral authority as a nation which apparently can profess but cannot practice democracy.

The injustices that have been done, that are being done the Negro, are obviously recognized throughout the country. But the implications of this treatment, I am certain, are not generally realized. We have too long accepted discrimination to achieve in any short time or with any determined resolution the will to change an injustice that has to some extent formed the pattern of habit. I do not mean that the need is agitation, which but tends to accentuate the bitterness; or any campaign for immediate reform of every evil on all sides at once. But the agitation is here already, emerging from the flame of the war which has suddenly brought out the difference to which I have referred—the difference between our profession and our performance.

I suggest that what is greatly needed is a broader and more intelligent use of the moral and educational influences of the community. Most Americans are honest in their belief in equality of opportunity. But intellectual honesty in such a field of prejudice and ancient folk ways can be achieved only by the slow and steady impact of education.

Just as the responsibility for existing conditions cannot be fixed in any one group, or in any single section of the country, so the change must come from the efforts of all stable and progressive elements of our society. The recent outbreak of anti-Semitism among Boston public school children shows how great is the part educational institutions must play in the picture. One of the striking features of the Detroit riots was that there were no racial clashes in the plants where a well-disciplined union had insisted that it would not tolerate the refusal of whites to work side by side with Negroes. But in some unions discrimination against Negroes is practiced by not permitting them to vote; from some unions they are excluded, and in others prevented from rising into skilled jobs.

The government—national, state and local—must of course bear its share of responsibility for existing conditions.

I cannot tonight take time to discuss in any detail the steps which the Department of Justice is taking to help the situation. Our particular field is the enforcement of the Federal criminal statutes which may be violated. On this score there seems to be a very wide misunderstanding, particularly among these minority groups, as to the extent of our jurisdiction. Briefly considered there are two types of Federal statutes that are sometimes applicable. The first includes the so-called "civil rights" sections of the criminal code which make it a crime to conspire to deprive citizens of their rights guaranteed by the Federal Constitution, and for officers of the law, acting under color of law, to deprive them of such rights. These statutes were adopted soon after the Civil War, and have been very seldom invoked until the last three or four years. The Civil Liberties Section of the Criminal Division was organized to enforce them. We have obtained a number of indictments, though less convictions, under their provisions. Ordinary crimes of violence by individuals such as criminal assaults, murder and mob violence generally, do not come within the Federal jurisdiction. I shall presently cite one striking instance where this Federal jurisdiction was successfully invoked.

The other group of Federal offenses to which I refer deals with the war, such as resisting selective service and sedition. Anti-racial acts and utterances are not seditious in this criminal sense. As far as criminal enforcement is concerned, therefore, most acts of racial or mob violence are punishable under the laws of the state where they occur. Of course if it can be shown that these acts are the result of a conscious effort or conspiracy intended to hamper the war effort, or to use a current phrase, are "Axis inspired," the Federal courts would have jurisdiction. There has been no evidence or even indications of this in any of the recent riots and lootings in Los Angeles, Detroit or New York.

In any event government, Federal or state, must have the support of public opinion. But let me go further. It must have not only the indignation of the public generally against racial discriminations and outrages, but the insistence of the leaders of public opinion in the particular community involved, where the trouble occurs, that it is vital for their good to enforce the law and to prevent violations of law. And it is at this point that the influence of the church, of the press, of local leaders in all walks of life, can be felt. Ultimately government can do little without the support of that *community* public opinion. And the problem is not only national, it is necessarily local as well.

Let me give you two instances of what I have in mind. I have referred to the Federal statute that makes it criminal for law enforcement officers acting under the color of law to deprive anyone of his rights guaranteed under the Constitution of the United States. Recently a jury in Newton, Baker County, Georgia, convicted the county sheriff, a deputy sheriff and a Newton policeman under this statute for beating a Negro to death under cover of a forged warrant charging larceny of an automobile tire.

Newton is the county seat of Baker County. The county has a population of seven or eight hundred people. It is one of the few counties in the United States where there is no railroad.

Bob Hall, a Negro, owned a pearl handled automatic forty-five pistol. Deputy Sheriff Jones wanted it, and got it. After a month Hall appealed to the sheriff, and finally to the grand jury, who under instructions from the Solicitor General of the Circuit Court ordered the gun returned. But the sheriff would not return it. On the morning of January 29 of this year the sheriff received a letter from Hall's lawyer demanding the return of the gun. On the evening of January 29th Hall met his death at the hands of the three defendants. The State brought no prosecution. The Federal Government did. And on October 7, 1943, a local jury in this little town in Georgia, all of whom must have personally known the sheriff, his deputy, and the policeman, convicted all three. The defendants were sentenced by Judge Bascom S. Deaver to the maximum penalties under the law, three years' imprisonment and a fine of $1,000 each. It is significant that the Judge, the members of the jury, the United States Attorney and his staff, my special assistant whom I detailed to help the United States Attorney, and even the Federal Bureau of Investigation Agents who collected the evidence, were all native Georgians.

The government showed that on the day of the killing the defendants had been drunk for nearly six hours; that they boasted they were "going to get" a Negro who had "lived too long," who had got too smart and gone before a grand jury and employed a lawyer to recover his gun; that they arrested Hall, handcuffed his hands behind his back, brought him to the courthouse square and there beat his head with a blackjack; and that they dragged Hall by the feet through the Square into the jail where he was left in a dying condition. Hall died a few minutes after he was taken from the jail to a hospital.

The defendants tried to show that they had arrested Hall under a warrant, that Hall tried to shoot them, and that in self-protection they had to use a blackjack. The jury did not believe this; but what is more, the jury were not carried away by the arguments of defense counsel who tried to inflame their prejudices by injecting into the case the issues of race and "Yankee interference" in their community. This is the first time a conviction of this kind has ever been obtained in Georgia.

I take this occasion to say all honor to these twelve white men, who saw their duty and did it, under a wise and courageous charge from Judge Deaver, enforcing *their* law, the Federal law of *their* Government.

The *Atlanta Journal* said, commenting on the result: "Georgia's justice must become a synonym for equal justice for all, colored or white, humble or mighty." And the *Atlanta Daily World*, in another editorial: "The determination of Baker County's most distinguished white citizens . . . lends a new and encouraging stand against mob violence and brutality in the South."

While the punishment in this case scarcely fits the crime, it is the maximum under the Federal law involved, and the action of this Federal judge and jury is what I mean by leadership exercised within the community.

I suggest another example. The Federal Public Housing Authority is vitally interested in building homes for low-wage workers particularly in congested areas in the great and often dangerously overcrowded industrial centers. It is often very difficult to get the local authorities to agree on locations for housing for Negroes.

Often delays of many months intervene while the housing situation becomes more acute, as recently in Baltimore where a decision to select four sites, agreed on by the city authorities, after many months of negotiation, has been finally worked out. The program totals 1750 units, both temporary and permanent. The final plan had the approval of the city and county authorities and was developed to complement plans contemplated by private builders for Negro housing. The importance of community leadership in such practical and urgent problems is readily apparent. Without such leadership accomplishment becomes well nigh impossible.

Axis propaganda in this country took the form of vicious anti-Semitic teachings. There were a number of Fascist groups preaching disunity and race antagonism in the name of patriotism. Some of their members have been convicted of sedition, more are presently under indictment. Not all of these groups were directly Axis-inspired; but, led by violently bitter and prejudiced persons, they deliberately aroused in their publications and at their meetings the hatreds of the crowd against Negroes, against Jews, against foreigners, against liberals, against all who believed in a tolerant and generous democracy. They appealed to the maladjusted, to the ignorant, to the prejudiced. And their activities were not unprofitable. Contributions flowed in from frightened souls who believed the lies about Jewish domination or labor dictatorship, and from the thousands of little people who saw themselves saving their country, seizing a pathetic color of importance by joining movements and starting imaginary crusades.

Most of these wretched little pools of discontent and hatred have been dissolved or have disappeared under the great forward sweep of the country united in the war effort. But the fruit of their teaching is still with us. For all of them under different labels of patriotism or Americanism advocated hatred and violence, directed against one minority group or another. Our democratic institutions have at other times had to contend with similar attacks—the A.P.A., the Know-Nothings, the Ku Klux Klan. Today as in the past they incite men's hatreds into channels of violence and mob action against the orderly processes of the law. They set one group against another—Catholic against Jew—white against Negro. They try to disrupt the very essence of our democracy. They occur, where misunderstanding and prejudice have the first play; where these weaknesses have been stirred from the dark places of human nature into need for violent expression, and whipped into action; where the forces of education and religion have been unable to persuade or to control. Violence can be swiftly roused; reason and tolerance are the products of patience and the background of a decent way of living.

I have spoken tonight chiefly of the Japanese and Negroes, and have said almost nothing of the increase of anti-Semitism which so particularly concerns a Jewish audience. By this omission I do not mean to indicate that I am not deeply concerned with the cruel and dangerous form it is taking. It is profoundly shocking that it should have developed among school children, who, left to themselves, could hardly have turned against other children merely because they were Jewish. The desecration of Jewish cemeteries is hideously like what we have seen in those countries which have been conquered by the Germans. As Americans we must not tolerate this outbreak of the Axis pattern in our own country. It must be met, as it occurs, by firm law enforcement, at the same time that efforts are directed towards the eradication of its underlying causes.

But the efforts of government, whether in the field of law enforcement or elsewhere can do little, as I have said, without the support of public opinion. The President when he created the Committee on Fair Employment Practice, whose practical duty it is to remove barriers of discrimination which deny war jobs to available and needed workers, had this in mind when he stated, in the Executive Order, "that the democratic way of life within the nation can be defended successfully only with the help and support of all groups within its borders."

It has been suggested from time to time that there should be established by the Administration a council which should deal with these crucial minority problems. Basic to all these suggestions is the idea of research and education for the formation of public opinion. But I do not believe that the government should in any way attempt to mold public opinion, even in this field, by any such organized approach. It is said that if men of outstanding reputation were appointed on such a council or committee their work would be unpolitical and objective. Perhaps; and yet I do not think that government should institute or organize such a movement.

The idea has creative possibilities for good. But the impulse should rise from the private sources. The idea warrants exploration in these terms. The purpose of such a group would be primarily one of education. A good deal of research has been done. Possibly more is required. The need as I see it is not merely to collect the information and to distribute it, as objectively as possible, but by discussion, teaching, education, and cooperation on the community level to bring to our people an immediate realization of the tragic implications of these disunities. Already local groups have done effective work, as for instance at the Durham, Atlanta and Richmond conferences. The need is for a sustained effort, and a national approach.

I have great faith in the effectiveness of discussion and negotiation, particularly when it involves the leaders of the community itself, and where it is grounded on local interests, cleared from agitation and pulled out of the clouds of any philosophy, or theory of government. The men of Baker County, Georgia, whose action I have described, have done more for their community and for their state than anyone outside of Baker County could have accomplished.

I remember when I was chairman of the National Labor Relations Board in 1934-1935 we laid great emphasis on settlements of labor disputes by negotiation locally before they reached the stage of formal presentation to the board, when they were often overcharged with emotion. In several of the great cities we organized local panels of the leaders of industry and of labor, with a public chairman, who acted promptly and were immediately available to prevent labor disputes before they came to an issue, or to settle them after the disputes broke out. It was day-to-day work; and you could see the way representatives on each side grew to respect the other point of view, as prejudices gradually fell away under the impact of disinterested and humane cooperation for a common end—industrial peace.

If such a committee or council were formed to deal, let us say, with the minority problem of the Negro, it should be of course bi-racial in membership, with Negroes playing an equal part with whites. For the reason for its being would not be that whites were doing something *for* Negroes, but that both Negroes and whites were working for the common good of their country. And although it should be national in scope, and have in its ranks men and women from every section of the country, it must build through those who are the leaders of the local communities in the schools, in the labor unions, in groups of employers, in women's clubs, in churches of all faiths. It would seek to develop a local pride of tolerance and fair play that would not permit such assaults in our American way of life.

We have talked much of democracy, of the American way of life, in these last few years. But surely it cannot grow into the fullness of realization, as long as we, through indifference or through fear, permit these bitter injustices to continue. What we do today will write the history of the years to come. Do you remember what Walt Whitman said:

"We have frequently printed the word Democracy. Yet I cannot too often repeat that it is a word the real gist of which still sleeps, quite unawakened, notwithstanding the resonance and the many angry tempests out of which its syllables have come, from pen or tongue. It is a great word, whose history, I suppose, remains unwritten, because that history has yet to be enacted."

# Intolerance[3]

## Eric A. Johnston

*Born December 21, 1896, Washington, D.C.; died August 22, 1963; LL.B., University of Washington, 1917; U.S. Marine Corps, 1917-22; founder, director, Brown-Johnston Co., 1923-63; founder, chairman of the board, Columbia Electrical and Manufacturing Co., 1933-63; president, U.S. Chamber of Commerce, 1942-46; president, Motion Picture Association of America, 1945-63.*

### Editor's introduction

In 1941, the Treasury Department created the Writers' War Board to enlist the aid of writers in the selling of war bonds. As World War II progressed, the Writers' War Board wrote articles, scripts, stories, poems, slogans, pamphlets, and books in support of the Allied cause. Members of the Writers' War Board included William L. Shirer, author of *The Rise and Fall of the Third Reich*; Clifton Fadiman, noted essayist, critic, and anthologist; and Thornton Wilder, Pulitzer Prize–winning playwright. In this widely reprinted address, Eric A. Johnston, former president of the United States Chamber of Commerce, described to the Writers' War Board a rising American intolerance of foreigners. He theorized that this had emerged during the years between the World Wars. Johnston believed that this intolerance was a threat to both individual freedom and economic stability. To counter it, Johnston asserted that we must first understand it as a reality, and then gradually develop, and adhere to, a moral and ethical idealism that places all individuals on an equal plane.

---

I like to look on my presence here as a sign that the Hatfields of business and the McCoys of the writing world have ended their old-time feud. Maybe business is beginning to see more clearly that art has its practical aspects; and maybe the artist is beginning to realize that industry has its artistic values. More importantly, maybe both are beginning to understand that each is part of America and that neither has a right to pluck the mote out of the other's eye until he has first extracted the beam from his own.

Your subject tonight is "The Myth That Threatens America." Surely, the business man and the artist share responsibility in eradicating the myth of group or class superiority. Those who pretend that it does not exist are kidding themselves.

Of all the social problems that face our great country in this era of crisis, that of national unity seems to me the most challenging. Most other problems will not be solved if the American people are divided into mutually hostile and suspicious groups, sections and classes. More than that; even if solutions were possible under such conditions, they would hardly be worth achieving. They would be empty victories, utterly meaningless, if the character of our American civilization were changed in the process.

And the core of that civilization, it seems to me, is in the sacred dignity of the human being, regardless of race or class or place of birth. Individual freedom—liberty within a framework of law—is essential to the America we know and love. Without these elements it would no longer be *our* America, except in the geographical sense. In the deeper moral sense it would be an alien country, where those of us who cherish ideals of freedom would be exiles in our own homes.

We are all of us, in our several ways, seeking to preserve America. Millions of our sons are doing it on battlefields with bombs and bayonets. You who write and inspire and propagandize do it with the weapon of words. Those of us who build and manufacture do it with machines and goods. But what all of us have in mind is not simply the physical preservation of

[3]Delivered to the Writers' War Board, in New York, New York, on January 11, 1945.

our country. It is the preservation of those human values which are implicit in the word America—the freedom, the opportunities, the equalities, the democratic ideals celebrated in our national songs and poetry and books and holiday speeches.

I know there are the clichés of American patriotism and after-dinner oratory. But we do not discount them for that reason. On the contrary, we accept them and cherish them as proof positive that the American Dream is a dream of free men living together in a spirit of harmony and trust.

I regard as profoundly significant the fact that the average American, whether he be a blasé business man or a cynical writer, looks on these so-called clichés as desirable even when he doesn't live up to them. Equally significant is the fact that even the salesmen of dissension must disguise their sales talks in the phraseology of American freedom.

Race hatreds and group intolerance simply do not jibe with any of the formulas of freedom so dear to the American heart. To the extent they are allowed to flourish, they threaten to change the American Dream into another European nightmare.

Let's not underestimate the threat. There is a tendency to soft-pedal the spread of alien doctrines of intolerance. The theory, I suppose, is that the best way to treat a disease is to pretend that it doesn't exist. That is a cowardly theory and worse, a futile one. It seems to me that honest diagnosis is the first and indispensable measure in meeting the challenge of propagandas and whispering campaigns directed against foreigners, against Jews, against Catholics, against Negroes.

Equally dangerous, but not so dramatic, and therefore not so well understood, are the campaigns of intolerance and vilification that are directed against economic groups such as business, labor and agriculture—sometimes by one another, and sometimes by the enemies of one or all. To the extent that business has been guilty of such intolerance in any direction I deplore it. I have set my face against it, and I shall continue to denounce it. To the extent that you, as writers have been guilty of this same type of intolerance with respect to any of these groups, including business, I invite you to have another look to see if the beam in your eye has gotten you off the beam of tolerance.

I have been privileged to travel widely in our country, and I do not hesitate to offer my personal testimony that the tremendous tension of race and group animosities is warping the very foundations of American democratic life. Men and women who should know better—who do know better—allow themselves to mouth the catch phrases of anti-Semitism and anti-foreignism, of anti-business, or anti-labor, anti-farm. Most of them are not themselves aware that they have been infected by the virus of intolerance which already has the whole world writhing in the fatal fever of war.

When there's a riot in Detroit or Harlem, when racial antagonisms break into the open in Boston or Brooklyn, it's more comfortable to shrug them off as local incidents. But the truth must be faced. These episodes of violence are symptoms of pressures and emotions and maladjustments which are nation-wide.

The first thing we must do, it seems to me, is to confront the reality. Obviously the most violent and deep seated of our antipathies are racial and religious. Widespread though these expressions of group hatred are, it is a hopeful fact that they still afflict only a small minority of the American population. That minority can be curbed and re-educated if conscious and organized efforts are undertaken.

At the very worst, that minority can be frightened into desisting. Not by legal threats—you can't legislate the golden rule as you can the gold standard. I mean that Americans can be made sharply aware that intolerance endangers not merely the small groups against whom it is directed but the country as a whole. The obstreperous hate-mongers and their foolish or frivolous fellow travelers who think it is smart to rock the American boat may drown with the other passengers.

If they achieve the calamity of race persecutions, they will drag our beloved America down to the barbarian level of Nazi Germany and we will pay for it in death and suffering and national degeneration, precisely as the Germans are doing today. We need to emphasize, day in and day out, that the spread of intolerance is not primarily a threat to the intended victims but to the whole country. Once the poison enters a nation's bloodstream, the entire population is doomed. Only six hundred thousand German Jews suffered through the triumph of Nazi barbarism—but the non-Jews who suffered from it include the more than eighty million Germans!

If the day ever comes in this country when tolerance gives way to internal enmities and persecutions and discriminations, it will be the end of American civilization. Remember this: The dictates of intolerance cannot be enforced finally without the connivance of government. Should intolerance triumph, it will mean, as a matter of course, that free government is stamped out. Racial persecutions—whether in the old Russia or the present day Germany—have always been conducted under the protection of a tyrannical governmental regime.

Viewed from the narrowest vantage point of the nation's well-being, quite aside from human and moral considerations, the growth of doctrines of race and group hatreds represents a major economic threat. America has prospered because it has provided avenues of economic expression to all men who had the urge and the capacity to advance themselves. Wherever we erect barriers on the grounds of race or religion, or of occupational or professional status, we hamper the fullest expansion of our economic society. Intolerance is destructive. Prejudice produces no wealth. Discrimination is a fool's economy.

Freedom of the individual is the most vital condition for creative life in economy as in every other department of human existence. Such freedom is impossible where men are restricted by reason of race or origin, on the one hand, or on the other, paralyzed by fears and hatreds of their neighbors.

There are some in our country—industrialists, white collar workers, laboring people—who hold to the myth that economic progress can be attained on the principle of an unbalanced seesaw. They think that if some groups can be forever held *down*, the others will forever enjoy economic privileges and prosperity at the end which is up.

Fortunately it does not work that way. Any advantage thus gained must be paid for out of the fruits of the productive plant. The withholding of jobs and business opportunities from some people does not make more jobs and business opportunities for others. Such a policy merely tends to drag down the whole economic level. You can't sell an electric refrigerator to a family that can't afford electricity. Perpetuating poverty for some merely guarantees stagnation for all. True economic progress demands that the whole nation move forward at the same time. It demands that all artificial barriers erected by ignorance and intolerance be removed. To put it in the simplest terms, we are all in business together. Intolerance is a species of boycott and any business or job boycott is a cancer in the economic body of the nation. I repeat: Intolerance is destructive. Prejudice produces no wealth. Discrimination is a fool's economy.

These are things that should be made manifest to the American people if we are to counteract the pestiferous labors of race and group hate-mongers. The job lies to a large extent in the hands of you writers, in your colleagues in the movies, the theater, radio, the press. You are the people with direct access to the mind—and what is more important, to the heart and emotions—of the American people.

You must somehow take words like freedom and democracy and unity and lift them to the level of religious fervor. We require more than a broad acceptance of these American concepts. We need an eager enthusiasm. And you, in particular, have the power to arouse it and to keep it alive. I want to emphasize that.

If eternal vigilance is the price of liberty, the writer and the artist generally have a prime duty in keeping the vigil. It is for them to dramatize the strength and beauty that resides in America's multiplicity of races, religions, national origins and social backgrounds. The totalitarians who looked on us as "mongrels," as a chaos of clashing cultures, have learned their mistake. We always must remember that America is a nation made up of the peoples of all lands.

Any metallurgist will tell you that the toughest, most resistant metals are not "pure" ores but alloys that blend the most valuable qualities of many ores. It is thus with the American, who fuses in his blood and his spirit the virtues and vitalities of many races, creeds, and cultures—giving us an amalgam that is new, unique, and immeasurably strong.

That is why tolerance is necessarily and rightly a supreme American characteristic. In truth, we must continue to cultivate our native American tolerance for everything except intolerance.

Our enemies have learned in this war the toughness of our fiber. It now remains for the American people, likewise, to absorb that lesson. It was Walt Whitman who celebrated the diversity that is America's strength. "This is not a nation," he proclaimed, "but a teaming of nations." In some measure every poet sensitive to the nature of our still young American experiment has felt and expressed that diversity. Russell Davenport has just done it in "My Country." Perhaps the poet, more than the economist or historian, senses the absurdity in attempts to hammer all Americans into a single national type and discriminate against the minorities who do not conform to an arbitrary creation.

Let's not apologize for the amazing variety of our human material here in America. Let us rather glory in it as the source of our robust spirit and opulent achievements. Let's not deny that there are differences in race and that our country has all the fifty-seven varieties of God's humanity. Let us merely make clear that these differences cannot be measured on any scale of good, better and best. They are all equally valid and all must continue to contribute to the magnificent mosaic of American life.

Subtract from the grand total of America the contributions of our racial and religious and economic minorities—and what remains? Subtract foreign-born Andrew Carnegie from our metallurgical industry; or David Sarnoff from American radio; or George Gershwin and the Negro composers from our native music; or Norwegian-born Knute Rockne from our football; or Dutch-born Edward William Bok from publishing; or Danish-born William S. Knudsen from the automotive industry; or Russian-born Major de Seversky from American aviation; or Belgian-born Leo H. Baekeland from American chemical achievements; or slave-born Dr. George Washington Carver from biological developments. The temptation is to list hundreds and thousands who have thrown their particular genius into the American melting pot.

And behind those whose names we know are the nameless legions of immigrants, generation after generation, whose labor and lives went into every bridge, and tunnel, every mine and factory in these United States.

Too many Americans—indeed, too many of the immigrants themselves, whatever their race or land of birth—behave as if America only *gave* things to newcomers. We need to be reminded that America *received* more than it gave. After all, our country let the strangers in because it needed their muscle power, their purchasing power, their fecundity and their brains.

It is this vision of a society wonderfully rounded by reason of its many racial contributions—of an *inter*nation within the borders of a vast nation—that should be brought home to every American child and adult. The cooperation of these multiple elements—the unity of a powerful amalgam—has given a peculiar destiny and genius to our country. In pointing out our achievements to our preachers of division and distrust we are protecting that part of our history that still lies in the future.

But it seems to me that all of us who fight against intolerance can hurt our own cause by expecting too much too soon. The simple human fact is that prejudice is latent in all of us. The average Protestant, Catholic, Jew is normally prejudiced in favor of his own kind and against the others. The underprivileged are prejudiced against the well-to-do. The strong are prejudiced against the weak and vice versa. Men are prejudiced against women and women, alas, are even more prejudiced against men. The saintly soul who goes through life devoid of all prejudices is rare indeed.

These attitudes cannot be wished away or talked away or smothered with fine phrases. They are the products of centuries of history which must be taken into account in any functioning society. Those who would eliminate such things overnight may deserve good marks for their intentions, but they do not rate high in common sense. Let me say frankly that the bigotry and impatience of the right-minded can do as much harm as good. There is always the danger that their unrestrained zeal may sharpen animosities and stimulate unrealistic demands. I for one would caution such people that in clamoring for what is impossible they are sacrificing what is possible. A counter-propaganda that is divorced from living usually creates more tension than its cures.

On the whole, America, through the generations, has shown itself capable of preventing natural prejudices from spilling over into unnatural intolerance. On the whole the trend has been towards greater equality. Even the worst manifestations of prejudice have been gradually tempered.

The danger today comes because the normal prejudices are being stimulated by deliberate propaganda. Watered by hate they flourish in more and more places as outright intolerance and discrimination. What is a mild and natural disaffection is being turned into a malignant disease. It is that which we are called upon to combat with all the skills, with all the energies that we possess.

Ill abused and unjustly treated are the victims of intolerant hate, but the dupes who follow the intolerant leader are unmercifully betrayed. Look at Nazi Germany. Intolerance is a hideous beast with an insatiable appetite. When it has devoured its unhappy victims, it turns upon its guilty followers. The strong Nazies liquidated the weak Nazis.

The inevitable cycle of organized intolerance is that it destroys the individual, the family, the community, and finally the state. In contrast, tolerance is constructive. It creates, builds, unifies. It gives strength and nobility to the individual, to the family, the community, the state. The fight against intolerance is not merely our duty as decent human beings, it is the indispensable condition of our survival as free individuals and as a prosperous nation.

More than all this, it is a condition of happiness and a guarantee of spiritual enlargement. The very word tolerance itself derives from the same Latin stem as the words to lift up and to bear.

"Bear ye one another's burdens," said a clear voice long ago. This counsel should have been remembered by us during the past generation.

We all recognize that the two decades between the two world wars was a period of cynicism and little faith. In the enslaved and dictated countries, this cynicism found its most complete and ugliest expression.

But this degradation was not confined within the borders of totalitarian countries alone. Even among us in America there were symptoms of moral decay. During these two decades it was smart to question moral values, to debunk traditional virtues, to rationalize brutalities, to make excuses for moral indignities. During this period we heard men sneer at freedom and make light of democracy. A lot of us forgot that our code of morals, respect for truth and fair dealing are not arbitrary laws imposed upon us from without. They are the products of thousands of years of human experience—the quintessence of the wisdom of the ages. To violate these codes brings disaster as surely as the violation of physical laws of nature brings disease and death.

To the extent that we yielded to this wave of cynicism, we have contributed to the greatest crisis of our epoch which came to a head in the most destructive war of all time. It has not been merely a political or economic crisis. It has been a spiritual and moral crisis. An evil wind has swept throughout the world and its havoc is all about us.

But in spite of this destruction, I know that the physical ingredients for a better, a happier and nobler America are at our disposal. Raw materials, machinery, skills, manpower in abundance. Can we match these with intelligence, good-will, social idealism and tolerance?

In the perspective of history, it will appear that ours is the tragic privilege—the tragic privilege of living in the greatest military crisis since Napoleon, the greatest economic crisis since Adam Smith, the greatest moral crisis since the fall of the Roman Empire. But if ours is the tragic privilege, history will also show that ours is the magnificent opportunity—the magnificent opportunity to understand that in unity there is strength; in good-will there is prosperity; in tolerance there is progress—progress towards a better, a healthier and a happier America. In fact, this is the only way we may have peace at home or abroad in our lifetime.

# The Challenge of Human Relations[4]

Ralph J. Bunche

*Born August 7, 1904, Detroit, MI; died December 9, 1971; B.A., University of California, 1927; M.A., 1928, Ph.D., 1934, Harvard University; professor, Howard University, 1928-41; analyst, Office of Strategic Services, 1941-45; associate chief, State Department division of dependent area affairs, 1945-46; principal secretary, United Nations Palestine commission, 1947-55; winner of Nobel Peace Prize, 1950; undersecretary general, United Nations Office of Special Political Affairs, 1955-67; undersecretary general, United Nations, 1967-71.*

## Editor's introduction

Sharing the stage with Eleanor Roosevelt, noted professor and United Nations official Ralph J. Bunche spoke on race relations at a tribute to Abraham Lincoln. Later that year, Dr. Bunche would be the first African American to win the Nobel Peace Prize for his efforts in constructing and mediating the 1948 Arab-Israeli truce. It follows that Dr. Bunche was not only, a professor of political science, well studied in race relations, but as a high-ranking United Nations official, equally well practiced. In this address, Dr. Bunche lamented the state of human relations throughout the world. Asserting that humans are by nature good and just, Dr. Bunche felt that people should acquire the "universal common denominator" that religion and education had failed to provide. Such a bond should be the common goal of peace, which Dr. Bunche believed must be espoused on both governmental and individual levels if it is to be realized.

---

We are gathered here tonight to pay tribute to a man of rare greatness—one of the most stalwart figures of our nation's history. But it is not within our feeble power to do honor to Abraham Lincoln except as we may dedicate ourselves to the fulfillment of the imperative objectives which he sought.

Lincoln, the man, was mortal, and being mortal was fallible. History records his moments of indecision, his groping, his bows to political expediency. But in the crucial hours of decision, he found a boundless strength which flowed from his unwavering faith in the "plain people," from the equalitarianism of the West in which he was born and reared, from his undecorated belief in the equality and dignity of man.

I am impelled to deviate for a moment and to say that on this platform tonight there is another great American personality, whose greatness history will also record, and from whose untiring efforts posterity will reap an abundantly rich harvest. A great lady, who walks unerringly in the hallowed tracks of Jefferson and Lincoln, and whose greatness, like theirs, is grounded in the dedication of her life to the high principles of true democracy. Mrs. Roosevelt, herself identified with a group—women—which is still not fully emancipated from traditional and unjust inequalities, is, in her own right, a twentieth century emancipator.

I have been chosen to speak tonight to the topic—The Challenge of Human Relations—for two reasons.

In the first place, it seems to me to be a rather appropriate subject for this occasion. Lincoln, himself, was called upon to save this nation from as great a crisis and conflict in human relations as has ever confronted any nation. And though he met the challenge and saved the nation, even Lincoln could not avert a cruel, tragic, devastating internecine war. Indeed, eighty-five years later, that war is still not fully liqui-

[4]Delivered to the City Club of Rochester, at an Abraham Lincoln celebration, in Rochester, New York, on February 11, 1950.

dated, and at times it may seem not entirely clear who won it.

In the second place, the greatest danger to mankind today, in my view, is to be found in the sordid human relations which everywhere prevail.

Were Lincoln alive today, he could scarcely avoid taking a dark view of the relations among peoples the world over, not by any means excluding his own country. It would be understandable if even a quick view of the situation should induce in him one of those occasional moods of melancholia which some historians have attributed to him.

For what is the situation? The relations among peoples are broadly characterized by dangerous animosities, hatreds, mutual recriminations, suspicions, bigotries and intolerances. Man has made spectacular progress in science, in transportation and communication, in the arts, in all things material. Yet, it is a matter of colossal and tragic irony that man, in all his genius, having learned to harness nature, to control the relations among the elements and to direct them as he sees fit—even to the point where he now has the means readily at hand for his own complete self-destruction—has never yet learned how to *live* with himself; has not mastered the art of human relations. In the realm of human understanding the peoples of the world remain shockingly illiterate. This has always been and today remains man's greatest challenge: how to teach the peoples of the world the elemental lesson of the essential kinship of mankind and man's identity of interest.

We live in a most dangerous age—an age of supersonic air-speeds, of biological warfare, of atomic and hydrogen bombs, and who knows what next. In no exaggerated sense, we all today exist on borrowed time. If we of this generation deserve no better fate, surely our children do. They, certainly, can never understand why we could not do at least as well as the animal kingdoms.

We need peace desperately. But the world has always needed peace. Today, however, the question is not peace or war, as it has been in the past. The question now is sheer survival—survival of civilization, survival of mankind. And time is short, frighteningly short.

How is the question to be answered! We may improvise, we may build diplomatic dams, we may pile pact upon pact. The United Nations, as it is doing, may scurry about valiantly with its fire-fighting machinery and put out a war-fire in Indonesia today, in Palestine tomorrow, and in Korea or Kashmir or Greece the next day. But new war-fires will continue to flare up, and one day one of them, fanned by a furious windstorm of human conflict, may very well get out of hand. And then the final havoc will be upon us. Indeed, it is a sign of the deplorable state of human affairs in our time that unless we blind ourselves to the realities we must always think and speak of the future in terms of sound and fury, of fire and brimstone. Yet I do not believe that either the present or the future is by any means irretrievably lost, that all is hopeless.

No strength is ever to be gained from sheer imaginings and escapisms. Let us be not like the figures in Plato's parable of mankind in the dark cave. We must see and face reality and truth rather than shadows and images, distortions and illusions on the wall of the cave. The truth is that there can be but one really secure foundation for peace in the world. And that foundation must be in the attitudes which reflect the state of the hearts and minds of man. Without great changes in human attitudes, without massive strides toward human understanding and brotherhood, the most perfect international machinery for peace will ultimately be unavailing. No mechanical device, no international charters or pacts, no diplomacy however ingenious, can serve to save mankind from itself if man in his relations with man remains mean and brutish.

It is ourselves that we must fear more than the atomic or hydrogen bomb. It is in man's perversities, in his brooding suspicions, in his arrogances and intolerances, in his false self-righteousness and in his apathy that the real danger is to be found. In the final analysis, there is but one road to peace and that is the road of human understanding and fellow-feeling, of inflexible determination to achieve peaceful relations among men. That, clearly, is a long, hard road, and today it is too little traveled.

I repeat that the fundamental weakness and danger of the world today is the universality of bad human relations. If these relations were everywhere, or let us even say *almost* everywhere, internationally and domestically, good, there would be little to fear. For then the free peoples of the world would have unassailable strength, and more than that, unwavering confidence in their ability to protect themselves collectively and fully against any maverick who might go on the loose. On the other side of the coin, bad human relations are, indeed, an encouragement and stimulus to the adventures of mavericks. It is on the disunity of peoples that Hitlers prey.

By "human relations" I mean simply the ability—or inability—of mankind to live with itself in peace and order, in harmony and understanding, in honor and mutual respect.

I am optimistic enough about my fellow beings to believe that it is human *attitudes*, not human nature, that must be feared—and changed. On the international scene, it is these attitudes which have brought the world to the menacing state of affairs of today—the "cold war," the maneuverings for power and dominance, the dangerous rivalries, the propaganda battles—cannibalistic struggles in which ethical principles, and moral law are often callously jettisoned. If peoples could not be induced to suspect, to fear, and finally to hate one another, there could be no wars, for governments, from whatever motivations, can only lead peoples into wars—the peoples must fight them. And in these wars, countless numbers of human beings—by nature essentially good, whatever their immediate attitudes—must be sacrificed solely because the peoples of one society or another embark, or permit themselves to be embarked, upon fatal adventures of conquest or domination. On the domestic scene, it is human attitudes, not human nature, which nurture the racial and religious hatreds and bigotries which today permeate many societies, and even in democracies thrive in the fertile soil of complacency.

The picture is foreboding and the future looms ominously. But perhaps there lies the hope. Can man, a thinking animal, capable of both emotion and cool calculation with regard to his self-interest, be brought to his senses in time? Can he see the black doom which awaits him at the end of the path he now follows? I have enough faith in the potentiality of mankind for good to believe that he can save himself.

Certainly, there is nothing in human nature which renders it impossible for men to live peacefully and harmoniously with one another. Hatred, intolerance, bigotry, chauvinism are never innate—they are the bad lessons taught in society. Despite the fact that in recorded history, mankind has been as much at war as at peace, it cannot be concluded that war is inevitable—a natural state of mankind. Nor do I believe that because hatreds, bigotries, intolerances and prejudices loom large in the pages of history, these are the natural conditions of man's societal existence on earth.

I am under no illusions about mankind and I do not for a moment underestimate his capacity for evil doing. All of us, no doubt, are painfully aware of some individuals who live up to the hilt—and then some—to the Hobbesian characterization of man as "nasty, poor, mean and brutish." Yet, I am persuaded that such persons are the exception rather than the rule, and in any case, they are the unfortunate end-products of society. I believe, with Julian Huxley, that there is a sharp distinction between human nature and the *expression* of human nature. War and bigotry are not reflections of human nature but rather collective expressions of it in the particular circumstances in which man finds himself at a given time. Ironically enough, modern man has given some of the best demonstrations of how peoples can work together in a close bond of understanding during the adversities of war itself. Human nature may be relatively constant, but its expression is subject to change. That man has the *ability* to change the circumstances which influence the expression of his nature and lead him down disastrous paths is undoubted. The great decision involves his *will* to do so.

It may be that man's will can be activated only by an impending sense of catastrophe; that only on the brink of disaster may he turn to human solidarity as his last chance for salvation. If so, he finds himself today precariously on that brink.

I think it no exaggeration to say that unfortunately, throughout the ages, organized religion and education have failed miserably in their efforts to save man from himself. Perhaps they have failed because so often they have merely reflected the mean and narrow attitudes of the very peoples they were striving to save.

Human understanding, human brotherhood and solidarity, will be achieved, if at all, only when the peoples of many lands find a common bond through a compelling sense of urgency in achieving common goals. The purposes and principles of the United Nations—with peace as the universal common denominator—afford that bond and the common goals. The implements of modern warfare afford the urgency, if people once understand the frightful implications and elect to survive.

Lincoln, instinctively a true democrat, believed deeply in the essential justice of the plain people, whose better impulses and good will he trusted ultimately to prevail. Given half a chance, I believe that the peoples of the world today, in their collectivity, will justify Lincoln's faith.

It is not necessary to seek to transform people into saints in order that impending disaster may be averted.

Throughout the world today, thinking and psychology have not kept pace with the times. That people inevitably think in terms of their self-interest is something very little can be done about. But is it not equally tenable that a great deal can be done about influencing people to think and act in terms of their *true* self-interest? In this dangerous age, notions of exalted and exaggerated nationalism, of chauvinism, of group superiority and master race, of group exclusiveness, of national self-righteousness, of special privilege, are in the interest of neither the world nor of any particular group in it. They are false views of self-interest and carry us all toward the disaster of war. And in the war of tomorrow there can be no victor; at best there will be only survivors. The old concepts and values are no longer valid or realistic. The future may well belong to those who first realign their international sights.

I sincerely believe that the generality of peoples throughout the world really long for peace and freedom. There can be no doubt that this is true of the American people. If this is true, it is the one great hope for the future. The problem is how to crystallize this longing, how to fashion it into an overpowering instrument for good. The United Nations recognizes acutely the desperate need, but has not yet found the ways and means of mobilizing the peace-loving attitudes of the peoples of the world over the stubborn walls of national egoisms.

I sincerely believe that the generality of peoples throughout the world really long for peace and freedom. There can be no doubt that this is true of the American people. If this is true, it is the one great hope for the future. The problem is how to crystallize this longing, how to fashion it into an overpowering instrument for good. The United Nations recognizes acutely the desperate need, but has not yet found the ways and means of mobilizing the peace-loving attitudes of the peoples of the world over the stubborn walls of national egoisms.

Every nation, every government, every individual, has a most solemn obligation to mankind and the future of mankind in the fateful effort to rescue the world from the morass in which it is now entrapped and to underwrite a future of peace and freedom for all. This is a time of gravest crisis. Constructive, concerted actions—not negativism and recrimination—are called for. There are many motes in many eyes. There is no nation which can stand before the ultimate bar of human history and say: We have done our utmost to induce peoples to live in peace with one another as brothers.

It must be very clear that what the world needs most desperately today is a crusade for peace and understanding of unparalleled dimension; a universal mobilization of the strong but diffused forces of peace and justice. The collective voice of the peoples of the world could be so irresistible as to dwarf into insignificance both A and H bombs and to disperse and discourage the warlike and war minded.

In the existing state of affairs, societies admittedly owe it to themselves to be prepared and protected against any eventuality. With that, given the international circumstances, reason and reality might perceive no quarrel. But it would also appear that reason and reality would dictate that since armament is never an end in itself and must expand itself, if at all, only in war, the only way peace-loving societies might cover their mounting losses from the tremendous expenditures on armaments would be to exert an effort of at least equal magnitude for peace—to the end that the armaments would never have to be used. This, it seems to me, would be at once good economics, good humanitarianism, and good self-interest.

And now, if I may take advantage of my nationality and speak for a moment simply as an American citizen, I may ask where do we, as Americans, stand with regard to the challenge of human relations?

The United States is in the forefront of international affairs today. The eyes of the world are focussed upon us as never before in our history. A great part of the world looks to us for a convincing demonstration of the validity and the virility of the democratic way of life as America exalts it. It would be catastrophic if we should fail to give that demonstration. We cannot afford to fail.

But it is only too apparent that our democratic house is not yet in shipshape order.

There are yawning crevices in our human relations; the gap between our democratic profession on the one hand, and our daily practices of racial and religious intolerance on the other, while less wide than formerly, is still very wide.

Race relations is our number one social problem, perhaps our number one problem. It is no mere sectional problem; it is a national—indeed an international—problem. For any problem today which challenges the ability of democracy to function convincingly, which undermines the very foundations of democracy and the faith of people in it, is of concern to the entire peace and freedom loving world. Surely, it must be abundantly clear that it is only through the triumph of democracy and the determined support of peoples for it as an imperative way of life that secure foundations for world peace can be laid.

That race relations are gradually improving, both in the South and elsewhere in the nation, cannot be doubted. But neither can it be doubted that these relations remain in a dangerous state, that they are a heavy liability to the nation, and constitute a grave weakness in our national democratic armor.

Certainly the costs of anti-racial and anti-religious practices are enormously high. Attitudes of bigotry, when widely prevalent in a society, involve staggering costs in terms of prestige and confidence throughout the rest of the world, not to mention the contamination and degradation resulting from the presence of such psychological diseases in the body of the society.

Throughout the nation, in varying degree, the Negro minority—almost a tenth of the population—suffers severe political, economic and social disabilities solely because of race. In Washington, the nation's capital, Lincoln, the Great Emancipator, sits majestically in his great armchair behind the marble pillars, and overlooks a city which does not yet admit his moral dictum that the Negro is a man; a city in which no Negro can live and work with dignity; a city which, administered by Congress itself, subjects one fourth of its citizens to segregation, discrimination and daily humiliation. Washington is this nation's greatest shame precisely because it is governed by Congress and is the capital of a great democracy. Washington, of all American cities, should symbolize and vitalize that democracy.

Lincoln saw that slavery had to be abolished not only because as an institution it was contrary to human morality, but also because it was inimical to the interests of the "plain people" of America. By the same token, present-day practices of racial segregation and discrimination should be outlawed as inimical to the interests of all who believe in and derive benefit from democracy, whatever their race or religion.

The most valuable resources of any country are its people. But in our country today, and in the South particularly, our human resources, white and black alike, are being recklessly squandered. They are being squandered in interracial conflict, in prejudices and animosities among two groups of citizens—Americans all—which prevent that unity of purpose and that cooperative effort which alone could insure the full realization of the nation's potential in its human resources; and this at a time when it vitally requires its maximum strength.

The vitality of this great country derives from the unity of purpose and the devotion to its democratic ideals of the diversified peoples—by race, religion and national origin—who make up its population. Disunity and group conflict constantly sap that vitality.

As a nation we have also found strength in the fact that we have always been able and willing to face our shortcomings frankly and attack them realistically. It is in this spirit and in this knowledge that I, as an American, take occasion to point to our shortcomings. I do not imply, in any sense, that the rest of the world is free of such imperfections, or in given instances, even greater ones.

To enjoy our maximum strength, we need more *applied* democracy. We need to live up to the principles which we believe in and for which we are hailed by the world. We too need a mobilization—a mobilization throughout the country of men and women of good will, of men and women who are determined to see American democracy fulfill its richest promise, and who will ceaselessly exert their efforts towards that end.

This nation, by its traditional philosophy, by its religious precepts, by its Constitution, stands for freedom, for the brotherhood of man, and for full respect for the rights and dignity of the individual. By giving unqualified expression to these ideals in our daily life we can and will achieve a democratic society here so strong in the hearts and minds of its citizens, so sacred to the individual, that it will be forever invulnerable to any kind of attack.

Because I believe in the reason and essential goodness of human beings; because I have deep respect for and faith in my fellow man, I look to the future of race relations in our country with reasonable optimism. I know that there are very many men and women of good will in the North, South, East and West, that their ranks increase daily, that their influence is being widely felt, and that this influence is gradually clearing away the race-relations fog which has enshrouded us. But I must add that where rights and birthrights are concerned, gradual progress can never be rapid enough for those deprived, since rights and birthrights can never be enjoyed posthumously.

If I may be pardoned for a personal reference, I am proud to be an American and I am proud of my origin. I believe in the American way of life, and believing in it, deplore its imperfections. I wish to see my country strong in every way—strong in the nature and practice of its democratic way of life; strong in its world leadership; strong in both its material and spiritual values; strong in the hearts and minds of all of its people, whatever their race, color or religion, and in their unshakable devotion to it. I wish to see an America in which both the fruits and the obligations of democracy are shared by *all* of its citizens on a basis of full equality and without qualification of race or creed.

The United Nations ideal is a world in which peoples would "practice tolerance and live together in peace with one another as good neighbors." If this ideal is far from realization it is only because of the state of mind of mankind. Man's reason and calculated self-interest can be powerful forces for changes in that state of mind. No ideal could be more rewarding. Every individual today has it in his power—in his daily living, in his attitudes and practices—to contribute greatly to the realization of that ideal. We must be strong in our adherence to ideals. We must never lose faith in man's potential power for good.

# For the Federal Fair Employment Practices Act[5]

Adam Clayton Powell, Jr.

*Born November 29, 1908, New Haven, CT; died April 4, 1972; B.A., Colgate University, 1930; M.A., Columbia University, 1932; D.D., Shaw University, 1938; minister, Abyssinian Baptist Church, 1937-71; councilperson, New York City, 1941-45; representative (D) from New York, 1945-70.*

## Editor's introduction

Confronted by well-organized opposition from southern representatives, New York representative Adam Clayton Powell, Jr., gave this speech in support of the Federal Fair Employment Practices bill. The setting was quite dramatic, with crowds packing the House galleries and people waiting in long lines for admission. No doubt, such drama was fueled by the nature of the bill, which was one of the first designed to prevent employers from discriminating against applicants because of race, color, religion, ancestry, or nationality. Adhering closely to the methods of argument, yet instilling his speech with emotion and vigor, Powell controlled the entire debate. While the bill did not pass, it is considered one of the forerunners of the 1964 Equal Employment Opportunities Commission, and Powell himself is regarded as a pioneer of the Civil Rights movement.

---

Mr. Chairman, I would like to express my thanks to the members of the FEPC [Fair Employment Practice Committee] subcommittee for the cooperation they gave me in the hearings on this bill. I would like to publicly thank our colleague from Ohio [Mr. Brehm], whose cold has been plaguing him and developed into laryngitis. His actions on the subcommittee were greater than any words he could utter today. Also I want to thank members of the full committee on Education and Labor, and I refer to Members on both sides, those who agreed and disagreed, for the cooperation and understanding that we had in committee. I trust that further debate on this bill will be in an atmosphere of dignity, even though we may oppose it bitterly or we may be in favor of it wholeheartedly.

I have allotted myself only five minutes because there are scores of members who want to talk and I do not want to cover myself with any personal glory.

I would like to say one or two things concerning the bill so that we can remove from our minds anything that we may not know concerning the details . . . .

I. Does job discrimination exist? There can be no serious question that employment discrimination is widespread. In its final report, the wartime FEPC predicted that even such gains as it had made were dissipating and predicted further, accelerated dissipation . . . .

II. Should it be eliminated? Without going into the vast wealth of detail available in answer to this question, it should suffice here to indicate briefly some of the areas adversely affected by employment discrimination.

(a) The democratic principles on which the nation was founded are flaunted by discrimination. Any violation of these principles has an adverse effect. Furthermore, the general moral code to which we pay allegiance, demands that all men be considered as individuals and rated according to their individual worth. As the bill states, "it is essential that this gap between principle and practice be closed."

(b) Our foreign relations are hampered by the publicity our enemies give to our discriminatory practices. Secretary of State Acheson describes discrimination as "a handicap in our relations with other countries." Senator Dulles when a United States delegate to the UN said that FEPC is necessary to "erase what today is

[5]Delivered to the United States House of Representatives, in Washington, D.C., on February 22, 1950.

the worst blot on our national escutcheon." The United States is bound by its international agreements to eliminate discrimination—for example, the Inter-American Conference in Mexico City, 1945; the Charter of the UN; and the Universal Declaration of Human Rights proclaimed by the General Assembly.

(c) The economic waste of discrimination cannot be totally computed. One economist estimated before the House subcommittee that we send at least $15 billion annually down the drain because of discrimination. Contributing to this total is the cost of training those whom we will not allow to use their training; the cost to industry of using artificially limited pools in selecting what should be the most skilled manpower; the creation, in minority populations, of a disproportionate degree of unemployment, resulting in an island of depression which affects its surroundings—"a man who can't earn can't buy"; the breakdown in morale among those who know that no matter what their skills, they cannot compete on an equal basis with those whom they are taught to believe are their equals; the personality difficulties resulting from lack of home life when mothers are forced to work to supplement inadequate income brought in by fathers.

The only remaining question, then, is—

III. Can S. 1728 [the FEPC bill] properly do the required job? Since the testimony at the various hearings in support of FEPC, combined with the analysis of the S. 1728 above, seems to make out a prima facie case for an affirmative answer to this question, it would appear sensible to put the burden on the objections raised.

The chief ones are as follows:

(a) "The bill is unconstitutional; it violates States' rights."

But, first, the Federal Government has the right to impose any reasonable regulations regarding its own employment relations, including regulations against discrimination—United Public Workers against Mitchell.

Second, it can do likewise re employment relations of those who contract with it—Perkins against Lukens Steel Co.

Third, it may regulate the employment relations of private businesses engaged in commerce—NLRB against Jones & Laughlin Steel Corp.

Fourth, it can therefore impose regulations against discrimination in such businesses, (i) logically, from first, second, and third above, and (ii) on the basis of cases like New Negro Alliance against Sanitary Grocery Co.

(b) "Even if constitutional, this matter should be left to the states; it is a Southern problem."

But, first, the problem is not a Southern problem—nor a Negro, or Jewish, or Catholic, or Mexican problem. Discrimination exists in the North, South, East, West, and middle of America; it is an American problem.

Second, cutting across State lines as it does, discrimination is of national legislative concern.

Third, in general, the greater number of discriminators in a given area, the more difficult to enact local antidiscrimination laws; so the areas which do practice the most discrimination will be just those with no statutory inhibition.

Fourth, many large businesses have their affairs spread out into many states; where one sells may not be where it hires. Federal legislation is the only feasible way to meet this problem.

As an impartial study made by the Library of Congress states, education alone is not sufficient to do the job.

These various studies, together with the testimony presented during the hearings on H. R. 4453, demonstrate all too strikingly that in virtually every section of this country qualified workers are being denied an opportunity of making a living—and a life—solely because of their race, color, religion, or national origin.

Gentlemen, let us conduct this debate in dignity. Let us now proceed to the business of restoring integrity to this body. Both parties and presidential nominees pledged this in their platforms and we will now show the world that at least the House of Representatives is a place that keeps its word.

# Labor's Responsibility for Human Rights[6]

David J. McDonald

*Born November 22, 1902, Pittsburgh, PA; died August 8, 1979; B.S., Carnegie Institute of Technology, 1932; clerk, Wheeling Steel Products Co, 1923; secretary to the vice president, United Mine Workers of America, 1923-36; secretary-treasurer, 1936-52, president, 1952-62, United Steelworkers of America.*

## Editor's introduction:

David J. McDonald, then president of the United Steelworkers of America, was a dynamic and fluid speaker. In this speech, McDonald outlined labor's responsibility to human relations and human rights. McDonald also extolled the United Steelworkers of America's prior record in improving race relations, including its establishment of an "equal pay for equal work" policy. Yet despite such successes, McDonald readily admitted that more had to be done. To that end, he proposed a series of programs to be undertaken by the union, all designed to facilitate cooperation between the races.

---

I want to express my appreciation to everybody who has come here today to join with Governor Leader and me and my colleagues in this National Conference for Human Rights.

It is indeed rewarding to know that so many prominent leaders of our national community, representing almost every facet of American life, have been willing to take this time from their very busy lives to help make this Conference a historic occasion, a historic step to what I believe is America's progressive effort to solve the problems of human relations.

I think you all will agree this is a novel experiment, perhaps the first of its kind to be conducted under the auspices of the government of a great industrial state and the leadership of a large labor union.

The problems for which we seek solutions affect the lives of every citizen in our country and are in some way related to the things that affect the people who live in all other countries of the world.

Governor Leader and Mr. Morrow have spoken on the responsibilities of government and industry in the business of protecting human rights. I am going to try to outline what I believe to be labor's role in this particular field.

The whole broad subject of human relations and the protection of human rights is one that labor must of necessity give attention to every day. It is broad in the sense that we are obligated to negotiate contracts with employers which incorporate within their framework certain provisions which govern wages, hours and conditions of employment. In essence, these contracts provide equality of treatment for all employees regardless of race, creed, color or national origin.

And within this framework we have made real progress, particularly during the last twenty years. During this period the American trade union movement has grown from 3.5 million to over 17 million members. It is obvious that these workers are now in a position to include provisions in their agreements which will guarantee equality of treatment for all people under the contract.

And, of course, it is significant to note that in our own union, the United Steelworkers of America, racial and intergroup relations have continued to improve from year to year as the workers' economic status has improved.

It is also significant that there have never been any outbreaks due to racial conflict in any of the plants where we have labor contracts. And this, in spite of the fact that serious breakdowns in race relations have occurred in the very communities where the plants are located.

[6]Delivered at the National Conference for Human Rights, in Philadelphia, Pennsylvania, on February 3, 1958.

I am justly proud of what we have done to date to free the steelworker from the economic and social restrictions which combine to prevent the full enjoyment of a happy life.

I would like to enumerate some of these accomplishments.

(1) We have established equal pay for equal work in the steel industry, regardless of race, creed, color or national origin.

(2) The North-South wage differential which existed for so many years has been eliminated.

(3) We have negotiated pension and insurance plans which permit steelworkers to retire under conditions providing substantial financial security, regardless of race, creed, color or national origin.

(4) We have developed educational facilities for training our members to assume the responsibilities of holding local union offices and for participating in community service work.

(5) Our Committee on Civil Rights, which was created in 1948, has played an important role in carrying the union's policy and program against discrimination into the local, state and national community. It has promoted a program within the union to prepare our members for dealing with the multitude of human relations problems which are a part of everyday union life. We have no segregated locals and many Negroes hold local union office. They are holding positions of great importance in our organization not because of the fact that they are Negroes, but because of the fact that they have demonstrated their ability to hold these offices.

(6) Enforcement of the union's basic policy of equal rights and representation has opened up many categories of employment heretofore closed to members of minority groups. Moreover, regional progress is now being made to establish on-the-job apprentice training programs in the crafts (which Mr. Morrow has made reference to) giving people an opportunity to rise up through these apprentice training programs.

(7) Union support and guidance has played an important part in the enactment of fair employment practices legislation in fifteen states and forty cities, the majority of which are located in heavily industrialized areas.

(8) We have participated in almost one hundred district and national conferences on matters of human relations since 1954. We are affiliated with twenty-five state and national committees and organizations whose programs on human rights, civil rights and civil liberties conform to the policy of the United Steelworkers of America.

(9) Our nationally televised monthly union meetings have served to direct public attention to many of the things we are here to discuss today.

You now have some idea of what we have been doing in the field of human rights and civil liberties. But we do not propose to stand on our record. Up to now we have attacked only the fringes of the problem as it affects the average citizen.

It is largely true that segregation ends when men and women enter the mill or the factory for there is literally no segregation in a mill or a factory. And for that we feel that the energies that we have expended have not been in vain.

But the other sixteen hours of a man's day are also important. Constitutionally and psychologically can a man be expected to work equally if he is not permitted to eat equally, reside equally, relax equally, improve his knowledge equally, play equally, travel equally—in short, if he is not permitted to live equally?

This is where we are falling short in America. This is the chink in our armor. Compassionate people everywhere feel the pull of this tainted weight. But the need for action has not manifested itself in those who are right-thinking and compassionate. And unless it does, we will not carry out our purpose.

Unions have their frailties—and that includes the United Steelworkers—because they are human in nature and in character. Just as human as the leaders in the business world, and in religion, and education, and other walks of life.

There is still too much idle talk about what kind of a country we should have and the way society should be organized, and too little done in the practical application of the things which make freedom and justice meaningful.

I do not mean to infer that any one segment of our society is solely responsible for our failure to measure up to our role as leader among the democratic nations of the world.

For while I am the nominal head of a strong trade union numbering about a million and a quarter men and women, I would be guilty of misrepresentation if I said there was complete unanimity of opinion among all our members on the subject of human rights. Unfortunately, we still have in our union those who get quite worked up about equality of opportunity, and they get quite vocal about this subject, but they never practice it themselves.

We haven't been able to break down completely employment practices and community patterns which still deny minority members of our union the opportunity to work and live as full-fledged, law-abiding citizens. But we are trying.

Let me say with emphasis that the United Steelworkers of America and other great unions have dedicated themselves to the orderly attainment of equality of opportunity for all Americans. We are pledged to work for the elimination of discrimination in all its ugly manifestations and the prejudices upon which it feeds. We are going to attain this goal if it is humanly possible to do so. And to this we dedicate ourselves.

But while the responsibility of the forces of labor in America looms large in this enterprise, ours is not the sole responsibility. We have done what we have done because we believe in the Fatherhood of God, the Brotherhood of Man, the tenets of the constitutions of our union and of the United States.

I have said this before, and I say it again today, that the National Association of Manufacturers and the National Chamber of Commerce, together with the local bodies of these associations, must speak out firmly and give their support for compliance with the Supreme Court's ban on segregation, for fair practices in employment and in housing, and in support of legislation which will guarantee all Americans equal protection under the law.

And I would like to call upon those who formulate the policies of the great industries of America to use their wide influence to help set the pattern in which these things can be realized. I think the leaders of American industry can do this far better even than the leaders of labor.

The policy and administrative procedures under which industry operates are largely made in the North. It is the obligation of those who formulate and enforce these policies to institute an educational program for management personnel so that they can join with us in helping to establish real American democracy in the North as well as in the South.

We have already shown that all categories of men work well together if given a chance. With the help of industry, we can make the mills and factories of this country the real classrooms of democracy.

If we are losing our prestige and our position of leadership among the countries of the world, we can attribute it in part to the fact that we have failed to avail ourselves of the tremendous human resources we have at our disposal.

In the light of our failure to practice what we preach, people in other countries tend to forget the things that are truly America. They forget the magnificent contributions of individual initiative and cooperative enterprise. They forget the engineering and scientific skills that have made our way of life the goal of all men. They forget the enormous economic assistance we have poured into their countries. And they forget that this nation, twice in the past half century, has risen up as one to help defeat potential world dictatorship. They prefer to look at our weaknesses.

Our treatment of minorities is one of the chief obstacles we face in our efforts to achieve world peace. World peace is a moral ideal and our highest political ambition. It can be established only on the basis of high moral principle.

A nation's morals is not conjured up in legislative halls and judicial chambers. Morals is a substantive thing, rooted deep in the lives and homes of every citizen. On a moral issue, in world council, our diplomats can be only as effective as the moral standards of the people they represent. Consequently, our elected and appointed government officials in their efforts toward world peace are being hamstrung by our national attitude toward minorities.

If we are losing the battle in the court of world opinion on this point, what is the effect upon ourselves here at home?

I believe that race and religious prejudices are a cancer on our social, economic and political fortunes. The problem of the Negro is especially acute. Negroes unwanted in the South are moving to the North where they are equally unwanted. School districts in many parts of the country are being gerrymandered to assure the separation of whites and nonwhites. Newly-built suburban developments are restrictively white. Older urban sections are filled to overflowing with nonwhite and foreign-born—through their sheer inability to go elsewhere.

No Negro in America has full social, economic and political freedom. He may acquire one, or even two, of these freedoms but never all three. The Civil War made his political freedom attainable. FEPC laws make a stab at economic freedom. One doubts that social freedom can ever be legislated.

The northerner takes a smug attitude as he ponders the Negro situation in the South. But he has nothing to be smug about. To all intents and purposes, there is as much segregation in the North as there is in the South. In general, the northerner accepts the Negro as a race but not as an individual. In the South the Negro is accepted as an individual, but not as a race. From a Negro's point of view he is as bad off in one section as another.

In spite of all the serious questions that demand our attention today, the problem of racial minorities is still our number one problem, as it was ninety-five years ago when the Emancipation Proclamation was signed.

We have failed to meet the challenge of building good human relations and establishing strong moral values, in keeping with our unprecedented material and technological progress.

In failing to provide equality of opportunity and equal protection under the law for all Americans, we have contributed to a tragic waste of manpower, talent, intellectual and moral energy, all of which are so necessary if our nation is to continue to progress and to remain strong.

Our crying need today is for strong, courageous, intelligent leadership which realizes that we face the most weighty problem of the century, a problem so complex that it can only be dealt with by men and women who are dedicated to the principles of justice and freedom.

As the leaders of American culture, religion, education, industry, labor and affairs of state, we have willingly or unwillingly inherited this responsibility. It is ours. The problem is here, now, and it is alive, and it needs immediate attention.

We in labor accept our responsibility. Some measures we can take alone, and we will take them. In others, we will need the help of everyone gathered here today and all of your constituencies.

In brief, let me review our union's program:

(1) We propose to set up a million-dollar-a-year scholarship reservoir. These scholarships will not be restricted to science and engineering, but will embrace a wide range of educational opportunity. Students will be selected from every walk of life without regard to race, color, religion or national origin.

(2) We propose to select representatives from our membership to visit NATO nations as ambassadors of good will.

(3) We propose to work out a program with industry which will insure upgrading the qualified employees without respect to their creed, color or national origin. We propose to broaden the in-plant training programs for apprentices to qualify members of minority groups to work in presently restricted categories.

(4) We shall expand opportunities in the union for minorities, making more positions of leadership available.

(5) We shall support demands for Federal aid and finance for additional aid to education and equal educational opportunities.

(6) We propose to work more closely with community leaders in broadening the influence of minority groups.

(7) We shall support a program to abolish slums and provide badly needed low-cost and middle-income homes.

(8) We propose to see to it that all citizens are accorded equal protection and justice under the law.

Because we believe these eight points are sound, reasonable, honest and worthy of attainment, we pledge ourselves to their fulfillment.

Never before have so many influential leaders met to deal with this grave and urgent problem. Is it too much to hope that we will do more toward solving the problem than at any other event in our history?

The spelling out of precepts and a heightened understanding of human relations by leaders are only the preliminary step toward achieving the objectives we discuss today. But we all have a solemn obligation to convert sound precept into effective practice among those we represent.

The opportunity is ours.

In the words of my good friend, Dr. Howard McClusky, at our first human relations seminar at Penn State University in 1951:

"No one knows how much time we have, but it can't be long. It would be fatal to assume that somehow we will muddle through our inhumanities into some form of ultimate accommodation. Fate will not be so kind. On the contrary, it must be the responsibility of free men of good will to work increasingly for satisfying relations among people everywhere.

"It would not be extravagant to hope that the experience and example of our meeting here today will contribute materially to that goal."

Please God, let it be so.

# Economic Injustice in America Today[7]

## Shirley Chisholm

*Born November 30, 1924, Brooklyn, NY; B.A., Brooklyn College, 1946; M.A., Columbia University, 1952; director, Friends Day Nursery, 1947-53; director, Hamilton-Madison Child Care Center, 1953-59; educational consultant, New York Bureau of Child Welfare, 1959-64; assemblyperson, New York State Legislature, 1965-68; representative (D) from New York, 1969-82; professor, Mount Holyoke College, 1983-87; chair, National Political Congress of Black Women, 1985–; author,* Unbought and Unbossed *(1970),* The Good Fight *(1973).*

### Editor's introduction

In her characteristically blunt fashion, Representative Shirley Chisholm explained to students that the American political process has failed to empower women and many ethnic groups. In an earlier speech at the University of Tennessee, Chisholm declared "Because I am a woman, because I am black, I, Shirley Chisholm, am a part of these two segments, and I will lead the women into the political arena to preserve our most important resource—our people." Such fierce determination in the face of great odds allowed Chisholm to become both the first African-American congresswoman and a revered leader in the fight for racial equality. Commenting on the speech below, the *New York Times* described Chisholm as a "commanding and imperious presence . . . . Her syntax and delivery are flawless."

---

Political participation has been and continues to be the way individuals gain access to Government in this country. But . . . there has been a failure in the process of political participation—we all know this—and I think most of us are now aware that the failure has done its damage in Government, so that individuals in this country now feel powerless and out of control of their own lives. We have a Government that is remote. We have a Government that is responsive to other institutions that are equally remote: large corporations, conglomerates, powerful interest groups, and an uncaring or condescending financial establishment. We have a Government that has, in short, lost its credibility.

There are a lot of theories about why this Government of ours has lost touch with its own people. But if we were to wait until we had a total agreement about exactly what is wrong to try to make changes, we could all be sitting here for two or three centuries and we would still probably be without answers, no changes would have been made, and the problems would be worse.

We don't have time to sit and wait. We have to make an input. This is why you see me here in New Jersey today—a black woman from Brooklyn, New York—as a candidate for nomination to the United States presidency.

I have my own theory about what we can do to improve this United States Government. And my theory is easy to understand. We have to expand the base of political participation in this country so that the decisions made reflect the thinking of more than just a small segment of the population. For I believe that you *cannot* exclude over one half of the population—women—and one tenth of the population—black people—and exclude in addition the points of view represented by young people, poor people, the Spanish-speaking and other minorities—you cannot exclude all of these groups from influence over governmental decisions and social policy without finding that the Government is out of touch and that its policy

[7]Delivered at the Newark College of Engineering, in Newark, New Jersey, on April 15, 1972. Reprinted with permission of Shirley Chisholm.

is narrow and damaging to the majority of people it is intended to serve.

Let's take the American economy for an example of what I mean by "narrow and damaging" policy. Today, we have no economic bill of rights, and we need one. We must renegotiate the basic terms of our economic relationships in this society.

The American Indian knows that the capital he needs to start basic economic development in Indian communities is not available in significant amounts through public agencies of Government, yet he knows that without that capital he will continue to be exploited on and near reservations, in urban centers, and wherever he lives.

Ask him and he will tell you that the American economy denies his citizenship.

Ask the Chicano in East Los Angeles, in which 35 percent of the housing is substandard, whether President Nixon's announcement of a record 2 million housing starts in 1971 had anything to do with improvement of housing in East Los Angeles.

Or talk to the Spanish-speaking migrant worker in California, or Texas, about the abundance of good health and medical care which this Administration proclaims: That migrant worker knows that infant and maternal mortality among his or her people is 125 percent higher than the national rate; that influenza and pneumonia death rates are 200 percent higher than the national rate; that death from tuberculosis and infectious disease is 260 percent higher: And life expectancy itself for the migrant worker is 49 years—compared with 67.5 years for the members of the silent majority.

Talk to the young black man or woman in our urban areas.

In urban poverty neighborhoods the unemployment rate three years ago was almost 6 percent—on the average—and that is the figure which today the President's economic policies have bestowed on the entire nation—on the average. Yet today in the urban black ghetto unemployment averages 12 percent and rising! Is that where President Nixon plans to take the nation during the next four years? He has made this entire nation an unemployment disaster area comparable to conditions which existed only in ghettos three years ago.

In the city of Seattle the Nixon economic policy has created a whole new class of involuntary poor—middle-class Americans who five years ago never thought they would have to know what the bitter sting and emptiness of unemployment feels like.

I mention the systematic exclusion of the Indian, the Chicano, and the ghetto black from the American economy only as examples of a much broader and more disturbing pattern.

They are not the only ones who live outside the system. Children under sixteen comprise 38 percent of the poor; and households headed by persons aged sixty-five and older make up 23 percent of all the poor in America today. Women, regardless of race or class, find themselves the victims of economic discrimination so consistently on the basis of their sex alone that they are uniting across a broad front to fight for basic economic equality.

The coalition women have formed—in which the white college graduate links arms with the black household domestic worker whose only education may be life itself—is the beginning of the union of the disenfranchised peoples of America. As the American labor movement discovered years ago there is no better or quicker way to bring people together than the common experience of economic injustice!

Economic injustice, however, is now no longer the exclusive possession of the poor.

A union of the disenfranchised, a coalition of those who are on the outside of the American economy, will not be purely a union of racial minorities, the young, and women. For economic injustice has shown its ugly head in millions of American homes where five years ago it was unknown.

If unemployment is not enough, there is the question of interest rates on home loans, the price of food and clothing, the price of gasoline and heating oil, and the ever-increasing cost of everyday public transportation in city after city.

The Administration's sensational price control program, in the face of repeated and categorical statements by the President that he would never use such controls, was at best an effort to close the barn door after the horse of runaway inflation had long gone. In fact, the door was never even half closed.

I have been particularly concerned about the rent control aspect of Phase II. The rent controls were highly publicized by the Administration—so highly publicized in fact that they amounted to an open season on tenants by landlords who declared that the President had said,

"Now is the time for a rent increase, so get it while you can."

Or look at food prices now that we're into Phase II. The Consumer Price Index for food showed an increase of four tenths of a percent in December after the conclusion of Phase I controls: The December figure, according to a recent article entitled "Higher Prices Ahead for Groceries" in *U.S. News & World Report*, translates into a 4.8 percent annual increase in food prices—double the rate which occurred under Phase I.

And in some notable specific items, food prices skyrocketed immediately after the end of Phase I: tomatoes up 50 percent a pound from 43 cents to 60 cents on the average; lettuce per head up from 34 to 47 cents, an increase of 38 percent. Across the board, the cost of food in grocery stores went up 1.3 percent in December, twice what is usual for that month.

And Dr. Herbert Stein, chairman of the President's Council of Economic Advisers states that he wouldn't be surprised if the "bulge" in prices would *increase* in the future. He did not mention the increases in other areas as well—the cost of new cars and gasoline during December for one.

The cost of living is first on all of our minds this important year. Yet the President has decided that it is a year for travel.

But I ask—when is he going to make a "Trip to Peking" in regard to the basic problems facing us in the United States this year? He is willing to go halfway 'round the world—yet he doesn't have time to walk ten blocks from the White House in Washington and look at the lives people are living under Phase II.

While the President was in Peking, almost 21 million Americans over sixty-five—roughly 10 percent of our population—faced the rising costs of food and services with fixed incomes—fixed at a median of $2,800 a year if you are an old man, fixed at $1,400 a year if you happen to be an old woman. The most recent survey—published in 1970—showed that 90 percent of these citizens over sixty-five subsist on retirement benefits of which the bulk is Social Security payments.

In the President's State of the Union Message January 20 of this year he laid special emphasis on "action for the aging" and urged Congress to enact a 5 percent across-the-board increase in Social Security. That my friends is just two tenths of a percent above the 4.8 percent increase in food prices we are now experiencing in Phase II.

And I think it is very significant that President Nixon lied to the American people when he spoke to the nation on January 20 and said that "our program of wage and price controls is working," and cited as evidence for that statement the fact that the Consumer Price Index, and I quote him again, " . . . which rose at a yearly rate of slightly over 6 percent during 1969 and the first half of 1970, rose at a rate of only 1.7 percent from August through November of 1971."

The next day, January 21, the White House released the figures which showed what the President deliberately omitted from his State of the Union Message: that during December 1971 and into the month of January consumer prices rose by 4.8 percent, well on their way back to the previous outrageous levels.

Older Americans know what these figures mean. They mean taking scarce funds from this month's meager food budget and putting it into clothing if it's winter; or they mean less for medical care or medicine these months in order to buy food.

But since the President has decided this year to try to turn our attention to his foreign policy grandstanding, I would say a few words about the impact of international economic decisions as they affect you and me.

Our economic bill of rights should set forth certain basic principles regarding foreign economic policy. If I am elected President, one of the first acts of my Administration would be high-level reconsideration of the relation between our international economic decisions and their impact, in particular, on the poor people of America.

Every day the President virtually by himself makes decisions on foreign trade, surcharges, tariffs, and balance of payments which have direct consequences on the lives of millions of Americans, but neither the Congress nor the American public share in a great many of those decisions.

As part of the President's Annual Economic Report, I would submit to the Congress an "Economic Impact Statement" similar to the environmental impact statements required now under Federal law. The Economic Impact Statement would show how, for example, foreign trade quotas or changes in tariff rates impact on various groups in our national economy at home. Today this is not done. President Nixon acts on the assumption that what is good for the international bankers and corporations on Wall Street will inevitably trickle down to the middle-class consumer and the unemployed person.

Yet the only things trickling down from this Administration are taxes and increased costs of goods and services.

Take for example the so-called value-added tax which the Nixon economists are now promoting. It is nothing other than a thinly disguised sales tax on a national level, designed to add taxes at each stage of the journey from manufacturer (or importer) to the consumer.

Now in theory, says the President, this spreads the tax load on that item and indeed it would if rigid price controls existed at the retail level, so that the item could not be increased in cost along the way. But what do you think will really happen? The pattern under Phase II is that *costs*, not savings, are being passed along to the consumer.

A sales tax is the enemy of the poor person. It is the enemy of the elderly couple who live on fixed income. And it is the enemy of the everyday American consumer, poor or not.

I am completely opposed to increasing the debt ceiling without basic tax reform. What we need in this country today is leadership which has the courage to call for *income tax reform* to put the burden where it must be placed, on those who can afford to pay.

It makes me sick to read every year the "honor roll" of all the wealthy Americans who avoided paying income taxes this year or last because of loopholes and special subsidies. Yet in the face of chronic and continuing inequities, the Administration suggests raising the debt ceiling while creating the value-added tax to bring in new revenues from the people at the bottom of the economic ladder.

I say the time to force tax reform is now, and the way to force it is to keep the lid on the debt ceiling and end the system of special privilege which *is* the tax system of this country today.

The American people don't need college degrees to understand the phony arithmetic of the Nixon economy. In 1971, individual citizen taxpayers paid in $86.2 billion in taxes, while corporations—which control 90 percent of the wealth of this nation—paid in $26.8 billion in income taxes.

In other words, you and I collectively paid in roughly $60 billion more than all the great corporations of this country.

Well, where did President Nixon put that money? He spent $77.6 billion on national defense, $3.5 billion on outer space, almost $20 billion on interest to pay off previous extensions of the debt limit, $12 billion on commerce and transportation, and about $20 billion on programs which are designed to help people get on their feet in our economy.

In the national defense budget, just under $19 billion was spent on procurement of hardware in 1971—in short, the corporations did not quite break even, they took a $7 billion loss in the speculative market on paying income taxes to the Federal Government. Of course, the corporations actually got back considerably more than the $26.8 billion they paid in taxes, when you look at the money in every sector of the budget which goes not to the citizen but to private producers of Government services.

In the last year we have seen a whole series of incredible Government welfare subsidies for the huge corporations: the supersonic transport, the C-5A giant aircraft, and most recently the President's endorsement of a multibillion expenditure on the space shuttle. A space shuttle to where? Mars, Jupiter, or Saturn?

I know a lot of Americans who would be glad to settle for better bus service from their home to their jobs, or from poor neighborhoods to areas of the city where jobs are to be found. Repeated studies of riots in urban ghettos show that lack of adequate transportation was a big factor in the discontent and bitterness which caused riot conditions to erupt, but President Nixon's answer is to build a space shuttle or an SST with precious public funds, to serve a tiny elite of the population or to stimulate the economy of a state or region by creating massive and useless technological public-works projects.

Why don't we get this country to work again at things which need to be done?

I would start with the construction and maintenance of a good subway system in every city over 250,000 population. Our city streets and basic public facilities are badly dilapidated in huge areas of inner cities—even in suburban areas for that matter: many cities have no public sidewalks, bad street lighting, poorly maintained public parks. And perhaps one of the biggest items of unfinished business is the rehabilitation of existing housing—this in itself would be a prime stimulus to the revitalization of our basic economy and job market.

I am fully aware that there are important aspects of the economy which are served by technological industry. For example, in Japan the best engineers and scientists perfected high-speed rail transportation which could be a model for this country. But we waste our best minds on outer space! And our slow train service between major cities is a disgrace to a society which thinks of itself as the most technologically advanced in the world.

We have come to the point where we have allowed our economic well-being to wither away and rot in order to support a few highly specialized and remote kinds of activity, much of it defense-oriented.

The price you and I have paid is not necessarily better protection at home or less involvement in foreign and distant wars, as the availability of this hardware seems to often beg for its use: The real price we pay is in shoddy consumer goods, rotting cities which can no longer pay their share of taxes, increased property taxes in suburban areas to pay for the declining revenue base in the older parts of cities, and collapse of school systems because taxpayers revolt and say they have had enough. And the basic reason, the underlying cause, of this cycle is the fundamental lack of balance in national priorities. If the priorities were set by the people for a change, some of this imbalance would be removed.

# Let Candles Be Brought[8]

Sol M. Linowitz

*Born December 7, 1913, Trenton, NJ; B.A., Hamilton College, 1935; J.D., Cornell University Law School, 1938; lawyer, Sutherland and Sutherland, 1938-41; assistant general counsel, Office of Price Administration, 1942-44; U.S. Navy, 1944-46; partner, Sutherland, Linowitz, & Williams, 1946-58; director, 1947-51, vice president, 1951-59, chairman of the board, 1959-66, Xerox Corp.; senior partner, Harris, Beach, Wilcox, Dale & Linowitz, 1958-66; ambassador, Organization of American States, 1966-69; senior partner, 1969-84, senior counsel, 1984-94, Courdert Bros.; chair, Academy for Educational Development, 1992–; author,* World Hunger, a Challenge to American Policy *(1980),* The Making of a Public Man *(1985),* The Betrayed Profession *(1996).*

## Editor's introduction

To an audience of distinguished leaders in business, education, government, and religion, Sol M. Linowitz, a prominent lawyer, spoke of the precarious position he believed the world to be in at the time this speech was given. In part, this understanding stemmed from Linowitz's belief that technology and international relations have allowed a "global society" to emerge. The tenets of such a society include the notion that the problems and difficulties of one group are not limited to that group, but are shared by the world. Consequently, whether it be from "Africa or Asia or Latin America or New York or Detroit or Washington," hunger, disease, suffering, and pain can no longer be tolerated.

---

As I look around this room and see so many who have done so much over the years for so many, I must admit that I have a sense of kinship with William Howard Taft's great-granddaughter who in her third-grade autobiography wrote: "My great-grandfather was President of the United Sates, my grandfather was a United States Senator, my father is an ambassador, and I am a Brownie."

I want you to know that in your presence, I am a Brownie.

I am truly grateful to you for the award this evening, for the spirit in which you have tendered it, and for the auspices under which you have presented it. Let me express my special appreciation to the General Electric Company for the generous contribution which they have made on my behalf in the name of that distinguished American, Charles E. Wilson.

With your permission I would like to take a few minutes just to say a few things which are on my mind and my heart.

We are met at a moment in history which is uncertain, fearful and indeed, dangerous. While it is true as Professor Whitehead once said that "it is the business of the future to be dangerous," nonetheless there is reason for concern as we look about us.

We are at a time that has been called both the Age of Anxiety and the Age of Science and Technology. Both are accurate, for indeed one feeds upon the other. As our scientific and technological competence has increased, so have our fear and anxiety.

In a real sense we are at a time of paradox—a time when we have learned to achieve most and to fear most. It is a time when we seem to know much more about how to make war than how to make peace, more about killing than we do about living. It is a time of unprecedented need and unparalleled plenty, a time when great advances in medicine and science and technology are overshadowed by incredible achievements in instruments of destruction. It

[8]Delivered at the Religion in American Life annual dinner, in New York, New York, on March 8, 1977. Reprinted with permission of Sol M. Linowitz.

is a time when the world fears not the primitive or the ignorant man, but the educated, the technically competent man, who has it in his power to destroy civilization.

It is a time when malaise hangs heavy, when we can send men up to walk the moon yet hauntingly recall Santayana's words that people have come to power who "having no stomach for the ultimate, burrow themselves downward toward the primitive."

No one needs to remind us that this moment may be the most fateful in all the long history of mankind. And that the outcome will depend on whether the human intellect which has invented such total instruments of destruction, can now develop ways of peace that will keep any man, no matter what his ideology, his race or his nation, from pushing the fatal button.

In the past men have warred over frontiers, they have come into conflict over ideologies. And they have fought over ideologies. And they have fought to better their daily lives. But today each crisis seems to overlap the other and we are engaged in a vast human upheaval that touches upon every phase of our existence—national and international, religious and racial.

Part of that upheaval is as old as hunger. Part is as new as a walk in lunar space. The overriding fact is that today we are all part of a global society in which there no longer is any such thing as a separate or isolated concern, in which peace is truly indivisible.

And the fact is that whether we like it or not, either we will all survive together or none of us will. Either we will all share the world's bounty, or none of us will.

We must, therefore, ask what chance we have of accepting our shrinking world with its fewer and fewer natural frontiers, or of transcending our ideological struggles unless we are prepared finally to get to the roots of the problem—the roots that are dug so deep in injustice and resentment in a worldwide contrast between wealth and misery. And the answers are vital not only to a sound foreign policy, but to a compassionate domestic policy. Indeed, both are interrelated in an interdependent world. For there is no escape any longer from what I believe is surely the central fact of our time: That whether it be Africa or Asia or Latin America or New York or Detroit or Washington—human beings can no longer be condemned to hunger and disease and to the indignity of a life without hope.

Who are these human beings that make up this world in which we live—the millions upon millions no longer thousands of miles away, but not just down the runway? Here they are in microcosm: During the next 60 seconds, 200 human beings will be born on this earth. About 160 of them will be black, brown, yellow or red. Of these 200 youngsters now being born, about half will be dead before they are a year old. Of those that survive, another half will be dead before they are sixteen. The 50 of the 200 who live past their sixteenth birthday, multiplied by thousands and millions, represent the people of this earth.

They, like their fathers and forefathers before them, will till the soil working for landlords, living in tents or mud huts. Most of them will never learn to read or write. Most of them will be poor and tired and hungry most of their lives. Most of them—like their fathers and their forefathers—will lie under the open skies of Asia, Africa and Latin America watching, waiting, hoping. These are our brothers and sisters, our fellow human beings on this earth.

What kind of a tomorrow does the world offer these, the people of this earth? Two diametrically opposed philosophies are being presented. One we call Communism—the other Democracy. Each asks acceptance of a basic idea; each offers a larger slice of bread.

Make common cause with us, say the Communists, and accept three basic premises: First, *dialectical materialism*—all that matters is matter itself. Second, *godlessness*—accept the notion that there is no spiritual being who determines your destiny. Third, accept the idea that the *State is supreme* and determines the will of the individual. Believe these things and accept them, say the Communists, and we promise you more food in your stomachs, more clothes on your backs, a firmer roof over your heads.

And what about Democracy? Because Democracy rejects absolutes, it tends also to resist precise definition. But when you and I think of Democracy, we think of a system dedicated to the preservation of the *integrity, dignity* and *decency* of the individual person.

We talk of all men being created equal but what we really mean is that all men are created with an equal right to become unequal—to achieve the glorious inequality of their individual talent, their individual capacity, their individual genius. We don't talk of the common man because what we believe in is not man as common, but with a common right to become uncommon—to think uncommon thoughts, to believe uncommon beliefs, to be an uncommon man.

We like to say that in a Democracy every person has a right to life, a right to a decent life, which comes not from government, not from his fellow citizens, but from God. We say that in a Democracy it is the individual who matters; and because we count by ones and not by masses or by mobs, we believe that in a Democracy each human being, regardless of his race, his creed, his color, has the right—the God-given right—to stand erect with dignity as a child of God.

I submit to you that that is the essence of what we really mean when we talk about the impact of religion on American life—our deep faith in *every man's* right to stand erect and with dignity as a child of God. That is the basic principle to which we are committed as a nation and as a people; that is the foundation on which our system rests; and that is what distinguishes us in the eyes of the world—in the eyes of the world—in the eyes of those millions who are searching for hope of a better *future.*

From the beginning there has been an expectation about us as a nation. From the beginning the world has looked to us to live up to certain standards of integrity, decency, dignity and humanity—to involve ourselves deeply in moving humankind toward a more humane world of freedom and justice.

Archibald MacLeish once wrote: "America is promises." America is, indeed, promises. We started with a promise over two hundred years ago. At the time when we were but a loose group of weak and scattered colonies of 3 million people, we lit up the western sky with a promise based on faith and hope—the promise of a free and compassionate society committed to the preservation of fundamental human values.

From the beginning we have always treasured the human and the humane and we have always cared about what happened to other human beings. The promise we held out to the world—saying we did so "out of a decent respect to the opinions of mankind"—is still the promise of America to the millions on this earth.

And today as never before in our history we have the opportunity to redeem that promise. Today we have the science and the technology, the skills and the resources to make it happen, to put an end to the hunger and disease and privation that have for so long been the scourge of mankind.

The question is whether we have the will, whether we are prepared to do what we should and must if we are to be the kind of nation we have said we are.

We have a great responsibility to ourselves, to our heritage and to our children. We are not going to discharge that responsibility by building larger missiles or making more powerful warheads. We will not do it by issuing new and eloquent statements. We will only do it by remembering who we are and what we are—by tapping the very deepest within us as a people—by dedicating ourselves to the fulfillment of our mission as a beacon of hope for ourselves and for the other people of this world, not only as Americans but also as Christians and Jews, drawing upon the richest within our faiths.

As I indicated earlier, this is a time of uncertainty, of deep concern. But there is a moment in our history which I think suggests the temper in which we must approach whatever challenge is before us. On May 19, 1780, the Connecticut State Legislature was in session. For days there had been prophecies that it was to be the day of doom. Then suddenly in mid-morning the sky turned from blue to grey to black. Men fell on their knees in fear and in prayer and there were many shouts for adjournment. Then a state Senator, Abraham Davenport, came forward to the podium, banged the gavel and said, "Gentlemen, either the day of judgment is approaching or it is not. If it is not, then there is no need to adjourn, and if it is, I choose to be found doing my duty. I therefore ask, let candles be brought."

I suggest this is a time for all of us to make that commitment. Let us also determine that no matter what lies ahead we will be found doing our duty to God and our country. Let us together ask that candles be brought.

# Universal Declaration of Human Rights[9]

## Jimmy Carter

*Born October 1, 1924, Plains, GA; B.S., United States Naval Academy, 1946; U.S. Navy, 1947-53; member, Georgia Senate, 1963-67; governor of Georgia, 1971-75; president of the United States, 1977-81; professor, Emory University, 1982–; author,* Why Not the Best? *(1975),* A Government as Good as Its People *(1977),* Keeping Faith: Memoirs of a President *(1982),* Negotiation *(1982),* Everything to Gain *(1987),* Turning Point *(1992),* Talking Peace *(1993),* Always a Reckoning *(1995).*

### Editor's introduction

In 1948 the United Nations issued the "Universal Declaration of Human Rights," which asserts the indivisibility of human rights, that certain rights cannot take precedence over others, and that development and democracy must go hand in hand. Speaking to a group of 200, which included civil-rights leaders, human-rights activists, and elected officials, President Jimmy Carter expressed his desire to reinstall the "beacon of human rights in American foreign policy." Recalling how African Americans in Georgia, his own home state, were historically denied the most basic human rights, Carter reminded his audience that the basic function of any government is to ensure the safety and well-being of its citizens. This speech echoed the Carter administration's consistent stress on the value of human rights, first signaled in his inaugural address, where he declared, "Our commitment to human rights must be absolute."

---

What I have to say today is fundamentally very simple. It's something I've said many times, including my acceptance speech when I was nominated as President and my inaugural speech when I became President. But it cannot be said too often or too firmly nor too strongly.

As long as I am President, the government of the United States will continue throughout the world to enhance human rights. No force on earth can separate us from that commitment.

This week we commemorate the 30th anniversary of the Universal Declaration of Human Rights. We rededicate ourselves—in the words of Eleanor Roosevelt, who was the chairperson of the Human Rights Commission—to the Universal Declaration as, and I quote from her, "a common standard of achievement for all peoples of all nations."

The Universal Declaration and the human rights conventions that derive from it do not describe the world as it is. But these documents are very important, nonetheless. They are a beacon, a guide to a future of personal security, political freedom, and social justice.

For millions of people around the globe that beacon is still quite distant, a glimmer of light on a dark horizon of deprivation and repression. The reports of Amnesty International, the International Commission of Jurists, the International League for Human Rights, and many other nongovernmental human rights organizations amply document the practices and conditions that destroy the lives and the spirit of countless human beings.

Political killings, tortures, arbitrary and prolonged detention without trial or without a charge, these are the cruelest and the ugliest of human rights violations. Of all human rights, the most basic is to be free of arbitrary violence, whether that violence comes from government, from terrorists, from criminals, or from self-appointed messiahs operating under the cover of politics or religion.

But governments—because of their power, which is so much greater than that of an indi-

[9]Delivered in the East Room of the White House, in Washington, D.C., on December 6, 1978.

vidual—have a special responsibility. The first duty of a government is to protect its own citizens, and when government itself becomes the perpetrator of arbitrary violence against its citizens, it undermines its own legitimacy.

There are other violations of the body and the spirit which are especially destructive of human life. Hunger, disease, poverty, are enemies of human potential which are as relentless as any repressive government.

The American people want the actions of their government, our government, both to reduce human suffering and to increase human freedom. That's why—with the help and encouragement of many of you in this room—I have sought to rekindle the beacon of human rights in American foreign policy. Over the last two years we've tried to express these human concerns as our diplomats practice their craft and as our nation fulfills its own international obligations.

We will speak out when individual rights are violated in other lands. The Universal Declaration means that no nation can draw the cloak of sovereignty over torture, disappearances, officially sanctioned bigotry, or the destruction of freedom within its own borders. The message that is being delivered by all our representatives abroad—whether they are from the Department of State or Commerce or Agriculture or Defense or whatever—is that the policies regarding human rights count very much in the character of our own relations with other individual countries.

In distributing the scarce resources of our foreign assistance programs, we will demonstrate that our deepest affinities are with nations which commit themselves to a democratic path to development. Toward regimes which persist in wholesale violations of human rights, we will not hesitate to convey our outrage, nor will we pretend that our relations are unaffected.

In the coming year, I hope that Congress will take a step that has been long overdue for a generation, the ratification of the Convention on the Prevention and Punishment of the Crime of Genocide. As you know, the genocide convention was also adopted by the United Nations General Assembly 30 years ago this week, one day before the adoption of the Universal Declaration. It was the world's affirmation that the lesson of the Holocaust would never be forgotten, but unhappily, genocide is not peculiar to any one historical era.

Eighty-three other nations have ratified the genocide convention. The United States, despite the support of every President since 1948, has not. In international meetings at the United Nations and elsewhere, when I meet with foreign leaders, we are often asked why. We do not have an acceptable answer.

I urge the United States Senate to observe this anniversary in the only appropriate way, by ratifying the genocide convention at the earliest possible date.

This action must be the first step toward the ratification of other human rights instruments, including those I signed a year ago. Many of the religious and human rights groups represented here have undertaken a campaign of public education on behalf of these covenants. I commend and appreciate your efforts.

Refugees are the living, homeless casualties of one very important failure on the part of the world to live by the principles of peace and human rights. To help these refugees is a simple human duty. As Americans, as a people made up largely of the descendants of refugees, we feel that duty with special keenness.

Our country will do its utmost to ease the plight of stranded refugees from Indochina and from Lebanon and of released political prisoners from Cuba and from elsewhere. I hope that we will always stand ready to welcome more than our fair share of those who flee their homelands because of racial, religious, or political oppression.

The effectiveness of our human rights policy is now an established fact. It has contributed to an atmosphere of change—sometimes disturbing—but which has encouraged progress in many ways and in many places. In some countries, political prisoners have been released by the hundreds, even thousands. In others, the brutality of repression has been lessened. In still others there's a movement toward democratic institutions or the rule of law when these movements were not previously detectable.

To those who doubt the wisdom of our dedication, I say this: Ask the victims. Ask the exiles. Ask the governments which continue to practice repression. Whether in Cambodia or Chile, in Uganda or South Africa, in Nicaragua or Ethiopia or the Soviet Union, governments know that we in the United States care. And not a single one of those who is actually taking risks or suffering for human rights has ever asked me to desist in our support of basic human rights.

From the prisons, from the camps, from the enforced exiles, we receive one message: Speak up, persevere, let the voice of freedom be heard.

I'm very proud that our nation stands for more than military might or political might. It stands for ideals that have their reflection in the aspirations of peasants in Latin America, workers in Eastern Europe, students in Africa, and farmers in Asia.

We do live in a difficult and complicated world, a world in which peace is literally a matter of survival. Our foreign policy must take this into account. Often, a choice that moves us toward one goal tends to move us further away from another goal. Seldom do circumstances permit me or you to take actions that are wholly satisfactory to everyone.

But I want to stress again that human rights are not peripheral to the foreign policy of the United States. Our human rights policy is not a decoration. It is not something we've adopted to polish up our image abroad or to put a fresh coat of moral paint on the discredited policies of the past. Our pursuit of human rights is part of a broad effort to use our great power and our tremendous influence in the service of creating a better world, a world in which human beings can live in peace, in freedom, and with their basic needs adequately met.

Human rights is the soul of our foreign policy. And I say this with assurance, because human rights is the soul of our sense of nationhood.

For the most part, other nations are held together by common racial or ethnic ancestry, or by a common creed or religion, or by ancient attachments to the land that go back for centuries of time. Some nations are held together by the forces, implied forces of a tyrannical government. We are different from all of those, and I believe that we in our country are more fortunate.

As a people we come from every country and every corner of the earth. We are of many religions and many creeds. We are of every race, every color, every ethnic and cultural background. We are right to be proud of these things and of the richness that lend to the texture of our national life. But they are not the things which unite us as a single people.

What unites us—what makes us Americans—is a common belief in peace, in a free society, and a common devotion to the liberties enshrined in our Constitution. That belief and that devotion are the sources of our sense of national community. Uniquely, ours is a nation founded on an idea of human rights. From our own history we know how powerful that idea can be.

Next week marks another human rights anniversary—Bill of Rights Day. Our nation was "conceived in liberty," in Lincoln's words, but it has taken nearly two centuries for that liberty to approach maturity.

For most of the first half of our history, black Americans were denied even the most basic human rights. For most of the first two-thirds of our history, women were excluded from the political process. Their rights and those of native Americans are still not constitutionally guaranteed and enforced. Even freedom of speech has been threatened periodically throughout our history. Only in the last 10 to 12 years have we achieved what Father Hesburgh has called "the legal abandonment of more than three centuries of apartheid." And the struggle for full human rights for all Americans—black, brown, and white; male and female; rich and poor—is far from over.

To me, as to many of you, these are not abstract matters or ideas. In the rural Georgia country where I grew up, the majority of my own fellow citizens were denied many basic rights—the right to vote, the right to speak freely without fear, the right to equal treatment under the law. I saw at first hand the effects of a system of deprivation of rights. I saw the courage of those who resisted that system. And finally, I saw the cleansing energies that were released when my own region of this country walked out of darkness and into what Hubert Humphrey, in the year of the adoption of the Universal Declaration, called "the bright sunshine of human rights."

The American Bill of Rights is 187 years old, and the struggle to make it a reality has occupied every one of those 187 years. The Universal Declaration of Human Rights is only 30 years old. In the perspective of history, the idea of human rights has only just been broached.

I do not draw this comparison because I want to counsel patience. I draw it because I want to emphasize, in spite of difficulties, steadfastness and commitment.

A hundred and eighty-seven years ago, as far as most Americans were concerned, the Bill of Rights was a bill of promises. There was no guarantee that those promises would ever be fulfilled. We did not realize those promises by waiting for history to take its inevitable course. We realized them because we struggled. We realized them because many sacrificed. We realized them because we persevered.

For millions of people around the world today the Universal Declaration of Human Rights is still only a declaration of hope. Like all of you, I want that hope to be fulfilled. The struggle to fulfill it will last longer than the lifetimes of any of us. Indeed, it will last as long as the lifetime of humanity itself. But we must persevere.

And we must persevere by ensuring that this country of ours, leader in the world, which we love so much, is always in the forefront of those who are struggling for that great hope, the great dream of universal human rights.

# These Things We Know[10]

John Hope Franklin

*Born January 2, 1915, Rentiesville, OK; A.B., Fisk University, 1935; A.M., 1936, Ph.D., 1941, Harvard University; instructor, Fisk University, 1936-37; professor, St. Augustine's College, 1939-43; professor, North Carolina College, 1943-47; professor, Howard University, 1947-56; chair, Department of History, Brooklyn College, 1956-64; professor, University of Chicago, 1964-82; professor, Duke University, 1982–; author,* From Slavery to Freedom *(1947),* The Militant South, 1800-1860 *(1956),* Reconstruction After the Civil War *(1961),* Racial Equality in America *(1976),* The Free Negro in North Carolina *(1995).*

## Editor's introduction

As James B. Duke Professor of History at Duke University, Dr. John Hope Franklin became the first African American to speak at a Louisiana State University commencement. In this address, he noted that it is no longer possible to envision one civilization, or society, as in any way superior to another. In fact, according to Franklin, our own society has many of the problems—poverty, apathy, and debt—that we typically attribute to the more "backward" nations. Franklin urged the graduates before him to allow their lives to focus on the fundamentally important issues of human rights and human dignity.

---

Mr. President, Members of the Graduating Classes and their loved ones, Members of the Faculty and Administration, Friends and Alumni, Ladies and Gentlemen:

First of all, permit me to say that it is a great honor and pleasure for me to be here and to participate in the commencement exercises of this great institution. I have been in and out of Louisiana State University for more than forty years. I did research here, for the first time, in 1945; and I have returned to use the rich resources of the library and archives on several occasions. In 1972 I delivered the Walter Lynwood Fleming Lectures here, and the Louisiana State University Press has graciously published my works from time to time. In several divisions and departments of the University, there are personal and professional relationships that I greatly cherish. Indeed, in the city, and at Southern University, I have friendships and associations that have been sustained for more than fifty years. For many reasons, therefore, I am delighted to be here.

Secondly, permit me to extend to the members of the graduating classes, their parents, loved ones, and friends, my heartiest congratulations for reaching this significant milestone. By your arrival at this juncture, you have indicated a capacity and a willingness to pursue additional studies or to take up the duties and responsibilities of a constructive contributor to some aspect of life here—or elsewhere. I hope that the members of the graduating classes will join me in expressing thanks to the officers and instructional staff of the university and to the parents and others who have made this day possible by their sacrifices, patience, dedication, and contributions in numerous ways. For their help I know that the graduates are truly grateful.

There are those, moreover, whom you have never seen and will never know who have contributed much to the enormous fund of knowledge from which you have drawn and will continue to draw. They are the dreamers, the gifted scientists, the talented humanists, the poets and philosophers, the great men and women who,

[10]Delivered at the Louisiana State University commencement exercises, in Baton Rouge, Louisiana, on May 18, 1988. 

through the ages, have stimulated our thinking, inspired moments of grandeur for us all, and moved us to work even beyond our own capacities to fulfill the dreams that each of us holds for tomorrow. We are grateful to them for helping us to see and appreciate the distinction between ourselves and lower orders of beings.

On this occasion, if I had the talent, I would not speak at all, but I would do something like Johannes Brahms did when he wrote the "Academic Festival Overture" to mark his attendance at the commencement exercises at the University of Breslau in 1879. Or, perhaps, I would like to have already composed a piece such as Aaron Copeland's "Fanfare for the Common Man," with which Copeland was serenaded as he rose to speak at the commencement exercise at Brooklyn College in 1975. Unfortunately, I can provide you with neither an academic festival overture nor a musical fanfare of any kind. You will, therefore, have to bear with me as I attempt to make some very brief remarks on this important and exciting occasion.

Perhaps this is one of the last times that you will have an opportunity to reflect in any formal way on what you have learned during your sojourn here. At the risk of delaying your celebrations—but only for a short while, I can assure you—I invite you to think about what you have learned and what you now know as you go down from this place. The sheer volume of information that the members of this class have been able to acquire would put to shame the knowledge available to college graduates of a mere half-century ago. For those of us who are separated from this graduating class by a half-century or more, it is difficult not to envy you for the wonderful academic fare on which you have been able to feast. With a curriculum much richer in so many ways than ours was, you who graduate today have been exposed to new sciences such as nuclear energy and space technology and a completely new language of the computer, to say nothing of the availability to you of numerous African, Asian, and exotic languages from the four corners of the earth. These areas have brought within your reach the great civilizations as well as the immortal wisdom of the great sages of China, Japan, India, Russia, and Egypt, to name a very few.

I assure you that I do not envy you for your academic achievements, whatever they may be. I can only congratulate you for what you have done here and hope that you will use what you have learned in a way that will bring great credit to you and the society of which you are a part. Indeed, it is about those things you know that I wish to speak quite briefly.

Since you have mastered the curriculum of this university—or at least have successfully coped with it—you know the fundamentals set forth in the core curriculum. You have learned a foreign language and some of you, hopefully, have become fluent in it. You have become familiar with some of the world's great writers and thinkers, and some of you have arrived at the point where you not only can appreciate them but can also view them critically and constructively. Many of you have mastered the language of the computer and have gained some understanding of the scientific world. All of you have achieved some specialization whether in an undergraduate major or in a graduate or professional area. For your efforts and for your success you have earned the commendation of us all.

There are some other things you know. You have doubtless learned to look at the world in the breadth and depth that it deserves to be viewed. This means, of course, that it is no longer feasible or even becoming to look at the world as an appendage to this country and thus to be judged solely by western or American standards and traditions. You should certainly be beyond the royal sovereign in "The King and I." You will remember he ordered that in his country geography had to be taught so that it showed Siam as the largest land mass not only in Asia but in the western world as well. This appears to be absurd, on the face of it; but you must be certain that you know it is absurd. Your knowledge of this matter has significant implications for the way you view certain current developments. For example, we are in the midst of what some regard as a great debate over the future curriculum of the university. At Stanford University it centers on whether students should be exposed to a larger slice of non-western studies in order to understand what the rest of the world is like. Even before the issues became clear there were those who opposed the very idea of an undergraduate curriculum embracing, say, African, Hispanic, Asian, or Afro-American studies. The United States Secretary of Education severely criticized Stanford and other institutions for yielding to the pressure of what he called "trendy lightweights." Regardless of the outcome of that debate, we need to know much more about the world in which we live. If we can learn more about the Soviet Union, the People's Republic of China, the emerging third world, and the multifaceted aspects of our own ethnic and racial diversity, we can arrive at a more intelligent understanding of how we should frame our own agenda as we react and respond to peoples in other parts of the world.

We also know that we in this country do not have a monopoly on creativity and ingenuity. It should be easy for us to appreciate what others can achieve as we witness the inundation of our markets with foreign automobiles, electronic products, clothing, and other manufactured goods. These are areas in which we formerly claimed a superiority that could not be challenged; but we have surely been overtaken in many of them. That is all right, we say to ourselves, for we have already made the transition from an industrial economy to a service and information economy. But even as we make the declaration, we witness gains being made by other countries in the new areas that we propose to claim as our very own.

If that is not sobering enough, we need only to remember that thirty years ago the capability of producing nuclear weapons was limited to less than a half dozen countries. Today, the number has more than doubled, and some of those are countries that we previously regarded as too backward, too small, or too poor to belong to the nuclear club. Many among us, including our leaders, condemn other countries for doing what we did almost a half century ago. Their priorities are all confused, we insist. Instead of developing a nuclear capability they should use their resources to feed their poor, develop their economy, and build a social and political system that will sustain them in the long run.

Before we sermonize too much, however, about what other countries should do with their resources, it is well to remember that we have our own very serious social problems. Today millions of Americans live below the poverty level, hundreds of thousands of Americans have no home, we have the largest trade imbalance in the history of our country, and our great-grandchildren will do well if they can pay off the federal budget deficit that we have amassed in the past eight years! Perhaps some of *our own* priorities are confused or misplaced. As we go about the world, flexing our muscles by invading Grenada, telling the Angolans what kind of government they can have, insisting that Central Americans model their governments on ours, and proceeding to militarize outer space, we would do well to reexamine our own priorities. Perhaps if we used our great resources in feeding the hungry, housing the poor, and healing the sick around the world, we might go far in dissolving the specter of ideological conflict that seems to haunt us endlessly.

Perhaps the best thing that we can do for an ailing world is to make our way of life work in such a way that it will be a shining example for the rest of the world. This means that we will not be moved to celebrate the anniversary of our invasion of one of the great powers of the world, Grenada, whose location is a bit hazy to many of us. Rather, it means that we should make certain that our economic and social system is working at a level that will inspire the Grenadans to follow our example, and that it works so well that we can assist Grenada and other countries in their quest for a better life. It means that perhaps our best approach to the problems of Angola is not to cheer the rebels, but to seek a policy toward Angola *and* South Africa that will make that part of the world a place of peace as well as a land of plenty. And we should make certain that we know where it is. (A few years ago when I returned from Senegal some solicitous friends said they hoped I was not exposed to the fighting. I assured them that I was not, since the nearest fighting to Senegal was, perhaps, among the gangsters of New York. After I returned from a later trip to Zimbabwe, some solicitous friends expressed relief that I had not been near the area where South Africa had been dropping bombs! One of the places I visited in Harare, the capital, was the headquarters of the African National Congress which South Africa had bombed a few weeks earlier.) I suppose one must excuse the citizens of a great world power if they do not know where the places are that help shape our foreign policy. We are too busy shaping theirs!

The examples we set before the world would be more impressive and attractive if they were marked by consistency as well as logic. We encourage in every way possible the striking workers in Poland, and it is well that we do. But you know, and even the workers in Poland must know, how inconsistent we are in doing so. When the air traffic controllers were in a similar situation in this country in 1981, our government destroyed their union by firing its members because they were striking against the government, which is precisely what the Polish workers have been doing. Why is a strike against one's employers for higher wages and better working conditions in Poland a legitimate pursuit, and a similar undertaking here an illegitimate pursuit?

Because of our long and tumultuous history of human rights and race relations, we know much more about the factors and considerations that are involved in improving them. It is reasonable if other countries look to us for leadership, and we give it willingly, if unevenly. Indeed, we issue a report card annually on which we grade countries on the basis of improvement or retrogression in these areas. We are loud to condemn certain acts of terrorism in the Middle East, but if we act at all about the reign of terror in South Africa, it rarely exceeds a gentle rap on the knuckles. Meanwhile, our own careful and discreet steps toward improved human relations have been challenged if not nullified by an administration and a President who has emasculated the United States Commission on Civil Rights, reluctantly signed the extension of the Voting Rights Act, belittled social programs ranging from school lunches to health insurance for the poor, and just a few weeks ago vetoed the Civil Rights Restoration Bill, only to have it overridden by an aroused Congress. Small wonder that there has been a significant increase in racial incidents on university campuses, largely northern incidentally, an increase in local terrorist groups, and a distressing rise in racial violence in urban centers. One wishes that we had a better record and a better example to present to the world.

You know, even if you did not major in political science, that our adulation of the rights and duties enshrined in our democratic form of government is not reflected in the attention we pay to the political process. We seem to be so busy praising the democratic process and recommending it to others, that we do very little about it ourselves. Thus, we leave elections to a small, highly interested segment of the population. If we get out fifty percent of the eligible voters in an election in this country, it is a rare and remarkable achievement. Two weeks ago, when the primaries were held in the county in which I live in North Carolina, a resounding 21.5 percent of the eligible voters bothered to participate. Compare this with an average of more than 80 percent in the Philippines and in other third world countries with multiple party systems and where voting is not compulsory. We talk about democracy a great deal but we practice it much less than some so-called benighted countries on whom we look with condescension if not loathsomeness.

As you reflect today on what you do know, I suspect that you will conclude that you do not know enough. If you reach that conclusion, you have acquired a distinguishing characteristic of an educated person. You know enough to care; you know enough to want to know more; and you know enough to appreciate the fact that it is in such places as Louisiana State University that the difference will be made between a self-centered, underdeveloped social order and one that is sensitive to the needs of our society and informed about the things that can be done to supply those needs. As you go down from this place today and as you take stock of what these years in this university have meant to you, this is a good time to renew your faith in the process with which you have been concerned here, and by which you have come to know what you do know.

It would be a lavish display of public service if you rallied others, especially the general citizenry, to renew their faith in this major vehicle for the improvement, preservation, and transmission of the very best that our civilization has to offer. It would be an act of courage, moreover, if you insisted that the resources of this country could not be spent better than in the building of an effective, successful educational apparatus for the benefit of our children at every stage of their development. Tell everyone, including our political leaders, that you will bear any burden, pay any price (including taxes), to protect and strengthen the educational institutions of this land.

As you say farewell to this university and to those who have become a part of your lives here, I invite you to join the company of those who believe in and work for the improvement of the human condition through the pervasive power of education and its related enterprises. If you do, you may discover that the company is ever growing and that with your renewed faith the battle for a world in which we can live in peace, prosperity, and wisdom, may, indeed, be won.

# Cultural Pluralism[11]

Henry Louis Gates, Jr.

*Born September 16, 1950, Keyser, WV; B.A., Yale University, 1973; M.A., 1974, Ph.D., 1979, Clare College; lecturer, Yale University, 1976-79; professor, Cornell University, 1979-90; professor, Duke University, 1990-91; professor, Harvard University, 1991- ; director, W.E.B. DuBois Institute, Harvard University, 1991- ; author,* Figures in Black *(1987),* The Signifying Monkey *(1988),* Loose Cannons *(1992),* Colored People *(1994).*

## Editor's introduction

In this speech, Dr. Henry Louis Gates, Jr., then W. E. B. DuBois Professor of Literature at Cornell University, addressed the notion of expanding curricula to include those groups not commonly considered part of the Western tradition. For some time, at selected universities throughout the United States, new initiatives in African-American and women's studies have been discussed and instituted. In the speech below, Gates defended such a multicultural college curriculum on the grounds that liberal, humanistic education must, if it is to adhere to its premises, understand the Western tradition as part of a larger, more encompassing whole.

---

I grew up in a little town on the eastern panhandle of West Virginia, called Piedmont, population two thousand, supposedly (we could never find the other one thousand people). I started school in 1956, two years after the *Brown* v. *Board* decision, and in that year, 1956, my father bought a full set of the *World Book* encyclopedia. He was working two jobs then, he did for thirty-five years—his idea was that his two sons wouldn't have to work in the same paper mill he did—and I guess it took a couple of years to pay off all the installments on those *World Books*, but he was determined that his kids would have them: and he made sure we used them. We always turned to them whenever we got in an argument about who did what when or where. It was quite a while before I realized there was a world not found in the *World Books*.

And it's that world I'd like to say a few words about today. As a scholar and teacher in a university, I am a fervent believer in the humanities, very broadly conceived. But it's that breadth of conception I want to address.

Many thoughtful educators are dismayed, even bewildered, when students say they feel like foreigners in relation to a traditional canon that fails to represent their cultural identities. I'm not interested in simply endorsing that sentiment: it's not a reasoned argument, this reaction, but it is a playing out—a logical extension—of an ideology resident in the traditional rhetoric about Western Civilization. And I want to consider it in that light.

Once upon a time, there was a race of men (always men) who could claim all of knowledge as their purview. Someone like Francis Bacon really did try to organize all of knowledge into a single capacious but coherent structure. And even into the nineteenth century, the creed of universal knowledge—*mathesis universalis*—still reigned. There's a wonderful piece of nineteenth-century student doggerel about Jowett, the Victorian classicist and master of Balliol College, Oxford, which rather nicely sums up this philosophy:

"Here stand I, my name is Jowett,
"If there's knowledge, then I know it;
"I am the master of this college,
"What I know not, is not knowledge."

The question this raises for us, of course, is: how does something get to count as knowledge? Intellectuals have been defined as experts in le-

[11]Delivered at the *New York Times* President's Forum on Literacy, in New York, New York, on December 5, 1989. Reprinted with permission of Henry Louis Gates, Jr.

gitimation: and the academy, today, is an institution of legitimation, establishing what counts as knowledge, what counts as culture. In the most spirited attacks on the movement toward multiculturalism in the academy today, there's a whiff of this: We are the master of this college—What we know not, is not knowledge. Straddling the sixteenth and seventeenth centuries, Bacon thought he could know everything. Today, we see a constriction, a narrowing, of what counts as even worth knowing. And beyond the cartography of Western culture? A cryptic warning: Here Be Monsters.

I got mine: the rhetoric of liberal education remains suffused with the imagery of possession, patrimony, legacy, lineage, inheritance, heritage. How often have you heard these terms, these metaphors for transmission?

Unfortunately, the rhetoric of possession and lineage subsists upon, and perpetuates, a division: between us and them, we the heirs of *our* tradition, and you, the Others, whose difference defines our identity.

What happens, though, if you buy into that rhetoric, if you accept its terms and presuppositions? Then you will say: yes, I am Other, and if the aim of education is to reinforce an individual's rightful cultural legacy, then it looks like I don't really belong here; I am a guest at someone else's banquet. How can you resolve this dispute? So long as we retain a vocabulary of heritage and inheritance in defining our putative national cultures, it cannot *be* resolved.

What this means is that the old fogey and the young turk have a lot more in common than they realize; that they may, in fact, be two sides of the same debased coin; and that those of us who really care about humane learning should convert to another currency. The argument has been made that cultural nationalism has been a constitutive aspect of Western education. As humanists, our challenge today is, simply, to learn to live without it. Indeed, it saddens me that there should be any perceived conflict between the ideal of humanistic learning and what I think of as the truly human, and humane, version of the humanities, one that sees the West not as some mythical, integrative Whole, but as a part of a still larger whole.

In the resonant words of W. E. B. Du Bois: "I sit with Shakespeare, and he winces not. Across the color line, I move arm in arm with Balzac and Dumas, where smiling men and welcoming women glide in gilded halls. From out the caves of evening that swing between a strong-limbed earth and the tracery of the stars, I summon Aristotle and Aurelius and what soul I will, and they come all graciously with no scorn or condescension. So, wed with Truth, I dwell above the Veil."

Which is then to say, I believe we can change the terms of argument; I believe we can rethink the role of a liberal education without the conceptual residue of cultural nationalism or geneticism. I believe it, because I do think many scholars have already begun to do so.

I've suggested that moving toward this human notion of the humanities moves us away from the divisive us/them implications of traditional defenses of the humanities, and removes a source of cultural alienation that is clearly breeding disenchantment and disillusionment among those for whom the experience of higher education may matter the most. But I also think, and here my Whiggish triumphalism is revealed, that it's the natural conclusion of scholarly enlightenment, in which ethnocentric presuppositions have fallen under scholarly critique—auto-critique—and been found wanting.

Such an embracive posture honors the best, the noblest traditions and ambitions of the academy; and while I've decried cultural nationalism, I hope you'll permit me to bow to it in citing something Ishmael Reed has said on the subject of multiculturalism: he said it's impossible here "because the United States is unique in the world: *the world is here.*"

Or listen to the great, canonical author, Herman Melville, writing a century earlier: "There is something in the contemplation of the mode in which America has been settled, that, in a noble breast, should forever extinguish the prejudices of national dislikes. Settled by the people of all nations, all nations may claim her for their own. You can not spill a drop of American blood, without spilling the blood of the whole world . . . . We are not a narrow tribe, no; our blood is as the blood of the Amazon, made up of a thousand noble currents, all pouring into one. We are not a nation, so much as a world."

Let me pinpoint and forestall a source of unease. Amy Gutmann said something important in her recent book, *Democratic Education:* "In a democracy, political disagreement is not something that we should generally seek to avoid. Political controversies over our educational problems are a particularly important source of social progress because they have the potential for educating so many citizens." I think that's true: I think a lot of us feel that any clamor or conflict over the curriculum is just a bad thing in itself, that it somehow undermines the legitimacy of the institutions of knowledge. A sort of no-news-is-good-news attitude on the subject of education; they think if you even look at a university cross-eyed, it'll dry up and blow away and then where will you be? Whereas I think one of the most renewing activities we can engage in is to rethink the institutions where we teach people to think; we invest in myths of continuity, but universities have constantly been molting and creating themselves anew for the last millennium, and there's no reason to think that'll change in the next.

Some people say, where there's no consensus—and there is no consensus—teach the conflicts. In fact, I think at the better colleges, we do. We don't seem to be able not to. And that's nothing to be embarrassed about: college isn't kindergarten; our job isn't to present a seemly, dignified, unified front to the students. College students are too old to *form*, we shouldn't delude ourselves; but they're not too old to challenge. I'm reminded of something that the great college president and educator Robert Maynard Hutchins wrote in a book he published during the height of the McCarthy era. He recounted a conversation he'd had with a distinguished doctor about the attempt of the Board of Regents of the University of California to extort (as Hutchins put it) "an illegal and unconstitutional oath of loyalty from the faculty of that great institution." "Yes, but," the doctor said, "if we are going to hire these people to look after our children we are entitled to know what their opinions are." And Hutchins grandly remarks: "I think it is clear that the collapse of liberal education in the United States is related as cause or effect or both to the notion that professors are people who are hired to look after children." Wise words, those.

Obviously, the simple embrace of cultural pluralism doesn't put you home free. But it does allow you to frame the hard questions and challenges ahead. As a great American philosopher of pluralism put it: "How are we going to make the most of the new values we set on variety, difference, and individuality—how are we going to realize their possibilities in every field, and at the same time not sacrifice that plurality to the cooperation we need so much? How can we bring things together as we must without losing sight of plurality?"

Well, how do we do it? And where? It's a question I take seriously; but for me, there's nothing vaporous about the form the answer takes: it's made of brick and mortar, and sometimes a little ivy about the architrave. For us, the educators and the educated, it is the university, whose constant refashioning is our charge, our burden, and our privilege.

# Democracy in an Age of Denial[12]

## Taylor Branch

*Born January 14, 1947, Atlanta, GA; A.B., University of North Carolina, 1968; staff writer,* Washington Monthly, *1970-73; staff writer,* Harper's, *1973-75; staff writer,* Esquire, *1975-76; winner of Pulitzer Prize in history, 1989; author,* The Empire Blues *(1981),* Labyrinth *(1982),* Parting the Waters *(1988),* Pillar of Fire *(1997).*

### Editor's introduction

In this speech, Pulitzer Prize-winning author Taylor Branch addressed over 300 members of Congress, their aides, and numerous Federation of State Humanities staff members. Speaking one week after the 1992 Los Angeles riots, Branch, an authority on the civil rights movement, asserted that we must find ways outside history books and federal documents to understand the many different groups of people who constitute the United States. Democracy, he maintained, is really faith in another. Such faith can only exist if we listen to one another and hear the clamor of all groups, so that ultimately we expand our "public consciousness." In order for this to occur, we must cease denying information from alternative sources.

---

I'm happy to be with you this morning. You're good people assembled here in war council in bad times. My work is in history, and I call upon you partly as witnesses to a dilemma that I fear I will have when the second part of my history of the civil rights movement appears, whenever that is. I fear that few readers will believe that I began working on the book's opening scene three years before the Rodney King case. It is a 1962 police action in Los Angeles in which the LAPD raided a house of worship, beat and shot thirteen people, one of whom died, three of whom were shot in the testicles, all black men. Afterwards the victims were arrested and charged with riot, mayhem, and resisting arrest. All were criminally convicted. In effect it was what would have happened in the Rodney King case had there been no videotape. That happened in 1962. I treat the episode as a turning point in the life of Malcolm X and the life of black America. Yet one of the reasons that I spend so much time trying to recover the event is that it passed almost completely without notice in the world at large. That a trauma of that size could occur in a city like Los Angeles in 1962 without public notice is part of the history of this time. It's sobering in the sense that we see the recycling of this violence not just in 1965 in the Watts riot and again last week in the Rodney King riots, but also in 1962. It's hopeful in another sense, that in 1962 you could have even worse outrages and miscarriages of justice and not even have them noticed by the world at large. At least we've come some way from there.

The riot and the racial upheavals of the 1960s generally marked the beginning of the end of a democratic renewal that was the hopeful upsurge of the early civil rights movement. We here have to ask the difficult question, if the riots of 1992 follow the path of history and mark another inward turning in our time, where was the renewal that should have gone before? We've already started the withdrawal before we had the great expansion of hope. That is indeed a sobering thought.

Twenty-five years ago, I was a kid at Princeton, at graduate school, with a bare inclination that we had passed through a period of democratic renewal in the civil rights movement, which had forced a change in my life's interest against my will. My father is in the dry cleaning business, he brought me up to believe that all people who are interested in politics, and espe-

[12]Delivered at the annual "Humanities on the Hill" breakfast, in Washington, D.C., on May 7, 1992.

cially politicians, are those who cannot find honest work. The 1960s forced me to change that. In graduate school at the Woodrow Wilson School at Princeton, I wanted one chance to experience the civil rights movement before it faded away, and I persuaded my faculty review board, much against its will, to allow me to go down and work for John Lewis' voter education project in southwest Georgia. The faculty committee did not want me to go because they said noninstitutional work was not policy relevant to experience; they wanted me to work for the Congressional Budget Office or preferably the Bureau of the Budget, which was and is considered the Taj Mahal of crisis management—that's what we called it back then. My proposal was considered an existential lark: I wanted to go down by myself, register these voters. The professors finally agreed that if I would agree to write a five-page memorandum on the policy implications of my existential experience for monopsony in the local labor markets of the agrarian counties of southwest Georgia. Back then, all freedom issues were considered a subsidiary of economic development. So I stepped off the end of the known world in going by myself into those rural counties. This is a personal story to tell you how my fascination with democratic history began only after I became a very disoriented young man.

In the summer of 1969, on the day men first landed on the moon, I was in a tiny little county, Schley County, in Georgia. After one month's work, I had given up on men. I decided that if there was any hope for voter registration in southwest Georgia, it was with the women. And in this tiny county I'd been told there was an old, old matriarch, 90 years old, and that if she could find it in her heart to say a kind word about voter registration in this county, where there were no black registered voters, that something might happen. So I was on her porch on July 20 [1969], the day Neil Armstrong had set foot on the moon. And I was trying to get her interested in voter registration, to receive a grant to register voters. She was in a rocking chair and had a lip full of snuff, and all of a sudden she said to me, "Young man, do you think we really landed on the moon this morning?"

And I said, "Yes," and she said, "How do you know?"

I said, "Well, I saw it on Walter Cronkite back at the motel before I came over here this morning."

She just rocked and she didn't say anything, and the next thing she said was, "Have you seen the Simonize wax commercial?"

And I said, "What Simonize wax commercial?"

She said, "The one where the little children float across the kitchen on an invisible shield of Simonize wax and don't scuff the floor."

Actually, I remembered that, it was a very vivid commercial. I said, "Yes, I've seen that."

She said, "Well, do you believe that?"

I realized she had an agenda going here, and I said, "Well, yes, I believe that they can make it look like that, but that's a commercial. I saw the moon landing on the news program. That's different than a commercial."

She didn't say anything, she kept rocking. The next thing she said was, "Have you ever been in a fist fight?"

Every time she threw me off balance I found myself talking more and more in the language of policy. I said, "Unfortunately, I have, I don't see it as a very good way of settling disputes," and so on and so forth.

She said, "I mean the kind of fist fight when more than one tooth gets knocked out at a time."

I said, "No, I've never been in one like that," and she said, "Well, I've been in some, and I've seen plenty of them, and people don't get up and talk again the way they do on 'Have Gun Will Travel.'"

She kept rocking for awhile, and I kept talking more and more about policy, getting more and more nervous, and finally she said, "Young man, I can prove to you that we didn't land on the moon this morning."

I said, "How can you do that?" She said, "Well, God wouldn't allow it." Now being in the depth of a heathen period at that time, I said, "What does God have to do with whether we landed on the moon?"

She said, "You have not thought about it. If we could land on the moon this morning, all we have to do is fill up our tank once on the moon and on the next jump we could probably make it into heaven without God's permission, without dying. And you know that could never happen."

By that time, she really had me. I didn't know what to say, but a number of lessons were dawning on me. One of them was that she was not interested in voter registration in Schley County. I perceived that. Another was that she was telling me in her own way a very profound lesson about what is fear, what is real, who can teach what to whom. Here was a lady almost 90 years old who literally went back to the end of slavery, lived in a county with no black registered voters and where her whole life has taught her that questions of voting and race go to the very nerve of survival and identity and being. And all of a sudden, here on her porch one morning comes a young white man talking about economic development and voter registration, telling her, encouraging her to do something that she knows might mean life or death in that county. At her age she was not ready for it. She was asking me questions about what is real, what is hope, what is dangerous, what you can perceive, what is fear.

I also sensed something else: there was absolutely no way that I could capture the reality of that moment or that conversation, or a thousand other things that happened to me that summer, in the language of a policy memorandum for that faculty review committee back at Princeton. The language of policy does not reach the wisdom and experience of the common people in a democracy like ours. The old lady's presence made me feel this lesson in my bones long before I could articulate it, which is the point. I kept a diary that summer, as never before or since, just trying to record the experiences that I had traveling around. That became the basis of the first article I ever published, which occurred before it dawned on me that writing might be something for me to pursue as a career.

The old lady taught me a good deal about narrative, about democratic experience and where movements came from. "Movement" is a trivial word today. But a social movement is a fundamental faith in strangers and an encounter with new possibilities, always involving discovery and a step in the unknown. A fresh sense of democratic movements led to my strong, strong belief in narrative history, particularly in cross-cultural affairs. We make discoveries at the human level and not at the analytical level, although many people fool themselves into thinking that they can cross barriers between culture by analysis. It's an insight as old as the Book of Genesis that the truth of even the most complex abstractions is best communicated in stories about brothers quarreling with sisters or fathers quarreling with sons. We need narrative history. I think we especially need it in a democracy. We lose sight oftentimes of just how terrifying, how bold democracy really is. Democracy, in its best form, is a stark, public encounter with the inner nature of the human condition. It is by definition a faith in strangers, faith that the greatest issues of the day can turn on the vote of the last wino to come to the polls. We have more faith in strangers embedded in our tradition and in our fundamental philosophy than most of us care to contemplate. But this democracy, this vision, this movement, this opening of the public space, is basically what will save us and what will renew us if we hope to have another democratic renewal of the public faith in strangers to renew the democratic spirit in our time.

I like to think of what I've learned in studying movement history, civil rights history, cross-racial history, religious history in the last ten years, as a fundamental primer in democracy. The democratic faith in strangers requires a disciplined vision. It is a faith balanced by the discipline of self-control. We lose sight of the elementary fact that the heart of it is self-government, to govern ourselves without benefit of external authority. So a basic definition is that democracy is where the discipline of faith in strangers meets the disciplines of self-control. This is a sobering thought for these times, when we by and large have very little of either. In the generation since I met the lady rocking on her porch, white Americans have basically evacuated all large cities in the United States. We have turned inward. It is an era of white power, of suburban power, of Jewish power, black power, turning inward to tribal constituencies, rather than reaching out towards strangers. We have turned inward, we have very little faith in one another, and obviously, we have very little self-control. All we have to do is look at the budget, at schools and cities, at the environment, at some of the issues that make people concerned about the health of democracy today.

This is not the era for triumphalism, for crowing that democracy stands victorious at the end of history because the competing systems have fallen, particularly communism. There are other forms of government that are much older and better established, not only in history but in most parts of the world—than democracy, and those forms are tyranny, and chaos. Democracy will not survive unless people give it renewals of spirit. When Ben Franklin came out of the Constitutional Convention, he was asked, "What form of government have you conceived?" He said, "A new one, a democracy, if you can keep it." It was considered a bold and risky venture to conceive of a government without some external authority treating citizens like children and telling them what to do.

The under side of modern progress is that we have lost many of the natural forms of discipline that once governed humankind. Famine, war, weather, crop failure, competition: many of these things checked our excesses through tragedy and hardship. We've triumphed over some of them, but we need to substitute a new source of discipline. The democratic belief is that it must come from within, sustained by our faith in one another and our belief in fundamental practices of citizenship. American history teaches that whenever the meaning of our democratic intuition is tested, when it is expanded, when leaders perform like geniuses and people perform like citizens, the focus has almost always been over the race issue. The race issue tells us how democratic we are becoming, in the age of the abolitionists as well as the age of Martin Luther King. Unfortunately, in the past generation, race has driven presidential politics in this inward turning period. The unspoken, prevailing message has been that government is evil because government exists to help poor people, which mainly means black people, and therefore we want to avoid it altogether. That subliminal message, in a sophisticated form, has driven our presidential politics to the degree that we have made government the enemy in a country dedicated to the notion that the government is us. How can we live with this kind of contradiction? It faces the Congress, it faces the humanities councils, so that we see democracy nowadays in these riots and in the budget questions, we see it drift, lost from its fundamental principles.

I see this to some degree in my own research in the secrecy issue. Some of the most ridiculous classifications and secrets going back to the 1930s and 1940s are still maintained today. The real Berlin Wall crumbled, which is a great miracle, but the paper Berlin Wall that separates our government from our people still stands proud. If you don't believe me, go to the F.B.I. reading room, which has no windows and where you can't go to the bathroom without an escort, and see some of the documents that still remain classified there, four, five decades later.

Another area where there is very little thinking about the fundamentals of democracy is the telltale realm of private vices. We are all over the place on the conflict between democracy's desire to protect people, to protect their freedoms, against its equivalent, competing goal of protecting people from harm by others. Cigarettes are terrible; they kill 350,000 people a year. We say that it should be against the law for children to smoke, but we sell cigarettes in vending machines. We say that drugs are a terrible thing, such that even a government premised on the notion that people can govern themselves also operates on the premise that those same people can't resist self-evidently self-destructive devices without police to tell them what to do. Vices are monarchical in the response that they call out of people. At the same time, we have state governments promoting lotteries, telling people that vice is not only something that they don't need to avoid, but that it is their civic duty to participate. The ethos of the lottery advertisement is very similar, almost identical, to the ethos of your street corner drug dealer, which is "forget reality, forget your obligation to the society, forget your children and take a chance that you might hit and get high." Evocations in those ads of what people should do and ought to do if they hit the lottery are so antisocial that it mocks reality that they exist in a democracy. The fantasies portrayed have to do with buying castles or your own personal moon rocket, escaping into material bliss, getting away from the futility of work and the wretchedness of your fellow creatures. Nothing that Donald Trump ever thought of doing would embarrass the role models in lottery ads, who make rubber barons look like models of civic virtue.

To recapture and renew the basics of democracy requires clear thought, faith, discipline, and to some degree an enlargement of the public space. As the world shrinks we have to face the fact that we Americans are rich, we have to speak plain, like the lady in the rocking chair, we have to understand that we can't all be middle class, that by world standards anybody who makes $10,000 or $15,000 is rich. We have a country that is paralyzed because we have a large number of people who are too puffed up to realize that the great challenge in the modern world is what sacrifices we are willing to make for our future, for our progeny, for our public space. Marginal private consumption of people even at the middle-class level is not as important as whether we pass on the democratic experiment alive and well in spirit. To do so requires enormous discipline and connection with strangers.

In the period I'm writing about now, one of the most moving displays of such disciplined faith occurred in the final moments of Mickey Schwerner. I've spoken with several of the FBI agents who took the confessions of the Klansmen who killed Schwerner and two other civil rights workers in June '64. The agents were struck by something: that all the Klansmen remembered the same haunting words from their victim. When he was dragged out into the Mississippi night, knowing that he was about to be lynched, facing people full of hate, Schwerner's last words before he was shot were "Sir, I know just how you feel." The discipline of the movement was that even when confronting death itself and your worst enemies, you never broke hope of establishing human contact with your fellow citizens. Such incandescent faith cannot last long. Within two years of that remark by Schwerner, which was fully in keeping with the preaching and the discipline of the freedom riders, people who had built a movement by reaching out for common ground with their enemies were instead chopping off ground even among their own allies, saying "you're not militant enough for me," or "you're only a liberal, I'm a radical," and they started turning inward. People can't afford to do that. It is rejecting the discipline and the hope of the democratic spirit.

Looking back after ten years' research, I have a number of odd thoughts on the historical challenge of renewing the democratic experience. I'll mention just two. Number one, the last time the United States had a balanced budget was in 1968, the year of the Tet offensive, the Martin Luther King riots, the Robert Kennedy assassination, the King assassination, the peak year of the Vietnam war, and the only major year of the war on poverty. The President who introduced that budget and who got it through was Lyndon Johnson, the father of the Great Society. If we have accepted the political paradox that only a bedrock conservative can have the potential capital to open the door to communist China, perhaps we need to begin to entertain the notion that only a social liberal who aches for the poor can have the discipline to regain our sense of budgetary discipline in our country. How many trillions of debt must we heap on our children before that possibility occurs?

The second odd thought has to do with women, like the old woman in the rocking chair. If the periods of renewal, of movement spirit, of expansion in the public consciousness occur most often in American history around the race issue, it also seems true that those movements have been built upon the sensibilities of women in alliance with the maverick clergy. When you're looking for people to go to jail, when you're looking for plaintiffs, they are more likely to be women. And when you need a public spokesman, that spokesman is going to speak the language of Isaiah, the language of Amos and of the other justice prophets of Hebrew scripture. That's true of the age of Theodore Parker, and true in the age of Martin Luther King, who quoted Parker: "The arc of the moral universe is long, but it bends towards justice." That message, and the purity of the notion that democratic intuition is married to something that's very close to the heart of both our religious impulses and of our highest civic duty, seems to come through the sensibilities and the manpower, if you will, of women. From this perspective, it is a tragedy that the abortion issue in the last 25 years has to some degree divided women from the clergy. We need either more women clergy or more of the prophetic clergy in consultation with women, to restore a coalition that has wrestled illumination and hope for eras far more gloomy than our own.

Finally, for your humanities councils and in the spirit of democratic renewal, I would like to recommend something that I have grown with in conviction ever since I met the woman in the rocking chair, which is the value of oral history. My interview with her was of oral history. I would not have found her lessons in a library. Cultures tend to preserve what they are comfortable with. Fifty years from now, if someone wants to write about the impact of Asian-American immigration in the United States in the '80s and '90s, they probably will not find the documents to bring it alive in libraries. Oral history is important not just for the raw materials of living history but as an antidote to television and other forces in our modern age that shear us from one another, generation from generation, grandparents from grandchildren, black from white, Asian from European, all these divides that are so crucial and so paralytic to democratic change and to understanding our history. I believe that oral history is a rectifying force not just in overcoming the great tragedy of vanished, unrecoverable history. If you go to Alabama today and ask for the oral histories of the bus boycott in Montgomery or the Selma march, they will look at you like you're nuts, but as teaching tool for the people, like myself, who go and do those oral histories. In your state humanities councils, I encourage you to explore the notion of having teenagers and little school children in American history courses do oral histories with their own grandparents or other relatives, to rekindle, to rediscover the human sinews of family, these differences within the generation. They may move on to do an oral history of a grandparent of somebody else's family, particularly from a different culture. Then you've got the beginnings of what a movement is—a discovery that the world is larger than its material boundaries, and that they themselves can make it larger. That sense of stepping into the unknown is the beginning of faith in strangers, and I hope that it will renew the democratic spirit as has constantly occurred when people really apply themselves to that central intuition of our American history.

If democracy is all that's left, we must try it. And never, never take it for granted.

# VII. Civil Rights

## Editor's introduction

From the 1787 Constitutional Convention to the present, American leaders have debated the degree to which the Constitution guarantees and protects basic personal liberties. The 13th, 14th, and 15th amendments, passed in 1865, 1868, and 1870 respectively, abolished slavery and guaranteed civil rights to all United States citizens. Yet over 130 years later, the manifest reality of these guarantees is still questioned. Such questioning is the focus of the speeches contained herein. In all of these speeches, American leaders, embodying a variety of perspectives, debate the American government's ability to ensure civil rights for citizens, regardless of their race, religion, gender, age, or other traits or conditions.

In this century, the fight for civil rights has been both dramatic and powerful. A. Philip Randolph, an early civil rights and labor leader, accelerated the African-American effort for equal protection and opportunity under the federal law as he organized workers to demand equal pay, regardless of race or color. In a similar vein, Dr. Martin Luther King, Jr.'s successful boycott of the Montgomery, Alabama public transportation system (1955-56) helped to desegregate that system. In 1957, 1960, 1964, and 1965, Congress passed laws to both ensure the minority right to vote and guarantee equal access to public accommodations. During that period, courts placed their concern on the degree to which businesses, organizations, and universities could instill "affirmative action" in their day-to-day operations.

Without doubt, the parties involved in the fight for civil rights have disagreed on both the goals of their particular causes and the means of reaching those goals. Such debate is crystallized in speeches by Bayard Rustin and Robert S. Browne, both of which are reprinted below. Brown, an economist, believed that African Americans must preserve their "own group individuality." He thus advocated separatism, the notion that African Americans should not attempt to integrate into a "mainstream society." In contrast, Rustin supported a middle way, with African Americans developing "black institutions and a black image," while at the same time "going downtown into integrated work situations."

Many other ethnic groups have waged battles for a guarantee that their civil rights will be both respected and maintained. These groups want to defy a racism that is undoubtedly evoked by both ignorance and indifference. They include, among others, women, Native Americans, Jews, Chicanos, and the physically challenged. Their road has been difficult, and each step has been a hard-earned success. Not only have they had to strive for the right to sit on a bus in a seat of their choosing, but also to be considered for certain jobs and certain responsibilities. The speeches reprinted below reflect only a small part of that struggle, as it continues for a significant portion of the American population each and every day.

# Fifty Years of Zionism[1]

Stephen S. Wise

*Born March 17, 1874, Budapest, Hungary; died April 19, 1949; B.A., 1891, Ph.D., 1901, Columbia University; rabbi, Madison Avenue Synagogue, 1891-1900; rabbi, Temple Beth Israel, 1900-06; president, American Jewish Congress, 1917-49; founder, rabbi, Free Synagogue of New York, 1907-49; founder, Jewish Institute of Religion, 1922; author,* The Great Betrayal *(1930),* As I See It *(1940),* Challenging Years *(1949).*

## Editor's introduction

In this speech, Stephen S. Wise, rabbi of New York City's Free Synagogue and an important leader of both Zionism and Reform Judaism, provided a history of the Jewish quest to achieve a Jewish national state. At the time this speech was given, the Jewish state of Israel had not yet been formally established (1948). Here, Wise outlined the persecution endured by the Jews, as well as the culmination of that persecution in the Nazis' systematic genocide of over six million Jews.

---

To dwell in this hour upon the great Day of Herzl is not to ignore the significant men and movements that went before, nor yet the equally significant developments of the cause and movement within the half century that has passed since we first met within this to us little less than sacred city of Basle, Switzerland.

Herzl's predecessors were unknown to him: his successors are not unknown to us. Before him stood some historic Jewish figures though he knew them not: Moses Hess, author of *Rome and Jerusalem*, which despite its obvious limitations and defects remains one of the classical operas of our immortal enterprise, and Leo Pinsker, author of *Auto-Emancipation*, a title which reveals the deepest meaning of the Zionist purpose. Not only books and their authors went before Herzl, but a number of indeflectibly faithful groups, the earliest pre-Herzlian groups, including Chibath Zion, that admirable company of for a time ineffective Zionist dreamers, the memorable *Bilu*, and other Russian, Rumanian, Hungarian companies of men and women. With prescience these foresaw and with prophecy they foretold, chiefly to themselves, that as it was later to be expressed in the formula of the great Achad Haam, there was no other way, that despite a thousand years of residence in Eastern and South Eastern Europe, it could not and never would be their home, their permanent and inalienable home, that their home was and must for ever be *elsewhere*, and that elsewhere was Erez Israel.

They were not impatient in reaching this conclusion. A thousand years during which dispersed Israel had tested itself and the mood of its hosts had in its own sight throughout been a watch in the little relieved darkness of the night. Never in history had a people been so long alienated from its own land and retained its unaltered and unlessened love for the land, nor sustained its hope for the restoration of its nationhood. These trends of discontent, these tendencies to abandon at last an unendurable way of life, found understanding and voice in the person and Jewish genius of him whom history has come to know as Dr. Theodor Herzl. His little more than one-hundred-page brochure, *Der Judenstaat*, marks one of the turning points of Jewish history. In order to appraise and evaluate it, it is necessary to say no more than that it has changed Jewish history, which, having changed its course, can never be the same again. A new epoch began, not to be without its evil days and its terrible years, but these were to come to a people, which under the impact of *Der Judenstaat*, had, without losing faith in humankind, resolved to be the master of its fate and the captain of its soul.

[1]Delivered to the 22nd World Zionist Congress, in Basle, Switzerland, on December 9, 1946.

What did Zionism as propounded by Herzl mean? Much, everything, but one thing supremely! We had lived throughout the centuries on decisions, permissions, or inhibitions by others,—rulers, governments, nations. The world had too long said to us, you may or you must, you can or you cannot. Herzl at last spoke the magic word—you can, we can. We may fulfill our own prayers and purposes. The answer to our prayers lies with, even within, us. At one and the same time every need of the Jewish people was or was to be fulfilled—faith, people, nation.

It was not quite extraordinary for Herzl to predict the continuance of Jewish oppression, the intensifying of wrong inflicted upon the Jew. But it was more than extraordinary that Herzl should have seen what the world begins to see, namely, that "The Jewish State is essential to the world: it will, therefore, be created." What he could not easily have foreseen was that the last supreme effort to destroy the Jewish people grew out of the understanding by Nazism that mankind cannot be enslaved as long as Jews survive, that Jewish survival must forever signify revolt against human enslavement and inhuman injustice.

It may be that the nations slowly begin to comprehend the role of the Jew on the world's stage, as the indestructible servant of eternal faith and freedom. If so, why do not the nations, led by Britain and the United States, offer to the decimated but undestroyed Jewish people, the one supreme reparation which it merits, the creation of the Jewish State of Palestine as healing for the almost immedicable wounds of the "tribe of the wandering foot and weary breast" of which Byron sang "How shall you flee away and be at rest?"

Herzl was a Titan, one of a race of giants, which includes glorious and resounding names in Jewish history: Max Nordau, David Wolfsohn, Otto Warburg, Nahum Sokolow, Menachem Ussischkin, and the one figure, who has functioned as leader throughout two wars, happily before and after both, whose stature has grown with the years, to whom the Institute bearing his name is a scientific tribute, to whose political genius and statesmanship our cause is under deep and uncancellable indebtedness, Dr. Chaim Weizmann.

Unimaginably electric was the effect upon us, upon world Jewry, upon the world, of the publication of *Der Judenstaat.* The day after the opening session of the first Zionist Congress, the then Mr. Brandeis, temporarily staying in San Francisco, said to a member of his family as he read the opening address of Dr. Herzl, "Now that is a cause for which I could work and give my life."

The twenty years before the day of Herzl had not been wholly unlike these last twenty years of horror. In the then largest Jewish settlement of the world instead of Nazism there was Pobiedonostoff. The measure of the effect of Herzl and the first Zionist Congress it is not wholly impossible to appraise. After every other calamity in Jewish history, some manner of escape complete or partial had been come upon—from Jerusalem to Rome, from Spain and Portugal to Holland, France, and Germany, from Russian-Rumanian pogroms to America, flight, escape, refuge for self-preservation, always Exodus without Palestine. For the first time in twenty centuries, Herzl had dared to propose that there be no more escape, no more retreat, no more refuge—but *going home* and thus the end of dependence upon others, the substitution of our own will for the good or ill will of other peoples, other nations, other faiths, no further extension of the boundaries of the Golah. Herzl's discovery and thesis was that the mission ideal of Israel, as urged for half a century or more especially among the German-speaking Jewish peoples, could not be carried out by an Israel which had ceased to be; in a word, a non-existent Israel was least able to serve and to bless the world.

It was not as if another way, every other way, had not been tried, the kindly and the ruthless regimes, the benevolent and maleficent rulers of States alike, all alike, and the Dreyfus affair was not more than the final and unanswerable proof of Herzl's faith, that for a people proud and honourable, a people not made up of gypsies, the status of permanent guest is not tolerable, least of all secure. Herzl's was a true mission theory as well. All that Israel scattered, dispersed, impotent, could not be or do, Israel in its own land, Israel in its own National Home, could be and must do.

The terrible persecution of Jews in Eastern Europe in Herzl's day no more explains Zionism than the shocking surprise of the Dreyfus affair. There was a combination of causes and circumstances, which together explain Herzl and the Zionist movement—a sense of Jewish life's lack of dignity and adequacy, loneliness, spiritual loneliness, a world arranged for or against us, whether good or bad, instead of being determined by us, a deep nostalgia organizing itself at last the transcendent effect of an unsatisfied yearning and love for Palestine, plus a sense of the urgent need of the substituting for the shadow of perfunctory emancipation by an alien world, the substance and truth of a passionately eager and voluntary self-emancipation.

No story of these fifty epic years dares fail to pay tribute however inadequate to our Jewish youth, verging upon and reborn in Palestine, our Chaluzim and Chaluzoth, pioneers, whose labor, devotion, sacrifice, did more than all else to make their and our precious dream come true.

Many and grievous were the crises which befell the Movement beginning in 1920. There were the first terrible disorders, though the unnumbered political crises antedate and postdate all disorders. Later there ensued the crisis of 1929, resolved only in part by the Ramsay MacDonald dissent from the lamentable and still inexplicable Passfield Document. Happier days came too: the year 1935 with its blessed immigration figure of more than 60,000, followed, alas, by the renewed Arab disorders, and the attitude on the part of the attacked, which was their moral glory but not their complete physical saving, *Havlagah.*

Nothing worse befell us throughout the two generations of resettlement than the White Paper, the failure to reject which out of hand was a terrible blunder on the part of all of us. That evil, the White Paper, has dogged our footsteps since the day it was framed, and, far graver, hardened a line of policy, which by its limiting of immigration to 75,000 over a period of five years, including a narrowly fixed "bonus" of refugees, committed one of the most terrible of crimes against the Jewish people, crime of crimes, for hundreds of thousands of these crushed, slaughtered martyrs might have become the living and creative members of the household of Israel instead of the victims of inexpiable crime.

Herzl was no more the creator of Zionism than Moses was the creator of liberation. Each was, we devoutly believe, a human instrument in the hands of divine purpose, and, above all, equal to that purpose. Herzl focused, expressed, glorified the spirit of his people. The symphony of his people had been writing itself in blood and tears throughout nearly 2000 years. The magic hand of a great conductor was needed. Others before him had essayed to interpret that Jewish symphony of the ages—Moses Hess with deep intuition, withal an inadequate sense of the human drama; Pinsker, it may be, too near to the unfolding tragedy to envisage its majestic outlines. Herzl came at last, deeply troubled albeit unconfused and daring to direct the rendition of the symphony of his people for centuries, to utter the protest of his people's soul, in the terms of heroic and noblest prophecy.

We Jews had throughout the ages been pessimists with respect to ourselves, as if we could not do for ourselves, as if it were unthinkable that we could help to save ourselves; and yet, strange to say, we had always been optimists with regard to the world which least justified our optimism. We could not have lived without acquiring the high habit of forgetting wrongs and forgiving the hurt which we suffered, even when our honor was no less hurt than was the life of the wounded and the slain. To forget and to forgive was easier for us than to plan hopefully and to labor creatively for ourselves. Herzl was the first to see that the roles must be reversed, namely, we were to be meliorists if not pessimists with respect to the world, and optimists with regard to ourselves. History has borne out and abundantly vindicated the revolutionary view, which in a sense merely substituted enriching self-trust for the ancient and impoverishing self-distrust, a view which voiced the renascent faith of a people still equal to greatness of spirit and achievement.

There came the joyous day, November 2, 1917, with its issuance of the Balfour Declaration to which the Jewish people have almost ever since been equal even when and though England was not. Five years later the Jewish Agency was established, the Hebrew University of Jerusalem created some years after that, with its unalterable ideal, students of all peoples, races, and faiths shall be welcomed within its walls. In 1919 the Agency was enlarged, the value of such enlargement yet to be proved, though the non-Zionist leaders of the enlarged Agency met the crisis of 1929 with utmost strength.

Sorrowfully, we recall the Vienna Congress of 1925, when, twenty years after Herzl's death, in his own city, you and I heard thousands of paraders marching to one raucous tune, "Juden

Heraus." Only one answer to that cry was possible: "Anybody might have heard it, but God's whisper came to me—'Juden Herein.'" But most cowardly of all the answers to "Juden Heraus," to the anti-Semitism of Central Europe, and in the end most cruelly punished was the pitiful plea of them that sought not to accuse others but to excuse themselves in the lamentable words, "We are not Semites nor even Jews; we are merely citizens of the Jewish faith."

One needs do no more than contrast these fifty years of Zionism with the fifty years that had gone before, confused, groping, pulseless, with the assault of Chassidim upon the bulwark of Rabbinism not yet wholly spent, with Jews of Central Europe still groping towards a mild and disguised assimilation, little redeemed even by the fruitful creativeness of *Jüdische Wissenschaft*, Reform Judaism, lapsed into the grievous blunder of minimizing the difference between Synagogue and Church, as if there were no other differentiation of Israel from the world than that inherent in religion, with the implication that if we Jews minimize the religious or credal differences, we shall be more and more like the rest of the world, and the last surviving difference will finally have vanished.

I will be forgiven if I dwell for one moment upon the incredible growth of American Jewry and American Zionism in these fifty years, especially throughout the last decade. Best of all, this growth of American Zionism has been the token of American Jewish awakening and of American Jewish understanding of all that Zionism means. Again, I know I will be forgiven if I make mention of the names of two great American Zionists, each of whom made a precious contribution to Zionism, Justice Louis D. Brandeis and Henrietta Szold. Brandeis great as American, as Jew, as Zionist, and Henrietta Szold, who gave nothing to the Zionist cause equal to the purity and nobility, I had almost said holiness, of her own life.

Invited to essay the role of historian, it is not for me to deal with current political situations, and yet the present crisis of crises can hardly be ignored. Certain it is that a situation has been reached which admits of only two ways of dealing therewith. Palestine is not an independent Dominion, nor yet a dependent Colony. Mandate and Mandatory mean one thing, Trustee and Trusteeship. Either England will cancel the White Paper, the blighting White Paper, and resume as genuine Mandatory over Palestine, or it must be assumed that it has resolved to abandon the Mandate.

This brief sketch of Zionism over a period of fifty years can hardly come to a fitting close without a twofold appeal alike to the mandatory power and to the British people. It is barely credible that the British Government should within a generation descend from the heights of the Balfour Declaration to the depths of Yagur and Cyprusism.

Surely the British Government, which long stood as a friend to the Jewish people, will not be satisfied to accept the role of the betrayer of Zionism. After all the infinite woe of the Jewish people—one of every three of whom has been most foully and unnaturally murdered—the Jews returning to Palestine merit a kinder fate than to be transshipped from its shores to Cyprus or to any place on earth outside of Palestine. The hand of Britain that wrote the Balfour Declaration should not now be used to drag war-weary and disinherited refugees away from Palestine instead of facilitating their pilgrimage to the heart of Palestine, which is the heart of their heart.

To our fellow Jews we appeal in another key. Resist, resist, resist the oppression of our brothers but let no deeds of our own soil the blameless record of a long unsullied history. We Zionist dare never forget "What thou wouldst have highly thou must have holily." Zionism was ever a cause of moral and social standards, of ethical and spiritual regeneration. If these moral standards of ideals are foresworn, Zionism will have sunk to the low level of a rabble-rousing chauvinism.

These fifty years of Zionism must fittingly end with the proclamation of the tenth verse of the twenty-fifth chapter of the book of Leviticus:

" . . . and ye shall hallow the fiftieth year and proclaim liberty throughout the land unto all the inhabitants hereof: it is to be a Jubilee to you; and ye shall return every man unto his possession and ye shall return every man unto his family."

As if interpretation were necessary, Sifra adds the significance of the word *deror*, liberty, is *cherut*, freedom.

Let mankind unite to make it a year of Jubilee for the Jewish people. We have made and we shall keep Palestine Jewish and free. We call upon the nations of the world to guarantee never to suffer that freedom to be violated, to make

Jews free wherever they dwell and to make free all the inhabitants of the earth.

And when this Zionist Congress after celebrating the close of fifty years shall have been ended, let it stand as the reaffirmation of the unwithstandable purpose, the unbreakable unity, the unimpairable faith of the Zionist movement—and with God be the rest.

# I Have a Dream[2]

Martin Luther King, Jr.

*Born January 15, 1929, Atlanta, GA; died April 4, 1968; A.B., 1948, L.H.D., 1957, Morehouse College; B.D., Crozer Theological Seminary, 1951; L.H.D., Central State College, 1958; Ph.D., 1955, D.D., 1959, Boston University; pastor, Dexter Avenue Baptist Church, 1954-68; president, Southern Christian Leadership Conference, 1956-68; winner of Nobel Peace Prize, 1964; author,* Stride Toward Freedom *(1958),* Why We Can't Wait *(1964),* Where Do We Go from Here *(1967).*

## Editor's introduction

During the centennial year of the Emancipation Proclamation, Dr. Martin Luther King, Jr. succeeded in bringing together over 200,000 people to march on the Capitol and demand equitable opportunities for African Americans. In the speech reprinted below, King asks that the African-American quest to achieve equality not "degenerate into physical violence." For his adherence to peaceful methods, his eloquence, and his bravery in the face of backward thinking and repressive policy-making, King is remembered as perhaps the greatest leader of the civil rights movement, and one of the most profoundly powerful speakers of his age.

---

Five score years ago, a great American, in whose symbolic shadow we stand, signed the Emancipation Proclamation. This momentous decree came as a great beacon light of hope to millions of Negro slaves who had been seared in the flames of withering injustice. It came as a joyous daybreak to end the long night of captivity.

But one hundred years later, we must face the tragic fact that the Negro is still not free. One hundred years later, the life of the Negro is still sadly crippled by the manacles of segregation and the chains of discrimination. One hundred years later, the Negro lives on a lonely island of poverty in the midst of a vast ocean of material prosperity. One hundred years later, the Negro is still languished in the corners of American society and finds himself an exile in his own land. So we have come here today to dramatize an appalling condition.

In a sense we have come to our nation's Capital to cash a check. When the architects of our republic wrote the magnificent words of the Constitution and the Declaration of Independence, they were signing a promissory note to which every American was to fall heir. This note was a promise that all men would be guaranteed the unalienable rights of life, liberty, and the pursuit of happiness.

It is obvious today that America has defaulted on this promissory note insofar as her citizens of color are concerned. Instead of honoring this sacred obligation, America has given the Negro people a bad check; a check which has come back marked "insufficient funds." But we refuse to believe that the bank of justice is bankrupt. We refuse to believe that there are insufficient funds in the great vaults of opportunity of this nation. So we have come to cash this check—a check that will give us upon demand the riches of freedom and the security of justice. We have also come to this hallowed spot to remind America of the fierce urgency of *now.* This is no time to engage in the luxury of cooling off or to take the tranquilizing drug of gradualism. *Now* is the time to make real the promises of Democracy. *Now* is the time to rise from the dark and desolate valley of segregation to the sunlit path of racial justice. *Now* is the time to open the doors of opportunity to all of God's children. *Now* is the time to lift our nation from the quicksands of racial injustice to the solid rock of brotherhood.

[2]Delivered at the March on Washington for Jobs and Freedom, in Washington, D.C., on August 28, 1963. Reprinted by arrangement with the Heirs to the Estate of Martin Luther King, Jr., c/o Writers House, Inc. as agent for the proprietor. 

It would be fatal for the nation to overlook the urgency of the moment and to underestimate the determination of the Negro. This sweltering summer of the Negro's legitimate discontent will not pass until there is an invigorating autumn of freedom and equality. 1963 is not an end, but a beginning. Those who hope that the Negro needed to blow off steam and will now be content will have a rude awakening if the nation returns to business as usual. There will be neither rest nor tranquillity in America until the Negro is granted his citizenship rights. The whirlwinds of revolt will continue to shake the foundations of our nation until the bright day of justice emerges.

But there is something that I must say to my people who stand on the warm threshold which leads into the palace of justice. In the process of gaining our rightful place we must not be guilty of wrongful deeds. Let us not seek to satisfy our thirst for freedom by drinking from the cup of bitterness and hatred. We must forever conduct our struggle on the high plane of dignity and discipline. We must not allow our creative protest to degenerate into physical violence. Again and again we must rise to the majestic heights of meeting physical force with soul force. The marvelous new militancy which has engulfed the Negro community must not lead us to a distrust of all white people, for many of our white brothers, as evidenced by their presence here today, have come to realize that their destiny is tied up with our destiny and their freedom is inextricably bound to our freedom. We cannot walk alone.

And as we walk, we must make the pledge that we shall march ahead. We cannot turn back. There are those who are asking the devotees of civil rights, "When will you be satisfied?" We can never be satisfied as long as the Negro is the victim of the unspeakable horrors of police brutality. We can never be satisfied as long as our bodies, heavy with the fatigue of travel, cannot gain lodging in the motels of the highways and the hotels of the cities. We cannot be satisfied as long as the Negro's basic mobility is from a smaller ghetto to a larger one. We can never be satisfied as long as a Negro in Mississippi cannot vote and a Negro in New York believes he has nothing for which to vote. No, no, we are not satisfied, and we will not be satisfied until justice rolls down like waters and righteousness like a mighty stream.

I am not unmindful that some of you have come here out of great trials and tribulations. Some of you have come fresh from narrow jail cells. Some of you have come from areas where your quest for freedom left you battered by the storms of persecution and staggered by the winds of police brutality. You have been the veterans of creative suffering. Continue to work with the faith that unearned suffering is redemptive.

Go back to Mississippi, go back to Alabama, go back to South Carolina, go back to Georgia, go back to Louisiana, go back to the slums and ghettos of our northern cities, knowing that somehow this situation can and will be changed. Let us not wallow in the valley of despair.

I say to you today, my friends, that in spite of the difficulties and frustrations of the moment I still have a dream. It is a dream deeply rooted in the American dream.

I have a dream that one day this nation will rise up and live out the true meaning of its creed: "We hold these truths to be self-evident; that all men are created equal."

I have a dream that one day on the red hills of Georgia the sons of former slaves and the sons of former slaveowners will be able to sit down together at the table of brotherhood.

I have a dream that one day even the state of Mississippi, a desert state sweltering with the heat of injustice and oppression, will be transformed into an oasis of freedom and justice.

I have a dream that my four little children will one day live in a nation where they will not be judged by the color of their skin but by the content of their character.

I have a dream today.

I have a dream that one day the state of Alabama, whose governor's lips are presently dripping with the words of interposition and nullification, will be transformed into a situation where little black boys and black girls will be able to join hands with little white boys and white girls and walk together as sisters and brothers.

I have a dream today.

I have a dream that one day every valley shall be exalted, every hill and mountain shall be made low, the rough places will be made plains, and the crooked places will be made straight, and the glory of the Lord shall be revealed, and all flesh shall see it together.

This is our hope. This is the faith with which I return to the South. With this faith we will be able to hew out of the mountain of despair a stone of hope. With this faith we will be able to transform the jangling discords of our nation into a beautiful symphony of brotherhood. With this faith we will be able to work together, to pray together, to struggle together, to go to jail together, to stand up for freedom together, knowing that we will be free one day.

This will be the day when all of God's children will be able to sing with new meaning

"My country, 'tis of thee,
Sweet land of liberty,
Of thee I sing:
Land where my fathers died,
Land of the pilgrims' pride,
From every mountain-side
Let freedom ring."

And if America is to be a great nation this must become true. So let freedom ring from the prodigious hilltops of New Hampshire. Let freedom ring from the mighty mountains of New York. Let freedom ring from the heightening Alleghenies of Pennsylvania!

Let freedom ring from the snowcapped Rockies of Colorado!

Let freedom ring from the curvacious peaks of California!

But not only that; let freedom ring from Stone Mountain of Georgia!

Let freedom ring from Lookout Mountain of Tennessee!

Let freedom ring from every hill and molehill of Mississippi. From every mountainside, let freedom ring.

When we let freedom ring, when we let it ring from every village and every hamlet, from every state and every city, we will be able to speed up that day when all of God's children, black men and white men, Jews and Gentiles, Protestants and Catholics, will be able to join hands and sing in the words of the old Negro spiritual, "Free at last! free at last! thank God almighty, we are free at last!"

# Separation or Integration: Which Way for America?[3]

Robert S. Browne

*Born August 17, 1924, Chicago, IL; A.B., University of Illinois, 1944; M.B.A., University of Chicago, 1947; instructor, Dillard University, 1947-49; industrial field secretary, Chicago Urban League, 1950-53; economist, U.S. Foreign Aid Program in Cambodia and Vietnam, 1955-61; consultant, Phelps-Stokes Fund, 1963-69; assistant professor, Fairleigh Dickinson University, 1967-71; director, Black Economic Research Center, 1969-80; research fellow, Howard University, 1982-85; director, House Banking Subcommittee on International Development, 1987-91; author,* Race Relations in International Affairs *(1961).*

## Editor's introduction

Central to civil rights is the notion of whether or not one culture should assimilate into a dominant culture or remain a distinct and separate entity from that dominant culture. In the following two speeches, Robert S. Browne and Bayard Rustin debate the issue of separatism versus assimilation with regards to the African-American community. Browne, a former professor of economics, believed that African Americans should remain "significantly distinct from the majority culture." Browne further argued that separatism would allow African Americans to preserve an identity that is entirely independent from the surrounding, dominant culture.

---

There is a growing ambivalence in the Negro community which is creating a great deal of confusion both within the black community itself, and within those segments of the white community that are attempting to relate to the blacks. It arises from the question of whether the American Negro is a cultural group, significantly distinct from the majority culture in ways that are ethnically rather than socioeconomically based.

If one believes the answer to this is yes, then one is likely to favor emphasizing the cultural distinctiveness and to be vigorously opposed to any efforts to minimize or to submerge the differences. If, on the other hand, one believes that there are no cultural differences between the blacks and the whites or that the differences are minimal and transitory, then one is likely to resist the placing of great emphasis on the differences and to favor accentuating the similarities.

These two currents in the black community are symbolized, and perhaps oversimplified, by the factional labels of separatists and integrationist.

The separatist would argue that the Negro's foremost grievance is not solvable by giving him access to more gadgets, although this is certainly a part of the solution, but that his greatest thirst is in the realm of the spirit—that he must be provided an opportunity to reclaim his own group individuality and to have that individuality recognized as having equal validity with the other major cultural groups of the world.

The integrationist would argue that what the Negro wants, principally, is exactly what the whites want—that is, that the Negro wants "in" American society, and that operationally this means providing the Negro with employment, income, housing, and education comparable to that of the whites. This having been

[3]Delivered at the National Jewish Community Relations Advisory Council Plenary Session, held from June 30 to July 3, 1968, in New York, New York. Reprinted with permission of Robert S. Browne.

achieved, the other aspects of the Negro's problem of inferiority will disappear.

The origins of this ideological dichotomy are easily identified. The physical characteristics that distinguish blacks from whites are obvious enough; and the long history of slavery, supplemented by the postemancipation pattern of exclusion of the blacks from so many facets of American society, are equally undeniable. Whether observable behavioral differences between the mass of the blacks and the white majority are more properly attributable to this special history of the black man in America or are better viewed as expressions of racial differences in life style is an arguable proposition.

What is not arguable, however, is the fact that at the time of the slave trade the blacks arrived in America with a cultural background and a life style that was quite distinct from that of the whites. Although there was perhaps as much diversity amongst those Africans from widely scattered portions of the continent as there was amongst the European settlers, the differences between the two racial groups was unquestionably far greater, as attested by the different roles which they were to play in the society.

Over this history there seems to be little disagreement. The dispute arises from how one views what happened during the subsequent 350 years.

The integrationist would focus on the transformation of the blacks into imitators of the European civilization. European clothing was imposed on the slaves; eventually their languages were forgotten; the African homeland receded ever further into the background. Certainly after 1808, when the slave trade was officially terminated, thus cutting off the supply of fresh injections of African culture, the Europeanization of the blacks proceeded apace. With emancipation, the national Constitution recognized the legal manhood of the blacks, United States citizenship was unilaterally conferred upon the ex-slave, and the Negro began his arduous struggle for social, economic, and political acceptance into the American mainstream.

The separatist, however, takes the position that the cultural transformation of the black man was not complete. Whereas the integrationist is more or less content to accept the destruction of the original culture of the African slaves as a *fait accompli*, irrespective of whether he feels it to have been morally reprehensible or not, the separatist is likely to harbor a vague sense of resentment toward the whites for having perpetrated this cultural genocide and he is concerned to nurture whatever vestiges may have survived the North American experience and to encourage a renaissance of these lost characteristics. In effect, he is sensitive to an identity crisis which presumably does not exist in the mind of the integrationist.

To many observers, the separatist appears to be romantic and even reactionary. On the other hand, his viewpoint strikes an harmonious chord with mankind's most fundamental instinct—the instinct for survival. With so powerful a stimulus, and with the oppressive tendencies congenitally present in the larger white society, one almost could have predicted the emergence of the burgeoning movement toward black separatism. Millions of black parents have been confronted with the poignant agony of raising black, kinky-haired children in a society where the standard of beauty is a milk-white skin and long, straight hair. To convince a black child that she is beautiful when every channel of value formation in the society is telling her the opposite is a heart-rending and well-nigh impossible task. It is a challenge that confronts all Negroes, irrespective of their social and economic class, but the difficulty of dealing with it is likely to vary directly with the degree to which the family leads an integrated existence. A black child in a predominantly black school may realize that she doesn't look like the pictures in the books, magazines, and TV advertisements, but at least she looks like her schoolmates and neighbors. The black child in a predominantly white school and neighborhood lacks even this basis for identification.

This identity problem is not peculiar to the Negro, of course, nor is it limited to questions of physical appearance. Minorities of all sorts encounter it in one form or another—the immigrant who speaks with an accent; the Jewish child who doesn't celebrate Christmas; the vegetarian who shuns meat. But for the Negro the problem has a special dimension, for in the American ethos a black man is not only different, he is classed as ugly and inferior.

This is not an easy situation to deal with, and the manner in which a Negro chooses to handle it will be both determined by and a determinant of his larger political outlook. He can deal with it as an integrationist, accepting his child as being ugly by prevailing standards and urging him to excel in other ways to prove his worth; or he can deal with it as a black nationalist, telling the child that he is not a freak but rather part of a larger international community of black-skinned, kinky-haired people who have a beauty of their own, a glorious history, and a great future. In short, he can replace shame with pride, inferiority with dignity, by imbuing the child with what is coming to be known as black nationalism. The growing popularity of this latter viewpoint is evidenced by the appearance of natural hair styles among Negro youth and the surge of interest in African and Negro culture and history.

Black power may not be the ideal slogan to describe this new self-image that the black American is developing, for to guilt-ridden whites the slogan conjures up violence, anarchy, and revenge. To frustrated blacks, however, it symbolizes unity and a newly found pride in the blackness with which the Creator endowed us and which we realize must always be our mark of identification. Heretofore this blackness has been a stigma, a curse with which we were born. Black power means that henceforth this curse will be a badge of pride rather than of scorn. It marks the end of an era in which black men devoted themselves to pathetic attempts to be white men and inaugurates an era in which black people will set their own standards of beauty, conduct, and accomplishment.

Is this new black consciousness in irreconcilable conflict with the larger American society?

In a sense, the heart of the American cultural problem always has been the need to harmonize the inherent contradiction between racial (or national) identity and integration into the melting pot which was America. In the century since the Civil War, the society has made little effort to find a means to afford the black minority a sense of racial pride and independence while at the same time accepting it as a full participant in the larger society.

Now that the implications of that failure are becoming apparent, the black community seems to be saying "Forget it! We'll solve our own problems." Integration, which never had a high priority among the black masses, now is being written off by them as not only unattainable but as actually harmful—driving a wedge between those black masses and the so-called Negro elite.

To these developments has been added the momentous realization by many of the "integrated" Negroes that, in the United States, full integration can only mean full assimilation—a loss of racial identity. This sobering prospect has caused many a black integrationist to pause and reflect, even as have his similarly challenged Jewish counterparts.

Thus, within the black community there are two separate challenges to the traditional integration policy which long has constituted the major objective of established Negro leadership. There is the general skepticism that the Negro, even after having transformed himself into a white blackman, will enjoy full acceptance into American society; and there is the longer-range doubt that even should complete integration somehow be achieved, it would prove to be really desirable, for its price may be the total absorption and disappearance of the race—a sort of painless genocide.

Understandably, it is the black masses who have most vociferously articulated these dangers of assimilation, for they have watched with alarm as the more fortunate among their ranks have gradually risen to the top only to be promptly "integrated" off into the white community—absorbed into another culture, often with undisguised contempt for all that had previously constituted their racial and cultural heritage. Also, it was the black masses who first perceived that integration actually increases the white community's control over the black one by destroying black institutions, and by absorbing black leadership and coinciding its interests with those of the white community.

The international "brain drain" has its counterpart in the black community, which is constantly being denuded of its best trained people and many of its natural leaders. Black institutions of all sorts—colleges, newspapers, banks, even community organizations—are experiencing the loss of their better people to the newly available openings in white establishments, thereby lowering the quality of the Negro organizations and in some cases causing their demise or increasing their dependence on whites for survival. Such injurious, if unintended, side effects of integration have been felt in almost every layer of the black community.

If the foregoing analysis of the integrationist *vs.* separatist conflict exhausted the case, we might conclude that all the problems have been dealt with before, by other immigrant groups in

America. (It would be an erroneous conclusion, for while other groups may have encountered similar problems, their solutions do not work for us, alas.) But there remains yet another factor which is cooling the Negro's enthusiasm for the integrationist path: he is becoming distrustful of his fellow Americans.

The American culture is one of the youngest in the world. Furthermore, as has been pointed out repeatedly in recent years, it is essentially a culture that approves of violence, indeed enjoys it. Military expenditures absorb roughly half the national budget. Violence predominates on the TV screen and the toys of violence are best-selling items during the annual rites for the much praised but little imitated Prince of Peace. In Vietnam, the zeal with which America has pursued its effort to destroy a poor and illiterate peasantry has astonished civilized people around the globe.

In such an atmosphere the Negro is understandably restive about the fate his white compatriots might have in store for him. The veiled threat by President Johnson at the time of the 1966 riots, suggesting that riots might beget pogroms and pointing out that Negroes are only 10 per cent of the population was not lost on most blacks. It enraged them, but it was a sobering thought. The manner in which Germany herded the Jews into concentration camps and ultimately into ovens was a solemn warning to minority peoples everywhere. The casualness with which America exterminated the Indians and later interned the Japanese suggests that there is no cause for the Negro to feel complacent about his security in the United States. He finds little consolation in the assurance that if it does become necessary to place him in concentration camps it will only be as a means of protecting him from uncontrollable whites. "Protective incarceration" to use governmental jargonese.

The very fact that such alternatives are becoming serious topics of discussion has exposed the Negro's already raw and sensitive psyche to yet another heretofore unfelt vulnerability—the insecurity he suffers as a result of having no homeland which he can honestly feel is his own. Among the major ethnocultural groups in the world he is unique in this respect.

As the Jewish drama during and following World War II painfully demonstrated, a national homeland is a primordial and urgent need for a people, even though its benefits do not always lend themselves to ready measurement. For some, the homeland constitutes a vital place of refuge from the strains of a life led too long within a foreign environment. For others, the need to reside in the homeland is considerably less intense than the need merely for knowing that such a homeland exists. The benefit to the expatriate is psychological, a sense of security in knowing that he belongs to a culturally and politically identifiable community. No doubt this phenomenon largely accounts for the fact that both the West Indian Negro and the Puerto Rican exhibit considerably more self-assurance than does the American Negro, for both of the former groups have ties to an identifiable homeland which honors and preserves their cultural heritage.

It has been marveled that we American Negroes, almost alone among the cultural groups of the world, exhibit no sense of nationhood. Perhaps it is true that we do lack this sense, but there seems to be little doubt that the absence of a homeland exacts a severe if unconscious price from our psyche. Theoretically, our homeland is the U.S.A. We pledge allegiance to the Stars and Stripes and sing the national anthem. But from the age when we first begin to sense that we are somehow different, that we are victimized, these rituals begin to mean less to us than to our white compatriots. For many of us they become form without substance; for others they become a cruel and bitter mockery of our dignity and good sense; for relatively few of us do they retain a significance in any way comparable to their hold on our white brethren.

The recent coming into independence of many African states stimulated some interest among Negroes that independent Africa might become the homeland which they so desperately needed. A few made the journey and experienced a newly found sense of community and racial dignity. For many who went, however, the gratifying racial fraternity which they experienced was insufficient to compensate for the cultural estrangement that accompanied it. They had been away from Africa for too long and the differences in language, food, and custom barred them from experiencing that "at home" sensation they were eagerly seeking. Symbolically, independent Africa could serve them as a homeland: practically, it could not. Their search continues—a search for a place where they can experience the security that comes from being a part of the majority culture, free at last from the inhibiting effects of cultural repression and induced cultural timidity and shame.

If we have been separated from Africa for so long that we are no longer quite at ease there, then we are left with only one place to make our home, and that is in this land to which we were brought in chains. Justice would indicate such a solution in any case, for it is North America, not Africa, into which our toil and effort have been poured. This land is our rightful home and we are well within our rights in demanding an opportunity to enjoy it on the same terms as the other immigrants who have helped to develop it.

Since few whites will deny the justice of this claim, it is paradoxical that we are offered the option of exercising this birthright only on the condition that we abandon our culture, deny our race, and integrate ourselves into the white community. The "accepted" Negro, the "integrated" Negro, are mere euphemisms, hiding a cruel and relentless cultural destruction which is sometimes agonizing to the middle-class Negro but which is becoming intolerable to the black masses. A Negro who refuses to yield his identity and to ape the white models finds he can survive in dignity only by rejecting the entire white society, which ultimately must mean challenging the law and the law-enforcement mechanisms. On the other hand, if he abandons his cultural heritage and succumbs to the lure of integration he risks certain rejection and humiliation along the way, with absolutely no guarantee of ever achieving complete acceptance.

That such unsatisfactory options are leading to almost continuous disruption and dislocation of our society should hardly be cause for surprise.

A formal partitioning of the United States into two totally separate and independent nations, one white and one black, offers one way out of this tragic situation. Many will condemn it as a defeatist solution, but what they see as defeatism may better be described as a frank facing up to the realities of American society. A society is stable only to the extent that there exists a basic core of value judgments that are unthinkingly accepted by the great bulk of its members. Increasingly, Negroes are demonstrating that they do not accept the common core of values that underlies America—whether because they had little to do with drafting it or because they feel it is weighted against their interests.

The alleged disproportionately large number of Negro law violators, of unwed mothers, of illegitimate children, of nonworking adults *may* be indicators that there is no community of values such as has been supposed, although I am not unaware of racial socioeconomic reasons for these statistics also. But whatever the reasons for observed behavioral differences, there clearly is no reason *why* the Negro should not have his own ideas about what the societal organization should be. The Anglo-Saxon system of organizing human relationships certainly has not proved itself to be superior to all other systems and the Negro is likely to be more acutely aware of this fact than are most Americans.

This unprecedented challenging of the conventional wisdom on the racial question is causing considerable consternation within the white community, especially the white liberal community, which has long felt itself to be the sponsor and guardian of the blacks. The situation is further confused because the challenges to the orthodox integrationist views are being projected by persons whose roots are authentically within the black community—whereas the integrationist spokesmen of the past often have been persons whose credentials were partly white-bestowed. This situation is further aggravated by the classical intergenerational problem—with black youth seizing the lead and speaking out for nationalism and separatism whereas their elders look on askance, a development which has at least a partial parallel within the contemporary white community, where youth is increasingly strident in its demands for thoroughgoing revision of our social institutions.

If one were to inquire as to who the principal spokesmen for the new black nationalism or for separatism are, one would discover that the movement is essentially locally based rather than nationally organized. In the San Francisco Bay Area, the Black Panther party is well known as a leader in the tactics of winning recognition for the black community. Their tactic is via a separate political party for black people, a format which I suspect we will hear a great deal more of in the future. The work of the Black Muslims is well known, and perhaps more national in scope than that of any other black nationalist group. Out of Detroit there is the Malcolm X Society, led by attorney Milton

Henry, whose members reject their United States citizenship and are claiming five southern states for the creation of a new Black Republic. Another major leader in Detroit is the Rev. Albert Cleage, who is developing a considerable following for his preachings of black dignity and who has also experimented with a black political party, thus far without success.

The black students at white colleges are one highly articulate group seeking for some national organizational form. A growing number of black educators are also groping toward some sort of nationally coordinated body to lend strength to their local efforts for developing educational systems better tailored to the needs of the black child. Under the name of Association of Afro-American Educators, they recently held a national conference in Chicago which was attended by several hundred public school teachers and college and community workers.

This is not to say that every black teacher or parent-teacher group that favors community control of schools is necessarily sympathetic to black separatism. Nevertheless, the general thrust of the move toward decentralized control over public schools, at least in the larger urban areas, derives from an abandoning of the idea of integration in the schools and a decision to bring to the ghetto the best and most suitable education that can be obtained.

Similarly, a growing number of community-based organizations are being formed for the purpose of facilitating the economic development of the ghetto, for replacement of absentee business proprietors and landlords by black entrepreneurs and resident owners. Again, these efforts are not totally separatist in that they operate within the framework of the present national society, but they build on the separatism that already exists in the society rather than attempting to eliminate it. To a black who sees salvation for the black man only in a complete divorce of the two races, these efforts at ghetto improvement appear futile—perhaps even harmful. To others, convinced that coexistence with white America is possible within the national framework if only the white will permit the Negro to develop as he wishes and by his own hand rather than in accordance with a white-conceived and white-administered pattern, such physically and economically upgraded black enclaves will be viewed as desirable steps forward.

Finally, those blacks who still feel that integration is in some sense both acceptable and possible will continue to strive for the color-blind society. When, if ever, these three strands of thought will converge toward a common outlook I cannot predict. In the meanwhile, however, concerned whites wishing to work with the black community should be prepared to encounter many rebuffs. They should keep ever in mind that the black community does not have a homogeneous vision of its own predicament at this crucial juncture.

# Toward Integration as a Goal[4]

Bayard Rustin

*Born March 17, 1910, West Chester, PA; died August 24, 1987; student, Cheney State Teachers College, 1930-31; student, Wilberforce University, 1931-33; student, City College of New York, 1933-35; field and race relations secretary, Fellowship of Reconciliation, 1941-53; executive secretary, War Resisters League, 1953-55; special assistant to Dr. Martin Luther King, Jr., 1955-60; organizer, March on Washington for Jobs and Freedom, 1963; executive director, 1964-79, chairman, A. Philip Randolph Institute, 1979-87.*

## Editor's introduction

To counter Robert S. Browne's theory of separatism, Bayard Rustin, then executive director of the A. Philip Randolph Institute, supported the notion that African Americans should, at least in part, integrate with the mainstream, majority culture. Ultimately, Rustin advocated a balance between strict separatism and full integration. He argued that African Americans should "develop black institutions and a black image," while at the same time engaging in the political process and participating in integrated work situations.

---

Dr. Browne dealt with the concept of separation in psychological rather than sociological terms. The proposition that separation may be the best solution of America's racial problems has been recurrent in American Negro history. Let us look at the syndrome that has given rise to it.

Separation, in one form or another, has been proposed and widely discussed among American Negroes in three different periods. Each time, it was put forward in response to an identical combination of economic and social factors that induced despair among Negroes. The syndrome consists of three elements: great expectations, followed by dashed hopes, followed by despair and discussion of separation.

The first serious suggestion that Negroes should separate came in the aftermath of the Civil War. During that war many Negroes had not only been strongly in favor of freedom but had fought for the Union. It was a period of tremendous expectations. Great numbers of Negroes left the farms and followed the Union Army as General Sherman marched across Georgia to the sea; they believed that when he got to the sea they would be not only free but also given land—"forty acres and a mule." However, the compromise of 1876 and the withdrawal of the Union Army from the South dashed those expectations. Instead of forty acres and a mule all they got was a new form of slavery.

Out of the ruins of those hopes emerged Booker T. Washington, saying in essence to Negroes: "There is no hope in your attempting to vote, no hope in attempting to play any part in the political or social processes of the nation. Separate yourself from all that, and give your attention to your innards: that you are men, that you maintain dignity, that you drop your buckets where they are, that you become excellent of character."

Of course, it did not work. It could not work. Because human beings have stomachs, as well as minds and hearts, and equate dignity, first of all, not with caste, but with class. I preached the dignity of black skin color and wore my hair Afro style long before it became popular; I taught Negro history in the old Benjamin Franklin High School, where I first got my teaching experience, long before it became popular. But in spite of all that it is my conviction that there are three fundamental ways in

[4] Delivered at the National Jewish Community Relations Advisory Council Plenary Session, held from June 30 to July 3, 1968, in New York, New York.

which a group of people can maintain their dignity: one, by gradual advancement in the economic order; two, by being a participating element of the democratic process; and three, through the sense of dignity that emerges from their struggle. For instance, Negroes never had more dignity than when Martin Luther King won the boycott in Montgomery or at the bridge in Selma.

This is not to say that all the values of self-image and identification are not important and should not be stimulated; but they should be given secondary or tertiary emphasis; for, unless they rest on a sound economic and social base, they are likely only to create more frustration by raising expectation or hopes with no ability truly to follow through.

The second period of frustration and the call for separation came after World War I. During that war, 300,000 Negro troops went to France—not for the reason Mr. Wilson thought he was sending them, but because they felt that if they fought for their country they would be able to return and say: "We have fought and fought well. Now give us at home what we fought for abroad."

Again, this great expectation collapsed in total despair, as a result of postwar developments: Lynchings in the United States reached their height in the early twenties; the Palmer raids did not affect Negroes directly but had such a terrifying effect on civil liberties that no one paid any attention to what was happening to Negroes; the Ku Klux Klan moved its headquarters from Georgia to Indianapolis, the heart of the so-called North; and unemployment among Negroes was higher at that period than it had ever been before. It was at that time, too, the Negroes began their great migration to the North, not from choice but because they were being driven off the land in the South by changed economic conditions.

The war having created great expectations, and the conditions following the war having shattered them, a really great movement for separation ensued—a much more significant movement than the current one. Marcus Garvey organized over two million Negroes, four times the number the NAACP has ever organized, to pay dues to buy ships to return to Africa.

Today, we are experiencing the familiar syndrome again. The Civil Rights Acts of 1964 and 1965 and the Supreme Court decisions all led people seriously to believe that progress was forthcoming, as they believed the day Martin Luther King said, "I have a dream." What made the march on Washington in 1963 great was the fact that it was the culmination of a period of great hope and anticipation.

But what has happened since? The ghettos are fuller than they have ever been, with 500,000 people moving into them each year and only some 40,000 moving out. They are the same old Bedford-Stuyvesant, Harlem, Detroit, and Watts, only they are much bigger, with more rats, more roaches, and more despair. There are more Negro youngsters in segregated schoolrooms than there were in 1954—not all due to segregation or discrimination, perhaps, but a fact. The number of youngsters who have fallen back in their reading, writing, and arithmetic since 1954 has increased, not decreased, and unemployment for Negro young women is up to 35, 40, and 50 per cent in the ghettos. For young men in the ghettos, it is up to 20 per cent, and this is a conservative figure. For family men, the unemployment is twice that of whites. Having built up hopes, and suffered the despair which followed, we are again in a period where separation is being discussed.

I maintain that, in all three periods, the turn to separation has been a frustration reaction to objective political, social, and economic circumstances. I believe that it is fully justified, for it would be the most egregious wishful thinking to suppose that people can be subjected to deep frustration and yet not act in a frustrated manner. But however justified and inevitable the frustration, it is totally unrealistic to divert the attention of young Negroes at this time either to the idea of a separate state in the United States, or to going back to Africa, or to setting up a black capitalism (as Mr. Nixon and CORE are now advocating), or to talk about any other possibility of economic separation, when those Negroes who are well off are the two million Negroes who are integrated into the trade union movement of this country.

This is not to belittle in any way the desirability of fostering a sense of ethnic unity or racial pride among Negroes or relationships to other black people around the world. This is all to the good, but the ability to do this in a healthy rather than a frustrated way will depend upon the economic viability of the Negro community, the degree to which it can participate in the democratic process here rather than separate from it, and the degree to which it accepts methods of struggle that are productive.

I would not want to leave this subject without observing that while social and economic conditions have precipitated thoughts of separation, it would be an oversimplification to attribute the present agitation of that idea exclusively to those causes. A good deal of the talk about separation today reflects a class problem within the Negro community.

I submit that it is not the *lumpen-proletariat*, the Negro working classes, the Negro working poor, who are proclaiming: "We want Negro principals, we want Negro supervisors, we want Negro teachers in our schools." It is the educated Negroes. If you name a leader of that movement, you will put your finger on a man with a master's or a Ph.D. degree. Being blocked from moving up, he becomes not only interested in Negro children, but in getting those teaching jobs, supervisory jobs, and principal jobs for his own economic interest. While this is understandable, it is not true that only teachers who are of the same color can teach pupils effectively. Two teachers had an effect upon me; one was black, and the other was white, and it was the white teacher who had the most profound effect, not because she was white, but because she was who she was.

Negroes have been taught that we are inferior, and many Negroes believe that themselves, and have believed it for a long time. That is to say, sociologically we were made children. What is now evident is that the entire black community is rebelling against that concept in behalf of manhood and dignity. This process of rebellion will have as many ugly things in it as beautiful things. Like young people on the verge of maturity many Negroes now say, "We don't want help; we'll do it ourselves. Roll over, Whitey. If we break our necks, okay."

Also, while rebelling, there is rejection of those who used to be loved most. Every teenager has to go through hating mother and father, precisely because he loves them. Now he's got to make it on his own. Thus, Martin Luther King and A. Philip Randolph and Roy Wilkins and Bayard Rustin and all the people who marched in the streets are all finks now. And the liberals, and the Jews who have done most among the liberals, are also told to get the hell out of the way.

The mythology involved here can be very confusing. Jews may want now to tell their children that they lifted themselves in this society by their bootstraps. And when Negroes have made it, they will preach that ridiculous mythology too. That kind of foolishness is only good after the fact. It is not a dynamism by which the struggle can take place.

But to return to separation and nationalism. We must distinguish within this movement that which is unsound from that which is sound, for ultimately no propaganda can work for social change which is not based in absolute psychological truth.

There is an aspect of the present thrust toward black nationalism that I call reverse-ism. This is dangerous. Black people now want to argue that their hair is beautiful. All right. It is truthful and useful. But, to the degree that the nationalist movement takes concepts of reaction and turns them upside down and paints them glorious for no other reason than that they are black, we're in trouble—morally and politically. The Ku Klux Klan used to say: "If you're white, you're right; if you're black, no matter who you are, you're no good." And there are those among us who are now saying the opposite of the Ku Klux Klan: "He's a whitey, he's no good. Those white politicians, they both stink, don't vote for either of them. Go fishing because they're white."

The Ku Klux Klan said: "You know, we can't have black people teaching," and they put up a big fight when the first Negro was hired in a white school in North Carolina. Now, for all kinds of "glorious" reasons, we're turning that old idea upside down and saying: "Well, somehow or other, there's soul involved, and only black teachers can teach black children." But it is not true. Good teachers can teach children. The Ku Klux Klan said: "We don't want you in our community; get out." Now there are blacks saying: "We don't want any whites in our community for business or anything; get out." The Ku Klux Klan said: "We will be violent as a means of impressing our will on the situation." And now, in conference after conference a small number of black people use violence and threats to attempt to obstruct the democratic process.

What is essential and what we must not lose sight of is that true self-respect and a true sense of image are the results of a social process and not merely a psychological state of mind.

It is utterly unrealistic to expect the Negro middle class to behave on the basis alone of color. They will behave, first of all, as middle-class people. The minute Jews got enough money to move off Allen Street, they went to West End Avenue. As soon as the Irish could get out of Hell's Kitchen, they beat it to what is now Harlem. Who thinks the Negro middle classes are going to stay in Harlem? I believe that the fundamental mistake of the nationalist movement is that it does not comprehend that class ultimately is a more driving force than color, and that any effort to build a society for American Negroes that is based on color alone is doomed to failure.

Now, there are several possibilities. One possibility is that we can stay here and continue the struggle; sometimes things will be better, sometimes they will be worse. Another is to separate ourselves into our own state in America. But I reject that because I do not believe that the American government will ever accept it. Thirdly, there is a possibility of going back to Africa, and that is out for me, because I've had enough experience with the Africans to know that they will not accept that.

There is a kind of in-between position—stay here and try to separate, and yet not separate. I tend to believe that both have to go on simultaneously. That is to say there has to be a move on the part of Negroes to develop black institutions and a black image, and all this has to go on while they are going downtown into integrated work situations, while they are trying to get into the suburbs if they can, while they are doing what all other Americans do in their economic and social grasshopping. That is precisely what the Jew has done. He has held on to that which is Jewish, and nobody has made a better effort at integrating out there and making sure that he's out there where the action is. It makes for tensions, but I don't believe there's any other viable reality.

Furthermore, I believe that the most important thing for those of us in the trade union movement, in the religious communities, and in the universities is not to be taken in by methods that appeal to people's viscera but do not in fact solve the problems that stimulated their viscera.

We must fight and work for a social and economic program which will lift America's poor, whereby the Negro who is most grievously poor will be lifted to that position where he will be able to have dignity.

Secondly, we must fight vigorously for Negroes to engage in the political process, since there is only one way to have maximum feasible participation—and that is not by silly little committees deciding what they're going to do with a half million dollars, but by getting out into the real world of politics and making their weight felt. The most important thing that we have to do is to restore a sense of dignity to the Negro people. The most immediate task is for every one of us to get out and work between now and November so that we can create the kind of administration and the kind of Congress which will indeed bring about what the Freedom Budget and the Poor People's Campaign called for.

If that can happen, the intense frustration around the problem of separation will decrease as equal opportunities—economic, political, and social—increase. And that is the choice before us.

# This Is Our Quest: To Fight for the Right[5]

Armando M. Rodriguez

*Born 1921, Durango, Mexico; U.S. Army, 1942-44; A.B., 1949, A.M., 1951, San Diego State College; instructor, San Diego State College, 1947-49; teacher, Memorial Junior High School, 1949-54; guidance consultant, San Diego city schools, 1954-57; principal, Wright Brothers Junior-Senior High School, 1965; chief, Bureau of Intergroup Relations, California Dept. of Education, 1966-67; chief, Mexican-American Affairs unit, Dept. of Health, Education, and Welfare, 1967-74.*

## Editor's introduction

In this speech, Armando M. Rodriguez, former head of the Department of Health, Education, and Welfare's Mexican-American Affairs unit, countered the "myth of the lazy, jealous, passive, fatalistic Mexican" and asserted the reality of the Mexican-American's presence in America. Given this presence, Rodriguez argued that America must reassess its educational policy and practices and that Mexican-Americans must learn to seize educational opportunities and use them to their advantage.

---

It is a privilege for me to be the keynote speaker at the first annual Mexican-American Youth Adelante Conference. I would like to congratulate the United Mexican-American Students, the University of Colorado and the Great Western Sugar Foundation for their interest in promoting the education of the Spanish-speaking youth of Colorado. It is through education that we will find the knowledge, the strength, the inspiration to fully realize our goals, our dreams, in this land of opportunity. First, we have to recognize that we are full-fledged Americans with the same rights and privileges as any other American. We have to understand who we are, what our historical past is, our surroundings, our weaknesses, our assets. We are here to discuss the problems of Mexican-American youth of the Southwest and in particular Colorado. We are here to discuss what help can be given to assist you in your higher education. We are hopeful that this conference will benefit you in promoting your educational aspirations.

It would be well to clarify the hyphenated term *Mexican-American* as herein to include an ethnic as well as a national concept describing the Spanish-speaking group of Mexican ancestry. This obviates the problem as to when his parents arrived in this country or where he may live.

There are those who raise the academic question of denying belonging to this ethnic group. Fortunately, history cannot be denied or changed by wishful thinking of wanting to be different. What difference does it make if a group migrated to this country some thirty years ago or [was] included as an integral social unit in the territory ceded to the United States by Mexico at the Treaty of Guadalupe in 1848? The people and culture found in what is now the Southwest were but an extension at this particular period of the Mexican nation. Therefore, for all practical educational purposes, and if we are to think in terms of this ethnical and national concept, the Mexican-American is a well-defined social group whose ethos and cultural pattern differ very little from Texas to California.

We must recognize that the Mexican-American is a reality. Many of you represent families who have been in this territory for more than four centuries. Unfortunately, in many parts of the Southwest, the Mexican-American is still not considered a full-fledged citizen. Foreign immigrants to the United States, particularly immigrants from northern

[5]Delivered at the 1st annual meeting of Mexican-American Youth Adelante, at the University of Colorado, in Boulder, Colorado, on May 8, 1969.

European countries, came to be referred to as Americans within one or two generations. In the American Southwest, however, a different situation exists. When Texas became part of the United States, for example, Texans became citizens of the United States and were thereafter, called Americans. Mexican-Texans remained, and still are, in the everyday language of Texans, Mexicans rather than Americans. *Mexican* does not properly describe those whose residence north of the Rio Grande predates the existence of both Mexico and the United States as nations.

But it is less the geographical inaccuracy of the term *Mexican* that invites comment than the meaning with which the term is invested. As used and understood in the Southwest, *Mexican* is a descriptive term and carries with it an entire complex of moral and physical attributes. It excludes such commonplace notions of Americanism as godliness, cleanliness, a sense of justice and fair play, Yankee know-how. This may be denied, but proof that *Mexican* is used as a disparaging term lies in the fact of its careful avoidance on the part of those who do not at the moment wish to offend.

The term *Mexican-American* ostensibly bestows a measure of Americanism on the recipient, yet balks at acknowledging unqualified American citizenship. Another alternative, prompted sometimes by misled notions of tact or kindness, sometimes by irony, is *Spanish*. If *Mexican* is geographically inaccurate, *Spanish* is even more inaccurate: there are relatively few Spaniards in the United States, and those that are here, by virtue of education or by virtue of being Europeans, generally move in higher circles than so-called Mexicans. We do not call Canadians *English*, nor Brazilians *Portuguese*. Yet we use *Spanish* in spite of its obvious inaccuracy and in tribute to the *evocative* power of *Mexican*. The tragedy is that many *Mexicans* resort to the same hypocrisy: bona fide Americans in every sense other than name, they assent to the stigma of *Mexican* by their disavowal of it. Tacitly, they concur with their detractors—not of their own choice, of course, but generations of conditioning has convinced them that they are indeed as the dominant society has portrayed them: different and inferior, unworthy of sharing the name *American*.

Popular American usage does not expressly distinguish between the Mexican national and the American-born citizen of more or less remote Mexican ancestry. The popular imagination mixes them both into a stereotype that is at once quaint and threatening. Across the length of the United States, the symbol of the Mexican is the peon, asleep against the wall of his adobe hut or at the foot of the saguaro cactus. At best he wears only sandals. He is lazy and given to putting things off until *mañana*. This picturesque fellow and his inevitable burro adorn the menus and neon signs of restaurants and motels all across the United States. At some point in his life, the peon wakes up, takes a drink of tequila, puts on his wide-brimmed sombrero, and emigrates to the United States—by swimming across the Rio Grande, of course. Once here, he loses his picturesque and harmless ways and becomes sinister: he is now proud and hotblooded, easily offended, intensely jealous, a drinker, cruel.

The myth of the lazy, jealous, passive, fatalistic Mexican is perpetuated in literature in such books as *Tortilla Flat, Rio Grande, The Oregon Trail*. In a *Treasury of American Folklore*, edited by B. A. Botkin, there is the following celebrated peroration, attributed to Judge Roy Bean, "The Law West of the Pecos":

"Carlos Robles, you have been tried by twelve true and good men, not men of yore peers, but as high above you as heaven is of hell, and they've said you're guilty of rustlin' cattle. Time will pass and seasons will come and go; spring with its wavin' green grass and heaps of sweet-smelling flowers on every hill and in every dale. Then will come sultry summer, with her shimmerin' heatwaves on the baked horizon; and fall, with her yeller harvest-moon and the hills growing brown and golden under a sinking sun; and finally winter, with its bitin' whinin' wind, and the land will be mantled with snow. But you won't be here to see any of 'em, Carlos Robles; not by a dam' sight, because it's the order of this court that you be took to the nearest tree and hanged by the neck till you're dead, dead, dead, you olive-colored son-of-a-billy-goat!"

The prisoner, it is said, did not know a word of English, and missed the flavor of Roy Bean's oratory.

Only rarely in American literature of the Southwest does one encounter a portrayal of Mexicans that is both sympathetic and unsentimental. One sympathizer was Bret Harte. In a short story entitled, "The Devotion of Enriquez," Harte's sympathetic treatment of Mexicans is probably due, at least in part, to the fact that he sets his story in California at a time when Mexicans still held large tracts of land and mixed socially with the newer Californians. Mark Twain, too, had a brief word to say about Mexicans and he shared with Bret Harte an open admiration for their horsemanship. Despite the fact that it is in this area of horsemanship and horseraising that the Mexican contributed so much to the American West, Mark Twain's admiration has few echoes in later literature. Nevertheless, the Mexican horseman left his mark on the everyday English of the West: *bronco, lariat, lasso, rodeo, mustang, buckaroo.*

Yet, in spite of broncos and buckaroos, in spite of place names, in spite of architectural and musical influences, in spite of the millions of people who are a living reminder of the part that Spain and Mexico played in forming the character of the Southwest—in spite of all this, the American-Mexican is an alien, unknown in his own land. Our history and culture are either ignored or romanticized. The Mexican is pictured on the one hand as the peon, who, hat in hand, holds the reins for the rich rancher in the movies, or is the Frito Bandito on TV. On the other hand, he is the glamorous *hidalgo,* the ambassador of goodwill for the city of San Diego and a participant in the Rose Bowl Parade. Between the fanciful extremes of the peon and the hidalgo is the ordinary American-Mexican. Probably the most telling observation ever to be printed about the Mexican came from the pages of *Newsweek* (May 23, 1966): "We're the best-kept secret in America."

The secret is kept against considerable odds. There is, for example, the visibility of the Mexican, which, paradoxically, works against him: he is easily identified and, once identified, easily categorized and ignored. It is a complaint of Mexicans that they are seen only when they do wrong; otherwise, they don't exist—they are secret. In the words of a recent television special report (April 20, 1969), they are the "Invisible Minority." It is this nonexistence within American society that gives the Mexican the "furtive and uneasy look" that Octavio Paz perceived in the *pachucos* of Los Angeles in his book *El Laberinto de la Soledad.* The Mexican-American is neither truly American nor truly Mexican; he is suspended between the two cultures, neither of which claims him. As a result, he withdraws into himself and away from the larger society. An observation similar to that of Octavio Paz is made by Jack London in a short story entitled, "The Mexican." The hero of the story is a young Mexican boy in the United States as an alien; the reactions that he provokes in those about him have a significance beyond the limits of the story itself; "And still they could not bring themselves to like him. They did not know him. His ways were not theirs. He gave no confidence. He repelled all probing."

This furtive, secretive air is adopted early in life. Shortly after entering the primary grades, the Mexican child begins to realize that he is different and that this difference is taken by society at large as a sign of inferiority. And it is not only his schoolmates that teach him: frequently the teachers themselves betray an ill-disguised contempt for the schools and neighborhoods in which they work. The opinions of the teacher are seconded by history books, wherein the youngsters read of the cruelty of the Spaniard toward the Indians, of the Spaniard's greed for gold, of the Spanish Inquisition, of Mexican bandits, and of the massacre of the Alamo.

The result of this kind of teaching, or lack of teaching, by school and society is that Mexican youngsters are kept ignorant of the contribution that their forebears made to the so-called winning of the West. At a time when they should be learning pride in their history and in their own peculiar kind of Americanism, these children are made to feel that they do not rightly participate in the American enterprise, that they are intruders in their own land. Mexican-American children can do and do well scholastically, but only in schools that not only help them adjust to Anglo society but also foster pride in their origin, history, culture, and bilingual background. A high school girl from the barrio in East Los Angeles said:

"We look for others like ourselves in these history books, for something to be proud of for being a Mexican, and all we see in books, magazines, films, and TV shows are stereotypes of a dark, dirty, smelly man with a tequila bottle in one hand, a dripping taco in the other, a sarape wrapped around him, and a big sombrero."

An area for immediate and forceful action in our quest to fight for the right is in the use of the negative image of the *Chicano* in advertising. I need not identify the specific cases—there are too many to enumerate. Let's get rid of them, or organize a massive boycott of these products.

Mexican-Americans cannot be described according to a simplistic formula, despite the strident assertions made by social scientists, assertions that insist upon the antiquated idea of a bipolar process of change beginning at one point and leading all Mexican-Americans in the same direction, like sheep—from stagnant fatalism to assimilation and creativity. But actual history itself reveals this formulation to be a grand hoax, a blatant lie. Witness the seemingly endless decades of labor conflict initiated by Mexicans and Mexican-Americans—conflict which involved literally tens of thousands of people of Mexican descent and which at one time spread to eight different states in the nation—conflict which was met with massive military counteraction. Social scientists have never asked themselves just why such massive military action was necessary in order to deal with a resigned, passive, fatalistic, nongoal-oriented people with lax habits and no plans for the future. The concept of the traditional culture as presently used by social scientists must be totally dropped. Instead, the concept of the historical culture must be adopted. Unfortunately, many of these books have become the authoritative sources of information about Mexican-Americans for a wide variety of institutional agencies, from schools of medicine, departments of social welfare, to departments of employment and other governmental agencies. In this way, thousands upon thousands of people, many of them Mexican-Americans themselves, have been indoctrinated with the historically perverted notion that Mexican-Americans are a historical people who have had no history except that of a long and tedious siesta.

Despite the constant reinforcement of his native culture at every turn, and the powerful forces that pull him in two directions, the Mexican-American has his loyalty to this country. His loyalty is unquestionably to the Stars and Stripes, as an enviable military record demonstrates in Vietnam. Mexican-Americans have never had a turncoat—not even in the Korean War. We won more Medals of Honor during World War II than any other ethnic group. The late U.S. Senator Chavez from New Mexico once said:

"At the time of war we are called 'the great patriotic Americans,' and during elections politicians call us 'the great Spanish-speaking community of America.' When we ask for jobs we are called 'those damn Mexicans!'"

If, then, Mexican-Americans are not Americans, what are they? What is an American? Regardless of what we call ourselves or are called: *coloniales, manitos, hispanos, mexicanos, espanoles,* Spanish-American, Mexican-American, Latin American, we are Americans. Who is more American? Carlos Garcia whose ancestors came aboard the Santa Maria or Paul Smith whose forebears arrived on the Mayflower? We should have pride of our Hispanic-Mexican background. History in this continent predated the arrival of Columbus and the Pilgrims. We still need to give full account of the contributions of the Mayan and Aztec civilizations. We should know that the first printing press was established in Mexico City and that the University of Mexico was founded one hundred years before Harvard University. We are proud of being Americans, we have roots in this continent. Who should be ashamed of this past? If you are ashamed of being what you are, then you are ashamed of being a man. The important thing is that you are accepted and respected. This is our fight, our quest. We must correct it.

"Who am I? [asks a young Mexican-American high school student]. I am a product of myself. I am a product of you and my ancestors. We came to California long before the Pilgrims landed at Plymouth Rock. We settled California, the southwestern part of the United States including the states of Arizona, New Mexico, Colorado and Texas. We built the missions, we cultivated the ranches. We were at the Alamo, in Texas, both inside and outside. You know we owned California—that is, until gold was found here. Who am I? I'm a human being. I have the same hopes that you do, the same fears, the same drives, same desires, same concerns, same abilities; and I want the same chance that you have to be an individual. Who am I? In reality I am who you want me to be."

This inner struggle of the Mexican-American, searching for roots is well portrayed in the characters of the play by J. Humberto Robles, *Los Desarraigados* (The Rootless Ones). This same concern for dignity and respect is found in Corky Gonzalez' "Crusade for Justice" and in the poetry of Alberto Alurista:

"Mis ojos hinchados
  flooded with lagrimas
de bronce
  melting on the cheek bones
of my concern
  razgos indigenos
the scars of history on my face

and the veins of my body
that aches
vomito sangre
y lloro libertad
I do not ask for freedom
I am freedom."

And this freedom means education. This freedom means that you and I must become bold, skilled, tough fighters for the educational opportunities that our society says—in abstract, at least—are ours. This means that we must be the advocates, the demanders of a society that honors—not rejects—bilingual, bicultural citizens. We have a great struggle ahead of us—for the basic battleground is the attitude of the dominant Anglo society. A society that equates Anglo-American origin and Anglo-American ways with virtue, with goodness. Other cultures are not merely different: they are inferior. We might have an official language in the United States, but certainly not an official culture. And in the Southwest, according to the much maligned Treaty of Guadalupe Hidalgo, we do have two official languages—Spanish and English.

The time has come for all of us to squarely face the challenge we have avoided or skirted too long. The real problem in our society today—and therefore the real problem in education is not the Negro problem nor the Mexican-American problem nor the Puerto Rican problem—it is the Anglo point-of-view problem. This point of view determines what happens in the school—what emphasis will be given or denied racial, cultural and language values. It is this point of view that through educational activities, social relations in the school, through the subtle, but devastating actions of education personnel, tells youngsters that they are not beautiful because they are different. This is the process that systematically makes it clear that this different youngster is unworthy and unwanted—and so are his parents.

The basic question which you and I must raise again and again—until the issue is resolved is: Is only a monolingual, monocultural society acceptable in America? The answers to this question are streaking across the entire fabric of our society right now. It is very obvious that the melting-pot ideology that we speak of so proudly has not produced a moral climate in which all citizens are accepted on the basis of individual worth. The conflict between youth and the society we have provided for them clearly illustrates the failure of our society—and especially the failure of our schools—to reflect the needs of today's youth. And this failure can be traced directly to the prevailing point of view that to be American is to erase all cultural identity through an education "brainwash." No institutionalized process can make us Anglo. It is imperative that we get this point across loud and clear so the United States will recognize this and we'll begin to fulfill the destiny of a country whose strength lies in its human diversity.

Many of you are here today to explore educational directions and hopefully determine some educational goals. I urge that you exhaust every avenue to secure the maximum education possible. Every *Chicano* is needed. We must become experts in the guerrilla warfare of attitude and behavior change. We must become experts in the psychology and sociology of human relations. We must become bicultural catalysts for a revolution in dominant cultural complacency. We must become experts in the politics of human rights and equal educational opportunities. I can't think of a tougher, but more rewarding role. And your preparation and training for these tasks must begin with your presence and participation in the educational opportunities available right now.

To those of you who have the responsibility of bringing education to our impatient, demanding young people, let me make a couple of observations. You must immediately examine, reexamine and reexamine again your philosophical and practicing basis on which your real and equal educational opportunities are based. And such examinations must be done with full participation of your students. To do less than this, or to delay doing this, will result in only one course—violence and revolution.

Dr. Eugene Smoley, a high school principal in Montgomery County, Maryland, comments on student militancy:

The activists represent a real challenge educationally by questioning the foundations of the society. They're looking for ways to be helpful, pushing for a way for their actions to have some influence, pressing for more meaningful lives. The movement is a very positive thing, because it can only be compared with the apathy of an earlier time.

The United States Office of Education, at the request of Secretary Finch, has set up some task forces to examine some of the critical issues of education. I have been serving on the group dealing with student unrest. Last week I took a whirlwind tour of several cities in the West and Southwest. I spent time talking to college students, teachers, and community people. Whether the responses I received are right or wrong they represent the beliefs and feelings of people. It is interesting to note in identifying the major causes of student unrest as seen by the students, that all of us must accept some part of the blame. Here are the major causes:

1. Failure to accept brown and black community in the educational community.

2. Students see the university as a reject system that is not willing or able to provide educational opportunities for the brown and the black.

3. Special Federal and state programs designed for the high risk students are not functional and cause conflict.

4. Teachers and students are not allowed to participate in determining their own future.

5. The news media have developed an inaccurate picture of student-university conflicts which has escalated the conflict.

It is interesting to note what the students then propose as their role in reducing or preventing conflict and confrontation.

1. Confrontation should only be used when all other alternatives are exhausted.

2. Students should become aware of the lines of authority in order to more adequately present their concerns to the right authority.

3. Students should learn how authority works in order to deal with it adequately.

4. Students should learn how to use the courts as a process of law and order.

5. Students should learn how to use the media to reflect their concerns.

Since the evaluation of the findings is not completed, I wish to refrain from any specific observations on the preliminary information collected. I do feel, however, that there is a wide area for exploration by the university, the student, and the community that holds hope for a relatively peaceful solution to the present educational crisis. I urge that all groups involved take time and effort to find those areas where common agreement can be reached.

The institutions of higher education must meet the challenge. They will have to reassess their very existence: Is their very existence to maintain power? Or is it to meet the demands of the changing times? Institutions of higher learning cannot perpetuate the outmoded methods of the past. They will have to align themselves with the present and with the future.

To date, colleges and universities have made little or no effort to reach the minorities. More effort should be made in disseminating information to the various high schools regarding their programs. The institutions of higher learning must play an active and aggressive role to encourage the Mexican-American to attend their schools, and help must be provided to assure the youth success to compensate for present and past failures of the public school system.

All institutions of higher learning must play a more active and aggressive role in seeking out, assisting in college decisions, and financially supporting the Mexican-American student. It is only through such vigorous movements that the entrance of the Mexican-American will bring to our country the strong fabric of cultural cognizance and thereby enrich our entire society. The *Chicano* is coming out of Tortilla Flats—*now*—you here today represent that movement. Our educational system better be ready—it must do for all of us what it says it is doing for some. *Viva la Causa, Viva la Raza. Gracias.*

# Indian Affairs—What Has Been Done and What Needs to Be Done[6]

Wendell Chino

*Born 1923, Mescalero Indian Reservation, NM; graduate, Western Theological Seminary, 1950; president, National Congress of American Indians, 1960-65; chair, New Mexico Commission on Indian Affairs, 1965-69; president, Mescalero Apache Tribe, 1969–.*

## Editor's introduction

The story of the Native American plight in the New World casts a blemish on American history. As Richard Nixon noted in 1970, "The first Americans—the Indians—are the most deprived and most isolated minority in our nation. On virtually every scale of measurement—employment, income, education, health—the condition of the Indian people ranks at the bottom." In 1969, as N. Scott Momaday won the Pulitzer Prize in fiction for *House Made of Dawn*, Native Americans began a cultural reawakening which continues to the present day. Reverend Wendell Chino, the first Apache minister and president of the Mescalero Apache Tribe, reiterates this reawakening as he demands that Native Americans receive both greater autonomy and a fuller share of the nation's bounty.

---

In the face of the agony of the Vietnam war, revolution for relevance, and revolution of racial hatred, our country has made tremendous progress in the fields of science and technology. We can send a man to the moon, we can go to the depths of the sea and probe its darkness. We have learned to harness the energy of the sun and use its energy, and we can build giant computers. So—we stop and take stock of our achievements—a technology that very few nations of the world can match. In spite of progress and advancements—we are failing in, and have neglected our primary duty to our people, and especially among our people—the American Indian.

I share the very deep common concern we all feel and have felt for these troubled and terrible conditions in our country and the world. Today, we, the American Indian people are faced with many problems—political, economic, financial, racial, and many more. As an individual, I am a concerned citizen of this country—the country, which, in spite of its failings, that I love so very much. Indeed, I want to do everything that I can to promote its welfare and to see that it does not neglect its people.

Therefore, I want to address myself to: Indian Affairs—what has been done and what is remaining to be done.

From that first historic encounter between the American Indians and the "white men," our Indian lands have been diminished, leaving only certain allotted lands and established reservations as the remaining land base for the American Indians.

The Congress of the United States assumed responsibility for the Indian people. That responsibility included their education, health, and their general welfare. After almost two hundred years, we are even more cognizant of this responsibility and the commitment to our people and the great job which still needs to be done.

In addition to the concern and the responsibility of the Federal Government, certain Indian-interest groups and non-Indian individuals

[6]Delivered at the 25th annual convention of the National Congress of American Indians, in Albuquerque, New Mexico, on October 6, 1969.

have made numerous reports on the administration of Indian affairs. We have been studied to death by reports and task forces representing the expenditure of vast sums of money. With this expenditure to improve our conditions you would think that we ought to be better off than we are today with all the reports and recommendations made in our behalf, suggesting ways and means of improving our conditions and welfare.

The changes in the Administration of this country have made the Indian people and their problems a political football resulting in vacillating policies. Some Administrations advocated keeping the status quo by leaving Indian matters and policies like they have been for a good many years. Some Administrations have initiated action requiring premature withdrawals of Federal services to the Indian people in several states—perhaps in more of the states, if the National Congress of American Indians and their friends had not intervened in certain cases in behalf of the Indian people. A review of the present condition of certain "terminated tribes" does not speak well of the Federal Government and its termination policy.

In view of these seemingly adverse and weak efforts by all parties concerned, we need now to look ahead and ask ourselves, What needs to be done in Indian affairs?

Since all of the studies and reviews reflect the weakness of the Bureau of Indian Affairs and the reticence of the Congress to deeply concern itself with the Indian people and their problems, then, in line with our theme, we must become involved! There is no other recourse but to stress the need for a strong, positive leadership among our Indian tribes, pueblos and groups. If you see a need or a job that is waiting to be accomplished—put your hands to the plow, then having put your hands to the plow, request assistance if you need it. The need of this hour among Indian people is for strong, positive leadership that must come to grips with local problems leadership that must be heard on state and national levels. It is not enough to speak only of our ills and the shortcomings of the Bureau of Indian Affairs—let us provide the leadership to provide the motivation and the stimulation to attack those areas needing our time, energy and effort.

Whether we are reservation or urban Indians—radicals or conservatives, we are Indians—let us not knock one another or seek personal aggrandizement. Let us, with common interest and energy make united efforts to attack those problems affecting our people. Unite we must—lest we divide and lose our strength.

Another thing that needs special attention is to secure from the Congress, an annual appropriation that is realistic, and large enough to attack and combat our problems. At the present rate of appropriation for Indian programs, it will take centuries to accomplish the task mutually facing all of us.

Turning our attention to the new national Administration, I have some remarks to address to it:

The "New Federalism" advocated by the new Administration has no appeal or interest for me as presently enunciated and I'll tell you why. The concept of the New Federalism that I hear is that all grants-in-aid and all Federal funding of projects and programs are going to be channeled through the states. By channeling funds through the states, the Federal Government will be abrogating its responsibility, a primary and a constitutional responsibility, to the several states for administration. I do believe that this form of the New Federalism will not work to the benefit of the American Indians, in fact, it will work against them. It will put all of us out in the cold!

New Federalism could work for the Indian people if it is handled in the right way. For New Federalism to work among the Indian tribes, those tribes must be dealt with on the same basis as the several states. Federal assistance must be granted to the Indian tribes in the same way that it is granted to the states—directly! For Federal Indian help to be channeled through the states will result in only tokenism. We need only to look at the administration of funds appropriated under the Omnibus Crime Law. Have any of our tribes really gained or received *any* benefits from this law, a law which grants funds to the several states for administration? At Mescalero, we have not received one iota of service or benefit from the Federal grant to the state of New Mexico.

Instead of New Federalism and tokenism for Indian people, there must come and there must be direct funding to tribes for Indian programs. The Indian desks now existing in the various departments of the Government must remain and continue; in fact, we need more of them.

The Congress of the United States must, without question, proceed immediately to enact

Senate Concurrent Resolution 34, a resolution enunciating a new national Indian policy which is being spearheaded by Senator McGovern and his other senatorial colleagues. This proposed national Indian policy statement by the Congress concerning the First American must be enunciated very clearly and positively. It is a new policy that will lay to rest all the hidden and known fears manifest to us because we just do not know where we stand in our unique relationship with the Federal Government. I do not believe that this decade should come to a close without a marked improvement for our Indian people!

The Congress, through this resolution, and its disavowal of the Termination policy will restore the confidence of the Indian people in the Federal Government, making it possible for the Indian tribes and the Federal Government to go forward together to a brighter future for our people and all people of this great country. The Indian must have the right of self-determination on the selection of his way of life!

Let us not be lulled into accepting programs from the states!

Most of our Indian people do not now have, nor have we ever had political or legal relations with state governments. We do not now receive state assistance in any form except for those Federal funds given to the states specifically for Indians. Our experience with the states' administration of Federal funds in behalf of Indians has not been good. Only recently have we been allowed the vote in many states and today few of our Indian people do vote in state elections and have no power base in the state political machines.

The first Congress of the United States reserved unto itself, the power to deal and negotiate with Indian tribes, showing a wisdom thereby which was not fully appreciated until recent times. The Indian tribes were then, and are now legally considered as pseudosovereign nations—exercising the powers of residual sovereignty. As early as 1775, Article IX of the Articles of Confederation asserted: "The United States in Congress assembled shall also have the sole and exclusive right and power of . . . regulating the trade and managing all affairs with the Indians . . . ." This Article was approved in Congress in 1777. In 1887, the Constitution clearly established the Federal relationship to Indian tribes in the "commerce clause," which reads in part . . . "to regulate commerce with foreign nations, and among the several states, *and with the Indian tribes.*"

Subsequently, Congress passed a series of Federal laws "to regulate trade and intercourse with the Indian tribes, and to preserve peace on the frontier," such laws were commonly known as the Indian Trade and Intercourse Acts which served to further clarify the *absolute* relationship between the Federal Government and the Indian tribes, *and excluded the interference of any state.* The Federal Government was anxious then to promote Indian friendship and prosperity because it needed the might of the Indian warriors allied with the Government in the fight against European colonialism. The few thousand American whites could not stand against several million Indians at their backs and several million Europeans at their shores.

Recently, a brief article appeared, stating, and I quote—"Approximately $525 million has been allotted by the Government for Indian Affairs for fiscal 1970. If that money were given directly to the heads of Indian households, they would be receiving an annual income of almost $6,000. (There are about 100,000 Indian heads of households and not more than a half million Indians in the United States.) At present, their average annual income is under $2,000." End of quotation. That is a nice thought, but the writer failed to realize that the major portion or share of the $525 million will go to maintain, sustain and perpetuate an empire of the Federal Government—the empire of the Bureau of Indian Affairs. Parenthetically, we have offered, through our NCAI position paper, ideas that we believe could provide solutions to the problem of getting more funds into the hands of the tribes, and the elimination of a bureaucracy.

This great country which we call the United States of America would not have been created without Indian participation and Indian help. During the Revolutionary War, the Federal Army invited the assistance, the cooperation and the participation of the Six Nation Confederacy, the Delawares, Wyandots, Chippewas, the Ottawas and the Shawnees to protect the northern and western fronts, and the Cherokees, Choctaws, Creeks and Chickasaws to protect the southern front against the invasion of the British army.

The Indians did such an outstanding job that it resulted in total victory for the United Colonies. Thus, was the foundation of this country saved by the Indians. Had the Federal Army been defeated, then, there would never have been a United States of America. The early colonists looked to the Iroquois Confederacy for the formation and framing of the United States Constitution—one of the greatest and mightiest documents this world has ever known. Again, it was Indian help and Indian influence through the Iroquois Confederacy that provided the mold for the Constitution of the United States of America.

In the war with Japan, the Japanese could not decode the Navajo language, this was one code that they could not break. What a vital role the Indian language played in the Second World War—not to mention the large percentage of Indians who served in that war.

This is the kind of Indian involvement that we need. We will not accept anything less!

Now, how sad, how ironic, that our people—the American Indians, who have certainly played a viable and vital role in the shaping of this great country—can be given only lip service by the leaders of our country, and in many cases, by the leaders of our states.

We are sick, tired, and disappointed with tokenism, political platitudes and promises that were never intended to be kept! It is going to take more than lip service from our Government, more than political tokenism from the leaders of our country to improve and accomplish the needed programs existing among our people today.

What about the pledges given to the American Indians at last year's convention in Omaha, Nebraska? How many, can we truthfully say have been kept or fulfilled to the satisfaction of our Indian people? We are sad that all of our pleading, prodding, and requests have been shrugged off and fallen on deaf ears to be ignored.

Our pleas on behalf of our people aren't shallow or slight, they affect the basic well-being of our people. Our request for better and greater service is not welfare or tokenism! We are asking that the historic commitment of 1775 to the Indian people be fulfilled in this century.

Finally—I say to our Indian leaders and our Indian people, let *your* people see *you* take an active part in Indian affairs, and be involved in salvaging the ideals of our people, the traditions of our people. Fight the non-Indian values that would destroy our culture, and *oppose* the platitudes of our time and of the dominant society. Our mutual concern and protection will preserve and sustain our Indian heritage and culture for generations to come.

Thank you.

# Do Not Refuse Us[7]

Martha J. Sara

*Born 1945, Bethel, AK; A.A., 1965, R.N., 1965, East Los Angeles College; assistant, Public Health Service Hospital, Bethel Prenatal Home, 1966-67; assistant, Social Services Department, Bureau of Indian Affairs, 1967-69; student, University of Alaska, 1969-73; staff assistant, Medical-Surgical Research Department, Veterans Administration, 1970–.*

## Editor's introduction

Representing some 50,000 Aleuts, Eskimos, and Indians, the Alaska Federation of Natives claimed from the United States government 40 million acres of native lands, payment of $500 million for other lands they historically occupied, and a 2 percent royalty on revenues from gas, oil, and other indigenous resources. Speaking on behalf of the Alaska Federation of Natives and the claim made by them, Martha J. Sara, an Eskimo, and at the time this speech was given an undergraduate sociology major at the University of Alaska, announced that the Eskimo people were capable of managing their own affairs and were therefore capable of governing their lands, as well as any money obtained from them. The statements that follow combine grace and dignity with a compassionate appeal, as they successfully voice the fervent hope and aspiration of the young Alaskan native for a humane settlement to a practical request. In 1971, the U.S. government satisfied the claim by granting native Alaskans full title to 40 million acres and paying them $962 million.

---

Mr. Chairman, members of the board, my name is Martha J. Sara. I'm an Eskimo. I was born and raised in Bethel. I'm a junior at the University of Alaska. My major is sociology and I plan to go on and become a social worker.

On behalf of the Theata Club, which is an organization of native students on the University of Alaska campus, and on behalf of myself, I would like to say that I'm grateful for the right and am happy to take the responsibility to testify on behalf of the Native Land Claims.

Along with hundreds of other native young adults, I've taken the responsibility of becoming educated to better equip myself for our coming responsibilities in the management of our own affairs.

This is not an easy undertaking.

Although I am not the best example available, I will use myself. After high school I entered a school of nursing in Los Angeles. It was difficult for me because I had to overcome handicaps not faced by most American youths. I entered a different culture. Along with the dynamic process of learning what the school offered, I also had to adjust to new values and surroundings. I graduated and became a registered nurse at the age of nineteen. I was filled with a sense of accomplishment and I applied for employment at the Public Health Service Hospital in Bethel. Never before had they employed an associate in arts degree registered nurse—and so young. They had to get permission from Washington; permission was granted. I worked only one year when our community decided to open a prenatal home in Bethel through the assistance of the Office of Economic Opportunity. A director was needed with the qualifications of a registered nurse. I enthusiastically wrote a letter of application even before applications were printed. I knew the people and a lot of the future clients having worked most of the year in the maternity ward in our hospital. To my delight I was hired. Complications arose, however, because someone pointed out that in order to be a director of a prenatal institution in the state of Alaska one had to be twenty-five years old, and I was not yet even twenty-one. Letters were written on my behalf

[7]Delivered to the congressional subcommittee on Native American affairs, in Fairbanks, Alaska, on October 17, 1969.

and permission was granted from Juneau for me to keep and fill the position. The funding was unsure because the deadline for occupancy was nearing and the building was unfit for expectant mothers as far as the state sanitarian, state fire marshal, and child welfare institution directors were concerned. Complete renovation of the physical plant and procurement of necessary equipment was urgent. Needless to say, I became an amateur painter, plumber, carpenter, electrician, diplomat, beggar, and petty larcenist. Local men did the plumbing, carpentry, and electrical work in conjunction with the BIA. Local boys under the neighborhood youth program did the painting. Used furniture was procured from the hospital through GSA. Supplies were ordered and opening day saw us admitting our first lady! We struggled and worked for what we wanted and got it. Of course we had the assistance and backing of the agencies, but the native peoples involved made it work. We were competent and proved it.

I am here representing a body of eager, willing young adults ready to learn, work, and show our capability in the management of our own affairs. I am just one of many who are willing to struggle for an education, who are willing to work hard, the way we worked on the Bethel Prenatal Home.

We are not asking for all our land—just a portion of it and if you grant it to us, we will have to strive very hard because what we are asking for is less than what we believe is fair. But we are capable of striving very hard.

And how shall you refuse us? You who have centuries of learning, education, civilization, colonization, expansion, domination, exploitation behind you? How shall you refuse us?

Do not refuse us because we are young! In youth there is energy, drive, ambition, growth, and new ideas. Do not refuse us because we are young! For we shall mature!

Do not refuse us because we are undereducated! We are learning fast; and utilizing our newly gained knowledge, comparing and weighing the truths and benefits of this knowledge. We know that the 40 million acres we are asking for will provide a minimum protection to hunting and fishing. We understand that we need the identification with, and the feeling for our *own land.* We also realize that we need this land as an economic base for our people. The land will be used as a commodity in our economic base. We can accomplish this with 40 million acres. Five hundred million dollars is a lot of money. We understand what a vital role this can play in the economic base of our people. We realize that with proper and careful handling and investment of this money we can make it work for us. We do not plan to make improvements without first establishing a sound economic base which will provide for growth and return. After this is established, then we can begin our improvements. We will then be able to maintain and expand these improvements. We realize that we can not only benefit our people, but *all* of Alaska. All this for $500 million. Do not refuse us because we are still learning! For we are fast learning!

Do not refuse us the chance to progress! We too have a dream for the progress of our land. We hold a superior position to develop our country because it is our country, and we love it. We will be more cautious in its utilization—and I deliberately use the word "utilization" instead of "exploitation." We will weigh each prospect carefully to assure ourselves that we are making the best decision for our generation and those generations to come. We are not here to grab; we are here to live with the growth of our native land. Do not refuse us the chance for progress. For we too share the dream of progress.

Do not refuse us because you are afraid we don't have competent leaders! I represent a generation of paradoxes. We are paradoxes in the fact that we are the closest links to the parties farthest separated in this issue. One of these groups is our beloved elders whom we left back home only a short time ago, who, along with others, still cling to the old ways and depend upon the land for subsistence. Another group is made up of our able leaders, native and white, who are presently in positions of decision. We are close to the old ones and the people back home because, having recently left them, their problems, worries, and fears burn deep in our hearts. We know what makes them happy; we know what can fill them with contentment; we know what gives them hope. At the same time we are close to our leaders in the fact that we are striving and aspiring to their positions of decision. Native young people are rising up to meet the demands and expectations of a foreign and sometimes hostile society. The day of our leadership is not too far off. When that day of fulfillment comes, I would like to think that we can proudly take our places side by side with the present leaders to direct the affairs of our own people. In their wisdom they can quell our fears, channel our energy, help shape our innovative ideas, direct our aggression, and interpret our anxieties. Together we can provide able leadership! Do not refuse us for fear of poor leadership! For we are capable leaders.

Do not refuse us simply because you purchased the sovereign right of our land! Our fathers since time began have paid dearly for our homeland every generation. They struggled against the harshest environment known to man and survived to teach us to do the same. Each generation paved the way for the next. Do not refuse us because you purchased this right! For our forefathers paid for it long before your forefathers had the money.

Do not refuse us because we are a minority! For this is America! We have proved in many ways that, not only do we take advantage of our rights and freedoms along with other Americans, but we are willing to, and have, fought equally for all its privileges. Our native soldiers fought and died for the United States in World War II, the Korean War, and in the present war in Vietnam. As American citizens, we have equal rights and have taken on equal responsibility. So do not refuse us because we are a minority! For this is America!

In closing I would like to say that competence is something that has to be proven. And as young native adults we have demonstrated our abilities and are now proving it.

I would like to add that we are deeply grateful to you all for taking time out of your busy schedules to come and hear our testimonies. It is deeply appreciated. Thank you! Quyana cakneq!

# Beyond the Dilemma[8]

Kenneth B. Clark

*Born July 24, 1914, Panama Canal Zone; A.B., 1935, M.S., 1936, Howard University; Ph.D., Columbia University, 1940; lecturer, Howard University, 1937-38; assistant professor, Hampton Institute, 1940-41; assistant analyst, Office of War Information, 1941-42; professor, College of the City of New York, 1960–; author,* Desegregation *(1953),* Prejudice and Your Child *(1955),* Dark Ghetto *(1965),* Argument *(1969),* Pathos of Power *(1975).*

## Editor's introduction

Kenneth B. Clark a respected leader and scholar of civil rights, and a former professor of psychology at the City College of New York, supplied much of the scientific data upon which the Supreme Court based its landmark *Brown* vs. *Board of Education* decision (1954). In this decision, the Court ruled that separate schools for African-American and white students were unconstitutional. In this speech, Clark expounded on the depth of racism in America, as well as its negative effects on all of American society. Working from the belief that racism will remain unchanged if it is understood as affecting only African Americans, Clark asserted that racism wreaks both psychological and economic havoc from the ghetto to the affluent suburb. For this reason, Clark declared that "whites must cope with racial problems for their own sake."

---

In terms of what has happened to the country—and to me—in the interim, it seems a very long time ago that I agreed, as a young graduate student, to work with my former teacher, Ralph Bunche, and Gunnar Myrdal on the project that was to result in *An American Dilemma.*

Much of the data in that report is now superseded; many of the findings may seem naïve in terms of our new realism about the depth of American racism. But the basic truths of that study have not been superseded and there is still an American dilemma, more frightening now than it seemed even then—and still unresolved.

The pathology of the ghetto is now clear and recognized—the statistics of infant mortality, disease, rat infestation, broken plumbing, littered streets, consumer exploitation, riot-burned buildings that have not been replaced, inefficient schools, a discriminatory system of police and court procedures. The litany of pain and despair is the same in every dark ghetto and, despite the antipoverty programs, Title I funds, model cities, and so on, the ghetto is still dark and still desperate.

We must now go beyond that litany to think, and conceive, and plan alternatives. If one assumes that the ghetto cannot survive as a ghetto if our cities are to survive, and that our nation cannot survive if the cities die, we have no choice *but* to create alternatives. We must face certain hard questions: Should we seek to disband and disperse the ghetto or reinforce it? What will be the possibilities of choice for human beings who are now confined to the prison of the ghetto? Will Scarsdale, White Plains, Bethesda, Grosse Point, or Newton make room for them? Or will scattered-site ghettos be built in the suburbs near the highways, or dumps, inconvenient to transportation lines, isolated from residential property? There is considerable evidence that the suburban Negro finds himself once again isolated or evicted in behalf of urban renewal, pushed out to another less affluent town that cannot afford to exclude him.

We need to consider *all* of the costs of the ghetto—whether it is more costly to retain or to abolish the ghetto; whether it is more costly to reinforce separatism—perhaps with a cor-

[8]Delivered at a joint conference of the Academy of Religion and Mental Health and the Metropolitan Applied Research Center, Inc., held on June 29-30, 1970, in New York, New York. Reprinted with permission of Kenneth B. Clark.

doned force—or to choose genuine integration. It may be that there is no choice between these two stark alternatives. We may well find that the answers are surprising—that the ghetto costs more than an integrated society even simply in terms of financial burden to the city—in terms of property that cannot support an adequate tax base, unproductive land, decaying utilities, damaged and unproductive persons.

It has always been apparent that the human costs of the ghetto could not be borne. What has been less clear is the extent of the human costs of the segregated affluent suburb too often corroded by its artificial isolation. The pathology of the ghetto itself has been recorded and does not need to be recorded again. No one who knows this tragic record can accept the fallacy and glib slogan of benign neglect—to relate that concept to America's dark ghettos betrays a profound deficiency and distortion of perception. It betrays the failure of many whites to understand that the ghetto will be neglected at their own peril, that whites must cope with racial problems *for their own sake.* The solution of the ghetto is tied to their own survival. *This* is the dilemma beyond the dilemma.

The price of racism in America is high and all must pay it—the victimizers as well as the victims, for the pathology of the ghetto cannot be contained. The drugs which lulled Harlem youth into a false euphoria have spread to Westchester; urban blight is creeping toward the suburbs like a steady plague. The riots and disruptions that burned the heart of many of the nation's largest cities from 1965 to 1967, spread to smaller cities and suburbs in 1968 and 1969.

Racism has many distinguishing characteristics, but none among them is more deeply necessary to the racist psychology than self-deception. The black nationalist who tells himself that he is "together" and proud—but who fears to face whites in competition in the classroom or the job; the black "militant" leader who exploits the frustrations of his own people in cynical alliance with segregationists; the white segregationist who justifies his rejection of other human beings, citing alleged evidence of Negro inferiority; the white liberal who defends his double-standard support of black separatism on benevolent grounds; the white public official who recommends benign neglect of the poor and the despairing—all these share in a dangerous fantasy that leads to self-destruction of the spirit, and corrupts and subverts a free society. This pattern of fantasies is the core of the contemporary American dilemma.

The American dilemma, as defined by Gunnar Myrdal, was the dilemma of ideals betrayed in practice. The dilemma beyond the dilemma is also essentially a dilemma of America's whites, who have the power to turn America around but have so far been unwilling to assume the costs of justice even in behalf of their own survival.

To focus on the dilemma as it is exemplified in the area of education: On May 17 of this year it will be sixteen years since the United States Supreme Court concluded, in *Brown v. Board oj Education of Topeka*

" . . . That in the field of public education the doctrine of "separate but equal" has no place. Separate educational facilities are inherently unequal."

In arriving at this conclusion, the Court cited modern psychological knowledge as to the detrimental effect of racial segregation in public schools on minority-group children. It stated:

"To separate them from others of similar age and qualifications solely because of their race generates a feeling of inferiority as to their status in the community that may affect their hearts and minds in a way unlikely ever to be undone."

With these words the United States Supreme Court established the basis and rationale for subsequent discussion of, and actions and evasions related to, the desegregation of the public schools—namely, that segregated schools violated the constitutional rights of Negro students—to equal protection of the laws—by damaging them, educationally and psychologically. The evidence of such detriment and damage had received judicial sanction.

Nevertheless, during the fifteen years that followed, this approach failed to touch the conscience of the masses of American people—and failed to arouse the type of serious action and social change designed to save human beings from sustained cruelty and damage.

Instead, public officials and educational officials sought a variety of ways of procrastination, evasion, tokenism. Some talked of "cultural deprivation" and decided that the schools could not assume the burden of teaching reading until the "deprived culture" was transformed. Some, like President Nixon, decried the effort to "demand too much of our schools . . . . not only to educate, but also to accomplish a social transformation."

Some flirted with the speculations of the new, and regressive racial geneticists who claim to have confirmed innate Negro inferiority. Some gave priority to the racial anxieties of whites and hence opposed programs of school pairing or bussing or educational parks.

I repeat—with a sense of profound concern about the humanity and morality of my fellow Americans—that the knowledge that segregated schools inflicted permanent damage upon Negro children was not enough to compel the American people to plan and implement a massive and effective program for the desegregation of our public schools.

For the masses of white Americans, it appears that Negro children are clearly expendable.

As the desegregation struggle moved from the South to the North it resulted in white backlash and in black separatism—two sides of the same coin—and it resulted in a tragic series of urban ghetto disruptions.

Recent urban riots and racial polarization in America can be viewed as symptoms of the increased frustrations resulting from unfulfilled promises inherent in the *Brown* decision. These disturbances and more overt forms of racism are a more intense and focused sign of the detrimental consequences of the continuation of racially stigmatized segregated schools in a segregated society.

But it is my considered judgment—based upon the evidence of the past fifteen years—that American society will not effectively desegregate its schools—or mount a serious attack against racism and racial polarization generally—as long as it views these problems primarily in terms of their damage to Negroes, and to Negro children. The history of racism has prepared many, if not the majority, of Americans psychologically to accept injury to—or the outright expendability of Negro children.

The argument for desegregation of our public schools must, therefore, be presented now in terms of the damage which racially segregated schools—and racism as a whole—imposes upon privileged white children.

There is strong evidence to suggest that racial segregation—the institutionalization of racism—is flagrantly and insidiously detrimental to white children, as well as to black. And I do not believe that the masses of American whites wish to inflict damage upon their own children.

Ironically, the United States Supreme Court, in the *Brown* case, had before it evidence suggesting that segregation did damage white children. In the social science brief appended to the legal brief it was stated in discussing the detrimental effects of racism on white children:

" . . . The culture permits and, at times, encourages them to direct their feelings of hostility and aggression against whole groups of people, the members of which are perceived as weaker than themselves. They often develop patterns of guilt feelings, rationalizations, and other mechanisms which they must use in an attempt to protect themselves from recognizing the essential injustice of their unrealistic fears and hatreds of minority groups."

The report indicates further that confusion, conflict, moral cynicism, and disrespect for authority may arise in majority-group children as a consequence of being taught the moral, religious and democratic principles of the brotherhood of man and the importance of justice and fair play by the same persons and institutions who, in their support of racial segregation and related practices, seem to be acting in a prejudiced and discriminatory manner. These ideas were first examined in 1950 and written in 1952. They may be viewed as prophetic of the current youth rebellion.

Let us examine some of the moral confusions posed for individuals who are required to cope with the dilemma of racism in a verbally democratic society:

1. The attempt to escape personal guilt, through the use of a variety of forms of self-protection and rationalizations—including reinforcing racism and blaming the victims of racism for their predicament
2. Moral cynicism and rejection of all values—the development of a dog-eat-dog philosophy of life
3. The effort to avoid a sense of moral and ethical emptiness which a racist—racially segregated—society imposes upon all sensitive human beings
4. Rejection of authority
5. The moral and ethical conflict created when one is compelled to serve as an accessory to racial segregation and cruelty imposed upon others; when one is forced to be an involuntary beneficiary of such cruelty

These are merely some of the symptoms of cruelty—the moral schizophrenia inflicted upon sensitive individuals as they struggle to avoid the personal disruptions inherent in this socially imposed ethical conflict.

It is a realistic and accepted tragedy that the majority of American youth accommodate to the normative hypocrisy, accept the rationalizations, the explanations, the excuses for the racism of the larger society. These "adjusted" young people function in terms of the philosophy of dog-eat-dog and every man for himself. They may experience an intensification of feelings of hostility and contempt toward minorities—and all others who are perceived as weak—and often act out these feelings in cruel, insensitive and at times immoral behavior.

On the other hand, a growing but critical minority of white American youth appear to be suffering from intense personal guilt feelings, and, therefore, seem compelled to rebel against parents, established leaders, institutions. Some of these young people sometimes adopt a cynical rejection of all moral values, all ethics as having no value other than the verbal and the exploitative. For these anguished young people, moral values and even rationality are seen as inevitably contaminated—as tools of immorality—for the hypocritical establishment and therefore must be rejected. This poses a most critical danger for a stable democratic society.

The contemporary racial dilemma, now mocking or challenging America, comes in the forms of the illusive malaise of the privileged—the affluent—white youth:

—The hippie movement with its random, chaotic, search for ethical clarity and consistency;

—The drug cult of the middle-class youth who seek escape from intolerable ethical emptiness;

—The hostility and aggression expressed toward parents and other authorities who inflicted, or permitted this conflict to be inflicted, upon them;

—The new-left-quasi-anarchistic movement among youth; with its hostile, often self-destructive expressions that seek to destroy that which is perceived as a social process systematically destroying the ethical substance and potential within them;

—The campus rebellions which, like urban ghetto riots, may be seen as the counterattack by a critical minority of American youth against a system of intolerable moral hypocrisy and ethical inconsistency.

For these young people, the system is not made tolerable by their affluence—by parental indulgence, by educational permissiveness—even by owning their own car; nor is it made tolerable by the deadening law and order offered by many homogeneous suburban communities in lieu of ethical substance and demonstrated democracy.

Segregated schools, and the tyranny and barbarity of American ghettos, are the institutionalized inescapable immorality of American racism. And, as such, segregated schools are stultifying and destroying the ethical and personal effectiveness of American white children more insidiously than they are destroying the personal and human effectiveness of America's black children—who, at least, understand what is done to them and many, therefore, can continue the struggle against this type of dehumanization.

If colleges and universities understood this, they would reorganize, modifying their governance structure if necessary in order to intervene directly to improve dramatically and rapidly the quality and efficiency of education for rejected black children. They would find a way to move into deprived public schools in a supervisory, accountability and evaluative role. They would demand that elementary and secondary public schools cease to be educational disaster areas.

They would, in addition, develop to help white students—the white student from the less privileged background and more privileged whites from affluent families—to help them broaden their perspective of man away from the constricted racist perspective of their parents and peers.

The anxieties and insecurities of blue-collar and white-collar whites are important factors in the random hostilities and cruelties of racism. Colleges and universities must assume the specific task of education to liberate white youth from this important form of moral and ethical disadvantage.

If public officials understood the special needs of ethically disadvantaged white youth, they would be less prone, I believe, to procrastinate, to equivocate and mouth the hypocrisy against "bussing" or transporting children for integrated education.

If they understood this, they would be less prone to talk the rhetoric of black capitalism or white supremacy—subtle or flagrant—support segregated black studies, pay out meaningless reparations at the same time that they fail to change American society; to talk compensatory education and cultural deprivation and all other language of narrow racial identity without planning for serious change.

If they understood this, they would build an agenda for a future—their own future, a future for all Americans.

America has the resources to move beyond the stagnant dilemma of the present. An America who could mobilize resources to land men on the moon, could mobilize its financial, material, intellectual and human resources to wage a serious war against slums and poverty and eliminate all institutionalized forms of racism within the decade of the 1970s.

There could be no more fitting goal in the celebration of America's bicentennial than to make the egalitarian promises of Jefferson real for all Americans—black as well as white—by 1976. The specific targets essential for attaining this goal are:

—effective nonracial schools, with teachers who teach and children who learn

—housing, worthy of human beings, in our urban and rural areas

—jobs—consistent with human dignity

—an elimination of the need and concept and stigma of welfare

—health services in terms of need rather than ability to pay.

# In These Present Crises[9]

Martha Peterson

*Born June 22, 1916, Jamestown, KS; A.B., 1937, M.A., 1943, Ph.D., 1959, University of Kansas; teacher, Kansas high schools, 1937-42; instructor, University of Kansas, 1942-46; dean of women, University of Kansas, 1946-57; dean of women, 1957-63, dean of student affairs, 1963-67, University of Wisconsin; president, National Association of Women Deans and Counselors, 1965-67; president, Barnard College, 1967-75; dean, Beloit College, 1975-81.*

## Editor's introduction

On June 17, 1970, Dr. Martha Peterson, then president of Barnard College, spoke to a group of junior and senior undergraduate women whose leadership and academic achievement had earned them a membership in Mortar Board, a national recognition society. Addressing the "second-class citizenship" to which she believed women have been assigned by American culture, Dr. Peterson called for the elimination of gender bias. While her solution to the plight of the American woman, being the "elimination of discrimination based on sex," has been called vague, Peterson's speech was in keeping with Mortar Board tradition as it emphasized rationality and responsibility. Peterson spoke with deference to the volatile nature of the times as she called for action tempered with reason.

---

Members of Mortar Board:

Being asked to be the keynote speaker for the 1970 National Convention of Mortar Board at the University of Nebraska, has special meaning for me.

In the first place, I welcome any excuse to return to the Midwest; New York City is magnificent and exciting; I wish everyone could have the experience of living there. But this is Home. Even as a loyal Jayhawker I am pleased to be at the University of Nebraska. I can, if hard pressed, sing "There is no place like Nebraska" although natural loyalty makes me prefer the verse of "I'm a Jayhawk" that ends—

"Talk about the Huskers, those old cornhusking boys. But I'm the bird that makes them weep and wail."

Secondly this is a Mortar Board Convention and I have never forgotten being tapped for membership in Mortar Board. As a member of Torch Chapter I learned the poem "The Torch"; I think I could improvise my way through "Thy Ideals" and "We Mortar Board Receive You." At least Kansas and Wisconsin Mortar Boards did their best to teach me.

But quickly, very quickly, lest those of you of the Class of '71 think you've got a real cornball from the rah-rah days of Betty Coed and Joe College on your hands, let's move to the present. And what a present it is!

Your theme "Rock—The Foundation" attests to that.

My title "In These Present Crises" confirms it.

If I had any hesitation about this assignment it came from wondering what on earth I could say to individuals like you, strong-minded, able, forceful—of differing ages, political persuasions, heritages—that might stimulate you to more effective action at a time when crises seem to rock the foundations on which our beliefs, thoughts and actions rest.

A number of years ago I went with a friend for a ten-day canoeing and camping trip in the Quetico-Superior Wilderness area on the border between Minnesota and Ontario, Canada. My companion was an experienced camper and a physician; we both could paddle a canoe reasonably well; we were eager to know what it meant to be self-dependent away from the con-

[9]Delivered at the National Convention of Mortar Board, at the University of Nebraska, in Lincoln, Nebraska, on June 17, 1970.

veniences of modern living. Our outfitter in Ely, Minnesota, assured us that we had adequate supplies for comfortable survival with one warning:

"There are bears in the area where you are going; they won't hurt you, but they have learned to like campers' food supplies better than what they can forage for themselves, so keep your food up high out of their reach unless you want an exceedingly restricted diet."

A bear appeared at our camp site on the first day out; we immediately built what is known in that region as a bear pole, hung our food pack on it and went confidently about fishing, exploring islands, resting and the other activities of the seven days we stayed there. It was only when we were en route home and saw a real bear pole at another campsite that we realized how inadequate the bear pole we had built was. It might have deterred a bear the size of a beagle dog, but Quetico-Superior bears could have gotten our food with no great exertion. Our days of wilderness camping had been a success because we had lowered our level of anxiety without adequately coping with a real and present crisis.

Let us consider briefly the nature of crises. They are commonplace in all our lives right now. We live in a time where a discussion of economics, politics, environment, health care, the disillusionment of youth, must always be examined under the rubric "in the present crisis."

There are catastrophes, acts of God if you will, the true accidents—crises in an environment over which we have no immediate control—to which as individuals, communities and nations we rise, first to meet the immediate problem, then to see how such an event can be controlled in the future. Hurricanes, tornadoes, floods, the bombing of Pearl Harbor, the earth quake in Peru, Asian flu, the explosion of the oxygen tank in Apollo 13, the appearance of cancer in a friend or patient, are examples of such crises. These events may change an individual's, a family's, a community's life pattern, but since no one can really be held responsible, since we really cannot turn the clock back, we adjust as best we can and direct our energies toward rebuilding, preventing recurrences, and readjusting. The mentally and physically healthy individual accepts risk as part of life and may even be stimulated to greater productivity by it.

Then there are the crises that are humanly induced without any apparent uncontrollable change in the environment itself. Mass hysteria, individual or group paranoia, are pathological examples of such human-induced crises. Physicians are prepared to treat psychosomatic illnesses; bankers to cope with rumors that might lead to a run on the bank; police to handle crowds reacting to a speech by Jerry Rubin. On the personal level each individual knows there are limits of personal tolerance: the neighbor's TV; the sassy saleslady or the strange discoloration of a spot on one's leg may alarm any one of us. The stranger walking behind us in the street can create within us, no matter the innocence of his intention, a crisis situation influencing his behavior. We cope with these by trying to "cool" the situation, reduce the level of anxiety, create a new, more rewarding kind of activity; we turn to psychiatry, either home style or professional—in order to learn how to continue to meet each day's frustrations. Whether what we do is appropriate may not be as important as how we see what we do. On our camping trip we really didn't cope adequately with the bears in the Quetico-Superior area but we thought we did, and fortunately that was adequate on that occasion.

Not all personally induced crises need to be controlled or subdued for they can produce more positive results. Elizabeth Blackwell, the first woman M.D. in the United States, had a passion to become a physician. Gauguin's was to be a painter, Hillary's to climb Everest. These internal crises created a source of energy to accomplish the impossible; personal crises can lead to public good.

But the crises that face us and discourage us in this summer of 1970 grow out of both the situations over which we have no control and the individual reactions to these situations.

Margaret Mead in her recent book *Culture and Commitment* quotes a fifteen-year-old boy who says "things just aren't right and we must do something about it." That was a reasonable quotation in early spring. Now it seems almost too mild to describe our current state of mind. Our environment has changed so politically, economically, socially, internationally, ecologically, and we are so tightly wrapped up in these changes that we all seem to be saying "things are terribly wrong and we wonder if they can ever be fixed."

It is this kind of world in which each of us here who has been labeled as a woman leader, lives. We are in a time of crisis that cannot be set right by calming fears or learning to accept reality, much as that might be useful to the overstimulated. It is a crisis that mandates real change in the public process, on the college campus, in our commitments and neighborhoods, in our attitudes toward each other, our capacity to effect change, if we are to cope with the frenzy and depressing pall under which we live.

Your questions and mine relate to our part in the present crisis. To despair or to preach doom is not helpful; it apparently does little good to march about carrying signs proclaiming where we stand on peace or smog or General Motors, or Bobby Seale. We may have signed a petition for peace daily since May 1; we may also have begun to wonder if petitioning cannot be overdone. It's just possible we have reached a point of diminishing return in issuing the less than pungent statements of position written by committees. Writing statements and circulating petitions may produce a personal sense of release, and as a first expression can be helpful, but what more is there to do. Should we curtail our spending to curb inflation; certainly we can stop littering without much effort; some of us will become involved in political campaigns and undoubtedly will continue to write, wire and visit Washington if for no other reason than to give credence to a statement in the *Times* a few Sundays ago that indicated that long-time observers of the Washington scene are beginning to suspect that the nation may be in the throes of a fundamental political trauma.

Many of us do believe we are in a state of crisis and will seek means to express our personal convictions as nonviolently as possible. Only somehow or other this is not totally satisfying; or rewarding. It is what any interested citizen can and probably should do, no matter what the crisis. Each of us wants, seeks, a more personal expression of her values, her concerns, her personal worth.

Let me speak now to the role of the educated woman leader in the 1970s. In modern rhetoric one of the nonnegotiable demands on you is that you are a woman, educated and recognized by your peers as a leader, else you would not be here.

There is a new feminism abroad these days that may create some crises for you as a woman, and that may also alter your effectiveness in the other crises. You may wish to reject this new feminism because its stridency shocks you, to ignore it because it does not apply to you; you may believe in the long-range value of personal victories to legal decision; you may believe in the steel hand in a velvet glove, or you may just prefer velvet. But will you or can you afford such disdain, disengagement or high-minded nobility in regard to woman's role if you are to be as effective a woman and a leader as you have the potential to be.

The new battle for Women's Rights appears in a variety of forms.

Recently the National Conference of Christians and Jews and the Women's Unit from the Governor's Office in New York sponsored a conference in New York City. A resolution was adopted at the conference demanding $100 million from one hundred top advertising firms to support child care, free abortion and legal services for women.

Later in the week a group of women picketed the Playboy Club asking that it be converted into a Day Care Center for Children to repay partially the exploitation of women inspired by the Playboy philosophy. Kate Millett's book on *Sexual Politics* which will appear in July, published by Harper & Row, will further stress the current emphasis of the Women's Liberation group on this exploitation of women because of the biological and cultural consequences of being female and therefore the bearer of children.

Where do you stand on legalized abortion, child care centers, exploitation of women as a sex symbol in advertising? You may not really care about these issues; you may insist that these are crises fabricated in the minds of the members of the Women's Liberation movement. But that does not mean they are not real or worthy of concern.

There are other concerns among the new feminists.

On June 9 the Labor Department issued guidelines designed to eliminate discrimination against women in jobs paid for with Federal funds. The new guidelines prohibit newspaper advertising labeled "male and female" unless sex is "a bona fide" occupational qualification; forbid penalties for women employees for taking time off to bear children and the denial of employment to women with young children "unless the same exclusionary policy" exists for men.

These new guidelines were recommended by a task force of distinguished men and women who reported six months ago to the President on women's rights and responsibilities. This report has just been released by the White House; it indicates that the United States "in its two hundredth anniversary lags behind some newly emerging countries in the role ascribed to women." You should read it even if you really do not believe that you want to work when you are pregnant and don't mind that jobs are labeled "male" or "female." You may say, "Any woman with ability and energy can accomplish whatever she is willing to sacrifice enough to do, and so what is the problem."

But are you sure?

A recent survey by The American Association of University Women of their members and their husbands or male colleagues, produced these findings:

A quarter of the women reported experiencing sex discrimination; the same proportion of men reported seeing discrimination against women.

Eighty-four per cent of the women and 77 per cent of the men felt that job discrimination because of sex existed.

The Women's Bureau reports that the salary of the median woman wage earner in 1968 was 58.2 per cent of that of the median male wage earner. And the gap has been widening; women were better off in 1955 when their median wages were 63.9 per cent that of men's.

And what about college women.

At Columbia University Commencement two weeks ago, the Columbia Women's Liberation distributed a leaflet to parents of Barnard graduates that said:

"Congratulations on your daughter's graduation.

But can she Type?"

With some restraint the leaflet pointed out that a woman graduate's prospects for employment, for graduate or professional school admission, were different from the man graduate's, usually to the disadvantage of women.

Only 11 per cent of the doctorates in the sixties were women; only 6.7 per cent of the physicians are women; only 35 per cent of the lawyers are women; and only one half of 1 per cent of working women earn over $10,000 a year.

Is there a kind of second-class citizenship for women, professionally and economically after graduation from college? Statistics and studies seem to point to this. Are the differences based on the necessities of being a wife and mother? Or are the crises in some women's lives created by unnecessary restriction on women which we accept unquestionably?

We may decide that the way things are for women is natural or at best should be accepted. Then as women leaders we have a real battle ahead with the new feminists. Or we may decide that this is a crisis of the seventies in which our leadership and ability is sorely needed, and seek to give the solid kind of leadership that is needed. To paraphrase awkwardly "As long as there is discrimination that denies one individual opportunities for which she is qualified, no other responsible individual can refuse to act."

I asked earlier how each of us could prove her personal worth in these overwhelming and sometimes discouraging times. I have suggested one responsibility we cannot ignore—the elimination of discrimination based on sex. Let me suggest another area in which there are crises we cannot ignore.

The volatility on the college campus and the disenchantment of people in general with the academic community is of crisis proportions. There may be less polarization of individuals on campus as they face attack and criticism from outside, but no real progress in achieving the values the academic community represents without the support and respect of alumnae, trustees, politicians, parents and the general public.

The Mortar Board Chapter may decide to enter positively into improving the status of women or the reading level of the third grades in whatever ghetto area is nearby, or in registering voters for the November election, but if they are not trusted, they will talk only to each other. Faculty and students may redouble their efforts to give new life to the liberal arts curriculum, but if the principles of academic freedom and inquiry are seen as synonyms for anarchy and irresponsibility, the efforts will have to go into self-defense rather than creative thought. And those who so desperately wish to be a part of the public process this fall may notice a wariness on the part of politicians lest the new manpower be a kiss of death.

Commonly held views of what colleges and students are like these days may be based on accurate assessment of some campus events. But to dismiss the contributions of colleges and universities as unnecessary, or to assume that only stringent measures of reform should be applied from outside, are self-defeating steps which only increase the crises. The colleges will turn increasingly inward, stifling the all-important exchange with the real world that makes learning relevant; and the world outside the colleges will lose that dynamic and reasoned leadership only education can supply.

Alexander Bickel in a recent issue of *The New Republic* puts it this way:

"There is a crisis in this country and it went from bad to worse this spring. But it is not only, it is not even chiefly, the crisis that fashion requires us to shake our heads about. The war has got to stop, the march into Cambodia is a gruesome error, the cities are a mess, our rivers and our air smell awful, and the blacks will not and ought not stand for being forgotten again. But there is another crisis that will incapacitate us from dealing with the ones I have just mentioned. It is not the crisis of allegiance on the part of downtrodden blacks and not the tinderbox of conflict between them and the lower-class whites who confront them, but the crisis of abandonment of reason, of standards, of measure, the loss of balance and judgment by intellectuals and their audiences. The symptoms of this crisis are the incivility and even violence of rhetoric and action that academics and other intellectuals have domesticated into their universe of discourse, and the interdiction of objective discussion of certain problems that they have increasingly tolerated."

This does not minimize the crises in the country but indicates that unless the crisis on the campus can be solved, the other crises won't be. It is this interdependence between campus and community to which I urge you to give your time and efforts.

To begin to find the way through there must be changes on the campus, perhaps first, Mr. Bickel suggests in the same article:

"No more vandalism; no more assaultive, vicious speech; no more bullying, simulated or actual. If the reassertion of this minimum of authority should bring strife and violence in the short term, as it may, it will be less strife and less violence than is otherwise in store for us."

Mr. Bickel suggests college and university presidents must achieve this return to sanity. I know, as do all of you, that it will be a joint effort of student leaders, faculty and administration, and when we have found a way we will then be able to bring back the interest and support of others.

A few weeks ago when I was beginning to work on these remarks I came across these notes on a 3 x 5 card: Lowell Crisis. I decided this had to do with a quotation from a Robert Lowell poem for I had been reading some of his poems in the past year. I could not find anything that seemed related in the books I had so I went to the college library and asked if Lowell had a poem on The Crisis. The librarian said—"of course"—and produced "The Present Crisis" by James Russell Lowell, written in 1844, to support abolition of slavery. You remember it from the verses of the hymn that starts: "Once to every man and nation comes the moment to decide."

I quickly took the book—embarrassed that I had confused Robert Lowell and James Russell Lowell, pleased that the librarian had not caught on to my ignorance. Then I began to wonder about these present crises. Are they so new? Are we living through catastrophes over which we have no control? Or are we becoming sensitized so that we do have the necessary energy to effect change?

Having stumbled onto James Russell Lowell, let me close these remarks with one more line from his poem "The Present Crisis":

"They have rights who dare maintain them;"

That seems to me to be adequate for our crisis, ladies of Mortar Board.

# Inaugural Address of the Chief of the Cherokees[10]

W. W. Keeler

*Born 1908, Dalhart, TX; B.S., University of Kansas, 1928; chemist, Phillips Petroleum Co., 1924-71; special consultant, U.S. Secretary of Interior, 1961; chief executive officer, Phillips Petroleum Co., 1971; principal chief of the Cherokees, 1971–.*

## Editor's introduction

In May 1838, federal troops forced members of the Cherokee tribe to leave their land in the southeastern United States. On what became known as the "Trail of Tears," nearly one-third of the tens of thousands of Cherokee died of starvation and disease while making their way to what eventually became the state of Oklahoma. Once there, they established Tahlequah as their capital. W. W. Keeler, former chief executive officer of the Phillips Petroleum Company, gave this address as the first chief of the Cherokees to be elected in 64 years. Since 1907, the United States government had appointed chiefs. Upon being inaugurated as chief of the Cherokees, he celebrated the autonomy that had been restored to his tribe and recalled the indomitable spirit of his people.

---

Deputy Commissioner Crowe, Chaplain Ketcher, Senator McSpadden and chiefs of the Indian tribes of Oklahoma who honor us by their presence here today, fellow Cherokees, friends, ladies and gentlemen.

This is a historic moment for all Cherokees, Delawares, and Shawnees. It marks the return of the management of their tribal affairs into the hands of the people. We have not had this responsibility of self-determination for more than threescore years. I am proud and happy to see this day. I am honored to be your elected leader.

The Cherokees were a free and independent nation, with a constitutional government elected by the people, almost a century and a half ago.

In the years between then and now, our forebears and we suffered internal strife, removal to an alien land, a civil war that was not of our making, loss of our land without fair compensation, discrimination because of our color, and indignity because we were few in number.

Our Delaware and Shawnee brothers joined us by purchase agreement to share in our hopes and sorrows and in the lean production of the rocky hillsides to which the Cherokees had been driven.

But we are a dauntless people. Our fathers would not bow to a stronger force. Neither have we ever bowed to it. Not when we were penniless; nor when we were without food to fill our children's stomachs.

Not when we were without clothing to shield us against bitter winds that howl in the forgotten hollows between these hills; nor when these hallowed grounds on which we stand were a place of mockery and contempt for those who had herded us onto them.

We were dauntless in our defeat. We remembered the hardships of those who gave us our heritage. We took courage from their example. We would not be overcome. The blood of our fathers beats strongly in our veins; and we can still hear the distant drums that echo against the mountainsides of the lost and lonely memories that whisper along the byways of our hallowed heritage.

Today we see the beginning of the realization of everything that was only a dream during the lifetime of most of us here today.

The Cherokee nation was never dead; only asleep. Today it stirs and begins to awaken. Today our children see the dream that you and I have had for so many bleak years.

[10]Delivered at the inauguration of the chief of the Cherokees, in Tahlequah, Oklahoma, on September 4, 1971.

We are again entrusted with the management of our own affairs. We are now free to elect our own leaders. We are free to train our people for jobs; to improve the educational opportunities of our children; to provide adequate medical care for all who need it; to record and promote our noble heritage.

We must be united if we are to accomplish the heavy work that lies ahead. We must join hands with all of our brothers as never before in the history of our people.

Past mistakes and animosity must be laid aside. All of us have been mistaken at some time in the past. We must learn from those mistakes. If we fail in this, the opportunity of this moment will be lost—perhaps beyond recall.

We must think of the work to be done in the future; not of what we should have done in the past.

My opponents in the election came forward with many good proposals. I intend to ask their help and support in making them part of the goals of my administration for the coming four years. I ask everyone to join with me in bringing about their benefits for the Cherokees and their brothers, the Delawares and the Shawnees.

We must develop the human resources of our people. We must end any inequities of tribal activities that may have developed in the past years. All of our programs must be fair to all of our people. The tribal rolls must be brought up to date to include our children as well as our fathers. We must standardize the Cherokee language. I agree that the chief or vice chief should speak Cherokee.

I recognize that our Cherokee executive committee, of which I have been a member, has been criticized. But I also know that they have given great service to the Cherokees. I want to express my thanks to them for their unselfish assistance to me. Certainly they should be continued until we have had time to rewrite our Cherokee constitution and make it possible for tribal leaders to be more responsive to individual Cherokees. I would like to see an executive and a legislative branch based on the pattern of our early-day constitution. The tribal government must reflect the will of all of the people.

I pledge to you today, in this historic setting, my time and the best of whatever talents I have.

I thank you for your support in years past; and for your confidence in me to lead the tribe for the next four years.

I humbly and sincerely ask for your support and for your best advice in the years ahead.

Together, we can accomplish even greater things than have been accomplished in the past. With God's help, we can bring about miracles even greater than the accomplishment of this day.

Cherokees! Give me your trust and your united support. Thank you.

# Seeking a Link with the Past[11]

Patsy T. Mink

*Born December 6, 1927, Paia, HI; B.A., University of Hawaii, 1948; J.D., University of Chicago, 1951; professor, University of Hawaii, 1952-56, 1959-62; lawyer, private practice, 1953-65; member, Territory of Hawaii House of Representatives, 1956-58; member, State of Hawaii Senate, 1962-64; representative (D) from Hawaii, 1965–.*

## Editor's introduction

Before an audience of 350 Japanese Americans, Hawaii Representative Patsy T. Mink deplored the poverty and racial prejudice she saw as part of the Asian experience in America. Mink spoke from experience, having grown up Japanese in the 1930s and 1940s and having witnessed the detainment of Japanese Americans during World War II. Mink urged Americans to relish the diversity of opinions that exist in America. She also asserted that Japanese Americans must maintain their heritage through disciplined study of their native culture.

---

I would like to thank President Kanegai and the other officers and members of the West Los Angeles Japanese-American Citizens League for this opportunity to be with you at your thirtieth anniversary banquet and installation. I am delighted to participate in this memorable occasion.

It must be difficult to look back thirty years to 1941 and relive the pains and agonies that were inflicted upon you as citizens, unloved and unwanted in their own country of their birth. Loving this land as much as any other citizen, it is difficult to fathom the despair and fury which many must have felt, yet who fought back and within a few years had reestablished their lives and their futures. Most of us remember these years vividly. Our faith in justice was tested many times over. Our patriotism was proven by blood of our sons upon the battlefields.

Yet today, thirty years later to many even in this room, it is only a part of our history. Our children, thirty years old and younger, cannot follow with us these memories of the forties. They tire of our stories of the past. Their life is now, today . . . tomorrow. Their youthful fervor was poured into the symbolism of the repeal of Title II of the Internal Security Act of 1950, portrayed by its title, Emergency Detention Act. That Act became law nearly ten years *after* the Japanese were evacuated from the West Coast into "relocation camps." Yet, it stood as a reminder of what could happen again. Of course, despite the successful repeal, it could happen again, as it did indeed to the Japanese-Americans who were rounded up without any statutory authority whatsoever. It was not until 1950 that Title II became law.

It is quite evident that I am standing before an affluent group whose surface appearance does not reveal the years of struggle and doubt that have ridden behind you.

Sociologists have generally described the Japanese-Americans as an easily acculturated people who quickly assimilated the ways of their surroundings. This has always been in my view a friendly sort of jab at our cultural background, for what it has come to mean for me is a description of a conformist which I hope I am not!

I still dream that I shall be able to be a real participant in the changing scenario of opportunity for all of America. In this respect, I share the deep frustration and anguish of our youth as I see so much around us that cries out for our attention and that we continue to neglect.

[11]Delivered to the West Los Angeles Japanese-American Citizens League, in Playa Del Rey, California, on November 6, 1971. Reprinted with permission of Patsy T. Mink.

Many factors have contributed towards a deepening sense of frustration about our inability to solve our problems of poverty and racial prejudice. Undoubtedly the prolonged, unending involvement in Vietnam has contributed to this sense of hopelessness. At least for our youth who must bear the ultimate burden of this war, it seems unfair that they should be asked to serve their country in this way when there are so many more important ways in which their youth and energy can be directed to meet the urgent needs at home. They view our Government as impotent to deal with these basic issues.

It is true that Congress has passed a great many civil rights laws. The fact that new, extra laws were found necessary to make it easier for some people to realize their constitutional guarantees is a sad enough commentary on the American society, but what is even worse is the fact that the majority of our people are still unready, personally, to extend these guarantees to all despite the Constitution and all the civil rights laws, and despite their protestations to the contrary.

Certainly, no one will admit his bigotry and prejudice—yet we always find ways to clothe such feelings in more presentable forms—and few will openly advocate suppression or oppression of other men, but nevertheless, it exists.

Although Congress has repealed the Emergency Detention Act, the fight for freedom is not over. We now see a new witch hunt proclaimed in which all Government employees will be examined for their memberships and organizations. It seems that we have not yet succeeded in expunging the notion that "dangerous" persons can be identified by class or group relationships and punished accordingly.

I believe that nobody can find safety in numbers—by huddling with the larger mass in hopes of being overlooked. Those who seek to suppress will always find ways to single out others. Instead, we must change the basic attitude that all must conform or be classed as renegades and radicals. Our nation was founded on the idealistic belief in individualism and pioneering spirit, and it would be tragic for our own generation to forswear that ideal for the false security of instant assimilation.

It seems to me that our society is large enough to accept a wide diversity of types and opinions, and that no group should be forced to try to conform to the image of the population as a whole. I sometimes wonder if our goal as Japanese-Americans is to be so like the White Anglo-Saxon Protestant population as to be indistinguishable from it. If so, we will obviously never succeed!

There has been and continues to be prejudice in this country against Asians. The basis of this is the belief that the Oriental is "inscrutable." Having such base feelings, it is simple to stir up public outrage against the recognition of the People's Republic of China in the United Nations, for instance, even though reasoned judgment dictates otherwise, unless of course a Yellow Communist is really worse than a Red one!

The World War II detention overnight reduced the entire population of one national origin to an enemy, stripped of property, rights of citizenship, human dignity, and due process of law, without so much as even a stifled voice of conscience among our leading scholars or civil libertarians. More recently, the Vietnam war has reinforced the view of Orientals as something less than fully human. All Vietnamese stooping in the rice fields are pictured as the enemy, subhuman without emotions and for whom life is less valuable than for us.

During the trial of Lieutenant Calley, we were told about "MGR," the "Mere Gook Rule" which was the underlying basis for Calley's mindless assertion that the slaughter of defenseless women and children, our prisoners of war, was "no big thing." The "Mere Gook Rule" holds that life is less important, less valuable to an Oriental.

Laws that protect other human beings do not apply to "gooks." One reporter noted before the verdict became known that the essence of the Calley case was to determine the validity of this rule. He described it as the "unspoken issue" at the trial.

The issue was not as unspoken as most would prefer to believe. The indictment drawn up by the Army against Lieutenant Calley stated in six separate charges that he did at My Lai murder four "Oriental human beings" . . . murder not less than thirty "Oriental human beings" . . . murder three "Oriental human beings" . . . murder an unknown number of "Oriental human beings" not less than seventy . . . and so on numbering 102. Thus, the Army did not charge him with the murder of human beings as presumably would have been the case had Caucasians been involved, but instead charged the apparently lesser offense of killing mere "Oriental human beings."

The Army's definition of the crime is hardly surprising inasmuch as the Army itself could have been construed as on trial along with Calley for directing a genocide against the Vietnamese. Indeed, the Lieutenant pleaded he was only doing what he thought the Army wanted. It seems clear to me that the Army recognized the "Mere Gook Rule" officially by distinguishing between the murder of human beings and "Oriental human beings." When Calley was convicted, the resulting thunder of criticism verified that many in the public also went along with the concept of differing scales of humanity.

Somehow, we must put into perspective Dean Rusk's dread of the "yellow peril" expressed as justification for a massive antiballistics missile system on the one hand, and on the other, a quest for improved relations with Peking. This latter event could have a great meaning in our own lives as Japanese-Americans. We could help this country begin to deal with Asians as people. Just the other day in a beauty parlor, I heard a congressional secretary discuss China and say, "An Asian is different, you can never figure out what he's really thinking. He has so little value for life!"

Instead of seeking refuge, we should seek to identify as Asians, and begin to serve America as the means by which she can come to understand the problems of the East. Our talents have not been used in American diplomacy, I suspect, largely because we are still not trusted enough.

We must teach our country that life is no less valuable, and human dignity no less precious, in Asia than elsewhere. Our detractors point to the large-scale killings that have occurred in China, Vietnam, Pakistan, and elsewhere in Asia, but we hear remarkably few references to the mass-slaughter of six million Jews in Nazi gas chambers in World War II—that was done by Aryans, not Asians, and the total far exceeds the loss of life in the Orient that has been used to justify the debasement of "mere gooks." I am not trying to compare one group against another, but merely to point out that a lack of appreciation for the value of human life can occur wherever totalitarian government exists. This makes it more than vital for us to oppose such influences within our own country wherever they may occur. The war in Vietnam has lasted for seven years. If Americans believed there was the same worth in the life of an Asian, this war would have ended long ago. If Americans were willing to concede that the Asian mind was no different than his, a peace would have been forged in Paris long ago. I am convinced that racism is at the heart of this immoral policy.

I know that many of you are puzzled and even dismayed by actions of some of your sons and daughters who have insisted on a more aggressive role in combating the war and other evils that exist in our society. I plead with you for understanding of this Third World movement in which not only young Japanese-Americans but many minority groups are so deeply involved.

We are confronted with what seem to be many different revolutions taking place all over the world . . . the black revolution, the revolution of emerging nations, the youth revolution here and in other countries as well—and something that was even more unheard of, the priests challenging the Vatican on the most basic issues of celibacy and birth control. It is no accident that these things are all happening at the same time, for they all stem from the same great idea that has somehow been rekindled in the world, and that is the idea that the individual is important.

All of the systems of the world today have this in common: for they are mainly concerned with industrialization, efficiency, and gross national product; the value of Man is forgotten.

The children of some of you here tonight are involved in the great protests of today—are they chronic malcontents and subversives? I think not—I think they are probably fairly well-educated, thoughtful people who see certain conditions they don't like and are trying to do something about it. I'm not sure they know exactly what they want to do. I do know they are clearly dissatisfied with the way their world has been run in the past.

So, the problem is not what to do about dissent among our young people—the problem is what to do about the causes of this dissent. The question is not "how to suppress the dissent" but how to make it meaningful . . . how to make it productive of a better society which truly places high value on individual human beings *as* human beings and not merely as so many cogs in the great, cold and impersonal machinery of an industrialized society.

I, for one, believe that the grievances of our youth are real and that they are important. Merely because the majority of students are not involved . . . merely because the dissidents are few . . . should not minimize the need for serious efforts to effectuate change. Our eighteen-year-olds now have the right to vote. Whether we like it or not, we will have to take better account of their wishes. Their acceptance as adults will bring into policy making eleven million new voters next year. Their cause for identity must be encouraged.

Our sons and daughters seek to establish a link with the past. They want to discover who they are, why they are here, and where their destinies are to take them. So many of our children are growing up in complete isolation in a society that places a premium on conformity, in middle-class homes where parents still want to play down their differences, and prefer to homogenize with society. Some of these children are rebelling and are seeking ways to preserve their uniqueness and their special heritage. I see pride and strength in this.

One of the most promising avenues for this renewed search for one's heritage is in our school systems—the logical place for instructing children in the knowledge they need. Programs of Ethnic Heritage Studies are needed in our schools. I feel that this would be particularly valuable in Hawaii, California and other areas where there are large numbers of children of Oriental descent.

It seems to me that we as Asians have a large stake in encouraging and promoting such a program. We cannot and must not presume knowledge about Asia merely because we are Asians. This requires concentrated study and dedicated determination. Of course, we do not need to become scholars cloistered in the ivory tower of some campus. We need to become aware of the enormous history of Asia and through our daily lives, regardless of what our profession, translate it to all the people with whom we deal. We have not fully met our responsibility to educate the public about Asia and its people.

I hope that all Japanese-American organizations and others with strong beliefs in the magnificent history and culture of the Orient will now help lead the way to a more enlightened America. We have an immense story to tell, for as I have said the public at large too often assumes that all civilization is Western and no worth is given to the human values of the East. As long as this belief persists, we will have future Vietnams. The way to counteract it is to build public knowledge, through school courses, travel, and dedicated emphasis on increased communications, so that our people will know and appreciate all that is Asian.

Last Thursday night in a display of utter ignorance and contempt for diversity, the House of Representatives killed the ethnic heritage studies program by a vote of 200 ayes to 159 noes. And so you see, I speak of an urgent matter. We are so few and they who do not care to understand us are so numerous.

It is fine for all citizens to pursue the good life and worldly goods on which our society places such emphasis, but there is increasing recognition that all will be ashes in our mouths unless our place as individuals is preserved. This is what the young are seeking—and I am among those who would rejoice in their goals.

They need the guidance and support of their parents to succeed, but in any event with or without us, they are trying. It behooves us to do all we can to accept their aspirations, if not all of their actions, in the hope that this new generation will be able to find a special role for themselves in America, to help build her character, to define her morality, to give her a depth in soul, and to make her realize the beauty of our diverse society with many races and cultures of which we are one small minority.

# Survival[12]

## Vernon E. Jordan, Jr.

*Born August 15, 1935, Atlanta, GA; B.A., DePauw University, 1957; J.D., Howard University Law School, 1960; field secretary, N.A.A.C.P., 1962-64 ; director, Southern Regional Council Voter Education Project, 1964-68; president, United Negro College Fund, 1970-71; executive director, National Urban League, 1972-81; senior partner, Akin, Gump, Strauss, Hauer and Feld, 1981–.*

### Editor's introduction

Vernon E. Jordan, Jr., former president of the National Urban League and noted African-American leader, gave this speech in Cleveland shortly after Carl Stokes had been elected the first African-American mayor of that city, and inlew of any major city. Jordan believed that the root of America's problems springs from racism. In this speech he asserted the necessity of change, which he believed would only occur through bold leadership and an "affirmation of belief in the principles of equality."

---

Last week the President of the United States, in his State of the Union address, very accurately described the mood of the nation. "We have been undergoing self-doubts, self-criticism," he said. "But these are only the other side of our growing sensitivity to the persistence of want in the midst of plenty, of our impatience with the slowness with which our age-old ills are being overcome."

The prevailing mood of self-doubt and self-criticism is without parallel in our times. We ask, "Are we a sick society?" The Gallup Poll reports that nearly half the people fear "a real breakdown in this country." The Roper organization finds that nearly two thirds of the American people believe the nation has lost its proper sense of direction. The country is in the throes of a deep-seated crisis of spirit, a crisis whose resolution calls for a harnessing of the moral energies of the society and for bold leadership that will carve a righteous path out of the wilderness of the soul.

The core of America's problems are racial. So long as black people suffer disproportionate disadvantage in almost every sphere of life, our society will be racked by guilt and agitation. So long as poor black people and poor white people are set against each other, scrambling for the crumbs from the table of an affluent society, this nation shall be troubled in mind and in spirit.

The time has come for America's dispossessed to come together, to formulate strategies that will unite and not divide, that will mobilize and not polarize. Black people, by forging solidarity and a spirit of pride, have inspired other Americans to rediscover their heritage and to treasure their ethnic backgrounds. It is my hope that black people, by forcefully exposing the inequities and the exploitation in our society, will similarly inspire other groups to focus their prime attentions on bringing about the changes that will benefit all Americans.

Cleveland is a microcosm for all America. It too suffers from the current economic depression. It too is polarized and torn by suspicion and dissent. It too stands at the brink of fiscal bankruptcy, a victim of the moral and social bankruptcy of a nation that spends billions on a jungle war or on space trips but cannot afford to insure full employment and schools and housing. Cleveland too has high barriers to black achievement. Its black citizens are confined to ghettos, its black workers are unemployed at a rate two and three times those for white workers, and many of its white citizens shrink from the kind of full and equal partnership with blacks that could help bring this city together again.

[12]Delivered at the 54th anniversary luncheon of the Cleveland Urban League, in Cleveland, Ohio, on January 28, 1972. Reprinted with permission of Vernon E. Jordan, Jr.

If change is to come, it will require the kind of bold leadership and human skills possessed by the city's business, labor and civic leaders. It will take above all a deep and abiding commitment to social change by the very people who have the power to bring about change. It will take an affirmation of belief in the principles of equality and concern with making this a truly open, democratic society. We in this nation will continue down the bitter path of racial strife and division until the men and women who hold responsible positions in this society—those who have made it—care about those who have not.

The Urban League is a vehicle for change, just as it remains a vehicle for those who must channel their energies and resources into building a better community. We have been and will continue to be:

"forceful advocates for the cause of black people and other minorities

a result-oriented, issue-oriented organization dedicated to serving the people

a bridge between the races, forging unity and harmony in a land torn by strife and friction

forthright believers in an open, pluralistic, integrated society"

The Urban League's task is a grave one, especially at this time of growing despair that this nation can ever solve the racial divisions that have so torn and bloodied the fabric of our society. Much of white America's attitude seems to be frozen in sullen resentment against what it interprets as a capitulation to blacks in the sixties. Many middle Americans seem to be complaining that: "They've got their laws. We've more clearly defined their rights. We've hired a few; voted for one. A black doctor just moved into our suburban neighborhood. We eat with them in restaurants; sit beside them in buses; and even allowed a few to desegregate our schools—on a token basis, of course. What more do they want?"

But while black Americans are saying "a little bit of freedom won't do," the apparent response is "thus far for black folk—and no further." Hence, there appears to be a national impasse founded on the reluctance of white Americans to complete the moral and social revolution started in the sixties, and their widespread inability to fully understand that the issues of that decade are no longer the civil rights issues of the seventies.

The civil rights issues of the sixties have changed. In the sixties, the issue was the right to sit on the bus; today the issue is where that bus is going and what does it cost to get there. In the sixties, the issue was the right to eat at the lunch counter; today the issue is the hunger and malnutrition that stalk the land. In the sixties, the issue was fair employment opportunity. Today, that can no longer be separated from full employment of minority people and equal access to every kind and level of employment up to and including top policy-making jobs.

The central civil rights issue of the seventies then, is the restructuring of America's economic and political power so that black people have their fair share of the rewards, the responsibilities, and the decision making in every sector of our common society.

This demands a more sophisticated strategy than the marches and demonstrations of the past. We are no longer engaged in a moral struggle for the conscience of the nation, nor is the civil rights thrust still focused on the Old Confederacy. If we've learned anything about the new issues, it is that racism is not just a southern phenomenon, but that it is endemic to all America. And we have learned, too, that other sections of the country can react with as much violence, repression and irrationality today as the South has historically.

Black people in the seventies will no longer be comforted by the stirring resolve sung in the sixties: "ain't gonna let nobody turn us 'round," because when they see the new Supreme Court, they'll know we've been turned around. Black people will no longer find the same inspiration in the words of the black woman walking in the Montgomery bus boycott who said: "My feets is tired but my soul is rested." The fact today is that not only are her feet tired, but they hurt, and her soul is not rested, but tested, 'cause her spirit is broken and made low.

Marches on Washington won't pass a fair and equitable welfare reform bill, but blacks marching to the ballot box might. Irrational opposition to busing and lawsuits are no guarantee to stop the school buses, but integrated suburbs and neighborhoods and quality education for all might. Corporate responsibility won't amount to much if it's limited to signing up as equal opportunity employers, hiring a few black workers, and donating a bit less to the Urban League than to the company president's alma mater. But it might take on a new meaning if corporate executives left their offices and went into the ghetto to see for themselves what it is like to be poor and black in this America in 1972. And that goes too, for the Administration in Washington.

It must understand the human suffering and the human aspirations behind the walls of the rotting tenements and crumbling shacks. It must understand that the Federal resources made available to the Urban League must go hand in hand with a dramatic commitment to change, and with steady and relentless positive action on the broad range of issues affecting minority people.

Yes, this new civil rights era will be less dramatic and, perhaps at first, less popular. It will be an era of trench warfare, requiring, instead of charismatic leadership, knowledgeable technicians skillfully monitoring and exposing racism in the twilight zone of America's institutional policy-making processes. The battle has shifted from the streets to the deliberations of legislative committees, zoning boards and school boards. This new era is one of hard work, selfless sacrifice, and the sophisticated techniques of planning, analysis, and synthesis.

And the Urban League must embark upon new strategies fitting to this new era. One of the first programs we will undertake in the coming year will be to institute a new program of voter registration in the North and West to help bring about the "political browning of America" that we hope will be a giant step toward redressing the powerlessness of urban minorities. The great strides made by black southerners in recent years have been directly related to their growing use of the right to vote, and it is their example we hope to bring north.

Our concern goes beyond the mere placement of blacks in some local elected offices. Cleveland knows from first-hand experience that the election of a black mayor does not necessarily bring with it the kinds of state and Federal resources that will allow the mayor to create the jobs, housing and education his constituents so desperately need. If the cities are in trouble today, it is because of the flagrant neglect of the basic needs of the poor by a nation whose war on poverty has been shamefully ended by an inglorious cease-fire.

Our concern is with the involvement of black people in the democratic process; with the achievement by black people of the kind of political power that will ensure that officeholders of whatever race are sensitive to the issues and interests affecting the black community. This is the democratic way. This is the way all other groups in our society ensure that government is responsive to their needs. This is the way of nonviolent peaceful change in a society that cries out for constructive change and for the revitalization of the democratic process.

The systematic deprivation of black people from the seats of this society's power is all-embracing. Across the country, there are some 1,800 black elected officials, but that figure is impressive only if we ignore the fact that there are 522,000 such positions at all levels of government. That means that black people, who make up 12 percent of the population, hold only three tenths of 1 percent of the elected positions in America's many levels of government. Senator Brooke, the only black man in the Senate, represents a 1 percent black share of that body's 100 senators. The crusading black caucus in the House of Representatives comes to 3 percent of the 435 congressmen. And even these figures look good when we try to find blacks at the Cabinet and sub-Cabinet level, or at the helm of regional departments or regulatory agencies.

The system continues to be stacked against black ballot power. Some of our handful of black congressmen are in danger of losing their seats through reapportionment by conservative state legislatures. In many northern cities, minorities and poor people are virtually excluded from the political process through antiquated registration procedures.

So a major civil rights objective now must be to mount a major drive to get neighborhood registration teams, weekend and night registration office hours, community registrars, and a simplified system of permanent registration.

The drive for political empowerment must go hand-in-hand with the drive for economic empowerment. It's not enough to point with pride at black income figures creeping slowly, point by point, to levels still less than two thirds of white income. Economic empowerment means putting green dollars into black pockets and filling jobs at all levels with skilled black workers. Economic empowerment also means opening up the suburbs to blacks of all income levels so they can be near the new jobs that are coming on stream in suburban offices and plants. It means overcoming the irrational opposition heard from Forest Hills to Cleveland to scatter-site housing for the poor, so that they too can escape the imprisonment of slum housing and benefit from the schools and facilities of good neighborhoods.

And economic empowerment is what the Cleveland Urban League is bringing to thousands of minority citizens in this community, in the face of a job drain that has hit this city harder than many others. The Urban League has found jobs for eight hundred returning veterans. It was a driving force in the coalition that helped get the Cleveland Plan agreement and has already placed apprentices in five construction trade unions. Although it's only been in operation for fifteen months, the storefront Street Academy Program has enrolled 160 students. These are young people the public schools have pushed out and they bear the label of dropouts and failures. But of the first fifteen Street Academy graduates, fourteen are now in college. In the crucial field of housing, the Cleveland Urban League's Operation Equality has brought about agreements with the managers of some 15,000 houses and apartments that will open these units up to black renters and black building workmen.

Impressive as this record is, it is but a mere indication of the kinds of things the Urban League could do if it were adequately funded and staffed. The truth of the matter is that the problems facing black people in Cleveland are so deep and so profound, that the League is literally inundated by cries for help, some of which must, of necessity, go unanswered. Every single day of the week about one hundred people come to the Urban League's office seeking jobs, housing, help with local bureaucracies, help for the teenager on drugs, help for the crushing burdens that press down upon anyone who is poor and black in this America of ours.

The Urban League deals on a daily basis with America's failure to respond to the needs of its black and poor citizens. It has helped thousands to win better jobs, housing, and education, and it has been the catalyst for community coalitions and joint efforts to make this a better, healthier city. If it has done so much with so little, how much more it could do if it had the resources and the increased support of the responsible, concerned leaders of this region.

The Urban League movement must continue to be effective. We must deliver. We cannot fail.

For if the Urban League fails in its mission, America fails in its purpose. But the Urban League cannot fail for another reason—there is a constituency out there depending on us. There are black folk out there who never heard our name and don't understand what we do who are depending on us.

Depending on us are those black people who have no hope or hope of hope.

Depending on us are those black people who cry out today, not for freedom and equality, but for a crust of bread and a morsel of meat.

Depending on us are little black children who cry out not for Black Power but for medicine for their festering sores and for protection from the rats and the roaches.

Depending on us is the junkie in the ghetto.

Depending on us is the unemployed father, the underemployed daughter, the welfare-dependent mother, and the son home from Vietnam who can't find work.

Depending on us are black folk like Grandpa Jim Griggs who, when he was seventy years old sat talking with me on the porch of his broken-down roadside shanty in southwest Georgia, where he spent his life as a sharecropper. "Pa," I asked, "What is it that you want most out of life at seventy?" And Pa said, "Junior, I just want to go to the bathroom indoors in a warm place one time before I die."

Depending on us are black people just like Pa who can't deal with the issues that galvanize those more fortunate than they—issues like integration or separation, pan-Africanism and nation-building, voting Republican or Democrat. The issues for these black folk boil down to one big issue—SURVIVAL!

It is for these black Americans that the Urban League exists. It is to their cause that the Urban League is dedicated. It is their agenda and their needs that must shape our policies. And it is their interests we must advance as we seek to forge a future that is more just and humane.

Like the tree planted by the rivers of water, we shall not be moved from our sacred mission to make this a land of freedom, justice and complete equality.

# A New Kind of Southern Strategy[13]

Bella S. Abzug

*Born 1920, New York, NY; B.A., Hunter College, 1942; LL.B., Columbia University, 1947; editor,* Columbia Law Review, *1947; lawyer, Civil Rights Congress, 1947–; lawyer, American Civil Liberties Union, 1947–; founder, Coalition for a Democratic Alternative, 1968; representative (D) from New York, 1971-76; author,* Bella! Ms. Abzug Goes to Washington *(1972),* Gender Gap *(1984).*

## Editor's introduction

Regarded as having a striking personality and a commanding presence, Bella S. Abzug, the first Jewish woman to win a seat in the House of Representatives, addressed a group of 357 people on the political silence of American women. Abzug remarked that despite having had the right to vote for more than 50 years, women had achieved little or no representation in Washington. Abzug believed that such representation could be accomplished if women worked collectively and picked their contests wisely.

---

As cochairwoman of the National Women's Political Caucus, I welcome you to the women's political power movement.

I am not an authority on the South, but I suspect that this is the first time a conference such as this has ever been held here. You are making history today.

You are creating a new kind of "southern strategy" for 1972 . . . a political strategy for women who have been shut out of power and who are determined that this is the year to win full citizenship and participation in political decision making for the women of the South—white and black.

As you come together here to study the techniques of electoral politics, you are part of a nationwide movement. You are doing what women all across the country are doing, and I predict that the male politicians are in for some real surprises in this election year. Reports are coming in of women turning out in unexpectedly large numbers at political meetings not just the big rallies, but the small precinct meetings where the political process starts. And I hear that the women are asking sharp questions of the candidates and they're not satisfied with platitudes or with having their babies kissed.

I think we can take some credit for that. We've been doing a lot of political consciousness-raising. Since the National Women's Political Caucus was organized in Washington last July, women have organized caucuses in more than forty states, North, South, East and West—and they're learning fast.

Our women are as diverse as America itself, as diverse as you who have come here today. Women who are young and old, rich and poor, white, black, Chicanas, Puerto Ricans and Indians, women who come from all parties and no parties, women who are in the United States Congress and women who have never held office.

Your presence here indicates the conscious unity that binds you together with thousands of women across the country and the sense of common wrongs and injustices that exists among millions of women, whether they work in universities, factories, offices or in the home.

We are women with many different life styles. Television and the other media which thrive on the offbeat and the sensational have tried to depict the women's liberation movement as an assembly of bra-burning, neurotic, manhating exhibitionists. Don't let them fool you.

[13]Delivered at the Southern Women's Conference on Education for Delegate Selection, in Nashville, Tennessee, on February 12, 1972. Reprinted with permission of Bella S. Abzug.

I have been to hundreds of women's meetings and I have yet to see a bra burned.

But I have met and talked to women who were burning with indignation at the wastefulness and stupidity of a society that makes second-class citizens of half its population.

Women, in fact, are 53 percent of the electorate. Yet throughout our history and now, more than a half century after we won the vote, women are still almost invisible in government, in elected posts, in high administrative decision-making positions, in the judiciary.

We are determined to change that. And we intend to do it by organizing ourselves and by reaching out to women everywhere.

I would like to read to you from the Statement of Purpose adopted by the National Women's Political Caucus at its founding meeting. It addressed its appeal to:

" . . . every woman whose abilities have been wasted by the second-class, subservient, underpaid, or powerless positions to which female human beings are consigned

To every woman who sits at home with little control over her own life, much less the powerful institutions of the country, wondering if there isn't more to life than this

To every woman who must go on welfare because, even when she can get a job, she makes about half the money paid to a man for the same work

To every minority woman who has endured the stigma of being twice-different from the white male ruling class

To every woman who has experienced the ridicule or hostility reserved by this country—and often by its political leaders—for women who dare to express the hopes and ambitions that are natural to every human being."

To all these women—and they are nearly all of us—we said that it is time for us to join together to act against the sexism, racism, institutional violence and poverty that disfigure our beautiful land.

We said it is time that women organize to get an equal share of representation and power in the political structures of government.

It is time that we organize to see that women's issues, the priorities of life, not war, are taken seriously and become the policy of government, a government that represents us.

Wherever I go, and I have traveled a great deal in the past year, I have found a strong community of interest among huge numbers of American women, a strong commitment to changing the direction of our society.

Women are in the forefront of the peace movement, the civil rights and equal rights movement, the environment and consumer movements, the child care movement. This is part of your tradition too. It was southern ladies who organized the Committee to Stop Lynching here in the South many years ago, and it was a woman who sat in the *front* of a bus in Montgomery, Alabama, and made history.

Just a few weeks ago I sat in Congress and heard the President give the State of the Union address. There were more than seven hundred of us seated on the main floor of the House. You may have heard the President say, Here we have assembled the Government of the United States, the members of the House, the Senate, the Supreme Court, the Cabinet.

I looked around and of these 700 leaders of Government, there were just 12 women. Could anything be more disgraceful? Eleven women out of 435 members of the House. One woman out of 100 in the Senate. No women in the Cabinet. No women on the Supreme Court, although the President has had four separate opportunities to appoint one.

In fact, there were more women up in the balcony than on the floor, and as onlookers their role was to look pretty, to applaud dutifully and to be silent.

But we have come to the end of silence. There is too much to say. The men haven't done such a great job by themselves. Women look at a nation run by a male executive branch, a male Congress, male governors and legislatures, a male Pentagon, and male corporations and banks, and they rightly ask:

If we shared equally with men the authority of government, would we condone the spending of more than a trillion dollars in the past twenty-five years for killing and useless weapons—

when our cities are dying of neglect

when families go hungry in Appalachia

when children in South Carolina suffer from malnutrition and are afflicted with worms

when people live in shacks or are forced to go on welfare because there are no jobs for them

when there are not enough hospitals, doctors and schools

when our young people are becoming more and more alienated from a society they regard as without soul or purpose

I think not.

I believe that shutting women out of political power and decision-making roles has resulted in a terrible mutilation of our society. It is at least partly responsible for our present crisis of lopsided priorities and distorted values. It is responsible too for the masculine mystique, the obsession with militarism that has made the nuclear missile the symbol of American power and that equates our national honor with continuing the senseless killing in Indochina, continuing a war which American women—in even larger numbers than men—say must be ended.

As you know, some of the most powerful men in the House are from the South. They hold the leadership posts. They head the most important committees—Armed Services, Appropriations, Ways and Means, and others. They are the ones who decide whether we are to build more bombs or more schools. They are there because of the seniority system and because they are reelected year after year without any significant opposition. Women help elect these men, and then men use their power to deny women their most basic needs.

I hope that this is the year when some of you women will begin to challenge these men and put them on notice that they don't have a lifetime hold on those congressional seats.

Don't get me wrong. I am not saying that the men in Congress are totally indifferent to the needs of women. Many are genuinely concerned. Others are catching on to the fact that they had better be concerned, and still others are now pretending to care.

But it is also a fact of life that it is the victim of discrimination who feels most deeply the injustice of discrimination and who is most determined to end it.

Consider what is happening in Congress in connection with the Equal Employment Opportunities Commission. A filibuster in the Senate has just defeated an attempt to equip the EEOC with effective cease-and-desist power to stop employers from discriminating against women, blacks and other minorities. We lost the same fight in the House, too.

The shameful facts of discrimination against black people have been set before the nation, but I wonder how many are fully aware of the scandalous and all-pervasive discrimination against women of all colors.

Do you know that women now make up 37 percent of the labor force . . . that almost thirty million women work, most of them because they need the money . . . that seven out of ten work at menial clerical jobs, and most of the others at service or factory jobs?

Do you know that only 7 percent of doctors are women, earn less than $5,000 a year? Do you know that even when they are better educated than men, they wind up with worse jobs . . . that even when they perform the same work as men, they usually get paid less, and that promotions usually go to men, not women?

Do you know that only 7 percent of doctors are women, and that we have only a toehold in the other professions? Do you know that the number of women in college and university teaching is actually declining?

Do you know about the 4.5 million mothers in the labor force who have youngsters under six? Nearly 6 million preschool children whose mothers have to work to help buy their food and clothing, but in all of this great land we have only enough child care centers to accommodate a half million children. And when we finally passed a child care act at this last session, the President vetoed it. He said it was fiscally irresponsible, and yet a few weeks later he asked for twice as much money—$4 billion—to increase military spending. And he also vetoed it because he said it was a threat to family life!

I would suggest that women are greater authorities on family life than is the President. It is they who bear the children and raise them, many as heads of the family. It is they who work as waitresses, secretaries, hospital aides, factory hands, and in the fields. And it is they who come home and have to clean and cook and care for their children and worry about getting baby sitters when they go to work the next day or night.

If we had more of these real experts in Congress, they would not let the President get away with pious invocations of a nonreal world. They would insist that instead of raising our military budget to $80 billion, as the President proposes, that we allocate money for child care centers, for training programs and more educational opportunities for women, for basic human needs.

And I believe that if we had a truly representative Congress, with at least half of its members women and with much greater representation of blacks and other minorities, we would get real, effective action to end discrimination. We would have not a filibuster, but an EEOC with teeth in it. We would have an Equal Rights Amendment.

I am not elevating women to sainthood, nor am I suggesting that all women share the same views, or that all women are good and all men are bad. But I do believe that because they have been excluded from political power for so long, they see with more clairvoyant eyes the deficiencies of our society. Their work in the voluntary organizations has made them the compassionate defenders of the victims of our distorted priorities. They know intimately the problems of the aged and the sick, of the neglected, miseducated child, the young soldiers returning home wounded in body or spirit.

There are only eleven of us women in the House. Some of us are Democrats, some Republicans, some liberals and some conservatives. But all of us supported the Mansfield Amendment which requires all American troops to be withdrawn from Indochina within six months. I find that very significant and an encouraging omen of things to come.

What is to come? Is this the year when women's political power will come of age? Or are we just going to make noise but no real progress?

I believe that in the seven months of our existence, the National Women's Political Caucus has already achieved a great deal.

As you know, in 1968 only 13 percent of the delegates to the Democratic convention were women. The Republicans did only slightly better, with 17 percent. Only 1 of the 180 delegations at both conventions was chaired by a woman.

This time we're going to do much, much better.

As standards for reasonable representation at the conventions, the women's caucus has voted that each state delegation should be comprised of no less than 50 percent women. It has also voted that racial minorities and young people should be present in each delegation in percentages at least as great as their percentage of the total state population.

We have set up task forces within the Caucus to meet with representatives of the Republican and Democratic parties to press the issue of representation. Our task force of Republican women is following up on this pledge. We do have a number of Republicans in the leadership of our caucus, including Elly Peterson, formerly head of the GOP's women's division, and Virginia Allen, who headed the President's Commission on the Status of Women. This is the commission that issued the report called *A Matter of Simple Justice*, which documented the pervasive discrimination against women in our society and made very specific proposals on how to end it. That report is gathering dust, and that is why Republican women find they have so much in common with the rest of us.

As for the Democratic party, it has a specific commitment to honor the guidelines of the McGovern-Fraser party reform commission which would ensure reasonable representation at the convention of women, youth and minorities. At a meeting which we held in Washington with Democratic Party Chairman Larry O'Brien and Patricia Harris, temporary chairman of the Credentials Committee (Carleen Waller was present, too), we obtained a definite statement that any delegation which does not contain at least 50 percent women and proportional representation of the young and minorities will be deemed in *prima facie* violation of the guidelines and subject to challenge.

We intend to hold the Democratic party leadership to that commitment. We are now engaged in a national effort to ensure that at least half of the delegates are women, and we are prepared to challenge the credentials of delegations that are not representative.

So what you are doing today is part of an ongoing campaign for political recognition of women. You will find that the delegate selection process varies from state to state. It is highly complicated in some states and simple in others. Many of you have already found that out.

Learn the procedures, and go back to your states determined to settle for nothing less than your full share. Whether they run on slates committed to specific candidates or to no candidate, women must join together at every stage of the delegation selection process—and form their own caucuses across slate lines to guarantee that women are not squeezed out, to make sure that male politicians don't try to use their wives or aunts as stand-ins and to agree on common goals and state their demands. They must do this at the precinct level, at the legislative district level, and at the state level. *We must be visible as women.*

Women will be wearing Muskie buttons, Humphrey buttons, McGovern buttons, Lindsay buttons and I predict that a surprising number will be wearing Chisholm buttons. The more the better—because Shirley Chisholm's candidacy offers us one of the most effective ways to press our demands. But we are also going to be wearing *Womanpower*—'72 buttons and ribbons because no matter what slates we're on, we're going to act together as women.

Let no one take us for granted.

I am recommending to the NWPC that on the opening day of the convention we cross slate lines and get women delegates to meet together, demonstrate our unified presence, and state our demands. We will serve notice that we want an equal share in leadership. We want a party and a platform actively committed to eradicating discrimination and making women first-class citizens in every aspect of their lives.

We want a party and a platform committed to working for a peaceful and humane society that meets the needs of all its people. And to make sure that this comes to pass, we want guarantees that women share equally in committee posts in the party and at the convention.

We want guarantees from the nominee, whoever he or she may be, that women will have an equal share in Government—an equal number of Cabinet posts and high administrative offices. And we want an end to the exclusion of women from the Supreme Court and their almost total exclusion from the lower courts.

We are prepared to use every means at our disposal to remove the "for men only" sign from American politics and to open wide our political institutions to women and to all underrepresented groups.

We intend to do this not only at the conventions, but in political contests all over the country. We will have more women running this year for local office, for the state legislature, for Congress. Some will run for the experience, and some will run to win. Some are already running. I have been getting phone calls from around the country. A woman is running for governor of Texas. Black women are running for Congress from Texas and California, and there are others who are planning to do so or who have already announced. At some point we're going to get all our women candidates together and introduce them to the nation.

We in the women's political movement have a responsibility to see that we do get some winners and that we pick out contests wisely. I would urge that in every state or region you get together, the sooner the better, and pick your concentration points. Choose your strongest candidates to run against the weakest incumbents. Try to select areas in which you can build coalitions with other underrepresented groups.

Remember, this is the year when the outs—all of us—are demanding "in."

Representatives of young people with a potential strength of twenty-five million new voters met in Chicago recently to organize a Youth Caucus, and they are now setting up caucuses in all the states. The black caucus is well organized, and other minority groups are also joining together to make their political power count.

I believe that with the organization of these groups we have the components of a New Majority—a majority of women, young people, minority groups and other Americans—small businessmen, working people, farmers, poor people—who share in our concerns and needs.

Working together, this New Majority has the capacity to change America, to lead us away from war and to work together instead for a society in which human needs are paramount, in which all people—men and women—who can work will have meaningful employment, in which women will have full citizenship and dignity as individuals, in which our children can learn and live free from the atmosphere of hatred and violence that has despoiled our land for so many years.

These are goals to which I believe most women will respond. What you do here this weekend at this historic first political meeting of southern womanpower will help create that kind of America.

# We Can Do It[14]

Patricia Schroeder

*Born July 30, 1940, Portland OR; B.A., University of Minnesota, 1961; J.D., Harvard Law School, 1964; field attorney, National Labor Relations Board, 1964-66; professor, Community College of Denver, 1969-70; professor, Regis College, 1970-72; hearing officer, Colorado Dept. of Personnel, 1971-72; representative (D) from Colorado, 1972-96; president, Association of American Publishers, 1997–; author,* Champion of the Great American Family *(1989).*

## Editor's introduction

Patricia Schroeder, former United States Representative (D) from Colorado, was one of six new women representatives to enter the House of Representatives in 1972. In this speech, she announced that "women can no longer be mere spectators of the political process." Instead, Schroeder urged, they must become participants within, and therefore shapers of, that political process. Drawing upon her own success, she offered suggestions on how to successfully run for office.

---

Senator Robert Kennedy once said of his brother, John, after the President's assassination, "If there is a lesson from his life and death, it is that in this world of ours, we can no longer be satisfied with being mere spectators, critics on the sidelines."

And surely that must be the continuing message for all of us here today. Women especially can no longer be mere spectators of the political process, critics on the sidelines; but active participants, playing an important and vital role out on the field.

By your presence here today, each of you is demonstrating her interest in the political process. Many of you have no doubt taken active roles in community and civic organizations, political activities and campaigns, or business and professional activities. You can *do* the job—but first, you have to *get* the job. For those of you, and I hope there are many, who may be contemplating a run for office—whether it be party, city, state, judicial, or federal—let me offer a few suggestions from my own experience.

First: Assess critically your own qualifications. It is probably fair to say—although certainly unfair in practice—that a woman running for public office should be "overqualified." Having been chairman of your church's women's club may not carry the same clout as being program chairman of the local Rotary Club.

It is interesting to note that all five of this years' new congresswomen are lawyers. Perhaps this is because, as lawyers, we have necessarily been thrust into an adverse, and often competitive, role with members of the male establishment. Furthermore, we have come into constant contact with many of the problems that face our communities, and worked on possible legislative solutions.

Second: Examine carefully the real base of your support. The support of one's family, close friends, and associates is indispensable. But what contacts, or qualifications do you have that will enable you to gain the confidence and backing of other groups and allies? In my own case, an extensive labor law background was valuable in helping eventually obtain both organizational and financial support from many labor unions. Teaching contacts with three major colleges in Denver were also important. Finally, it is essential to take the pulse, and constantly stroke the brows of many of the key party leaders and workers in your area. Many of these veterans of the political wars often will make astute judgements about prospective candidates. Every candidate honestly believes he

[14]Delivered at the National Women's Political Caucus Convention, in Houston, Texas, on February 9, 1973. Reprinted with permission of Patricia Schroeder.

or she is in fact *the* best candidate. If none of the pros agree, best reexamine your position.

Third: Build credibility. Because you are a woman, you will constantly confront the attitude that you are not "a serious candidate." At our County nominating convention it is customary for candidates to have booths, give away courtesy coffee, distribute literature, placard the walls with posters, etc. I had a basic feeling of aversion to that sort of thing; but we decided it was probably more important that I do some of the traditional things, simply because I was the untraditional candidate.

Because you are a woman you may have the ability to gain more than your fair share of press and media coverage, because you are the different candidate. But the other side of the coin is that you will often be more severely cross-examined on your views and statements by newspeople than is the average male candidate.

Fourth: Develop a strong "grassroots" organization. You will find that there are great reservoirs of dedicated, talented women who will really work for another woman. This is especially true of many older, retired women; and many younger gals, such as students and working girls.

You will probably have a very hard time raising money. My husband often said that the money "is controlled by male chauvinist pigs." Organization and union money is controlled by men, and they will usually have little confidence in the chances of a woman candidate. Hence, the bigger and better volunteer group you can muster, the better chance you will have of putting your scarce dollars into essential items like printed materials and media time.

Fifth: Use innovative and hard-hitting media. Because a woman candidate is "different," don't be afraid to run a different kind of campaign, utilizing original and different media techniques and content. Let me give you one example: the standard political brochure. You know what I am talking about—the picture of the candidate with family, with coat over the shoulder, in front of the Capitol, etc. with the standard one-liners: "X is honest; X is against pollution; X is for fiscal responsibility." We were able to achieve real impact—and also ruffle some feathers—with colorful miniposters.

And finally, Sixth: Be issue-oriented. Running for public office is too time-consuming and too expensive to embark on such a venture merely for the experience, or for the ego satisfaction. If you run, take a stand. Get out front on the issues that concern you, your family, your community, and the nation. The risk, of course, is great; but so are the rewards.

And again, being a woman has both its advantages and disadvantages. I think a woman can more easily take a strong position on the war, on gun control, or education, than perhaps can a man. Isn't a mother going to be against wholesale bombing, for tougher gun control, for better schools? However, you must also guard against being pushed into unreasonable or irresponsible extreme positions by your erstwhile supporters. I was the only major candidate running in Denver last fall who would attend and speak at an abortion panel hearing held at a local college. But I was criticized by some women there when I tried to emphasize my support for birth control and family planning programs, rather than an "abortion on demand" policy. It is all too easy to become a "Kamikaze candidate"—crashing and burning on one or two emotionally packed issues.

So, it can be done. Women can run. And win. "You can do it!" I hope there will be questions later, and I look forward to talking with many of you individually later on today. Thank you.

# Women in Politics[15]

Shirley Chisholm

*Born November 30, 1924, Brooklyn, NY; B.A., Brooklyn College, 1946; M.A., Columbia University, 1952; director, Friends Day Nursery, 1947-53; director, Hamilton-Madison Child Care Center, 1953-59; educational consultant, NY Bureau of Child Welfare, 1959-64; assemblyperson, New York State Legislature, 1965-68; representative (D) from New York, 1969-82; professor, Mount Holyoke College, 1983-87; chair, National Political Congress of Black Women, 1985–; author,* Unbought and Unbossed *(1970),* The Good Fight *(1973).*

## Editor's introduction:

Like Patricia Schroeder in the prior speech, former New York representative Shirley Chisholm urged the 800 delegates at the National Women's Political Caucus Convention "to plunge into the world of politics and battle it out toe to toe" with other candidates. Drawing from her own political experience, Chisholm stated that all women, regardless of race or political orientation, should get involved in the fight to achieve more equal political representation. To that end, she recommended that the National Women's Political Caucus broaden its base and make a greater effort to include women from all ethnic backgrounds.

---

When it was arranged that I should speak to you today, Liz Carpenter wrote me a note and suggested my speech should be, "Can a Woman Become President?" Knowing Liz, she probably thought this would be a wonderful occasion for me to exhort an audience of potential candidates to plan their own onslaughts on the pinnacle of elective office.

As I look back on the past year and a half, I think my campaign did help to break the barrier against women seeking the presidency and other elective offices but, my experiences also made me acutely aware of some of the problems women candidates face as well as particular problems which the women's movement, and especially the National Women's Political Caucus, must face up to.

One of my biggest problems was that my campaign was viewed as a symbolic gesture. While I realized that my campaign was an important rallying symbol for women and that my presence in the race forced the other candidates to deal with issues relating to women, my primary objective was to force people to accept me as a real viable candidate.

Although many have compared my race to that of Victoria Woodhull, I specifically rejected that comparison. Mrs. Woodhull was a feminist candidate running on a feminist party platform. I specifically rejected this feminist candidacy as I did the projection of myself into a black candidacy or an antiwar candidacy. I chose to run for the nomination of one of the major national parties.

I did this because I feel that the time for tokenism and symbolic gestures is past. Women need to plunge into the world of politics and battle it out toe to toe on the same ground as their male counterparts. If they do not do this, they will not succeed as a presidential candidate or in any other campaign for political office.

First and foremost, it is essential that you believe in yourself and your ability to handle the job you are seeking. If you don't, it is difficult to persuade others to support you. While pretty obvious to anyone who has run for office, I found that the press, the public, and even those in the women's movement found it difficult to understand this key point. Over and over in the

[15]Delivered at the National Women's Political Caucus Convention, in Houston, Texas, on February 9, 1973. Reprinted with permission of Shirley Chisholm.

campaign, I was asked, "But why are you running, Mrs. Chisholm?" Over and over I would reply, "Because I think I can do the job," "Because I think I am better than the rest of the candidates in the field."

One of the stumbling blocks I encountered was the fact that many people, including feminists, thought that since I "didn't have a chance" it was foolish to work for me.

For those who genuinely preferred another candidate, one can have no quarrel. But for those who thought I was the best candidate but chose to work for someone else because they viewed my campaign as hopeless, they will need to reexamine their thinking for truly, no woman will ever achieve the presidency as long as their potential supporters hold this view.

As the effect of the Wallace phenomenon in this last election points out, a campaign becomes truly effective when those who believe in their candidate pull out all the stops.

One of the other most difficult problems I faced was that many of my wonderful women's movement supporters did not understand that I both wanted and needed to talk about issues other than equal rights, abortion and child care. As you know, I am a strong supporter of all of these issues but in a campaign, there is a great deal of other ground to cover. Senior citizens don't really give a hang about abortion and homosexuals are more concerned with their own situation than the status of the Equal Rights Amendment.

Further, and this is critical to the discussion we will enter into at this convention, different women view different segments of the women's movement agenda as priority items.

The movement has, for the most part, been led by educated white middle-class women. There is nothing unusual about this. Reform as movements are usually led by the better educated and better off. But, if the women's movement is to be successful you must recognize the broad variety of women there are and the depth and range of their interests and concerns. To black and Chicano women, picketing a restricted club or insisting on the title Ms. are not burning issues. They are more concerned about bread-and-butter items such as the extension of minimum wage, welfare reform and day care.

Further, they are not only women but women of color and thus are subject to additional and sometimes different pressures.

For example, the black experience in America has not been one of unbridled success for black men. Indeed, there have been times when discrimination and the economic situation were such that it was easier for a black woman to get a job than her husband. Because of this, anything that might be construed as anti-male will be viewed skeptically by a black woman.

Indeed this is a problem not only for black women but most women.

If this caucus is to have a real impact, we must have a broad base and appeal to the average woman.

Unfortunately, the movement is currently perceived as anti-male, anti-child, and anti-family.

Part of this is bad press. The media does not concentrate on the blue-haired lady in pearls testifying on behalf of the equal employment opportunities bill. It trains its eyes on the young girl shaking her first and screaming obscenities at an abortion rally.

Part of it is that many of the leaders of the movement have down-graded traditional roles in their attempts to show abuses and to affirm the right of a woman to have a choice of roles to play.

Finally, there have been excesses. Not all sexual advances are sexist. Children are more than a pile of dirty diapers, and families while they have often restricted women, have also provided warmth, security, and love.

If we are to succeed in uniting ourselves and in attracting the typical woman who is likely to be a housewife and mother who likes living in suburbia, we are going to have to make a concerted effort to articulate issues so that everyone will want to be identified with and active in the movement.

With this in mind, the function of the National Women's Political Caucus is not to be the cutting edge of the women's liberation movement but the big umbrella organization which provides the weight and muscle for those issues which the majority of women see as concerns.

One of the critical items on the convention agenda is to put the National Women's Political Caucus on a sound financial basis. I don't know if you realize it or not but most of the time the women in our national office have to pay for the privilege of being screamed at, accused of doing things without authorization, or not doing enough. Yet, in a real sense these gals are the

Caucus. They get the mailings out, they do the nitty grittying of organizing meetings and conventions. Most of the time they work long hours and are lucky to get reimbursed for carfare. If we accuse others of ripping off and abusing women, we should begin by rectifying our own house.

It is time we rose above the cake sale mentality of financing. In this country we spend $6.4 billion on cosmetics. If we can spend that much on our faces, we can spend ten dollars a year for a membership fee—that is less than one dollar a month. Newsletters are also an enormous expense and should be put on some kind of paying basis.

Finally, we should set aside money to hire one full-time paid legislative lobbyist for the Caucus, and set up legislative lobbying leaders in every state and major subdivision. What is the point of having a National Women's Political Caucus and working at electing women to office if we ignore the simplest and most obvious methods of effecting this political process—that of lobbying? Without this we will lose everything we have gained. Right now the Equal Rights Amendment is stalled in the ratification process. Without effective lobbying, it will die after over a half a century of effort. The minimum wage bill, which affects a vast number of women was killed last year for a want of five votes to send it to conference committee. The National Women's Political Caucus could provide the margin of votes necessary for passage. After we passed a child care bill, the President vetoed it saying that day-care centers were destructive to families. The White House needs to know this is a vital issue for women all over America and that we disagree.

Another issue this convention must grapple with is the form and format of this organization and the composition of the new policy council. I, for one, believe that the Caucus will never be completely effective unless we develop a strong grass roots organization.

As I traveled around the country, I met hundreds of bright, capable, articulate women. These are the people who ought to be projected into the positions of authority and leadership.

We don't need any more of the "superstar" syndrome. Indeed, I am sure that Betty, Gloria, and Bella are as sick of seeing their faces as I am of seeing mine. What we need is to thrust new people into the limelight and to show the range and breadth of talent among women all over the nation.

I, therefore, propose that you do not place my name in nomination for the policy council and I hope that the others in the policy council, who are in the same position, will do likewise. This does not mean breaking our association with the Caucus. You can establish some sort of honorary advisory council or hall of fame or something and we can remain "on call" when we are needed but, what is necessary now are new faces.

In closing, I would like to make one observation: normally our meetings go on endlessly with much shouting, haranguing, grandstanding, and discussion of extraneous issues. Could we all try to be respectful and understanding of each other's views, concise, to the point, and mindful of the clock.

# In Pursuit of Equality in Academe: New Themes and Dissonant Chords[16]

Eleanor Holmes Norton

*Born June 13, 1937, Washington, D.C.; B.A., Antioch College, 1960; assistant legal director, American Civil Liberties Union, 1965-70; chair, New York City Commission on Human Rights, 1970-77; chair, Equal Opportunity Employment Commission, 1977-83; representative (D) from Washington, D.C., 1991–.*

## Editor's introduction

Eleanor Holmes Norton, then commissioner of the New York City Department of Human Rights, asked the academic administrators, graduate students, and government and foundation officials of a national conference on higher education how "in a land where mobility seemed mandated and came to all but the damned, America's dark-skinned immigrants remain at the bottom." A civil rights activist since her days at Antioch College, Norton condemned both government and the universities for failing to provide equal opportunities in academia for women and minorities. At the close of the speech, she was given a standing ovation.

---

Ladies and Gentlemen:

I knew I was speaking before a group of hardy academic souls when I learned that you unfailingly come to Chicago each March for this conference, apparently willingly, choosing it out of all the more gentle places in other parts of the country. Were you from some other sectors of our society, you might not be so hipped on Chicago. You would alternate between Puerto Rico and Miami. Anyway, I am pleased as a dyed-in-the-wool New Yorker to welcome you to Chicago.

A new equality has emerged during the past twenty years. It has been very much discussed but too little analyzed. It has been negatively associated with everything from the development of permissiveness to the demise of law and order. Its positive accreditations have sometimes been similarly exaggerated, as the use of the language of liberation to describe significant but modest moves toward equality would suggest. It has annoyed or exhilarated every significant and most insignificant parts of our society, not the least of them higher education.

The emergence of black people out of the shadows as darkies and into the light as blacks is of course the throbbing center of the newest impulse toward equality. But the nation is still unraveling its oldest, most torturous, most redundant riddle—the settlement of its black people. For they, alone among America's immigrants, remain unsettled after three hundred years. Over these centuries they moved from slave plantations to rural hovels until they emerged in the twentieth century as a profoundly urban people still searching for their place in America. What changed slowest about them was their status in America. In a land where mobility seemed mandated and came to all but the damned, America's dark-skinned immigrants remain at the bottom. Only in the past two decades, beginning with the *Brown* decision, has there been any serious challenge to the permanency of the subterranean status of America's blacks and its other people of color.

So elastic was this new equality that it readily reached to accommodate women, the nation's unequal majority, as well. Following the

[16]Delivered at the 31st National Conference on Higher Education, in Chicago, Illinois, on March 7, 1976. Reprinted with permission of Eleanor Holmes Norton.

pattern of the black revolution, women began rapidly redefining the meaning of equality for themselves and thus for all of us in the 1970s. Should they fully succeed they could by the force of their numbers and the inherent radicalism of their demands cause society itself to make fundamental alterations.

But the open struggle of blacks for equality influenced many more than those who saw themselves as similarly situated. The original social energy of the period in which we still live derives from the civil rights movement. The anti-war movement, the women's rights movement, the anti-poverty movement, the struggles of other minorities—all patterned themselves in one fashion or another on the extraordinarily fertile civil rights struggle.

Most of the developments toward deeper equality took shape and substance from the 1960s, a period characterized by the upset of social convention and injustice. The decade of the sixties was in deep reaction to the spirit of the fifties, a decade rooted more in the notion that all men should be alike than that they should be equal. The young people of the sixties were a quintessential movement generation. They were as shaped by social movements as the generation of the fifties was shaped by none.

Some changes that characterize the new equality appear fairly permanent. The black struggle for equality has changed America as much as it has changed the status of blacks. White Americans today are the first white people in the nation's history to be decisively influenced in their values by the experience, aspirations, and actions of black Americans. Martin Luther King Jr. influenced America as much as John F. Kennedy. Aretha Franklin and James Brown shaped the style of this period in the way that Dinah Shore and Bing Crosby influenced their parents' youth.

Such changes may be new, but they emerge from a special historic context. The recent vintage of changes in matters of equality sometimes serves to obscure the fact of a much longer American obsession with this subject. Historians may differ as to when to date its beginnings. But the nationalization of the anti-slavery controversy with the Missouri Compromise surely demarks a point when slavery and thus equality became truly national concerns tied to the destiny of the nation itself. At least since 1820, then, I think it fair to say that Americans have had an unparalleled and unceasing struggle with themselves over the meaning and the virtue of equality.

For no other people has equality required such sustained attention for so long a time. Nowhere else in the world has the struggle over this single question been so intense, so dynamic, so costly.

I would include within this more than 150-year period not only the perplexing and omnipresent struggle of black men and women. For mounted on the same canvas are the collages of others, including the old women's-suffrage movement, the women's-equality movement of today, and the largely successful struggle of European immigrants for inclusion on terms of equality and mobility. The very diversity of the actors who have played out equality themes in America has contributed to the preoccupation of Americans with this subject.

The American experience with equality has been both tortured and exhilarating. At the most promising end of the scale, successive waves of poor immigrants—most entering as illiterate peasants—found spectacular economic success in one or two generations, a phenomenal mobility unprecedented in world history. Somewhere in between are white women who, with the right to vote, won a new sense of themselves after a long struggle. While their transformation in equality terms is incomplete and disappointing, no one can doubt what the past fifty years have done to make the American woman more equal, both in her home and in her transformed role as member of the workforce. At the low end of the scale, the national experience with black people has been a unique tragedy, characterized first by sustained oppression and then by furtive progress. Still the past two decades have raised uncommon hopes and produced unprecedented gains. At the very least, black people have come from psychological depths to which it would seem impossible to return.

In any case Americans have had more diverse and concentrated experience with the dynamics of equality than any other people in the world. This has given America the opportunity to disproportionately influence the very meaning of the world. The American experience has done as much to define equality for the world as the Russian Revolutionary period did to give reality to Marxism.

Examples of American leadership on matters of equality, leadership often carved out of painful experience, are legion. The choice of Martin Luther King Jr. for world recognition as recipient of the Nobel Peace Prize in 1964 did not come because of his leadership of an indigenous freedom movement in the United States. King's world status derives from the same process that made world and not merely national leaders of Gandhi and Lenin. All staged essentially national movements with such universal force and applicability, that they moved men and women across the face of the earth. King made the idea of racial equality plainer to millions than it had ever been before, just as Gandhi moved peasants everywhere to demand freedom from colonialism.

One could cite other examples of American pace setting in the conception of equality. The women's movement appears better developed in this country than in most others. The French have a new cabinet post for the *condition feminine* but underdeveloped notions of feminism and no strong activist movement. Russian and other East European women have won significant access to male jobs but very little change in sex roles. By contrast, American women, with historically better developed notions of equality to work with, are pursuing change in magnificent proportions from carefully circumscribed issues such as equal employment and universal child care to weighty philosophical issues whose resolution could virtually redefine womanhood and remake entire areas of human experience.

All of these developments toward greater equality in America have been influenced in no small measure by American higher education, both in its functional educational role and in its role as a social force. But Academe, like most other sections of our society, is experiencing some difficulty today, when pressure for equality implementation has succeeded the simple demand for common justice. New and more complicated equality themes have replaced easier notions of simple justice from the days of "Freedom Now."

Thus, you do well to hold a conference concerned with equality and quality in what appears to be a congenial and truly searching atmosphere. I think it fair to say that in a very real sense the country has traditionally depended on American higher education, more than on most others, for leadership on issues of equality. But in recent years there have been some uncharacteristically discordant chords emanating from Academe on matters of equality, seeming to challenge the applicability of equality principles to the university setting. These arguments have been made in such a way as to undermine the preeminent place of the American university as a locus for pushing the society toward the realization of its own highest ideals.

I do not fault academic voices for their criticism of this or that government approach to affirmative action in university employment, for example. There is, I assure you, much room for criticism. Moreover the university is in a position to offer the most useful of criticism, because of its own research and scholarly functions. Affirmative action should not be exempt from criticism from Academe simply because the university is affected.

Rather I would argue just the opposite: that the academic community is in a unique position to contribute to the perfection of techniques for achieving equality but has inexplicably hung back from this natural function in recent years. This can be seen both in areas where the university has some self-interest and in areas where it does not.

Let me cite just one where universities themselves are not implicated, simply for the purpose of making my point about the university lag in contributing to the resolution of increasingly difficult equality issues in America today. Consider busing, a technique encountering deepening trouble and unpopularity throughout the country. When Professor James Coleman recently suggested that busing had spurred white flight from the cities and had thus hurt school integration, something of a furor developed. This deepened when it was learned that the cities he had studied had indeed experienced flight but not busing. Many who believe in school integration now simply discount Dr. Coleman's view as that of just one more turncoat liberal adversary to integration. This, of course, is unfair to Professor Coleman. Busing, like any controversial technique, needs criticism if we are to have any hope of making improvements. But in the context of today's chilled climate for racial equality, a finding that comes out of a decidedly negative context will only contribute to controversy. The need is not so much for less criticism of the mechanisms of integration as it is for a more forthright search for answers to complicated new issues that arise as we untangle our tortured racial past.

Indeed the need for clear analysis suggesting pathways to permanent equality solutions is especially great today, particularly in light of the inadequacy of a number of techniques in use. But when the thrust is one of complaint, rather than of searching—that a technique, busing for example, is not working, without more—many hear only the sound of retreat. If not busing, what is proposed? In a country where racial degradation and separation have been the rule, few blacks are prepared to consider arguments based on the utility of various approaches to equality—not when whites have so often found the entire exercise of equality unuseful. This may not be a wholly rational response, but it is understandable. Professor Coleman's conclusions concerning busing might have been received differently had they arisen within a more balanced study. In the absence of a committed search for alternatives, civil rights advocates feel they will be a part of their own undoing if they acquiesce in doubts about busing or other integration techniques.

Who is in the best position to search for alternatives to this troublesome issue? Politicians who find the issue especially treacherous in the political marketplace? The government which feels the day-by-day pressure from both sides? Judges sworn to expand constitutional principle and ignore popular reaction? None is in a better position than the university where detachment and time are afforded to think through society's most difficult problems—from cures for diseases to, yes, school integration. How are we to account therefore for the scant study of the actual experience of children in integrated settings, except for the search for magical improvement in test scores many somehow expected school integration to produce? There is a danger that one hopeful technique, the magnet school—one with special features or additional resources designed to attract a ballanced role-mix—will fall by the way because of lack of study of what specific features make a school able to attract white students in this way. I have seen such magnets thrown together so carelessly that they fail, giving the hopeful magnet concept a bad name as just one more failed integration technique. And I have seen others that succeed brightly. One would think that some professor would be busily cataloging success and failure factors in magnet schools and by this time would be well on his way to developing a success model. My own Commission, hard pressed by budget cutbacks, is considering undertaking such a study in the absence of this kind of assistance from the academic community to meet urgent problems of school integration.

Busing is only one of a litany of issues produced by the new complexities of race, ethnicity, and sex in America where the need for thoughtful study is as clear as the neglect of scholarly attention. Just to mention two others among the most serious: The conflict between the values of seniority and affirmative action, a most difficult question, is greatly in need of the best conceptual treatment. Another is the awesomely complicated question of encouraging racially and economically diverse cities in the face of white flight, the flight of other middle income people, and the resulting catastrophic effect on the viability of the American city itself. Both of these are issues on which my small government agency, without a single Ph.D., has been struggling without federal or academic leadership.

Why problems of such magnitude have inspired so little academic attention is not altogether clear. But this failure on large issues of equality has not helped to create an affirmative and hospitable atmosphere once these issues have come closer to home.

And they have come home to roost in Academe on both faculty and student selection. The faculty discrimination issues have provoked much more hostile reaction from administrators and faculty than student selection matters, although the issues are at least of equal moment. The society has at least as great a stake in fair student selection as in fair faculty selection. Of course, the matter of self-interest is, I think you will agree, a bit clearer in one than in the other. In any case, the cries from college and university presidents and professors, almost all of them white men, have not been received by the public as disinterested laments.

I do not mean to imply that their points of criticism are totally without merit. What I am saying is that they have no right to ask what amounts to an exemption for the university from many of the procedures of the civil rights laws. While today most academic institutions have found their way toward a posture of compliance, the early out-cries, especially from the university presidents, called for a virtual exemption of colleges and universities from many of the only effective procedures that have been developed, all of which apply to every other large employer in the country. These techniques include an evaluation of confidential personnel records, a matter not without difficulty, but one also not beyond the reach of those interested in compliance with the civil rights laws. And goals and timetables for rectifying exclusion within universities have also been subject to special displeasure. This issue, which continues to plow discord in Academe, is also capable of resolution if compliance rather than avoidance is the goal.

The fact is that the blame for the way the controversy between the universities and HEW developed belongs with both sides. When compliance was first attempted, the universities responded like wounded deer, the victims of a predator that did not understand the sensitivity of the beast. Its traditional strong concern for equality was not summoned in this, its own personal equality crisis. No galaxy of professors presented themselves as a technical task force to bring some reason into the process. The university chose noncompliance until persistence by the federal government appeared to destroy that option.

In the same way HEW, which had seen the face of recalcitrance before, identified this as just another garden variety. The agency was mindful that women professors had filed a massive class action against the entire university community, to prod the Department into a more forthright discharge of its anti-discrimination duties. In this atmosphere the question of whether some serious work might be done by the Department to adapt its procedures to college and university employment systems did not arise until negotiations occurred, often only after painful confrontation and then, at least until recently, on an *ad hoc* rather than a systematic and comprehensive basis.

I believe that a sound case can be made that universities constitute a special case when it comes to anti-discrimination enforcement and therefore are in need of special assistance and perhaps even a system of race and sex analysis and implementation of remedies attuned to the peculiar contours of the university work place. As a technician with some experience in this field, I accept the view that factors which in other situations must be rigidly controlled, such as credentialism and broad discretion to evaluate a candidate, must have fuller sway in the selection of faculty. Moreover, I believe this need not lead to more lenient application of the anti-discrimination laws to universities than to other employers, a wholly unfair and unacceptable result. By not looking at the university system in this particularized way, HEW may have sown the seeds that have made enforcement so tough and controversial in colleges and universities.

But if the government should have developed and provided better technical assistance to the universities, it is universities themselves, which, ironically are the richest resource for creating the appropriate technology. No other employer in the nation was in a position to influence government equal opportunity policy in the way the university was and is. By merely playing the role society expects of it, Academe had within its hands the power to shut down the controversy over the procedures of compliance and, through research and scholarly study, submit alternatives.

I am not suggesting that the university might have designed its own mode of compliance to equal opportunity laws. I am saying that by regarding the matter of compliance adversarily and not as an honest question of considerable technical difficulty, the university defaulted in its commitment to equality and encouraged needless and harmful controversy. No group of professors undertook to look at these as serious questions for study. Instead some formed themselves into a committee to oppose affirmative action.

One professor has authored a recent book designed to show that court decisions and other government actions to enforce the civil rights laws have themselves discriminated against the majority, a work whose deficiencies begin with the author's failure to read and digest the relevant court decisions or to understand the basic law of remedies in our system of jurisprudence. Nowhere in all of corporate America, with its historic lack of identification with equality and association with prejudice, has so negative a development toward equality emerged. It has fallen to the university to speak for the recalcitrant employer.

Problems of equality in the university promise to accentuate, not diminish in the years ahead. While faculties doubled in the 1960s, with 30,000 new hires a year, in the 1980s only 6,000 new hires annually are expected, a replacement rate that itself may diminish, as the years of fantastic expansion are followed not even by stabilization, but, as likely as not, by retrenchment. Last month the U.S. Office of Education reported that in 1975 faculty women lost ground in both salary increase and rank. According to the report, "The average salaries of men continue to exceed the average salaries of women at every academic rank and at every institutional level, in both publicly and privately controlled institutions." If the university is to avoid becoming a haven for racial and sex discord, it must summon its own best traditions, marshall its decided skill, and absorb itself in designing strategies for genuine equality in Academe.

In the same way student selection policies need urgent attention. If student admission procedures have upset administrators and professors less than faculty selection, they have been of considerable concern in the society-at-large. Again, part of the blame rests squarely with government. Colleges and universities have been left almost totally to their own devices in designing techniques for the admission of disadvantaged minority students. The government encouraged the opening of opportunities but, as in the case of university affirmative action, provided no technical assistance.

The result was the *DeFunis* case and a number of others like it. These cases demonstrate that universities had considerably more good will than expertise in criteria for evaluating disadvantaged minority students, who have been historically excluded from their student population. That good will has substantially diminished in the face of budgetary cutbacks and the controversy emanating from these very cases. But the problem will remain until someone decides to consider it an issue worthy of serious research and study. As with affirmative action technology, I cannot avoid asking again, who is in a better position than academicians themselves.

Neither the university nor the government has chosen to move toward rational problem solving here either. Instead court cases continue to make this explosive issue more so. The adversarial route has been chosen over the scholarly search.

Here the government is particularly at fault, for there has been a persuasive appeal for help on this matter before HEW for almost two years. After the inconclusive Supreme Court decision in the *DeFunis* case I talked with the heads of six national racial and ethnic organizations, all with headquarters in New York, who had been on opposite sides of the case. The following letter to then HEW Secretary Caspar Weinberger resulted:

"Dear Dr. Weinberger:

"While the undersigned organizations have taken varying positions on the *DeFunis* case, we have, over the years worked closely in support of civil rights and human freedom.

"We all recognize that the process of creating affirmative action is not an exact science. It is only in the past few years that the nation has begun the development of procedures for dismantling discrimination.

"All of us wish to avoid polarization. We agree that a primary goal for all of us is the elimination of all forms of discrimination and the establishment of affirmative actions and processes that will provide equal opportunity within our constitutional framework.

"Since the issues raised by the *DeFunis* case remain, we believe that an early response from HEW, within whose jurisdiction such matters lie, is indicated. We are therefore requesting that you direct the issuance of non-discriminatory guidelines clarifying how educational institutions can best develop appropriate tools for special efforts to recruit persons from previously excluded groups."

This letter was signed by the heads of the Anti-Defamation League of B'nai Brith, the American Jewish Committee, the American Jewish Congress, the NAACP, the National Urban League, and the Puerto Rican Legal Defense and Educational Fund.

Mr. Weinberger reacted immediately and a departmental study and letter of guidelines to college and university presidents were promised. Over a year later, when Dr. Weinberger was about to resign, I wrote to remind him that all were awaiting the promised guidance and was assured that the matter would be carried on by his successor in the department. Now almost another year has passed with no resolution of these issues.

This is inexcusable neglect from the federal government. The standards are theirs to give. Still government default need not have been decisive on the question. The knowledge and skills to develop the fair admission devices are found in special abundance among various disciplines in the very universities that now must commit resources instead to fighting court cases. Once again Academe has lost its way on issues that were thought to be of special concern.

In a very special way the country needs you who teach and administer higher education today. Rearrangements among the races and sexes and classes appear too complicated for many. The swirling events of our time seem to many not the inevitable content of modern change but a signal of endemic instability in American life. The line between rapid, dynamic change and meandering, perplexing instability has always been thin. But that line is not drawn entirely by events. It is drawn also by those who shape and react to events.

At such times, education is or should be a valuable hedge against bewilderment and panic. More than most Americans, educational leaders understand the reasons for the fear of change. After all, until the twentieth century most of the world's people lived virtually changeless lives. Change was a matter of the seasons or of youth mellowing into old age, which often came by forty. Change itself is a twentieth century phenomenon. Change has made all our lives more difficult. But it has also made them more rewarding. We are richer but we are also more burdened.

I would be the first to agree that higher education cannot and should not always pursue the utilitarian. You are not society's anointed problem-solvers. But you have always ventured special concern for equality in America. It is time to step forward once again. Someone needs to stand with both reason and justice. If not you, who?

# The Future Is Now: A Zest for Living[17]

Walter F. Stromer

*Born 1920, Iowa City, IA; U.S. Army, 1943-45; B.A., Hastings College, 1949; M.A., 1950, Ph.D., 1953, University of Denver; professor, Cornell College, 1954–.*

## Editor's introduction

Dr. Walter F. Stromer, a blind professor of speech communication at Cornell College, addressed a conference for the parents of students at the Indiana School for the Blind. After reviewing how disabled people have been treated throughout history, Dr. Stromer noted that employment of the physically challenged is still a major problem. He also remarked that it should not be assumed that the handicapped are unhappy. Given a little independence and a little faith, Stromer asserted, he had confidence that the handicapped, in particular the blind children of those present at this conference, could have successful careers and lead fruitful, rewarding lives.

---

When a man has to travel four hundred miles to find an audience to listen to him you have to wonder how things are going for him back home. But my excuse for being here is that some wonderful people who heard me speak years ago have been kind enough to invite me back and that kind of flattery is hard to resist.

When I was told that the title of this talk was to be "The Future Is Now," I was puzzled. When I was also told that it had been suggested by a psychiatrist, my first impulse was to turn the tables and to analyze the analyst. On second thought, I decided that this was a topic I could live with and that it expresses something which I truly believe. I feel strongly that we should learn from the past and that we have a responsibility to those who come after us, but that the most important task for us is to live this day and this moment to the best of our ability.

Since many of you here are parents of blind children, I want to talk first about what has been done in the past for the blind and other handicapped. Then I want to make some tentative suggestions that may be of help to you in the future, which begins now.

Those wonderful Greeks of twenty-five hundred years ago, to whom we owe so much, used to put defective babies in clay jars beside the road and let them die. In Rome such children were put into wicker baskets and put out on the Tiber river, to be swept away and drowned somewhere downstream. In many countries defective babies were staked out on the mountains to die of exposure or to be eaten by animals.

These earlier ancestors of ours were not entirely lacking in compassion; but, they were often in real danger of being exterminated by famine or flood or marauding enemies, and survival of the group had to be put ahead of the weakest members who could not help themselves. Caring for the handicapped, as we know it, could not really take place until societies became somewhat stable and had some surplus food and some leisure time for some members.

Lack of resources was not the only factor that kept society from humane treatment of its disabled members. Attitudes were also involved. Epilepsy was once thought to be caused by the moon. To be moonstruck was to be deranged or insane. What we call mental illness was once attributed to possession by demons, who in one case in the Bible were driven out of the man into a herd of swine. Blindness and other conditions were connected with sin, as when the disciples asked Christ, about the blind man, "who sinned, this man or his parents?" As long as the causes of disability are thought to

[17]Delivered at the Indiana School for the Blind, in Indianapolis, Indiana, on April 23, 1982. Reprinted with permission of Walter F. Stromer.

be supernatural, either godly or satanic, the only cure will have to be supernatural, such as prayers, incantations or exorcisms; but, not much will get done at the local human level.

Slowly attitudes began to change. In the 4th century A.D., a Christian bishop urged compassion for the retarded. In the 9th century in Baghdad, the Caliph ordered that those getting out of hospitals should be given a sum of money to tide them over until they could go to work. Yet, at this same time, in other parts of Europe people were being blinded for committing such crimes as poaching, that is hunting on land which they did not own. Ironically the church fathers of that day approved of blinding instead of putting the person to death because they felt that blinding would give the victim more time to repent of his sins.

Centuries later the defectives—the stutterers, those with pointed heads, the grossly deformed—were exhibited in cages, in carnivals and sideshows for the amusement and amazement of the public. After that, came they asylums and the institutions where the defectives were locked away. Others were locked away in attics or back bedrooms until their tortured bodies became torturing skeletons in the family closet.

As late as World War II, the federal government did not include blind people in this country as eligible for rehabilitation funds. It was thought that they could not be rehabilitated but would simply have to exist on welfare. Consider how far we have come. Last year was the International year of the Disabled Person. This year has been declared the National Year of the Disabled Person in this country. We know that there are between 30 and 40 million disabled persons in this country and about 450 million in the world. Just the fact that we can count them, even approximately, is a mark of our progress. In the Middle Ages young children were not even counted in the census because it was assumed that most of them would die by the age of twelve. Why bother counting?

Another indication of concern and our openness to the subject is the fact that there are 120 organizations for disabled. There are more than 130 wheelchair basketball teams. A totally deaf woman holds the world speed record for driving a vehicle on land. The president of Hofstra University is a man with cerebral palsy. Recently a young blind woman was involved in a down-hill skiing competition in Switzerland, while two other blind skiers and four sighted companions set out to ski across Lapland.

In the area of entertainment, we have had the play "Butterflies are Free," about a blind young man, and "Whose Life Is it, Anyway?" about a quadraplegic veteran. The movie "Inside Moves" deals with disabilities. The television movie, "Elephant Man," dealt with one who was grossly deformed. A retarded boy was permitted to play himself in a movie about the retarded instead of having the role played by a professional actor. From Seattle, you can rent a film about a boy who lost both legs and went on to become a football coach. In Dallas, a television station devotes several minutes each day to advertising available children. These children are not for sale for immoral purposes but they are handicapped children available for adoption.

Yet with all this progress we must admit that there are still problems. Many of them are in the area of employment. Of those who are paralyzed, almost 90 percent are unemployed. Of the blind, Job Opportunities for the Blind estimates that 70 percent of the blind are unemployed or underemployed. Harold Krents, graduate of Harvard Law School, and inspiration for the movie and play, "Butterflies are Free," applied to forty law firms before he got a job.

Taking it all together, the good and the bad, I think it is not unreasonable to say that if one must live as a handicapped person, this time and this place is one of the best that history has known.

Next, I would like to talk especially to those of you who are parents of blind children about some tentative suggestions as to how you can help your child and yourself. I do this with some hesitation because I knew so much more about child rearing before we had children than I do now.

One of the first things you can do is to believe sincerely that raw fish tastes good. I use this example because we have a Japanese student who has stayed with us often who assures me that raw fish is delicious. My mind says it's true. My stomach says, don't touch it. It is hard for us really to believe that people can enjoy food which we consider repulsive. In the same way, it is hard for us to believe that others can be happy without all the things that make us happy. For example, people will look at one who is blind and say, "How terrible, how tragic, how miserable it must be without sight." Yet, I can assure you from my personal experience and from contact with many blind people, that blindness need not result in constant unhappiness. Keep in mind that we have no reliable external measures of happiness, no brain scan, no blood test. About the best we can do is to ask people if they are happy. While I may be better informed on the happiness of blind people than you, still when it comes to deaf-blindness, my own reaction is very similar to yours. I find myself thinking, "How tragic, how difficult." I read recently about a man and wife, both deaf-blind, taking training at the Helen Keller Center on Long Island. When they want to communicate, one goes to the kitchen table and pounds on it to make the floor vibrate. Then they meet at the table and if they are angry they spell words into each others hands rapidly. My reaction was, "How tragic, how inadequate, how frustrating. How much better it would be if they could shout at each other, or better still if they could see each other and make faces." Or would it be better? Who are we to say that their way of communicating feelings or frustration is better or worse than ours? This same deaf-blind man laid tile for his basement floor; he hung paper on the walls of his kitchen, and he travels around the city by subway. Is he less happy than we are? I doubt it. Yes, he does miss out on things you and I take for granted. Is he aware of what he is missing? Yes, to some extent I am sure the deaf-blind are aware that life could be simpler and less frustrating if they could see or hear, or both. But I doubt that they spent much time fretting about it. In general, it seems to be the nature of living organisms to adapt as best they can to the circumstances that exist. Does the worm wish it could fly like the robin? Does the robin regret not having the wings of an eagle? But you will say people are different from the lower animals. Yes, they are. Yes, humans can worry and envy and regret. Still, it is amazing how people with stable personalities can have their bodies broken and pick up the few remaining pieces and make a life of them.

You and I can help handicapped people by letting them define happiness for themselves. We can make life more miserable for them if we constantly remind them of how terrible we feel because of what they are missing. When we do that we are really saying to them, "Please get rid of your handicap because it makes me so uncomfortable."

Let me illustrate how disabled people can be happy in their ignorance. Sometimes during a long Iowa winter I walk to class in the morning and decide it's a nice day because I can feel the sun warming my back. Then some sighted person comes along and says, "It's such a dull, depressing day." To him it is dull because the sun is under the clouds. That doesn't really destroy my happiness, and I do need to be aware that other people perceive the world in ways other than I do. I need to recognize that, just as I need to turn on lights in a room for the benefit of others even though I don't need them. So I will continue to be happy about the warm sun while my friend is depressed by the gray clouds. And, on other days, I will be depressed by the cold while he enjoys the bright, but cold, sunshine. We can each find happiness in our own way.

Is this so different from what happens to any of you? You are all missing out on some success or happiness. You fathers are all disabled in some ways. Some of you are too short to be successful basketball players, and others of you are too scrawny to be professional football players. Do you cry yourselves to sleep every night because of what you are missing? I doubt it. And, you mothers who are lacking the face or the figure to appear on a movie screen, do you beat your fists on the kitchen counter all day and moan about the things you can't do? I'm sure you go on with the business of living and do the best you can. Allow handicapped persons to do the same. If they like raw fish, let them eat it.

My next suggestion for you as parents is that you be like the character in magazine ads for Hastings piston rings years ago. They showed a picture of a big muscle man with a scroungy beard with a friendly smile, and the caption was, "Tough, but oh so gentle." That is a good motto for parents—to be tough, but gentle. It is especially apt for the parents of handicapped children. Just being a parent, of any child, means that you have to be gentle and protective or the child will not survive the first few years of life. Yet, somewhere along the way, you have to be as tough as the mother bear who cuffs the cubs on the snout to let them know that now is the time to leave home and get out on their own. It will be especially hard for you as parents of a blind child to watch your child bump into things or get cut and bruised and still to sit back calmly and say, "live and learn." But handicapped children, more than others, need to have such toughening experiences if they are to grow up as sturdy oaks instead of delicate African violets. All through life, society will tend to overprotect and shelter those who are disabled. They will need a little extra measure of toughness, of assertiveness, of independence if they are to get their fair share of rights and freedoms. It may help you in learning to be tough if you will remember that most of the accidents that happen to blind people are not serious, and almost never fatal. The greatest damage is always to the loved ones who watch things happen, and to the pride of the blind or disabled person.

Last winter I was hurrying to the chapel for a convocation program. I took a short cut along a narrow sidewalk, got too far off to the left side, and got clipped just above my left eye by a tree branch stump where it had been cut off. The branch drew blood, and I knew it. I had no more than sat down in the chapel than one of my students came along and said, "Oh, you're hurt; are you all right?" I said, "Yes," and I wanted to tell him to go away and let me suffer in silence. After chapel, I did not want to go back to the office because I knew the secretary would notice and make a fuss. I didn't even want to go home for lunch because I thought my wife would wrap me in bandages and keep me in the house for a month. What was hurt was my pride. I had demonstrated to others that I was careless, or worse, that blind people can't walk across the campus without bumping into things.

You can help most if you will encourage your child to be independent, to move out, to take risks. If there is a cut or a bruise, be cheerful about cleaning it up and applying a Bandaid and then go about your business. If you can do that, you will be saying most eloquently to your child, "I have confidence in you; keep trying."

My last suggestion to you is to believe in yourself. You are here at this conference to get help and reassurance from various experts. I am sure they have much to offer and I hope you will learn from them. Never forget that in one way you are more expert than any teacher, counselor or psychiatrist you will ever meet. You are expert in knowing how it feels to have your life and your life blood wrapped up in a handicapped child, and to live with that investment twenty-four hours a day, every day of the year. That is very different from being a professional helper who deals with the problem for an hour a week, or an hour a day, or even six hours a day. We need professionals who can be detached and objective and sometimes we, as parents, need to learn some of that detachment of perspective. If ever the professional helpers get so detached that they forgot the depth of our feelings, please feel free to remind them that you, too, have some expertise. Some years ago, I came across a book by a French psychoanalyst, Alfred Adler. In the first chapter of his book he wrote, "When parents come to me with a problem about their child and they tell me what they have been doing, my first response is to say,' I think you're on the right track,' because parents carry a heavy burden and they need all the support they can get." I wish I could meet that psychoanalyst and hug him and say, "Thank you for understanding."

I want you to learn all you can from the professionals here or wherever you are. I might even agree with them that you need to change your behavior in some ways. I do not want you to feel that you are stupid and worthless and that you are not doing anything right. If you do that, you won't be a good role model for your child. I want your child to be happy, but part of that will come about if your child sees you as parents who find life enjoyable and challenging. So—listen to the experts, but also trust yourself.

If I may summarize briefly, let me remind you how far we have come in a mere two thousand years, such a little time in the long history of the world. Next, believe in raw fish; that is, give handicapped people much freedom in deciding what they enjoy. Try to be both tough and gentle; and, finally, listen to others but also trust yourself. I think the greatest gift you can give your child is a zest for living, a spirit of wonder and adventure, and a confidence that the problems of life can be solved or endured.

In the words of a Chancellor who was both a tyrant and a romantic, Otto von Bismarck, "With confidence in God, put on the spurs and let the wild horse of life fly with you over stones and hedges, prepared to break your neck, but always, always, without fear."

If that is a bit too romantic, let me suggest two lines from a Kipling poem. A Russian who spent seven years in Siberia said that these lines helped sustain him. And, if you will update the sexist language to make it "man or woman," perhaps these lines will help you begin the future now: "If you can fill the unforgiving minute with sixty seconds worth of distance run, yours is the world and all that's in it, and which is more, you'll be a man, my son."

# Days of Remembrance[18]

Elie Wiesel

*Born September 30, 1928, Sighet, Romania; foreign correspondent,* Yedio Ahronoth *and* Jewish Daily Forward, *1949–; professor, City University of New York, 1972-76; professor, Boston University, 1976–; winner of the Nobel Peace Prize, 1986; author,* Souls on Fire *(1972),* The Town Beyond the Wall *(1981),* The Golem *(1983),* Somewhere a Master *(1984),* The Jews of Silence *(1987),* The Night Trilogy *(1987),* From the Kingdom of Memory *(1990),* The Forgotten *(1995),* The Trial of God *(1995),* Twilight *(1995),* All Rivers Run to the Sea *(1996),* A Beggar in Jerusalem *(1997).*

## Editor's introduction

To honor the six million Jews murdered during the Nazi holocaust, the United States Holocaust Memorial Council leads the nation in an annual Day of Remembrance. At the 1984 Day of Remembrance, Elie Wiesel, a recognized spokesperson for survivors of the Holocaust, and a concentration camp survivor himself, spoke to senators and representatives from both political parties. In his speech, Mr. Wiesel reminded his audience that then recent events, including the Soviet imprisonment of Cambodian refugees and the Iranian persecution of the Baha'i people, demonstrate that the world is not yet free from the conditions that led to the Holocaust.

---

Mr. Vice President, Congressman Yates, distinguished members of the House and Senate, fellow survivors, friends:

For some of us, this is the most solemn and awesome day of the year. We delve into the darkest recesses of our memory only to confront and evoke a vanished universe surrounded by flames and penetrated by silence. The living and the dead locked together as they are during Kol Nidre services, young and old, pious and secular, princes and madmen, sages and wanderers, beggars and dreamers. On this day, Mr. Vice President and friends, we close our eyes and we see them—an eerie procession which slowly, meditatingly, walks toward angels of death carried on wings of night into night. We see them as you see us. We are the link between you and them.

And, therefore, we thank you, members of the House and Senate, and Mr. Vice President, for allowing us to be that link. We thank you, people of the United States, for creating a framework in which we could share visions and memories that intrude, defy language and comprehension. On behalf of the Holocaust Memorial Council, its members, its Board of Advisers, its Second Generation Advisers, its staff, its friends and allies, we thank all of you for joining us today.

It is symbolic that our commemoration takes place in this August hall of legislation and commitment to law, and commitment to humanity. What we are teaching the world from this room, thanks to you, Members of the House and the Senate, is that laws must be human. Laws are to serve humanity and not destroy it. Laws are given to human beings to perfect life and not to profane it. Laws, too, became corrupt once upon a time. And here with your deed and our words, we shall shield laws in the future.

And so once more, as we have done since 1979, on this Day of Remembrance we gather from all the corners of exile to tell tales—tales of fire and tales of despair and tales of defiance—tales that we must tell lest we are crushed by our memories. In remembering them, remembering the victims in the ghettos and camps and the prisons, we become aware

[18]Delivered in the Rotunda of the Capitol, in Washington, D.C., on April 30, 1984. Reprinted with permission of Elie Wiesel.

of man's singular vulnerability but also of his stunning ability to transcend it.

We remember the killers and we lose our faith in humanity. But then we remember the victims and, though scarred, our faith is restored—it must be. The fact that the Jewish victims never became executioners, that they never victimized others, that they remained Jewish to the end—human to the end—that inside ghettos and death camps, my God, inside gas chambers, they could speak of God, to God. They could say: *S'hma Yisroael Adonai Elohenu, Adonai Echad*—God is God and God is One and God is the Lord of Creation. To say those words there on the threshold of death and oblivion must restore our faith in them and therefore in humankind. We think of the victims and we learn that despair is not the solution. Despair is the question. And that is why we gather year after year—to fight despair; and not only mine—ours.

As a son of the Jewish people, as a citizen who is proud to be a member of the American people, I live with a memory of Jewish children and their parents. It has been our task, it will remain our task, to maintain that memory alive. But then we remember not because we seek vengeance; we don't believe in it. We only seek justice. We do not aim to hurt, only to sensitize. We believe that by retelling our tales we might help our contemporaries by making them aware of what could happen to human beings when they live in an inhuman society surrounded and penetrated by indifference on one hand, evil on the other, with so few opposing evil and indifference. That is why I allow myself at times to see in the Holocaust an analogy only to itself, meaning that nothing should be compared to it but that everything must be related to it. It is because of what we endured that we must try to help victims everywhere today: the Baha'is in Iran who are being murdered by the dictatorship in Iran; the Miskitos on the border of Nicaragua; we must help the Boat People who are still seeking refuge; the Cambodian refugees; and the prisoners, so many of them, in Communist jails. It is because we remember what has been done to our people that we must plead at every opportunity, in this House and in all other houses, for Anatoly Scharansky, Iosif Begun, Vladmir Slepack, and all the dissidents and prisoners who are in jail waiting for someone to shake off humankind's indifference. If they were to lose faith in us, we should be damned. It is because we remember the solitude of Jews in those times that we feel so linked to and proud of the state of Israel today. We survivors, our friends and allies, are grateful to Israel, grateful to a people simply for existing, for inspiring us to keep faith in a certain form of humanity and tradition.

While we remember the victims we also remember those who tried to help us—the Raoul Wallenbergs and the Oskar Shindlers, as Congressman Yates said. They were so few and they were so alone. It breaks our heart to think of their solitude, of their sacrifice. Memory is not exclusive. Memory is inclusive. It is because we remember the singular aspect of the tragedy that we remember its universality. We must also think of tomorrow as though it would be part of our memory. I think the world unleashed madness forty years ago and that madness is still dominating spirits and minds of too many countries. There are too many signals of danger—racism, anti-semitism, bigotry, fanaticism. We are scared of what humankind could do to itself. Therefore, we tell the story.

In conclusion, Mr. Vice President, may I quote to you a legend of the great masterwork of human civilization and culture, the Talmud. The Talmud tells us that when God gave the law to the people of Israel he lifted up Mount Sinai over the heads of the Jewish people and said: "If you accept the law, you shall live. If not, you shall die." And so, we accepted the law.

I have the feeling today, Mr. Vice President and friends, that God has lifted above our heads a mountain of fire, and it is as though God were to say to us: If you obey the law—if you remember that we are all children of one father, if you remember that whatever happened to one people must affect all other people, if you remember that stupid cruelty is absurd and grotesque, and it is not in hurting people that one can redeem oneself—if you remember, you shall live and if not—but we must remember.

# We've Just Begun[19]

Eleanor C. Smeal

*Born July 30, 1939, Ashtabula, OH; B.A., Duke University, 1961; M.A., University of Florida, 1963; secretary-treasurer, Allegheny County Council, 1971-72; chairwoman, Equal Rights Amendment (ERA) Strike Force, 1977–; president, National Organization for Women (NOW), 1977-83, 1985-87; co-founder, president, Fund for the Feminist Majority, 1987–; author,* Why and How Women Will Elect the Next President *(1984).*

## Editor's introduction

Eleanor C. Smeal, former president of the National Organization for Women, addressed over 300 NOW members and journalists in this speech. In the address, Smeal reiterated the central theme of her campaign for the NOW presidency, being the degree and type of activism the organization should adopt. Contending that the political Right has long been an enemy of the women's movement, Smeal urged feminists to take a more aggressive role in opposing what she perceived to be the rising tide of conservatism.

---

If I ever doubted whether it was time to raise hell, all I had to do was read today's newspapers. The three-judge panel of the Ninth Circuit Court said that the 1964 Civil Rights Act does not obligate the state of Washington to eliminate an economic inequality which it did not create. That's the great principle in jurisprudence of Adam and Eve. Take it to your creator. God knows that man, who created this system of injustice that we work under, has no responsibility.

A lot of people would ask me what my reaction to that decision is. I say it's only fighting mad. We intend to break out of the ghetto of low wages that has been created for us one way or another.

What the Washington case shows is that we have to fight simultaneously on several fronts. While we were fighting in the court, we were also fighting in the state legislature in Washington state. The Washington state legislature has passed a law there that says by 1993 they are going to have pay equity in the state system and, in fact, the legislature has passed a $42 million back pay appropriation to help correct the inequity. There would have been no gains there if we had not fought the court case.

I believe the Washington state case set off a revolution in the fight to break out of the wage ghetto for women. And right now, throughout this country, in some 100 jurisdictions, similar pay equity cases are being fought through the courts. Or we're pursuing legislation at the state level. Or we're pursuing county commission ordinances to change the inequities.

And, as we fight in these arenas, where the real battle is taking place is in the court of public opinion. This three-man panel in the Ninth Circuit did not make this decision in a vacuum. They read the newspapers. They read what the right wing is saying, what business is saying. They know only too well what the opposition is saying about comparable worth and equal pay.

The lines about a "cockamamie" idea, about "looney-tunes," have gotten out there far more than the fight for justice, and that's why I think it's time to raise hell, to spread the word, to organize women. Because there's no question in my mind but that rights are never won unless people are willing to fight for them.

In 1848, some women and men met in a very, very small little town, Seneca Falls, and they wrote a Declaration of Human Sentiments.

[19]Delivered to the National Press Club, in Washington, D.C., on December 5, 1985. Reprinted with permission of Eleanor C. Smeal.

The Declaration of Human Sentiments was modeled after our own Declaration of Independence, and it was very, very, simple. They said, "We hold these truths to be self-evident, that all men and women are created equal. That they are endowed by their Creator with certain inalienable rights, and among these are life, liberty, and the pursuit of happiness." I think it's time for the feminist movement, for the progressive movement, to review history and declare their own independence. It is time that we stop thinking about what is fashionable and what is not fashionable in this city, what's in and what is not in. I am told that when I say it's time to go into the streets these are the politics of the '60s.

The politics of the '60s . . . you know we could have one decade, those of us who are concerned about human rights in this century, but God forbid if we take a little more. We can have that little decade. But, when we're trying to fight to make sure that there is forward movement, and progress, and that the great gains of the civil rights decade of the '60s are not lost, then we are told that we are passé.

We want to use terms like equal opportunity employer, but we don't want them to mean anything. We want to just feel good. Well, the job of a person fighting for equality is not to make anybody feel good while there's injustice in our system, but to make us all uncomfortable.

The right wing, I feel, is being given a honeymoon, an outrageous honeymoon. Jerry Falwell just took a whirlwind, five-day trip to South Africa in the pursuit of the myth of the happy slave. Jerry Falwell went there and, no question about it, he found a few blacks who didn't agree with Bishop Tutu. In fact, he could once again pursue the classic defense of injustice, by justifying no change or ever-so-imperceptively-small change, on the basis that change will hurt the victims of injustice.

Well, we know that there was a huge uproar over Jerry Falwell's trip. His thinly veiled racism was seen by many of us for what it was. But that thinly veiled racism and, in my opinion, sexism, is running rampant in this country, and we are hardly questioning it.

In reviewing all the articles about what the president is going to do about the sanctions, we constantly see that little phrase, "He'll veto it if he thinks it will hurt the blacks." The only time we ever care about what the victims of injustice think is when we try to change the injustice itself.

After 15 years of fighting for women's equality, the only time I'm ever asked what women think is when I'm asked, "Mrs. Smeal (and they do generally say' Mrs.'), how many women agree with you anyway?" And invariably, as we march down the street, some woman is interviewed who thinks we're all nuts. She thinks it's just perfectly fine the way it is. And that's it. Dismiss it. If we don't represent huge numbers, if there's not an instant poll right now, whatever the injustice is, it's okay.

Look at what this three-judge panel did. They are very educated men. They ruled that you don't even have to deal with injustice as long as everybody else does the same thing. That's called the free market system. You get away with discrimination if everybody else practices discrimination. Justifying the injustice.

We have a lot of experience in justifying injustice. In fighting it, we have ever so little experience. We recall the great names who have fought injustice. But we make sure of one thing—that they're all dead. Well, there's a lot of us around and we've got a lot of kick left in us, and we intend to raise hell while we're still living. And I don't think we can overcome any too soon.

We are fighting, I believe, for fundamental liberty and justice in our lives. Look at the abortion issue—the right to determine when and if you're going to be pregnant—really, the right to survive. Oh, I do love the great intellectual questions, such as, "Does a fertilized egg have more rights than I do?"

You know, I'm not debating that very much. I can't get over the fact that most people who want to debate this question are men. I'm not a sexist, and I generally do not call attention to the sex of my opposition, but I can't help noticing that most of the people picketing abortion clinics also are males. The Jerry Falwells, the Jesse Helmses, the Orrin Hatches—they never will have to face this decision. But we do.

I feel, without question, that we are dealing with life and death, that women have a right for their lives and their opportunities. And more importantly, every person on the face of this earth has an obligation to make her or his own decisions that impact on her or his own life.

Right now we are, I think, abandoning one of the great principles of our country: freedom of religion. The Pope has just visited Kenya and he said to that starving nation that birth control is wrong, a country whose average size of family is seven, that is racked by starvation. You know, in the sub-Saharan Desert area, nine million people will starve this year and 150 million people are at different levels of starvation. The average age of death is four. And he preaches no birth control.

We hardly can feed the people we have, and he preaches no birth control. That message is not just a message for Kenya. That message is having world-wide impact, and it's having an impact right here in this country.

The fight to outlaw abortion is fundamentally an attack on birth control. Let there be no mistake about that. It's fundamentally an attack on freedom of religion, and it's fundamentally an attack on a woman's right to her life and her pursuit of happiness.

I believe that every woman and every man who cares about a quality of life worth fighting for had better stand up, while they can still stand up, and join with us in a fight to keep abortion and birth control safe and legal. That's why I am organizing a mass mobilization in the spring of 1986 for abortion and birth control. I hope hundreds of thousands of people come here to Washington, but that will be only the first of many marches and many acts.

You know, there are a lot of people who want to advise us, who think we should operate only within the system of passing laws and getting Supreme Court decisions. Well, we did that with abortion. There is a Supreme Court decision that legalizes it, and, as you know, the opposition is not accepting that ruling as permanent. They are mobilizing. They are in the streets. They are threatening life and safety. They are using the tactics of the '60s in 1985. They're using tactics that they claim are those of civil rights (violent and non-violent), and they're fighting for what they believe in. They are very loud for a very small minority. Those of us who believe that women have the right to birth control and abortion must fight back. The Supreme Court alone cannot stand and defend the fundamental rights of people.

Thomas Jefferson once said that "the price of liberty is eternal vigilance." We also must be prepared to march, prepared to fight, and prepared to defend our liberty. We also must be prepared to fight to expand our liberties. We cannot just fight for the gains of yesteryear. We must fight for full equality.

The fight for the Equal Rights Amendment, I am told, is something we should give up. Well, we're not about to give it up. We're not about to give it up because we have a job to complete and the dream of full equality for all women to fulfill. The case-by-case approach is intolerable. Full equality is essential. But, if we don't fight for the dream of full equality, we will watch it be eroded statute-by-statute and case-by-case. So, we are going to make sure that we mount a campaign, this time at the state level in Vermont that will show that, indeed, there is plenty of fight left in the Equal Rights Amendment.

When the suffragists were stopped at the state level, they went to the federal level. And when they were stopped at the federal level, they went back to the state level. And they kept it up. For 56 state referendum campaigns, 480 legislative campaigns, 470 state constitutional campaigns, 277 state party campaigns, 30 national party conventions, 19 campaigns, and 19 successive Congresses, they kept it up. They kept it up until suffrage was theirs. And I believe we must keep it up, and keep it up, until equality is ours.

And I don't think we should step back from any hard or tough question. The opposition has a way of throwing every issue of the day at us, and a way of pretending that they are the only righteous people on this earth.

They claim we are the destroyers of the family, that we are the people without morals, and without concerns for the future. They make claims such as. "ERA leads to AIDS." They try to make this great connection. And we either laugh, because we don't know what to do with it, or we avoid the issue. I say it's time to stop avoiding these issues. They're not joking matters.

The right wing has a way of always singling out some class of people in our society and making them the untouchables, claiming God's wrath is upon them. They teach bigotry and hate, and we've got to recognize that for what it is. When they say ERA leads to AIDS, they are going after an oppressed class of people, lesbians and gay men. They are spreading ignorance and hate that could lead to the demise of all of us, because this is a dreadful disease that is spreading throughout the population of the world.

We are proud of fighting for the liberty of all people, and we are proud that we fight for gay and lesbian rights. We won't allow this issue to be distorted or to be used against women's equality. We won't step back from any issue. We will recognize bigotry for what it is, wherever it raises its ugly head. And we intend to wrap it around the neck of the right wing as we fight for liberty and justice for all.

I feel that one of the biggest problems that we have is that we haven't taken the right wing, fascist opposition seriously enough. In 1957 to 1961, I was at Duke University. I didn't know very much about the South. I was raised along the Great Lakes, around Erie, Pennsylvania. When I went to college, I decided to go to Duke. I didn't know that it was segregated. I had read about segregation, but I didn't know what it meant. I was first generation Italian-American. I could tell you all about discrimination against Italians, but I didn't know very much about discrimination against black people in the South.

But I got a crash course. Before you knew it, I was on the picket line at some movie theater in downtown Durham. It outraged me that black people were only allowed to sit in the un-air-conditioned balcony. So, when they asked for volunteers, I ended up there. The thing I will never forget is being called a "nigger-lover" and being spat on, because I believed people had a right to sit anywhere they wanted when they bought a ticket. I couldn't get over that hatred. I couldn't get over what made them think it was all right to call me such names.

The reason I bring this up now is because we're about to fight all over again unless we make a stand today. The Civil Rights Restoration Act is in Congress, and it's being tied up by all kinds of amendments. It's being called an abortion issue.

You know, when they want to kill something these days that deals with civil rights or women's rights, they slap on an abortion amendment. They make it an abortion issue. The great Civil Rights Act of 1964 is in trouble. Title IX for educational rights for women is in trouble. The Older American Discrimination Act is in trouble as well as protection for the physically disabled. Why? Because the Supreme Court and the Reagan administration have ruled that the federal government can fund discrimination. We're about to see the unraveling of all the gains of the last 30 and 40 years.

Well, there's no way we're going backwards.

We're going to launch an emergency campaign to save the Civil Rights Act, and I don't want to hear any American praise Martin Luther King or any other great civil rights leader if that person isn't doing anything to save the Civil Rights Act in 1985. It's time to show where you stand today, not to recall the great triumphs for human progress of yesterday. I want to see a campaign that will stir the soul of this country again for justice.

I don't want to hear that we don't have idealism in this country, that the young kids only are interested in the almighty dollar and don't really care about the fight for equality and justice. I believe they do, so we're launching a campus campaign to save the Civil Rights Restoration Act, to save women's rights, and to move forward.

There's a movie out now called "Back to the Future." I can't say I'm a movie buff, but I think it's about time we went back to the business of the future of this country and stopped romanticizing the eighteenth and nineteenth centuries. We must look to the future of this nation and work to make this world safe for justice.

I also believe that we're on the verge of a major comeback in the women's movement. You should know that, according to a Lou Harris survey, 43´of the American people believe we have just begun. Now, there's one American who I don't quote much, but there's one thing on which I agree with him: "You ain't seen nothing yet."

We've just begun. We are going to lead a movement that will be big enough, and proud enough, to do justice to the dream of equality for all people.

# Columbus Plus 500 Years: Whither the American Indian?[20]

David Archambault

*Born 1947, Fort Yates, ND; B.S., Black Hills State College, 1976; M.Ed., Pennsylvania State University, 1983; principal, Little Wound School, 1976-84; professor, United Tribes Technical College, 1984-87; president, Standing Rock College, 1987–; president, American Indian College Fund, 1991–.*

## Editor's introduction

David Archambault, president of the American Indian College Fund, spoke to some 150 people attending a weekly meeting of the Murray, Utah Rotary Club. Mr. Archambault is a member of the Hunkpapa Band of the Lakota Tribe and the Sioux Nation. As president of the American Indian College Fund, he tries to obtain grants for tribal colleges, of which there are 26 in the United States. On this occasion, being the 500th anniversary of Columbus's voyage to the New World, Archambault stated that he viewed Columbus as neither good nor bad, but rather as a symbol of a "world forever transformed." Archambault asserted that the time has come to move past the pain and anguish that Native Americans have endured since Columbus's arrival, and begin the process of education and economic development that will allow Native Americans to preserve history while having a satisfying existence in the New World.

---

Thank you and good afternoon. *Hau kola.* That is how we Lakota say "Greeting, Friends." I am happy to be here today to represent Native American people. I am a *Ikoeya Wicaska*, an ordinary man. We think of an ordinary man as not superior to anyone else or for that matter to anything else. We, all people and all things, are related to each other.

We begin our spiritual ceremonies with the phrase *Onitakuya Oyasi*, which means all my relations. We believe that all people are ultimately part of one nation, the nation of mankind, but that this nation is only one of many nations that inhibit the mother earth. To us all living things are nations: the deer, the horses, things that crawl, things that fly, things that grow in and on the ground. All of these nations were created by the same power, and none is superior to another. All are necessary for life. We are expected to live and work in harmony.

In my travels I have learned that many Americans in mainstream society are uninformed or ill-informed about American Indians. So let me begin by responding to questions people most often ask about us, or questions people might most like to ask.

No, we don't consider that Christopher Columbus discovered America. Estimates of the number of people who lived in the so-called New World at the time Columbus arrived run from 40 to 100 million or more. Hey, we knew we were here. It was Columbus who was lost. Maybe that poem ought to say, "When Columbus sailed the ocean blue, it was he, not America, who got discovered in fourteen hundred ninety-two."

Yes, American Indians are American citizens. After World War I, a nation grateful for the contributions of Indians to the war effort made all American Indians full citizens.

No, we are not prisoners on the reservations. We can leave any time. Many have. But the rest of us don't want to. We don't want to be assimilated into the dominant culture. We want to preserve our own culture and traditions. I'll tell you later how I hope to do that.

[20]Delivered to the Rotary Club, in Murray, Utah, on April 6, 1992. Reprinted with permission of David Archambault.

Yes, we have a unique status in the United States. We are both citizens and sovereign people. That comes from our history as nations, or tribes, defeated by Europeans, who, after giving up on trying to Christianize and civilize us, recognized our right to self-determination. I'll come back to this, too.

No, not all Indians are alike. There is diversity among tribal nations just as there is among European nations. American Indians in 500 or so tribes speak more than 200 languages and dialects.

Yes, many Americans have an especially tough time of it today with alcohol and other health problems, with poverty and inadequate education and job opportunities, and with just trying to figure out their own identity. Only we Indians can provide the leadership needed to solve these problems.

Finally, no, we don't care, at least most of us don't, whether you call us Indians, Native Americans, Indigenous People, or Amerinds. An Indian comedian tells it this way: "I know why white people call us Indians," he says. "when Columbus got here, he thought he had arrived in the Indies, so naturally he called the inhabitants Indians. I'm just thankful he didn't think he arrived in Turkey."

Today I want to share with you some of our history and culture and hopes for the future. It is important to American Indians, and I think to you as well, that *all* Americans know more about the first people to come to this land, about where we are and what we are doing and where we are headed. If we are to respect our differences and value what we have in common, we just begin with understanding.

During this quincentenary of Columbus' voyage, attention is once again focused on what the white man brought to this land and on Columbus himself. The man who made such a remarkable journey has become the stuff of legend as well as history. He is admired and detested, exalted and condemned. Columbus day will surely never be a favorite holiday among Indians, but we should consider Columbus for what he was, not for what we may wish he had been.

Columbus was a skilled and courageous mariner who led his ships across unchartered waters. He found land and people unknown to Europeans. He discovered a sea route between Europe and America. Never mind that Norse explorers and perhaps others had made the trip earlier. It was Columbus who recorded ways for others to make it across the waters, and back again.

Columbus came here, however, not to trade, but to conquer; he came here to enrich himself and enslave his captives. His mission, in the words of his royal charter, was to "discover and acquire" all new lands as well as "pearls, precious stones, gold, silver," and other valuables. He would write back to Spain, "From here, in the name of the Blessed Trinity, we can send all of the slaves that can be sold."

Columbus was a man of his time. He felt inspired by his god, empowered by his monarch, and reassured by the rightness of his cause. He was sailing, as the saying had it, for "God, glory, and gold." If he objected to enslaving others and taking their lands, someone else may have gotten that royal charter. To me, Columbus is neither hero nor villain, but rather a symbol of a world forevermore transformed. His culture and mine have never fully made peace.

Tens of millions of native people would die during and after the years of Columbus's four voyages to our shores: die of gunfire from soldiers who wanted their lands and precious metals; die of maltreatment while forced to work as slaves; die of white man's diseases, such as smallpox and typhoid, for which they had no immunity.

These native people had been hunters and fisherman and gatherers and farmers and weavers and traders. They had created stable, even advanced societies. They had highly developed agricultural and trading systems. It was they who had grown the first potatoes and had the first corn and the first tomatoes. They understood mathematics and architecture and calendar systems. They were rich in art and culture as well as in gold and silver. The Incas, the Mayans, the Aztecs, and many others, civilizations all destroyed, their people subjugated.

In North America, too, Indians lost their lands, their economy, and their freedom to Europeans. At times, the new settlers were not quite sure what to do about these native people. The Indians had welcomed them, fed them, traded with them. They were people who respected their environment. They had developed intricate political and social systems. The Iroquois, for example, had the world's oldest true democracy: a Supreme Chief, a legislative council, and a judicial branch as well as universal suffrage and direct representation. It was a system the Founding Fathers of the new nation would study and learn from.

But the Indians were in the way, in the way of new settlements and new riches. So for a long time, the objective was to get rid of the Indian. "The only good Indian is a dead Indian," the saying went. Whites even slaughtered the buffalos so the Indian could not hunt. The Indians fought back, often ferociously, but they lacked the manpower and the arms to resist.

Sometimes they pleaded. In a remarkable speech in 1879, Chief Joseph of the Nez Indians addressed his conquerors with these words: "All men were made by the same great Spirit Chief," he said. "They are all brothers and all should have equal rights . . . . Let me be a free man, free to talk and think and act for myself, and I will obey all of your laws."

Often they made treaties: 800 of them, in fact, nearly half of which were ratified by the U.S. Senate in full accord with the federal Constitution. Each of these treaties—every one—was violated by a nation that prides itself on keeping its word.

The Indians could not resist, but they could not be exterminated either. And so the government moved them to reservations, a movement with a long and sordid history. One of the most notorious chapters in that history was recorded in the 1830s when tens of thousands of Cherokees, Choctaws, and Creeks were forcibly moved from the southeastern United States to what is now the state of Oklahoma. The Cherokees called it the "trail of tears." Along the way, nearly one-quarter of them died of starvation and disease.

The reservations were run by those who believed the way to "civilize" us was to take away our language and culture and religion. Our children were called savages and taken from us. They were put in boarding schools where they were educated—dare we say "brainwashed"?—with the white man's ways. Their teachers vowed to "kill the Indian and save the child." The idea was that if the white man couldn't get rid of the Indian, perhaps he could at least get rid of the Indian's culture.

Not until the 1930s was an effort made to give Indians limited sovereignty, allowing them to carry on their traditions and pass along their culture to their children.

By the 1950s, the new watchword was assimilation: break up the tribes, move Indians into mainstream society. In other words, make them "real Americans." Once again the emphasis was on destroying Indian culture.

Only during the past several decades has there been a growing realization that we American Indians must determine our own destiny. We must be free to cherish our traditions and our culture, but also learn to live and work with society around us. We must learn to walk in both worlds.

Can we do it? Yes, we can. It will require education and economic development and self-sufficiency. It demands that we create opportunity and hope for future generations.

This idea is not original with me. It was taught to us by a great leader of the Lakota people, my people, the great chief Sitting Bull. He taught us that Indian children could succeed in modern society and yet retain the values of their culture, values such as respect for the earth, for wildlife, for rivers and streams, for plants and trees; and values such as caring for each other and for family and community.

He taught us that we must leave behind more hope than we found. "Let us put our minds together," he said, "and see what life we can make for the children."

That is why there is an American Indian College Fund. It is to carry out the dream of Sitting Bull: to bring together the best mind in the Indian and non-Indian world to build a better future for our children. Our mission is two-fold: to raise the badly needed funds, of course, but also to help the general public understand the heritage of American Indians.

There are 26 colleges located on or near reservations in the United States. They were created by and for Indians. Three are four-year colleges; the others, two-year schools. Most are fully accredited and the rest are earning accreditation.

In these schools, our children are prepared for both worlds. The schools maintain a rigorous academic discipline while preserving Indian heritage and culture. Our students study math and science and business management as well as American Indian philosophy, traditions, and language. They learn what it means to be Indian, and gain a greater understanding of the world around them.

And it's working. Young American Indians who attend our colleges go on to further education and employment. They become productive, active citizens with confidence and pride to their tribal heritage. Many return to the reservation to work. Above all, they learn to value learning, and to value the wisdom of those who came before us.

The colleges do something more. They serve their communities. They offer job training and day care, health clinics and counseling services, public-affairs and literacy programs. They provide leadership and support for economic development of the reservations. In short, they are committed to service and renewal.

Not long ago researchers from the Carnegie Foundation for the Advancement of Teaching spent two years studying our colleges. The schools, the Foundation concluded, "are crucial to the future of Native Americans and to the future of our nation." The foundation called accomplishments of the schools "enormously impressive" and said they "give hope to students and a new life to their communities."

But the report also pointed to the need for expanded science labs and libraries and urged the federal government to keep the promise it has made. Congress had authorized payment of nearly $6,000 for each full-time equivalent student at tribal colleges. But the amount actually appropriated is only about half that.

I feel a special commitment to the work of these colleges, not only because I temporarily head the effort to raise private funds and public awareness for them but, more important, because of what they mean to my life and the lives of my people.

More than 100 years ago, our great chief Sitting Bull was murdered. His people, frightened that they too would be killed, set out on foot across South Dakota along with Chief Big Foot. Carrying their children, they fled across the frozen prairie through the bitter subzero cold 200 miles to seek refuge on the Pine Ridge reservation in southwestern South Dakota.

On December 29, 1890, near a creek now known to all the world as Wounded Knee, Chief Big Foot and his followers were massacred. No one knows who fired first, but when the shooting was over, nearly 300 Indians—men, women, and children—lay dead and dying across the valley. Their bodies were dumped into a mass grave. The survivors were unable to hold a burial ceremony, a ceremony we call the wiping away of tears. It meant the living could never be free.

On the 100th anniversary of the Massacre at Wounded Knee, several hundred of us on horseback retraced the journey of Big Foot and his band during those final days. We arrived at dawn at the site of the mass grave at Wounded Knee and completed the wiping of the tears ceremony. The Si Tanka Wokiksuye, the Chief Big Foot Memorial Ride, was a mourning ritual that released the spirits of our ancestors and closed a tragic chapter in our history.

We have the opportunity now to help rebuild our nation. And I do not mean just the Indian nations. On this 500th anniversary of Columbus's voyages, we together can build a better America, a nation enriched by the diversity of its people and strengthened by the values that bring us together as a community.

Let us make this anniversary a time of healing and a time of renewal, a time to wipe away the tears. Let us, both Indian and non-Indian, put our minds together and see what life we can make for our children. Let us leave behind more hope than we found. I think Sitting Bull would be proud of us all.

Thank you. *Tosha Akin Wanchin.*

# When Communities Flourish[21]

## Hillary Rodham Clinton

*Born October 26, 1947, Chicago, IL; B.A., 1968, M.A., 1969, Wellesley College; J.D., Yale Law School, 1973; attorney, Children's Defense Fund, 1973-74; legal counsel, Carnegie Council on Children, 1973-74; assistant professor, University of Arkansas, 1974-77; partner, Rose Law Firm, 1977–; lecturer, University of Arkansas Law School, 1979-80; first lady of the United States, 1992–; author,* It Takes a Village and Other Lessons Children Teach Us *(1996).*

### Editor's introduction

In this speech, Hillary Rodham Clinton, first lady of the United States, addressed the United Nations Fourth World Conference on Women. More than 4,000 delegates attended the 10-day meeting, the purpose of which was to help correct inequities confronted by women throughout the world. Here, Ms. Clinton linked the fate of women with the fate of the world, proclaiming that "if women are healthy and educated, their families will flourish . . . And when families flourish, communities and nations will flourish." In response to her statements The *New York Times* asserted that Ms. Clinton "spoke more forcefully on human rights than any American dignitary has on Chinese soil."

---

Mrs. Mongella, Under Secretary Kittani, distinguished delegates and guests:

I would like to thank the Secretary General of the United Nations for inviting me to be part of the United Nations Fourth World Conference on Women. This is truly a celebration—a celebration of the contributions women make in every aspect of life: in the home, on the job, in their communities, as mothers, wives, sisters, daughters, learners, workers, citizens and leaders.

It is also a coming together, much the way women come together every day in every country.

We come together in fields and in factories. In village markets and supermarkets. In living rooms and board rooms.

Whether it is while playing with our children in the park, or washing clothes in a river, or taking a break at the office water cooler, we come together and talk about our aspirations and concerns. And time and again, our talk turns to our children and our families. However different we may be, there is far more that unites us than divides us. We share a common future. And we are here to find common ground so that we may help bring new dignity and respect to women and girls all over the world—and in so doing, bring new strength and stability to families as well.

By gathering in Beijing, we are focusing world attention on issues that matter most in the lives of women and their families: access to education, health care, jobs and credit, the chance to enjoy basic legal and human rights and participate fully in the political life of their countries.

There are some who question the reason for this conference.

Let them listen to the voices of women in their homes, neighborhoods, and workplaces.

There are some who wonder whether the lives of women and girls matter to economic and political progress around the globe.

Let them look at the women gathered here and at Huairou—the homemakers, nurses, teachers, lawyers, policymakers, and women who run their own businesses.

It is conferences like this that compel governments and people everywhere to listen, look and face the world's most pressing problems.

Wasn't it after the women's conference in Nairobi ten years ago that the world focused for the first time on the crisis of domestic violence?

[21]Delivered at the United Nations Fourth World Conference on Women, in Beijing, China, on September 5, 1995.

Earlier today, I participated in a World Health Organization forum, where government officials, NGOs, and individual citizens are working on ways to address the health problems of women and girls.

Tomorrow, I will attend a gathering of the United Nations Development Fund for Women. There, the discussion will focus on local—and highly successful—programs that give hardworking women access to credit so they can improve their own lives and the lives of their families.

What we are learning around the world is that if women are healthy and educated, their families will flourish. If women are free from violence, their families will flourish. If women have a chance to work and earn as full and equal partners in society, their families will flourish.

And when families flourish, communities and nations will flourish.

That is why every woman, every man, every child, every family, and every nation on our planet has a stake in the discussion that takes place here.

Over the past 25 years, I have worked persistently on issues relating to women, children and families. Over the past two-and-a-half years, I have had the opportunity to learn more about the challenges facing women in my own country and around the world.

I have met new mothers in Jojakarta, Indonesia, who come together regularly in their village to discuss nutrition, family planning, and baby care.

I have met working parents in Denmark who talk about the comfort they feel in knowing that their children can be cared for in creative, safe, and nurturing after-school centers.

I have met women in South Africa who helped lead the struggle to end apartheid and are now helping build a new democracy.

I have met with the leading women of the Western Hemisphere who are working every day to promote literacy and better health care for the children of their countries.

I have met women in India and Bangladesh who are taking out small loans to buy milk cows, rickshaws, thread and other materials to create a livelihood for themselves and their families.

I have met doctors and nurses in Belarus and Ukraine who are trying to keep children alive in the aftermath of Chernobyl.

The great challenge of this Conference is to give voice to women everywhere whose experiences go unnoticed, whose words go unheard.

Women comprise more than half the world's population. Women are 70 percent of the world's poor, and two-thirds of those who are not taught to read and write.

Women are the primary caretakers for most of the world's children and elderly. Yet much of the work we do is not valued—not by economists, not by historians, not by popular culture, not by government leaders.

At this very moment, as we sit here, women around the world are giving birth, raising children, cooking meals, washing clothes, cleaning houses, planting crops, working on assembly lines, running companies, and running countries.

Women also are dying from diseases that should have been prevented or treated; they are watching their children succumb to malnutrition caused by poverty and economic deprivation; they are being denied the right to go to school by their own fathers and brothers; they are being forced into prostitution, and they are being barred from the bank lending office and banned from the ballot box.

Those of us who have the opportunity to be here have the responsibility to speak for those who could not.

As an American, I want to speak up for women in my own country—women who are raising children on the minimum wage, women who can't afford health care or child care, women whose lives are threatened by violence, including violence in their own homes.

I want to speak up for mothers who are fighting for good schools, safe neighborhoods, clean air and clean airwaves; for older women, some of them widows, who have raised their families and now find that their skills and life experiences are not valued in the workplace; for women who are working all night as nurses, hotel clerks, and fast food cooks so that they can be at home during the day with their kids; and for women everywhere who simply don't have time to do everything they are called upon to do each day.

Speaking to you today, I speak for them, just as each of us speaks for women around the world who are denied the chance to go to school, or see a doctor, or own property, or have a say about the direction of their lives, simply because they are women. The truth is that most women around the world work both inside and outside the home, usually by necessity.

We need to understand that there is no formula for how women should lead their lives.

That is why we must respect the choices that each woman makes for herself and her family. Every woman deserves the chance to realize her God-given potential.

We also must recognize that women will never gain full dignity until their human rights are respected and protected.

Our goals for this Conference, to strengthen families and societies by empowering women to take greater control over their own destinies, cannot be fully achieved unless all governments—here and around the world—accept their responsibility to protect and promote internationally recognized human rights.

The international community has long acknowledged and recently affirmed at Vienna—that both women and men are entitled to a range of protections and personal freedoms, from the right of personal security to the right to determine freely the number and spacing of the children they bear.

No one should be forced to remain silent for fear of religious or political persecution, arrest, abuse or torture.

Tragically, women are most often the ones whose human rights are violated.

Even in the late 20th century, the rape of women continues to be used as an instrument of armed conflict. Women and children make up a large majority of the world's refugees. When women are excluded from the political process, they become even more vulnerable to abuse.

I believe that, on the eve of a new millennium, it is time to break our silence. It is time for us to say here in Beijing, and the world to hear, that it is no longer acceptable to discuss women's rights as separate from human rights.

These abuses have continued because, for too long, the history of women has been a history of silence. Even today, there are those who are trying to silence our words.

The voices of this conference and of the women at Huairou must be heard loud and clear:

It is a violation of human rights when babies are denied food, or drowned, or suffocated, or their spines broken, simply because they are born girls.

It is a violation of human rights when women and girls are sold into the slavery of prostitution.

It is a violation of human rights when women are doused with gasoline, set on fire and burned to death because their marriage dowries are deemed too small.

It is a violation of human rights when individual women are raped in their own communities and when thousands of women are subjected to rape as a tactic or prize of war.

It is a violation of human rights when a leading cause of death worldwide among women ages 14 to 44 is the violence they are subjected to in their own homes.

It is a violation of human rights when young girls are brutalized by the painful and degrading practice of genital mutilation.

It is a violation of human rights when women are denied the right to plan their own families, and that includes being forced to have abortions or being sterilized against their will.

If there is one message that echoes forth from this conference, it is that human rights are women's rights and women's rights are human rights. Let us not forget that among those rights are the right to speak freely—and the right to be heard.

Women must enjoy the right to participate fully in the social and political lives of their countries if we want freedom and democracy to thrive and endure.

It is indefensible that many women in nongovernmental organizations who wished to participate in this conference have not been able to attend—or have been prohibited from fully taking part.

Let me be clear. Freedom means the right of people to assemble, organize, and debate openly. It means respecting the views of those who may disagree with the views of their governments. It means not taking citizens away from their loved ones and jailing them, mistreating them, or denying them their freedom or dignity because of the peaceful expression of their ideas and opinions.

In my country, we recently celebrated the 75th anniversary of women's suffrage. It took 150 years after the signing of our Declaration of Independence for women to win the right to vote.

It took 72 years of organized struggle on the part of many courageous women and men. It was one of America's most divisive philosophical wars. But it was also a bloodless war. Suffrage was achieved without a shot being fired.

We have also been reminded, in V-J Day observances last weekend, of the good that comes when men and women join together to combat the forces of tyranny and build a better world.

We have seen peace prevail in most places for a half century. We have avoided another world war.

But we have not solved older, deeply-rooted problems that continue to diminish the potential of half the world's population.

Now it is time to act on behalf of women everywhere.

If we take bold steps to better the lives of women, we will be taking bold steps to better the lives of children and families too.

Families rely on mothers and wives for emotional support and care; families rely on women for labor in the home; and increasingly, families rely on women for income needed to raise healthy children and care for other relatives.

As long as discrimination and inequities remain so commonplace around the world—as long as girls and women are valued less, fed less, fed last, overworked, underpaid, not schooled, and subjected to violence in and out of their homes—the potential of the human family to create a peaceful, prosperous world will not be realized.

Let this Conference be our—and the world's—call to action.

And let us heed the call so that we can create a world in which every woman is treated with respect and dignity, every boy and girl is loved and cared for equally, and every family has the hope of a strong and stable future.

Thank you very much.

God's blessings on you, your work, and all who will benefit from it.

# VIII. Media

## Editor's introduction

During the last 60 years, the media, and our perception of them, have undergone vast changes. Perhaps these changes are felt most acutely when the number of sources of information, and the changes wrought upon them, are brought to light. Individually owned hometown newspapers, having collected into near monopolies, compete fiercely with television for both audiences and dollars. Major television networks are not immune to competition, as the number of cable channels increases annually. The Internet has spread from business to home and school, and so it is with good reason that ours has been called the information age. Yet despite, or perhaps as a result of, the large and ever-growing number of information suppliers, the public, being the consumers of this information, increasingly question the content and nature of the information they are offered.

While media technology and the speed of communication have changed spectacularly over the period, some old issues have persisted, including the role and responsibility of journalists in a democratic system. Many contend that as the media wield a greater presence in society, journalists must assume more accountability for their initiatives. As early as 1937, Carl W. Ackerman, dean of the Columbia School of Journalism, noted that "through the press and the radio, ideas are traveling with the speed and force of lightning. . . . This makes public opinion today probably the most powerful force in world affairs." In essence, Ackerman questioned the relationship between the media and the public they serve. He asserted that the validity of the media lay in the extent to which they are trusted by their audience.

The permeation of television into society has only intensified the debate surrounding the media's responsibility. In 1961, Newton N. Minow, former chair of the Federal Communications Commission, told broadcasters that "your industry possesses the most powerful voice in America. It has an inescapable duty to make that voice ring with intelligence and with leadership." History, he warned, would reveal whether the media have been an asset or a liability to the American people. Minow's stress on the increasingly large presence of television within society was underscored by George Gerbner, then dean of the University of Pennsylvania's Annenberg School of Communications. Gerbner believed that television "has become the functional equivalent of a new religion." It has replaced "most stories told by parents," he continued, "and has either replaced or reorganized what we learn in school or in church. It has become the norm, the standard to which we all have to relate." Anne Rawley Saldich, a professor of government and communications, claimed that "television has openly usurped certain functions that are traditionally governmental." In this usurpation, she argued that there is a clear potential for a destructive "tyranny" that is bound to neither truth nor law. Perhaps the possibility of such tyranny is owed to the fact that many believe that the media are subservient to what Norman Lear once called "the vagrant, highly imperfect whims of the marketplace." Lear accused the media of placing the acquisition of our dollars, rather than an obligation to truth or morality, as their main goal.

# The Role of the Press as a Factor in Public Opinion and Economic Changes[1]

Carl W. Ackerman

*Born January 16, 1890, Richmond, IN; died October 9, 1970; B.A., 1911, M.A., 1917, Earlham College; B.Litt., Columbia University, 1913; correspondent, United Press, 1915; correspondent,* New York Tribune, *1917; writer,* Saturday Evening Post, *1918; reporter,* New York Times, *1918-19; director of foreign news,* Philadelphia Ledger, *1919-21; president, Carl W. Ackerman, Inc., 1921-27; dean, Columbia University School of Journalism, 1931-56; author,* Germany, the Next Republic *(1917),* Mexico's Dilemma *(1918),* Trailing the Bolshevik *(1919).*

## Editor's introduction

Carl W. Ackerman, dean of Columbia University's Graduate School of Journalism, is remembered as a vigorous champion of freedom of the press. In this speech, Ackerman attempted to link the press with public opinion by asserting that it is the role of the press to make public opinion "dynamic" or more widely perceived. However, it is clear that he believed that the press is no longer understood as a true revealer of public opinion. It follows that Ackerman desired "a scientific study of public opinion" so that its complexities could be better understood, and the press could renew its understanding of the very thing Ackerman believed it should be devoted to revealing.

---

We are all aware, I think, of a new force in public affairs. That force, which we call public opinion, is directly related to economic and social changes in the United States and throughout the world. This is a challenging situation because practically all the information available anywhere resolves itself into someone's opinion of public opinion.

I wish to emphasize those two points at the beginning. Public opinion is a literally stupendous force which many of us believe is determining the course of civilization, while our knowledge of how it functions, how it is influenced, how it is related to the press and radio, whether on specific issues its source is Washington, Moscow, Rome or in the homes of workers and farmers, is largely a matter of personal observation and opinion.

Since 1911 I have had some opportunity of observing, reporting and studying public opinion throughout the United States and in thirty-four foreign countries. It has been my good fortune to have had this experience as a newspaper man, as a public relations officer of several large corporations and as an educator. The substance of this experience may be stated in one proposition: That the time has come for journalism, industry and education to cooperate in bringing about a transition from casual observation to a scientific study of public opinion. That is the only justification for the acceptance of your hospitality and for the privilege of participating on your program.

One significant aspect of contemporary affairs is the widespread interest in the printed and the spoken word. From the White House to the mines and farms, from the mills and factories to executive offices of industry, labor and finance, the press and the radio are actively in the consciousness of the people.

This interest is much deeper than a routine desire for news and entertainment. It is fundamentally related to economic and social changes in the United States and abroad.

[1]Delivered at the 21st annual meeting of the National Industrial Conference Board, in New York, New York, on May 27, 1937.

Through the press and the radio, ideas are traveling with the speed and force of lightning. The printed and the spoken word are the agencies of public communication. Mankind is thinking and is articulate. This makes public opinion today probably the most powerful force in world affairs. Because it affects all of us personally, because it is directly related to the problems of management and the development of industry, and their relation to our national economy, we are all searching for information upon which we can base a judgment and plan a course of action. Industry, journalism and education have a common interest in public opinion because they are composed of independent units dependent upon democratic institutions.

If politics were the only approach to an understanding of public opinion and if participation in political party activities were the sole means of influencing the trends of public thinking and action, our chance of escaping control of our national affairs by either the extreme right or the radical left would be too limited to be comfortable. The trend of public thinking appears to be in the direction of the socialization of activity and the centralization of authority. It is doubtful, I think, whether property rights and liberty, as we have been considering them, can be successfully defended, in the future, in the courts or before legislative assemblies. It is problematical whether the momentum of mass opinion can be stopped in Washington, either at the White House or by the United States Supreme Court. Whether this movement originated in the capital or because of capitalism, is an academic political question it is not my prerogative to debate.

In discussing the role of the press as a factor in public opinion and economic changes, I am confronted with the realities of today and the trends leading to tomorrow. These manifestations indicate that history today is being made in the realm of public thought and that the future character of our property rights and liberties will be determined by public opinion.

This would be a terrifying picture if politics were the only approach to an understanding of mass opinion, or if free publicity in the press or on the radio, the platform and the screen were the only instrumentalities available to religion, education, industry and the professions to maintain their respective rights in democracy.

Our perspective of the fundamental problem involved will be clearer, I think, if we eradicate from our minds the fixed notion of so many business men that publicity, public relations and public opinion are synonymous. I am not concerned here with the desirability or the technique of obtaining favorable publicity for individual leaders or with the building of good will for industry. Our concern, it seems to me, should be with the causes of the trend toward socialization and centralization; with the reasons for the momentum of mass opinion; with the methods which have been used and are being utilized to separate our people into suspicious and hostile groups. The national state of mind which considers the opinions of citizens outside of government, labor and agriculture as being dominated by selfish interests and motives and thereby contrary to the public welfare is becoming as dangerous to democracy as the united front of the totalitarian state. Therefore, the whole relationship of public opinion to recent changes in the economic policies and the administrative practices of government is of the greatest moment to all of us.

Until the outbreak of the World War it was everywhere assumed that public opinion, clarified by general education, assured the continuation of representative government and free institutions in the United States. Democracy was regarded as public opinion made dynamic by free speech. Since the armistice, although the circulation of newspapers and periodicals has increased and radio broadcasting has expanded, these confident assumptions are challenged or denied.

Is this because public opinion has been turned from its true purpose or is it because public opinion has been suppressed? If public opinion simply is being or has been suppressed and, if liberated, would be expressed again as it was prior to 1914 in devotion to the same ideals, then our task is one of uncovering and defeating the influences that stifle public opinion and thereby destroy free institutions. If, on the other hand, public opinion has been turned to the willing acceptance of the Fascist or the Communist theory of the state, then it is of the utmost importance to study the stimuli and their relation to the press and the radio.

The approach to the study of the larger aspects of public opinion must, for these reasons cover more than the mere physical channels or the utilization of these channels by governments or by militant minorities. There must be a scientific study. These problems cannot be solved by casual observation, or by the expansion of industrial public relations, or by the concentration of legal forces in Washington or by multiplying the readers of Kent, Thompson, Sokolsky and Lippmann or by group meetings.

These problems are not exclusively American. In South America, in the Orient, in the Scandinavian countries, Holland, Switzerland, Czechoslovakia and the British Empire public opinion is one of the important national concerns. In a lecture at the University College of Wales recently Professor E. H. Carr discussed it in relation to foreign policies and peace.

"The intellectual," he said, "has an immense role to fill as the leader of public opinion. But in order to lead it, he must keep in touch with it. The political thinking of the intellectual once it divorces itself from the political thinking of the man in the street, is sterile."

Is it not possible that one of the reasons for the cleavage of public opinion in this country is the sterility of individual opinions of public opinion?

To develop the proposition that journalism, industry and education should cooperate in bringing about the transition from casual observation and opinion to a scientific study of public opinion, I shall endeavor to present my point of view by examining two specific situations:

I. The relation of the government, particularly the White House, to the press and the radio as factors in public opinion and economic and social changes;

II. The relations between business and journalism.

In 1933 and 1934 when the newspaper publishers and editors of the United States believed that the freedom of the press was endangered by the proposed NRA code, they received no support from education, religion, the professions or industry. They fought alone, without aid or comfort from their readers or advertisers, and were widely accused of the desire to protect the publishing industry by the blanket application of the Bill of Rights. In the end they succeeded in obtaining a freedom of the press provision in the code. At the time it was repeatedly pointed out by the newspapers that the government was building a formidable publicity machine which was destined to have a profound influence upon public opinion. This machine was organized to serve every opinion-making group in the country, and to utilize the press, the radio, the screen, and the public forum. How many business men sensed the significance of this warning at that time, when public emotion was being forged into public opinion?

This situation had an important bearing on the relation of the press to public opinion, on the relation of the White House to the press and the newspaper publishers to politics. In this complex situation the President discovered, if he did not know it, that he could circumvent the political and personal partisanship of the publishers, by three equally effective and coordinated courses of action. First, by creating and dominating the news of the day, secondly by utilizing the radio for public addresses, and thirdly by building up in the public mind the thought that there was a distinction between what was printed about the President and what he himself said.

It is unnecessary to expand these statements other than to direct attention to a fundamental factor common to all the instrumentalities of public communication, namely, that news, editorial comment and interpretation, radio news broadcasting, comment and interpretation, and news-reel releases, all are chiefly concerned with the newest development of timely public interest. By giving thought to this factor and by acting accordingly, the President's point of view, his intentions and his arguments were brought to the attention of the people daily. This situation prevailed throughout the first administration and the campaign.

I have outlined this relationship between the government and public opinion not because of the political implications but because the role of the press in public opinion must be considered first of all from the standpoint of the distribution of news. The press is not the few newspapers you or I read, or the two or three large chains of daily newspapers. The press consists of nearly two thousand independent units and upward of eleven thousand independent weekly newspapers. It is also three large press associations and correspondents and syndicates serving dailies and weeklies with the newest developments of timely public interest. The influence of the daily flow of news is undoubtedly very great because statisticians can chart, with considerable degree of accuracy, the impact of the news on public opinion.

Since the election there has been considerable discussion of the question of the influence of the press because it is claimed that the great majority of daily newspapers opposed President Roosevelt's re-election. These claims are largely based upon publisher opposition, without giving any weight to the character and distribution of news. The claims can be disproved by additional evidence. First, there is the obvious fact that there is a difference between the number of newspapers which opposed the President and their circulation which is the point of public contact. Secondly, throughout the campaign the President averaged a larger share of editorial support, even in the newspapers whose owners were opposing him, because the bulk of editorial comment was based upon news developments not upon partisan or personal politics. Thirdly, the Gallup studies of public opinion throughout the campaign revealed that the people were making their decisions along economic, rather than political lines. By separating editorials into these classifications, a study of editorial comment in several hundred newspapers throughout one month of the campaign, showed that the President's arguments dominated the editorial interpretations and comment.

It would be most unwise, I think, for business men to conclude that President Roosevelt's re-election was due to a decline in the public influence of the press.

Furthermore, in 1936 and at the present time, the daily editorial reiteration of the *Daily News* is having probably as profound influence on public opinion and economic and social changes in New York City as the activities of the Federal government. If you will read the *Daily News* editorials which reach a larger daily audience than the *Times, Herald Tribune, World Telegram* and *Sun* combined, I think you will agree with me that circulation is a better basis for measuring the influence of the press on the thinking of mankind, than the addition of publication units, even when they are as eminent and powerful as the four I mentioned.

"We are making history in these days faster than ever before," James Truslow Adams said recently. Personally, I think it is being made in the realm of public thought and the newspapers, and radio broadcasting stations which newspapers own and operate, are having a literally stupendous influence. But what business men should have is not my opinion based on personal observation but the facts, which can be obtained through scientific study. What industry needs are facts which scientific research in the field of public opinion will bring to light.

The second specific situation to be examined is the relation between business and journalism. Newspapers also need more facts about public opinion and their own obligations and responsibilities to the public. Studies should be made of the impact of news and editorial policies and practices on the social and economic consciousness of the people.

Every citizen in the United States today is participating in a world war of ideas. This war may be as destructive of property rights and individual freedom, of institutions and of family life as a war involving material resources. In this modern warfare the printed and spoken word may in the end be the decisive weapons. Therefore, every man or woman who reports, edits or interprets facts and ideas today which are directly or indirectly related to the social and the political sciences, has a public responsibility superior to either professional or commercial interests. In the case of democratic nations, this involves the necessity for new orientation within the profession and industry of journalism because the claim of the press in totalitarian states that it is economically free is known and is being discussed in the United States. As public opinion in this country is divided on economic lines this foreign argument may someday be used effectively to substitute economic freedom of the press for our present interpretation of the Bill of Rights.

Unfortunately, both for the press and for the people, newspaper publishers, editors and writers are sensitive to criticism of their practices and policies. This lack of informed public criticism retards professional progress because it places the necessity for changes largely on a circulation or advertising basis. Unfortunately, also, as you are doubtless aware, no business man today would dare to criticize, even in a friendly way, journalistic practices and judgment which result so frequently in inaccuracies and distortion.

This relationship between business and journalism, between the church, the state and the professions and journalism must be changed or the movement toward the socialization of activity and the centralization of authority will dispose of a free press. And when that comes, the freedom of business and of religion will follow.

I mentioned inaccuracies and distortion. These are harsh words. Because of my admiration for the achievements of the press, for the character and integrity of the personnel, and my faith in the future of the profession, I use those words only because the responsibility for discussing the role of the press imposes the obligation of criticism as well as defense. Most of the inaccuracies today are due to carelessness or to traditional news practices. Only an insignificant fraction of the inaccuracies is due to any other cause. The distortion of news is largely due to re-write practices within newspaper offices resulting all too frequently in incorrect emphasis upon incidental facts or expressions of opinion which convey, under prevailing headline practices, a distorted perspective of the subject matter or the individual involved.

Every time specific instances have been brought to my attention and I have investigated them, I have absolved the individual from any intentional wrongdoing. The faults of the press today are due to the prevailing system of reporting, rewriting, headline writing and make-up. These involve technical problems as much as they do news judgment and editorial policies.

If inaccuracies and distortion were solely due to the press these matters could be dealt with by newspaper men behind closed doors and could be changed within a measurable period of time. But the politician, the business man, the preacher and teacher, the labor leader, the lecturer, the movie star, the racketeer, the sportsman, the speculator, the doctor, the lawyer, the engineer and in every community federal, state and local public officials, legislative, executive and judicial departments are all competing with each other for public attention. To achieve their objective they "create news." In many instances they are themselves responsible for inaccuracies and distortion. They overemphasize their own facts and overplay or exaggerate their own expressions of opinions for publicity purposes. Newspaper men are confronted every day by such a volume of material that editing and publishing is an endless vigil to sift intelligible news from this glut of matter. If you could see what is discarded daily by a single newspaper or press association I think you would be amazed to find how good the selection really is when compared with the material submitted for publication.

But whether the selection is good or bad, the prevailing relationship between business and journalism results in too many inaccuracies and in too frequent instances of distortion. During periods of industrial disorder the trend of the news and photographic display tends to become so fixed to one point of view, as to raise a serious question in regard to the objectivity of the press. Should there not be a scientific study of this whole situation to determine the causes and the effects of the relationships between industry and journalism which at present may be accelerating the thinking of mankind in a direction hostile to the freedom of business and of the press? Scientific research, it seems to me, gives the only promise for a true perspective of our common problems. They cannot be accurately analyzed by casual observation or solved by emergency action. To understand the causes of the present momentum for economic and social changes we must study the press and the radio, not from the superficial point of view of how to utilize them to build good will for industry, or to maintain our individual or group philosophies, but from the standpoint of their relationship and their responsibilities to the thinking of mankind. The continuation of the status quo will lead inevitably to chaos or to centralized control. Based upon our present knowledge of public opinion we cannot chart a course to reach a predetermined goal. We all have faith in scientific research in materials and matter. Is it not time for us to attempt a scientific approach to the study of the intangibles and the imponderables of public opinion which are responsible for the mass movement demanding hasty action and immediate change?

Politics cannot stop the momentum of mass thought in any direction to the right or to the left. Politicians can only yield. Science can and must lead. The hope for our civilization to escape the disastrous consequences of centralized authority and expression, is for science to endeavor to substitute the discipline of scientific knowledge for the opportunism of politics.

Science holds the key to the future of independent industry as well as to the freedom of the press. Industry and the people have a common interest in the printed and spoken word. Science can bring them together more rapidly and more peacefully than economic arguments or political action because science is fundamentally impartial, impersonal and reliable.

This, I think, is a realizable ideal.

Twenty-four years ago Dr. Edwin E. Slosson, author of "Creative Chemistry" and one of the pioneer interpreters of science, lectured at the School of Journalism on the necessity for an understanding between science and the press. Science, he repeated, is news, not the freakish and the sensational stories which were currently printed, but the truth about science and scientists. In the intervening years there was a complete change in the perspective of the press and of science. Scientific developments and the interpretation of science moved simultaneously in the same direction, contributing, through cooperation, to the social and economic welfare of mankind. This year Columbia University awarded the Pulitzer prize for reporting to five reporters for their distinguished services to science at the Harvard University Tercentenary. Within a brief span of years, Dr. Slosson's ideal was realized.

It is my conviction that a similar change can be brought about between industry and journalism. Through cooperation and with the aid of science, I think the role of the press as a factor in public opinion and economic and social changes can be of infinite benefit to mankind.

# "Checkers"[2]

## Richard M. Nixon

*Born January 9, 1913, Yorba Linda, CA; died April 22, 1994; B.A., Whittier College, 1934; LL.B., Duke University, 1937; lawyer, Wingert & Bewley, 1937-41; attorney, Office of Emergency Management, 1941-42; U.S. Navy, 1942-46; representative (R) from California, 1947-51; senator (R) from California, 1951-53; vice president of the United States, 1953-60; lawyer, private practice, 1961-63; president of the United States, 1968-74; author,* Six Crises *(1962),* Real Peace *(1983),* No More Vietnams *(1986),* 1999 *(1990),* Leaders *(1990),* In the Arena *(1991),* Seize the Moment *(1992),* Beyond Peace *(1994).*

### Editor's introduction

For his 1952 presidential campaign, General Dwight D. Eisenhower selected Senator Richard M. Nixon as his vice presidential running mate. In what became a classic "mudslinging" campaign, Nixon was accused of drawing $18,000 from a secret slush fund. While Nixon's actions were by no means unprecedented, the tense climate of the campaign made the accusations exceptionally embarrassing and politically damaging. Republican leaders urged Eisenhower to drop Nixon as his running mate. Before making this decision, Eisenhower decided to let Nixon defend his personal character over national television. In the defense that follows, Nixon insisted that none of the money went for his personal use. Seated with his wife and in front of a picture of Abraham Lincoln, Nixon made a strong appeal to his viewers' emotions, discussing many personal details, including a story about a dog named "Checkers." It is not too much to say that the speech saved Nixon's candidacy, and in doing so demonstrated for the first time television's unmistakable power.

---

My fellow Americans: I come before you tonight as a candidate for the vice presidency and as a man whose honesty and integrity has been questioned.

Now, the usual political thing to do when charges are made against you is to either ignore them or to deny them without giving details. I believe we have had enough of that in the United States, particularly with the present Administration in Washington, D.C.

To me the office of the vice presidency of the United States is a great office, and I feel that the people have got to have confidence in the integrity of the men who run for that office and who might attain them.

I have a theory, too, that the best and only answer to a smear or to an honest misunderstanding of the facts is to tell the truth. And that is why I am here tonight. I want to tell you my side of the case.

I am sure that you have read the charge, and you have heard it, that I, Senator Nixon, took $18,000 from a group of my supporters.

Now, was that wrong? And let me say that it was wrong—I am saying it, incidentally, that it was wrong, not just illegal, because it isn't a question of whether it was legal or illegal, that isn't enough. The question is, Was it morally wrong? I say that it was morally wrong—if any of that $18,000 went to Senator Nixon, for my personal use. I say that it was morally wrong if it was secretly given and secretly handled. And I say that it was morally wrong if any of the contributors got special favors for the contributions that they made.

And now to answer those questions let me say this:

Not one cent of the $18,000 or any other money of that type ever went to me for my personal use. Every penny of it was used to pay for

[2]Broadcast nationwide, from Washington, D.C., on September 23, 1952.

political expenses that I did not think should be charged to the taxpayers of the United States.

It was not a secret fund. As a matter of fact, when I was on "Meet the Press," some of you may have seen it last Sunday—Peter Edson came up to me after the program and he said, "Dick, what about this fund we hear about?" And I said, Well, there's no secret about it. Go out and see Dana Smith, who was the administrator of the fund. And I gave him his address, and I said that you will find that the purpose of the fund simply was to defray political expenses that I did not feel should be charged to the Government.

And third, let me point out, and I want to make this particularly clear, that no contributor to this fund, no contributor to any of my campaign, has ever received any consideration that he would not have received as an ordinary constituent.

I just don't believe in that and I can say that never, while I have been in the Senate of the United States, as far as the people that contributed to this fund are concerned, have I made a telephone call for them to an agency, or have I gone down to an agency in their behalf. And the record will show that, the records which are in the hands of the Administration.

But then some of you will say and rightly, "Well, what did you use the fund for, Senator? Why did you have to have it?"

Let me tell you in just a word how a Senate office operates. First of all, a senator gets $15,000 a year in salary. He gets enough money to pay for one trip a year, a round trip that is, for himself and his family between his home and Washington, D.C.

And then he gets an allowance to handle the people that work in his office, to handle his mail. And the allowance for my state of California is enough to hire thirteen people.

And let me say, incidentally, that that allowance is not paid to the senator—it's paid directly to the individuals that the senator puts on his payroll, that all of these people and all of these allowances are for strictly official business. Business, for example, when a constituent writes in and wants you to go down to the Veterans Administration and get some information about his GI policy. Items of that type for example.

But there are other expenses which are not covered by the Government. And I think I can best discuss those expenses by asking you some questions. Do you think that when I or any other senator makes a political speech, has it printed, should charge the printing of that speech and the mailing of that speech to the taxpayers?

Do you think, for example, when I or any other senator makes a trip to his home state to make a purely political speech that the cost of that trip should be charged to the taxpayers?

Do you think when a senator makes political broadcasts or political television broadcasts, radio or television, that the expense of those broadcasts should be charged to the taxpayer?

Well, I know what your answer is. The same answer that audiences give me whenever I discuss this particular problem. The answer is, No. The taxpayers shouldn't be required to finance items which are not official business but which are primarily political business.

But then the question arises, you say, "Well, how do you pay for these and how can you do it legally?"

And there are several ways that it can be done, incidentally, and that it is done legally in the United States Senate and in the Congress.

The first way is to be a rich man. I don't happen to be a rich man so I couldn't use that.

Another way that is used is to put your wife on the payroll. Let me say, incidentally, my opponent, my opposite number for the vice presidency on the Democratic ticket, does have his wife on the payroll. And has had her on his payroll for the ten years—the past ten years.

Now just let me say this. That's his business and I'm not critical of him for doing that. You will have to pass judgment on that particular point. But I have never done that for this reason. I have found that there are so many deserving stenographers and secretaries in Washington that needed the work that I just didn't feel it was right to put my wife on the payroll.

My wife's sitting over here. She's a wonderful stenographer. She used to teach stenography and she used to teach shorthand in high school. That was when I met her. And I can tell you folks that she's worked many hours at night and many hours on Saturdays and Sundays in my office and she's done a fine job. And I'm proud to say tonight that in the six years I've been in the House and the Senate of the United States, Pat Nixon has never been on the Government payroll.

There are other ways that these finances can be taken care of. Some who are lawyers, and I happen to be a lawyer, continue to practice law.

But I haven't been able to do that. I'm so far away from California that I've been so busy with my senatorial work that I have not engaged in any legal practice.

And also as far as law practice is concerned, it seemed to me that the relationship between an attorney and the client was so personal that you couldn't possibly represent a man as an attorney and then have an unbiased view when he presented his case to you in the event that he had one before the Government.

And so I felt that the best way to handle these necessary political expenses of getting my message to the American people and the speeches I made, the speeches that I had printed, for the most part, concerned this one message—of exposing this Administration, the communism in it, the corruption in it—the only way that I could do that was to accept the aid which people in my home state of California who contributed to my campaign and who continued to make these contributions after I was elected were glad to make.

And let me say I am proud of the fact that not one of them has ever asked me for a special favor. I'm proud of the fact that not one of them has ever asked me to vote on a bill other than as my own conscience would dictate. And I am proud of the fact that the taxpayers by subterfuge or otherwise have never paid one dime for expenses which I thought were political and shouldn't be charged to the taxpayers.

Let me say, incidentally, that some of you may say, "Well, that's all right, Senator; that's your explanation, but have you got any proof?"

And I'd like to tell you this evening that just about an hour ago we received an independent audit of this entire fund.

I suggested to Governor Sherman Adams, who is the chief of staff of the Dwight Eisenhower campaign, that an independent audit and legal report be obtained. And I have that audit here in my hand.

It's an audit made by the Price, Waterhouse & Co. firm, and the legal opinion by Gibson, Dunn & Crutcher, lawyers in Los Angeles, the biggest law firm and incidentally one of the best ones in Los Angeles.

I'm proud to be able to report to you tonight that this audit and this legal opinion is being forwarded to General Eisenhower. And I'd like to read to you the opinion that was prepared by Gibson, Dunn & Crutcher and based on all the pertinent laws and statutes, together with the audit report prepared by the certified public accountants.

"It is our conclusion that Senator Nixon did not obtain any financial gain from the collection and disbursement of the fund by Dana Smith; that Senator Nixon did not violate any Federal or state law by reason of the operation of the fund, and that neither the portion of the fund paid by Dana Smith directly to third persons nor the portion paid to Senator Nixon to reimburse him for designated office expenses constituted income to the Senator which was either reportable or taxable as income under applicable tax laws. (Signed). Gibson, Dunn & Crutcher by Alma H. Conway."

Now that, my friends, is not Nixon speaking, but that's an independent audit which was requested because I want the American people to know all the facts and I'm not afraid of having independent people go in and check the facts, and that is exactly what they did.

But then I realize that there are still some who may say, and rightly so, and let me say that I recognize that some will continue to smear regardless of what the truth may be, but that there has been understandably some honest misunderstanding on this matter, and there's some that will say:

"Well, maybe you were able, Senator, to fake this thing. How can we believe what you say? After all, is there a possibility that you may have feathered your own nest?"

And so now what I am going to do—and incidentally this is unprecedented in the history of American politics—I am going at this time to give to this television and radio audience a complete financial history; everything I've earned; everything I've spent; everything I owe. And I want you to know the facts. I'll have to start early.

I was born in 1913. Our family was one of modest circumstances and most of my early life was spent in a store out in East Whittier. It was a grocery store—one of those family enterprises. The only reason we were able to make it go was because my mother and dad had five boys and we all worked in the store.

I worked my way through college and to a great extent through law school. And then, in 1940, probably the best thing that ever happened to me happened, I married Pat—sitting over here. We had a rather difficult time after we were married, like so many of the young couples who may be listening to us. I practiced law; she continued to teach school. I went into the service.

Let me say that my service record was not a particularly unusual one. I went to the South Pacific. I guess I'm entitled to a couple of battle stars. I got a couple of letters of commendation but I was just there when the bombs were falling and then I returned. I returned to the United States and in 1946 I ran for the Congress.

When we came out of the war, Pat and I—Pat during the war had worked as a stenographer and in a bank and as an economist for a Governmental agency—and when we came out the total of our savings from both my law practice, her teaching and all the time that I was in the war—the total for that entire period was just a little less than $10,000. Every cent of that, incidentally, was in Government bonds.

Well, that's where we start when I go into politics. Now what have I earned since I went into politics? Well, here it is—I jotted it down, let me read the notes. First of all I've had my salary as a congressman and as a senator. Second, I have received a total in this past six years of $1,600 from estates which were in my law firm at the time that I severed my connection with it.

And, incidentally, as I said before, I have not engaged in any legal practice and have not accepted any fees from business that came into the firm after I went into politics. I have made an average of approximately $1,500 a year from nonpolitical speaking engagements and lectures. And then, fortunately, we've inherited a little money. Pat sold her interest in her father's estate for $3,000 and I inherited $1,500 from my grandfather.

We live rather modestly. For four years we lived in an apartment in Park Fairfax, in Alexandria, Va. The rent was $80 a month. And we saved for the time that we could buy a house.

Now, that was what we took in. What did we do with this money? What do we have today to show for it? This will surprise you, because it is so little, I suppose, as standards generally go, of people in public life. First of all, we've got a house in Washington which cost $41,000 and on which we owe $20,000.

We have a house in Whittier, California, which cost $13,000 and on which we owe $10,000. My folks are living there at the present time.

I have just $4,000 in life insurance, plus my GI policy which I've never been able to convert and which will run out in two years. I have no life insurance whatever on Pat. I have no life insurance on our two youngsters, Patricia and Julie. I own a 1950 Oldsmobile car. We have our furniture. We have no stocks and bonds of any type. We have no interest of any kind, direct or indirect, in any business.

Now, that's what we have. What do we owe? Well, in addition to the mortgage, the $20,000 mortgage on the house in Washington, the $10,000 one on the house in Whittier, I owe $4,500 to the Riggs Bank in Washington, D.C. with interest 4.5 per cent.

I owe $3,500 to my parents and the interest on that loan which I pay regularly, because it's the part of the savings they made through the years they were working so hard, I pay regularly 4 per cent interest. And then I have a $500 loan which I have on my life insurance.

Well, that's about it. That's what we have and that's what we owe. It isn't very much but Pat and I have the satisfaction that every dime that we've got is honestly ours. I should say this—that Pat doesn't have a mink coat. But she does have a respectable Republican cloth coat. And I always tell her that she'd look good in anything.

One other thing I probably should tell you because if I don't they'll probably be saying this about me too, we did get something—a gift—after the election. A man down in Texas heard Pat on the radio mention the fact that our two youngsters would like to have a dog. And, believe it or not, the day before we left on this campaign trip we got a message from Union Station in Baltimore saying they had a package for us. We went down to get it. You know what it was?

It was a little cocker spaniel dog, in a crate that he had sent all the way from Texas, black and white, spotted, and our little girl, Tricia, the six-year-old, named it Checkers.

And, you know, the kids, like all kids, loved the dog, and I just want to say this, right now, that regardless of what they say about it, we are going to keep it.

It isn't easy to come before a nation-wide audience and bare your life, as I have done. But I want to say some things before I conclude, that I think most of you will agree on.

Mr. Mitchell, the Chairman of the Democratic National Committee, made the statement that if a man couldn't afford to be in the United States Senate, he shouldn't run for the Senate. And I just want to make my position clear.

I don't agree with Mr. Mitchell when he says that only a rich man should serve his Government, in the United States Senate or in the Congress. I don't believe that represents the thinking of the Democratic party, and I know it doesn't represent the thinking of the Republican party.

I believe that it's fine that a man like Governor Stevenson, who inherited a fortune from his father, can run for President. But I also feel that it is essential in this country of ours that a man of modest means can also run for President, because, you know—remember Abraham Lincoln—you remember what he said—"God must have loved the common people, he made so many of them."

And now I'm going to suggest some courses of conduct.

First of all, you have read in the papers about other funds, now. Mr. Stevenson apparently had a couple. One of them in which a group of business people paid and helped to supplement the salaries of state employees. Here is where the money went directly into their pockets, and I think that what Mr. Stevenson should do should be to come before the American people, as I have, give the names of the people that contributed to that fund, give the names of the people who put this money into their pockets, at the same time that they were receiving money from their state government and see what favors, if any, they gave out for that.

I don't condemn Mr. Stevenson for what he did, but until the facts are in there is a doubt that would be raised. And as far as Mr. Sparkman is concerned, I would suggest the same thing. He's had his wife on the payroll. I don't condemn him for that, but I think that he should come before the American people and indicate what outside sources of income he has had. I would suggest that under the circumstances both Mr. Sparkman and Mr. Stevenson should come before the American people, as I have, and make a complete financial statement as to their financial history, and if they don't it will be an admission that they have something to hide.

And I think you will agree with me—because, folks, remember, a man that's to be President of the United States, a man that is to be Vice President of the United States, must have the confidence of all the people. And that's why I'm doing what I'm doing, and that is why I suggest that Mr. Stevenson and Mr. Sparkman, if they are under attack, that should be what they are doing.

Now, let me say this: I know that this is not the last of the smears. In spite of my explanation tonight, other smears will be made. Others have been made in the past. And the purpose of the smears, I know, is this, to silence me, to make me let up.

Well, they just don't know who they are dealing with. I'm going to tell you this: I remember, in the dark days of the Hiss trial, some of the same columnists, some of the same radio commentators who are attacking me now and misrepresenting my position, were violently opposing me at the time I was after Alger Hiss. But I continued to fight, because I knew I was right, and I can say to this great television and radio audience that I have no apologies to the American people for my part in putting Alger Hiss where he is today. And as far as this is concerned, I intend to continue to fight.

Why do I feel so deeply? Why do I feel that in spite of the smears, the misunderstanding, the necessity for a man to come up here and bare his soul, as I have—why is it necessary for me to continue this fight? And I want to tell you why.

Because, you see, I love my country. And I think my country is in danger. And I think the only man that can save America at this time is the man that's running for President, on my ticket, Dwight Eisenhower.

# Television and the Public Interest[3]

Newton N. Minow

*Born January 17, 1926, Milwaukee, WI; B.A., 1949, J.D., 1950, Northwestern University; U.S. Army, 1944-46; attorney, Mayer, Brown and Platt, 1950-55; law clerk to Associate Supreme Court Justice Fred M. Vinson, 1951-52; administrative assistant to Adlai E. Stevenson, 1952-53; partner, Stevenson, Rifkind & Wirtz, 1957-61; chair, Federal Communications Commission, 1961-63; vice president, Encyclopedia Britannica, 1963-65; partner, Sidney and Austin, 1965-70; chair, RAND Corporation, 1970-81; chairman of the board, Jewish Theological Seminary, 1974-77; professor, Northwestern University, 1987–; author,* Equal Time: The Private Broadcasters and the Public Interest *(1965),* How Vast the Wasteland *(1991).*

## Editor's introduction

Addressing over 2,000 people, Newton N. Minow, chair of the Federal Communications Commission, observed that "Ours has been called the jet age, the atomic age, the space age. It is also, I submit, the television age." Given the amount of time the average American spends in front of the television (4 to 6 hours per day), Minow's statement has held true to the present day. Describing a considerable part of television programming as "a vast wasteland," Minow conveyed what he thought was wrong with television, what he believed to be the broadcasters' obligation to their audience, and what he thought should be done to improve television.

---

Thank you for this opportunity to meet with you today. This is my first public address since I took over my new job. When the New Frontiersmen rode into town, I locked myself in my office to do my homework and get my feet wet. But apparently I haven't managed to stay out of hot water. I seem to have detected a certain nervous apprehension about what I might say or do when I emerged from that locked office for this, my maiden station break.

First, let me begin by dispelling a rumor. I was not picked for this job because I regard myself as the fastest draw on the New Frontier.

Second, let me start a rumor. Like you, I have carefully read President Kennedy's messages about the regulatory agencies, conflict of interest, and the dangers of *ex parte* contacts. And of course, we at the Federal Communications Commission will do our part. Indeed, I may even suggest that we change the name of the FCC to The Seven Untouchables!

It may also come as a surprise to some of you, but I want you to know that you have my admiration and respect. Yours is a most honorable profession. Anyone who is in the broadcasting business has a tough row to hoe. You earn your bread by using public property. When you work in broadcasting you volunteer for public service, public pressure, and public regulation. You must compete with other attractions and other investments, and the only way you can do it is to prove to us every three years that you should have been in business in the first place.

I can think of easier ways to make a living.

But I cannot think of more satisfying ways.

I admire your courage—but that doesn't mean I would make life any easier for you. Your license lets you use the public's airwaves as trustees for 180 million Americans. The public is your beneficiary. If you want to stay on as trustees, you must deliver a decent return to the public—not only to your stockholders. So, as a representative of the public, your health and your product are among my chief concerns.

[3]Delivered at the 39th annual convention of the National Association of Broadcasters, in Washington, D.C., on May 9, 1961. Reprinted with permission of Newton N. Minow.

As to your health: let's talk only of television today. Nineteen sixty gross broadcast revenues of the television industry were over $1,268,000,000; profit before taxes was $243,900,000, an average return on revenue of 19.2 per cent. Compared with 1959, gross broadcast revenues were $1,163,900,000, and profit before taxes was $222,300,000, an average return on revenue of 19.1 per cent. So, the percentage increase of total revenues from 1959 to 1960 was 9 per cent, and the percentage increase of profit was 9.7 per cent. This, despite a recession. For your investors, the price has indeed been right.

I have confidence in your health.

But not in your product.

It is with this and much more in mind that I come before you today.

One editorialist in the trade press wrote that "the FCC of the New Frontier is going to be one of the toughest FCC's in the history of broadcast regulation." If he meant that we intend to enforce the law in the public interest, let me make it perfectly clear that he is right—we do.

If he meant that we intend to muzzle or censor broadcasting, he is dead wrong.

It would not surprise me if some of you had expected me to come here today and say in effect, "Clean up your own house or the government will do it for you."

Well, in a limited sense, you would be right—I've just said it.

But I want to say to you earnestly that it is not in that spirit that I come before you today, nor is it in that spirit that I intend to serve the FCC.

I am in Washington to help broadcasting, not to harm it; to strengthen it, not weaken it; to reward it, not punish it; to encourage it, not threaten it; to stimulate it, not censor it.

Above all, I am here to uphold and protect the public interest.

What do we mean by "the public interest?" Some say the public interest is merely what interests the public.

I disagree.

So does your distinguished president, Governor Collins. In a recent speech he said,

"Broadcasting to serve the public interest, must have a soul and a conscience, a burning desire to excel, as well as to sell; the urge to build the character, citizenship and intellectual stature of people, as well as to expand the gross national product . . . . By no means do I imply that broadcasters disregard the public interest . . . . But a much better job can be done, and should be done."

I could not agree more.

And I would add that in today's world, with chaos in Laos and the Congo aflame, with Communist tyranny on our Caribbean doorstep and relentless pressure on our Atlantic alliance, with social and economic problems at home of the gravest nature, yes, and with technological knowledge that makes it possible, as our President has said, not only to destroy our world but to destroy poverty around the world—in a time of peril and opportunity, the old complacent, unbalanced fare of action-adventure and situation comedies is simply not good enough.

Your industry possesses the most powerful voice in America. It has an inescapable duty to make that voice ring with intelligence and with leadership. In a few years, this exciting industry has grown from a novelty to an instrument of overwhelming impact on the American people. It should be making ready for the kind of leadership that newspapers and magazines assumed years ago, to make our people aware of their world.

Ours has been called the jet age, the atomic age, the space age. It is also, I submit, the television age. And just as history will decide whether the leaders of today's world employed the atom to destroy the world or rebuild it for mankind's benefit, so will history decide whether today's broadcasters employed their powerful voice to enrich the people or debase them.

If I seem today to address myself chiefly to the problems of television, I don't want any of you radio broadcasters to think we've gone to sleep at your switch—we haven't. We still listen. But in recent years most of the controversies and cross-currents in broadcast programing have swirled around television. And so my subject today is the television industry and the public interest.

Like everybody, I wear more than one hat. I am the chairman of the FCC. I am also a television viewer and the husband and father of other television viewers. I have seen a great many television programs that seemed to me eminently worth while and I am not talking about the much bemoaned good old days of "Playhouse 90" and "Studio One."

I am talking about this past season. Some were wonderfully entertaining, such as "The

Fabulous Fifties," "The Fred Astaire Show," and "The Bing Crosby Special;" some were dramatic and moving, such as Conrad's "Victory" and "Twilight Zone;" some were marvelously informative, such as "The Nation's Future," "CBS Reports," and "The Valiant Years." I could list many more—programs that I am sure everyone here felt enriched his own life and that of his family. When television is good, nothing—not the theater, not the magazines or newspapers—nothing is better.

But when television is bad, nothing is worse. I invite you to sit down in front of your television set when your station goes on the air and stay there without a book, magazine, newspaper, profit and loss sheet or rating book to distract you—and keep your eyes glued to that set until the station signs off. I can assure you that you will observe a vast wasteland.

You will see a procession of game shows, violence, audience participation shows, formula comedies about totally unbelievable families, blood and thunder, mayhem, violence, sadism, murder, western badmen, western good men, private eyes, gangsters, more violence, and cartoons. And, endlessly, commercials—many screaming, cajoling, and offending. And most of all, boredom. True, you will see a few things you will enjoy. But they will be very, very few. And if you think I exaggerate, try it.

Is there one person in this room who claims that broadcasting can't do better?

Well, a glance at next season's proposed pro graming can give us little heart. Of 73.5 hours of prime evening time, the networks have tentatively scheduled 59 hours to categories of action-adventure, situation comedy, variety, quiz, and movies.

Is there one network president in this room who claims he can't do better?

Well, is there at least one network president who believes that the other networks can't do better?

Gentlemen, your trust accounting with your beneficiaries is overdue.

Never have so few owed so much to so many.

Why is so much of television so bad? I have heard many answers: demands of your advertisers; competition for ever higher ratings; the need always to attract a mass audience; the high cost of television programs; the insatiable appetite for programing material—these are some of them. Unquestionably, these are tough problems not susceptible to easy answers.

But I am not convinced that you have tried hard enough to solve them.

I do not accept the idea that the present over-all programing is aimed accurately at the public taste. The ratings tell us only that some people have their television sets turned on and of that number, so many are tuned to one channel and so many to another. They don't tell us what the public might watch if they were offered half a dozen additional choices. A rating, at best, is an indication of how many people saw what you gave them. Unfortunately, it does not reveal the depth of the penetration, or the intensity of reaction, and it never reveals what the acceptance would have been if what you gave them had been better—if all the forces of art and creativity and daring and imagination had been unleashed. I believe in the people's good sense and good taste, and I am not convinced that the people's taste is as low as some of you assume.

My concern with the rating services is not with their accuracy. Perhaps they are accurate. I really don't know. What, then, is wrong with the ratings? It's not been their accuracy—it's been their use.

Certainly, I hope you will agree that ratings should have little influence where children are concerned. The best estimates indicate that during the hours of 5 to 6 P.M. sixty per cent of your audience is composed of children under twelve. And most young children today, believe it or not, spend as much time watching television as they do in the schoolroom. I repeat—let that sink in—most young children today spend as much time watching television as they do in the schoolroom. It used to be said that there were three great influences on a child: home, school, and church. Today, there is a fourth great influence, and you ladies and gentlemen control it.

If parents, teachers, and ministers conducted their responsibilities by following the ratings, children would have a steady diet of ice cream, school holidays, and no Sunday school. What about your responsibilities? Is there no room on television to teach, to inform, to uplift, to stretch, to enlarge the capacities of our children? Is there no room for programs deepening their understanding of children in other lands? Is there no room for a children's news show explaining something about the world to them at their level of understanding? Is there no room for reading the great literature of the past, teaching them the great traditions of freedom? There are some fine children's shows, but they are drowned out in the massive doses of cartoons, violence, and more violence. Must these be your trademarks? Search your consciences and see if you cannot offer more to your young beneficiaries whose future you guide so many hours each and every day.

What about adult programing and ratings? You know, newspaper publishers take popularity ratings too. The answers are pretty clear: it is almost always the comics, followed by the advice to the lovelorn columns. But, ladies and gentlemen, the news is still on the front page of all newspapers, the editorials are not replaced by more comics, the newspapers have not become one long collection of advice to the lovelorn. Yet newspapers do not need a license from the government to be in business—they do not use public property. But in television—where your responsibilities as public trustees are so plain, the moment that the ratings indicate that westerns are popular there are new imitations of westerns on the air faster than the old coaxial cable could take us from Hollywood to New York. Broadcasting cannot continue to live by the numbers. Ratings ought to be the slave of the broadcaster, not his master. And you and I both know that the rating services themselves would agree.

Let me make clear that what I am talking about is balance. I believe that the public interest is made up of many interests. There are many people in this great country and you must serve all of us. You will get no argument from me if you say that, given a choice between a western and a symphony, more people will watch the western. I like westerns and private eyes too—but a steady diet for the whole country is obviously not in the public interest. We all know that people would more often prefer to be entertained than stimulated or informed. But your obligations are not satisfied if you look only to popularity as a test of what to broadcast. You are not only in show business; you are free to communicate ideas as well as relaxation. You must provide a wider range of choices, more diversity, more alternatives. It is not enough to cater to the nation's whims—you must also serve the nation's needs.

And I would add this—that if some of you persist in a relentless search for the highest rating and the lowest common denominator, you may very well lose your audience. Because, to paraphrase a great American who was recently my law partner, the people are wise, wiser than some of the broadcasters—and politicians—think.

As you may have gathered, I would like to see television improved. But how is this to be brought about? By voluntary action by the broadcasters themselves? By direct government intervention? Or how?

Let me address myself now to my role not as a viewer but as chairman of the FCC. I could not if I would, chart for you this afternoon in detail all of the actions I contemplate. Instead, I want to make clear some of the fundamental principles which guide me.

First: the people own the air. They own it as much in prime evening time as they do at six o'clock Sunday morning. For every hour that the people give you—you owe them something. I intend to see that your debt is paid with service.

Second: I think it would be foolish and wasteful for us to continue any worn-out wrangle over the problems of payola, rigged quiz shows, and other mistakes of the past. There are laws on the books which we will enforce. But there is no chip on my shoulder. We live together in perilous, uncertain times; we face together staggering problems; and we must not waste much time now by rehashing the chichés of past controversy. To quarrel over the past is to lose the future.

Third: I believe in the free enterprise system. I want to see broadcasting improved and I want you to do the job. I am proud to champion your cause. It is not rare for American businessmen to serve a public trust. Yours is a special trust because it is imposed by law.

Fourth: I will do all I can to help educational television. There are still not enough educational stations, and major centers of the country still lack usable educational channels. If there were a limited number of printing presses in this country, you may be sure that a fair proportion of them would be put to educational use. Educational television has an enormous contribution to make to the future, and I intend to give it a hand along the way. If there is not a nation-wide educational television system in this country, it will not be the fault of the FCC.

Fifth: I am unalterably opposed to governmental censorship. There will be no suppression of programing which does not meet with bureaucratic tastes. Censorship strikes at the tap root of our free society.

Sixth: I did not come to Washington to idly observe the squandering of the public's airwaves. The squandering of our airwaves is no less important than the lavish waste of any precious natural resource. I intend to take the job of chairman of the FCC very seriously. I believe in the gravity of my own particular sector of the New Frontier. There will be times perhaps when you will consider that I take myself or my job *too* seriously. Frankly, I don't care if you do. For I am convinced that either one takes this job seriously—or one can be seriously taken.

Now, how will these principles be applied? Clearly, at the heart of the FCC's authority lies its power to license, to renew or fail to renew, or to revoke a license. As you know, when your license comes up for renewal, your performance is compared with your promises. I understand that many people feel that in the past licenses were often renewed *pro forma.* I say to you now: renewal will not be *pro forma* in the future. There is nothing permanent or sacred about a broadcast license.

But simply matching promises and performance is not enough. I intend to do more. I intend to find out whether the people care. I intend to find out whether the community which each broadcaster serves believes he has been serving the public interest. When a renewal is set down for hearing, I intend—wherever possible—to hold a well-advertised public hearing, right in the community you have promised to serve. I want the people who own the air and the homes that television enters to tell you and the FCC what's been going on. I want the people—if they are truly interested in the service you give them—to make notes, document cases, tell us the facts. For those few of you who really believe that the public interest is merely what interests the public—I hope that these hearings will arouse no little interest.

The FCC has a fine reserve of monitors—almost 180 million Americans gathered around 56 million sets. If you want those monitors to be your friends at court—it's up to you.

Some of you may say, "Yes, but I still do not know where the line is between a grant of a renewal and the hearing you just spoke of." My answer is: Why should you want to know how close you can come to the edge of the cliff? What the Commission asks of you is to make a conscientious, good-faith effort to serve the public interest. Every one of you serves a community in which the people would benefit by educational, religious, instructive or other public service programing. Every one of you serves an area which has local needs—as to local elections, controversial issues, local news, local talent. Make a serious, genuine effort to put on that programing. When you do, you will not be playing brinkmanship with the public interest.

What I've been saying applies to broadcast stations. Now a station break for the networks:

You know your importance in this great industry. Today, more than one half of all hours of television station programing comes from the networks; in prime time, this rises to more than three quarters of the available hours.

You know that the FCC has been studying network operations for some time. I intend to press this to a speedy conclusion with useful results. I can tell you right now, however, that I am deeply concerned with concentration of power in the hands of the networks. As a result, too many local stations have foregone any efforts at local programing, with little use of live talent and local service. Too many local stations operate with one hand on the network switch and the other on a projector loaded with old movies. We want the individual stations to be free to meet their legal responsibilities to serve their communities.

I join Governor Collins in his views so well expressed to the advertisers who use the public air. I urge the networks to join him and undertake a very special mission on behalf of this industry: you can tell your advertisers, "This is the high quality we are going to serve—take it or other people will. If you think you can find a better place to move automobiles, cigarettes and soap—go ahead and try."

Tell your sponsors to be less concerned with costs per thousand and more concerned with understanding per millions. And remind your stockholders that an investment in broadcasting is buying a share in public responsibility.

The networks can start this industry on the road to freedom from the dictatorship of numbers.

But there is more to the problem than network influences on stations or advertiser influences on networks. I know the problems networks face in trying to clear some of their best programs—the informational programs that exemplify public service. They are your finest hours—whether sustaining or commercial, whether regularly scheduled or special—these are the signs that broadcasting knows the way to leadership. They make the public's trust in you a wise choice.

They should be seen. As you know, we are readying for use new forms by which broadcast stations will report their programing to the Commission. You probably also know that special attention will be paid in these reports to public service programing. I believe that stations taking network service should also be required to report the extent of the local clearance of network public service programing, and when they fail to clear them, they should explain why. If it is to put on some outstanding local program, this is one reason. But, if it is simply to carry some old movies, that is an entirely different matter. The Commission should consider such clearance reports carefully when making up its mind about the licensee's over-all programing.

We intend to move—and as you know, indeed the FCC was rapidly moving in other new areas before the new Administration arrived in Washington. And I want to pay my public respects to my very able predecessor, Fred Ford, and my colleagues on the Commission who have welcomed me to the FCC with warmth and cooperation.

We have approved an experiment with pay TV, and in New York we are testing the potential of UHF broadcasting. Either or both of these may revolutionize television. Only a foolish prophet would venture to guess the direction they will take, and their effect. But we intend that they shall be explored fully—for they are part of broadcasting's New Frontier.

The questions surrounding pay TV are largely economic. The questions surrounding UHF are largely technological. We are going to give the infant pay TV a chance to prove whether it can offer a useful service; we are going to protect it from those who would strangle it in its crib.

As for UHF, I'm sure you know about our test in the canyons of New York City. We will take every possible positive step to break through the allocations barrier into UHF. We will put this sleeping giant to use and in the years ahead we may have twice as many channels operating in cities where now there are only two or three. We may have a half dozen networks instead of three.

I have told you that I believe in the free enterprise system. I believe that most of television's problems stem from lack of competition. This is the importance of UHF to me: with more channels on the air, we will be able to provide every community with enough stations to offer service to all parts of the public. Programs with a mass market appeal required by mass product advertisers certainly will still be available. But other stations will recognize the need to appeal to more limited markets and to special tastes. In this way, we can all have a much wider range of programs.

"Television should thrive on this competition—and the country should benefit from alternative sources of service to the public. And—Governor Collins—I hope the NAB will benefit from many new members.

Another and perhaps the most important frontier: television will rapidly join the parade into space. International television will be with us soon. No one knows how long it will be until a broadcast from a studio in New York will be viewed in India as well as in Indiana, will be seen in the Congo as it is seen in Chicago. But as surely as we are meeting here today, that day will come—and once again our world will shrink.

What will the people of other countries think of us when they see our western badmen and good men punching each other in the jaw in between the shooting? What will the Latin American or African child learn of America from our great communications industry? We cannot permit television in its present form to be our voice overseas.

There is your challenge to leadership. You must reexamine some fundamentals of your industry. You must open your minds and open your hearts to the limitless horizons of tomorrow.

I can suggest some words that should serve to guide you:

Television and all who participate in it are jointly accountable to the American public for respect for the special needs of children, for community responsibility, for the advancement of education and culture, for the acceptability of the program materials chosen, for decency and decorum in production, and for propriety in advertising. This responsibility cannot be discharged by any given group of programs, but can be discharged only through the highest standards of respect for the American home, applied to every moment of every program presented by television.

"Program materials should enlarge the horizons of the viewer, provide him with wholesome entertainment, afford helpful stimulation, and remind him of the responsibilities which the citizen has towards his society."

These words are not mine. They are yours. They are taken literally from your own Television Code. They reflect the leadership and aspirations of your own great industry. I urge you to respect them as I do. And I urge you to respect the intelligent and farsighted leadership of Governor LeRoy Collins, and to make this meeting a creative act. I urge you at this meeting and, after you leave, back home, at your stations and your networks, to strive ceaselessly to improve your product and to better serve your viewers, the American people.

I hope that we at the FCC will not allow ourselves to become so bogged down in the mountain of papers, hearings, memoranda, orders, and the daily routine that we close our eyes to the wider view of the public interest. And I hope that you broadcasters will not permit yourselves to become so absorbed in the chase for ratings, sales, and profits that you lose this wider view. Now more than ever before in broadcasting's history the times demand the best of all of us.

We need imagination in programing, not sterility; creativity, not imitation; experimentation, not conformity; excellence, not mediocrity. Television is filled with creative, imaginative people. You must strive to set them free.

Television in its young life has had many hours of greatness—its "Victory at Sea," its Army-McCarthy hearings, its "Peter Pan," its "Kraft Theaters," its "See It Now," its "Project 20," the World Series, its political conventions and campaigns, the Great Debates—and it has had its endless hours of mediocrity and its moments of public disgrace. There are estimates that today the average viewer spends about 200 minutes daily with television, while the average reader spends 38 minutes with magazines and 40 minutes with newspapers. Television has grown faster than a teen-ager, and now it is time to grow up.

What you gentlemen broadcast through the people's air affects the people's taste, their knowledge, their opinions, their understanding of themselves and of their world. And their future.

The power of instantaneous sight and sound is without precedent in mankind's history. This is an awesome power. It has limitless capabilities for good—and for evil. And it carries with it awesome responsibilities, responsibilities which you and I cannot escape.

In his stirring inaugural address our President said, "And so, my fellow Americans: ask not what your country can do for you—ask what you can do for your country."

Ladies and Gentlemen:

Ask not what broadcasting can do for you. Ask what you can do for broadcasting.

I urge you to put the people's airwaves to the service of the people and the cause of freedom. You must help prepare a generation for great decisions. You must help a great nation fulfill its future.

Do this, and I pledge you our help.

# Electronic Democracy: How TV Governs[4]

Anne Rawley Saldich

*Born November 20, 1933, Orange, NJ; B.A., University of Detroit, 1958; M.A., Wayne State University, 1962; Ph.D., University of Paris, 1971; professor, College of Notre Dame, 1962-65; professor, College of San Mateo, 1965-72; professor, San Jose University, 1972-73; professor, University of Santa Clara, 1973–; assistant editor,* Journal of Economic Literature, *1980–; author,* Electronic Democracy: Television's Impact on the American Political Process *(1979).*

## Editor's introduction

In this speech, Anne Rawley Saldich discusses her book *Electronic Democracy: Television's Impact on the American Political Process*, in which she asserted that television does in fact have a "potential for tyranny." One example of such tyranny, according to Saldich, is seen when television journalists and broadcasters interpret events. Such interpretation is traditionally the privilege of those elected to public office. Consequently, Saldich believes that students should be taught "electronic literacy" and that interest groups should "form media evaluation centers." Saldich's interest in the power of television developed as she researched her doctoral dissertation, in which she analyzed Charles de Gaulle's use of television to augment his control of France.

---

Last December when TV's coverage of the mideast crisis was at full flood an Iranian was quoted as saying: "We've got America right by the networks." What he meant was that our hearts and minds soon would follow. That idea just about sums up two centuries of journalism's growth in the United States: our once-penny sheets are now powerful institutions. Perhaps because it is accepted political practice in his country, the Iranian seems to have understood better than we that television does govern. That is the pivot around which I will develop three problems in electronic democracy: how TV governs, why the First Amendment should apply differently to television than to print, and the need for public accountability.

My context is commercial network news, specifically ABC, CBS, and NBC. Although technological innovations, such as cable and satellite communication, now challenge their leadership it is instructive, nonetheless, to trace how television gradually moved beyond reporting events and influencing the government to functioning as government itself.

By network TV I mean national television. Hundreds of local stations throughout the country choose to affiliate with one of several conventional broadcast networks from which they get much of their programming, including the network's news feed of national and international events. Some stations are independent of networks. They pick and choose their programming from a wide variety of suppliers, but most stations are affiliated with one of the big three.

In deference to the practice of defining one's scope and terms, I would like to say what I mean by "government" and by "sovereignty of the people."

"Government" is used here in two ways: the institutionalized government that we think of on the national, state, and local levels which, in all cases, is divided into three branches: executive, legislative, and judicial. The other definition of "government" is all-encompassing. To use Thomas Jefferson's phrasing, it means the people themselves acting in their political capacity.

The other term that can do with a bit of citation is "sovereignty of the people." I am told by a well-known political scientist who specializes in American government that this country has

[4]Delivered as a public lecture, at Stanford University, in Palo Alto, California, on February 7, 1980.

no sovereign. That may be modern but I have decided it is inaccurate. I believe Alexis de Tocqueville's interpretation of this phrase is still valid. In Part II of his *Democracy in America* he wrote that "above all the institutions, and beyond all the forms, there is a sovereign power, that of the people [because] they can abolish or change them as it will." This classic definition is the one that I use.

Let me begin, now, to crystallize the three points that I make. First, observation shows that television has openly usurped certain functions that are traditionally governmental. In addition, TV continually shapes our political values and most of our electoral process in ways that are far from open.

Second, freedom of the press belongs to the people, not to journalists. Therefore, it seems to me that the First Amendment should not protect TV in the same way that it protects print because the airwaves are public property, legally. Broadcasters would like us to think television news is an extension of print but it is not. It is different, intrinsically and profoundly.

My last point is that television has a potential for tyranny. We can guard against it only if TV's vast powers are checked and balanced through public accountability, just as all political power is checked and balanced wherever democracy is strong.

Well, in what way does TV govern? The ways are numerous and subtle but four are obvious. Network executives have taken over what political scientists call gatekeeping, setting the nation's political agenda, being a court of last resort, and a conduit for TV diplomacy. Television's bid for a fifth governmental function collapsed when the networks tried to control the start of TV's presidential campaign last fall.

Gatekeeping is just what it sounds like, control of access to power. In this context it means control of the airwaves. No one may appear on national TV without network permission. That includes presidents. Until recently presidential requests were quickly met, usually without question. However, after Nixon and Watergate gave us the journalist-as-hero, network executives began to flex their political muscle. They have denied access to President Carter on more than one occasion. An example will suffice. CBS turned down the president's proposal for a nationwide speech on energy in 1977. The White House wanted to broadcast "live" but CBS decided the subject did not warrant interruption of their programming. Since the big three march in lockstep, it surprised no one when ABC and NBC followed suit. So, for the first time since his inauguration, Carter formally requested broadcast time, citing national urgency as his reason. Face was saved on all sides: he got access and the networks demonstrated independence.

Consider the political implications, even the absurdity of this situation. Who gave network executives this gatekeeping function? Ours is an electronic democracy, by which I mean much of the information in our society is transmitted electronically, and democracy assumes an informed citizenry. Presidents must have access to the viewing public because they comprise a majority of the body politic. It is not unusual for eighty million people to watch a televised presidential address and millions more listen on radio. After all, the public owns the airwaves and the president is our duly elected representative. No one elected or appointed broadcasters to control presidential access to the nation's electorate or our access to the president.

Another governmental function that networks exercise every day is this: on their evening news they set the country's political agenda, which simply means they pick and choose what is important for us to know about public affairs. We have no nationwide, general newspaper in the United States except for electronic news on radio and television. Of the two, TV has the greater impact.

Historically it was a nation's leaders, whether religious or secular, who decided what the people would know about public affairs. I am not saying that that was a better system. There was a great deal of deception in the good old days just as there has been in our recent past and as there may be now. But that is how government did work and in a democratic society such as ours people could at least vote their leaders out of office if they thought they were wide of the mark. Today, however, broadcasters pick and choose what many people will know and when they will know it. Despite the fact that TV has a long, well documented track record of not telling us what we need to know, in order to make intelligent political choices, broadcasters cannot be voted out of this governmental function. Furthermore, they think that we the people should have no say about news content. This attitude reflects a certain arrogance of power. Journalists have forgotten that freedom of the press belongs to the people. It does not belong to a particular profession. Furthermore, the airwaves are public property, legally. They are licensed to stations for three years and are relicensed on condition that the public's interest, convenience, and necessity is ascertained by the station and met. Otherwise the Federal Communications Commission, an arm of Congress, may reassign the license to another station manager. The conclusion is obvious: the public has a right to influence news standards that govern content because they have a right to influence the use of their property.

Because democracy requires an informed citizenry news sources receive special privileges. Print is posted at lower rates than otherwise would apply and broadcasters are awarded monopolies when they are assigned space on the TV spectrum. But TV news is superficial, fragmented, and often irrelevant to the needs of its viewers. Its prime mover is not the public's interest but the public's pocketbook. TV's "half hour" news is twenty-two minutes long. The other eight are sold to advertisers for rates that swing widely between eighty to a hundred and fifty thousand dollars, or more, for every thirty seconds of publicity, depending on how many warm bodies a network delivers to advertisers. X number of viewers are sold for Y number of dollars, like so many bales of hay. Therefore, networks try to build up massive audiences by having something for everyone. The result is that we learn very little about a lot. This has serious consequences for democracy because most Americans use TV as one of their information sources about public affairs and a majority of that group use it as their sole source. That alone is impressive. But TV also enjoys the highest credibility rating of all media, not because the quality of the news is good but because it reaches a national audience and people tend to believe what they see. We often forget that cameras can lie and there are myriad ways to distort reality on television, intentionally or inadvertently. The superficiality of TV news is a disservice to democracy because it is unsuitable as a source of information for participation in the political process. As long as broadcasters control the nation's daily political agenda the public should oblige them to produce quality news that is relevant.

Ironically, it is news coverage which gave network executives another governmental function. TV has become a court of last resort, a corridor to power, for many people who are normally shut-out of our political process. When the have-nots decided to have more they took their case to the viewing public. Through massive demonstrations and occasional violence anti-war protestors, blacks, American Indians, women, the aged and infirm dramatized their problems to the nation as a whole and this forced authorities to respond. Street politics became a carefully honed fine art as each group taught others how to manipulate public opinion, via TV, with the same skill and insight as advertisers, government leaders and media managers.

The story of democracy in America parallels closely the development of communications. New technology facilitates the flow of information and allows the underprivileged to see how the other half lives. This has led to an electronic revolution of rising expectations. Although we live in the age of future shock the same maxim is true today that was true in biblical times: knowledge is power. In this context, television's contribution to democracy cannot be overestimated. Ordinary people have used TV to widen and deepen the meaningfulness of America as a land of opportunity for themselves. They have learned that the political process is not limited to an occasional turn at the ballot box. Four years separate one presidential election from another, but TV's combined network news reaches 55 million people night after night during those intervening 208 weeks. Now, that's what you call raw political power.

With regard to television's role as diplomat, the benchmark year was 1977 when Walter Cronkite facilitated an Israeli-Egyptian rapprochement. On a news program that was carried overseas by satellite he helped to arrange an historic visit between the leaders of two nations whose previous relationship had been one of war and bitterness. The most recent sample of TV diplomacy is the Iranian crisis, but that is so familiar it needs no recounting.

Still, it is worth asking: what is the significance of TV diplomacy? In one sense the simple answer is: not much. There's a long history of business serving as a conduit for diplomacy when normal channels of official communication break down. While I wouldn't say that broadcasting is a business like any other (because it has more power than any governmental, economic, or social institution) it is, nonetheless, a multinational corporation with profit motives and business interests that are much the same as Mobil Oil, IBM, or IT&T. Like them, networks have governmental contacts in nations where they station personnel, who are similarly subject to temptations of privilege and corruption. So, in this regard, journalists trod a well worn path when they were chosen as a conduit for information exchange by both governments. (We've heard a great deal about the Iranians manipulating television, but the White House spokesman for the Iranian crisis was Hodding Carter III, whose professional credentials include seventeen years as a reporter and editor. That is not a coincidence.)

The yet undefined significance of TV diplomacy allows one's fantasies to roam. Perhaps modern warfare could be ritualized on TV as global theatre. Why not a war of words? Why not a holocaust of orchestrated street demonstrations any video frenzy? We could have a military draft system that would train an army of camera crews to fight on foreign soil, shooting film instead of missiles. Staging centers could be set up, under allied protection, where other military personnel study intensively for starring roles as tyrants or government negotiators. Instead of the classic infantry we could have a sort of televised Greek chorus, chanting in unison: The whole world's watching! Then, if a Canadian camera crew comes along to film, the chorus could salute or exploit that country's separatist tendencies by switching to French: le monde entier nous regarde!

Ridiculous? Sure. But not more so than many a ridiculous war that is now part of history.

The point is this: television received a lot of instant criticism for filling a function that is normally governmental, even though there is a long tradition of business becoming an information exchange when diplomatic channels break down. Perhaps it would be worthwhile to consider the positive possibilities of international TV as a forum, an electronic United Nations, through which nations could let off steam when the pressure builds up.

Is there a conspiracy among networks to take over the government? I doubt it. Most broadcasters have been slow to understand the nature of their vast political power and few admit they threaten or have taken over certain facets of governing. Television acquired political power gradually, almost imperceptibly, without plotting and scheming, as a spillover effect from video technology. However, a recent move by the networks to take on another governmental function did seem to be calculated.

In the fall of last year television executives decided they would not sell half hour time segments to political candidates. They said it was too soon to start TV's presidential campaign. Again, the question arises: should broadcasters control the start of a governmental function of this magnitude? As it happens, they did not succeed because candidate Carter appealed to the FCC and the commission overruled the networks.

The issues surrounding this event are enormously complex. One can sympathize with broadcasters because the fairness rule and equal time provision require them to make air time available to all candidates once one has appeared on television. At first glance it does seem "unwarranted," as the networks put it "to interrupt their regularly scheduled programming" for the campaign. But if we look at that explanation from a different angle it doesn't make any sense. After all, TV programs are designed to be interrupted, by advertisements that are sold at a princely sum. The CBS news magazine, "60 Minutes" earns $200,000 per minute of advertising. And specials are really special when it comes to the bottom line. When the Steelers and Rams met in the Rose Bowl this year advertising sold for $476,000 a minute. With twenty-two commercial minutes during that game we're talking about really big money. Therefore, we could reinterpret the networks' position as follows: presidential campaigns do not warrant the interruption of our regularly scheduled profits. Now they may be right. Surely more people would watch the Rose Bowl than a political candidate. But the start of TV's presidential campaign, in an electronic democracy, is a decision about governing America and it is far too important to be left solely to broadcasters. While the excessive length of our campaigns is worthy of debate it is one in which the public should participate since it is the use of public property that is being discussed.

These are the obvious ways that TV governs. There is no time to elaborate on the subtle ways in which TV affects our political values and how it restructures the electoral process. All I can do is mention a few in passing.

Personalizing power is one that comes to mind. Whoever is before the camera's eye gains ground for that episode of Who Governs? During Watergate it was the Congress; in the era of street politics it was the protestors; often it is the president; at the end of last year it seemed to be the Ayatollah. There are a few notable exceptions where TV is impressively destructive (for instance, Ted Kennedy's televised condemnation of the Shah) but these prove the rule rather than weaken it.

Another example of subtle shaping is immediacy. Electronic news is hard and fast. Its negative impact on democracy is that it conditions viewers to want immediate answers. But democracy is a bumbling, stumbling, inefficient form of government. It was designed that way to guard against tyranny. Dictatorships seem to be efficient. When journalists ask questions of a dictator the answers can be given immediately and without qualification because few people need to be consulted. In fact, the answers might be given to journalists before they are asked along with a list of questions from which reporters are not to deviate. But in a democracy the best way to preserve freedom is to have an open exchange of ideas, a public debate on matters of consequence. Democracy therefore takes time, whereas television is intolerant of reasoned discourse. Its emphasis is visual and visceral, not rational.

Officials know this. They often think they will look foolish or uncooperative if they don't answer a question put by a TV journalist and so they almost always do. That quickly but imperceptibly reverses the leadership role, putting the journalist in charge. It also reinforces the viewers' impression that there are immediate answers to all issues, no matter how complex, and if officials don't supply them they are guilty of some misdoing.

This kind of thinking ties in with another hidden governmental power that TV exercises daily. Whenever important public policy is decided for the nation the TV factor is always weighed: how will it play on the home screens? This means that TV personnel participate in the government's decision-making process even when they are not there personally. It's a kind of Orwellian remote control, a sort of grey eminence that subtly shapes policy with an invisible hand.

As for restructuring the electoral process, television coverage has weakened parties and conventions and it has caused campaign costs to skyrocket. It is not simply that politicians buy expensive air time, if stations will sell it to them. It has to do with candidates entering as many primaries as possible, with the hope that they will get TV coverage and therefore win national recognition on the nightly news. Every primary costs money, lots of money. If there were a neck and neck race here in California among Brown, Carter, and Kennedy, the state Democratic headquarters tells me that each candidate might be expected to spend between two and three million dollars. In other states where there's not much of a fight (for example, Georgia would probably go to Carter) the contestants might spend as little as a few hundred thousand dollars or less. As Mary Ellen Leary pointed out, the political significance of this is that candidates spend a large part of their time fundraising instead of dealing with issues. For those candidates who already hold office this getting and spending of money takes time away from their governmental responsibilities. For everyone who makes politics a career it is important to accommodate TV by maintaining a good rapport with its reporters and managers. Again, the Orwellian syndrome: even after an office is won there is always the next election to think about, and this gives television personnel additional leverage in day-to-day government. Although much more could be said on this subject it's time to move on to the First Amendment and why I think it should apply differently to television than to print.

Television's immense political power flows from a combination of several qualities that are not found elsewhere. Its powerful imagery gives viewers a you-are-there feeling, which tends to shut down one's critical, analytical faculties. This, in turn, gives the medium high credibility. People are inclined to believe what they see even if it contradicts their knowledge or experience. Because television news has the highest credibility of all media it also enjoys the kind of authority that every institution in America envies. Credibility is the keystone of all power relationships because belief is the engine of action.

Another unique quality that TV enjoys is its vast audience, which can be compared with radio. While the combined network news reaches 55 million viewers on week nights the space shots, President Kennedy's funeral, the Watergate hearings, and President Nixon's resignation, as well as many other TV specials, were seen by billions throughout the world.

And, television news is received more or less simultaneously, depending on time zones. This is unlike newspapers and magazines whose readers read at their convenience, rather than having their news consumption orchestrated nationally as TV's is. Still another characteristic of television is that it is a continuum and cannot be scanned. Just as the TV set dictates at what time people will get their nightly news so it also dictates that everything must be viewed if one is looking for a particular report.

While radio shares many of these characteristics it does not have the visuals, or the highest credibility, nor does it personalize power in the same way. The source of TV's impact is the mix of all these qualities. That is why all of the still photos in all of the print media did not create the same degree of furor that TV's coverage of the Iranian hostages did. To cite one source, *Newsweek* had dramatic color photos of two Iranians carrying garbage in a large American flag, they showed a black hostage against a wall poster that was covered with anti-American propaganda, other hostages were photographed in humiliating positions—on the floor with hands bound. This kind of picture was not confined to *Newsweek*. Why, then, was there such an outcry when similar images appeared on the home screen? It is because of the medium's unique combination of qualities which are also its source of potential for tyranny: immediacy, moving pictures, a vast audience, and more or less simultaneous reception. The impact has a terrific effect that strains a democratic process because viewers want instant solutions. But international diplomacy is a ritual that takes time.

Freedom of the press is a great tradition in America, and ours has been a model for many countries. Journalists are quick to defend themselves against tendencies to abridge that freedom and they are right to do so. However, the press controls most information sources in the U.S. but media managers seldom admit that they have unmatched political power for that very reason. Others may spend as much time, money, and talent in advancing their interests but no institution has the media's power to investigate for publication, and do so with social approval. Even the FBI, CIA, and the police need media cooperation in order to round off their investigations with publicity. Big business may influence policy at home and abroad, as do the multinational broadcasting networks, but they cannot tell their story to the American people unless the press will sell or give them space and time. Similarly, television executives almost never allow their network or station problems to be aired and in this way the public is cleverly manipulated.

Let's consider the case of free TV. Americans who visit Western Europe are often surprised to learn that an annual tax is paid on each television set. For color it is about $50 a year and for black and white it is about $35. Figures vary from country to country and are subject to change. Everything about this is fairly straightforward but American tourists are almost always shocked and they usually tell their European friends: Why in our country we have free TV. But that isn't true. We pay a hidden TV tax, because prices of all TV-advertised products are raised a few cents so that we may have the pleasure of viewing commercials. It's a simple little system. Broadcasters use our airwaves at no cost to themselves. Consumers (not just people who own television sets) pay for them to have this opportunity. Manufacturers use our airwaves at no cost, also, because they have passed the advertising bill on, and it is from that fortune in advertising revenue that broadcasters make their enormous profits, enough to pay Barbara Walters a million a year, and to budget eighty thousand dollars annually so that Charlie's angels will have their hair nicely combed when you watch that program. In short, what we have in America is an undeclared system of pay-TV, or, in political terms, of taxation without representation. Why don't most Americans realize this? Because broadcasters have carefully controlled that information. For the same reasons the networks don't like to have themselves discussed as multinational big business. But they are. Nor will their managers readily admit to having governmental power. But they do. And certainly journalists are unlikely to tell us that their role as guardians of the public interest is a self-appointed one. But it is. The First Amendment on which they base their claim also protects religion. Using the same logic that the press has used, there is no reason why legitimate religious leaders and their less respectable counterparts should not appoint themselves as the public's watch dog.

The First Amendment is a part of the Bill of Rights that was written for the people, not for the press. Its wording is clear and simple: "Congress shall make no law abridging the freedom of speech, or of the press . . . " Note, there is no mention of this nation's sovereign, the people. If the First Amendment is not taken out of context, if we keep in mind that the overall purpose of the Constitution is to separate and divide power so that it cannot become tyrannous, then simplicity gives way to complexity. Then, a strong argument can be made that television has staggering political power which should be checked and balanced. Naturally, this interpretation of the Constitution is not the broadcasters' favorite.

Tyranny is the arbitrary use of power in the absence of accountability. This describes television before 1968, which is when Paul Simpson founded this nation's first television news archive for public use. Speaking politically, what he did was to provide us with the means of checking TV's tyrannous potential by documenting how its power is used and making it accountable to the public.

To set the tone for this last theme on accountability I would like to quote Freeman Dyson, an eminent physicist, from his new book, which is titled *Disturbing the Universe:* What he says is this: "Through science and technology, evil is organized bureaucratically so that no individual is responsible for what happens." Think of that in connection with television. A dozen years ago, when there were no TV archives, broadcasters were fond of saying their medium is merely a neutral conduit of information, that their reporters are objective, without bias, that TV is simply a window on the world. What they did not tell us is that what we see depends on where they put the window. Objectivity does not exist but it is a wonderful thing if we can convince others that it does because that frees us from responsibility.

Usually when we think about making TV accountable to the public the first thing that comes to mind is regulation through institutionalized government, such as the FCC. That is not what I advocate. The public accountability that I am thinking of would find expression in press councils, classroom instruction in electronic literacy so that we learn how to watch and listen to television with a new awareness; I would like television archives to expand and proliferate and I would like to see citizens' groups influence standards for news content. That last one is bound to raise the ire of broadcasters for they have accustomed themselves to think that freedom of the press means freedom to do what they please, even though we the people pay them to use our property for their profit. It is a favorite axiom in business that "there ain't no free lunch." I think it is time to let the wealthy multinational networks pick up the tab for some part of this accountability process. Unlike most other businesses they have never had a year without profit since 1940. Wall Street analysts tell us that NBC had a bad year in 1978 when its pre-tax profits bottomed out at $122 million. In the language of transactional analysis that would come under the game called: "Ain't it awful?" We should all have such a bad year.

Teaching electronic literacy should be done in the schools and over the air. Everyone should learn about the absence of truth in advertising, when it occurs, and how to recognize it. We should know how TV shapes values and what the mechanics are for distorting reality. For instance, when blacks rioted in Watts, California, during the sixties TV did not have the fast film that they now have, which allows crews to shoot in the dimmest of light. So, to accommodate the technology that was then available TV photographers, filming at night, sought out available light sources, most of which were fires set by arsonists. Without intending to they distorted reality because the televised version of Watts gave the impression of an entire city aflame, which was not the case, though it did provide good visuals. Electronic literacy would also teach us to find out the source of video materials. Much of the TV film that we saw during the early years of our war in Indochina came from the government in the form of "handouts" which were used by broadcasters without telling us that we were viewing propaganda instead of reports filmed by TV journalists. If Watergate gave us the journalist as hero those early years of fighting in Southeast Asia gave us the journalist-as-dupe. We should all learn how TV technicians can splice together bits and pieces of what a person says so that it bears no resemblance to the actual event. Some astute interviewees prevent this by insisting that they be taped to time, which means that if they grant a ten minute interview the broadcasters must agree to air all ten minutes of it. Or, they might refuse an interview altogether unless it is broadcast "live," thereby circumventing the lab where so much of reality ends up on the cutting room floor. We should also learn to see what is not on our TV screens. Broadcasters keep telling us that TV mirrors society. Really? Where are the American Indians? Where are the Mexican Americans? The Puerto-Ricans? Where and when do we see on our home screens images of intelligent, capable, hardworking people with physical infirmities? Where are the analyses of media's influence on every facet of our lives?

In addition to press councils and electronic literacy much can be done on behalf of public accountability by encouraging interest groups to form media evaluation centers. This has already been done with success by Action for Children's Television and by the United Church of Christ which is to television what Nader's Raiders are to car manufacturers. Many other organizations have also been effective media activists but TV managers don't like people to know what a lot of power we have. For example, in the spring of 1978 the Parent Teachers Association met in Chicago with nearly twenty executives whose products are advertised on children's programs. The PTA had a simple message: use your influence to get sex and violence off of children's programs or we will lead a nationwide boycott of your products and we have the clout to get others, such as churches and medical institutions, to join us. Their threat was successful. This was a giant step for grass roots democracy. It was an extraordinary coming together of issues and events but network news gave it the silent treatment. They invoked that principle of journalistic folklore that says: if it wasn't reported it didn't happen.

The fourth expression of public accountability is television archives and all the others are really based on their existence, but most particularly on adequate access to their resources.

It was while doing research here at the Hoover Institution that I began to appreciate how important TV archives are to the vitality of electronic democracy. They are as important as the public library system was in the linear era when most information came through print. When I was doing that research I wanted to analyze how each network had reported the American Indians' takeover of Wounded Knee as a protest against injustice. I was able to do this efficiently, at minimal cost, because there is an excellent television news archive at Vanderbilt University in Nashville, Tennessee, which was started by a private citizen with his own funds in 1968. This is not the place to tell you the story of that remarkable institution and how CBS tried to put it out of business. What you want to know is that it exists, that it is service oriented, and that its materials are accessible because that TV archive has troubled itself to put out an index and abstract of its resources that is comparable in comprehensiveness and quality to the *New York Times Index*. Both the Hoover and the Green libraries have these, here at Stanford. To get videotapes from Vanderbilt you simply go through their indices, select news segments that you want to see, list your selections (which are really a reflection of your editorial judgment), and mail it off to Nashville. You will pay a modest user fee, a refundable deposit for the tapes, and you will sign a promise that you will not have public showings of the materials except under certain conditions. In Tennessee the archive technicians will splice together the selections that have been made and in short order you will receive a compiled video subject tape that can be studied with ease. Or, you can request an entire evening's broadcast, as well as certain documentaries and public affairs programs.

There are few video archives in America. The Vanderbilt Television News Archive is the only one that sends materials from its institution to the user, so that research can be done wherever a playback facility exists, whether in libraries, business offices or homes. This gives the researchers considerable flexibility because they do not have to conform to an institution's business hours. Here at Stanford playback machines are available in the Communications library, at the Hoover, in the Education department and probably in several other places of which I have no knowledge.

It is important to know that Vanderbilt's is the only archive that will compile a subject tape for you. The other major video archive is our National Archives in Washington, D.C. Unwisely, they have let CBS dictate the terms of government policy with respect to their collection and how it is used. CBS, whose whole empire turns on the ability to sell, simply sold the director of the National Archives a bill of goods that prevents the archives from compiling subject matter tapes or sending tapes directly to users. Materials are mailed only from one institution to another. If your library in northwestern Alaska does not have a playback machine, too bad. Try Seattle. In return for letting CBS dictate its policy, the National Archives gets CBS news free of charge and CBS has issued nationwide press releases to advertise its generous gift to the nation.

The political issues involved here are essentially these: CBS is making government policy which denies public access to public events that were broadcast over public property from which activity CBS accrued considerable revenue. Let me give you an example of what I mean by denying access. When I did my research on Wounded Knee it took me three hours to run through those segments of the networks' news coverage that I had asked the Vanderbilt Television News Archive to splice together. Had Vanderbilt signed one of CBS' agreements about the use of video tapes I would have had to request 9 weeks of evening news for each of the networks. That's a total of 135 video cassettes. Imagine retrieving all that from the shelves, packaging it up, mailing it out, being handled by me. Think of the expense in terms of retrieval time and postage. Think of how long I would tie up a playback machine in order to get to one 45 seconds or three minute news segment. Think of how awkward and cumbersome that makes the mechanics of doing research. This is what Dyson means when he says that evil is organized bureaucratically through science and technology.

At this point you are not surprised to learn that NBC and ABC have followed CBS' policies in lemming-like fashion. What the networks are doing is not unlike techniques that were used to keep blacks from voting in the South. This is the broadcasters' version of the poll tax and unreasonable literacy laws. It denies access while appearing to be in the public's interest.

Researchers and educators who understand the importance of television archives should take the lead in petitioning Congress to change our National Archives' policy so that big business (the networks) do not dictate access to public resources. And we should take the lead in working out a system whereby the networks help to support and multiply archives. They can well afford to do this from their profits, as part of their legal commitment to the public interest. There is not much point in knowing about all this unless someone takes action, and I think that burden falls on scholars who understand how documentation is related to accountability, and how accountability is related to freedom.

In closing I want to say again that television has been a great asset to democracy. Sure, there are problems but there are problems everywhere: in education, religion, government, business, and volunteer associations. Broadcasters have not cornered the market on imperfection. The medium is no longer in its infancy but it, and we, are on the learning curve. While we must have the courage to study its political power and governing functions with care, we should do this with the intention of building on its strengths in such a way that future communications technology will continue to protect not only freedom of the press but the people for whom that press is free.

# Does TV Have the Courage to Pioneer a New Commercial Ethic?[5]

Norman Lear

*Born July 27, 1922, New Haven, CT; H.H.D., Emerson College, 1968; U.S. Air Force, 1942-45; comedy writer for television, 1950-59; president, American Civil Liberties Foundation, 1973–; founder, Act III Communications, 1987–; executive producer, creator, director, "Henry Fonda and Family" (1964), "All in the Family" (1971), "Maude" (1972) "Sanford and Son" (1972), "Good Times" (1974), "The Jeffersons" (1975), "One Day at a Time" (1975), "Mary Hartman, Mary Hartman" (1976), "I Love Liberty" (1982), "The Powers That Be" (1992).*

## Editor's introduction

In this speech, Emmy award winning director, producer, and writer Norman Lear addressed a group of 300 television executives and academics at a two-day seminar entitled "Television and Ethics: Who's Responsible?" Admitting that his own company, Act III Communications, has made mistakes, Lear charged that there is "too little consideration for the ethics" of programming decisions. Lear further asserted that television's obligation to "public taste" prevents it from being a medium capable of leading its viewers to new awarenesses and understandings.

---

It is very good to be here this morning and I am grateful to the New England Chapter of the Television Academy of Arts and Sciences and Emerson College for convening this conference.

I attended Emerson College, class of 1944, so I take special pleasure in being here. Today, Emerson students studying communications work in a complex of TV studios and other facilities that were, in 1942, the Emerson Theatre, just off the Esplanade behind 130 Beacon Street. It was in that little theatre that I made my first appearance as an actor, playing "Uncle Stanley" in the Emerson production of "George Washington Slept Here." And, thanks to that experience and the specific advice of our director, Gertrude Binley Kay, it was my last appearance as an actor.

I have many memories of Boston, too, dating back long before I attended Emerson. As a child, we lived in Chelsea, Winthrop, Everett, and my father, who was my prototype for the character of Archie Bunker, wasn't paid by Everett to live in Chelsea, by Chelsea to live in Winthrop, and by Winthrop to live in Brookline.

Our subject for this conference is "Television and Ethics: Who's Responsible?" As I thought about this, preparing for these remarks, the very linkage of those two notions, television and ethics, struck me as some kind of bizarre juxtaposition of terms. Like "supermarket music" or "airline food." For almost fifty years, the companies introducing new communications technologies have promised that their new inventions would lead to a cultural renaissance. General David Sarnoff, the founder of the Radio Corporation of America and one of the founders of the television industry itself, predicted that "television drama of high caliber and produced by first rate artists will materially raise the level of dramatic taste of the nation." That was in 1939. In 1951, another pioneer, Edward R. Murrow, said of television: "This instrument can teach. It can illuminate. Yes, it can even inspire. But it can do so only to the extent that humans are determined to use it to those ends. Otherwise it is merely lights and wires in a box."

[5]Delivered on December 6, 1984, in Boston, Massachusetts. Reprinted with permission of Norman Lear.

In Sarnoff's words, have we been seeing television drama of high caliber that raises the level of dramatic taste of the nation? And in Mr. Murrow's words, is the instrument of television being used to teach, to illuminate, to inspire?

May I state quickly and remove from doubt that I understand that television is not entirely a wasteland. I am well aware of the many fine Movies-of-the-Week and miniseries that appear on all three networks. I applaud with you "The Dollmaker" and "A Streetcar Named Desire" and "Live From Lincoln Center" and "Nova" and "The MacNeil-Lehrer Report" and "Brideshead Revisited" and the Shakespeare plays and the distinguished "Dance in America" series; and I stand behind no one in my appreciation for "Hill Street Blues" and "Cheers" and "Family Ties" and "St. Elsewhere," and that latest gift of laughter, "The Bill Cosby Show," which also illuminates the nuances of familial interpersonal relations and inspires.

But average American viewers are currently watching 7 hours and 34 minutes of television every day of their lives. Children between the ages of 6 and 11 are watching an average of 27 hours a week, 1400 hours a year. By the time a youngster graduates from high school, he or she will spend more time in front of the tube than in the classroom—and I ask you, how much of what is available for them to view do you believe can materially raise the level of their taste? How much of it do you believe serves to teach, illuminate, and inspire?

My references thus far have only been to entertainment on television. Think about news and public affairs. How much of the news and public affairs available to the average American, seven days a week, meets the challenge? To my mind, the answer is simple: precious little.

I believe that the manufacturer of television entertainment, news, and public affairs, and those responsible for preparing and broadcasting it, proceed with very little consideration of the ethics involved. I believe that there is too little consideration for the ethics involved in most American businesses today.

Why are we reading so much about new toxic waste sites; about the increasing hazards of old toxic waste sites; and the continued do-nothing attitude of local, state and federal government?

Why are we reading so much about the further pollution of the air we breathe and the water we drink; of the do-nothing attitude toward acid rain and the contamination of our lakes and streams?

Why are the breakfast cereals sold on supermarket shelves that scientists tell us should be labelled candy?

Why are so many unsafe automobiles sold to American consumers by companies fully aware of their products' defects, only to be recalled later?

Why are drugs that could cost the consumer pennies, sold and advertised under multitudinous brand names at many hundreds times their costs?

Why is American business so consumed with short-term thinking—so obsessed with the need for a profit statement this quarter larger than the last—that it is losing its position of world leadership in industry after industry?

Business forever condemns people like me—writers for the stage, theater, television or books—for portraying business and business people too often in an unflattering light. Well, this writer believes that American business earns every bit of that. And if I am wrong and we writers do overdo it, America won't die of our sins. I believe America is dying, slowly, of theirs.

I feel better for having said that because I don't think television should ever be considered out of context with the rest of American business. As a matter of fact, I am perpetually angered by the way television is lashed at and berated and heaped on by the print media—raked over the coals daily for its sins—while the rest of American business goes relatively scot-free. Now, having said that—where its ethics are concerned—I would like to lash at, berate, and heap on television, too!

And let me confess, sadly, that I do not exclude myself or my company, Embassy Communications, from the problem. Despite all the awareness herein expressed, Embassy, too, must plead guilty.

Commercial television's moral north star, from which nearly all bearings are set, is quite simply: "How do I win Tuesday night at 8 o'clock?" That is the name of the game, the only thing that matters.

When television producers and/or production companies decide what ideas should be developed, their sole criterion is, too often, "What will the networks buy?" And, when deciding what programs are worthy of air time, network television program executives, locked in an overwhelming competitive race that is reported by the print media day in and day out across the nation, have no charter from management to take risks. They have no character to nurture innovation, to seek the kind of quality that might teach some, illuminate some, and inspire. The need to win quickly is too great. Winning in the short-term, beating your competitor's brains out, half-hour by half-hour, that is the ethic that prevails in TV today.

It is an ethic I call the "binary imagination." By "binary" I am using a computer metaphor, the computer habit of reducing everything down to binary codes, either one or zero. If something cannot be captured in that code, it doesn't exist as far as the computer is concerned. Television has come to a place where it, like any other business, insists upon reducing everything down to its own binary code of numbers. Television, in fact, is a cult of numbers: Nielsen ratings, market share percentages, viewer demographics, audience research demographics—did you know that television has now taken to researching program *ideas* for new series before a script is even written?

This reduction of everything to numbers results in a stunted, number-based mentality that impoverishes our understanding of the world by screening out the non-quantifiable facts of life. If something cannot be distilled into a number—or a sliding scale of numbers—the subtler value-laden facts that also constitute reality are disenfranchised, and the wondrous resources of the human mind and soul and spirit are replaced with the binary imagination.

Now I submit that it is one thing to apply the binary imagination to pork bellies, toothpaste, and tires, and quite another to apply it to television, the nation's largest-by-far marketplace of ideas and values, whose product springs largely from the creative impulse of the writers and other artists who serve it.

Asking a writer to conceive to please the machines and tests and graphs that measure audience response to his ideas, is like imagining Michelangelo and a hundred other painters painting the Sistine Chapel from their Sistine Chapel Paint-by-Numbers Kits.

And so, television shows, which have the potential to teach, illuminate, and inspire—shows that have the potential for raising the dramatic and general level of taste of the nation—are too often forfeited to the vagrant, highly imperfect whims of the marketplace, as measured by some highly deceptive numbers. If a show cannot make a 20 market share with the 18-34 year-olds or jump through some other set of arbitrary numerical hoops, it is dropped within a matter of weeks. No opportunity exists for something innovative and different to become an acquired taste. Of course there are exceptions, but we are dealing with the rule. It is the rule, not the exception, that defines ethical behavior.

Television's rationale for this is, of course, that its obligation is to give the viewer what it wants. So if television is serving up a diet that is largely junk and the viewer is watching that junk, television is off the hook, it is the viewer's fault. Let's stop and examine the ethics of that proposition.

When television insists it is merely responding to public taste, it effectively renounces any obligation to lead and places the viewer in charge. Now does that really make sense? Does the television executive who asserts that really believe it? Are we to assume that these highly educated men and women, people who attended major universities and received their masters in communication, then made their way slowly up the television industry ladder to positions where they are the ones who decide what will play on television in American homes—are we to assume that they came that distance, just to take a seat on the back of the bus and let the viewer do the driving? No, I believe that they adopted that attitude when they arrived at their positions of power, because it goes with the territory.

Now, let's look at it from the angle of the average American viewer. The average viewer is the average American, and we know that he or she is leading an emotionally embattled life somewhere in the country, harassed by the economy, by concerns for the future, struggling just to get from Monday to Friday—somewhat under-educated, and probably underpaid and overtaxed. Do you really believe that that individual—who uses television as a means of escape from an otherwise cruel day—could even imagine himself in the job of a television programmer, making such sophisticated determination as what America will see on TV? Uh-uh.

The average TV viewer doesn't run for mayor, doesn't seek a seat in the Congress and isn't looking to program television. He or she is looking, however, in all those places, for leadership. Life and fate and circumstance place leaders in positions of overview, which means that they are able to see things that others can't, and in those positions of overview, responsible leaders will suggest a direction that may not be popular in the short-term, but will benefit *everyone* long-term. Politicians fail this ethical question in leadership when they sacrifice that long-term interest of the electorate, for the immediate gratification of casting a more popular vote now. And, similarly, television programmers ignore the opportunity, if not the obligation, to select programming that will, in the long-term, teach, illuminate and inspire as it entertains, for the sake of yet another instant carbon copy ratings success, short-term.

Grant Tinker, Chairman of the Board at NBC, told the *New York Times* recently, "I think it's criminal of people to stare at television so uncritically." The man who created NBC, General Sarnoff, said that "television drama of high caliber . . . will materially raise the level of dramatic taste of the nation." What has happened to us in 50 years? General Sarnoff wasn't satisfied to blame the consumer for the product. He obviously believed that the proper role of leadership was to continually improve upon the product and help the consumer reach for it.

It is only television executives who insist that television merely responds to public taste. Educators, sociologists, and other observers of the media tell us it is shaping public taste. Both positions are right, but this is one situation where the chicken comes squarely before the egg.

Yes, three networks will respond to the success of MTV by creating their own music video shows. But it was all those years of sharply edited, highly expensive, musically sophisticated TV commercials that paved the way and weaned the viewer to an appetite for what became MTV. Yes, they were responding to the success of the prime-time soap opera, "Dallas," when the competition created "Dynasty" and "Hotel" and "Falcon Crest" and "Knots Landing" and "Glitter"—but it was all those years of daytime soap operas that weaned a major portion of the viewing public toward the acceptance of a glossier kind of soap opera in prime time.

If television will accept the responsibility for weaning generations of Americans to programs that most television executives will tell you privately shame them—or as they put it, are "not my personal cup of tea"—television might at last be ready to fulfill the promise held for it by the men who created the medium.

But television has weaned several generations of Americans to accept more than just the style and content of its programming. America's esthetic sense, its sensibilities and much of its behavior has been shaped by television, too.

How many adult family members can we watch on game shows—jumping up and down like little children, under instruction from the producers—clapping their hands and shrieking wildly at the sound of a bell that tells them they have guessed right and won $80—before we begin to believe that it is proper and normal to explode in front of millions of your peers, in a kind of foolish and herd-like ritual of childish abandon?

How many people will we have to see on the evening news—in a moment of consummate grief, just having learned of the death of a loved one—responding politely to the voyeuristic questions of an aggressive TV newsperson, before we begin to believe that it is our obligation, even in moments of unspeakable pain, to stand still and answer the media's questions?

And how many little white lies do we have to hear—such as "We'll talk to so-and-so when we come back after this message"—only to sit through not only one commercial message, but two or three before "so-and-so" appears—how many of these little white lies do we have to hear before we become so deadened by them that we are ready to accept larger ones?

If these examples stretch your belief, remember that there are many examples of TV influencing behavior that have been documented. When the Fonz on "Happy Days" got his first library card, thousands of youngsters everywhere visited libraries the next day for theirs. When the father on "Good Times" was diagnosed as suffering from hypertension, thousands of black males across America sought similar help after the broadcast. Of course, television influences behavior—and of course, that should be a matter of ethical concern for every individual in a leadership role in the medium.

Most television programming executives will not buy this. And yet, ironically, they have been victims of the weaning process themselves. A young writer of the situation comedy that I had mentored sent me this note not too long ago:

"I don't think the networks understand the real people. Most of the programming executives are only 32 or 33, like me—and we all grew up watching a lot of television—I mean, *really* a lot of television. Then we all went to college and studied communications. I don't know how I escaped this, Norman—maybe it's because I always knew I wanted to write—but I swear, most of those guys at the network are all confused about what real human behavior is. They ask us to write stupid things for people because the only thing they know about how people talk and behave is what they've seen all their lives on television. Sometimes I think TV is not so much a reflection of society as a reflection of other TV shows. *And they don't know that.*"

It is arrogant of television to accept so little responsibility for the nature of its programming and for its effect on society. And if that attitude isn't certifiably lacking in ethical considerations, it's awfully close. Especially when you consider that the binary imagination and the obsession with ratings applies as much to news and information as it does to entertainment.

Don't believe for a minute that the top priority of Dan Rather, Tom Brokaw, and Peter Jennings and their staffs is to present the news in a way that helps the American viewer understand the world and events around him. These are earnest and talented people and they would hope to achieve that end, but their broadcasts are in a life-or-death struggle with the competition, and the name of the game for them is to win Monday through Friday at 7:00 P.M. This is as true in every city with more than one local independent station as it is at the networks.

We all know that violence has a very special place in the evening news. Murder, rape, fire, a highway accident—especially those that provide terrific photo opportunities—are premium items on America's newscasts. The people responsible will tell you that that's what the viewers want. As a matter of fact, a recent piece of research conducted on behalf of the Radio Television News Directors Association, revealed that when viewers were asked what they remembered most on news, "Murders and murderers totally outdistanced foreign wars . . . homicidal maniacs as a class proved seven times as memorable as the brutal war between Iran and Iraq."

The research concluded, in part, with: "Violent crimes are more memorable as news events than all but the most dramatic political occurrences." I am not shocked by that report. Why wouldn't a hot local murder or a major traffic accident—especially as photographed with the zeal and zoom lens of one of our macho, staccato, late-breaking news teams—be more memorable than the same two minutes or less allotted to the coverage of a war between Iran and Iraq?

The problem with the research conducted for the News Directors Association, among television viewers nationwide, was: one-quarter of the respondents said that they had never heard of presidential advisor Ed Meese; 64% replied that they never knew that Gary Hartpence had changed his name to Gary Hart. Of this the Radio Television News Directors Newsletter said smugly: " . . . The public enthusiastically exhibited the right not to know."

Okay, so the average viewer doesn't remember some of the more important stories covered by TV news as well as he does the lesser reports of local violence. The same Gary Hart, in a television interview during the primary campaign, didn't know who Louis Farrakhan was, or the news reporter he had threatened with death just that week. During the recent campaign, your own very able Congressman, Ed Markey, was asked to name the Prime Minister of Israel on a Boston show, admitted he didn't know, and then guessed wrong.

If the truth be known, your keynote speaker—this Talmudic-looking fellow who stands here working hard to impress you with his depth of knowledge—is sadly lacking in information on many of the more pressing domestic and international problems that confront us today. If I had to state a quick opinion on aspects of the situation in Nicaragua and El Salvador or participate in a discussion on some of the more sophisticated problems concerning the Middle East, I would turn privately to people I consider experts in the field to get the information needed before I could perform.

Now, I think you will grant that Gary Hart and Ed Markey and Norman Lear, by virtue of fate, fortune, and circumstance, lead less emotionally-embattled lives than the average American I described earlier. We are better educated, have more time and better opportunity to learn about the issues, and we suffer less *angst* than that citizen who is simply struggling to get from Monday to Friday. And yet, often enough, *we* don't know. The wonder is we don't get caught at it more often.

Why then are the self-appointed arbiters of taste and judgment so quick to put down the average television viewer? How dare television interpret his confusion at the complexity of the issues that confront him—and his inability to recall the myriad of names and events with which he is constantly bombarded—as evidence that it has no responsibility to them? Ethically, those in positions to lead must accept that obligation or, ethically, it is a case of the blind leading the blind.

Television has, of course, had an effect on the political scene, too, and I am again sorry for the viewer. I am not sorry for the politicians. In the 1984 election, they were co-conspirators in a ten-month television extravaganza that sacrificed everything to the binary imagination. The issues, the ideas and the candidates themselves were largely sacrificed to an obsession with numbers and percentages, statistics and polls. Here was the binary imagination run amok.

TV coverage of the 1984 presidential campaign was a triumph of images over substance. It was the horse race and hoopla of the campaign, not the ideas and merits of the issues, which received the most attention. From the primaries through to November 6th, the big story most evenings was the result of the latest poll. Again and again, the candidates were seen on the evening news, responding to the same tired questions: "The polls show you so many points behind, Mr. Mondale. How are you going to catch up?" "The polls show you slipping a little among this or that constituency, Mr. President. What are you going to do about it?"

And talk about being *weaned* by the media: convention delegates no longer complain if their view is obstructed by TV cameras and crews. The real floor manager at political conventions is the man who points the camera. "Spontaneous" demonstrations are scheduled to last twelve minutes, *precisely*, to satisfy the needs of the convention floor, Olympus-like, and senators of great renown scurry like beggars from booth to booth hoping that Dan Rather or Tom Brokaw will think them worthy of an interview.

I had the privilege of traveling with a presidential candidate in the 1980 primary campaign, and I was fascinated to observe the minuet for news coverage that was danced by the politician and the TV journalist. It took place each afternoon, when everyone paused, the TV lights were on, the cameras pointed, and every Sam Donaldson on the tour sought to ask that provocative fifteen-second question which would elicit a sharp twenty-second response that would assure *him* a place on the evening news along with the candidate.

Television news, like television entertainment, is a business. And business today, all businesses, perform for the bottom line. Is there anything ethically wrong with this? Not on the surface, I suppose. But I believe our society is threatened by an unhealthy emphasis on success in the short-term, as measured by The Numbers. Much has been written to indicate that the American motor car ceased to be the standard of the world when Detroit, all those years ago, thought it could not and should not diminish a current profit statement to meet the challenge of the smaller, less expensive, foreign imports. In recent years, we have witnessed the same phenomenon in consumer electronics, steel, and many other industries.

Americans have been shaken by these losses. Across the country, in city after city that were once known as "company towns," the compact between the family and the company—a compact that had been carried forward from generation to generation, where fathers and uncles and brothers and nephews all worked in the same plant—has been broken. When we talk about the breakdown of the American family and try to list its probable causes, how much should we attribute to this overwhelming loss of continuity and stability?

Was there an ethical responsibility to attempt to prevent this from occurring? And if so, whose responsibility? Certainly the union chieftains, responsible for the long-term interests of the work force, saw the handwriting on the wall at some point, but they never blew the whistle. On the other hand, they were only representing their workers, who were interested only in increased wages and a larger package of benefits. Then what about management? Certainly they could see trouble down the road if they didn't diminish a current profit statement to modernize, or otherwise meet the threat of foreign competition. Yes, but they were tied to contracts that demanded they produce in the short-term, so they couldn't blow the whistle either.

Those who run television are in the same boat. It is no secret that the networks have been losing their share of audience steadily for years; the largest of the capable enterprises, HBO, is losing share precipitously now, and all of the broadcast television is beginning to lose to the videocassette. They are in a trap, not of their own devising.

And so it is very hard to pin down where ethical responsibility lies. We have created a kind of climate in our country, a climate in which leadership everywhere—in the Congress, federal agencies, business, labor, the universities, television—leadership everywhere glorifies instant success—whether in profit margins, ratings, or polls—and refuses through indifference or myopia to make adequate provisions for the future. All the while, committing suicide in the long term.

Because television probably affects us more profoundly than any other of America's businesses, and because its profile is certainly higher than any other American business, it would be helpful to see it lead in accepting its ethical responsibilities. It would be helpful to see those television executives, who have been content to let the viewers do the driving, finally take the wheel. General Sarnoff was driving when he said that what he envisioned for television drama would raise the taste of the American viewer, and Edward R. Murrow was driving when he told us that television had the capacity to teach, illuminate and inspire.

We can't let that kind of leadership end with the pioneers. Television needs some new pioneers: men and women in every area of the industry who will resist the inexorable commercial logic of the present day television which tends to trivialize everything that comes in its path; men and women who will strive for more than seeking to win Tuesday night at 8 o'clock; writers, directors, producers, actors, and executives who will not forfeit their moral judgment to the Bottom Line.

When I grow up, I hope to be just such a writer and executive myself.

# Children's Television: A National Disgrace[6]

George Gerbner

*Born August 1919, Budapest, Hungary; B.A., University of California at Berkeley, 1942; M.S., 1952, Ph.D., 1955, University of Southern California; reporter, assistant financial editor,* The Chronicle, *1942-43; U.S. Army, 1943-46; instructor, Pasadena Junior College, 1948-51; instructor, El Camino College, 1951-56; professor, University of Illinois-Urbana, 1956-64; dean, University of Pennsylvania Annenberg School of Communications, 1964-89; author,* Mass Media Policies in Changing Cultures *(1977),* Violence and Terror in the Mass Media *(1988).*

## Editor's introduction

Delivering the keynote address at a "Television and Children: Facts vs. Fiction" symposium, George Gerbner, then dean of the University of Pennsylvania's Annenberg School of Communications, condemned the violence on television, the lack of minority and senior citizen representation on television, and the poor quality of children's programming. As the title to the speech indicates, Gerbner asserted that children's television is a "national disgrace of world-class proportions." In addition to his vehement criticism of children's programming, Gerbner conveyed the fundamental significance of television to American society, as he remarked that watching television is perhaps the most common way by which Americans define themselves.

---

I'd like to reach my destination in five steps and I'll tell you what they are so you can keep me on course. First, I'd like to make some comments about what I think the age of television means. Secondly, I'd like to describe its main characteristics. Third, I will present some highlights of our research of eighteen years' standing, an ongoing project attempting to analyze the symbolic environment into which our children are born and in which they grow up. Fourth, I'd like to focus attention on so-called children's television, and I say "so-called" because only one-fifth of children's viewing goes into children's television. For the first time in human history children are plunged into an accelerated version of the adult cultural environment. I don't think we've ever fully grasped the significance of that. And fifth, I want to make some comments about the political situation that surrounds the issues we are talking about.

So now to begin. You must have heard the story about the teacher who asked, "Children, what does this century owe Thomas Edison?" One child raised his hand and spoke and said, "Teacher, without Edison we would still be watching television by candlelight!"

It is inconceivable to most of our children and grandchildren that there was an age before television. Television has become as much a fabric of our life as a pre-industrial religion and ritual must have been. Television has ushered in not just another medium but a new era. It has created a new symbolic environment into which our children are born.

The significance of that symbolic environment can be best reflected in the word that to me sums up the most distinctive element of human life, the most crucial distinction between humans and other creatures, and that word is storytelling. We experience the world through our stories about it. Whoever tells stories of a culture defines the terms and the agenda of human discourse and the issues we face in common.

There are three major ways in which human beings have told stories throughout our history. The first and certainly most lasting period, the pre-industrial, was a period of face-to-face sto-

[6]Delivered at the Yale University School of Medicine, in New Haven, Connecticut, on October 3, 1985. Reprinted with permission of George Gerber.

rytelling. There was no way of saying, "Well, I don't have to tell you about this, you can look it up." Stories about the origin of life, the nature of the universe, and the modes of right and wrong conduct had to be remembered, rehearsed, and repeated in something we now call ritual mythology, even religion.

It was only relatively recently, with the coming of the industrial revolution, that the method of storytelling has changed. The first mechanical device putting out standardized commodities, the first machine, was the printing press. The first manufactured commodity was the book. Indeed, that was necessary for all the rest of the upheavals of the industrial revolution to come.

With the book you record and mass-produce the stories of the culture. You make it possible for people to get off the land, to go into other countries and continents, and to take much of their culture, much of their world, much of their mythology, much of their community with them. The book breaks up the ritual. It ushers in the Reformation. It makes it possible for people to go anywhere in the world and no longer be dependent on the local culture. The ministration of the chief or the priest is no longer necessary just to convey the word. The early Protestants could say, "Here is the Book, read it for yourself." Others could say: take it with you, develop your own interpretation, your own tastes. Different cultures, different religions could begin to live side by side.

The book made possible the plurality of storytelling, the plurality of "worlds" that storytelling builds for different people.

A modern mass public is a community that never meets face-to-face. It is created through publication. The notion of self-government itself is predicated on the ability to be reasonably free, to cultivate competing and conflicting conceptions of life of society side by side, competing for attention, competing for support, competing for votes.

In the last forty years or so, the situation has fundamentally changed. The change is due to television. Television, unlike all other previous media, is not a selectively used medium. Most people use television relatively non-selectively. They watch not by the program but by the clock.

Television is on an average of 7 hours a day in the typical American home. In half of our homes, typically homes that cannot afford a great variety of cultural activities, it is turned on in the morning and turned off at night. It is used as a ritual. It has become the functional equivalent of a new religion. It reaches those whom no previous central authority could reach, such as children, and reaches them at home, quickly and continuously. It incorporates most of what we know in common such as art, science, and government. It has replaced the church in that historic nexus of power which used to be state and church.

Television presents a common world to all our people, the only common denominator in an otherwise heterogeneous nation, the first true melting pot of our country. That common world is the largest single source of information. Most of it comes from entertainment. I call entertainment the education we choose for its immediate rewards.

We have studied the effects of television on our health habits, on images of science, on conceptions of medicine, on orientation to politics, on occupational choices, on educational and intelligence test scores, on violence, religion, and other issues. (Write me and I'll send you some reports.)

Now I go into my second step. What are some general features of the world of television? For the first time in history children are born into a symbolic world that does not originate with parents, church, or school, and requires no literacy. Television has replaced most stories told by parents, and has either replaced or reorganized what we learn in school or in church. It has become the norm, the standard to which we all have to relate. We use it as a measure of our own behavior and of the behavior of people around us. We use it as a way of defining ourselves. Even if you don't watch television, you get it through other people who do.

The process of presenting a common world to an otherwise heterogeneous community has for many people enormous attractions. These are people who never read books, people who never participated in the riches of culture, people who never saw anyone who was famous or powerful or beautiful or infamous, people who are isolated, parochial, removed from the centers of action. These people are now all in the mainstream. That is the enormous attraction of television. No one is out in the sticks. You can be in the hospital or in a prison, you can be very young or very old, you can be anywhere and anybody—you are now part of the mainstream.

You can be very poor and still many of the same famous and rich and beautiful and ugly people come into your own home as they come into the homes of rich people.

For many this is a tremendous enrichment of cultural horizons. They will not give it up. They will not turn it off. Even to ask them is an arrogance that does not respect the genuine attraction of being a part of the mainstream to people who have always been out of it. What we should do is to ask about its dynamics, ask about its lessons, because that is not a private business. It has become a major, central, public issue and problem of our times.

Now the third step. A typical viewer of prime time sees a cast of about 300 characters each week. A very stable cast. We have been monitoring it for 18 years. What kind of cast is this? Well, about 41 characters a week are engaged in law enforcement. Protecting society is the main preoccupation of the largest single occupation on the air. Prime time is a time of power. That is why it has so much violence. (Daytime is a time of *internal turbulence.* For all its melodramatic qualities it has much more relevance to things that are close to people than the feverish macho rituals of prime time.) While 41 characters enforce the social order, about 23 criminals threaten it each week, week in and week out. There are about 12 doctors, 6 lawyers and 3 judges engaged in enforcing the rules of the game.

All-in-all, men outnumber women 3 to 1. The representation of young people (under 18) is one-third of their true proportion in the population. The representation of old people (65 and above) is less than one-fifth. These are marginal markets and thus marginal people; television unwittingly favors the world of its best customers.

The question of representation is not just a question of numbers, like a census. It is a question of the range of opportunities that people growing up in the cultures learn about. If you are white, male, in the prime of life, there are no limits. You can do almost anything. If you are a woman, non-white, young or old or in any sense some member of a minority, you are under-represented not only in number but also in opportunities, save one: You are over-victimized.

Violence is a demonstration of power. On TV it is a dramatic device to demonstrate what happens between different kinds of people in a conflict. Who tends to get away with what against whom? That is the principal lesson of violence. To reduce that to the question of aggression alone as an isolated behavior is sheer obfuscation. It is the favorite media question because, as the programs themselves, it has a repressive control function. Although true on a low level, it is not the major lesson.

The more we're exposed to violence-laden television, the more we exhibit what we call the "mean world syndrome." We absorb a sense of mistrust and insecurity, a sense of living in a mean and dangerous world in which we must protect ourselves and in which we must depend on strong people and measures for protection. If anything, it's a device that tends to put people in their place according to their status. It makes those who are lower in status feel weaker and more vulnerable and more easily controlled.

There is a direct correlation between amount of exposure and expressions of insecurity, vulnerability, and dependence. The slight, if often tragic, relationship to actual imitated violence is the fallout from this vast social control exercise. I submit that we should be equally concerned with the kind of debilitation that increases feelings of vulnerability, powerlessness, feeling of dependence, especially among those who are already more vulnerable, who are already lower on the scale of power, namely women, children, minorities. This is the mechanism that maintains and exacerbates the injustices and the inequities of our society. That is how violence really works.

Now my fourth step. One would think that in what has been called a wasteland (it's not a term I like because it doesn't give full justice to its rich dynamism) children's television would be an oasis. Unfortunately, the opposite is true. It's the real desert. It is called the "kidvid ghetto" in the industry. Like a ghetto or slum, it is the high profit, quick turnover, most exploited sector of a market.

There is no other civilized country that I know that doesn't have at least a half hour of high quality programming for children in prime time. We don't have a single network that has any kind of regular children's programming even once a week. Public broadcasting used to provide most quality children's programs. But for the first time in our television history, the fall schedule will be devoid of any original programming produced for PBS by an American producer. Instead, the schedule will be composed of foreign acquisitions and repeats.

Where do quality children's programs come from? They come from PBS and from abroad. The BBC, the Italian, French, Scandinavians, Germans, or Japanese TV systems have between four and six times the number of hours of new programming we have. Many of the highest quality programs that win international festival prizes of children's programming come from the Soviet Union and other countries of Eastern Europe. That's where you will find some of the most popular productions, the classics, the highest-paid talents, and the most compelling stories of family, friendship, and cooperation on television. Unlike our situation of not having any decent programs, the Soviet Union has several major studios engaged only in producing children's films and programs.

In the transfer of controls from partly public to mostly private hands, in the shift of controls from one set of large conglomerates to another set of even larger conglomerates, otherwise called deregulation, and under the impact of the "merger mania," the previously existing mechanisms of citizen participation and consumer protection are being dismantled. The first to suffer is always the weakest and most vulnerable. The situation is a national disgrace of world-class proportions.

Now the fifth and final step. The Wirth-Lauterberg bill, which would mandate five hours of children's programming during the week, is not censorship but its opposite; it is a step toward liberation of television from the constraints of the marketplace selling children to the greediest and highest bidder.

We need a new environmental movement, addressed at the environment that is most crucial to our humanity, the environment of stories we tell our children, the environment that shapes so much of what we think and do in common. This environmental movement has to be a coalition of parents, health professionals, educators, and citizens. It is designed not to censor but to *liberate* from the iron censorship of a market of manufactured daydreams that debilitate and hurt so many. That, at least, is a dream that heals.

# The Intimidated Press[7]

Anthony Lewis

*Born March 27, 1927, New York, NY; A.B., Harvard University, 1948; deskman,* New York Times; *reporter,* Washington Daily News, *1952-55; reporter,* New York Times *Washington, D.C., bureau, 1965-72; columnist,* New York Times, *1969–; author,* Gideon's Trumpet *(1964),* Portrait of a Decade: The Second American Revolution *(1964).*

## Editor's introduction

*New York Times* columnist Anthony Lewis gave the 11th annual Frank E. Gannett lecture to some 400 journalists and government officials in 1988. The speech was made possible by a grant from the Gannet Foundation to the Washington Journalism Center. The grant is intended to provide "an annual lecture . . . on a journalistic subject of importance and interest to thoughtful laymen as well as to media leaders." Due to a record low voter turnout (50.16 percent) for the 1988 presidential election, Lewis's "subject of importance" was the relationship between the media and the executive office. Lewis believed that media had, particularly during the Reagan years, retreated from an adversarial relationship with the president and begun a deferential, nearly symbiotic relationship with political leaders. In essence, Lewis asserted that it is the media's responsibility to place the president under "unstinting scrutiny," as had been the norm during Vietnam and Watergate.

---

Seventeen years ago *The New York Times* and then *The Washington Post* published the Pentagon Papers, and fought off the Nixon Administration's attempt to stop further publication. Examining that episode afterward, a law review article by Professors Harold Edgar and Benno Schmidt, Jr., of the Columbia Law School said it marked "the passing of an era" for the American press. It was an era, they said, in which there was a "symbiotic relationship between politicians and the press." But now, by printing the secret history of the Vietnam War over strenuous official objections, establishment newspapers had "demonstrated that much of the press was no longer willing to be merely an occasionally critical associate [of the government], devoted to common aims, but intended to become an adversary. . . . "

A year after the Pentagon Papers, *The Washington Post* began looking into Watergate. What it published, in defiance of administration pressures, set in motion a process of law and politics that ended in the resignation of the President. That surely seemed to confirm what Professors Edgar and Schmidt had said. The symbiotic relationship was over. We now had an independently critical press.

I thought about Professors Edgar and Schmidt this past September when I read an editorial in *The Washington Post.* It was about the statement by the Speaker of the House, Jim Wright, that the C.I.A. had admitted, in secret testimony, helping to arouse anti-government protests in Nicaragua in order to provoke repression that would harm the image of the Sandinistas. The editorial was critical—of Speaker Wright, not the C.I.A.

The Speaker's statement was harmful to the Nicaraguan opposition, the *Post* said. It noted Mr. Wright's claim that what he said had already appeared in other news reports. But that explanation, it said sternly, failed to consider "the crucial authority that a Congressional figure can add by his confirmation." Finally, the editorial came to the question whether the C.I.A. had in fact sparked the Nicaraguan protests. That would have been "incredibly stupid," it said, and public testimony in Congress had absolved the C.I.A. of the charge.

[7]Delivered as the Frank E. Gannett lecture, in Washington, D.C., on November 28, 1988. Reprinted with permission of Anthony Lewis.

The C.I.A. has in fact done some "incredibly stupid" things, in Nicaragua among other places. I think a genuinely critical press would have taken a hard look at the facts before chastising a Congressional leader for improper leaking or abuse of authority in this case.

But what struck me about the editorial, and the reason I mention it now, was not so much its factual assumptions as its reverential tone. Its premise was that legitimacy rests in the executive branch of the United States government, not the legislative. Congress, along with the rest of us, owes respect to the secrecy that the executive, with its special knowledge and expertise, deems necessary in the interest of national security.

Ladies and gentlemen, those were the very attitudes that the *Times* and the *Post* and other newspapers rejected when they published the Pentagon Papers. As a result of the Vietnam War they had come to realize that executive officials did not always have superior knowledge and expertise, and did not always tell the truth. They were not entitled to reverence, from the press or Congress. The country would be better off—more wisely led—if policies were subject to unstinting scrutiny, including a good many policies covered up by secrecy.

Of course my point does not lie in the particular editorial, and I know that there were reasons to question Speaker Wright's wisdom in speaking out when he did. But I think the tone of the editorial reflected a general trend. The established press in this country has to a large extent reverted to the symbiotic relationship with the executive branch. We are an adversary only on the margins, not on the fundamentals that challenge power. We have forgotten the lessons of Vietnam and Watergate.

Think about press treatment of the presidency in the 1970s and, by comparison, in the last eight years. In Ben Bradlee's phrase, there has been "a return to deference." We are all uneasily aware that something like that has happened. We are not sure why it came about. But we can place the change in the Reagan years.

When President Reagan took office in 1981, the press at first reported with gusto on the gaps in his knowledge and interest, the confusion of fact and fancy. The evening television news noted his mistakes at press conferences, and newspapers detailed them the next day. But it turned out that the public did not care about Mr. Reagan's flubs. James David Barber, the scholar of the presidency, said the public treated his contempt for facts "as a charming idiosyncrasy." So the press's gusto for recording Mr. Reagan's wanderings from reality waned. More important, the press did not give the public real insight into the working of the Reagan White House—into the confusion and vacuity that have been described so convincingly now in books by former insiders.

After Mr. Reagan had been President for about a year, I wrote a column puzzling over why the press seemed to hold back from giving us an unvarnished picture. The reporting was gingerly, sometimes almost protective. Why? I ventured a few guesses on the possible reasons.

One was Mr. Reagan's political standing. He had won in a landslide in 1980, and rolled over Congress in the tax and budget battle of 1981. He had the most convincing validation a democracy can give, and the public was not interested in carping at the details. Who was the press to challenge that? To put it another way, I thought some in the press were subconsciously asking themselves what our critics like to ask: Who elected us?

Second, some in the press may have felt uneasy because they were liberals. If they did tough stories, they might be accused of treating Mr. Reagan unfairly for that reason—accused, that is, of being insufficiently "objective."

Third, I guessed that some reporters and editors who watched Mr. Reagan were reluctant as citizens to speak out about what they saw. They saw the most powerful of offices occupied by a man with an anecdotal view of the world, giving simplistic answers to complicated questions, or tuning out. They found it upsetting to acknowledge, to the public or to themselves, that American leadership was in such hands.

My friends in Washington did not think much of my speculations; they denied that they were holding back for any such reasons. But looking back now, I still think that my concern had a basis. I believe there were unacknowledged constraints on the vigor of the press in covering the Reagan White House, including the three I mentioned. To them I would now add a weightier fourth reason: in a word, fear.

For nearly 20 years now the political right in this country has been working to intimidate the press and arouse public feeling against it. Spiro Agnew may be taken as the starting point, with his denunciations of the liberal elitist press and the nattering nabobs of negativism. We treat him as a joke figure now, with his notion that someone should start a good newspaper; and, after all, he did turn out to be a particularly cheap crook. But the resentments he touched and aroused were not a joke, and they have not gone away. There are a good many Americans who use the phrase "elitist press." I get letters from them, and I imagine many of you do.

Watergate fed the resentment, the anger. Nixon had his supporters to the end; and they were enraged at the part played in his fall by an unelected press. A certain amount of press hubris about its role made the feelings worse. After the President resigned, even some citizens and politicians who knew he had to go resented what they considered the display of the power of the press. So there was a Watergate backlash against the press. We felt it, we worried about it, and we tried to compensate for it.

Most important of all, in these historical causes, there was Vietnam. Millions of Americans, including some in high office, are convinced that we lost that war because the press showed us the horrors of it in graphic detail, and somehow favored the other side. What the press actually did, in its noblest tradition, was to show the reality that it was an unwinnable war. But the anger remains.

Today intimidation of the press is a standard item on the agenda of the organized political right. There are self-appointed monitors who circulate denunciations of articles and television programs that depart from their ideology. There are groups that support libel suits. And there is Jesse Helms, threatening to buy up a network that is not far enough to the right for his taste.

People in our business tend to have more than the usual amount of courage. But we kid ourselves if we think that pressure from the right has no effect on us, or on the companies that own media institutions. All things being equal, most of us prefer to avoid trouble in life. And editors and publishers know that tough journalism, journalism that may embarrass conservative interests, means trouble.

There was an important example of the effectiveness of intimidation in the election campaign. When Vice President Bush appeared on the CBS Evening News, Dan Rather tried to question him about his role in the Iran-Contra affair. Mr. Bush ducked, weaved, barracked, picked a fight. It was a beautifully staged performance, well prepared by Mr. Bush and his handlers. The purpose was to make it seem that Rather was leaning on the Vice President improperly, and to frighten others away from asking him questions about Iran. And it worked. After that evening nobody in the press went after Mr. Bush about his role in a sustained way, though there is every reason to believe that he was more deeply involved in the affair than he said.

Lately one of the right-wing extremists who goads the press has again denounced Mr. Rather over that episode. It showed, he said, what an unfair liberal Mr. Rather was that he pressed such questions on the Vice President of the United States. *Lèse majeste!* That is where we are: The price of pressing a question of fundamental importance on a political candidate who will not answer is to be denounced as "liberal." And I repeat: it works.

There was another example of the effectiveness of intimidation in the 1988 campaign. That was the handling of the press in the Dan Quayle affair.

I hardly need to remind you what happened. When George Bush chose Senator Quayle as his running-mate, reporters at the Republican Convention soon discovered that Quayle had avoided military service in Vietnam by getting himself public relations duty in the National Guard. How did he get it? By all indications, through family influence. Then came the counterattack. Republicans compared the reporters to sharks in a "feeding frenzy." Senator Quayle staged a press conference in the middle of a political rally in his home town, Huntington, Indiana. When reporters tried to ask questions about the Guard, people in the audience booed. When Ellen Hume of *The Wall Street Journal* stood her ground, the crowd shouted against "the redhead."

On television, that made a wonderful piece of "press harassment," all planned, I repeat, by the Quayle handlers. And then there was another perfect television clip. A few days later Quayle was shown taking the garbage out of his home, and reporters surrounded him and shouted questions. An outrageous invasion of privacy, right? Wrong. What television did not say in showing that episode was that the Bush-Quayle campaign had listed the trash dumping on its schedule as that day's only press availability for Quayle.

There were a lot of questions about Senator Quayle that never got answered in the campaign. How did he graduate from college without meeting the requirements that all other political science majors had to meet? Why was he given a second general examination when he failed the regular one, and what was the nature of the second exam? How did he get into law school when his grades were below the levels expected of other applicants? His academic records would have told us the answers, but Senator Quayle refused to let anyone see the records. I know some reporters were interested, but somehow the questions were not pressed hard enough or often enough to make the refusal to answer an issue, which it properly was.

I wonder what part the intimidating effects of the attacks on the press had in the way the Quayle story trailed off into nothingness. I wonder whether the press would have let such a story about a Democratic candidate trail off. Nowadays, at least, Democrats are not much good at bullying the press. And bullying has its effect.

The 1988 campaign left some reporters who covered it, and their editors and producers, feeling uncomfortable. One said she thought she had been complicit in a fraud on democracy. Another said: "I feel dirty." I think we can identify a number of reasons for those feelings: a number of press failures in the campaign.

One was the failure to make clear how Vice President Bush was insulated from the press, kept away from unprogrammed questions. It was the same kind of insulation practiced in the Reagan campaigns, but this time without the excuse of Mr. Reagan's personal aura to disarm the press. Yet the press essentially accepted the role assigned to it by the Bush campaign, grumbling but in the end largely passive. There was hardly any effort to describe what was going on.

After the election I had a letter from a reader saying that, yes, this had been a frustrating campaign for voters, one in which the candidates had not grappled with the real issues facing the country; but that was not just the fault of the candidates or their handlers. They can only be "handled," the reader said, if the press cooperates. Why didn't reporters traveling on the candidates' planes at least have the backbone to demand weekly press conferences? That would work, he said, "because no candidate can afford to risk the concerted antagonism of his mouthpieces."

I doubt that that remedy would work so easily. It is difficult to get reporters to work in concert, and it should be. The media men have ways to get around us, at least for a considerable time. But surely we in the press ought to be putting up a fight against the insulated campaign, describing it, focusing on it in a sustained way, instead of shrugging our shoulders. The problem was particularly acute this time for television. While George Bush was refusing to meet the press, Michael Dukakis at first held daily press conferences. He was rewarded by having embarrassing bits shown on the nightly news up against sound bites staged by the Bush campaign. Paul Friedman, executive producer of the ABC World News Tonight, said he was aware of the problem but did not know how to deal with it. He and the rest of us had better start trying to figure out how.

A second problem in this year's coverage was fascination with the process of the modern campaign, and with its manipulators: process, not substance. And not values. We celebrated Roger Ailes for his craft as a maker of television ads that created a picture of Michael Dukakis as a friend of murderers and rapists. There were lots of stories about the superiority of the technicians on that side: value-free stories. One newspaper political analyst even wrote a piece arguing that the inferior quality of Governor Dukakis's television ads had "disturbing implications about Dukakis's leadership."

I wonder how Thomas Jefferson, an introspective man, would rate as a political leader by that standard. Perhaps our democracy has been so corrupted by technology that a sensitive person, a Jefferson, can no longer hope to lead it. That may be. But I do not think the press should be cheering the corrupters for their efficiency. I say all that not out of concern for Michael Dukakis, who should have replied to the smears long before he did. My concern is for our business. There were times in this campaign when we looked like theater critics—critics interested only in the artfulness of the scenery, not in the message of the play.

Third, the press in this campaign actually participated in the degradation of the democratic process. It did so by taking up, as if they were real, the non-issues invented to distract voters from the hard economic and other problems ahead. The two so-called presidential debates provided embarrassing examples. I say so-called because of course they were not debates, not head-to-head confrontations like the Lincoln-Douglas debates. They were games, in which members of the press played stage roles. I think CBS News people were right when they decided not to participate in the second.

In that second debate Governor Dukakis was told by one of the journalists that the public didn't seem to like him; he was asked whether a President should be likable. That was one of the questions in the supposed focal point of our great democratic process. Then there was the opening question, put by the moderator, Bernard Shaw of CNN: Would Governor Dukakis favor the death penalty if his wife Kitty were raped and murdered? I leave it to Roger Ailes to comment on that. In an interview in the *Gannett Center Journal*, just published, he says: "It was an outrageous . . . question."

A fourth disturbing feature of the 1988 campaign was the press's inability to deal with lies. For example, the Bush campaign had a highly effective ad blaming Dukakis for the polluted state of Boston Harbor. It showed a sludgy pool of water with a sign saying: "DANGER/RADIATION HAZARD/NO SWIMMING." The picture was in fact not of Boston Harbor, and it had nothing to do with Dukakis. It was taken at an abandoned nuclear submarine repair yard.

What is the responsibility of the press when it is paid to carry such flagrant distortions? As a general rule it is sensible not to try to edit political advertising for truth. *The New York Times* used to print, once a year, full-page ads containing the thoughts of Kim Il Sung, the dictator of North Korea. I think we were right to take the money and let him say whatever he wanted. But it is another thing to refrain from comment on advertising that directly affects the American political process and that is deliberately false. Run the ad, yes, but say something.

That leads to a fifth problem. It is the press's desire to look "objective," which I think has become a dangerous obsession of American journalism.

Go back to Boston Harbor. George Bush took a cruise around it one day during the campaign, and said its condition proved that he was a better environmentalist than Dukakis. Most television networks and stations used the nice visual and a Bush sound bite, without any critical analysis. The simplest check would have shown that Dukakis had a fairly good record on environmental issues, while Bush as Vice President had a negative record and indeed had often pointed with pride to his activity in pushing development over environmental interests. But to report that would not have been "objective."

Some of us remember when we had a hard lesson on the limits of "He said, She said" journalism, when we learned that just repeating what a politician said was not "objective" in the true sense. Senator Joe McCarthy taught us the lesson. When he denounced 57 or 22 people as Communists, the wire services would flash what he said. For a long time they maintained that it would not be right to add any perspective: to tell the readers what had happened to his last charges, and the ones before that. But eventually the services understood that their obligation went beyond carrying the propaganda of a demagogue; they had an obligation to truth.

Serious reporting has to provide perspective on events. That obligation is not to be left to comment on the editorial and op ed pages. In a complicated world the reporter must try to make sense of things for the viewer or reader.

Reporters today are equipped to analyze events. They have had a liberal education, and many have had special training in their fields. In political reporting, certainly, there are men and women with wide knowledge and acquaintance. We need their perspective. But I had the feeling in this campaign that we were not getting enough writing by political reporters following their instincts for the deeper springs of politics. It was only very late in the campaign, for instance, when attention began to be paid to what is surely one of the determining factors in national voting patterns: race.

Instead of old-fashioned political reporting we had more of what could be called market research. The press has generally been using marketing surveys to find out what people want to read and watch. The surveyors, I am told, attach little flashlights to the heads of newspaper readers and note how long the light shines on different parts of the paper. Then the marketeers advise the paper to give readers more of what they like.

Political campaigns have used market research methods since 1968, when the Nixon campaign did so well with them. You know the technique: survey the voters, find out what they want in a candidate, then reshape the image of your man to fit that desire. Now the press seems to have become entranced by market research for campaign coverage. We had "focus groups" of our own, collections of voters whose impressions we reported. We all had polls, and devoted enormous space and time to reporting the results of our own and others'. It all left the impression that the press's main interest was in what tactics were working, who was winning and who was losing, not in the substantive choices facing the country, and not in truth.

We have less individual flavor in our political reporting today: less of the writer with a distinctive style and background and point of view. Those qualities are suspect, I think, because they are not "objective." It is safer to write about polls and focus groups, which are "objective."

The craving for objectivity was carried to great lengths in this campaign. One television report did try to deal with the low road of the Bush campaign. It showed the falsehoods in a Bush ad stating that "Michael Dukakis had opposed virtually every defense system we have developed." But the report went on to show a Dukakis ad that slightly exaggerated Bush positions. The story had to be "balanced." Even editorial pages balanced their criticism of the Bush smears with comments on this or that in the Dukakis campaign, as if its faults remotely approached the impugning of Dukakis's patriotism.

The notion that journalism should be "balanced" goes against the grain of American history and the Constitution. When the Constitution and the First Amendment were written, there was no such thing as a "balanced" newspaper. There were highly partisan, opinionated sheets. That was "the press" that Jefferson and Madison knew and wanted to protect. They didn't love it. After he had been President for a few years, Jefferson wrote a friend: "The man who never looks into a newspaper is better informed than he who reads them, inasmuch as he who knows nothing is nearer the truth than he whose mind is filled with falsehoods and errors." They just thought the press was necessary, to keep the government honest and the republic free. The First Amendment did not guarantee the freedom of the press as a mere common carrier, printing whatever politicians said "objectively." It guaranteed the freedom of independent, opinionated, quarrelsome, irritating newspapers.

For those reasons I find the current fetish of "objectivity" troublesome. Press institutions are much larger now than in Jefferson's day, and they have reasons to carry different points of view. But it does not follow that they should find two sides to every question or regard it as a triumph to be bland.

There are two other points that should concern us as journalists. They go beyond the campaign. They are cultural trends of which the press is a part, and of which the press should be wary.

The first is the growth of a political class in Washington, D.C. That has happened in my lifetime. Before Franklin Roosevelt this city did not amount to much in our national life. It was a sleepy Southern town—a segregated one—that housed a small government with little impact on the daily life of most Americans. Now it is the headquarters of a powerful government that affects us all in myriad ways: our health, our housing, our jobs and so on. It is the center of a vast military-industrial complex. And it has a permanent society of men and women concerned with government, and with the names and numbers of the players. The popular phrase for the phenomenon, awkward but perhaps unavoidable, is the Inside the Beltway Mentality.

Journalists are part of that Washington society: a leading part. And just as the word "Washington" casts a certain spell on the American public now, so the press corps here has a larger influence than ever before on the way the country's newspapers and magazines and broadcasters see things. My concern is that the press is becoming too Washington-centered in its thinking. I say that as an outsider, but not only for that reason.

There is always a danger of seeing the world in too small a circle of acquaintance and thought. I think that is a particular danger now in Washington: a city where access to the great is easy, where quotes can be picked from every tree, where members of the press have almost the dignity of office. Joan Didion did a remarkable piece on the campaign in *The New York Review of Books*. One of her striking insights was how much the press has become part of a new class, a managerial elite. She heard people at the conventions speak of "the process," and she realized what they meant: not the democratic process but the reverse. "The process," she said, was this:

"A mechanism seen as so specialized that access to it is correctly limited to its own professionals, to those who manage policy and those who quote them, to those who ask and those who answer the questions on the Sunday shows, to the media consultants, to the columnists, to the issues advisers, to those who give the off-the-record breakfasts and those who attend them; to that handful of insiders who invent, year in and year out, the narrative of public life."

To be an insider is wonderful fun. But it carries with it the danger of talking to yourself.

My final subject of concern follows from the one just mentioned. It is the worship of the Presidency. Here again the press is in danger of following a cultural trend. Worship may seem too strong a word. I do not think it is.

Since 1933, gradually but inexorably, Americans have come to invest their hopes and fears in the President. He will solve our problems. He alone represents us all: a national view as compared to the narrow parochialism of members of Congress. Along with this mythic popular image has gone a strange ideological strand in contemporary conservatism, arguing that the President should have total power over everything that touches foreign affairs or national security, with Congress as an illegitimate outsider.

All this would astound the makers of our Constitution if they could see it. They did not think of the President as a tribune of the people, not at all. It was Congress, in particular the House of Representatives, that was to represent the popular will. The President was to be a manager, carrying out the policies established by the legislative branch. What a wonderful irony it is that conservatives who want the Supreme Court to be bound by Original Intent in interpreting the Constitution are also devoted to exalting presidential power, which is a mockery of the Framers' intention.

The trouble with myths is that you may come to believe them. When the press looks to the President to solve all problems, when it assumes the legitimacy of his power in all situations, it creates a mystique about the presidency that may be difficult to penetrate. I think that has happened. I think the press finds it very hard to challenge the President of the United States on things that matter.

But there was Watergate, you will say. Yes. But the man in the White House then was a peculiarly vulnerable President, elected but not loved, given to self-destruction. It certainly required courage to challenge, and the courage was there. But the example does not convince me that the press is bold enough to challenge a secure, popular President.

Consider this question: What was the boldest action by the press in the politics of these last few years? I think it was the investigation of Gary Hart's sexual behavior. There again the target was a loner of a politician, without strong personal links to his colleagues in the Senate or to state politicians. And he was not a friend of the press.

What is needed is not confrontation for confrontation's sake. It is the will to press unwelcome questions into the center of presidential policy. It is the persistence to demand answers from Vice President Bush about his role in the trading of arms for hostages, not the brashness to ask Senator Hart: "Have you ever committed adultery?"

We were at fault in not smelling the arms for hostages deal and the transfer of funds to the *contras* before the story leaked in the Middle East. Something had been known about Colonel North's character and activities: enough to arouse the curiosity of skeptical journalists, I would have thought. And that is what we are meant to be: skeptical.

The press cannot do its job if it is bemused by the presidential mystique: That is the argument I make to you most forcefully. If we must learn again what we learned in Vietnam and put into practice in the Pentagon Papers, let us do so. Officials may act in what they sincerely believe is the interest of national security but be wrong—dangerously wrong. The greatest danger, Justice Brandeis said, lies in "men of zeal, well-meaning but without understanding." Some degree of secrecy is necessary in national security matters, but officials will always try to expand secrecy beyond the necessary because it is so comfortable—because it relieves them of the duty to justify their policies. But it is exactly that duty of justification that is at the heart of our system of government. Our premise is that policy will be wiser if those who make it are forced to consider conflicting views and account for their choice.

Executive officials like to argue that those are old-fashioned ideas, that in a world of nuclear weapons a President needs secrecy. But those officials often see it differently when they leave office. David Gergen spoke in this forum two years ago, and he said he thought we had too little reporting on national security matters, not too much. He spoke of the value of accountability and said "the quest for secrecy has led more than one Administration astray."

The press has a critical function to play in our scheme of government. Madison, the author of the First Amendment, defined that function. It was to give information to the sovereigns of this country, its citizens, so they could freely examine "public characters and measures."

The public relies on the press more today than ever. People feel remote from national politics and governance. They feel it has become not a participatory but a spectator sport. They count on us to penetrate the shams and speak the truth to power. They are often angry at us, but they need us. We should not let them down.

Shortly after Watergate, Justice Potter Stewart of the Supreme Court made a speech at Yale about the press. Its performance in the Pentagon Papers affair and Watergate, he said, had brought on the press charges that it was arrogant and exercised illegitimate power. He disagreed. In the last few years, he said, the American press had "performed precisely the function it was intended to perform by those who wrote the First Amendment."

Justice Stewart said it was a great mistake—a constitutional mistake—to see the press "as a *neutral* conduit of information between the people and their elected leaders." Those who framed the Constitution did not intend the press to be "a neutral vehicle" for "balanced discussion." To them "the free press meant organized, expert scrutiny of government. The press was a conspiracy of the intellect, with the courage of numbers."

That is a rather grand description of our business. But we should try to live up to it.

# Values Deserving Our Attention[8]

William A. Hilliard

*Born 1927, Chicago, IL; U.S. Navy, 1945-46; B.A., Pacific University, 1952; editor-in-chief,* Portland Oregonian, *1952–; vice-president, 1992-93, president, 1993-94, American Society of Newspaper Editors.*

## Editor's introduction

William A. Hilliard, long-time editor-in-chief of the *Portland Oregonian*, addressed some 800 members of the American Society of Newspaper Editors attending their national convention in 1994. Hilliard discussed First Amendment abuses as they relate to managing a newspaper. Drawing upon his own experience with racial discrimination, Mr. Hilliard cautioned the newspaper can only be of value to its community if it reflects the values, concerns, and hopes of that community. In short, a newspaper must appear as "a cross-section of the community it serves." Hilliard called for cultural diversity, greater civility, and an end to First Amendment abuses during a time when many had described news columns as "'gotcha' efforts to embarrass public figures" (*New York Times*, April 1994).

---

I hope all of you agree that a man can do worse than be remembered for his consistency and perseverance. If you agree with that premise, you won't be disappointed if I stick to what I know best and care about most.

I have composed my remarks around three points. I want you to remember them whenever you think about what it takes to run a good newspaper. And I want to express these points as values that need to be accommodated when newspaper managers make decisions: news decisions, editorial decisions, and people decisions.

These are the values I believe are most deserving of that accommodation:

*Cultural diversity.* Assurance that the people newspapers hire and promote mirror the community's cultural demographics.

*Civility.* It seems to me there is a cancer of mean-spiritedness festering in the journalistic gut today. It troubles me. It troubles thoughtful readers. I think it should trouble you.

And last, *First Amendment abuses* of our profession's most vulnerable and least protected practitioners: high school, college, and university newspaper staffs.

First, the issue of cultural diversity.

Our profession took giant strides toward cultural diversity when professors in our schools of communication and journalism stopped telling people of color, especially young blacks, as one professor told me: that big newspapers wouldn't hire them. We took an additional step forward when ASNE [American Society of Newspaper Editors] announced publicly that by the year 2000, its member newspapers' staffs would reflect the percentage of minorities in the population.

But cultural diversity is more than just race or color. Cultural diversity in American newspapers means that all components of our buildings will accommodate the wheelchairs, guide dogs, and unique accouterments of our employees with disabilities.

It means that white reporters and photographers don't dress down when they visit tribal officials in Native American communities.

And it means that our employees' sexual orientations are irrelevant to who gets hired, who gets fired, who gets the "good" assignments, and who gets promoted. We will have achieved true diversity when the differences among us don't make any difference.

[8]Delivered at the national convention of the American Society of Newspaper Editors, in Washington, D.C., on April 13, 1994. Reprinted with permission of William A. Hilliard.

But we are not there yet. And, in my view, a newspaper that does not look like a cross-section of the community it serves will not, and cannot, serve that community as it wants and deserves to be served.

No newspaper can claim immunity from a role in helping to build and maintain the cultural collaboratives that comprise rich and successful societies. And a successful society's greatest virtues, the wellsprings of its greatness, are tolerance, respect, and unyielding commitments to common values.

And such are the values of great newspapers.

What would most of the newspapers in our large cities look like if they had circulation wards and the readership had say in the newspaper's racial, ethnic, gender, and age mix? Would they look different? Probably.

And what if ASNE itself chose arbitrarily to forfeit some of the rich diversity it has? What if our membership excluded newspapers from, say, Wisconsin, Michigan, Illinois, Indiana, Ohio, and Iowa?

Would ASNE represent newspaper America? Of course not. Would we be poorer for our omission? Of course we would. Would newspaper editors in those states hold ASNE in much regard? I doubt it.

Without those editors, important regional values and perspectives would be missing from key ASNE policy discussions and decisions, much less from our college basketball coverage. And if those editors' principles and perspectives were not sought out and valued by ASNE, then ASNE would be of no value to them.

So it is with minority elements among our constituent readers.

Any newspaper editor still in denial about our nation's cultural evolution may, sometime in the next century, be part of a displaced institution when people of color comprise the majority in America.

To those few who are threatened by that prospect, let me remind them that this is not a case of winners and losers. No one has to be disenfranchised when we accommodate and nourish cultural diversity everywhere—in our newsrooms, in our communities and in our nation.

*The Oregonian* did not fire a white male reporter to make room for me. And I was not promoted at the expense of more competent or deserving colleagues. Nobody lost because I succeeded.

On the contrary, I want to believe that, over the years, scores of young people of color have looked at me and said, "It can happen."

With that responsibility in mind, I have tried to make sure that when any prospect applies for work at *The Oregonian*, that person's only cause for anxiety should be: Am I good enough? Not, am I man enough? Or white enough? Or young enough? Not, can I cut it as a black reporter? Or a lesbian reporter? Or a disabled reporter? Just, can I cut it as a reporter? That is all that counts.

In 1978, ASNE set a goal. We gave ourselves 22 years to make our news and editorial rooms reflect America's racial makeup. It is projected that by the year 2000, 30 percent of our news and editorial staffs must be people of color, one out of every three, if we are to meet this goal.

That was 16 years ago. We have less than six years in which to reach our goal. We are only one-third of the way there. The first one-third was somewhat easy. The last one-third will be even more difficult. But nobody said it would be easy.

On civility. According to my *Webster*, civility is courtesy. It is "a polite act or expression." Civility implies maturity and respect for other people and other opinions, or at least calm restraint in the fact of contentiousness.

It follows that incivility is a discourtesy, an impolite act or expression, a lack of maturity, a lack of respect for other people and other opinions, and the inability to exercise restraint.

Not too long ago, James J. Kilpatrick, one of my favorites, wrote about President Clinton's nomination of Ruth Bader Ginsburg for the Supreme Court. I frankly do not know why Kilpatrick felt compelled to write, and I quote: " . . . Given his repeated vows before the gods of diversity and multiculturalism, Clinton could not have nominated a white male to the court."

To my ear, Kilpatrick's choice of words "gods of diversity and multiculturalism" deliberately holds in cold contempt sincere comments to end discrimination in this country. Kilpatrick is not a frequent offender, although in my view, he missed an opportunity to give young writers a lesson in cool persuasion and civility.

Many of you read the op-ed piece by Thomas R. Roeser, a conservative activist and founder of the Republican Assembly of Illinois. In the piece, Roeser wrote about President Eisenhower's "tragic judgment" in abandoning

Berlin instead of capturing the city at the close of World War II. Years later, in 1953, the first year of the Eisenhower presidency, the Berlin judgment came back to haunt the new president.

Wrote Roeser: "TV news features it endlessly. Ike's approval numbers plummet. The partisan advantage is clear."

But, according to Roeser, the feeding frenzy failed to bring down the president, thanks to bipartisan support from Congress. "Frankly," Roeser observed, and I quote, "we had better men then." "In contrast," he continued, "in our decadent age of sensationalistic incivility, whoever can manipulate media facts and put them to political use can cause reputations to fall like dominos."

Continuing from the Roeser piece, and again I quote:

"It crested with Watergate—where opportunism on all sides caused Richard Nixon, a successful foreign policy president, to fall. Bill Safire and others vowed to get even. Watergate-era rules maimed the administrations of Jimmy Carter, Ronald Reagan, and George Bush . . . and now, Bill Clinton,"

concluded the Illinois conservative.

If Roeser is right, and I think to a great extent he is, American politics seem destined to be awash in blood feuds that rank retribution above common decency, above accountability, and above the salvation of the republic.

The question then becomes: are American newspapers independent, objective chroniclers of events? Or is our future mortgaged to grotesque one-upmanship where news stories begin and end with an empty headline?

There may or may not be perfect parallels in the 1950s and the 1990s. The 1950s were different times, and to some perhaps better times.

But I think we misjudge our readers' capacity to tolerate the media's sometimes manic and ill-tempered self-indulgence.

I do not believe American newspaper readers have an infinite capacity to tolerate incivility. And I believe that the newspaper executive who expects infinite indulgence does so at his or her peril.

I want to commence the last of my remarks with a question. When is the First Amendment kid stuff?

I think the answer is never.

I am certain, however, that every one in this audience, at one time or another, defended his or her or someone else's right to free speech protection under the First Amendment.

In our business, the quickest way to rally the troops is to challenge free speech. Nothing is as righteous and heroic as an embattled newspaper editor exercising and defending his or her sacred duty to resist being told what he or she can print and what he or she can't.

Well, there is a need to rally the troops when the local college or university suspends the campus newspaper for offending some ivy-covered moral protocol, almost always ill-defined. There is a tendency for most of us to report the incident as news and too often to forego an editorial opinion.

It is my view that it was not the intent of our founding fathers that the First Amendment be held in abeyance through one's adolescence. If the American newspaper establishment fails to defend free speech for high school and college journalists, how can we claim it for ourselves?

Can we be credible models and leaders in our profession and condone censorship at the same time?

ASNE has, in my view, done some important work in this emotionally charged and not altogether rational journalistic area. We have urged hometown, mainstream newspaper editors to get involved in hands-on, community-level workshops for high school journalism advisers. We have urged managers to send professional staffers to meet and talk with campus newspaper staffs.

Last year we published and distributed *How to Rescue High School Journalism* to editors of every daily newspaper in the country and to high school journalism teachers. These are meaningful steps, but are they enough?

I believe ASNE needs to step into the campus journalism censorship fray every time a meritorious opportunity arises. I cannot conceive of an ASNE-member newspaper not intervening in this most fundamental constitutional issue.

Because I am an individual who has suffered personally from the indignities of discrimination, I am extremely sensitive to the feelings of those around me, so these values have a special meaning for me.

I believe the daily newspaper is indispensable to the survival of a free society. It can show best the need to celebrate one's ethnicity and its benefits to a multicultural society: the achievements of women, black Americans, Native Americans, Hispanics, and Asians.

In doing so, we must be careful to move more toward a unified America, without divisions along racial, economic and cultural lines.

# IX. Education

## Editor's introduction

Between 1937 and 1997, educational institutions at every level in the United States underwent significant change. Much of this change was in response to our evolving understanding of education's purpose, as well as to the calls of women and minority groups for fair representation in the modern curriculum. While *Brown* vs. *Board of Education of Topeka, Kansas* officially ended segregation in 1954, African Americans, women, and other groups have only recently undertaken the fight to have their accomplishments included in the more "mainstream," Western-based curriculum. In addition, many public school systems have expanded their curricula to include not only courses that prepare students for college but also those that provide them job training. The very role of the school has undergone a fundamental alteration, as public schools in particular have been asked to help shoulder the mounting burden of social problems, including drug abuse, violence and sexual abuse.

Many of the changes endured by the educational system were accompanied by a significant amount of debate and conflict. In many ways, this conflict and debate are represented in the controversy that erupted between William J. Bennett and C. Everett Koop. These speakers disagreed on as to how the nation should prepare its youth to survive in an increasingly changing and often dangerous environment. Bennett, then United States secretary of education, contested Surgeon General Koop's endorsement of an explicit sex education curriculum. Troubled that "words of . . . morality seem to have been banished from" many sex education curricula, Bennett insisted that adults should explain and "defend . . . moral standards and the formation of character," both at school and in the home. Koop countered that given the emerging prevalence of AIDS, open and frank discussions on sex must occur if we hope to control the damage being wrought by the disease.

In all of the debate, the importance of education to a prosperous and secure society has never really been at issue. Academic leaders have consistently urged that students use their knowledge to direct and improve our society. For example, Matina S. Horner, former president of Radcliffe College, maintained that institutions of higher learning should foster a woman's ability to both realize her skills and talents and assist her in using them for the purpose of improving the world in which we live. In a similar vein, graduating senior Brittain Rogers reminded his fellow graduates of the importance of actively employing what they had learned if they hoped to effect change.

# Farewell for Students[1]

Robert Maynard Hutchins

*Born January 17, 1899, Brooklyn, NY; died May 14, 1977; A.B., Yale University, 1921; J.D., Yale Law School, 1925; dean, Yale Law School, 1927-29; president, 1929-45, chancellor, 1945-51, University of Chicago; director, Ford Foundation, 1951-54; president, 1954-69, chairman, 1969-74, Fund for the Republic; founder, chairman, 1959-74, president, 1975-77, Center for the Study of Democratic Institutions; author,* No Friendly Voice *(1936),* Education for Freedom *(1943),* St. Thomas and the World State *(1949),* The Conflict in Education in a Democratic Society *(1953),* The University of Utopia *(1953).*

## Editor's introduction

Robert Maynard Hutchins, former chancellor of the University of Chicago, gave this farewell address to students at a special reception given in his honor on the occasion of his retirement. In the address, Hutchins advised students that their central goal should be moral and intellectual, being the achievement of the "feeling that you have made the most of yourselves, that you have done the best you could, and that you have not let down yourselves or your fellow-men." On a much more ominous note, Hutchins warned of the power of television, which he asserted has the potential to eradicate all forms of civilized communication and render its audience "indistinguishable from the lower forms of plant life."

---

One of the saddest aspects of my life is that I have not organized it so that I could know the students better.

It would be outrageous presumption on my part to suppose that my presence here has anything to do with yours or that my departure can make the slightest difference to you. I cannot even claim that I have been what Mr. Justice Holmes said the common law was not, a brooding omnipresence in the sky. I have had no chance to brood, I cannot by any extension of the word have been said to be omnipresent unless it means to be everywhere else, and I have spent more time in Wall Street than in the sky.

Yet, though seldom nourished by the sight of you, and sometimes not even by the thought of you, I have perhaps some right to say farewell to you, because you have been the inspiration of my life and have given to it such meaning as it has had. Here I do not refer to you as individuals sitting here tonight, but to the hundreds of thousands of young people who have passed through these halls while I have presided over the University and who have symbolized for me the rising generation and the hopes of mankind. If it had not been for you, and what you stood for, I should never have had the impulse to carry on my modest and intermittent efforts in higher education.

I must confess that this process of abstraction whereby some thousands of different individuals each with his individual constitution, background, and desires become equivalent to the rising generation and are treated as such, however valuable it is for the person making the abstraction, may not be so agreeable to the individuals abstracted. We have been struggling to create here a model university. A model university is not one that asks, "What is good for these individual students?" but "What is good for all students?" For a model is useless unless it can be imitated. Some aspects of this are not so serious as might at first appear. It is more than a verbal twist to say that a model university will do its best to see to it that each individual student has the greatest opportunities and the chance to make the most of them. But other aspects of the effort to create a model university

[1]Delivered at the University of Chicago, in Chicago, Illinois, on February 2, 1951.

are as serious for the students as they seem to be.

If a model university is needed, it must be because the educational system and the public attitude toward it need in some degree to be changed. The students in such a university come out of the educational system and the public attitudes that exist. The student in the Chicago College comes from the American high school and may go into an American graduate or professional school. The University of Chicago is trying to change the American high school and the American graduate and professional school. So far it has been wholly successful only in changing its own. The result is that Chicago students may encounter difficulties that those of other institutions seldom hear of.

A model university in America at this time is necessarily at war with the public, for the public has little or no idea what a university is or what it is for. I do not need to tell you what the public thinks about universities. You know as well as I, and you know as well as I that the public is wrong. The fact that popular misconceptions of the nature and purpose of universities originate in the fantastic misconduct of the universities themselves is not consoling. It shows that a model university is needed; it shows how much one is needed; but it also suggests the tremendous difficulty of the enterprise upon which a model university embarks and the strength of the tide against which its students have to contend.

It is clear to me that you are very superior and that you come from very superior families. Otherwise you could not have come to or stayed in so independent an institution. Some of you and some of your predecessors have tried to divert the University from its course and make it more like other universities. This I attribute to the contagion of the reforming spirit of the University itself and not to any desire on your part for an easier life. All students should want to reform their university. If the University is already unconventional, the only way to reform it is to make it conventional.

Your views on other matters through the years I have fully shared. I wish it were possible to eliminate the mechanics of institutional life. In a large institution, for some reason, the rooms can never be nice enough, the food can never be good enough, the lights can never be bright enough, the buildings are either too hot or too cold, the processes of registration, examination, and graduation are too protracted and too complicated.

I have carefully studied the various expressions of student opinion on these subjects as they have appeared since 1929 and have agreed with them all. There must be something refractory about the material out of which a university is made, or perhaps my efforts have been too modest and too intermittent. At any rate I have concluded that there is something about institutional life, at least on a large scale, that makes it impossible to do anything about it, just as I have concluded that the food in the various faculty clubs is identical, even though the clubs are as far apart as New York and Palo Alto, and that nothing can ever be done about it. One of the reasons why I would favor the development here of the Oxford and Cambridge system of small residential colleges that are federalized into a university is that I believe the smaller the unit the less institutional the institution.

Perhaps the greatest difference between your time in college and my own is the popularization in the intervening years of the works of Freud. Far be it from me to decry the significance of this writer. But I must say that he has had, as it seems to me, an unfortunate effect upon your conversation and upon the standards by which you judge yourselves and others. A graduate student in psychology told me last year that in her opinion 99 per cent of the people of this country were abnormal. In addition to providing an interesting definition of normality, this suggested to me that the ordinary difficulties of growing up and being human, from which the race has suffered for a million years, had taken on a kind of clinical character that I could not help hoping was exaggerated. Whenever I have visited with student groups, I have been impressed by your determined insistence that you were neurotic and your resentment at my suggestion that you looked perfectly all right to me.

On the principle laid down by Gilbert and Sullivan that when everybody is somebody, nobody is anybody: if everybody is abnormal, we don't need to worry about anybody. Nor should I be prepared to admit that a serious interest in being educated, the characteristic that distinguishes the students of the University of Chicago from all others, is necessarily neurotic. It may be in these times in this country somewhat eccentric, but it seems to me an amiable eccentricity, and one that should be encouraged. The whole doctrine that we must adjust ourselves to our environment, which I take to be the prevailing doctrine of American education, seems to me radically erroneous. Our mission here on earth is to change our environment, not to adjust ourselves to it. If we become maladjusted in the process, so much the worse for the environment.

If we have to choose between Sancho Panza and Don Quixote, let us by all means choose Don Quixote. The flat conformity of American life and thought, toward which all pressures in this country converge, raises the only doubt one may have about democracy, which is whether it is possible to combine the rule of the majority with that independence of character, conduct, and thought which the progress of any society requires.

One of the most interesting questions about the higher learning in America is this: Why is it that the boy who on June 15 receives his degree, eager, enthusiastic, outspoken, idealistic, reflective, and independent, is on the following September 15, or even on June 16, except at Chicago, dull, uninspired, shifty, cautious, pliable, and attired in a double-breasted blue-serge suit? Why are the graduates of the great American universities indistinguishable, even by their grammar, from the mass of the population who have never had their advantages? Their grammar may perhaps be accounted for by the deficiencies of the American schools, the ineradicable marks of which are borne by our fellow-countrymen to their dying day. But what about the intellectual interest, the willingness and ability to reason, the independence of thought and character, the

"Spirit of youth, alive, unchanging,
"Under whose feet the years are cast,
"Heir to an ageless empire ranging
"Over the future and the past—"

what about that? Why are the alumni organizations of the country, except that of Chicago, dedicated to the affectionate perpetuation of all the wrong things about their universities? Why do the massed graduates of American universities behave in the same way on the same kind of occasions as the massed followers of the most celebrated cultural institution of my native city, the Dodgers?

The answer must lie in the relative weakness of higher education compared with the forces that make everybody think and act like everybody else. Those forces beat upon the individual from his birth up on almost a twenty-four-hour-a-day basis and constitute the greatest obstacle with which the schools have to contend; so that it can now be seriously argued that since education cannot cope with the comic book it should absorb it and substitute elevating and instructive comic books for textbooks.

The horrid prospect that television opens before us, with nobody speaking and nobody reading, suggests that a bleak and torpid epoch may lie ahead, which, if it lasts long enough, will gradually, according to the principles of evolution, produce a population indistinguishable from the lower forms of plant life. Astronomers of the University of Chicago have detected something that looks like moss growing on Mars. I am convinced that Mars was once inhabited by rational beings like ourselves, who had the misfortune, some thousands of years ago, to invent television.

The forces that beat upon the American citizen from infancy become really serious when he finishes his formal schooling and has to think about earning a living and getting along in the world. How will those who have jobs to offer and prestige to confer feel about him if he does not merge imperceptibly with the scenery? How far will he get if he does not adjust himself to his environment? I hasten to say that I am for tact, politeness, and good manners, I would not for the world be taken as urging you to be offensive or holier-than-thou or carry a chip on your shoulder or fail to distinguish between matters of etiquette and matters of principle. You may even wear a double-breasted blue-serge suit if you find it becoming. But to adjust yourselves to brutality, inhumanity, injustice, and stupidity, of which the world is full, though it is easy, and may look profitable, is, I must warn you, habit-forming, and will make out of you at the last characters that you would shudder to think of now.

My observation leads me to think that happiness lies in the fullest use of one's highest powers. Of course it is folly to talk of the fullest use of a man's highest powers if he is starving to death. You are in little danger of starving to death, at least you are if a world catastrophe can be avoided. Your advantages are such that you have a decided superiority over the great majority of your fellow-citizens when it comes to the sheer business of staying alive. Your problem lies in the moral and intellectual realm, in achieving the feeling that you have made the most of yourselves, that you have done the best you could, and that you have not let down yourselves or your fellow-men.

Here I hope that you will follow the example of your university. I still think, as I have thought for many years, that the motto of the University should be that line from Walt Whitman, "Solitary, singing in the West, I strike up for a new world."

Our lives are overshadowed now by the threat of impending doom. If you were neurotic, I could not blame you. To what extent the threat of impending doom grows out of our ignorance and immorality, and to what extent it grows out of the ignorance and immorality of the Russians, I do not pretend to know.

I confess, too, that I have a lifelong hatred of war that perhaps makes it impossible for me to have a rational view of the present situation. War has always seemed to me the ultimate wickedness, the ultimate stupidity. And if this was true in less enlightened days, when the best we could do was to slaughter one another with TNT, it is plain as day now, when, thanks to the progress of the higher learning, we can wipe out thousands of innocent people at one blow, and be wiped out ourselves in the same way. I am not a pacifist. I would echo the sentiments of Patrick Henry. I grant that, when a great power is loose in the world seeking whom it may destroy, it is necessary to prepare to defend our country against it.

Yet the goal toward which all history tends is peace, not peace through the medium of war, not peace through a process of universal intimidation, not peace through a program of mutual impoverishment, not peace by any means that leaves the world too frightened or too weak to go fighting, but peace pure and simple, based on that will to peace which has animated the overwhelming majority of mankind through countless ages. This will to peace does not arise out of a cowardly desire to preserve one's life and property, but out of a conviction that the fullest development of the highest powers of men can be achieved only in a world at peace.

War, particularly modern war, is a horrible disaster. If this is the destiny prepared for us, we must meet it as best we can. But at least we should have no illusions about it. There is a certain terrifying lightheartedness underlying the talk about war today. Each political party is belaboring the other not because it is too warlike but because it is too peaceful. Men in public life are being crucified because they are suspected of trying to keep the peace. The presidents of the greatest universities have met and enthusiastically voted to abandon the higher learning so that the universities may become part of the military establishment. By endless reiteration of the slogan, "America must be strong," we have been able to put a stop to our mental processes altogether and to forget what strength is.

We appear to believe that strength consists of masses of men and machines. I do not deny that they have their role. But surely the essential ingredients of strength are trained intelligence, love of country, the understanding of its ideals, and, above all, a conviction of the justice of our cause.

Since men of good will can regard war as conceivable only as a last resort, they must be convinced that all channels of negotiation have been kept open until the last moment and that their own government has sought in good faith, and without consideration of face or prestige, to prevent the outbreak of war. Men of good will must be convinced that they are not fighting to maintain colonialism, feudalism, or any other form of intrenched injustice. And since it is obvious to the merest simpleton that war must come sooner or later to a world of anarchy, men of good will would hope that their own government would proclaim its desire to transform the United Nations from a loose association of independent states into an organization that could adopt and enforce world law.

There seems to be something about contemporary civilization that produces a sense of aimlessness. Why do university presidents cheerfully welcome the chance to devote their institutions to military preparations? They are of course patriotic; but in addition I think they feel that education is a boring, confusing, difficult matter that nobody cares very much about anyway, whereas getting ready for war is simple, clear, definite, and respectable. Can it be that modern men can have a sense of purpose only if they believe that other men are getting ready to kill them? If this is true, Western civilization is surely neurotic, and fatally so.

You are getting an education infinitely better than that which my generation, the generation that now rules the world, had open to it. You have had the chance to discern the purpose of human life and human society. Your predecessors in this place, now scattered all over the world, give us some warrant for hoping that as you go out to join them you will bear with you the same spark that they have carried, which, if carefully tended, may yet become the light that shall illumine the world. I shall always be proud and happy that we were here together.

# Opportunity for Educational Innovation[2]

Matina S. Horner

*Born July 28, 1939, Roxbury, MA; B.A., Bryn Mawr College, 1961; M.S., 1963, Ph.D., 1968, University of Michigan; teaching fellow, University of Michigan, 1962-68; professor, Harvard University, 1970-72; president, Radcliffe College, 1972-89.*

## Editor's introduction

Upon being chosen as Radcliffe College's sixth president, Dr. Matina S. Horner gave this address to students, faculty, and various supporters of the college. At the time this speech was given, there had been much talk about phasing out special colleges for women. Horner argued that Radcliffe College, a college specifically for women, still had a vital role to play in the changing society. This role, according to Horner, is to provide an environment that will help prepare young women to meet the demanding academic and social pressures which change has brought. By the creation of such an environment, Horner asserted that the Radcliffe both would be able to women realize their talents and successfully employ them in the world at large.

---

I come before you today with high expectations and, to a certain extent, some anxiety. You have entrusted Radcliffe's future to me, and I hope that I shall prove worthy of your confidence and trust.

Together we celebrate this moment in Radcliffe's history as a family. My only sense of regret is that *all* our students could not be here with us. It is for us all an opportunity for serious contemplation about and thanksgiving for the nature and quality of our "Acre for Education."

It is an opportunity to pause from the busyness of the day's activities, to reflect upon the traditions of the past, to recognize and respond to the needs of the present, and to consider the possibilities of the future.

These are exciting and challenging times for those of us concerned with higher education in general and with the education of women in particular. We are aware that today many social, sexual, and vocational changes are occurring in society with such awesome acceleration that many more questions are raised than we can immediately answer. Among other questions under consideration, one of particular importance to Radcliffe is what role women will play in the new society. Her relation to work, study and family is under close scrutiny and review, and reactions of both sexes toward her new social importance are varied. In the light of Radcliffe's long tradition of improving opportunities for women who have "the taste and talent for higher education," we at the College must now enter a new and intensely self-critical period, directing our attention toward reevaluating our goals and defining our objectives. If we do so, mindful of the issues of our times, we can shape and provide an environment here that will help prepare young women and men to meet the demanding academic and social pressures which change has brought. It will not be easy. The new demands on the educator to assist students to surmount the many educational and psychological Mount Everests they now face in college and beyond will require new and unpracticed skills. Our aim is to create a living and learning environment in which each student can experience the joy of discovering her own capabilities. Our hope is to create a community in and out of which each student—past, present and future—can realize the fulfillment of her talent and the fullness of her spirit. I will be happy when we have reached the point in society that a woman is ap-

[2]Delivered at Radcliffe College, in Cambridge, Massachusetts, on November 16, 1972. Reprinted with permission of Matina S. Horner.

pointed or gains admission to respected, high-level positions not in spite of, nor because of the fact that she is a woman but because she is, feels, and is recognized to be a talented human being with something important to give.

Your Eminence, I am delighted that you could be here today—not only because of the fond memories your presence evokes for me personally, but also because it serves as a reminder to us all of how far we have come. The clergy, as you know, has not always looked kindly on women educators and speakers. In 1837, the General Association of Congregational Churches in Massachusetts issued a Pastoral Letter in which they declared quite firmly:

"We cannot . . . but regret the mistaken conduct of those who encourage females to bear an obtrusive and ostentatious role and who countenance any of that sex to so far forget themselves as to itinerate in the character of public lecturers and teachers."

I shudder to think of their reactions to the events of this day.

Despite the presence of such attitudes, not only in the clergy but even among members of the Harvard faculty and Governing Boards, Radcliffe's early leaders remained undaunted. Committed to the idea that women could, and therefore should, be educated like men, Mr. Gilman and Mrs. Agassiz organized a plan for providing "private, collegiate instruction for women . . . " equal to the best available for men: namely, that at Harvard. They sought instruction that was not only to be of Harvard quality, but to be given by Harvard teachers and lead to certification recognized as equal to a Harvard degree. Because they challenged the existing stereotypes and expectations of their time, they met considerable resistance. The resistance was based on arguments such as the one that female education could only be gained at the expense of woman's reproductive function, and that academic and public achievement could only be realized at the expense of a woman's femininity, marriage and family. These are not unlike the arguments one hears today.

Dr. Edward Clarke, for instance, a Professor of Medicine at Harvard and later an Overseer of the College, argued at that time that while a boy could study for six hours a day, if a girl spent more than four, her "brain or special apparatus" would suffer.

Similarly, President Eliot remained firm in his conviction that the physique of woman was unfit for higher education despite the statement from Vassar in 1873 that "four hundred healthier women can hardly be found than those at Poughkeepsie."

And yet, our predecessors persisted and ultimately established a college for women in Harvard's backyard, in a location described as "up the river from Boston and down through the forest from Watertown." The founders won President Eliot's support for their plan when they assured him that they all opposed coeducation and that the plan would in no way strain Harvard's finances. It would, they argued, enhance the College's attraction for outstanding faculty members by providing an additional source of income. I am amused, in the context of today's fiscal crisis, to learn that at one time Radcliffe was considered a "financial temptress." But, I am digressing. . . .

Arguments that Radcliffe was founded in quicksand and doomed to end in failure or complete coeducation proved to be unfounded. Instead, "gradually, steadily, miraculously, with no convulsion of nature, the quicksand hardened into rock," proving that women could be educated with, and on the same campus as, men without suffering the severe physical or mental aberrations predicted, and even without introducing an "element of frivolity into the serious business of education."

Times and attitudes have changed. President Bok's remarks to the Class of '76 attest to that fact. Commenting on this year's historic event—the official introduction of two hundred freshwomen into the Harvard Yard—he said:

"I am confident that the civilizing influence of these two hundred pioneers will produce an aura of graciousness and scholarly dedication never before achieved upon that hallowed ground."

For ninety years, Radcliffe's historic and continuing contribution has been to make accessible to women the opportunities afforded by a Harvard education—an education anchored in more than three centuries of excellence. Our connection with Harvard was then and continues to be essential to our progress. I, for one, am glad that she is there and that she has the kind of leadership she does in men like Derek Bok and John Dunlop.

With courage and foresight, my predecessors met the challenging problems of educating women in their time and succeeded in opening the doors of quality education to them. This goal is no longer sufficient. The challenge to our generation is different and, in some ways, considerably more complex. Many of the issues at stake involve intangibles. We have, for instance, a culture and an educational system that ostensibly encourage and prepare men and women identically for educational programs and careers which, evidence indicates, other social and psychological pressures really limit to men.

We pride ourselves on being completely free of the prejudices of the age in which Radcliffe was founded, and yet experience and recent research, including my own, tell us differently.

I remind you that it was *1968* when Anthony Storr stated in his highly acclaimed and respected book, *Human Aggression*, that:

" . . . it is highly probable that the undoubted superiority of the male sex in intellectual and creative achievement is related to their greater endowment of aggression . . . . The hypothesis that women, if only given the opportunity and encouragement, would equal or surpass the creative achievements of men is hardly defensible."

And it was *1970* when Dr. Edgar Berman said of women:

"Their physical and psychological disabilities render them unfit to make important decisions or hold positions of power."

With the existence of such attitudes, it is not surprising to find that young men and women of today still tend to evaluate themselves and behave in ways consistent with age-old stereotypes and expectations. These stereotypes argue that independence, competence, intellectual achievement and leadership are all positive attributes of maturity and mental health. These very characteristics are at the same time viewed as synonymous with what is male and as basically inconsistent with what is female. The implication is that a feminine woman cannot be a healthy, mature adult and Margaret Mead's statement that "each step forward as a successful American is a step back as a woman" is very much to the point.

Thus, one of the challenges to our generation will be to help women resist and dissolve the persistent myth that the development of their intellectual capacity and the fulfillment of any of their nontraditional aspirations is a denial of their femininity and proof of their inadequacy as potential wives and mothers. This myth prevents educated women from walking through doors now open to them, from exercising their skills in personally meaningful and satisfying ways, and from taking advantage of opportunities now available to them. What a tremendous waste of both human and economic resources this represents! The price is too high. It is paid for by our students and by women in general in an easily recognizable loss of confidence and self-esteem, in an attrition of aspirations, in a persistence of low expectations for the future, and in the presence of a pervasive, often self-defeating sense that they are second-class citizens. These are impossible conditions for personal and intellectual growth and development.

It has become increasingly clear that only if all our students (both men and women) leave here feeling confident about their own abilities and about their capacity to *freely* determine the directions of their future lives, will they be stimulated toward creative involvement with the world about them. Only then will society be able to meet the steadily increasing demand for the talent necessary to identify and solve some of the major problems of the day—problems like pollution, overpopulation, health and child care delivery, and changing styles of life and learning in the community.

Obviously we cannot undo the impact of child-rearing practices that families have followed and that our institutions have reinforced for years. I do believe, however, that it will be possible, though not easy, with imaginative educational programs to help our students develop a strong sense of their worth, gain confidence in themselves as they master academic and social skills, and ultimately counteract the tendency to withdraw from the mainstream of thought and achievement in our society. In essence, this is the task I see before me.

Since I have assumed this office, one of the questions I have been asked most frequently is: What do I do and how do I spend my day?

From the perspective of my six-year-old, I was intrigued to learn last week that I spend my time writing "dumb speeches," and when not so creatively occupied, am in my office "making ideas." I then remember hoping that his perception of today's effort was not prophetic and that the opportunity for "making ideas" could be more frequent.

Another perspective on the job of a modern college president comes from Henry Wriston of Brown University. He said in 1946 that:

"the president is expected to be an educator, to have been at some time a scholar, to have judgment about finances, to know something of construction, maintenance, and labor policy, to speak virtually continuously in words that charm and never offend, to take bold positions with which no one will disagree, to consult with everyone and follow all preferred advice, and do everything through committees, but with great speed and without error."

I must say that there are times when I am certain Mr. Wriston anticipated the true dimensions of my job, *except* for the additional expectations that arise if the president is a woman. To paraphrase Marya Mannes, no one will object to a woman being president *if*, in addition to her official duties, she manages to "be a good wife, a good mother, good looking, good tempered, well dressed, well groomed, and unaggressive."

In the wake of such fulsome observations and expectations, you may wonder, as so many have, why on earth I took on this job. I must admit that I was tempted not *in spite of* but *because* of the unique nature of our present relationship with Harvard.

Our two institutions resisted the temptation to follow national trends or to succumb to pressures—political, financial and federal—for complete coeducation—total merger. They have thus given us an especially great opportunity for educational innovation. I, for one, am grateful for and excited by it. Ours together is a unique "experiment in education," as Mrs. Agassiz called it—*unique* in the possibility it provides (if only we take advantage of it) for identifying and bringing together the best aspects of independent single-sex and coeducational institutions—and of developing here the kind of living and learning environment that sufficient time, effort and adequate information will tell us are not only helpful but essential in preparing our extraordinarily talented students for their roles in the rapidly changing world about them.

There are at the moment many more questions than there are answers. But only if we consciously and actively take the time and effort—*now*—to raise the questions, to pursue the answers and to evaluate their implications will we be able to have a valuable and valid input in the lives of our students and through them to the wider society and toward the solution of its many problems.

I feel a particular responsibility to respond to this exciting challenge and to bring to fruition what three invigorating years of research, teaching and learning in this faculty have taught me. Observing the exciting young men and women in our student body engaged in vital dialogue with the intriguing questions of life and learning, I have become convinced that the full development and achievement of our students depends not only on the quality of the *academic* programs we offer them but also, and perhaps even more importantly, on the subtle attitudes and expectations held by those around them—by the faculty that teach them, by the advisors that counsel them and by the administrators that admit them. The time has come to ask the vexing questions—whether, when, or how one teaches men and women differently, *not* in standards of accomplishment *nor* in content, but in pedagogical technique. We must do so, so that the energy and talents of the students are not exhausted in a struggle against either overt and covert discrimination in such areas as admissions, curricular or extra-curricular opportunity, and that they are not frustrated because certain activities and behavior carry masculine or feminine label, either explicitly or implicitly.

In the end, the success of our "educational experiment" and the quality of the programs we create will be judged by their ability to give all students, male and female alike, the freedom to develop and employ their talents and energies in harmony with self-determined life goals. Our students can give their best to society only if they are able to pursue programs, careers and ways of life they find personally rewarding and socially worthwhile—and to do so in an atmosphere free of the pressure to conform to existing stereotypes—*past* and *present*.

The days have gone when Sophocles could have his player say: "Woman, a woman's ornament is silence." The world that permitted a woman to live, in Robert Frost's words, "Hopeless of being known for what she has been, failing of being loved for what she is" has perished, or soon will. In its place, Radcliffe, and other institutions like it, must mold and shape and found a world where the opportunities open to men and women, the hopes they can share and the new society they can create together will flourish. What we do here will be seen and studied by many. As we join together today as a family, we find ourselves with an important challenge, the challenge of shaping the intellectual and personal development of the young men and women who will ultimately determine the new directions of this society.

You have made me responsible for answering this challenge, and I look forward to your help in this effort.

In conclusion, as I formally accept my new responsibilities, I must say a word of thanks and praise to the members of my family—to my parents and especially to my husband Joe and my children, Tia, John and Chris. It is only with their constant reassurance that I have been able to enjoy the task of the presidency, and only with their unending support and patience that I can carry its burdens.

I thank you all for the support, help and confidence with which you have welcomed me both for Radcliffe and for women everywhere. I gladly await the opportunity to work with you in the years ahead and hope that in the not too distant future we shall be able to come together once again as a family and rejoice in what we have accomplished.

# Sex and the Education of Our Children[3]

William J. Bennett

*Born July 31, 1943, Brooklyn, NY; B.A., 1964, M.A., 1965, Williams College; Ph.D., University of Texas, 1970; J.D., Harvard University, 1971; assistant professor, University of Southern Mississippi, 1967-68; assistant to the president, Boston University, 1972-76; executive director, National Humanities Center, 1976-79; associate professor, North Carolina State University, 1979-81; chair, National Endowment for the Humanities, 1981-84; U.S. Secretary of Education, 1985-87; director, National Drug Control Policy Office, 1989-90; co-director, Empower America, 1991–; author,* Our Children and Our Country *(1988),* The Book of Virtues *(1993),* The Devaluing of America *(1994),* The Index of Leading Cultural Indicators *(1994),* The Moral Compass *(1995),* The Book of Virtues for Young People *(1996),* What Works *(1996),* Our Secret Honor *(1997).*

## Editor's introduction

In this speech, William J. Bennett, then United States secretary of education, argued against former Surgeon General C. Everett Koop's endorsement of explicit sex education (also reprinted in this volume) in America's public schools. Bennett believed that sex education could not be value-free or without a "moral guidance." He further argued that AIDS education should be "value-based," and aimed at teaching abstinence as the only sure means of protection. As is typical with many of Bennett's speeches, a sharply divided reaction was evoked. Faye Wattleton, then president of the Planned Parenthood Federation, called his speech fodder for "the anti-sex-education elements in this country," whereas the California Superintendent of Public Instruction welcomed Bennett's emphasis on character-building as a key element of any sex education course.

---

I've spent a good deal of my time as Secretary of Education talking about character. I've said that schools, teachers, and principals must help develop good character. I've said that they don't have to reinvent the wheel, we don't have to add special courses or devise new materials for the purpose of instilling character in the young. There is no great mystery or trick to this task: parents and teachers have been doing it for centuries. We simply need to put students in the presence of adults of sound character, adults who know the difference between right and wrong, who will articulate it to children, who will remind them of the human experience with that difference, and who will live that difference in front of them. Aristotle gave us this prescription more than two thousand years ago: In order to teach good character, expose children to good character and invite its imitation. It has been the experience of mankind, confirmed by the findings of contemporary psychology, that this prescription works, that it still works.

Today I would like to talk about one place in which attention must be paid to character in an explicit, focused way. That is in the classroom devoted to sex education. It would be undesirable, but a teacher could conduct large portions of a class in English or history without explicit reference to questions of character. But to neglect questions of character in a sex education class would be a great and unforgivable error. Sex education has to do with how boys and girls, how men and women, treat each other and themselves. It has to do with how boys and girls, how men and women, *should* treat each other and themselves. Sex education is therefore about character and the formation of character. A sex education course in which issues of right

[3]Delivered at the National School Board Association's conference on "Building Character in Public Schools," in Washington, D.C., on January 22, 1987.

and wrong do not occupy center stage is an evasion and an irresponsibility.

Sex education is much in the news. Many states and localities are considering proposals to implement or expand sex education curricula. I understand the reasons why such proposals are under consideration. And indeed, polls suggest that a substantial majority of the American people favor sex education in the schools. I too tend to support the idea. It seems reasonable to the American people, and to me, for the schools to provide another opportunity for students to become both more knowledgeable and more thoughtful about this important area of life. To have such matters treated well by adults whom students and their parents trust would be a great improvement on the sex curriculum available on the street and on television.

For several years now, though, I have been looking at the actual form the idea of sex education assumes once it is in the classroom. Having surveyed samples of the literature available to the schools, and having gained a sense of the attitudes that pervade some of this literature, I must say this: I have my doubts. It is clear to me that some programs of sex education are not constructive. In fact, they may be just the opposite. In some places, some people, to be sure, are doing an admirable job. But in all too many places, sex education classes are failing to give the American people what they are entitled to expect for their children, and what their children deserve.

Seventy percent of all high school seniors had taken sex education courses in 1985, up from 60 percent in 1976. Yet when we look at what is happening in the sexual lives of American students, we can only conclude that it is doubtful that much sex education is doing any good at all. The statistics by which we may measure how our children, how our boys and girls, are treating one another sexually are little short of staggering:

More than one-half of America's young people have had sexual intercourse by the time they are 17.

More than one million teenage girls in the United States become pregnant each year. Of those who give birth, nearly half are not yet 18.

Teen pregnancy rates are at or near an all-time high. A 25 percent decline in birth rates between 1970 and 1984 is due to a *doubling* of the abortion rate during that period. More than 400,000 teenage girls now have abortions each year.

Unwed teenage births rose 200 percent between 1960 and 1980.

Forty percent of today's 14-year-old girls will become pregnant by the time they are 19.

These numbers are, I believe, an irrefutable indictment of sex education's effectiveness in reducing teenage sexual activity and pregnancies. For these numbers have grown even as sex education has expanded. I do *not* suggest that sex education has *caused* the increase in sexual activity among youth; but clearly it has not prevented it. As Larry Cuban, professor of education at Stanford University, has written, "Decade after decade . . . statistics have demonstrated the ineffectiveness of such courses in reducing sexual activity [and] teenage pregnancy . . . . In the arsenal of weapons to combat teenage pregnancy, school-based programs are but a bent arrow. However, bent arrows do offer the illusion of action."

Why do many sex education courses offer merely the illusion of action? When one examines the literature and materials available to the schools, one often discovers in them a certain pervasive tone, a certain attitude. That attitude is this. Offer students technical information, offer the facts, tell them they have choices, and tell them what the consequences of those choices could be, *but do no more.* And there is the problem.

Let me give you a few examples. And let me say that these are not "worst case" examples, that is, they are not examples of the most controversial and provocative material used in some sex education courses. These are, rather, examples of approaches commonly used in many schools.

A curriculum guide for one of the largest school systems in the country suggests strategies to "help students learn about their own attitudes and behaviors and find new ways of dealing with problems." For example, students are given the following so-called "problem situation," asked to "improvise dialogue" and "act it out," and then discuss "how everyone felt about the interactions."

"Susan and Jim are married. He becomes intoxicated and has sex with his secretary. He contracts herpes, but fails to tell Susan.

"What will happen in this situation?

"How would you react if you were Susan and found out?"

The so-called "Expected Outcome" of this exercise of "acting out" and "interacting" is to get the student "to recognize sexually transmitted diseases as a threat to the individual."

Another lesson presents a situation of an unmarried girl who has become pregnant. Various parties in her life recommend various courses of action, from marriage to adoption to abortion. Having described the situation, the teacher is then supposed to ask the following questions:

"Which solution do you like best? Why?

"Which solution do you like least? Why?

"What would you do if you were in this situation?"

And the "Expected Outcome" of this exercise is "to identify alternative actions for an unintended pregnancy." Now we know what will likely happen in the classroom discussion of this lesson. Someone will opt for one course of action, others will raise their hands and argue for something else, more will speak, the teacher will listen to all opinions, and that will be that. The teacher will move on, perhaps saying the discussion was good, that students should be talking about this, and that as long as they are talking about it, even if they do not arrive at a clear position, they are somehow being educated.

Now the point I would like to make is that exercises like these deal with very complex, sensitive, personal, serious, and often agitated situations, situations that involve human beings at their deepest levels. But the guiding pedagogical instruction to teachers in approaching all such "Sensitive and Personal Issues" is this, and I quote: "Where strong differences of opinion exist on what is right or wrong sexual behavior, objective, informed and dignified discussion of both sides of such questions should be encouraged." And that's it—no more. The curriculum guide is loaded with devices to help students "explore the options," "evaluate the choices involved," "identify alternative actions," and "examine their own values." It provides some facts for students, some definitions, some information, lots of "options," but that's all.

What's wrong with this kind of teaching? First, it is a very odd kind of teaching, very odd because it does not teach. It does not teach because, while speaking to a very important aspect of human life, it displays a conscious aversion to making moral distinctions. Indeed, it insists on holding them in abeyance. The words of morality, of a rational, mature morality, seem to have been banished from this sort of sex education.

To do what is being done in these classes is tantamount to throwing up our hands and saying to our young people, "We give up. We give up. We give up on teaching right and wrong to you. Here, take these facts, take this information, and take your feelings, your options, and try to make the best decisions you can. But you're on your own. We can say no more." It is ironic that, in the part of our children's lives where they may most need adult guidance, and where indeed I believe they most want it, too often the young find instead an abdication of responsible moral authority.

Now I ask this: Do we or do we not think that sex for children is serious business, entailing serious consequences? If we do, then we need to be more than neutral about it in front of our children. When adults maintain a studiously value-neutral stance, the impression likely to be left is that, in the words of one twelfth-grader, "No one says not to do it, and by default they're condoning it." And a sex education curriculum that simply provides options, and condones by default, is not what the American people want, nor is it what our children deserve.

It is not that the materials used in most of our schools are urging students to go out and have sexual intercourse. In fact, they give reasons why students might want to choose not to have intercourse, and they try to make students "comfortable" with that decision. Indeed, you sometimes get the feeling that, for these guides, being "comfortable" with one's decision, with exercising one's "option," is the sum and substance of the responsible life. Decisions aren't right or wrong, decisions simply make you comfortable or not. It is as though "comfort" alone had now become our moral compass. These materials are silent as to any other moral standards, any other standards of right and wrong, by which a student might reach a decision to refrain from sex and which would give him or her the inner resources to stick by it.

It seems to me, then, if this is how sex education goes, that we should not wonder at its failure to stem the rising incidence of teenage sex, teenage pregnancies, teenage abortions, and single teenaged parents. One developer of a sex education curriculum recently said, "If you measure success in terms of reduction of teen pregnancy, I don't know if it has been successful. But in terms of orientation and preparation for students to comfortably incorporate sexuality into their lives, it has been helpful." There's that telltale "comfortable." But American parents expect more than that from their schools. Americans consistently say that they want our schools to provide reliable standards of right and wrong to guide students through life. In short, I think most Americans want to urge not what might be the "comfortable" thing, but the right thing. Why are we so afraid to say what that is?

I believe the American people expect from sex education courses in the schools that their children will be taught the basic information, the relevant biology, the relevant physiology, what used to be called the "facts of life." But they also expect that those facts will be placed in a moral context. In a recent national poll, 70 percent of the adults surveyed said they thought sex education programs should teach moral values, and about the same percentage believe the programs should urge students not to have sexual intercourse. And, believe it or not, the sense of adults on this matter is actually confirmed by the young people who take the sex education courses. According to a recent survey, seventh and eighth graders say that the single greatest influence on their intention to engage or not to engage in intercourse is the fact that "It is against my values for me to have sex while I am a teenager." Social science researchers report that mere factual "knowledge alone has little impact, and that even peer pressure is less powerful" than what they call "the student's internalized beliefs and values."

How, then, might sex education do better in shaping the beliefs and values of our children? It could do better by underpinning the whole enterprise with a frank attention to the *real* issues, which has to do with responsibility for oneself and for one's actions. In the classroom, as at home, this means explaining and defending moral standards in the area of sex, and offering explicit moral guidance. For example, why not say in schools to students exactly what most American parents say at home: Children should not engage in sexual intercourse. Won't our children better understand such a message, and internalize it, if we say it to them—and if we say it in school as well as at home? Why isn't this message being taught in more classrooms? Why isn't this said?

In general, there seem to be three common excuses as to why the schools cannot teach such lessons in character.

First, it is said that, given the diversity of today's society, you could never determine whose values to put into the sex education curriculum, and anyway you should not indoctrinate the young with your beliefs or anyone else's. Apparently being "comfortable" with one's decision is the only consensual value left.

I cannot buy this reasoning because it seems to me that, when it comes to the well-being of our children, there are certain precepts to which virtually all Americans adhere. For example, I have never had a parent tell me that he or she would be offended by a teacher telling a class that it is better to postpone sex. Or that marriage is the best setting for sex, and in which to have and raise children. On the contrary, my impression is that the overwhelming majority of parents would gratefully welcome help in transmitting such values. And I don't think they would view this as indoctrination. It is simply ethical candor. To put students in the presence of a mature adult who speaks honestly and candidly to them in this way is not to violate their rights or to fail to respect their diversity.

Second, it is said by some that teenage sex is so pervasive now that we should simply face reality and surrender any quaint moral notions we continue to harbor about it. The kids are going to "do it" no matter what, so we ought to be trying to head off pregnancies by making sure they have contraceptives. As a member of one Washington lobbying organization said last month, "All of us wish teenagers wouldn't have sex, but Reagan and Bennett are dealing with the world as they would like it and we're looking at it as it is." Well, Reagan and Bennett *are* talking about the world as it is, and I would like to assert that it violates everything a school stands for simply to throw in the towel and say, "O.K. We give up. It's not right, but we can't seem to do anything about it, so we're not going to worry about it any more." That is no lesson in good character, either. Yes, sex entices from many parts of the culture. So does violence. So do drugs. But school is supposed to be better, and do better, and point to a better way. After all, we can accept reality while also trying to shape it and improve it. If school were no better than TV, parents would just leave their children to sit at home and watch the tube all day long. School is supposed to be better. Parents who are trying to do better for their children, who are trying to shape their children's character, need an ally in the schools. They do not need another opponent, or, almost as bad, an unprotesting "option" provider. And furthermore, not "everybody" is doing it, and we might wish to give those youngsters, half of our seventeen-year-olds, support and reinforcement, too.

There is simply no reason to assume that efforts to shape character in matters of sex are doomed to failure. In fact, there are encouraging signs to the contrary. A teen services program at Atlanta's Grady Memorial Hospital, for example, found that of the girls under age 16 it surveyed, nine out of ten wanted to learn how to say "no." Let me underline this. This is not just Reagan and Bennett talking, it's girls under 16 talking. Well, one way to help them say "no" is for adults who care to teach them the reasons to say "no," and to give them the necessary moral support and encouragement to keep on saying it.

The third excuse for giving up on the teaching of character in sex education was stated most recently by a panel of scientific experts. The much publicized report on teenage pregnancy by the National Research Council of the National Academy of Sciences draws one conclusion that few, I think, would disagree with: sexual activity among teenagers is intimately connected with issues of self-image. As the report states, "Several studies of social and psychological factors associated with adolescents' sexual behavior conclude that self-perception (not self-esteem)—that is, the sense of what and who one is, can be, and wants to be—is at the heart of teenagers' sexual decision making."

This would be a good starting point for any educational project aimed at helping our children understand ways in which premature sex hinders the possibilities of becoming who they can be, who they want to be. But, strangely enough, the National Research Council reverses course, saying, "[W]e currently know very little about how to effectively discourage unmarried teenagers from initiating intercourse." Rather than drawing a conclusion from the studies on self-perception, the council simply accepts the inevitability of teenage sexual activity, and urges "making contraceptive methods available and accessible to those who are sexually active and encouraging them to diligently use these methods" as "the surest strategy for pregnancy prevention."

I have a couple of observations about this. One, there is no evidence that making contraceptive methods more available is the surest strategy for preventing pregnancy, to say nothing about preventing sexual activity. Nor is it true that "we currently know very little about how to effectively discourage unmarried teenagers from initiating intercourse." It is true that what we know about such matters is not easily amenable to being measured and quantified. Nevertheless, we *do* know how to develop character and reinforce good values. We've known for quite a long time. As columnist William Raspberry has said, you do it the old-fashioned way. You make it clear to young people that there are moral considerations in life. You make it clear through habit, example, precept, and the inculcation of priorities. This is not only possible, it has been tested and proven through centuries of experience. It seems to me that the National Research Council is acting with an extravagantly single-minded blindness when it simply, in the name of science, ignores such experience, and offers instead a highly mechanical and bureaucratic solution: more widely available contraceptives in the schools.

The National Research Council's solution betrays a view of sex, and of life, that is dangerous for our children. For to suggest to our children that really the only things that matter about sexual activity are pleasure, or "comfort," or getting pregnant, or getting a sexually transmitted disease—to suggest that the act of sexual intimacy is not significant in other ways—is to offer them still another very bad lesson. Why? Because it's false. It's false because, as every adult knows, sex is inextricably connected to the psyche, to the soul, or if you don't like that term, to personality at its deepest levels. Rarely is it a mere riot of the glands that occurs and then is over and meaningless thereafter. Sexual intimacy changes things: it affects feelings, attitudes, one's self-image, one's view of another. Sexual activity never takes place outside the wider context of what is brought to it or left out of it by the persons who engage in it. It involves men and women in all their complexity; it involves their emotions, desires, and the often contradictory intentions that they bring with them, whether they mean to or not. It is, in other words, a quintessentially moral activity.

All societies have known this and have taken pains to regulate sexual activity. All societies have done so, sometimes wisely, sometimes not, because they have recognized that sex is fraught with mystery and passion, and that sex involves the person at the deepest level of being. As John

Donne wrote, "Love's mysteries in *souls* do grow." Poets, novelists, philosophers, saints, and most psychiatrists have known that the power and beauty of sex lie precisely in the fact that it is *not* like anything else, that it is not just something you like to do or don't like to do. Far from being value-neutral, sex may be among the most value-loaded of any human activity. It does no good to try to sanitize or deny or ignore this truth. The act of sex involves deep springs of conduct. It is serious. It has complicated and profound repercussions. And if we're going to deal with it in school, we'd better know this and acknowledge it. Otherwise, we should not let our schools have anything to do with it.

Our children, too, ought to know this. We ought to tell it to them. Not to tell them, to make sex out to be something less special and powerful than it is, is a dodge and a lie. It is just as much a dodge as denying the importance of sex or silencing a child who is awakening to an interest in sex. We serve children neither by denying their sexuality nor by making it a thing of no moral account.

With these thoughts in mind, I would like to offer a few principles that speak to the task of educating schoolchildren about sex, principles which I believe should inform curricular materials and textbooks, and by which such materials could be evaluated. These principles are, I believe, what most American parents are looking for in sex education.

First, we should recognize that sexual behavior is a matter of character and personality, and that we cannot be value neutral about it. Neutrality only confuses children, and may lead them to conclusions we wish them to avoid. Specifically: *sex education courses should teach children sexual restraint as a standard to uphold and follow.*

Second, in teaching restraint, courses should stress that *sex is not simply a physical or mechanical act.* We should explain to children that sex is tied to the deepest recesses of the personality. We should tell the truth; we should describe reality. We should explain that sex involves complicated feelings and emotions. Some of these are ennobling, and some of them, let us be truthful, can be cheapening of one's own finer impulses and cheapening to others.

Third, *sex education courses should speak up for the institution of the family.* To the extent possible, when they speak of sexual activity, courses should speak of it in the context of the institution of marriage. We should speak of the fidelity, commitment, and maturity of successful marriages as something for which our students should strive.

To the girls, teachers need to talk about readiness for motherhood. And they must do more. They must not be afraid to use words like "modesty" and "chastity." Teachers and curriculum planners must be sure that sex education courses do not undermine the values and beliefs that still lead most girls to see sexual modesty as a good thing. For it is a good thing, and a good word. Let us from time to time praise modesty. And teachers must not be afraid to teach lessons other girls have learned from bitter experience. They should quote Lani Thompson, from T. C. Williams High School in Alexandria, Virginia, who says of some of her friends: "I get upset when I see friends losing their virginity to some guy they've just met. Later, after the guy's dumped them, they come to me and say, 'I wish I hadn't done it.'"

And the boys need to hear these things too. In discussing these matters, teachers should not forget to talk to the boys. They should tell the boys what it is to be a father, what it is to be ready to be a father, what the responsibilities of being a father are. And they should tell them how the readiness and responsibility of being a father should precede or at least accompany the acts which might make them fathers.

Fourth, *sex education courses should welcome parents and other adults as allies.* They should welcome parents into sex education classrooms as observers. If they do not, I would be suspicious. They should inform parents of the content of these courses, and they should encourage parents and children to talk to each other about sex. Studies show that when parents are the main source of sex education, children are less likely to engage in sex. This should come as no surprise when one remembers that the home is the crucible of character, and that parents are children's first and foremost teachers.

Many parents admit that they do not do enough to teach their children about sex. But still parents, more than anyone else, make the difference. Sex education courses can help remind those parents of their responsibilities. And these courses should encourage the individual counsel of priests, ministers, rabbis, and other adults who know a child well and who will take the time and offer the advice needed for the particular child. For it is the quality of the care and time that individuals take with other individuals which means the most in the formation of character.

Finally, schools, parents, and communities should pay attention to who is teaching their children about sex. They should remember that teachers are role models for young people. And so *it is crucial that sex education teachers offer examples of good character* by the way they act, and by the ideals and convictions they must be willing to articulate to students. As Oxford's Mary Warnock has written, "you cannot teach morality without being committed to morality yourself; and you cannot be committed to morality yourself without holding that some things are right and others wrong."

These, then, are some of the principles I would like to see standing behind our schools' sex education courses. The truth, of course, is that what I think in this matter isn't as important as what you think. I don't have any schools. You've got the schools, and part of your job is to help inform the philosophies that guide them. Above all else, then, I would urge you, as you think about those philosophies, to make sure your schools are teaching our children the truth. Sometimes the simplest way to recognize the truth is to consult common sense. Let me urge you to follow your common sense. Don't be intimidated by the sexologists, by the so-called sex-ed experts, by the sex technicians. Character education is mostly a matter of common sense. If sex education courses are prepared to deal with the truth, with reality in all its complexity, with the hard truths of the human condition, then they should be welcome in our schools. But if sex education courses are not prepared to tell the truth, if instead they want to simplify or distort or omit certain aspects of these realities in this very important realm of human life, then we should let them go out of business. If sex education courses do not help in the effort to provide an education in character, then let them be gone from the presence of our children.

# Educating Our Children About AIDS[4]

C. Everett Koop

*Born October 4, 1916, Brooklyn, NY; A.B., Dartmouth College, 1937; M.D., Cornell University, 1941; professor, University of Pennsylvania School of Medicine, 1949-70; surgeon-in-chief, Children's Hospital of Philadelphia, 1948; U.S. Navy, 1964; deputy assistant secretary of health, Department of Health and Human Services, 1981; U.S. surgeon general, 1982-89; author,* The Right to Live, The Right to Die *(1976),* Whatever Happened to the Human Race? *(1983),* The Health of the Nation *(1992),* Koop: The Memoirs of America's Family Doctor *(1992),* Sometimes Mountains Move *(1994).*

## Editor's introduction

By 1987 more than 32,000 Americans had been diagnosed with AIDS. Sixty percent of that number have since died from the disease. Notions on how to avoid infection range from distributing condoms in schools to promoting sexual abstinence. U.S. Surgeon General C. Everett Koop advocated a program of explicit sexual education. Conservatives immediately regarded him as having "failed in moral courage," while those on the political Left regarded him as a hero. William J. Bennett's speech "Sex and the Education of Our Children," also reprinted in this volume, was given on the same day, and the two speeches provide a good summary of the challenge the AIDS virus has posed to our educational system.

---

I'm pleased to have the chance to speak to this group of key government officials. Over the past couple of months, ever since I released *The Surgeon General's Report on AIDS*, I've felt that my office—of any office I know—is "where the action is." But in my more sober moments, I have to admit that each one of you has the "action" in our country. I can produce a report on AIDS and have it be a good one—and I truly believe it is—but the people who actually have AIDS are in your cities. They're your constituents, and they look to you and to your colleagues in local public health agencies for the help they need. I know that. And so, I'm pleased to talk with you and, if possible, offer you some insight into what this problem is all about.

First of all, as you know, our experience with AIDS is only six years old. The first reports of the disease were sent from some of your cities into our Centers for Disease Control in Atlanta in June, 1981. You already know the rest of the history of the disease since then, so I won't go into it.

I want to emphasize, however, that we're talking about a disease that's spreading. The number of victims is doubling in little more than a year. For example, as of January 1986, we had a cumulative total of 16,000 reported cases. Today that cumulative total is 30,000, and over half of them have already died of the disease. And the rest apparently will.

Last year we had over 13,000 new cases added to the total. This year we expect another 23,000 new cases. By the end of 1990 a quarter of a million people will have contracted AIDS. Make no mistake about it. AIDS is spreading among more people, and it is fatal.

Now, even though scientists have had a look at the AIDS virus itself, we don't really know what it is, and unless we know that, we have no way of permanently stopping it. Yes, we're making progress in the research effort, but it's very slow going.

People ask, "When will we have an effective vaccine available?" And I have to tell them that I don't see one in the foreseeable future. I will

[4]Delivered at the annual mid-winter meeting of the United States Conference of Mayors, in Washington, D.C., on January 23, 1987. Reprinted with permission of C. Everett Koop.

remind you that it took 19 years to develop the hepatitis B vaccine, and that was a comparatively easy virus to understand.

There are a lot of things we don't know about AIDS. But we do know with complete certainty that the AIDS virus is transmitted from one person to another either in blood or in semen. It's a peculiar trait of a virus, I'll admit. But there it is.

And while it may be peculiar, it is also the most serious piece of information we have. It explained, for example, why AIDS has been so prevalent among homosexual and bisexual men. Some homosexual sex practices not only produce semen but they also cause some bleeding.

The second largest group of AIDS carriers are drug abusers who borrow dirty intravenous needles from other addicts who already have AIDS.

When we first began to confront the AIDS epidemic, the people at highest risk were homosexual and bisexual men. I'm afraid they still are, even though homosexuals have apparently become much more cautious about their sexual practices. This is clear from the downward trend-lines of other diseases, such as gonorrhea, herpes, and syphilis, in the gay community. However, the virus has a long incubation period and many men who are more cautious today and show no signs of the disease are nevertheless carrying the virus in their bloodstreams.

Make no mistake about this: homosexual and bisexual men are still the primary high-risk group, and they are also the primary group transmitting the disease as well. But lately we've been seeing a rise in the reports of AIDS occurring among heterosexual men and women who are not I.V. drug abusers. In fact, their heterosexual activity seems to be their only risk factor. As of last week, about 4 percent of all AIDS reports involved heterosexual men and women. That's not much. However, while we anticipate that the overall numbers of AIDS cases will increase about 9-fold over the next five years, the number of AIDS cases involving heterosexuals will increase about 20-fold.

So far, we've beamed virtually all our information and education efforts at homosexual and bisexual men. But now that the disease is occurring more and more among heterosexual men and women, we need to direct our information and education efforts out to the whole society, which, of course, is predominantly heterosexual. This new development also means that the geography of this disease is changing. At one time we were concerned primarily—almost exclusively—with the homosexual communities in San Francisco, Los Angeles, and New York City, and these are still the cities with the highest numbers of AIDS cases.

But they're no longer alone. Other cities and states are showing a rise in cases, too. You've probably heard some of these figures already, but let me offer just a couple: Houston had 77 cases in 1983, but it reported 345 last year; Dallas had only 26 AIDS cases in 1983—it had 208 last year; Atlanta had 25 in 1983—it had 185 last year; Boston had 38 in 1983 and 155 last year.

Now, for the benefit of some people here from state capitols, let me add these figures: Colorado reported 167 new cases during 1986, but only 63 new cases in 1985; Ohio had 173 new ones last year, but only 64 a year ago; and Arkansas had 40 new cases last year, but only 27 in all of 1985.

These broadly geographic trend-lines were already appearing, when President Reagan asked me—back in February of 1986—to pull together everything we knew about AIDS and put it in a plain-English report to the American people.

I met with individuals and groups from across the spectrum of society: groups like the National Education Association and the National P.T.A.; the Christian Life Commission of the Southern Baptist Convention and the Synagogue Council of America; with the National Coalition of Black and Lesbian Gays and the Washington Business Group on Health. I had good meetings with the representatives of local, county, and state and territorial health officials, also, 26 groups in all. They were extraordinarily helpful, and each one pledged to do whatever was necessary to distribute my report across the length and breadth of America.

After 8 months of listening and writing, I delivered my report to the White House. Late last September the cabinet heard it and accepted it, the Domestic Policy Council heard and accepted it, and, of course, the President accepted it. I want to assure you that at no time did anyone suggest a little change here and a little something there. I'm happy to say that the final published report I released on October 22 was the exact same report that I personally wrote between February and September of last year.

I think the report has done two things: First, it has impressed the country generally that AIDS was indeed everybody's problem. We had said that before, but nobody really wanted to believe it. Now they must.

Second, the report makes it clear that we have to stop the disease not by waiting around for the development of a vaccine but by teaching our young people the facts about AIDS and—hopefully—thereby ending the chain of transmission once and for all with the help of a new generation of enlightened, cautious Americans. Heterosexual as well as homosexual young people are now at high risk. How they live out their sexuality over a long period of time will determine whether our society can survive this devastating disease or not. And this is the difficult part. What we have to do over the next several years is educate and inform young people about AIDS, about their own sexuality in such a way that they can become a little more responsible than their elders have been.

I know you're all wondering what educational messages you should plan in your communities. I won't be prescriptive, but let me offer a couple of suggestions.

The first one is simple enough: It's monogamy. In other words, short of total abstinence, the best defense against AIDS is to maintain a faithful, monogamous relationship, the kind of relationship in which you have only one continuing sexual partner, and that person is as faithful as you are. This may sound like a morality lesson, but it also happens to be good science. In containing the epidemic of AIDS, science and morality walk hand-in-hand toward the same goal.

My second message is for people who don't yet have a faithful monogamous relationship for whatever reason. My message is caution. You need to know with absolute certainty that neither you nor your partner is carrying the AIDS virus. If you are not absolutely certain, then you must take precautions. In such situations I advise the following:

Don't have sex with someone who already has AIDS. Period.

Don't have sex with someone who could carry the virus of AIDS, a person who, for example, practices high-risk behavior. That includes homosexuals, intravenous drug users, prostitutes, and other persons who have many different sex partners. Obviously the same message goes to any of those high-risk individuals.

And finally, if you do decide to have sex with such an individual anyway—a decision that could have serious health consequences—then, if you're a man, at least use a condom from start to finish. If you're a woman, make sure your male partner uses a condom. A condom won't provide 100 percent protection—few things in life do—but so far it seems to be the best protection short of monogamy.

If sexually active people will heed these two messages, they will achieve a high degree of protection and will most likely not be infected with the AIDS virus.

What else can we do to combat this terrible disease?

In my report on AIDS, I also advise people to avoid those sex practices which can cause cuts or tears in the linings of the rectum, vagina, or penis. I say, don't have sex with female or male prostitutes. I strongly advise young people to stay clear of drugs and alcohol, because these substances lower your ability to think clearly and protect yourself from danger, especially the danger of having sex with an AIDS-infected partner.

And I also suggest that we educate our young people about AIDS and about sexuality. Young people are curious and eager for such knowledge. They're still learning about their bodies and their emotions, they're still unsure about their own sexuality, and they still have that priceless optimism about the world and the people in it. I prefer to speak about the need for "AIDS education," and I truly believe we need such education at the appropriate age level in the schools of America.

But I also recognize that, for many young people, such education may be frightening, or puzzling, or both. Hence, I believe that the most significant action our society might take to protect its young people from the mortal threat of AIDS is to provide them with education concerning their own sexuality that is factually correct, personally sensitive, and morally strong.

The term "sex education" is one I'm not at all comfortable with because it immediately polarizes any audience. Also, in my view, "sex education" usually means a course of instruction that is much too limited. Let me explain what I mean by that.

Most of the time, when you hear the phrase, "sex education," you think of class time devoted to human reproductive biology, including carefully phrased explanations about the use and abuse of the male and female genitalia. I'm told that young people call these classes "organ recitals."

Most schools now offer this minimum kind of sex education some time during the junior high or middle school years and that's a good thing, although it might be a little late. I personally would urge that the material be presented earlier, among 9-, 10-, and 11-year-olds.

Of course, developmental age is more important than chronological age. Also, community standards, which vary from place to place, must be taken into account. Grade-school children are extremely curious about themselves. They are also kinder and more generous than older children, or even most adults, for that matter. And they are, above all, susceptible to being loved and to offering much love in return. And sex education without the concept of love and responsibility is like a piece of pie that's all crust and no filling.

My own preference, therefore, would be to have our elementary schools introduce children to the subject of reproductive biology within a more general discussion of the nature of sensitive and affirmative human relations. That's easier to say than to do, I know. And furthermore, some parents get uneasy about having the schools impart certain human values to their children. They think that such instruction should be done at home.

And I agree. My advice to parents has always been the same: the social and spiritual development of your children is your business. Don't pass it up, don't pass it by, pass it on. Parents agree with me 100 percent. But most of them, I have to confess, never do much more than agree with me. Nevertheless, I encourage parents to talk openly, clearly, and affirmatively with young people about their developing physiology. But I want them to give some other information, too.

As I indicated earlier, "sex education" means more to me than just an "organ recital." "Sex education" ought to deal with relationships between men and women that are loving, caring, respectful, and tolerant. Such relationships include some fulfilling sexual activity, but they are not defined only by that activity. There's much more to human relationships than just "good sex." And young people ought to be advised of that.

But for many people, such a balanced relationship is an ideal. "Real life" isn't always like that. Grown-ups know about human imperfection. But children don't. And grown-ups can deal with human imperfection. But children can't unless we help them. Without a compassionate understanding of the imperfect nature of many human relationships, a child's education will be, itself, very imperfect.

So if parents are to educate their children about human relationships—sexual and otherwise—they must first understand and accept the nature of their own. For many of us, that's hard to do. And then they must be able to tell their children about that relationship. I'd like parents to do this with compassion, with respect and love, and with some understanding not just of the child who is listening, but also of the adult who is speaking. And that's even harder to do.

I'm sharing these thoughts with you today because I want you to know that my deepest wish is still for the parents of this country to be the primary teachers of sex and human relations to their children. And I say that, knowing full well that this may be an assignment that some parents simply can't handle. When that's the case, then I believe there is a compelling social need for our schools, churches, synagogues, and other communal institutions—including our local governments—to do whatever they can to provide our children with the most helpful kinds of information.

Our children don't live in a vacuum, as we all know. They live in a real world of pleasure and danger, along with the rest of us. But we have some experience with it and some sense of how to survive in it, with our lives and our values intact. And I believe, therefore, that each of us—in our homes or in our schools—has the moral responsibility to pass that information on to our children. We can't leave it by default to the movies, television, or the street-corner. Not if you value the young lives that are now at stake.

This has been a grim message, and I guess I am a grim courier. I only hope that everyone who hears it or reads it will also believe it and do his or her part to stop the spread of AIDS, protect and save the lives of people at risk, including unsuspecting young people, and return human sexuality back to its rightful place: part of the total complex of human, caring interpersonal relations.

# Benefits and Responsibilities[5]

Britt Rogers

*Born 1976, Tupelo, MS; winner, Robert C. Byrd Scholarship, 1995; winner, Cambridge College Scholarship, 1995; student, Rhodes College, 1995–.*

## Editor's introduction

Brittain ("Britt") Rogers gave this salutatory address at the 1995 Tupelo High School commencement ceremonies. Speaking to over 2,000 people, Rogers urged his fellow graduates to take an "active role" in determining America's future course. As told to the editor of this volume, Rogers wanted to "address the many different backgrounds and interests that the families of the Tupelo Public School system share" by employing "cultural icons to capture [his] audience's attention." The speech was broadcast on a local Tupelo radio station and excerpted in the *New York Times* (June 11, 1995).

---

Dr. Mike Walters, Superintendent of Education; Members of the School Board; Administrators at Central Office; Mr. Dale Dobbs, Principal of Tupelo High School; Administrators, Faculty, and Staff of Tupelo High School; Parents, Guests, and fellow classmates of the graduating class of 1995.

Mom awakened me extra early that morning to start preparing for my big day. I carefully stowed my brand new Trapper Keeper, decorated on all sides with baseball stickers, inside my backpack. I checked my supplies: three pencils (meticulously sharpened), one bottle of Elmer's glue, and a pair of the blunt scissors because Mom said I wasn't old enough to use the good kind yet. I put on my best pair of red shorts, my favorite green shirt, and my blue striped socks that came up past my knees. After a breakfast of Froot Loops and milk, Mom marched me down the street to the bus stop. After a few minutes, the pungent odor of carbon monoxide filled the air as the bus pulled to a stop and opened its doors. With a tearful goodbye, my mother waved at me as I rambled off toward my first day of school. I can still remember arriving at Church Street Elementary School, staring wide-eyed at the enormous building, and wondering how many wonderful mysteries were held inside.

Now, twelve full years later, we have all uncovered the countless mysteries that school has offered us: from comma splices to the quadratic equation to finding out that Dr. Weeks really doesn't have an electric paddle that plugs into the wall. Here we now stand, at the pinnacle of our high school career—the consummation of twelve years of hard work. I want you each to pause and remember all the struggles and triumphs that have brought you here: the time your team won in kickball, the time you stayed up all night working on that paper and somehow got an A, and the time all your friends were jealous because your lab partner was the cutest girl in school. Let us never forget these moments, for this has been a magical time for us—we were the last class ever to spend our freshman year in the unique atmosphere of Carver School and under the compelling leadership of Mr. Harry Grayson. Our senior year has given us State Championships in Cross Country, Golf and Tennis and strong showings in all other sports; these victories have combined with everything from DECA to Decathlon to make our years at Tupelo High School unforgettable. Never again will we live like this. So, before we plunge into the "real world," let us make sure that we hold tightly to these memories. For no matter how hard life may become in the future, you will always be third place in the science fair and that cute guy or girl in your English class will always be in his or her seat, waiting for you to get enough nerve to talk to him. Yes, this has

[5]Delivered at the Tupelo Coliseum, in Tupelo, Mississippi, on May 24, 1995. Reprinted with permission of Britt Rogers.

truly been a magical time, but we could not have done it alone.

It has long been said that "Behind every good man is a great woman." Now, while some may question this theory, no one can deny that behind all of us students here tonight are hundreds of very hard working parents, grandparents, and guardians. Through their prompting, prodding, and sometimes pleading, they have pushed us to our fullest potential. They shared our defeats and our victories—they consoled us when we lost our lunch money, and they rejoiced with us when we passed our spelling test. Truly, our parents deserve more credit than we can ever give them, nevertheless I now ask all of the proud parents and guardians here tonight to stand and, classmates, please join me in applauding those who have brought us here tonight. (Applause.)

Our teachers are a group of people who deserve an equally immeasurable amount of credit. From the minute we stepped into elementary school, our teachers have shaped and molded us into thinking, feeling, and questioning human beings. They are special people who care enough about our futures to devote their lives to ensuring our success. Each day our teachers pursue the enormous task of preparing America's youth to become productive members of society. Although they receive little pay and often less recognition, our teachers continue to dedicate themselves to building and educating our youth. So I would like all teachers and administrators here tonight, from kindergarten to grade twelve, to please stand. Let's recognize our outstanding teachers and administrators. (Applause.)

The work of teachers, parents, and countless others has brought us here to this great threshold. Beyond lies a labyrinth of relationships, salaries, and W-2 Tax forms—of job interviews, car payments, and mothers-in-law. No one path leads through this maze of humanity. Each one of us must travel his own road to adulthood. Some of us will head directly into a workplace that is the backbone of today's society. Others will p[ur]sue further education in college or perhaps service in the United States Armed Forces. Whatever our plans may be, we all have one thing in common—tonight is the ceremonial end to our childhood. No longer will Mom or Dad be there to remind us of meetings or deadlines. No one will tell us when to wake up, how to dress, or when to come home at night. The freedoms and responsibilities of independence are ours. It is our obligation to make the best of them.

The American journalist Sydney J. Harris once said that "We have not passed that subtle line between childhood and adulthood until we move from the passive voice to the active voice—that is until we have stopped saying,' It got lost,' and say, 'I lost it.'" No statement can more accurately describe the situation which we now face. We can no longer turn on the television, hear a report about the declining state of our country, and turn passively from the problem. This country belongs as much to us as it does to any adult here tonight. It is not "up to our parents" to decide which direction this country will take—it is up to us. And if we want to insure that our children will have all the opportunities that we have had, we must take an active role in our country's government now by educating ourselves and voting. Freedom is a double-edged sword: its benefits are many, but its responsibilities are great.

We have no excuse for failure. There is an entire world full of opportunities out there. New frontiers are discovered almost daily that will improve our lives and provide thousands of jobs. Our responsibility is to seek these opportunities and to reap all the benefits they may offer. The quality of our lives—and this world—depends solely on our efforts.

So, tonight, as we say our final farewell to Tupelo High School and the leadership of Mr. Dale Dobbs and Dr. Mike Walters, I urge all of us to meet the world with chins high and chests out. We have come a long way in twelve years, but the vast majority of our lives still remains uncharted. There are many roads yet to be traveled, many questions yet to be answered. I charge us to venture boldly into the world, living every day of our lives by the creed of Tennyson's "Ulysses"—"To strive, to seek, to find, and not to yield"—and above all, to meet every new opportunity with the wide-eyed enthusiasm of that first grader in all of us.

# The Imagination of Prepared Minds[6]

Neil L. Rudenstine

*Born 1935, Ossining, NY; B.A., Princeton University, 1956; B.A., 1959, M.A., 1960, Oxford University; Ph.D., Harvard University, 1964; professor, administrator, Princeton University, 1968-88; executive vice president, Andrew W. Mellon Foundation, 1988-91; president, Harvard University, 1992–.*

## Editor's introduction

This speech was given by Neil L. Rudenstine, president of Harvard University, at that university's 344th commencement ceremony. Speaking to an audience of approximately 20,000, Rudenstine expressed concern that the United States had "reached what may be a critical turning point in its commitment to the creation of important new knowledge and understanding." Rudenstine called for continued increased financial support of university teaching and research. Research and education, he reminded his audience, are indispensable if we are to maintain and protect "our health, prosperity, and security as a nation in the modern world."

---

Fifty years ago, as World War II was coming to an end, Harvard graduates and their families gathered in this Yard for Commencement. The occasion was the same as today. But the mood was very different. Victory had been declared in Europe, but we were still at war in the Pacific. The Commencement audience was much smaller than usual, and so the gathering was held not here, in this space, but in the Sever Quadrangle, off to my left. President Conant explained that more than 25,000 Harvard graduates and students were still in uniform. The Harvard Commencement of 1945, he told the audience, was a purely local gathering because of national restrictions on wartime travel. The usual daylong activities of Commencement were condensed into two hours.

And yet the day—while in some ways solemn—was essentially one of affirmation and hope. One of the honorary degree recipients—and the principal speaker—was Sir Alexander Fleming, the renowned British bacteriologist. It was Fleming, in 1928, who had discovered penicillin. And it was penicillin that had saved thousands and thousands of lives during the war: a war in which so many Harvard students, faculty, and alumni served with great courage and distinction—and in which so many gave their lives.

But on Commencement Day fifty years ago, Fleming did not speak about conflict and destruction. He spoke instead about the importance to society of scientific discovery. He talked in an unassuming and personal way about the role of chance—of serendipity—in research, as well as in his own life.

As a young man, Fleming had spent five years as a shipping clerk. He couldn't afford the medical education he wanted. Then fortune intervened: a relative left him a legacy that was enough to launch him in his medical studies. He earned his degree, served in World War I, and went on to a career in biological research, studying bacteria.

Within a decade, fortune intervened again, this time as Fleming was working in his laboratory. "I did not ask for a spore of *penicillium notatum* to drop on my culture [plate]," he said. "[And] when I saw certain changes [take place there], I had not the slightest suspicion that I was at the beginning of something extraordinary. . . . That same mould [spore] might have dropped on [any one] of my [other] culture plates, and there would have been no visi-

[6]Delivered at Harvard University commencement exercises, in Cambridge, Massachusetts, on June 8, 1995. Reprinted with permission of Neil L. Rudenstine.

ble change to direct [my] special attention to it. . . . However, somehow or other, everything [fit] in. . . . There was an appearance which called for investigation—with the result that now, after various ups and downs, we have penicillin."

Why did Fleming tell this story on that particular Harvard Commencement day? He said he wanted to offer some advice to young researchers in pursuit of new knowledge. "Never," he said, "never neglect an extraordinary appearance or happening. It may be a false alarm and lead to nothing. But it may, on the other hand, be the clue provided by fate to lead you to some important advance."

We can now see, from our own vantage point, that there was also another significance to Fleming's remarks: he was already helping to shift our focus from the war that was ending, to the peace that was about to begin. His own personal experience reminded everyone that research and discovery could lead to dramatic and unpredictable advances by society, and by all individuals.

In fact, as we know, our own nation began to invest heavily in basic and applied research during the war years, and increased that investment afterward. Our major universities were seen as senior partners in this enterprise—and not only in research, but in the training of graduate and professional students in many different fields. We need to remember (and it can hardly be stressed enough) that advanced education—providing the constant stream of physicians and health professionals, educators, architects, business leaders, religious leaders, lawyers, government officials and other public servants—such advanced education depends most of all on a creative faculty engaged in significant research and discovery at major universities.

Without such a faculty, and without support for its research, neither Harvard nor any other university can carry out its fundamental mission, or achieve its own goals and those of society. Research and advanced education are inescapably linked to one another. Neither can flourish without the other.

I want to stress this point today because we have reached what may be a critical turning point in our nation's commitment to the creation of important new knowledge and understanding. Decisions now being made in Washington will have a profound effect on the future of research and education in this country. The stakes are very high. And the issue is not receiving the urgent and widespread attention it deserves—because this is certainly the most hazardous moment with respect to federal support for higher education in this country during the postwar period.

In the fifty years since Alexander Fleming spoke at Harvard—it is no exaggeration to say—basic research at universities has done much to transform our world.

We should remember, for example, the discovery of the structure of DNA—in 1953—which has increased our understanding of almost every aspect of our biological nature, which began the revolution in genetics, and which led to the creation of the entire new industry of biotechnology.

We should consider the computer revolution—the ways in which it has changed how we learn, how we transmit and access information, how we solve problems that were previously insoluble.

Think about microwaves, plastics, optical fibers, laser discs, superconductors, weather and communications satellites, and many other devices and new materials that have become so much a part of our daily lives that we hardly even notice them any more.

Or the advances in understanding cancer, heart disease, and other illnesses including mental illnesses. Think how much has been accomplished, but how much more work there is still to be done.

How we travel, how we communicate, what we eat, what we do with our free time, how we protect our environment, how we make a living—all these aspects of our lives have increasingly come to depend in essential ways on the discoveries that flow from our basic and applied research.

The driving force behind this steady advance—as I suggested—has been the cooperation, for a full half-century and more, between our universities and the federal government. This joint enterprise has been based on a simple premise that was spelled out in a famous report whose fiftieth anniversary we are also marking this year. The report was titled *Science: The Endless Frontier*. Its author was Vannevar Bush—who also received a Harvard honorary degree, in 1941, when he was the principal speaker at our Commencement.

"Progress in the war against disease depends upon a flow of new scientific knowledge," Bush wrote in 1945. "New products, new industries, and more jobs require continuous additions to knowledge . . . and the application of that knowledge to practical purposes. Science . . . provides no panacea for individual, social, and economic ills," he continued. But "without scientific progress, no amount of achievement in other directions can insure our health, prosperity, and security as a nation in the modern world."

These words are no less true today than fifty years ago. But our national mood, and certainly our sense of perspective, have changed. Today, we are more skeptical about institutions and what they can achieve. As a society, we have much less patience for long-term investments and long-range solutions. In fact, we have less patience for many things that require it. It is true, in addition, that the financial resources at our disposal are more constrained, and we face difficult choices about how to spend these resources. In such a climate, basic research—which has no broad or obvious constituency in our national politics—finds itself very seriously at risk.

A scientist spends weeks, months, even years studying the genetic make-up of baker's yeast. It sounds completely irrelevant, and might at first seem to be an easy target for ridicule. Later, we find out that the results of this work can help pave the way for a breakthrough in understanding the basis of colon cancer.

A team of physicists studies how protons shift energy levels inside the nuclei of atoms—not something that most of us worry about very much in our daily lives. But years later, the work leads to magnetic resonance imaging—MRI—an astonishingly precise tool that allows us to picture and to study normal and abnormal structures inside the human body. With other imaging devices, we can now watch parts of the brain and other organs in action; and we can begin to diagnose many diseases in ways that we could hardly have imagined before.

This is only the smallest handful of possible examples, illustrating what has been accomplished in the last half-century—thanks to our national conviction that discovery and increased understanding will constantly lead to real and tangible benefits, of many kinds, for all of us. Now, at a time when our ability to solve increasingly complicated problems—in the economy, in international affairs, in health, in ethnic relations, in technology—depends so much on intelligent leadership; on people who can both analyze and act; on research that can illuminate patterns in behavior, or the deepest puzzles in nature: at such a time we cannot afford to give up on the basic commitments and investments that have been so much a source of our collective human and economic strength.

The question many people are asking today is whether we can *afford* to make such investments in research and education. This is now—and always—an essential question to keep before us. But the other question we must ask—as we look to the future of our society as a whole—is whether we can afford *not* to make such investments.

We dare not underestimate the dangers—even if they are not immediately apparent. If, for instance, the enterprise of basic science is seriously damaged at the National Institutes of Health, the National Science Foundation, and other agencies, we may not see or feel the most profound effects either today or tomorrow. After all, it has taken fully forty years since the discovery of the structure of DNA to begin to realize what it will finally yield in terms of medical, social, and economic benefits. So we may well persuade ourselves into thinking that today's budget cuts will really have no profound impact. But that would be a very great mistake. The total impact will be felt later—in a decade, or even two. And then, it will be too late to turn back the clock—and it will cost a very great deal more to rebuild something that now needs only to be kept in good repair.

Many people in the Congress and the Executive Branch understand this. Many have been working hard, helping to follow the thoughtful, careful approach that is needed—and they have done so courageously, and with some real effect. The effort is bipartisan, and continuous. But our many leaders in Congress need to know that all the rest of us care, and that we too want to help. They cannot, in the current national climate, manage this entire formidable job on their own.

With them, we should remember another of Alexander Fleming's remarks fifty years ago. "The unprepared mind," he said, "cannot see the outstretched hand of opportunity." Curiosity alone does not produce new knowledge. Fortuity alone does not produce new knowledge. Rather, significant new knowledge depends on the rigorous work and imagination of *prepared* minds. It depends on excellent education. It depends on a climate of free inquiry, in which individuals have the flexibility and support that they need to follow their deepest insights and intuitions, in discovering new knowledge about human nature and the natural world.

In closing, let us remember, too, that Alexander Fleming almost did not make it to medical school. A small legacy from a relative happened to come his way. Without that financial help, we might well never have heard of Fleming—and we might never have had the benefit of his own well-prepared mind.

In the years since World War II—though we sometimes forget this fact—higher education in America has become far more accessible than ever before. Our society's conviction about the importance of educational opportunity—as expressed in our public policy and in the constant generosity of so many individuals—has steadily opened doors to women and men of talent and energy, from all backgrounds and walks of life, even when their financial means have been very modest. The commitment to provide financial aid to students in need—the commitment to openness and inclusiveness in our colleges and universities—has been one of the defining achievements of American society in the last fifty years.

For example, the Harvard class of 1945 included the first Harvard graduates who were supported by scholarships under the GI Bill of Rights—one of the great steps forward in expanding access to American higher education. In the following decades, we have seen even broader efforts to open the doors of our colleges and universities. Here, as in the case of scientific research, the key to progress has been a powerful partnership between educational institutions and the government—as well as generous private donors and, of course, our students and their families.

Here, too, we have arrived at a major crossroads. There are proposals on the table in Washington that would turn back the clock in significant ways. There are deeply troubling signs that an immensely productive investment in financial aid and access to education is in increasing danger.

For instance, the idea of beginning to charge interest on student loans from the moment a student enrolls in college would—if adopted—add very substantially to student debt: for graduate students as well as for undergraduates. The proposals to freeze or cut campus-based aid programs such as work-study, or to freeze the Pell Grant program, are no less disturbing.

We must not let these and similar reversals take place. President Conant told us why, when he spoke here, fifty years ago. Broad access to education, he said, "is the great instrument created by American democracy to secure the foundations of a republic of free [people]." He remembered the many Harvard alumni who had given their lives to secure that freedom. And he pledged that we would honor their sacrifice—that we would work even harder, in times of peace, to serve society by continuing to advance knowledge, and by keeping the doors of educational opportunity open to everyone.

We must not, at this important moment, turn our backs on that pledge—for *all* of our sakes, and for the health of the nation. We have made good on our shared commitment to education, year after year, decade after decade, for these past fifty years. Let us not begin to falter now.

Honored guests, graduates, family, friends—I would now like to ask you all to rise. I ask that you join me in paying tribute to the Harvard men and women who gave so much of themselves—and especially the many who gave their lives—in the cause of freedom during the Second World War, and in later wars. I ask that you join me in honoring the Class of 1945, celebrating its 50th reunion today; and the Class of 1970, celebrating its 25th reunion. Let us celebrate the spirit of freedom that they did so much to protect and defend—and that *we* must protect and defend. We shall honor them, in the traditional way, by observing a moment of silence as the bell of Memorial Church tolls—in memory, and in thanks.

# X. The Arts

## Editor's introduction

Between 1937 and 1997 American leaders discussed the role, function, and propriety of the arts and humanities within American society. Many denounced the message they perceived a given art work conveyed. Some opposed using tax dollars to fund what they deemed to be obscene works. Recently, several members of Congress endorsed ending public funding of artists, which meant terminating the National Endowment for the Arts. Yet, just as some were quick to label certain artistic expressions as "obscene," many others were equally quick to defend an artist's right to her or his artistic expression. In the speeches below, two professors, an elected official, a writer, and an artist examine an artist's responsibility to society, public support of the arts, and the contribution that artists make to communities and culture.

Esther M. Jackson, former professor of Speech and Theatre at Adelphi University, criticized the art community for not fulfilling its responsibility to society. She maintained that unlike the sciences, "the arts in general have seemed least prepared to cope with the major social, political, and cultural changes of the sixties." Jackson believed that the American drama community had failed to create an indigenous, American style of acting. For Jackson, the arts are a means by which many of society's problems be confronted and solved. Failure to create a peculiarly American way of confronting the problems of American society through drama therefore represents the inability to use art to the maximum benefit of society.

Other speakers whose speeches are reprinted in this chapter also examined the vital importance of art to individuals and society. Arthur M. Schlesinger, Jr., professor of Humanities at the City University of New York, made a strong case for public support of artists. Schlesinger began by refuting the notion that accepting public funding for art necessarily means that government will control the artist. Drawing upon historical illustrations, he insisted that "public support does not restrict professional independence." Art must therefore be publicly supported, according to Schlesinger, as it is a means by which America is undoubtedly enriched and strengthened. For Schlesinger, a culture is judged by its art. Representative Barbara Jordan wholeheartedly agreed with such a notion. She argued that "the arts are an integral part of us" and should be understood as "a response to our individuality and our nature." This sentiment was also echoed by Pulitzer Prize winning author David McCullough, who in the speech contained herein, asserted that "in the arts, we show who we are."

# The American Theatre and the Speech Profession[1]

Esther M. Jackson

*Born 1922, Pine Bluff, AR; B.S., Hampton Institute, 1942; M.A., 1946, Ph.D., 1958, Ohio State University; teacher, Clark College, 1949-56, 1961-64; teacher, U.S. Office of Education, 1964-65; director, New York Shakespeare Festival, 1965-66; professor, Adelphi University, 1965-67; lecturer, Free University of Berlin, 1967-68; professor, University of Wisconsin, 1969–; author,* The Broken World of Tennessee Williams *(1965).*

## Editor's introduction

As a professor of Speech and Theatre at Adelphi University, Esther M. Jackson contended that the theatre "has been among the last professions to respond to the challenge of the sixties." This, according to Jackson, is quite ironic in light of the theater's common association with the "vanguard of change." Consequently, issues of magnitude—family disintegration, racial conflict, and the threat of nuclear war—are interpreted for the American people by the "communication media," while the theater concerns itself with "the world of purely private dreams and longings." As a counter to the theater's artistic and professional problems, Jackson called upon the speech profession to help strengthen the role of the arts within the community at large.

---

The American theatre of the sixties appears to have entered a period of transition which may have a decisive effect on its subsequent history. This marked alteration in the course of American theatre arts may be traced to the kinds of social and political changes which are taking place in the nation at large. For America of the sixties is a society characterized by the rapid extension of human possibilities; particularly, by the expansion of opportunities for hitherto unrecognized social, economic, and professional classes.

One result of this extension of opportunity has been the assignment of a greater level of societal responsibility to the theatre, as to the arts community in general. As in earlier periods of history, the assumption of increased societal responsibility on the part of the arts has had both fortunate and unfortunate results. Certainly, the theatre stands to reap the benefits of that increased financial support offered by Federal legislation in support of the arts. But such responsibility must inevitably create new problems for the theatre, not only in regard to its fundamental relationship to the society, but in regard to the kind of artistic context in which it exists. It is not surprising, therefore, that at this point of confrontation, the American theatre seems momentarily to be without a clear sense of professional purpose.

Oddly enough, the arts in general have seemed least prepared to cope with the major social, political, and cultural changes of the sixties. The sciences, reinforced by massive funding and by decades of organized activity, have responded brilliantly to the often painful realities of this era. Indeed, it may be claimed that the sciences—with their image of man against the unknown of space—have usurped the ancient function of epic, creating new myths which capture the spirit of twentieth-century man perhaps more effectively than the contemporary theatre. But even more conservative professions such as religion, medicine, and public education have begun the revision of many of their traditional practices and have evolved

[1]Delivered at the Speech Association of America's annual convention, in New York, New York, on December 29, 1965.

new methodologies, techniques, and goals consistent with the new shape of our society. Certainly, the response of the religious community to the pattern of political and social action initiated in the past decade, marks a change in our understanding of the principle of separation of Church and State. Even more significant may be the evolution of a new theology which attempts to provide new insights relevant to the context of crisis in which most Americans live today. One of the most impressive adjustments to change has been that of a relatively new complex of disciplines: the social sciences, which have, in a relatively brief period, moved to build conceptual, methodological, and practical support for the programs of the Great Society. In reward for this decisive use of professional resources, the social sciences have earned virtual control over a vast professional empire, including programs in education, technology, and the arts.

It is, therefore, disappointing to note that the theatre—traditionally in the vanguard of change—has been among the last professions to respond to the challenge of the sixties. Though the complex theatre community has acknowledged the effect of change upon its own national role, it has, as yet, arrived at nothing resembling a clear purpose in regard to the function which it should assume in this period of political and social transition. The failure of the theatre community to clarify its new responsibilities is all the more distressing, since many of the acute problems which characterize this period can be alleviated only through the appropriate and effective use of the theatre arts. It is, for example, no exaggeration to claim that one of the primary roots of permanent cultural disadvantage is insufficiency of those complex imaginative faculties which fine theatre develops most fully. Psychologists of learning tell us that the ability to perceive relationships between image, symbol, concept, and reality is fundamental to the total pattern of the individual's intellectual, social, psychological, and cultural growth. The theatre is not primarily a recreational device; it is a powerful and sensitive instrument in the total process of human growth, the source of basic understandings, available in no other form of knowledge.

In this context, it is a matter of concern that the record of the American theatre in responding to the crises of the sixties is less than admirable. Although substantial funds are today available for the support of theatre through the National Foundation for the Arts, the Office of Education, and the Office of Economic Opportunity, the theatre community has yet to propose any program comparable to that in operation in behalf of the sciences, social sciences, or education. Unlike the sciences, the social sciences, medicine, religion, or—for that matter—professional sports, the theatre community has simply allowed its facilities, personnel, and basic contents to be requisitioned to social and political uses without assurances for the validity or integrity of that use.

We might be persuaded to offer excuses for this reluctance in assuming responsibility for the use of the drama in the pursuit of social, political, and intellectual objectives, except that the central failure of the American theatre in the sixties is, in fact, artistic. An examination of the history of the past decade indicates that its reputation rests on the achievement of the twenties, thirties, forties, and early fifties. Although our theatre productions demonstrate a technical excellence which is virtually unmatched in Western theatre—except perhaps for those of Germany and Poland—we have as yet developed no acting company which can compete successfully with the great ensembles of England, France, Russia, Germany, or, for that matter, Canada. We have been unable to apply our celebrated ingenuity to the creation and development of an indigenous American style of acting appropriate to the interpretation of classical works. The creative achievement of our great playwrights of the thirties, forties, and fifties—of O'Neill, Wilder, Miller, Williams, and others—remains unchallenged by the leading playwrights of the sixties, Albee, Baldwin, or LeRoi Jones. Our hope for the resuscitation of the theatre—the repertory company—has not proven to be an immediate answer to the problem. In a melancholy note on the current season, the *New York Times* reporter Lewis Funke commented on the difficulties affecting three valiant experiments in repertory theatre: at Seattle, Pittsburgh, and Lincoln Center.

The problems of these three companies are not singular. Rather, they are symptomatic of our failure as a profession to deal with basic problems in a systematic way. For many difficulties in acting which plague these theatres have developed as the repertoire demanded by audiences has become more difficult. Basic problems in acting cannot be solved by a single company, any more than the problems incident to producing space scientists can be solved by a single institution.

Lillian Smith, writing in a recent issue of the *Saturday Review* (October 2, 1965), traces the present difficulties of the American theatre to its failure to engage the great social and political issues of our time. Miss Smith writes that the American theatre has avoided the very themes out of which great and vital drama might emerge: the struggle for human rights, the growing conflict between youth and age, the clash between radical and conservative movements in the political arena. Instead, Miss Smith charges, the new playwrights have become more and more immersed in the expression of narrow personal desires. Our theatre today is concerned primarily with themes relating to interpersonal conflict, ego fulfillment, and the search for pleasure. Although these motives represent an aspect of the drama in all ages, they cannot be interpreted as the foci of our primary concerns in the sixties. The agonizing issues—family disintegration, racial conflict, and the threat of nuclear war—have been left to the interpretation of the communications media, while theatre has, increasingly, removed to the world of purely private dreams and longings.

It is clear both artistic problems and professional failure are related to the way in which the theatre has chosen to confront the realities of our time. How does it happen that the American theatre—a pioneer in the intellectual revolution of the twenties, thirties, and forties—should have failed to respond to such profound social changes? Undoubtedly, the theatre community was badly frightened by the attacks it suffered during the so-called McCarthy Era. Some of its new conservatism may be traced to the hostility which has in the past characterized the attitude of segments of the society to the performing arts community. But more of the problem of the sixties may be traced to misapprehensions within the theatre community itself. Perhaps the most apparent barrier to the formulation of a relevant national policy is the kind of fragmentation which exists within the theatre world. The deep antagonisms and suspicions which characterize the relationship between educational theatre and the professional community have thus far precluded cooperation in regard to professional and preprofessional training. Similarly, many of the difficulties in style which beset both New York and regional companies might have been alleviated through a national program of apprenticeship.

A more serious kind of fragmentation appears in the emergence of a protest theatre, whose aim is the exacerbation of racial and class conflict. It is curious that this "theatre of hatred" should be encouraged and sponsored by elements of the larger theatre community as an alternative to full opportunity in the arts for all people. The folly of continued splintering, the danger to theatre and to the society in general, can be measured by the speed at which a new cult of violence is developing in connection with the new minority theatre movement.

How does it happen that the American theatre today reflects such limited understanding of its new responsibilities? Perhaps the problem may be traced to a lack of true professionalism. By this, I do not mean a lack of technical excellence and occasional bursts of brilliance; but rather a failure to impose upon the theatre activity, in any consistent fashion, that discipline which has characterized all periods of great artistic achievement. The fact is that the larger theatre community does not recognize theatre as a discipline: neither as a serious academic discipline, nor as a disciplined artistic form. Rather, the American theatre community itself is responsible for the impression that theatre is a platform for unfettered personal expression. The American theatre community, unlike its counterparts in other Western nations, protests that the presence of standards is a limiting and restricting influence upon its creativity. The effect of this doctrine of subjectivity may be seen, not only in the increasingly private concerns of our playwrights, but also in the erratic performances which this approach elicits from many of our acting companies.

The source of such misapprehensions about the nature of the theatre arts is not difficult to trace. They have origin in the intellectual history of our country. They are holdovers from those Romantic theories current at the time of our beginning as a nation; but they also reflect a kind of anti-intellectualism which has characterized much of our artistic endeavor. It is interesting, however, to note that no such claims mark the work of our major creative talents in other fields. The work of Martha Graham for example is characterized by exceptional regard for training, discipline, and the unflinching application of stringent standards.

I wish today to suggest that the key to the solution of these problems may rest in the possibility of leadership from the academic community; particularly, in the possibility of national leadership on the part of the speech profession. In the same way as the university has functioned to accelerate the advancement of the sciences and social sciences, so the speech profession may transform the sixties into a new period of growth for the American theatre arts.

A look at our past history of the American theatre would suggest that we should be recovering a function which the academic community has formerly assumed. American forms of drama, dance, and theatrical design were forged in the workshops and scene-shops of Harvard, Yale, Wisconsin, and North Carolina, as in the dance studios of Bennington and Mills. The rudiments of a new grammar of playwriting were evolved and disseminated in seminars at Yale, Iowa, and Michigan. The decisive steps toward the development of public policy in theatre were precipitated by Hallie Flanagan, who evolved much of the theory and practice which she was to put into national operation at Vassar College. In recent years, our most successful repertory theatre began as a kind of experiment, designed by a former professor of dramatic literature at the University of Michigan.

What are some of these problems for which the speech profession should help to find solutions? Perhaps the most immediate task is that of helping to reestablish unity within the theatre community; to arrange for the creation of task forces which shall engage the resources of the entire theatre community. The speech profession should, in this connection, seek to bring to bear upon these problems the considerable resources of other theatre arts, particularly, of dance, cinema, radio, and television. Clearly, many of the theoretical and practical problems which face the drama also involve these related professions. Moreover, these professions hold answers to many problems of theatre. Perhaps the greatest stylist in the American theatre today is Martha Graham who has, in her dance forms, worked out both theoretical and practical solutions to many of the problems which yet elude directors in the spoken drama.

Further, the speech profession might accelerate the solution of problems in professional training by launching a series of pilot programs to test new concepts of training. History has shown that the gifted playwright, actor, or director is likely to be found where the societal conflict is at its height. The theatre requires first-rate acting schools, playwriting workshops, and apprentice programs, not only on eastern university campuses, but at every class level. While some of these workshops should be placed in the colleges of the South, and Middle West, others should be located outside of the university setting, in centers of social and political activity. Such a program would differ from the kinds of activity presently sponsored by the Office of Economic Opportunity, in that it should undertake to establish conditions which could lead to serious professional careers.

Fortunately, Actors' Equity is now engaged in attempting to establish a pilot program for the training of actors. Again, the speech profession has an important role to play if this venture is to succeed. For the establishment of a national academy requires an extensive program of testing, experimentation, and evaluation before we can arrive at the codification of those principles which will support the development of an American classic style.

A third problem to which the speech profession will need to give systematic attention in the next decade is that of developing new curricula in teacher education and new programs in audience education, which will take advantage of the resources of the theatre and, which will at the same time, provide a kind of laboratory for the training of young professionals. Again, we should hope that the speech profession will seek to develop concepts affecting curricula, teacher preparation, and the development of theatre facilities which will revolutionize the teaching of theatre at elementary, secondary, and undergraduate levels. We should hope that through such programs theatre will come to occupy a place in the curriculum as a basic form of knowledge rather than as a kind of recreation; a form of knowledge on par with science, mathematics, languages, and the humanities. In this connection, new methodologies are required for the use of the theatre as an instrument for the eradication of intellectual, cultural, and psychological disadvantage.

A final problem area in which the speech profession can offer the theatre critical assistance is the development of public policy in the arts, at national, state, and local levels. The speech profession has a clear obligation to assist in the training of administrators, teachers, and specialists who can implement those governmental programs in operation, as well as those which are planned. This would suggest that some retraining of personnel is in order. The speech profession might follow the example of the scientific and business communities in the use of short-term seminars, fellowships, and grants, for professionals whose abilities to administer arts programs might be enhanced by an opportunity to explore ideas in a systematic way. It is of equal importance that the speech profession help to supply that kind of research required for the development of a sound national policy for the arts. New methodologies and new research areas should result not only in the accumulation of substantial data, but also in the development of those historians, critics, and methodologists which theatre in the seventies will require.

Undoubtedly, the implementation of these objectives will require a major reappraisal of graduate studies in theatre and indeed of the entire relationship of the speech profession to the theatre. It is my impression that such a reexamination will not result in the narrowing of the scope of theatre studies. On the contrary, I should predict a new alignment. It seems clear, for example, that many of the functions presently maintained by theatre departments should no longer be handled by academicians. Increasingly, the conduct of practical courses must be ceded to the professional actor, director, or designer. It seems likely that we shall increasingly have a university-based theatre, rather than a university theatre. What then will be the new role of theatre in the university? It will be to provide basic education together with those kinds of training which are critical to the advancement of theatre in America. Certainly, the university, particularly, the speech profession, will remain concerned with the general education of the artist. But beyond this, the educational theatre will, it seems to me, be forced to concern itself more and more with research, education, and planning; specifically, with the systematic gathering of data, with the training of scholars and specialists, and with the development of policy and standards.

It would appear to me appropriate, therefore, that the speech profession, in conjunction with other interested organizations, might now elect to establish a national study group for the purpose of reexamining the relationship of university programing to the theatre. One effort is already under way which will undertake to study needs in theatre research. But a second task force is needed to examine the goals, methods, and standards of curricular offerings in speech and theatre departments throughout the country.

Today, it seems clear that the arts, particularly the art of the theatre, may have a critical role to play in establishing those conditions which insure orderly social change. It is reassuring to know that such have been the conditions under which the art of the theatre has always flourished. I believe that the speech profession can offer major impetus to the growth of American theatre by helping to solve its basic problems in a systematic, efficient, and thoroughly reliable way.

Nothing could be more central to the academic function. For we in America believe that the chief use of knowledge is to accelerate human achievement and to improve the fundamental conditions of human existence, so that every man may aspire to grasp the total riches of human existence within his own lifetime.

# America, the Arts and the Future[2]

Arthur M. Schlesinger, Jr.

*Born October 15, 1917, Columbus, OH; B.A., Harvard University, 1938; LL.D., Muhlenberg College, 1950; professor, Harvard University, 1946-61; special assistant to the president of the United States, 1961-64; professor, City University of New York, 1966–; winner of Pulitzer Prize, 1945, 1965; author,* The Age of Jackson *(1945),* The Vital Center: The Politics of Freedom *(1949),* The Coming of the New Deal *(1958),* Kennedy or Nixon: Does It Make Any Difference? *(1960),* The Politics of Hope *(1963),* A Thousand Days *(1965),* The Bitter Heritage *(1967),* The Crisis of Confidence *(1969),* The Origins of the Cold War *(1970),* The Imperial Presidency *(1973),* Robert F. Kennedy and His Times *(1978),* The Cycles of American History *(1986),* The Politics of Upheaval *(1988),* The Disuniting of America *(1992).*

## Editor's introduction

In honor of Nancy Hanks, Pulitzer Prize winning author and historian Arthur M. Schlesinger, Jr. addressed a group of 500 people, which included artists, art administrators, patrons, leaders of government and business. Nancy Hanks (1927-83) was president of the American Council for the Arts, and chair of the National Endowment for the Arts from 1969 to 1977. Schlesinger asserted that history will judge the United States in terms of her "character, and achievement as a civilization." Such character he argued, "depends on activities that enrich the nation even if they do not meet the box-office test." It follows that Schlesinger believed the arts to possess a singular importance, which clearly warrants public support.

---

It is a high honor to be invited to inaugurate this series of annual lectures in memory of Nancy Hanks and in support of the cause she so nobly served—the sustenance and enrichment of the arts in America. And it is appropriate that this series should be sponsored by the American Council for the Arts, an organization that for twenty-eight years has given the artistic condition of our diverse and combative society searching analysis and vigorous advocacy; all the more appropriate because Nancy Hanks was president of the ACA before she moved on to become the brilliantly effective leader of the National Endowment for the Arts.

Our concern this evening is the arts and public policy; and we meet, I believe, at a propitious time for stock-taking. For it was almost exactly twenty-five years ago that the first presidential Special Consultant on the Arts, August Heckscher, rendered his report to President Kennedy on "The Arts and the National Government"—a report that decisively advanced the movement which culminated two years later in the creation under President Johnson of the National Endowment for the Arts. Today, the more than two decades of practical experience under the Endowment afford us the opportunity to see where we have been, what we have learned and where we should go from here. The establishment of a governmental role in support of the arts has not taken place without argument. Still such a role is not some hideous novelty of the 20th century. The idea that the arts are so vital to society that they are entitled to public support is an old one on the continent of Europe. Princes and prelates commissioned Leonardo, Raphael and Michelangelo, Haydn, Mozart and Wagner. Louis XIV subsidized the *Comedie Francaise* and the *Opera.* Joseph I built the great opera house in Vienna. The small states of Germany nurtured music, theater and museums. The continental tradition

[2]Delivered as the first Nancy Hanks Lecture on Arts and Public Policy, at the National Academy of Science, in Washington, D.C., on April 13, 1988. Reprinted with permission of Arthur M. Schlesinger, Jr.

of court patronage was readily adopted to the modern nation-state.

In Great Britain, they ordered this matter differently. There 17th century puritanism instilled suspicion of the arts, and 19th century laissez-faire left the arts to fend for themselves. As a result, public support, at least for new as against old art, took much longer to emerge. But Lord Keynes persuaded the British government to set up the Arts Council in 1945. The idea of the council, Keynes said,

"is to create an environment, to breed a spirit, to cultivate an opinion, to offer a stimulus to such purpose that the artist and the public can each sustain and live on the other in that union which has occasionally existed in the past at the great ages of a communal civilised life."

Forty years later Sir William Rees-Mogg, Mrs. Thatcher's non-Keynesian chairman of the Arts Council, could declare that Britain has firmly "adopted the principle that the arts, like education, health and social security, are universal goods that ought to be generally available regardless of ability to pay."

The United States has lagged behind both the continent and Britain in public support of the arts. Here the case against the public role has rested on four propositions:

That public subsidy lacks constitutional authority;

That public subsidy endangers the autonomy of the arts by making the artist dependent on government and thereby vulnerable to government control;

That public subsidy represents a net transfer of income from the poor to the high-income and educated classes;

That public subsidy represents a paternalistic and elitist effort to dictate popular taste; if a cultural institution cannot please consumers and earn its way in a free market, then it has no economic justification, and, if no economic justification, no social justification.

I would suggest that the experience of the last quarter century has demonstrated these four propositions to be misleading, overwrought or simply wrong.

The constitutional objection is entirely devoid of merit. No one has seriously challenged the constitutionality of the 1965 act establishing the National Endowments. In view of the fact that Article I, Section 8, of the Constitution empowers Congress to provide for the general welfare, such challenge would be ill-advised. Enthusiasts for the jurisprudence of original intent might note that George Washington himself told Congress in his first annual message, "There is nothing which can better deserve your patronage than the promotion of Science and Literature." The father of his country proposed especially the creation of a national university for instruction in the arts and sciences and even left money in his will toward the endowment of such an institution. The founding fathers were influenced by the tradition of civic republicanism—a tradition that laid central emphasis on the inculcation of public virtue. Madison in the *Federalist Papers* held up the "public good"—"the permanent and aggregate interests of the community"—as the supreme goal of legislation.

John Adams, as we all remember, said he had to study politics and war so that his sons could study philosophy and science and his grandchildren painting, poetry, music and architecture: not a bad prediction, in fact, of the evolution of the Adams family. His son John Quincy Adams in his first annual message defined the "great object" of government as "the improvement of the condition of those who are parties to the social compact," described "moral, political, intellectual improvement" as duties assigned "to social no less than to individual man" and called for "laws promoting . . . the cultivation and encouragement of the mechanic and of the elegant arts, the advancement of literature, and the progress of the sciences." Failure to exercise constitutional powers for the elevation of the people, the younger Adams said, "would be treachery to the most sacred of trusts."

The civilized 18th century hopes of the men who founded the republic were disappointed in the 19th century for much the same reasons in America as in Britain, the dispiriting combination of a puritan heritage with a laissez-faire creed. Only undertakings like the Smithsonian Institution, defensible because both educational and practical, secured congressional and presidential support. But our contemporary policy toward the arts can be reasonably seen as a belated fulfillment of the expectations of the founding fathers.

Nor need we fear, I believe, that public support is per se corrupting or threatening for the artist. The argument that political pressure is bound to dominate any relationship between the state and intellectual or artistic endeavor is refuted every day. The record of the two Endowments and of such agencies as the National Science Foundation and the National Institutes of Health shows that public support does not restrict professional independence.

The last two propositions—that public funding of the arts is income redistribution from the poor to the rich; and that it is an elitist attempt to prescribe popular taste—raise more interesting questions. "What justification is there," the Nobel laureate economist Milton Friedman has asked, "for imposing taxes on low-income people to finance luxuries for high-income people?" Note the assertion that the arts are luxuries like yachts and Rolls-Royces, and therefore inessential to civilized society. The argument further implies that public support of these luxuries violates the sacred principle of consumer sovereignty for the benefit of a snobbish minority and that only those things that can "earn their way" in the competition of the marketplace are worth having.

A moment's reflection shows, I think, how absurd these contentions are. I do not believe, by the way, that the defense of public support need rest on the spill-over effects of the arts boom—tax revenues, jobs, business relocation, urban renewal, tourism, general commercial stimulus. These "vulgar benefits," as Professor William Baumol calls them, are all very well. But the case must be made on the intrinsic value of the arts to society as a whole. If the arts are worth pursuing at all, they are worth pursuing for their own sake.

And here one must ask: is it not the real elitism to suggest that low-income people have no interest in the arts and can derive no benefit from public support of the higher arts? Surely the poor as well as the better-off have appetites to be awakened, yearnings to be clarified, lives to be illuminated. The arts are, in Rees-Mogg's phrase, universal goods.

As for the argument that the arts, if they deserve to survive, must contrive to earn their own way, one can argue the reverse more persuasively: that the most precious institutions in society—our schools, universities, hospitals, clinics, libraries, museums, churches—are precisely those that do not earn their own way. All are characterized by the fatal gap between earned income and operating costs. Our civilization depends on activities that enrich the nation even if they do not meet the box-office test.

Government is, among other things—or should be—a trustee for future generations: a trustee of the national interest not only for the protection of military security and economic prosperity but for the protection of cultural legacies, choices and opportunities. Artistic creativity does not yield instant pay-offs. Sometimes decades pass before a society appreciates its own best art. The public obligation is to safeguard the integrity of the artistic process and heritage. Surely government has as strong an obligation to preserve the cultural environment against dissipation and destruction as it has to preserve the natural environment against pollution and decay. "We inherit a cultural structure," Professor Ronald Dworkin has well said, "and we have some duty, out of simple justice, to leave that structure at least as rich as we found it."

We owe that duty to ourselves and to generations to come, and we owe it to the glory of the nation. The United States will be measured in the eyes of posterity not by its economic power nor by its military might, not by the territories it has annexed nor by the battles it has won, but by its character and achievement as a civilization. In the third year of the Civil War, Abraham Lincoln ordered work to go ahead on the completion of the dome of the Capitol. When critics protested the diversion of labor and money from the prosecution of the war, Lincoln said, "If people see the Capitol going on, it is a sign that we intend this Union shall go on." Franklin Roosevelt recalled this story in 1941 when, with the world in the blaze of war, he dedicated the National Gallery in Washington. And John F. Kennedy recalled both these stories when he asked for public support of the arts in 1962. Lincoln and Roosevelt, Kennedy said, "understood that the life of the arts, far from being an interruption, a distraction, in the life of the nation, is very close to the center of a nation's purpose—and is a test of the quality of a nation's civilization."

Our political process is often halting and untidy in its operations. But it seems indisputable that, over the last quarter century, the constitutional polity has weighed the various objections to public support for the arts and found them all wanting. In these twenty-five years the republic has at last made an apparently irreversible commitment to the goal of cultural improvement for the public good—the goal contemplated two centuries ago by the founding fathers.

The great depression first made arts and artists a concern of the national government. Early in his administration Franklin Roosevelt appointed the painter Edward Bruce as head of the Fine Arts Section of the Treasury Department charged with improving decoration and design in public buildings. Then on 10 May 1935, four days after his creation of the Works Progress Administration, FDR sent Harry Hopkins, the WPA chief, a historic, one-sentence memorandum: "Will you and Bruce try to work out a 'project' for artists." The WPA Arts Projects were emergency programs, regarded by many legislators with dark suspicion and abolished as soon as unemployment began to decline. In retrospect, however, the Arts Projects are accounted as among the New Deal's notable achievements, and their memory has done much to invigorate later proposals for federal support of the arts.

These proposals came in the 1950s, paradoxically, from Congress, the very body that killed the Arts Projects a dozen years before. It is invidious to signal out individuals; but no historian can overlook the role played in these years by Frank Thompson and Charles Howell of New Jersey and Jacob Javits of New York, and in later years by Sidney Yates of Illinois, John Brademas of Indiana, and Clayborne Pell of Rhode Island, among so many others. A majority of Congress soon came to see intrinsic value in the cultivation of the arts as a means of promoting the general welfare. In 1958 a young second-term congressman from Texas named Jim Wright observed,

"All of us like to portray ourselves as real, sure enough corn-fed, home-grown log cabin boys . . . . In striking such a pose, it is always kind of easy to ridicule and poke fun at things of a cultural nature. I plead guilty to having done my share of it, but I think, Mr. Speaker, that we have reached a state of maturity in this nation where that kind of attitude no longer becomes us. Sooner or later we have to grow up and stop poking fun at things intellectual and cultural."

With the advent of John F. Kennedy in the White House in 1961, congressional advocates of national arts policy received enlightened presidential collaboration and leadership. The Heckscher report of 28 May 1963 led on to the establishment of the Endowments in 1965 and President Johnson's designation of Roger Stevens as the first chairman of the National Endowment for the Arts. Roger Stevens avowed that his intention was to make Washington the artistic as well as the political capital of the United States; and, in the view of this envious if admiring New Yorker, I can testify that he has done his wicked work all too well. His labors in organizing the NEA and his benevolent dictatorship of the Kennedy Center have transformed and vitalized the cultural atmosphere of this city in ways the cliff dwellers of my youth could hardly have imagined.

The federal role in the arts thus began as a legislative-executive partnership, with each branch of government offering usable ideas on structure and program. At the same time, however, arts policy seemed the child of the Democratic party, originating in the New Deal and revived thereafter by Democratic legislators in alliance with lonely liberal Republicans like Jacob Javits and John Lindsay, men too often shunned by their own party. Republican members of the House Committee on Education and Labor denounced the 1965 bill for "creating Federal czars over the arts and humanities." In 1968 Republicans in the House voted nearly 2-1 against the reauthorization of the NEA; among the opponents were such future party leaders as Gerald Ford, Robert Dole, and George Bush. The crucial test of the new national cultural policy came when the 1968 election brought a Republican president to the White House.

President Nixon had hardly been the candidate of the artistic and intellectual community. Many in that community feared that his victory portended the end of the Endowments. Instead, as we all know, the Nixon administration embraced the new cultural policy and gave the Endowments solid support and status. We owe this happy result to two people in particular—to Leonard Garment, a persuasive and public-spirited presidential special assistant who made the arts his special charge, and above all to Nancy Hanks, who in September 1969 became the new chairman of the NEA.

Nancy Hanks was not only a great North Carolina lady. She was also a tough, tenacious, resolute and resourceful public servant who skillfully deployed southern charm, northern determination and astute political instincts to achieve her objectives. Before coming to the ACA, she had worked for the Rockefellers in New York; and, as an administrator, she was reared in the Nelson Rockefeller school, which is to say that her creed was expansion. Leonard Garment persuaded President Nixon that support for the arts was good politics. Nancy Hanks then used White House backing to strengthen her case for bigger budgets and enlarged and diversified programs. The endowment budget under her seductive ministrations grew tenfold, and its challenge grants increased incentives for private giving. Most important of all, her leadership, cordially supported by Presidents Nixon and Ford, gave national arts policy firm and enduring bipartisan support. That policy now expressed partnership not only between the executive and legislative branches but between the two major parties as well.

Partnership between the two branches of government and between the two political parties was accompanied by a third partnership—between the NEA and the state arts councils. Legislation setting aside 20 percent of NEA funds for state arts agencies stimulated state and community development, promoted local initiative and gave the public role in the arts the balance enjoined by our traditional federalism. The states have risen to the challenge. The aggregate budgets of state arts agencies now surpass the NEA budget by $245 million to $167 million for fiscal year 1988.

And the fourth, and most vital, partnership was with the arts community itself, cemented by the award of grants and the cherished NEA imprimatur through juries composed of artists, the so-called peer panel review process.

These four partnerships form the basis for the quiet revolution of the last quarter century in the relationship between government and the arts, an incremental revolution shaped by experiment, participation and consent, and resulting in a complex and ingenious system of public support. The intricate network of national, state and local arts agencies has further benefited from invaluable supplementary initiatives proposed and enacted by Congress, such as the Institute of Museum Services and the Arts and Artifacts Indemnity Act, the latter facilitating the exhibit in American museums of art from abroad (an act that should be accompanied by a domestic version for the circulation of works of art within the United States).

The evolving national policy has been most effective when vitalized by concerned presidents or at least by White House assistants with a keen sense of responsibility for the arts. Presidential interest is the surest guarantee of a strong and lively arts policy. But arts policy can now survive even the indifference or hostility of presidents—as demonstrated in 1981 when the arts programs withstood the severe budgets cuts demanded, ironically, by the first president who was himself by vocation a performing artist. (All politicians are by avocation performing artists.) Congress even in the conservative 1980s has remained steadfast in its belief in the centrality of arts to a civilized society. Both political parties have joined to defend the Endowment budgets against drastic retrenchment as well as the Institute of Museum Services against total abolition. The four partnerships have survived a time of adversity.

As late as 1958, William Faulkner could write,

"The artist has no more actual place in the American culture of today than he has in the American economy of today, no place at all in the warp and woof, the thews and sinews, the mosaic of the American dream as it exists today."

I doubt that anyone would so depose thirty years later. The policy of public support certifies the value the republic has come to place on the arts.

But the consensus that sustains the policy of federal support does not by itself resolve difficult questions of priority—questions rendered the more difficult by budgetary deficits that will cramp and constrain the federal role for years to come. In considering these questions, we can draw once more on the experience and wisdom of Nancy Hanks. In a panel discussion at Columbia University on 30 September 1980, three years before her death, Nancy Hanks gave her view of the major issues facing the arts community in the decade ahead.

"First and foremost" among the problems confronting the cultural development of the republic, Nancy Hanks said, is "our lack of understanding of the individual artist" and of "the importance of creating an environment in which the artist can flourish. How right she was! It is banal to remark that the source of art is the artist; but it is a banality too often forgotten in our overorganized society. Universities and foundations are splendid institutions, and so too is government. But art results from the confrontation of experience by a disciplined, sensitive, and passionate individual possessed of an intense interior vision and capable of rendering that vision in ways that will heighten and deepen the sensibility of others.

It is this individual, the artist, who must always remain in the forefront of our consideration. Creativity cannot be institutionalized. Art arises in conditions of individuality and diversity, even of doubt and estrangement. "Beauty will not come at the call of a legislature," said Emerson. "It will come, as always, unannounced, and spring up between the feet of brave and earnest men."

The creation of an environment in which the artist can flourish involves not only such lofty matters as the degree of honor accorded artists in a commercial society but such mundane matters as income, time, work space, health insurance, postal rates, and the tax law. We must pay more attention to the unintended consequences of legislation indirectly affecting the arts. Sometimes these consequences can be benign. I suspect that the great subsidy to artists today is the system of unemployment compensation set up by Franklin Roosevelt in 1935, a result that might have surprised FDR but would certainly have gratified him. And for a long time the major subsidy to artistic institutions came from provisions in the tax code permitting deductibility on gifts to non-profit corporations. Writing in the *Economist* in 1984, Simon Jenkins argued that the American system of financing the arts indirectly through tax expenditures was far superior to the British system of direct subvention. Among other considerations, a diversity of funding sources is itself a guarantee of artistic freedom.

Alas, sometimes the unintended consequences of legislative action are malign. Congress, generally solicitous when dealing with direct support of the arts, has too often been cavalier when dealing with the impact on artists of revisions in the tax code. In the tax revision of 1969, Congress eliminated tax deductions for the donation of works of art and literature by the original artist or author to museums and libraries, while peculiarly retaining the deduction for collectors. And the Tax Reform Act of 1986, whatever its other merits, is notably harsh in its treatment of writers and artists, thereby erasing much of the superiority that impressed Simon Jenkins two years earlier.

This act abolishes the charitable deduction for non-itemizers. It also contains the notorious provision placing writers and artists under a uniform capitalization rule designed for industrial manufacturers and forbidding them to deduct business expenses in the year when the expenses were incurred. I understand that no one has been able to find out how the footnote applying the capitalization rule to writers and artists ever got into the act. Congress last fall was prepared to include a writers' exemption in a technical tax corrections bill, but this exemption was dropped under Treasury pressure in the budget reconciliation act. One must hope that Congress will act speedily to repair the grievous harm this provision will do to literary, scholarly and artistic productivity.

I might add that since the start of the republic writers have provided a direct subsidy to the government by permitting the free circulation of their books in public libraries, and it is surely time to correct this inequity by following the example of Britain, Canada and the Scandinavian countries and passing an Authors' Lending Royalty law. The same principle calls for the enactment of Senator Kennedy's Visual Artists Rights bill assuring painters resale royalties. Government, instead of carelessly discriminating against writers and artists, should at least give them a fair shake in the tax code and elsewhere, especially when most writers and artists (and their families) live from hand to mouth anyway.

Other problems confront the artistic community in the years ahead. To list some of them is to illustrate the dilemmas of a national cultural policy. One of the proven successes of the NEA, or so one had supposed, is the process of peer panel review. This procedure relieved the artistic community's fears of bureaucratic control, extended participation, and solidified a constituency in support of the Endowment. Current proposals to confide grant-making to the computer raise disturbing questions about the virtue of trying to quantify aesthetic judgment.

Then there is the problem cogently posed by August Heckscher twenty-five years ago and still unresolved—the problem of mobilizing government across the board in support of aesthetic quality. For government, in Heckscher's words, "is the great builder, the coiner, the printer, the purchaser of art, the guardian of great collections, the setter of standards for good or for bad in innumerable fields where it is itself hardly aware today of its great influence"—hardly aware in 1963; much less aware in 1988.

There is the problem of maintaining a high level of discretion and expertise in arts administration, both private and public, remembering always that the function of the bureaucrat is to serve the artist and not the other way round. In this connection presidents and Congress must be considerably more conscientious and exacting about appointments to the National Council of the Arts. Not all our recent presidents have resisted the temptation to use these appointments as rewards for political or financial support. These places must be reserved for persons with serious interest in and experience of the arts.

There is the perennial problem of decentralization, that is, the division of labor and harmonizing of functions among federal, state and community arts agencies and striking the appropriate balance between established arts capitals and artistically impoverished outlying areas. There is the problem of meeting the needs of an ever more ethnically diversified population without lowering standards, fostering ghettos, encouraging politicization, rip-offs and cultural babble and diluting the precious artistic heritage of the west that we in America are especially obligated to preserve and transmit.

There is the problem, recently dramatized in the understandable protest against the horrid Tilted Arc in New York City, of reconciling the rights of the artist and the rights of the audience. There is the problem, dramatized by the "colorization" controversy, of preserving the artist's control over his own creations. There is the problem of assessing the artistic impact and exploiting the artistic possibilities of wondrous new technologies, television, the videocassette recorder, the compact disc.

All these problems arise, we must understand, at a time of crisis in the state of the arts. There is a crisis of funding. Federal budget deficits both foreclose an increase in subsidy and invite further discrimination against the arts in tax legislation, with tax exemption for non-profit institutions and the charitable deduction itself becoming likely targets. Major foundations, like Ford and Rockefeller, which have contributed so much to the nurture of the arts, are withdrawing from the field. Economic uncertainty on top of tax changes will reduce individual giving. Aggregate corporate giving has levelled out and may be declining; the merger mania reduces the number of corporate givers; and many corporations are shifting their charitable dollars from cultural activities to other worthy areas that more directly advance business interests. So Exxon is abandoning "Great Performances" on public television and New York Philharmonic concerts in order to put mathematics specialists in public schools.

Leisure time, according to the Louis Harris poll, is contracting, and audiences for theater, opera, classical music, and dance are diminishing. Observers report a falling-off in artistic interest among business and community leaders and also among younger people. "My judgment in 1988," W. McNeil Lowry, whose intellectual leadership has contributed so much to the arts in America, said in a speech ten weeks ago, "is that . . . the reservoirs of good will on which non-profit institutions largely relied have begun to dry up." And this retrogression in finance and audience and attention and priority and participation is taking place in an age of implacably rising costs.

Yet the future is not entirely bleak. The Harris survey shows a surprisingly high degree of respect for artists, popular support for federal assistance to the arts, and readiness to pay extra taxes for this purpose. It shows also an emphatic majority in favor of giving the arts a basic and continuing role in the school curriculum along with a mournful conviction that our schools presently fail to give our children adequate cultural opportunities. As one whose painter daughter teaches in New York City public schools in the Learning through an Expanded Arts Program, I know through her testimony of the responsiveness of even the children of poverty to artistic challenge. "Toward Civilization," the recent NEA report, makes a powerful case for action in the field of arts education. What better way to create not only an audience but a civilization.

I have a deeper reason for a measure of optimism. As I have argued elsewhere, our political life, at least in the view of this historian, flows in cycles and displays a fairly regular alternation between private interest and public purpose as its governing orientation. From this perspective the private-interest 1980s are a reenactment of the private-interest 1950s, as the 1950s were a reenactment of the private-interest 1920s. In the same fashion, the nation turns at 30-year intervals—the span of a generation—to public purpose, idealism and affirmative government: Theodore Roosevelt ushering in the Progressive period in 1901, Franklin Roosevelt the New Deal in 1933, John Kennedy the New Frontier in 1961. If the rhythm holds, and all indications are that it is holding, the 1990s should be a decade of innovation, experiment and idealism, a turn in the cycle of which the arts, which have thrived in earlier eras of public purpose, will again be a major beneficiary. As we prepare to seize these new possibilities and as we contemplate the dilemmas of our present cultural situation, surely the time has come, if we are to renew and elevate the public commitment to the arts, for a serious reconsideration of national arts policy. The last thing we need or want is official state doctrine on artistic matters. But we do require, after these last rather static years, a rebirth of purpose and a clarification of destination. We do require an uncompromising rededication to artistic quality as the supreme object and justification of a national arts policy. We do require fresh thought on the enlargement of artistic opportunity for our multifarious country and our variegated people. We do require the raising of the national consciousness and priority on the issues of our cultural future. The time for revaluation is upon us, and it should take place at the highest level.

Congress has recently established a National Economic Commission to seek remedies for our manifold forms of economic anguish. I would hope that the next president of the United States would ask Congress to establish a counterpart National Commission on the Arts. This Commission should be composed of eminent scholars, writers, artists and arts administrators and also business and labor leaders with special artistic concerns. Its charge would be to examine the range of governmental activity affecting the arts, to propose a comprehensive arts agenda and to set goals for national arts policy in the 1990s.

You are here in Washington today because you deeply believe in the arts as vital to fulfilled lives, to civilized society and to the glory of the republic. Your devotion in the months and years ahead can do a great deal to persuade our masters to restore momentum and meaning to a national arts policy. Government cannot create civilization. Its impact is at best marginal on the adventure and mystery of art and on the creative solitude of the artist. But public leadership reinvigorates the understanding of art as a common participation, a common possession and a common heritage.

It may be too much to support with Walt Whitman that the salvation of the republic will come from "prophetic" art "radiating, begetting appropriate teachers, schools, manners, and, as its grandest result, accomplishing (what neither the schools nor the churches and their clergy have hitherto accomplished, and without which this nation will no more stand permanently, soundly, than a house will stand without a substratum) a religious and moral character beneath the political and productive and intellectual bases of the States." Art will be only one, if an indispensable, strand in our salvation, if we are to be saved at all.

But we may at least more soberly conclude with George Washington: "The Arts and Sciences essential to the prosperity of the State and to the ornament and happiness of human life have a primary claim to the encouragement of every lover of his Country and mankind."

# The Arts and the American Dream[3]

Barbara Jordan

*Born February 21, 1936, Houston, TX; died January 17, 1996; B.A., Texas Southern University, 1956; LL.B., Boston University, 1959; lawyer, private practice, Houston, 1959-66; member, Texas State Senate, 1967-72; representative (D) from Texas, 1973-79; lecturer, University of Texas, 1979-96.*

## Editor's introduction

On "Arts Advocacy Day," representatives from more than twenty organizations convened with elected officials to assess the status, function, and needs of art. At the time this speech was given, public support of artists and their work was a highly controversial topic because of a group of senators who, in 1989, accused the National Endowment for the Arts of supporting what they believed to be obscene and pornographic material. In this speech, Barbara Jordan, former representative from Texas and professor of National Policy at the University of Texas, discussed the importance of the arts for individuals and society. Speaking at the Kennedy Center, Jordan reminded her audience that "art has the potential to unify" and thereby reinvigorate our collective national spirit. Its importance to the nation should therefore never be underestimated.

---

I am most delighted to be included among the list of distinguished persons who have presented the Nancy Hanks Lecture. Thank you for the honor.

In 1988, Arthur Schlesinger, Jr. gave this lecture. He referred to the well-regarded work he and his father have done in developing and promoting the idea of the cycles of American history. I quote now from his book, which bears that name:

"Wise men have remarked on a pattern of alternation, of ebb and flow, in human history. 'The two parties which divide the state, the party of Conservatism and that of Innovation,' wrote Emerson in 1841, 'are very old, and have disputed the possession of the world ever since it was made. . . . Now one, now the other gets the day, and still the fight renews itself as if for the first time, under new names and hot personalities'. . Innovation presses ever forward, Conservatism holds ever back. We are reformers spring and summer, in autumn and winter we stand by the old; reformers in the morning, conservers at night. 'Innovation is the salient energy; Conservatism the pause on the last moment'."

Continuing, from Professor Schlesinger:

"Half a century later, Henry Adams applied a more precise version of the cyclical thesis to the first years of the American republic. 'A period of about twelve years,' he wrote, 'measured the beat of the pendulum.' After the Declaration of Independence, twelve years had been needed to create an efficient Constitution; another twelve years of energy brought a reaction against the government then created; a third period of twelve years was ending in a sweep toward still greater energy; and already a child could calculate the result of a few more such returns."

We are properly positioned in time, in this year, 1993, to begin a new cycle. Optimism is fairly dropping from the air. A new generation of leaders struggles, at first somewhat awkwardly, to find its sea legs. Old words are coming out of new mouths as we seek to find our niche. This is not a time to be shy. One way to guarantee that this sense of hope will not be lost is to act on it now.

If your thing, that is, your interest, concern, involvement, or passion is the arts, you are

[3]Delivered as the Nancy Hanks Lecture on Arts and Public Policy, at the Kennedy Center for Performing Arts, in Washington, D.C., on March 16, 1993.

probably at this moment in time somewhat reluctant to speak too loudly. With all the rhetoric of budget deficits and sacrifice perhaps you feel that it would be somehow sacrilegious to talk about the arts. Wrong! The arts are an integral part of us and have been often pivotal in reinvigorating our national spirit.

The primary thesis of my remarks today is that the arts, instead of quaking along the periphery of our policy concerns must push boldly into the core of policy. The arts are a response to our individuality and our nature and help to shape our identity. Or as a young student in my class at Laguna Gloria Art Museum in my hometown of Austin, Texas, wrote, "Every feeling comes out on my paper and in my drawings." The arts are not a frill, and should not be treated as such. They have the potential to become the driving force for healing division and divisiveness.

I would guess that few of you in this room think that the arts are a frill. I doubt that you would be here if you held that view. But each of us knows that to further what progress the arts have made as an integral part of American life, we must reason with those who are inclined to consider the arts as one of those things to be dealt with seriously much later on.

I want to offer to you today a premise, with which I hope you agree, that in this time of change in American life, in this new administration of hope, in this time of putting people first, it is the arts that are uniquely placed not just to tag along in the changes, but to be part and parcel of every bold new step we take.

I submit to you the idea that the arts can be the validation of the American life. We heard President Clinton in his address to a joint session of Congress last month speak about renewing our economy so that the American dream can be a possibility for everyone. No one disputes that a healthy economy is part and parcel of the American dream. But it is our job to teach emphatically that the arts are more than just the decorations on that dream.

And what precisely is the American dream? It is: That we are one people.

*E Pluribus Unum.* The Latin phrase on the great seal of the United States literally translated means one from many. We need to reattach pluribus to unum—the many to the one. That motto challenges our diversity. No nation on the face of the earth had tried so bold an experiment until us, the Americans. No one thought that success would come easily. Even though the founders were aggressive in pursuing liberty, their quest for equality failed to include all. They envisioned no role for former slaves and deferred for a century even thinking about the issue. Even the great democrat of Monticello, Thomas Jefferson, was apprehensive. He, quoting now from a recent *Wall Street Journal* article, "feared that a simple biracial America, white and black as equals, would not long endure. He advocated black freedom, but remained paralyzed by its implications."

Jefferson articulated his quandary regarding slavery when he said, "We have the wolf by the ears and we can neither hold him, nor safely let him go." What frustration!

The arts can help us painlessly to articulate and showcase our oneness. The arts have no pigmentation. The American dream has survived many attacks from our deadliest war to Rodney King. That's a long stretch. To borrow a phrase from William Faulkner, I remain confident it will continue not just to survive, but to prevail over the attacks from extremists of every ilk. Today, we are made uncomfortable by newly awakened conditions of "ethnic cleansing." Why the discomfort? Perhaps we are haunted by our past. Again, we do not know what to do with that wolf.

Assimilation was never the goal of the diverse ethnic groups in America. Inclusion without discomfort is now and ever will be the goal. Maybe one day we will be comfortable enough with each other to drop the hyphens. There should be no hyphenated Americans. The idea of a melting pot was and remains a myth. Universal inclusivity is not a racial idea. The President's Committee on the Arts and the Humanities, writing under the Bush administration, concluded that "American culture incorporates the heritage of many people and thereby provides a unique context for multicultural understanding."

But what is there that can transcend deep differences and stubborn divisions? I suggest: the arts. They have a wonderful universality. Art has the potential to unify. It can speak in many languages without a translator. Art does not discriminate: it ignores external irrelevancies and opts for quality, talent and competence. Let me quote again from the children attending the class at the Austin museum, children who could not have attended without scholarships. When asked if they were surprised at what their classmates had made, as well as what they had made themselves, some of the responses were, "Yes, because I didn't expect to see some of the things I could do," and "Yes, I didn't think I could do it that good," and "I was surprised that all the art work turned out great." Again, art unifies, it does not discriminate.

We are concerned about the economy. We know it has been in a deep rut and President Clinton is struggling mightily to find the tools to get us out. We need to make our voices heard with the measure that the arts should not be overlooked in the economic decisions being made today. I applaud our President for seeking to avoid the quick-fix mentality that got us where we are today. It is only in long-term solutions that we will thrive. And I think the arts offer one of these long-term solutions. Yes, this is one of those "radical" ideas spelled out by none other than the last administration's Committee on the Arts and Humanities.

There is no reason, patrons of the arts, to apologize for beauty. But it is important in this time of economic worries to articulate what is obvious to each of us: that art does more than stimulate and please the senses. The arts, in the words of the President's committee, are integrally related to the U.S. economy and contribute to our nation's wealth, competitiveness, and growth. If we look just at the copyright industries of broadcasting, records and tapes, motion pictures, theatrical productions, newspapers, periodicals, and books, plus computer programming and software, we find a contribution of more than $173 billion, or 3.3 percent of our gross national product. Add art, photography, and architecture and you find a contribution of almost 6 percent to the GNP from the arts, more than food, apparel, chemical, and retailing industries combined.

These figures don't include the economic impact of increased tourism and revitalization of downtown urban areas. Nor do these figures speak to a vital part of the American dream: the arts provide a passage out of poverty for thousands of economically disadvantaged individuals. Professional sports may capture the imaginations of many economically impoverished young people, but the arts—historically more open to all of the diverse segments of our society—provide the careers that can lift young men and women out of poverty.

And why is it that the arts can work this economic magic? It isn't magic, it's common sense. There is a direct relationship between the arts and self-esteem. Again, quoting from the children in the Laguna Gloria museum school: "No one can say your art is ugly because it is in the eyes of the beholder." One child learned "that I could be productive." Self-esteem is a good that each individual cherishes. An artist creates beauty and others enjoy it. He or she gets pleasure in knowing that he is the source of that pleasure and thus, regard for self is enhanced.

Self-esteem is a value which forecloses destructive tendencies; that is, you cannot feel good about who you are and where you are and simultaneously destroy your neighborhood. Such a contradiction is inherent and would be personally painful and debilitating.

I have just echoed the thoughts of Jacques Barzun, who in the 1973 Mellon Lectures in Fine Arts, declared that "art is power." He said that art "influences the mind, the nerves, the feelings, the soul" and that it "carries the message of hope, hostility, derision, and moral rebuke. It can fight material and spiritual evils and can transmit the ideals of a community now living, long past, or soon to be born." The arts are a multigenerational communicator.

In order for the arts to live up to the ambitious agenda I have prescribed, those of us who are patrons and supporters must be more than distant observers and appreciative spectators. We need to seek a permanent place in public school curricula for arts education. I commend the *New York Times* for its attention in a number of recent articles entitled "Missing Muses." Those articles point out that art classes teach the very qualities educators can reinvigorate American schools: analytical thinking, teamwork, motivation, and self-discipline.

In Austin, an elementary school teacher is quoted as saying, "Fine arts is where every child can succeed. It doesn't matter if the child is a genius or a slow learner. You have a natural at-risk program at every school." A school board trustee said, "Public school arts programs are the only outlet that poor people have. While some families can afford private lessons, there are thousands who can't." That trustee was obviously not in the majority when two years ago, the Austin school board cut art and music and physical education classes out of its kindergarten curriculum as one way of balancing its budget. Some of the district's schools have managed to re-institute those classes, but only through extraordinary efforts by teachers, parents and private contributions.

The arts deserve a higher place on America's public policy agenda. Sondra Meyers, the cultural advisor to Pennsylvania's governor, recently wrote:

"At this moment of political change—which offers the promise of a people-centered political agenda—we must wake up to the realities of our rich cultural resources and make the case for the integration of culture into public policy. We need to use every asset at our disposal to restore a sense of community and humaneness to our society and culture."

We must, to borrow a phrase from the 1960s, seize the moment that has been handed to us. We are embarking on the first movements in a new cycle in American history. We have just completed a cycle during which the arts survived but only by scratching and clawing to hold the gains of the previous cycle. It is up to those of us in this room to lead the way. We must be sure that our President and the Congress—and the American people most of all—understand that the arts can lift us all up.

I listened on January 20, to Maya Angelou as she captured beauty in language. She said:

"Here on the pulse of this new day
You may have the grace to look up and out
And into your sister's eyes and into
Your brother's face, your country
And say simply
Very simply
With hope
Good morning."

I listened; I heard; I believed. Patrons, practitioners, supporters of the arts, I say to you, very simply, with hope, Good morning. Have a very good day.

# A Sense of Proportion[4]

David McCullough

*Born July 7, 1933, Pittsburgh, PA; B.A., Yale University, 1955; writer, editor, Time Inc., 1956-61; writer, U.S. Information Agency, 1961-64; editor, American Heritage Publishing Co., 1964-71; host,* Smithsonian World, *1984; host,* The American Experience *television series, 1988; narrator,* The Civil War, *1990; winner of Pulitzer Prize in nonfiction, 1993; author,* The Path Between the Seas *(1977),* Mornings on Horseback *(1981),* The Great Bridge *(1982),* The Johnstown Flood *(1987),* Brave Companions *(1991),* Truman *(1992).*

## Editor's introduction

Pulitzer Prize winning author David McCullough asserted that the best way to teach the arts is to allow them to be seen by the student as a revealer of who that student is. According to McCullough, the arts, be they dramatic, written, or visual, are a living and breathing testament of our concerns, hopes, and dreams. While history tells us who we *were*, the arts "transcend time," giving us vivid glimpses into our identities and presenting what matters most to our society and our culture.

---

This is a great honor to be the Nancy Hanks Lecturer on the Arts and Public Policy, to have the opportunity to speak to you.

Art and history, culture and history, must not be seen as separate, any more than science and history. Dividers are imposed too often. We have the history of art over here, the history of science over there, the history of medicine, the history of music made separate, with walls between, as if music isn't medicine. Plain history, too often, winds up with only politics and wars.

But it is all part of human experience. To leave painting and song out of the story, theater, architecture, poetry, is to leave out too much of life, too much that matters above all.

Creativity, innovation, invention are impossible without imagination and without risk. This was true in times past. It is true today. Yet we do too little in educating our children to encourage and reward imagination and the willingness to take risks.

"How many things can you think of to do with a brick?"

It's a question I like to ask students in writing courses. "Take out a piece of paper, make a list. There's no right or wrong answer. Use your imagination." It's wonderful to see how liberating many find that.

History is about who we were. In the arts we show who we are. History is about time. Art transcends time. "Who's statue is that, there in the park, with the pigeon on his hat?" How many politicians have strutted their stuff here down the years—hundreds, thousands—confident they were taking their place in history? How few are remembered at all.

But Gershwin lives. Every time everywhere his music is played, Gershwin lives. Whitman and Willa Cather, Thomas Eakins, Louis Sullivan, Martha Graham, Langston Hughes speak to us still, touch our lives. Take away our art, our music, the best of our buildings, take away Mark Twain and Julia Ward Howe and Woodie Guthrie and Scott Joplin and who are we? Take from this our capital city Daniel Chester French's Lincoln or that greatest of the city's works of abstract art, the Washington Monument by Robert Mills, take away the great collections of the Library of Congress, and how then would we feel?

Culture might be defined as what matters to a society. And certainly a good measure of what matters is how we spend our money.

Nearly everywhere in the country libraries are shortening their hours, laying off staff, put-

[4]Delivered as the Nancy Hanks Lecture on Arts and Public Policy, at the Kennedy Center for the Performing Arts, in Washington, D.C., on April 17, 1994.

ting a freeze on book purchases, or closing their doors. The explanation always is that there's not enough money.

Yet in all the years of the Great Depression, not one library is known to have closed its doors anywhere in all the country. Not one. And in the worst of times when our material abundance individually and as a nation was nothing like what it is today.

In Massachusetts, where I live, twenty libraries have closed in the last three years alone. In California since 1980 more than half the public school libraries have closed. Libraries in Los Angeles are open now only a few days a week. This in California, golden California.

The Library of Congress, too, has lately cut back its services, closing the main reading room plus six other reading rooms on Sundays, a severe blow to anyone wishing to use the Library on weekends.

As a personal note I might add that it was on a weekend at the Library of Congress in the early '60s that I happened to see a collection of newly acquired, rare old photographs taken in Johnstown, Pennsylvania, soon after the calamitous flood of 1889. Photographs that led me to write my first book, that led me to writing history as I had never anticipated I would. So I am particularly sympathetic to those with full-time jobs who can only make use of the Library on weekends.

How do we spend our money? For all public libraries nationwide: $4.3 billion a year, which is considerably less than we spend on potato chips or sneakers. Less than we spend on our lawns or for cellular phones. Last year, we spent $7.5 billion on our lawns, $9 billion on cellular phones.

Have we changed so much in our regard for libraries since the Great Depression? Not to judge by the demand for library services. Library use, even with the cutbacks, is up substantially. What is not up is our willingness to pay the price, or more specifically to vote the taxes to pay the price for a measure of civilization that has long been standard to our way of life and that so many benefit from in ways beyond anything determinable by cost-accounting.

Still more serious, even more shameful, is what is happening to programs in the arts in our schools. And it is this especially that I want to talk about.

All across the country arts programs in the schools are being cut or eliminated altogether, and it's a disgrace. We are cheating our children!

"We hold these truths to be self-evident." We teach them from history books that all men are created equal, that they are endowed by their Creator with certain inalienable rights, that among these are Life, Liberty, and the pursuit of happiness. But how will they have any idea of happiness, of all that Thomas Jefferson had in mind when he used that word, if they are shut off from art and architecture and music and theater and dance and literature, if they are denied that part of life, that vital center, if they have only a limited chance at the experience of self-expression, or no chance at all?

There are new figures for what's to be spent by the federal government on the arts. And for the first time there is a specific allotment for art and music in the schools. For fiscal 1995 it's to be $75,000,000. Federally funded cultural programs including money for the National Endowment for the Humanities, the National Endowment for the Arts, and education in the arts comes to approximately $600,000,000, while the overall figure, the grand total, which includes money for the Smithsonian, museums, art galleries, and the like is $882,000,000. And what's that? It's a pitance is what it is.

$882,000,000 is one sixth-hundredth of one percent of the federal budget.

We need to recover a Jeffersonian sense of proportion. Jefferson, whose passion for education exceeded that of any of our political leaders, worked out his own guide "to the faculties of the mind," as he called it, in his classification system for his library. This was the private collection of 6,500 books assembled over fifty years that Jefferson sold to the government at half its value to create a new congressional library after the British burned the capitol during the War of 1812. It took eleven wagons to haul the books here. And what a picture that must have made as they left Monticello and started through the countryside.

There were three main categories and he gave them equal importance.

First was *memory*, by which he meant history: history civil, history ecclesiastical, natural history, history ancient and modern.

Second was *reason*, which included philosophy, the law, and mathematics.

The third category, titled *imagination*, was the fine arts. And on this lovely spring evening in the city he helped design, I would like to mention that within fine arts, along with painting, sculpture, architecture, music, poetry, drama, oratory, and criticism, he included gardening.

Three parts equally weighted, and history and the arts are two of the three: history, philosophy, and the fine arts.

I grew up in Pittsburgh, Pennsylvania. I was number three in a family of four sons. My father worked with his father in a family-owned electrical supply business, McCullough Electric, now run by my brother George.

I began public school in kindergarten in 1938, about the time when the National Gallery was being built here. The building, along with a surpassing collection of old masters, were a gift from the late Andrew Mellon of Pittsburgh, about whom I knew nothing, of course, but whose generosity to his country I've come to appreciate more and more. The paintings alone were the largest gift of any individual to any government.

Like McCullough Electric, the Linden Avenue School is still in business, a fine two-story, yellow brick building about mid-way between Point Breeze and Squirrel Hill, if you know Pittsburgh. To me then, its marble halls and great sweeping double stairway to the second floor were grand in the extreme. When I returned last year for the school's 90th anniversary celebration, I was delighted to find that those marble halls and sweeping stairs are in fact just as grand as I remembered.

We had music at Linden School, lots of music, and Miss Polichio, our music teacher, was perfectly beautiful. For quite a while I was in love with Miss Polichio. We had music several times a week in a room reserved for music. We played tambourines, woodblocks, and the triangle. (I thought myself something of a woodblock virtuoso.) We sang, learning by heart most of Stephen Foster, who came from Pittsburgh. There was a school orchestra. My oldest brother played the violin in the school orchestra.

There was an auditorium with a stage and real pull curtains and we were all in plays, the whole way along. There was an art room and an art teacher, Miss Bridgewater, and the day she took her chalk and with a few fast strokes demonstrated two point perspective on the black board, is one I've never forgotten. She had performed pure magic right before our eyes. I had to be able to do that. I had to learn how. I began drawing and painting and I'm still at it at every possible chance. (One of the particular pleasures of painting is you don't have to work with words.)

By now these were the World War II years, when the steel mills were going at capacity and at night the sky pulsed red from the flames of the blast furnaces.

There was a library at school, with books on every wall except for where the windows faced the street. It is still that way. The first morning we were declared sufficiently advanced to go to the library—a very great step in the upward march at Linden—we were told we could each go to the shelves and choose any book we wished. What a moment! I remember especially one called *Ben and Me* written and illustrated by Robert Lawson. It was about a mouse who lived in Ben Franklin's hat and who consequently had much to report.

When my oldest brother, Hax, went to Peabody High School, he both played the violin in the Peabody Symphony orchestra and stole the show in a Peabody production of *Arsenic and Old Lace.* He was Teddy Brewster, the one who thought he was Theodore Roosevelt and was kept busy down in the cellar—down in "Panama"—digging the canal and burying the supposed yellow fever victims. It was the most marvelous stage production I had ever seen and my first realization of there ever having been anyone like Theodore Roosevelt or a place like Panama.

"How do you pick the subjects for your books? "I'm asked." Whatever made you decide on Theodore Roosevelt? The Panama Canal?"

There's no telling, I suppose, when the seed of an idea takes hold. But on the first day I went to the Carnegie Library—in Pittsburgh this means *the* Carnegie Library, the mother church as it were—and with my new, first library card took out a book, I was perhaps eleven years old. It was *A Tree Grows in Brooklyn.* About that same time, as I remember, our wonderful science teacher at Linden School, Miss Schmeltz, had arranged an exhibit of bridges of all kinds. They were made of match sticks and I can see them still, lined up along the window sills, flooded with sunlight.

At a party, long afterward, when I told her what I was working on, a Washington socialite boomed loud enough for everyone to hear, "Who in the world would ever want to read a book about the Brooklyn Bridge?"

August Wilson, whose best-known plays are set in Pittsburgh, has described how, in boyhood, the Carnegie Library became his preferred classroom, where he read Ralph Ellison, Richard Wright, and Langston Hughes. "Just the idea black people would write books," he has said. "I wanted my book up there, too."

Art, music, science, history, putting on plays, it was all part of school and childhood and I loved school, almost every day. Nor was there ever a thought that the arts were frills. Or that everyone had to stay stuck in the same interests, at school or at home.

Brother Hax had his music; George, engineering; I had my painting; brother Jim, astronomy. We were not rich, certainly not by Pittsburgh standards. I suppose we could be described as comfortable. Except for engineering, my father had no interest in any of these other pursuits. Neither my father nor my mother played a musical instrument, or, as far as I know, ever painted a picture or had a part in a play. When Hax tuned the radio to the Metropolitan Opera on winter Saturday afternoons, the volume cranked up full throttle, it about drove my father crazy. "Who's getting murdered now," he'd call out. And while my father and mother willingly paid for paints and music lessons, concert tickets, and the like, and mother welcomed such activity, it was really at school that we got the bug, got the chance. And I say this because I think it so important to understand that it is not just children who are economically deprived who benefit from school libraries, from arts programs, from community commitment to the arts for children. And to argue for support of the arts on that basis primarily is to miss the point. All boats rise with the incoming tide.

What I didn't know then was how exceptional the arts program was throughout the Pittsburgh school system; indeed how exceptional it had been for years. And many of the results were exceptional, too, as we now know.

A who's who of those in the arts who attended the public schools of Pittsburgh is strong testimony to just how the whole country benefits from that kind of education: Andy Warhol, Earl Hines, Erroll Garner, Mary Lou Williams, August Wilson, Rachael Carson, composer Henry Mancini.

From Peabody High School alone came Malcolm Cowley, Gene Kelly, Billy Eckstine, Fritz Weaver, novelist John Edgar Wideman.

Gene Kelly, the son of a sales executive, was a football and baseball star at Peabody. He excelled in gymnastics, played the violin and banjo, edited the school paper, wrote poetry, and was praised on his report card for his "vivid imagination."

Erroll Garner, a mill worker's son, played the tuba in the Westinghouse High School band. Henry Mancini, whose father was a steel worker, started on the piccolo at age eight, by twelve turned to the piano. The 1942 Aliquippa High School yearbook says of him: "a true music lover, collects records, plays in the band, and has even composed several beautiful selections. He wishes to continue his study of music and to have an orchestra of his own some day."

I thought I could also include Martha Graham, who was born in Pittsburgh, but damn, she moved away at age 3.

Willa Cather once taught high school English in Pittsburgh. "So vivid was her personality," remembered a student, "so unforgettable her method of making us see the picture (as she read aloud), that even yet I hear her voice . . . ."

Selma Burke lived, worked, and taught in Pittsburgh through the 1960s and 70s, founding her own art center for children. She is a sculptor and one of the country's most respected black artists and teachers. If you have a dime with you, you own one of her works. She did the sculpted profile of Franklin Roosevelt.

And then there was Carolyn D. Patterson, a name you don't know. She was the principal of Linden School and a force, unforgettable, tall, severe-looking. A woman who brooked no nonsense whatsoever. My friend Richard Ketchum, the historian, who also went to Linden, remembers her looking at least six foot eight. Just the sound of her approaching steps could freeze you cold in your chair. She wore stout, black, lace-up shoes with thick high heels hard enough to drive a ten-penny nail. And down those marble halls she would come, making her rounds.

"Boys and girls," she would say, "Remember always you are a reflection on your parents." I'm not sure any of us knew what that meant exactly, except that we'd better tow the line. Yet, I think deep down inside we knew she was right: that our education mattered, that we mattered, each of us, and that we had potential beyond anything we might imagine.

Miss Patterson, I now appreciate, ran an outstanding school. She was dedicated, far-seeing. A pioneer. She helped found the country's first educational television station. Pittsburgh's WQED, the beginning of public television, and the station that would introduce to Pittsburgh and ultimately to the entire country, Fred Rogers, "Mister Rogers," who in his years on the air has touched and influenced the lives of more children than any teacher who ever lived. The longest running national program in the history of public television, *Mister Rogers' Neighborhood*, broadcast still from WQED, reaches more than 8,000,000 households on some 318 public stations.

I feel I had a huge advantage growing up in Pittsburgh, *because* I grew up in Pittsburgh. For along with the schools, besides all the programs in art and music, went the Carnegie Library, the Carnegie Museums, and Carnegie Music Hall, all in one great complex in the Oakland section of town, close by Carnegie-Mellon University and the University of Pittsburgh, and, in those days, Forbes Field. I can hardly overstress the importance of this: that art, science, music, literature, history, the world of books, were joined, all together, to be taken as parts of the same whole, all under one roof. There were school trips to the Carnegie Museum of Natural History, free Saturday morning art classes at the Carnegie Museum of Art.

Or you could go on your own in perfect safety, "down" to the library or museums by bus or streetcar, though the streetcars were preferable. They were more fun. Annie Dillard, who grew up in my neighborhood, has described them as "orange, clangy, beloved things—loud, jerky, and old." That they were.

The looming stone exterior of the Carnegie then was black as coal, from the smoke in the air, and a lot inside seemed gloomy and boring. But not the dinosaurs, or the big scale model of the Parthenon, presented as it looked in its prime. There were some paintings in the permanent collection that I fed on, Edward Hopper's *Cape Cod Afternoon*, for example. And year after year, the great Associated American Artists exhibition came to the Carnegie Museum of Art, with paintings by Andrew Wyeth, Burchfield, Benton, Raphael Soyer, Grant Wood, Horace Pippin, Georgia O'Keeffe, Joe Jones, Walt Kuhn, Reginald Marsh. There was something about those Reginald Marsh girls that was beginning to interest me.

I remember also coming into one of the galleries and seeing at the far end, bigger than life, John Stuart Curry's painting of John Brown, his arms flung out, great beard flying in the wind, a cyclone roaring out of the background. How could anyone not want to know about that man, the story there?

The Kaufmann family, owners of Kaufmann's Department Store and staunch supporters of the arts, brought a string of eminent artists to Pittsburgh to paint the city, then staged an exhibition of their work. Something that ought to be done again and not only in Pittsburgh. The Kaufmann family also sponsored exhibitions of the work of school children and believe me to go downtown with your family to see one of your own paintings hanging in Kaufmann's window, *that* was something!

Private benefactors like the Kaufmann's should get all the credit they deserve. And so should the many corporations that support the arts.

What is so important to understand about education in the arts, is that there especially you learn by doing. Think of the lesson in that.

You learn to play the piano by playing the piano. You learn to paint by painting. It's not just a way to learn; it's the only way.

"She knew that the only way to learn to write was to write, and she set us to writing," remembered a student of Willa Cather.

Especially in the arts you learn how very much can be learned from a teacher, and that a great teacher is a true God-send, an opener of doors, giver of gifts, a star to steer by. Especially in the arts, you learn to bring out what is unique in you, to express yourself, your feelings, and to experience the incomparable, high-octain lift of that. But you learn about working with others, too, of being part of something larger than yourself, as anyone knows who has ever played in an orchestra, ever taken part in a theatrical production.

And—*and*—maybe it's in the arts above all that we learn most directly, discover for ourselves most immediately in the doing, that the reward *is* the doing, that the payoff for the effort is the effort.

"I want to show the children that art is not money," Selma Burke has said. "It's a life."

Selma Burke is in her 94th year.

"You can see beauty and creation without ever drawing a line—if you just look . . . You can see the beauty of creation in an apple. To many people it's just an ordinary red object. But if you take a bite into it, you transform it. Now you see the white solid juicy inside. If you bite deeper you get to the core and you see the black seeds from which the apple came. Then, if you take that seed and lay it down on paper—it's almost magic! That such a big red apple could come from that seed. It's the fascinating process of creation. The art teacher has to find a simple way to teach that.

"I'm hard on my students—to get them to see how important that apple is.

"To see that—right in your hand—you have the beauty of creation."

"Do all you can—and then some," she would tell her students. "Do all you can—and then some."

Coaching his young son Andrew, talking of the world around them, N. C. Wyeth would say, "You must be like a sponge. Sponge it up. Soak it up."

Andrew Wyeth describes how, at 15, he learned anatomy:

"He got me a skeleton. Had it there and had me draw it from every angle. Every bone. And I did that for about a winter and towards spring he said, 'Now you've drawn this enough. Now . . . I want to see how much you can remember.' So he took the skeleton away. 'Now I want you to draw that figure at all angles—what you remember'."

Learning to appreciate the miracle of creation . . . learning to observe and remember . . . learning to see beneath surface appearances to the essential: and yet some deride education in the arts as frivolous, irrelevant.

But listen please to one more teacher. Ann Marshall has been teaching the visual arts at Peabody High School for 20 years and is herself a graduate of Peabody:

"You can teach all of life with art. You learn the lessons of life. You learn that you are unique and that what you make is unique. You learn self-worth. You learn to make decisions, to make mistakes. You learn to take risks. You learn that sometimes what you think are big mistakes can turn into big successes."

Yes, but we must be practical, argue the naysayers. Alright, let's be practical.

Consider that in Pittsburgh the new Andy Warhol Museum, scheduled to open next month, will bring an estimated 200,000 people to the city this year. With more than 3,500 pieces in its collection, it will be the largest art gallery in the world devoted to one person. Andy Warhol, the son of a coal miner, excelled in the free Saturday art classes at the Carnegie Museum.

Or on a national level, consider the astonishing transformation of Chrysler Corporation. In less than three years Chrysler went from being the "basket case" of the American automobile industry to "leading the resurgence" of the American automobile industry. Chrysler is suddenly the most profitable car maker in the country. And the reason? Above all? Design. Inspired design. The "alchemy of design," as *The New York Times* reported. If there are heroes to the story they are Chrysler's vice president in charge of design, Tom Gale, and his extraordinary young staff. And yes, Gale remembers being inspired first by a fourth grade art teacher. Designer Michael Santoro remembers looking down from a seventh floor window at New York City's High School of Art and Design, and studying the cars waiting at the red light. "You look out the window and all the cars look the same," he told a reporter for the *Times*. "I said, 'If I ever get the chance, my car's going to look different . . . .'"

How do you appraise the "practical" value of a program like the Saturday art classes at Carnegie Museum or a school like New York's High School of Art and Design? How do you calculate the return on such public dollars as it takes to educate an Andy Warhol or a Tom Gale or Michael Santoro?

The nation needs artists and designers to work in the automobile industry, in advertising, publishing, fashion, interior design, television, the movies. And musicians and singers and dancers and actors for all the so-called entertainment industry. And teachers. And teachers to teach teachers. Teachers, teachers, teachers for all the arts and not just for those who will perform but for all who will learn to care and enjoy the arts all their lives. Surely that is obvious.

Talent doesn't just happen. Training, craft, experience can't be summoned willy-nilly out of nowhere as needed. It has to be developed, brought out, brought along with education. And the process has to begin early. The earlier the better.

"Would the gentleman be opposed to federal funding to assist in educating school children in the arts and music?" asked Representative Sidney Yates of Illinois of Representative Philip

Crane, also of Illinois, in an exchange on the floor of Congress last summer.

"To educating school children, making art a part of the curriculum?" asked Crane.

"As the arts Endowment does," affirmed Yates.

"It should not be doing that," said Crane.

"Is the gentleman opposed to federal funding of such institutions as the Lincoln Memorial?" asked Yates.

"National statues, basically, I would not have a problem with that," replied Crane.

In Pittsburgh now the prospect is shadowed. The number of teachers in the visual arts has been cut. Music programs have been cut. Two high schools have no music program at all. Saturday art classes at the Carnegie Museum continue, but where in years past thousands enrolled, the number now is about a hundred.

Instead of a separate budget for the arts in the schools, there is a large overall allotment for "support services" which includes the arts but a lot else besides, general equipment for example. And how the money is spent is left to the principal of each school. Instead of $800 being spent, say, for musical instruments, it buys a new office typewriter.

Pittsburgh, according to a former director of art education in the public schools is "slowly, but surely decimating its art programs."

The arts, as Fred Rogers says, give children ways to say who they are, how they feel, to say whether they are happy or sad or angry, and without hurting anyone.

The late Margaret McFarlan, professor of child development at the University of Pittsburgh and an inspiration for three generations of specialists in child studies, including Fred Rogers, liked to say:

"We don't teach children. We just give them who we are. And they catch that. Attitudes are caught, not taught. If you love something in front of a child, the child will catch that."

So what is our attitude to be here in America? What do we love? What do we want our children to see that we love?

And who will be the leaders with both the spirit and courage of a Theodore Roosevelt, who loved the poetry of Edward Arlington Robinson and on hearing that Robinson was in financial straits, found him a job in the Treasury, then sent him a note saying, "Think poetry first, Treasury second."

I am an optimist, by nature and from reading history. I am also of that generation raised on the belief that we Americans can do anything we set our hearts and minds to. I still believe that.

A new set of national standards for education in the arts has been drawn up and approved by Secretary of Education Richard Riley. The standards are voluntary and national in name only, but a step in the right direction.

We should be grateful for what's being done for the arts here in Washington by people like Jim Wolfensohn, like Sidney Yates in the House, Claiborne Pell, Jim Jeffords, and Alan Simpson in the Senate. Jane Alexander is magnificent. But we mustn't count on government only. Congress is always slow catching up with what the country wants. The energy, the commitment, the determination must come from us. That's how the system works. And money, too, that has to come from us.

*We* must be "the public policy" on the arts.

If we want libraries open again, if we want a generous, exciting, creative education for our children, if we want a culture that counts for something, it's up to us. We must get busy and make it happen: "Do all we can, and then some."

# Worth Defending[5]

Kenneth Lauren Burns

*Born July 29, 1953, Brooklyn, NY; B.A., Hampshire College, 1975; co-founder, Florentine Films, 1975–; producer, director, writer,* The Brooklyn Bridge *(1982),* The Shaker *(1985); producer, director,* Huey Long *(1985),* The Statue of Liberty *(1985),* Empire of the Air *(1992),* Baseball *(1996); co-producer, director,* The Civil War *(1990); executive producer,* The West *(1996).*

## Editor's introduction

Acclaimed documentary filmmaker Kenneth Lauren Burns, speaking alongside several representatives and senators, made this plea to maintain funding for the National Endowment for the Humanities (NEH). In the speech, Burns noted that all of his award-winning documentaries were made with the support of the NEH. Without such organizations and their funding, Burns argued, projects such as educational documentaries will simply not be made. In this sense, funding allows the "excruciatingly wise messages" taught by history to reach the ears and eyes of an interested audience.

---

Good morning. It is an honor for me to come down from New Hampshire today to express my whole-hearted support for the National Endowment for the Humanities. Let me say from the outset that I am a passionate supporter of the Endowments and their unique role in helping to stitch our exquisite, diverse, and often fragile culture together.

Few institutions provide such a direct, grass-roots way for our citizens to participate in the shared glories of their common past, in the power of the priceless ideals that have animated our remarkable republic and our national life for more than two hundred years, and in the inspirational life of the mind and the heart that an engagement with the arts and humanities always provides. It is my sincere belief that anything which threatens these institutions weakens our country. It is as simple as that.

For nearly 20 years I have been producing historical documentary films, celebrating the excruciatingly wise messages American history continually directs our way. The subjects of these films range from the construction of the Brooklyn Bridge and the Statue of Liberty to the life of the turbulent Southern demagogue Huey Long; from the graceful architecture of the Shakers to the early founders of radio; from the sublime pleasures and unexpected lessons of our national pastime to the searing transcendent experience of our Civil War. I even made a film on the history of this magnificent building and the much maligned institution that is charged with conducting the people's business.

In nearly every instance, these films have been produced with the support and encouragement of the National Endowment for the Humanities, either at the state or national level. In every instance, I have produced these films for national public television broadcast, not the lucrative commercial networks or cable. For each film project we have worked on, we have willingly submitted to the Endowment's unique and rigorous proposal process, sometimes producing documents running to several hundred pages of detailed scholarly interpretation, budgetary analysis, and scrupulous preplanning. The months-long application process includes, among many difficult requirements, the engagement of nationally recognized scholars who advise at every juncture of the production, insuring balance, adjudicating differences in historical interpretation, offering a variety of perspectives and modes of inquiry.

Without a doubt, my series on the Civil War or Baseball could not have been made without

[5]Delivered at the annual "Humanities on the Hill Day," in Washington, D.C., on May 2, 1996. Reprinted with permission of Kenneth Lauren Burns.

the National Endowment for the Humanities. The Endowment not only provided some of these project's largest grants, thereby attracting other funders, but also, through unrelated grants to other institutions, helped restore the archival photographs we would use to tell our story.

As I produced my own documentaries over the years, I have watched the Endowment fund literally thousands of other projects that have touched Americans, that have engaged Americans, that have made a difference in American lives that belie the relatively small outlay of public funds necessary to sustain these fundamentally good works. I have watched the Endowments save critical archival documents from decay and destruction, bring great art to the high plains of South Dakota, send professors from Nebraska and Georgia on important research trips their own universities could not underwrite, and I have watched a man bring Thomas Jefferson to life in the little towns of my own conservative State of New Hampshire to the delight and inspiration of all.

But now, and sadly not for the first time, I hear critics saying that these remarkably efficient Endowments must be scrapped, that our government has no business in the arts and humanities, that we must let the marketplace alone determine everything in our cultural life, that these huge broad based institutions are essentially elitist, that a few controversial projects prove the leftist political bias of not only the Endowments but the entire artistic and academic communities. I feel strongly that I must respond to these charges.

Since the beginning of this country, our government has been involved in supporting the arts and the diffusion of knowledge, which was deemed as critical to our future as roads and dams and bridges. Early on, Thomas Jefferson and the other founding fathers knew that the pursuit of happiness did not mean a hedonistic search for pleasure in the marketplace but an active involvement of the mind in the higher aspects of human endeavor—namely education, music, the arts, and history. Congress supported the journey of Lewis and Clark as much to explore the natural, biological, ethnographic, and cultural landscape of our expanding nation as to open up a new trading route to the Pacific. Congress supported numerous geographical, artistic, photographic, and biological expeditions to nearly every corner of the developing West. Congress funded, through the Farm Securities Administration, the work of Walker Evans and Dorthea Lange and other great photographers who captured for posterity the terrible human cost of the Depression. At the same time, Congress funded some of the most enduring writing ever produced about this country's people, its monuments, buildings, and backroads in the still much used and universally admired WPA guides. Some of our greatest symphonic work, our most treasured dramatic plays, and early documentary film classics came from an earlier Congress' support.

With Congress' great insight the Endowments were born and grew to their startlingly effective maturity echoing the same time-honored sense that our Government has an interest in helping to sponsor Art and Education just as it sponsors Commerce. We are not talking about a free ride, but a priming of the pump, a way to get the juices flowing, in the spirit of President Reagan's notion of a partnership between the government and the private sector. The NEH grant I got for the Civil War series attracted even more funds from General Motors and several private foundations; money that would not have been there had not the Endowment blessed this project with their rigorously earned imprimatur.

When I was working more than ten years ago on a film about the Statue of Liberty, its history and powerful symbolism, I had the great good fortune to meet and interview Vartan Gregorian, who was then the president of the New York Public Library, and who is now the president of Brown University. After an extremely interesting and passionate interview on the meaning behind the statue for an immigrant like him—from Tabriz, Iran—Vartan took me on a long and fascinating tour of the miles of stacks of the New York Public Library. Finally, after galloping down one claustrophobic corridor, he stopped and gestured expansively. "This," he said, surveying his library from its guts, "this is the DNA of our civilization." He was saying that that library, indeed, all libraries, archives, and historical societies are the DNA of our society, leaving an imprint of excellence and intention for generations to come. It occurs to me, as we debate the very existence of the Endowments, that they, as well as public television, are also part, a critical part, of the great genetic legacy of our nation. They are, in the best sense, modern educational institutions first and foremost.

But there are those who are sure that without the Endowments, the so-called "marketplace" would take care of everything; that what won't survive in the marketplace, doesn't deserve to survive. Nothing could be further from the truth, because we are not just talking about the commerce of a nation, we are not just economic beings, but spiritual and intellectual beings as well, and so we are talking about the creativity of a nation. Now, some forms of creativity thrive in the marketplace and that is a wonderful thing, reflected in our glorious Hollywood movies and our globally popular music. But let me say that the marketplace could not have made and to this day could not make my Civil War series, indeed any of the films I have worked on.

That marketplace does not produce, by the way, the most respected news program on television; that marketplace does not produce the most respected children's, history, and science programs on television either. These are but a small part of the legacy of the Endowments and PBS, institutions supported by 70% of Republicans, 80% of Independents, and 90% of Democrats across the country.

That marketplace does not save the old papers of a founding father, it doesn't fund research into that which enriches our heritage—not necessarily our pocketbooks or what is fashionable at the moment, and it does not fund the local poetry reading, or dance recital, or symphony group, or lecture on great books that take place daily from Maine to California. The Endowments are like posterity's spies—moles penetrating farther and deeper into our political and social landscape than any agent of the so-called marketplace.

No, the marketplace will not produce the good works of the Endowments. Just as the marketplace does not and will not produce a B-2 Bomber, something we are told that is essential to the defense of our country. It has taken government involvement, government sponsorship, government encouragement, government oversight, government absorption of overuns, and government procurement to build a B-2 Bomber. Interestingly, the total cost of both endowments plus the Corporation for Public Broadcasting does not equal the cost of one B-2 Bomber. It is obvious, too, that the National Endowment for the Arts, the National Endowment for the Humanities, and the Corporation for Public Broadcasting have nothing to do with the actual defense of our country, I know that—they just make our country worth defending.

It is a sad commentary when the richest nation on earth cuts its cultural funding 40% and threatens much worse, forcing institutions which serve as the bedrock of our community life to curtail their activities. Don't these over-zealous critics realize that 200 years from now whether the military budget increases or decreases a few percent, whether a tax was imposed or repealed will be less important than the quality of our schools, the symphonies we have written, the new museums we have opened. Only in retrospect will they see clearly what we see clearly now: the palpable truth that the aesthetics of living are as important as the standard of living to human life.

Even during the Great Depression when some towns were forced to shoot the animals in their zoos and distribute the meat to the poor, even in the Great Depression, public libraries were not forced to shorten hours, as they must do now, during a period of unparalleled prosperity, growth, and riches.

Do not be persuaded by the feeble argument that this is all elitist, that we are funding the superfluous; "opera for the rich." The meat and potatoes of the Endowment's work reaches out to every corner of the country and touches people in positive ways the Federal Government rarely does. Indeed, it would be elitist itself to abolish the Endowments, to trust to the marketplace and the "natural aristocracy" that many have promised over the last two hundred years would rise up to protect us all—and hasn't.

Many have recently criticized the Endowments for certain controversial or political projects; many believe the Endowments and public television are hot-beds of radical thinking. I wonder, though, have they ever applied for an Endowment grant, worked with their staffs or been to a council meeting? I doubt it. These are essentially conservative institutions, filled with people who share the concerns of most Americans. One need only remember that the Endowments are criticized just as vigorously from the far left, to realize at once what a tough job they have, and what a good job they are doing. And in a free society, the rare examples of controversial scholarship that may run counter to our accepted canon, need not be the occasion for a new reactionary Puritanism, but ought to be seen as a healthy sign that we are a nation tolerant of ideas, confident—as the recent tide of geo-political history has shown—confident that the best ideas will always prevail.

One hundred and fifty eight years ago, in 1838, well before the Civil War, Abraham Lincoln challenged us to consider the real threat to the country, to consider forever the real cost of our inattention: "Whence shall we expect the approach of danger?" he wrote. "Shall some transatlantic giant step on the earth and crush us at a blow? Never. All the armies of Europe and Asia could not by force take a drink from the Ohio River or make a track in the Blue Ridge in the trial of a thousand years. No, if destruction be our lot, we must ourselves be its author and finisher." As usual, Mr. Lincoln's words speak to us today with the same force he spoke to his own times.

Most of us here, whether we know it or not, are in the business of words, and we hope, with some reasonable expectation, that those words will last.

But alas, especially today, those words often evaporate, their precision blunted by neglect, their insight diminished by the sheer volume of their ever-increasing brethren, their force diluted by ancient animosities that seem to set each group against the other.

The historian Arthur Schlesinger, Jr. has said that we suffer today from "too much pluribus and not enough unum." Few things survive in these cynical days to remind us of the Union from which so many of our personal and collective blessings flow. And it is hard not to wonder, in an age when the present moment consumes and overshadows all else—our bright past and our dim unknown future—what finally does endure? What encodes and stores the genetic material of our civilization, passing down to the next generation—the best of us—what we hope will mutate into betterness for our children and our posterity? This Endowment provides one clear answer. Please do not be the author of its destruction, the finisher of its important good works. The NEH is the best thing we have to remind us why we all still agree to cohere as a people. And that is a good thing.

# XI. Religion

## Editor's introduction

Religious discourse between 1937 and 1997 took place in a wide variety of venues, and adopted a range of forms. It was heard in the academy, during political campaigns, in the courtroom, and on the streets. At times it could be described as theological postulating, but it was often more akin to evangelizing. Just as the holocaust loomed throughout the speeches contained in Chapter VI (Human Rights), it also permeated the addresses contained herein. Leaders of established religions discussed ways of caring for their congregations and expanding the breadth of their message, while evangelists increasingly utilized television to attract larger followings. Central to most discussions on religion has been the extent to which spiritual concerns are manifest in daily life.

In the speeches in this chapter, two theologians, a Methodist preacher, a Rabbi, an evangelist, and a government official consider the spiritual needs of modern human beings. They also discuss what can be done to satisfy those needs. Reinhold Niebuhr, prominent theologian and former professor of Applied Christianity at Union Theological Seminary, described a despair that he believed the "optimism of modern culture" cannot cure. Keenly conscious of the then recent dropping of the atomic bomb on Japan, Niebuhr warned that "the defense of a civilization requires military strategy but it also requires political and moral strategy." Such a strategy, according to Niebuhr, must be concerned with world-wide "community building," and must therefore "cease to identify God with any particular culture." In a similar criticism of the modern world's religious failings, Charles E. Shulman, rabbi of the Riverdale Temple in New York City, suggested that "Americans should emphasize the things of the spirit that have been so greatly neglected in recent years." Like Niebuhr, Shulman believed that "individual and national character" arises from neither military strength nor economic power, but rather from spiritual awareness.

Further recalling the value of spirituality to everyday life, the Reverend Billy Graham observed that "America, possessing all the economic affluence for enjoying life, virtually leads the world in crime, narcotics abuse, pornography, immorality, and even debts." In essence, Graham proclaimed that economic strength does not always foster spiritual health, but often a division between morality and everyday life. It is exactly this disparity between reality and the goals and tenets of most religions that dominates many of the speeches reprinted in this section.

# An Adequate Faith for the World Crisis[1]

Reinhold Niebuhr

*Born June 21, 1892, Wright City, MO; died June 1, 1971; B.D., 1914, A.M., 1915, Yale Divinity School; ordained, Evangelical Synod of North America, 1915; pastor, Bethel Evangelical Church of Detroit, 1915-28; associate professor, Union Theological Seminary, 1928-71; co-founder, Fellowship of Socialist Christians, 1935-40; author,* Does Civilization Need Religion? *(1927),* Moral Men and Immoral Society *(1932),* Reflections on the End of an Era *(1934),* Beyond Tragedy *(1937),* Christianity and Power Politics *(1940),* The Nature and Destiny of Man *(1943),* The Children of Light and the Children of Darkness *(1944),* Discerning the Signs of the Times *(1946),* Faith and History *(1949),* The Irony of American History *(1952),* Christian Realism *(1953),* Interpretation of Christian Ethics *(1953),* The Self in Its Dialogues and Dramas *(1955),* The Godly and the Ungodly *(1959),* The Structure of Nations and Empires *(1959),* A Nation So Conceived *(1963),* Man's Nature and His Communities *(1956),* The Democratic Experience *(1969),* Reminiscences *(1972),* Justice and Mercy *(1996).*

## Editor's introduction

Acclaimed theologian Reinhold Niebuhr gave this speech at a forum entitled "The Spiritual Contributions to the Strength of Man." In response to the dropping of two atomic bombs on Hiroshima and Nagasaki, Dr. Niebuhr declared that "we are experiencing tragic realities for which the optimism of modern culture has not prepared us." His argument illuminates the two-fold nature of technology—both capable of making life easier, and capable of ending life. In response to this reality, Niebuhr asserted that we must come to understand God as a unifying force, one that is not owned by a particular culture but rather fosters the creation of a world community.

---

We might profitably distinguish between three dimensions of the world crisis and consider what resources are required to meet our situation in each of these dimensions. In the narrowest dimension, the crisis we confront consists of the peril in which a democratic civilization stands.

The second dimension of the crisis consists of the peril in which the whole of civilization stands, whether democratic or no. It is the dimension of the crisis which would exist, even if Russia were not a difficult partner in the world community. It would exist in any event because we have not yet developed the moral imagination or the political instruments for creating a world community.

The third level of the crisis is more explicitly religious and spiritual. It is created by the fact that the vicissitudes of our generation were not anticipated in our culture. We are experiencing tragic realities for which the optimism of modern culture had not prepared us, and we are consequently threatened by despair and the sense of the meaninglessness of life. Our perils are most obvious and most immediate in the first dimension and least so in the third: but the perils in the third dimension may be ultimately the most serious.

Perhaps it may seem foolish to speak of moral or religious resources for overcoming the peril in the first dimension. We face a truculent and ruthless foe, who is probably not as intent upon world dominion as some people imagine but who is certainly driven by peculiar dogmas and by a probable inferiority complex to defend himself against fancied or real enemies by re-

[1]Delivered at the *New York Herald Tribune*'s 16th annual forum, in New York, New York, on October 21, 1947. 

jecting every offer of cooperation and by stirring up as much confusion in the world community as possible.

It would seem that what is required to meet such a foe is not some great resource of imagination but simply common sense: the common sense which counsels us to be well armed and not to allow the foe to gain the strategic advantages in any part of the world which might prompt him to risk a martial adventure against us. But though the bitter experiences of the last decade have taught us that power is inevitably a factor in international relations, we would lack wisdom if we followed these precepts of common sense alone.

The defense of a civilization requires military strategy but it also requires political and moral strategy. The best political strategy is prompted not so much by ordinary common sense as by humility—if you will, by religious humility. We call our civilization a democratic one and believe it worth defending. And so it is. But no civilization is as just, and no cause is as persuasive as it seems to its defenders and proponents. Our business is to make our cause more deserving of defense, even though we must defend it strategically without reference to its virtues but because it is ours.

This is particularly true in facing a great center of power, a nation which has become a holy land of a secular religion. To millions of devotees, including many in our Western world, Russia has falsely become a fixed point of international virtue. This is a highly implausible faith. It is made the more implausible by the fact that this holy land seems increasingly involved in every kind of political chicane and skulduggery which we once attributed only to Nazi tyrants. The fact that millions should still hold to this faith must be partly attributed to generosity of the dream of a classless and just society which originally animated the Marxist cause.

Modern communism is a corruption of utopianism and is thus different in principle from the moral cynicism of Nazism. We are therefore in a more difficult ideological battle than when we engaged the Nazis. It is a battle which we cannot win among the impoverished and insecure people of Europe and of Asia if we do not make it clearer than we have done that we stand for freedom and justice, and not for the preservation of privilege. To win the ideological battle against communism it is not enough to point to the crass corruptions of the original dream of justice which we see in the police states of Eastern Europe. It is more important to make our cause so just that it will win the allegiance not of the comfortable but of the insecure and the impoverished.

It is particularly important that America, as the most powerful and wealthiest of the nations in the Western World, should acquire a higher degree of humility. Without it we will insist upon political creeds and political forms which Europe regards not as the creed of democracy but as the characteristic prejudice of a very wealthy nation. Europe is a vast ideological middle ground between communism and American libertarianism. We are quite wrong if we think that it does not cherish freedom as much as we do.

But it needs economic security more desperately than we. Its creeds are colored by that fact even as our creeds are colored by the fabulous character of our productivity and our immediate, though not ultimate, lack of anxiety about economic security. Without the humility and the imagination to think beyond the characteristic prejudices of American life we cannot win the ideological battle against communism.

But even if the world's hopes had not been frustrated by the irrelevancies and the truculence which the Communist creed has introduced into our situation, we still would have been in a world crisis. For there is another dimension of the crisis. A technical civilization has produced a potential world community, but not an actual one. There would be great centers of power in the world not easily brought under the dominion of a law higher than their own will, even without this conflict between a Communist and capitalist, a totalitarian and a democratic world. Even if we survive the present tensions we will face for decades the problem of achieving moral strength and political imagination to bring moral and political order in a world now related only by technics.

Our immediate perils tempt us to forget our more ultimate danger, caused not by Russian policy but by the inability of all nations and peoples to face new responsibilities. By clinging to ancient securities they make themselves increasingly insecure in a new situation. It is a tragic aspect of human history that men learn so little from the lessons of history. They are, as one of the prophets observed, wounded by the Divine Judge but they do not grieve; they are consumed but they will not receive correction.

An adequate faith for such a day as this must be a faith which induces repentance on the part of all nations and all peoples; and a consequent readiness to sacrifice any privilege or prestige, incompatible with community on the new and wider level of human community. No dreams of world constitutions or contrivances of international law will avail if there is not a wider and more resolute will to achieve world community than is now apparent.

The first and the second level of the world crisis—the peril in which a democratic civilization stands and in which civilization as such stands—engage the minds of our generation. These perils are obvious and immediate. I should like to suggest, however, that there is a third level or dimension of the crisis which is not so obvious but which may be more important than the others. It is the crisis in our culture caused by the fact that the faith of modern man has not prepared him for the tragedies which he experiences and does not help him to interpret his urgent tasks as meaningful.

Our culture has been dominated by one idea: the idea that history would solve all our problems. We hoped that historical growth and development would eliminate methods of force and bring all politics under the dominion of reason; that it would bring victory to democracy everywhere and eliminate tyranny; that it would abolish poverty and injustice; and that it would move inevitably toward a parliament of mankind and a federation of the world. These are false hopes.

Contemporary experience proves that history creates as many problems as it solves by creating human power and freedom. A technical civilization created a vast interdependence of nations but not a world brotherhood or even world community. It did not abolish methods of force but ushered in total wars, engaging the total resources of nations. It did not insure man's increasing security. Rather it transmuted the perils of nature into perils of history and society. It made us safer against death by epidemic and less safe against death by atomic destruction. It did not gradually change our position from that of slavery to historical process to mastery over our own destiny. We remain now, as we have always been, both masters and tools of history. We are moved by forces vaster than our own power and are yet called upon to make fateful decisions.

It is because we had so completely miscalculated the character of human history that we are so frequently threatened by despair in this day of frustration and disappointed hopes. We fear atomic destruction partly because it is a great peril but also because it is the old peril of death in a new form. We thought we had banished the peril of death. We are driven to despair because the last war did not result in a stable peace, because we falsely thought that every task had to be justified by some completely new tomorrow. But no tomorrow is ever completely new. We must learn all over again not only that "sufficient unto the day are the evils thereof" but also the duties thereof and the hopes thereof also. We must learn to exploit the qualitative meaning of our duties and tasks today without too much regard for what tomorrow may bring forth.

We are driven to despair because we cannot build out of hand the kind of stable world we desire, having discovered that recalcitrant forces in history stand against our will and our purposes. We must again acquire a faith which finds meaning in human life, even though no person or generation ever has the power to complete the ideal meaning of life. Our modern culture moved from a too simple optimism to a too deep despair: This cultural and religious confusion is dangerous for us, even on the lower levels of the crisis, because the distraction of alternate moods of unjustified hopes and unjustified pessimism prevent us from doing our duties amidst the pressing and urgent tasks of today.

An adequate faith for a day of crisis will contain what modern men have completely dismissed, namely, a tragic sense of life and a recognition of the Cross as the final center of life's meaning. The Scripture describes the works of the night, as those of sleep and drunkenness: "They that sleep, sleep in the night and they that be drunken are drunken in the night." Let us who are of the day watch and be sober. We cannot afford either the sleep of complacency or the drunkenness of hysteria. We must watch and be sober. But this watchfulness and sobriety is the fruit of a profounder sense of the meaning of our existence, than any of the credos which have recently guided us. A much more modest estimate of human power and of human virtue might bring us nearer and quicker to the goal of a tolerable peace and a sufferable world order for all nations.

Finally, we had hoped that it was a fairly simple matter to achieve a universal culture or a universal religion as the basis of a universal community. Now we realize that the universal community remains full of partial and particular elements. It is characterized by differences in political, moral, and religious ideas. There is no possibility of achieving complete unity or identity of conviction. We must learn therefore that community with our fellow men and other nations requires not so much a common culture as a recognition of the partial and particular character of our truth and our interest.

A religion adequate for community building on a world scale must cease to identify God with any particular culture or civilization, but sense, as the prophets of Israel did, that the judgment of God stands over all nations and that His mercy is available to all who are moved by that judgment. We can achieve accord with our fellow men in the proportion in which we recognize that both they and we hold facets of the truth and are loyal to aspects of justice imperfectly.

The wide variety of human aspirations is an old fact. We now face it in the new dimension of a world community. Every form of fanaticism has achieved new proportion of evil in this wider dimension. Religious forbearance of our fellow men has become even more urgent than when the words were spoken, "Let us judge not that we be not judged."

# Loneliness and Solitude[2]

## Paul J. Tillich

*Born August 20, 1886, Starzeddel, Kreis Guben, Prussia; died October 22, 1965; Ph.D., University of Breslau, 1911; Th.D., University of Halle, 1926; chaplain, German Army, 1914-18; professor, University of Marburg, 1924-25; professor, University of Dresden, 1925-29; professor, Leipzig University, 1928-29; professor, University of Frankfurt, 1929-33; ordained, Evangelical Lutheran Church, 1932; lecturer, Union Theological Seminary, 1933-54; professor, Harvard Divinity School, 1955-62; professor, University of Chicago, 1962-65; author,* The Interpretation of History *(1936),* The Protestant Era *(1948),* The Shaking of the Foundations *(1948),* The Courage to Be *(1952),* Love, Power, and Justice *(1954),* The New Being *(1955),* Dynamics of Faith *(1957),* Systematic Theology *(1963).*

### Editor's introduction

In this speech, Paul J. Tillich, professor of Theology at the Harvard Divinity School and considered the "most discussed Protestant theologian" of his age (*Time*, June 10, 1957), addressed the subject of loneliness. Within solitude, Tillich argued, we are able to "penetrate into the limits, where the mystery of life appears." Citing solitude as a universal condition of all nature, Tillich believed that it can be a rewarding and rich opportunity if we use it as a time to look inside ourselves and come to a greater understanding of the potential that lays within us all.

---

"He was there, alone" . . . so are we. Man is alone, because he is man! In some way every creature is alone. In majestic isolation each star travels through the darkness of endless space. Every tree grows according to its own law, fulfilling its unique possibilities. Animals live, fight and die for themselves, caught in the limits of their bodies. Certainly, they appear as male and female, in families, in flocks. Some of them are gregarious. But all of them are alone! Being alive means being in a body—a body separated from all other bodies. And being separated means being alone.

This is true of every creature, and it is true of man more than of any other creature. He is not only alone, he also *knows* that he is alone. Aware of what he is, he therefore asks the question of his aloneness. He asks why he is alone and how he can overcome his being alone. He cannot stand it; but he cannot escape it either. It is his destiny to be alone and to be aware of it. Not even God can take away this destiny from him.

In the paradise story we read: "Then the Lord God said, It is not good that man should be alone." And he creates the woman from the body of Adam. An old myth is used showing that originally there was no bodily separation between man and woman. In the beginning they were one; now they are longing to be one again. But although they recognize each other as flesh from their own flesh, each remains alone. They look at each other and although longing for each other, they see their strangeness. In the story God himself makes them aware of this when he speaks to each of them separately, when he makes them responsible each for his own guilt, when he listens to their excuses and mutual accusations, when he pronounces a different curse over each of them and leaves them to the experience of shame in face of their nakedness. They are alone. The creation of the woman has not conquered the situation which God describes as not good for man. He remains alone, and the creation of the woman, although providing a helper for Adam, has only added to the one human being who is alone another hu-

[2]Delivered to the Federated Theological Faculty, at the University of Chicago, in Chicago, Illinois, on January 6, 1957.

man being who is equally alone, and out of them all the others each of whom is also alone.

But is that really so, we ask? Did not God do better than that? Is our aloneness not largely removed in the encounter of the sexes? Certainly it is for hours of communion and moments of love. The ecstasy of love can absorb one's own self in its union with the other self. Separation seems to be overcome. But after such moments the isolation of self from self is more deeply felt than before, even to the point of repulsion. We have given too much of ourselves and now we want to take it back. An expression of our desire to protect our aloneness is the feeling of shame. We are ashamed if our intimate self is opened, mentally as well as bodily. We try to cover our nakedness as Adam and Eve did after they had become conscious of themselves. Man and woman remain alone even in the most intimate union. They cannot penetrate each other's innermost center. If this were not so, they could not be helpers to each other; they could not have human community.

And this is the answer to the question of why God himself could not liberate man from his aloneness: It is man's greatness that he is centered within himself. He is separated from his world and able to look at it. Only because this is so can he know the world and love it and transform it. God, making him the ruler of the earth, has to separate him and put him into aloneness. Therefore, man can be spoken to by God and by man; therefore, man can ask questions, give answers and make decisions. Therefore, he has the freedom for good and evil. Only he who is alone can claim to be a man. This is the greatness and this is the burden of man.

The wisdom of our language has sensed these two sides of man's being alone. It has created the word loneliness in order to emphasize the pain of being alone. And it has created the word solitude in order to emphasize the glory of being alone. In daily life these words are not always distinguished; but we should do so consistently, thus deepening the understanding of our human predicament.

In the Twenty-fifth Psalm we read: "Turn thou to me and be gracious; for I am lonely and afflicted." The psalmist feels the pain of loneliness. We do not know the character of *his* loneliness but we know about the many facets our loneliness can have. We all have experienced some of them.

Most widespread is the feeling of loneliness when those who helped us to forget that we are alone leave us, be it by separation, be it by death. This refers not only to those who are nearest to us, but also to the groups which gave us the feeling of communion, groups with which we worked, groups with which we had social contact, groups with which we had spiritual communication. For many people, such loneliness has become a permanent state and a continuous source of melancholy feeling and profound unhappiness. The sighing of numberless lonely people all over the world and in our nearest neighborhood fills those ears which are opened by love.

And now let us turn to those among us who are surrounded by friends and neighbors, by coworkers and co-citizens, who live in a family group and have the communion of the sexes—all that the others do *not* have! And here we ask: Are they without the pain of loneliness? Is their aloneness covered up by the crowd within which they move? Perhaps this is our own situation and we may be able to give an answer to this question. And this might be our answer: I never felt so lonely as in a particular hour when I was surrounded by people and suddenly realized my ultimate isolation. And I became silent, I retired into a corner and left the group in order to be alone with my loneliness. I wanted my external predicament to match my internal one. Do not minimize such an experience by saying that people often do not feel strong enough to obtain a significant place with a group and that their withdrawal is nothing but an expression of their weakness calling for counseling or psychiatric help. Such people certainly do exist in large numbers, and they need help. But I am speaking of the strong ones who have their place within the crowd and who nevertheless have this terrifying experience of ultimate loneliness. They are aware in a sudden breakthrough of man's real predicament. Do not minimize such an experience by saying that people often feel misunderstood in spite of their urgent desire to make themselves understandable; and that this gives them the feeling of loneliness in the crowd. No one can deny that there are such people and even more, that they are not altogether wrong; for who is really understood, even by himself? The mystery of a person cannot be dissolved into a neat description of his character. But those who feel always misunderstood confuse the mystery of every person with imaginary treasures they believe they possess within themselves demanding of others that they recognize them. But the others don't, and so they feel lonely and withdraw. They also need help; but let us instead consider those people whose real treasures are great enough to find expression and who are understood and received, but who nevertheless have the terrifying experience of ultimate loneliness. In such moments they break through the surface of their average life into the depth of man's predicament.

Many feel lonely because their love is rejected, although they try hard to love and to be loved. Often this loneliness is self-created. There are people who claim as their right what only can come to them as a gift. They withdraw into a self-chosen loneliness, taking revenge through bitterness and hostility upon those by whom they feel rejected, enjoying at the same time the pain of their loneliness. There are many such persons and they greatly contribute to the growth of neurotic loneliness in our days. They, above all, need help; for they easily become the prey of a demonic force which keeps them completely secluded within themselves. There is also the genuine experience of rejected love. No claim was made, but hope was at work. And the hope was disappointed. A community of love came to an end or never came into existence. Such loneliness cuts the ties with our world, it becomes manifest that we are ultimately alone, and that even love cannot take this burden from us. He who can stand the loneliness of disappointed love without bitterness has experienced the depths of man's predicament in a most radical and creative way.

There are two forms of loneliness which do not permit any cover or any escape: the loneliness of guilt and the loneliness of death. Nobody can take from us what we have done against our true being. We feel our hidden and open guilt as *ours*, and ours *alone*. We cannot make anybody else responsible for what has happened through us. We cannot run away from our guilt, we cannot honestly cover it up. We are alone with it; and it is this loneliness which permeates all other forms of loneliness, transforming them into experiences of judgment.

Above all, this is true of the loneliness in which we have to die. We remain alone in the anticipation of our death. No communication with others can remove this loneliness, as no presence of others in the actual hour of our dying can hide the fact that it is *our* death, and *our* death *alone*, that we die. In the hour of death we are cut off from the whole universe and everything in it. We are deprived of all things in the encounter in which we forgot our being alone. Who can stand this loneliness?

Loneliness can be conquered only by those who can bear solitude. We have a natural desire for solitude because we are men; we want to feel what we are, namely alone, not as a matter of pain and horror, but as a matter of joy and courage. There are many ways in which solitude can be sought and experienced. And every way is that of "religion"—if it is true what a philosopher has said, that "religion is what a man does with his solitariness."

One of these ways is the desire for the silence of nature. Here we can speak without voice to the trees and the clouds and the waves of the ocean. They answer without words in the rustling of the leaves and the moving of the clouds and the murmuring of the waves. This can be solitude. But only for a brief time. Then we realize: the voices of nature have no answer to the questions of our mind. Our solitude in nature easily becomes loneliness, and we return to the world of man.

Solitude can be found in the reading of a poem, the hearing of music, the seeing of a picture, the thinking of significant thoughts. We are alone, perhaps in the midst of multitudes, but we are not lonely. Solitude protects us like an armor without isolating us. But life calls us back to its empty talk, its unavoidable demands, its daily routine, its loneliness and the cover it spreads over our loneliness.

There can be no doubt: this is not only a description of man's general predicament. It is also, and emphatically so, a description of our time. Today more than in preceding periods man is so lonely that he cannot bear solitude. So he tries to become a part of the crowd. And everything in our day supports him. It is a symptom of our disease that everything is done by teachers and parents and the managers of public communication to deprive us more and more of the external conditions for solitude, the simplest aids to privacy. Even our houses, instead of protecting the solitude of every member of the family or the group, are built in such a way that privacy is almost excluded. And the same holds true of the forms of communal life in school, college, office and factory. A never-ceasing pressure tries to kill even our desire for solitude.

But sometimes God pushes us out of the crowd into a solitude which we did not desire, but which takes hold of us. As the prophet Jeremiah says: "I sit alone, because thy hand was upon me." God sometimes lays hands upon us. He wants us to ask the question of truth which may isolate us from most men, and which can be asked only in solitude. He wants us to ask the question of justice which may bring us suffering and death, and which can grow in us only in solitude. He wants us to break through the ordinary ways of man which may bring disrepute and hate upon us, a break-through which can happen only in solitude. He wants us to penetrate to the limits of our being, where the mystery of life appears, and it can appear only in the moments of solitude.

There are some among you who want to become creative in some realm of life. You cannot become and cannot remain creative without solitude. One hour in conscious solitude does more for your creativity than many hours of learning how to become creative.

What is it that happens when we are in solitude? Let us hear the few words of Mark about Jesus' solitude in the desert: "And he was in the wilderness forty days, tempted by Satan; and he was with the wild beasts, and the angels ministered to him!" He is alone, facing earth and sky, the wild beasts around him and in him, he himself the battlefield of divine and demonic forces. This is what first of all happens in our solitude. We meet ourselves, not as ourselves, but as the battlefield of creation and destruction, of God and the demons. Solitude is not easy. Who can bear it? It is not easy even for Jesus. We read: "He went up into the hills to pray. When evening came, he was there alone." When evening comes, loneliness becomes more lonely. We feel this when a single day, or a period, or all the days of our life come to an end. Jesus went up to pray. Is this the way to transform loneliness into solitude and to stand solitude? We should not answer this question too easily. Most prayers have not such power. They make God into the partner of a conversation, useful in *preventing* the only true way to solitude. They go easily from the mouth of ministers or laymen. But they are not born out of a solitary encounter of God with man. This certainly is not the prayer for which Jesus went up to the hills. We had better remain silent and let our soul, which is always longing for solitude, sigh without words to God. And this all of us can do even in a crowded day and in a crowded room, even under most difficult external conditions; this can give us moments of solitude which nobody can take from us.

In the moments of solitude something is done to us. The center of our being, the inner self which is the ground of our aloneness, is elevated to the divine center and taken into it. Therein we can rest without losing ourselves.

And now we have reached the point where we can answer a question which you may have already asked: how can communion grow out of solitude? We have seen that we can never reach the innermost center of another being. We always are alone, each for himself. But we can reach it in a movement which rises first to God and then returns from him to the other self. In this way man's aloneness is not removed but taken into the community with that in which the centers of all beings are resting, and so into a community with all of them. Even love is reborn in solitude. For only in solitude are those who are alone able to reach those from whom they are separated. Only the presence of the eternal can break through the walls which isolate the temporal from the temporal. In one hour of solitude we may be nearer to those we love than in many hours of communication. We take them with us to the hills of eternity.

And perhaps if we ask what is the innermost nature of solitude, we should answer: It is the presence of the eternal upon the crowded roads of the temporal. It is the experience of being alone but not lonely, in view of the eternal presence which shines through the face of the Christ and which includes everybody and everything from which we are separated. In the poverty of solitude, all riches are present. Let us dare to have solitude: to face the eternal, to find others, to see ourselves. Amen.

# Four Philosophies of Modern Life[3]

Charles E. Shulman

*Born July 25, 1900, Ukraine; died June 3, 1968; LL.B., Ohio Northern University, 1920; LL.B., University of Cincinnati, 1922-23; Ph.B., 1924, A.M., 1927, University of Chicago; lawyer, New York Central railroad, 1920; lawyer, Santa Fe railroad, 1921; rabbi, Johnston, PA, 1926-27; rabbi, Wheeling, WV, 1927-31; rabbi, Glencoe, IL, 1931-47; U.S. Navy, 1943-47; rabbi, Riverdale Temple, 1947-68; author,* The Problems of Jews in the Contemporary World *(1934),* Europe's Conscience in Decline *(1939),* The Test of Civilization *(1947).*

## Editor's introduction

Charles E. Shulman, former rabbi of the Riverdale Temple in New York City, discussed cynicism, nihilism, materialism, and idealism as the "four philosophies of modern life." In order to achieve the inner "peace" he believed the modern age so desperately seeks, Shulman advocated reinvigorating a philosophy of idealism, or a belief in the innate potential of human beings. Shulman also asserted that we must take our focus away from simple material concerns and begin to understand the value of those less tangible but fundamentally important aspects of existence, which include spiritual well-being and peace of mind.

---

This period of world's history which the poet W. H. Auden has called "The Age of Anxiety" has had its effects upon American citizens. We cannot live in a world of confusion and tension without being disturbed by the course of events. Some of the effects on Americans indicate that they may have forgotten the paths their fathers trod in the search for adequate living. They are seen in the things we value, in the thinking we do, in the manner in which we view our world, in the purpose or lack of purpose in our lives, in the kind of gods we serve, in the way we face the nations across the seas.

We do not lack bread in America. Nor shelter. Nor comfort. Our standard of living is the highest in the world. Our basic problem in these times is not economic—not when over sixty million Americans are employed and our national income is well over four hundred billion dollars annually; not when business flourishes and trade unions are firmly established and respected. These signs of well being are physical ones. They might be called evidence of the quantitative character of our American civilization. But these external symbols of national development cannot hide some of our present deficiencies. The richer we get the more tense we become, the more insecure we feel. Here we are, wealthier than ever before, more powerful than ever before, yet we devote less and less of our great wealth and concern to public welfare. Our national income rises, our stores are filled with gadgets and staples of life, our consumer goods are enormous in quantity. But our schools are more crowded and dilapidated. Our teachers are more weary and underpaid. Our playgrounds are more jammed and dirty. Our national parks are more neglected. Our law enforcement bodies are more overworked. And we wonder why we have more prejudice, more selfishness, more juvenile delinquency than formerly.

We have physical abundance—houses, automobiles, televisions and frozen foods to suit every conceivable taste. But our spiritual problem is greater than it was a generation ago. We are desperately looking for peace of mind, peace of soul, peace of heart and peace of all else; we are buying popular religious books by the thousands to give us the inner security we so badly need. We definitely need to better the quality of our lives to match our physical quantitative

[3]Delivered to the Ad-Sell League, in Omaha, Nebraska, on February 5, 1957.

blessedness and to teach us how better to use our gadgets of the new atomic age. We need aid of the kind that will help us be a noble influence for freedom and justice and decency both in our wonderful country and in lands abroad. It is high time that we went beyond the necessities of living which our national abundance offers us so well, beyond the physical preoccupation with a job, a square meal, a new suit of clothes, an automobile and a house in the suburbs, and thought some about individual dignity and individual character in our society in this period when we tend to become indifferent to our neighbors' existence. It is time we added some vision to our life, that we remember clearly that where there is no vision the people perish.

Our real problem in this period of physical change in our living due to wonder drugs and airplanes that fly fifteen hundred miles an hour and television and hydrogen bombs in a shrunken world is to know what to do with what we have, to help others to live so that this abundant physical life may be shared more, to emphasize the things of the spirit that have been so greatly neglected in recent years, to turn our minds to the primary purpose of our existence, to develop individual and national character. We must think more about such things as education and religion which stress intelligent and noble living and turn our gaze on such individual and social needs as more equal opportunities for minority groups, better planning for our cities and suburbs, slum clearance, decent housing, improvement of life for the sick and the aged, a sense of justice toward people abroad who long for the good life we possess and the necessity of helping democracy in other places on earth. Let us face up to our responsibilities as free people. Our treatment of the Negro in this country must sooner or later honor the decisions of our own Supreme Court of the United States if we are to survive as a nation. Our concern for the freedom of Jewish people in the state of Israel must be as important as our respect for the income from Arabian oil and Arabian dictators who purchase arms from the Soviet Communists for war purposes that could conceivably be turned against us. Our interest in Asia must be governed by more enlightened policies than pure trade and commerce if we are to have the good will of the people of India and Indonesia and others who can be our friends and allies in making this earth a free world.

If we concentrate only on the material things, if we persist in thinking only of the quantitative factors of our national life that give us physical comfort and pleasure we will forget the warning that one of America's distinguished poets, the late Stephen Vincent Benét, uttered a few years ago:

"You will not be saved by General Motors
You will not be saved by prefabricated houses
You will not be saved by dialectic materialism
You will not be saved by the Lambeth Conference
You will not be saved by Vitamin D
You will not be saved by the expanding universe
In fact you will not be saved!"

There are four philosophies in our time followed by men. One of them is cynicism. One is nihilism. One is materialism. And one is idealism. In our brief survey of these philosophies we may be able to see more clearly the causes that underlie some of the confusions and tensions of the day.

1. The philosophy of cynicism is tied to an ancient group called the Cyrenaics, founded by the Greek philosopher Aristippus of Cyrene. Their course was called hedonism—self-indulgence. The end and aim of existence of such people is pleasure. They are indifferent to their neighbors, indifferent to their civic duties, indifferent to world events. Their religion is one of comfort. Their attachment to any cause is only in terms of their own convenience. As free men they will exercise the ballot on election day if it is not raining or if it is comfortable for them to do so. They are not aroused by the social ills of their time. They put their faith in gadgets and more gadgets. Of such people a clergyman, the Reverend Edward Ziegler of Roanoke, Virginia, thought when he rewrote the Twenty-third Psalm in terms of the gadgets of our day (cynic's version):

"Science is my shepherd
I shall not want
He maketh me to lie down on foam rubber mattresses
He leadeth me beside six-lane highways
He rejuvenateth my thyroid glands
He leadeth me in the paths of psychoanalysis
For peace of mind's sake.
Yea, though I walk through the valley
Of the shadow of the Iron Curtain

I will fear no Communist for thou art with me.
Thou preparest a banquet for me
In the presence of the world's billion hungry people.
Thou anointest my head with home permanents
My beer glass foameth over
Surely prosperity and pleasure shall follow me all the days of my life
And I will dwell in Shangri-la forever."

2. The philosophy of nihilism. This is a philosophy of power leading nowhere socially or politically. There are individuals who live and dream of naked power for its own sake. They constitute one of the problems of our time because of the shrunken character of the world. And they vitally affect our life and thinking in America because of the instability they can create in the life of peoples. We fought World War II because of this philosophy in Germany under Hitler and Italy under Mussolini and Japan under Tojo. If you would appreciate the consequences of this dreadful philosophy when it assumes authority you can find it in Norman Cousins' evaluation of Hitler's book *Mein Kampf* which was the Bible of Nazi Germany. Cousins tells us that for every word in that book 125 lives were lost in the world. For every page in that book 4,700 lives were lost. And for every chapter in that book 1.2 million lives were lost.

We are witnessing the recrudescence of this philosophy of nihilism in Egypt ruled by a handsome young power-driven dictator, Gamal Nasser, and the dictators of the Arab states who are in league with him. How else can we judge the cynical course of these Arab nations in the Middle East whose rulers turn one face toward the oppressed and illiterate masses and tell them that Communist Russia is their only friend because it is supplying millions of dollars' worth of arms with which to destroy the young state of Israel, who spend millions of dollars of the royalties for oil paid them by the Arabian American Oil Company to set up antidemocratic and anti-Semitic propaganda agencies in the United States accusing my people of double loyalties in their American citizenship because they sympathize with their brethren in the state of Israel and help them in their needs and guide them in their difficulties? The second face these Arab dictators turn to America and to the free world and piously claim that they have bought arms from the Communists to protect themselves against the tiny state of Israel. But if you make a pact with the devil you will not easily escape from the clutches of the devil. Communist Russia does not grant favors without demanding something in return. And the Arabs with their philosophy of Nihilism enjoying their power and their new toys of destruction will awake one day to find they are puppets of Soviet Russia.

3. The philosophy of materialism. This is the twisted heritage of Karl Marx that today rules half the population of the earth—in Russia and its satellites in China, in Indo-China, in parts of France, and Italy, in North Africa and in the Mediterranean. What is it that Marxism stands for?

Its philosophy is that the history of all existing society in the world is the history of class struggles, freeman and slave, patrician and plebeian, lord and serf, guild master and journeyman, oppressor and oppressed—all carry on perpetual warfare. Also: the production of the immediate requisite material means of existence and therewith the extant economic development phase of a nation or an epoch constitutes the foundation upon which the state institutions, the legal outlooks, the artistic, even the religious ideas of those concerned have been built up.

The trouble with this philosophy is that it fails to account for the obvious differences between people which are in the same stage of economic development. It leaves out of account such vital factors as race, religion and nationality. It does not reckon with the vast importance of human personality. It is doubtful whether a single historical event could be interpreted in terms of this theory.

But this philosophy of materialism has been buttressed by dictatorship and slavery and oppression and cruelty and violence and bloodshed. The state as an octopus has swallowed the individual. The dictator is supreme. The few rule the overwhelming majority and the majority is silenced. The whims of the dictator prevail. One day it is Lenin. Another day it is Stalin. Today it is Khrushchev.

We have learned a great deal about the way in which this philosophy is forced upon people from above. The silent masses can do little about it without suffering torture and death. The dictators will not brook questioning of their course of conduct. When Khrushchev was challenged by the British labor people during his visit to England to release the prisoners who differ with him he grew furious and told the English people to mind their own business. The American Protestant mission of churchmen who just returned from Russia reported to their fellow Americans that the antireligious campaign is not quite as crude as it was twenty years ago, that Mr. Khrushchev has just issued a directive to the Communists stressing the importance of using more subtle means of oppression against all religion in the country. And like the smiles of Khrushchev and Bulganin in their meetings with Western leaders this policy of deceit is all the more dangerous than outright hostility. And now these godless Communists who are so cruel and intolerant of the religions of men are posing as the protectors of the religion of the Arabs, the religion of Mohammedanism in the Near East.

We have a way of measuring the success of the materialistic philosophy of communism as it is practiced by the dictators who rule with an iron hand. That way is through the stories that filter out of the Iron Curtain from time to time. One of them used to be told about the Fascists in the thirties. It tells about Khrushchev coming to a movie and sitting incognito in the back row. Suddenly his picture was flashed on the screen and everyone stood up in salute. Khrushchev sat back enjoying the scene when an usher tapped him on the back and whispered ominously: "Listen, you'd better get up too. I don't like him any better than you do. But better get up. It's safer." Another story concerns the school teachers in Soviet-dominated lands. They have had to postpone the history examinations in all schools and colleges because they won't know the correct answers for a while. Still a third one concerns the classroom where each child was given a picture of Prime Minister Bulganin and told to take it home and hang it in a corner of her home. The next day a little girl appeared with the picture. She had brought it back. "What's the matter?" asked the teacher. "Don't you like Bulganin?" "Oh yes," she answered, "I like Bulganin, but we don't have any corner in our room. We live in the middle of the room." A fourth story concerns a new jet plane that transported a citizen in Russia from Pinsk to Minsk in four minutes thirty-two seconds. The citizen was overwhelmed. He rushed to the home of his friend in Minsk and cried: "What a nation Russia is? What a government! Not only the greatest constitution, the greatest leader, the greatest army, but now we have a wonderful plane that brought me here from Pinsk in less than five minutes!" The friend refused to be impressed. "So you got here from Pinsk in less than five minutes. What good did it do you?" "What good? It enabled me to be the first in line to buy a pack of matches!"

4. The philosophy of idealism. It is the philosophy of the potential in each human being as an individual. It is the philosophy on which this nation, America, was founded and built. Thank God it still prevails in our midst as a guide to us and our children in days to come. So much has been said and written about American shrewdness and inventiveness, American concentration on material things, that it would be good to weigh our national achievements in our brief history on the scales of their true merit.

In the year 1897 Dr. Charles Eliot of Harvard University, one of our truly great educators and the originator of the famous five foot bookshelf of Harvard classics, spoke on America's five great contributions to civilization. He pointed out that under our philosophy of idealism property has never been safer in any form of government, that no people have ever welcomed so ardently the new machinery and new inventions generally, that religious toleration was never carried so far and so universally, that nowhere have the power and disposition to learn been so general, that nowhere has government power been more adequate or more freely exercised to levy and collect taxes, to raise armies and to disband them, to maintain public order, to pay off great public debts—national, state and town, that nowhere has property been so widely diffused, that no form of government has ever inspired greater affection and loyalty or prompted to greater personal sacrifices in supreme moments. This is essentially true of America and American idealism . . . .

America's philosophy of idealism has guided our inventions and our free enterprise. America's moral aspiration has touched and inspired the peoples of the world in days past. We must not forget this as we contemplate our present-day association with the nations of the world—the people who are still free and who look to us as examples of the kind of free men and women they would like to follow if given the opportunity. We must help the world to know better what America stands for. The defense of this great nation, as Norman Cousins has reminded us in a stirring editorial in the *Saturday Review of Literature*, rests today as it did all along, not on arms, but on what we stand for in the world. The first front is the moral front. What other people see when they look at America. The kind of hope that comes to life at the mention of our name. The crisp conception of justice inside America and in our dealings as a nation; any ideas we may have about the pooling of sovereignty in the creation of effective world law—all this is what counts. Military preparedness without it is motion without action.

When we become weary of things, confused by the conflicting philosophies of our time, when we wonder about the future of democracy in a world of such disintegration and tension and change it would do us good to read our immortal American documents once more. Among these is the Constitution of the United States and its famous preamble which says:

"We the people of the United States, in order to form a more perfect union, establish justice, insure domestic tranquillity, provide for the common defense, promote the general welfare, and secure the blessings of liberty to ourselves and our posterity, do ordain and establish this Constitution for the United States of America."

The philosophies of cynicism and nihilism and materialism ignore the general welfare. Our problem today and tomorrow is to revive strongly in this nation the conception of the general welfare, a conception that has tided us over many wars and crises in the nearly two centuries of our existence. It was dear to the Founding Fathers of this Republic. It is indelibly stamped in the preamble to the Constitution of this nation. It teaches us under this general welfare clause we have developed from small colonies to the greatest power on earth. But we must heed its instruction. We cannot expect equality abroad to be taught by us if we restrict equality at home. We cannot expect to teach others the blessings of opportunity if we deny it at home. We cannot export democracy elsewhere unless it functions here at home. We must have a fighting faith in our philosophy of idealism as did those who preceded us on these shores. And in God's time that faith will kindle a flame that will light up the fires of democracy everywhere on earth.

# Our Bicentennial[4]

Billy Graham

*Born 1918, Charlotte, NC; Th.B., Florida Bible Seminary, 1940; B.A., Wheaton College, 1943; ordained, Southern Baptist Convention, 1939; minister, First Baptist Church, 1943-45; evangelist, 1944–; vice president, Youth for Christ, 1945-48; president, Northwestern College, 1948-52; founder, president, Billy Graham Evangelistic Association, 1963–; author,* Revival in Our Times *(1950),* America's Hour of Decision *(1951),* Peace Aflame *(1965),* The Challenge *(1969),* The Jesus Generation (1971), Approaching Hoofbeats *(1983),* Till Armageddon *(1983),* A Biblical Standard for Evangelists *(1984),* The Secret of Happiness *(1985),* Facing Death and the Life After *(1987),* Hope for the Troubled Heart *(1992),* Storm Warning *(1992),* Unto the Hills *(1993),* The Faithful Christian *(1994),* Angels *(1994),* Breakfast with Billy Graham *(1996),* Just as I Am *(1997).*

## Editor's introduction

Since 1944, the Reverend Billy Graham has evangelized to audiences worldwide, both in person and via radio and television. Perhaps the most respected and popular Christian evangelist of his day, in this address, Graham, having recently returned from a preaching tour in Asia, the Middle East, and Europe, expressed a kind of outsider's astonishment at what he perceived to be a breakdown in the American values system. Although America enjoys unprecedented economic power, Graham noted that the nation also "leads the world in crime, narcotics abuse, pornography, immorality, and even debts." Recalling the religious influences which have shaped the United States since early times, and helped forge such documents as the Declaration of Independence and the Constitution, Graham advocated recalling those inspirations and bringing God back into the political sphere.

---

Good evening!

I have just returned from a three-month trip around the world that took me through Asia, various countries in the Middle East and Europe. I have talked with church leaders, political leaders, educators, and military leaders. I visited with a number of heads of state. I wish that every American could have been with me on this trip. It has been an eye opener! For example, someone has said that if you haven't been in Asia in the last six months you don't know Asia. The world is changing so rapidly that I hardly know it anymore.

At midnight we enter 1976, the year of our two hundredth birthday, with a paradox of moods on the part of the American people. On the one hand, many are excited, thrilled, and optimistic about the next year. On the other hand, as a news magazine says, "Americans are in a bitter and fearful mood." There is no doubt that many are confused, discouraged, cynical, afraid, and disillusioned—with our scientists warning us of an all-out atomic war before the end of the century.

While we Americans will be glued to our television screens tomorrow watching the football games, the rest of the world is reeling and rocking from crisis to crisis. Dangerous explosions are almost everywhere. We are on the edge of a precipice. One newspaper reports that over twenty-five wars have been fought this past year or are now being fought. Most of them do not make the headlines, but people are being wounded and killed. When I hear so much talk of peace, I am reminded of what God said through Jeremiah to the false prophets of his day. God said they were "shouting peace, peace, when there is no peace." The Psalmist

[4]Broadcast nationwide, on December 31, 1975. 

warned about dealing with those whose words are smoother than butter—those who say, "I am for peace," but . . . are for war. Let's face it. There has never been so much talk of peace, nor such a preparation for war as there is today.

Here at home many of our problems are getting worse with every passing day. The crime rate jumped faster than any other year in history. Drug addiction continues to soar as stronger drugs arrive daily by the planeload. Massive debts threaten some of our major cities with bankruptcy. Family life falters, and thousands of children are made orphans every month from broken homes. Abortion has brought the population growth to a standstill.

As I return home, I have a feeling that the American people are almost drugged and are oblivious to the events at home and abroad that cause the Atomic Clock to move closer to midnight.

What is wrong? It is almost a paradox that America, possessing all the economic affluence for enjoying life, virtually leads the world in crime, narcotics abuse, pornography, immorality, and even debts. We seem to be naive to what is happening in the real world. So we watch spectator and entertainment events on television and try to forget it all, hoping that it will go away. Or we take another highball and try to relax.

The rest of the world watches our self-inflicted wounds with amazement. They cannot understand why we wash so much dirty linen in public.

Tonight, before we take a look at the future, we should look at the past and remind ourselves of the roots from which we sprang two hundred years ago.

I do not see how anyone could study the history of America without recognizing religious influences that have helped mold this nation from the beginning.

In 1835, an astute French visitor to the United States reported, "Upon my arrival in the United States, the religious aspect of the country was the first thing that struck my attention."

In no other nation's founding documents can we find so many declarations of allegiance to God. Time after time in our history there have been appeals to the "Supreme Judge" in seeking to build a new nation. This idea of freedom as a "right" of all men everywhere is absolutely unique among nations.

But where did it come from? Any search for its origin takes us back to "our fathers' God . . . Author of liberty." It takes us to the creation of man, whom God made in His own likeness, free to roam and replenish the earth. Free to decide *how* or even *whether* he would serve his Creator. And man chose rebellion. Today because of that choice by our first parents, we are alienated from God. Because of this alienation we are a "suffering" planet, with the ultimate result of "death" for every generation.

But this idea of freedom also takes us back to the Old Testament prophets, proclaiming in the face of kings and shouting from dungeons man's God-endowed right to freedom under God.

It takes us back to an angry Moses, daring Pharaoh's wrath to demand, "Let my people go!" and later leading a great army of the enslaved into a new country where they could, at God's behest, "proclaim liberty throughout the land and to all the inhabitants thereof." These words from Leviticus 25:10 are inscribed on America's Liberty Bell in Philadelphia.

It takes us back to Jesus Christ who, standing in Nazareth, boldly declared His destiny—"to preach deliverance to the captives, to set at liberty them that are bruised."

Liberty and freedom—these were the flaming revolutionary words the early followers of Christ cast again and again into the tinderbox of men's hearts and hopes.

Now, the thing tyrants feared was this ideal of the Free Man in God. That ideal has always been terrifying to tyrants and that is why religious liberty is being curtailed in so many parts of the world today. Give men the Bible and freedom to proclaim its message, and they will soon be free.

It was in pursuit of this ideal that those 102 brave men and women clambered aboard a tiny vessel called the Mayflower one chill day in 1620 and, with prayers on their lips and visions of a new "nation under God," set sail for a far, unknown land.

The night before that historic dawn when the Pilgrims landed, they had crowded into her tiny hold to sign their "Mayflower Compact" (based on Biblical principles as they saw them)—later to be called "the birth certificate of American democracy."

And the Puritans who followed during the great migrations of 1630-1640 also "laid it on the line"—their reasons for coming to Massachusetts Bay. The opening sentence of their "New England Confederation" says, "We all came into these parts of America with one and the same end, namely, to advance the Kingdom of the Lord Jesus Christ." Not all, of course, were dedicated Christians. After the Puritans, there came a diverse lot of adventurers, slave traders, ex-prisoners and unbelievers. But it is a mark of the Puritans' vitality that their ideals largely prevailed in early America.

Americans who scoff at their straight lacedness and earlier intolerance should never forget that it was the Puritan's religious faith and his passion for self-rule that gave us much of our system of political and social democracy—that has lasted these two hundred years.

But both patriotism and Puritanism tended to wane and weaken in the third generation. By the middle of the eighteenth century, problems for the young country began to mount. Many of them are the problems we face today. For example, inflation is nothing new in American history. In the late 1700s, during the days of the American Revolution, they too faced inflation. In 1779, ducks and chickens were sold for a few pennies each. In just two years' time they were costing $250 each. There came a time that money was hardly worth the paper it was printed on. That money, issued by the Continental Congress, had become valueless.

We should remember, as we face inflation today, that it's not nearly so bad as was faced by our forebears, and they licked it by sheer courage, discipline, hard work, and faith in the future of America.

Remember, the people that founded America did not have telephones, radio, television, electricity, automobiles, airplanes, inside plumbing, or refrigerators. They had no tractors or bulldozers. They had no supermarkets. They had no Social Security or guaranteed welfare. The fastest they could travel was by horseback. Yet they succeeded—where we seem to be failing. They scratched, dug, worked, sweated, and prayed to build a nation from New York to San Francisco.

Many times during American history there have been great spiritual awakenings that have affected the nation and strengthened its moral and spiritual fabric. One of those was called "The Great Awakening" of the 1740s. It strengthened the nation for the bitter days of the Revolution. Great evangelists like George Whitefield and Jonathan Edwards proclaimed judgment and grace, calling on the people to turn to God.

This Great Awakening, say historians, cradled and paved the way for the Revolution. Under such eloquent preaching sat those young people who would soon be called "the Founding Fathers" of America. And from under such preaching came men like John Adams who wrote, "Statesmen may plan and speculate for liberty, but it is religion and morality alone upon which freedom can securely stand. A patriot must be a religious man."

The Declaration of Independence reflects the feelings of men to whom religious faith was all-important. There was not an atheist or an agnostic among the fifty-six who signed that Declaration, though some were deists. Before they strode forward to append their signatures, each bowed his head in prayer. The Declaration's giant step was being taken, they affirmed, "with a firm reliance upon the protection of Divine Providence." In declaring themselves free, they said, they were assuming "the separate and equal station to which the laws of God entitled them." The self-evident truth they voiced was that men were "endowed by their Creator" with inalienable rights. And before the world they appealed to "the Supreme Judge of the world" for the source of their intentions.

Such expressions were no mere polite gestures to God. They were a firm commitment to the principle that God must be central to any plan of government. Because they signed that document, some of those men were captured and hanged. Some were stripped of their possessions, some were jailed. I have to ask myself tonight, at another hour of American crisis, do we have that kind of courage? Would we be willing to sign? How many people today would be willing to put their life on the line for freedom?

Eleven years later, *after* the Revolution was won, there assembled in Philadelphia men from thirteen colonies charged with creating one of the most revolutionary political documents of all time.

Yet there were flaws. They were men who had never known the concept of democratic liberty and freedom. For example, slavery was a part of the social structure, both North and South. Catholics could vote in only three of the thirteen states. Jews were not permitted to vote in New Jersey or in New Hampshire. Women could not vote anywhere in America. In the hindsight of two hundred years, they made many mistakes, but what they produced was nothing short of a miracle of God.

When the Constitution was submitted for ratification, the people demanded a Bill of Rights that would settle certain fundamental freedoms once and for all. They were implied in the Constitution, but the people wanted them in black and white. In the Amendments making up the Bill of Rights, where was religion? *First!* In top place! Speech, Assembly and Petition followed Religion in the First Amendment. These were quickly approved. But for three and a half months the House and Senate debated the phrasing of Religious Freedom, changing the words around, adding, deleting, clarifying. At no time in history has so much care and attention been lavished on one sentence of legislation.

The final wording: "Congress shall make no law respecting an establishment of religion, or prohibiting the free exercise thereof." It was not government renouncing religious faith; it was government protecting our religious faith by forever removing "religious rights" from tampering by any public authority or self-seeking hierarchy. Here we have a guarantee that America would never have a civil religion. But we would have freedom of religion—not freedom from religion as some have mistakenly interpreted this Amendment.

In every area of American life, the "faith of our fathers" has left its indelible imprint. And nowhere more so than in its educational system. When our forefathers stepped ashore in the New World, their first act was to establish a home. Next, they erected a church. Then they started a school.

The Puritans and the Pilgrims came to the New World determined to provide education for their young. In the lands they'd left, education was the privilege of the few. Therefore, those early Americans flung up their rude schoolhouses all along the advancing frontier. Their first textbook was the Bible, their first task to teach children to read.

Founded also by the churches were America's first institutions of higher learning. A few years after the Pilgrims landed, Harvard College came into being—its motto: "For Christ and the Church"; its main purpose: a training center for clergy. In 1701, Yale College was founded by a group of evangelical clergymen for the same purpose. Princeton was brought into being by the Presbyterian "revivalist party." The University of Pennsylvania stemmed directly from George Whitefield's electrifying preaching during the Great Awakening.

It was in America's churches too that women first came into their own. The Pilgrim woman was a new breed. Along with her man she stepped onto those free shores with freedom shining in her eyes. At home, in her community and church, she began her God-given fulfillment as a woman.

We may be a vastly different people today than we were two hundred years ago. Our society is far more complex, more pluralistic. But of this we can be sure—God has not changed. His laws have not changed. He is still a God of love and mercy—but He is also a God of righteousness and judgment. Any individual or nation which ignores His moral and spiritual laws will ultimately face His judgment.

I believe that every problem facing us tonight as Americans is basically a spiritual problem. Crime is a spiritual problem. Inflation is a spiritual problem. Corruption is a spiritual problem. Social injustice is a spiritual problem. The lack of a "will" even to defend our freedoms is a spiritual problem.

The Lord, speaking through His servant, the prophet Isaiah, said,

"I was ready to be sought by those who did not ask for me. I was ready to be found by those who did not seek me. I said, Here am I, to a nation that did not call on my name. I spread out my hands all the day to a rebellious people who follow their own devices. A people who provoke me to my face continually . . . . When I spoke, you did not listen, but you did that which was evil in my eyes."

And judgment came!

The great question before us tonight, on the eve of our two hundredth birthday and on the eve of 1976—a crucial election year—is: will this nation survive this century as a free society, or even the next five years as a free society? As I came home from my three-month world tour, this is how crucial and how critical the problems of the present hour seem to me. I do not believe that we will be a free democracy twenty-four years from now in the year 2000, unless a dramatic change takes place within the hearts of the people of this nation.

It was James Russell Lowell, American poet of the last century, who put the challenge to us. When asked by a French historian, "How long do you think the American republic will endure?" Lowell replied, "So long as the ideas of its Founding Fathers continue to be dominant!"

One of the ideas was that the Bible was true, and that our entire social and political structure was to be built upon its laws and teachings.

Another idea that our Founding Fathers had was that God was supreme. That is why they put on our coins, "In God We Trust."

Another early idea, not shared by all by any means, was that every person needed Jesus Christ in his heart.

As tonight we enter a historic year, America is troubled. Our people are filled with frustration, fear, and confusion. According to a series of articles in the Los Angeles *Times* in October [1975], thousands of radicals are highly organized from coast to coast with the determination to overthrow this country. We have heard testimony before Congress recently that highly trained terrorists have arrived in the United States to begin terror tactics during the Bicentennial year.

Will they succeed? It will depend on the patriotism, courage and faith such as those early Americans had, when they landed on these shores. Is God going to allow a cataclysmic judgment to fall upon this nation as has fallen upon nations of the past who have turned from God and forgotten Him? Or will God send to us another great spiritual awakening that has saved us in the past?

During the last twelve months, thousands of Americans have been turning to God. Prayer groups and Bible study groups have been springing up all over the nation. Churches and other religious organizations are reporting that millions are living a more disciplined Christian life. This is encouraging—even though it only involves a minority.

In a time similar to ours, when only a minority were true believers, Isaiah the great Hebrew prophet said, "Except the Lord of hosts had left unto us a very small remnant, we should have been like Sodom, and we should have been like unto Gomorrah."

But God is warning us tonight that judgment is going to fall upon us in a very short time unless we as a nation repent and turn to God. In pleading with ancient Israel, God said,

Come now, and let us reason together, saith the Lord: though your sins be as scarlet, they shall be as white as snow; though they be red like crimson, they shall be as wool. If ye be willing and obedient, ye shall eat the good of the land. *But* if ye refuse and rebel, ye shall be devoured with the sword; for the mouth of the Lord hath spoken it."

Will America turn to God at this late hour, or will America continue on the broad road that leads to destruction? It will soon be too late to decide—already the storm clouds are gathering.

I am calling Christians everywhere to a time of humiliation, prayer, and fasting during this two hundredth anniversary. There is no possible solution to the problems we face apart from a change in the spiritual atmosphere.

You who are listening to me tonight are asking the question, "What can I as an individual do? I feel so helpless in the midst of the present crisis. I want to do something—but what?"

What did those early pastors, teachers and evangelists proclaim? The heart of the message of Whitefield, Edwards, Wesley, Tennent and hundreds of other clergy along the frontier was basically the same message I offer to you tonight.

*First*, recognize that God loves you. The Bible says that He is not willing that any should perish but that all should come to repentance.

*Second*, be honest before God. Admit that you have broken His laws and chosen to go your own way instead of His way. Be willing to let Him change your life.

*Third*, receive Jesus Christ into your heart as Savior and Lord.

*Fourth*, be a living example by your good works. The apostle James said, "Faith without works is dead." This proves that you mean business with God. Pray for those in authority—be a good citizen—help the poor—help the distressed and help the oppressed of the world.

*Fifth*, get involved in the political process. This coming year is an election year. I would like to challenge every deeply committed American who is qualified to think about running for political office. I do not believe that we as Christians should withdraw. We need men and women of integrity and Christian commitment who will run for political office this coming year—no matter to which political party you belong. On this New Year's Eve, if you will do these things you could have a part in helping America be the kind of country you want for your children and grandchildren.

America is too young to die. She is only two hundred years old. During the last few weeks

I have been in countries that date their history back thousands of years. We are a young country and should be just getting started. But unless we wake up and accept the challenge handed to us by our forefathers, we will die, like countries and civilizations of the past.

During this past year [1975] Alexander Solzhenitsyn visited the United States. While he was here, he told a little story that bears repeating tonight. He said that only once during his long imprisonment in a Soviet Union labor camp did he become so discouraged that he contemplated suicide. He was outdoors on a work detail, and he had reached the point where he didn't care whether the guards killed him or not. When he had a break, he sat down, and a perfect stranger sat down beside him—someone he had never seen before and never saw again. This stranger took a stick and drew a cross on the ground for no explainable reason. Solzhenitsyn sat and stared at that cross and then said, "I realize therein lies man's freedom." At that point, a new courage and a will to live and work returned.

Tonight you can come to that same cross and find forgiveness, peace, joy, and eternal life. Life takes on a new meaning, a new hope, a new song. This could be your commitment tonight.

May God help you to make this commitment, and may 1976 be a joyous and blessed year for each of you.

# Political Pluralism and Religious Absolutism[5]

Patricia Roberts Harris

*Born May 31, 1924, Mattoon, IL; died March 23, 1985; B.A., Howard University, 1945; J.D., George Washington University, 1960; program director, YWCA, 1946-49; assistant director, American Council on Human Rights, 1949-53; executive director, Delta Sigma Theta, 1953-59; trial attorney, Department of Justice, 1960-61; associate dean, 1961-63, professor, 1963-65, 1967-69, Howard University; ambassador to Luxembourg, 1965-67; secretary of Housing and Urban Development, 1977-80; secretary of Health, Education, and Welfare, 1980; secretary of Health and Human Services, 1980-81.*

## Editor's introduction

In this speech, Patricia Roberts Harris, the first African-American woman to hold a cabinet position, addressed the American Whig-Cliosophic Society, which is Princeton University's student debating organization. She opposed what she perceived as the adverse impact of fundamentalism. Without questioning the Constitution's guarantee to freely practice the religion one chooses, Harris asserted that the sudden political presence of certain fundamentalist ministers, occurring at the time this speech was given, posed "a serious threat to the American democratic process." Harris believed that "fundamentalist politics" by their very nature excluded many and, if taken to an extreme, would polarize opinion to an unmanageable extent.

---

In recent weeks newspaper columns and the television airwaves have been filled with the allegedly new phenomenon of the entry of American Evangelicals into the elective political process. The news-cum-entertainment program (or is it the other way around) "60 Minutes" this week gave us the unedifying spectacle of overt threats to targeted political figures because they failed to agree with the political position of putative religious leaders on several issues.

That "60 Minutes" has reported the phenomenon confirms its reality and, indeed, its pervasiveness. What we need to remember is that this invasion of the political process by those purporting to act in the name of religion is neither new nor a matter for entertainment.

Two hundred and one years ago, in 1779, Thomas Jefferson condemned such activity by religious leaders, saying in the preamble to a bill on religious freedom which he had introduced in the Virginia legislature:

"Our civil rights have no dependence on our religious opinions, any more than our opinions in physics and geometry; therefore, the proscribing of any citizen as unworthy of the public confidence by laying upon him an incapacity of being called to office of public trust . . . unless he profess or renounce this or that religious opinion, is depriving him injuriously of those privileges and advantages to which he has a natural right."

Thomas Jefferson was born into a society acutely aware of the danger of an official relationship between religious and political institutions. Requirements of religious orthodoxy had caused churning of the political life of England from which the early settlers derived so much of their political perception. Every school-boy and girl is taught that the pilgrims came to Plymouth seeking religious freedom. Few understand how little there was for those who refused to accept the orthodoxy of the dominant Protestants who led the Massachusetts Bay colony.

[5]Delivered to the American Whig-Cliosophic Society, at Princeton University, in Princeton, New Jersey, on September 23, 1980.

Anne Hutchinson's belief that God's love is communicated immediately to the regenerate and that this love serves as a guide to action without mediation of the clergy was considered politically subversive and she was banished from the Massachusetts Bay colony by John Cotton.

Thus our founding fathers had early and significant experience with the demand of religious leaders and their flocks for acceptance of a particular theology, and the insistence that political punishment would result from failure to accept the orthodox religious opinion.

The result was the adoption of George Mason's eloquent provision for religious freedom in the first Virginia Bill of Rights adopted in 1776, which was the forerunner of the first amendment to the Constitution of the United States. His provision read:

"That religion, or the duty which we owe to our creator, and the manner of discharging it, can be directed only by reason and conviction, not by force or violence; and therefore all men are equally entitled to the free exercise of religion, according the dictates of conscience; and that it is the mutual duty of all to practice Christian forebearance, love and charity towards each other."

George Mason would undoubtedly be appalled today—two hundred and four years after Virginia adopted this statement of tolerance—to discover the following:

—An organization called "The Moral Majority"—founded just a little over a year ago by a fundamentalist minister from Virginia—has 400,000 members nationwide and is forming political action committees in all 50 states to distribute $1.5 million to political candidates who it determines favor a "pro-Christian" viewpoint.

—During last spring's "Washington for Jesus" rally, a number of participants visited the office of a southern senator and they informed him that he scored only 23 percent in a "morality rating" prepared by Christian Voice, a political committee organized by right wing Californians. They demanded that he fall on his knees and pray for forgiveness. When he refused, he was targeted for defeat in the fall elections.

—Evangelical leaders and conservative politicians gathered last month in Dallas for two days of oratory and political activism strategy sessions. At that meeting in Dallas, the New York *Times* quoted one leader as saying:

"It is interesting at great political rallies how you have a Protestant to pray, a Catholic to pray, and then you have a Jew to pray. With all due respect to those dear people, my friends, God Almighty does not hear the prayer of the Jew."

He has refused to withdraw the statement.

There is none of the "Christian forebearance, love and charity towards each other" urged by George Mason in these three examples.

These three reports do illustrate the nature of the growing involvement of fundamentalist religious organizations in the political process. Furthermore, the preponderance of this involvement is on the right, rather than the left, side of the political spectrum.

Now before going any further in my examination of this phenomenon and its danger to previously accepted political values, let me make several important points.

*First* of all, I do not intend to become involved in any discussion of the personal religious beliefs of any individuals or groups. The freedom to hold religious convictions and to worship freely is fundamental to both the constitution and the very soul of this nation. I do not propose to talk about religion per se, but only about the nature of religious participation in the secular, partisan political process.

*Second*, I do not imply that all "born again" Christians reflect a right-wing, or even conservative, political outlook. Any number of evangelical Christians—President Carter, Senator Mark Hatfield and former Senator Harold Hughes, for example, hold decidedly different views. The vast majority of such individuals believe in and practice toleration of opposing views and vote as most of us vote—on the basis of deeply felt beliefs about priorities and goals, parties and candidates—and their votes are therefore widely distributed all across the political spectrum.

Nor do I imply that all evangelical Christians want their churches or other religious organizations to participate in a direct and particular way in political campaigns.

There is evidence, however, that significant numbers of evangelical Christian organizations are moving toward intense involvement in elective politics and that they have become a major factor in energizing right-wing politics in our country.

The terms "born again" and "evangelical" have been popularly applied to individuals who attest to having had a personal religious experience which has changed their lives. A large number of these individuals, in addition to experiencing a personal conversion, also hold to a stricter or more "fundamental" interpretation of the scripture.

The American religious tradition is a rich and varied one, and the distinction between the evangelical and more "establishment" religious experience is as old as the country. What is significant about the trend today is that the number of "born again" Christians seems to be steadily on the rise. Public opinion polls have tried to measure the number of Americans in that category, and although they do not agree on a number, they variously estimate it to be between 35 and 60 million.

In the last few years we have seen evidence of the trend in large rallies like the one held in Washington last May. We have also seen rapid growth in the so-called "Christian oriented" media—several hundred television and radio outlets which are now devoted primarily to religious programming.

The growing activism of such religious groups can also be seen in the political arena. At the session of fundamentalist leaders in Dallas last month, one evangelist said, "not voting is a sin against Almighty God," and he urged his audience to "crawl out from under those padded pews." According to one newspaper account, "attentions swung widely from theology and scripture to instruction on how to organize without violating tax laws, the practicality of registering a congregation to vote during the Sunday service and the importance of keeping a 'moral score card' on the voting records of elected representatives."

I have no quarrel with the right of individuals and groups—no matter what their political positions—to become involved in the political process. I have sought such involvement all my life. At the same time, however, there are aspects and implications of these particular efforts which pose a serious threat to the American democratic process and tonight I want to discuss my reasons for believing this to be the case.

My chief concern is that fundamentalist politics as practiced at this time is at best exclusionary and at worst a dangerous, intolerant, and polarizing influence in our political system.

At the recent Dallas conference speaker after speaker denounced "perverts, radicals, leftists, communists, liberals and humanists" who presumably have taken over the country and are actively seeking its destruction. This kind of overt "us against them" appeal—the "God-fearing" against the "heathen"—has roots in virtually every generation in American history. At various times it has made victims of Catholics, immigrants, Jews, blacks, Indians and countless others who failed to fit into neat patterns of acceptability. In my judgment, at least, there are undercurrents of many of the same prejudices in much of the new right rhetoric today.

One slightly more subtle example of exclusionary practices is the so-called "Christian yellow pages"—a telephone directory, similar to the one in popular use, that lists only "born again" merchants and exhorts Christians to restrict their business to those establishments.

George Will—a columnist, a graduate of Princeton, and a man few regard as a radical, a leftist, or even a humanist—described such an appeal as "an act of aggression against a pluralistic society." He added "discrimination condoned—indeed, incited—in commerce will not be confined to commerce."

Although the majority of the people of the country classify themselves as Christian, the nation has consistently, painfully, and with great success moved from intolerance to toleration of both political and religious dissent.

We Americans have, in this century, truly come to agree with Voltaire that we may "disagree with what you say, but we will fight to the death for your right to say it" because we recognize the value of both political dissenters and of non-Christian traditions. Our democracy has functioned because, as a rule, we have sought out common ground—shared values and beliefs, rather than an orthodoxy espoused by any particular group. The end result may not have pleased everyone, but it has offered to each individual a reasonable measure of freedom in which to exercise his or her civil and human rights.

That consensus orientation is profoundly threatened by those who advocate a "Christian crusade" or who want our leadership narrowed to include only "pro-Christian" public officials.

In this particular campaign, fundamentalist organizations seek to identify "pro-Christian" candidates with a measuring stick of very specific issues. More often than not, the connection between Christian scripture and such concerns is mystifying.

I am sure that I need not remind this audience of the positions fundamentalist groups have taken on our most pressing and most controversial social issues.

In a time of rapid and often disconcerting change in social and moral values, right wing political operatives are working hard to cultivate votes among the distressed. Direct scriptural guidance is cited in determining the "Christian position" on such issues as equal rights for women, gun control, abortion, sex education in schools, and pornography. I grant the existence of profound moral issues in the debate on the legality of funding of abortion, but I can find only a political basis for being opposed to gun control.

Earlier, I mentioned a senator's meeting with a group who rated him "poor" on a moral score card. His so-called "morality rating" took into account his positions on such issues as recognition of Taiwan as the legitimate Chinese government, prayer in the public schools, a balanced budget, sanctions against the former Rhodesian government, and creation of the Federal Department of Education.

A 1978 candidate for Congress in Virginia, himself an evangelical minister, saw a direct biblical admonition against welfare programs, called the income tax "unscriptural" and declared that "the free market is the biblical approach to economics."

A senator who was defeated in 1978, largely because of his vote in support of the Panama Canal treaties, said an astonishing number of letters from his constituents admonished him "as a Christian" to vote against ratification.

In sheer exasperation, another former senator, Harold Hughes—a Christian evangelist himself—said recently, "I have searched the scriptures diligently and I have not found one word in them on Jesus Christ's position on the Panama Canal. To say you've got to believe this or that in the political arena or you are not a Christian is absolute blasphemy."

Whether you agree or disagree with the position fundamentalist organizations have taken on these issues is beside the point. What is important are the underlying premises which serve as the basis for their views: that this is a "Christian" and not a pluralistic society; that the nation must achieve its "Christian" destiny by adhering to a specific set of positions derived from scripture as interpreted by a particular theological school and that the imposition of those beliefs on the nation as a whole is not only permissible, but desirable.

The consequences of the demand for orthodoxy enforced by the political process are found throughout history, from Socrates to the victims of the Ayatollah Khomeini. For those who assert that their restrictive interpretations are essential to the well-being of this country, I would remind them that the theory that the world was round was denied by certain theologians as little as 50 years before "Columbus sailed the ocean blue." If we could speak to Galileo about whether the "Christian" position on Copernican theory and his own work on astronomy was in the best interest of that genius or the world he served, he might well suggest that if the fundamentalism of his time had prevailed, its modern U.S. proponents would live in Europe, and Indians would still own this land. The association of church and state, the identity of interest of Aristotelian professors who disagreed with Galileo's ideas, and their ability to end his freedom and halt his work are some of the inevitable consequences of the achievement of the kind of identity of theology and public policy that our political evangelicals appear to seek today.

We have conveniently forgotten that Scopes was convicted of violating the law when he taught the theory of evolution, which some fundamentalists still oppose. That conviction was in this century.

On one issue which the radical right refuses to leave alone—prayer in the school—the lack of respect for difference, and the insistence upon using government to achieve particular Christian theological ends is most blatant and most intolerant. That Jews, Moslems, Buddhists or non-believers must have the time and nature of their relationship with the deity determined by the state runs counter to George Mason's Virginia Bill of Rights and to the Bill of Rights of the Constitution. Such a position is blatantly intolerant of both of the religious and non-believers and takes us back to days of religious inquisitions that I thought we had rejected in this country with the adoption of our Bill of Rights.

The damage such viewpoints do by excluding large numbers of people from full participation in the nation's present and future is difficult to assess, but the problem of exclusion is exacerbated by the righteous fervor with which these political fundamentalists approach the debate.

This is especially painful for other Christians who do not share a right wing viewpoint.

Public officials today regularly encounter citizens who tell them how "real Christians" would vote or act—or how "real Christians" will repay an errant representative for his sins. This offends me because I care about what my Jewish and Buddhist and Bahai brothers and sisters believe about an issue and I want to be sure that what I do is as broadly acceptable to their ethical system as I can make it.

Republican senator Mark Hatfield wrote: "During my opposition to the Vietnam war, the religious segment of the radical right attacked not only my patriotism, but the authenticity of my personal Christian faith."

When the argument is so presented, there is no room for discussion of the issues. Politics—that crucible of ambiguities and compromises, choices and alternatives—degenerates into a raw power struggle in which one side impugns the other's religious sincerity and the judgment of how to act is based on numbers of votes, and not the validity of the idea. To argue that there is a single "Christian" viewpoint or even a religious point of view on every issue in foreign and domestic policy is to say no debate is necessary or desirable—that all that is required is unquestioning obedience of "God's will" as revealed to a single individual or group. I thought that was what the last 400 years had rejected.

That kind of moral absolutism is alien to the best of the American experience, and it is sobering to note that one country in which such a totalitarian interpretation of "God's will" is today practiced is Iran. In that nation the rich variety of Islamic culture has been trampled by religious zealots who profess to know the one truth and who are willing to impose their narrow interpretation of Moslem principles on the entire nation.

Our own country has been nurtured and sustained in a more tolerant atmosphere. Even in the darkest days of the Civil War, Abraham Lincoln reminded the country that both North and South pray to the same God, and when he invoked the deity, he understood that we see the right only "as God gives us to see the right."

That spirit of humility and tolerance which so characterized Lincoln is much needed today. The absolute certainty with which some individuals approach the political battle—and the arrogance with which they propose a crusade to "re-Christianize" America—is dangerous for our democracy. I am beginning to fear that we could have an Ayatollah Khomeini in this country, but that he will not have a beard, but he will have a television program.

I would argue that the politicization of evangelical Christianity is bad for religion. As Paul Tillich reminded us, "Doubt is not the opposite of faith; it is an element of faith." Those who measure their piety and the piety of others with "moral score cards" are the modern day pharisees, and they do themselves, as well as their nation, no service. We may find that equating religious position with particular political positions will lead to rejection of both. The founding fathers of this nation were religious men, and they did not seek to divorce religious, moral, and ethical beliefs from the practice of politics. They knew that such beliefs are the foundation on which political philosophies are based. But at the same time, they pointedly chose to separate church and state because they did not want one particular group, or one particular point of view, to dominate all the others. They knew the result of failure to separate church and state could be excommunication from the polity as well as excommunication from the church, as happened to both Galileo and Anne Hutchinson.

Our society—infinitely more pluralistic today than was the America of 1789—needs to reexamine that premise and reaffirm our commitment to that principle.

Pluralism requires political discipline on the part of the majority. Any majority has the power in a democracy to eliminate the minority or to eliminate the expression of the ideas of the minority. It is the essence of democracy that the majority protects, respects and listens to its minorities.

Neither political nor religious absolutism is consistent with the United States democratic assumption that unfettered debate may lead to a change of mind on issue.

It is ironic that the political absolutism with which we are faced today finds its center of support in Protestant groups. That very name is a reminder that these denominations grew out of a protest against religious absolutism.

Reinhold Niebuhr reminded us that "we must never confuse our fragmentary apprehension of the truth with the truth itself." Our political system rests on our having the humility to remember that fact, and act accordingly.

None of us knows a single truth which closes the debate and dictates our actions in the political world, but in a democracy we can work together in the search for truth and in doing so create the just and humane society which all of us seek.

Although the first amendment directs itself to the Congress in its prohibition of the establishment of religion, the history out of which it came, and the intent with which it was adopted were clearly part of the movement of this country to a toleration of differences and encouragement of dissent. That these two concerns must live side by side with the right of the majority to make decisions if no consensus can be reached, and no compromise adopted, does not say that the majority has the right to refuse to seek consensus and compromise.

There is hope that for all the attention garnered by the religious absolutists in this campaign, the people of this nation have understood and accepted the admonition of religious freedom of George Mason and Thomas Jefferson. In Boston last week, voters backed candidates denounced from the pulpit of their church.

The Des Moines, Iowa *Register* reported on September 14 that a new Iowa poll showed the Iowans overwhelmingly disapprove of religious leaders urging their followers to vote for specific candidates, and only four percent of those polled said they would be persuaded to vote for a candidate if their religious leader asked them to do so.

Before we become too optimistic about these results, it should be pointed out that four percent would be enough to determine a close election.

The solution, of course, is for the majority that supports rationality and consensus to go to the polls, vote their informed consensus, and, in so doing, again overwhelm the forces of bigotry and polarization.

If they stay home, absolutism will win and we may be required to begin again the battle for humanism, rationality, and the democratic spirit which we thought had been won with the Declaration of Independence and the Bill of Rights of the United States Constitution.

# XII. Business, Industry, and Labor

## Editor's introduction

Business, industry, and labor have been on a veritable roller-coaster ride during the past 60 years. In 1937, the American work force languished in the depths of the greatest economic depression the world has yet known. Currently, we are in a period of relative prosperity. Yet even during these supposed "good" times, company mergers, "downsizing," and "restructuring" have decreased job security and caused wide-spread anxiety for many individuals and their families. The rapid advances made in computer and industrial technologies have had perhaps the most significant impact on the work force. While such progress has opened avenues for many, it has threatened the jobs of those unprepared for the change. Bill Bradley, a former New Jersey senator, explained how "for centuries, the determinants of national wealth have been capital, natural resources, and an abundance of labor. Today none of them is as important as knowledge." In short, technology has created what we now term the "information age," and the ability to access, control, and direct information is of prime importance to both American business and the American work force.

Dramatic technological advance and its effect on the economy have been the focus of oratory throughout the twentieth century. John I. Snyder, Jr., an industrialist who manufactured automation machinery, correctly anticipated the presence of automation. He argued that automation, while it will inevitably displace workers, is also a necessity if the United States is to compete in the world market. Mr. Snyder ended his speech by suggesting ways in which employment in an automated economy could actually be increased.

With Roosevelt's National Industrial Recovery Act of 1933, unions that experienced significant setbacks during the Great Depression gained government protection. Such protection allowed unions to select their own leaders and organize themselves free from any influence or intimidation by business owners. In the early 1940s, union membership increased substantially. Wages also improved, as did working conditions. However, by the late 1970s and into the early 1980s, union membership became less prevalent, a trend which persists to the present day. George Meany, former president of the American Federation of Labor, spoke out strongly on the role of the union and such issues as inflation, profiteering, housing, social security, health care, and education. "Congress," he warned, "will not act on any . . . of these problems until . . . the people of this country demand action." Victories won by workers, he insisted, did not occur automatically, but rather through unions' "struggle against stubborn opposition." James B. Carey, former president of the International Union of Electrical, Radio and Machine Workers, echoed Meany's praise of the union, as he recalled earlier days when union workers' "heads" were "clobbered" and their "arms and legs" broken. Now, however, he said, "labor . . . continues to grow larger and stronger." At the same time, he noted that corruption in unions, particularly in the form of labor racketeering, must be eliminated. Yet the depiction of union strength and power, as extolled by Meany and Carey, is no longer a reality. On November 16, 1981, Lane Kirkland, former president of the AFL-CIO, noted that the strength of unions was declining. He promised to "preserve unity within the family of labor." "We can survive adverse public opinion," he contended, by "pursu[ing] our duty."

The extent of government constraint on business and labor is also treated in several of the speeches contained herein. Ms. Ruth Alexander, a newspaper columnist and radio debater, castigated business leaders for not confronting government interference on labor issues. She declared that executives should "speak up for themselves," as they, not the state, create goods and provide jobs. Defending the role of government in labor, and in American life in general, Barbara Hackman Franklin, former commissioner of the Consumer Product Safety Commission, said that she understood the widely held belief that the federal government has "gone overboard" in regulating American lives and labor. In short, she recognized that people, particularly at the time the speech was given, wanted a "more affordable government." At the same time, however, Jordan defended what she considered to be necessary public health and safety programs. On October 7, 1993, former senator Bill Bradley agreed that "government has a role in this time of transformation" to assure all citizens "basic health coverage, an opportunity for lifetime education, and a guarantee of pension security." In order for government regulation of labor to be worthwhile, Bradley believed that it must provide substantial and tangible benefit to those who constitute the work force.

# Labor's Contribution to American Democracy[1]

Matthew Woll

*Born January 25, 1880, Luxembourg; died June 1, 1956; B.A., Lake Forest University, 1904; president, International Photoengravers' Union of North America, 1906-29; vice president, American Federation of Labor (AFL), 1919-35; president, Workers Education Bureau, 1935-41; president, Union Labor Life Insurance Company, 1941; vice president, American Federation of Labor/Congress of Industrial Organizations (AFL/CIO), 1942-56; author,* Labor, Industry and Government *(1935).*

## Editor's introduction

Matthew Woll, former vice president of the AFL/CIO, gave this speech in which he provided an interpretation of labor's relationship to American government. He began this address by praising labor's contributions to civil rights and restating the importance of labor's fight against "tyranny and dictatorship." However, he insisted that even in the United States citizens must oppose "excessive regulation by legislation—a policy that . . . will surely undermine the very foundation of personal freedom." Woll thus took a notably conservative standpoint, asserting that goals and agendas of unions should not be hampered by excessive federal intervention.

---

William Gladstone, more than three generations ago, said: "The trade union is the very bulwark of democracy." Democracy is in fact the rock upon which the movement of labor has been founded—it is in turn the very foundation of a truly democratic society. Labor's contribution to American democracy has been impressive, far reaching and continuous. It is a contribution synonymous with the beginning of America—it will continue to the end of time with America.

One may judge of the constancy of any movement to the democratic objective by a number of criteria.

First of all, democracy rests upon a spiritual principle—the worth of the individual, what Thomas Mann has called "the inalienable dignity of man." The Christian religion rests upon the sanctity of the individual as a child of God. Democracy depends for its being on the recognition of the same spiritual principles.

In the second place, democracy rests upon a respect for the minority. Majority rule requires the balance wheel of opposition. Beneath this principle of respect for the rights of minorities, for tolerance for the minority point of view, rests another principle—the obligation of the strong to help the weak—whether it be a strength of numbers or of the weight of ideas.

The third principle is that society is a living body composed of individuals, not of robots or automatons. In such an organic conception of society individuals have rights and duties which arise out of their membership in society. Such individuals must live and serve one another, if they are to have any life worth living.

In the fourth place, democracy rests upon the rule of law rather than the rule of force—of persuasion over compulsion. This voluntary character of a democratic society stands in sharp contrast to the coercive power of a police state.

Finally, a truly democratic society rests upon the freedom of the individual to speak, to associate, to print or to worship, those things which we think of as civil liberties. Unless men are free to speak their minds, unless they are free to exercise those other basic freedoms, there can be no democracy, there can be no truly free society.

It is upon these five principles that any democratic society rests. By these basic principles,

[1]Delivered to the *New York Herald Tribune's* ninth annual forum, in New York, New York, on October 24, 1939.

which we may describe as a measuring rod, what has been labor's contribution to democracy?

First and foremost labor has accepted from the very start the principle of the spiritual nature of men. Man is not an automaton, a commodity or article of commerce, nor an economic abstraction. Labor believes so much in the uncommon fineness of the common man that it has protested from the days of its earliest foundation down to the present whenever it has believed that the worker was being exploited or compelled to labor under conditions which undermined his health and endangered the nation's well being. In spite of all its verbiage and all of the rhetoric of labor policy, labor's protest against the exploiting of children and women in industry rests upon this central concern. But labor has continued its efforts far beyond the mere protest against those conditions in industry which have done violence to the human spirit. Indeed, there is no reason why we should not realize the highest hopes of an ideal life, where man's worth shall be measured by his utility to his fellows, where his generosity and sympathy, rather than his cupidity and rapacity will receive the encomiums and rewards of a nobler manhood, a more beautiful womanhood and a happier childhood.

Labor's contribution to democracy has been positive as well as negative. In particular labor's insistence on the development of a great system of free public education, which has today become our greatest single business enterprise, is an indication of the positive and constructive way in which labor has tried to see to it that all people should be given an opportunity to develop to the fullest their personality. Today perhaps as never before we are realizing that universal democracy is impossible without universal education. Labor conceived that principle more than a hundred years ago and has valiantly supported it for more than a century.

Labor has likewise stood unhesitatingly in support of the rights of the minority. It has understood the mental attitude of the minority because it has been a member of the minority. It has asserted with great persuasion that the final test of a democracy is not in the manner in which the will of the majorities is made to prevail but in the manner in which the rights of the minority are respected. Labor has fought against every tyranny and dictatorship because they have ruthlessly suppressed all minority rights. It was labor that first sounded the note of warning against Communism and all that this philosophy and practice implied and at the time its voice was held up to public ridicule. Again it was labor that first called attention to the menace of fascism. It was likewise labor that received the first brutal and murderous assaults of naziism. It is no mere coincidence that wherever dictatorships have come they have begun by suppressing labor, because they have known that the most valiant defenders of the rights of minorities have been the organized wage earners. Although we have sought amongst us those who are endeavoring to capture our trade unions and subordinate them to alien doctrines, the overwhelming number of our organizations have successfully repudiated these destructive elements in our society.

Labor has always conceived of society as made up of free individuals who have free wills and should have the opportunity to express them in accordance with their own convictions. It has opposed the growth of state-ism because it believes that as the state is magnified in power and importance it inevitably minimizes the dignity and sovereignty of the individual citizen. The virile spirit that has given our nation a foremost place among the nations of the world is the spirit of aggressive initiative and independence, the ability of our people to grapple with hard problems and to solve them for their own benefit and for the benefit of the nation. We must not as a nation allow ourselves to drift or venture upon a policy of excessive regulation by legislation—a policy that eats and will surely undermine the very foundation of personal freedom. It should be remembered that the American labor movement is the only movement in the world that has consistently and effectively repudiated both communism and socialism. Labor has held steadfast to the principles and ideals of democracy. It has remained uninfluenced by the false philosophies of the day, which envisage society as divided either into hostile economic classes, waging everlasting war with one another or into fixed racial groups with nothing but contempt in their hearts for one another.

Labor firmly believes in the American principles of our constitutional democracy. It has built the structure of its organization to correspond to the frame of our American Republic. It has developed a body of constitutional law for the guidance and conduct of its own organization patterned in many respects after our basic constitutional documents. Labor has not sought immunity from the law but equality before the law. It asks no special privileges, it seeks only those rights which should be enjoyed by all. Democracy cannot continue or survive as a healthy state so long as there are inequalities either in law or in economic or political conditions.

Finally, labor has stood valiantly and courageously in support of civil liberties in our land. As the distinguished American historian James Truslow Adams asserted, the Bill of Rights was in truth "a charter of liberty for the common man." These civil liberties were sought by the artisans and farmers in the closing years of the eighteenth century, they have been jealously guarded and supported by labor down through the years. Some months ago a study was made of civil liberties and it was pointed out that labor in a period of approximately sixty years has passed no less than 243 different resolutions or pronouncements in support of civil liberties both at home and abroad. No institution in our American life has more consistently supported the right of men to speak, to print, to assemble or to worship than have the representatives of labor. No group has and no group will more fearlessly contend against any force or agency that would strip away this protection for the freedom of our nation.

However much we may condemn Hitler for his methods and his objectives, it is important to remember that Hitler was a result of conditions and causes in post-War Europe. So too the menace to American democracy is perhaps not so much from without, but from within. We are immensely rich in natural resources and not seriously dependent upon other countries for our own prosperity. Yet we have a great problem of unemployment. We cannot hope indefinitely to shift the burden of carrying ten millions or more of unemployed and with an increasing number of aged and disabled upon the shoulders of an ever lessening number of employed without serious reckoning. We cannot look forward with complacency and unconcern to the two and one quarter million youngsters released each year from our schools, colleges and universities into community life without hope of doing something useful—something which potentially enlarges the possibilities of human happiness, comfort or knowledge. It is evident the movement of destruction is abroad. The philosophy of despair has its fantastic adherents. The lean body is easy prey to the teachings of re-action masked under pretense of progress. Those who see wisely into the future, must, if we are to be saved from fires more consuming than those we have known, so shape our course as to offer this hideous wraith of destruction no foothold.

American labor is making a contribution to the economic foundation and security of our democracy which can hardly be overestimated. However, labor cannot uphold the banner of democracy alone. It is but part of the great process of American industry. Unless management can and will cooperate with labor in translating the ideals of democracy into relations in the workshop, then much of the work of labor is prejudiced if not actually nullified.

If we are to have democracy in the maintenance and operation of our government, if we are going to have the substance as well as the theory of political democracy, we must do something more than merely provide opportunities for people to vote once a year. It was labor that early recognized the fact that a man cannot be politically free until he is economically free, that it is not possible to build a great society until the economic foundations of that society have been soundly laid. And the foundations of that society must rest in the possibilities which are present for all to enjoy adequate returns for honest work under good working conditions.

Labor early recognized the fact that the American people were the best customers of its products, that here indeed we had a vast free trade area larger in extent and more effective as a consuming market than any other comparable market in the world. Labor sought high wages and shorter hours not for material satisfaction alone but because they were enabled thereby to become the purchasers of the goods and services that were made available by the creative genius of American industry.

In coming to a close—let us not forget that America itself is a nation the inhabitants of which are drawn from many races and many parts of the earth. It in a sense is the microcosm of the world. To America have come immigrants drawn from different stocks, whose dreams of a new society have in part been fulfilled by the America of today. In the Americanizing of these newcomers to our shores the trade union itself has played a role of great importance and one I am bound to say that is seldom fully appreciated. I can speak about this with some right and with some feeling, for I, too, came to this country as a young boy from Luxembourg and early found myself enrolled in American schools for a brief time and then in American industry, and finally in an American trade union. And what I say of myself can be said of countless other men from Samuel Gompers down. I think you would agree with me that Gompers was not only the greatest leader of labor that this country has ever developed, but I am sure you would also agree that he was a great American. For he could say upon his deathbed what is in the heart of the workingmen of America, native as well as adopted sons of America: "God bless American institutions. May they grow better day by day."

# Which Way America?[2]

Ruth Alexander

*Born Chicago, IL, 1899; A.B., 1920, M.A, 1921, Ph.D., 1933, Northwestern University; concert pianist, 1929-30; associate editor,* Finance, *1941-44; columnist,* New York Mirror, *1944-45; host,* Wake Up, America *radio show.*

## Editor's introduction

In this speech, in fervid, colloquial, and dramatic fashion, Ruth Alexander, a well-respected columnist and crusader for the free-enterprise system, debunked socialism and attested to the benefits of capitalism. Admonishing business persons for a lack of bravery, Alexander insisted that executives must "speak up for themselves." She charged those who led the socialist cause in the United States with "fak[ing] love for humanity" for their own economic and political gain. The liberal economy planner, she stated, "likes to play God with other people's money." In contrast, "producers" are "the most important group in our nation." They, and not the "state," create goods and provide jobs, according to Alexander.

---

Which way America?

Don't let the title fool you. It's not in the nature of a prediction—any man's folly. It won't tell you which way the international wind blows—any man's guess. It will tell you which way the flag at home—namely, where we stand; where we're headed; who pointed our nose in that direction and what we can do about it.

In other words, the content of this talk is an analysis of present trends—and inquiry into their origins and objectives. The purpose of this talk is to persuade businessmen to throw off their occupational timidity and speak up for themselves.

What have you got to lose?

Your good name has been taken from you. Your incomes have been pilfered and are on the way to confiscation. Your shelter is often on a thirty-day basis. Your children have been indoctrinated with communism in the name of a "liberal" education. And now your wives are to face the hazards of childbirth under doctors who are politically certified.

What are you waiting for?

I think I know. I think you are waiting for the answer to the $64 question—"But what can I do about it?"

You'd be surprised. You can do a great deal. You got yourselves into the dog house because you "scare easy." You can get yourselves out by refusing to scare at all.

Certainly there is no use talking about it if we don't intend to do anything about it. And if we can't—or won't—do anything about it now we might as well call it a day for the grand old USA, lie down, roll over, and purr at the feet of those who fake "love for humanity" in order to get power over humanity.

First, where do we stand?

By the terms of the President's messages, fulfilling his campaign promises with unprecedented fidelity, we have assumed the mantle of socialism. For fifteen years we hung by our eyelashes over the precipice of the police state. We are no longer on the brink. We are within the borders. A planned economy is inconceivable without Gestapo eyes and ears and jails to insure fulfillment of the plan—which, however wise, can never be unanimous.

I had hoped that the end result of the second war to spread Democracy would be as advertised. I thought that this time our shots for freedom might go home. But again they went wild. We set out to Americanize Europe. Instead, we Europeanized America. We set out to reverse

[2]Delivered to the Northeastern Retail Lumberman's Association, in New York, New York, on January 26, 1949.

the Socialist "trend of the times." Instead, we climbed on the band wagon. We set out to lead a "liberated" world away from a planned economy. Instead, we embraced it ourselves.

Of course it doesn't make sense. But there it is.

For better or worse, now—but not necessarily forever—the President's program makes us an integral part of the Socialist world. Our attitude toward property, privacy, and personality is based on the universal orthodox Socialist concept of the relationship between the individual and the state. Namely, the dominance of the state—defined as a living tissue, a pseudo-biological organism—over its subordinate and component parts, the individual citizens.

I am talking to you as producers—the most important group in our nation. I want to tell you something about your competitor—the state as producer. You may think you're in competition with one another, but the great menace to you all is the monopoly state. Let me read you my column for the New York *Mirror* of Sunday, January 30 [1949], on this subject and then you won't have to get it! (Just be sure you get all other Sundays to come!)

"Last Sunday I said it made no difference who owns the instruments of production as long as the product or 'national dividend' is large and is consumed by the people.

"I want to elaborate that today.

"It makes no difference whether one, a few, or many own our tools as long as they are in private hands. When they are owned or operated by the state that is something else again, and it makes all the difference in the world.

"In any society the state is merely the name used to describe a group of men in power—for the time being or life, as the case may be.

"These men, the state, do not make their living by creating and exchanging goods and services in the market place.

"They are not 'in trade,' as the British snobs used to say. They are in politics. They are not producers. They are parasites who live off the productive efforts of the citizen taxpayers.

"There is nothing wrong about that unless government becomes so swollen with bureaus, and their administrators, "bureaucrats," that the taxpayers are bled white.

"In any case, the state produces nothing. Everything it has it gets. Everything it gives away it first must take away.

"If the state decides to give Mr. Voteright Smith free room and board, free education, hospitalization, etc., etc., it must first take away the money to pay for these services from Mr. Taxpayer Jones. THERE IS NOTHING FREE.

"When the state owns or operates industry it can afford to operate it at a loss. It has access to unlimited tax money with which it can subsidize its losses.

"But private industry cannot operate at a loss for long. Unless it can keep its cost of production low enough to make an annual profit it must shut up shop.

"Which do you think will operate more efficiently—the state which has no incentive to make a profit or private industry to which profit is a matter of life and death?

"And which will result in the largest product, the greatest national dividend, the biggest piece of pie to be cut by us all? Efficiently operated industry, looking for a greater and greater reward, or inefficiently operated industry, indifferent alike to profit or loss? You don't need me to answer that. Just use your own common sense."

That's the story for January 30. I wish I could write every day instead of every Sunday. As a matter of fact, I do write every day! It takes me six days to compress an economic earthquake into five-hundred words and on the seventh I rest—just like the Bible says.

According to the President's proposals, which I assume will become laws, property, defined as producers' goods, is to be publicly owned and/or operated in key industries. Privacy—defined as the right of the individual to buy or sell; to labor or loaf; to spend or save—at his discretion—is to fall by the axe of the tax collector. Personally, defined as valuable variations in opinions, in choice of livelihood, education or association, is to be standardized by over-all conformation to the plan.

The outlook is grim. But there's always another chance. What are twenty years to history?

As of today, however, we are embarking upon a Yankee version of the current British experiment.

Our self-styled "liberals" thought it would be just dandy to try socialism over here in keeping with the "trend of the times." In fact, the lunatic fringe thought so-called "Democratic socialism" might ward off Soviet socialism! They wanted to cuddle up to the Russian baby bear to keep the Russian papa bear away! But the child has the potential characteristics of the parent and Democratic socialism is identical with Lenin's "Democratic centralism"—the transitional stage between capitalism and communism!

But what has socialism of any kind—British or Russian, or German or Italian—produced that makes it so hot? Why should we imitate a non-productive economy? What makes England tick, for instance, when millions of people are getting something for nothing? We, a productive economy, are providing something. That's what makes England tick! We are subsidizing socialism.

Nearly two hundred years ago, the great British philosopher, Jeremy Bentham, pointed out that that government which provides the "greatest good for the greatest number" is the most desirable.

In the machine age Bentham's statement must be amended to read, "the greatest goods to the greatest number." Capitalism provides the greatest goods to the greatest number. Compare the relative scales of living in our capitalist democracy and any Socialist country throughout all history.

The voluntary exchange of goods and services in a free competitive market provides the greatest goods to the greatest number.

A free market is outlawed by the terms of Socialist over-all planning. No matter how wise the plan or how considerately enforced, compulsion is its essence and maximum productivity its despair.

Russia, England, and France are paying the price of compulsory exchange of goods and services. The incentive of personal gain for personal labor has been reduced in England and removed in Russia—a difference in degree, not in kind. Result. The people's scale of living is at subsistence level, consumers' goods are so scarce they must be rationed, and producers' goods are at the mercy of politicians.

What is there in that setup that is worthy of imitation? Yet we asked for it. Our record, if nothing else, should have demonstrated that capitalism is the most productive system and must be preserved for that reason if no other. Yet we deliberately chose a system of socialism with its inevitable by-products of compulsory labor, allocation of jobs and goods, and taxation without cessation.

Even if our socialism should prove "successful," it would mean merely an equality of poverty—as in England and Russia today. Poverty is an unworthy and uneconomic aim. Capitalism inherited poverty from its predecessors, primitive socialism and feudal socialism, wherein the top "looked after" the bottom and the bottom "looked up" to the top for its daily bread.

But capitalism has done more to alleviate poverty than any system known to mankind. It is the "wunderkind" of history. And we want to scrap it!

Sometimes we even apologize for it and, like the apostle Peter, deny our allegiance to it. "Who, me? Oh no, I'm not a capitalist, I'm a liberal!" Even businessmen have been known to say things like that—in their off moments, of course! Even businessmen's wives have been known to sabotage the very system which provides food, clothing and shelter for them and their children. They will do a marvelous job of budgeting and marketing to get the most for their dollar and then go straight down the street and vote away half their husband's entire income because they think it is fashionable to be a "liberal"!

But what is a modern "liberal"? A man who likes to play God with other people's money. Liberal with others' earnings—no relation to liberty—but first cousin to regimentation. A liberal is one who poses against special privilege for the businessman—a producer—in order to get special privilege for himself—a parasite. For privilege can never be abolished, though the personnel of the princes of privilege may change.

Finally, a liberal is one who says—and who may believe—that he does not want socialism and its derivative, communism—but who supports freedom of speech for Socialists and Communists because of a deformed interpretation of liberty.

But back to our socialism, vintage 1949—How did we get that way? What appeal could socialism, a scarcity economy, have to us, luxuriating in the economy of plenty provided by capitalism?

Well, I'll tell you. It appealed to minority pressure groups who itched to get their hands in the tax gravy and their signatures on the law books.

Some of these groups were organized—like labor and the city bosses. Some were technically unorganized but occupationally amalgamated. Some were ideologically knit, soul mates of socialism—like the penthouse pinks who sling the political slang of ragamuffins but who live the life of Riley.

The next time one of your defeatist friends shrugs his shoulders and says, "But what can we do? It's what the people want?" Please reply, "It's what what people want?" Then name the above mentioned minority pressure groups which obviously are not the people.

I doubt if all these knew what they voted for or what they want. I further doubt if the President, himself, realized the fatal implications for freedom in his messages. I have great respect for his personal integrity, and I only wish his information were comprehensive regarding socialism.

For a man's judgment is no better than his information. And the public mind has not been informed on the program upon which they are embarking. In fact, I'll go so far as to say that if an unmistakable majority of fully informed and fully aware voters had passed reasoned and sober judgment on socialism and voted for it by name, I, for one, would put up and shut up.

I emphasize by name. For, hitherto, we have been sold a Socialist bill of goods piecemeal. This time we went the whole hog and it should have been tagged, so the voter would have known the contents of the package he bought.

I have long advocated a fair trade practices act in the field of ideas. So many things are put over on us under assumed names. It might have spared us the economic cannibalism of socialism. Opponents of capitalism have called it contemptuously a dog-eat-dog economy. But for real juicy cutthroat practices the monopoly state of socialism has no equal. Under capitalism, there is always recourse to the state if the going gets too rough and monopoly rears its ugly head. But under socialism the state itself is the monopoly—the sole producer, the sole distributor, the sole employer.

But the state is not the creator. That is the unforgivable sin of socialism.

Let me tell you in a nutshell the line where capitalism ends and socialism begins. In a free capitalist economy, exchange of goods and services takes place between the two interested parties—buyer and seller. They determine the conditions of the bargain—if any. Whatever is offered, each can take it or leave it—there is no cracking down, no coercion, no hard feelings.

In a planned socialist economy, the state steps in and determines the terms of the bargain, from which there is no appeal. The case for this economic interventionism rests off the assumption that the state will enforce better terms as to price. Better terms for whom? For the poor man who may be undeserving? For the rich man who may contribute heavily to campaign funds?

No one can tell. But X marks the spot where capitalism ends and socialism begins; where a non-productive but not disinterested third party—the state—steps in, determines the conditions of exchange and enforces its decision by violence.

As for the place where socialism ends and communism begins, there is no signpost. That is the terrible danger. One merges into the other by a series of gradual changes. The qualitative break is made between capitalism and socialism. From then on, the breaks are quantitative and creep imperceptibly inch by inch upon an indifferent or ignorant people.

I could talk forever on this subject. But the time is getting short and I know you have important appointments. Let me conclude with some specific suggestions which are my answers to the question—"Now that I know where we stand, where we are headed, and who pointed our nose in that direction, what can I do about it?"

Speaking broadly, you can organize and you can become class conscious. Class warfare was not of our choosing, but our survival depends on its outcome.

Organization is inevitable in the machine age. Modern industry and agriculture demand skill. Organization is the social expression of technical skill. Labor figured that out and has acted with more dispatch than business. Take a page from labor's book. Be intolerant of those who sabotage your team by refusing to join your organization. For the only hope of survival is for business to organize from attic to cellar. Organization does not mean monopoly. Your own great associations—the least monopolistic in the nation when it comes to restricting production or influencing the market—stand as a beacon light to business in general.

Further, specifically, disabuse the public mind of the propaganda that there is any economic antagonism between so-called "big" business and "little" business. "Big" depends on "little" for parts and "little" depends on "big" for a market. They are mutually dependent, but "big" business has taken the biggest beating from the politicians who feed at its hands. "Little" business has been courted by the same men who have tried to discredit its market, "big" business.

Third, contribute money to your organization without stint. A man can't fly on one wing and an organization is helpless without a well-filled pocketbook for participation in public affairs. It is staggering to realize that "the combined legislative expenditures for all business organizations of all trades do not match the legislative appropriations of one of the two rival labor organizations."

What do you expect for a dollar—and a two-bit dollar at that?

Fourth, go class conscious. Be proud and loud about the fact that you belong to the middle class—the creators and preservers of our two-edged sword, capitalism and democracy.

When "liberals" accuse your capitalism of boom-and-bust shenanigans, remind them that the universe itself is characterized by periodicity. Why not the market? It is not an isolated phenomenon but is dependent on the physical phases of life, such as the crops, and on the social phases, such as wars and peace. Nobody can predict Mother Nature or human nature. And they are beyond control.

Fifth, speak out in meetings. When the cracker barrel Socialist yaps about profits being too high, ask him, "Too high for whom? Too high for the employer who must plow them back into the business or put them away for a rainy day? Too high for labor when employment always follows the trend of profits? Or just too high for politicians who want to make hay out of them?"

Sixth, above all, take pen in hand! Never underestimate the power of a single letter. It sounds trite to say, "write your Congressman." So I say, "Wire your Congressman and write everybody else." Much of our freedom of speech has been all freedom and no speech. Write blistering letters to forums whose "neutrality" exists in name only. Let radio stations and advertisers know when their stooges offend your class patriotism. Send love and kisses to that small lonely band of Americans who have been fighting your battles so long and with so little encouragement from you. Meaning, among others, John T. Flynn, Fulton Lewis, Jr., Westbrook Pegler, Henry J. Taylor, George Sokolsky, Isaac Don Levine, Sam Pettingill—and Ruth Alexander!

It may be too late. But it's worth trying.

If you will forget your fears which brought you to this lowly state and remember your magnificent and unsurpassed production which brought our nation to its high state you will hold your heads up once again.

It is your turn now to wake and rise. "You have nothing to lose but your chains!"

# Labor Day Message[3]

George Meany

*Born August 16, 1894, New York, NY; died January 10, 1980; plumber's apprentice, 1910-15; journeyman plumber, 1915-22; business representative, Plumbers Local Union, 1922-34; president, New York State Federation of Labor, 1934-39; secretary-treasurer, 1939-52, president, 1952-55, American Federation of Labor (AFL); president, American Federation of Labor/Congress of Industrial Organizations (AFL/CIO), 1955-79.*

## Editor's introduction

Regarded as a philosophical "heir" to the father of organized labor, Samuel Gompers, George Meany, former president of the American Federation of Labor (AFL), gave this forceful and altogether direct Labor Day address. In a rigid chain of reasoning, Meany asserted that to deal with the threat of the Soviet hydrogen bomb, we must have efficient production. Efficient production, according to Meany, depends upon efficient labor, which depends upon proper conservation of the labor supply. To conserve the labor supply, i.e. to use it as effectively and as efficiently as possible, inflation must be controlled, housing and social security must be guaranteed, medical costs must be reduced, and proper educational facilities must be devised.

---

Labor Day is the one national holiday which does not commemorate famous heroes or historic events. It is dedicated to the millions of men and women who work for wages, the people who have built America's towns and cities, the skilled and unskilled laborers who are responsible, in large measure, for the miracle of American industrial progress.

As the representative of nine million of these working men and women, it is my purpose to report to you on the issues which are of supreme importance on this Labor Day.

First comes the issue of war or peace. It was not resolved by the truce negotiated in Korea. That event has failed to ease the growing international tension caused by Soviet Russia's relentless determination to dominate and control the entire world.

Since the death of Stalin, sweet words have been broadcast by his successors in the Kremlin, but they mean absolutely nothing in the way of concrete assurance of peace. The grim facts are clear. The Russian dictators may change their tactics, but they have not changed their objective. They still refuse to enter into any enforceable agreement for disarmament. They still refuse to give up the use of war of aggression. They even refuse to work out reasonable peace treaties necessary to end chaotic conditions left over from the last World War.

To these ominous factors, something new had been added. The Communists have proved they now possess the secret of the hydrogen bomb—the world's most dreaded weapon.

What does atomic war mean? It means that a million people—men, women and children—can be wiped out of existence in a few seconds by a single bomb blast. It means that whole cities, with most of their population, can be reduced to ashes overnight.

To us that kind of warfare is unthinkable. Labor builds. It does not destroy. The thought of having our entire civilization go up in smoke appears to us nothing short of madness.

How can we prevent such a war? Our national leaders have explored every conceivable way to induce the Communists to listen to reason and used every possible approach to bring about peace by negotiation without concrete results. It would be folly to suppose that ap-

[3]Broadcast nationwide, from Washington, D.C., on September 7, 1953. Reprinted with permission of The George Meany Memorial Archives.

peasement would provide a solution. No dictator in history has ever been converted to human decency by appeasement. Partial surrender to the insatiable demands of the Communists can only lead eventually to total surrender.

The only thing they fear or respect is superior power. The only factor that will deter them from plunging the world into another war is the knowledge that they will have to contend against superior power.

How does America stand? Do we possess greater power than the Soviet empire? If not, how can we achieve it?

It is not my purpose to compare the military might of the free world with that of the Communists. That is not my field. In modern warfare, the prime factor actually is the ability to produce. And in that respect, America enjoys at this time definite superiority.

When reduced to essentials, production depends upon men and machines and raw material. We have the skilled manpower. We have the machines. And we possess, or have thus far been able to import from the free world, all the materials we need.

Some of our military strategists believe that the production problem of greatest concern is access to raw materials. I disagree. All the materials in the world and all the machines in the world put together would produce nothing without a capable, a loyal and a willing work force.

Thus the human element is obviously the main element in the national defense picture. And that is why, by all means, we should concentrate on strengthening the status and the security of the working men and women who serve in the front lines of our defense production program.

On this Labor Day, the American worker stands head and shoulders above the workers of any other land. His wages and working conditions are better. He and his family have better homes to live in, better food to eat and better clothing. These advances did not come to the workers of our country automatically. They were won by organizing into trade unions and by struggle against stubborn opposition.

Because they are better off, the workers of America produce more than workers in other countries, who do not possess the skill, the training nor the incentive to get ahead. By the same token, the high standards enjoyed by American workers create the mass purchasing power which has made it possible for industry to grow and expand to a productive capacity unmatched anywhere on earth.

This is the bright side of the picture. But there is another side. There are glaring weaknesses in our national life which require immediate action, vulnerable spots which demand correction if we hope to muster our total strength for the long-drawn-out struggle ahead.

Let's get down to cases. First is the basic problem of inflation. Higher wages don't buy any more groceries when the cost of living keeps climbing to record heights. When the Eighty-third Congress abolished economic controls and killed rent controls, we were told that prices could more effectively be stabilized by indirect methods. Well, those methods haven't worked. The working people of this country and the farmers as well, are being victimized by unjustifiable profiteering. It must be stopped. It is up to Congress to halt inflation if the nation is to be kept strong.

The second problem is housing. At least eight million of our people are still living in the worst kind of slums—slums that breed disease, juvenile delinquency and crime. Yet the Eighty-third Congress cut off the low-cost, public housing program which is the only effective method of replacing slums with decent housing for those in the lowest income brackets.

Even families with moderate incomes cannot buy the homes they need at prices they can afford. The government increased interest rates to the bankers on home loans, but it took no action to meet the housing shortage. At the rate our population is growing, the country will need 12 million new housing units in the next six years. To prevent needless suffering and to keep the American people strong, Congress should act promptly to encourage the building industry to meet this acute deficiency.

Another field, in which we have gone backward instead of forward, is social security. This is the self-insurance program through which our country has sought to protect the American people from fear of unemployment and fear of destitute old age. It has served also as a powerful bulwark to economic stability and the security of the free enterprise system itself.

But what has happened to social security? Millions of Americans are still left unprotected. Inflation, with its fifty-cent dollar, has cut benefits below the minimum subsistence level. Almost 10 per cent of our people have now reached the legal retirement age of sixty-five. Millions more are approaching old age in fear of poverty.

To afford them the security which they were promised and for which they paid insurance, through payroll taxes, Congress is duty-bound to improve the social security program. Yet it has done nothing but to postpone action.

The record of the Eighty-third Congress on health problems is even worse. It refused to give any consideration whatsoever to the growing need for a national program to insure the American people against the high cost of medical care. It took no action on bipartisan appeals for aid to medical schools so that the alarming shortage of doctors, nurses and hospital facilities could be overcome.

Obviously, Congress has failed to meet human needs in the vital field of social security and health. It has failed to strengthen the nation.

When it comes to the need for education, there can be no controversy. The facts speak for themselves. The Federal Commissioner of Education only a few days ago reported shocking conditions in American schools due to reopen this month, after summer vacations. There is a tremendous shortage of school space for our children. One out of every five will be exposed to the danger of fire-traps. There are not enough teachers to go around. The shortage of 72,000 teachers is due to the fact that teachers' salaries have been allowed to sink shamefully low.

This is the official record. Congress knows all the facts. The members of Congress understand, as well as you or I, the prime importance to our national vitality and safety of good education for the nation's children. Yet what has it done about this basic problem of Federal aid to education? Absolutely nothing. Surely, in the field of education, our nation must be greatly strengthened.

Finally, we are still faced with the serious problems arising from the manifest unfairness of the Taft-Hartley Act to the nation's workers. Because it is weighted against labor, this law can—at any time—throw production schedules out of balance. This fact is clear to the responsible leaders of our nation. In his first message to Congress, President Eisenhower said that the law must be changed to eliminate union-busting provisions and to provide a fair and just code for the guidance of labor-management relations. Yet, after months of public hearings, Congress did nothing. Unless Congress fulfills its responsibility to act constructively on this issue at its next session, our nation will not be able to achieve its maximum production strength for survival against the threat of Communist dictatorship.

Let me make one thing clear. Congress will not act on any or all of these problems until and unless the people of this country demand action. Your Congress represents you. Under our democracy, you can make your government carry out your wishes or you can vote it out of office. The power to give America the power it needs is in your hands.

This is not the situation behind the Iron Curtain. Under the Soviet dictatorship, the people of Russia and its satellites have no will of their own. They must obey orders or die.

As we see it, the fatal weakness in Soviet Russia's armor is the enforced slavery of its people. When the test comes, slaves will never stand up under pressure like free men. This is not wishful thinking. It was proven in the last World War. It was proven all over again on June 17.

On that date, the whole world caught its first glimpse of the true conditions behind the Iron Curtain. Through the open window of East Berlin, we saw slave workers rise up against their oppressors and dare to fight guns and tanks with their bare fists. Since then, resentment of the workers against intolerable conditions has spread like wildfire throughout the satellite states. As soon as one uprising is suppressed, another springs up. The Communists cannot depend upon the loyalty and support of the people they have enslaved. They are hated.

We, in the American Federation of Labor, want no part of communism. Experience has taught us that free labor can exist and make progress only in a free land. There is no stronger enemy of communism in the world than the nine million men and women who make up the A.F.L.

Our hopes and objectives on this Labor Day can be summed up briefly. We want to make America strong so that it can continue to be free. We want to build up the whole fabric of our national life, so that the freedoms which all of us cherish can survive and endure.

# Enemies Within the House of Labor[4]

## James B. Carey

*Born August 12, 1911, Philadelphia, PA; died September 11, 1973; electrical worker, 1929-34; national organizer, American Federation of Labor (AFL), 1934; national secretary, Congress of Industrial Organizations (CIO), 1938; president, United Electrical, Radio, and Machine Workers of America, 1936-41; president, International United Electrical, Radio, and Machine Workers of America, 1950-65; secretary-treasurer, American Federation of Labor/Congress of Industrial Organizations (AFL/CIO), 1938-55; vice president, AFL/CIO, 1955-73; labor representative, United Nations, 1965-72.*

### Editor's introduction

The significance of this address by labor leader James B. Carey lay in its strong voicing of the AFL/CIO's determination to establish a code of ethics. At the time the speech was given, the United States Senate Committee on Improper Activities in the Labor or Management Field had been hard at work finding corrupt union leaders and forcing them into an early "retirement." In this speech, Carey told laborers that American labor was confronting a crisis from "within"—being "labor racketeering." Unlike business and industry, which are committed solely to profit, "labor," according to Carey, "aspire[s] to the highest moral and ethical ideals, and proclaim[s] . . . brotherhood, economic justice, human dignity, and the national welfare." Corruption within the union is therefore particularly inexcusable, given the mission of the union, as described by Carey.

---

This, the twentieth and last regular convention of the Pennsylvania State CIO, is both a solemn and portentous occasion.

I am extremely proud of having had the opportunity of addressing both the first convention of the Pennsylvania State CIO and its last convention. And if, in this final convention, we are inclined a bit toward sentimentality that indulgence is not only justified but appropriate. We would be less than human and we would be unfeeling toward our own hectic history if we did not, during these two climatic days, glance backward over the long, long path we have traveled during the past two decades. It would be surprising if we didn't look back even with a touch of nostalgia to the excitements and turbulences of our early years.

Those years have already started to take on something of a rosy, romantic glow. It's an astonishing thing but today, looking back over the receding years, it somehow doesn't seem so terrible that we had our heads clobbered by Pearl Bergoff goon squads or took beatings efficiently administered by Pinkerton thugs. The pain somehow seems to have disappeared from our recollections of broken arms and legs handed out by Baldwin-Felts professional strikebreakers. Today we look back on bloody noses given us by Railway Audit detectives or by Chowderhead Cohen almost as the equivalent of a merit badge or a distinguished service medal.

One reason, I believe, for the slightly romantic glow with which we are beginning to surround those early years is the fact that we won and our enemies were defeated. True, we lost battles—that is to say, we lost strikes and lost organizing campaigns—but we won the war. We are here today, but the once-powerful union-busting outfits and labor spy rackets have fallen into unmourned oblivion.

This twentieth convention of the Pennsylvania State CIO demonstrates that labor in this state, as in others, continues to grow larger and stronger. But the once-feared Pearl Bergoff?

[4]Delivered at the Pennsylvania Industrial Union Council's 20th convention, in Philadelphia, Pennsylvania, on February 27, 1957.

He's now a footnote in the histories of labor. The Pinkerton thugs? They're now embalmed in the pages of the La Follette Committee Reports. The Baldwin-Felts strikebreakers? I understand there are one or two of them left in wax museums. The Railway Audit detectives and Chowderhead Cohen? They are lost in ancient history as completely as Herbert Hoover's high celluloid collars and belief in the divine right of millionaire robber barons.

Yes, the world has changed in the nearly twenty years since the Pennsylvania CIO was born, but it's not enough to say merely that. The world has changed because we changed the world. The upsurge of the American labor movement in the depths of the Great Depression became one of the greatest moral and ethical crusades in history, a crusade that authoritative historians have termed "a second American revolution."

We of the labor movement more than any other group changed the moral and ethical climate of our country. We made employers moral and made the government moral.

We made employers moral by compelling them to abandon their ancient dog-eat-dog economic philosophy and forcing them to accept the fact that labor is not a commodity but a grouping of individual human beings with the same rights, privileges and capacities as employers. We made employers moral by compelling them to understand that their responsibilities did not begin and end with profits but that they had inescapable social and economic obligations to the workers who created their wealth, their leisure and their luxuries.

We made the government moral by helping elect an administration responsive to the needs of the people and by erasing forever the concept of government as an instrument in the service of big business and industry. We made the government moral by insisting successfully, for the first time in history, that government has a responsibility to alleviate the mass unemployment, hunger and homelessness created by the free enterprise system. We made government moral by establishing its obligation to bring humanity and decency to the cut-throat economic jungle created by big business and industry. We made government moral by demonstrating that it had both the right and the duty to intervene in the prescription of minimum wages, maximum hours, healthful working conditions, the prohibition of child labor, the right to bargain collectively, old age security, and a host of other benefits and protections.

Pennsylvania was the birthplace of the CIO; therefore, it must be counted as the birthplace of the moral and ethical crusade that became the "second American revolution." Your organization, therefore, has special reason for pride. When the CIO held its first constitutional convention in Pittsburgh in November 1938 your Pennsylvania Industrial Union Council was its host. In addition, Pennsylvania achieved the first successful unionization of such industries as mining, electrical, radio and machine manufacturing, and steel.

If we are investing those early years of the CIO with something of a romantic aura we may also be starting to forget the enormity of the strides we made in those early days.

For example, next Saturday, March 2, will be the twentieth anniversary of the signing of the first contract between the United Steelworkers of America and the United States Steel Corporation.

That first contract was a revolution in steel. Among other things, it jumped the pay rate for common laborers to 62.5 cents an hour. The significance of this lies in the fact that during the previous thirty-seven years—from 1900 to 1937—the rate for common laborers had increased only 15 cents, up to 47 cents an hour in 1937.

No wonder, therefore, that one of my sharpest recollections of that First Pennsylvania CIO Convention nearly twenty years ago is that we were people in a terrible hurry back in 1938. We were in a hurry to change the face of the American labor movement and in a hurry to change the world we were living in.

God knows the world we were living in did need changing and changing in a hurry. One of the resolutions passed by that historic first convention pointed out that there were at that time 13 million American workers unemployed. The American economy in 1938 was only slowly dragging itself out of the most devastating and degrading depression in history; mass unemployment, homelessness and hunger still stalked the richest land on earth.

It's a fascinating fact that today, almost twenty years later, most of the moral and ethical issues that occupied your first convention are still moral and ethical issues for American workers in 1957. To mention just a few of them:

Improved unemployment compensation; expanded social security; better minimum wage legislation; a national housing program; an equitable Federal labor law; and effective civil rights statutes.

I said these were moral and ethical issues, and indeed they are. They involve economic and social morality and such ethical concepts as justice, decent living standards and human dignity. They are moral and ethical issues, moreover, because they affect not simply trade union members but all the nation's wage earners, the economic health of their communities and the economic health of the nation as a whole.

I want to suggest that your forthcoming creation of a great, new, unified labor movement in Pennsylvania should be the occasion for a fresh evaluation of the moral and ethical responsibilities both of trade unionism and of business and industry.

Such a reappraisal is vital for two reasons:

First, the essential purposes of establishing a new, unified trade union movement are moral and ethical insofar as we seek to create a more effective instrument in the service of human welfare and social good. Second, a reappraisal of business ethics and morality may disclose whether unionism and business share, to any degree, common ethical and moral objectives.

Turning first, therefore, to trade unionism, let me put the problem to you—as I see it—as frankly and as bluntly as I possibly can.

The American labor movement today is faced with a moral and ethical problem as crucially important as the problem that produced the CIO and the "second American revolution" in the mid-1930's.

Very possibly it is an even bigger problem, because this one has arisen not outside the labor movement but from within. This is a problem—a crisis, if you wish—that has emerged not from any external situation, not from defects in our economy, not from union-hating employers, not from antilabor legislation.

On the contrary, this problem, this crisis, has been generated almost entirely from within the labor movement. We cannot, justifiably, blame others. Whatever eventuates—for good or for evil—the labor movement must accept the responsibility.

The cancer of labor racketeering, of corrupt unionism, menaces not only the good name, the prestige and reputation of the labor movement today; it also threatens the very future of our development as a free labor movement.

By itself labor racketeering is immoral and unethical. But it may also have three other direct effects.

First, labor racketeering—no matter how limited—smears all labor with the foul taint of corruption.

Second, labor racketeering places incomparable propaganda weapons in the hands of union-hating employers to render organizing work either impossible or enormously more difficult.

Third, labor racketeering provides the excuse and justification for savagely repressive antilabor laws in Congress and state legislatures.

But here let us make one thing extremely clear. We do not and cannot confine our definition of union corruption to statutory crimes, to indictable offenses. Corruption is not demarcated by such felonies as bribery, extortion, theft of union funds, shakedowns of employers, financial alliances with the underworld of gambling and vice, or kickbacks from the investment of welfare and pension funds.

There is such a thing as venal corruption. There can be crimes in the labor movement that are not illegal but morally reprehensible.

Venal corruption, I think, can arise when union officials are men who view their organizations not as a sacred trust, not as a brotherhood, not as the preliminary realization of an ideal, but rather as a business enterprise, a cold-blooded commercial undertaking.

Venal corruption can arise when enormous gaps develop between the living standards of union members and the living standards of union leaders, when union officers start to own large business enterprises, apartment houses, stables of race horses.

Venal corruption can arise when union officials come—consciously or unconsciously—to think of the labor movement as a means to personal enrichment, huge bank accounts, swimming pools in their front yards and artificial waterfalls in their living rooms.

Those who, either legally or illegally, use unionism solely as a means to personal enrichment deserve to be hounded out of the American labor movement as fast, as furiously and as finally as we can find the means to do it!

Such men are not unionists, but antiunionists! They are not labor, but antilabor! They are more dangerous to the democratic labor movement than the worst of union-hating managements! They are more poisonous than professional spies and strikebreakers! They are more destructive than the union-busting goon squads of two decades ago! They are more contaminating than any kind of decay that can afflict a labor union!

Because they betray us and our ideals from within the labor movement, they are doubly abominable and doubly dangerous. Because they exploit the sanctuary of union brotherhood to despoil the very name and idea of brotherhood, they bring a loathsome contagion into our midst.

We can fight reactionary employers and we can hold our own in combat with union-hating managements because we know pretty thoroughly where they stand. They don't pretend to be the opposite of what they are. They don't (at least not often these days) attempt to betray our organizations from within. Our fighting with management in recent years has become increasingly above-board. We know who our enemies are in the arena of economic conflict.

But we're not so sure today that we know who our enemies are within the labor movement. We know, however, that they are there, using the labor movement as a shield for their despicable practices. We know that trade unionism has been and is still perverted into a protective cover for criminal activities.

The undeniable fact is that the House of Labor has termites and, therefore, needs a fumigation!

There's no sense in trying to reassure ourselves with the fact that the number of termites is limited. We risk self-deception by repeating to ourselves that only a very small percentage of unions and workers are involved in racketeering.

But the fact of the matter is that we do not know today how far the termites have eaten into the foundations, nor actually how extensive the infestation is.

Of one thing we are certain, however. One single national union that is corrupt is one too many! One single local union that is run by racketeers is one too many!

Corruption anywhere in trade unionism is morally indefensible. Perhaps in only one other institution in contemporary society—our religious bodies—is there a greater obligation to moral purity than in the labor movement.

Business and industry are institutions erected frankly to the purpose of profit. They make little or no pretense of being either altruistic or humanitarian. Hence there is a minimum of hypocrisy when business and industry operate unethically or for immoral ends. The public has been conditioned to accept business immorality—and even business criminality—as an inevitable part of the dog-eat-dog world which business and the free enterprise system have created for themselves.

But there's no such immunity for organized labor, because labor professes to be an altruistic and humanitarian movement. More than that, we aspire to the highest moral and ethical ideals, and proclaim that our only motivations are brotherhood, economic justice, human dignity, and the national welfare.

Within such a spiritual framework as this, consequently, there can be no room for moral laxity or lapses from high principle.

More than any other organizations in our society, trade unions ought to be able to live inside out. They should be able to disclose themselves fully to public view, to scrutiny by friend and foe alike. More and more unions find it possible to do so. It is to be regretted that in other instances the complete disclosure of union finances and resources might very well become an open invitation to employers to risk a strike or undertake a decertification campaign.

Yes, it is true that only a very limited area of trade unionism—as far as we know—is affected by corruption, and only a small percentage of unions and workers are victimized by racketeering.

But that fact doesn't mean a thing to big business and industry. The truth is that every union represented in this convention is finding that new organizing has been made immeasurably tougher by the continuing disclosures of corruption and racketeering in the labor movement.

Organizing has become tougher because: (1) unorganized workers have read the newspaper stories and concluded that because one union or two unions are corrupt all unions must be, or (2) employers are actively exploiting the corruption disclosures as antiunion propaganda.

Either way I'm afraid that for thousands upon thousands of unorganized workers the tremendous accomplishments of organized labor over many decades can be obliterated by a few screaming headlines dealing with isolated cases of labor racketeering.

We cannot know, for example, but we can easily guess what psychological balance was achieved by two different occurrences here in Philadelphia last week.

One was the dedication of a splendid new $1.5 million union health and medical center, the realization of a longtime dream of twenty-eight Philadelphia unions. Here was a manifestation of union brotherhood, humanitarianism and social conscience at its best.

The headlines were fair; however, it was a one-shot news story for the local press.

But in one or more Philadelphia newspapers on that same day—and every day since, as far as I can ascertain—there has been another kind of headline and another kind of news story dealing with labor.

This running news story has recounted the sordid and sickening history of a flagrantly racket-controlled local union here in Philadelphia, a union run by criminals and ex-convicts for the sole purpose of defrauding workers out of tens of thousands of dollars while at the same time extorting additional thousands from their employers.

Here is one of the foulest stenches ever to afflict the city of Philadelphia where the American labor movement was born and where so much union history has been made.

Discussing as we are the question of union morality you will, I am sure, find particularly interesting the moral safeguards established by the constitution of this local union.

This, if it were not so tragic and vicious, could be comic. The ex-convicts, the goons who run this racket union, who offer kickbacks from members' dues to employers, who seek sweetheart and sell-out contracts, who employ coercion and terror on employees and employers alike, these men who represent virtually everything that is hateful to honest unionism, these creeps had the brazen effrontery to write a local union constitution which declares in Article 1—and get this!—"An applicant for membership must be of good moral character. . . . "

Which do you think has made the deeper and more permanent impression on the average, nonunion citizen of Philadelphia—the dedication of the wonderful new union health center or the disclosures of a rotten racket outfit masquerading as a labor union? Which will be remembered? Which will do most to shape and color public attitudes toward labor? I'm afraid we know only too well.

In the face of screaming outrages like this one are we to console ourselves with the recollection that, still and all, only a tiny portion of labor is involved? In the face of similar abominations dredged up by congressional investigating committees, are we to take refuge in percentages and in pious hope that such conditions will remedy themselves?

No, of course we can't. The labor movement has already waited far too long to cut out these festering sores. We are paying a heavy penalty already for allowing them to continue, and we are likely to pay even heavier penalties in the future.

Probably every union represented in this convention, as I remarked earlier, has had organizing made tougher by these revelations of union corruption. Antiunion employers from coast to coast and from Canada to the Gulf of Mexico have jumped gleefully on these disclosures and now are using them as clubs with which to clobber union organizing campaigns.

Our IUE organizing campaigns, for example, have recently had to confront that type of propaganda weapon in the hands of huge corporations and small companies alike. The stories of union corruption are being hurled at us by officials of the billion-dollar General Electric and Westinghouse companies, among others.

To cite only one instance, the IUE is currently conducting a determined campaign to organize a new General Electric plant in Hendersonville, North Carolina. GE, it is clear, would like to brainwash its employees into believing that union dues are entirely devoted to providing union leaders with luxuries and the means for riotous living. The GE employee newspaper in Hendersonville reported in a recent issue, for example, that a congressional committee discovered that one union leader had:

"used union funds to pay his personal bills; another official allegedly used money from the membership to finance his stable of race horses and pay for the upkeep of horse vans, and additional union money was used to buy and repair this same official's personal automobile."

And so it goes. GE hopes, of course, that some of the mud it flings will stick to the IUE, and that a majority of workers will associate the charges of misused union funds with our international union.

Make no mistake, we're going to have more of this kind of vicious propaganda thrown at us. Management likes it; management believes it works. I'm afraid that maybe it does; so are other union officials I've talked to.

There, then, is part of the picture of how employers can use—and do use—a few instances of union corruption to smear the entire labor movement.

But that doesn't end it. Those few instances have also put potent antiunion weapons into the hands of reactionaries in Congress and in state legislatures. Yesterday as the Senate Select Committee on Improper Activities in the Labor or Management Field opened hearings in Washington we learned for the first time that the investigation is now scheduled to continue for a full year. Its chairman has been quoted as saying, even before the hearings opened, that legislation is necessary because "working people must be protected from a form of extortion, theft and embezzlement. . . . "

In nearly a score of state legislatures new and more repressive antilabor laws are being prepared, more often than not at the instigation of industrial employers. And the excuse for these new laws will be, more than ever before, the disclosures of union corruption and racketeering.

The influential *New York Times*, for example, in an editorial on abuses in the administration of union welfare funds, first demanded that Congress pass legislation to outlaw these abuses, then added, "And state legislatures throughout the country should enact their own laws. . . . "

We can well imagine what kind of laws will be proposed in states that already have right-to-scab laws in operation, states that encourage municipalities to enact statutes requiring union organizers to buy licenses and pay daily fees for the right to organize.

Those are the penalties under which we're suffering today because we allowed a handful of racketeers and businessmen masquerading as unionists to continue their criminal careers inside the labor movement.

Let me emphasize right here that I have no intention nor desire to paint a picture that is entirely dark. On the contrary, there are dramatically bright aspects, features in which the labor movement can take pride.

We can, for example, ask ourselves: what other movement has set out voluntarily to eradicate the evil elements inside itself, even at the risk of weakening its organizational strength?

What other institution or major organization in American society has undertaken to police itself, to cleanse its own ranks of wrong-doing and wrong-doers?

What employer organization, such as the United States Chamber of Commerce or the National Association of Manufacturers would expel, suspend or even denounce an affiliated company found guilty of corruption or other crimes?

The extent to which trade unionism is determined to drive the termites from the house of labor was shown earlier this month when the AFL-CIO Executive Council, with only one dissenting vote, approved a set of Codes of Ethical Practices. In this unprecedented action, the AFL-CIO in effect declared war on corruption and racketeering. At long last the entire American labor movement was provided the means with which to free itself from corruption and the perversion of union ideals.

I am personally proud that a week before this announcement, the IUE adopted its own Code of Ethical Practices designed, as we declared, "to prohibit any conduct that would countenance racketeering, racism, corruption or undemocratic practices of any kind."

Our Code of Ethical Practices set new precedents as a comprehensive document, covering such areas of union operations as organizational work, administration of health-welfare-pension programs, the conduct of local union affairs including membership rights and elections, the management of local union funds, and enforcement.

Among other requirements, the IUE Code calls for strict financial accounting and control of union funds. In general it is intended "not only to promote the principles and practices of trade union democracy but also to encourage the expansion and diversification of democracy within our union."

The IUE, therefore, is determined to erect every possible barricade against the invasion of unethical practices or corruption. The adoption of similar codes of ethical practices by other unions, I feel, is inevitable.

Let me point out that both the AFL-CIO Codes of Ethical Practices and the IUE Code of Ethical Practices deal not only with illegal activities but also with activities that are simply unethical. Both Codes, therefore, seek not merely to penalize criminal actions but also to establish higher principles and standards of conduct for unions and union officials.

We have got to make these Codes of Ethical Practices work. They must be made to function swiftly and vigorously against corruption and racketeering wherever they are proved to exist.

The Codes can and should also be employed to eliminate the businessmen disguised as union leaders, or at the very least convert them into unionists. The Codes can and should have the effect of making union leadership more sensitive and more responsive to rank-and-file needs. They should help narrow whatever unreasonable gaps have grown up between the membership and leadership of unions.

The labor movement has delayed overlong the decisive action necessary to its renewal as a great moral and ethical crusade. The labor movement can make up for that lost time and for the indulgence of corruption in its ranks by hitting hard and fatally now at labor racketeering wherever it can be found.

We can redeem our mistakes and insure a healthy and accelerated growth for American trade unionism by not waiting for grand juries, state legislatures of congressional committees to do our work for us.

We can justify the vast trust placed in us by millions of American workers and prove worthy of the heritage of sacrifice and dedication bequeathed to us by the men and women of labor who have preceded us only if we guide this greatest of all free labor movements to new high levels of morality and integrity.

In that lies both the hope and the need of the labor movement's future; the need of our nation's future, also.

# The Total Challenge of Automation[5]

## John I. Snyder, Jr.

*Born 1909, Chicago, IL; B.S., New York University, 1933; student, London School of Economics, 1934-36; lawyer, Kuhn, Loeb & Co., 1936-48; chairman, board president, U.S. Industries, Inc., 1948-71.*

### Editor's introduction

In 1964 legislation was introduced by Senator Hubert Humphrey to investigate the impact of automation upon employment. Immediately preceding Senator Humphrey's call for an investigation, John I. Snyder, Jr., chair and president of U.S. Industries, Inc., pointed out that "automation is here to stay." An industrialist who manufactured automation machinery, Snyder was fully aware that if America hoped to compete in world markets, automation was a necessity. He also readily admitted that automation would undoubtedly create unemployment. Expressing dismay at the placidity with which the country viewed the unemployment crisis occurring at the time, Snyder discussed five myths about automation and then suggested possible ways of creating more jobs in the automated society of the future.

---

I am deeply moved and honored to have been invited here today to address this vitally important convention representing our nation's organized labor force.

I know it is highly unusual for an employer to speak at any union convention, much less one as significant as this. Just to keep the record straight, I want you to know I addressed a major labor union convention once before—seven years ago, to be exact, in September 1956. The place was the Civic Auditorium in San Francisco and the occasion was the 24th Grand Lodge Convention of the International Association of Machinists. I believe I was the first employer ever to appear before that body of men.

My subject then was collectively bargained health and welfare programs—specifically the work of an organization called the Foundation on Employee Health, Medical Care and Welfare. This Foundation had been jointly established by the company I work for and the Machinists. Its purpose was to study ways and means by which labor and management could get the greatest possible benefits for their collectively bargained health and welfare dollars. I discussed with the Machinists in San Francisco exactly how we proposed to do this, and I believe that in the subsequent years the Foundation proved its worth many times over, not only to our company and the IAM, but to many other companies and unions as well.

Today my subject is very different. It is automation—a much more controversial and stormy topic than health and welfare benefits.

Before starting on that subject, I want to say a few words about a man well-known to you all—Al J. Hayes, international president of the IAM, and vice president of the AFL-CIO.

Al Hayes and I have known each other and have sat across bargaining tables from each other for many years. I am proud to number him among my closest friends. I also regard him as one of our most enlightened and farsighted labor leaders. He has been speaking for machinists for more than forty-five years and, lest anyone misunderstand these remarks from an employer, let me assure you that he also *fights* for them. I am sure you know this about Al at least as well as I do.

As you know, Al Hayes and I were co-chairmen of the Foundation on Employee Health, Medical Care and Welfare. Today, we are co-sponsors and co-chairmen of another foundation—the American Foundation on Au-

[5]Delivered at the AFL/CIO's 5th Constitutional Convention, in New York, New York, on November 15, 1964.

tomation and Employment; and it is in this latter context—as co-chairmen of our automation foundation—that I was asked to address you today.

Now I want to make it clear immediately that I do not regard myself as being particularly pro-labor—that is not my reason for being here. I am a manufacturer and an employer and in fact my company produces automation machines. I do *not* agree that automation is an evil. I believe automation is necessary for this nation today if we are to produce and sell goods in the face of world competition, and that ultimately it can do greater good for mankind, relieving man of much drudgery he has had to perform before.

However, I also believe it is in the best interests of all businessmen to work hard to solve the very real and immediate human problems that automation is creating. I want to sell the automation machines my company makes, and if our economy turns sour, if the unemployment problem is not solved, I will have difficulty selling them.

Let me repeat, I feel strongly that all business should share this view—that the unemployment problem and the automation problems are at least as serious for business as they are for labor.

Now, one of the main concerns of our Foundation has been to promote the automation dialogue—to call attention constantly to automation and its attendant human problems. We have felt from the beginning that if we are to solve the grave human problems that automation is creating and will continue to create, in increasing orders of magnitude, for some years to come, we are going to need really new ideas, genuine innovations; we have also felt that the more people become involved in conscientious discussion of these problems, the better our chances of finding the new ideas we need. And to this end, I've been doing quite a lot of talking on the subject of automation over the past few months.

The paradoxical age we live in is well illustrated by the opening of Dickens' *Tale of Two Cities:*

"It was the best of times, it was the worst of times [Dickens wrote]; it was the age of wisdom, it was the age of foolishness; it was the epoch of belief, it was the epoch of incredulity; it was the season of light, it was the season of darkness; it was the spring of hope, it was the winter of despair."

Dickens, of course, was writing about the time of the French Revolution but he could have been setting the stage for a thesis on the automation revolution.

On the one hand, Americans are earning more, spending more, and enjoying more material wealth than any other peoples in the history of the world. In these respects we are living in "the best of times . . . the season of light . . . the spring of hope."

On the other hand, as you've been hearing all week, more than 4 million of our people—or more than 5 per cent of our labor force—are without jobs, and more than 2.5 million have completely exhausted all of their unemployment benefits. For these people, it is "the worst of times . . . the age of foolishness . . . the epoch of incredulity . . . the season of darkness . . . the winter of despair."

Now I don't want to bore you with statistics—from my reading about your deliberations I gather that you've had plenty thrown at you in the past few days—but I would like to make the point that the "official" unemployment figures don't tell the full story. Professor Charles Killingsworth of the University of Michigan, who has been working closely with our Foundation, feels that the official statistics are below the *real* unemployment rate, which in 1962, he says, was not 5.5 per cent but closer to 8 per cent. He arrives at this figure by including a group whom he calls "the invisible unemployed," those who have run out of unemployment benefits and have stopped reporting in, and those who've got tired of looking for jobs and who tell the census taker "no" when asked if they're looking for work.

The point, however, is not which statistics are the right ones, but that whichever statistics we choose to use, the end result, if we are sane and humane men, should be a firm determination to remedy a frightening situation.

The reasons why our unemployment rates are high seem clear. Over the past ten years or so our labor force has been growing faster than new jobs have been created. This trend has been accelerating and will continue to accelerate for some years to come as our so-called "war babies" move into the labor market at a phenomenal rate. As an example, in the decade between 1950 and 1960 only 7.5 million young workers entered the labor market; in the current decade, in contrast, some *26 million* new young workers will enter the labor force and only 4.5 million of these intend to go to college. President Kennedy has said that nearly 8 million of them will not even have finished school—they are the "dropouts" we hear so much about.

Now to these facts we must obviously add the impact of technological change, or automation, depending upon which phrase you prefer. There is no question that automation *is* displacing workers. There is some question, however, about the rate at which machines are taking jobs away from men—without wanting to, I personally seem to have got myself into a debate on this point with some of the country's leading economists. Well, what they may not know is that I was an economist once myself, before I had to earn a living, and I can work with economic equations as well as the next man.

I read in the paper yesterday that the President's Council of Economic Advisers had concluded, on the basis of a recent examination of the figures, that blue-collar workers have been less affected by automation from 1957 to 1962 than they might have been from 1948 to 1957. This is an interesting conclusion. As far as I am concerned it really supports the theory that statistics can be shown to prove almost anything. I don't think such conclusions would be of substantial interest to the longshoremen who have had three cuts in job crews over the past ten years due to automation; to the railroad firemen whose services are no longer required on diesel engines; to the flight engineers whom modern technology has eliminated; to the men on the engine production lines in Detroit where new tooling of a sophisticated nature has directly replaced them; or to any other one of a thousand groups of people who know better than the statistics.

I will tell you right now what I have not told anybody before—that the formula we've been using in the Foundation to arrive at an estimate of how many people are losing their jobs to automation is almost exactly the same as one of the basic statistical formulas used in the past by the Department of Labor. Most of you know this formula. It isn't very dramatic. It involves simple multiplication of the over-all employment figure by the rate of increase of output per man-hour in any given year.

Thus in 1962 the total employment figure in the United States was roughly 67 million and the average rate of increase of output per man-hour was a little over 4 per cent, and if you multiply these you come up with more than 2.5 million jobs lost to automation last year. That would be 51,000 jobs a week. To allow for a margin of error we have maintained—we think realistically—that automation has been a major factor causing the loss of jobs at the rate of 40,000 per week.

Since I used this figure before a Senate Committee this fall, no one has come forward with any evidence to refute this staggering figure. In fact, your president, George Meany, has information that the figure may run as high as 80,000 jobs a week in the next year! And I'm inclined to agree that the rate of loss *will* accelerate unless something is done to stop it.

Now there is nothing sacred, or even exact, about our finding that automation is causing the loss of jobs at the rate of nearly 40,000 a week. As Secretary Wirtz has said, this statistic—how many jobs are machines taking over from men—is "a hard figure to arrive at."

What I *do* regard as sacred is the necessity for this country to face up to two hard and brutal truths. The first of these truths, with due apologies to President Meany, is that automation is here to stay. I don't think he issued a clarion call for a Luddite uprising. As I've said, this nation needs automation if it is to compete in world markets. The second truth is that automation is putting a hell of a lot of people out of work this year, and will continue to do so, increasingly, for a long time to come. These people are not confined to any single group. As we know, they include so-called blue-collar workers. They include white-collar workers—bookkeepers, clerks, statisticians, and accountants—who are also rapidly being replaced by sophisticated electronic brains of one kind or another. Even the ranks of what we know as "middle management" are starting to be thinned out by computers which make minor decisions automatically. In the insurance industry alone one study found that in the five years from 1952 to 1957 employment had increased by 200,000, or 23 per cent, while in the next five-year period, after computers began to move in, employment by insurance companies went up only 80,000, or 8 per cent.

And perhaps most important, there are the minority groups—in particular the Negroes. Their unemployment rate is higher than anybody's. As Whitney Young, executive director of the National Urban League, has pointed out, Negro workers constitute only 11 per cent of our total work force but *22 per cent* of the unemployed—largely in the "hard core" category. In the 14-to-24-year-old group, 10 per cent of our white boys but *17.5 per cent* of our Negro boys are unemployed; and 9.5 per cent of the white girls but *23 per cent* of the Negro girls are unemployed. As a friend of mine has put it, Negroes should be allowed at least to gain equality in unemployment. Today, the only way they seem to be able to enter the labor market is through attrition, death, retirement or disability of white workers.

Now to all of us here these facts, taken together, are appalling. In a time of great prosperity, we are faced with great and mounting unemployment. We are faced with the prospect of millions of our young people entering a labor force which is already overcrowded. We are faced with a Negro revolution at the very moment when we are also faced with an automation revolution which at best can only compound and aggravate all of the other problems.

Yet the country as a whole remains singularly unaroused and I can't help but wonder why. Is it because today we have so many benefits that we did not have back in the thirties—social security, welfare, unemployment compensations, and all the other desirable, necessary, and good benefits which we fought so hard to win? Is it because the unemployed aren't organized or represented by any spokesmen? The unemployed would make a pretty big union.

I don't know the answer. I do know that I find myself wondering about our placidity in the face of such challenges. And I do know that I find myself angry about the emergence of a whole series of delusions, or fallacies, with which we seem to have surrounded ourselves—not you gentlemen here, who know better, but the public at large, and in particular a large part of the business community of which I am a member. As Albert Camus, the Nobel Prize-winning novelist once said, "Truth, like light, blinds. Falsehood, on the contrary, is a beautiful twilight that enhances every object." Or as one of our humorists put it a hundred years ago: "It ain't what a man don't know that makes him a fool, but what he does know that ain't so."

I've been hammering away at these delusions—or myths, as I've sometimes called them—almost all of this past year, and I want to hammer at them some more right now. They are widely accepted and, it seems to me, they have had a deep tranquilizing effect on many men and women who otherwise might help us solve the human problems automation is creating. Therefore I think that they must be exposed as the fallacies they are. One way or another, they are all interrelated.

*Fallacy Number One* goes like this: that automation really is not going to eliminate many jobs, all things considered. Here, I will stand on some of the statistics I gave to you before, and on the flat statement I made earlier that automation is indeed eliminating jobs. I'm sure that all of us can think of examples to prove this point. Detroit, as we all know, is the center of automation, and largely as a result of this fact it is also one of our country's largest and most critical unemployment areas. A business magazine ran a survey on automation and employment this past June and came up with some frightening figures, of which I will give you only a few random samples: the number of employees in one major automobile company dropped 43 per cent between 1957 and 1962; in the chemical industry in the same period one leading company's employee roster was off by 8 per cent, another by 6 per cent, another by 5 per cent; a leading defense contractor in the same period had reduced its employees by 12 per cent; in the food industry the number of employees in three major companies were off 25 per cent, 17 per cent, and 12 per cent; and in the oil industry one leading company's employees were down 28 per cent, another's by 25 per cent. And so on. In almost all of these cases, the sales of the companies involved in the same period of time had increased rather substantially—or put another way, productivity was up.

It is important to remember in this context that automation is not only displacing people directly, but also indirectly through "silent firings." You all know what that phrase means—workers who without automation would eventually have been hired for specific tasks that are now automated. There are also those workers who lose their jobs through vertical integration due to automation, as in the case of a company which formerly supplied a third of Ford's body parts. When Ford automated its stamping plants, no Ford employees were displaced, but five thousand employees of the body company were obliterated from the payroll.

*Now for Fallacy Number Two:* this one holds that automation will create jobs, not only in the running of machines, but in the building and maintenance of them. Of course this is true to a degree, but not nearly to the degree that some would have us believe. Experience has shown that after the initial "debugging" of automated machines, they require relatively very little maintenance. If this weren't true, it would not make economic sense to automate. And if the equivalent number of workers replaced by automation were required to build the machines and systems, there would also be no point in automating. The automatic machines would cost too much.

*Fallacy Number Three* has to do with retraining: according to this dreamy fallacy, all of those nice people who lose their jobs to machines can be rapidly retrained and placed immediately in other jobs requiring higher skills and, naturally, paying more money. Most of our experience so far refutes this claim. Unfortunately, many of our workers appear to be simply not retrainable by present techniques. The Armour experiment of 1960 is already a classic of its kind: out of 433 packing-house workers displaced by machines in 1960, only 170 were at all interested in learning new skills, only 60 were eligible for the program, only 58 actually took the course, and *fewer than 20* wound up working at jobs relating to their retraining experience. In Huntington, West Virginia, more than 1,000 hard-core unemployed were notified about an Area Redevelopment Administration training program, but only 640 took the aptitude tests, and only 240 qualified. Up in Connecticut, some 3,500 semi-skilled applicants were screened for training for a state project and only 84 completed the course. Perhaps the most dramatic example along these lines has been California, where some 50,000 unemployed were eligible to take thirteen-week training courses, and yet only 38 applied for retraining, of whom 26 actually took the courses.

Our list of examples illuminating the fallacies of the retraining myth is a long one. I could go on and on reciting the grim case histories of dozens of companies whose experiments with retraining have failed for one reason or another. You just cannot force people into retraining, and after you retrain them you can't manufacture jobs out of thin air. We have not yet discovered a satisfactory system for retraining and reemploying a significant number of workers.

There is another matter which must be examined in any discussion of retraining. It has to do with the actual retraining methods employed. As we have been told over and over again, our country is in the middle of a teacher crisis. With overflowing classrooms providing half-day schooling, our teacher shortage is staggering.

If in the face of an appalling lack of teachers we attempt to provide retraining, how can we do it? For one thing, we can't do it by traditional teaching methods. Yet those public officials charged with the responsibility for retraining cannot use modern machine teaching techniques unless they are sure we will all accept them. Quite simply, if we don't accept them—little meaningful retraining is possible.

*Fallacy Number Four is as silly as Number Three:* this one has to do with relocation and holds that workers displaced by machines in one part of the country will find jobs with comparative ease, and with some help, in other areas. I know that Governor Rockefeller proposed this as a viable solution last week, but in my opinion—and I believe that our experiences to date bear me out—workers who lose their jobs due to automation or anything else are usually just those who are least able to move in the first place. They are generally the lower paid, the older, the unskilled workers who either cannot afford to move from an economic standpoint, or who are psychologically incapable of beginning a new life in a strange area. One sociologist studied a number of cases in which companies built new automated plants in new areas, offered employees jobs in their new plants, offered them moving allowances and many other services to insure a smooth transition. In one such case, a plant closing eliminated 325 jobs and it was found that of these, 265 had average debt liabilities of over $900 each. More than 100 owned houses. For those in debt and with those of homes of their own, moving was virtually an impossibility.

*Fallacy Number Five* concerns the Negro and his problem which I mentioned earlier: this fallacy holds that there is no relationship between the automation revolution and the Negro revolution. This is patent nonsense. *Fortune* magazine recognized this fall that the key issue involved in the Negro protest movement in this country today is jobs, and that automation has played a role in aggravating this problem. It certainly is clear to me, as a businessman, that the message spelled out by the freedom rides, the street demonstrations, the sit-ins and the boycotts, is that the gap between the column of figures running down the balance sheet and the column of Negroes marching down an embattled street is a slim one indeed, for what happens to one can gravely affect the other. As labor leaders, I think you must recognize that this is true also as it applies to your membership lists. All are interrelated and interdependent, and we are already feeling the enormous impact of the clash of what I regard as the two surging forces of our time: the growth of automation—sometimes inaccurately referred to as the Second Industrial Revolution; and the eruption of the Negro's demand for equality—sometimes referred to as the Second American Revolution. It seems to me there is little doubt that in eliminating the jobs of men who have been working and of millions of others who have not yet even come into the labor market, the technological revolution has intensified the social revolution.

Now, those are what I have come to think of as the Five Fallacies of Automation; and let me repeat that I mention them now because I feel they are serving as deep sedation for those who either cannot or will not come forward to grapple with the human problems caused by automation. It is much easier to look for proof that these problems do not exist than to admit their existence and move ahead towards a solution.

How do we move ahead towards such a solution? How do we generate the 3 to 4 million new jobs each year which we must generate if we intend to lick the unemployment problem? This is what we must all address ourselves to—you on the labor side; men like me, representatives of industry, on the management side, and representatives of government. We must somehow initiate a thoroughgoing search for solutions that will work.

Is tax reduction a solution? In my opinion if it creates enough purchasing power to stimulate enough additional production to stimulate additional employment, it *can* be a *partial* solution—but only partial. I do believe that a tax cut is necessary for the well-being of our economy but I also believe that we must remember that a tax cut won't help a worker who doesn't have any salary left to tax because he is unemployed.

At the very least a tax cut now of the proportions the Administration has proposed will help preserve the jobs of those now employed. If an early tax cut is not forthcoming, the effects on business will be adverse enough so that our numbers of unemployed will undoubtedly rise.

In your own terms as labor leaders, you must ask yourselves whether collective bargaining will provide a solution. In view of the threat of automation I believe the answer is obvious. In the hardest terms of automation, how can you negotiate the elimination of yourselves or of your members who are principal parties at the bargaining table? This is a serious problem, not only for you but for business leaders and the nation as well. Back in 1942, Winston Churchill said he hadn't become the King's first minister "in order to preside over the liquidation of the British Empire." Today no American in his right mind wants you to preside over any liquidations either. If that day ever comes, our nation is in very serious trouble.

Leaving aside all other considerations about collective bargaining, I don't believe that—*at least as we have known it in the past*—it can help us to solve the human problems created by automation. On the other hand, I *do* believe that the collective bargaining process will prove invaluable if it is employed with the kind of wisdom and vision which resulted in both the Kaiser steel agreement and in the industry-wide steel agreement. I think too that it is important to note that these agreements were arrived at without a timetable and without a deadline, which may indicate that collective bargaining in the future ought to become a round-the-year process instead of a round-the-clock, deadly deadline process.

How about the shorter work week—will it be the solution to the problems of automation? Well, as we all know, this one is something of a hot potato. Both my friend Al Hayes and Mr. Meany have specific views on the subject. They're for it. Harry Van Arsdale, that intrepid New York fighter in the cause of labor who sits on the board of our Foundation—Harry certainly has specific views on that subject, too. He is also for it. But other men in some very high places have other views.

In the context of the shorter work week, I want to quote from a brochure put out by the AFL-CIO:

"Under the most typical and likely circumstances [this brochure says] a company reducing its work week by several hours ordinarily will have to immediately hire additional workers to provide those hours of work if it wants to maintain approximately the same output or service as before.

"The longer-run effects then hinge on productivity movements [the brochure continues] and on whether demand for its products increases sufficiently to enable savings from economies of increased production to finance continued payment to workers. In principle, the combination of the new hiring by this and other companies will build aggregate worker income and, in turn, demand for the products.

"[Your brochure goes on to say that] the pivotal question is to what extent, by serving to maintain and often to increase employment, shorter hours will be the dynamic new ingredient to bolster demand and increase it to the point where more and more companies have to expand employment further and thereby carry along an accelerating rate of economic and employment growth."

I will tell you what I think. We have been studying the pros and cons of the shorter work week within the Foundation and on the basis of our studies, I *do* believe it has merit as a solution in the absence of other solutions—and if only because of some long-term benefits that it may produce. A shorter work week clearly means more leisure time. More leisure time requires means of constructively using it. A constructive use of leisure time will require new leisure time industries to be created. This means more total jobs.

Now, I want to propose other solutions to you. We need to act now, we need to become totally preoccupied with this problem—all of us in industry, labor and government—if we intend to solve it. I can't stress this too much. It is our greatest domestic problem. I am convinced that as a result of automation, as a result of our new relationship to machines, the relationship of the worker to both management and his union will also have to change somewhat now. I am also convinced that because the problem is so enormous, we have entered into an era in which we must court totally new ideas and totally new ways of approaching our problems—ideas and techniques that will be very far removed from any approaches we have known before. All such ideas should get fair hearings, no matter how outlandish they may seem. Our very salvation, in my opinion, depends on innovation—innovation and the cooperative will of us all.

As I've said, I believe that President Kennedy's tax reduction proposal, while vitally important, is only a partial solution. I believe that Governor Rockefeller's labor market program is also, at the very best, only a partial solution.

Total solutions to our unemployment problem, I believe, are going to depend on total planning directed towards two major ends: first, the creation of new industries in this country; and second, the creation of new markets for our products.

We *can* create new industries. The other day Secretary Wirtz proposed to you that education be built into new, vast, and more meaningful and useful dimensions than ever before. He is right, of course, and his suggestion it seems to me is one of the most brilliant that has been presented to you during your deliberations here.

Similarly other new industries can be created and old ones can be expanded. The service industries have been growing at a phenomenal rate in recent years—services like the installation of instant heat lines and fuel oil lines, among others. We should study this growth carefully and figure out how to accelerate it beyond its present pace. There are real jobs in service industries.

Also, as I've said, leisure-time activities—the kind of activities which have become so important and will become even more important if the shorter work week becomes a reality—also will lead to new industries. All such leisure-time activities are directly associated with one or more industries or businesses which are constantly expanding as more and more people have more and more time for leisure. This is an area which also should be studied. Here, too, there are jobs.

I believe we have not yet applied ourselves with proper diligence to the matter of relating the industrial techniques and skills of our defense and aero-space efforts to the field of consumer products and services. I am convinced on the basis of what knowledge I have that we could study these enormous and largely secret industries and, without revealing any secrets, we could create very sizable new consumer industries out of what we would learn. Here again we could find new jobs, and in view of our clear and pressing need to find such jobs I think it would be ridiculous to let any bogus considerations of national security stand in the way of releasing secrets which could not possibly have any adverse effect on the security of our nation. I seem to recall that the nuclear secrets learned at the time of the Manhattan Project were still buried about twenty miles underground long after there was a need for them to be buried there, and that it was years before they were released to enable commercial atomic energy to become a reality insofar as industry was concerned. I believe that today the Defense Department is the repository of a thousand secrets that could be translated into consumer products and goods and services without affecting our national security. And I believe that the Administration must attempt to secure the release of some of these secrets for the creation of new industries and of new jobs—particularly at a time when unemployment is our most pressing domestic problem.

All these new industries either have now, or would have, domestic markets. We must create other new markets as well. Recently, I have found myself increasingly thinking of the needs of the developing nations of the world—of their imperative requirement for industrialization, for new products, for new machines. I really don't believe that up to the present time we have studied this market with the kind of depth that is needed—taking into consideration both the points of view of the developing nations themselves and our own unemployment situation at home. We must become true partners in progress with the developing nations, for we need them just as much as they need us—not only as allies in our cold war with the Soviets but in direct relation to our unemployment problem. This is one market we will not obtain, however, if President Kennedy doesn't get his foreign aid requests through Congress. These are many-sided problems, as you can see, and they represent matters of grave importance not only to businessmen like myself, but to you labor union leaders as well. New markets mean new jobs.

I do not pretend to know how these apparently disparate needs and aspirations and problems can be related. I do believe strongly that with proper study and with proper application they can be *made* to relate, to the benefit of all. To meet the needs of the developing nations, and at the same time to compete vigorously in the international marketplace, there is no question in my mind, as I said earlier, that we need automation at home. We also need more jobs. And it has been going through my mind that if through some superhuman effort of cooperative effort, study and will we could relate all these factors, then we would be able to find more jobs than we realize both at home and abroad—more of the jobs we need so badly.

Now, I hasten to say that these may not all be proper and sound solutions, they might not all work out, but they are examples of the kind of far-out thinking that I am convinced is required if we are ever to solve the unemployment problem as we have it today, as well as some of the other mammoth problems which exist all around us on the globe.

If we are to grapple effectively with such theories, if we are to find *new* theories and make them work for us, it seems to me there is no question that we have already entered upon a time which requires a far greater degree of whole-hearted cooperation between labor, management, and government than mankind has ever known before. Obviously, this means some unlikely joinings. In the long run—and we all might as well face it—it would probably be in the very best possible interest of all of us to have working in the closest possible harmony together, the AFL-CIO, the National Association of Manufacturers, the Department of Labor, and the Department of Commerce—and probably some others as well. Our Automation Foundation—representing the Machinists and our company—is a sign pointing in this direction. Such cooperation is possible.

This may seem far-fetched to some of you. It may seem far-fetched, if they hear of it, to some of the stonier faces in the NAM. It may seem impractical to some members of government. Indeed, it may be—like the streamlined car that came out in the early thirties—far ahead of its time. But like the streamlined car, such cooperation must happen and I think we will all be better off the sooner it happens. If it does not happen, I believe we will have entered the "winter of our despair."

# Consumer Safety and Health[6]

Barbara Hackman Franklin

*Born March 19, 1940, Lancaster, PA; B.S., Pennsylvania State University, 1962; M.B.A., Harvard Business School, 1964; vice president, First National City Bank, 1969-71; assistant to the president of the United States, 1971-73; commissioner, Consumer Product Safety Commission, 1973-92; U.S. secretary of commerce, 1992-96; president, Barbara Hackman Franklin Enterprises, 1992–.*

## Editor's introduction

In this speech, Barbara Hackman Franklin, former commissioner of the Consumer Product Safety Commission, defended the commission against the charge that it fostered unnecessary regulations and therefore complicated the lives of the American people. While aware that the public felt that the government had "gone overboard" in regulating their lives, Franklin defended certain public health and safety programs she believed necessary to the overall well-being of American citizens.

---

As a federal regulator, I accept speaking engagements these days with more and more trepidation. The trepidation turns to outright fear as the day of the speech arrives and the experience of Winston Churchill comes to mind.

On one of his trans-Atlantic tours, a student asked, "Mr. Churchill, doesn't it thrill you to know that every time you make a speech the hall is packed to overflowing?"

Churchill pondered the question for a moment. Then he replied, "Of course, it is flattering. But always remember that if I were being hanged, the crowd would be twice as big."

Churchill's point is not lost today. In view of predictions that government regulation is an idea whose time is passing, the prospect of a public lynching is very intimidating—especially to a potential "lynchee."

I'll take my chances this evening. In fact, I welcome this opportunity to discuss the issue of regulation with those of you who ultimately will decide where it goes—consumers, the business community, and government officials.

Across the country and across the political spectrum, the American people are saying they want less—but better—government.

The rallying cry is this: Government has gone overboard; overhaul the machinery, and stop the wasteful spending. The specifics are more complex: a government which fosters competition and social goals at a reasonable cost; a government which is accessible and responsive, but less intrusive and sluggish; a government more accountable to the people, yet freer from the pressures of narrow special interests.

It is a tall order.

It is sending seismic waves through the White House, the Congress, and the agencies.

And it is a bread and butter issue for every American.

The burden of regulation, once only a burning issue in business forums, today is on the tip of everyone's tongue. The message is being repeated in ways that graphically underscore the impact of regulation upon our basic economic health and social well-being:

—the direct costs to business, consumers, and the government.

—the indirect costs of business investments not made, plants not opened, job opportunities lost, reduced productivity, and new technologies dampened.

—the international costs, typified by the devalued dollar.

—the psychological costs of weakened leadership and the loss of consumer and taxpayer confidence.

[6]Delivered at the Conference for and about the Conspicuous Consumer, in Boston, Massachusetts, on November 29, 1978. Reprinted with permission of Barbara Hackman Franklin.

In short, government is a dominant force in our lives. It is said to be the nation's biggest employer, its biggest consumer, and its biggest borrower. Government today exercises direct regulation over much of everything bought and sold in the US and indirect regulation over almost every other sector of the private economy. The now-defunct Commission on Federal Paperwork estimates the total cost of federal paperwork is $100 billion a year—or about $500 per person. Already, *Newsweek* suggests that each year's harvest of administrative regulations is so large that it defies quantification.

Do we have a regulatory monster?

More and more people believe that we do and that it is long overdue for a leashing. The concern is fueled by the toll inflation is taking and an awakening of the press and the general public to what some businesspeople have been saying all along: that regulation, however intended to protect consumers and competitors from the marketplace abuses of a few, doesn't always work that way.

The critical issue is where we go from here and how.

Frankly, I am encouraged with the public demand for a better, more affordable government. It is too early to pinpoint precisely when results will emerge—but soon enough to predict that they will and that the impact had better be more substantive than symbolic.

For those of us in this room who have long been tilting at certain regulatory windmills, it is already heartening to feel the fresh winds of change.

I would be deluding you, however, if I did not admit to some concern, especially in the area of health and safety regulation.

I am a proponent of reform in this area, too—in order to better protect the public in a way business can live with, government can live with, and most of all, that the American people can live with. But in the current rush to give all government a bad rap, the great temptation is to forget why many important public health and safety programs exist.

The Consumer Product Safety Commission is a classic example.

One businessman put it this way: "Let's face it. CPSC is another federal agency that probably wouldn't be in existence if those of us in business had been doing our jobs properly."

He has a point.

The creation of the Commission was not an accident. It was born during the rising tide of consumerism, the first wave of product liability suits and legitimate concern about the safety of products consumers buy and use. It was said 20 million consumers were being injured each year—many needlessly, at an annual cost to the national economy of some $5.5 billion.

So Congress created the agency in 1973, giving us jurisdiction over the safety of some 10,000 consumer products.

Today, the familiar Washington formula—find a problem, pass a law, and set up a new agency—seems to be running out of steam. But make no mistake: public demand for a better quality of life has not.

A Harris public opinion poll this summer underscores the point.

Controlling crime, according to the survey, is seen as very important in improving the quality of life. So is better education, conserving energy, and curbing air and water pollution. More and more people emphasize safety in the workplace, and 74 percent place a high priority on making products and services safer, up almost ten percent over the last two years.

To me, the message of 1978 is this: CPSC, like other agencies whose job involves the public health and safety, has a responsibility to see that it happens—at a price that is reasonable.

In this spirit, I am recommending the Commission take four steps.

*First*, we must take a closer look at precisely when safety regulation makes sense, under what circumstances and to what extent.

In other words, we need to rethink safety regulation—to make it better, to make it work and to make it stick—in those cases where it is necessary.

In those instances where government intervention isn't needed, we should stay out. And in the vast majority of cases which fall somewhere between the two extremes, we must not hesitate to explore promising alternatives to regulation.

Personally, I'd like to see the Commission sign more agreements along the lines of the one we have with the Chain Saw Manufacturers Association. If a timely, effective standard addressing the safety of chain saws is written in the private sector, then everybody stands to benefit—the Commission, industry, and consumers.

Consumer education and information is another tool which too often is underestimated. The plain truth of the matter is that many, many accidents can be prevented only with changes in human behavior.

*Second*, the Commission should review its overall strategy to achieve greater consumer safety.

It may be that a vigorous campaign directed at top corporate managers is a wise expenditure of everybody's time and money. When the person at the top is tuned in to product safety, so is everyone else in the organization.

The Commission also should convene regional conferences so that companies can learn, firsthand, what others are doing to make and sell safer products, the organizational mechanisms they've put in place, and the procedures they follow to get defective products off the production line, off retail shelves, and out of consumers' hands.

Then, too, the Commission must find, in the very near future, special ways to work with small businesses—those companies who lack the time and resources to deal with every finite detail of regulation. A major first step would be to assure that the concerns of small companies are reflected in our regulatory decision-making early in the process.

*Third*, we must reduce unnecessary delay.

Frankly, as many representatives of companies as consumer groups complain whenever our work becomes unduly protracted. Predictability in public policy is thwarted. The ability for businesspeople to plan ahead is stymied. Protection for consumers can be denied. Scarce resources, public and private, are squandered.

An issue coming before the Commission next month is a vivid case in point.

The Commission now is in its fifth year of developing a mandatory safety standard for power mowers—five years in which consumers have received no uniform protection from some hazards which the agency, a major trade association, and a national consumer group agree exist.

The fault, in my judgment, rests heavily on the Commission's shoulders. Only this summer did we decide to stagger consideration of the complex problems—in order to reduce the burden on industry and to try to hasten the day when consumers could receive some protection.

Other factors, however, also contributed to the delay, not the least of which is an expensive publicity campaign waged by the industry to discredit the proposal almost from the moment it was drafted.

All in all, the years invested in the project have taken quite a toll, literally and figuratively. Surely it was in everybody's best interests to find a better way to protect consumers.

*Fourth*, cost/benefit analysis.

Let's say it right up front: Product safety costs, and somebody's got to pay.

That "somebody" is called the consumer or the taxpayer—depending who passes along the costs, business or government. Then, too, if an accident occurs, the consumer and his or her family get it in the pocketbook in another way. There are staggering medical and hospital bills, lost income, higher insurance rates—to say nothing of the extensive pain, suffering, and possible loss of life.

In my judgment, the Commission needs to get a better handle on issues like these.

Already, by law, we are required to establish the need for and general impact of our regulations. But more is needed. Indeed, the courts seem to agree—if we expect our proposals to withstand judicial scrutiny. So does President Carter. He is urging a hard look at the goals, benefits, and costs of all regulatory proposals, adding that he wants the "consumer protected . . . with the least adverse inflationary effect."

Addressing safety issues in the cost/benefit context is not a panacea. Precise determination of the benefits and burdens is difficult, especially in the area of health and safety regulation. Our present ability to consider the full range of costs is elementary. On the benefit side of the equation, it is downright primitive.

But even with what we know now the cost/benefit way of thinking is useful. It sets up a real-life framework for regulators to ask the hard questions, make the tradeoffs, and set priorities.

I believe this is what the American people expect from their government. Indeed, the majority of Americans, according to a new study by Cambridge Reports, Inc., want the benefits and burdens considered and the tough tradeoffs made.

All of us share the same goals—economic well-being and a healthy, safer environment in which to live. But to reach these goals, we must use our resources well, trying to obtain the most benefit and leverage for every dollar—public and private—we spend.

When it comes to consumer safety and health, my own feeling is that in certain circumstances, government does need to step in. On the other hand, optimal protection of the public requires vigorous attention to safety factors long before products reach the store shelves or the hands of consumers. Thus, the onus really is on business. Putting it another way, the point is this: it's wiser and cheaper to design and sell safer products or to locate and correct defects early on than to be the defendant in product liability suits, mount expensive recall campaigns and endure the sales-wrecking publicity and weakening of consumer confidence.

The challenge to all of us—and I believe, the opportunity—is to make America work better again.

When I say "better" I do not mean a bigger government which crowds out the private sector or the individual.

I do not mean a more meddlesome government, burrowing deeper into the affairs of business "to fix things that ain't broke."

But I also do not believe that we can turn back the clock, championing only those solutions which fit other times in our national life 50, 30, or even 20 years ago.

We must learn from our mistakes of the past—so that we can do better in the future. Our country was not built by complacency or excessive caution, but by boldness, innovation, and competition.

Now it is up to us to carry on in the same spirit. Where we go from here really is up to us.

# Solidarity, Indispensable Key to the Future[7]

Lane Kirkland

*Born 1922, Camden, SC; B.S., U.S. Merchant Marine Academy, 1942; B.S., Georgetown University School of Foreign Service, 1948; U.S. Navy, 1947-48; research staff member, American Federation of Labor (AFL), 1948-53; director, Union Operating Engineers, 1958-60; assistant director, 1953-58, executive assistant to the president, 1961-69, secretary treasurer, 1969-79, president, 1979-95, American Federation of Labor/Congress of Industrial Organizations (AFL/CIO).*

## Editor's introduction

Traditionally the president of the United States is invited to speak at the AFL/CIO's biennial convention. Conservative Republican president Ronald Reagan, however, was not invited to address the 1981 convention, as his election to office was generally understood as having sharply negative consequences for organized labor. In his place, noted Democrats, including House Speaker Thomas P. O'Neill, Senator Edward Kennedy, and former vice president Walter Mondale were invited to address the delegates. Aware of the criticism directed at organized labor, Kirkland, then president of the AFL/CIO, refused to go on the defensive. Instead, he vowed to "preserve unity within the family of labor" and asserted that organized labor would survive the "adverse public opinion" which Reagan's election signaled.

---

Reverend clergy, distinguished guests, members of the Executive Council, delegates, brothers and sisters, two years ago, George Meany left us this charge:

" . . . the labor movement cannot be content with defending the status quo, or reliving past glories. We must constantly look to the future, develop new leadership, adapt policies to changing conditions and new technologies, but—always, always—with unswerving loyalty to the mission of the trade union movement as the instrument for improving and enhancing the working and living conditions of those who work for wages."

Yesterday, November 15, 1981, we made the crossing into our second century as a confederated trade union movement. We are here, at the conclusion of our first hundred years, not just to honor the past, but to prepare ourselves to serve the future.

There is an old church anthem which instructs us as follows: "New occasions teach new duties. Time makes ancient good uncouth." That is not a call to pursue novelty for its own sake, nor to bend and trim to the shifting winds. It is a message, rather, of the need to acknowledge essential change and to respond to its requirements.

We are here in strength and vigor because those who went before us and built this great instrument of progress did indeed adapt its role and structure to the needs and demands of their times. The makeup of this body bears little resemblance to the Horse Collar Workers, the Architectural Cornice Makers, the Box Sawyers and Nailers, and the Umbrella and Walking Stick Makers who gathered into the Federation a hundred years ago. This body will bear as little resemblance to those who assemble under our banner a hundred years hence.

Throughout its history, labor has reflected all the trends and events—sometimes harmful, sometimes enriching—of its times, at home and abroad. Like our nation, we have been enriched by refugees from strife and tyranny in other lands. Like our nation, we have been compelled to grapple with the consequences of vast technological, social, and economic changes that have taxed our wits and capacities.

[7]Delivered at the 14th biennial convention of the AFL/CIO, in New York, New York, on November 16, 1981. 

At times we have lagged behind the path of the curve of change; at times we have surged ahead. Too often to recount, we have been written off and left for dead by the fashion-mongers of the day, only to see them come and go while we remained steadfast on the field of action. Through it all, we have never abdicated our role of leadership in the struggle for human freedom and human progress and we shall not do so now.

Conversely, we are often taken to task because we do not confine our role to the most narrow interests of the dues-paying members, but assume responsibility for the broadest range of human concerns. Seafarers understand their duty, not only to their immediate shipmates, but to all castaways and drifting souls at sea. Last summer, the SS President McKinley was steaming through a stormy night in the China Sea. She came upon a small boat in distress and rescued ten persons fleeing from tyranny on the mainland. When the captain was asked why he felt obliged to risk his ship to rescue these forlorn refugees, he responded:

"Shall we ship's masters just leave refugees or seamen or others to drift hopelessly at sea until their ultimate death because they have no passports or seaman's papers?"

Our answer, like his, must be "no."

We are honored to have as our guests most of the leaders of the trade union centers of the free world and we welcome them as comrades-in-arms. We share their problems and concerns. I pledge to them, in your name, our cooperation and commitment in our common universal struggle for the rights of working men and women, for bread and freedom, everywhere. To that end, with the support of this convention, we shall apply for re-affiliation, effective January 1, 1982, with the International Confederation of Free Trade Unions.

You have before you the comprehensive Report of the Executive Council which details the work of the federation since our last convention. It will tell you all that you might want to know about that work and probably more. Without trying to retrace all of that ground, let me note some of the ways in which we have sought to address the challenge of the times in keeping with our historic mandate.

We have a permanent mandate to seek and preserve unity within the family of labor, and we rejoice in the re-affiliation of a great union, the United Automobile Workers. We warmly welcome its delegates here, as we welcomed its President, Brother Doug Fraser, to the Executive Council last August. We welcome, above all, the addition to our ranks of the force and vigor of the UAW's role and voice in the fight for social and economic justice.

This old church will remain wide open at all hours. Our mission will not be completed until all of labor's flock is brought within the fold, to work and move together in solidarity. We have an enduring mandate to bring all working people the message of trade unionism and we have pursued that instruction. The officers and members of the Executive Council of this federation are deeply committed to the proposition that there is no matter of more constant urgency than to organize the unorganized.

The past two years have witnessed important breakthroughs against major strongholds of resistance by the Steelworkers, the Amalgamated Clothing and Textile Workers, the Food and Commercial Workers, the Teachers, AFSCME, CWA, and other affiliates, in testimony to the quality of their leadership and dedication. We have initiated an ambitious campaign in the Southwest, with the Houston Cooperative Organizing Program, and we intend to see it through to a solid result.

The strides we have made have been masked in part by offsetting historical factors. A deep recession; the decay of the nation's industrial base, infrastructure, and urban services; the export of jobs; and profound occupational, geographic, and demographic shifts in the work force, have taken their toll.

In the face of these trends, the fact that the labor movement at large has more than held its own and continued to grow is a remarkable achievement. It is evidence, not of weakness, but of inherent strength and vigor. It is a tribute to the capacity of modern labor to respond, to adapt, and to move with the times into new areas of service and growth.

I assure you now that the AFL-CIO stands ready to explore any method of approach and to offer any service that you, the affiliates, desire or will allow in pursuit of our common mandate to organize the unorganized. We have an age-old mandate to educate and agitate and we have over these past months sought to do it justice.

Democratic trade union education is a two-way street and we ignore that at our peril. All channels of information-communication and participation must be open and active throughout and at both ends or they fail altogether.

We can survive adverse public opinion because—being so often the agents of controversy in the pursuit of our duty—we always have. Samuel Gompers summed it up, in 1913, when he wrote:

"Until all elements exert proportional influence in determining public opinion, until all individuals that make up the public become genuinely and unselfishly desirous of continuously striving for justice to all mankind, public opinion will not become an infallible dispenser of justice."

But we cannot long survive the erosion of support for programs and policies on the part of the membership. Without cultivation and conservation, erosion must surely follow.

Last spring, through a series of regional conferences extending over several weeks, the officers and department heads of the Federation met with state and local trade union leaders for face-to-face discussions on any and all issues, no holds barred. We committed ourselves to bring the ideas and opinions that emerged from those two-way conversations to the attention of the Executive Council, and we have fulfilled that commitment. Some of the steps we have since taken, as well as some that will be proposed to this convention, are the product of those meetings. We found them of such value that we shall repeat them next year and in the future. I strongly commend such a practice to every constituent organization.

From those sessions emerged the concept of Solidarity Day and the conviction that the spirit required for its success was there, waiting for an opportunity of expression. On that day, there gathered in Washington the greatest protest demonstration in our history. Over 400,000 members of the main stream of the trade union movement and their allies spoke with one great voice against the course of their government and for the human values we represent. My only regret is that many thousands more who wished to come had to be turned away because all available means of transport were exhausted. I am convinced that every member who assembled in Washington on Solidarity Day went home a better trade unionist, more ready, willing, and able to speak and work for the cause.

What can we fairly say now of these engaging, amiable, and persuasive men of power in Washington, whose measures drew our forces there in protest?

The President, we are told, is the Great Communicator; but so were many other heads of state in history whose policies left suffering and distress in their wake. Herbert Hoover was known as the Great Engineer, but wreckage was his legacy. Communication is scarcely enough, particularly for a President of the United States. Though he "speaks with the tongues of men and of angels, and has not charity," he is "but sounding brass and tinkling cymbals." He has shown a cold heart and a hard fist, but, where, indeed, is the rest of him?

It is one thing to use the full force of government to break a small union of hard-pressed public employees. That, I suppose, does express the harshest construction of the law and is, perhaps, popular. But is it then just and fitting to go out upon the field and shoot its wounded?

As for his brilliant and tireless team, drawn from the service of avarice, they promised us a boom and brought us a bust. They have drained the public purse to lavish welfare on the greedy rich, in the name of "incentive." They have stripped the poor and jobless of welfare, food stamps and unemployment insurance, also in the name of "incentive." That is known as the carrot-and-stick policy: for the rich, the carrot; for the poor, the stick.

What is the net result so far of their genius and masterful command of the Congress? Eight and one-half million workers are now unemployed, the largest number since 1939. Unemployment among blacks and other minorities has reached 15.5 percent; eleven percent of all blue collar workers are unemployed. Unemployment has increased by one million in the last three months alone. The real earnings of workers are down 4.4 percent in the last year. Bankruptcies are up 40 percent. The housing, automobile and related industries are being strangled by sky-high interest rates.

Mr. Paul Volcker, high priest of monetarism at the Federal Reserve Board, is a very kind and engaging man—until he goes to work in the morning. Then something happens. For the past few weeks, in public and private discourse, he has been blaming the terrible harm that his policies have already done the nation's economy on next year's wage bargains. To grapple for such a flimsy alibi is a sure sign of the final bankruptcy of monetary doctrine. It calls to mind an old, old ditty:

It's the same the whole world over,
It's the poor that get the blame,
It's the rich that get the gravy.

Ain't it a bleeding shame?

What can we who opposed the domestic policies of this Administration from the beginning now say that is one-half as devastating as the recorded fleeting spasms of honesty of its leading hatchet-man, Mr. David Stockman? What provoked his candor one can only guess. But you don't have to be an old sailor to know what it means when the smartest rat on board heads for the hawse pipe. Lest you feel a twinge of human sympathy for his public embarrassment, let me remind you that this is the man who once coldly declared that no one is entitled to anything from one's government. He even now boasts, as his proudest achievement, of the destruction of public service employment and trade adjustment assistance.

He was the original interior decorator of this economic house of ill repute. Now that the sirens are sounding and the bust is due, he has his story ready. He was only the piano player in the parlor. He never knew what was going on upstairs.

The aftermath also tells us a lot about this Administration. Was he chastised by the President for cooking the books, rigging the computer, over-feeding the tax hogs, conning the Congress and duping the public? No—he was taken to the White House woodshed for, at long last, telling the truth. So far have we come from young George Washington and the cherry tree. Now, after his scolding, he tells us that it was all a foolish mistake, that he was only guilty of being the south end of a north bound Trojan horse.

It is hard to decide which is worse about the social and economic policies of this Administration—the array or the disarray. If this is the direction of the New Beginning that President Reagan promised, God save us from the End.

When we turn to consider the course of our foreign and defense affairs we find the same pattern repeated.

We were promised a more vigorous and consistent role of American leadership and a more coherent and sustained approach to the revival of our forces in freedom's defense. We welcomed that prospect, for labor has always believed that our values are worthy of a strong defense in the face of external danger. But what is the objective record, stripped of the fog of rhetoric?

We have, in the past year, witnessed the following:

The growing dismay and division of our allies;

The feeding of our deadliest adversaries on easy credit, making lighter their growing burden of lethal arms;

The appeasement of the Saudi-financial-industrial complex with gifts of costly and exotic weapons, paid for in higher oil prices, by the American consumer;

The destruction of domestic support for necessary defense expenditures through the exemption of the rich and the drafting of the poor in the service of its cost, and they have the nerve to call previous administrations soft.

On the vital issue of human rights, they have sought to pose a fine choice between lice who are totalitarian and lice who are authoritarian. We reject such a choice and we call instead for a freedom of association everywhere as the keystone of a genuine human rights policy.

On that record, as regards this Administration's team of foreign and defense policymakers, one need say no more than did the Duke of Wellington when he observed his own troops in a state of disarray: "I don't know if they frighten the enemy—But Gad, sir, they frighten me!"

We shall endure and survive all these afflictions, as we have so many others during the ebb and flow of the changing tides and the entrances and exits of great communicators, great engineers, and other flickering lights and shooting stars. Our fortunes depend, not on the stars, but upon ourselves.

As we approach a new election year, we must prepare now for the next battle in our long campaign. Tools and tactics may change, people may come and go, but one element remains essential to our prospects. That is, as always, true and lasting solidarity. Solidarity yields to the common wealth, to build the store of strength that each of our parts will surely need to draw upon, late or soon. Solidarity requires, not blind submission to command, but the free and timely exchange of views in search of consensus. Once that is gotten, it then requires of all the character and forbearance to defer one's own pride or preference to the general good.

The officers of this Federation will seek the advice, consult the wisdom, and promote the expression of the views of all quarters of this movement, so that its great and rich variety may be fairly and fully summoned to our common struggle. When we gain a goal together, there will be enough honor and recognition to go around to each organization that makes up this body. None will be slighted or deprived of its due.

As we go forth into our second century, solidarity remains the indispensable key to the future.

And now to work.

# An Economic Security Platform[8]

Bill Bradley

*Born July 28, 1943, Crystal City, MO; B.A., Princeton University, 1965; M.A., Oxford University, 1968; U.S. Air Force Reserve, 1967-78; professional basketball player, New York Knickerbockers, 1966-77; senator (D) from New Jersey, 1979-96; author,* Life on the Run *(1976),* The Last of the Great Stations *(1979),* The Fair Tax *(1984),* Pirate's Guide to Lake St. Clair and Surrounding Waters *(1986),* Time Present, Time Past *(1997).*

## Editor's introduction

On October 7, 1993, Bill Bradley, then a senator from New Jersey, addressed the Center for National Policy, a "liberal" think-tank that studies social issues. The audience of some 150 persons included Center for National Policy staff members and Bradley supporters, ambassadors, and several members of President Clinton's staff. Senator Bradley first recognized that millions of citizens found "economic security" to be an "unattainable dream" and had come to believe that hard work would not guarantee a high standard of living. Bradley argued that the federal government must reduce spending and begin to provide a system of economic security that would allow the next generation of Americans to attain a higher standard of living than the previous one.

---

George Fatemi went to work for a major U.S. steel company when he was 19. He lost that job when big steel couldn't compete with new technology from Japan during the 1970s. He got another job with a glass company, but they laid him off during the 1982 recession. In both cases, he couldn't take his pension benefits with him because he hadn't worked long enough to vest. George then hooked up with a defense contractor making missiles until 1992, when the defense cutbacks axed him. Three jobs and three layoffs. George was left with a minuscule pension and payments of $460 a month if he wants to continue health coverage for his family.

Five years ago, Mary and Charles Jones lived the American dream in New Jersey. Mary did marketing for AT&T; Charles was a lawyer with IBM. They had a house in the suburbs, two children, and a three-week family vacation every August. Then both of them lost their jobs.

Today Charles works for a small business selling computer software, and Mary consults, but not often. No more vacations, no health benefits from the jobs. Mary's father lost his pension benefits due to an LBO and a loophole in the pension law. The two kids are now in high school, and the oldest wants to go to MIT, but the family can't afford it.

Louise Pearl is a single mother who works as a secretary to the president of a construction firm. The office construction boom of the early 1980s has turned into a construction depression in the '90s, and in the last 18 months, the firm has shrunk from 46 workers to 15. If the company goes under, Louise will need training to get a new job, but she won't have the money to pay for it.

These composite portraits of Louise Pearl, George Fatemi, and the Joneses are not unusual. There are millions of Americans who find economic security an unattainable dream. It is as if Americans are adrift on a gigantic river of economic transformation that carries away everything that resists the swirling currents of its mighty flow. Americans are being buffeted by new economic forces as surely as the communities along the Mississippi last summer were being hit by a 100-year flood. Not since the age of democratic revolution coincided with the industrial revolution, nearly 200 years ago, has the river of economic change flowed so powerfully. What makes the experience so

[8]Delivered at the Center for National Policy, in Washington, D.C., on October 7, 1993.

hard is that we have to cope with four fundamental transformations taking place in the world simultaneously.

The first is the end of the age of ideology. With the fall of Marxist-Leninist communism and the triumph of democratic liberalism, the content of the U.S.-Russian conflict disappears.

Yet peace doesn't reign. Ask any ethnic or religious warrior in Bosnia, or Georgia, or Tibet, or Northern Ireland. But conflict has a less cataclysmic implication. The garrison state of the Soviet Union, with its missiles aimed at the United States, has evolved into a nationalist Russia whose hopes of meeting human needs take precedence over its bombast in preparing for Armageddon.

With peace breaking out, people feel more secure, and the arsenals of the United States and Russia can be dramatically reduced. But for millions of people who work in the defense sector, peace has an even more personal consequence than freedom from first strike. It has cost them their jobs. In 1987, there were 7.2 million people working in what President Eisenhower called the military-industrial complex. In 1992, it was 6.3 million, and in 1997, it will be 4.4 million. The economic impact of the West's triumph is the downsizing of an entire sector of our economy.

The second transformation is the explosion of world markets. There are three billion more people in the world market today than just ten years ago, and most of them will become our customers by the turn of the century. That means thousands of jobs.

During the last decade, not only have communist societies crumbled and their replacements opened up to the world, but authoritarian and protectionist regimes in Latin America and Asia have also fallen. Instead of billions of people living in closed economies, unwilling to trade and bent on producing everything they need domestically, with a politics that argues over which subsidies go to which monopolists, country after country—Poland, Mexico, Argentina, India, Vietnam—has liberalized economically. They are encouraging exports, accepting imports, and seeking capital worldwide.

A market of three billion more people represents billions of potential sales of computers, cars, Coca-Colas, and CDs, as well as capital goods to electrify a continent, to build more ports and highways, to equip new hospitals, and to build new homes. But it also means a billion more workers ready to challenge our own workers in the production of tradeable goods. Clearly, some American workers will lose their jobs. But far more will be created by a competition that not only provides higher quality and lower prices to consumers, but also demands greater efficiency from our own companies and more complex skills from our work force.

Not since the end of the 19th century has the world economy been as open or the potential for worldwide human betterment through open markets been as great. Since political openness usually follows economic openness, democracy's roots are extending deeper and deeper into more societies than ever before. And yet there are dangers too.

In the early 20th century, ethnic tension and nationalist fervor snuffed out the flame of hope represented by open trade. Both irrational impulses remain alive today. Ethnic tension threatens to engulf more and more nations in costly conflict: witness Bosnia. Nationalistic fervor in its Ross Perot-Pat Buchanan form calls for protection from international competition and advocates trade only with developed countries "like us." Witness the debate over NAFTA.

It's possible that we will be closed off to this wider market and not accept the challenge, but to do so has consequences: a lower standard of living, a fraying social fabric, and a refusal to lead in a new world.

The third transformation is driven by man's advancing ability to shape his world. It is the knowledge revolution. Through knowledge applied to telecommunications, we communicate without travel. Through knowledge we combine elements in new ways to make materials that don't exist in nature to do jobs with less energy and less assembly. Through knowledge we transform genetic material and worry less about pest control.

For centuries, the determinants of national wealth have been capital, natural resources, and an abundance of labor. Today none of them is as important as knowledge, which has changed the production process and multiplied the types of services available. Applied knowledge can make society cleaner, wealthier, and more humane.

Manual labor serving a machine, whether it's in Detroit or Kuala Lumpur can never produce as efficiently as a computer serving man. It's just that simple. That's why in the future the biggest economic problems will be found in countries where the most unskilled workers live.

America is further through that revolution than most people imagine. Manufacturing remains essential to our economy. We continue to make things, but we do it with fewer people. When George Fatemi lost his job at the steel company, there were 721,000 steel workers in America, and today there are only 374,000. But those 374,000 are highly efficient. Partly as a result, imports today supply only 15 percent of the U.S. market. This story is being told over and over again in our economy as companies in order to compete become leaner, producing more with less.

To resist the trend toward knowledge-based production is to give the future to those in other countries who capitalize on the inexorable transformation. Yet the challenge to our economy is clear. If we produce the same product with less labor, then there have to be more, not fewer, jobs, producing more new products or serving more new needs.

An exploding knowledge sector built on a sound economic foundation can create these jobs, but the skill requirements will be higher. A worker tomorrow will require a substantial amount of formal knowledge and the capacity and opportunity for continuous learning. Successful work careers will exist only for those who can match what they know to what needs to be done. The days of the 40-year career on the assembly line of one company making one product are over. Sequential jobs with different companies, even sequential careers, will be the norm.

The fourth transformation has to do with the connection between economic growth and debt. America is mired in a five-year period of low growth. After the collapse of 1980s' false optimism, people are reluctant to spend or to invest. Usually a government would jump start an economy out of recession either by lowering interest rates, or by giving a tax cut or spending more money on government projects. But interest rates are at a 30-year low, and increasing the deficit to stimulate the economy risks a no-confidence vote from millions of world-wide investors. In short, the gigantic national debt has robbed us of savings just when we need them most for new investment and new training.

America got hooked on the narcotic of debt in the 1980s. It became our worst addiction. Between 1980 and 1987 consumer credit increased 95 percent. Government debt went from $800 billion in 1980 to $4 trillion in 1992. Personal debt began to decrease in the early 1990s as companies and individuals slammed on the brakes. Government kept spending. As 1993 began, the debt over the next five years was expected to go from $4 trillion to $5.4 trillion, and even after the 1993 Clinton budget, it will go to $4.9 trillion. The thing that most appalls me is the public and social policy consequences that these numbers imply. The General Accounting Office told me that if nothing were done about the debt, by 2020 every American's income would be 40 percent less than it otherwise would be. We will get poorer as we send more and more of our tax dollars to creditors and invest less and less in job-creating, wealth-producing assets. The existence of the debt literally transforms our prospects. It mortgages our children's future and robs them of the expectation that hard work usually yields reward.

So there they are: the end of the ideological cold war, the explosion of world markets, the knowledge revolution, and the gigantic debt. We feel so unprepared, even disoriented, by these four transformations, because no one predicted their cascading impacts on our prospects. No one told us, not even the best of our intelligence analysts, that the Soviet Union would disappear without a whisper and leave us little need for a vast military machine. No one told us that Adam Smith would replace Marx on the third world's best-seller list. No one told us that companies resisting change would stumble even if their names were AT&T or IBM. No one told us that gigantic American budget deficits would be financed gladly by the rich of the world and that Americans would continue merrily and irresponsibly consuming our future. No one told us that we could spend more than anyone else in the world on health care and still have millions with no coverage. No one told us that just as we educated more Americans to college level than any other country, the mediocre quality of many American elementary and high schools would be apparent to all. No one told us that the Japanese would be accepted into ASEAN or that China would be burgeoning forward to become an economic superpower. No one told us that the Europeans of Brussels could not displace the French of Paris, the British of London, and the Germans of Berlin as the centers of tribal action, political and economic drama.

Each of these events has shaped what we produce, how we trade, and pushed us further into uncharted economic waters, with more workers anxious that it will be their job that the swirling river of economic transformation will sweep away next. To survive, we must lighten our load, fix our steering wheel, and get used to living without the certainties of another time. General Motors, General Electric, Dupont no longer assure lifetime jobs. Natural resources won't be decisive in the coming economic competition. Workers can't be seen as simply discardable cogs in a machine. The cheap labor of larger and larger numbers of unskilled workers won't produce economic growth or generate higher productivity any place in the world for long. Military might won't provide substantial benefits for an economy. A democracy in time of peace and in absence of clear threat won't ever spend $310 billion on defense again. Ethnic and racial tension can't be viewed as irrelevant to the economic potential of our workers or the collective capacity of our citizens.

What we've always assumed about each generation of American's having a higher standard of living is not guaranteed. New realities can prevail. Our leaders must be honest with us, and we must be honest with ourselves. Above all, we have to resist the temptation to believe that the only course is to hold on to what we have and how we do things now. To hold on means to lose, as individuals, as companies, and as a nation. No matter how good a worker George Fatemi was in his third career, when the missile orders stopped, so did his job. The Joneses who worked for IBM and AT&T couldn't have secure employment when IBM failed to see the technology shift, and AT&T, with deregulation, stood unprepared for worldwide competition. To believe that a labor-intensive apparel shop can compete with a modernized factory is, however well-intentioned, a delusion. The idea that we should trade only with countries "like us" of equivalent living standards ignores that other nations "*like us*" have absolutely no intention of limiting their trade and economic interaction *to us*. Underfunded pensions; deficits that can only be financed abroad; educational concepts that presume formal learning ends at 24; personal behavior that leads to skyrocketing health care costs: all of these cannot continue. If we hold onto these misconceptions and destructive patterns, we risk awaking one morning like a town after the river's flood recedes to find our communities broken and the health of our families failing.

For those in the midst of the turmoil, our heart must go out to them. They aren't interested in theories. They have to worry about putting food on the table and a roof over the heads of their families. For too long policy makers have ignored their needs and mistaken their loyalty for indifference. But the morning after, when the tears of compassion dry up, what people want most is a direction to follow that makes sense, a path to take that leads to a job. We must get about the business of dealing with our reality, not hiding from it or denying it or cursing it.

Without minimizing the difficulty, we need to see these transformations as part of a consistent and continuing American saga. We always were a nation suspicious of ideology (as Alexis D'Toqueville said). We always did seek competition to protect liberty (as James Madison stressed). We have always sought to be recognized, not for our muscle, but for our wit and agility and values (as Thomas Jefferson argued). We hate being in debt and desperately want to pay our own way (as Andrew Jackson demanded). These transformations are then "in character" for America (as they are not for much of the world). They are at once fundamental to the American crisis and at the same time a key to America's renewal. We simply have to know where we want to go and to build a platform that can allow us successfully to navigate the currents of our present economic waters.

I believe government has a role in this time of transformation. It must assure all Americans access to an "economic security platform." Given our gigantic national debt, we must build this platform with precision and hard-headedness, conserving our resources at every juncture. As platform designers, we must not respond to the siren calls of political expediency or short-term palliatives; we must steer between too many government interventions, subsidies, and entitlements and too few to liberate Americans from feeling so vulnerable and paralyzed. We must establish a set of initiatives that does not hobble the efficiency of market forces, but liberates our workers so they can realize their potential.

Who among us doesn't believe that Mary and Charles Jones have a lot more to contribute to our economy than their current employment would allow? Can we afford to let a worker like

George Fatemi not work? Does any of us believe that our economy should be deprived of Louise Pearl's talents just because she cannot afford to update her 1970s' skills for a 1990s' job?

What specifically do I mean by an economic security platform? My economic security platform has three planks. It consists of, and is limited to, a guarantee of basic health coverage, an opportunity for lifetime education, and a guarantee of pension security.

First is health care. It should be available to all Americans. If any American loses a job, changes a job, grows old, experiences a serious illness or a difficult childbirth, confronts an injury to a spouse, or needs regular checkups, that American should be guaranteed access to quality health care. And we simply must control its costs. We cannot compete economically if we pay a health "tariff" of 4 to 7 percent more of our GNP for health costs than in other developed countries. This premium amounts to a giant health tax on all our goods.

Second is lifetime education. We can't survive with 40 percent of Americans with high wages, 40 percent with low wages, and 20 percent unemployable. The only sure way that America will guarantee its workers higher wages is if they have higher skills. The more American workers with superior talents, the higher productivity will be, and the higher worker productivity, the faster the economy will grow.

Given the demands of a knowledge economy, the opportunity to advance and learn anew must be available for workers at every stage of a career. Lifetime education means counseling, training, and relocation. Counseling means making it clear that sequential careers will be the norm; that changing a job usually won't be the worker's fault and might not even be the company's; that is just in the nature of things in an economy that rewards innovation during a time of rapid change. Counseling also means deciding on the skill to be obtained and determining where to get it. Training means actually learning a new skill and using government financial assistance to help pay for it. Relocation means finding a new job that employs the newly acquired skills. Access to lifetime education can be assured with income contingent self-reliance loans where any American can get a loan if he or she agrees to pay a small percentage of future income to the government until it's repaid. Other times access amounts simply to assuring adequate information and coordinating the 123 existing education programs so that people know how to apply for them.

Third is pension security. One hallmark of the new age must be labor mobility. That means that when someone works and gets pension benefits, they should be portable. The worker should have his or her benefits guaranteed, companies should fund their pensions adequately, and government should assure that promises of income security for the aged are kept. The trends toward defined contribution plans and stagnating participation levels challenge this promise, as does the state of the Pension Benefit Guarantee Corporation. Greater participation in the system would provide more security and increase our private savings rate.

Our current patchwork pension system is failing large numbers of our workers. Too many are facing uncertainty in their later years. One sharp correction in the stock market, and our current federal insurance program would be in grave danger and the budget deficit would skyrocket. With the lessons of the S&L debacle in mind, we need to strengthen the pension system today rather than wait for it to falter tomorrow. It may take public funds; it will at the very least require government ingenuity. But we must begin.

With an economic security platform, people can live with less anxiety because job loss won't be fraught with the danger of catastrophic health costs or lost pensions, and lifetime education will offer the chance to start anew if you want to work for it. The economic security platform is individual and family focused. It deals with issues that erupt in people's faces. It assumes that failure has some limits and bad luck can't run its full course. It gives the middle class, as well as working people who are poor, a place to stand—a foundation from which they can regroup and then move forward on their own behalf.

But the economic security platform is limited. It is not a slippery slope back to expanded government entitlements. It does not attempt to avoid all risks. It does not guarantee income or prevent failure or oversee how people live. The nest level of both security and opportunity must come from building strong communities where people live and work.

Government programs do not create self-worth; that's what families, neighbors, and communities do. That's why neighborhood leadership and community structures are so important and should be encouraged. This is as true for the problems of rebuilding urban America as it is for the problems of small towns whose factories have closed. Communities are to humane living what markets are to international competition; both work optimally when given the freedom and the incentives to find paths that meet specific needs best.

In this sense, the economic security platform is different from a social safety net. The safety net of government subsidies is where you end up if everything is falling out from under you and you're about to hit bottom. The economic security platform is where you rest before you advance. It gives reassurance before a continued pursuit of success within our national community.

Health care, lifetime education, and pension security. "Is that it?" one asks. "Aren't there hundreds of anecdotes about failed lives that, if only there had been this or that government program, someone could have pursued happiness or someone else could have avoided tragedy?" Perhaps. But the economic security platform is strictly and intentionally limited because of resources—we have a gigantic debt—and because of theory—the market's dynamism must not be lost. I have tried only to build a platform on which a nation can steer through troubled waters. To add a house of additional new programs, mandates, and work rules would create a structure that would not be seaworthy.

What America should not do is emulate Europe. In America, overall wages have been stagnant since 1973. During the 1980s, the knowledge superstars arrived. Vast salaries went to the brightest, and no raises went to the unskilled. In Europe, unemployment has been high. Today it's 11 percent. The joblessness is caused in part because European governments have created a rigid labor market that discourages the hiring of new workers and prevents the shedding of incompetent workers, while at the same time it burdens business with cumbersome work rules even to the point of determining the required number of vacation days. In addition, income-support payments go on forever and fearsome restrictions confront anyone who wants to start a new business. Such overregulation stifles an economy's ability to adjust to new circumstances. America's challenge is to raise take-home pay and to reduce the disparity of income without creating the disincentives to job creation that exist in Europe. Only a healthy economy that creates jobs will dampen people's worries. Only an economy that creates new businesses will create new jobs.

Beyond finding a balance between encouraging business and job creation, and providing every American some security in times of transformation, government needs to get its own fundamentals correct.

Government needs to spend less money overall with more of the money it does spend going to public investment in infrastructure, education, and R&D, which stagnated even as our population grew over the last two decades. Less money should go to transfers from one group of taxpayers to another, particularly if those transfers are unrelated to need.

Taxes should not penalize job creation, but rather hit consumption. Payroll taxes should be replaced by consumption taxes. With less tax penalty for hiring, more workers can be hired and wages can rise too.

All government spending programs should be sunsetted—presumed to expire unless reauthorized. The President should have a line-item veto both for appropriations and for special interest tax loopholes, both of which increase the debt.

International markets should stay open and competition fierce so that the highest quality and lowest price can be assured and export jobs can grow. That means assigning absolute priority to approving the North American Free Trade Agreement and completing the GATT round, which reduces barriers to worldwide trade.

I cannot help but see NAFTA as the test case of whether we hold on and lose, or transform and win. To defeat NAFTA will solve none of the problems generated by the four transformations. To pass NAFTA will improve the chances for more jobs in America and a stronger economy to deal with the real threats to American jobs coming from Europe, Japan, and China. To defeat NAFTA will darken the chances for GATT, and the defeat of both will deny America its major source of job creation during the next few years. Ultimately, if world trade expands, everyone can win. To pass NAFTA is to take the challenge head on.

People such as Louise Pearl, George Fatemi, and the Joneses will be helped by the economic security platform. Their children will be helped by keeping the market open and businesses unburdened by excessive regulation. Their children will be helped by more public investment and less transfers. Their children will be helped by reducing payroll taxes and increasing taxes on consumption. Their children will be helped by a major reduction of the national debt.

With an economic security platform to help us navigate the surging river of economic change and a healthy, dynamic market awaiting us at our destination, we all have reason to hope. America is relatively better off than our competition. We've turned transformations to our advantage before. Remember the ages of industrialization and automation. We are more flexible than the rigidified economies of Europe and more ethnically diverse than the economies of Asia. Because of those strengths, we are better able to penetrate markets worldwide with goods that are high quality and reasonably priced. What is needed for us to catch the next wave of growth is national leadership that levels with the people, that tells the hard truths as well as the good news, that guides as well as empathizes, and that sees our path clearly and shows the energy to persevere.

One final image. Odysseus, when he was sailing where the siren songs were sure to be too seductive, plugged the ears of his sailors and had them tie him to the mast so that neither they nor he would plunge into the water and drown. I have painted a picture of turbulent waters where many people on their own, without a security platform, will in fact drown. I have suggested that we cannot fail to get into the middle of this new world of international competition or knowledge production because each promises hope as well as anxiety. I have said that if we heed the siren song of every new idea of what government should do, we will never navigate these waters. If we tie ourselves to the mast of efficient government, which does what has to be done and jettisons the rest, we will not need to plug our ears in order to survive and prosper.

I continue to believe in a strong, intelligent, and caring America—one that sets its compass and pursues a course that can provide leadership by example to the world as well as sustenance and security to ourselves. A national economy free of the burden of debt, populated by educated citizens ready to work and to care for their neighbors must be our goal. A dynamic, market-driven economy that remains open to the world must be our destination. A transformed and transforming America can get beyond the river's turbulent waters with our optimism intact and our future prospects bright.

# XIII. Science, Technology, and Space

## Editor's introduction

Technological advancement, while it provides an array of conveniences and abilities, also prompts questioning and debate. Such debate is typically an attempt to understand the potential effects of a new technology. For example, atomic energy can both warm the human race and exterminate it. Consequently, we must decide whether its negative effects outweigh its positive benefits. Ultimately, it is a question of application, i.e. how we are going to actually use that which science has provided us. Or, as Nobel Prize winning scientist George D. Snell explained, "the immediate end product of applied research is options. At some point the decision must be made as to whether and how each option is to be exercised." In this chapter, a variety of scientists and American leaders discuss the "options" that technology has made possible, while keeping an eye on the long-term consequences of implementing those options into everyday life.

The ethical debate on the use of particular military, medical, and communication technologies has always lagged behind the headlines which announce the capabilities of those technologies. In 1949, Dr. Harrison S. Brown, a scientist at the University of Chicago's Institute of Nuclear Studies, worried that humanity too often "accepted science and technology as its benefactors, seldom questioning . . . where it was leading." He noted the dual nature of technology, remarking that it was capable of creating "total catastrophe" or aiding "in the molding of a balanced world in which men may have the opportunity to live in reasonable harmony with their environment and with each other." Dr. George D. Snell echoed Brown's claims, asserting that "the question of whether and how to use a given technology can bring us face to face with questions of right and wrong." Clearly, the technological explosion has created new situations for which we are ethically unprepared. Jeremy Rifkin affirmed this notion, insisting that while "nuclear power and petrochemical technology" have provided benefits in the "short run," they have "created tremendous long-term environmental, economic and social dislocation."

Our efforts in space have contributed greatly to twentieth century technological advancement. When the Soviet Union placed *Sputnik* in Earth's orbit in 1957, the United States accelerated its own space research. On February 20, 1962, astronaut John H. Glenn, Jr. became the first American to orbit the Earth in a space capsule. As American astronauts came to shuttle to and from space on a regular basis, and the National Aeronautics and Space Administration (NASA) planned for a permanent research facility in space, leaders and citizens debated the cost, scope, purpose, and benefits of these initiatives. Glenn felt the need to assure the arrival of "dividends" for the dollars already invested in the program. In 1967, James E. Webb, former NASA administrator, declared that technologies used to get people in space can in fact serve people on earth. Webb rightly understood that many of the advances needed for space travel would have an application to everyday life.

# Science and Religion[1]

Arthur Compton

*Born September 10, 1892, Wooster, OH; died March 15, 1962; B.S., 1913, M.A., 1914, College of Wooster; Ph.D., Princeton University, 1916; professor, University of Minnesota, 1916-17; research engineer, Westinghouse Lamp Co., 1918-19; professor, Washington University, 1920-23; professor, University of Chicago, 1923-45; winner of Nobel Prize in physics, 1927; professor, chancellor, Washington University, 1945-61.*

## Editor's introduction

Nobel Prize winner Arthur H. Compton cautioned that technology can be used either for the harm or the benefit of the world. Following a theme that would be a topic of discussion throughout the twentieth century, Dr. Compton stated that "the social unit has become the world, in which each person's welfare affects that of each other." In effect, technology has created a global village. It follows that "without cooperation, our store of human knowledge cannot be fully effective." Science and religion, he concluded, could cooperate to provide the "moral and ethical outlook" required to temper technology, allow it a morality, and thereby make it better suited to benefit both individuals and society as a whole.

---

This is Thanksgiving Eve, when it is customary for the American people to pause, consider, and be grateful for whatever love, success, beauty, peace, happiness and comfort may be in our lives.

Probably a great number of thoughtful people tonight, as they reflect upon the common life we all share, will choose as one reason for gratitude the fact that they have been born into the modern instead of the ancient or medieval world. For, despite some of the horrors and barbarism of modern life which appall and grieve us, life in the twentieth century undeniably has—or has the potentiality of—such richness, joy and adventure as were unknown to our ancestors except in their dreams.

Comfort and beauty in our homes, increased health and longevity, ease of transportation from one place to another, a succession of miracles about us every day—these are some of the good things which we can enjoy in our modern world. If we are grateful for any of those things on this Thanksgiving Eve, we must be indirectly grateful to the science which has given them to us.

Science has made the world a smaller place and brought all human beings closer together. As never before in human history, science and technology have made men closely dependent upon each other. We think of the Stone Age, the Bronze Age, the Iron Age and the Machine Age, and thus in quick outline catch a view of man's technical growth. Any one of us produces only a small part of the things we require. We are specialists, each supplying his own small part to the life of the community. We depend upon the other man for most of our food, clothing, transportation and entertainment. This sharp specialization and intense interdependence of men on each other has been made necessary in order that the achievements of the Machine Age should give us the things we want.

These great new powers given to man by science and technology may be used either for his good or his harm. The airplane may be a swift and convenient vehicle of the skies, or the most potent weapon of death ever invented. The science of chemistry can be used in countless ways in the creation of food, clothing, and shelter, or it can be employed in the manufacture of death-dealing gases and poisons. Elec-

[1]Broadcast nationwide, from Chicago, Illinois, on November 22, 1939.

tricity can be used to make a night-time fairyland of a great modern city—or it can be sent through barbed wire for an Oriental blockade of innocent women and children.

Thus we see that without cooperation, our store of human knowledge cannot be fully effective. When men divide into antagonistic groups, knowledge can be put to desperately destructive uses.

Twenty thousand years ago, the family was the social unit. Now the social unit has become the world, in which it may be truthfully said that each person's welfare affects that of every other.

In such a civilization, the importance of good-will among men becomes a matter of unprecedented urgency. In the absence of such good-will, we can expect only increasingly terrible strife. Hostilities pile up between nations and nations; and within nations battles are in progress between business and government, labor and capital, union and union. The need for mutual respect and consideration, both among individuals and organized groups, has become so evident that only those who want to be blind can fail to see it. With wars and threats of wars darkening the world on this Thanksgiving Eve, it has become literally a matter of life and death for men to become inspired with the spirit of fellowship.

I have been strongly impressed by the way in which science can be interpreted to give a moral and ethical outlook closely parallel with that taught by the highest types of religion. The language and mode of thought are different, but the correspondence between their conclusions is close. Far from being in conflict, science has become an ally of religion. By increased knowledge of nature, we become better acquainted with the God of nature, and with the part we have to play in His cosmic drama.

Science represents but one aspect of human experience. I find myself unsatisfied without at least a careful attempt to relate the various aspects of experience with each other in my own mind, thus formulating a philosophy which I can use for guiding my own life. Science does not pretend to interpret all aspects of life. Yet few in this age would willingly base their lives on a philosophy which to a man of science is demonstrably false.

And for a way of life inculcating good-will and service—so vitally essential for the continuance of our civilization—nothing has been found comparable with true religion.

A democracy such as ours needs leaders with vision and skill to carry forward the accomplishments of the past and chart the course of the future. But we can prosper in peace only if our leaders are men and women with both good-will and the knowledge necessary for expressing that good-will in effective service to their fellows.

Our democracy can be extended and made truly great only if the youth of our nation are imbued with devotion to an ideal of work for the welfare of mankind, and to this end are implemented with the education required in bringing that ideal to reality.

It is the distinctive purpose of the Christian college to inspire that devotion and to supply the needed training. Now the need for sound training has become so evident that the attendance of high schools and colleges has rapidly increased during the score of years that I have been in the teaching profession. Here, young people feel, is the way to learn to make a living.

But some see farther than the mere means to a livelihood. They realize that man is not really human unless he takes some part in creating and enjoying the beauty of life and in understanding the world of which he is a part.

What is needed most, of course, is an objective. Ambition for preferment and fame and wealth—how soon we know the disappointment that comes with failure, and the disillusionment that comes with what small successes we may gain! Where then shall we find that driving spirit?

Viewing fairly all the lives of those who have achieved great things in advancing the lot of humankind, we cannot fail to see how frequently the impetus has been given by religion. Religion tells us that our lives are not our own to waste. We owe our existence to the great Power that made us. We know what it means to be free to shape our ends. We learn that true freedom means effort toward the better life, toward the greater welfare of man. We know that in doing this work we are carrying on the design of God that made us, and we have faith that His encouraging hand is on our shoulder as we try to do our part.

It is something of this spirit that the Christian college tries to inculcate in its students—the spirit of devotion of *all* of life to the great cause of serving man's needs.

True it is that such a spirit can be effective only when combined with an understanding of the things that are vital, and a knowledge that enables us to put ideals into effective action. That is why education is needed. Saint Paul once described a religious man as one who is "alive to all true values." Here likewise is one of the great objectives of education: to make people "alive to all true values." But how frequently education falls short of the goal! How often our schools teach the technique of living, leaving unmentioned the objectives of life as a matter of no concern!

In recent generations, education has been placed more and more in secular control. Rightly fearing to coordinate church and state, we have leaned over backward by denying most of our children any opportunity of learning the great truths of religion. If each learns to make his own way in the ruthless competition of a hardened world, that is all we have asked.

I vividly recall a remark of one of my brilliant Chinese students, who had spent five years in American universities.

"In China," he said, "our teachers consider themselves responsible for the moral as well as for the intellectual development of their students. In your country, it seems that the teachers consider a student's moral development of no proper concern to them."

He could hardly believe that his own observation was correct. But who, that has a wide acquaintance with our universities, would deny that the majority of their teachers assume no responsibility for the principles of life and action adopted by their students, as long as their actions do not create a scandal.

We are now beginning to learn once more that self-preservation is not the first law of life, that nature is not concerned with the welfare or even the survival of the individual, except as his life contributes to the growth of his species. We are finding that he is biologically good who works for the welfare of his group—and today that group is all mankind.

It is for training men and women, inspired by such a vision that they may do their work with the highest skill and the deepest understanding of human problems, that Christian colleges exist. Where else can we search for the leaven that will lighten the lump? The nation needs such leaders.

In these days of reduced income from endowments, of diminished fortunes in the hands of donors, of growing tax funds supporting the secular universities which offer a subsidized education to all, it becomes increasingly difficult to support the private college. Yet there are those who see these colleges as one of the nation's greatest assets. Because of the resolute faith of such individuals, these Christian colleges have been able to grow in keeping with the rising educational standards of our day.

If our free nation is to have the strength that can come only with cooperation, if we would grow in that strength that comes with straight thinking, if we would enrich our lives by a fuller appreciation of beauty and understanding of nature, if we would give our children a heritage for which in years to come they may be genuinely grateful, we must encourage and support that education which strives to awaken youth to life's true values, and which seeks to inspire a love implemented by knowledge and guided by a sense of what is vital.

# Social Responsibility of Science[2]

Harrison S. Brown

*Born September 26, 1917, Sheridan, WY; died December 8, 1986; B.S., University of California, 1938; Ph.D., Johns Hopkins University, 1941; researcher, University of Chicago, 1942-43; assistant director, Clinton Engineer Works, 1943-46; professor, University of Chicago, 1946-51; professor, California Institute of Technology, 1951-84; editor-in-chief,* Bulletin of Atomic Scientists, *1985-86; author,* Must Destruction Be Our Destiny? *(1946),* The Challenge of Man's Future *(1954),* Learning How to Live in a Technology Society *(1979).*

## Editor's introduction

Noted scientist Harrison S. Brown, who did pioneer research in the origin and chemical analysis of meteors, was known for his ability to interpret scientific problems clearly and simply for the layman. In this address, he remarked that in the past an often uninformed humanity "accepted science and technology as its benefactors, seldom questioning where it was leading." Given the creation of the atomic bomb and the consequent ability to annihilate life on Earth, Brown asserted that technology can no longer go unchecked by society. "Technological expansion," he warned, "may bring total catastrophe, or it may aid in the molding of a balanced world in which men may have the opportunity to live in reasonable harmony with their environment and with each other."

---

Whenever I am asked to speak before a group of young men and women, my thoughts drift back to the days when I graduated from high school and a prominent business man in my home town spoke at our commencement. "The world is in a sorry plight," he told us. "It is up to you—the citizens of tomorrow—to mold the world into a globe fit for human habitation. It is up to you to abolish war and to see to it that the necessities of life are made available to all mankind."

Such graduation speeches were given that year throughout the United States and throughout the world, and for all I know they are still being given.

But what happens when the high school graduate goes out into the world and attempts to change things for the better? He suddenly finds himself called "naive," "rash," "inexperienced." He learns that the oldsters really don't want the youngsters to remake the world after all. The soreness of the tops of many young heads (resulting from much battering against stone walls) testifies amply to the resistance that confronts them.

Yet if we look back a few years we find that the majority of the soldiers who fought and died in the last war were in their early twenties and younger. The majority of the scientists who contributed actively toward the development of the atomic bomb were in their twenties. Youngsters, we are told, are old enough to fight and die; they are old enough to help figure out how to make atomic bombs—but they are too young to have anything to say about what to do about the frightening problems that face the modern world and threaten to destroy it.

In speaking today about the social responsibilities of science, I will speak of things which are relatively easy for young people, but difficult for older persons, to understand. This is because young people possess a quality that in general diminishes with years: the quality of imagination. Imagination is a quality which is an integral part of science, and naturally endowed to young people. It is a quality which sadly enough evaporates with advancing age, yet it is a quality which our unhappy world needs in abundance at the present time.

[2]Delivered to the *Herald Tribune* High School Forum, in New York, New York, on March 5, 1949. Reprinted with permission of Harrison S. Brown and *The Bulletin of Atomic Scientists.*

For the last three centuries the findings of science have had marked impact upon society, but people on the whole have not understood just how our world has been affected, nor have they cared. From the time of Newton men began to realize that through technology, which is based upon the findings of science, substantial comforts and profits could be gained. From the time of Pasteur men began to realize that through the application of science to medicine they might be able to live longer.

From the time of Leonardo da Vinci, men appreciated that science could materially aid in winning wars. As years went by a technological materialism was developed; demands for new technical knowledge became greater and greater; more and more men became scientists and technologists. The scientist came to be looked upon as the creator of a new and abundant life. To make substantial profits, to work less, to live longer, to win wars—what more could the people of a nation desire? In the valor of its ignorance humanity accepted science and technology as its benefactors seldom questioning, seldom asking where it was leading.

And where has it led? To a large part of the world it has brought unprecedented comfort. To an even larger part of the world it has brought unprecedented agony.

To the world of the future (the world in which you young people must live) technological expansion may bring total catastrophe, or it may aid in the molding of a balanced world in which men may have the opportunity to live in reasonable harmony with their environment and with each other. The end result will depend upon the wisdom and imagination with which we plan for the future—upon the wisdom and imagination with which we integrate our scientific and technical knowledge from other fields of human endeavor, into a pattern for a peaceful and stable world.

Let's look at the record. It is not a happy one! Science and technology have placed in the hands of the rulers of nations tools of coercion and persuasion of unprecedented effectiveness. Modern implements of war make it possible for small groups of men to enforce their rule over large groups of people. In modern totalitarian states, the weapons in the hands of rulers make impossible successful popular revolts.

In the past, uprisings against despotism by masses of people armed only with crude weapons were possible. Today, applied science makes despotism invulnerable to internal overthrow by violent means.

Improvements in transportation and communications have increased the effectiveness of police action. Revolutionary methods of mass communication, rotary presses, radio and motion pictures provide powerful tools for persuasion. Today, when propaganda can be spread to millions of people when the governed can be unknowingly fed with untruths and kept in ignorance of the truth by government control of communications outlets, the people become powerless.

It would be pleasant to believe that by creating new techniques in transportation and communication, thus making the world effectively smaller, some sort of a dent might have been made in minimizing the concept of intense nationalism. But the reverse has been true. The creation of vast industrial nations, competing with one another, and the creation of centralized national authorities of ever increasing power have more than overbalanced the effect upon nationalism of increasing communication and education.

History has taught us that intense nationalism sooner or later results in wars between nations. Today wars are, more than ever before, wars of competing technologies. The first half of the twentieth century will go down in history as the period within which technological developments took place which converted destruction from a difficult operation into a fantastically easy one. But as yet, we have seen only the crude beginnings of what can be done, should circumstances dictate. Now that nations, each in the interest of its own military security, have mobilized science, we can expect developments in the technology of war to proceed at an accelerated pace.

Even our good intentions have brought trouble. The spread of sanitation measures and the control of disease to ever-increasing bodies of humanity has created the problem of overpopulation. With the population check of disease removed, we are now confronted with the gigantic task of finding ways to feed people and to keep populations in check.

Increased populations and wars have, in turn, placed tremendous drains upon our natural resources, upon our power reserve, upon our arable land.

Indeed, it is not a pretty picture that confronts us. It has caused many persons to say that perhaps, like the dinosaur, mankind is doomed to extinction.

But fortunately our position is somewhat different from that of the dinosaur, whose size, which once permitted him to survive, destroyed him when his environment changed. The dinosaur did not create the environment that destroyed him. Man, through his thoughtless misuse of science, has created his. The dinosaur had no control over his environment. Man, if he wishes and if he is willing to apply science and technology properly, may have control over his.

Science and technology offer man important tools that may enable him better to control his environment and as a result enable him to control his destiny. Man must learn how to use those tools properly and he must apply his imagination to the task of devising the social and political institutions that will permit him to utilize the tools with maximum effectiveness.

As we have not thought sufficiently far into the future, the net result of our haphazard and unplanned use of science and technology has been disastrous to society. We should now, realizing the danger that confronts us, study the future, plan accordingly and utilize those aspects of science that can aid us in moulding a more hopeful destiny than that which now confronts us.

The first social responsibility of science is to shout from the housetops whenever it sees science and technology being used in the dangerous ways in which they have been used in the past.

The second responsibility is to develop wherever possible constructive solutions to the political problems that now confront mankind: the production of food, clothing and shelter.

A third, and in many respects an even more important responsibility exists, and that is to disseminate far and wide an attitude that I like to call the "scientific attitude."

The scientific attitude is at once a way of thought, a way of conduct and a way of life. It is an attitude that has been found essential for constructive scientific progress—an attitude which, if it were to be more widely disseminated, accepted, appreciated and used, would go a long way toward helping mankind resolve the many dilemmas that now confront it. A scientific attitude has many component parts, the most important of which are straightforward and easy to understand:

The scientist must avoid dogmatism. He must always insist upon valid argument. He must proceed cautiously, yet he must be ready for change. He must insist upon the truth. He cannot permit national fetishisms to influence his judgment. And above all, he must insist upon complete, undistorted and uncompromising freedom of speech.

The assimilation of a scientific attitude will enable all of you to build the kind of world you want to live in—a world free of fear, free of war and free of want.

# A Scientific Society—The Beginnings[3]

Glenn T. Seaborg

*Born April 19, 1912, Ishpeming, MI; A.B., 1934, Ph.D., 1937, University of California at Berkeley; professor, 1941, professor, 1945-61, chancellor, 1958-61, University of California at Berkeley; associated with development of atomic bomb, Manhattan Project, 1942-46; co-winner of Nobel Prize in chemistry, 1951; associate director, Lawrence Radiation Laboratory, 1954-58; chair, Atomic Energy Commission, 1961–; author,* The Chemistry of the Actinide Elements *(1957),* Elements of the Universe *(1958).*

## Editor's introduction

In this speech, Glenn T. Seaborg, chair of the Atomic Energy Commission, Nobel Prize winning chemist and the discoverer of plutonium, concluded that the "scientific society has arrived." His meaning is simple—government, business, and industry are now dependent upon research and technology as science is no longer limited to labs and research centers. Science is, as Seaborg noted, a fundamental part of all our lives. Given this he argued that we must not become victims of technology but rather remain free by allowing education to increase our knowledge of science and therefore our mastery over it.

---

John Wesley Powell was a man who stands large in the history of American science. He believed in the frontier, and he lived on it vigorously and adventurously, whether exploring the Colorado or insisting upon good science policy in Washington. Powell was a man of great vision. He saw clearly how science and engineering could develop the vast potential of the West to help make ours a great nation. He understood the nature of science and technology, and his Geological Survey demonstrated the usefulness of properly administered Government science. It is with pride, therefore, that I speak in Powell's name, here in the West he knew so well.

As I prepared for this lecture and considered some of the developments in science since Powell's time, my thoughts drifted to personal reminiscence. I recalled that in this season twenty-one years ago, my colleagues and I were doing the experiment which resulted in the discovery of plutonium. Needless to say, my world has not been the same since. Nor has my experience been unusual. The same forces operating in my case have markedly altered the lives of many millions of people and, indeed, society itself. Allowing for the lack of perspective that accompanies our closeness to the events, it still seems most pardonable to judge the past two decades to be one of the most portentous periods in human history. And this has been made so by science and technology.

I believe these things to be true not alone because of the novel dilemma revolving about nuclear weapons and the very survival of modem civilization; but also because of the general scientific-technological progress most dramatically exemplified by the peaceful atom and space exploration.

What is perhaps more important in the long run, granted our ability to avert total nuclear war, is the fact that in these two decades science and technology have become a dominant force in our social order. Much has been written about the scientific society, usually in the future tense. I believe we are warranted in changing the tense to the present. Although it is in its infancy, the scientific society has arrived; it has crossed the threshold in its relationship to society as a whole.

Science and technology are now part of the fabric of Government, industry and business,

[3]Delivered to the American Association for the Advancement of Science, in Denver, Colorado, on December 27, 1961.

and of our social institutions. The destinies of individuals and peoples are irrevocably associated, from day to day, with the growth and use of scientific knowledge.

As was to be expected, the birth of the new infant has not been an easy one. Nor will its development be untroubled. It seems clear that science and technology are the most powerful forces for material advancement unleashed by man. The changes these forces bring—and will continue to bring—run wide and deep through society. Men as a whole are not friendly to such changes and forces. But to scientists, these developments may seem clearer than to most men.

The conception of our infant scientific society can best be assigned to the Renaissance. At that time, men challenged authority and the dogma that had ruled for centuries, and questioned the nature of the universe and man's place in it. The spirit of questioning in the Western world occurred on many fronts—in religion and philosophy and political theory, in art and literature, and in science. One important result was the expression in the Declaration of Independence and the Bill of Rights of the Constitution of the idea of individual personal, political, and intellectual freedom as controlling in an organized society. The same forces that liberated men politically, and in other ways, also produced the scientific method. With the growth of freedom of inquiry and the development of techniques for discovery, there began an acceleration of our ideas about nature. And the knowledge gained became highly significant when translated by technologists into tools.

Through our privileged perspective, we can see that—given the conditions of the last five centuries—everything that has happened has been virtually inevitable. For the achievement by men of the right to search for truth was the critical breakthrough. When this right was established on a continuing basis, it was only a matter of time until bacteria were discovered, electricity identified, and nuclear fission revealed. In a word, modern scientific knowledge and its application are a consequence of the vigorous exercise of the freedoms that arose in Western Europe and America. I should like to introduce my stock-taking of the twenty years now ending by recalling some personal experiences to illustrate, in an anecdotal way, something of the changes within science and its new relationships to society.

In the fall of 1940, I was a young chemist at the University of California. We had been trained to believe that a deep gulf ran between pure and applied science. I was "pure," of course, searching for knowledge for its own sake. We were also poor—a property which followed purity like the night the day. But, being pure, we could accept poverty in good grace and even with some pride. Our poverty, of course, pervaded our research operations. Research funds were almost unknown. We built as much of our own equipment as we could, or coaxed our more talented friends into helping with it. Laboratory space was hard to come by. I can recall, as a graduate student, adopting the squatter's rights technique to obtain some space in an abandoned and condemned old wooden structure. But these were the accepted conditions of research science in those days, and we were hardly aware that our difficulties were difficulties.

The Lawrence Radiation Laboratory was a new kind of thing on the scientific horizon. It gave us a foretaste of things to come in some fields. The equipment was huge—by 1939, there were two cyclotrons that were giants among scientific equipment. Scientists from a variety of fields found it profitable frequently to pool their talents in working with the cyclotrons and their products. In this way, many of us encountered the emerging concept of group research. The laboratory budget, mostly from private sources, was considered enormous for the time, although it might arouse some amusement today.

Of course, we were not unaware of what was happening in the world—of the war that had started, and of the power-mad dictator who was a threat to our ideals and who aspired to engulf humanity in his medieval social order. But, like many research scientists, I did not then relate my work very much to practical things, and certainly not to war.

Until 1940, my research had been concerned with the identification—with J. J. Livingood, primarily—of new radioisotopes. In the spring of that year, Edwin M. McMillan and Philip H. Abelson opened the transuranium field with their brilliant discovery of element 93, neptunium. It is an interesting commentary on the thinking and the priorities of the time that McMillan, who had started work aimed toward the discovery of the next higher element—element 94—was called away to do defense research on radar at the Massachusetts Institute of Technology.

With the assent of McMillan, three of us, my associate, the late Joseph W. Kennedy, Arthur C. Wahl, at that time a graduate student, and I, undertook to continue the research. It seems doubtful that many theses have been written that contained significance to rival that of Wahl's. A few days before Christmas, in 1940—just twenty-one years ago—the cyclotron bombardment was made which, in the succeeding few weeks resulted in the chemical identification of plutonium. Plutonium may be said to have "come of age" as this meeting takes place.

Even at Christmastime in 1940, our work was not done in an atmosphere heavy with historical import, but rather in the carefree manner of young adventurers breaking new ground. It is true that fission and its implications were then known, and that some steps were being taken to learn how to exploit this discovery, using uranium-235. It was theoretically postulated, too, that an isotope of element 94 might be fissionable. Yet there was not, twenty-one years ago, any clear idea of how the then-identified element, if discovered, could be practically made in quantity and how it could be put to use as a military weapon.

Subsequently, with Emilio Segre, we created and identified the fissionable isotope, plutonium-239, in March 1941. And a way was soon visualized to make this element in quantity and to use it as a weapon. In a short time, the knowledge gained in the search for truth became a formidable bulwark of national defense.

We crossed the divide between science and technology, and our work became useful in many ways, including its significant contributions to our arsenal of defense. We went from poverty to relative riches. Instead of working alone or with a colleague or two, we banded together in the team research pattern now so well established.

At times, during the war, we dreamed of a kind of scientific V-Day, after which we would return to the old ways, most especially the pursuit of knowledge for the sake of knowledge alone and divorced from application. Some of you probably were with me in the great hegira to fundamental research which actually did occur at the end of the war.

However, a large number of us found that the conditions of science had changed, in varying ways and to varying degrees. Perhaps the central point is that two decades ago science was called up, as it had been in the Civil War and World War I, to fight a five-alarm blaze. But this time, in a sense, science did not return to the firehouse.

The use of the nuclear bomb crystallized, as never before and on a world stage, the enormous power of science and technology. But this power was not to be confined to war alone, but was to be used for man's benefit in the expansion of industrial productivity and the advancement of our economic system generally. Later in the two decades of which I speak, Sputnik further dramatized the lesson.

Moreover, the realization grew among us and among industrial and political leaders that the time fuse between discovery and application had become short and was growing shorter. The gulf between basic and applied science had narrowed, and in some instances had become imperceptible. This realization was expressed in many ways: for example, while the government after World War II continued the development of nuclear weapons, it dared not risk failure at the same time to support the fundamental research in particle physics. In addition, under the conditions of modern competition between great nations, the prestige and power of a society came to be measured in part by its accomplishments in the growth of all knowledge.

In the past two decades, then, science has come to stay, as a regular, essential and pervasive activity in modem society. The signs that ours has become a scientific society are all around us. Suffice it to say here that Government, business and industry are dependent for survival and expansion not alone on technology, but upon an accelerating growth of knowledge deriving from research that once was sometimes described as "pure." Moreover. it appears that nearly everyone is aware of this fact.

Let me give just one example of these developments, relating to the governmental agency of which I have the honor to be chairman. In 1940, there was no such thing as atomic energy. Today, atomic energy is one of our biggest enterprises. The capital investment of the Atomic Energy Commission is $7.5 billion before depreciation. Its annual budget is $2.5 billion. It is true that approximately 75 per cent of this is devoted to defense activities. Yet, some $600 million per year are also dedicated to peaceful arts—to the development of productive industries for the present and the future, such as power reactors and research on controlled fusion; to the advance of medicine and its application; to the growth of knowledge in many areas of fundamental research; to the export of materials and techniques as a part of our international relations program. In addition, there is the private atomic energy industry, involving nongovernmental expenditures of $50 million annually on development, and with a capital investment of $400 to $500 million. And we can hardly visualize the ultimate potential of this great private industry. And yet, all of this emanated from one discovery in basic research.

The new relationship between society and science is also reflected in the spectacular growth of the numbers of people who are doing research and development or who play supporting roles in these efforts. It is to be seen in the Federal budget for research and development—some $9 billion annually, today, compared with about $400 million in 1940. Even more important are the new attitudes—of society in general toward science, and of scientists toward society.

The former is symbolized by the policies of Government and industry. Recognition by the Government of the need to support research across a broad spectrum was slow and spotty after World War II. The tendency has been—and continues to be to a large extent—to support fashionable or dramatic areas and those that might have some early, foreseeable technological value. Considerable progress was made, however, in the early postwar days as a result of the enlightened policies of the Office of Naval Research and the later policies of the Atomic Energy Commission. The National Science Foundation has significantly expanded the concept of governmental support for broad advances in fundamental knowledge, and I believe this trend will continue and will increasingly embrace the policies of special agencies that support research. Today, about 12 per cent of the Federal funds for research and development are used to support basic research fields. In other words, we can detect a fairly general recognition of the fact that the growth of fundamental knowledge, even though it may not have specific foreseeable application, contributes to the general welfare. Perhaps we can even hope for an appreciation for the more subtle cultural values of basic research.

The enormous impact of the past two decades on the scientific community reflects significant integration of science into society. I do not detect any qualitative change in the spirit of scientific inquiry, fortunately. But it would appear that there is an important alteration in the attitude of scientists about the relationship of their work to the larger social environment. Many of us can recall a fairly general feeling of pride among scientists in the isolation of their work from the practical affairs of men. Indeed, it was not difficult to find resentment at any implication that a piece of research should have more than the remotest connection with application. Now, with the reduction of the time gap between basic and applied research, and with growing general appreciation of the value of knowledge, scientists seem more willing to relate themselves and their work to social objectives.

The material conditions have been modified, too. More and more, scientists find that they are supported adequately, if not opulently, and for sustained programs. Funds are available for "elegant" equipment that saves time and gives greater power to investigators. Money can be obtained for assistants to do detailed work, giving researchers more time for creative effort. The improvements are not uniform, of course. Space to work is still in short supply, especially in our graduate schools; yet, new governmental policies promise some alleviation. And the personal rewards are still relatively less for those who train our scientists and generate much of our knowledge, than for many others in our society who play much less significant roles.

The consolidation of science into society is striking in the field of governmental policy and international relations. The Government has become increasingly dependent upon scientists for advice. This is true not only in the sphere of the administration of Government science, but in a much more comprehensive way. Any evaluation of the future of the economy must embrace scientific and technological knowledge. Decisions in military matters are intimately involved with science and technology. And any commitment of portions of our national resources for science and technology themselves must be decided with the help of men of wide knowledge in these fields.

The entry of scientists into important national advisory capacities is an inevitable concomitant of the events of the last twenty years.

I believe it is a healthy and essential development, and I have advocated it for many years. It does not seem to me that the influence of scientists in this respect is greater than it should be; indeed, in the national interest, I believe it must increase.

The question of the place of science in Government touches upon some of the critical questions about the future evolution of a scientific society in a democratic context. Our aim must be to use science to strengthen democracy, not weaken it; to expand the potential fulfillment of the individual, not decrease it. We must avoid any erosion of the broad base of informed participation by the electorate. In the past two decades, our democracy has ingested science, but has not yet digested it—a measure of the infancy of our scientific society. This is not surprising, since our previous experience had not prepared us for anything like the explosion of those twenty years. We must expect the next twenty years to be even more dynamic. Therefore, it is urgent that we accelerate the process of assimilation.

A central problem in assimilation, it seems to me, is the extent to which men, including the otherwise well-educated, fail to identify freedom of scientific inquiry with our political and other freedoms. In the somewhat less complicated world of the eighteenth century, a great thinker like Thomas Jefferson could be all at once a political theorist and practitioner, a philosopher and a scientist. His mind could embrace and integrate a very large part of human knowledge. He had, therefore, a clear appreciation of the broadly humanistic values which are the common heritage of all men who pursue the truth.

But, as knowledge grew and fragmented, the specialties went their separate ways. Science has seemed to walk more apart than other fields, perhaps because the details of scientific truth touch infrequently a community of intellectual experience. Science became a stranger even to many intellectuals.

This estrangement has resulted in the paradox with which we are familiar: as science became more important to society, it apparently became less important in the curricula of liberal education. This fact was noticed as long ago as the last century by Thomas Huxley, who pleaded with contemporaries holding a narrow view of humanism to include a more generous helping of science in liberal education. A cultured, or liberally educated person, Huxley maintained, is one capable of making a criticism of life—of evaluating the environment and making enlightened judgments.

Thirty years ago George Sarton wrote in the same vein in his volume *The History of Science and the New Humanism.* He stated the issue, which remains central for our nascent democratic-scientific society, as follows:

"The main issue does not simply concern humanism but the whole of education from the cradle to the grave. And the real question is: will education include science, or will it exclude it? The intellectual elite is at present divided into two hostile groups—which we might call for short the literary and scientific—who do not speak the same language nor think in the same way. If nothing is done, the gap separating them must necessarily increase, together with the steady and irresistible progress of science. Shall we deliberately widen the gap as the old humanists would have it, or shall we take special pains to reduce it as much as we can?"

In our own time, C. P. Snow has eloquently drawn attention to the same problem, in his discourses on the "two cultures."

To summarize the matter, I should like to ask a question paraphrasing Huxley: Who in our times can make an adequate criticism of life without knowledge of the ideals, the methods, and the dynamics of science?

The remedies have been widely discussed: a larger content of science in the lower schools and in the universities and colleges; a wide range of efforts to give the public some appreciation of science; a greater effort by scientists to explain their work in popular terms.

All of these measures are needed. It is necessary to bring about a larger understanding of scientific principles. But in striving toward this goal, it may be even more important to promote a greater consciousness of the common heritage of all who pursue the truth. The philosopher, the social scientist, the artist, the writer, the natural scientist—all are intellectual brothers under the skin. Whether their technique involves the distillation of human experience or the ordering of measurable phenomena into statements of principles, their motivations, the quality of their experiences, and their satisfactions are rooted in a broadly defined humanism.

I am sure intellectuals generally know this to be true. Yet it would appear that it is often far back in the consciousness. I wonder if this fact is not responsible for much of the inability of Snow's two cultures to communicate? I wonder if there is not a common language, deriving from a community of basic ideals and purposes, whatever the details of different bodies of knowledge, that is the foundation for communication? I wonder if the barriers are not superficial, even as language is a superficial obstacle between men who share common bonds?

The achievement of a conscious, working realization of the common heritage of truth-seekers—among scientists as well as other intellectuals—can be significant in the successful evolution of our new kind of society. It should make it clearer that the free and uninhibited pursuit of truth in science is a natural part of the right of free inquiry that is inherent in democracy. It should do much to abolish fruitless discussions over whether we should continue doing science and whether scientists should not withhold scientific truths that may be used destructively. It should give wider acceptance of the inevitable growth of knowledge and of its continual change. It should force us to a greater awareness of the need to prepare for and to cope with the hazards that are a paradoxical by-product of the expansion of knowledge.

It has seemed natural to lay some emphasis on science in this discussion of the society that has developed in the last twenty years. I do not wish to give the impression, however, that I believe this new kind of society is the property of science. We cannot, of course, proceed intelligently without integrating into our thinking and our acting the full range of human wisdom. If you have noticed carefully, I have asked primarily for men generally, and intellectuals in particular, to return science to the fold of humanism. It is unthinkable that a democratic-scientific society could evolve constructively without a wide endowment among its people of art, music, history, literature and social dynamics.

We can hardly discuss the future of the scientific society without relating it to the world struggle and the terrible dilemma confronting man as the result of the development of nuclear weapons.

I am reminded of the reaction of many scientists, including some of us who worked on nuclear weapons, to this dilemma—when it became a reality in 1945. Natural scientists sometimes have been called too optimistic and naive by social scientists. As a group, they are not lacking in idealism. Perhaps it was natural that many of us, recognizing from close at hand the significance of nuclear weapons, set out to advise the world that nuclear war was out of the question. To us, the data were unequivocal, the conclusions indisputable, and the course of action clear. We felt the world would quickly see this—and, seeing it, do something about it.

The half-life of disillusionment varied from individual to individual. Few have changed their minds about nuclear war. But, many have become more sophisticated, if less idealistic. Much of what has been described as naivete has rubbed off. But we should remember that idealism, happily, has not been limited to scientists. In the period following World War I, experienced statesmen, imperceptibly influenced by scientists, solemnly signed unrealistic treaties outlawing war. Perhaps sophisticated statesmen, aided by sophisticated scientists in an age of science, may be able to combine realism and idealism.

My own instruction in these matters includes the experience, earlier this year, of being appointed by President Kennedy to head the U.S. delegation to the Fifth Annual Conference of the International Atomic Energy Agency in Vienna. This is an agency established to spread the peaceful uses of atomic energy throughout the world. Its problems, I found, are hardly less difficult than those of the United Nations.

I was impressed with the enormous difficulty of finding common solutions to problems—when the effort had to be made with individuals who seem to speak a different language, not only linguistically, but ideologically, and some of whom appear to possess a deterministic faith that is alien to our humanism.

While I found no basis for arrant optimism, neither did I find reason to stop trying. In the absence of any foreseeable breakthrough in diplomacy, it would appear that the best condition of the world we can hope for is a continuing crisis. In the competition of ideas which will accompany the crisis, the victory may be won by the successful evolution, here, of a society combining science and freedom.

Scientists and engineers can continue, as they have in the past, to make a major contribution in this contest, not only by achievements in the laboratory but also by their participation in exchange programs and international meetings, and other contacts with Iron Curtain nations through the medium of basic research when and if the occasions arise. All of these activities are essential to help keep the channels of communication and understanding open.

I believe each of us, scientist and nonscientist alike, must be aware of the importance of his own effort to the preservation of a libertarian society in the continuing crisis. Each of us needs a sense of responsibility and urgency—for the total of our efforts will be decisive, however remote from combat our work may seem. We must not do too little. We cannot delay. We must have both determination and good intentions; and what is most important—*we must act.* As I have advocated in the past, we must expand and raise the level of education all along the line. We must, especially, search out and cultivate the gifted and creative—for it is these that usually make the great breakthroughs in knowledge and understanding. We must mine every vein of our human resources and exploit our talents in the fullest measure.

The democratic-scientific society has taken root in the past two decades, combining the values of freedom and individual worth with the promise of growing material well-being. Can we preserve it—not only for ourselves, but as a choice for other peoples?

I believe we can and will, partly because of the moral strength of freedom and partly because of the material power of our new society. We cannot be blind to the fact that freedom needs strength and determination as well as a good heart. Generosity has its place in relations between men, but it is, unfortunately, a quality not uniformly respected by all nations in relations between themselves. This is why, for example, we must be prepared to negotiate from a position of unquestioned strength as well as undoubted good faith; and negotiate we must: to turn our back on this most hopeful and sensible solution of the differences between East and West would be as foolish as it could perhaps be fatal. But we must recognize that until all nations can proceed from the same definition of right and truth, international agreements which involve our vital interests must incorporate provision for adequate controls against violations as well as provision recognizing the other's rights. We must be firm when our own security is at stake, as well as fair when another's is. I cannot help but recall, in this vein, that eloquent passage from President Kennedy's Inaugural Address: "Civility is not a sign of weakness, and sincerity is always subject to proof. Let us never negotiate out of fear. But let us never fear to negotiate."

Beyond these principles, my confidence in freedom is based upon a personal faith, originating in my interpretation of human experience, to which one must appeal when scientific data are absent or inconclusive. Many times in history the future has not looked bright. However, the things most feared have not always come to pass. Man's native faith and hope in his own destiny have motivated solutions to awesome problems. History does, we know, repeat itself—both in crises and in their resolution—and so, we must trust it will again.

# Address to a Joint Meeting of Congress[4]

## John H. Glenn, Jr.

*Born July 18, 1921, Cambridge, OH; U.S. Marine Corps, 1943-56; test pilot, Navy Bureau of Aeronautics, 1956-69; astronaut, National Aeronautics and Space Administration (NASA) Project Mercury, 1959-64; vice president, Royal Crown Cola Company, 1962-74; senator (R) from Ohio, 1975–; author,* P.S., I Listened to Your Heartbeat *(1976).*

### Editor's introduction

On February 20, 1962, Lieutenant Colonel John H. Glenn, Jr., became the first American to orbit Earth in a space capsule. In this address, at one of the many ceremonies held in his honor, Glenn spoke to a joint session of Congress, the Supreme Court, the diplomatic corps, the Cabinet, and representatives from 97 nations. Recalling his remarkable mission, Glenn spoke of his experiences on the flight, the importance of the team effort, and the need for extensive space exploration. To justify the cost of the trip, Glenn asserted that "exploration and the pursuit of knowledge have always paid dividends."

---

Mr. Speaker, Mr. President, Members of the Congress, I am only too aware of the tremendous honor that is being shown us at this joint meeting of the Congress today. When I think of past meetings that involved heads of state and equally notable persons, I can only say I am most humble to know that you consider our efforts to be in the same class. [Applause.]

This has been a great experience for all of us present and for all Americans, of course, and I am certainly glad to see that pride in our country and its accomplishments is not a thing of the past. [Applause.]

I still get a hard-to-define feeling inside when the flag goes by—and I know that all of you do, too. Today as we rode up Pennsylvania Avenue from the White House and saw the tremendous outpouring of feeling on the part of so many thousands of our people I got this same feeling all over again. Let us hope that none of us ever loses it. [Applause.]

The flight of Friendship 7 on February 20 involved much more than one man in the spacecraft in orbit. [Applause.] I would like to have my parents stand up, please. [Mr. and Mrs. John Glenn, Sr., stood and received the rising applause of the Members.]

My wife's mother and Dr. Castor. [Dr. and Mrs. H. W. Castor stood and received the rising applause of the Members.]

My son and daughter, David and Carolyn. [David and Carolyn Glenn rose and received the rising applause of the Members.]

And the real rock in my family, my wife Annie. [Mrs. John H. Glenn, Jr., rose and received the applause of the Members.]

There are many more people, of course, involved in our flight in Friendship 7; many more things involved, as well as people. There was the vision of Congress that established this national program of space exploration. Beyond that, many thousands of people were involved, civilian contractors and many subcontractors in many different fields; many elements—civilian, civil service and military, all blending their efforts toward a common goal.

To even attempt to give proper credit to all the individuals on this team effort would be impossible. But let me say that I have never seen a more sincere, dedicated, and hard-working group of people in my life. [Applause.]

From the original vision of the Congress to consummation of this orbital flight has been just over three years. This, in itself, states eloquent-

[4]Broadcast nationwide, and delivered to a joint meeting of Congress, in Washington, D.C., on February 26, 1962. Reprinted with permission of John H. Glenn, Jr.

ly the case for the hard work and devotion of the entire Mercury team. This has not been just another job. It has been a dedicated labor such as I have not seen before. It has involved a crosscut of American endeavor with many different disciplines cooperating toward a common objective.

Friendship 7 is just a beginning, a successful experiment. It is another plateau in our step-by-step program of increasingly ambitious flights. The earlier flights of Alan Shepard and Gus Grissom were steppingstones toward Friendship 7. My flight in the Friendship 7 spacecraft will, in turn, provide additional information for use in striving toward future flights that some of the other gentlemen you see here will take part in. [Applause.]

Scott Carpenter here, who was my backup on this flight; Walt Schirra, Deke Slayton, and one missing member, who is still on his way back from Australia, where he was on the tracking station, Gordon Cooper. A lot of direction is necessary for a project such as this, and the Director of Project Mercury since its inception has been Dr. Robert Gilruth, who certainly deserves a hand here. [Applause.]

I have been trying to introduce Walt Williams. I do not see him here. There he is up in the corner. [Applause.]

And the Associate Director of Mercury, who was in the unenviable position of being Operational Director. He is a character, no matter how you look at him. He says hold the count-foul, and one thing and another.

With all the experience we have had so far, where does this leave us?

There are the building blocks upon which we shall build much more ambitious and more productive portions of the program.

As was to be expected, not everything worked perfectly on my flight. We may well need to make changes—and these will be tried out on subsequent three-orbit flights, later this year, to be followed by eighteen-orbit, twenty-four-hour missions.

Beyond that, we look forward to Project Gemini—a two-man orbital vehicle with greatly increased capability for advanced experiments. There will be additional rendezvous experiments in space, technical and scientific observations—then, Apollo orbital, circumlunar and finally, lunar landing flights.

What did we learn from the Friendship 7 flight that will help us attain these objectives?

Some specific items have already been covered briefly in the news reports. And I think it is of more than passing interest to all of us that information attained from these flights is readily available to all nations of the world. [Applause.]

The launch itself was conducted openly and with the news media representatives from around the world in attendance. [Applause.] Complete information is released as it is evaluated and validated. This is certainly in sharp contrast with similar programs conducted elsewhere in the world and elevates the peaceful intent of our program. [Applause.]

Data from the Friendship 7 flight is still being analyzed. Certainly, much more information will be added to our storehouse of knowledge.

But these things we know. The Mercury spacecraft and systems design concepts are sound and have now been verified during manned flight. We also proved that man can operate intelligently in space and can adapt rapidly to this new environment.

Zero G or weightlessness—at least for this period of time—appears to be no problem. As a matter of fact, lack of gravity is a rather fascinating thing.

Objects within the cockpit can be parked in midair. For example, at one time during the flight, I was using a hand-held camera. Another system needed attention; so it seemed quite natural to let go of the camera, take care of the other chore in the spacecraft, then reach out, grasp the camera and go back about my business.

It is a real fascinating feeling, needless to say.

There seemed to be little sensation of speed although the craft was traveling at about five miles per second—a speed that I too find difficult to comprehend.

In addition to closely monitoring onboard systems, we were able to make numerous outside observations.

The view from that altitude defies description.

The horizon colors are brilliant and sunsets are spectacular. It is hard to beat a day in which you are permitted the luxury of seeing four sunsets.

I think after all of our talk of space, this morning coming up from Florida on the plane with President Kennedy, we had the opportunity to meet Mrs. Kennedy and Caroline before we took off. I think Caroline really cut us down to size and put us back in the proper position. She looked up, upon being introduced, and said "Where is the monkey?" [Laughter.]

And I did not get a banana pellet on the whole ride.

Our efforts today and what we have done so far are but small building blocks in a huge pyramid to come.

But questions are sometimes raised regarding the immediate payoffs from our efforts. What benefits are we gaining from the money spent? The real benefits we probably cannot even detail. They are probably not even known to man today. But exploration and the pursuit of knowledge have always paid dividends in the long run—usually far greater than anything expected at the outset. [Applause.]

Experimenters with common, green mold, little dreamed what effect their discovery of penicillin would have.

The story has been told of Disraeli, Prime Minister of England at the time, visiting the laboratory of Faraday, one of the early experimenters with basic electrical principles. After viewing various demonstrations of electrical phenomena, Disraeli asked, "But of what possible use is it?" Faraday replied, "Mister Prime Minister, what good is a baby?"

That is the stage of development in our program today—in its infancy. And it indicates a much broader potential impact, of course, than even the discovery of electricity did. We are just probing the surface of the greatest advancements in man's knowledge of his surroundings that has ever been made, I feel. There are benefits to science across the board. Any major effort such as this results in research by so many different specialties that it is hard to even envision the benefits that will accrue in many fields.

Knowledge begets knowledge. The more I see, the more impressed I am—not with how much we know—but with how tremendous the areas are that are as yet unexplored.

Exploration, knowledge, and achievement are good only insofar as we apply them to our future actions. Progress never stops. We are now on the verge of a new era, I feel.

Today, I know that I seem to be standing alone on this great platform—just as I seemed to be alone in the cockpit of the Friendship 7 spacecraft. But I am not. There were with me then—and with me now—thousands of Americans and many hundreds of citizens of many countries around the world who contributed to this truly international undertaking voluntarily and in a spirit of cooperation and understanding.

On behalf of all of those people, I would like to express my and their heartfelt thanks for the honors you have bestowed upon us here today.

We are all proud to have been privileged to be part of this effort, to represent our country as we have. As our knowledge of the universe in which we live increases, may God grant us the wisdom and guidance to use it wisely.

# From Runnymede to Ganymede[5]

James E. Webb

*Born October 7, 1906, Tally Ho, NC; died March 27, 1992; A.B., University of North Carolina, 1928; U.S. Marine Corps, 1930-31; J.D., George Washington University Law School, 1936; secretary-treasurer, Sperry Corporation, 1943; U.S. Marine Corps, 1944-45; U.S. under secretary of treasury, 1946; director, Bureau of the Budget, 1946-48; U.S. under secretary of state, 1949-52; deputy governor, International Bank for Reconstruction and Development, 1949-52; president, Republic Supply Company, 1953-58; assistant to president, Kerr-McGee Oil Industries, 1952-61; administrator, National Aeronautics and Space Administration (NASA), 1961-68.*

## Editor's introduction

On May 27, 1967, James E. Webb, former administrator of the National Aeronautics and Space Administration (NASA), spoke on the occasion of the Prelude to Independence. This annual event commemorates the Fifth Virginia Convention (May 15–July 4, 1776), during which the Independence Resolution of May 15, the Declaration of Rights of June 12, and the Virginia Constitution of June 29 were drafted. Webb, who was appointed to the post of NASA chief by President John F. Kennedy, recalled Kennedy's near direct order to have a man placed on the moon by 1970. Webb described such a feat as the "most complex nonmilitary undertaking of all time." In answering those who asked how funds invested in space research could serve those on Earth, Webb described how satellites provide information on weather conditions in order to better depict space exploration as part of the age-old search for a better understanding of both ourselves and our environment.

---

It is a great honor to share with you the privilege of meeting here in Williamsburg to recall the concepts of individual liberty, self-government, responsible leadership, and public service breathed into life by the great American patriots who did their work here in the fifty days from May 15 to July 4, 1776. Time and again on these occasions Governor Winthrop Rockefeller and his distinguished guests have pointed out that independence for the United States was accomplished because the leaders of Virginia based their work on a deep understanding of man as an individual and as a collection of individuals making up society.

While the main events that we commemorate here today took place in fifty days, there was a long period in which, to use Woodrow Wilson's words,

"the great continent lay "a veiled and virgin shore" inflaming desires that could not be gratified, stirring dreams that only enticed brave men to their death, exciting to enterprise and adventure, but never to substantial or lasting achievement."

Then came a colonial development prelude that lasted more than fifty years. Even the Byrds of Virginia had to submit to the rigors of this period. In fact, in 1717, having lost his first wife, William Byrd of Westover was in London paying ardent suit to a young lady named Mary Smith whose father required that he set down an analysis of his property and income. He did this, adding a statement of his honorable descent from the Byrds of Cheshire. But Mr. Smith replied coldly that property on the moon was as acceptable as an estate in Virginia. So Byrd lost Mary Smith.

Today, the moon seems much nearer, and samples of it are eagerly awaited by scientists all over the world. It is nearer because over 400,000 men and women have worked hard to develop every scientific discipline, every major area of technology, and every engineering and management requirement to succeed in the

[5]Delivered at the Prelude to Independence celebration, in Williamsburg, Virginia, on May 27, 1967.

largest and most complex non-military undertaking of all time. Our nation has mobilized for this project within a decade about the same number of people required to build our transcontinental railroads. As independent individuals, these people have cooperated to use gravity, inertia, thermodynamics, and celestial mechanics in extraordinary new ways. They have constructed a rocket-powered transportation system that is already being used again and again, not only to the moon, but to almost any place in the solar system.

Property from the moon will soon become a more acceptable asset than even an estate in Virginia. Today, communications satellites and weather satellites are serving to tie the peoples of Europe, Asia, North America, and Australia together and to provide to the entire world useful weather information.

On June 25 [1967], the people of twenty-four nations, completely girdling the earth, will simultaneously watch the same television program—which will tell millions of men what other men are doing at many, many points around the world. It is an interesting fact that communications satellites of both the United States and the Soviet Union will make this possible.

Thirty-nine nations currently receive cloud-cover pictures on a routine basis from our weather satellites.

During the period from February to April, a combination of surface-based, airborne, seaborne, and satellite observations were taken in the Pacific which will be used to study fundamental meteorological problems.

Observing the earth from satellites will soon provide a powerful means for us and other nations to locate potential areas of mineral and oil resources.

Man is not only looking toward how space can serve him here on earth, but is also continuing to look further outward into space, eagerly awaiting the time when he can travel to the moons of planets other than his own earth. One such moon revolves around Jupiter, that distant and little-known planet. Its name is Ganymede, and it was discovered by Galileo 150 years before the famous fifty days we celebrate here today.

The capability man now has to project himself or his instruments to our own nearby moon or a distant moon of Jupiter is, of course, dependent on that developed intellectuality which flourishes on man's independence nourished by individual liberty, and freedom of choice. This is less well stated in our history books than is the story of that great turning point in man's struggle for independence and liberty that occurred at Runnymede in the thirteenth century. Runnymede means to most of us an epoch in man's struggle for his natural rights and for self-fulfillment. Ganymede means an intellectual concept and an object so distant that we can hardly reach it in this century. But both are symbolic. Therefore, I have chosen for my topic today, "From Runnymede to Ganymede."

The men who labored here in 1776 took the long view of man: man in space, if you will, since to the best of their knowledge—and ours—man has always been in space and always will be. He was in space when King John at Runnymede made his giant step toward guaranteed human rights. He was in space at Padua in the seventeenth century when Galileo Galilei made his giant step toward understanding his place in space with the aid of free scientific thought. And he will be in space at Ganymede in the twenty-first century if he chooses to stop there to do a detailed spectroanalysis of Jupiter to see if life exists. (This is an important concept because no one has yet figured out a way to land on Jupiter itself. Already, here on earth, we are performing experiments which show the possibility that some life could evolve even on that hostile planet.)

Thus, while this century will bring us the capability to travel to our moon and the nearby planets, Venus and Mars, man already begins to dream of going on to the distant planets in the next century. If Jefferson were alive today, he would without doubt be an enthusiastic participant in this thought process. In Jefferson there was a happy marriage of physical science and political science. Through him both were joined for good at Williamsburg in 1776.

Jefferson knew about Runnymede, and he was deeply committed to extend the progress man had made in the intervening five centuries. Interestingly enough, Jefferson also knew about Ganymede. More than this, he understood the profound importance of the interaction between the physical and the social sciences. He knew the sequence that plays itself out as man's attention is drawn to a phenomenon of nature and begins to think about it, to refine his observations, and to analyze them in depth. He understood that given enough motivation, enough intelligence, and enough time, man would then begin to identify the important elements and to perceive their relationships one to another. Jefferson recognized that through this scientific method there would come understanding, and that with sufficient understanding man could achieve the power to make predictions about the phenomenon to which his attention had been drawn.

Many who explain science and interpret the scientific method today stop at this point. But Jefferson, a close student of Bacon, recognized that with a deeper and more profound understanding, man discovers the basic principles that enable him to predict related phenomena, and that in time he will discover he can control some of these and put them to work.

The term we use today for man's ability to capture and put to work the forces of nature is "technology." Since technology frequently gives birth to better means for making new scientific observations, it continually provides the beginning of a whole new cycle of discovery, understanding, and practical use of knowledge.

As Jefferson thought deeply on the lessons of history in the spring of 1776, it seems to me hardly possible that he did not reflect on the fact that the most dramatic examples of man's scientific success had derived from his centuries-old interest in the vast regions outward from the earth. Jefferson was aware, for example, that almost two hundred years earlier, the famous Danish astronomer, Tycho Brahe, and his collaborators perfected the quadrant and made a long and especially accurate series of observations of the motions of the stars and planets. He was aware that a short time later Galileo Galilei applied the telescope to the more detailed study of our moon and the planets of our solar system. He knew that the observations of Brahe and Galileo cast great doubt on the then current theory which placed the earth at the center of the solar system and which had been man's egocentric view since the time of the ancient Greeks. Jefferson also knew that Johannes Kepler, a student of Brahe's, had achieved greatness by analyzing Brahe's data in detail and deducing his famous laws of planetary motion. And Jefferson knew well that Newton, who was described as "he who in genius surpassed human kind," had surveyed the work of Kepler on planetary motions and of Galileo on falling bodies and had concluded that the dynamics of these phenomena were really but manifestations of a universal principle which became his law of gravitation. Jefferson knew that Newton had gone on to enunciate his three famous laws of motion, and had become thereby, apart from relativistic considerations, the architect of dynamics and celestial mechanics as we know them today.

Here in Williamsburg two hundred years ago, Jefferson undoubtedly pondered the massive impact on man and society of this sequence of events. What did it mean, what could it mean to the new nation being born, that those literary and religious positions which had rallied around the fallacious earth-centered universe of Ptolemy, and were made vivid in the epic poems of Milton and Dante, had been so recently and so sorely shaken by advancing intellectual processes?

Could Jefferson have foreseen that man's lesson in humility and objectivity in the face of such a vast unfolding physical universe had only begun, and that the forces of a freethinking science would shortly bring man to conceive that the solar system itself was nowhere near the center of the universe? Indeed, that the universe itself is an immense space-time continuum in which energy and mass are interchanging on a grand scale?

We know today that if knowledge is to be of benefit to mankind, it must be put to work through organized society. Jefferson knew this, too. He had read John Locke, and had placed his picture in his home. Indeed he had made Locke's *Essay Concerning Human Understanding* a subject of careful study. He knew what Galileo's great accomplishment had contributed to Newton's work and that it had also provided an inspirational basis for Newton's friend, Locke, in the fields of philosophy and government. The effect of Locke's works defining and defending human rights were strongly reflected in the Declaration of Independence and in much that came thereafter.

And so, it is today hard to imagine a grander consequence of the cross-fertilization of ideas in the history of man than that represented by Locke and Newton, as seen by Jefferson.

In our early days Washington, Hamilton, Jefferson, and Franklin built in concert on the knowledge of each other, and they did this with all the effectiveness that characterized the work of Brahe, Galileo, Kepler, and Newton. This was no small feat. Washington, the soldier, had to know government as he knew war; Hamilton, the lawyer, had to know banking as he knew jurisprudence; Jefferson, the philosopher, had to know men as he knew logic; and Franklin, the scientist, had to know diplomacy as well as he knew electricity. There was no assumption underlying their work more important than that individually free men would become collectively responsible men. They set a pattern of collective action and governmental framework that has enabled a growing society of free men to effectively exercise initiative in exploiting new knowledge through new technology on a scale never before attained. Our free society has become a select haven for freethinking science and advanced technology, with the result that its search for and application of new knowledge has been successful on a scale that challenges all the rest of mankind.

But let us return to Newton and recall that his third law of motion, equating action and reaction, is especially suited for providing vehicles that move in the vacuum outside our atmosphere. This possibility was recognized by Robert Goddard, who conceived and developed the first small liquid rocket over thirty years ago. He laid the foundation for today's large space boosters that have already succeeded in taking man far away from the earth, where he may make even more revealing observations and find new ways to make use of his environment.

Truly, then, we are witnessing the full measure of John Wesley Powell's penetrating observation in 1888 when, as president of the American Association for the Advancement of Science, he stated,

"In man's progress from savagery to enlightenment, he has transferred the laws of beast evolution from himself to his inventions, and relieved of the load, he has soared away to the goal of his destiny on the wings of higher law."

It may be instructive to mentally blast off from earth and look at ourselves as an *entity in the totality of this space region which we can now traverse.* Either individually or collectively as an element of mass or energy, man's presence in space can easily be calculated to be of trivial significance. On the grand scale of space, man appears to be a physical triviality.

As an intellectual entity, however, he is as uniquely significant in the totality of space as he is in the locality of earth. By all odds his destiny appears to be the destiny of his intellect. He appears to have no recourse but to engage by all means available in the endless search for new food for thought—new information which he digests to form the new knowledge that enables him to continue the search for better understanding of himself and of his environment.

This search then is the greatest continuing adventure known to man, and it is uniquely his in the physical universe. It is uniquely suited to constructively consuming all of his resources, mental and physical. Thus, if man so chooses, he does indeed have an outlet for all the effort now expended in conflict or wars, an outlet vastly more noble and rewarding.

But the events of the day make it clear that the existence of conflict and of war still provides dramatic evidence of the animal that remains in man; that man himself is the one animal that man has far from fully mastered.

George Mason penned in Article XV of the Virginia Declaration of Rights, "That no free government, or the blessing of liberty can be preserved to any people but by . . . frequent recurrence to fundamental principles."

What then are these principles as they apply today? To get at this question, let us take another view of ourselves, paying special attention to the impact of science and technology. It is important to note first that we have become a nation composed largely of specialists, both as individuals and as professional groups. This has been necessary in order to cope with the increasing number and complexity of the functions which must be performed, each of which must be tractable for the individual, for his professional or associated group, and for those who must fit them together to provide an effective total operation of society. In a very real sense, then, we have evolved into a highly complex, interconnected, and interdependent system of people, groups, functions, and interests. This is in contradistinction to our early period when the advancing frontier provided opportunity and fluidity, and the pattern of settlement consisted of a relatively small number of loosely connected groups which could enjoy a quasi-independent existence.

Now perhaps the most remarkable thing about this evolution is that our fundamental principles and rules of law and order have been able to adjust and to evolve at more or less the same rate. Within our constitutional frame of government this has served to preserve the essential independence and freedom of the individual and to maintain a balance of forces and positions between existing and new groups.

Increasingly, science and technology have been important forcing functions of this evolution. It is the prime purpose of science to enlarge our understanding of known phenomena and to begin our understanding of new phenomena. The output of this effort is new knowledge, which is put to work in improving the way we do things we already know how to do and in developing ways of doing things we never knew how to do before. Accordingly, science and technology facilitate the development of new and improved functions in our society, and the most effective management techniques for exploiting these functions have largely involved the specializing of peoples and groups.

More generally, however, the essential product of science and technology is *change*—that is, *change in the attitudes and interests of people* through the acquisition of new knowledge, and *change in the methods of action and interaction of people* through the application of this knowledge. It follows that the larger the effort in science and technology, the larger those changes will be and the more rapidly they will occur.

Is this sufficient background against which to ask if we today are participating in a prelude to independence or the loss of it in the twenty-first century? Can we now grasp the basic problem posed for the individual by big science and big technology as major continuing elements in the same way the problems of 1776 were grasped by the men we honor today?

We know that the effect of science and technology is to upset the dynamic equilibrium of society. The bigger the effort of science and technology, the bigger and more rapid these perturbations are likely to be.

The hard fact of life for organized society and its leaders today is that if dynamic equilibrium is achieved at any one time it becomes increasingly difficult to maintain. This is especially true when it is upset by a number of large innovations not introduced with the most careful consideration of their second- and third-order effects.

We have now, also, significant evidence that new and improved methods must be brought into play to analyze and prepare for the introduction of major innovations. These methods must include not only consideration of the direct benefits which the innovations are primarily intended to provide, but also the intellectual response-time of humans, the inertia of human systems, and the interaction of human endeavors with their supporting physical and social environment.

In the National Aeronautics and Space Administration our experience to date indicates that for success we must make the most careful analysis of all factors at the start and still be prepared to adjust to meet reality when conditions turn out to differ from those that were foreseen. When we proceed this way the "integrated systems" approach developed for defense systems and for space exploration is vastly more effective for specific purposes than the "independent components" approach to the solution of problems in complex dynamic systems.

We all know, I believe, that goals for society and the projects to achieve them are realistic only as they are achievable with existing systems or desirable modifications of such systems.

This means that goals, projects, and systems must, in the last analysis, be viewed as interdependent elements, and goals that depend on undesirable systems are undesirable goals. Cooperation is desirable; loss of independence or individuality is not. The classic and continuing goal of our society is to preserve those basic freedoms and rights that have been won for responsible individuals, and the essential bases for cooperation between responsible groups within the framework of representative government.

The problem of choosing goals in our society depends on both our capabilities and our desires. From a capability point of view, we have long since passed the stage of surviving in our natural environment. To be sure we are creating problems of environmental pollution, but these are in no sense intractable to scientific and technological solution. We are in the process of pulling up the rearward displaced elements of our society, and we are extending assistance to provide security and opportunity to many other peoples throughout the world. All of this we are doing, and yet there is still capability left over. Some desire is left over, too, and we are satisfying this desire by applying some of our remaining capability to the enlargement of our science and technology effort, on earth and out in space. Many important factors contribute to this, but there is one that stands out. This is the fact that the carefully conceived methods of science and technology provide the only proven means known to man for consistently enlarging and applying his understanding of himself and his environment. Moreover, man alone of all creatures has learned to develop and use these methods for these means.

In this setting, the opening of the space regions to man's exploration and use is an epoch of vast significance. It is a prelude to a new and endless quest for enlarging and applying our understanding of ourselves and our environment. It is uniquely our quest—our unique destiny, and our unlimited adventure.

And so, we arrive back at the starting point of the evolution of our free society from eighteenth-century Willamsburg toward an unknown but beckoning twenty-first century. The challenge at Williamsburg was to establish an *independent order of free and responsible men* whose physical frontier would then move north, south, and west, but whose intellectual expansion would be bounded solely by their individual capacities and their ability to cooperate. This challenge was met so magnificently that the physical frontier is not now measured in the horizontal but by the vertical—it is out in space away from earth. We are exploring this frontier with Mariner and Surveyor, and also with Glenn and Schirra, as Jefferson probed north and west with Lewis and Clark. Today's frontier is limited only by our ability to maintain individual freedom and yet join many minds and hands in concerted action. Independence must continue to find a way to include interdependence in spite of complexity. Interdependence is the root of the nonlinearity which marks the safe limits of our over-all systems and of our individual lives.

Can we as individuals be *essentially free and yet interdependent?* This is Zeno's paradox of the twentieth century and it may continue into the twenty-first. Can we remain free and still put a governor on society that will stop us short of war? Can we remain independent and still go to Ganymede? How we answer it today and tomorrow will make up the character of any prelude to independence for man in the twenty-first century.

Much of what we can contribute to the answer lies in a fact that is obvious. This fact is the essential requirement for each of us to do what we can as individuals and as groups to make our system of representative government work, and then work better. More and more this means that each of us must find a way to reach through complexity and organized prejudice to organized facts and trusted sources of information. We must not do less than to make sure we understand the *fundamentals in the many important disciplines* of human activity.

Without this understanding of at least the fundamentals, from the golden rule to the laws of gravity and natural selection, today's citizen will not play the role only he can play in representative society, cannot bridge the gap from one discipline to another, from the old to the new. Without this, a citizen today cannot be a fully effective participant in a free society. Indeed, without this basic understanding on a large scale at all levels our nation is likely to forfeit the capability of collectively responsible action, and thus the opportunity and capability for an effective free society.

This is the heritage of the tremendous intellectual and cooperative effort made here in Williamsburg in the fifty days that were the prelude to independence in 1776. If we can now build on this heritage to achieve the same kind of success in the face of the massive complexities of our times, I am confident that free men of the twenty-first century will look as well upon us as we do upon the men whom we honor here today.

# A Time for Decision[6]

## John H. Glenn, Jr.

*Born July 18, 1921, Cambridge, OH; U.S. Marine Corps, 1943-56; test pilot, Navy Bureau of Aeronautics, 1956-69; astronaut, National Aeronautics and Space Administration (NASA), Project Mercury, 1959-64; vice president, Royal Crown Cola Company, 1962-74; senator (R) from Ohio, 1975–; author,* P.S., I Listened to Your Heartbeat *(1976).*

### Editor's introduction

Ohio senator John H. Glenn Jr., the first American to orbit Earth in a space capsule, delivered this keynote address to the 1,300 members of the National Space Club, an organization of individuals and companies who promote space research. Glenn's primary concern in this speech was a mounting criticism from those who believe that the United States spends too much money on space exploration. Once described as "the clean-cut Marine who showed the Russians America was still in the space race" (*New York Times*, Feb. 21, 1982), Glenn, to justify the funds going towards space research, remarked that "The loss of our once commanding lead in space should both embarrass and frighten us."

---

Thank you, Jim (Hart) for that most gracious and generous introduction. You know, I find it almost unbelievable that we are fast approaching the 20th anniversary of my flight in Friendship 7. Twenty years! Although I was reminded tonight that my own adventure in space is now almost two decades old, I am delighted to be here and am deeply honored that the National Space Club asked me to participate in this year's Goddard Memorial Dinner. Tonight's dinner is particularly special, since we are standing on the threshold of the Space Shuttle launching. It is altogether fitting that the calendar has brought these two events together. For just as Robert Goddard's rocket experiments in 1926 ushered in the Space Age, so the launching of the Space Shuttle will open a whole new era—an era in which man will probe ever deeper into this Last Frontier.

With the Space Shuttle, the possibilities are as exciting as they are unlimited. It is the largest, most powerful and most complicated space vehicle ever launched. Because it is reusable and can return from space to land like an airplane, it is both versatile and economical. It will dramatically increase our knowledge of Earth and its resources—and perhaps even provide us with clues as to how we can someday become independent of the Earth's environment. In 1983, the Shuttle will launch the Space Telescope, a 22 thousand-pound piece of equipment that will enlarge our view of space seven-fold and bring us closer to answering age-old questions concerning the origins and nature of life, matter and energy. And as important as these cosmic questions are, the principal justification of our space program lies in the benefits it provides not just to us in the future alone, but to us in the here and now—benefits which will enhance the lives of each and every one of us. And, although estimates vary, some experts have suggested that the space program has had a cost-benefit ratio as high as 8 to one. But, perhaps equally important, the Space Shuttle will signal America's return to space after an absence of almost six years—an absence that has not gone unnoticed in the world community.

Let us reflect for a moment on the theme of this evening's program: "A Time for Decision." In the Spring of 1981, that theme is particularly appropriate. It is appropriate because America today truly stands at a critical crossroad—not

[6]Delivered at the National Space Club's 24th annual Goddard Memorial Dinner, in Washington, D.C., on March 27, 1981. Reprinted with permission of John H. Glenn, Jr.

only with respect to space, but also with regard to the broader issue of all U.S. research and development. And like the traveler in Robert Frost's immortal poem, the road we choose will have enormous impact on our future—and that of our children today.

Today, man's most fundamental tool in the quest for knowledge—basic research—is under sharp attack. Evidence of this hostility is all around us. It manifests itself in the shrinking number of research grants available to our universities. It is apparent in the devastating slashes that have been proposed in the NASA and National Science Foundation budgets. And it shows up even in the halls of Congress where important basic research is often cynically disparaged and presented with facetious" awards" which imply that it is little more than a clever rip-off.

Similarly, many Americans greet our return to space with something less than enthusiasm. For these people, space exploration is too costly, too visionary and too far removed from such "real world" problems as hunger, disease and poverty.

Does research sometimes seem unrealistic? To those enmeshed in the complexities of the "real world," it is bound to seem that way at first—just as it always has in every historical epoch. But let us remember that we ourselves live in a "real world" created by previous generations of emigrants who set sail from another "real world" in pursuit of a dream.

Is exploration of the unknown merely an "escape" that we can no longer afford? Was our first human ancestor who rose on two legs to discover new horizons "escaping" the problems of his age? We could go back in our minds to see a group of cavemen. Perhaps we could see one adventurous caveman in the group who is sitting with his peers, wondering what's over that nearby hill. And his fellow cavemen are telling him he's crazy to think about going beyond the hill. "We have enough food here, and only 15 percent of our people died in the cave last year. Why go over there?" they're asking him. Well, he goes over the hill anyway, and he finds some different types of food; there's even more sun than he had in his own valley. He returns home with his treasures, finding years later that his people are living longer, becoming more healthy because of the treasures he brought them.

Did Columbus, Vespucci and Cabot "escape" the problems of their age or contribute to their resolution by going beyond that next hill or ocean? Again and again history demonstrates that when solutions at hand don't solve the problem, it is time to reopen the quest. Only by doing so can we reap those marvelous byproducts of the inquisitive, innovative and inventive mind and discover the unexpected possibilities that emerge when we encounter unknown worlds either at the end of a telescope or a microscope.

Does research and development seem a fanciful extravagance unlikely to produce tangible results? Let us remember that the one thing we know about research is that it is not amenable to the rigors of cost accounting. How can we know in advance what we're looking for? Or, what we'll find? Rarely can we see at the outset what ultimate benefits research will bring us. If you doubt that, listen to what the astronomer, William Pickering, said about air flight after the invention of the airplane:

" . . . the popular mind often pictures gigantic flying machines speeding across the Atlantic carrying innumerable passengers . . . . It seems safe to say that such ideas (are) wholly visionary, and even if a machine could get across with one or two passengers, the expense would be prohibitive."

Or, let us recall that the Edison Power Company once offered Henry Ford a managerial job, but only, as Ford put it, "on the condition that I give up my gas engine and devote myself to something really useful." And before we condemn specific scientific undertakings as foolish, let us recall that in 1945, Admiral William Leahy chided the development of the atom bomb by telling President Truman:

"That is the biggest fool thing we have ever done . . . . The bomb will never go off, and I speak as an expert in explosives."

Or, we could go back and look at the technologists' record at forecasting the future. Their long-range record is even worse than that of today's economists. Technology forecasters in the 1930s, for example, missed the development of the computer, atomic energy, antibiotics, radar, and the jet engine.

I'm also reminded of a statement Daniel Webster made in the U.S. Senate when the Senate was trying to decide whether to spend more money to get west of the Mississippi River. His statement was to the effect that he could see no reason why to go out into this area of prairie dogs and wild savages, of howling winds and blowing sands. He finished his remarks by saying:

"Mr. President, I would not devote one cent from the U.S. Treasury to bring the West coast one inch closer to Boston."

It will be twelve years ago this summer that Neil Armstrong and Buzz Aldrin walked the cratered barrens of the moon. Many people assumed that the sole practical value of our space program lay in the political victory we achieved in beating the Soviets to the lunar surface. Many regarded our space effort as a cosmic drag race with the Soviets. And, if the moon was the finish line in the minds of those Americans, then we won the race and could quit our space efforts.

But, there was a significance to our landing on the moon that goes far beyond the satisfaction which comes from a dramatic and spectacular victory in international competition.

The success of the Apollo program gave mankind initial access to the literally infinite resources of the universe. Few Americans fully realize the extent to which the uses of space have already affected our daily lives since we achieved that initial success. Consider the following:

We now make quick, clear intercontinental telephone calls at half of what it cost 10 years ago, thanks to the ever more versatile and reliable communications satellites pioneered through our space program.

Satellite technology also permits us to transmit sharp, full-color television coverage of events transpiring anywhere on the globe having a mammoth impact on how man relates to man around the world. I think it would be fair to say that we've lived in a time when television stopped the first war—as we found in Vietnam.

Countless thousands of human lives and many millions of dollars have been saved through satellite warning of hurricanes, typhoons and other severe storms. The increased knowledge of Sun-Earth relationships acquired through such efforts as the Space Shuttle will permit far more accurate weather forecasts in the future and perhaps even the ability to modify weather and climate. We have found, for example, that during times of high solar activity, the Van Allen Belts moved, changing the heating of the upper atmosphere as well as the flow of the jet-streams. The result was a change in our weather here on Earth.

Our digital watches, hand-held calculators and desk-top computers are direct derivatives from the integrated circuit technology developed for the Apollo spacecraft.

We can now navigate ships and aircraft to within yards. This equipment is even available for pleasure craft on the Chesapeake Bay, providing navigational fixes with the help of satellites.

Aircraft, automobiles, ships and even buildings are now more structurally sound and thus safer, due to the use of a computerized structural analysis technique developed for the construction of spacecraft.

And, worth every penny spent on the entire space program is the increased security our nation has because reconnaissance and early warning satellites make a surprise attack on the United States more costly, less feasible and, therefore, much less likely.

And yet, despite these life-enhancing spin-offs, despite the fact that space research and development, even in its infancy, has provided the cutting edge of our technological superiority for almost 20 years, we are not pressing our advantage in space. We are all but abandoning portions of our civilian space program. The Administration's proposed NASA budgets for 1981 and 1982 will provide even less money, given inflation, than that agency had in 1969, the year Apollo 11 landed on the moon. The depressing result is that, except for the shuttle, the only new space missions that will be undertaken between now and 1986 are two that had been planned but previously deferred.

This is especially disturbing in light of the stepped-up space activities of other nations. Since the last manned American Flight in 1975, there have been 21 manned Soviet flights. During that period, America remained earthbound while Soviet cosmonauts accumulated two years of space-flight time.

The Soviet Union plans to orbit a permanent, 12-man space station by 1985. And some observers believe that the U.S.S.R. will soon announce its intention to send a man to Mars by the end of the decade. In addition, France and West Germany are hard at work on a low-cost booster that could corner the launch business. In a joint venture, China and Japan hope to orbit two astronauts for a full week by the end of 1986.

The loss of our once commanding lead in space should both embarrass and frighten us.

We should be embarrassed because we are consciously choosing to default rather than to compete. We are consciously choosing that we will let other nations be the "first to know, to discover the new, to have available to them, first, the new information on potential energy source, of earth resources analysis, of space weightless manufacturing, and of so many other things."

And we should be frightened because that default could some day prove literally fatal. Many experts are convinced that much Russian work aboard Salyut has been directed toward military applications of space research—applications such as electronic surveillance and satellite interception. Although I'm not one who sees a threatening Soviet behind every lamp post, but, given what we see going on in the world, God help us should we ever reach a decidedly inferior position in space while the Soviets develop not only "eyes and ears" in space but weaponry systems as well.

Currently, the Soviets are believed to devote 2 to 3 percent of their GNP (Gross National Product) on space—six times more than we spend. If we allow these trends to continue, we may soon find ourselves worrying about far more than balanced budgets or the relative wisdom of supply-side economics.

But a crucial point I wish to emphasize tonight is that the challenge confronting America in the areas of research and development is by no means confined to our space program. On the contrary. Whether we speak of national defense, industrial strength or energy independence, research and development is an indispensable tool for realizing our objectives.

Historically, America's willingness to facilitate and invest in research has been the touchstone of her pre-eminence. This point is well-understood by our international neighbors. In 1969, for example, Jean Jacques Servan-Schreiber, the French author and politician, wrote a book entitled, *The American Challenge.* One of his central themes was that the United States surpassed the rest of the world economically and industrially not simply because of our waving fields of grain or purple mountains' majesties but because from our inception as a nation we have always promoted and financed inquiry into the unknown. We had devoted a larger part of our GNP to research than any other nation in history.

Piece by piece, increment by increment, new advances in knowledge multiplied—until, finally, a quantum leap forward was made possible. Research, and the technology we developed to exploit the fruits of that research, made America the wealthiest, most powerful and most productive nation on Earth in a tiny time frame in history.

In the 12 years since the publication of *The American Challenge*, however, there is mounting evidence that we are killing the proverbial goose that laid the golden egg. Over the past 15 years, the proportion of America's GNP invested in research has steadily declined, dropping over 20 percent between 1965 and 1979. During that same period, West Germany's investment in R & D (Research and Development) climbed by 41 percent of her GNP, Japan's rose 27 percent and the Soviet Union's increased by 21 percent. These figures take on added economic significance when it is recognized that 50 percent of all U.S. research is defense-related, while less than 1 percent of Japan's and only 8 percent of Germany's is spent in the same fashion.

It is, therefore, hardly an accident that since the close of World War II, other nations have become alternative sources of industrial innovation. We're seeing employment leave our nation far too often. Nor is it coincidental that U.S. productivity and economic growth have lately been falling. Studies by such renowned economists as Edward Denison have shown that "advances in knowledge" constitute the single most important source of productivity gain, as well as of overall economic expansion. So while the U.S. economy may still be the world's largest, it is no longer the most efficient or the fastest growing.

Fortunately, American industry has recognized the danger and has been moving to meet it. According to a recent study by the National Science Foundation, industrial research and development has been rising in real terms since 1972. In January, Battelle's Columbus Laboratories forecast a continuation of this trend in 1981 and predicted that industrial R & D funding would climb 13 percent over last year's level.

Welcome as this news is, we must not be lulled into a false sense of security. For one thing, much of our industrial R & D is devoted simply to meeting the requirements of government regulation, rather than to the kind of risk-taking research that promises true technological breakthroughs. Historically, American industries have concentrated their efforts on applied R & D, leaving basic research mostly to the government and academia.

Each side works in relative isolation and collaborative research is often studiously avoided. In contrast, our competitors in Europe and Japan link industrial research to government and academic science. The result is that they are now surpassing us in a growing number of fields, perhaps the most conspicuous of which is the production of new scientific instruments. In my view, America can simply no longer afford a continuation of our traditionally "armslength" research relationships. If we are to meet the challenges ahead, it is vital that we begin to encourage cooperative research ventures between the public and private sectors.

But even that will not be enough. We must also recognize that expanding industrial R & D does not mean that the federal government can now begin to reduce its own commitment to research. Much of the basic research needed to achieve energy independence, for example, is of so large a scale and requires so long a development period that it is simply unrealistic to expect the private sector to shoulder the burden alone.

America's dependence on foreign energy sources cost us about $100 billion last year—and it is estimated by some economists to account for between 40 and 60 percent of the increased inflation we have suffered over the past four years. Because our energy dilemma threatens both our national security and our national economy, involvement by the federal government is, to my way of thinking, clearly appropriate.

So, I am appalled that under the Administration's latest budget proposals, energy R & D has been mercilessly slashed. If these proposals are adopted, by 1982 conservation programs will be cut by 79 percent and solar energy development by 66 percent. Similarly, research on electrical energy storage—which could make solar, wind, geothermal and other alternative energy sources practical and usable—is being cut by 28 percent in 1981 and by almost 33 percent in 1982.

If I had one energy wish tonight, it might surprise you what it would be. My wish would be for better electrical energy storage that would enable us to take the power generated by wind, wave, tidal and solar power and store it for later use. If we could store this electricity, and bring it back when needed, as some research indicates we could do in the near future, we would have one of the biggest breakthroughs we've had for some time.

Electrical energy storage would also enhance development of the electrical automobile which could take care of 92 percent of the noncommercial driving we do within 20 miles of our homes. If we let the Japanese and the Germans beat us to the world's first practical electrical automobile, we will have nobody to blame but ourselves. And if that happens, we won't be bailing out Chrysler, we'll be asking for money to make Detroit a great national park on a scenic river.

Now, I fully recognize the need for budgetary restraint in these inflationary times and I support these efforts. But let us not be pennywise and pound-foolish to what is going to happen to this country in 1985. Let us not seek fiscal frugality by mortgaging our future. And let us recognize that if the energy crisis constitutes the moral equivalent of war, as Jimmy Carter called it, failing to develop alternative energy sources could well be the economic equivalent of suicide. There are many areas today in which it is desirable and necessary to reduce federal involvement. But surely research and development is one area where even greater government support is clearly justified.

In today's world, failing to meet the R & D challenge is the surest way to forfeit our claim to world leadership. It's just that simple.

Let me close this evening with one final thought. In 1962, just before Wally Schirra's Mercury flight in Sigma 7, President Kennedy declared that:

"The exploration of space will go ahead, whether we join it or not . . . . It is one of the great adventures of all time, and no nation that expects to be the leader of other nations can expect to stay behind in the race for space."

I submit that those words are equally applicable today—not just with respect to the space race, but also with respect to the global competition in research and development. For that competition may be the most compelling challenge of our age. History has shown that missing or retreating from such challenges almost inevitably leads to a loss of national eminence. Perhaps that is what the Immortal Bard, William Shakespeare, sensed nearly 400 years ago when he wrote:

"There is a tide in the affairs of men which, taken at the flood, leads on to fortune; omitted, all the voyages of their life is bound in shallows and in miseries. On such a full sea we are now afloat, and we must take the current when it serves or lose our ventures."

Thank you very much.

# Technology and Moral Responsibility[7]

George D. Snell

*Born December 19, 1903, Bradford, MA; died June 6, 1996; B.S., Dartmouth College, 1926; Sc.D., Harvard University, 1930; instructor, Dartmouth College, 1929-30; instructor, Brown University, 1930-31; assistant professor, Washington University, 1933-34; research associate, 1935-37, senior staff science administrator, 1949-50, senior staff scientist, 1957-96, Jackson Laboratory; co-winner of Nobel Prize in physiology or medicine, 1980.*

## Editor's introduction

George D. Snell, who won the Nobel Prize for his pioneering work in genetics, called for a renewal of moral and ethical responsibility in making decisions regarding technological innovations that affect the environment. Snell noted that "While many conscientious and intelligent decisions have been made, we also have made decisions incompatible with the preservation of a free and livable world." Historically, Snell asserted, scientists have failed to balance technological advancement with a concern for the consequences inevitably wrought by that advancement.

---

In the last 100 years, technology has undergone an enormous expansion, in the process, altering our lives and our world. Dozens of miraculous devices, undreamed of in 1881, are commonplace today. Many of these technological developments have occurred in my lifetime.

The Wright brothers made their first flight at Kitty Hawk on December 17, 1903. This was two days before I was born. For at least another ten years, airplanes were still a rarity of primitive construction. Automobiles were invented in the last century, but were uncommon when I was a small boy. My first recollections of an auto are of an electric vehicle, more like a carriage than what we now think of as an auto, that a middle-aged lady used to drive by our house. The milkman and the iceman still brought their wares in horse-drawn wagons. The street lights outside our house were gas; a lamp lighter went by every evening to turn them on. Our house was still lit by gas, though newer houses were equipped with electric lights, still Edison's original carbon filament bulb. Wireless telegraphy was in existence, but it had little effect on our lives, and broadcasts of the human voice and of television were part of the future. The first computer was built in 1944.

Back of each of the technological marvels produced by applied research has lain a long and complex history of basic research. The pathways by which basic research leads to usable methods or products are often winding and full of surprises. I can testify to this from my own experience; that is part of the fun and excitement of science. The essential point here is that the basic and applied aspects of research are both necessary ingredients in the progress of technology.

Looking to the future, I think we must assume that the expansion of science and technology which we have witnessed in the past century will continue. Nature still hides many secrets from us, and there is much to learn. The pace of discovery may indeed accelerate rather than slacken. I see no barriers in natural law to further developments, though shortages of natural resources may limit some applications. The institutionalization of science, both in the universities and in industry, to which much of the past century of progress is due, is firmly in place and provides the necessary setting for continuing discovery. There may be ups and downs due to fluctuations in financing, but the long range prospect is for further advances in technology, medicine, and human understanding.

[7]Delivered at the University of Maine commencement exercises, in Presque Isle, Maine, on April 18, 1981.

While technology has brought us great benefits, it also is a source of great risks. It is to these risks that I now turn.

The immediate end product of applied research is options—ways of doing new things and new ways of doing old things. At some point the decision must be made as to whether and how each option is to be exercised. The multiplicity of options also is expanded on down the line. We have, in our daily lives, more ways of doing things, more products on the market to choose from, a greater diversity and complexity of jobs. The decision whether or not to exercise a given option is often far from trivial. Do we market a new drug which has proven benefits but also known deleterious side effects? Do we equip a new coal burning facility in Ohio with scrubbers, thereby reducing the risk of acid rain in Maine and Canada? In the ultimate military crisis, do we use the atomic bomb? And in our personal affairs, what line of work do we seek to enter? No one, I think, can doubt the importance of the correct exercise of these options.

We are faced, in this matter of options, with a third domain, the domain of value judgments. It is a domain with very different properties from the two already discussed, the domains of basic and applied research. It is not and never can be a science, although science interacts with it in important ways. It is, however, akin to ethics or morals. The exercise of an option we are evaluating can have significant effects on the welfare of others and, insofar as it does, our judgment takes on moral qualities. The question of whether and how to use a given technology can bring us face to face with questions of right and wrong.

Let me interject here a story which I heard when I spent some time in Texas many years ago. A Texan, so the story goes, was driving in southwest Texas between San Angelo and San Antonio when he noticed a hitchhiker and stopped to pick him up. The hitchhiker turned out to be a young New Zealander who was seeing the United States on a shoestring budget. The part of Texas through which they were driving was flat as a pancake and so covered with cactus and thornbushes that even a goat would hardly manage a living. It was also scorching hot. As they were driving along, the hitchhiker noticed a bird running across the road.

"What's the bird? he asked.

"That's a bird of paradise," replied the Texan.

"A bird of paradise? Gosh! He's a hell of a long way from home!"

Despite the comment of the hitchhiker, we *do* live in a paradise. Nature has given us a world both unique and beautiful, its diversity being part of its beauty. The more I learn about life and evolution and, from space probes, about other worlds in our solar system, the more convinced I am that planet Earth is a very rare and special place, adapted in extraordinary ways to the development and support of complex forms of life. We are indeed blessed with a priceless inheritance.

In the United States, a free and democratic society is also part of our inheritance. This social component of our environment, like the natural component, can be tarnished or destroyed by unwise or unethical decisions. If we, as free citizens, fail to cope with the complex problems created by modern technology, we will become the puppets of those who offer authoritarian and ultimately totalitarian solutions.

It would be a tragedy beyond belief if we lost either our freedom or the loveliness of the world that nature has given us. The preservation of these inheritances is the greatest single task which we face.

My generation, now largely retired, and the succeeding middle-aged generation, have done a very imperfect job in carrying out this task. While many conscientious and intelligent decisions have been made, we also have made decisions incompatible with the preservation of a free and livable world. The technological explosion created new situations for which we were philosophically and ethically unprepared. Of course there were warning voices and we did, at times, listen to them, as in the creation of the National Parks, but like all generations before us we did not face up to major and novel problems in time to institute orderly and adequate solutions before substantial damage had been done.

The great need, I submit, was and is a renewed sense of moral responsibility. The increase in our options requires a realization that, although basic ethical principles have not changed, the complexity of their applications has changed. It may be, too, that the consequences of moral failure have expanded. The areas of past deficiency and future need are many, but a few deserve especial emphasis.

The ethical obligations created by technology rest on all of us, not just on our leaders who have to make the most momentous decisions. The fabric of mutual confidence on which a free society depends is woven from the honest and considerate choices made by each and every one of us. The fabric is weakened whenever dishonesty and selfishness are condoned.

All of us, but especially those in positions of major responsibility, need to expand our circle of consideration. We need to think not only of our friends, our business associates, our state, our nation, but of people everywhere. In the world as it exists today, ethics must be universal, not parochial.

We need to expand our circle of consideration in time as well as in space, thinking of the welfare of people decades, centuries, or, as in the case of the disposal of long-lived radioactive wastes, even millennia beyond our time. Only a long-range point of view can insure that the powers conferred on us by technology are well used.

We need to realize that many of the decisions we face are enormously complex, and prepare ourselves to deal with these complexities. This requires the assembling of all possible relevant facts. This is an area where the basic sciences impinge on the domain of value judgments. They can help us, by adding to our knowledge, to foresee the outcome of our acts, and hence to choose wisely.

If your generation has inherited problems, it has also inherited and, indeed, has helped to generate, encouraging trends.

You begin your careers in a world made beautiful by Nature and enriched by the wonders of technology, yet a world which we, its inhabitants, have defiled and not so often through ignorance as through greed. It is a very different world from the one I remember as a boy. Those were simpler times and we tend to look back on them with nostalgia. But they also were times when many essential undertakings, now done by machine, were done in sweat shops or by underpaid manual labor and when diseases now almost forgotten were still prevalent and dreaded.

But have we traded our past problems for permanent disillusionment and disaffection? I reject that conclusion. Along with the disillusionment has come a ferment of intellectual and civil involvement, a ferment directed to the discovery and implementation of solutions.

In the past few decades, an extraordinary number of organizations have been formed, seeking to help the consumer, protect the environment, reform the government, or in some other way deal with the problems which we face. The multiplication of these voluntary organizations and their success in enlisting public support recalls the comment of Alexis de Tocqueville in his classic, *Democracy in America*, that "whereas at the head of some new undertaking you see the government in France, or a man of rank in England, in the United States you will be sure to find an association." Even though the accomplishment of these associations is still far short of the need, the spirit of active citizen involvement in the search for solutions which they represent will not be thwarted in the long run.

Though the times you face are not easy, they are nevertheless challenging times, times full of hope. Problems that have been recognized can be solved. I think I can say for members of my generation, you carry our warm good wishes, our cheers, and our faith.

# The Challenger Astronauts[8]

## Ronald Reagan

*Born February 6, 1911, Tampico, IL; B.A., Eureka College, 1932; sports announcer, radio station WHO, 1933-37; motion picture and television actor, 1937-1966; U.S. Army, 1942-55; president, Screen Actors Guild, 1947-52, 1959-60; program supervisor, General Electric Theater, 1952-62; governor of California, 1967-74; president of the United States, 1981-88.*

### Editor's introduction

On January 28, 1986, six American astronauts and school teacher Christa McAulife were killed when the space shuttle *Challenger* exploded shortly after liftoff from Cape Canaveral, Florida. Later that day, Ronald Reagan gave this eloquent eulogy in place of the State of the Union Address he was supposed to have given. Reagan recognized the great pain caused by the astronauts' deaths, and he praised their actions as those of brave pioneers who had devoted their lives to the exploration of new and unseen worlds. To the children throughout the nation who had watched the explosion with horror, Reagan said that "painful things" are often "part of the process of exploration and discovery." To the nation, Reagan declared that despite this tragedy, "we'll continue our quest in space."

---

Ladies and gentlemen, I'd planned to speak to you tonight to report on the State of the Union but the events of earlier today have led me to change those plans. Today is a day for mourning and remembering.

Nancy and I are pained to the core by the tragedy of the shuttle *Challenger*. We know we share this pain with all of the people of our country. This is truly a national loss.

Nineteen years ago, almost to the day, we lost three astronauts in a terrible accident on the ground. But we've never lost an astronaut in flight; we've never had a tragedy like this. And perhaps we've forgotten the courage it took for the crew of the shuttle; but they, the *Challenger* Seven, were aware of the dangers, but overcame them and did their jobs brilliantly. We mourn seven heroes: Michael Smith, Dick Scobee, Judith Resnik, Ronald McNair, Ellison Onizuka, Gregory Jarvis, and Christa McAuliffe. We mourn their loss as a nation together.

For the families of the seven, we cannot bear, as you do, the full impact of this tragedy. But we feel the loss, and we're thinking about you so very much. Your loved ones were daring and brave, and they had that special grace, that special spirit that says, "Give me a challenge and I'll meet it with joy." They had a hunger to explore the universe and discover its truths. They wished to serve, and they did. They served all of us.

We've grown used to wonders in this century. It's hard to dazzle us. But for 25 years the United States space program has been doing just that. We've grown used to the idea of space, and perhaps we forget that we've only just begun. We're still pioneers. They, the members of the *Challenger* crew, were pioneers.

And I want to say something to the schoolchildren of America who were watching the live coverage of the shuttle's takeoff. I know it's hard to understand, but sometimes painful things like this happen. It's all part of the process of exploration and discovery. It's all part of taking a chance and expanding man's horizons. The future doesn't belong to the fainthearted; it belongs to the brave. The *Challenger* crew was pulling us into the future, and we'll continue to follow them.

I've always had great faith in and respect for our space program, and what happened today does nothing to diminish it. We don't hide our space program. We don't keep secrets and cover things up. We do it all up front and in public.

[8]Broadcast nationwide, from the White House, in Washington, D.C., on January 28, 1986.

That's the way freedom is, and we wouldn't change it for a minute.

We'll continue our quest in space. There will be more shuttle flights and more shuttle crews and, yes, more volunteers, more civilians, more teachers in space. Nothing ends here; our hopes and our journeys continue.

I want to add that I wish I could talk to every man and woman who works for NASA or who worked on this mission and tell them: "Your dedication and professionalism have moved and impressed us for decades. And we know of your anguish. We share it."

There's a coincidence today. On this day 390 years ago, the great explorer Sir Francis Drake died aboard ship off the coast of Panama. In his lifetime the great frontiers were the oceans, and an historian later said, "He lived by the sea, died on it, and was buried in it." Well, today we can say of the *Challenger* crew: "Their dedication was, like Drake's, complete."

The crew of the space shuttle *Challenger* honored us by the manner in which they lived their lives. We will never forget them, nor the last time we saw them, this morning, as they prepared for their journey and waved good-bye and "slipped the surly bonds of earth" to "touch the face of God."

# Biotechnology at a Crossroads[9]

Jeremy Rifkin

*Born January 26, 1945, Denver, CO; B.A., University of Pennsylvania, 1966; M.A., Tufts University, 1968; founder, People's Bicentennial Commission, 1971-76; founder, co-director, People's Business Commission, 1976-77; founder, president, Foundation on Emerging Technologies, 1977–; founder, Foundation on Economic Trends, 1977–; author,* How to Commit Revolution American Style *(1972),* Own Your Own Job *(1977),* Who Should Play God *(1977),* The North Will Rise Again *(1978);* The Emerging Order *(1980),* Declaration of a Heretic *(1985),* Time Wars *(1989),* Biosphere Politics *(1992),* Voting Green *(1992),* Beyond Beef *(1994),* The End of Work *(1995).*

## Editor's introduction

In this speech Jeremy Rifkin, social activist, author, biotechnology critic, and head of the Foundation on Economic Trends, expressed concern over the potential dangers of genetic engineering practices. Rifkin suggested that "gene splicing, engineering and rearranging the code of plants, animals and microbes is more adventurous and extreme" than "prudent." Rifkin, who sparked much of the present controversy surrounding genetic engineering, asserted that nature's ways are largely unpredictable. It follows that experimenting with the living code of all existence could create consequences we are neither prepared for nor able to handle. Rifkin advised that before acting impetuously, one should always ask, "How does the decision we make today affect seven generations removed?"

---

Good morning! I'd like to try and place into context some of the issues that we think are important in dealing with the public policy implications of biotechnology. First of all let me try to place it within a larger anthropological perspective.

The world community is making a long-term transition. We are moving out of fossil fuels, the energy base for industrial technology, and we're now moving into renewable resources, the energy base for biological based technology. This transformation will be as significant, in my opinion, as the transformation from Medieval agriculture to the industrial, urban way of life of the last 200 years.

And, certainly, it's going to raise profound environmental, social, ethical and economic questions for the whole world family to have to grapple and deal with. I think there's two broad philosophical approaches to organizing renewable resources. The first is an ecological approach, a stewardship approach. The idea is to develop a philosophy of science that works with the environment, that is empathetic to the natural resource base rather than a philosophy of science based on exploitation and short-term gains only.

The ecological approach would be based on a technology assumption where we use new tools to develop sustainability with our resources rather than short-term expedient use. And the ecological approach to the age of biology would be based on an economic theory, based on justice for the homo sapien species and equity and justice for all the other creatures that we have to live with in this small planet. So, there's an ecological approach to the age of biology. There's also another approach to the age of biology, very different in philosophy and in application: genetic engineering. Genetic engineering simply means placing engineering principles into the gene pool. That's why we call it genetic engineering. We're learning how to map genes, program genes, turn on and off

[9]Delivered to the United States Agricultural Communicators Congress, in Washington, D.C., on July 12, 1988. Reprinted with permission of Jeremy Rifkin.

genes. We're learning how to recombine genetic traits between unrelated species. We're learning how to apply engineering assumptions into the blueprint for microbes, plants, animals, and the human race.

What are those engineering assumptions that we used during the industrial age? Quality control, the ability to reduce phenomena to a quantifiable standard of measurement, predictability of outcome, utilitarianism, and efficiency. Those are the kinds of industrial-based assumptions that we used for the last two hundred years in organizing inanimate materials during the fossil fuel era.

And, now the talk in the scientific community and among corporate policy makers is to take those engineering assumptions and apply them directly into the blueprint—microbes, plants, animals, homo sapiens. Now, many scientists have said to me," Well, Jeremy, gee, lighten up. I mean we're just, this is just a more sophisticated approach to the kind of domesticating technologies we've been using since neolithic agriculture. We've been breeding and domesticating for a long time—this is just a more precise way of doing the same old thing we've always been doing." I have to take exception to that.

You see, in nature it is possible to do a lot of manipulation, but you are constrained by biological boundary walls. For example, you can cross a donkey and a horse and get a mule. Correct? But, as far as I know, there's no breeder in history that can cross a donkey and a dandelion and get a damned thing. Now, we have a technology called gene-splicing that allows us in both theory and practice to eliminate the idea of a species as an identifiable being with an egos and telos, you Latin scholars, an essential nature. Now we can perceive of a horse as a series of genetic programs, any one of which can be snipped out and recombined and placed into the germ line of a totally unrelated species. As you know, scientists have taken human genes and placed them in the permanent genetic code of mice, pigs, and sheep. There's no breeding technology in history, my friends, that can do that. Scientists have taken carp genes—trout genes—and placed them into the genetic code of carp fish. Scientists have taken the gene that emits light in a firefly, injected that gene into tobacco plants and those leaves glow 24 hours a day. There is no breeding technology in history that allows us to bypass species borders with this kind of abandon. So, it's going to create a whole new set of questions—environmental questions for sure, but also ethical and philosophical questions. Is there any limit to the amount of manipulation that we ought to be able to do in rearranging the genetic programs between species?

Now, I'm 43 years old. I grew up in the United States in the 1950s. We had two great technology revolutions: nuclear power and petrochemical technology. The scientific establishment and the corporations and the policy makers said "Trust us, we have a technology revolution here with many benefits and with minimum risks." Back in the 50s and 60s we as a society did not ask the hard questions up front. We rushed pall mall into these technology revolutions hopeful that we would be able to resolve all of the problems of society by these tools and we didn't ask tough environmental, social, ethical and economic questions. They simply were not raised. The result—to be perfectly honest—we benefited immensely in the short run from nuclear power and petrochemical technology. We'd all admit that. But, I think every person in this room would also acknowledge that we have also created tremendous long-term environmental, economic and social dislocation as a result of rushing in with these technologies without asking the hard questions up front. Genetic engineering—only benefits, no problems? I doubt it. Now, let me go through several issues we're dealing with to give you an idea of the kind of questions that need to be raised.

Deliberate release of genetically engineered organisms into the environment. Whenever you release a genetically engineered organism into the environment for agricultural purposes, you have to realize that the environmental consequences are quite different than if you introduce a petrochemical into an agricultural environment. First of all, genetically engineered organisms are alive. So, they're inherently more unpredictable in terms of what they will do when interacting in the eco-system.

Secondly, genetically engineered organisms—many of them can reproduce and they mutate and they can migrate off site. They have much greater mobility than any chemical product.

And, finally, third, if you don't like what a genetically engineered organism is doing out there in your agricultural field, you can't simply say "My fault" and recall it to the laboratory.

Would you like to try and recall a virus, or a bacteria or even a plant back to the laboratory if it does do damage?

Now, please understand the level of risk and we've perceived it, up to now. Whenever you introduce a genetically engineered organism into the agricultural field, be it plant, animal, or microbe, there's only a small chance that it's going to do any damage. I know you were expecting I'd come here and talk to you about "killer tomatoes" moving on Iowa and andromeda strains heading toward Kansas. Now, we've never said that although we've been accused of it. There's only a small chance that any given introduction is going to cause a problem. But, if it does cause a problem, the long-term impact on your agricultural environment can be extreme and potentially catastrophic. The analogy is exotic organisms. You people that have covered the farm beat for a long time know we've brought a lot of exotic organisms over to North America—many of them fit into our ecosystem, but some of them, quite frankly, become pests and we can't get rid of them. Kudzu vine in the South—anybody here from the South. Anybody here from the South? That doesn't make you too comfortable. We can't get rid of that. We brought that over from somewhere else. Dutch elm disease—remember those beautiful tree-lined streets through the Midwest? No more. Chestnut blight. Do we have enough starlings? Gypsy moth. You know how that happened? Some schmuck brought the gypsy moth over—did you hear this story?—for the silk industry. One night it was hot and he was up in Massachusetts. He opened up his bedroom window and the eggs blew out. And, we can't get rid of gypsy moth.

And, these exotics cause hundreds of millions of dollars a year in damage. Now, please understand the scale. In the next ten years industry would like to develop scores, perhaps hundreds of products, to release into the agricultural field.

In the 21st century, our children's century, the ambition is to introduce thousands of genetically engineered viruses, bacteria, transgenetic plants, and animals in massive commercial volumes all over the planet earth. They hope it'll be comparable to the introduction of chemicals. We introduced thousands of chemical products into the earth.

Now, my friends, you don't have to be a molecular biologist, merely a statistician. Let's assume most of these introductions are safe. If only a tiny fraction turn out to be pests, because of the scale of introductions, the biological pollution could well exceed chemical pollution because these products are alive, many of them reproduce, they mutate, migrate and you cannot recall them once they're out there. You're stuck for centuries, perhaps, millennium. Now, many other countries have taken a very sophisticated, prudent approach to the release of genetically engineered organisms. I think in this country a lot of the folks in this country just think it's just Jeremy Rifkin and a few folks. Let me tell you about other countries.

In Germany, one of the three biotech powers, de Vuntegstag commission on biotechnology has recommended a five year prohibition—a moratorium—on any release into Germany because the scientific questions are yet to be dealt with seriously.

In Denmark they have voted legislation that prohibits any release into the environment because these questions are still unredressed.

Japan, which we always point to "if we don't do it they will get ahead of us." No, Japan has never released an organism into the environment and they have a moratorium now, ostensibly they're doing a three-year study to assess the scientific impact.

There are a few countries that have rushed ahead—the United States, France and England—without seriously raising the problems of a risk-assessment science. The botton line, my friends in the agricultural community, is this. There is no science of predictive ecology. It doesn't exist. There is no science of risk-assessment with which we can judge these introductions. We've been asking for such a science for years. There is none. So, we're in the very uncomfortable situation of regulating a technology in this country on the one hand and on the other realizing there is no science to adequately do it with. I think we should heed the call of other countries and impose a five-year moratorium worldwide so that we can bring the best environmental sciences together with our molecular biologists to see if we can hammer out a reasonable risk-assessment science. To do less than that would be a disservice to our children's generation. Deliberate release into the environment.

Second issue: let's examine bovine growth hormone for a minute because it is a classic example of why the blessings of biotechnology turn out to be a curse when you look at them with more serious attention.

Bovine growth hormone, as you know, is the first major product being researched to introduce into agriculture. Two chemical companies, Monsanto and Cyanamid, two pharmaceutical companies, Eli Lilly and Upjohn, are spending tens of millions of dollars in research, field trials in fifteen countries, I think, to introduce a product which they claim will be a 500 million dollar to one billion dollar a year product.

Now, as you know, bovine growth hormone increases milk production between what? Ten and forty percent per cow. Normal increase in milk production, as you know, is what? About two percent a year with breeding. Now, we're talking ten to forty percent. If you measure progress narrowly in terms of more output and less time, this is the most progressive product in the history of animal husbandry. But, if you mark, if you define progress by enhancing the well-being of society, this is the silliest product that's ever come down the pike. That's why we have to redefine our concepts of progress.

The last thing we need is more milk. Every industrial nation in the world is awash in milk surpluses and now these companies come along with a product that will massively increase the surpluses. Parenthetically, this product cannot be used in the third world because in the southern hemisphere at high temperatures, the cows overheat. You do not get as good a production out of them.

So, we have a product that has literally no redeeming social values: it hurts the farmers, it will hurt the taxpayers, it might hurt the consumers. The farmer—one study done by Cornell which they've later kind of back-tracked on—Culture and Bowman study that they did, I think with Monsanto—they predicted that if, I think, you eliminate price supports, that within three years of the introduction of BGH up to 30 percent of the American dairy farms may be out of business. Any way you look at it, that's the biggest dislocation in a short period of time in U.S. agricultural history.

Let's say they change their study. Let's say it's only half that. Imagine the devastation to certain regions of the country by introducing this hormone: Wisconsin, western New York, Missouri, Washington state, etc.

A study was just released in Wisconsin. The University of Wisconsin, your alma mater, Chuck, was commissioned by the state legislature to do a study on biotechnology and BGH. The study made the following conclusion: within four years of the introduction of BGH into Wisconsin and around the country, that Wisconsin dairy farmers by year four would lose one hundred million dollars. We have a—by the way there are health hazards to the cows—I don't have a lot of time today to go into it but there have been studies that have shown now that the cows are facing sterility, mastitis, a whole range of production stresses and it stands to reason. If you're going to put massive injections of a hormone into an animal beyond what it was biologically designed for it's naive and disingenuous to believe that won't stress that animal. Many of you are farmers. You know just what I'm talking about with stress related production diseases. Will the taxpayers want to pay to buy up all of the surpluses? You want to see how this is going to float in Washington when it gets in front of the dairy, poultry and livestock committee? Last Monday, we have a coalition—the international coalition against BGH—we're determined that this product will never enter the market place. Last week our international coalition in Europe—we have seven countries organized—farmers, environmental groups, consumer groups. We did a lobbying effort at the European parliament last Monday to vote. The European parliament has voted and recommended to ban commercial use of BGH and to recommend that it only be used by veterinarians for therapeutic purposes which is ostensibly a ban. That recommendation is going to the counsel of the European community. Germany, one of the three big biotech powers, is on record opposing the introduction of BGH.

Now let me give you a little sneak preview of something that's going to come next year. The international coalition against BGH is fully prepared to launch a consumer boycott worldwide if BGH is introduced in any market in the world in the next year and we have prepared the first series of TV, radio spots and print ads which will be used all over Europe and the United States—if you want to hit the lights—let me just give you—you'll be the first to see this. This is what we will be prepared to launch in the spring of 1989. Can we get the lights?

[Radio to television spot:]

"With so many chemicals and additives in our food, there's still one that's one hundred percent natural—pure milk. But, now chemical companies want to inject cows with a genetically engineered growth hormone that forces them to produce more milk creating a milk surplus and putting thirty percent of America's dairy farmers out of work. It could be a health hazard to cows and the milk you drink will contain that hormone. What are they doing to our milk?"

We will have those available to anyone who would like to see them afterward. We have copies of the TV and radio spots. We're going to ask, demand that labelling be placed on all milk products—BGH, non-BGH—so that the consumers worldwide will have a choice.

Let me try to talk about one more issue. What I'm trying to point out here is there's no fait accompli about the technology. Just because it can be done doesn't mean it will be done. Parts of the biotechnology revolution make sense, they should go ahead. There are other parts that probably have very little socially redeeming value and we as a citizenry have a responsibility to pick and choose. There is an issue tomorrow coming to a vote in the House of Representatives that we've been working on for fourteen months. Back in April of 1987, the U.S. Patent Office issued a policy decision. The decision was that you can now patent any genetically-engineered animal on the planet. If you place a human gene into the genetic code of a pig, since that can't be done through natural breeding, that whole pig is now considered a human invention. In one regulatory stroke, a handful of bureaucrats in the patent office reduced the entire animal kingdom to the lowly status of a commercial commodity indistinguishable from microwave ovens or automobiles or tennis balls. Those are all patented inventions.

Now, I for one, I think there are philosophical, environmental, and economic reasons to oppose the patenting of animals. By the way, I should tell you that by this decision, any number of human genes can be placed into the genetic code of animals and they can be patented. The patent office did offer a reprieve. They did say that we cannot patent a homo sapiens because the 13th amendment and the 14th amendment forbids slavery. So, that was nice of them. By this decision, our children would grow up in a world where they would come to think of all animals as patented inventions indistinguishable from inanimate materials, from chemical materials that we have patented over the years.

Now, don't get me wrong. I'm like a lot of people: I'm not a purist. I do believe you have to manipulate nature to survive. I don't want to take us back into the stone age. I do believe we have to go ahead and proceed on into the future and we have to manipulate and tinker and organize nature, and especially agriculture in order to make a better way of life for us and our kids. But, I do believe there's a margin between mutual give and take so we can sustain a healthy, vibrant, economic agricultural system on the one hand and on the other reducing all of life to strict, utilitarian expediency. The farmers don't want patenting animals. The National Farmers Union, the American Agricultural Movement, Save the Family Farm Coalition—they have all joined in our coalition with many of the animal welfare groups like the Humane Society, the ASPCA—that's an interesting coalition isn't it?—animal rights and farm groups. Things are changing. And, other groups have called for a moratorium on patenting animals. The Wildlife Federation of America, the Consumer Federation of America, the 27 religious leaders of every major protestant denomination in the United States and several Jewish. They're all saying," Let's look at patenting before we rush ahead." And, all of these organizations are in favor of a short moratorium so that the Congress of the United States can take a long, hard, careful look as to whether this is the road we want to pursue. It makes no sense for two of three men at the patent office to dictate the entire future control of the gene pool of this planet. Whoever controls the gene pool will be effectively as powerful as whoever controlled the oil in the way of minerals in the industrial age—you with me?

So, this a decision that we as a people ought to respond to collectively through our elected representatives. Tomorrow morning two bills will be voted for markup in the House Judiciary Committee on Patents and Trademarks. Both bills I expect will pass and we anticipate that to be a major for our coalition against patenting animals—both bills.

The first bill introduced by Congressman Charles Rowles with 64 congressional sponsors calls for a two year moratorium on patenting animals so Congress can look at this question. The second bill introduced by the chairman of the committee, Congressman Kastenmeyer, calls for major exemptions for farmers and for researchers. You see, under existing patent policy, if you buy a patented animal from a chemical company, and that animal gives birth, you have to pay a royalty because every birth is considered a reproduction, now. You see why farmers are not happy with patenting? It'll mean a few chemical, and pharmaceutical and biotech companies in the next twenty years literally taking over animal husbandry as they have poultry. By this exemption, Congressman Kastenmeyer has put on the table and I think because of the effective lobbying of this coalition for 14 months, farmers making under $2 million gross a year will be exempted from paying royalties and researchers will be exempted from paying royalties for pure research reproduction. Again, when this patent policy was announced, everyone assumed it would be a fait accompli. And, what I'm here to say to you today is that today as Chuck I think mentioned earlier, we're entering a new chapter in our relationship to technology, especially in agriculture. Now, we're going to, as a society, debate the pros and cons of each new technology so we can have a more sophisticated analysis of cost benefit. So, that when we proceed into these new areas we do so with a sense that we've taken care.

You know, when you intervene into the environment, you can never anticipate all of the consequences. Right? There's no fail-safe method of knowing the future. So, the rule of thumb ought to be when intervening in nature, always intervene the most gently, the most careful, and the most prudent course. Never take the most radical and the most adventuresome approach because you can never foresee all the consequences.

Gene splicing, engineering and rearranging the code of plants, animals and microbes. Is that prudent, caring, thoughtful? Or, is that radical, adventurous, and extreme?

Finally, you'll notice in those press releases that we handed out that there's mention of the greenhouse effect. In 1980 I wrote a book called *Entropy* and we developed a project called the Entropy project. We predicted that this would happen. And, the reason I'm glad to speak with you this morning is because it points out the problems we faced and the approach to science and technology we have used in the past. In the last two weeks you've all been reading about the greenhouse effect. My friends, that's the bill for the industrial age. I've often been accused of being against progress and being a Luddite. Well, I'm here to tell you this morning that the real obstacle to progress has been the pursuit of an industrial policy and an agricultural policy that has created now a change in climate so severe that we'll be paying for it for thousands of years in the future. You might have noticed on the cover of *Newsweek* and the congressional testimony NASA, the Goddard Space Institute, the Volagia report—they are now saying in the next fifty years, as a result of industrial pollutants on this planet, the temperature change in the next 40 to 75 years, that's the range, will increase by a greater margin than in the last 18,000 years since the end of the ice age. And, all the eco-systems of the planet will be affected in ways we can't begin to measure. It's being called the greatest social, environmental crisis in world history. And, it will force a readjustment across this planet of the entire way we do business—our science, our technology, our public policy—how we develop our infrastructures and finally how we grow our plants and raise our animals. Because the surveys that I've been reading from the National Academy of Science, the CEQ, EPA suggest agriculture is going to be the first to be affected you've seen the drought this year. According to these studies, between the early 21st century and the end of that century our entire agricultural areas of this country will be increasingly unavailable for agriculture. That's a big adjustment to make in less than 75 years.

We are initiating, by the way, and you know the major cause of the greenhouse effect is auto emissions and coal burning plants. You know what the third greatest cause is? Of the greenhouse effect? How many know? Ten percent of the greenhouse effect is caused by you know what? Fertilizers—the green revolution. Ten percent nitrous oxides in all the studies the third major cause of the greatest crises facing humanity is the green revolution of modern agriculture that we have pursued with great benefit for three decades at the expense of the survival of our planet for the next millennium.

We are initiating a global network, a global coalition which we announced this fall of farm organizations working together with environmental groups, food and consumer groups, religious leaders from around the world and we're going to announce this fall a global coalition of groups. We will seek whole new approaches to orient our agriculture in the future so that it's based on sustainability, it's based on diversification and it's based on a working partnership with our environment so that in 500 years from now and 1,000 years from now our children's children's generation will look back and say we made some wise choices for the future because at this point it's not a matter of who's right and who's wrong and pointing blame. We're all going to be part of this problem in the next 50 years. How will we choose the future of agriculture? An extension of green revolution philosophy, genetic engineering of those plants and animals, or new, sophisticated ecological science based on sustainability?

Finally, let me leave you with the words of the Iroquois Indians. Lest we snicker at the thought of the Iroquois remember Thomas Jefferson was quite enamored with the Iroquois. He borrowed quite liberally from their philosophy to pen his own. When the Iroquois Indians made decisions, they asked "How does the decision we make today affect seven generations removed?" "How does the decision we make now affect our children's children's children's children's children's children's children?" The Iroquois didn't live just for the moment, the quick fix, the short run. They heard their ancestors speak from the grave saying, "Honor the past. We have to have continuity between the generations." But, they also heard their unborn children and all other life not yet here saying, "Speak for us. We're not there yet." So, when the Iroquois made decisions, they did so as part of the continuum of history from the beginning to the end time. Now, I've been in Washington 17 years. You know what the attention span here is? The two-year general election. And in New York on Wall Street, the attention span is the three month profit and loss quarterly statement. Who is more sophisticated: us or the Iroquois? In winning in the short run we lose in the long run. So, together we have a tremendous opportunity and challenge and that's why I'm so grateful to even get this time to speak with you this morning. We have a tremendous opportunity and challenge to learn from the past and to develop a critical analysis of former agricultural practices so that we can move ahead with a new vision of agriculture that can allow us not only to deal with and adjust to the current greenhouse crisis, but could allow to plan a new agricultural policy for the world in coming centuries that will be based on resacrilizing our relationship with life. Because the new politics of the next century are not going to be based on right wing-left wing. Kids don't understand that politics anymore. The new politics is going to be based on resacrilizing our relationship to living things on the one hand or on the other reducing all of life to programs and chemicals and engineered genes that can be manipulated and rearranged for short term expedient purposes. So, I'm hoping that when we look back 50 to 75 years from now we can look back and say we carved a new course out, a course based on all of us working together to resacrilize our relationship to life and develop an agricultural policy that can allow future generations to not only survive but to prosper. Thank you.

# Science and the American Future[10]

Donald Kennedy

*Born August 18, 1931, New York, NY; A.B., 1952, A.M., 1954, Ph.D., 1956, Harvard University; professor, Syracuse University, 1956-60; professor, Stanford University, 1960-72; editor,* Journal of Experimental Zoology, *1965-71,* Journal of Comparative Physiology, *1965-76,* Journal of Neurophysiology, *1969-75,* Science, *1973-77; senior consultant, Office of Science and Technology Policy, 1976-77; commissioner, Food and Drug Administration, 1977-79; president, Stanford University, 1980-91; author,* Academic Duty *(1997).*

## Editor's introduction

Donald Kennedy, former president of Stanford University, gave this keynote address to begin a meeting of the American Association for the Advancement of Science. At this meeting, thousands of the nation's scientists gathered to discuss some of the most critical scientific and technical issues facing the nation. In this speech, Kennedy expressed concern over the public's apparent "mistrust" of scientists' practices. He argued that scientists must confront whatever misconceptions have arisen, as these views inhibit the growth of science and impede its ability to solve problems.

---

We begin the last year of a decade; and the next decade we start will be the last of a century. It is tempting at such times to review the past, but much more important to prepare for the future. So what can the *fin de siècle* of the twentieth century say to us about the twenty-first?

Much of what the future portends for our society will, I think, be determined *first* by the scientific preparations for it that we are undertaking now, and *second* by the public attitudes that will govern the extension of such work as a form of social investment.

In the first domain there is every reason for encouragement. Our accomplishments have been extraordinary, and in dozens of research areas we are poised for a kind of progress of which we would not have dared to dream at the midpoint of this century. Not only have we enriched our knowledge of the natural world at a breathtaking rate; we are also beginning to assault some of the great practical problems that burden society. Yet in the second domain we encounter a paradox: despite its stunning successes, American science finds itself increasingly inhibited by negative public attitudes—views of the scientific venture that are full of suspicion and doubt. These views translate readily into political constraints that are already stunting the growth of our science, and cutting into its capacity to help us resolve our other problems.

That paradox will be my subject this evening. I will begin with an account of our scientific potential, and then move to the perplexing phenomenon of social inhibition. Finally, if you have the patience, I will suggest some ways in which we might overcome the latter.

The good news is that by any intellectual measure our science has never been more vigorous, nor has it ever offered more hope for future advances. Somewhat to my dismay I note that in my own field, loosely defined as behavior and the neurosciences, progress in the ten years since I left it has been much greater than in the previous 30 when I was in it! The recent accomplishments seem remarkable to a lapsed practitioner: one can analyze currents at the level of single ionic channels, molecular probes can be constructed for the major classes of channel proteins, and we are beginning to learn about the molecular basis for plasticity and long-term changes in synaptic efficacy. Perhaps

[10]Delivered at the 155th meeting of the American Association for the Advancement of Science, in San Francisco, California, on January 14, 1989. Reprinted with permission of Donald Kennedy.

even more dramatic, the signals that guide axons to their proper terminations during development are beginning to be unraveled at the biochemical level, so that at last we may begin to penetrate the fundamental mystery of how the brain becomes connected in the right way. These stunning findings on experimental animals are being complemented by the new ability to analyze the genetic nature of the lesions in human neurological and behavioral disorders, from color blindness and muscular dystrophy to depression and perhaps schizophrenia. Just around the corner lies an interplay between these two different levels of approach, an interplay that may be productive beyond our wildest imaginings.

Such visions are arising not just in one or two fields, but everywhere. A couple of decades ago most of the popular attention given to physics was directed at the exciting world of new particles and high energies. None of that is any less interesting now, but condensed-matter physics and materials research have become hot topics as well. The recent breakthroughs in superconductivity are a striking example. These events are reforming the structure of the physical sciences: at Stanford, for example, "advanced materials research" will be one of the main elements in the new science campus, but it will involve researchers from at least three schools and more than seven academic departments. They will take advantage of all the new tools that permit analysis of materials at the atomic level—synchrotron radiation, tunneling scanning electron microscopy, short-wavelength lasers, and so on—turning these to the analysis of phenomena as diverse as the formation of ore at rock-water interfaces and electron migration to quantum effects in artificially synthesized semiconductors.

It is difficult to know why things are moving so fast. There are more people working in science, and I think they're smarter (although I hope maybe they're only better trained). But also, and perhaps as a result, something else is happening: research is developing new tools or technologies, and these are then being applied more quickly to new research problems. Consider, for example, how rapidly the recombinant DNA techniques were applied to a whole family of analytical challenges in genetics and biochemistry. Their application in the basic sciences, in fact, was much more extensive than their much-heralded application to commercial uses. Similarly, laser technology has transformed physical chemistry by permitting it to operate in a new time dimension—the femtosecond scale. We work in a time of tight coupling between the invention of tools and their application to new domains of analysis.

It is an exciting time, and as a result we are in a position to make science work for the betterment of the human condition in a way that is unparalleled in our history. We had better be, because the human condition had never been in greater need of help in *its* history!

Just consider the predictable extensions of what we already know. Genetic engineering techniques not only offer medicine new ways in which to produce pharmaceuticals and to diagnose disease; they also hold out the hope of replacement therapies for a number of congenital conditions. Although most of the popular attention given to recombinant DNA technology has emphasized these medical opportunities, some of us believe that its most dramatic successes will be in the other great area of applied biology, agriculture. There, the new methods are likely to improve crop yields by altering plant responses to environmental factors, or by creating new symbiotic relationships or improving old ones between seed and forage crops and bacteria with engineered nitrogen-fixing capacity. Success in the latter area could relieve us of much of our dependence on commercial chemical fertilizers, the enormous energy cost of their production, and the ecological destructiveness of their use. The same kind of opportunity awaits us through the development of insect-resistant crop strains that could unhook us from the grip of ever-increasing dependence on chemical pesticides.

These last two possibilities illustrate another aspect of the breakthroughs in modern biology. They promise to solve important problems in environmental quality—not to exacerbate them, as many of the technological developments of our century have done. Consider just two prospects:

*First*: bacteria can be developed to attack many of the compounds that have created toxic waste dumps in the industrial nations. We are finding new and exciting properties in naturally-occurring microorganisms that can transform pesticides, PCB's, chlorinated solvents and other persistent hazardous chemicals into innocuous products. Through gene manipulation it should be possible to "evolve" cost-effective detoxifying schemes.

*Second*: population biologists are now adducing principles that may contribute to the design of wiser and more effective strategies of conservation and preserve design. New applications of population genetics and advances in the analysis of population viability are being combined with biogeographic theory derived from the study of island populations. The prospect is that we might hold back the wave of extinction that is sweeping our planet of its biological diversity—burning our genetic library, book by book.

I am particularly excited by these prospects, because they represent science in the very mode that attracted many of us to our work in the first place: a humane calling, proffering relief from suffering and a better world in which to live. Most of you, I suspect, would find expressions somewhat like those on your list of motivations for doing scientific work.

And yet, despite an abundance of good will and a truly extraordinary record of contemporary success, science in contemporary America finds itself in the midst of a paradox—a situation in which its work, however emphathetic with public need, finds itself inhibited by public mistrust. What forms does the inhibition take?

The first version you will hear from most scientists involves the level of public support. In real-dollar terms, this has not been a bad decade for the federal support of basic research—if you look at the program side only. But the physical infrastructure is crumbling, and most of us know it. That decay is contributing most of the upward pressure on the indirect cost of doing research; indeed, at my own institution space-related costs constitute over 40´of the indirect cost rate, and have been increasing at least four times as fast as administrative costs. Until this last Congress there had been no significant federal program to fund the facilities needs of universities since the 1960s. Although Congress did take the important step of authorizing a facilities program in the National Science Foundation last year, it is by no means clear that any money will actually be appropriated for that purpose. More disturbingly, the institutions responsible for most of the nation's basic research, the universities, have encountered one blockade after another in their efforts to recover the indirect costs of sponsored research or to develop other funding sources for infrastructure maintenance and improvement. The 1986 tax law revision, meanwhile, exacerbated the situation by reducing the incentive for important kinds of private capital gifts and by restricting the access of private research universities to the tax-exempt bond market. In recent years, our work with the Congress on these and related matters has suggested a growing impatience with the needs of the scientific community. Indeed, there is a suggestion that we are now regarded—whether we approach Washington as university representatives or as groups of investigators represented by discipline—as "just another interest group."

There is another and much more local manifestation. It takes the form of a generalized fear and mistrust of the perceived external costs of scientific work. You have come for this meeting to an unusually beautiful and admired part of the United States, and one that has an exceptional concentration of distinguished research universities. But I can say, speaking for the leadership of all of them, that you are also visiting the nation's capital of activist, single-issue, "not-in-my-backyard" politics when it comes to the externalities of science.

During the past two years, for example, facilities for the housing of research animals have been held up at the University of California at Berkeley and at Stanford by objections on the part of animal rights activists. The delays were accomplished by different means: challenge to a state legislative appropriation and lawsuits in one case, objections to the building permit at the county level in the other. The two together cost the universities in excess of two and a half million dollars. At Stanford the construction of a new animal facility designed to house rodents was held up for over a year by the delayed imposition of an environmental impact report—the first ever required for an academic building on the campus. A similar delay was imposed on the construction of a new biological sciences building. In both the Stanford cases, concerns about recombinant DNA research and toxic waste discharge were brought forward by objecting groups. But it is interesting to note that the leaders who used environmental concerns to force the construction delay of the animal facility were the same ones who had earlier opposed its construction on animal rights grounds. I think it is fair to suggest that the real agenda at work was not the stated one.

Meanwhile, in this city, residents succeeded in blocking the relocation of some University of California research programs from its campus on Parnassus Avenue to new facilities in

Laurel Heights. What began with neighborhood concerns about traffic and other routine planning impacts escalated into some of the worst science-bashing and fear-mongering of recent times. Exaggerated and distorted information about hazardous materials and toxic wastes, combined with false rumors of the University's intentions in the neighborhood and the ludicrous charge that germ warfare research would be conducted at Laurel Heights, created an ugly community relations problem that threatened the viability of this splendid university's program.

The controversy eventually found its way into the courts where California's complicated and well-intended environmental quality act received its most thorough test to date with respect to university research facilities. A trial court and the Court of Appeals reached differing conclusions, leaving the matter to be resolved by the California Supreme Court.

Just over a month ago, the California Supreme Court handed down what I think will be a landmark decision. While the Court did find aspects of the University of California's Environmental Impact Report to be deficient on planning grounds, it gave strong endorsement to the University's research programs and restored reason to the discussion about research safety and risk assessment.

More importantly, the Court arched its judicial eyebrows and delivered some badly needed plain talk about the unreasonable positions taken by objectors to the Laurel Heights project. Scattered through its opinion, one finds the Court employing pithy phrases like these to describe the opponents' arguments on issues related to research safety: "entirely unreasonable," "gross misstatement of the record," "unsupported by the record," "greatly exaggerated," and "clearly untenable." This high court ruling is of enormous importance to research in California; and the welcome, sensible language of the Court will be of help in continuing efforts to educate the public and public officials on issues related to science, research, and the environment.

Although these incidents occurred in a region especially hospitable to special-interest local politics, they bespeak a more general phenomenon: a new and corrosive popular mistrust of scientists and their work. The media popularity of the issue of scientific fraud is a barometer that bears careful watching in this connection. A year ago my friend David Baltimore, a Nobel laureate who is as justly renowned for his personal qualities of scientific leadership as he is for his own pathbreaking work, delivered the address I am privileged to give this evening. Now he is the victim of an unprecedented attack, based on a rather narrow difference of scientific interpretation that has been transmuted—through the alchemy of politics—into allegations of misconduct. This attack, shameful though it is, will probably not in the end damage David Baltimore's career. But it tells us something when the United States Congress is prepared to enact legislation to create fraud-catching offices in Federal agencies that support science—based upon hearings at which the accused persons were not even invited to testify. Taken with the other evidence, it tells us much about the paradox of which I spoke. The American public believes in progress, believes in science, and admires you as its practitioners. It knows what a first-rate scientific enterprise has brought us. It is happy to consume the products—technical, social, economic—of that enterprise. But it is much less confident than it once was about what you and I are up to, and it displays an alarming level of mistrust about our motives.

So much for the paradox. I suspect you already believed, without any prompting from me, in the future science promises us. And I hope I have convinced you that we nevertheless face serious inhibitions in the form of public reservations about the external costs of science and the trustworthiness of scientists. Now let me close with a few thoughts about how we might try to cope with the latter problems.

First, I think we must deal in a straightforward way with some misconceptions about the nature of scientific work and its promised outcomes. If what we do has no chance of matching the expectations of those who support us, we are in for real trouble. A particularly important set of misconceptions has to do with the relationship between science and money. It is widely believed that you can buy good science if you spend enough; the corollary is that it doesn't matter where, or on whom, you spend it. This belief has underlain the dramatic growth of the scientific pork barrel in the recent history of federal appropriations. It is fatally wrong, and we owe Senator Nunn a large debt for his recent performance of liposuction on the defense budget. But I fear he has given us only temporary respite, not permanent relief.

A belief of a different kind is that improvement in basic science will by itself make us more economically competitive with other nations. It can help all right, but recent analyses suggest that our deficit position with respect to Japan, for example, owes much more to such factors as product engineering, production management, the opportunity to form industry consortia, and advantages in the cost of capital than it does to research—even applied research. After all, only about one-tenth of the investment in product creation represents research. Nine-tenths represents product development activities that take place outside university settings.

Second, I think we need to examine some reasons behind the public perception of us as human beings. We are seen, I think, as having become more absorbed in our research, and much less concerned with communicating its meaning and its implication to others who are not scientists. This had led to a gradual erosion in our relationship to the polity in this country, an alienation that we can ill afford in a future that promises severe resource constraints. One aspect of this alienation, and I'm afraid it has gone unrecognized, is the increasingly popular belief that those of us who do science in the universities are neglecting our own undergraduate students. My own faculty colleagues—many of whom are devoted undergraduate teachers whom I hasten to exempt from this charge—point out that it is much harder to get grants, to manage the administrative burdens and the reporting requirements of contemporary research management, and to discharge the increasingly time-consuming burdens of faculty citizenship. There is a good deal of evidence for that view; for example, the average science faculty member at Stanford today has half again as many sources of support for a constant real-dollar research volume as a decade ago. However valid the reasons, though, it will be unacceptably costly if the consequences fall heavily on this extraordinarily capable cohort of bright students. Their disillusionment will spread quickly; worse still, we will not have them around to succeed us when the time comes.

Third, we need a lot more resolve in the face of the special political interests that are hostile to American science. We all recognize, and occasionally do battle with, the creationists, the right-to-life advocates who would ban all forms of research with fetal tissues, the animal liberation crowd. But we don't give it much of our time unless we are especially threatened. Such groups, furthermore, are often easy to identify and to dislike because of their tactics, which are often mean-spirited and sometimes violent. Sometimes it seems harder to oppose those forces hostile to science that arise from sources with which many scientists are naturally sympathetic—the environmental movement, for example. Yet the implacable opposition of some environmental organizations to all recombinant DNA research, and the local no-growth movements that reflexively oppose new research facilities, are no less the enemies of scientific progress. If organized science entered the battle against all these forces with the same invigorated self-interest they annually bring to the appropriation cycle of the National Institutes of Health and the National Science Foundation, we would all be better off.

Finally, I have a few thoughts about how we state our case to our public patrons. To the extent that the 1980s have been kind to science, it has been for the most practical of reasons. International competitiveness has become the research buzz-word of the decade, and it is small wonder that we have been willing to link our own future to the powerful political energy it has provided. Thus we have tended to justify, and sometimes to oversell, our science on utilitarian grounds.

Therein lie several traps for the unwary. First, it is not nice to disappoint people, and it is downright dangerous to disappoint your Congressman. To the extent that we persuade policymakers of the economic utility of our work, we risk being held to account if the federal investment in research doesn't produce tracking responses in the index of leading economic indicators. The political fallout from the failure of the well-advertised "war on cancer" is a recent lesson that we could all ponder with profit. Some years ago when I called that war a biomedical Vietnam, it provoked some objections even from my friends. I wasn't trying to be mean; I was just trying to point out that raised expectations turn to frustration and outrage when they aren't met.

Second, the utilitarian argument encourages a pernicious notion, now circulating widely among our policymakers, that if one appropriates research money geographically, economic prosperity will distribute itself along with it. That is the way to convert science to another form of public works project, with all the propensity for haggling and horse-trading we have come to associate with the appropriations process for rivers and harbors.

Third, we unwittingly encourage our patrons to adopt a procurement model for research when we place it on a utilitarian footing. That is not a model with which most basic scientists are familiar, and certainly not one with which they would be comfortable. It includes intensive monitoring of performance, is guarded and suspicious with respect to the Three Devils of Waste, Fraud and Abuse, requires competitive bidding procedures that consider price and quality as tradeable, and generally takes a more regulatory approach. Try it; you *won't* like it.

There is another way, and I think it is better. We should be perfectly willing to point to the economic benefits of science, and to the wonderful opportunities it presents us for improving the quality of human life. But we should say, at the same time, that we do it for love; that is, we are engaged in a search for understanding of the physical world and the nature of living systems because we share a passion to know such things and to teach them to others. We should approach our public patrons with some humility, and a grateful acknowledgment that they have made a society that can afford to subsidize discovery—not because it can make us richer or healthier but because it can make us better for knowing these wonderful and mysterious things. The people who make this possible have shown time and again that they are willing to share in that excitement. To suppose that they are only in it for gain is to underrate them, and to disadvantage ourselves.

# In Today Walks Tomorrow[11]

Randall L. Tobias

*Born March 20, 1942, Lafayette, IN; B.S., Indiana University, 1964; U.S. Army, 1964-66; vice president, AT&T, 1981-82; president, American Bell Consumer Products, 1983-84; chairman, chief executive officer, AT&T Communications, 1985-91; chairman, chief executive officer, AT&T International, 1991-93; chief executive officer, Eli Lilly & Co., 1993–.*

## Editor's introduction

Randall L. Tobias, then chief executive officer of AT&T, gave this McDonough Caperton lecture at the University of West Virginia's College of Business and Economics. McDonough Caperton, a large insurance group based in West Virginia, sponsors a series of lectures to increase public awareness of business and economic systems and the contributions and social responsibilities of business. Aware that technology is considered by some "a promise" and by others "a threat," Tobias reviewed the basic technologies that he believed would accompany citizens into the 21st century.

---

It's a pleasure to be back at West Virginia University and an honor to be presenting the McDonough Caperton Lecture.

My topic today is shaping the future through technology. But it will not be a technical talk. My interest lies less in the technology itself, though I am fascinated by how it works. My interest is more in how technology can be used to benefit AT&T's customers.

The topic is a risky one because it touches on some of society's deepest hopes and fears. Our literature is filled with conflicting views of technology and the future, from Edward Bellamy's utopian "Looking Backward" to Aldous Huxley's bleak" Brave New World." We've been exposed enough to both extremes to regard technology as a promise and a threat.

A lighthearted story I heard from a scientist-colleague illustrates this point.

A theologian asked the most powerful supercomputer, 'Is there a God?" The computer said it lacked the processing power to know. It asked to be connected to all the other supercomputers in the world. Still, it was not enough power. So the computer was hooked up to all the mainframes in the world, and then all the minicomputers, and then all the personal computers. And eventually it was connected to all the computers in cars, microwaves, VCRs, digital watches, and so on. The theologian asked for the final time, "Is there a God?" And the computer replied: "There is now."

I heard some nervousness in the laughter. Don't worry. I can assure you, with a tinge of regret, that the information industry is a long time away from that kind of computer connectivity. But I can report we are making rapid progress with computers that understand spoken language and answer in kind.

In fact, progress in communications and computer technology has become so rapid that as much as you've seen in the 1980s, you haven't seen anything yet. As John Scully, CEO of Apple, put it: "We've been racing to the starting line. The really interesting stuff begins in the 1990's."

The next decade or so we will see: computers that speak and understand spoken language; personal telephone numbers that allow you to be reached anywhere; pocket-size personal communicators that combine computer and communication technology; high definition TV and hundreds of cable channels; two-way videophones; and computerized virtual reality.

Today, I'll describe these remarkable devices and capabilities. I'll discuss them in the

[11]Delivered at the University of West Virginia, in Morgantown, West Virginia, on October 14, 1992. Reprinted with permission of Randall L. Tobias.

context of overcoming four limitations on communications: the limits of geography, mobility, sense perception, and the human-machine interface. And I'll comment on how over the decade communications technology will change our work, home, and leisure lives.

And when I'm done I hope you will agree with the British poet Samuel Coleridge who said, "In today, already walks tomorrow."

But first, let's ignore the warning label on the back of communications devices: you know, the one that says only qualified technicians should open. Let's figuratively remove the cover and peek inside at two underlying technologies: microelectronics and fiber optics, for these are the basic technologies driving communications "warp-speed" into the 21st century.

Foremost, is microelectronics: transistors and other electronic components etched on a sliver of silicon. Thanks to the small-is-beautiful movement in electronics, there are more microprocessors—that is, computers on a chip—than there are people on earth.

Over the last few decades, the rate of progress in microelectronics has been fantastic. The number of components on a chip has been doubling every 18 months, without a substantial cost increase. To put that in perspective, if we had similar gains in automotive technology, today you could buy a Lexus for about $2. It would travel at the speed of sound, and go 600 miles on a thimble of gas. It would be only three inches long, but easy to parallel park!

Today we can squeeze about 32 million transistors on a chip. By the year 2000, we will shoehorn 256 million onto a chip, allowing us to pack the power of today's supercomputer on a desktop. By the year 2010, with a billion transistors on a chip, we will have exhausted the limits of the current technology. And we may well tap the ultra-small world of quantum physics. I'm told by our scientists at Bell Laboratories that quantum technology might permit chips with a trillion transistors.

While microelectronics has the raw power to process huge amounts of information, information only gains its full value when communicated. Enter fiber optics, the technology of communicating with light.

Fiber optics systems combine lasers as small as grains of sand with glass fibers as thin as strands of hair. Unlike ordinary glass, it's ultrapure. If oceans were made of this glass, you could see to the bottom.

In fiber optic systems, lasers transmit billions of light pulses each second as bits of data through these glass strands. The bits represent conversations, computer data or images. Currently, we transmit about 3.4 billion bits a second, equal to 50,000 simultaneous phone calls on a pair of fibers. But with not-too-distant developments in the technology, we expect to transmit one trillion bits per second, of about 70 million simultaneous conversations on a single pair of fibers. Such advances in these well-matched technologies are helping us to overcome the limitations on communication.

First, geography. For the last hundred years, most of our effort has been in shrinking distance, making it as easy to call another continent as it is to call another state. And we've largely succeeded. We now have global networks that allow you to directly dial up not only Peoria and Paris but even remote Pitcairn Island where the Bounty's mutineers landed. There's virtually no country or territory a consumer can't reach, no market a business can't access by telephone.

These global networks have been a spur to the world economy. Fiber cables under the oceans have evolved into the new trade routes of a global economy that prizes information as the most precious of all cargos.

Using global networks, corporations are able to establish farflung world operations. For example, today Mazda offers a sports model designed in California, financed in Tokyo, and assembled in Michigan and Mexico with advanced electronic components invented in New Jersey but fabricated in Japan. To say the least, it takes tight communication linkages worldwide to pull this off. And Mazda is but one of thousands of global companies doing it every day.

With international networks in place we can now tackle individual mobility. When people left their homes or offices, they used to be hard to reach. And if on the road traveling, impossible to reach. But that has changed with wireless technology, through-the-air communication.

It began with cellular phones that could allow you to, theoretically, carry on a running conversation as you drove from New York to LA. It gained even greater popularity with cordless phones at home and in business.

Over the decade, we'll cut the cord for good with affordable personal communication networks that operate on radio waves. People will have a personal telephone number for life and will be tracked as they move from one service area to another. You could be reached anywhere. Whether in a cab, walking on the street, or waiting on line in a supermarket. Whether in West Virginia, California, or on the European continent. But only if you want to be reached, as I'll explain shortly.

You will receive calls with "personal communications devices," or "pocket phones." More than just miniature phones, personal communicators could combine telephone service with computer technology such as electronic mail and facsimile. You will be able to easily store notes in these devices by writing with a special pen on a computer screen. I know it sounds futuristic. But, in fact personal communicators will hit the market this year.

You can imagine the impact devices will have on the way we do business. For example, if you can pack an office in a briefcase, or even in your pocket, do you need an office?

The answer was "no" for 500 AT&T salespeople in ten states. They traded their offices for car phones, portable computers, printers and modems that transmit data over the telephone lines. The results have been overwhelmingly positive, more direct contact with customers and higher productivity. We plan to extend the concept to thousands of other salespeople.

Communications mobility may force even more sweeping changes in the workplace. An estimated 5.5 million people "telecommuted" in the U.S. last year, and we expect the number to double by 1995. Converging with home office technologies, social forces are putting pressure on companies to further expand work at home.

Traffic and pollution, for example. As more persons per household work, traffic gets worse. The average length of a commute is expected to double in the 1990s from about 37 minutes today to one hour and 15 minutes, and that's just one way. As car pollutants double and traffic jams increase, federal and local governments will pressure business to expand work at home.

The social ramifications of work-at-home are enormous. For example, people who telecommute could choose to live in remote, rural locations, though probably not too far from the office since occasional face-to-face meetings will still be required.

On the downside, working at home may cause social isolation, one reason why face-to-face meetings will still be a fairly frequent part of worklife. On the other hand, some people may overcome the isolation by becoming part of a "virtual community." People who have never met but have common interests may communicate regularly with each other over computer networks.

Of course, being on-call, anytime, anywhere has its drawbacks. But even as technology creates a privacy problem, it offers a solution. When you want to, you can choose not to answer and still get the message by directing the telephone network to take your calls, like having an answering machine constantly at your disposal. You can retrieve the messages at your convenience, from anywhere and in any form you want, whether voice, print or electronic mail.

Most of us don't think of a telephone conversation as unnatural communication, but in a way it is. People prefer to see people when they talk. It adds an extra dimension of feeling and understanding. Conventional telephone service is an unnatural separation of our senses of sight and sound.

But we're working on bringing them back together again. Indeed, visual communication may well be to telecommunication in this decade what facsimile was in the '80s, an explosive technology.

Video communication used to require an expensive investment in equipment. Moving images eat up an enormous amount of telecommunications capacity. But scientists have developed compression techniques, a bit like the electronic equivalent of concentrated orange juice, that remove much of the visual information for transmission and restore it at the receiving end to constitute the picture.

As a result, AT&T has just introduced affordable videophones that use the standard telephone lines. The response has been so great we already have thousands on back order. Who is buying them? People with particularly strong incentive to see their family or friends. For example, grandparents who live far from their grandchildren and want to be able to see them grow up. Or parents sending children off to college who want to lessen the sense of separation and at the same time nervously monitor changes in hair and clothing styles.

Video will really take off in the mid-to-late 1990s when high-definition television, or HDTV, hits the market. High-definition television uses twice as many lines as standard television to create a moving image, in essence doubling the clarity. An HDTV picture has the color and the crispness of a 35 millimeter slide and the sound of a compact disc. Because the image is so well defined, it's possible to make larger TV screens without degrading the image quality. And, with digital technology, it's possible to get special effects, like zooming in on the pass receiver during a football game.

Over the decade, too, public demand for more video channels likely will prompt local cable or telephone companies to begin installing high capacity fiber optics to the home. Then 150 channels, and the potential for 10 times more, will be possible. And your TV guide may weigh as much as your telephone directory.

Within the next 20 years, we'll move beyond sight and sound with "virtual reality." Virtual reality uses specially designed goggles and gloves with computer chips embedded in them and communicates directly to a computer with radio transmitters. It can give the user the impression of being in a particular setting. The user's hand and eye movements are detected and the scene is moved to create the perspective being looked at. Not only is there dimensional perspective possible, but also the sense of motion and even smell.

At first blush, this might seem a trivial technology with sensational entertainment value only, an attraction in a pinball arcade. But virtual reality may prove to be practical.

For example, you may have heard about the murder trial in California where a video tape using virtual reality techniques was used to reenact the crime. In a less sensational illustration, Chrysler engineers have been testing the dashboard and steering wheel of a 1997 model car, still in the blueprint stage, using an experimental virtual reality system.

You can imagine other uses. Architects could give home buyers the experience of walking through a house still on the drawing board, allowing them to experience the effect of changing a room's size, ceiling height, or style of windows. Students could explore the moon's surface in a lunar vehicle or walk unharmed through a reenacted battle of Gettysburg.

And, as costs go down, virtual reality will settle into the home entertainment market. VCRs and cable TV have proven how enormous that market is.

The last frontier I'll discuss today is the human-machine interface: communicating with computers. Computer command systems have evolved from the punch card to the keyboard to the "mouse" and now special pens used to write instructions on a computer screen. But all this is less natural than simply telling a computer what you want.

Well that day is not far away. At the current rate of progress, we probably will have a talking computer by the year 2001, although it will be a pale imitation of the "Space Odyssey's" HAL.

At AT&T's Bell Laboratories, a computer has been programmed to understand 1,000 words. Our scientists believe in the mid-90s, we will have computers with 5,000-word vocabularies that could take simple dictation. By the turn of the century, computers may have 20,000-word vocabularies, more than the average person, and will be capable of translating foreign languages.

In fact, AT&T and Spain's telephone company demonstrated a rudimentary translation system at the summer Olympics. With a vocabulary of about 450 words relating to money, the system was able to translate requests about the exchange rate of dollars and pesetas in English and Spanish.

Closer to home, a speech recognition system that pulls information from a database is being trialed right now in Arizona. There highway police phone into a computer and speak the driver's license and plate numbers. In seconds, the computer checks a data base and tells them whether the car is stolen or if the driver is wanted.

In the very near future, you will be able to dial your phone by telling it who you want to talk with, and it won't just ring but will tell you who is calling.

Which brings me to the other half of this human-machine equation: computer-synthesized speech. It's a very well developed technology. In fact, you may have talked with such a system already. Speech synthesis and recognition systems are now handling some telephone operator services, such as collect calls, across the country. By the way, if you have any problems talking to the computer, the system will connect you with a human operator at the touch of a button.

For all this progress, it's not clear just when we'll be able to throw away our computer keyboards and converse with a computer as easily as with a person. As complicated as computers are, it turns out human beings are much more complex. But on a pretty basic level we will be conversing with computers and other appliances in ten years or so.

As you've probably noticed, almost all that I've described is off the drawing board and in the laboratory or the marketplace. As Coleridge said: "In today, already walks tomorrow." What I've described is not so much a prediction—what is possible—but rather a technology forecast—what is probable.

And if some of this still seems improbable to you, consider that fifteen or so years ago we didn't have portable phones and fax machines, PCs or CDs, VCRs or microwaves. They've burst on the scene and changed our lives immeasurably.

Arguably, not all of the technological change in that time has been for the better. But, on balance, I'd think most of us would agree technology has improved our lives. Whether the future will be better yet is beyond prediction. It's more a matter of faith.

The progress of communications leads me to cast my lot with the optimists. Over the past 100 years, communication technology had drawn our nation closer together, and helped create a single marketplace, possibly even a single national identity.

Now communication is helping to create a global village, truly democratizing information, making it accessible to everyone, everywhere. The downfall of communism was brought about in good measure because information media penetrated the Iron Curtain, and made the people behind it aware that in other countries people led richer, freer lives.

So while it's wise to regard technology with some suspicion—to accept the Luddite within us—I hope we will keep faith in ourselves because we ultimately control how technology is used.

And I hope you would agree with the philosopher John Dewey who said, "The future is not ominous but a promise; it surrounds the present like a halo."

# XIV. Environment

## Editor's introduction

Threats to the earth's land, water, and air have accompanied many technological advances in the areas of transportation, communication, agricultural production, and the packaging and distribution of goods. In a speech reprinted herein, Dr. Jessica Tuchman Mathews, vice president of the World Resources Institute, detailed some of these threats, which include soil erosion, deforestation, loss of species, greenhouse warming, and ozone depletion. In response to these problems, a "new environmentalism" emerged in the late 1960s and early 1970s. The annual Earth Day celebrations (April 22) are one outcome of this new environmentalism. It has also sparked extensive leglislation, including the National Environmental Protection Act (1970) and the 1970 and 1990 Clear Air Acts. Despite these efforts, however, industry and technology still pose serious threats to the environment as government and private business continue to debate over who is ultimately responsible for protecting it.

August Heckscher, special presidential consultant on the arts, argued that we must maintain "beauty and fitness in the environment," as such qualities can be considered the true mark of a civilized society. Yet the maintenance of such beauty and fitness has not been the focus of our "progress," according to Heckscher. Instead, we have focused on technology alone and given little attention to the effect of that technology on the natural world. Barry Commoner, professor of plant physiology at Washington University, warned that our stress on technology amounts to a massive environmental intervention. Moreover, such intervention is being performed without an awareness of its "biological consequences." Gus Speth, president of the World Resources Institute, echoed these concerns, as he maintains that "pollution is occurring on a vast and unprecedented scale around the globe." If this pollution continues, Speth warned that life on Earth will be irrevokably altered.

According to speakers represented in this chapter, to ensure the sanctity of the environment, we must reorient our thinking so that the natural world is in fact a major consideration in the planning and execution of all subsequent technological advances. Rene Dubos, a microbiologist and experimental pathologist at Rockefeller University, prescribed a new "Theology of the Earth" in which citizens would "reject the attitude which asserts that man is the only value of importance and that the rest of nature can be sacrificed to his welfare and whims." Anthropologist Margaret Mead similarly advised changing our "present way of life." Dr. Jessica Tuchman Mathews maintained that people have to "change how [they] think, and how [they] behave, especially as a global community" if they have any hopes of preserving the environment.

# The Challenge of Ugliness[1]

August Heckscher

*Born September 16, 1913, Huntington, NY; B.A., Yale University, 1936; M.A., Harvard University, 1939; instructor, Yale University, 1939-41; Office of Strategic Services, 1941-45; editor,* Citizen Advertiser, *1946-48; chief editorial writer,* New York Herald Tribune, *1948-56; director, Twentieth-Century Fund, 1956-61; special White House consultant on the arts, 1962; author,* These Are the Days *(1936),* The Woods Are Large *(1945),* A Pattern of Politics *(1947),* The Politics of Woodrow Wilson: Selections from His Speeches and Writings *(1956).*

## Editor's introduction

On April 3, 1962, August Heckscher, special White House consultant on the arts, addressed leaders of government, architecture, art, and business at the First Conference on Aesthetic Responsibility. The conference was held to help "save the face of America from further ugliness." To do so, Heckscher asked that citizens look "beyond the search for security and for material benefits," and instead place their concern on the nation's "beauty and fitness in the environment." Heckscher also asserted that the condition of the environment is indicative of the culture which resides in that environment. According to Heckscher, the extent to which a society cares for its environment is a gauge by which the overall quality of that society is judged.

---

Let me say, first of all, that it is a pleasure to be here, in this company, and concerned with this subject. Since being named by the President, I have received many good wishes and many encouraging expressions of support, not only from individuals but from groups and organizations. I am glad to be able to acknowledge them and to say how much they have meant to me and to others involved in this work. The New York Chapter of the American Institute of Architects has been particularly considerate and cordial. I thank them especially.

Now it seems to me that the Challenge of Ugliness is a good topic to begin on—for in declaring myself against ugliness I am certain to be on safe ground. In denouncing ugliness roundly and resolutely, I am hardly likely to lose any of these new-found friends. And I really don't want to lose them: I am going to need them all as we go forward along a path where troubles and perplexities are bound to accumulate. Indeed, I trust that as the work progresses I may continue to earn your good will.

Having said this, I should perhaps conclude and sit down. But I am constrained to confess that opposition to ugliness is not the whole of my platform—nor is a simple declaration the end of my discourse. I believe that our twentieth-century American society is entering upon a new phase, where the concerns and controversies of the past several decades are going to be muted or supplanted and a whole new range of interests is going to excite the public. Leaving aside the ever-present problems of the cold war, what has been the central preoccupation of our common life? It has been Welfare. It has been the satisfaction of the private desires of the citizenry: the increase in their comforts and the multiplication of their possessions. But there is surely an end of the state more noble and enduring than welfare. The old measures in this field have reached a point beyond debate; new measures may still divide us, but they are destined to take their place, in one form or another, in the anthology of accepted reforms. Meanwhile the people begin to look beyond the acquisition of private possessions and indulgence in personal pleasures.

It is hard to know how to formulate these new and larger interests. I have used elsewhere

[1]Delivered at the First Conference on Aesthetic Responsibility, in New York, New York, on April 3, 1962.

the phrase "The Public Happiness." I like to think that this in some sense describes the satisfactions men find significant when they reach out beyond the search for security and for material benefits.

The arts and cultural activities form an important part of this realm. The widespread, lively interest in the development of the arts—you can discern it in the press, you can feel it amid the public and even in the Congress—is a symptom of a deep movement in public opinion, one of those transformations in our habits and ways of thinking which, once in a generation or so, create wholly fresh demands and possibilities.

Sometimes this enthusiasm for culture seems a little overwhelming. One fears that where such winds are blowing nice distinctions are going to get lost and the highest standards will prove difficult to maintain. The difference between the excellent and the second-rate, between the genuine and the spurious, between the artist and the amateur, are perhaps now in more danger of becoming blurred than in periods when the arts are neglected.

But the capacity to appreciate and enjoy, and the energy to create, certainly exist in a high degree among us. They may yet bring us out into an age of cultural achievement such as our country has not known before.

Now I would like to maintain today, before this audience, that the maintenance of beauty and fitness in the environment—a sort of comeliness in the world around us—is wholly as important as other forms of culture in determining the quality of a society. The things that are created by men working together, consciously or unconsciously, are the most durable facts about a civilization. They outlast the living generation; they carry forward, to be modified by time and by new men, the body of an age. Where we find that men have built meanly, without common purpose or a sense of the ideal, we can be sure that they lived meanly also—or at the very least that they lived with a disproportionate emphasis on the private sphere of life, neglecting the influences which can make a civilization out of an accumulation of individual existences.

What, after all, do we mean by a civilization? It is surely not the accumulation of private things. Not is it, necessarily, the building of public things. In the *Republic*, Plato complained of those who had heaped up physical structures and yet missed the most important aspects of a true civilization. They have filled the city, Plato complains, "full of harbors and docks and buildings and all that," and have "left no room for temperance or justice." Many of those arguing today that we have overdeveloped the private sector while neglecting the public sector fall into this fallacy; they seem to suggest that money spent in the public realm is necessarily and in all circumstances a boon.

Granted there are public needs poorly met and some not met at all, still a transfer of funds from the private to the public budget is no assurance of a higher degree of maturity and civilization. A civilization requires "temperance and justice" at the core—an inner sense of values in the light of which decisions are made. It implies an external order of things which are not only beautiful in their own way but correspond to a people's intrinsic sense of what is good.

The next decades will be a period of vast building and of great physical transformations of the American scene. It is not only that goods will pour from the factories. New highways will crisscross the country. Cities will be torn down and rebuilt. The countryside will be made over into new forms of urban and suburban communities. Yet all this activity will not in itself mean that a civilization is being shaped. A civilization begins to manifest itself when men and women have begun to take thought about what it is they construct, and why, and to what end. It begins to be a living whole when the idea of beauty has found its place alongside the pressure of utility and the spur of need.

In the past history of this country, the outward pattern of things has, to an extraordinary degree, been left to chance—to the haphazard actions of special interests and groups. Sometimes it has seemed that as a nation we simply did not concern ourselves with the face of the land. The American continent was so huge, its resources of land and forests and water so unbounded, that though men chopped away at them with only their own interests in mind we trusted that the great bulk of things would remain unspoiled. Sometimes we have assumed that private interests working competitively would create their own kind of fitness.

In strange ways this has often happened. The farming landscape, whether tightly knit in New England or spread across the midwestern miles, has its peculiar beauty. The New York skyline reveals a spirit that no sculpture could have matched. But there are limits beyond which this faith in automatic artistry cannot be pushed. Where these limits are passed over, as in the sprawling roadside slums or the monotonous housing developments, the results have often been appalling. And the public has appeared to stand by helplessly.

Public agencies undertaking to mold the landscape or drastically alter the environment, have most frequently acted with a single interest in mind—to speed up traffic, to stop floods, to put roofs over needy people. All these separate things may be to the good. But the fact that these interventions were the work of lonely enthusiasts, or of bureaucratic experts, suggests that something has been amiss. Where was there a concern for harmony? Where was that sense of the whole which alone can give beauty and meaning to what men accomplish by their common toil?

When we look about us at the natural environment today we are struck by the degree to which it is subject to human designs. No part of it is safe from the bulldozer, from the land speculator, from the engineer and road builder. When Theodore Roosevelt and Governor Pinchot started the conservation movement in 1908, their problem was essentially that of preserving a few key areas, or of instituting practices which allowed natural resources to endure and to reproduce themselves. Since then, the power of man over nature has increased enormously. The great advances in human organization, in science and technology, have literally put into our hands the fate of a vast continental expanse. What we do with it is for us to decide. The forests that sheltered our grandfathers we now shelter and preserve. The land that kept them is now in our keeping. We possess the earth as in no sense could it have been said of any previous generation.

Alas, what we do with it is often discouraging enough. The natural scenery may survive in its grander aspects; the great parks and monuments have been preserved and are appreciated yearly by increasing numbers of citizens. Elsewhere, however, the rash of cities spreads ominously from what were once tight and focused settlements; the roads bring their burden of stretched-out, undefined structures and habitations. These suburbs are strip cities, seen from within, bear out the disturbing impression gained from the sky: too often they are defilements of the natural scene, wasteful desecrators of what have been free space and green land.

On sentimental journeys, on campaigns and outings of a summer season, the Americans show themselves still affectingly aware of the values implicit in a noble environment. If only they could heed as attentively the landscape which surrounds them through the rest of the year! It is one thing, they seem to feel, to retreat into the silence and loneliness of a forest (at least as much silence and loneliness as their ever increasing numbers afford)—but another thing to expect beauty or fitness in their everyday surroundings. They want a national park three thousand miles away; they do not seem to care—or to care enough—if there is no park to which they can motor on a Sunday, or one to which they can walk in their lunch hour. They want the wilderness to be forever wild; but they seem unheeding if the roadsides are forever cluttered with billboards.

Judged by the apparent attitude of too many present-day Americans, there is doubt whether we shall ever be able to extricate ourselves from a descending spiral of ugliness and irrationality. What is required is readiness to undertake on a large scale the kind of public works which are truly *public*—in the sense that they serve the highest interests of the citizenry; and truly *works*—in the sense that they are made to endure and to be judged by future generations. Yet it is this kind of undertaking for which it is often most difficult to muster support among the people. No foreign threat is so intangible but it can evoke a readiness to sacrifice and even a positive enthusiasm for the ordeal. No project, however costly or tenuous its returns, will be seriously challenged by the public if it can be shown that undertaking it will increase our material power. But if it is proposed that something be done by the people for their own delight and for the enhancement of their common life, a dead silence ensues. If someone suggests elegance in a public building, the matter is hushed up as if it were a scandal.

We have been prepared to call on the best architects in the country when it has been a matter of building abroad. The embassies and consulates that have been constructed in various countries over the past decade remind us what the United States can do—and what government can do—when it sets beauty and excellence as a goal. The cultural center built by the nation for the people of West Berlin shows that we are not unmindful of the value of a setting in which great public events can be fittingly held. At home, however, the story is different. We still wait to see accomplished a national cultural center in Washington. We might well feel impelled to ask, in regard to our own public buildings, whether we consider ourselves to be so backward or uncivilized that we cannot enjoy the kind of beauty which we prepare for others.

We feel impelled to ask such a question—and yet in some dim way we sense an answer more hopeful than the face of things might seem to warrant. For there is certainly an influence taking shape which promises for the America of tomorrow a more sane appreciation of the true values which make a civilization. The environment can be man's greatest work of art; and it cannot be that while we strive for excellence and beauty in specific forms of culture—in painting, in sculpture, in literature, in poetry and music—we shall permanently minimize the significance of the outward world which surrounds us from our birth and insensibly makes us what we are.

Yet I would remind you in closing of the other side of the coin. It would be all too easy to fall from the error of underestimating the importance of beauty in the environment to the opposite error, assuming that environment by itself creates men and citizens. In *The City in History*, that monumental book which has just won for Lewis Mumford the National Book Award, the author has some interesting things to say about the outward aspect of Athens in the classic age of Pericles and Plato. The picture we have in our minds, he says, is of a town with "a marmoreal chastity, a purity and rationality." This did not exist in fact. If the *polis* existed in this form it was afterwards, in the third century B.C., when the impetus of the great age had been spent and men were settling down into an existence no longer fired by ardor and creativeness.

The Greek mind at the top of its bent possessed, besides its love of abstract perfection and its strong inner order, "the violent, tormented and irrational aspects . . . one finds in the tragic dramatists or in the rude horseplay and barnyard smut one encounters in Aristophanes." The Greek city reflected all this.

No one has been more scathing than Mr. Mumford in his denunciation of modern ugliness; yet Athens, he reminds us, kept in the period when life was at its highest development a "casual jumble and sprawl." "The visible, tangible city," Mr. Mumford tells us, "was full of imperfections: the disorders of growth, the fermentations and secretions of life, the unburied refuse of outlived forms, not yet decently removed, the relics of rural ways not yet adjusted to the continued ordeals and challenges of urban life." Yet the Acropolis crowned it all, its serene form reaching above the town below, finding completion as part of the landscape of rock and blue sky.

In this tension between the old and new, between the perfection of the isolated form on the hill and the seething city below—between, as it were, earth and sky—Greek life found its moment of fulfillment. When that moment passed, Mr. Mumford tells us, "buildings began to take the place of men."

Let us make sure, as we build for ourselves, that men and their cities prove of equal worth. It is not, after all, only beauty itself, but also the striving for beauty that lifts up men and makes a civilization. We shall strive in our own way, as this second half of the century moves toward its meridian. Who shall say that the striving will not bring its own rewards? Who shall know where the greatest achievement will ultimately lie—within ourselves, or upon the enduring face of the things we have created?

# Scientific Statesmanship[2]

Barry Commoner

*Born May 28, 1917, Brooklyn, NY; A.B., Columbia University, 1937; M.A., 1938, Ph.D., 1941, Harvard University; instructor, Queens College, 1940-42; U.S. Naval Reserve, 1942-46; associate editor,* Science Illustrated, *1946-47; associate professor, 1947-53, professor, 1953-65, chairman, 1965-66, Washington University; director, Center for the Biology of Natural Systems, 1966–; author,* Science and Survival *(1974),* The Politics of Energy *(1979),* Making Peace with the Planet *(1990).*

## Editor's introduction

Professor Barry Commoner, who is considered one of the elders of the environmental movement, asserted that because of the rapid advance of technology, "we can no longer exert a sufficient mastery of our environment." According to Commoner, technology has allowed us to interfere with the very processes of the natural world, without giving us any knowledge of the consequences of such interference. Regrettably, many of those consequences may be irreversible. It follows that Commoner believes that citizens, not scientists, "must serve as the final arbiters of social good." This can only become a reality if those citizens are willing to learn and understand the many effects of technological advancement.

---

That science should require the guidance of statesmanship and statesmanship the discipline of science is a special mark of these disjointed times. Science, which is at its source an encounter of a single mind with the stern reality of nature, would appear to have no cause to weigh the wisdom of its inevitable course. The affairs of state, which are guided by values that are remote from natural law, have seemingly little need for the discipline of science.

Why then have science and statesmanship become—as they now are—so closely intertwined? Seventy years ago Pasteur could advise students, "Whatever your career may be, do not let yourselves be discouraged by the sadness of certain hours that pass over nations. Live in the serene peace of laboratories and libraries." Why has the serenity of the laboratories been swept away by intruding social problems? Why has the discipline of science now intervened in the councils of state? Where in this tangled design lies the duty of the scientist to society, to science, to himself?

The answer, I believe, lies in understanding the paradoxical effects of scientific progress on the welfare of man. Nowhere is this paradox more acutely revealed than in the problem of environmental pollution.

This conference is concerned with finding ways to free the air of its growing burden of pollution. That such a conference should be necessary at this time sharply illuminates the conflicting effects of science on society.

We are living in a time of astonishing scientific progress. Scientific research has become a powerful tool for analyzing the natural world, from the depths of the earth to the outer reaches of space. Evidence of its success—the wonderful harvest of technological applications—is all around us: space vehicles, nuclear power, numerous new synthetic chemicals, great improvements in the practice of agriculture, medical advances which have significantly increased the length and usefulness of human life.

But we also see some sharp contrasts. At this moment, in some other city, a group may be meeting to consider how to provide air for the

[2]Delivered at the National Conference on Air Pollution, in Washington, D.C., on December 10, 1962. Reprinted with permission of Barry Commoner.

first human inhabitants of the moon. Yet, we are meeting here because we have not yet learned how to manage our lives without fouling the air that man must continue to breathe on mother earth. We hear of masterful schemes for using nuclear explosions to extract pure water from the moon; but in some American cities the water that flows from the tap is no longer an entirely palatable fluid, and the householder will find it instead in bottles on the market shelf. Science in 1962 is radiant with far-flung success, and—it would seem—clouded by growing difficulties in providing for the necessities of life.

Why should this be so? Is the pollution of the air that we breathe and of the water that we drink only a passing imperfection in human society? Or is it a more serious matter—a warning that despite all the new powers of science, or perhaps because of them, we can no longer exert a sufficient mastery of our environment?

Air pollution is only one of a number of new and unwelcome problems: the pollution of water, not only by human waste, but by synthetic chemicals; unwanted loss of animals and plants, and possible health hazards from widespread dissemination of pesticides and herbicides; confusion about tolerable levels of chemical food additives; the hazards of radioactive wastes from nuclear reactors and of fallout from nuclear explosions.

These problems have in common a set of relationships to science, and a troublesome involvement in public controversy.

1. Each of these difficulties is a result of scientific and technological progress. The new synthetic chemicals, which are the fruits of remarkable advances in chemical technology since World War II appear in a multitude of useful forms—but also as pollutants of air and water. The development, just twenty years ago, of self-sustained nuclear reactions has given us not only new weapons and sources of power—but radioactive debris as well.

2. Many of these problems seem to crop up unexpectedly. The photochemical conversion of hydrocarbons, which produces smog, was discovered not in a chemical laboratory but in the air over Los Angeles, long after the technological practices that disseminated the hydrocarbons were well entrenched in our economic life. The resistance of synthetic detergents to bacterial degradation was apparently discovered only when the resultant accumulation in water supplies became noticeable, by which time detergents were already a common household item. The absorption of certain radioisotopes in the human body became known only some years after the establishment of massive programs of nuclear testing. All of these problems have been imposed on us—sometimes with a considerable surprise—well after the causative activity was in full swing.

3. It is also characteristic of the pollution problem—whether of air, water or food—that the most serious difficulties arise in the realm of biology. Unfortunately, the processes which are the biological targets of modern pollutants are singularly intractable to scientific analysis. The hazards from certain air pollutants and from radioactive wastes are due to the possibility that they may induce cancers. The origin of cancerous growth and the mode of action of chemicals and radiation in promoting it, remain, of course, one of the great unsolved problems of modern science. The mechanism of action of DDT on insects, or its effects in mammals are poorly understood. Despite very considerable investigation the basic mechanism of plant growth, with which the new synthetic herbicides interact, remains unknown.

There is, then, a remarkable incongruity between the two ways in which science enters into modern pollution problems. On the one hand scientific research has produced chemical and radioactive pollutants hitherto absent from the surface of the earth. But at the same time modern science appears to be poorly prepared to understand the particular biological damage that these new materials may cause.

The recent history of the sciences reveals some of the reasons for these conflicting consequences of scientific progress. Nuclear technology results from laboratory experiments on fission reactions first reported some thirty years ago; and behind this discovery lay the great revolution in our basic understanding of the structure of matter which took place at the turn of the century. One reason for the remarkable growth in the number of synthetic organic chemicals is that chemical engineering, which was once an empirical technology has now become firmly based on the theoretical knowledge of the mechanisms of chemical reactions—which is in turn elucidated by the new physical theories.

While physics and chemistry and its technological offshoots have been radically reformed by the theoretical revolution that began about fifty years ago, biology—or at least those areas related to the effects of the new pollutants—has proven to be considerably more resistant to change. Anyone who wishes to be convinced of this, need only compare the present textbooks of physics, chemistry and biology with those of, let us say, twenty-five years ago. A twenty-five-year-old text in organic chemistry is a densely packed summary of empirical knowledge about a vast array of organic reactions; but the modern text is a logically organized consideration of the electronic structures of atoms and molecules, and describes how this knowledge can guide the chemist in controlling reactions and in synthesizing new molecules to specification. On the other hand, current textbook discussions of the physiology of plant growth, or of the mechanism of carcinogenesis, while they may be couched in the language of present fads in experimentation lead to the same final answer offered by a twenty-five-year-old text: The mechanism of growth, whether of plants or of neoplasms, remains unknown.

If basic theories of physics had not attained their present power we would not be confronted with massive dissemination of man-made radioactive isotopes and synthetic chemicals. If biological theory had by now become sufficiently advanced to master the problems of normal and neoplastic growth we might be better prepared to cope with these modern pollutants. We are in difficulty because of a wide disparity between the present state of the physical and biological sciences.

Trouble arises because the separation of the laws of nature among the different sciences, is, of course, a human conceit; nature itself is an integrated whole. We classify nuclear explosions as experiments in physics, representing a step in a progression of growing knowledge about nuclear reactions. Yet every nuclear explosion is also a vast experiment in biology, but one which is only remotely connected with earlier biological research. Thus, modern physics was ready to detect strontium 90, to analyze its nuclear structure and to understand its origin in the fission reaction. In contrast, modern biology was quite unprepared for the entry of strontium 90 on the scene, for until the fallout problem revealed the necessity for such studies, *normal* strontium metabolism was an almost completely neglected subject.

The same pattern can be found in most of our pollution problems. The development of highly efficient new insecticides reflects an impressive mastery of chemical synthesis and of methods of dissemination. But the intrusion of a new insecticide into the biosphere may lead to rude surprises.

The current debate about insecticides reminds me of my own education in this matter. During World War II, I served as project officer in the Navy's development of aircraft dispersal of DDT—which proved to be of great importance in the Pacific battles. The project made meticulous studies of aerosol production, aerodynamic distribution, insect kill, meteorological effects, and problems of flying tactics. Toward the end of our work, when we were justifiably proud of a system ready for fleet operations, we received a request for help from an experimental rocket station on a strip of island beach off the New Jersey coast. Urgent experimental work was severely hampered by flies; would the Navy please get rid of them. We doused the island with DDT. Within half a day the beach became a flyless paradise and the rocketeers went about their work with renewed vigor. But a week later they were on the telephone again. A mysterious epidemic had littered their beach with tons of decaying fish—and all the flies in New Jersey had come to enjoy the fun. This is how I learned that DDT kills fish.

I believe that the history of modern pollution problems shows that most of them result from the same general fault. We have been massively intervening in the natural world, without being aware of many of the biological consequences until the act has been performed, and its effects—which are difficult to understand, and sometimes irreversible—are upon us. We can produce and widely disseminate radioisotopes, but do not fully comprehend how they will affect life. We can synthesize and disseminate a marvelous variety of synthetic chemicals before we have sufficiently mastered what they will do in a living organism. Like the sorcerer's apprentice, our education is dangerously incomplete.

It will be argued, I know, that this is nothing new—that it is the grand purpose of science to move into unknown territory, to explore and to discover. It can be said that similar risks have been taken before, and that science and technology cannot move forward without taking some risks.

But these arguments overlook an important element which *is new.* In the past, the risks taken in the name of scientific progress—boiler explosions on the first riverboats, or the early experiments with X-rays—were restricted to a small place and a brief time. But the processes which we now strive to master are neither local nor brief in their effects. Air pollution covers vast urban areas. Fallout is world-wide. Synthetic chemicals may remain in the soil for years. Radioactive pollutants now in the biosphere will be found there for generations, and in the case of carbon 14 for thousands of years. The size and persistence of possible errors has grown with the expanding power of modern science.

One can also argue that the hazards of modern pollutants are small compared to the dangers associated with other human enterprises—such as automotive traffic. But no estimate of the actual harm that may be done by smog fallout or chemical residues can obscure the sober realization that the risk was taken before it was fully understood. The importance of these issues to science lies not so much in the technical difficulty of estimating the associated hazards, but in that they warn of an incipient abdication of one of the major duties of science—prediction and control of human interventions into nature. The true measure of the danger is not represented by the present hazard, but by the disasters that will surely be visited upon us if we dare to enter the new age of science that lies before us without repairing this basic fault in the scientific enterprise.

Having examined some of the scientific difficulties associated with modern pollution, what can be said about the scientist's relationship to the social problems that follow in their wake? Each of the issues that I have mentioned has been marked by public confusion and controversy, severe legislative debate and enormous administrative difficulties. They represent a veritable jungle in which science, industry, economics, local politics, foreign affairs, religion and morality intermix in uproarious confusion. No scientist who enjoys the quiet of his laboratory or the reasonableness and objectivity of scientific discourse, is likely to walk into this wilderness voluntarily—or to emerge from it unscathed.

That thousands of scientists—including those present at this conference—have been willing to devote their skill and energy to bring order out of this chaos reflects, I believe, the serious impact which these problems have had on the inner life of science.

In no area has there been a more serious concentration of effort than in the problem of low-level radiation from fallout, particularly under the aegis of the United States Public Health Service. The recent history of this issue provides a clear picture of how the social problems emerge from scientific ones and can illuminate some general aspects of environmental pollution as a whole.

Until a few years ago the possible effects of low-level radiation were guided by the assumption that doses below a particular level would cause no discernible medical effects. Since the estimation of the threshold dose is a purely scientific matter it was possible for groups of scientists, such as the International Committee for Radiation Protection, to deliberate on the problem and recommend some permissible level of radiation which ought not to be exceeded if medical hazard is to be avoided.

However, evidence has since accumulated which suggests that one cannot safely assume any threshold in the relationship between radiation dosage and the resultant biological effects. Consequently, beginning in 1958 scientific agencies charged with the responsibility of setting radiation protection standards uniformly adopted the assumption that any increment in radiation exposure, however slight, is accompanied by a comparable increase in the risk of medically undesirable effects. If this is the case, and there is no *absolutely* safe limit, how can one determine what dosage is to be tolerated?

This judgment requires a balance between the risk associated with a given dosage and some possibly countervailing benefit. The agency now responsible for setting radiation standards in the United States, the Federal Radiation Council, has explicitly stated this position.

"If . . . beneficial uses were fully exploited without regard to radiation protection, the resulting biological risk might well be considered too great. Reducing the risk to zero would virtually eliminate any radiation use, and result in the loss of all possible benefits. It is therefore necessary to strike some balance between maximum use and zero risk. In establishing radiation protection standards, the balancing of risk and benefit is a decision involving medical, social, economic, political and other factors. Such a balance cannot be made on the basis of a precise mathematical formula but must be a matter of informed judgment." [Report No. 1, May 13, 1960.]

This approach is, I believe, equally applicable to most other pollution problems. Since they are all large-scale effects and influence a wide variety of living organisms, on statistical grounds alone, it is probable that the smallest detectable pollutant level represents some hazard, however slight, and that the risk will increase roughly with the level.

What is the proper role of the scientists in such a judgment? What *scientific* procedure can determine, for example, whether the benefits to the national interest of nuclear testing outweigh the hazards of fallout? What is the "importance" of fallout, determined scientifically? Some scientists have stated, with the full dignity of their scientific pre-eminence, that the fallout hazard while not zero is "trivial." Nevertheless I have seen a minister upon learning for the first time that acts deliberately performed by his own nation were possibly endangering a few lives in distant lands and a future time, become so incensed at this violation of the biblical injunction against the poisoning of wells, as to make an immediate determination to oppose nuclear testing. What science can gauge the relative validity of these conflicting responses to the same facts?

How can scientific method determine whether the proponents of urban superhighways or those who complain about the resultant smog are in the right? What scientific principle can tell us how to make the choice—forced upon us by the insecticide problem—between the shade of the elm tree and the song of the robin?

Stated in this form, the answer to these questions becomes apparent. Certainly science can validly describe what is known about the information to be gained from a nuclear experiment, the economic value of a highway, or the hazard of radioactive contamination or of smog. The statement will usually be hedged with uncertainty, and the proper answer may sometimes be: "We don't know"; but in any case these separate questions do belong within the realm of science. However, the choice of the balance point between benefit and hazard is a value judgment; it is based on ideas of social good, on morality or religion—*not on science.*

There can be no scientific agreement on such judgments; answers will differ according to religious or political outlook. Scientists who present their own judgments on these matters as though they *were* scientific evaluations are simply forcing a disagreement which can never be resolved by scientific means. Such a disagreement appears as a perplexing exception to scientists' vaunted skill at winning truth. The citizen will be driven to ask a question which is now heard with increasing frequency, "How do we know which scientist is telling the truth?" This doubt can only impair confidence in the validity of the excellent methods which science possesses for getting at the truth—about scientific questions.

In the "informed judgment" of which the Federal Radiation Council so properly speaks, the scientist can justly claim to be "informed," but in my opinion he can make no valid claim for a special competence in "judgment." To act otherwise, is to corrupt the meaning of science and to undermine its usefulness to society.

I believe that once the scientific evidence has been stated, or its absence made clear, the establishment of a level of tolerance for a modern pollutant is a *social* problem and must be resolved by social processes. In these processes the scientist has one vote and no claim to leadership beyond that given to *any* person who has the gift of moving his fellow men. But the government official, whose task is to make these judgments, and the citizen—who must provide the social ideology which guides administrative decision—require for these purposes the necessary facts and the relevant evaluations. Where these are matters of science, the scientist as the custodian of this knowledge has a profound duty to impart as much of it as he can to his fellow citizens. But in doing so he must guard against false pretensions, and avoid claiming for science that which belongs to the conscience.

In this discussion I have tried to show that the scientific and social difficulties that encumber the problems of modern pollution reflect a basic flaw in the present relations between science and social processes. We have not yet learned how to apply modern science in a manner which is consistent with its enormous power and its present inadequacies. We have not yet learned to discern in these complex problems, the proper roles of scientific knowledge and social judgment.

It seems to me that until effective means for dealing with these questions are developed we will be in continuous danger from unanticipated and poorly understood hazards, which will grow in magnitude as the power of science advances. If we are to live securely with the new discoveries and inventions of modern science, we shall need as well new inventions to govern the relation between science and society.

Although the task of developing such new procedures is formidable, there are some useful guidelines in our recent experience. I believe, for example, that the scientific community might have done a great deal to mitigate the present conflicts about insecticides, fallout and smog, if it had applied the customary principles of scientific inquiry to these problems *at the right time.* Clearly, the decisive time to evaluate the risks associated with a new technological program is *before* it is put into effect. The longer such an evaluation is delayed, the less its value to society, for once the process has become embedded in a vast economic or political commitment, it may be nearly impossible to alter.

In this task, the scientist's duty is plain, for it is no different from his responsibilities toward the development of all scientific knowledge. The scientist must examine all the evidence and summarize it in a statement of what is known, what is assumed, what is doubtful, and what is possibly erroneous. He must also describe the limits of the relevant knowledge, for these will reveal what new knowledge is needed and indicate when a proposed technological application may expose us to the dangers of acting in ignorance.

I make this proposal quite conscious of the obstacles which may block scientific evaluation of risks and benefits *in advance* of a proposed technological innovation. Perhaps the most serious of these is that the Government's military or political necessities, or an industry's competitive position may dictate secrecy. A recent scholarly review of the toxicology of herbicides, written to enlighten the scientific community and to encourage new work on this difficult problem states in its opening paragraph:

"Many of the toxicological data underlying assessment of the risks involved by using them [weed killers] in practice originate from confidential, nonpublished reports placed at the disposal of the authorities concerned. Such data have not been included in the present survey." [Dalgaard-Mikkelsen and Poulsen, *Pharmacological Reviews*, v. 14, no. 2. Je. '62.]

We pay a steep price for this kind of secrecy. Scientific knowledge is not created whole in one man's mind, or even in the deliberations of a committee. Each separate scientific analysis yields an approximate result and inevitably contains some errors and omissions. Science gets at the truth by a continuous process of self-correction, which remedies omissions and corrects errors. In this process, the key elements are open disclosure of results, their general dissemination in the community of scientists and the resultant verification, criticism and correction. Anything that blocks this process will hamper the approach to the truth. The basic difficulty with secrecy in science is that mistakes made in secret will persist. Every attempt to keep a scientific problem secret is paid for in the most expensive currency in the world—knowledge.

Science has great power to serve society. But it cannot properly perform this function if deprived of access to the facts. The time has come, I believe, for Government and industry alike to consider with great care the relative benefits and risks associated with the avoidance of full and early disclosure of scientific evidence relevant to large-scale processes that may result in environmental pollution. I believe that the present confusion and controversy about these problems is part of the price paid for secrecy, and in my opinion the price is uneconomical for both industry and the nation.

It should be possible, I believe, to find ways of bringing the full force of scientific knowledge—which is something that only the total community of scientists possesses—to bear on these problems. An important first step might be the organization, *in advance* of any large-scale technological innovation of an open *scientific inquiry* to consider the state of knowledge about the associated benefits and hazards. This, or any other, procedure must be established soon, for new proposals are being advanced constantly. Suggestions have been made for the use of mutagenic (and therefore also carcinogenic) chemicals for controlling insects by inducing sterilization. This may entail new biological hazards. Surely the scientific community can arrange to discuss these openly and widely *before* the proposal is put into effect.

If we develop such new means for orderly consideration of the problems of environmental pollution they will have a much wider usefulness. Consider, for example, a proposal which is about to be considered by the Government to develop airliners designed to fly at two or three times the speed of sound. Such an airliner flying across the United States will produce in a zone twenty-five miles wide a continuous series of intense sonic booms. Where in our social processes have we weighed whatever benefit is involved in traveling from coast to coast in two hours against the hazards associated with the effects of sonic booms?

I can report that in my own city the resolution of this balance has taken a rather curious form. For a period of weeks earlier this year St. Louis endured sonic booms sometimes at hourly intervals and often in the small hours of the night. The hazards were clear: The Air Force was besieged with claims for broken windows, cracked walls and fallen ceilings. Citizens complained about children awakened or frightened while awake. Protests began to mount, but not enough to counterbalance the military benefits of the flights—for they continued. I offer as a possibly useful piece of evidence regarding the weight to be accorded such benefits and hazards that when two gazelles in the St. Louis Zoo became so startled one night as to die in the ensuing upset—the flights were abruptly halted.

Is this the proper measure of the sonic boom hazard? Do we know enough about the number of babies that will be awakened every night by a supersonic airliner to make an "informed judgment" on its social usefulness? Do we really understand the physiological effects of the rather sudden compression associated with a sonic boom to be capable of evaluating the basic medical hazard? If these factors are not yet understood how can a Government agency, or the citizen, make the necessary informed judgment? If we invest nearly $1 billion in an airliner before we have determined whether its social usefulness will outweigh its social harm, will the step become thereby an irreversible one? Surely we need a scientific inquiry into this project before it is committed to action.

But no amount of advance information will suffice if it is not in the hands of those who must serve as the final arbiters of social good—the citizens. Can this be done? Can we expect our citizens to comprehend the benefits and hazards of nuclear reactions? Can they understand the relationship between hydrocarbons, sunlight and smog?

I am convinced that this is possible—providing citizens accept the duty to learn, and scientists accept the duty to teach. The task will not be an easy one, but I believe that we have the resources at hand. This vast educational task is not one that ought to be delegated alone to those scientists who have already devoted their professional energies to the problems of environmental pollution. These problems are so large and range so widely across the spectrum of science, that *all* scientists, regardless of their immediate professional interest are intimately concerned with them. Pollution of the environment touches the work of every meteorologist, ecologist, or chemist; the possible hazards are of interest to every biochemist and to every specialist in the biological and medical sciences.

Knowledge of these problems, and the willingness to explain them to the public, should, I believe, be the responsibility of each of the more than 100,000 scientists of this nation. Given this army of teachers, which is available to almost every community in the country, this educational task can surely be accomplished. Already in a number of cities, groups of scientists are educating their fellow citizens about radiation problems; I believe that given adequate support and the broad participation of all scientists, such groups should be capable of expanding their work to encompass the broad range of problems of environmental pollution.

Nor should we be discouraged by the difficulties and disagreements that now burden these problems. The attention which these controversies generate can serve as a timely warning that we must learn—now, before the hazards of unwitting action overtake us—how to live in the new world that science is creating. Science has placed enormous new powers at the hand of man. If we accept with these powers, the new responsibilities which must govern their use, science can serve its true goal—the welfare of man.

# A Theology of the Earth[3]

Rene Dubos

*Born February 20, 1901, Saint-Brice-sous-Forêt, France; died February 20, 1982; B.S., Institut National Agronomique, 1921; professor, Harvard Medical School, 1942-44; Ph.D., Rutgers University, 1927; professor, Rockefeller University, 1927-82; co-winner of Pulitzer Prize in nonfiction, 1969; director, State University of New York College, 1971; author,* Bacterial and Mycotic Infections of Man *(1948),* Mirage of Health *(1959),* Pasteur and Modern Science *(1960),* The Dreams of Reason *(1961),* The Touch of Life *(1962),* The Cultural Roots and the Social Fruits of Science *(1963),* The Unseen World *(1962),* Man Adapting *(1965),* Health and Disease *(1965),* Man, Medicine, and Environment *(1968),* So Human an Animal *(1968),* A God Within *(1972),* Only One Earth *(1972),* Celebrations of Life *(1981).*

## Editor's introduction

Rene Dubos, an experimental pathologist at Rockefeller University in New York and discoverer of the first commercially produced antibiotic, called upon citizens to "reject the attitude which asserts that man is the only value of importance and that the rest of nature can be sacrificed to his welfare and whims." Dubos further asserted that we should balance our own needs with a concern for "the health of nature." For Dubos, humanity and the environment are inextricably linked, and to harm one is to harm the other.

---

Ladies and gentlemen, the title of this lecture would be pretentious if it did not express profound feelings that I experienced a few months ago at the time of the Apollo 8 mission. Shortly after the return to earth of Apollo 8 the science editor of the Columbia Broadcasting System, Earl Ubell, interviewed the crew over the CBS network. Through skillful and persistent questioning he tried to extract from the astronauts what had been their most profound impression during their trip through space. What turned out was that their deepest emotion had been to see the earth from space. The astronauts had been overwhelmed by the beauty of the earth as compared with the bleakness of space and the grayness of the moon.

On the whole, I have been rather skeptical concerning the scientific value of the man-in-space program. But, while listening to the Apollo 8 crew, I became interested in that effort because I felt that it would pay unexpected dividends—namely, make us objectively aware, through our senses as it were, of the uniqueness of the earth among other bodies in the sky.

The incredible beauty of the earth as seen from space results largely from the fact that our planet is covered with living things. What gives vibrant colors and exciting variety to the surface of the earth is the fact that it is literally a living organism. The earth is living by the very fact that the microbes, the plants, the animals, and man have generated on its surface conditions that occur nowhere else, as far as we know, in that part of the universe that we can hope to reach. The phrase "theology of the earth" thus came to me from the Apollo 8 astronauts' accounts of what they had seen from their space capsule, making me realize that the earth is a living organism.

My presentation will be a mixture of the emotional response of my total being to the beauty of the earth, and of my mental processes as a scientist trying to give a rational account of the earth's association with living things. The phrase "theology of the earth" thus denotes for

[3]Delivered at the Smithsonian Institution, in Washington, D.C., on October 2, 1969. Reprinted with permission of The Smithsonian Institution.

me the scientific understanding of the sacred relationships that link mankind to all the physical and living attributes of the earth.

I shall have to touch on many different topics because I want to convey my belief that we have collectively begun to engage in a kind of discovery of ourselves—who we are, where we belong, and where we are going. A few lines from T. S. Eliot in his poem *Four Quartets* seems to me the ultimate expression of what I shall try to express emotionally and to analyze scientifically:

"We shall not cease from exploration
And the end of all our exploring
Will be to arrive where we started
And know the place for the first time."

All archaic peoples, all ancient classical cultures, have practiced some form of nature religion. Even in our times a large number of isolated, primitive tribes in Australia, in Africa, and in South America still experience a feeling of holiness for the land in which they live. In contrast, respect for the earth and for nature has almost completely disappeared from industrialized people in most of the countries that have accepted the ways of Western civilization.

Primitive religion, with its sense of holiness of the environment, was always linked with magic. It is easy to understand how there can be links between primitive religious beliefs and the attempts to control nature through the mysterious influences of the world. Even though they always have coexisted among primitive people, religion and magic represent two very different kinds of attitudes.

In the words of the anthropologist Malinowsky: "Religion refers to the fundamental issues of human existence while magic turns round specific, concrete and practical problems."

Most of my remarks this evening will be based on the conviction that the ecological crisis in the modern world has its root in our failure to differentiate between the use of scientific technology as a kind of modern magic and what I shall call modern religion, namely, knowledge as it relates to man's place in the universe and, especially, his relation to the earth.

All ancient peoples personified a locality or a region with a particular god or goddess that symbolized the qualities and the potentialities of that place. Phrases such as "the genius of the place" or "the spirit of the place" were commonly used in the past. All followers of ancient cultures were convinced that man could not retain his physical and mental health and fulfill his destiny unless he lived in accordance with the traditions of his place and respected the spirit of that place. I believe it was this attitude that helped ancient peoples to achieve rich and creative adjustment to their surroundings. Now you may say: "Spirit of place; genius of place? This is no longer for us. We are far too learned and sophisticated."

Yet, rationalistic and blasé as we may be, we still feel, deep in our hearts, that life is governed by forces that have their roots in the soil, in the water, and in the sky around us. The last part of Lawrence Durrell's book *Spirit of Place* deals with this very topic. There is not one among us who does not sense a deep meaning in phrases such as "the genius of New England" or "the spirit of the Far West." We still sense that there is some kind of uniqueness to each place, each location, which gives it a very special meaning in our minds. But while we pine for the sense of holiness in nature, we do not know how to introduce this sense in our social structure. I am convinced that this has much to do with the ecological crisis.

I am not the first to express the feeling that we shall not be able to solve the ecological crisis until we recapture some kind of spiritual relationship between man and his environment. Some two years ago, for example, the learned American scholar Lynn White, Jr., a professor at the University of California in Los Angeles, delivered before the American Association for the Advancement of Science a special lecture titled "The Historical Roots of Our Ecologic Crisis." This lecture must strike a very sensitive chord in the minds of Americans because it has been reproduced again and again in several journals—ranging from *The Oracle*, the organ of the hippie movement in San Francisco, to the plush magazine *Horizon.* Among the many interesting and important things White says, I single out a particular item with which I disagree in part. He stated that, in his opinion, the lack of reverence for nature on the part of modern industrial man, especially in the United States, and the desecration of nature by technology are consequences of biblical teachings. He traced them to the first chapter of Genesis in which it is said that man and woman were given the right and the duty to replenish the earth, subdue it, and have dominion over all living things. According to White, this biblical teaching has had such a profound and lasting influence on Western civilization that it has made modern man lose any feeling for nature and to be concerned only with the conquest of nature for his own benefit. Also, White sees no hope of retracing our steps through science and technology because both exemplify the authority expressed in that statement in the first chapter of Genesis. The only solution to the ecological crisis, therefore, is to try to recapture the worshipful attitude that the monks of the Franciscan order had toward nature in the thirteenth century. The last sentence of White's lecture is, if my memory serves me right, "I propose Francis as a patron saint for ecologists."

All of us have some kind of sentimental, romantic sympathy with Lynn White's thesis. All of us are happy that there have been practical expressions of this attitude in the development of the national parks and in the attempts to preserve as much wildlife as possible. By preserving the state of certain wilderness areas, with their animals and plants, their rocks and marshes, mankind symbolizes that it has retained some form of respect for the natural world. In passing, it is not without interest that the United States—the country which has certainly been the most successful and has done the most toward achieving dominion over the earth through technology—is also the one country which is doing the most to save some fragments of wilderness. I wonder at times whether Glacier Park and Monument Valley do not represent a kind of atonement for God's own junkyard.

Despite my immense admiration for Lynn White's scholarship, I find it difficult to believe that the Judeo-Christian tradition has been as influential as he thinks in bringing about the desecration of the earth. One does not need to know much history to realize that the ancient Chinese, Greek, and Moslem civilizations contributed their share to deforestation, to erosion, and to the destruction of nature in many other ways. The goats of primitive peoples were as efficient as modern bulldozers in destroying the land. In any case, the Judeo-Christian attitude concerning the relation of man to nature is not expressed only in the first chapter of Genesis. The second chapter of Genesis states that man, after he had been placed in the Garden of Eden, was instructed by God to dress it and to keep it—a statement which has ecological implications. To dress and keep the land means that man must be concerned with what happens to it.

Man is rarely, if ever, just a worshiper of nature, a passive witness of its activities. He achieved his humanness by the very act of introducing his will into natural events. He became what he is while giving form to nature. For this reason I believe that ecologists should select St. Benedict as a much truer symbol of the human condition than Francis of Assisi. Most of you probably know little about St. Benedict, perhaps even less about the history of the Benedictine order. So allow me to elaborate on them for a few minutes because they represent a topic that is crucial to my personal attitude toward conservation.

St. Benedict created the first great monastery in the Western world on Monte Cassino, in Italy, in the sixth century. He must have been a wise man, because when he formulated the rules of conduct for Monte Cassino—rules which became a model for monastic life all over the world—he decided that the monks should not only pray to God but also should work. Moreover, he urged that the monastery be self-sufficient. The rule of work and the need for self-sufficiency led the Benedictine monks to master a multiplicity of practical arts, especially those relating to building and to architecture. The monks learned to manage the land in such a manner that it supplied them with food and clothing, and in such a manner that it retained its productivity despite intensive cultivation. Moreover, they developed an architecture which was lasting, well-suited to the country in which they lived as well as to their activities, and which for these reasons had great functional beauty. Those of you who have traveled over the world know that the Benedictine monasteries are marvels of medieval architecture.

It seems to me that the Benedictine rule implies ecological concepts which are much more in tune with the needs of the modern world than is the worshipful attitude of St. Francis. Perhaps most influential among the monks who followed the Benedictine rule were those of the Cistercian order. For reasons that I shall not discuss, the Cistercians established their monasteries in the lowlands and swamps; consequently, they had to learn to drain the land, and therefore they learned to use water power. And, through these technological practices, they converted areas of swamps and forests (that were not suitable for human habitation because of the prevalence of malaria) into wonderful fertile land which now makes up much of Europe's countryside.

If I have talked so long about St. Francis and St. Benedict it is not to give you a course in the history of medieval religion. Rather it is to illustrate two contrasting—but, I believe, equally important—attitudes toward nature: on the one hand, passive worship; on the other, creative intervention.

I have no doubt that the kind of worship symbolized by St. Francis helps man to retain his sanity by identifying himself with the totality of creation from which he emerged. Preserving the wilderness and all forms of wildlife is essential not only for esthetic and moral reasons but also for biological reasons.

Unfortunately, it will become increasingly difficult in the modern world to protect the wilderness from human use. In fact, no longer can there be any true wilderness. No fence is tight enough to shut out radiation clouds, air and water pollution, or noise from aircraft. Some ten or twenty years ago we could still escape from the insults of technological civilization by moving to the Rocky Mountains, to the Greek islands, or to the islands of the Pacific Ocean, but now the national parks and the isolated islands are almost as crowded and as desecrated as Coney Island. The only solution left to us is to improve Coney Island. In his short novel *Candide*, Voltaire pointed out that Candide discovered at the end of his adventures that the surest formula for happiness was to cultivate one's own garden. I believe that our Garden of Eden will have to be created in our own backyards and in the hearts of our cities. Just as the Benedictine monasteries had to apply, although empirically, ecological principles so as to remain self-supporting and viable, so must we learn to manage the earth in such a manner that every part of it becomes pleasant.

The achievements of the Cistercian monks serve to illustrate another aspect of modern ecologic philosophy. As I mentioned before, the swamps in which they established their monasteries were unfit for human life because of insects and malaria. But monastic labor, skill, and intelligence converted these dismal swamps into productive agricultural areas, many of which have become centers for civilization. They demonstrate that transforming of the land, when intelligently carried out, is not destructive but, instead, can be a creative art.

My speaking of medieval times in Europe was not meant to convey the impression that only then have there been great achievements in the management of the land. One need only look at the Pennsylvania Dutch country to see a striking demonstration of land that has been created out of the forest, that became highly productive, and that has been well preserved. One could cite many similar feats all over the world. But the tendency at present is to determine the use of lands and waters, mountains and valleys, only on the basis of short-range economic benefits. And yet one can safely assert that sacrificing ecological principles on the altar of financial advantage is the road to social disaster, let alone esthetic degradation of the countryside. I shall now present a few remarks about how we can create land. By this I mean taking nature as it is presented to us and trying to do with it something which is both suitable for human life and for the health of nature.

To do this it is essential that we identify the best "vocation" for each part of our spaceship. In Latin the word for "vocation" refers to the divine call for a certain kind of function. I wish we could apply this word, and indeed I shall apply it, to the different parts of the earth because each part of the earth has, so to speak, its vocation. It is our role as scientists, humanists, and citizens, and as persons who have a feeling for the earth, to discover the vocation of each part of it.

Certain parts of the earth, like certain persons, may have only one vocation. For example, there may be only one kind of thing that can be done with the Arctic country; there may be only a limited range of things that can be done with certain tropical lands. But in practice most places, like most persons, have several vocations, several options, and this indeterminism adds greatly to the richness of life. To illustrate with a few concrete examples what I have in mind, I ask that you consider what has happened to the primeval forest in the temperate parts of the world. I am not going to speak about the tropics, I am only going to speak of western Europe and the United States—the two parts of the world that I know best.

Much of the primeval forest in temperate countries has been transformed into farmland, but what is interesting is that each part of this primeval forest transformed into farmland has acquired its own agricultural specialization, social structure, and esthetic quality. On the other hand, the temperate forest need not become agricultural land. In Scotland and eastern England such lands progressively were transformed into moors—the famous moor country of the Scottish Highlands and eastern England. This happened largely through lumbering activities and also through the sheep grazing of the Benedictine monks. The moors are not very productive from the agricultural point of view, but their charm has enriched the life of Great Britain and played a large part in literature. In North America, much of the primeval forest was transformed into prairie country as a result of the fires set by the preagricultural Indians. The prairies have now been converted in large part into agricultural land, but they have left a lasting imprint on American civilization.

I have quoted a few transformations of the land from one ecological state to another which have been successful, but I hasten to acknowledge that many other such transformations have not been as successful. Much of the country around the Mediterranean has been almost destroyed by erosion, and very little is left of the famous cedars of Lebanon. The transformation from one ecological state to another has given desirable results, especially where it has occurred slowly enough to be compatible with adaptive processes either of a purely biological nature or when it involved the adaptation of man to the new conditions. This is the case for the moors in Great Britain. In this case the creation of romantic moors out of forest land took a thousand years, so there was a chance for all the adjustments that always occur in nature, when there is enough time, to come about. Contrast this with what happened in many parts of the United States where massive and hasty lumbering has been responsible for ghost towns and for eroded land.

From now on most of the transformations of the earth's surface will occur so rapidly that we may often create those terrible situations resulting in erosion and destruction of the land. It therefore is urgent that we develop a new kind of ecological knowledge to enable us to predict the likely consequences of massive technological intervention, and to provide rational guides as substitutes for the spontaneous and empirical adjustments that centuries used to make possible.

I have spoken so far chiefly of the transformations of the forest into new ecological structures that have economic value. But utilitarian considerations are only one aspect of man's relation to the earth. The widespread interest in the preservation of wildlife and primeval scenery is sufficient evidence that man does not live by bread alone and wants to retain some contact with his distant origins. In practice, however, the only chance that most people have to experience and enjoy nature is by coming into contact with its humanized aspects—cultivated fields, parks, gardens, and human settlements. It is, of course, essential that we save the redwoods, the Everglades, and as much wilderness as possible, but it is equally important that we protect the esthetic quality of our farmland, and to use this image again, that we improve Coney Island.

I wish there were time to discuss at length the factors that make for a beautiful landscape. Clearly, there is a kind of magic splendor and magnitude which gives a unique quality to certain landscapes. The Grand Canyon, the Painted Desert, and Niagara Falls are examples of scenery to which man's presence never adds anything, and may detract a great deal. In most cases, however, the quality of the landscape consists, in a sense, of fitness between man and his surroundings. This fitness accounts for most of the charm of ancient settlements, not only in the Old World but in the New World as well. The river villages of the Ivory Coast in Africa, the Mediterranean hill towns, the pueblos of the Rio Grande, the village greens of New England, and all the old cities so well organized around peaceful rivers represent many different types of landscapes that derive their quality not so much from topographical or climatic peculiarities as from an intimate association between man and nature.

Among the many factors that play a role in the sense of identification between man and nature, let me just mention in passing how history and climate condition the architecture and the materials of dwellings and churches. Also, how the climate determines the shape and the botany of gardens and parks.

The formal gardens of Italy and France didn't just happen through accidents or through the fancy of some prince or wealthy merchant. These wonderful parks and gardens were successful because they fitted very well into the physical, biological, and social atmosphere of Italy and France at the time of their creation. Such formal parks and gardens also flourished in England, especially during the seventeenth century, but the English school achieved its unique distinction by creating an entirely different kind of park. The great and marvelous English parks of the late seventeenth and eighteenth centuries were characterized, as we all know, by magnificent trees grouped in meadows and vast expanses of lawn. This style was suited to the climate of the British Isles, to the abundance of rain, and to the fact that insolation is sufficiently limited to permit certain types of growth. In France many attempts were made in the eighteenth century to create gardens and parks in the English style. Except in a few cases, however, English-type parks and gardens were not very successful in France.

On this topic, there is an interesting letter of Horace Walpole, who was one of the prophets of the English landscape school. He traveled in France and after his return he expressed a critical opinion of the attempts to duplicate the English park on the Continent. "The French will never have lawns as good as ours until they have as rotten a climate," he wrote in a letter. This witticism expresses the biological truth that landscape styles can be lastingly successful only if they are compatible with the ecological imperatives of the countries in which they develop. This is what Alexander Pope summarized in his famous line, "In everything respect the genius of the place." The word "genius" here express the total characteristics and potentialities of a particular area.

We should have Horace Walpole's phrase in mind when we look at what is being done in our large cities toward creating parks and gardens. Just as the climate in France cannot produce the green magnificence of the English parks, so in general the atmosphere in most of our large cities is unable to support most plant species. This does not mean that plant life is out of place in our cities, only that much more effort should be made to identify and propagate for each particular city the kinds of trees, flowers, and ground cover that can best thrive under its own particular set of climatic and other constraints. When I look on New York City parks and notice how their ordinary grass can appear so pathetic, and when I see how monotonous row after row of plain trees can be, I feel that botanists and foresters should be encouraged to develop other plant species congenial to urban environment. This is a wonderful field for plant ecologists because, in the very near future, pioneers of plant ecology are likely to be much more needed in the city than in the wilderness.

To summarize my remarks, let me restate that the "genius" or the "spirit of the place" is made up of all the physical, biological, social, and historical forces which, taken together, give uniqueness to each locality. This applies not only to the wilderness but also to human settlements—Rome, Paris, London, Hamburg, New York, Chicago, San Francisco—and I have selected these cities as representatives of very different types. Each of these cities has a genius that transcends its geographical location, commercial importance, and population size. The great cities of the world contribute to the richness of the earth by giving it the wonderful diversity that man adds to the diversity of nature. The "genius of the place" will be found in every part of the world if we look for it.

In the final analysis the theology of the earth can be expressed scientifically in the form of an enlarged ecological concept. Since this theology will be formulated by human minds it inevitably will involve man's interplay with nature. We certainly must reject the attitude which asserts that man is the only value of importance and that the rest of nature can be sacrificed to his welfare and whims. But we cannot escape, I believe, an anthropocentric attitude which puts man at the summit of creation while still a part of it. Fortunately, one of the most important consequences of enlightened anthropocentricism is that man cannot effectively manipulate nature without loving nature for her own sake. And here I shall have to summarize a set of complex biological concepts in the form of general and dogmatic statements which, I hope, will convey to you some feeling of what I would have liked to state more scientifically.

It is not just a sentimental platitude to say that the earth is our mother. It is biologically true that the earth bore us and that we endanger ourselves when we desecrate her. The human species has been shaped biologically and mentally by the adaptive responses it has made to the conditions prevailing on the earth when the planet was still undisturbed by human intervention. Man was shaped biologically and mentally while responding to wild nature in the course of his evolution. The earth is our mother not only because she nurtures us now but especially because our biological and mental being has emerged from her, from our responses to her stimuli.

Furthermore, the earth is our mother in more than an evolutionary sense. In the course of our individual development from conception to death, our whole being is constantly influenced by the stimuli that reach us from the environment. In other words, we constantly are being modified by the stimuli that reach us from nature and also from what we have done to the earth. To a great extent, we therefore come to reflect what we create. I shall restate here a phrase of Winston Churchill's that I quoted two years ago in this very room: "We shape our buildings and afterward our buildings shape us."

This means that everything we create, good and bad, affects our development and, more importantly, affects the development of children. In his *Notes of a Native Son* James Baldwin expressed even more vividly the influence of our environment on our biological and mental characteristics. Here are three phrases:

"We cannot escape our origins however hard we try, those origins which contain the key, could we but find it, to all that we later become."

" . . . means something to live where one sees space and sky, or to live where one sees nothing but rubble or nothing but high buildings."

"We take our shape within and against that cage of reality bequeathed us at our birth."

In the light of the remarks that I have presented to you, I have come to a sort of general philosophy about the meaning of the word "conservation"; and it is with a brief statement of this philosophy that I end my presentation. Conservation programs, whether for wilderness or for man-made environments, usually are formulated and conducted as if their only concern were to the human species and its welfare. Yet they can be effective only if they incorporate another dimension, namely, the earth and her welfare. This is not sentimentality but hard biological science. Man and the earth are two complementary components of an indivisible system. Each shapes the other in a wonderfully creative symbiotic and cybernetic complex. The theology of the earth has a scientific basis in the simple fact that man emerged from the earth and then acquired the ability to modify it and shape it, thus determining the evolution of his own future social life through a continuous act of creation.

# The Planetary Crisis and the Challenge to Scientists[4]

Margaret Mead

*Born December 16, 1901, Philadelphia, PA; died November 15, 1978; B.A., Barnard College, 1923; M.A., 1924, Ph.D., 1929, Columbia University; curator, American Museum of Natural History, 1926-78; professor, Columbia University, 1954-78; professor, Fordham University, 1969-71; author,* Coming of Age in Samoa *(1928),* Growing Up in New Guinea *(1930),* The Changing Culture of an Indian Tribe *(1932),* Sex and Temperament in Three Primitive Societies *(1935),* Male and Female *(1949),* New Lives for Old *(1956),* People and Places *(1959),* Continuities in Cultural Evolution *(1964),* Culture and Commitment *(1970),* Rap on Race *(1971),* Twentieth Century Faith *(1972),* Blackberry Winter *(1972).*

## Editor's introduction

In this speech, celebrated anthropologist Margaret Mead spoke to some 600 people about the gasoline shortage occuring at the time the speech was given. Mead attempted to soothe the hysteria associated with the "energy crunch." She believed that the crisis was, first and foremost, a signal that the way we manage our natural resources must change. More tangibly, Mead asserted that we can no longer exist in the current state of dependency on motorized transportation. Mead supported an utter transformation in lifestyle so that the excessive creation of waste, so much a part of current existence, is eradicated.

---

This is a meeting of members of all the different disciplines included in the New York Academy of Sciences. The members of each discipline are laymen and laywomen to each other. So we meet as scientists, as concerned lay people, and as concerned citizen members of our national and our world communities. But we are gathered together tonight because of our membership in the scientific community. I speak to you as a longtime member of the Academy, and also as a representative of the scientists' information movement represented in the Scientists' Institute for Public Information (SIPI), which was fostered by the New York Academy of Sciences. I am assigning the award money from the Lehman Award which you have given me tonight, to SIPI, to symbolize my adherence to the belief which the scientists' information movement stands for—that it is the duty of the citizen to make major political decisions, but that it is the duty of the scientist to clarify for the public the complex issues which the development of science continually presents today. I speak to you also as an anthropologist who has been honored by the presence of many of my colleagues and by the site of this meeting, the American Museum of Natural History, where I have been a member of the Department of Anthropology since 1926.

The energy crunch, which is being felt around the world—in Japan, in Europe, in the United States—has dramatized for us a worldwide situation and a worldwide opportunity to take stock of how the reckless despoiling of the earth's resources—here in America and all over the world—has brought the whole world to the brink of disaster. It also provides the United States, its citizens, its Government, its scientists, and its leaders of business and labor with a magnificent opportunity to initiate a transfor-

[4]Delivered at the New York Academy of Science's annual meeting, in New York, New York, on December 6, 1973. Reprinted with permission of The New York Academy of Sciences.

mation in our present way of life. Our present way of life was conceived in a spirit of progress, in an attempt to improve the standard of living of all Americans through the increasing capability of technological development to bring previously undreamed of amenities within reach of the common man. But this search for a better life has—especially since World War II—taken a form which is untenable, and which this planet cannot support. The overdevelopment of motor transport, with its spiral of more cars, more cement highways, more pollution, more suburbs, more commuting, has contributed to the near destruction of our great cities, the disintegration of the family, the isolation of the old, the young, and the poor, and the pollution not only of local air, but also of the earth's atmosphere. Our terribly wasteful use of electricity and of nonrenewable resources are likewise endangering our rivers, our oceans, and the atmosphere which protects the planet.

The realization that a dramic transformation is needed has steadily increased. But the problem has been how to turn around? How to alter our dependence on motor transport? How to persuade the individual citizen enmeshed in a system in which he and his wife and children are imprisoned without one car, two cars, three cars, that change is possible? How to stop building enormous, uneconomical buildings which waste electricity night and day, all year round? How to break the deadlock between environmentalists, bent upon enacting immediate measures to protect an endangered environment, and industry, itself caught in the toils of a relentless compulsion to expand? How to alter our own course and not injure the young economies of the developing countries, desperate to obtain the barest necessities of food and water and light for their hungry millions, clamoring for one percent of our gross national pollution! Even though the present rate of development of energy use and resource use is only some twenty-five years old, it has been so much taken for granted in the industrialized countries that it has seemed almost impossible to turn around short of some major catastrophe . . . some catastrophe which would destroy millions of lives.

The catastrophe has now arrived, not in the form of the death of millions in an inversion over a large city, but in the energy crunch. The causes may be debated, will be debated: how much blame to assign to government mismanagement, how much to the recent war in the Middle East, how much to the action of the oil-producing countries for whom oil represents their only bargaining resource, how much to manipulation by companies that control oil, natural gas, coal, and the processing steps between producer and consumer, how much to the intention of producers to defeat environmental measures, how much to the maneuvers of exporting countries to strengthen their currencies. But in a more basic sense, these triggering events do not matter and focusing on them can in fact divert our attention from a much more important issue—how we are to take advantage of the crisis to move toward a way of life which will not destroy the environment and use up irreplaceable resources, not destroy large sections of the country by ripping off the surface of land in strip mining and by killing rivers, lakes, and the smaller seas like the Baltic and the Barents Seas. We can easily be diverted into acrimonious accusations instead of concentrating on what measures must be taken.

The crisis is here and some kind of crisis activities will be undertaken. Some measures have been taken. More are underway. But we have the opportunity to use the crisis to transform our own economy, to take the lead in a transformation which is needed right around the world, to aim not for a shallow independence but for a genuine responsibility. We must not be content with half measures, with small, mean palliatives, following the Administration's assurance that all that is needed is fewer Sunday drives to visit mother-in-law and lowered lights on Christmas trees—to be followed very soon by a return to normal waste and pollution. We must not return to complacency over a situation in which our major nutritional disease is *over*-nutrition, while millions of Americans are on the verge of starvation and while we are only 6 percent of the world's population, we are using 30 percent of available energy resources. The crisis can and must be used constructively.

During the inevitable disorganization of everyday life, business, industry, and education, we will be taking stands, making decisions, learning new habits and new ways of looking at things, and initiating new research into alternative technologies in transportation, agriculture, architecture, and town planning. It is vital that these activities move us forward into a new era, in which the entire nation is involved in a search for a new standard of living, a new quality of life, based on conservation not waste, on protection not destruction, on human values rather than built-in obsolescence and waste.

As scientists who know the importance of accurate information, we can press immediately for the establishment of an enquiry with subpoena power to ascertain from the energy industries the exact state of supplies and reserves in this country. As scientists, concerned with direction of research and the application of scientific knowledge to a technology devoted to human ends, we can press for a massive project on alternative and environmentally safe forms of energy—solar energy, fusion, other forms. Such a project should be as ambitious as the Manhattan Project or NASA, but there would be no need for secrecy. It would be aimed not at destroying or outdistancing other countries, but at ways of conserving our resources in new technologies which would themselves provide new activities for those industries whose present prosperity is based on oil and motor transport and energy-wasting, expensive synthetic materials.

Those of us who are social scientists have a special responsibility for the relationship between measures that are to be taken and the way in which the American people and American institutions will respond. For example, we have abundant information on the responses of Americans to rationing during World War II. If there is to be gasoline rationing, we have to consider the importance of built-in flexibility and choice. In the United States, a rationing system will only be experienced as fair and just if it discriminates among the needs of different users; recognizes that workers have to get to work, that many people work on Sundays, that different regions of the country will need different measures. Without rationing, we will set one set of users against another, one part of the country against another, encouraging such narrowly partisan measures as severance taxes through which oil-rich states will benefit at the expense of the residents of oil-less states. Rationing is a way of making the situation genuinely national, involving each American in the fate of all Americans.

But while some form of rationing or allotment—or the same procedure by some other name—will be necessary, it will be important to consider that the American people have experienced rationing only as a temporary measure in wartime or as an abhorrent practice of totalitarian countries. There will be danger that rationing may simply accentuate the desire to get back to normal again, with "normal" defined as where we were when the shortage hit us. What we need to do is to define all measures taken not as temporary but as *transitional* to a saner, safer, more human life style. How can we make the present period into a period of tooling up for smaller cars, rapid research, and preparation for entirely new forms of transportation, of utilities, of energy generators? Such mechanisms can be found. In the past, war, revolution, and depressions have provided the dire circumstances within which society's technologies and social institutions have been transformed.

Our present situation is unlike war, revolution, or depression. It is also unlike the great natural catastrophes of the past—famine, earthquake, and plague. Wars are won or lost, revolutions succeed or fail, depressions grind to an end, famine and plagues are over after millions have died. A country rebuilds, too often in the same spot, after an earthquake. The situation we are in is profoundly different. An interdependent, planetary, man-made system of resource exploitation and energy use has brought us to a state where long-range planning is crucial. What we need is not a return to our present parlous state, which endangers the future of our country, our children and our earth, but a movement forward to a new norm—so that the developed and the developing countries will be able to help each other. The developing countries have less obsolescence, fewer entrenched nineteenth century industrial forms to overcome; the developed countries have the scientists and the technologists to work rapidly and effectively on planetary problems.

This country has been reeling under the continuing exposures of loss of moral integrity and the revelation that ubiquitous lawbreaking, in which unenforceable laws involve every citizen, has now reached into the highest places in the land. There is a strong demand for moral reinvigoration and for some commitment that is vast enough and yet personal enough to enlist the loyalty of all. In the past it has been only in a war in defense of their own country and their own ideals that any people have been able to invoke total commitment—and then it has always been on behalf of one group against another.

This is the first time in history that the American people have been asked to defend themselves and everything that we hold dear *in cooperation* with all the other inhabitants of this planet, who share with us the same endangered air and the same endangered oceans. This time there is no enemy. There is only a common need to reassess our present course, to change that course and to devise new methods through which the whole world can survive. This is a priceless opportunity.

To grasp it, we need a widespread understanding of the nature of the crisis confronting us—and the world—a crisis that is no passing inconvenience, no byproduct of the ambitions of the oil-producing countries, no figment of environmentalists' fears, no byproduct of any present system of government—whether free enterprise, socialist or communist or any mixture thereof. What we face is the outcome of the inventions of the last four hundred years. What we need is a transformed life style which will be as different from our present wasteful, shortsighted, reckless use of the earth's treasures as the present twentieth century world is from the agrarian world of the past. This new life style can flow directly from the efforts of science and the capabilities of technology, but its acceptance depends on an overriding citizen commitment to a higher quality of life for the world's children and future generations on our planet.

# Can the World Be Saved?[5]

## Gus Speth

*Born March 4, 1942, Orangeburg, SC; B.A., Yale University, 1964; B.Litt, Balliol College, Oxford University, 1966; LL.B., Yale University, 1969; law clerk to Associate Justice Hugo L. Black, 1969-70; senior attorney, Natural Resources Defense Council, 1970-77; member, 1977-79, chairman, 1979-81, Council on Environmental Quality; chairman, Task Force on Global Resources and Environment, 1980; professor, Georgetown University Law Center, 1981-82; board of directors, Natural Resources Defense Council, 1981-82; president, World Resources Institute, 1982–.*

### Editor's introduction

Gus Speth is president of the World Resources Institute, a non-profit organization which carries out interdisciplinary policy studies on issues related to natural resources. In this speech, Speth warned that "pollution is occurring on a vast and unprecedented scale around the globe" in part because of the unprecedented increase in manufacturing. In addition, the creation of radioactive and synthetic chemicals has contributed to the further destruction of our environment. Like Margaret Mead, Speth advocated "a technological transformation of unprecedented scope and pace."

---

In an amusing scene in a recent popular movie, the intrepid Captain Kirk awakes from the sleep of time travel and, gazing out, sees that his starship is, as hoped, orbiting Earth. "Earth!" he says, "but when?" To which the genetically unflappable Spock, checking his instrument panel, replies, "Judging from the pollution content of the atmosphere, I believe we have arrived at the latter half of the twentieth century." And indeed they had. And so have we. And there is plenty of pollution here to measure.

Today, in the latter years of the twentieth century, pollution is occurring on a vast and unprecedented scale around the globe. Trends since World War II have been in two directions: first, toward large releases of certain chemicals, principally from using fossil fuels, that are now significantly altering natural systems on a global scale and, second, toward steady increases in the release of innumerable biocidal products and toxic substances. These shifts from the "sewage and soot" concerns of the pre-war period to vastly more serious concerns pose formidable challenges for societies—challenges that today's pollution control laws just begin to address.

The dramatic changes in pollution in this century are best described in terms of four long-term trends.

First is the trend from modest quantities to huge quantities. The twentieth century has witnessed unprecedented growth in human population and economic activity. World population has increased more than threefold; gross world product by perhaps twentyfold; and fossil fuel use by more than tenfold.

With these huge increases in economic activity and fossil fuel use have come huge changes in the quantities of pollutants released. Between 1900 and 1985, annual sulfur dioxide emissions increased sixfold globally, while nitrogen oxide emissions increased about tenfold, perhaps more. Another gas formed when fossil fuels are burned is carbon dioxide, one of the greenhouse gases implicated in global warming and climate change. Annual global emissions of CO2 have increased tenfold in this century, and a dramatic 25 percent increase in the CO2 content of Earth's atmosphere has occurred.

Second is the trend from gross insults to microtoxicity, from natural products to synthetic ones. Paralleling the dramatic growth in the volume of older pollutants, such as sulfur

[5] Delivered at the Environmental Protection Agency seminar, in Washington, D.C., on June 21, 1988.

dioxide, has been the introduction in the post-World War II period of new synthetic chemicals and radioactive substances, many of which are highly toxic in even minute quantities and some of which persist and accumulate in biological systems or in the atmosphere.

One major product of the modern chemicals industry, pesticides, are released to the environment precisely because they are toxic. Projected global pesticide sales for 1990 are $50 billion, a tenfold increase since 1975. Ironically, another major product of the chemicals industry, the chlorofluorocarbons, found wide use in part because they are not toxic. Such are the pathways of our ignorance.

Third is the trend from First World to Third World. A myth easily exploded by a visit to many developing countries is that pollution is predominately a problem of the highly industrialized countries. While it is true that the industrial countries account for the bulk of the pollutants produced today, pollution is a grave problem in developing countries, and many of the most alarming examples of its consequences can be found there.

Cities in Eastern Europe and the Third World are consistently more polluted with SO2 and particulates than most of the cities in OECD countries. The rivers most severely contaminated by bacteria and other pathogens are in developing countries.

Third World populations now rank high in their exposure to toxic chemicals. In a sample of ten industrial and developing countries, three of the four countries with the highest blood lead levels of their populations were Mexico, India, and Peru; for the same ten countries, DDT contamination of human milk was highest in China, India, and Mexico. And what may be the worst industrial accident in history occurred not in New Jersey or West Virginia, but in India.

These first three trends combine, with others, to produce the fourth, the trend from local effects to global effects. When the volumes of pollution were much smaller and the pollutants similar to natural substances, impacts tended to be confined to limited geographic areas near sources. Today, the scale and intensity of pollution make its consequences truly global. For the first time, human impacts have grown to approximate and to affect the natural processes that control the global life-support system.

Nothing better illustrates this broadening of the concern about pollution from a local affair to a global one than air pollution. Local air pollution is improving in some cities in industrial countries, but it is worsening in others, principally in developing countries, and is hardly solved anywhere. Meanwhile, global use of fossil fuels, and emissions of traditional pollutants such as sulfur and nitrogen oxides that result from it, continue to climb. Acid rain, ozone, and other consequences of these pollutants are affecting plant and animal life—killing forests and fish, damaging crops, changing the species composition of ecosystems—over vast areas of the globe. Depletion of the stratosphere's ozone layer is a matter of such concern that an international treaty has been negotiated to reduce emissions of chlorofluorocarbons, but the latest measurements indicate the current protocol is already inadequate. And, probably most serious of all, the buildup of infra-red trapping "greenhouse" gases in the atmosphere continues. This buildup is largely a consequence of the use of fossil fuels and CFCs, deforestation, and various agricultural activities, and in now threatens societies with far-reaching climate change.

While the regional impacts of a global warming are uncertain and difficult to predict, rainfall and monsoon patterns could shift, upsetting agricultural activities worldwide. Sea level could rise, flooding coastal areas. Ocean currents could shift, altering the climate of many areas and disrupting fisheries. The ranges of plant and animal species could change regionally, endangering protected areas and many species whose habitats are now few and confined. Record heatwaves and other weather anomalies could harm susceptible people, crops, and forests.

These interrelated atmospheric issues probably constitute the most serious pollution threat in history. I say "interrelated" because these atmospheric issues are linked in ways that scientists are still discovering, and the scientists are far ahead of our policymakers. First, they are linked in time. The view is still common today that, initially, we should address local air pollution, then we should turn attention to regional issues like acid rain, and then, at some point in the future, we should address the global issue of greenhouse gases. But the failures of our clean air efforts make urban air quality an issue for today, forcing a 1970s issue from the past into the present. Simultaneously, the realizations that greenhouse gases other than CO2 double the urgency of the problem, and that societies may have *already* committed the planet to a 10 to 2.50 C global average warming—these realizations are forcing what was thought to be a "21st Century issue" into the present.

These atmospheric issues are also linked in the vast chemical reactor that is the atmosphere, where pollutants react with each other, other substances, and solar energy in a fiendishly complex set of circular interactions. Touch one problem, you may touch them all.

Third, they are linked in their effects on people and on the biota. What are the consequences of multiple stresses—a variety of pollutants, heat waves and climate changes, increased ultraviolet radiation—when realized together? Who knows? We are all still learning.

And these atmospheric issues are linked through the sources of the pollutants involved. CFCs, for example, contribute both to greenhouse warming and ozone layer destruction, but the dominant source of these problems is the use of fossil fuels.

In short, the time to address all these atmosphere problems—local, regional, global—is now. The way to address all these problems is together. And, in the long run, the key to these problems is energy.

What can we say about the U.S. role in causing these atmospheric problems? We should take pride in what has been accomplished to date under the Clean Air Act and various U.S. energy laws. But let's not overdo it. The United States still produces about 15 percent of the world's sulfur dioxide emissions, about 25 percent of NOx, 25 percent of the CO2, and we manufacture about 30 percent of the CFCs. While emissions of criteria air pollutants other than NOx have fallen over the last fifteen years, a period during which real GNP grew about 50 percent, emissions today still exceed two-thirds of 1970 amounts, particulates excepted. In other words, the bulk of the pollution that gave rise to the Clean Air Act in 1970 continues. Similarly, real strides have been made in increasing U.S. energy efficiency: between 1973 and 1985 per capita energy use in the U.S. fell 12 percent while per capita gross domestic product rose 17 percent. Still, the United States today remains a gas guzzler of a nation, consuming a fourth of the world's energy annually and producing only half the GNP per unit of energy input as countries such as West Germany, Brazil, France, Japan, and Sweden.

Beyond these atmospheric issues are other pollution concerns, and beyond them the challenge of the planet's biological degradation—deforestation, desertification, the loss of biodiversity—in short, the steady process of biological impoverishment. When we take all these challenges together, we see that we are witnessing nothing less than the emergence of a new environmental agenda. This new agenda encompasses the great life-support systems of the planet's biosphere. It is global in scope and international in implication. It is rapidly forcing itself on the attention of policymakers and the public at large.

Almost twenty years ago, U.S. leaders responded vigorously to the environmental concerns emerging then. Today, the new agenda faces us with challenges that are more disturbing and more difficult. It is not enough to say that we must hope that our leaders respond as they did before. We must ensure that they do.

Now, into this troubled present comes a message from the future. Not, this time, from Captain Kirk, but more reliably, from the World Commission on Environment and Development. Consider closely the following passage from the report of the commission, *Our Common Future*:

"The planet is passing through a period of dramatic growth and fundamental change. Our human world of 5 billion must make room in a finite environment for another human world. The population could stabilize at between 8 billion and 14 billion some time next century, according to UN projections . . . . Economic activity has multiplied to create a $13 trillion world economy, and this could grow five- or tenfold in the coming half-century."

Imagine, just as a simple thought experiment, what would happen if greenhouse gases, industrial pollution, and other assaults on the environment rose proportionately with the vast economic growth to which the commission refers. I am not suggesting that this will happen, but thinking this way does highlight the magnitude of the challenge ahead.

In the early 1970s the CBS Evening News with Walter Cronkite ran a series of environmental stories entitled "Can the World Be Saved?." I remember the globe behind this title was firmly grasped by a hand which seemed to come from nowhere. I was never sure whether this hand was crushing our small planet or saving it, but I was sure at least that Cronkite was out to save it. He dramatically presented the much simpler environmental problems of that period to a huge audience, and helped build the powerful environmental consciousness of the day. Today, the question "Can the World Be Saved?" is a much more serious and legitimate question than it was then.

Societies near and far have set two long-term goals for themselves: improving environmental quality, in part by reducing current pollution levels, and achieving a virtual order of magnitude increase in economic activity. Let us not deceive ourselves, or accept blithely the assurances of political leaders who say casually that we can have both. We know from sad experience that we can have economic growth without having environmental protection. But the stakes on the environmental side are much higher now, and they will only grow in the future. I predict that reconciling these two goals will be one of the dominant challenges facing political leaders on all continents in the 1990s and beyond. It will require constant attention at the highest levels of government. It will require strong, effective, smart government.

Enviromentalism began on the outside, on the periphery of the economy, saving a bit of landscape here, bottling up some pollution there. It will inevitably spread as creed and code to permeate to the core of the economies of the world. We will all be environmentalists soon.

If these are the challenges before us, what should be done? Let's rephrase Cronkite's question into a somewhat more answerable one: how can the world be saved? Certainly, we must strengthen the efforts already begun. The regulatory programs of the industrial countries have yielded definite results over the last two decades, and continuing challenges will require that these programs be enhanced. Monitoring and enforcement capabilities must be strengthened; new types and sources of pollution must be tackled; inter-media effects must be attended to; regional and global approaches to pollution control must become increasingly common; and the overall regulatory process must become more cost-effective, efficient, and streamlined. And much, much more attention needs to be paid to the pollution problems of the developing countries. They can learn from our successes and failures, and pioneer new development paths rather than repeat old ones.

Yet, something more fundamental will be needed. From its origins in the early 1970s, U.S. air and water pollution legislation has recognized that tighter standards could be applied to "new sources" of pollution, in contrast to existing plants, because new sources present the opportunity to go beyond "end of pipe" removal of waste products and to build in" process changes" that reduce or eliminate the wastes that must otherwise be removed. This concept—source reduction through changing the basic technologies of production and consumption—*writ large*, is fundamental to solving world pollution problems. "Pollution control" is not enough. Societies must work "upstream" to change the products, processes, policies and pressures that give rise to pollution.

I urged you a moment ago to consider what would happen if pollution increased proportionately with the five- to ten-fold expansion in world economic activity projected for the middle of the next century. That would indeed happen if this growth merely replicates over and over today's prevailing technologies, broadly conceived. Seen in this light, reconciling the economic and environmental goals societies have set for themselves will only occur if there is a thoroughgoing technological transformation—a transformation to technologies, high and low, soft and hard, that are solution-oriented because they facilitate economic growth while sharply reducing the pressures on the natural environment. We speak positively of "environmentally sustainable" development. What this means in the context of pollution is technology transformation.

In this limited sense at least, one might say that only technology can save us. This is a hard thing for a congenital Luddite like myself to say, but, in a small victory of nurture over nature, I do now believe it. I do not diminish the importance of lifestyle changes—some go hand-in-hand with technological change—and I await the spread of more voluntary simplicity in our rich society. But growth has its imperatives; for much of the world it is the imperative of meeting basic human needs. And, we must not forget it is sustainable economic development—growth that takes the pressure of mass poverty off an eroding resource base—that is an essential component of environmental progress worldwide.

For these reasons, we must think explicitly about society's need to accomplish a technological transformation of unprecedented scope and pace. And we must think as well about the interventions that will be needed to bring it about. Although many emerging technologies offer exciting opportunities, and some are moving us in the right direction, no "hidden hand" is operating to guide technology to reconcile environmental and economic challenges.

The two fundamental processes of this transformation are the process of discovery and the process of application. The first is the realm of science and technology, of research and development. Science and technology must have the financial support and the incentives to provide us with an accurate understanding of the Earth's systems and cycles and what our pollution is doing to them; it must deliver to us a new agriculture, one redesigned to be sustainable both economically and ecologically, which stresses low inputs of commercial fertilizers, pesticides and energy; and it must show us how industry and transportation can be transformed from an era of materials-intensive, high-throughput processes to an era that relies on inputs with low environmental costs, uses materials with great efficiency, generates little or no waste, recycles residuals, and is, hence, more "closed."

To guide and speed the application of solution-oriented technologies will require policy action in the form of both economic incentives and direct regulation. It will require institutional innovation at the national and international levels, particularly to speed the process of international agreement and concerted action. Today, the problems are coming faster than the solutions. We will need a new international law of the environment, environmental diplomats, and the integration of environmental concerns into our trade and other international economic relations.

I have become a believer in the ingenuity of individuals and companies to find efficient solutions and to meet challenging goals, if the incentives are there. We need performance standards and economic rewards and penalties that are powerful, that provide the needed incentives, but that do not micromanage the process of technological innovation. This agency is no stranger to technology-forcing. We need more of it. and we should consider economic rewards for those who exceed baseline requirements.

We need to make the market mechanism work for us, not against us. Today, natural resource depletion and pollution are being subsidized on a grand scale around the globe. We have got to get the prices right; to begin by removing subsidies and then to make private companies and governments "internalize the externalities" so that prices reflect the true costs to society, including the costs of pollution. We need an environmentally honest economy.

Let me illustrate these points further by referring to one area where the need for technology transformation is most pressing—the energy sector—and one area where the need for concerted international action is most pressing—the greenhouse effect.

Our energy problems are forgotten but not gone. Energy will return to our political landscape again in the 1990s, driven by a U.S. oil import bill that was $46 billion in 1987 and could reach $80 billion in 1995, and by the grave atmospheric pollution—local, regional, and global—that our use of fossil fuels causes. I talked earlier about the ways that urban air pollution, acid rain, and the greenhouse effect are all linked together, and linked to our energy use patterns. Addressing our nation's economic, security, and environmental objectives will require a careful process of long-term, integrated energy planning. Put simply, we can no longer safely make air pollution policy and energy policy independently, directed by separate executive agencies with little communication, under laws written and overseen by different congressional committees.

If we and other countries are to meet our economic and environmental challenges, what energy paths should we take? The coming energy transformation, I would argue, must have rapid energy efficiency improvements as its dominant feature, supplemented by increased reliance on renewable energy sources. The potential for energy efficiency gains through technological change is simply enormous. If the efficiency in energy use current in Japan today could be matched in the U.S. and around the world, total economic output could be doubled globally, and virtually doubled in the U.S., without increasing energy use.

Auto efficiency provides a good example of what is possible. Miles per gallon achieved by new cars sold in the U.S. doubled from 13 mpg to 25 mpg between 1973 and 1985. Ford, Honda and Suzuki all have cars in production that could double this again to 50 mpg, and Toyota has a prototype family car that could double efficiency again to almost 100 mpg. I am reminded here that there is a huge role for the private sector in the coming technological transformation. Those companies that see the future can profit from it.

One recent global energy analysis, built up from careful studies of energy use in industrial and developing countries, concluded "that the global population could roughly double, that living standards could be improved far beyond satisfying basic needs in developing countries, and that economic growth in industrialized countries could continue, without increasing the level of global energy use in 2020 much above the present level." In this technically and economically feasible future, total energy use goes up only 10 percent between 1980 and 2020 and fossil fuel use grows even less. In such a low-energy, high-efficiency future, the great energy supply debates, such as coal vs. nuclear, which preoccupy us so, lose much of their significance, and pollution problems are knocked down to more manageable proportions.

Large energy efficiency gains, and the consequent reductions in CO2 emissions, will be essential in addressing what is probably the most serious environmental challenge of all—the global warming, which seems to have already begun. I recognize the uncertainties remaining in characterizing the greenhouse effect, but given the risks, I would advocate consideration now of a series of international conventions responsive to the various aspects of the problem.

First, we need to secure swift international approval for the ozone layer protection protocol signed in Montreal last year. We need this for its own sake and to continue the momentum that can get the nations of the world back to the table so that a complete, swift phase-out of CFCs can be negotiated. The phase-out is fully justified on ozone layer grounds alone, but the fact is that a CFC phase-out is the fastest and cheapest way societies can do something major to contain the greenhouse effect.

Second, we need an overall global climate protection convention, the prime goal of which should be to stabilize atmospheric concentrations of greenhouse gases at safe levels. This convention should focus particularly on steps needed to secure reductions in CO2 emissions from fossil fuel use. Two facts stand out in this regard: the U.S. and the Soviet Union together account for almost half of global CO2 emissions today, and the U.S., the USSR and China together account for about 90 percent of the estimated coal reserves.

Third, the time is ripe for an international agreement to protect the world's tropical forests and to reforest the spreading wasteland areas in many developing countries. The industrial nations have a double stake in halting the now-rapid clearing of the tropical forests. Not only are these forests repositories for about half of the wildlife and genetic wealth of the planet, but CO2 emissions from biotic sources such as deforestation are estimated to be about a fifth of CO2 emissions from fossil fuels. Our stake in the salvation of these forests is sufficiently large that we should be more than willing to help provide financial incentives—incentives that will be necessary [if the] tropics are to turn their attention to what often appears as a low priority or even a threat to development and sovereignty. I suggest that we go far beyond the debt-for-nature swaps under way today and consider a global bargain as part of this international convention. This bargain would involve the easing and forgiving of international debts in exchange for forest conservation. Of the top 17 most heavily indebted countries, 12 are destroying their tropical forests at extraordinarily rapid rates, contributing to the world's annual loss of 27 million acres.

And fourth, we need international agreement on the protocol now being developed to limit nitrogen oxide emissions. Unless capped, increasing NOx emissions will lead to increasing ozone concentrations, and ozone is a greenhouse gas as well as a source of urban and rural air pollution. Many good reasons exist to control NOx emissions at the international level, and I urge the State Department and EPA to signal U.S. support for the proposed protocol by the fast-approaching July 1 deadline.

Some of you may be wondering: is he going to discuss nuclear power, an available non-fossil source of energy? My concern about nuclear power, as things stand today, is that it probably will not, in the end, provide a major part of the answer to global warming. Its public acceptability is too low and its price is too high. If we try to solve the greenhouse problem by cramming nuclear power down the throats of an unwilling public and unwilling investors, we will be setting the stage for prolonged confrontation and stalemate. And what is going to happen to nuclear power if there are one or two more major accidents like Three Mile Island and Chernobyl? Moreover, I believe there are safer and cheaper alternatives for the short run, including the vast potential for efficiency gains in how we generate and use electricity. For the longer run, I would favor research aimed at reinventing nuclear power in a way that could gain public and investor confidence; we may need it one day. My guess, however, is that before such a new nuclear system could be commercialized in the next century, the price of photovoltaic and other solar energy systems will be competitive. But who knows? We are all still learning.

In all these areas, in seeking these treaties and in setting an international example by acting on our own, U.S. leadership and EPA leadership could not be more important. The world is not exactly waiting on us, but neither will it get very far without us. I hope you will join with me in urging our Presidential candidates to give these issues the time and thought they deserve. We need to know, beyond the level of generalities, how each candidate would address the emerging environmental agenda of the 1990s.

Let me conclude with a word about why I am optimistic that the world can indeed be saved. This address, you have doubtless noted, reflects a deep appreciation of the importance of economic and technological forces in the modern world. One reason for optimism is that science and technology are presenting us with answers. We are in the midst of a revolution in earth science and a revolution in industrial and agricultural technology, both with huge potentials in the areas we have been reviewing.

But if solutions are found, they will come from another realm as well, from the hopes and fears of people, from their aspirations for their children and their wonder at the natural world, from their own self-respect and their dogged insistence that some things that seem very wrong are just that. People everywhere are offended by pollution. They sense intuitively that we have pressed beyond limits we should not have exceeded. They want to clean up the world, make it a better place, be good trustees of the Earth for future generations. With Thoreau, they know that heaven is under our feet as well as over our heads. Politicians around the globe are increasingly hearing the demand that things be set right. And that is very good news indeed.

# Man and Nature: The Future of the Global Environment[6]

Jessica Tuchman Mathews

*Born July 4, 1946, New York, NY; B.A., Radcliffe College, 1967; Ph.D., California Institute of Technology, 1973; director, National Security Council, 1977-79; vice president, World Resources Institute, 1982–.*

## Editor's introduction

The North American Conference on Religion and Ecology is an interfaith group dedicated to making citizens more aware of environmental problems. Jessica Tuchman Mathews, vice president of the World Resources Institute, spoke to some 2,500 persons gathered for this conference at the National Cathedral in Washington, D.C. She outlined the threats confronted by the world community, which include population growth, hunger, malnutrition, soil erosion, deforestation, loss of species, greenhouse warming, and ozone depletion. "Unless policies change," she asserted, "man's impacts on the planet are so profound . . . that irreversible damage could occur." In essence, Mathews advocated a fundamental change in both behavior and thought if we hope to alter our treatment of the environment.

---

The great French biologist and Nobel laureate Jacques Monod concluded not long ago, that "Mankind was mother nature's only serious mistake." A newspaper reader attentive to the health of the global environment in the 1980s, might almost have been tempted to agree.

Consider for a moment a few of the events of this past decade: the oil price rise and widespread shortages at its beginning; the chemical accident at Bhopal; the decimation of European and high-altitude U.S. forests from acid rain and other air pollutants; the explosion at Chernobyl; ozone depletion and the discovery of a "hole" in the ozone layer over Antarctica; drought and famine in Africa; the Rhine river chemical spill; the homeless freighter that sailed the world for two years without finding a place to unload its toxic cargo; steadily rising rates of tropical deforestation and of species extinction; closed beaches from Western Europe to the Baltic to New Jersey; the Exxon Valdez oil spill; and, as the decade closed, an outbreak of freakish weather—drought and record-breaking heat in the U.S., devastating floods in Bangladesh, the most powerful hurricane ever measured, and the warmest winter in Moscow in more than a century—all bringing intense new concern to the possibilities of global warming.

There were more hungry people on the planet as the 1980s drew to a close than ever before. Seven hundred to eight hundred million people, outside of China, eat fewer calories than are necessary for an active life. Malnutrition is a major factor in the deaths of twenty-five thousand infants and children under five each *day*. Even where adequate calories are available, clean water, which is equally essential, often is not. Waterborne disease, whose solutions are environmental, rather than medical, remains a scourge. Two hundred million people are sick with schistosomiasis, 175 million with malaria, 450 million with hookworm, river blindness and sleeping sickness affect 20 million each.

The 1980s also brought rich new scientific insights. As scientists studied the chemical elements essential to life—carbon, nitrogen, phos-

[6]Delivered at the North American Conference on Religion and Ecology, in Washington, D.C., on May 19, 1990. Reprinted with permission of Jessica Tuchman Mathews.

phorous and sulfur—they quickly found that their natural cycles through earth, air, water and living things were being affected on a global scale by human activities. Non-chemical changes are equally massive. On land, soil erosion and deforestation are accelerating the flow of sediments and nutrients to the ocean in some places, while dams built for irrigation and electricity interrupt the natural flow in others. The permanent loss of species—now estimated to stand at four per hour—utterly disrupts the natural balance between speciation and extinction.

The more closely scientists looked at the planet's structure and metabolism, from the top of the stratosphere to the ocean canyons, the more the evidence of rapid change accumulated. A sense of urgency gradually filtered through to governments that man is now the principal agent of environmental change on the planet, and that if humanity is to live successfully with its ability to alter natural systems it must first understand those systems and the ways in which human society depends on their normal functioning. Unless policies change, some scientists warn, man's impacts on the planet are so profound and are accumulating so rapidly that irreversible damage could occur—to put it bluntly—before we have any idea of what we are doing. Since man's ability to tinker inadvertently with the basic physiology of the planet is new in history, it is worth spending a few minutes to look at these changes in more detail.

At the core of all environmental trends lies population growth. It took 130 years for world population to grow from 1 billion to 2 billion; it will take just this decade to climb from 5 billion to 6 billion. Though the *rate* of growth is slowing, the human family grows by 93 million each year, a larger increment than ever before. Africa, already mired in poverty and struggling against a falling per capita GNP, will add more than the present population of the U.S. between 1980 and 2000. If fertility continues to decline at its present slow rate, demographers predict that the human population will level off at a staggering 14 billion, almost triple today's population, not at the 9 or 10 billion that seemed most likely just a few years ago.

No simple relationship links population levels and the resource base. Policies, technologies and institutions intervene between population growth and its impacts and can spell the difference between a highly stressed, degraded environment and one that could sustainably provide for many more people. Sometimes absolute numbers are crucial. Most often, though, the *rate* of growth is most important. Whereas a government might be fully capable of providing food, housing, jobs and health care for a population growing at one percent per year (and therefore doubling in 72 years), it might be completely overwhelmed by an annual growth rate of three percent, which would double the population in 24 years.

While the U.S. and the Soviet Union are each growing at just under one percent per year, and Europe only half that fast, Africa is expanding by about three percent annually and Asia and Latin America by about two percent. By 2025 the working age population in the developing countries alone will be larger than the world's current total population. Clearly these countries face an urgent choice. For many of them, current rates of growth mean that available capital will be swallowed up in meeting the needs of today's populations rather than invested in the job creation and resource conservation that will be needed to sustain their children. And of course, there are global impacts as well.

The most serious form of renewable resource decline is tropical deforestation. Globally, ten trees are being cut down for every one that is replanted, and an area twice the size of Austria is deforested each year. These luxuriant forests are deceptively fragile. Once disturbed, the entire ecosystem can unravel. The loss of the trees interrupts nutrient cycling; the soil loses fertility; plant and animal species lose their habitat and disappear; acute fuelwood shortages arise (especially in the dry tropical forests); without groundcover the soil erodes, and downstream rivers suffer siltation, causing both flooding and droughts, and damage to expensive irrigation and hydroelectric systems on which hopes for economic growth are pinned. Planned to last for 50-100 years, the dams can silt up almost overnight, leaving only foreign debt as a legacy. The record is probably held by a large dam in China which silted up completely in 4 years.

Traced through its effects on agriculture, energy supply and water resources, deforestation impoverishes about a billion people, and often leaves political as well as economic chaos in its wake. In Haiti, many of the boat people who fled to the U.S. left because of the brutality of the Duvaliers. But many were forced into the boats by the impossible task of farming the bare rock left behind by near total deforestation and soil erosion. Haitians are by no means the only environmental refugees. No one knows the true numbers, but in Indonesia, Central America, and sub-Saharan Africa, millions have been forced to leave their homes in part because the loss of plant cover and the consequent disappearance of soil have made it impossible to grow food. Where the refugees settle, they add to the local demand for food and put new burdens on the land, spreading the environmental stress that forced them from their homes like a disease. Resource mismanagement is not the only cause of these mass movements, of course. Religious and ethnic conflicts, political repression and other forces are at work. The environmental causes are simply the most often ignored.

The tropical forests also harbor most of the planet's genetic wealth, the heritage of 3.5 billion years of evolution. This diversity is therefore vanishing on a scale not seen since the disappearance of the dinosaurs. Extinction is a normal part of nature, but today's rate is 1,000 to 10,000 times greater than the natural rate. With the loss already at 100 species per day, one-fifth of all the species living in 1980 may be gone by the end of this decade.

The loss will be felt aesthetically, scientifically, and economically. Its costs are impossible even to estimate. A few years ago, a Mexican graduate student stumbled upon a primitive form of perennial corn which appears to exist nowhere else in the world but on that single hilltop, and which would have been quickly wiped out but for his alertness. If the perennial character can be bred into commercial corn its environmental and economic value will be enormous.

Genetic diversity is a virtually untapped resource. Man currently makes use of less than one percent of what is available. Among the vast numbers of unused types of edible plants, for example, are a great many with equal or greater potential than the few that now form the basis of the human diet. The bitter irony is that genetic diversity is being lost on a grand scale at the very moment when biotechnology makes it possible to fully exploit the resource for the first time.

The most truly global and potentially threatening of environmental trends is greenhouse warming. The greenhouse effect results from the fact that the planet's atmosphere is largely transparent to incoming radiation from the sun but absorbs much of the lower energy radiation re-emitted by the earth. The effect is a natural phenomenon that makes the earth warm enough to support life. But as emissions of greenhouse gases increase, the planet warms *un*naturally. Carbon dioxide, the product of all combustion and therefore of all fossil fuel use, is the principal greenhouse gas.

There are many uncertainties about greenhouse climate change, but a scientific consensus exists on its central features: the soundness of the theory; the identity of the greenhouse gases; the rate at which their concentrations are growing, and in most cases, the reasons for that increase. There is also agreement that global average temperature has risen by slightly more than half a degree centigrade since the industrial revolution began, at the low end of the range the theory predicts. The uncertainties arise over how much warming will result from added greenhouse gases, and how fast it will occur. The questions, in short, are not whether, but when and how much.

Hotter temperatures are only one of the expected results. Precipitation patterns would shift, perhaps causing Dust Bowl-like conditions in key grain producing areas. Ocean currents may also shift, dramatically altering climate. A diversion of the Gulf Stream, for example, would make Western Europe far colder than it is today. Sea level would rise due to thermal expansion of the oceans and the melting of land-based ice. The predicted rise would inundate large coastal regions, erode shorelines, destroy coastal marshes and swamps (both areas of very high biological productivity), affect water supplies through the intrusion of salt water, and put at high risk the vastly disproportionate share of the world's economic infrastructure that is packed along coastlines. The great low-lying river deltas, from the Mississippi to the Nile and the Ganges, would likely be flooded. Some island nations would disappear altogether.

There would be positive consequences as well. Some plants would grow more quickly (though many, alas, will be weeds), fertilized by the additional carbon dioxide. Rainfall may rise in what are now arid but potentially fertile regions. Conditions for agriculture may also improve in some northern regions. The net effect, however, is almost certain to prove costly to all countries because all depend so heavily on the normal, predictable functioning of the climate system. Adapting to a changing climate, where that is possible, and when the impacts can be predicted in time, will be very expensive. Developing countries, with small reserves of capital, few scientists and engineers, and weak central governments, will be especially hard hit. Many needed adaptations will be prohibitively costly, and some of the most severe impacts, such as those on wildlife and ecosystems, will be beyond the reach of human correction.

Greenhouse warming is closely linked to stratospheric ozone depletion, which is caused by a group of manmade compounds known as chlorofluorocarbons, or CFCs. These, it turns out, are also potent greenhouse gases. The increased ultraviolet radiation caused by ozone loss will produce an increase in skin cancers, eye damage, crop loss and other as yet unknown impacts on plants and animals, including perhaps the suppression of immune systems.

Ozone depletion is a valuable object lesson in environmental humility. Chlorofluorocarbons were thoroughly tested when first introduced and found to be completely benign. Their possible effect on the remote stratosphere was simply never considered. More than a decade after the effect was discovered, a related phenomenon came to light, that led to a continent-sized "hole" in the layer over Antarctica. This history reminds us that our present knowledge of planetary mechanisms is scanty. The possibility of surprise, possibly a quite nasty surprise, must be placed rather high on the list of likely outcomes. The greatest risk may well come from a completely unanticipated direction, for we lack both crucial knowledge and early warning signals.

Do all these trends mean that the human prospect is bleak? Certainly, we—the human species—cannot go on as we are without fundamental change. Without it there is no way the planet can accommodate a doubling or more of population, at least a fivefold rise in economic output and a tripling of energy use all by the middle of the next century. We will need to redesign our technologies from the inside out, rather than continue to fiddle with what comes out the end of the pipe. The new designs must follow nature's example in which there are few if any wastes, materials are used with high efficiency, and every byproduct is used as the starting point in other processes. Look in a biochemistry text and you will see that all of nature's systems are circular designs. Nothing is linear, as most manmade processes are.

Such change is well within our technological capacity. With only a modest effort many of our present practices could be made to look primitive. The U.S. could cut its energy use in half with presently available technologies, and there is no telling what could be achieved through a determined research effort. We use a billion pounds of pesticide each year, less than one percent of which reaches a target pest. It should not be beyond us to increase that number three, five or ten fold. Our transportation system uses marginal improvements on fifty-and one hundred-year-old technologies. The hottest thing in mass transit right now is so-called "light rail," which is just another name for the trolley car, a technology that was introduced in the 1880s. We have not begun to use the revolutionary power of information and communications technologies to transform transportation just as they have transformed banking, publishing, retailing and just about everything else. In short, we have not yet really tried to make technology serve nature instead of letting nature serve technology as a source of resources and repository for wastes.

Yet even with that ambitious goal, technological change will be the easiest part of the challenge that lies ahead. The difficult part will be understanding what we are doing to the planet before it is too late, summoning the will to choose a different future, and developing the new rules and institutions that will enable us to travel that different path. That is a tall order, I know, but notice what is not included. I do not believe that we need to change human nature or human values. We will have to change how we think—especially about the future—and how we behave, especially as a global community. But change in thought and behavior, even in deeply ingrained habit, is well within what history tells us is possible. Indeed, thought and behavior can change quickly and profoundly as conditions and institutions change. Human slavery once seemed essential to economic success, morally acceptable, even ordinary. Now it is unthinkable.

How we act is a function of what we see in the world around us, and what we see is a function of what we understand. Thus science is a powerful shaper of human behavior. From Newton to Einstein our concept of the physical universe changed our way of thinking. Darwin certainly did too. Perhaps now it is Lovelock's turn. Lovelock proposes a theory he calls Gaia after the Greek earth goddess. Gaia sees the earth as a living organism in which the non-living realm is continuously shaped by the presence of life. Not just species evolve in the Gaian view, but species and their living and non-living environment together. Thus, the apparent planning and sense of purpose that natural selection produces—and which has always been so hard to grasp—is broadened to include the entire planet. It is far too early to say that Lovelock is correct, but the theory has generated exciting research, which is always suggestive. If Gaia is correct, it will force us to shift our focus from an overriding concern for the welfare of our own species to that of the planet as a whole.

Science regularly makes a fool of anyone who tries to predict its future. Darwin himself wrote in his *Autobiography*, "I rejoice that I have avoided controversies." But I will take the risk and hazard a guess that the revolutionary sciences of our time (just as astronomy and physics have been in the past) will be ecology and the study of earth as a living whole.

From that science will come the realization that despite technology, and what our major religions have taught, beginning with Genesis, man does *not* exercise dominion over nature. The reverse may well be closer to the truth: nature rules man, both because it shapes our minds, bodies and spirit and because we are, and will always remain, so economically dependent upon it. Our world view now is that man is not only above, but separate from nature, which exists solely to serve his purposes. We do not need to go to the other extreme as some suggest, and see ourselves as no different from nor better than a chimpanzee or a guppy. We can continue to view ourselves as the peak of creation, but we must discard our misguided sense of separateness. In that endeavor lies a great task for organized religion.

Those whose work keeps them closest to nature understand this best. They learn that, except in a narrow sense, or over a short term, it is hard to do better than nature. Let me give you a very simple example. When foresters first began to plant trees where old forests had been cut, they had a terrible time. The new forests looked nice, full of young, healthy trees with clean trunks and without crumbling dead trees in the way, but they didn't grow well. Slowly the foresters learned that everything in the natural forest served a purpose: without the dead hollow trees for owls and woodpeckers to nest in, insect populations got out of control; without the lichen that coats the trunks of old trees, forests could not fix enough nitrogen from the air to fertilize themselves.

Usually, the connections are harder to trace. The human system appears to outperform nature, but only till we count the cost in some other place or at some later time. This is a lesson that will have to be learned again and again. As human demands on the planet accelerate, we will learn the lesson on a larger and larger scale, until eventually we learn to incorporate it into how we think and behave.

The influence of nature on man's spirit should also be a positive force for change. It is the source of man's creativity. Probably the original inspiration for stained glass, like the magnificence that surrounds us, came from someone who had seen how sunlight filters through the leaves of a high tree canopy. Each of us has experienced the force with which a beautiful day lifts the spirit even in the middle of a city. We know the strength of our connection to certain species: witness all the fuss over the three trapped whales a few years ago. And we need wilderness, not just for recreation, but as Wallace Stegner wrote, "for spiritual renewal, the recognition of identity, and the birth of awe." I may be too optimistic here, because of course these connections have always been with us and in recent centuries haven't been notably influential. But perhaps as nature grows ever more threatened, its value will seem more obvious and urgent. Or perhaps as we see less of nature, it will be all the easier to lose.

If science, religion, and man's emotional connections to nature can reshape how we perceive our role on the planet, then institutional changes can pave the way to new policies and economic behavior. Prosaic and rather simple changes will have a sweeping impact. For example, economic indicators currently ignore environmental costs. When countries calculate their national income accounts—their GNP—they value and depreciate everything man-made, even intangibles like knowledge. But the accounts completely ignore environmental resources. The result is policies that can not distinguish between using income—say, the sustainable yield of lumber or fish—and using up a capital asset, namely the forest or fishery itself. In the private sector, we have indicators that measure how efficiently labor and capital are used, but nothing that measures environmental productivity—how much resources are used and emissions produced per unit of economic output. Changing these and other signals, to which policymakers are exquisitely tuned, will automatically and effortlessly go a long way toward turning bad policies into good ones.

Global environmental trends all pose potentially serious losses to national economies, are immune to solution by one or a few countries, and render geographic borders irrelevant. The internationalization of finance and industry and the boundary-erasing effects of remote sensing technology and linked computers, have the same effect. Even the amount we travel makes health policy, once solely a domestic prerogative, into an international issue. These invasions of national sovereignty make governments less central than they once were. I don't mean to suggest that nation states will disappear, but some of the powers they have held will be inherited by other actors: by individuals, the business sector and international organizations.

Individuals have a particularly important role to play. First, because changes in thought and understanding come from people, not institutions. Individuals will also provide much of the impetus toward a functioning global community in place of today's collection of nations. Working through their own international communities—science, business, labor, citizen activism, and so on—people offset the centrifugal forces that govern relations among states. Jean Monnet, the father of the European Community, knew this when he described his intention as "not to form coalitions between states, but union among people." That Monnet's wild dream is now a reality, and that Europe is in the longest period of peace in its history, is to me another hopeful portent.

Whether each of our individual preferences is for scholarship or business, civic action or research, the nudge of a petition or the slap of a lawsuit, all of us must believe and behave as if, to paraphrase another famous Frenchman, the fate of the planet is too important to be left to governments. Individual efforts in the face of problems which have a global dimension may seem inadequate, even futile. But, in aggregate, they are not. "Your actions may seem insignificant," Gandhi said, "but it's crucial that you do them."

For all that can be achieved outside of government, changes in national policy are also absolutely vital. Looking at the United States today and over the past decade, one cannot be very hopeful about the prospects for leadership in the Executive or the Congressional branch. Despite the manifest flaws in our political system as it functions today, I cannot put all of the blame on politicians, because leadership is a two-way street.

Leaders need followers who are willing to be led. We Americans have given no sign that we would reward leadership no matter how enlightened or beneficial. We need to care a lot more about our federal government and demand a lot more of it. We should insist that it provide what we want, while being more honest in matching those expectations with our willingness to pay. We must stop being diverted by phony debates over manufactured symbols and images. We need to care more about the budget and less about flag burning. Let's get rid of those who are content to do nothing more than nurse along a manifestly inadequate status quo, and seek out those who are determined to do better. And when we find leaders like that let's do what's necessary to elect them and then hold them accountable.

You will have gathered by this time that I am optimistic about our ability as a species to develop a permanent *modus vivendi* with the earth. Being an intensely practical person I have no other option. But I do not underestimate the challenge. Indeed it is in part because present policies are so bad that I see so much room for improvement. I also believe that a positive outlook is an essential ingredient of success. If our aim is merely to make a bad thing marginally better, we will never unleash the necessary energy and motivation. We need to believe in something bigger than fear of the consequences of inaction.

The historian Barbara Tuchman wrote that "We cannot reckon on the better impulses predominating in the world, only that they will always appear." They are appearing now, in thousands of gatherings like this one that would not have taken place even a few years ago. Our job is to seize this fleeting opportunity and to blow the scattered sparks into a bonfire for change.

# To Protect the Whole of Creation[7]

Bruce Babbitt

*Born June 27, 1938, Los Angeles, CA; B.A., Notre Dame University, 1960; M.S., University of Newcastle, 1962; LL.B., Harvard Law School, 1965; assistant to the director of VISTA, 1965-67; attorney general of Arizona, 1975-78; governor (D) of Arizona, 1978-87; secretary of the interior, 1987–.*

## Editor's introduction

Speaking to an audience of 500 scientists and theologians, Secretary of the Interior Bruce Babbitt, in the words of the *Oregonian* (March 1, 1996), underscored "the link between spirituality and preserving the environment." Babbitt explained to the editor of this volume that his purpose in this speech was to "find a values basis for the USA beyond what is good for humans." Many, including Representative Helen Chenoweth, who also has a speech reprinted in this chapter, opposed Babbitt's linking of religion and environmental causes. Secretary Babbitt also criticized Republican members of Congress for threatening the 1972 Clean Water Act and the 1973 Endangered Species Act.

---

A wolf's green eyes, a sacred blue mountain, the words from Genesis, and the answers of children all reveal the religious values manifest in the 1973 Endangered Species Act.

I began 1995 with one of the more memorable events of my lifetime. It took place in the heart of Yellowstone National Park, during the first week of January, a time when a layer of deep, pure snow blanketed the first protected landscape in America. But for all its beauty, over the past 60 years this landscape had been an incomplete ecosystem; by the 1930s, government-paid hunters had systematically eradicated the predator at the top of the food chain: the American grey wolf.

I was there on that day, knee deep in the snow, because I had been given the honor of carrying the first wolves back into that landscape. Through the work of conservation laws, I was there to restore the natural cycle, to make Yellowstone complete.

The first wolf was an Alpha female, and after I set her down in the transition area, where she would later mate and bear wild pups, I looked through the grate into the green eyes of this magnificent creature, within this spectacular landscape, and was profoundly moved by the elevating nature of America's conservation laws: laws with the power to make creation whole.

I then returned to Washington, where a new Congress was being sworn into office, and witnessed power of a different kind.

First I witnessed an attack on our national lands, an all-out attempt to abolish our American tradition of public places—whether national parks, forests, historic sites, wildlife refuges, and recreation areas. Look quickly about you, name your favorite place: a beach in New York harbor; the Appomattox Courthouse; the great western ski areas; the caribou refuge in the arctic; or the pristine waters off the Florida Keys. For each of these places is at risk. Last month in the Denver *Post*, the Chairman of the House Subcommittee on Public Lands estimated that his committee may have to close more than 100 of the Park Service's 369 units. In these times, it seems that no part of our history or our natural heritage is sufficiently important to protect and preserve for the benefit of all Americans.

Next I witnessed an attack that targets the 1972 Clean Water Act, the most successful of all our environmental laws. Until that Act passed, slaughterhouses, pulp mills and factories from Boise to Boston to Baton Rouge

[7]Delivered to a joint meeting of the National Religious Partnership for Environment and the American Association for the Advancement of Science, in Weston, Massachusetts, on November 11, 1995. Reprinted with permission of Bruce Babbitt.

spewed raw waste into our waterfronts. Yet 23 years later, as I visited America's cities, I saw that Act restoring those rivers, breathing new life into once-dead waters. I saw people gather on clean banks to fish, sail, swim, eat and live. I saw that, as the Act helps cities restore our waters, those waters restore our cities themselves. And then I saw Congress rushing to tear that Act apart.

But finally, more than any of our environmental laws, the Act they have most aggressively singled out for elimination—one that made Yellowstone complete—is the 1973 Endangered Species Act.

Never mind that this Act is working, having saved 99 percent of all listed species; never mind that it effectively protects hundreds of plants and animals, from grizzly bears to whooping cranes to greenback cutthroat trout; never mind that it is doing so while costing each American 16 cents per year.

For the new Congress—while allowing for the above charismatic species, plus a dozen other species good for hunting and fishing, plus, just for good measure, the bald eagle—can find absolutely no reason to protect all species in general.

Who cares, they ask, if the spotted owl goes extinct? We won't miss it, or, for that matter, the Texas blind salamander or the kangaroo rat. And that goes double for the fairy shrimp, the burying beetle, the Delphi sands flower-loving fly and the virgin spine dace! If they get in our way, if humans drive some creatures to extinction, well, that's just too bad.

Over the past year that is, I think, a fairly accurate summary of how the new majority in Congress has expressed its opinion of the Endangered Species Act.

They are not, however, the only Americans who have expressed an opinion on this issue.

Recently I read an account of a Los Angeles "Eco-Expos" last April, where children were invited to write down their answers to the basic question: "Why save endangered species?"

One child, Gabriel, answered, "Because God gave us the animals."

Travis and Gina wrote, "Because we love them."

A third answered, "Because we'll be lonely without them."

Still another wrote, "Because they're a part of our life. If we didn't have them, it would not be a complete world. The Lord put them on earth to be enjoyed, not destroyed."

Now, in my lifetime I have heard many, many political, agricultural, scientific, medical and ecological reasons for saving endangered species. I have in fact hired biologists and ecologists for just that purpose. All their reasons have to do with providing humans with potential cures for disease, or yielding humans new strains of drought-resistant crops, or offering humans bioremediation of oil spills, or thousands of other justifications of why species are useful to humans.

But none of their reasons moved me like the children's.

For these children are speaking and writing in plain words a complex notion that has either been lost, or forgotten, or never learned by some members of Congress, and indeed by many of us.

The children are expressing the moral and spiritual imperative that there may be a higher purpose inherent in creation, demanding our respect and our stewardship quite apart from whether a particular species is or ever will be of material use to mankind. They see in creation what our adult political leaders refuse to acknowledge. They express an answer that can be reduced to one word: values.

I remember when I was their age, a child growing up in a small town in Northern Arizona. I learned my religious values through the Catholic Church, which, in that era, in that Judeo-Christian tradition, kept silent on our moral obligation to nature. By its silence the church implicitly sanctioned the prevailing view of the earth as something to be used and disposed however we saw fit, without any higher obligation. In all the years that I attended Sunday mass, hearing hundreds of homilies and sermons, there was never any reference, any link, to our natural heritage or to the spiritual meaning of the land surrounding us.

Yet, outside that church I always had a nagging instinct that the vast landscape *was* somehow sacred, and holy, and connected to me in a sense that my catechism ignored.

At the edge of my home town a great blue mountain called the San Francisco Peaks soars up out of the desert to a snowy summit, snagging clouds on its crest, changing color with the seasons. It was always a mystical, evocative presence in our daily lives. To me that mountain, named by Spanish missionaries for Saint Francis, remains a manifestation of the presence of our Creator.

That I was not alone in this view was something I had to discover through a very different religion. For on the opposite side of the blue mountain, in small pueblos on the high mesas that stretch away toward the north, lived the Hopi Indians. And it was a young Hopi friend who taught me that the blue mountain was, truly, a sacred place.

One Sunday morning in June he led me out to the mesa top villages where I watched as the Kachina filed into the plaza, arriving from the snowy heights of the mountain, bringing blessings from another world.

Another time he took me to the ceremonials where the priests of the snake clan chanted for rain and then released live rattlesnakes to carry their prayers to the spirits deep within the earth.

Later I went with him to a bubbling spring, deep in the Grand Canyon, lined with pahoes—the prayer feathers—where his ancestors had emerged from another world to populate this earth.

By the end of that summer I came to believe, deeply and irrevocably, that the land, and that blue mountain, and all the plants and animals in the natural world are together a direct reflection of divinity, that creation is a plan of God, and I saw, in the words of Emerson, "the visible as proceeding from the invisible."

That awakening made me acutely aware of a vacancy, a poverty amidst my own rich religious tradition. I felt I had to either embrace a borrowed culture, or turn back and have a second look at my own. And while priests then, as now, are not too fond of people rummaging about in the Bible to draw our own meanings, I chose the latter, asking: Is there nothing in our Western, Judeo-Christian tradition that speaks to our natural heritage and the sacredness of that blue mountain? Is there nothing that can connect me to the surrounding Creation?

There are those who argue that there isn't.

There are those industrial apologists who, when asked about Judeo-Christian values relating to the environment, reply that the material world, including the environment, is just an incidental fact, of no significance in the relation between us and our Creator.

They cite the first verses of Genesis, concluding that God gave Adam and his descendants the absolute, unqualified right to "subdue" the earth and gave man "dominion over the fish of the sea, and over the fowl of the air, and over every living thing that moveth upon the earth." God, they assert, put the earth here for the disposal of man in whatever manner he sees fit. Period.

They should read a few verses further.

For there, in the account of the Deluge, the Bible conveys a far different message about our relation to God and to the earth. In Genesis, Noah was commanded to take into the ark two by two and seven by seven every living thing in creation, the clean and the unclean.

He did not specify that Noah should limit the ark to two charismatic species, two good for hunting, two species that might provide some cure down the road, and, say, two that draw crowds to the city zoo.

No, He specified *the whole of creation.* And when the waters receded, and the dove flew off to dry land, God set all the creatures free, commanding them to multiply upon the earth.

Then, in the words of the covenant with Noah, "when the rainbow appears in the clouds, I will see it and remember the everlasting covenant between me and all living things on earth."

Thus we are instructed that this everlasting covenant was made to protect the whole of creation, not for the exclusive use and disposition of mankind, but for the purposes of the Creator.

Now, we all know that the commandment to protect creation in all its diversity does not come to us with detailed operating instructions. It is left to us to translate a moral imperative into a way of life and into public policy. Which we did. Compelled by this ancient command, modern America turned to the national legislature which forged our collective moral imperative into one landmark law: the 1973 Endangered Species Act.

The trouble is that during the first twenty years of the Endangered Species Act scientists and administrators and other well-intentioned people somehow lost sight of that value—to protect the *whole* of creation—and instead took a fragmented, mechanistic approach to preserve individual species. Isolated specialists working in secluded regions waited until the eleventh hour to act, then heroically rescued species—one at a time.

Sometimes the result was dramatic recovery, but often the result was chaos, conflict, and continuing long term decline. In the Pacific Northwest, for example, the spotted owl was listed even as federal agencies went forward with clear cutting. Efforts to save the alligator proceeded even as the Everglades shrivelled from diverted waters. They listed California salmon runs even as water users continued to deplete the spawning streams.

It is only in the last few years that have we recovered, like a lost lens, our ancient religious values. This lens lets us see not human-drawn distinctions—as if creation could ever be compartmentalized into a million discrete parts, each living in relative isolation from the others—but rather the interwoven wholeness of creation.

Not surprisingly, when we can see past these man-made divisions, the work of protecting God's creation grows both easier and clearer.

It unites all state, county and federal workers under a common moral goal. It erases artificial borders so we can see the full range of a natural habitat, whether wetland, forest, stream or desert expanse. And it makes us see all the creatures that are collectively rooted to one habitat, and how, by keeping that habitat whole and intact, we ensure the survival of the species.

For example, in the Cascades, the spotted owl's decline was only part of the collapsing habitat of the ancient forests. When seen as a whole, that habitat stretched from Canada to San Francisco. Not one but thousands of species, from waterfowl of the air to the salmon in their streams, depended for their survival on the unique rain forest amidst Douglas fir, hemlock and red cedar.

Our response was the President's Forest plan, a holistic regional agreement forged with state and local officials and the private sector. Across three state borders, it keeps critical habitat intact, provides buffer zones along salmon streams and coastal areas, and elsewhere provides a sustainable timber harvest for generations to come.

That's also the lesson of Everglades National Park, where great flocks of wading birds are declining because their shallow feeding waters were drying up and dying off. Only by erasing park boundaries could we trace the problem to its source, hundreds of miles upstream, where agriculture and cities were diverting the shallow water for their own needs. Only by looking at the whole South Florida watershed, could state and federal agencies unite to put the parts back together, restore the severed estuaries, revive the Park, and satisfy the needs of farmers, fishermen, ecologists and water users from Miami to Orlando.

This holistic approach is working to protect creation in the most fragmented habitats of America: from salmon runs in California's Central Valley to the red-cockaded woodpecker across Southeastern hardwood forests; from the Sand Hill Cranes on the headwaters of the Platte River in Central Nebraska to the desert tortoise of the Mojave Reserve. I'd like to say that the possibilities are limited only by our imagination and our commitment to honor the instructions of Genesis.

But more and more, the possibilities are also limited by some members of Congress. Whenever I confront some of these bills that are routinely introduced, bills sometimes openly written by industrial lobbyists, bills that systematically eviscerate the Endangered Species Act, I take refuge and inspiration from the simple written answers of those children at the Los Angeles expo.

But I sometimes wonder if children are the only ones who express religious values when talking about endangered species. I wonder if anyone else in America is trying to restore an ounce of humility to mankind, reminding our political leaders that the earth is a sacred precinct, designed by and for the purposes of the Creator.

I got my answer last month.

I read letter after letter from five different religious orders, representing tens of millions of churchgoers, all opposing a House bill to weaken the Endangered Species Act. They opposed it not for technical or scientific or agricultural or medical reasons, but for spiritual reasons.

And I was moved not only by how such diverse faiths could reach so pure an agreement against this bill, but by the common language and terms with which they opposed it, language that echoed the voices of the children:

One letter, from the Presbyterian Church, said: "Contemporary moral issues are related to our understanding of nature and humanity's place in them." The Reform Hebrew Congregation wrote: "Our tradition teaches us that the earth and all of its creatures are the work and the possessions of the Creator." And the Mennonite Church wrote: "We need to hear and obey the command of our Creator who instructed us to be stewards of God's creation."

And suddenly, at that moment, I understood exactly why some members of Congress react with such unrestrained fear and loathing towards the Endangered Species Act. I understood why they tried to ban all those letters from the *Congressional Record.* I understood why they are so deeply disturbed by the prospect of religious values entering the national debate.

For if they heard that command of our Creator, if they truly listened to His instructions to be responsible stewards, then their entire framework of human rationalizations for tearing apart the Act comes to nought.

I conclude here tonight by affirming that those religious values remain at the heart of the Endangered Species Act, that they make themselves manifest through the green eyes of the grey wolf, through the call of the whooping crane, through the splash of the Pacific salmon, through the voices of America's children.

We are living between the flood and the rainbow: between the threats to creation on the one side and God's covenant to protect life on the other.

Why should we save endangered species?

Let us answer this question with one voice, the voice of the child at that expo, who scrawled her answer at the very bottom of the sheet:

"Because we can."

# Preserving the Environment and Liberty[8]

Helen Chenoweth

*Born January 27, 1938, Topeka, KS; medical and legal management consultant, 1964-75; executive director, Idaho Republican Party, 1975-77; chief of staff for Congressman Steve Symms, 1977-78; vice president, Consulting Association Inc., 1978-94; representative (R) from Ohio, 1994–.*

## Editor's introduction

In this speech, Idaho representative Helen Chenoweth criticized Secretary of the Interior Bruce Babbitt's espousal of an "environmental religion," which is also reprinted in this volume. Chenoweth argued that Secretary Babbitt's "emotional spiritualism" not only violates the First Amendment but also "makes villains of hard working, productive citizens." In addition, she asserted that it ignores many scientific findings. Chenoweth told the editor of this volume that her purpose in giving this speech was "to draw public attention to the growing connection between religion and the federal government's environmental policy" as a means of demonstrating "how over-zealous environmental regulations are negatively impacting Idaho."

---

Mr. Speaker, it is a rare individual who does not want an effective environmental policy. Sometimes these policies, or the remedies thereof, have been called extreme, just like we heard from my friends on the other side of the aisle. I am one of the freshman Members, but I find it interesting that a party who has lost its vision can use only one word to define the other party, and that is the word "extreme." I beg of my colleagues on the other side of the aisle to come up with alternative programs that will benefit the American people.

I just have to say Mr. Speaker, this was not a planned part of my speech, but I do want to say that it is private individuals who risk and who invest who employ Americans. I join the gentle-woman from Ohio [Ms. Kaptur], a woman I admire greatly, about the fact that we do want to keep American jobs here in America. I do agree with her there. But, you know, we either have one of two employers: Either you, the taxpayers, are employing individuals through government, or we have private businesses employing people. I prefer private entrepreneurs in employing people and downsizing government.

Mr. Speaker, it is a rare individual who doesn't want an effective environmental policy. We all want to promote the wise use of America's natural resources, but the driving force behind our current policies have little to do with sound science, foresight, or reason. Instead, environmental policies are driven by a kind of emotional spiritualism that threatens the very foundation of our society, by eroding basic principles of our Constitution.

Mr. Speaker, if there is one quote I could center my remarks around today, I think it would be a personal statement made by Thomas Jefferson, who probably was the world's greatest articulator of man's heavenly endowed individual rights and liberties. Jefferson wrote in 1776:

"I may grow rich by an art I am compelled to follow, I may recover health by medicines I am compelled to take against my own judgment; but I cannot be saved by a worship I disbelieve and abhor."

Mr. Speaker, the very first clause of the very first amendment to our Constitution states that "Congress shall make no law respecting an establishment of religion," and yet there is increasing evidence of a government sponsored religion in America. This religion, a cloudy mixture of new age mysticism, Native American folklore, and primitive Earth wor-

[8]Delivered to the United States House of Representatives, in Washington, D.C., on January 31, 1996.

ship, (Pantheism) is being promoted and enforced by the Clinton administration in violation of our rights and freedoms.

Proponents of this new-environmentalism are the first to recognize its religious nature. Just to name a few: Sierra Club Director David Brower announced "We are a kind of religion." Scientist James Lovelock, author of the bestseller "Gaia," admits that "Gaia is a religious as well as a scientific concept." Bill McKibbon, author of "The End of Nature," proclaimed that "it is not in God's house that I feel his presence most—it is in His outdoors." According to columnist Alston Chase, nearly all environmental leaders have conceded that environmentalism is a religious movement.

The trouble is that these sentiments are not just expressed by leaders in the environmental movement, but frequently, by government leaders who influence and promulgate the regulations we live under. When Vice President Al Gore was invited to speak at the Episcopal Cathedral of St. John the Divine, he sermonized that "God is not separate from the Earth." Espousal of this environmental religion by political leaders and regulators carries profound constitutional implications.

I recently came across the transcript of a speech delivered by U.S. Secretary of the Interior Bruce Babbitt on November 11 to a joint meeting of the National Religious Partnership for the Environment and the American Association for the Advancement of Science. It was entitled "Between the flood and the rainbow: Our Covenant to protect the Whole of Creation." In this speech, Babbitt explains how he became disillusioned with Christianity because the commandment that man should have dominion "over every living thing that moveth upon the Earth" conflicted with his view of nature's supremacy. "I always had a nagging instinct," he explained, "that the vast landscape was somehow sacred, and holy, and connected to me in a sense that my catechism ignored." Babbitt explains how a young Hopi friend taught him "that the blue mountain was, truly, a sacred place," and he became "acutely aware of a vacancy, a poverty amidst [his] own religious tradition."

To fill this vacancy he adopted the new environmentalism, and he has every intention of regulating and enforcing his dream of utopia into reality.

You may ask, what is the harm of public officials maintaining deeply held beliefs? The problem, Mr. Speaker comes when those deeply held beliefs become the driving force for policy which that nonbelievers face persecution. Mr. Babbitt has made it clear that environmentalism—the religion—is driving this Nation's regulatory scheme. This is a violation of the establishment clause of the Constitution. It mothers our values and it threatens our liberties.

James Madison wrote his great "Memorial and Remonstrance" against a Virginia tax for the support of an established church. In it, he eloquently argued that a true religion did not need the support of law; that no person, either believer or nonbeliever, should be taxed to support a religious institution of any kind; that the best interest of a society required that the minds of men always be wholly free; and that cruel persecution were the inevitable result of government-established religions.

Madison was right. The backbone of America—workers, small businessmen, and property owners—are becoming victims of this new-environmentalism.

Businesses like Stibnite Mine in my district, whose mining operation was shut down for 2 years waiting for the National Marine Fisheries Service to determine whether they could haul supplies on a Forest Service road.

People like the Yantis family in my district, who were told by the National Marine Fisheries Service that they should just give up their right to irrigate for a fish that is not instream now, but could be one day.

People like a Minnesota farmer who had two 1-acre glacial potholes on his property. To make farming around them easier, the farmer filled one and expanded the other two acres. The U.S. Army Corps of Engineers objected, and the Federal Government ordered him to dig out the pothole he had filled and fined him $45,000.

Whole families throughout the Northwest who have lost their jobs because government restrictions and environmental lawsuits have shut down the region's ability to keep forests healthy.

Farmers in the Bruneau Valley whose livelihoods have been held hostage to a snail the size of a buck shot. The Fish and Wildlife Service has yet to scientifically prove that farming activities have an effect on the snail.

For those who still refuse to see the dangerous character of an established religious environmental movement, let me give you another example:

Wayne and Jean Hage bought a cattle ranch in Nevada in 1978. The former owner had been forced to sell because the regulatory pressure by the U.S. Forest Service had become unbearable. But Hage was confident that he could work with the Forest Service to resolve any problems that might occur. He was wrong. Problems started when, without warning or notification, a nearby Forest Service Ranger Station began to pump water from a critical spring on Hage's property into the ranger's cabin. The Forest Service maintained a fence around the spring so that cattle could not drink, but, Hage felt that if the Service needed the water an amicable agreement could be reached. The Forest Service refused to cooperate, and when Hage held a field hearing on the issue, they launched an all-out holy-war against the rancher.

For the sacrilege of questioning Forest Service actions, Wayne was contacted no less than 110 times with violations of bureaucratic regulations. Most, if not all, were wild goose chases, but each required time consuming and often expensive responses. The Forest Service even resorted to several armed raids on the ranch, confiscating 104 head of cattle and keeping the proceeds of their sale. Hage also faced felony charges for clearing brush from his own irrigation drains. The charges were thrown out by the courts, but this was the last straw—Hage filed a suit for the regulatory and physical taking of his ranch.

Unfortunately, CIGNA Corporation, the lender and lien holder on Hage's property is one of the environmentalist faithful, and has been attempting to foreclose on the property to effectively kill the case. CIGNA is a major corporate donor to the National Wildlife Federation which is acting as a friend of the court on behalf of the Forest Service. This is an organization that instructs environmental activists on how to use Forest Service and Bureau of Land Management regulatory power to "Make it so expensive for the rancher to operate that he goes broke."

Mr. Speaker, there is something seriously wrong with this picture.

Environmentalism need not be a religion. It could—and should—be based on science and logic and aimed at secular goals. But Secretary Babbitt rejects the protection of species for potential cures for disease, or new strains of drought-resistant crops, or bioremediation of oil spills, in favor of uniting "all state, county and federal workers under a common moral goal." He concluded his speech by affirming that "religious values remain at the heart of the Endangered Species Act, that they make themselves manifest through the green eyes of the grey wolf, through the call of the whooping crane, through the splash of the Pacific salmon."

The fact that this moral philosophy makes villains of hard working, productive citizens makes it repugnant to American values. The fact that it dismisses science prevents technological progress. The fact that it violates the Establishment Clause of the Constitution makes it an attack on our form of government. And the fact that it places obstacles in the way of American prosperity makes it a threat to our children's future.

Mr. Speaker, policies inspired by this new green religion are having devastating effects on my State. One example that I think exemplifies this new trend is unnecessary introduction of predators such as wolves and grizzlies against the will of the people and at great expense to the taxpayer.

Many people do not realize that the idea of releasing wolves in Idaho and in the west is not a new one. There were attempts as far back as 1982, when Senator Craig held the seat that I hold now. At that time, when the U.S. Fish and Wildlife Service introduced this idea, the plan was quickly shelved after then-Congressman Craig held hearings in which obvious flaws of artificially introducing the wolves were exposed.

In those hearings biologists admitted that the wolf was recovering naturally in Canada and Alaska, where there are currently as many as 40,000 to 50,000 of the grey wolves. Moreover, the plan was soundly rejected after it became clear what the consequences would be of introducing a dangerous predator into an area that was no longer completely wild, but in fact, where there are activities such as ranching, logging, mining, and recreation.

The mere suggestion of introducing wolves prompted the State legislature to pass a number of bills prohibiting the introduction of wolves unless it was under the terms and conditions of the State. I would like to insert into the *Record* the testimony of State representative Jo Ann

Wood, who came before the House Resources Committee and testified to the long history of Idaho's objection to Federal wolf introductions.

Nevertheless, when President Clinton was elected, Bruce Babbitt, the President's appointed Secretary of the Interior, again resurrected the idea of introducing wolves in the West. This time, instead of trying to establish a sound, practical, scientific basis for the program, the Government promoted wolf introduction as a romantic notion of restoring the western ecosystem to its pre-Colombian state. Indeed, Mr. Babbitt has gone as far as saying that it fulfills a "spiritual" void. Mr. Babbitt proclaimed in his November 11 speech that wolf introduction efforts were driven by the "elevated nature of America's conservation laws: laws with the power to make creation whole . . . ." in essence recover "our ancient religious values."

The Department of the Interior also responded differently to the avid opposition to wolf reintroduction by States of Montana, Idaho, and Wyoming. The Fish and Wildlife Service promised the States that no wolves would be released until an agreement of how these wolves would be managed was in place. The Department of the Interior, in conjunction with the many environmental groups also initiated a large scale nationwide advertising campaign—in places where nobody would have to worry about managing the critters—to sell the romantic notion of returning these animals to the west.

Very little has been mentioned during the governments publicly campaign blitz of the overall costs of the wolf introduction, which includes aircraft, ground vehicles, equipment such as kennels, shipping crates, sophisticated radar tracking devices, radio collars, tranquilizing guns, and extensive staff of biologists, veterinarians, technicians, and administrators—not to mention a massive publicity campaign. Added up, it amounts to about $1 million per wolf.

I first dealt with Mr. Babbitt's infatuation with the green eyes of the wolf just after I was sworn in to represent the citizens of Idaho's First Congressional District. It was apparent that after the fiscally austere Republicans won the majority in Congress, Babbitt determined that the release of the wolves must be greatly expedited or his chance "to make nature whole" would once agaln be jeopardized. We found that his attempts to work out an arrangement with the States were not only completely disingenuous, but merely used as a device to detour the legitimate concerns of the States while he found a way to implement his plan. When Babbitt realized that his costly wolf scheme could come under scrutiny by this Congress, he went into emergency mode, bypassing all the processes, including State laws and section 6(f) of the Endangered Species Act which specifically requires the Secretary to work in coordination with the States in any introduction effort. He did this while ignoring the pleas of Governors and legislators to not proceed, but by actually speeding up the capture of the wolves.

By early January, just days after the new Congress had been sworn in, Babbitt had his wolves ready to be released at Yellowstone and in Idaho. My office received a firestorm of pleas and concerns from constituents and State officials calling for an immediate halt to the releases. In fact, one of my first official acts as a Congressman was to send a letter to the Secretary requesting that he halt any releases, and at the very least let due process take place. Babbitt defiantly responded by immediately releasing the wolves into Idaho—and even forging a highly questionable agreement with the Nez Perce Indian Tribe to manage the wolves.

Despite all, Secretary Babbitt proceeded with the release of his imprisoned green-eyed friends—although I don't know how anyone can consider him a friend of the wolf considering the abrupt way these wolves were tracked down and shot by a tranquilizer gun, forced into a pen, had a collar placed around their neck, taken away from their native habitat, and released into unfamiliar and unfriendly territory. Moreover, problems resulting from the unnatural methods used became evident when wolves which were released into Yellowstone, that were under the care of humans for weeks, refused for a time to leave their newfound comforts and security. Even now the wolves, which in the wild steer clear of humans, are routinely seen—and quite possibly fed—by many of the tourists visiting the park. It is easy to see that the wolf program in Yellowstone Park has done nothing more than create more dependents on the Government dole.

The released wolves faced—and caused—even more dire consequences in Idaho. Shortly after the wolves were released in Central Idaho, a wolf was shot near Salmon after feeding on the carcass of a newborn calf. The body of the wolf was found on the property of a 74-year-old

World War II veteran and rancher by the name of Mr. Gene Hussey. The reaction of the Fish and Wildlife Service was to initiate a fullblown investigation that included a $500,000 autopsy performed on the dead wolf. The Fish and Wildlife Service obtained a search warrant, and without notifying Mr. Hussey or the local sheriff, proceeded to send several officers to investigate Mr. Hussey's property. In a hearing about this incident held jointly with the Resources and Agriculture Committees, on which I sit, Mr. Hussey testified that on arriving home from his neighbor's house, he discovered several armed Fish and Wildlife officers crawling over his gate—damaging the gate in the process—and refusing to heed his warnings to leave his property until the local sheriff arrived. The predicament escalated to the point that the Federal agents accused this 74-year-old man of throwing rocks at them, and rushed across a stream to confront him about it. In the meantime, the local sheriff, Mr. Barsalou was speeding to the scene—very concerned about the possibility of a violent confrontation. Fortunately, he was able to arrive in time to defuse the situation.

After some of the problems that we have witnessed with the release of only 14 wolves last year, I am amazed to see the media reporting the program as "remarkably successful." I was even more disappointed to find out that even during the Government shutdown, and before their appropriations were approved, the Fish and Wildlife Service was busy preparing to capture another 30 wolves in Canada for release in Idaho and Wyoming. The Service has spared no expense and has let nothing stop them including inclement weather, lack of appropriations, animal rights protesters, the continued disapproval of the State legislature, and another call by this Congressman to refrain from capturing and releasing more wolves.

Apparently one of Mr. Babbitt's green-eyed friends did not like the whole idea and bit one of his handlers before receiving the unlucky fate of being killed by one of the Fish and Wildlife officials. Of course, if I had just been tracked down from my home, snared, darted, caged, drugged, and jostled, I would have bitten someone too.

The truth of the matter is that there remain many unanswered questions and unaddressed concerns about the wolf introduction program. Despite the fact that the Government continues to disregard the wishes of the local citizens, to implement a program that serves no scientific purpose, creates the potential for more conflicts, and costs taxpayers a bundle, the Government and the national media continue to paint the program as a better than expected success with few hitches. I believe this is because the media, like Mr. Babbitt, are not focusing on the logic or scientific merits of the program, but on how well it has fulfilled their own spiritual expectations.

Some wonder why I have fought so hard against a Federal program that has little direct impact on most Americans. I fight because I believe that we should be practicing great fiscal constraint, because excessive deficits threaten the future stability of this country. I fight because the taxpayer deserves to know that millions of their dollars are being spent on aircraft outfitted with sophisticated radio equipment which daily track a handful of confused wolves meandering about and stirring up trouble in the mountains of Idaho, Wyoming, and Montana.

I also fight because I believe there are deep implications about the wolf introduction program that affects all Americans—and that is the precedent it has set.

Now the Federal Government is finalizing plans to introduce an even more dangerous predator into the Selway-Bitteroot mountain range located in Idaho and Montana—the grizzly bear. Mr. Speaker, only a few years ago—the very idea of introducing grizzlies into central Idaho was considered pure lunacy. Why? Quite frankly, the grizzly bear, a species that now numbers over 100,000 in Canada, Alaska, parts of Montana, and in Yellowstone, simply has a propensity for violence against humans and animals. Last year there were numerous incidents of bear maulings during unprovoked situations. In one case a hiker was merely taking his shoes and socks off to cool his feet in a mountain stream when the odor of his socks apparently caught the attention of a nearby grizzly. And in the State of Wyoming and Montana, there has been an epidemic of nuisance bears which have been killing cattle and sheep, and rummaging around human habitation. Some are even suggesting that the grizzly no longer needs the special protection of the Endangered Species Act.

Mr. Speaker, the response that I have received from my constituents—even some who do not normally agree with me—has been overwhelmingly against the introduction of the grizzly. I believe that some in the forest industry have been driven by fear or strong coercive tactics into supporting a program that simply will not work. Other than that, the reaction against the idea comes from all types of individuals and for many legitimate reasons. Campers and hikers are concerned for obvious safety reasons, and that many of the trails and areas would be made off-limits. Hunters are concerned about dramatic reductions in game animal population. Ranchers are concerned about the loss of cattle and road closures. Miners are concerned about the possibility of restrictions on their activity as well, and property owners are deeply concerned about bears foraging about their garbage, and around their homes. Overall, people are not only afraid of the potential danger of having the bears in their backyard, but also having severe restrictions in accessing the forests and lands, both for recreational and industrial purposes. In fact the public comments compiled by the Fish and Wildlife Service show overwhelming opposition to the grizzly introduction plan in the Selway-Bitteroot coming from places as far as California and Colorado.

Moreover, introducing the bear has little scientific merit. The Fish and Wildlife Service has not shown how the grizzly is vital to the survival of the ecosystem of the Selway-Bitteroot. In fact, no solid evidence proves that the bear once roamed there in great numbers. Some have pointed to a supposed journal entry by Lewis and Clark claiming that they shot around 20 grizzly in the area during their travels. Considering that no taxonomy was even in place at the time to distinguish between types of bears, it is ludicrous to use a journal entry almost 200 years ago as a solid basis of the facts. Finally, the small amount of data that does exist from previous attempts to capture and release grizzly into unfamiliar and rugged terrain shows that it is impossible to predict the behavioral response of the bear. I believe it is not worth the cost, both in human and budgetary terms, to find out. Mr. Speaker, considering the significant amount of opposition to, and the lack of scientific need for the proposed grizzly introduction, we must look again at what is clearly the real impetus behind this idea. Introducing the bears addresses only an emotional attachment to the romance of having grizzly bears roaming the wilderness. It contributes to Mr. Babbitt's realization of the spiritual dream that he envisioned with his Hopi Indian friend so many years ago.

If environmentalists get their way with the grizzlies, there will be a devastating impact on the freedoms and livelihoods of my constituents, and significant ramifications throughout this country. I have seen evidence lately of ambitious goals by the Fish and Wildlife Service and environmental groups to populate regions of the West with thousands of grizzly bears. This would have the drastic consequence of shutting down access to many of our lands and forests to all human activity, including hiking and camping which virtually all Americans enjoy from time to time.

This would be a giant step closer to the utopia religious environmentalists are striving to create—a utopia where human beings have only as much value as the razorback sucker fish, and possibly less.

Mr. Speaker, this religious vision is not shared by every American and no American should be forced to promote a religious vision contrary to their own beliefs. The environmentalists want a new Inquisition to eradicate those with opposing views, and they have the might of the Executive behind them. This threatens, in the most profound way, our entire way of life. It is thoroughly un-American, and I won't stand for it.

# XV. Urban Issues

## Editor's introduction

Often incorrectly described as over-populated and crime-ridden, American cities typically embody a highly diverse population and a range of modern conveniences and cultural possibilities. Recent public addresses concerning urban life have attempted to reconcile media depictions of city life with the unique opportunities and services found in the urban setting. In addition to the clear conveniences that come with living in a city, urban crime, in general, has been on a rapid decline. Boston recently reported that for the second straight year not a single person under the age of 17 was killed by a firearm, and New York City has reported drastic decreases in all types of crime. In addition, many other cities, particularly Baltimore and Philadelphia, have undergone vast renovations to make them not only more appealing to the eye, but also more profitable.

As the following speeches indicate, the upsurge of the American city is a recent event. Throughout the twentieth century, American cities have endured not only extensive criticism but high crime, extreme poverty, and low levels of government funding. In fact, central to the comments of many of the speakers included in this chapter is the belief that the federal government simply does not provide cities with adequate financial support.

In 1967, Whitney M. Young, Jr., executive director of the National Urban League, warned that unless necessary institutions were restored in large urban centers, life there could collapse. Young further asserted that the federal government, far from presenting workable solutions for urban problems, has provided "band-aids" for an "advanced cancer." Shirley Chisholm supported Young's assessment, as she spoke of the hunger, inadequate education, poverty, prejudice, and racism endured by urban residents. David Dinkins, former mayor of New York City, outlined how the attractive qualities of urban life were threatened by the federal government's cuts in housing, child care, mass transit, public education, and drug enforcement. John V. Lindsay, also a former mayor of New York City, called for increased employment opportunities for minorities and "a responsible wage." Progress, he said, would require revenue sharing, block grants, and urban funding. Common to all of these speeches is the belief that American cities, if properly supported and maintained, have much to offer the country as a whole.

# The Crisis of the Cities: The Danger of the Ghetto[1]

Whitney M. Young, Jr.

*Born July 31, 1921, Lincoln Ridge, KY; died March 11, 1971; B.S., Kentucky State College, 1946; M.A., University of Minnesota, 1947; U.S. Army, 1944-47; director, St. Paul Urban League, 1947-50; executive secretary, Omaha Urban League, 1950; instructor, University of Nebraska School of Social Work, 1950-54; dean, Atlanta University School of Social Work, 1954-61; executive director, National Urban League, 1961-71.*

## Editor's introduction

On February 28, 1967, Whitney M. Young, Jr., former executive director of the National Urban League, addressed a meeting sponsored by the Joint Center for Urban Studies and by the Massachusetts Institute of Technology. Young stated that America's urban centers are "threatened with collapse." If major initiatives were not taken, he warned that cities would become "centers of chaos" and violence. The United States government, he concluded, must "build into urban society the human institutions which will provide the experience of community."

---

Here at the outset I may as well state my central thesis, which is that the central cities of this increasingly urban nation are not only threatened with collapse but are, in fact, collapsing, in large part due to the fiscal drain of the ghetto. As a consequence, what we are confronted with in the civil rights struggle is no longer a problem for the Negro alone, but for the whole society.

Throughout the country, the major cities are in trouble, scarred by slums and ghettos, threatened by racial strife and crippled by inadequate finances. Predictions are that the nation's urban population will double by the beginning of the next century and unless adequate steps are taken to avoid disaster, so will the problems of the big cities. Without radical action, our cities are destined to become centers of chaos.

One speaks of the possibility of violence with caution. Too often, to predict the possibility of violence is interpreted as an incitement to violence. But I infinitely prefer to be called an alarmist than to stand by, a silent witness to impending crisis. If what I say is interpreted as the message of an alarmist, then I can only say that Paul Revere was an alarmist.

I assume that what we are really talking about here, in talking about the crisis of the cities, are the problems of people—that we are not confining ourselves simply to questions of bricks and mortar in our consideration of the urban scene—and that we are concerned with the problems of people living in an urban environment, an environment to which mankind did not come naturally. Many of these problems derive from tangible factors, many from intangibles—from feelings of anonymity, of being nameless and faceless, a feeling of being lost in the great urban mass. Most of these latter derive from rootlessness and the lack of a personal stake in the community.

The questions before us become questions of how to provide the urban resident, and most particularly the slum and ghetto resident, with a stake in his own community, how to diminish the sense of anonymity he feels, how to reduce the impersonality of the urban environment, and, in the process, how to approach all the problems affecting the society-at-large.

Urbanization, first of all, causes severe stresses both for the community and the indi-

[1]Delivered at the Joint Center for Urban Studies, in Cambridge, Massachusetts, on February 28, 1967.

vidual. Housing shortages are chronic in all our major cities. Educational facilities in our slums are inferior from the standpoint of social and welfare services. Urbanization perhaps has its most profound impact on the structure of family institutions. The old traditions and values of the original family unit disintegrate under the impact of urbanization. The problems of the ghetto invade every aspect of life. It is our responsibility, in this society, to insure that the same skills, genius and creative drive that have gone into brick-and-mortar progress throughout the world, into the building of bridges, highways and tunnels, and indeed into smashing the atom and flights into space, must and do, now, go into planning with people for their own social needs. Only in this way can our cities reflect viable functional modes of productive living rather than struggles for survival against despair, hopelessness and frustration. Children then are not walled off from grass and sky and adults need not be faced with a monotonous routine which, at best, becomes a matter of existing—and without much choice.

Man in the urban complex has more than just physiological needs—the needs for food, clothing and shelter. He also has psychological needs—the needs for attention, affection, status and a feeling of making a contribution to his community.

At one time a man was adequate and had status if he simply provided a roof over the head of his family and could give his children a piece of candy from time to time. To be able to perform these simple acts was sufficient to obtain physiological and psychological satisfaction and to provide him with status in the community where he lived.

But living in the city demands more in terms of skills and of sophistication and so, man, newly transplanted within the urban complex, faces, and feels, alienation, a sense of rejection and loneliness, which makes even more painful the vision of those who are more affluent than he in the affluent society he sees all about him; and he either reacts with hostility by concluding that he is being exploited by the forces that are making others affluent, or he is diminished in his own self-estimation and says to himself, "I'm a failure." Such self-devaluation carries over into his role as a husband and as a father and into his concept of his own status and dignity.

Under the burden of anxiety, individual urban man becomes apathetic, overwhelmed, withdrawn. Because he doesn't want to acknowledge that he himself is inadequate in a new setting, he must cite powers bigger than himself, and what he says to himself and the community is, "I don't care, I don't want to succeed anyhow, You can't beat the system, You can't fight City Hall." Apathy is hopelessness, powerlessness and the forgetting of the most important fact, the fact that money is not power, that status is not power, that color can never be power. That the greatest power is to be right. And if you're right and believe in that right, you can get power. The Negro cause in America today is right and that's why it upsets those who refuse to accept change.

The question before us is how, given all the factors that make up reality, we can build into urban society the human institutions which will provide the experience of community. The problem is how to make the urban environment human and humane, how to make the geographical entity in which so many people reside livable, how to guarantee that people do not live as part of an amorphous mass, as impersonal cogs in the urban complex where the size and formality and the impersonal quality of the urban setting tend to deprive the individual man of his sense of identity.

I am prepared to say without hesitation that, in large measure, this country's success of failure will be gauged by the success or failure of Negro Americans in their struggle for existence in the urban environment, and on the success or failure of white Americans in meeting the challenges posed by the circumstances in which the bulk of American Negroes live. The real test of the urban structure will be whether or not the Negro within it benefits and succeeds on a par with his white peer in the larger society.

The simple fact is that despite all the frenzied activity, despite all the well intentioned efforts, and all the signs of real progress in the last decade and more, the gap between nonwhite citizens in the United States and white citizens has not been closed. In most instances it is not even narrowing—it is widening.

The time is clearly past for halfway measures, token gestures, pilot programs and halfhearted, one-dimensional, small-scale efforts, no matter how well intentioned. The crisis of our cities defies any such simple solutions. The expanding ghettos are not only thoroughly destructive to the people who live in them, but they threaten the welfare of every major city with strangulation and dry-rot. As one mark of our urbanity today we now have more people living in slums than we have on farms. The United States Census shows 21 million on farms; 22 million in slums—and that was in 1960. There is little doubt but that current figures, if available as of today, would show a still more remarkable picture.

We are using a slingshot for a job that calls for nuclear weapons. We are applying band-aids in the curious expectation of stopping the growth of an advanced cancer.

Three things are obvious. First, it is obvious that, whatever specific approach to the problems of the cities, the job is too big for government alone. Success will require the fullest possible commitment from every segment of this society, from the private sector as well as the public sector, from industry, labor, Federal, state and local government, as well as from the nonprofit sector as represented by the foundations.

Second, we cannot confine ourselves to any single approach, or to any one method. There must be concerted and coordinated action on many fronts at once, in education, in housing, in employment and in health and welfare. The job requires the full application of American genius and imagination.

It is also essential to realize that the debate now raging over whether to disperse the ghetto or to rebuild it is a debate without substance. Housing stock in the ghetto must be redeemed or replaced no matter who lives there—this year or next. The schools in the ghetto must be made excellent no matter who attends them—this year or next. And neither can wait on solutions to other problems before the beginnings are made there.

Third, it is obvious that within the Federal sector, with many of the legislative battles now won, that the struggle in the immediate future will lie to a considerable extent in the struggle for appropriations massive enough to get the job done that must be done.

The overriding question is one of the *will* to achieve definitive solutions. The first imperative is that we devise programs appropriately scaled to the size and urgency of the problems we face.

Recently, we have seen a growing recognition of the need for a massive effort, as expressed in the "Freedom Budget," which calls for an expenditure of $185 billion over the next ten years to be derived from the nation's "economic growth dividend"—a plan which fleshes out, puts meat on the bones of the domestic Marshall Plan we in the Urban League enunciated several years ago. We support this, and other, proposals which actively serve the same ends. These are proposals which actively serve the same ends. These are proposals properly scaled to the size and urgency of the urban problems we face. Only when the need is understood on this scale and long-range programing is undertaken along these lines, will we be able to assume that we are on the road to adequate solutions.

Nothing short of action on the scale indicated in the "Freedom Budget" will allow us to rescue the cities from the problems that now beset them, restore a viable tax base to major municipalities, create a full-employment economy, and provide every American with a decent home and a decent education, all of which are essential objectives if the crisis of the cities is to be overcome. Otherwise we will have to face all the implications of finding our central cities more and more fully occupied by a dispossessed, undereducated, underemployed, embittered, angry, impatient, low-income population.

New York City is a good case in point. What is happening in one degree or another in every major metropolitan area in the country. New York's annual budget crisis occurs with the regularity of clockwork. It did not begin with the Lindsay administration and it will not end with the Lindsay administration. Where it will end may well determine the fate of the Republic.

A year ago, New York, deep in its desperate annual search for funds to make up the difference between public revenues and the cost of essential public services, faced a budget deficit of $518 million. The Mayor stated then "that without new revenues a major reduction of *all* city services will be necessary resulting in a drastic change in the quality of life in New York City." In the course of the crisis the New York Stock Exchange threatened to leave the city; the City University was threatened with seriously cutting back on the number of students it could accept and city hospitals were threatened with a catastrophic mass resignation of nurses for want of adequate pay and for a time municipal hospital doors were closed to all but emergency patients. New taxes were enacted and the city survived.

Today one year later, of course, the city is in the grips of this year's budget crisis and the Mayor has stated that "New York City is at a crossroads. We must find the revenues to keep city government financially viable or so cut back services that government provides that the city becomes less and less livable."

The New York Stock Exchange still has not resolved the question of where to settle, and this month Pepsico, the American Can Company, Corn Products, Flintcote, and Olin-Mathieson have announced that they will move their operations out of the city. More disturbing, Leonard C. Yaseen, board chairman of the Fantus Company, the world's largest location consultants, has said that "six years ago we might have done six relocation studies in an entire year, but in 1967 we may conduct forty such studies."

This is the kind of disruption of the normal business and civic cycle that American cities are experiencing now in the present moment and it is symptomatic of the price we as a nation are paying for our failure to resolve the problems of the ghetto.

Put another way, HHFA [Housing and Home Finance Agency] figures show that the average cost per citizen for municipal services in a blighted area is $7 but the area pays back only $4.25; whereas in a good area, the average cost of essential services is $3.60 per citizen and the area pays back $11.30. Because of the distressed conditions under which they live, the number of Negroes on the public welfare rolls is increasing and one third of the $3.5 billion we spend today as a nation for public aid, education and housing goes to Negroes who constitute only 11 per cent of the population. In light of these facts, the fiscal management of the cities becomes increasingly difficult and the plight of the ghetto resident becomes increasingly acute.

It is inconceivable to me that responsible legislators and leaders in industry and commerce should any longer deny strong support to all measures necessary to correct the evils that pervade ghetto life and drain the resources of American cities.

And yet, what, for instance, is the picture in Washington today, and what is the picture in the private sector? In both arenas, it is exceedingly mixed. In Washington, leadership in the Executive branch is strong. You can give Johnson hell if you like on Vietnam, but the commitment of the Executive to solutions to our number one domestic problem is beyond doubt. Added evidence accumulates every day. To talk to people at the policy-making levels in the Executive departments is often immensely rewarding. The best of them are creative, sophisticated in the nature of the problem, passionately committed to solutions and imaginative in the use of legislative tools already at hand.

The picture in the Congress is, in large part, another story altogether and this is not just a result of the elections in November. The elections in November only serve to make matters worse. They can't be said to have been all that good prior to November.

For one thing the pace of implementation of domestic legislation is dependent upon manipulation of the fiscal machinery of government. Much worthy legislation languishes for lack of adequate appropriations. The Model Cities legislation enacted by the last Congress, for example, is conceived to put the full resources of the nation—Federal, state and municipal, public and private—to work to achieve not only the physical, but the social, rehabilitation of the cities. To date, the total sum appropriated for Model Cities is $11 million and that is for planning. No monies have yet been appropriated for the implementation of the Model Cities legislation.

Moreover, it is interesting to ponder the fact that this appropriation is in the control of a subcommittee of the House Appropriations Committee which is composed of ten men, not one of whom comes from a major city. The chairman, Representative Joe L. Evins, is from Smithville, Tennessee, a town with a population of 2,348. The largest city represented on this committee is Springfield, Massachusetts, with a population of 174,463. Other members of the committee come from towns of 8,780; 2,428; and 5,699.

To the President's full credit, his budget message recommended appropriations for the implementation of the Model Cities legislation at the full level of departmental request. What the appropriations subcommittee will choose, in its wisdom, to recommend is anybody's guess.

A further part of the problem in the Congress is that, in general, the northern liberal representative in the Congress, the man who votes "right" on issues affecting the Negro, is neither as shrewd nor as committed to his objectives as the southern representative. In practice, the northern liberal tends to be completely outmaneuvered by the committed southerner and the key to effective implementation of legislation is inevitably tied to the Federal purse strings which are firmly in the grip of the Congress.

Quite aside from the deliberations of the ten small-town men who, by virtue of their seniority, sit astride the appropriations for Model Cities, I greatly fear what the record of some members of northern congressional delegations, for example, may be when they are called upon to vote on massive appropriation rather than on, say, the Civil Rights Bill of 1967. Many a northern congressman, whose heart isn't really in it, may find it thoroughly feasible to vote against an appropriations bill, which is poorly understood by his constituency, whereas he could never vote against a civil rights bill. As we enter into a new phase of the struggle, where appropriations massive enough to do the job under existing legislation are of the essence, the lack of commitment among many northern congressmen becomes a matter for serious concern.

It is further interesting to note that, at a time when it has become clear that dispersal of the ghetto is essential to the health of the central cities, that it was a congressman from New York City who required inclusion of language in the Model Cities bill which precludes use of the Model Cities program to effect dispersal of the ghetto. In the same vein, more than a decade after the Supreme Court decision desegregating the schools, the Elementary and Secondary Education Act was passed, but only after language was inserted which states that "desegregation shall not mean assignment to public schools in order to overcome racial imbalance."

The picture in the private sector is no less interesting. Hundreds of companies have voluntarily complied with the President's Plans for Progress, and many have proved imaginative and inventive in dealing with the problems of recruiting, training and motivating minority workers. But the job and the responsibility of the private sector does not stop there.

I like to cite the situation as it now exists in Hartford, Connecticut, where, I am informed, the most progressive element in the community is the Chamber of Commerce, and the most regressive elements are the two major political parties, the Democratic the more so in that it is the stronger. Now the reason for the progressivism of the Chamber of Commerce, I am told, is that being good Yankee businessmen, its members take the position that they don't care what color people are, they are concerned only with getting them back on the tax rolls. "If you have to educate them, educate them," these men say. "If you have to build them houses, build them houses. But let's get them back on the tax rolls." This is my idea of an enlightened outlook for business and businessmen, and I hope and pray that the business community generally rapidly accepts the wisdom of this approach—both for the welfare of the Negro community and for the sake of the future of the cities.

There are further encouraging signs on the horizon. Within the recent past, for example, the New York Board of Trade, which is a major business-civic organization in New York, has taken the position that it is deeply aware of the total environment in which business operates and that equal concern must be given in management's planning for environmental factors other than the purely economic. The Board of Trade has determined to take an active part in identifying management's rightful role in the solution of socioeconomic problems besetting New York City, including those of the ghetto. There are even rumblings from within the National Association of Manufacturers emanating from a deep urge to image-changing through a new examination of the role of the corporate structure in relation to the socioeconomic problems that haunt the entire society.

As the pressures of the urban crisis continue to mount, it is possible that the most significant pressures for change will come not from their accustomed sources but from a concerned, aware and affected private sector. It is also possible that the Model Cities program which requires the active cooperation of the private sector will effect the first happy marriage in the solution of the problems besetting urban areas between Federal, state and local government and private interests.

To revert now to the coming struggle for massive appropriations as opposed to new legislation at the Federal level. The need, of course, varies from area to area. In general, the necessary legislative tools already exist for a broadscale attack on the problems of housing and manpower training.

The Department of Housing and Urban Development has a battery of techniques available to it, prime among which are the Turnkey Housing formula for the rehabilitation and replacement of substandard housing stock, and the leasing program which makes it possible for local Public Housing Authorities to lease apartments at will for use as public housing units. Massive application of the Turnkey concept alone could serve to eradicate substandard housing, estimated at 5 million units nationally, within the next ten years, if a massive effort were undertaken, as indeed it must be.

In addition, HUD has the tools at hand to create broad opportunities for home ownership by low-income people, a proposition the Urban League stresses as essential to any plan for the physical and social redemption of the ghetto. Home ownership, and the pride of ownership, constitute the surest way to create a stake in the community for individual families and to guarantee the health and stability of the community over the long haul.

The Urban League has proposed that leases on all rehabilitated housing made available to low-income families be combined with an option to buy, either on a cooperative or a condominium basis. Under this proposal, as a family's income increases, the family could undertake purchase rather than being required to move. Present housing law contains a provision for private ownership of public housing in attached and semidetached houses, a device so far being utilized only in St. Louis.

We have also proposed that private ownership of low-cost housing be further encouraged through the introduction of a federally subsidized below-market interest rate of not more than 3 per cent for the purchase of rehabilitated substandard housing by low-income families, a precedent for which currently exists in the Model Cities Act, which authorizes the purchase of such mortgages by the Federal National Mortgage Association under its special assistance program. In this connection, we would further urge the extension of such a below-market interest rate to all returning veterans.

Thirdly, we have proposed that one component in any program for the mass rehabilitation of slum housing be a provision whereby slum residents can obtain a "sweat equity" in ownership, through contributing physical labor to the rehabilitation and construction process, and that this provision for "sweat equity" be coupled with on-the-job-training in the construction trades. A precedent for "sweat equity" in low-cost housing exists in HUD's Mutual Help Program which so far has been applied on only a limited basis, and never yet in an urban setting.

It is not my purpose to discuss these proposals at length here. The point I wish to make is that in the field of housing the question now is largely one of the imaginative and, most importantly, the *massive* use of presently available housing tools. What must be developed within existing legislation is a basic framework for action consisting of the fullest possible use of the credit and subsidy powers of the Federal Government on a massive and coordinated basis and in a fashion designed to involve the initiative and incentives of competitive free enterprise.

Again, the debate about whether to "gild" the ghetto or disperse it is irrelevant. The housing stock in the ghetto has to be redeemed or replaced *now* no matter who is to live there now or at a later date.

As in housing, the laws on the books affecting manpower training are generally adequate. Programs have been written to cover most contingencies in this field and there is adequate leeway for experiment. What is essential, again, is that these tools be utilized on a scale commensurate with the problem, with the need to train all those who need training in order to become gainfully employed.

In both education and welfare there is a continuing need for legislation if, on the one hand, quality and integration are indeed to become the hallmarks of our public school system, and if, on the other, poverty is to be eradicated in this affluent society.

It is still very early to tell what the results to date have been of Title I of the Elementary and Secondary Education Act in contributing either to the quality of education in the schools or to the integration of the schools. Present indications are that while some schools have been able to make very good use of the monies provided by this Act, many schools were unprepared to utilize the monies to full advantage and, in the eyes of concerned people, they have often resulted in what could be called "add on" programs, programs which have just provided the schools with more of the same old uninspired and uninspiring materials, equipment and program they have had before.

As for the progress of integration, the United States Civil Rights Commission has just reported that thirteen years after the Supreme Court decision desegregating the schools, 75 per cent of all Negro children and 83 per cent of all white children still go to schools that are 90 per cent or more segregated, whether the segregation be of Negro children or of white; that the achievement levels of Negro children have been only slightly affected by so-called "compensatory programs" in these segregated schools; and that they will continue to suffer academically unless legislation is enacted that requires racial balance in all the nation's public schools. Like the Supreme Court decision of 1954, the current report by the Civil Rights Commission holds that both Negro and white children suffer when isolated from the mainstream of society. It further states that even though state and local governments in the North do not decree segregated school systems, Negroes are nevertheless denied equal protection of the law through a subtle combination of assignment patterns, school board decisions and the selection of school sites, which affect them quite as severely as those practices which have permeated the South.

The problem, obviously, of desegregating the schools is not an easy one. No schoolman wants to turn his whole system inside out in order to desegregate, but, often, that's the only real solution. Some inspired efforts have been undertaken in cities and towns across the country including Xenia, Ohio, where white support was enlisted for desegregation with a demonstration school in the Negro neighborhood; in Irondequoit, New York, where Negro youngsters were successfully imported into the school system of an all-white community; in Evanston, Illinois, where a computer was used to redistrict school attendance areas and to redistribute white and Negro students in combination with a dynamic education improvement program for the whole district; in York, Pennsylvania, where Negro youngsters were gradually slipped into elementary schools, grade by grade, starting with kindergarten in combination with a human relations program for students, parents and teachers; in Teaneck, New Jersey, where developing *de facto* segregation was rooted out by converting an elementary school into a central school for all sixth-graders; and in Riverside, California, where a crisis situation paved the way for integration of the schools.

In Riverside, where schoolmen were committed to the concept of the neighborhood school, someone else in the community wasn't. So, he burned one of them down. With a Molotov cocktail. At midnight.

A crisis? Yes—and an opportunity, too, as it turned out. The school's destruction forced immediate integration of its students into other schools. And this integration went off so smoothly that, within a matter of months, the Riverside Superintendent of Schools was able to schedule integration of the city's remaining racially imbalanced schools and predict that "minority pupils will be as well received by staff members and other pupils as those who were integrated as a result of the fire."

Which is not to say that this school superintendent or any other sane schoolman recommends school burning as a desegregation catalyst. But the fact remains that, in this case, the fire stimulated fast and effective action. Within a month of the fire, Riverside's administration was able to announce a solid plan to desegregate totally within two years.

Or—consider the education plaza, or educational park, as it's being developed in Orange, New Jersey. The concept is simple enough. If small neighborhood grade schools are creating a *de facto* segregation problem, and the entire K-12 system is getting out of date to boot, the idea is to close the schools and consolidate. The first step toward an education plaza has already been taken in East Orange. A pilot group of 250 fifth- and sixth-graders is being introduced to nongraded, individualized instructional techniques which will be used in the projected school plant. Land purchase and construction of a $1.5 million base building is scheduled for completion in 1968. A large intermediate school, an upper school and a lower school, are scheduled to follow in that order. The base building will be used for new teaching programs for the plaza and will be integrated into that structure later. Total implementation time for the plaza, which will also include a resource tower and junior college, a "lively arts" center, gymnasiums, a covered stadium and a large parking lot—is pegged at fifteen years.

It has even been suggested that one way to desegregate the schools is to strip the ghetto of schools for a period of time. The rationale behind this suggestion is that given a situation where you have an all-black school here and an all-white school there and perhaps an integrated school in between, the logical movement of pupils would be from the all-black school to the all-white school, and vice versa, but that, in fact, this two-way movement doesn't work. You can get movement from the all-black school to the all-white school, but you can't get comparable movement from the all-white school to the all-black school as long as the latter is perceived by the white community as an all-Negro school. Hence the proposal is to strip the ghetto of schools by moving the student population out and leaving the buildings empty if need be until such time as the school in question is no longer perceived as an all-Negro school; at that time it can be reopened with an enriched curriculum designed to attract white students as well as black on the magnet theory. I am by no means facetious in seriously urging that this approach be explored fully where everything else seems to fail.

To be good, the schools of this nation have to be desegregated. Where the will to desegregate exists, the schools are being desegregated.

There are still other things that a given school district can do. The middle-school concept, or the 4-4-4 system can change perceptions of the all-Negro school so that schools attract a more representative student body. Shuttle lines can be established, so that kids can get to an integrated school in a ten-minute bus ride. Bussing, like the idea of Federal control of the schools, is a false issue. White parents, who can afford to, have been bussing their children to private schools for generations. The rural consolidated school has depended on bussing for decades. And as far as Federal control is concerned, out of the total spent on education in this country for education at all levels, including higher education, only 8 per cent comes from Federal sources. At the elementary and secondary levels, the percentage is a mere 4 per cent.

The legislative route to achieving integration of the schools might result from a happy marriage between certain provisions of bills introduced in the last session of the Congress by Senator Edward Kennedy and Representative Adam Clayton Powell. The Kennedy bill would amend Title IV of the Civil Rights Act of 1964 to authorize the Commissioner of Education to provide technical assistance and grants to school boards which have drawn up programs for overcoming racial imbalance in their public schools. In other words, it would provide monies, which present legislation does *not* do, to meet the costs of desegregation. There are no coercive provisions in this bill whatsoever. The Powell bill, on the contrary, provides that every school district shall report to the United States Commissioner of Education on the racial composition of its student population by building and if, by 1970, any building exceeds the minority population of the school district by more than 20 per cent, it would get no more Federal money. For instance, in New York City, where the minority public school population throughout the City is 33 per cent of the total, any school with a minority population of 54 per cent as of 1970 would be deprived of any further Federal aid. Solutions are possible. It is not beyond the genius of America to find solutions.

The major needs for welfare legislation are threefold. One most important step is legislation requiring that by a given date, the states pay in full their own standards of assistance, which at this point, numbers of them do not. Further legislation is required in order to establish a major training component for people now receiving Aid for Dependent Children plus incentives to work. At present, we give the needy income. And we take away most of that income if the recipient gets the smallest job, causing needless waste and demoralization. Worse still, public assistance as presently written and administered encourages the disintegration of the family. In most states, the main assistance program, Aid for Dependent Children, is not available if there is an able-bodied man in the house, even if he is not working. All too often it is necessary for the father to leave his children so that they can eat. It is bad enough to provide incentives for idleness but even worse to provide legislative incentives for desertion.

Perhaps the best solution would be for the Federal Government to assume the cost of providing a minimum income. Nothing is quite so certain to provide an antidote for poverty as the provision of definite and dependable income. Ideally, such income would derive from expanded job opportunities, including jobs on needed public works, but in the absence of sufficient job opportunities, a minimum income is eminently desirable.

Numerous arguments are raised against this solution, the foremost among which is the assertion that it would destroy individual incentive. Yet, nothing is more certain than that we now have a welfare system that could not be better designed to destroy incentives if it had been planned for that specific purpose.

Perhaps the best solution to the crisis of the cities would be for the Federal Government to assume the cost of providing a minimum income, and thus freeing the cities from the present burden of welfare costs. In the years of the farm crisis, Federal Government did this for agriculture. In these years of urban crisis, we need a system that directs funds not by some formula to the country at large, but to the points of greatest need, in short, to the large cities. The United States Conference of Mayors, for one, is convinced that the cities are being shortchanged in a period when their own taxing resources are manifestly too limited to halt urban decay.

To transfer income maintenance to the Federal Government, would be to free big city budgets of a large share of their welfare payments and would be an enormous step in the right direction, leaving the cities free to meet problems which can be met only on local terms.

Whatever the analysis of our urban problems, whatever combination of approaches are taken toward their solution, one point is clear and that is that there is no simple way. The problems that confront us are desperate problems, infinite in their complexity and interrelatedness, and we must use every tool in the social arsenal to achieve solutions.

As one additional tool, which requires no legislative action, just administrative decision in both the public and private sectors, I would draw your attention to the Urban League's proposal for Operation Urban Survival, first enunciated at our annual Conference in Philadelphia last August and predicated on the following facts.

The explosive increase of the Negro population in northern, central and western cities represents one of the most dramatic social changes in urban history. No other ethnic group has ever made up as large a proportion of the population as does the Negro today. In 1910, when the Urban League was founded, 73 per cent of all Negroes lived in rural areas. Today, 73 per cent of all Negroes live in cities. In just one decade, New York City lost a middle-class white population almost the size of Washington, D.C., and gained a nonwhite population almost the size of Pittsburgh.

The United States Civil Rights Commission has reported that if all of New York City were as jammed with people as several of the worst blocks in Harlem, the entire population of the United States could fit into three of the City's five boroughs, with two left over for expansion.

By 1970, it is estimated that there will be 18 million Negroes living in our urban centers and before long, ten of the major cities of the United States will be more than 50 per cent Negro. Washington, D.C. already is and has been for nearly a decade. Newark, which was 34.4 per cent Negro at the time of the 1960 census, is now over 50 per cent Negro.

In Detroit, Baltimore, Cleveland and St. Louis, Negroes constitute a third or more of the population and in Chicago, Philadelphia, Cincinnati, Indianapolis and Oakland, they constitute more than one fourth of the population. The impact of the expanding ghetto is being felt in smaller cities like New Haven and Gary, San Diego, Buffalo and Rochester, Toledo and Akron, Fort Wayne and Milwaukee, Kansas City and Wichita. Not even the South is immune. New Orleans is 41 per cent Negro, Memphis and Atlanta, 38 per cent.

Whether you accept or reject the basic immorality inherent in the existence and growth of the racial ghetto, it is clear that the emerging picture in the central cities has implications which overshadow past social and economic revolutions and make them pale into insignificance. As long as the ghettos continue to swell, the welfare of American cities is in jeopardy.

The welfare of the American city depends upon the stability of its fiscal base; its ability to finance those collective necessities which make it possible for large numbers of people to live close together, allow commerce to thrive and create those public facilities and services which make urban life tolerable. Blighted areas—and all the ghettos of our major cities are blighted—work intolerable hardships on the people who live in them and drain the total community of its financial resources. Such areas are utterly unable to make a satisfactory contribution to the city treasury in return for services. Taxable income diminishes as the ghettos expand and the cost of public services mushrooms. This is the vise in which most of our major cities are caught.

In light of these facts, the Urban League's Operation Urban Survival represents a major additional measure for the alleviation of these conditions.

Operation Urban Survival calls, quite simply, for public and private institutional building in the ghetto, for a nationwide program of locating new commercial, governmental, industrial, cultural and educational buildings and developments in slum areas in order to spearhead the transformation of the ghettos into viable, integrated communities. *Where* such facilities are located can have as much social meaning as the purposes they are intended to house and social costs to the community can be vastly reduced by just such enlightened measures as this.

Widely implemented, Operation Urban Survival would mean a vast upgrading of ghetto areas. Just as location of the United Nations upgraded a blighted area of the East Side of New York, just as location of Lincoln Center upgraded a blighted area of the West Side, and just as Rockefeller Center upgraded a deteriorating section of midtown Manhattan, the location of major commercial, governmental, cultural and educational institutions designed to service the total community, black and white, in the ghetto, would not only upgrade blighted areas but would have a multitude of tangential, and eminently desirable, effects.

This proposal addresses itself to the social, commercial, civic and cultural vitality of areas now alienated from the larger community. A major, though intangible, side effect would be the improvement of communications between the races, an essential to progress which is largely lacking at present.

Operation Urban Survival means creating jobs within the ghetto that will command a mixed working population and is conceived in the belief that a mixed working population will lead to a mixed residential population. Dispersal of the ghetto, essential to the health of the central cities, requires not only that Negroes move out of the ghetto but that whites have good reason to move in.

In one stroke, Operation Urban Survival can bring new life and vitality to a decaying part of the city. It will generate new hope in the slums as adults find jobs and youngsters see that education can lead to tangible results. It will generate many kinds of peripheral enterprise and development, further adding to the vitality of the community. Such projects in the hearts of the ghettos will provide visible evidence that the city cares, that neglect and abuse are at an end, and that integration is a living force in city life. Most important of all, it will end the isolation of the ghetto from the rest of the community and is essential to achieving healthy traffic in both directions.

For example, if the two million square feet now planned for consolidation of New York State Office space in the World Trade Center on a site in downtown Manhattan, were consolidated instead in Harlem, we would have a facility in the Harlem community that would meet all the standards of Operation Urban Survival. It would employ a mixed working population, it would establish a healthy in-and-out traffic in the area, it would lead to the development of peripheral enterprise and would create a standing reservoir of jobs in the ghetto, and it could be expected to lead to a mixed residential pattern.

In addition, it is more than probable that construction of the two million square feet of office space now scheduled for the World Trade Center downtown would prove significantly cheaper to build in Harlem.

There is every reason for state and municipal governments to respond favorably to this proposal inasmuch as substantial portions of their funds go to bridge the gap caused by the economic conditions of the ghettos. The private sector has a comparable stake in this means to establishing the future fiscal health of the cities.

In conclusion, it is obvious that the urban crisis stems in large part from the failure to resolve the problems that confront the Negro and it is obvious what the Negro wants. He wants what white Americans are able to take for granted. He wants the same opportunity to earn a living, the same freedom of choice in the selection of housing and the same quality of education for his children. He wants dignity as well as opportunity, performance on the part of white Americans as well as pledge.

If there is no genuine conviction about the rightness of integration and human relations and no will to arrive at solutions—then laws alone cannot solve the problem—and the future welfare of our cities is in serious jeopardy.

I hope I have made it utterly clear that nothing less than massive effort will produce significant results. We must marshal all our available resources for the job at hand and proceed on a scale commensurate with the task. We are in terrible danger, and our cities in desperate peril, if any among us permit ourselves the luxury of "thinking small."

# Reality and Rhetoric[2]

John V. Lindsay

*Born November 24, 1921, New York, NY; B.A., Yale University, 1943; U.S. Naval Reserve, 1943-46; LL.B., Yale University School of Law, 1948; partner, Webster, Sheffield, Fleischmann, Hitchcock & Chrystie, 1953-55; executive assistant to the U.S. attorney general, 1955-57; representative (R) from New York, 1959-65; mayor of New York City, 1966-74.*

## Editor's introduction

In this speech, John V. Lindsay, former mayor of New York City, cited the National Advisory Commission on Civil Disorder's 1968 conclusion that America was becoming "two societies, one black, one white." In response, he called "for performance" in the form of increased employment, and "a responsible wage" for minorities. Lindsay described the problems of cities at the time, including discrimination, inadequate housing, faulty education, welfare deficiencies, and stark hunger, as inherently complex. Given this set of problems, Lindsay declared simple solutions to be woefully inadequate.

---

Any elected official must now face a group like this with more worries and qualms than he would have had two months ago. Speaking to students used to be painless and unworrisome: they couldn't vote you out of office; they judged you more by the sophistication than by the substance of what you said.

Now you've changed all that. You went to New Hampshire and to Wisconsin and stunned the pros. You showed that in 1968 a political organization couldn't deliver the votes if it couldn't convince the people that what it stood for was right. You helped convince an incumbent President that it would not be wise to seek reelection.

And you've put a very high premium on honesty and courage for anyone who would offer to lead you.

Your generation showed the capacity for change and the dimensions of dissent. You picketed, boycotted, and sat in. And this winter you poured your energies and talents into traditional political channels and revolutionized that tradition.

The changes, the uneasiness, the questioning, the sense of critical choices—all these come to us now in part through the work you have done in the civil rights movement. Through action and debate on our involvement in Vietnam. Through your search for new roles and responsibilities for individual participation in the political and academic communities. Let us welcome the questions and the choices. And let us begin to define them and to answer them.

Less than two months ago the National Advisory Commission on Civil Disorders stated: "Our nation is moving toward two societies, one black, one white—separate and unequal." This was a harsh and straightforward assessment. It had been made long ago by the people who live in Harlem, Watts, and Roxbury. It may have surprised them that *this* statement was made without qualification by a group of predominantly white, middle-class Americans.

But many of the nation's political leaders saw it differently. They said it was an exaggeration, or overstatement, or worst of all, that it ignored the significant progress in race relations of the past decade. They squirmed, they quibbled, and they denied that it was so.

Then suddenly the death of Dr. Martin Luther King and its destructive aftermath made the Commission's findings all too real. Many of the same national leaders quickly began to talk about the problem of divisiveness. It was safe now for almost anyone to decry the split in the country and the division between the races.

[2]Delivered to the Harvard Republican Club, at Harvard University, in Cambridge, Massachusetts, on April 20, 1968.

Did we really need such overwhelming proof as disruptions in 110 additional cities? We had hoped that the Commission's report would end this debate, that the candor of the report would encourage others to adopt a new honesty in their discussions of the problems of the cities and the relationships between the races. But that honesty was not forthcoming.

Nor is it yet clear that we have seen that honesty in response to the killing of Dr. King. How many of the government officials who issued proclamations in city halls and state capitols across the nation on the death of Dr. King had ever bothered to meet with him during his life, to talk with him, speak out for him, or march with him? How many of the corporations that sponsored public memorials after his death had been willing to contribute those funds during his life to his organization or to the cause he championed? And how many of them even now understand that they must either choose to act, or face the terrible costs of inaction.

We face now a new test of our honesty and purpose in confronting the problems described in the Commission Report and exposed in the streets of our nation last week. We will not relieve the tension in the streets of American cities with vague calls for "national reconciliation" or a "searching of men's hearts and minds." This is not the time to design new slogans for America. The promise of this country is clear—the Constitution, the Bill of Rights, the civil rights laws—spell it out unmistakably. This is a time—once and for all—for performance. It is time to make real in our lives the promise that has so long been written in our laws.

Let us be candid and specific about our shortcomings. Twenty-two years ago, in the Employment Act of 1946, Congress established as the policy of this nation the goal of a useful job at a reasonable wage for all who wished to work. In 1964 the official platform of the Democratic party again stated that "Full employment is an end in itself and must be insisted upon as a priority objective." That language is unambiguous—but so is the persistence of chronic and excessive unemployment in every ghetto in this nation. In San Antonio's slums the subemployment rate is 47 per cent; in Boston's slums it is 24 per cent; in New Orleans', it is 45 per cent. Need we ask what any of those men would say if they heard another speech, or another promise, or another pledge? They need jobs. Let us make that our standard.

Let us measure each proposal for America not by its appeal but by its consequences. Let us place it on the streets and study its impact. How will it affect the life of the fifteen-year-old high school dropout at 125th Street and Lenox in Harlem, or the welfare mother with four children on Chicago's Roosevelt Road?

Let us focus on specific legislation—on funding levels, numbers of jobs, salary levels, and on rounding up the votes for passage. The Commission on Civil Disorders recommended specific targets:

The creation of 250,000 new public service jobs this year, and one million over the next three years

The creation of 300,000 new jobs in the private sector this year, and one million such jobs over the next three years

Emergency bills to implement these recommendations have been introduced by Senators Javits of New York and Clark of Pennsylvania. They are languishing in committee. They have failed, like so much other vital urban legislation, to gain the support of the majority of white America.

We must not forget that the crisis of the cities is a crisis for the white man too, and that pressure and fear and bitterness and uncertainty threaten to alienate him too.

Today Americans stand poised for a brief moment undecided, confused, and insecure. There is the danger of stampede toward simple primitive solutions: tanks, guns, firebombs. But these are instruments that cannot work in America, just as they have not worked in Vietnam. Peace cannot be imposed on our cities by force of arms. The social and economic ills that have brought desperation to the ghettos cannot be overcome by military might. We begin to relearn old truths. Violence begets violence. Fear begets fear. A gun in the hands of a policeman aimed at a black teenager will no sooner heal wounds than a brick in the hand of a black man will erase poverty.

There is no simple solution to the disorder of our cities. The problems are complex and so also the solutions. Above all else these are problems of people, and they must be dealt with in human terms and with humane commitments.

If we are to be honestly concerned about the quality of urban life, we must look not only at Harlem and Hough and Lawndale, but also at our Park Avenues, our Lake Shore Drives and our Wilshire Boulevards. These are the streets of white Americans—affluent, defensive and uncertain whether to stay in the city, or to rush to the suburbs to meet the same problems there. For there is no longer any escape for those who would run.

By now it should be clear to every citizen that cities that don't work for black men cannot work for white men. If schools in Woodlawn or Central Square do not work, the price of that failure will be paid by others in West Rodgers Park and Brattle Street in welfare checks and police costs.

But if this nation is not one and equal in its affluence, at least it has become one and equal in its despair. Not only are black and white trapped together in cities that no longer work, they are also trapped together in a senseless struggle overseas whose purpose is not clear. All Americans have heard the nation's highest leaders describe a war in Southeast Asia as consistent with this country's most cherished traditions. Yet we have seen on television a very different conflict. We have been told of success and seen defeat. We have been told of life and seen death. We have been told of tunnels of light and seen graves of darkness. We have been told of freedom and seen repression.

America has been guilty of deception and blindness in our involvement in Vietnam: in our refusal to acknowledge civilian casualties from our bombing of the North; in our unwillingness to admit the existence of the National Liberation Front; and in our stubbornly sanguine assessment of the progress of the military effort and the pacification program. The cost of such self-deception is incalculable. Throughout the world it has undermined the prestige and authority of America because it did not look as if we knew what we were doing or why we were doing it. At home it has forced increasing numbers of citizens to doubt the word of our government—while at the same time the government suggested that those who dissent from its policies are inciting division and guilty of disloyalty.

The price we are paying in lives and in dollars in Vietnam is extremely high. And it is directly related to the cost of inaction in our cities. For the truth, I'm afraid, is that we cannot achieve either the cities or the society we would like as long as we continue the war in Vietnam. We cannot spend more than $24 billion a year in Vietnam and still rebuild our cities. We cannot speak of nonviolence at home when we are displacing, maiming and killing thousands of Asians for the professed purpose of protecting the peace in a land halfway across the world.

These are not healthy signs. These are not the signs of a country that has debated and defined its goals and values at home or in the world, or faced honestly the ambiguity of its position or the limitations of its power.

Just as the Commission report and the death of Martin Luther King demand from all of us some straight talking on the subject of race and the cities, the inconsistencies and the pressures of the Vietnam situation demand some new thinking of all our traditional ideas on foreign policy.

Whatever the answers we find to these questions, whatever the policies we choose, abroad as well as at home, they must be put to the same test: What are the consequences?

We must look to what is accomplished, not what promised. We must discern and judge the reality, not the rhetoric.

You have made us do just that. The debate of the next seven months must continue on these terms—on the terms that you have helped to set.

I last visited Cambridge in the spring a year ago. Since then your faces have changed. Then there was hestitation and uncertainty. Your causes had few leaders and your actions few consequences. You were only vaguely aware that white and black America were deeply divided. And though increasingly threatened by personal involvement in a war many challenged as immoral, you could plan no course of action that seemed to make much difference.

But this year you went to New Hampshire. You have seen Atlanta and Memphis. You have seen men begin to talk more about issues and less about each other. You have read the report of a presidential commission which was candid, and which you could believe.

But although there is hope, nothing is yet certain. The President now talks of peace, but the war and the draft go on. Commitments have been renewed, but a man, and perhaps a movement, lie dead in Atlanta. And in our cities it is almost summer again.

So I think you had better keep moving. I think you had better demand more than what you have gotten so far until America comes home again.

# It Is Time to Reassess Our National Priorities[3]

Shirley Chisholm

*Born November 30, 1924, Brooklyn, NY; B.A., Brooklyn College, 1946; M.A., Columbia University, 1952; director, Friends Day Nursery, 1947-53; director, Hamilton-Madison Child Care Center, 1953-59; educational consultant, NY Bureau of Child Welfare, 1959-64; assemblyperson, New York State Legislature, 1965-68; representative (D) from New York, 1969-82; professor, Mount Holyoke College, 1983-87; chair, National Political Congress of Black Women, 1985–; author,* Unbought and Unbossed *(1970),* The Good Fight *(1973).*

## Editor's introduction

In this speech, former representative Shirley Chisholm's maiden speech before the House of Representatives, Chisholm criticized the Nixon administration for funding an antimissile system at the expense of the Head Start Program. The Head Start Program, which began under Lyndon B. Johnson's 1964 Economic Opportunity Act, provides educational, developmental, medical, and nutritional services to poor preschoolers. Given the rampant poverty in American cities at the time this speech was given, the benefits of the Head Start Program were particularly felt in urban centers. For Chisholm, spending money on "elaborate, unnecessary, and impractical weapons when several thousand disadvantaged children in the nation's capital get nothing" meant that the federal government's priorities were misplaced.

---

On the same day President Nixon announced he had decided the United States will not be safe unless we start to build a defense system against missiles, the Head Start program in the District of Columbia was cut back for the lack of money.

As a teacher, and as a woman, I do not think I will ever understand what kind of values can be involved in spending $9 billion—and more, I am sure—on elaborate, unnecessary and impractical weapons when several thousand disadvantaged children in the nation's capital get nothing.

When the new Administration took office, I was one of the many Americans who hoped it would mean that our country would benefit from the fresh perspectives, the new ideas, the different priorities of a leader who had no part in its mistakes of the past. Mr. Nixon had said things like this: "If our cities are to be livable for the next generation, we can delay no longer in launching new approaches to the problems that beset them and to the tensions that tear them apart." And he said, "When you cut expenditures for education, what you are doing is shortchanging the American future."

But frankly, I have never cared too much what people say. What I am interested in is what they do. We have waited to see what the new Administration is going to do. The pattern now is becoming clear.

Apparently launching those new programs can be delayed for a while, after all. It seems we have to get some missiles launched first.

Recently the new Secretary of Commerce spelled it out. The Secretary, Mr. Stans, told a reporter that the new Administration is "pretty well agreed it must take time out from major social objectives" until it can stop inflation.

The new Secretary of Health, Education, and Welfare, Robert Finch, came to the Hill to tell the House Education and Labor Committee that he thinks we should spend more on education, particularly in city schools. But, he said, unfortunately we can't "afford" to, until we have reached some kind of honorable solution

[3]Delivered to the United States House of Representatives, in Washington, D.C., on March 26, 1969. Reprinted with permission of Shirley Chisholm.

to the Vietnam war. I was glad to read that the distinguished Member from Oregon, Mrs. Green, asked Mr. Finch this: "With the crisis we have in education, and the crisis in our cities, can we wait to settle the war? Shouldn't it be the other way around? Unless we can meet the crisis in education, we really can't afford the war."

Secretary of Defense Melvin Laird came to Capitol Hill, too. His mission was to sell the antiballistic missile insanity to the Senate. He was asked what the new Administration is doing about the war. To hear him, one would have thought it was 1968, that the former Secretary of State was defending the former policies, that nothing had ever happened—a President had never decided not to run because he knew the nation would reject him, in despair over this tragic war we have blundered into. Mr. Laird talked of being prepared to spend at least two more years in Vietnam.

Two more years, two more years of hunger for Americans, of death for our best young men, of children here at home suffering the lifelong handicap of not having a good education when they are young. Two more years of high taxes, collected to feed the cancerous growth of a Defense Department budget that now consumes two thirds of our Federal income.

Two more years of too little being done to fight our greatest enemies—poverty, prejudice and neglect—here in our own country. Two more years of fantastic waste in the Defense Department and of penny-pinching on social programs. Our country cannot survive two more years, or four, of these kinds of policies. It must stop—this year—now.

Now I am not a pacifist. I am, deeply, unalterably, opposed to this war in Vietnam. Apart from all the other considerations, and they are many, the main fact is that we cannot squander there the lives, the money, the energy that we need desperately here, in our cities, in our schools.

I wonder whether we cannot reverse our whole approach to spending. For years, we have given the military, the defense industry, a blank check. New weapons systems are dreamed up, billions are spent, and many times they are found to be impractical, inefficient, unsatisfactory, even worthless. What do we do then? We spend more money on them. But with social programs, what do we do? Take the Job Corps. Its failures have been mercilessly exposed and criticized. If it had been a military research and development project, they would have been covered up or explained away, and Congress would have been ready to pour more billions after those that had been wasted on it.

The case of Pride, Inc., is interesting. This vigorous, successful black organization, here in Washington, conceived and built by young inner-city men, has been ruthlessly attacked by its enemies in the Government, in this Congress. At least six auditors from the General Accounting Office were put to work investigating Pride. They worked seven months and spent more than $100,000. They uncovered a fraud. It was something less than $2,100. Meanwhile millions of dollars—billions of dollars, in fact—were being spent by the Department of Defense, and how many auditors and investigators were checking into their negotiated contracts? Five.

We Americans have come to feel that it is our mission to make the world free. We believe that we are the good guys, everywhere, in Vietnam, in Latin America, wherever we go. We believe we are the good guys at home, too. When the Kerner Commission told white America what black America has always known, that prejudice and hatred built the nation's slums, maintains them and profits by them, white America would not believe it. But it is true. Unless we start to fight, and defeat, the enemies of poverty and racism in our own country and make our talk of equality and opportunity ring true, we are exposed as hypocrites in the eyes of the world when we talk about making other people free.

I am deeply disappointed at the clear evidence that the number one priority of the new Administration is to buy more and more and more weapons of war, to return to the era of the Cold War, to ignore the war we must fight here—the war that is not optional. There is only one way, I believe, to turn these policies around. The Congress can respond to the mandate that the American people have clearly expressed. They have said, "End this war. Stop the waste. Stop the killing. Do something for our own people first." We must find the money to "launch the new approaches," as Mr. Nixon said. We must force the Administration to rethink its distorted, unreal scale of priorities. Our children, our jobless men, our deprived, rejected and starving fellow citizens must come first.

For this reason, I intend to vote No on every money bill that comes to the floor of this House that provides any funds for the Department of Defense. Any bill whatsoever, until the time comes when our values and priorities have been turned right side up again, until the monstrous waste and the shocking profits in the defense budget have been eliminated and our country starts to use its strength, its tremendous resources, for people and peace, not for profits and war.

It was Calvin Coolidge, I believe, who made the comment that "the Business of America is Business." We are now spending $80 billion a year on defense—that is two thirds of every tax dollar. At this time, gentlemen, the business of America is War and it is time for a change.

# At Stake Is "A Vision of Our Country"[4]

Henry G. Cisneros

*Born June 11, 1947, San Antonio, TX; B.A., 1968, M.A., 1970, Texas A&M University; M.P.A., Harvard University, 1973; Ph.D., George Washington University, 1975; administrative assistant, Office of the San Antonio City Manager, 1968; assistant director, San Antonio Department of Model Cities, 1969; assistant to the executive vice president, National League of Cities, 1970; member, San Antonio City Council, 1975-81; mayor of San Antonio, 1981-90; secretary of Housing and Urban Development, 1992-96.*

## Editor's introduction

Former mayor of San Antonio Henry G. Cisneros gave this address concerning decreases in federal funding for urban centers to 3,500 city officials at a National League of Cities plenary session. Worried that spending cuts signaled a "disastrous dismantling of federal-local partnerships," Cisneros called upon the delegates to work for much-needed support of urban housing, transportation, and the environment. To achieve those ends, he advocated revenue sharing, block grants, and urban funding. Cisneros received a standing ovation at the end of the speech. In fact, his address was so effective that the next day hundreds of the same mayors and city council members who listened to him visited Capitol Hill in a "massive, organized lobbying effort aimed at persuading Congress not to sacrifice domestic spending in the fight against federal deficits" (Baton Rouge, Louisiana, *State Times*, March 11, 1986).

---

Representatives of America's cities have been gathering at this conference, in this very room, for over 15 years. If these walls could speak, they would tell a powerful story of America and of its city leaders.

In these seats where you sit now have sat leaders of the big cities and of the small communities, from the Northeast and from the Midwest, and the South and the West, from all across America. Recounting the history of this conference would tell a story of the places that we love and the dramatic story of America's cities.

Over the last 15 years since this room has been used in this way every year, we have seen miraculous turnarounds: stories such as those of Baltimore and Boston, and Indianapolis and Cleveland. We've seen smaller communities that have succeeded and that have given us leaders to the national organization, like Scotland Neck, North Carolina, and Sunnyvale, California. Communities like Lincoln, Nebraska, and Lancaster, Pennsylvania, Lowell, Massachusetts, Topeka, Kansas, Nitro, West Virginia, and Vancouver, Washington.

We've seen cities that were sort of in the second rung of cities and now are national powers like Tampa and Seattle and Atlanta, Minneapolis, Denver and Houston and San Jose and the second largest city in the country now—Los Angeles. We see the same cities that were struggling work to forge new roles for themselves to completely convert their economies and perform in this new era. Cities like Akron, Fort Wayne, Fort Worth, Rochester, Beaumont, and Tucson.

All in all, what we have seen are the performances of the finest public officials in American life. The jobs that they have done have been masterful, tough, independent, resourceful, financially responsible, and competent. All across those years that they have been here, you have been here. Sometimes, it was to build new partnerships as in the early 1970s when in this

[4]Delivered to the National League of Cities, in Washington, D.C., on March 10, 1986. Reprinted with permission of Henry G. Cisneros.

room, this organization met to celebrate the passing of revenue sharing signed by President Nixon. The mood then was excited and exuberant, optimistic and appreciative of the respect extended by the federal government.

Sometimes we met in years when the mood was more one of commiseration over the black clouds that loomed on the horizon far away—as in the Carter years—when the theme was high inflation. Or, in the early years of the Reagan presidency when we heard the first language of the New Federalism. The mood then was anxious and cautious.

But always we have been city officials first, Republicans and Democrats second, liberals, conservatives somewhere else, but city officials first.

This year all of us together face a new problem that none of those who sat in these chairs has faced before. It is a disastrous dismantling of the federal-local partnership. It is a meat-ax chopping of the domestic obligations of government.

These are not in the category of threats or distant storm clouds, but the realities of the next 90 to 120 days. The mood, our response, must not be gloom, or timidity, or uncertainty, or hang-dog apologetics.

We must be determined to stand up for what is right in the face of what I can only call disrespect: a disrespect for our cities, disrespect for the people who govern them, and disrespect for the people who live in them.

Now, if you think that the word "disrespect" is too strong, then I don't know any other word that describes what is happening. "Miscommunication" or "misunderstanding" doesn't explain it. The only word that I can find that fits the bill is disrespect.

How else can one account for the fact that in 1980 urban programs were $69 billion in our nation's budget, while today they are $17 billion, a dramatic cut? Yet over that same period of time, the deficit has grown from $27 billion to $200 billion. Picture that for a minute: a deficit that has grown from $27 to $200 billion, our programs have gone from $69 billion to $17 billion, and it is we who are blamed for the deficit! It is just not true, and don't you believe it!

I'll tell you what is true, though. What is true is that the loopholes in the tax codes are up 8 percent, while housing programs are down 67 percent. What is true is that foreign aid is up 8 percent, but job training is down 16 percent. What is true is that defense is up 12 percent, but municipal wastewater grants are down 25 percent.

Where is the balance, where is the equal sacrifice, where is the fairness in that? People of our cities will lose—not because there is a deficit—but because of the way the rules of the game have been set by the administration and the Congress.

When the rules of the game are set in this way, when you increase defense by 12 percent, when you leave the entitlements untouched so that they grow by 8 percent, when there are no new revenue sources at all, and when you hold tax reform revenue neutral and still try to balance the budget on the Gramm-Rudman timeframe, there is no way that you can win in the ball game.

The fact of the matter is that the numbers don't work. The only course when the rules of the game are set that way is to dismantle the domestic side of government, which may in fact have been the intent of some of those in the Congress and the administration all along.

In 1981, we had what was called the Gramm-Latta tax cut. It cut taxes on upper incomes with the supposed knowledge that it would invigorate the economy so that we would have a balanced budget in a few short years. Instead, we ended up with the worst deficit in the history of our country: $200 billion. So we now have Gramm-Rudman, which is supposed to solve what Gramm-Latta didn't, by dismantling the domestic side of government.

You may have seen a listing of some of the programs that are slated to be eliminated. It is a long list, and it includes a whole host of programs such as EDA [Environmental Development Agency], programs related to senior citizens' housing, FHA [Federal Housing Administration], and the Small Business Administration and countless others. Many of you have said that you want to know what we stand for. Before this meeting is out, we hope to set before you a priority list that indicates what programs this organization is going to fight for, recognizing that we can't fight for them all. But even as we are losing programs, we are also losing the capacity to generate revenues because of what is happening on the other side of the discussion—not the spending side, not the budget side, but with tax reform.

Tax reform [legislation] involves some $400 billion of incentives and credits in the tax code, and right now there is a Berlin Wall, if you will, placed between a tax code that is intended to be revenue neutral and the budget cuts that are being made. You end up with some really unfair contrasts.

For example, accelerated depreciation for office buildings went up from $10 billion in 1984 to $15 billion in 1986 in the tax code, while CDBG [Community Development Block Grant] was slated for a 32 percent reduction on the budget side.

Special capital gains treatment for timber went up by 150 percent in the tax code, while low-income housing will be down 67 percent in the budget.

Corporate tax breaks and subsidies are running at $140 billion in the tax code, while general revenue sharing will be cut out, aced out 100 percent in the budget.

The purchase price of a corporate plane can be recouped entirely through tax credits and deductions in the tax code, while city mass transit monies will be down 31 percent in the budget.

Again, where is the equality of sacrifice when we leave the tax code alone with some $400 billion and make all the cutting that needs to be made on the budget side?

But if that were not enough, tax reform goes even further and goes to the heart of the ability of cities to finance the self-reliance that is intended.

Of course the attack on state and local tax deductibility is one of those. We must remember that before there was a federal income tax, there were state and local taxes. These taxes already existed before there was a federal tax, and when the federal tax came into existence, it recognized the fact that people were paying state and local taxes.

So don't allow ourselves to be "walked into" the logic that says that we are just one other lobby group on the question of the tax code. Unlike other incentives built into the tax code to encourage some kind of spending or buying activity on the part of the American public, this is a fundamentally different thing.

The same thing is true of tax-exempt bonds. We've gotten ourselves into a situation where the enormity exists right now that the federal government mandates us to clean water, but calls the bonds that we'll need to do sewage treatment plants nonessential. That's the craziness, if you will, of this present situation, and so when I use the word "disrespect," that's exactly what I mean. There is no other way to describe it except as disrespect that is thoughtless and will result in years of damage.

The shape of our governmental system for 15 years is going to be set in the next 180 days, and I honestly don't believe that we can allow the dismantling of such a system that has been so productive: the breakup of working relationships that have been put together on a bipartisan fashion year in and year out, the closing of day-care centers, the termination of housing initiatives, the closing of senior citizen nutrition centers, the reduction of manpower training centers.

I honestly believe that you don't deserve to be portrayed as the inept managers who cut, slashed and chopped people programs because you didn't know how to manage. But that's the picture that will be facing urban America in another 180 days. No matter what size of city you come from, you have got to see that the homeless, the poor, and the old will not be going to the oakpanelled committee rooms in the Rayburn House Office Building to make their case. They're not going to be going to take their case to the white-gloved gentility of the West Wing of the White House. They are not going to penetrate the upper office suites of HUD [Housing and Urban Development] or the Treasury Department.

But they will be at your council offices. They will be at your offices at City Hall. And they will be even at your house.

You are the ones that are going to have to cut the parks in your community because there is no more revenue sharing. You are the ones that are going to have to cut day-care because there is no more community services block grant. You are the ones that are going to have to cut job training because there is no more Job Training Partnership Act.

You are the ones that are going to have to cut housing programs because CDBG has been reduced. You are the ones that are going to have to let sewer moratoria run a risk in your community because the Clean Water Act monies have been eliminated. You are the ones that are going to have to let traffic become congested because transportation programs are reduced.

And you are going to be the ones who raise taxes, because in 1986 the federal government decided to get out of the business of domestic America.

I've sensed some reluctance on the part of some of you over the course of the last days and weeks, some ambivalence, a sense even on the part of some that says, "I care about this program but not that program, and I'm here to work on mine and I'll make my arrangement with my congressmen, and as soon as we cut our deal then we'll sort of break away from the rest of the organization."

I understand some of that sense, because I come from a region where it is very difficult to articulate the kind of message that I'm trying to convey to you today. But this is one of those cases, ladies and gentlemen, where if we don't hang together, then we'll hang separately.

This is a time when we need to address some questions of attitude even before we get into tactics. I say one of the first things we need to address together and understand together is that there is no need to apologize because you run cities.

There is no need to apologize because you are sworn to uphold a city charter. It is an honorable place in our system; the cities of America are where 80 percent of the people of this country live. The cities of America are where the essential dynamics of modern American life occurs.

When the cure for cancer is found in this country, it is going to be found in the hospital of a great American city. When new ideas of government are advanced, it's in the neighborhood movements of American cities and towns. When new forms of art are advanced, it's in the galleries that exist in the cities. When new books and ideas in literature are contributed, it's in the university complexes that exist in your cities and towns.

All in all, the cities of America are important to this country, and as a result the city governments of America are important.

When people stop and think every night as they go to sleep, whether there is going to be somebody that they can depend on if their spouse should be walking across the bedroom floor and collapses of a heart attack, it's not some esoteric argument at that stage. It's a question of whether they can pick up the telephone and find that emergency medical service on the other end of that line that can get there in a reasonable span of time.

Or as one sleeps at night and worries about crime and burglary problems in the neighborhood, is there a police officer on hand that the city government put in place?

One sends one's children off to school in the morning in the knowledge that they are walking on sidewalks, through traffic signalization systems, on decent streets where the traffic flows safely, that the city made possible.

Even as they leave for their jobs, often it's to jobs in a restaurant or a retail center adjacent to something that the city government help put in place.

The point I'm making is simply that you have absolutely nothing to apologize for in fighting for these programs, nor for standing up for the place of cities in the American system of government.

This is not just another lobby group. The truth of the matter is that not one of you in this room will make one more penny next year in terms of what the charter salary is in your city, because you have fought to save CDBG.

This is not like someone who gets a bonus in their salary or who gets stock savings or stock options if they are successful in running their cities better. All you're trying to do is advocate for a place for people in the American system.

So there is no need to be defensive: in fact, we have a very good offense. Think about the business of running cities as defense and offense. Defense means protecting our cities against these kinds of incursions, whether they be budgetary or tax reform. On the other hand we have an offense which means what we do with our own capability in our respective towns.

We have one hell of an offense. We have an offense that includes Charley Royer and what he has managed to do to make Seattle an international city by developing that port capability and marketing that city. We have an offense that includes Bill Hudnut and what he's managed to do in Indianapolis, rebuilding that downtown and bringing back an older industrial city, and what Kathy Whitmire has done in Houston—despite the fact that the city is ravaged by the decline of oil and gas prices.

We have an offense that includes Mayor Schaefer in Baltimore and what he has been able to do with an old port city, or Buck Rinehart, mayor of Columbus, Ohio, and his unique relationships with the university there, and Bob Bolen in Fort Worth. And in the small communities, places like Lowell, Lancaster, and Fort Wayne, there are countless examples of people who have been competent and self-reliant. There is nothing to apologize for on that scale.

But at the same time, when we're called upon to play defense, we have a defense as well. It begins with the priorities on the national agenda for the nation's cities.

Top of the list: General Revenue Sharing reenactment, and after that, other priority program reenactments: Community Development Block Grants, Urban Development Action Grants, environmental programs, transportation programs and the housing assistance programs.

Our priority is to try also to educate our people about the Gramm-Rudman-Hollings process, and so that is listed as a priority for this year. Other priorities include: tax reform, tax expenditures (which is that $400 billion that I described earlier that's available, but at the moment not being used for deficit reduction), federal mandates (which require that we clean water, but give us no revenues to clean it), and the liability insurance issues. Stated in one succinct format, these are the priorities of the National League of Cities in 1986.

In preparation for testimony recently, Mayor Voinovich and I asked the staff to prepare the 10 toughest questions that we were likely to encounter. We have reproduced those questions and some answers for your use in meetings with your congressmen and senators.

**Question 1: Isn't it hypocritical for you to express concern about the federal deficit and then to oppose Gramm-Rudman because it will cut city programs?**

No. Gramm-Rudman substitutes nonelected officials to make critical budget priority decisions affecting our taxpayers in place of the accountability and responsibility on the part of people who are elected to make those decisions. Gramm-Rudman is not fair. It applies to only 13 percent of the budget. That portion could be cut out 100 percent, and the budget would still not be balanced. Congress and the administration need to adopt fair and balanced deficit reduction budgets. The NLC board has adopted a budget priority statement that would reduce the deficit, but without increasing your property taxes or cutting your services.

**Question 2: Aren't you really calling for a tax increase?**

No. Tax reform would lead to increased revenues to reduce the deficit. The federal budget included federal tax subsidies, benefits and loopholes totalling more than $500 billion next year. Just freezing federal tax expenditures would reduce the deficit by over $50 billion.

**Question 3: Won't a tax increase or increased revenues cause a recession, as the President insists?**

No. There is no general rule on that question; a recession depends on many economic variables. In fact, in 1981 there was a tax cut but a recession followed a tax cut. In 1982 federal taxes rose, but we have had a steady building of the economy since then.

**Question 4: What really has happened to federal aid in the last five years or so?**

Federal aid to cities has been cut from $69 billion in 1980 to about $17 billion proposed this last year. Gramm-Rudman and the new budget will likely result in the elimination of the federal partnership with cities and towns over its five-year life. Having rigged the game the way I described, the only outcome can be elimination of all federal programs over time.

**Question 5: What will happen to and in cities if Gramm-Rudman operates for five years without a major federal tax increase?**

If Gramm-Rudman continues for five years, all federal aid to local governments will likely be eliminated. But because such a small portion of the federal deficit is subject to Gramm-Rudman (only 13 percent), the federal deficit itself will remain after the dismantlement of the working relationship that has been so arduously and carefully built up over all these years.

**Question 6: How do you reconcile your call for closing tax expenditures and your vigorous lobbying to retain the deductibility of state and local taxes and the tax exemption for interest on bonds?**

Tax expenditures are incentives built into the federal tax code to encourage certain types of activities, but the deductibility of state and local taxes and the tax-exempt bonds were not put into the code to encourage constituents to pay property taxes. They were already paying property taxes. It was a constitutional recognition of a partnership, of a relationship; not an incentive device as all of the other provisions in the code, but a recognition of another level of government.

**Question 7: Federal aid is down, local taxes may go up. You call that passing the buck,**

**but isn't that really the best way to finance these activities so they address local need?**

No. Federal spending of money coming from our cities and towns is up, but aid back to our municipalities is down. There is a question of priorities. Why should we be spending more in foreign aid and eliminating domestic aid? Second, not all cities and towns have the same capacity to raise their own local taxes. Some cities and towns have to provide a disproportionate level of services, because they have a very poor community and also a poor tax base. So the structure of the tradeoff is just not fair. We will force, for example, people to rely less on a progressive income tax and more on regressive local fees.

**Question 8: More than a majority of cities seem to be doing all right. Why then are you so insistent about the dire effects of Gramm-Rudman and the loss of federal aid? Aren't you exaggerating and painting an unnecessarily bleak picture just in order to rationalize keeping federal aid programs for your constituency?**

The cities have sacrificed, have cut, and have raised taxes, year after year. Some cities are in good shape, but many (especially in regions beset by economic turndowns) are at the end of their ropes. Poverty is up in America, unemployment is up in America, and tax caps have been thrown in place. Cities truthfully, honestly have a more difficult time; and I think that point needs to be gotten across.

**Question 9: How can you support General Revenue Sharing, when there is no revenue to share—especially when General Revenue Sharing goes to so many wealthy jurisdictions?**

General Revenue Sharing was not created to share methodical federal revenues or surpluses. It was created to help comply with federal mandates, but it is shared according to need. The lower the average income of your city's taxpayers, the greater the revenue sharing amount. When President Nixon signed Revenue Sharing into law there was a federal deficit then. Since 1972, when revenue sharing was enacted, federal funding for revenue sharing has been cut, but the deficit has grown by 1,000 percent.

**Question 10: Finally, are the governors right when they say that the federal role should be basically national defense and Medicaid, but all other programs such as housing, environment, education and transportation should be left to the states?**

The answer, we feel, is no. Providing a decent, safe and sanitary house for all Americans has been a federal goal since 1937. Cleaning the nation's air and water is a national problem; we can't have 50 different sets of laws and standards for bodies of air and water that don't respect state borders because of their natural layout. Giving our children a quality education must be a national priority for the future of our country. Providing the American people access to schools and jobs and health care on the waters, highways, rails, and airs is fundamental to a national economy. So the states have an important role to play but so does the federal government. The proof of the need for federal aid is the costly mandates in each and every area imposed upon us.

In other words, the federal government cares enough about these questions to set down regulations and laws thereby defining its interest in the subject—defining a role for the federal government, but it's withdrawing from the financing of those activities.

As I said to you this morning, I think we have a tremendous opportunity.

I came away from Seattle [the 1985 Congress of Cities] totally depressed, beset by a feeling of gloom. I didn't see a sliver of daylight in an otherwise solid wall of obstruction and opposition. But it seems to me that as we get closer to the day of reckoning on these questions there is some reason for some measure of, if not open optimism, then at least a hard sense of determination.

First of all, I think we are going to get some movement on that re-enactment date on the bonds, on that effective date of the bonds as you heard Mr. Rostenkowski suggest this morning, but we have to work on that.

I think we will see some movement on state and local tax deductibility, but you have to work on that.

I think we'll see some movement on the tax-exempt bond question, but you can determine whether that actually happens. And on the question of the programs, I think that as the congressmen realize what is actually going to happen, you are going to see some opening of daylight for compromise.

But it's got to be in a spirit of clear determination on our part. There is not one moment that can be wasted, not one iota of energy wasted on apologizing for the cities' role in this country or for their place in this system.

We have a place to roam, to play; it is an honorable one, and I cannot tell you in words just how important. Because what I think is at stake here is a lot more than just the cities, as important as they are. I think what is at stake here is a lot more than some federal titles in a law, as important as that is. I think what is at stake is a lot more than some budgetary appropriations.

What's at stake here is an American way of life, in which we have set some ideals. This country works so that all its people have a measure of justice and opportunity, prosperity, and, yes, equality.

We teach little children at five years of age their first day in school to recite words that they don't even understand at that point, and that's the Pledge of Allegiance. We teach them as they say that to close with the phrase, "one nation under God, indivisible, with liberty and justice for all."

One nation, not the Sunbelt against the Frostbelt, not the big cities against the little cities, not the defense industry pitted against the needs of the homeless or day care.

One nation under God—a God who can see just as easily into the homes of those senior citizens, who wait in the cold scared about whether or not the programs that they depend on are going to continue—just as easily as he can see into the skybox suites of the modern stadiums.

Indivisible, not divided, white against black, rich against poor, with liberty and justice for all. And if we lose that sense, we lose something else in this country—a country that fundamentally believes in a sense of equality, so that people are willing to work their hearts out now knowing that there's something better out there for them and their children.

If we lose that quality of people sacrificing now for the future, then we will end up no more than a nation in a constant adversarial hostility, as people have to demand right this minute everything because there is no faith in the future.

Ladies and gentlemen, the stakes here are a lot bigger than our individual cities, or even laws, or even grant programs. The stakes are a vision of our country, and the cities have had and will continue to have a place in that system. A lot of how it comes out is up to you and what you do over the course of the next 24 hours.

# In Praise of Cities[5]

## David Dinkins

*Born July 10, 1927, Trenton, NJ; U.S. Marine Corps, 1945-46; B.S., Howard University, 1950; J.D., Brooklyn Law School, 1956; attorney, Dyett, Alexander, Dinkins, Patterson, Michael, Jones, 1956-75; district leader, New York State Democratic Party, 1967-72; assemblyman, New York State Assembly, 1966; president, board of elections, 1972-73; city clerk, 1975-85; president, borough of Manhattan, 1986-90; mayor of New York City, 1991-94; professor, Columbia University, 1994–.*

### Editor's introduction

In this speech, former mayor of New York City David Dinkins detailed the benefits of living in a city, which include close proximity to a plethora of cultural activities, sporting events, and universities. At the same time, he criticized the federal government's decrease in support for housing, child care, mass transit, public education, and drug enforcement. For Dinkins, federal spending cuts in city support constituted a "politics of antiurbanism" that, given the amount of money the federal government makes from cities, must cease.

---

Good morning.

I am deeply grateful to former Chancellor Ira Heyman and his successor, Chancellor Chang-Lin Tien, for inviting me to address the distinguished students, faculty, staff, and alumni at this great center of learning, the University of California at Berkeley, a symbol of freedom for universities throughout the world.

To step onto these historic grounds today is to fulfill an American pilgrimage. The most basic human impulse is to communicate; the Free Speech movement rescued the life of the mind of our country, and neither America nor the academy has been the same since.

It was at Berkeley that the academy emerged as America's searing conscience; it was from Berkeley that students spread throughout the Deep South to aid the Negro struggle for civil rights; and it was again at Berkeley that the first Asian-American was appointed to lead a major American university. Congratulations, Dr. Tien.

I am here today to do something that may be as unfashionable in 1990 as the defense of free speech in 1964: to praise cities. But although my voice may seem isolated, I'm in very good historical company, for human beings have sung in praise of cities for thousands of years.

I find the open air of the Hearst Greek Theatre an appropriate forum for my remarks, for the ancient Greeks believed deeply in their cities. Their passion has left its mark on our pattern of thought and on the language we speak.

The very words we use when we refer to cities belong to ancient idioms: "metropolis" comes to us from Athens, "urban" and "civic" from Rome, the twin pedestals upon which Western civilization was erected.

For without the spark provided by cities, the torch of human civilization stands as a dry sheaf. It is not by accident that we call the period between the decline of ancient urban centers and the rise of medieval Western cities "the Dark Ages."

When Athens and Rome collapsed, so did the West; and when cities rose again—Paris and Prague, London and Lyons, Freiburg and Florence—so did the West emerge from rustic feudalism and blossom anew with a million ideas and a bursting ambition to see beyond the horizon.

Medieval Germans used to say that "City air makes man free," and indeed, it was in cities

[5]Delivered at the University of California at Berkeley, in Berkeley, California, on September 13, 1990. Reprinted with permission of David Dinkins.

that democracy evolved and from them that it spread throughout the world. From Paris and the French Revolution of 1789 to Prague and the Velvet Revolution of 1989, cities have called their nations forth to the great work of freedom.

In America too, cities have led the way to freedom and democracy; "the shot heard 'round the world" was fired in defense of Boston, and it was followed by barrages in Philadelphia, New York, Trenton, Princeton, Charleston, and Yorktown.

Thomas Jefferson drafted the Declaration of Independence in a room at the corner of Market and Seventh Streets in Philadelphia and sent it to be printed in Baltimore, where the Continental Congress sat in session.

Eleven years later in Philadelphia, George Washington presided over the Constitutional Convention which gave birth to a document so momentous that, 202 years after it was written, it inspired Eastern Europeans to brush aside police states as they reached for its truth.

Cities liberated America, and they have continued to liberate us ever since. They serve as our commercial and intellectual marketplaces, where economics and philosophy, entertainment and art, science and technology, ideas and emotions, flourish and enrich the American experience.

Like a mighty engine, urban America pulls all of America into the future: 77 million Americans, almost one-third of our population, live within the limits of our cities.

And corporate America lives in our cities as well. For all the growth of suburban office parks and rural shopping malls, no self-respecting major bank or insurance company, no major law firm or hospital would be at home outside of our cities.

Our ballet companies and museums, theaters and sports teams, great restaurants and fine hotels, and our great halls of education—Harvard and Berkeley, Chicago and Austin—all depend on urban centers.

Our cities pulse with vitality and diversity. It is there that so much astonishing individual achievement flowers. But it can blossom only in an orderly social system that allows our people to plan for the future and compete for the bounty that surrounds us.

That is a fact. In the areas of housing and child care, in mass transit and public education, in drug enforcement and expanded medical services, the federal government retreats. In New York City ten years ago, federal funds constituted 19.4 percent of our budget; today, that share has shriveled to 9.7 percent.

More than billions of dollars, these figures represent the nutrition that might have saved a low-birth weight baby; they represent hospitals that might have cared for hundreds more AIDS patients; they represent drug treatment slots that might have helped thousands of junkies change from thieves to taxpayers.

Every American mayor has a litany of federal dereliction that has hamstrung our efforts to provide the fundamental services of government.

The national administration has punished urban America by transferring to us enlarged responsibility but denying us expanded resources. Indeed, the change involves more than neglect; it reveals hostility as well.

Yet, as our cities go, so goes America and our unique civilization. Why, then, does my song of praise find no accompaniment in Washington or in our state capitals?

It turns out that condemnation of cities is also a very ancient tradition. In one of the oldest stories in the book, cities are painted as bloody cauldrons of iniquity and despair, in contrast to the crisp virtue of the countryside.

Tension pulses in the relationship between town and country. In exchange for the corn and wheat of the countryside, cities have provided tractors and tools for the harvest as well as markets for rural products. This co-dependence makes the relationship uneasy.

Nations survive only as well as their cities. After New York City overtook London as the financial capital of the world in the 1920s, Great Britain lost its empire.

America had grown greatly in the preceding 50 years: we industrialized and challenged the world.

Huge numbers of immigrants kept the fires of American industry burning. In those years, our rural population doubled, but our urban population grew almost seven-fold.

As cities grew, so did friction with the countryside. An international depression just before the turn of the century threatened to turn that friction into a national schism.

Out of this tension arose populism, a political ideology that interpreted the legitimate grievances of farmers and other rural Americans hit hard by the economic contraction as a classic struggle between good and evil.

The populists felt the honest, hardworking farmer represented the highest good, while the Wall Street financier, more often than not an immigrant Jew, embodied the greatest evil, using such "tricks" as the Gold Standard to squeeze away the wealth of farmers.

The great metaphor of populist demonology belongs to that famous orator and presidential candidate, William Jennings Bryan. In his 1896 speech before the Democratic National Convention, Bryan warned, "You shall not crucify mankind upon a cross of gold."

Populism was an exceptional, ephemeral movement, for it set rural dwellers against urban, and no nation can long survive that sort of division. Progressive nations simply do not shoot themselves in the foot.

But cities survived and prospered, often with the enthusiastic support and cooperation of federal and state governments. In fact, until quite recently, the national administration stood alert as an honor guard at the gates of our cities.

John F. Kennedy spoke forcefully in their behalf: "We will neglect our cities to our peril," he said, "for in neglecting them we neglect the nation."

Lyndon Johnson expanded upon JFK's efforts to assist our cities, which had deteriorated enough by the time of his presidency that Johnson felt compelled to issue this dire warning to Congress:

"If we permit our cities to grow without rational design; if we stand passively by, while the center of each becomes a hive of deprivation, crime, and hopelessness; if we devour the countryside as though it were limitless while our ruins, millions of tenement apartments and dilapidated houses, go unredeemed; if we become two people, the suburban affluent and the urban poor, each filled with mistrust and fear one for the other, if this is our desire and policy as a people, then we shall effectively cripple each generation to come."

But with the passing of LBJ from the political stage, the federal government began its gradual abandonment of our cities—a great turning-point in American history.

This new epoch began with "the Southern strategy," a cynical revival of populist sentiments that exploited the tension between cities on the one hand and suburbs and rural areas on the other a tension already exacerbated by the great postwar migration of African-Americans and Latinos into our cities.

And those same African-Americans and Latinos have particularly suffered since the American presidency departed from the ideal of urban-rural harmony and played to the fears concerning our cities. For the division in our country has been much more than urban-rural, as the Willie Horton ads of 1988 demonstrated all too vividly.

This national cleavage has left our urban centers tattered and bruised, scrambling to fend for themselves in a hostile environment.

In 1975 the *New York Daily News* told it all in a now-famous headline: "Ford to City: Drop Dead."

But New York did not drop dead. It roared back in a way that took the breath out of those who would gladly have presided over its funeral. We shot dozens of towers into the sky and welcomed hundreds of thousands of newcomers from all over the world. We learned to eat streetside souvlaki and to trade stock index futures and barrels of oil made of paper.

In such an environment, New York managed its financial recovery without much help from Washington; but a quieter market was growing at the same time, one that was to change the scenery on the stage of history by the end of the decade. It was a market for a new drug that prodded its users to ever greater acts of violence.

And it appeared as a new president took office who felt that the only answer for America's cities was to neglect them in the hope that they would just go away.

Call it what you will—populism, the southern strategy, the sagebrush rebellion—the politics of anti-urbanism even propelled the current administration into the White House.

Yet, where do Americans go when they have a dream but not the opportunity to fulfill it? Where do Americans go when they have AIDS but no treatment center, or when the local community ostracizes them for their disease? Where do they go when they are down on their luck and need a roof over their heads?

Indeed, where do human beings from throughout the world go in order to escape the iron grip of dictators, to make a brand new start, to seek equality and opportunity? Six million of them arrived in America during the 1980's, and they went to our cities, about one million to New York alone.

And our cities welcome them: the sick, the suffering, the hungry, the homeless. We welcome them with open arms, whether they arrive in a first-class jet or an ambulance, whether they bring along Swiss bank accounts or just the shirts on their backs, whether they speak English or Swahili.

The city nurtures all who enter; we assume that in 5 months or 5 years or 50 years, our guests and their families will have become part of our great family.

Of course this steady stream of new arrivals requires an extraordinary array of services. But we would no more turn them away than a hospital would turn away a patient.

To my great pride, the Statue of Liberty shines its light on New York harbor; yet, the words inscribed on its pedestal belong to every city:

"Give me your tired, your poor,
Your huddled masses yearning to breathe free,
The wretched refuse of your teeming shore.
Send these, the homeless, tempest-tossed to me."

In the long run, American civilization and all humankind are served well by our cities. Yet the administration in Washington has made a virtue of bashing us and trashing us, so much that even state governments have abandoned their cities under cover of this anti-urban ideology. Our cities have been left to sweat and suffer for the last quarter-century.

If we are to reverse our fortune, we must expose anti-urbanism as a false and insidious ideology. We must demonstrate that, though it may win an election today, turning Americans against their cities will destroy our country tomorrow.

The media, too, have picked up a strain of anti-urbanism; in recent days they have deluged newsstands and airwaves alike with pronouncements and prophecies about our cities, especially New York.

Consciously or unconsciously, a national news magazine of enormous circulation distorted its own poll data to bring them into line with Washington's conclusion that American cities are crumbling around us, particularly our greatest city, New York.

*Time* magazine reported that 59 percent of New Yorkers would leave the city if they could. The article neglected to mention that its own data showed that 70 percent of our people feel that despite its faults, New York remains the greatest city in the world.

But in this, too, I am an optimist; not only do I hope the media will soon recover, but I also hope they will lead the way to curing our country of the same virulent disease, for none of us, least of all the media, can thrive unless our cities thrive.

My argument applies to all cities, but even more to New York because of its size. In fact, I hope you'll forgive me if I seem to be boosting New York, in defiance of the polls and newspapers. I am, after all, the Mayor.

To put New York's size in perspective: If one were to combine the populations of Los Angeles, San Diego, San Francisco, San Jose, Long Beach, Sacramento, Fresno, Oakland, and Berkeley, the total would still not add up to that of New York, no matter what the Census Bureau says about us. America's cities are its marketplaces, and New York stands as our nation's most important marketplace; in fact, it is the most important market in the world, by almost any measure.

A popular notion has it that with a computer and a FAX machine you can move to Montana and still keep your blood pressure high. Yet as large as our villages have become, we still make our best deals face-to-face over the back fence. And even when we do resort to electronic communication, the words and images flow through our great cities.

A study of American telecommunications earlier this year revealed that more than 35 percent of all international phone calls made from the United States originate in New York City.

An astonishing share of the world's wealth changes hands on Wall Street, whose markets trade more than half of all shares of stock bought and sold the world over, more than London, Tokyo, Brussels, Milan, San Francisco, and Chicago *combined.*

On any given day, financial transactions in New York City represent approximately one-third of the Gross National Product of the United States. That's a trillion and a half dollars *a day*, almost as much as it will cost to bail out the S & L's, at the rate the problem is growing.

And guess where governments go to levy their taxes? Remember Willie Sutton, the safecracker? When asked why he robbed banks, Sutton answered, "Because that's where the money is." Governments follow the same rigorous logic, and they are rewarded so well for their efforts that far from drain the American economy, cities *subsidize* that economy.

Our own analysis in New York suggests that we receive only 77 cents from the federal government for each dollar we send it, even after we account for our share of such national responsibilities as the armed forces.

Thus, when we insist on federal support for housing, transportation, health, and safety, we do *not* ask Washington and our state capitals for a subsidy; we seek only to cut our own subsidy, and that of other American cities, to the federal government. It is they who are the recipients of grants-in-aid from us.

If we could reduce that subsidy by even a fraction, we could cure almost all of our own urban problems with our own solutions.

In the days when New York City did not underwrite the federal and state governments, we built the Brooklyn and Queensborough bridges, the world's most extensive mass transit system, block after block of decent housing, reservoirs, aqueducts, and an extraordinary network of parks, boulevards, and roads, and we still took in the world's homeless and poor.

Our marketplace can meet its own social needs. But the anti-urban ideology emanating from Washington over the last 25 years has obscured these glorious achievements by depicting cities as recipients, not givers.

It has pitted cities against suburbs and the countryside. Yet we are not at war with the suburbs, and we have no quarrel with the countryside. We stand as ready as ever to serve as their partners.

For we depend on each other more than we know. The wheat of the farmer in Iowa ends up as bread in a supermarket in Little Rock; the advertising executive from New York buys a home in Fairfield, Connecticut, and sends her children to school there; the corn grown in Indiana is turned into fuel to run buses in Denver; the shrimp trawled by Vietnamese fishermen in Louisiana is flown to restaurants in Detroit, Phoenix, and Omaha.

The result of a quarter-century of antiurbanism is an economy on the verge of collapse, with our cities left to get by on a starvation diet. We are like tenant farmers, from whom the federal government takes so large a share that we cannot feed our own families.

The politics of antiurbanism, the ideological basis for the federal withdrawal from our cities, must be brought to an end. The gorgeous mosaic of America must be brought together again—city and country, black and white, rich and poor—all together.

That is why I have invited the mayors of America's largest cities to join me in an urban summit this fall. It is cities that must lead the way and reunite our divided country, for the future of America resides in its cities.

As I speak, America is undergoing its greatest ethnic and cultural change since the turn of the century. Thirty percent of the population of New York was born in another country: 170 different ethnic groups call our city home, making New York the most complex, diverse city in human history.

And not just New York; more than half of the public school students of Los Angeles are Latinos. Almost 30 percent of freshmen entering the University of California are Asians. Miami has become a Latino city and Milwaukee has seen a revival of its Polish neighborhoods. It is this great mixture of ethnic identities learning to live together that makes cities the nurseries of freedom and democracy.

To win our cause, and to halt the destruction of our cities, urban leaders must band together into the largest lobbying effort Washington has ever seen. And we must make our voices heard not only in Washington but in state capitals and throughout the country.

For unless our great cities prosper, the American civilization that inspired a whole world to freedom will itself not survive.

We must bring urban affairs back to the top of the list of priorities of both our state and federal governments, and to its rightful place in the curricula of America's great centers of academic excellence.

At the same time, we must realize that cities alone cannot effect the changes we seek. The political boundaries of New York City, for example, were fashioned well before it was evident that northwestern New Jersey, southern New York State, and eastern Connecticut would someday be drawn into our city's dynamic economy.

Thus when I speak of New York, I speak not only of our 8 million residents, I speak of the 25 million who comprise the metropolitan area. The same hold true for every metropolis. Our suburbs are the most important partners in our day-to-day lives.

If we are to succeed in reordering our nation's priorities, we must begin by building coalitions with our suburban neighbors.

For all the simplistic talk of Democratic-liberal cities and Republican-conservative suburbs, this alliance is a natural one, for when our cities prosper, so do our suburbs. And when our cities suffer and decay, suburban dwellers also feel an encroaching sense of insecurity.

Nevertheless, some still ask: Can we really achieve an urbansuburban alliance? What are our chances?

And I answer: What were the chances that a Haitian immigrant would become a leading student at one of America's finest law schools and at the same time be chosen Miss America? What were the chances that an African-American would be elected Mayor of the greatest city in the world, a city of whose population only one-fourth is African-American.

The challenges of our cities are the challenges of America. They must be met by all Americans. Together, all together, we will carry our message to Washington.

But even if we succeed in reducing our subsidy to the federal government—and I know we will succeed—even if we do, we will still require a final ingredient, and that is you, the young people of this great nation, soon to be our educators and our lawyers, our leaders in politics and business, our writers and our doctors.

Cities are the racing heart of our civilization, the home of our greatest ideas. Cities are where the problems of America are worked out. Cities are the soul of America, but good citizens are the soul of our cities.

The ancient Greeks fervently believed that human beings were political creatures, that is, creatures of the "polis" or city. They felt that human beings reached their fullest potential only in the city.

Three thousand years ago, the Greek poet Alcaeus remarked that, "Not houses finely roofed, nor the stones of walls well-built, nor canals and dockyards make the city, but human beings able to use their opportunity."

For your good, and for ours, use your opportunity: bring your talents and your skills, your ideas and your passions, your hopes and your dreams to our cities.

# Saving Our Cities[6]

Tom Gerety

*Born July 22, 1946, New York, NY; B.A., 1969, M.Phil., 1974, J.D., 1976, Ph.D., 1976, Yale University; assistant professor, Illinois Institute of Technology, 1976-78; professor, University of Pittsburgh, 1978-86; dean of law, University of Cincinnati, 1986-89; president, Trinity College, 1989-93; president, Amherst College, 1993–.*

## Editor's introduction

Speaking to 2,000 graduates, Tom Gerety, former president of Trinity College, prescribed healthy cities as a remedy for the "cynicism and apathy" he believed to exist in the American people. "We cannot lose our pride in our cities," he explained, "without losing some measure of our pride in our nation." Gerety asserted that the cultural fortune of a nation lay within the fate of its cities. If we abandon our cities to poverty and crime, he said, we are abandoning our desire to integrate the various races that constitute America. For Gerety, such abandonment is tantamount to foresaking our faith in democracy.

---

I grew up in the country, or what seemed to me the country. We had fields all around our house, with woods beyond them. In the spring, Mr. Ference came with his tractor to turn the ground and plant rows of corn and potatoes. All summer we would hide in the cornrows or make our way through them to their mysterious honeysuckled borders, near the stonewall at the edge of the woods. Three giant maples stood astride the fields, perhaps a quarter mile back from our yard.

To me the country meant solitude: there was no one to play with except my own brothers. Across the street from us lived Newton Hawkins and his sister, an ancient pair in an ancient house. Because of his name, I will forever associate them with the invention and production of what to me was the most exquisite delicacy of my childhood, the fig newton. They drew their water from a well and had no plumbing. They were reported to be the last of their line; they and their ancestors farmed land that, over two centuries, had been sold down to less than an acre.

On holidays we always went to the city. New York City was to me, in those first few years after the second world war, a splendid if somewhat daunting gathering of people, places, zoos, skyscrapers, museums and shops. My immigrant grandparents lived there with hot pretzels and strong brogues and close neighbors.

All my life I have loved cities, loved them as only a child of the country can love them, as a convert, a yearner, a dreamer for whom they live partly in fantasy and ideal. As soon as I could get away from the country, I did: to Paris for the last year of high school, to Lima, Peru, for one year of college, to New Haven and Chicago and Pittsburgh and Cincinnati—and now to Hartford. Cities have always held out to me the promise, even in their sounds and smells, of adventure, of ideas, of music and art, of markets and conversation.

Few of us can be blessed with the wisdom to know more than a portion of what really goes on around us. Was it Hegel who said that what is familiar is what is hardest to see and understand? For children, time meanders among a few landmarks: the corner store, the playground, the walk or ride to school. Later, time rushes by, or seems to, no longer a rivulet but a river.

Coming back to Connecticut after years away, I had the impression, on Hartford's

[6]Delivered at the 1992 Trinity College commencement ceremonies, in Hartford, Connecticut, on May 17, 1992. Reprinted with permission of Tom Gerety.

streets, that little had changed: the three-family houses on Crescent and Broad, the kids in the doorways, the bustle of commuters downtown; this looked to me like New Haven or Bridgeport twenty years before when I was still a student.

But in my lifetime, and in yours, a great shift has taken place in the life of cities.

My father and mother moved to the country to rear a family in green and quiet, near woods and fields. But my father was no country-person; he was a new variety of American: a suburbanite. He commuted by train to the city; all over the United States (and a little later over much of Europe) commuters in cars and trains were building houses farther and farther from the great centers of work and culture. Soon the farms began to disappear; both the Hawkins died; Mr. Ference no longer baled hay in the heat at the end of summer.

Millions and millions of us have participated in this process of transformation. What one scholar has called the "crabgrass frontier" has lured us on as irresistibly as the Western frontier did in the 19th Century.

"First, the people went to the suburbs to live, "someone said to me last year." Then the shops went to the suburbs; and now the jobs are moving to the suburbs."

What I saw as a child was a lush countryside and an equally lush, if very different, city.

What I did not see—and what now we cannot fail to see—is that the America of suburbs leaves neither the countryside nor the cities intact. And plainly it is the cities that suffer most.

Several days after the riot in Los Angeles, commentators began to compare what had happened there with the riots of the late 1960s. The photographs showed what had become of neighborhoods and streets in Newark and Detroit and Chicago, burned out and vandalized a long time ago. With few exceptions, they remain now, a quarter-century later, just as they were in the days *after* their riots. Stores that were burnt down often do not reopen; houses rarely go up again in a neighborhood destroyed in a night.

What happened in Los Angeles, in anarchy and anger, is striking and vivid to us now, as it should be. But it should be no more vivid or striking than what we see around us in nearly every city in the nation.

Those who can choose where they will live or work are choosing too often *against* cities. The result, should we let this go on much longer, will be that our cities will die. In their place will rise up' edge' cities, built up around a monotonous succession of malls—for shopping, for work, for schooling, for housing, for entertainment, and, above all, for parking.

What we will lose should America lose its cities is incalculable. Some, like Jane Jacobs, the great champion of street-life, believe that without cities a nation can have no economic future. She argues from history: great cities bring together the skills and energy and markets that foster industry and invention.

It is a good argument. Still it may prove false; perhaps we can have a strong economy without strong cities.

There are even better arguments for saving our cities.

Whatever our economic future, our cultural future without cities is barren and meager. If somehow invention and industry survive without cities, will theaters and museums and symphonies? Cities provide the one ecological niche where human beings push themselves to greater and greater achievements not only in commerce but in all the arts, especially the highest and most complex.

Patriotism, too, requires of us a standard of national achievement. We cannot lose our pride in our cities without losing some measure of our pride in our nation. To say of this country that it will someday soon have no great cities, nothing to compare to Paris or Budapest, to Delhi or Cairo, is to say that we will have no settlements of cultural and economic stature to stand alongside those of other nations.

Finally, America's cities are the great integrators of our people, of the new immigrant from Laos, Haiti or Nicaragua along with the old immigrant from Poland or Italy, Ireland or England. Cities bring us together and teach us new ideas and new possibilities. They teach us to live with one another; they permit us to see close up what we all share of the human condition, of its virtues, its vices, and its variable genius for everything from baking to poetry.

When I look out on your future, leaving school as you do in a time of some uncertainty, I have no fear for you as individuals. You are a sturdy, bright, and tenacious class. If the world does not at first open its arms to you, it will, in time, if you persevere.

But I do fear for America. We seem as a nation to have fallen into cynicism and apathy;

drift seems our only response to what ails us. On our urban frontiers we give way to a greater and greater divide between those who can make choices in their lives and those who cannot. In this direction lies an American South Africa, separated out into camps: to one side, the prosperous and choosing; to the other, those for whom there is no chance of prosperity and little to choose from. Our cities in this bleak vision will be the Sowetos of our South Africa: segregated, impoverished, disordered—and without much hope.

This need not happen; we have it in our power to stop it, you and I. *We* can call America to its senses and restore its pride in *all* its settlements.

I charge you, then, with the care of our cities and of their citizens. Athens, said Thucydides, was the teacher of Greece. Our cities, too, teach the glory and promise of America. In forsaking them we forsake the hope of our democracy.

# XVI. Crime and Terrorism

## Editor's introduction

In recent years, events such as the 1995 bombing of the Alfred P. Murrah Federal Building in Oklahoma City and the 1993 bombing of New York City's financial district have spawned a fiery debate on the presence of violence within our culture. In addition, the use of violence as entertainment is addressed in the speeches contained herein. Whatever form it takes, violence is and has been an unmistakable and lamentable feature of American society.

In addressing the nature and scope of crime, special prosecutor Thomas E. Dewey argued that New Yorkers had been "terrorized at the polls for years." Such "political violence" was often initiated by politicians who had resorted to forceful coercion of voters in their bid for election. While such violence is exceedingly rare today, at the time the speech was given it was a far more common practice. Adopting an argument that has recently received increased amounts of attention, Judge George Edwards blamed the large number of guns in America for increases in crime. He related how "fear of criminal attack and homicide is rampant in the mind of our urban dwellers." He considered such fear to be the greatest contributing force to the deterioration of American cities. To reduce the murder rate, Edwards advocated prohibiting the sale and possession of all handguns that can be concealed. He further advocated registering rifles and shotguns and banning the interstate sale of firearms.

Other speakers on the topic of crime in America discussed more theoretical ways to reduce or eliminate violence. Critical of the "diminishing emphasis on ethics and values within the family structure," Mark W. Cannon, former administrative assistant to the Chief Justice of the United States, advocated transmitting "positive values, norms, and attachments from one generation to another." Dr. C. Everett Koop asked fellow physicians to develop a greater understanding of the symptoms of a violent personality in both children and adults. In this way, Dr. Koop believed that physicians could isolate those individuals more likely to commit a crime. Through counseling and a more positive family environment, Dr. Koop believed that physicians could help prevent the occurrence of crimes.

# The Inside Story of a Racket[1]

Thomas E. Dewey

*Born March 24, 1902, Owosso, MI; died March 16, 1971; B.A., University of Michigan, 1923; LL.B., Columbia University Law School, 1925; attorney, Larkin, Rathbone & Perry, 1925-26; attorney, McNamara & Seymour, 1926-31; chief assistant to the U.S. attorney, Southern District of New York, 1933-35; special prosecutor, New York district attorney's office, 1935-36; district attorney of New York City, 1937-41; governor of New York, 1942-55; lawyer, private practice, 1955-71; author,* Journey to the Far Pacific *(1952),* Thomas E. Dewey on the Two Party System *(1966).*

## Editor's introduction

Thomas E. Dewey, then New York City special prosecutor, gave this speech as part of a five-part radio address in support of his candidacy for the position of New York City district attorney. Dewey, a Republican candidate, was opposed by "Tammany" candidate Hastings. "Tammany" was the popular name for the Democratic political machine, which many, including Dewey, believed to be a flagrantly corrupt organization. In opposing Harold W. Hastings, Dewey attacked Albert Marinelli, then New York's County Clerk, charging that he represented an "alliance between crime and politics." Dewey's accusations were effective, as he defeated Hastings by a majority of more than 300,000 votes, thus removing "Tammany" from an office it had held for more than 20 years.

---

Tonight I am going to talk about the alliance between crime and politics in the County of New York.

I am going to tell you about a politician, a political ally of thieves, pickpockets, thugs, dope peddlers and big-shot racketeers. Albert Marinelli, County Clerk of New York, powerful leader of half the second assembly district, dominates the whole. He attained power by staying in the dark and keeping his mouth shut. Tonight we turn on the spotlight.

The people in the second assembly district in downtown New York know what gorillas they have met at the polls, how they have been threatened, how their votes have been stolen; and I am going to tell them how it came about that gangsters roamed their neighborhood immune from prosecution.

For years racketeers used the name of Marinelli to frighten victims—and not in vain. Back in 1932 there was a pair of rising gangsters known as James Plumeri alias Jimmy Doyle and Dominick Didato alias Dick Terry. They had never driven a truck but they were handy with a knife or a gun. They decided to take over the downtown trucking industry. They started by forming a so-called truckmen's association at 225 Lafayette Street, which just happened to be the building where Marinelli had his office and his Albert Marinelli Association. They elected themselves President and Treasurer of this Five Borough Truckmen's Association, and were ready for the business of intimidating truckmen. For front men, and to help with the rough work they took on Natale Evola and John Dio. They went to work on the truckmen. They set themselves up as dictators. They told decent truckmen whom they could truck for and whom they could not. They enforced their rules by beatings, stench-bombs and the destruction of trucks. They boasted of their political connections.

William Brown was a typical victim. Together with his wife he ran a small trucking business on West Twenty-first Street. The Browns had three trucks. They were struggling along in 1933, making a fair go of it, until the racket got after them. As a result of their trou-

[1]Broadcast over radio, from New York, New York, on October 24, 1937.

bles, his wife had a nervous breakdown. Brown's brother was beaten black and blue, and their best truck was wrecked.

Brown and his wife were sitting in their trucking office one night working on the books. Terry and Doyle walked in. Brown had just got a new customer.

"What's the idea of your taking this account?" Doyle demanded. "We are from the Five Borough Truckmen's Association. You can't get away with taking any of these accounts around here."

Now, Brown had courage. He told them where to get off. Doyle threatened, "You know what happens to guys that don't play ball with us. They are pretty soon out of business."

Then they shoved Brown up against the wall and told him that unless he gave up that account they would put emery in his truck motors and beat up his drivers. Then Doyle said, "We've had a lot of complaints against us in the last year and we've beat every rap. All we got to do is call up Al Marinelli and the rap is killed. He's the man we got higher up that's protecting us."

Brown defied the gangsters, and within three weeks there was emery powder in the crankcase of his best truck. It wrecked the motor. Seven gorillas entered the office one night, threw monkey wrenches at Brown's brother and beat him with an ax handle. He was in bed for two weeks. A fellow worker was slugged at the same time.

Mr. and Mrs. Brown were terrified. They remembered what Doyle had said about protection from Marinelli. They were afraid to go to the District Attorney's office and so they kept quiet. Then one night in May, 1933, Brown was listening to the radio and he heard a speech by the man who was then the Police Commissioner who said racket victims should come in and he would see they were protected. The very next morning Brown was at the Police Commissioner's office, and he was sent at once to tell his story to the grand jury. Indictments for coercion and conspiracy were voted against Dick Terry, Jimmy Doyle, and Johnny Dio. Brown and his wife went home believing they had found justice.

But the case dragged on for a year with no trial. Finally Brown got a subpoena calling him to the Court of General Sessions for the trial. He handed his subpoena to the clerk and the clerk said, "Why that's a wrong date on that subpoena; your case was dismissed yesterday." And the record shows the dismissal on recommendation of the district attorney.

Last week the district attorney of New York County tried to explain away one of the turnouts his office gave this gang. This is what he said—and I am quoting him—"The defendant Didato died, I understand, in August 1933." Let me inform the district attorney, Didato was murdered by gunmen in the office of the Five Borough Truckmen's Association in the building where Al Marinelli's Association is, six blocks from the district attorney's office. It was a double shooting. When the smoke had cleared away, Didato, alias Terry, lay dying on the floor and Doyle was seriously wounded. But Doyle lived to go on with the racket, a racket immune from prosecution.

The ignorance of the district attorney of murders and racketeering in his own county is not confined to the trucking racket as we have shown before. But here's another example in that particular racket.

Less than a year before the turnout on the Brown complaint, a truckman named Blackoff had caused the arrest of Terry, Dio and Evola for threatening him with violence if he did not obey the mob. At the time of the arrest of these defendants police found right in their car a bottle full of emery. Emery is the same to a truck racketeer as a jimmy is to a burglar. It is the instrument of crime, poured into the crankcase to grind the motor to pieces. This case came to trial in 1932. The emery was right there in the court room. Twice the Court asked the prosecutor what significance the emery had. And the stenographic record of the trial shows that the assistant district attorney failed to advise the Court. The instrument of crime was there and the prosecutor stood silent. The best information the Court could get the prosecutor to disclose was that emery was used for grinding valves. So the case ended with an acquittal and the racket went marching on.

The murder of Dick Terry was just an incident in the growth of the racket. With him out of the way, Johnny Dio and Jimmy Doyle moved uptown. With the Brown indictment still open and hanging fire in the district attorney's office, they brazenly served notice on the Garment Center Truck Owners' Association. They said, "We are taking over your association. If you don't pay, we are coming uptown and there will be busted trucks and broken heads." The president of the Association consulted his directors. They were worried. Somebody suggested that they go to the district attorney of New York County. But everybody agreed that would be too dangerous. Nothing but turnouts had resulted from complaints to the district attorney. So the directors agreed that the only thing the association could do was pay up and shut up. And they did.

All of these charges, fumbled by the district attorney, together with others, were brought to trial in the spring of this year by my office. After a year of investigation we procured an indictment exposing the entire brazen history of the trucking racket. Finally Jimmy Doyle and Johnny Dio pleaded guilty on every count, after my assistants, Murray I. Gurfein and Jacob Grumet, had presented the people's evidence. The men the district attorney turned loose are now in state's prison.

Before that case came to trial, Evola was sought as a material witness by my office. The police went looking for Evola. But he couldn't be found. We did find that after his acquittal Evola had become a member of the County Committee in Al Marinelli's district, and while a member of that Committee, he became a fugitive and never was found. Perhaps that is why he was not designated as County Committeeman again this year.

Who is this Albert Marinelli? Officially he is your county clerk. You elected him four years ago. He survived the LaGuardia landslide because the people did not take the trouble to know who was running for county clerk, just as the machine controlled district attorney survived, with the help of Marinelli and his boys.

It was Marinelli's office which affixed his signature to the extradition papers for his friend, Lucky Luciano, which my office used to bring that worthy back from Hot Springs, Arkansas.

Al Marinelli today is one of the most powerful politicians in New York. This shadowy figure gives no interviews to the press. His history is shrouded in mystery. No one even knows just how he rose to power. In 1931 he took over the leadership of the second assembly district of Manhattan. Rapidly his power spread to other districts. In 1935 he put up a handpicked candidate named Joseph Greenfield and unseated David Mahoney as leader of half of the first assembly district. Mahoney charged that two notorious racketeers, Socks Lanza and John Torrio, were active in that election which led to Marinelli's triumph. Lanza was the gorilla who dominated the Fulton Fish Market for years. Complaints were made to the district attorney of New York County against Lanza but they were ignored. Lanza was the cause of one of those frequent scandals in the machine dominated district attorney's office which resulted in an investigation ordered by Governor Roosevelt. It took the Federal Government to catch up with Lanza and save the fish industry from his terrorism. Torrio, once the boss of Al Capone in Chicago, is now under indictment in Federal Court. When he was brought to Court, he put up $100,000 in cash for bail. Somehow or other, Torrio was also indicted on a forgery charge last year by the district attorney of New York County, but the indictment was quietly dismissed last December and Torrio walked out a free man.

Mysterious as he may be in New York, Marinelli's supporters may be interested to know that he has a luxurious estate surrounded by an iron fence, on Lake Ronkonkoma, way out on Long Island. From his several motor cars, he chooses to drive back and forth in a Lincoln limousine; and his Japanese butler, Togo, serves him well.

Regularly, you will find Al standing in the basement of the Criminal Courts Building in Manhattan, quietly chatting with bondsmen, lawyers, and hangers-on. Your county clerk has many, diversified interests.

In 1932, when Marinelli set out to attend a function in Chicago, there was with him a well-dressed, pasty-faced, sinister man with a drooping right eye. He had an air of quiet authority. Together, they turned up in Chicago, playing host in a suite at the Drake Hotel, and were constant companions at the race track in the afternoons. Marinelli's companion was Charlie Lucky Luciano, then almost as unknown as Marinelli, later revealed as the Number One man of New York's underworld, master of many rackets. Luciano is now in Dannemora Prison, serving a sentence of thirty to fifty years.

In January, 1935, the Marinelli Beefsteak Dinner was a colorful affair. Benny Spiller, loan shark for the Luciano mob, bought tickets and was there. So did Jesse Jacobs, the Luck mob bondsman. So had the bookers and other hangers-on in the prostitution racket. They knew they had better buy, for Davie Betillo was selling tickets—the same "Little Davie" who was a Capone trigger-man for five years, and later Lucky Luciano's chief henchman in New York. All of these boys are now in jail at last, as a result of the prosecution we completed last year.

Some of the facts about Al Marinelli and his organization are matters of record and you are entitled to know the kind of man who helps to pick your public officials—who helps select those who are in charge of criminal justice.

Back in 1933 while I was a chief assistant United States attorney, the United States Government conducted an investigation of election frauds under the Federal law. Election inspectors in various districts of the city were indicted and convicted but nowhere were conditions worse than in Al Marinelli's second assembly district. In that district alone, the records indicate, they had added 4,534 votes to their own set of candidates and stolen 3,535 from the others. You know, in some districts the dominant party will bribe or intimidate the officials appointed by the other party. And both become parties to the corruption of the ballot. Democrats and Republicans alike were indicted.

Let us take just two election districts in Marinelli's district. We'll see who was running the election for Al. In the 28th election district, the chairman of the election board was George Cingola. He was the man directly charged with preserving the peace at the polls and seeing that there was an honest count. He was imported into the district for the election and registered from the home of his sister. Back in 1927 he had once before been arrested for an election offense and "beat the rap." But less than a year before he was appointed to his 1932 election day job, he was arrested no less than three times—twice for assault and once for bootlegging and he served a term for one of the assault raps in the county jail in Mineola. And just a few months before that, three detectives of the Police Department Narcotic Squad, upon arresting him in his home found him sleeping with two loaded revolvers under his pillow. He was convicted in the Court of Special Sessions for his double violation of the Sullivan Law. He was let off with a $25 fine. And so he became qualified to serve as an election inspector. Marinelli made him the public official in charge of the polling place and graced him with the title of chairman of the local board of elections.

He was indicted by the Federal Attorney's office, but he has not been heard from since, and the indictment has now been dismissed.

Another expert election official in that assembly district that year was Charles Falci. He, too, was brought in specially for the occasion from Brooklyn. Marinelli made him an election inspector in the 23rd election district. Falci was indicted, but he also ran away.

For years Falci was a fugitive from justice. Last year, Falci was caught and the fact is that during the time he was a fugitive from justice he had been Al Marinelli's private chauffeur. He had been driving Marinelli's Lincoln limousine. He had been working around Al Marinelli's estate at Lake Ronkonkoma, sharing the work with Togo, the Japanese butler. On Christmas Eve of 1935 Marinelli had made a touching gift to his faithful servant of a chauffeur's livery and a pair of shoes, bought at Wanamaker's for $38.50.

The members of Al Marinelli's county committee faithfully elect him year after year and faithfully work for his candidates. They ratify the party choices and work desperately for them, this year most of all. You are entitled to know what kind of people some of them have been.

I have the official criminal records in front of me. Here is the first one. He has eight arrests to his credit, but the only charge which stuck was one in the Federal Court for selling dope. They sent him to prison for that one but on the other seven arrests, going way back to 1918 when he was locked up for robbery, he has "beaten the rap." These include two charges of robbery and one each of felonious assault, disorderly conduct, malicious mischief and grand larceny.

Here is another who has a great personal interest in law enforcement and municipal government in New York. He began in 1924 with a sentence to Atlanta for counterfeiting. Some years later he was picked up for extortion and carrying a gun, but it took him only two weeks to get out. Only a month later, he was again in the hands of the police, charged with homicide with a gun. But he "beat that rap" too. Last month he was named as a member of Al Marinelli's County Committee.

Here's one who started his criminal career with an arrest in Hoboken, New Jersey, as a horse thief. He got out of that rap and also a later one for felonious assault. A year later, the law finally caught up with him and he was convicted on an assault charge. For fifteen years then he kept his name off the police books, but in

1929 he was again arrested for assault and robbery. He "beat that rap," but fourteen months later he was caught peddling drugs and finally went to the penitentiary again. Known to the police as a public enemy, he was arrested in 1935, but was discharged. He joined Al Marinelli's County Committee that year and was handed another term last month.

Here's one who qualified back in 1928 by getting himself convicted for dope peddling and in due course graduated from a term in Atlanta Penitentiary. Last month he qualified as a County Committeeman for Al Marinelli.

Dope peddling is also the habit of another. He began by beating a homicide charge in 1923, and after that, arrests for robbery and manslaughter were turned out, but a narcotic charge did stick and this statesman of the second assembly district was fined $25. Later he was arrested, charged with the possession of a large quantity of opium, but a turnout resulted.

Here's another, with a record of two convictions, first for impersonating a police officer, and then for drugs.

Listen to this one. He started thirty years ago with a discharge on a pickpocket charge; five years were spent in a New Jersey prison for assault and robbery; he was dismissed on a charge of homicide with a knife in 1927.

Now here's one party who was never caught as a peddler of dope. He is just an ordinary exconvict, with an assault conviction.

Here's some more. But these men are probably not particularly important in the councils of the second assembly district. They've never been convicted of crime. But perhaps I'm wrong—it may be that their achievement in avoiding conviction entitles them to special honor in the Marinelli councils.

One of these was just selected County Committeeman last month. He has to his credit discharges on complaints of stealing an automobile, robbery with a gun, and vagrancy. Another of his fellows who was just chosen has a vagrancy discharge. A colleague of his, likewise selected last month, beat an attempted robbery charge. Another of his fellows was turned out on a grand larceny charge. Here is a precious pair who each beat two "raps." The first one on a felony assault charge and for stealing an automobile; another for toting a gun and for coercion. Here's another charged with being a fence for receiving stolen goods. Then we have one who ran up against the liquor law a couple of times and another who was in conflict with a policy charge. All of these, as members of the official county committee of the second assembly district! Aside from those who always "beat the rap," the exconvicts alone include a counterfeiter, a stickup man, and others convicted of assault, injuring property, gun toting, impersonation of a public officer and larceny, both grand and petty. Worst of all are the six convicted of dope charges. What an intense interest these men must have in electing the public officials who administer criminal justice! What an interest these men must have in decent municipal government! But that is not all. These criminal records on more than a score of Al Marinelli's county committeemen tell only part of the story. There are also the election inspectors.

Inspectors of election are public officials, certified to by the county chairman from a list provided by the leader. Let's look at Al Marinelli's election officials. Perhaps we will find out the reason for some of the things that have been going on in New York. Here are some of the men officially designated to keep the peace, certify to the honesty of the election and count the votes in the second assembly district. This faithful worker who counts your votes started as a pickpocket in 1908. He wasn't out long before he was convicted of grand larceny, and later of assault. But he won't serve as an election inspector this year. On June 1st he ran up against the Federal Government and a United States judge sent him to Lewisberg Penitentiary for a year and a half.

Here is another who counted your votes last year. His police record doesn't indicate whether he is in jail at this moment so I can't tell whether he will be an inspector this year. Starting with a conviction for grand larceny in 1922, he was arrested and convicted for petty larceny a year later. He was caught again two years later and again convicted on petty larceny but got a suspended sentence and went back to jail as a parole violator. He wasn't out long on that one before he was arrested and "beat the rap" for burglary. In 1930 he was arrested, charged with possessing counterfeit money, and turned over to the Federal Government.

Here are three more vote counters. The first has three arrests to his credit but went to jail only once. That was for petty larceny. Three years ago he was arrested for felonious assault but it took him only a day to get out.

Another was convicted of attempted grand larceny in New Jersey and still another, whose pedigree I have here was convicted on a policy charge. But he acted as an election inspector last year and you will probably see him at it this year too.

Of course some of the election inspectors in the second always manage to "beat the rap." Here is one who wiggled out of two burglary charges. Another was acquitted of burglary and a third was discharged on a grand larceny count.

Well, these are some of the county committeemen and inspectors of election in the 2nd assembly district. I have police records for thirty-two of them. Twenty of this fine assortment, who have been selected to serve on the county committee or to count votes, have been convicted at least once. The other dozen have thus far succeeded in "beating the rap." Their attainments include seventy-six arrests on a varied assortment of charges ranging from robbery to sex crimes, with dope peddlers heading the list. No wonder they are desperately fighting to keep the office of the district attorney in the same hands it has been for twenty years. No wonder Marinelli is joining with his pals, running the fight of his life.

The people of the second assembly district are entitled to know the facts about those who have been misrepresenting them in the political councils of New York. For years they have been terrorized at the polls and forced to submit throughout the year to the domination of the gunmen who paraded their streets. And don't for one moment believe these are the only cases.

On Wednesday night at 10:30, over WABC you will learn more about what we are fighting in this campaign. You will learn more of the reasons why the office of district attorney is the most cherished prize of the political leaders who want to continue their control of criminal justice.

These are the sinister forces who are fighting to keep the right to select assistants for the office of district attorney of New York County. These are the living obstacles to everything that's decent and clean in the conduct of our city.

This is not a political issue. There can be no difference of opinion on the questions involved. Gorillas, thieves, pickpockets, and dope peddlers in the political structure are not the subject of argument. There is nothing political about human decency.

The issue is defined. The decision is in your hands on election day.

# Murder and Gun Control[2]

George Edwards

*Born August 6, 1914, Dallas, TX; died April 9, 1995; B.A., Southern Methodist University, 1933; M.A., Harvard University, 1934; J.D., Detroit College of Law, 1949; director, Detroit Department of Welfare, 1938-39; director, Detroit Housing Commission, 1940-41; member, 1941-49, president, 1945-49, Detroit Common Council; lawyer, private practice, 1946-51; probate judge, Wayne County Juvenile Court, 1951-54; judge, Third Judicial Circuit, Wayne County, 1954-56; justice, Supreme Court of Michigan, 1956-62; Detroit commissioner of police, 1962-63; judge, U.S. Court of Appeals, 1963-85; author,* The Police on the Urban Frontier *(1968).*

## Editor's introduction

In this speech, George Edwards, a former Detroit police commissioner who was then judge of the United States Court of Appeals, linked increases in the murder rate with handgun possession. Possessing a handgun, he warned, "greatly increases the possibility that you . . . will be killed with, or as a result of, that weapon." Employing a variety of statistics, Edwards argued that a lack of gun control is the surest way to an increase in deaths, both intentional and accidental, by firearms.

---

In the United States in 1971 the topic of gun control and the topic of murder are inseparable. This speech could properly be called "Four Myths About Murder." They are:

1) That present conditions in this country justify the average citizen in living with a top priority fear of being murdered

2) That most murderers are premeditated killers for money

3) That the most likely murderer is a stranger—particularly one of another race

4) That you can protect yourself from murder by keeping a pistol handy

None of these myths are true.

The statistical chance of being murdered in any year is approximately one in 20,000. You can compare that to the chance of being killed in an automobile accident, which is one in 4,000.

The great majority of murders are products not of cupidity, but of high emotion. Anger, fear and jealousy are leading factors.

The great majority of murders are committed by someone closely related to or associated with the victim.

The possession of a handgun greatly increases the possibility that you or someone you love will be killed with or as a result of that weapon.

All present public opinion surveys indicate that fear of criminal attack and homicide is rampant in the mind of our urban dwellers. Such fear may indeed be the most destructive single force in the deterioration of the American city. Yet of all the causes of death, murder is an infinitesimal percentage, and even if we chose to deal only with violent death, criminal homicide rates as one of the smaller of the causes.

Automobile accidents, for example, cause five times as many violent deaths as does homicide. Home and industrial accidents cause two and one half times as many. Falls cause twice as many, and more than twice as many people commit suicide as are killed by the willful act of another. Almost as many people die by fire each year in these United States as are murdered, and very nearly as many people die by drowning to name just two other risks in our daily lives to which few of us ever give more than a passing thought.

[2]Delivered at the 12th annual meeting of the American Psychiatric Association, held during the week of May 3-7, 1971, in Washington, D.C.

Arthur Conan Doyle was one of my favorite authors as a boy. I read everything he wrote that I could lay my hands on—not the least of these being the Sherlock Holmes stories. But his detective novels and those of his successors gave me very poor preparation for what I was later to see of murder in real life. Six years as a trial judge, thirteen years as an appellate judge, and two years as police commissioner of Detroit have given me some very vivid contact with the crime called murder. There is almost no resemblance between ordinary murder as seen in the courts and the average murder mystery.

The murder-mystery writer hypothesizes a single evil malefactor who concocts a long-range plot to kill an innocent party for his (or her) money. There may be such murders. But I have had somewhat vivid contact with perhaps a thousand murders without ever seeing one which fits the pattern. The closest to this pattern in our day, of course, are the gangland executions of the Mafia. But here the evil purpose is sustained by numbers of conspirators and enforced by the discipline of the mob.

Most murder in real life comes from a compound of anger, passion, intoxication and accident—mixed in varying portions. The victims are wives, husbands, girlfriends, boyfriends, prior friends or close acquaintances (until just before the fatal event). The quarrels which most frequently trigger murders might well result in nothing more than bloody noses or a lot of noise, absent a deadly weapon—handy and loaded.

All the statistics show that if you choose with care the people who will share your bedroom with you or your kitchen, or the adjacent bar stool, you will improve your chances from one in 20,000 to one in 60,000.

As for the one third of murders committed by strangers, the overwhelming motive is robbery. Murder generally results from resistance and surprise. Police recommendations in every city are unanimous in counseling against a holdup or burglary victim attempting resistance. Reaching for a gun is the most dangerous possible gesture when confronted by an armed felon. Outside of the movies, there are few people who win in trying to draw when someone else has a gun in his hand.

Much of the current fear of being assaulted and killed by a stranger involves racial fears. Actually in the overwhelming majority of homicides the victim and the assailant are of the same race. Marvin Wolfgang put it this way in his book *Crime and Race:*

"National and official crime statistics do not provide data, but enough research has been conducted to permit the definite statement that criminal homicide, like most other assaultive offenses, is predominantly an intragroup, intraracial act. In a detailed five-year study of homicides in Philadelphia (1948-1952), it was noted that in 516, or 94 percent, of the 550 identified relationships, the victim and offender were members of the same race. Hence, in only 34, or 6 percent, of these homicides did an offender cross the race line: 14 were Negro victims slain by whites and 20 were whites slain by Negroes."

Nothing which I have said to this point is designed to minimize the problem of criminal homicide which we face in this country. We have a murder rate over ten times that of Great Britain—and as we will see, since the mid-1960s it has been increasing. I believe deeply in the sanctity of human life and in the duty of our country to guard and protect its citizens. But the mythology of murder has occasioned all too many people purchasing arms as a means of self-defense when in fact such measures greatly increase the hazard to them and their loved ones.

This brings me directly to the topic of gun control.

During the past three and one half years I have served as a member of the National Commission on Reform of Federal Criminal Laws. Recently this Commission sent its Final Report to the President and to Congress. The report deals, of course, with the whole of the criminal law and must be judged on more than just its recommendations on the most controversial topics. There was a substantial minority of the Commission which opposed any new gun-control laws. But this is what the report says concerning the majority position on gun control:

"[A] majority of Commissioners recommend that Congress:

"1) ban the production and possession of, and trafficking in, handguns, with exceptions only for military, police and similar official activities; and

"2) require registration of all firearms.

"Among the arguments supporting the majority view are the following. Crimes of violence and accidental homicides will be markedly reduced by suppression of handguns, which, on the one hand, are distinctively susceptible to criminal and impetuous use, and, on the other hand, are not commonly used for sporting purposes as are long guns. State control is ineffective because of differing policies and leakage between states. A comprehensive and uniform registration law will facilitate tracing a firearm when it has been used for criminal purposes."

The working papers of the National Commission on Reform of Federal Criminal Laws and the staff report of the Commission on the Causes and Prevention of Violence contain some compelling data concerning the relationship between murder and handguns:

1) Between 1962 and 1968 sales of long guns doubled while sales of handguns quadrupled (10 million sold in the last decade). Also note that since 1963 homicides involving firearms have increased 48 percent, while homicides by other means have risen only 10 percent.

2) Handguns are the predominant weapon in crime, although they comprise only 27 percent of firearms in the country. Of crimes involving firearms, handguns are used in 76 percent of homicides, 86 percent of aggravated assaults and 96 percent of robberies.

3) The commission studied three major areas of crime: homicide, robbery and aggravated assault. They found that: "Two out of every three homicides, over a third of all robberies, and one out of five aggravated assaults are committed with a gun, usually a handgun."

4) Regarding homicides, they observe that firearms are "virtually the only weapon used in killing police officers," and that handguns have been involved in eight of the nine assassination attempts on Presidents or presidential candidates.

5) Nineteen sixty-six data shows that the rate of accidental firearms deaths by geographic region parallels the pattern of firearm ownership. Over half of firearms accidents involving fatalities occur in or around the home, and about 40 percent of the victims are children or teen-agers.

6) Firearms were used in 47 percent of all completed suicide attempts.

7) The fatality rate of the knife (the next most frequently used weapon) is about one fifth that of the gun. A rough approximation would suggest that the use of knives instead of guns might cause 80 percent fewer fatalities.

No one who fairly contemplates the criminal carnage which occurs in the United States can fail to conclude that disarming the criminal element of our population is essential to our civilization. National statistics indicate that over 6,000 homicides occur in the United States each year with the use of firearms. Yearly we produce a murder rate more than ten times that of England—and that of many other European countries. I know of no way by which we can achieve disarming the criminal or the criminally inclined without accepting the flat prohibition of some weapons and the sale and use of others under some regulation.

The theory believed by many that as a nation we cannot legally accomplish reasonable firearm control because of the Second Amendment to the Constitution is simply not valid. The language of the amendment and its historic interpretation in the courts is not nearly as restrictive as is popularly believed.

The Second Amendment provides: "A well regulated Militia, being necessary to the security of a free State, the right of people to keep and bear Arms, shall not be infringed."

The basic United States Supreme Court interpretation of this amendment came in *United States* v. *Miller*, 307 U.S. 174, from which we quote the holding in the opinion of Mr. Justice McReynolds:

"In the absence of any evidence tending to show that possession or use of a 'shotgun having a barrel of less than eighteen inches in length' at this time has some reasonable relationship to the preservation or efficiency of a well regulated militia, we cannot say that the Second Amendment guarantees the right to keep and bear such an instrument. Certainly it is not within judicial notice that this weapon is any part of the ordinary military equipment or that its use could contribute to the common defense. *Aymelle v. State*, 2 Humphreys (Tenn) 154, 158.

"The Constitution as originally adopted granted to the Congress power—'To provide for calling forth the Militia to execute the Laws of the Union, suppress Insurrections and repel Invasions; To provide for organizing, arming, and disciplining, the Militia, and for governing such Part of them as may be employed in the Service of the United States, reserving to the States respectively, the Appointment of the Officers, and the Authority of training the Militia according to the discipline prescribed by Congress.' With obvious purpose to assure the continuation and render possible the effectiveness of such forces the declaration and guarantee of the Second Amendment were made. It must be interpreted and applied with that end in view. *United States v. Miller*, 307 U.S. 174, 178."

From this case (and other leading cases, such as *United States v. Tot*, 131 F.2d 261 [3d Cir. 1942], Goodrich, J; *Cases v. United States*, 131 F.2d 916 [1st Cir. 1942], and *Velazquez v. United States*, 319 U.S. 770 [1943]) these two conclusions follow:

First, the prohibition of the Second Amendment has been held to apply only to the Federal Government and not to the states.

Second, the right to carry arms is applicable to the sort of arms which "a well regulated militia" would carry.

While rifles and shotguns have legitimate relationship to the Second Amendment and have legitimate value for both hunting and home defense, handguns suitable for concealment are basically the weapons of the assassin, not of the militia.

Acquaintance with this problem as a judge, as a former police commissioner of the City of Detroit, as a former infantry officer, and at least an occasional hunter convinces me that these three steps should be taken to lessen our criminal carnage:

1) The manufacture and sale and possession of handguns suitable for concealed weapons should be prohibited by state and Federal law.

2) The purchase and possession of rifles or shotguns should in my judgment be a matter of right for any law-abiding citizen. Such weapons should, however, be registered under state law and sold only on proper identification.

3) Interstate mail-order sale or delivery of firearms of any kind should be banned by Federal law.

Let me close by telling the poignant story of my own home town of Detroit where the present Mayor (Mayor Gribbs) has just proposed a tough gun-control ordinance.

I was police commissioner of Detroit in 1962 and 1963. In those two years we watched murder figures with alarm at the possibility they might exceed one hundred. We did not know when we were well off. In the next few years race tensions increased markedly for reasons too long to tell here. In four years, starting in 1965, gun registrations in Detroit quadrupled.

In six years, starting in 1964, murders in Detroit more than tripled, from 138 to 488. Concerning these figures Inspector Delore L. Ricard, head of the Detroit Police Department's Homicide Bureau, said:

"There are more homicides in the city because there are more handguns in the city.

"The relationship is that clear. You can't go by the increase in registrations, either. The bulk of handguns used in violent crime are not registered."

These were not Conan Doyle type murders. Inspector Ricard also said:

"It usually involves people who know each other well or members of the family. They are sitting around somewhere—a home, a bar—and there is an argument.

"Suddenly someone has a gun in his hand. Then someone else is dead.

"The argument doesn't have to be important. Maybe it's about cards or politics or even baseball. I can show you homicides that were committed for reasons you could not believe."

Gun accidents increased too. The Violence Commission found that in 1967 more homeowners were killed in gun accidents than had been killed by burglars or robbers in the home over the previous four and one half years.

The problem spilled over into the suburbs too. In Dearborn handgun registrations tripled between 1967 (the year of the Detroit riot) and 1969. During those years the Dearborn police were advertising instructions for women on the use of handguns. From 1967 to 1969 the homicide rate in Dearborn went from zero to an all-time high of seven.

The Violence Commission report provides us with this summary:

"In our urbanized society, the gun is rarely an effective means of protecting the home against either the burglar or the robber; the former avoids confrontation, the latter confronts too swiftly. Possession of a gun undoubtedly provides a measure of comfort to a great many Americans. But the data suggest that this comfort is largely an illusion bought at the high price of increased accidents, homicides, and more widespread illegal use of guns."

Justice Oliver Wendell Holmes once remarked, "Taxes are the price we pay for civilization." In the seventies in this country gun control may well be the price we have to pay for civilization.

# Terrorism, the Ultimate Evil[3]

Clarence M. Kelley

*Born October 24, 1911, Kansas City, MO; died August 6, 1997; B.A., University of Kansas, 1936; LL.B., University of Kansas Law School, 1940; special agent, Federal Bureau of Investigation, 1940-61; U.S. Navy, 1943-46; Kansas City chief of police, 1961-73; director, Federal Bureau of Investigation, 1973-78; author,* Kelley: The Story of an F.B.I. Director *(1987).*

## Editor's introduction

According to the *FBI Police Bulletin*, 1975 saw 89 bombings that were attributable to terrorists. This represented a marked increase from previous years. Responding to criticism of his agency's practices and warnings about the growing problem of terrorism, Clarence M. Kelley, then director of the Federal Bureau of Investigation, concluded that terrorism is "the ultimate evil in our society. And no one can consider himself immune from terroristic acts." In order to combat terrorism, Kelley steered the FBI away from its campaign against Communism and had his agents adopt more modern crime-fighting tools.

---

As we Americans prepare to celebrate the two hundredth anniversary of our independence, I find myself increasingly concerned about the growing problem of terrorism.

It is a strange anomaly that we, the citizens of the freest major nation on earth, should find it necessary to concern ourselves with terrorism.

Yet we *must*—and that is the message I bring to you today. All Americans who cherish freedom, all Americans who would preserve orderly government and domestic tranquillity, must involve themselves in the effort to prevent terrorism from becoming a crisis problem in our society.

Some may say our concern *should* be directed toward failures in our society that spawn terrorism.

I disagree.

History is replete with instances where reforms did nothing to dissuade truly committed terrorists.

Alexander II of Russia in the 1860s emancipated the peasants and instituted land and other reforms beneficial to the poor and oppressed. By our standards those measures were not spectacular; but back then they represented genuine social progress. Yet the response of the revolutionaries, frustrated in their efforts to whip up popular support, was to intensify their campaign of bombing and assassination.

And Alexander II himself eventually was murdered by revolutionaries.

To achieve tranquillity and order by appeasing avowed terrorists is not only unworkable, it's unthinkable.

Their rationale is too mercurial, inconsistent and twisted.

How do you reason with an individual who considers the murder and mutilation of children an acceptable means to impose his will on others?

You don't.

The terrorist neither listens to reason nor engages in reasoning with others. His aim is to generate fear—to frighten people into submission.

He measures success by the magnitude of the fear he generates through brutal, savage acts of violence.

How proud those responsible must have been of the bombing at Fraunces Tavern in New York City last year—a bombing in which four persons were killed and scores were injured. Members of the Armed Forces of Puerto Rican Liberation crowed that they committed that vicious act and others.

[3]Delivered at the American Security Council Press luncheon, in Washington, D.C., on January 13, 1976.

Terrorists like these are prepared to kill men, women and children to further whatever cause they claim to be pursuing. And the heinousness of these murders is accented by the fact that they murder without passion. They murder with cool deliberation and careful planning.

Because they have no compunction whatsoever about killing human beings, they have no compunction about committing other crimes. They steal. They rob. They kidnap. They take hostages. They extort.

There are no depths to which they will not go to further their "cause."

Make no mistake about it, the true terrorist is *committed*—committed to an extent that is difficult for rational people to comprehend. A perverted sort of courage and profound dedication sustains them. They are humorless, insensitive and they are influenced by no truths other than those they perceive to validate their cause.

They are utterly amoral.

I have been in law enforcement thirty-five years. I have met and talked with murderers—murderers who have taken lives cruelly and viciously; but nevertheless, most of them have moments of compassion and gentleness.

The terrorist does not.

The law makes allowances for homicides that are committed without premeditation. The penalties are less severe. The law recognizes that there is an added evil in a murder that is planned and deliberate, with malice aforethought. And the penalties for such acts are more severe.

There is a dispassionate, impersonal cruelty in terroristic murders that adds an extra dimension of horror.

The terrorist's exploding bomb kills and maims indiscriminately—the young, the elderly, the robust, the infirm—people who have absolutely no inkling of the terrorist's perceived grievance or cause.

As far as I'm concerned, terrorism is, indeed, the ultimate evil in our society. And no one can consider himself immune from terroristic acts.

I've met a couple of terrorists. One of them was planning to bomb my home in Kansas City before his arrest. He admitted it. Take my word for it, nothing can bring the evil of terrorism in perspective more quickly for a person than to learn he is a target.

I wonder how the American people view the revolutionary terrorist.

I fear many people see them as a caricatured comical figure, a bearded, rumpled individual furtively clutching a round bomb with fuse sputtering. It would be folly to confuse this invention of some cartoonist's mind with the true revolutionary terrorist. He is not amusing. He is lethal. And Americans simply must realize this.

And Americans should be aware there has been strong evidence in the past couple of years that our terrorist problem is growing.

There were 89 bombings attributable to terrorist activity in our nation last year, as compared to 45 in 1974 and 24 in 1973.

During the past five years there have been 255 such bombings, 122 firebombings, 45 sniping incidents, 120 shootings, 24 ambushes and 21 arsons.

Eleven persons were killed in terrorist acts of violence in 1975. And 72 people were injured. Property damage amounted to more than $2.7 million.

I don't know how well statistics can convey the true extent of the terrorist menace; but one figure that is particularly revealing to me is the number of police officers attacked.

Since 1971, the deaths of at least 43 officers and the wounding of 152 more have been linked to terrorists.

Sometimes one terrorist group or another writes a letter to the news media boasting of successful ambush attacks on law enforcement officers.

Still, I think to most Americans, the terrorist threat is a remote and abstract thing—a problem that commands little, if any, of their attention in their understandable preoccupation with problems more immediate in the everyday business of living.

They may review with revulsion news reports of terrorist activities around the globe—the bloody atrocities in Northern Ireland, the Middle East, and elsewhere.

They may be momentarily dismayed by occasional news reports of such activity in the United States. But thus far this activity has been scattered across our nation; and the total impact of this activity is not easily perceived by the public.

But the families of those killed and maimed have perceived it. Nothing I could say, no figures I could cite, could speak more articulately of the terrorists' menace than the cold, still and mutilated bodies of their victims.

All right. Granted we have a growing terrorist problem, what is the FBI doing about it?

Everything we possibly can within the parameters of law.

The importance of our intelligence work in this area cannot be overstated. In our intelligence work we have striven—and have succeeded in many instances—to prevent bloodshed and property loss.

Unfortunately our successes are rarely publicized, nor is it possible to make public some of them; to do so could jeopardize the safety of innocent persons who helped us.

We also have worked arduously to bring to justice those who commit such acts. It is not an easy endeavor. And we have been criticized for taking so long to apprehend alleged terrorists who are fugitives.

But it should be recognized that we are dealing for the most part with small, closely knit, clandestine groups difficult to penetrate. Some have achieved expertise in preparing false identifications. And they are able to lose themselves in a subculture of communes that spans the United States.

Incredibly, some otherwise law-abiding people provide moral and material support to terrorists, apparently for idealistic reasons. The best that can be said about such people is that they are terribly misguided.

Terrorists are not idealists. They are without principle. They have no regard for human life. They pervert the freedoms this nation bestows upon its citizens. They defile American traditions. They are not political activists. They are criminals. And their numbers seem to be growing.

I'm not saying that our nation is in imminent danger of being devastated by terrorists. But I *do* consider terrorism a very *real and growing problem.*

And I think it's vital that Americans involve themselves in the effort to stem terrorist acts *before* they reach crisis intensity.

How can citizens combat terrorism?

First, by recognizing the true, despicable nature of the terrorist.

By supporting law enforcement in its efforts to frustrate these peddlers of death and destruction.

By promptly reporting information pertaining to terrorism.

By vigorously supporting the principle of rule by laws that has enabled our nation to flourish these two hundred years.

We are a nation of about 214 million people—heterogeneous, industrious, robust and peace-loving. No two of us are exactly alike. We usually differ, sometimes vehemently, on major issues and national priorities.

But we have at least one thing in common. *We cherish freedom.* We are unified in that. And let those terrorists who boast that they will bring the fireworks to our Bicentennial celebration take note of this: Americans will not permit themselves to be divested of that freedom.

Let the terrorists know that their mindless acts of violence can only strengthen Americans' resolve to preserve our democratic system that has served us so well these two centuries.

Thank you.

# Terrorism and Low-Level Conflicts: A Challenge for the 1980s[4]

Anthony C. E. Quainton

*Born April 4, 1934, Seattle, WA; B.A., Princeton University, 1955; B.Litt., Oxford University, 1958; foreign service officer, 1959-66; senior political officer, Department of State, 1969-72; deputy chief of mission, Kathmandu, 1973-76; ambassador to the Central African Empire, 1976-78; director, Department of State Office for Combating Terrorism, 1978-81; deputy inspector general, Department of State, 1987-89; ambassador to Peru, 1989-92; assistant secretary of state for diplomatic security, 1992–.*

## Editor's introduction

Anthony C. E. Quainton, former director of the Department of State's Office for Combating Terrorism, addressed more than 1,000 people at the annual convention of the American Society for Industrial Security. To an audience of security specialists, Quainton expressed deep concern over what he believed to be an unprecedented level of terrorist activities. It must be remembered that, at the time this speech was given, 52 Americans were being held hostage in Iran. To counter the increase in terrorist-related violence, Quainton reported that the State Department had "developed a strategy for combating terrorism" which is outlined below.

---

Violence abounds in our world. Governments and corporations are equally affected. The statistics for 1979 were horrendous: Worldwide, 293 major incidents including 47 assassinations, 20 kidnappings, 13 hostage-barricade situations, not to mention bombings and armed attacks. Seventy-seven of these terrorist incidents directly involved U.S. citizens or property. High on the list came the kidnapping and murder of our ambassador to Afghanistan in February, 1979, the seizure of our Embassy in Iran in November, and the killing of eight of our citizens in violent attacks in Turkey throughout the year.

The story for 1980 is even more alarming. In the first eight months alone, there have been 500 incidents, of which 101 have involved Americans. One American ambassador was taken hostage in Bogota and held for 61 days; another in Beirut narrowly escaped assassination a month ago. Americans have been kidnapped and held for ransom in Guatemala and Colombia. Overall, 58 countries have been the target of at least one attack. Even the Soviet Union, which many have thought to be immune, has had to face over 30 terrorist attacks putting it second in the listing of countries most frequently targeted. The United States, alas, remains in first place.

In 1979 and 1980, the private sector has been particularly hard hit. Let me cite the major incidents in 1979 of which I am aware which were directed against your corporations:

January 3—The General Manager of Texaco in Colombia killed, having been held hostage since the previous May.

February 13—The Cairo Sheraton bombed—17 people injured.

February 19—The Pan American office in Izmir, Turkey, bombed.

April 19—Explosives detonated at the Ford Motor Company showroom in Valencia, Spain.

April 23—A subsidiary of Babcock and Wilcox bombed in Dusseldorf, Germany.

[4]Delivered at the American Society for Industrial Security's annual convention, in Miami Beach, Florida, on September 25, 1980.

May 20—The IBM office in San Salvador strafed.

June 15—The Nicaraguan Manager of National Cash Register kidnapped in El Salvador.

June 20—An American Airlines jet hijacked to Ireland by a Serbian nationalist.

July 24—The offices of the Wells Fargo Bank in Istanbul, Turkey, bombed.

August 14—The factory of Apex Textile Company seized in El Salvador, its American General Manager held for nine days.

September 21—Two American executives of Beckman Instruments kidnapped in El Salvador.

October 26/28—Citicorp's Deputy Manager shot to death; the Bank of America office bombed. Both in El Salvador.

November 26—Armenian terrorists bomb Western Airlines and TWA in Madrid.

December 3—Morgan Guarantee Trust in Frankfurt bombed.

December 5—W.R. Grace Fertilizer Plant in Trinidad bombed.

December 14—Three Boeing contract employees killed in Istanbul.

December 23—TWA bombed in Rome.

December 25—Citibank and ITT bombed in El Salvador.

In 1980, there has been no respite. In Trinidad a Texaco refinery was bombed; so were TWA offices in Madrid. A Texaco regional vice president was abducted in Honduras. A similar attempt was made against a Colgate Palmolive executive in Cali, Colombia. And in the last month, a series of bombings have damaged banks and other American corporation premises in Manila. Finally, the month of August enters into the Guinness book of terrorist records as the month with the most hijackings, all of American aircraft.

I have cited for you only some of the more dramatic incidents which have directly affected U.S. interests. I have not mentioned, for example, the Corsican terrorists' attempt to blow up an oil refinery near Marseilles or the successful attack against South Africa's major synthetic fuels manufacturing plant. These two incidents have a particular significance since they represent attacks on highly sensitive facilities, rather than the more traditional symbolic attacks on airline offices and banks.

In the last year we have also seen a new phenomenon—systematic assassinations by states of their political enemies abroad. Assassinations have succeeded in 24 countries with 23 different groups involved. The assassinations have included Libyans and Iraqis in Europe, Syrians in Jordan, Iranians in the United States, and most recently the killing of ex-President Somoza in Paraguay. The international community is faced with a growing lawlessness, a diminishing respect for international law, a continuing erosion of the basic principles of diplomatic intercourse. There is no reason to suppose that these attacks will stop. We must anticipate increasing numbers of violent acts as the 80s advance.

What we did not see in the 1970s was any significant escalation of terrorist tactics. To be sure, in the last two years there have been more casualties than ever before. But the terrorists continue to kill with relatively unsophisticated weapons: homemade bombs, automatic weapons, and rocket propelled grenades. We have seen no evidence that terrorists are about to turn to esoteric weapons (nuclear, chemical or biological), recent novels such as the *Fifth Horseman* notwithstanding.

There are, however, some indications that we may see a change to new and more significant targets. If so, the private sector will be directly affected. It is evident to most of us that in modern society there are numerous vulnerabilities: computers, power generation and transmission systems, tankers, off-shore oil facilities, etc. Many of these are only lightly protected. Security for these installations will require the most careful attention in the years ahead and the closest possible cooperation between government and industry. The cost will be high.

I have attended several conferences in the last six months at which these issues have been discussed and at which industry and government representatives have begun to examine together ways in which we can address the next generation of problems. At this point in time, we cannot predict with any certainty which facilities or which industries are most likely to be attacked or threatened. However, given the high stakes and the potential costs of being unprepared, we must be sure that the best minds available are doing the contingency planning which is needed.

But before returning to the question of what needs to be done in the future, let me review for you what we have already achieved. In the last five years, we have developed a strategy for combating terrorism and other forms of low-level violence which has five elements: intelligence, physical security, contingency planning, crisis management, and international cooperation. None of these is new; all have been significantly improved and upgraded in recent years. In the crucible of events our competence has been refined. We have learned a number of lessons which should stand us in good stead as we approach the 21st century.

In some ways the most important lesson is that intelligence in the broadest sense is critical. Ten years ago we knew little about terrorist groups, their leaders or their *modus operandi.* This situation has dramatically changed, notwithstanding self-imposed restraints on some kinds of intelligence activity. We now do have computer data bases which enable us rapidly to factor information about terrorist groups into our crisis management system.

Most significantly we have information about terrorist plans. Almost every week somewhere in the world we are informed of a specific threat against one of our diplomats or embassies or against a private corporation, airline, or executive. Without exception, this information is passed to our embassies through diplomatic channels, or in the case of the private sector, through the State Department's Office of Security to the corporation concerned. Intelligence is worthless if it is not used. It is a highly perishable commodity. Although we must be concerned to protect sensitive sources and methods, I can assure you whenever we are aware of information which affects the security of your companies or your executives, you will be the first to know.

Unfortunately, intelligence provides only a partial answer. We will not have forewarning of all terrorist attacks. The problems of penetrating small, highly dedicated terrorist cells are enormous. The resources available are limited. We must therefore take other measures to deter attacks. The most obvious of which is physical security. I do not pretend to be an expert in this field, and certainly with so much talent and expertise in the audience, I am hesitant to offer any guidance. Nonetheless, I am convinced that security does pay off. Our ambassador in Beirut was saved in an assassination attempt last month because he was in a specially protected vehicle and had armed and trained professional security officers with him. Our embassy and ambassador's residence in Bogota were not attacked this spring because the M-19 concluded that the protective systems in place were too difficult to breach. They chose the Dominican Republic Embassy instead. Only once, in fact, in Kuala Lumpur in 1976 has an American embassy been taken over by a terrorist group. Everywhere else terrorists have been successfully deterred.

Unfortunately, the systems created to deter the entry of terrorists were insufficient to deal with the mob violence which we saw in Pakistan, Iran, and Libya in the last year. We are now embarked on a major upgrading of our embassy security at a cost of over $40 million to improve perimeter controls and to develop the concept of internal safe-havens. We must give our personnel abroad the protection which they need in a world of growing violence and in which governments may be unable or unwilling to come to our assistance promptly. No task has a higher priority for our security experts in the department.

In the last decade we have also made notable progress in deterring hijackings. With almost 20,000 weapons seized at American airports since 1974, we know that the system works. Only one plane in all that time has been hijacked in the United States with a weapon taken through screening. Now we are faced with a new weapon: flammable liquid. Improved screening methods will have to be devised. The FAA is already actively engaged in seeking a solution to this new threat.

We all know that security is only as good as its weakest link. We, as you, must be alert to any weaknesses so that we can enhance our protective systems and thereby diminish the vulnerability of those we are called on to protect. But weaknesses there will always be, and we must assume that occasionally terrorists will succeed in taking hostages or in carrying out some other violent act. When terrorists succeed, we must be prepared with adequate contingency plans and a crisis management structure that ensures that all appropriate resources are rapidly deployed toward the resolution of the incident.

We have given high priority to contingency planning. Every American embassy and consulate is required to have plans to cover bomb threats, internal defense, hijackings and hostage incidents. Every FBI field office in the United States has plans for handling terrorist incidents in collaboration with appropriate local law enforcement agencies. The Federal Government has a National Response Plan for Nuclear Emergencies including terrorist attacks. There now exists a credibility assessment system for all kinds of nuclear and other esoteric threats. Within hours through this system the Federal Government can obtain a succinct and technically sound appraisal of any threat received. We are looking as a priority at ways to improve our contingency plans for handling incidents in the maritime environment. The Counter-Terrorist Joint Task Force which the Department of Defense is creating as a result of Admiral Holloway's report, will provide yet another level of contingency preparedness. The purpose of all of these plans and preparations is to make certain that we have ready and clearly defined lines of command and control and the necessary supporting resources, including communications, which we will need to manage a crisis.

Plans only provide a framework within which crisis managers can act. They do not provide policy guidelines nor ensure the harmonious working of a system which ultimately depends on the personal relations which exist among representatives of various agencies and jurisdictions. In recent years we have worked to build experienced teams of area and intelligence experts, behavioral scientists, security professionals, public relations officers. They are used to working together. They understand the basic policy framework in which they must act. They have training in the basic principles of hostage negotiation and crisis management. When there are major policy issues to be addressed in the course of an incident, they are taken promptly to the Special Coordination Committee of the National Security Council. The SCC is the policy level group to which the Working Group on Terrorism and its Executive Committee report for guidance. Similarly, the lead agency responsible for managing an incident (the FBI/Justice domestically, the State Department abroad, the FAA in the case of hijackings) would also get its guidance from the SCC.

As part of our preparation for future terrorist attacks, we have given high priority to the training of all employees of all Federal Government agencies serving abroad. At the Foreign Service Institute in Washington we offer a course on terrorism and coping with violence which provides an introduction to such subjects as surveillance recognition, travel precautions and countering vehicular kidnapping, recognition of and defenses against letter and parcel bombs, residential security, protection against local crime, preparedness for riots and demonstrations, preparation for family separations and evacuations, and hostage survival. We are now paying particular attention to the needs of families; for our experience has been that they must be part of any emergency planning system. Spouses and other adult family members attend all our counter-terrorist and security training courses.

Increasingly, in our contingency planning and crisis management we have come to recognize that no one agency has all the answers. Crisis management is a team effort in which many agencies and many layers of state and local government are involved. In more and more incidents, the private sector is an essential element of this partnership. In hijackings the airline concerned is always a part of the government crisis network sharing in the decisions and listening and contributing to the analysis of the evolving situation. Similar structures may be needed in the future if we are faced with other kinds of terrorist attacks or hostage incidents involving corporate assets and personnel.

Because of the need for close cooperation, we must face squarely the fact that we do not always agree. In some terrorist incidents, the government and private industry may have conflicting interests, priorities and policies. For example, industry usually pays ransom: the government does not. Yet both are concerned for the lives at stake in the immediate situation and for the possibility that others will be at risk in the future. Both should be aware of the political radicalization which may result from giving in to terrorist demands. To the extent that ransom fuels the coffers of revolutionary groups, long-term government and corporate interests may suffer. On these issues we need to have a more vigorous dialogue so that each side understands the rationale for the other's policy and the problems which may result from different corporate and government strategies. I hope and believe that these differences can be minimized so that when we are faced with an actual incident we will be working together rather than at cross purposes.

The final aspect of our strategy for dealing with terrorism and its proliferation is international cooperation. Here too we have made progress although not as much as we would have liked. On a number of fronts the international community has demonstrated that it agrees with us that there are certain kinds of terrorist acts which are inadmissible in civilized society and which are contrary to the basic principles of international law. These include aircraft hijacking and sabotage, attacks on diplomats and the taking of hostages. All of these acts are now covered by international conventions drawn up in the 1970s. The most recent is the Convention Against the Taking of Hostages which was opened for signature last December and which the United States signed almost immediately thereafter. This Convention is before the Senate for ratification.

All of the Conventions impose upon states party to them the obligation either to prosecute or extradite the perpetrators of these crimes. Unfortunately, not all crimes are covered by conventions: assassinations, bombings, vessel hijackings are still outside this system of universal condemnation. In addition, none of the Conventions provides for enforcement measures against states which violate their obligations as Iran did so flagrantly in the seizure of American hostages last November. The only exception is the undertaking of seven leading aviation nations to cut-off air services to countries which harbor hijackers. The Bonn Declaration, as it is known, marks a significant turning point in international attitudes. We hope it will be extended to other areas, but we are realistic enough to realize that this process may take time and that some states will refuse to accept the limitations on their sovereignty which any system of sanctions implies.

As we look ahead to the last two decades of this century, we will undoubtedly see high levels of violence and turmoil. Increasing population pressures, growing competition for scarce resources, widening income disparities within and between societies will create uncertainty and lead to various forms of conflict. Some of the turbulence in the world will take the form of traditional terrorism—hostage taking, kidnapping, etc. Some will be in the form of urban unrest, revolution, and civil war. We must also anticipate continuing incidents of state-supported violence and terrorism. This phenomenon of state violence exercised through surrogate groups may, in fact, become one of the major political issues of the 1980s.

Nonetheless, high though the levels of violence may be, we need not despair. Government and the private sector have coped with violence in the past and can do so in the future. However, if we are to succeed, we will have to refine the tools which we have already identified—intelligence, security, crisis management, contingency planning, international cooperation.

Above all else, we must develop sound working relationships between government and industry. A close partnership is essential. Of especial importance will be research and development into techniques which will deter terrorists, protect executives, and deflect threats. One area which is already of great importance is the technological frontier represented by explosive taggants. Within the next decade we will be able to add to explosive materials both detection and identification taggants permitting us to spot bombs before they go off and to track down the perpetrators afterwards. This technology is of particular significance given the fact that bombs still represent the most numerous and most serious threat that we face. I have no reason to suppose that that situation will change in the years ahead.

If we are to cooperate more effectively, as I believe we must, we have to understand each other better and know where and how to get the information we need. This Convention is enormously valuable in bringing together so many professional security experts for a detailed exchange of views, information, and technology. ASIS makes a unique contribution to this process through its terrorism committee and its regional seminars.

In Washington, there is unfortunately no central point for information or assistance. However, I would like to commend to you a small pamphlet which the Department of Commerce has recently put out entitled *Combatting Terrorism: Sources of Federal Assistance for Business.* It describes a number of places you can go for assistance and the kinds of help which are available. I know I speak for my colleagues at State, Commerce, the FBI, FAA, and Defense in saying that one of our principal responsibilities is to support and collaborate with the private sector. We need to know your concerns and your problems. We welcome the contact which meetings such as this provide. For they are sure signs of that spirit of partnership through which we can jointly meet the challenges of terrorism and low-level conflict in the 1980s.

# Crime and the Decline of Values[5]

Mark W. Cannon

*Born August 29, 1928, Salt Lake City, UT; B.A., 1949, M.A., 1954, M.P.A., 1955, University of Utah; Ph.D., Harvard University, 1961; research analyst, Utah Foundation, 1953; secretary, Utah Scholastic Merit Study Commission, 1954; professor, Brigham Young University, 1961-64; administrative assistant to Representative Henry A. Dixon, 1956-61; legislative assistant to Senator Wallace F. Bennett, 1961-64; member, Institute of Public Administration, 1964-72; director, Venezuela Urban Development Program, 1964-65; director, International Programs Institute, 1965-72; administrative assistant to the chief justice of the U.S. Supreme Court, 1972-85; vice chair, Cannon Industries, 1989–; author,* The Makers of Public Policy *(1965),* The Challenge of Urban Government in Valencia *(1966).*

## Editor's introduction

Mark W. Cannon, the first person to hold the position of administrative assistant to the chief justice of the Supreme Court, gave this widely publicized speech at a very small, relatively obscure conference. To account for the unexpected publicity the speech received, Cannon remarked, "The apparent high interest in the speech may have derived from a growing apprehension that crime is threatening all that is of value in our society; and a massively growing unease and distress over a deterioration of the individual values which engender a lawful and responsible society." To prevent crime, Cannon advised, society must understand the importance of families "transmit[ting] positive values, norms, and attachments from one generation to another."

---

Justice Stanley Reed has reported that when the Supreme Court was deliberating over *Public Utilities Commission v. Pollock*, Justice Felix Frankfurter felt so strongly opposed to transit companies forcing audio advertising on their riders that he told the Justices he would disqualify himself. Justice Reed responded, "Felix, how can you feel so strongly about protecting captive audiences? You have been using the rest of us as a captive audience ever since you came here."

I appreciate the opportunity to address a captive audience of so many distinguished judges who are leaders in their states and communities.

Matthew Cossolotto, aide to Congressman Leon Panetta, wrote in the *Washington Post* about walking up to the front door of his home on Capitol Hill at 10:35 P.M.:

"It was then that I heard the gate squeak open behind us. . . . I felt the hard cool steel of a handgun against my head. . . . The handgun told me to open the door. . . . I realized that my world of values, of reason—in fact, my life itself—counted for little. I opened the door and, under the gun's command, turned off the burglar alarm. . . . was forced to lie face down. . . .

"We were at the mercy of the two feral men. We did not know what they wanted from us, nor whether the next few moments might be our last.

"Then suddenly they disappeared into the night, taking . . . $31 and credit cards. Such was the extent of our tribute to the terrible god of crime, who for some unknown reason spared us. . . . "

Early last Thursday morning one of the best loved gentlemen on Capitol Hill, delicatessen owner Charles Soloman, was beaten to death after he returned to his deli. He had become a foster father to many of his customers and they

[5]Delivered to the Southwestern Judicial Conference, in Santa Fe, New Mexico, on June 4, 1981. Reprinted with permission of Mark W. Cannon.

were left shocked and choked with tears at the tragic death of this kindly man.

Recently a 17-year-old youth of a loving black family failed to return home for dinner, or to sleep. The family members were beside themselves. Their fears were realized the next day when he was found strangled, victim number 27 in Atlanta.

Last year, virtually one-third of all homes were victimized and a reported 23,000 Americans were killed by criminals. This was up from 16,000 in 1970 and was four times as many Americans as were killed in combat per year in the Vietnam War.

If an illness suddenly struck one-third of our households, killing 23,000 Americans and costing us $125 billion per year, or if foreign-supported terrorists did the same, would we not rise up in alarm and mobilize our best intellects and harness our collective energies and resources to try to stop such devastation? We would devote ourselves unceasingly to the eradication of such an enemy.

A *Newsweek* survey revealed that 53 percent of Americans are afraid to walk in some areas within a mile of their homes at night. Although there is no panacea which will eliminate crime, anything which may reduce this malignancy requires our attention.

Instead of attempting to prevent crime, we rely on law enforcement. But as Cossolotto says, "Police are society's bouncers, there to rid us of anti-social behavior after it occurs." Thoreau long ago stressed prevention, saying "For every thousand hacking at the branches of evil, there is one striking at the roots." Yet to examine the roots of crime is perplexing.

Numerous theories attempting to explain the causes of crime and delinquent behavior have been advanced. Some assert that anti-social behavior is often "neurological" or "psychological" and, hence, uncontrollable. Others maintain that sociological and cultural factors, including poverty and class-based frustrations, contribute heavily to crime. Crime is even viewed by some to be a "rational response" to the inequities of our capitalistic economic system. The sheer profitability of crime is cited as a cause, as is the use of alcohol and drugs. One study showed that only 29 percent of offenders had taken neither drugs nor alcohol before the offense.

Though alcoholism, poverty, and perceived social injustice all contribute to crime, there is a deeper force that is causing a breakdown of our society. These merely tip the raft of social order, while a deep current is moving the entire raft at a startling speed. That deep current is our failure to transmit positive values, norms, and attachments from one generation to another.

As Justice Powell has observed: "We are being cut adrift from the type of humanizing authority which in the past shaped the character of our people." He was not referring to governmental authority, but to "the more personal forms we have known in the home, church, school, and community which once gave direction to our lives."

The U.S. Constitution, perhaps the most enduring product of western democracy, assumed two components of a well-ordered polity: a political system which prescribed *how* people should live and a metaphysical theory that explained *why* they should comport themselves thusly. Each component is inextricably bound to the other. James Madison, the architect of the Constitution, urged that in its adoption, people should "perceive a finger of that Almighty hand which has been so frequently . . . extended to our relief." But much of our intellectual community has in recent decades dismissed the metaphysical part as superstition or imagination.

We consequently live in a society where spirituality is denigrated. Arianna Stassinopoulous, former president of the Cambridge Union, wrote recently:

"The relegation of religion and spirituality to the irrational has been one of the most tragic perversions of the great achievements of Western Rationality and the main reason for the disintegration of Western Culture."

Similarly recognizing the tremendous effect of spirituality and religious commitment upon society is Alexander Solzhenitsyn. He stated at Harvard:

"How did the West decline? . . . I am referring to the calamity of a despiritualized and irreligious humanistic consciousness. . . . It will exact from us a spiritual upsurge."

Not only has spirituality declined, but families have been weakened. Thirty percent of all children under six years of age live with just one parent or no parents at all. Michael Novak noted in *Harpers:*

"The family nourishes 'basic trust.' From this spring creativity, psychic energy, social dynamism. If infants are injured here, not all the institutions of society can put them back together. Familial strength that took generations to acquire can be lost in a single generation, can disappear for centuries. If the quality of family life deteriorates, there is no 'quality of life.'"

Ironically, the very system that depends upon families for its subsistence too often undermines them through its institutions and legislation. "Almost everything about mobile, impersonal, distancing life in the United States—tax policies, real-estate policies, the demands of corporations, and even the demands of modern political forms—makes it difficult for families to feel ancient moral obligations," writes Novak.

Concomitant with the weakening of the family structure is the diminishing emphasis on ethics and values in our public schools. The Thomas Jefferson Research Center, a nonprofit institution studying America's social problems, reports that in 1775 religion and morals accounted for more than 90 percent of the content of school readers. By 1926 the figure was only six percent. Today it is almost nonexistent. A study of third grade readers reported that references to obedience, thoughtfulness, and honesty began to disappear after 1930.

A majority of parents have considered the private school alternative, according to *Newsweek.* The desire of parents to have a "clear moral framework" for their children's education is one of the factors contributing to declining public school enrollments and increases in private schools.

Is it mere conjecture that values relate to crime or is there evidence? Few people have studied this question. Searching for such studies is like panning for gold. However, since they are both little known and yet important to the curtailing of crime, they warrant more emphasis than would be usual in a speech.

Sean O'Sullivan of Columbia University, in a study of families in the Bedford-Stuyvesant area of New York, found that law abiding youth most often came from homes where the father was present and the mother was active in church. "Discipline in a family cuts the chances of drug addiction in half," reported O'Sullivan. He also found a close link between drug addiction and fighting, skipping school, drinking, and driving without a license. O'Sullivan concluded that the "complete nuclear family," combined with discipline and religious faith was the best insulation from anti-social behavior and, therefore, efforts at prevention of drug abuse and delinquency should concentrate on strengthening such families.

A thorough investigation by Peter O. Peretti indicates that when parents separate, youngsters tend to "lose interest" in their values. Peretti adds, "It might be assumed that religion does play a part in inculcating youth and adults alike with the socially desirable values of a society." Albert Rhodes and Albert Reiss, in their significant article "The 'Religious Factor' and Delinquent Behavior," after elaborate statistical analysis found that boys with no religious preference committed twice as many crimes per thousand as those "having a religious preference."

The vitality of traditional values is shown by their relationship to achievement. Many people are astounded to learn that most young achievers hold much more traditional values than others their age. A 1980 poll of *Who's Who Among American High School Students*, with 24,000 responding, revealed:

Eight out of ten belong to an active religion and 71 percent attend services regularly.

Nearly half don't drink and 88 percent have never smoked cigarettes.

A vast majority (94 percent) of these teens have never used drugs, including marijuana.

Eighty percent do not think marijuana should be legalized and 90 percent wouldn't use it if it were.

Seventy-six percent of these teens have not had sexual intercourse.

Some 87 percentof the survey group favor a traditional marriage.

A good number (52 percent) watch less than 10 hours of television a week.

Allen Bergin, former professor of clinical psychology at Columbia, observed:

"If one considers the 50 billion dollars a year we spend on social disorders like venereal disease, alcoholism, drug abuse, and so on, these are major symptoms of social problems. Their roots, I assume, lie in values, personal conduct, morality, and social philosophy."

Alberta Siegel of Stanford wrote,

"Every civilization is only twenty years away from barbarism. For twenty years is all we have to accomplish the task of civilizing the infants . . . who know nothing of our language, our culture, our religion, our values, or our customs of interpersonal relations."

The increasing number of student assaults on unfortunate teachers, under-reported at 113,000 last year, is a commentary on how America has been "civilizing" its children.

Historically, families, churches, and schools perpetuated societal norms and values. The deterioration of these institutions, however, has left a void which is being filled by such institutions as television and motion pictures. Do the mass media influence behavior?

Television brings into our homes such outstanding programming as the voyage of the space shuttle, Pavarotti and the Met, and in-depth features on most important issues. But these are not the shows primarily watched by youth. A child entering school has seen television more hours than would be spent in the classroom during four years of college. By the age of fourteen, the average child has witnessed on television the destruction of more than 12,000 people.

Many studies, reports, and articles on the audio-visual media's impact on our society underscore the concerns of many responsible analysts and leaders of the media.

An emerging body of scholarly literature indicates that violence is idealized on television; violent methods are the ones used most frequently for goal attainment. Many shows promulgate and encourage instant gratification. Deferment of gratification, often essential to the attainment of a larger reward later, is, on the other hand, subtly denigrated by many shows. One study showed that only half as many frequent television watchers were concerned about planning for the future as non-frequent watchers. Psychologist Victor Cline, editor of a collection of essays and empirical studies on values and the media, went so far as to state:

"Concerning probably no other issue in the social sciences has the evidence been so overwhelming or convincing as that regarding the influence of media violence on values and behavior. Television and motion pictures are powerful teachers of values, behavior, and social conduct."

The Surgeon General of the United States reported, "The overwhelming consensus and the unanimous Scientific Advisory Committee's report indicate that televised violence, indeed, does have an adverse effect on certain members of our society."

Alberta Siegel asks, regarding many television shows:

"How many instances are there of constructive interventions to end disagreement? What other methods of resolving conflict are shown? How many instances of tact and decency could an avid televiewer chronicle during the same hours? How often is reconciliation dramatized? What strategies for ameliorating hate are displayed? How many times does the child viewer see adults behaving in loving and helpful ways? What examples of mutual respect does he view? What can he learn about law and order? How many episodes of police kindness does he see? How frequently does the glow of compassion illuminate the screen?"

Self-indulgence is often promoted and sensitivity and sympathy belittled.

Shifting values may explain the increasing tendency of delinquents to blame others—society, other people, and their social and economic conditions—for their actions. Last fall I visited the Union Gospel Mission in Seattle, which provides free beds and meals to thousands of unfortunate, rootless people. The Reverend Stephen Burger said a significant difference from the past was that "older down-and-outers readily admit having 'messed up their lives.' But the younger men have no moral concept that they have done anything wrong."

In short, the decreased teaching of traditional values and mores in our society and the rise of mass media as teachers of values have produced results which challenge our ingenuity.

Crime and delinquency cost us at least 125 billion dollars per year, forcibly alter our lives, destroy people, frighten and demoralize us, and may even threaten our civilization. The vast resources we commit each year to law enforcement, the courts, correctional institutions, rehabilitation, and crime prevention efforts have unfortunately not curtailed the surge of crime. We must therefore regroup, and explore additional methods to reduce and prevent crime.

Institutions that encourage positive norms and a sense of personal responsibility should be strengthened. If Americans successfully fortify the foundations of pro-social behavior, rather than simply combat the symptoms of anti-social behavior, some embryonic crime will be eliminated. We must focus on the roots of the problem—some of which are the beliefs, values, and attitudes being adopted by the young.

An illustration of how an established institution can help the young was shown by the Harvard Public Health School. As part of its preventive medicine program, it targeted smoking in junior high schools. Dr. Albert McAlister worked with non-smoking student leaders who had classroom discussions on questions such as why people smoke, showed films, and set up role playing on such problems as resisting taunts. He found that in some schools the number of new smokers could be cut in half. He also reported positive results dealing with alcohol and drugs.

Since the family, the church, the school, and the community have traditionally encouraged pro-social behavior by teaching values of integrity, accountability, planning for the future, service, and respect for others' rights, efforts should be made to strengthen people's affiliations with these entities. Strong ties to one or more of these encourage adherence to rules. Theories which maintain that people "stay out of trouble" because of their association with traditional institutions, termed "bonding theories," are becoming increasingly accepted by sociologists and criminologists.

Schools should strengthen and expand programs encouraging broad student participation, particularly by those who generally hang back, thereby providing more students with a sense of personal success. Successful involvement in meaningful activities, with clear and consistent reinforcement for positive behavior, strengthens the bonds which help prevent delinquent behavior. Such activities may be athletics, music, student government, special-interest clubs, or drama and dance. Major goals of these activities should be to heighten each student's sense of personal success, attachment to teachers and to school, and belief in moral order. Committed and competent teachers can also encourage student involvement and satisfaction with learning. John Steinbeck put it well:

"In her classroom our speculations ranged the world. She breathed curiosity into us, so that each morning we brought in new questions, cupped and shielded in our hands like captured fireflies. When she left us we were sad, but the light did not go out. She had written her indelible signature on our minds. I have had many who have taught me soon forgotten things, but only a few who created in me a new direction; a new energy. I suppose, to a large extent I am the unsigned manuscript of such a teacher. What deathless power lies in the hands of such a person."

The Center for Action Research reports, "The only important conventional affiliations for most young persons are the school and the family. When these deteriorate, there is usually nothing left. In practice, many youth do not even have the luxury of two independent affiliations." The number of conventional ties open to young people should be increased. An obvious option is through employment. Though many "make-work" programs have demonstrated little success in deterring delinquent behavior, the Center reports that significant "employment that creates an affiliation that the young worker does not want to jeopardize through misconduct . . . should deter delinquent behavior."

Special benefits come from youth helping youth through such volunteer activities as tutoring, day care centers, and counseling their peers. The National Committee on Resources for youth has documented 1500 successful examples of such programs.

Community-focused youth participation projects can increase attachments to the neighborhood and community and thereby help prevent delinquency. Community planning committees should include youths, organize activities, and seek to provide an environment for pro-social behavior. A major goal should be to include young people who are not typically involved in leadership roles in their schools.

Another possibility for increasing ties is through organized religion and service groups. By providing programs for youth and adults in athletics, arts, crafts, music, and community service, religious affiliations could be broadened and involve an increased proportion of young people. This, of course, should be done by church groups, since public schools are prohibited from promoting religions.

In short, we must find ways to increase the number of meaningful "bonds" our youth have with institutions encouraging pro-social behavior. If we do not, many youth will find reinforcement from less worthwhile sources.

One of the most effective ways to offset negative norms and behavior is to promote values in our schools—even though this is difficult in a pluralistic society. Increased use of curricular materials and emphases that provide both the incentive and the resources for confronting problems of moral commitment and choice is a necessary first step. The Hon. Charles E. Bennett testified before a House sub-committee:

"The home and the church can no longer be solely relied upon. Today they are least available where most needed. These institutions today are no longer equipped to handle the job without help from our schools. Those children who are most in need of instruction are getting it least."

Congressman Bennett hopes that young people can "learn to formulate their own values in an open academic atmosphere where free discussion may improve and strengthen our culture."

A recent Gallup poll found that 79 percent of the public favored "instruction in the schools that would deal with morals and moral behavior." Only fifteen percent were opposed. As the Center for Action Research points out, such instruction could be carried out completely "within Constitutional limitations."

In 1967, Sandrah L. Pohorlak published a study conducted at the University of Southern California. She found that in over half the states, schools were required to teach ethics. Yet although many laws *required* instructors to teach ethics, states provided *nothing* in the way of texts, guides, or other materials to help teachers deal with ethics and character in the classroom.

*Amoral America*, a book published in 1975, summarized a study by political scientists George C. S. Benson and Thomas S. Engeman. "Contemporary western society," wrote Dr. Engeman, "suffers from inadequate training in individual ethics. Personal honesty and integrity, appreciation of the interests of others, nonviolence, and abiding by the law are examples of values insufficiently taught at the present time." Dr. Engeman continued, "Our thesis is that there is a severe and almost paralyzing ethical problem in this country . . . . We believe that we can demonstrate that unlawful behavior is in part the result of the absence of instruction in individual ethics."

The Thomas Jefferson Research Center has identified case histories where dedicated, competent teachers have achieved remarkable improvements in discipline and deportment by emphasizing ethics and character in the classroom. For example, the Character Education Curriculum, developed by the American Institute for Character Education is a systematic program in ethical instruction for kindergarten through sixth grade. It has been tested in more than 400 schools in 19 states with dramatic success in a number of instances.

The Character Education Curriculum has been in continuous use at Wendell Phillips Public School #63 in a poverty area of Indianapolis since September 1970. Principal Beatrice M. Bowles described the school before character education:

"The building resembled a school in a riot area. Many, many windows had been broken, and the glass had been replaced with masonite. . . . Most of the pupils were rude, discourteous, and insolent to the members of the faculty. . . . The children had no school pride, very poor self-image, and were most disgruntled because they had to attend 'that old school.'"

Mrs. Bowles reported surprising results during the six years after all of the teachers began using the character development program. "There has been less than $100 of glass breakage and this has been accidental. Student attitude has greatly improved. . . . There is a feeling of one for all and all for one." Mrs. Bowles reported that "discipline and vandalism are no problem. . . . Our children are well behaved, courteous, and with few exceptions, achieving at maximum potential. . . . The program has been a tremendous success for us and our children."

Literature reinforcing traditional values need not be dull. Far from it. Much adult literature has become nihilistic, empty of moral content, and reflective of the view that life is meaningless and purposeless. Nevertheless, it is interesting that an author who has been popular with young people is Ray Bradbury, who unabashedly believes America is a great success. His science fiction is cheerful and reflects a clear sense of moral order.

Research shows it is practical to teach ethics in junior high school, high school, and at college levels. Don Hutson, speaking before the Phi Alpha Delta Law Fraternity, said:

"You don't become ethical when you pass the Bar. You don't suddenly find integrity by turning a faucet. And you can't find honesty at the corner drug store. It has to be learned, and understood, at the law schools, in the undergraduate schools, and yes even down into the high schools of America. That is where you learn the basic principles that ought to guide you as a lawyer."

Encouraging results also appear to be coming from nearly 500 "law-related education programs" established in recent years. Under these programs, information about the law, both the benefits it provides and the responsibilities it requires, is being disseminated among participating students from kindergarten to twelfth grade. This increases their ability to make informed and responsible decisions. Equally important as teaching substantive law is providing students with an understanding of the moral foundations of our legal system. Having been taught by judges, law students, and lawyers, students better comprehend and appreciate law enforcement, the judicial system, and legal concerns relevant to their personal lives and the reasons the legal system should receive support. It has been generally observed that student participation and interest in these programs is high. The first Values Education Commission in America, recently established in Maryland, found that there is "nothing in court decisions that would preclude the teaching of ethical content. It has been made equally clear that the schools have both the right and the duty to instill into the minds of pupils those moral principles which are so necessary to a well-ordered society."

Thus Frank Goble, president of the Thomas Jefferson Research Center, concluded that, based upon tens of thousands of hours of research, "an increase in quality and quantity of ethical instruction in our schools and other institutions is the only practical method to bring present exploding crime, violence, and delinquency under control."

Similarly, Owen V. Frisby, vice president of the Chase Manhattan Bank, testified: "Without materials in the curriculum and much more emphasis on character building in the classroom and in our homes, we will not produce as many future leaders as we need to solve the enormous number of problems that will face the next generation." He continued, "The benefits of such an effort in the schools, in our homes and in the media would certainly be vast. It would mean less crime, less drug addiction, less alcoholism, less violence in the classroom, less cheating on exams, less inflation because of a reduction in retail theft, more productivity, and a much happier society."

It is interesting to note that during Chief Justice Burger's February speech in Houston, the audience burst into spontaneous applause when he stated: "Possibly some of our problem of behavior stems from the fact that we have virtually eliminated from public schools and higher education any effort to teach values of integrity, truth, personal accountability, and respect for others' rights."

A backup to the more immediate socializing institutions of our society—the home, school, and church—is the community. Communities influence the development of their citizens by offering general norms and expectations for either deviant or conforming behavior. Crime rates are associated with characteristics of community areas.

Nineteen thousand Neighborhood Watch Programs have been created, providing unique protection for residential areas. Their social strategy of engaging neighborhood members in shared activities around the common goal of crime prevention develops a community pride and establishes community norms against crime. A report by the Center for Law and Justice at the University of Washington hypothesized that these norms can "contribute to a climate in which criminal actions are viewed by community youths as both risky and unacceptable rather than as a routine part of growing up." Furthermore, some junior watch programs in schools have been highly effective against drug dealers. The National Neighborhood Watch Association has taken on the important challenge of expanding and strengthening these programs, which encourage close cooperation between law enforcement officials and citizens and allow communities to overcome sentiments of frustration and helplessness with regard to rising crime. A county police officer was quoted in the *Washingtonian* magazine as saying, "Ninety-nine percent of all arrests depend on citizens giving us information." Whatever the actual percent, the value of alert neighbors who inform police cannot be overstated.

In summary, violent crime and juvenile delinquency have been ascending. Attempts to explain and fight crime have been, at best, only partially successful. The diminished influence of traditional institutions and our failure to promote ethical standards suggest another explanation for crime. Audiovisual media have partially replaced the family, church, school, and community in conveying values to the oncoming generation and these often appear to encourage hedonism and the use of force. We are in jeopardy of becoming a valueless society and of encouraging decision-making by aggression instead of by reason and democratically established law. If this is the case, then possible avenues to pursue in the prevention and elimination of crime are: teach values in our schools; promote law related education so young people understand both the rights and the responsibilities of our Constitution and legal system; increase youth activities by constructive organizations; guide children to quality media productions; increase the number of potential bonds or attachments citizens have with prosocial institutions; strengthen families and communities; and educate and constructively counsel delinquents. We must, in short, revitalize and strengthen the moral and ethical foundation of our society.

The possibility of reducing the scourge of crime exists. In addition to skilled, often courageous law enforcement and speedy, just courts, achieving this goal will require devotion, creative energy, and a more widespread commitment to values. There is evidence that more youth can be reached. A $5 million study of schools included two conclusions—smaller schools do better than large ones and it makes a difference when the school's principal is strongly committed to and encourages basic learning—showing that students are far from impervious to effectively projected values of teachers.

Indeed, the stakes are high. Since decision-making power belongs to the entire citizenry, our system requires widespread responsibility and wisdom. Yet responsibility and wisdom are not ours by nature. They must be learned. If our society neglects this teaching, we do so at our peril. During the formative period of our nation, judges, particularly while circuit riding, helped explain and increase support for the new Constitutional system. So, like your predecessors, you also can educate citizens today to civic virtue, moral responsibility, and voluntary support of law. You should call their attention to the reasons to abide by the law and to make responsible, ethical contributions to improve our society. Hopefully, this will not only deter law breaking, but will also enrich the quality of life and happiness of our citizens. May we all rise to the challenge ahead!

# Violence and Public Health[6]

C. Everett Koop

*Born October 4, 1916, Brooklyn, NY; A.B., Dartmouth College, 1937; M.D., Cornell University, 1941; professor, University of Pennsylvania School of Medicine, 1949-70; surgeon-in-chief, Children's Hospital of Philadelphia, 1948; U.S. Navy, 1964; deputy assistant secretary of health, Department of Health and Human Services, 1981; U.S. surgeon general, 1982-89; author,* The Right to Live, The Right to Die *(1976),* Whatever Happened to the Human Race? *(1983),* The Health of the Nation *(1992),* Koop: The Memoirs of America's Family Doctor *(1992),* Sometimes Mountains Move *(1994).*

## Editor's introduction

C. Everett Koop, then surgeon general of the United States, called upon physicians, and pediatricians in particular, to address the problem of violence in American society. A "family environment that supports study and learning," he counseled, "that rewards the child that is successful in school, will produce children who do well in school and in life later on." In contrast, he said, "a family environment that is cruel and uncaring will send cruel and uncaring children into the world as aggressive, violent adults." Koop expressed the opinion that violent behavior is treatable, in the sense that pediatricians should know enough about the symptoms of a violent personality to make diagnostic, predictive, and preventative decisions.

---

The Academy has had 35 annual meetings since the day I sat with seven other surgeons in Atlantic City and founded the surgical section. Of the meetings since then, I've attended two-thirds. Of the seven surgeons, five have died.

I'm still here, and it is always a comfortable occasion coming back to be with you. In a sense, it's like a homecoming. It provides another opportunity for me to say "thank you" once again to the Academy for giving the pediatric surgeons a haven, a pulpit, and a future.

I appreciate this opportunity to speak to you this morning on a subject that is uncomfortable to raise: violence as a public health concern. It is uncomfortable because, when we do raise that issue, we are really admitting that mankind still has quite a distance to travel in its long march toward civilized living.

I'm not limiting my remarks just to child abuse this morning. Rather, this is a call to action on your part, individually and collectively, to address this issue of violence by discussion, study, and research.

We've got to do this because violence has grown to become one of the major public health problems in American society today. It is not new, of course. Violence of some kind—murder, suicide, assault, armed confrontation of neighbor against neighbor—these have appeared in our national history since the 17th century. In the past 80 years or so, as we improved our ability to collect vital statistics, we have been able to identify periods when there were changes in the incidence of morbidity and mortality caused by violence. We are coming through just such a period now.

Violence in this country surged in the late 1960s and into the 1970s. All the indicators went up, but the toll upon young people—preschoolers, early adolescents, and young adults—has been particularly high. The mortality rates have risen during this period and there seems to be little likelihood that they will return to the levels of the 1950s and early 1960s.

[6]Delivered at the American Academy of Pediatrics annual convention, in New York, New York, on October 26, 1982. 

Let me isolate the recent mortality history just for 15- to 24-year-olds in three different areas of trauma and violence:

In motor vehicle fatalities, the death rate per 100,000 of this age group in 1960 was 38. In 1970, it hit its peak of 47.2. By 1978, it had abated only slightly to 46.4. That is the history for all men and women ages 15 through 24. Among white males the numbers are far worse: from a 1960 rate of 62.7 to a 1978 high of 75.4 deaths per 100,000, nearly *twice* the rate for the entire age cohort. One-half of the fatalities are caused by the combination of driving and drinking. We can do something about that.

The story in homicide is the same. From a 1960 low of 5.9 murders per 100,000 men and women age 15 to 24, to a rate of 11.7 by 1970, and to a high of 13.2 in 1978. The carnage among black males, however, is particularly alarming: from a rate of 46.4 deaths by murder in 1960 to a high of 102.5 a decade later, and then down to a homicide mortality rate of 72.5 in 1978.

In suicide, my third and last example, the mortality rate for men and women ages 15 through 24 rose from 5.2 in 1960 to a peak of 13.6 in 1977 and then dropped slightly to 12.4 in 1978. The story among white males bears some study: their rate had been 8.6 back in 1960. It then rose in virtually a straight line to a level of 20.8 in the latest year we have, 1978.

Motor vehicle accidents, homicide, suicide—these violent death categories now have new and higher death rates per 100,000 population in almost *any* grouping of persons between 1 year and 24 years of age. I picked the 15- to 24-year-olds not only because their mortality trends are so clear or because they are about to cross the threshold to adulthood and become the workers and voters and leaders of this country. They are also the products of the pediatricians' efforts in the preceding decade and a half. If, of course, they have survived.

Something happened in this country about a decade or so ago. Or, maybe we should say some things, since no single cause or event could be responsible for results so widespread, so pervasive, and so destructive. And, it may be too soon for us to know with any certainty what those things were. We may not yet have the historic distance, the detachment, to come to any reasonably sound conclusions. But, we still must try to understand, even with our contemporary myopia, just what has been happening and why—and what the effects seem to be upon the American people. I am, by speciality and training, *not* a social historian. But, it *is* my job to monitor the health status of the American people. If I sense something wrong, I am obliged to bring it out into the open and talk about it.

And that's precisely what I'm doing right now.

Rather than resurrect much of the literature of violence, with which many of you may be familiar anyway, I want to take a few careful steps forward to see what the role of the physician might be in understanding and possibly preventing the loss of life—through these violent premature deaths.

I have chosen this particular occasion because, of all physicians, I believe the pediatrician has a unique relationship with children and with parents. You gain certain insights about individuals and families that other physicians may not have the chance to see.

I base that opinion, by the way, on the reflections of my own career of 35 years in pediatric surgery. Dealing with the young children who were my patients I saw firsthand the stresses of childhood and was aware of both the strengths and weaknesses of children trying to cope. I also had to understand the families of those children. I had to gain their confidence and win them as allies in the battle to help their children.

In the process, I think I began to understand a great deal about the contemporary American family.

I tried to absorb that information and then focus it upon the problem to be solved by surgery. Sometimes, when it was clear to me that I was gaining insights into a serious family problem not directly related to the surgery, I would be open and available to that family, just in case they wanted to talk it through. But, I knew that I lacked a clear understanding of the need for me to become involved and to what extent I should become involved and what I might hope to accomplish.

Now, after looking at the data from my new vantage-point as surgeon general, and appreciating the special access to and relationship with the American family that pediatricians do enjoy, I think my message to you today on violence in our society and its effects on children and families is appropriate and necessary.

Let me propose as a starting-point the proposition that physicians need to become more familiar with the symptoms of violent personality in child and parent alike. Unfortunately, we don't have available some stock, off-the-shelf profiles of persons who are disposed toward violence. But the research literature does provide us with some clues that seem sturdy enough to follow.

For example, according to the work done by Dr. Dorothy Otnow Lewis of the N.Y.U. School of Medicine, homicidally violent children also tend to have a history of attempted suicide. Many of them have a history of psychomotor seizures. Their fathers are usually characterized as "very violent," particularly to the mothers. These children also tended to have mothers who at some time had to have inpatient psychiatric care. Other studies indicate that violent adolescents had seen severe physical abuse occur at home or were themselves the victims of family violence.

High-risk families also tend to be socially isolated from their neighbors. This is the case across all social, racial, and economic lines. Such families lack strong friendships. They can't seem to get close to other families, particularly families that do *not* show evidence of stress or violent behavior. High-risk families have difficulty coping with pressures outside their own home—pressures on the job or pressures while looking for a job, or the internal pressures that may build up while trying to negotiate such social transactions as shopping or using public transportation. Such families also have difficulty coping with stress inside their own homes: children making noise—loud radios, television sets, or stereos—and a whole range of marital upsets, including those produced by alcohol and drugs.

We know that violence within the family, particularly parental violence toward children, tends to escalate during periods of economical stress. Indebtedness, lack of work, eviction, layoffs, repossessions, these are the stuff of trauma for many families. They can overwhelm parents and open them to the terrible impulses of violence against each other and against their children. In some areas of the country we are experiencing very difficult economic conditions and, if the research and the anecdotal material we have is any guide, those areas are also experiencing a rise in family violence.

These may show up in marks on battered spouses and abused children. They are never well explained. The victims are often embarrassed, evasive, or simply tight-lipped. The physician needs to understand how to "read" those intensely personal and human signals of the victim of family violence.

I have spent some time on the family because of its overwhelming influence in the shaping of individual behavior. Educational research has demonstrated again and again that a family environment that supports study and learning, that rewards the child that is successful in school, will produce children who do well in school and in life later on, all other things being equal. And the reverse is true, also. A family environment that is cruel and uncaring will send cruel and uncaring children into the world as aggressive, violent adults. These are not hard-and-fast rules. Human beings are not pigeons and don't fit into neat, consistent pigeonholes. But the weight of experience and evidence does indicate that some signals, such as the ones I mentioned, ought to be noted and respected by the physician.

The physician, suspecting that a patient may be predisposed to violent behavior, should provide the same kind of counseling or referral service as if the patient showed a predisposition to cardiovascular disease, obesity, or diabetes. With the patient's consent, it may be possible to involve a spouse or a child in the discussion of this health problem. This is a sensitive area and we need to give it our professional study and attention in order to provide guidance to pediatricians and other primary care physicians. The objective, let me repeat, is not to intervene into a patient's private family life for intervention's sake but to prevent violent behavior from occurring and endangering the health or the life of another.

I recognize that not all physicians would agree with that assessment of their role. They would object to it as being yet another example of the "medicalization of social problems." And I fully appreciate the uneasiness felt by many physicians and other health professionals with society's habit of casually turning to medicine to solve what may simply not be a health or medical problem. But with violence, I think there is a difference.

This point was also made at a workshop last summer by the Institute of Medicine. The subject was the prevention of violence. On this matter of the "Medicalization of Violence," the participants made several good points, which I will summarize:

*First,* there seems to be no other institutional focus for research into the causes of violence that takes into account the multiple biological, psychological, social, and societal dimensions of crime, its victims, and its prevention. The institutions closest to being able to provide a multidisciplinary approach to research in the prevention of family violence, for example, would be the National Institute of Mental Health and the National Institute of Child Health and Human Development.

*Second,* the National Institute of Law Enforcement and Criminal Justice, the research arm of the Justice Department, sees "prevention" as a way of stopping a *recurrence* of a criminal act. In effect, the Justice Department does not have what would be in our discipline of medicine a "primary prevention" strategy, and, on reflection, one would have to admit that such a strategy under the criminal justice system could very well come in conflict with traditional civil liberties.

*And, third,* the workshop participants agreed that the morbidity and morality from violence are extremely costly to society not only in productive years lost but in the hard dollar terms of the impact upon the health care system. This is particularly true in the cases of abused children, who frequently have chronic disabilities even after treatment. Young women who have been sexually abused by family members frequently develop chronic illnesses requiring repeated inpatient psychiatric care. They also make increased use of gynecological health services, as their total personal health status declines.

We might not want this very complicated issue to gravitate toward medicine for answers, but I believe we need to accept the fact that we may have a contribution to make. I believe that we do and we are obligated to make that contribution.

In addition to learning more about the issue of violence and how it manifests itself in patient behavior, I believe physicians need to see themselves as capable of prescribing some rudimentary, preventive behavior for such patients. This may be more easily proposed than done, but I think it's time we looked at this as a serious aspect of pediatric and family practice for contemporary American society.

I spoke before of seeing patients with predispositions toward violence as needing our help, as if they were patients predisposed to hypertension. As physicians, we do not hesitate to counsel patients to avoid salt and salted foods or to avoid simple sugars. And, I think we all would agree that there is a profound difference between advising a patient to avoid sugar and advocating that the government remove all sugared products from the marketplace. The former is good medical practice, the latter is bad government.

Similarly, if we have a patient with a predisposition for violent behavior, especially against family members, I think we need to advise that patient to get some professional counseling and also suggest that he or she monitor their entertainment "menu" and avoid the kinds of television or motion picture fare that stimulates and contributes to the violence in their personalities. I don't like the violence in so-called "entertainment" shows today, but I do not believe the answer is government censorship. That does not leave me powerless as a physician, however. I believe it would be completely within the canons of my profession to advise patients predisposed to violence to self-censor their entertainment diet.

I don't know how many times the government has to come out with yet another study of television violence to make the point that it is harmful to children. There has been an interminable amount of bean-counting to quantify the obvious:

"Children spend a least 2 hours and a half in front of a T.V. set each day;

"Many of today's high school graduates will have spent more of their lives in front of a T.V. set than in the classroom;

"By the age of 18, a young person could have witnessed over 18,000 murders on television. This does not count the documentation of violence that seems to be in every T.V. news report;

"Adults spend about 40 percent of their leisure time watching television, which ranks third—behind sleep and work—as an occupier of an adult's average day."

Last year the California Commission on Crime Control and Violence Prevention considered these and other facts and concluded that there *is* a relationship between the violence that is televised and the violence that takes place in the "real world." Not only are the specific details of a fictional crime re-enacted by viewers—often young children or adolescents—but there is a strong suspicion that the aggressive behaviors by the "heavies" on television are mimicked by viewers also, whether consciously or unconsciously, in a variety of relationships and settings.

This is directly related to another potential result from extensive viewing of television or motion picture violence: We begin to believe that violence is a socially acceptable and credible way of responding to frustration or insult or some other direct, personal hurt. And, frequently, violent behavior that stops just short of murder seems to go unpunished. Children especially become "desensitized" to violent interpersonal conflict and, when seeing another child being hurt, will tend *not* to do the thing that civilization requires be done—step in and protect the victim. Instead, they will watch, as if this too were dramatized entertainment.

I have not mentioned video games because I don't want to duplicate what another speaker on your program may present. Also, we are just beginning to assess the data. But I do know these games are not constructive. Whether they show soldiers or spacecraft or men from Mars or just from "the other side," we *zap* them—and that means annihilation.

It seems to me that the weight of evidence—whether it has a solid research base or is purely anecdotal—the weight of evidence strongly suggests that physicians ought to recognize that a diet of violent entertainment for the violence-prone individual is as unhealthy as a diet of sugar and starch is for the obesity-prone individual.

I have indicated the need for physicians to recognize the signals of the violent personality and the violent home and I have suggested that there are some things we can "prescribe." Such as a lower intake of violent entertainment. These are ways of responding to the phenomenon of violence as we see it develop or deal with its aftermath. But there are things we ought to do, as physicians, that are *pro*-active, as well as *re*active.

One task we have is to put the full weight of our profession on the side of strengthening positive, healthy family life in this society. In this matter of violence, as in other matters, we tend to look all about for other palliatives—magic potions of one sort or another, real or figurative, exotic therapies, all sorts of diverting possibilities keep cropping up.

But, that's what they are: diverting. We need to return to the business of holding the family together, the fundamental, irreducible social unit.

I believe that it is primarily and substantially within the limited physical and emotional space occupied by the family—its "home"—that one human being can get used to the work of loving and truly caring about the welfare of another human being. Of course, we know that the reverse is true, also. But the family violence we talk about is the *exception* to the human rule. We need to deal with those exceptions, but, in doing so, we must not cut adrift the healthy families from our constant support and attention.

The family relationship is rich, but it is also fragile. Physicians providing family care and concerned about the maintenance of peace as well as of health in a family, need to understand the influence of work—or the influence of the lack of work—upon family members; also understand the symbolism of material goods, which are supposed to convey a sense of well-being for the family but rarely do all by themselves; and also understand the healthy ways in which people grow up and grow old, and the possibility that some families face their own aging with anger and fear.

This is a very difficult request to make of any physician. Most have not been trained in these areas, which tend to be more the province of the sociologist, the psychiatrist, the psychologist, or the social services worker. The work of sociologists Murray Straus of the University of New Hampshire and Richard Gelles of the University of Rhode Island tends to be unknown among physicians, yet Straus and Gelles are among the leading researchers in the field of family violence.

Physicians tend to be unclear about the roles of these and other professionals. Communication between the practitioners of physical medicine and those who practice other disciplines tends to be limited and unclear. Physicians are also generally unfamiliar with the education and training of personnel engaged in the delivery of social services. Nor are they always aware of the similarity of ethical imperatives shared by both medicine and the social services.

Because of this, physicians, especially those in private practice, tend not to refer patients as often as they should nor do they seek the counsel of social services professionals when a possible incident of family violence comes to their attention.

This may be a problem now, but I believe it will be less of a problem in the future as physicians become more familiar with the total constellation of research and service becoming available for the protection of victims of family violence. Let me note just one example where we are making some progress. This is the work of Dr. Eli Newberger at Boston Children's Hospital.

Dr. Newberger is a pediatrician and editor of a new book on *Child Abuse* for the Little, Brown series on clinical pediatrics. With the support of the National Institute of Mental Health, he has been carrying out a program of interdisciplinary training and research in the detection and treatment of victims of family violence. In this program, Dr. Newberger brings together a group of professionals on the staff of Boston Children's Hospital. They include pediatricians, social workers, researchers, psychologists and psychiatrists, sociologists, and computer analysts.

Working as a team, they provide hands-on clinical care for children who have been abused. They also seek to understand the causes of the violence within the family, to prevent it from recurring. The result is a program that draws upon a variety of skills right at the time they are needed most. The program generates new information regarding family violence and this new information, plus other research data, are translated into direct patient care.

These are the kinds of projects that benefit not only the immediate persons under care, but can also benefit the practice of medicine itself. These projects are dedicated to the protection of innocent victims of violence, especially family violence. I hope to see more of these kinds of efforts begun, whether supported by government research funding or not. Eventually, the medical profession should be engaged, as a routine matter and without the benefit of research dollars, in such interdisciplinary practices as the treatment of victims of violence and the protection of potential victims as they come to our attention. When that time arrives, then we may indeed be close to understanding and controlling violence, which is one of the most extensive and chronic epidemics in the public health of this country.

I have talked of violence on the highways, and of the influence of alcohol and drugs on our escalating violence. I have given you some statistics on homicide and suicide, and I've once again underlined the destructive impact of T.V. on our children and I've added video games to the list. I know I have laid a great burden on you. I share it.

Can we handle it? When that question is asked, I am reminded of that point in the book called *The Little Prince*, by Antoine deSaint Exupéry, in which the Little Prince talks with the fox. The fox says, rather plaintively, "one only understands the things that one tames. Men have no more time to understand anything. They buy things already made at the shops. But there is no shop anywhere where one can buy friendship, and so men have no friends anymore. If you want a friend, tame me."

The fox can be tamed and it can become a friend. Violence can also be tamed and people who are disposed to violence can also learn how to live in peace with the rest of us—and all of us should feel secure. It's not a task that can be done easily or in a short space of time. But it has to be done.

# Combating Crime[7]

Janet Reno

*Born July 21, 1938, Miami, FL; A.B., Cornell University, 1960; LL.B., Harvard University, 1963; partner, Lewis and Reno, 1967; staff director, Florida House of Representatives judiciary committee, 1971; lawyer, Steel, Hector & Davis, 1976-78; attorney general, Dade County, FL, 1978-93; U.S. attorney general, 1993–.*

## Editor's introduction

The issues of crime, youth violence, and gun control dominated the Conference of Mayors at which this adddress was given. In the speech, Attorney General Janet Reno stressed the importance of creating a "true partnership" between the federal government and local and state law enforcement. Naturally, such a partnership would mean an end to the "turf battles" that typically occur when different enforcement agencies are asked to cooperate. Given the amount of crime in the United States, Reno declared, "We've all got enough to do."

---

I thank you so much for that warm applause. I thank you, too, for letting me know how difficult it is to be mayor. It is also difficult to be a prosecutor who has 26 mayors in her jurisdiction.

I learned a lot in 15 years. I learned that mayors have one of the toughest jobs of anybody in government, particularly in these last 5 years as the federal government has shifted programs to the states without monies, the states to the counties without monies, and the counties have said, "cities, you do it." And what is so exciting to me is that everywhere I have visited throughout this nation, and I have already had the chance to say hello to mayors who have made me feel welcome, Republicans and Democrats, cities are making such an incredible difference because you have your back up against the wall. You don't have money, but you are bringing people together and showing what Americans can do. With the spirit of innovation, of working together, you cut across lines of diversity to bring people together. And what is happening in American cities today is one of the most heartwarming, encouraging signs that I have seen.

You've made me feel like I was off on the right track. There were some people that were saying I was perhaps soft on crime for talking about prevention. On May the 4th of this year some mayors came to see me from your conference. I think there were six or seven mayors, balanced Republicans and Democrats, and they started talking about prevention. And I said, "Hey, I am not too far wrong."

You have led the way in your plan that you presented to the President, to myself, and to Dr. Brown this December. Every time I turn around you are doing incredible things, and I, for one, tell you all I know how difficult the job is and I appreciate it so very, very much.

I would like to talk to you today in response really to your plan. I've spoken to many of you in broader concepts, and I'd like to be as specific as I could today to give you information and to discuss with you and to develop thoughts for the future that might be helpful, first of all, with respect to funding for police.

Ladies and gentlemen, Mayor [Jerry] Abramson has already called for it, a number of you have already joined me in calling for immediate, swift passage of a good, sound crime bill that provides for police on the streets in ways that you can use them and use them as soon as possible.

Those of you who have community policing initiatives underway know what they have done—what they can do in terms of reducing

[7]Delivered at the winter meeting of the United States Conference of Mayors, in Washington, D.C., on January 27, 1994.

crime. You know how they can bring a community together as community police involve the neighborhood and create a spirit of cooperation that we have not seen for some time. We cannot let this bill get stalled in Congress. We have got to get it passed and we need everybody's help in getting it passed, to get drug courts, provisions for drug courts that can be seen throughout the land as evidence of what was done in Dade County and has now been expanded to 37 jurisdictions; more drug treatment monies, and Dr. Brown [Lee] will be expanding on that; boot camps that let our youngsters know that there is going to be punishment but also provide after-care and followup and jobs so they can return to the community with a chance of not becoming involved in a revolving door. Let's get that bill passed. Let's get the ban on assault weapons passed. The American people have spoken, and they have spoken so eloquently through you.

But let's go to the issue of police funding. First of all, with respect to the issue of rounds 2 and 3 on the $150 million supplement, I am going to revisit with our staff what we can do to speed that up. But we are trying to do it in as thorough a way as possible. We are learning a lot because apparatus was not there for its distribution.

I would welcome, mayors, the opportunity to have a continuing dialogue with you as to anything we can do to improve any process we have in which we deal with cities, whether it is in distribution of these monies or in other efforts, so that we can cut through red tape. What we tried to do in the police funding procedure was to develop hotlines so that communities throughout this country could call us directly, get immediate answers. We then tried to provide followup to see how these calls have worked to make sure that we are doing it the right way. And I invite you to work with us in every way possible to ensure a smooth dialogue between the cities and the Department of Justice.

In these next weeks, I am going to need your help in framing issues with respect to the flexibility you need to use the dollars as soon as possible, as wisely as possible, whether it be for new technology or overtime or for actual bodies on the streets. There are disputes and disagreements about that, but I understand that each city is different. There are problems in each city that don't match the others. We've got to be—I just don't think that we've got to say we're defeated because we're too big to be direct and personal in our contact with mayors, and I want to try to do everything I can.

On issues such as waivers and other methods that we might use to tailor grants to your community so that it can make a difference, on whether we also count as part of the 100,000 police officers prosecutors and the backup people to go with it, that's another consideration that's important. I don't know what the answer will be, but I understand just how important flexibility is.

With respect to firearms, it is because of your second point in your plan, it is because of your leadership and so many others, that the Brady bill is now the Brady law. Isn't that a nice sound?

We've tried to gear up working with the FBI to ensure smooth implementation and the prompt implementation of that bill without bureaucratic snags along the way. But we have got to move ahead and not rest on our laurels with Brady. We've got to get that ban on assault weapons passed. We have got to make sure that we develop attitudes and procedures that make sure that it is at least as difficult to get a gun as it is to get a driver's license in America and that you ought to be able to demonstrate that you know how to safely and lawfully use a weapon before you buy a weapon, just like you know how to safely and lawfully use a car before you get a driver's license.

It is leadership from amongst you that is leading the nation in saying let's get rid of the guns that police confiscate. When you look at the number of guns in your property rooms across this nation, and if you think what would happen if we'd start melting them down or start dumping them on the reefs what we could do in terms of beginning to get the millions out of circulation. Let us all join together and start now in getting rid of the guns that way.

Dr. Brown will be talking, too, about expanded drug control efforts. But I would like to describe for you what we have tried to do within the Department of Justice. When I was in Miami as a prosecutor, as some of you know, the DEA and the FBI would fight and everybody would fuss at each other and they would have turf battles. And I swore that if I didn't do anything else in Washington I wanted to try to end the turf battles, at least within the Justice agencies. I think we're well on our way to doing that.

But we're reaching out beyond the Justice agencies to say to other agencies, "Look, we don't want to take you over. We want to work hand in hand with you because there is too much to do in terms of crime and drugs in America. We've all got enough to do. If we use our resources wisely, if we share information amongst ourselves and with local law enforcement we can make a difference."

We have developed the Office of Investigative Agency Policy and we had the most remarkable ceremony, and it wasn't just ceremony because when I walked into the room they were all standing around talking together. With the announcement of Tom Constantine as the new Administrator of DEA we had all the federal agencies there. We had representatives of the police organizations, state and local prosecutors, the state attorneys general, it was one of the most exciting ceremonies that I have seen in a long time.

Lest I get carried away with ceremony, I'm also told by experienced career people in the Department of Justice that they had never seen such coordination in many, many years, and we want to continue to improve it. But as a local prosecutor in heart and soul, I think it is terribly important that the federal government form a true partnership with local and state law enforcement around this nation in sharing information and backing each other up, in doing what each does best but doing it in a coordinated way. And I commit myself to working with your law enforcement officials in every way possible in that regard.

One of the plans that you suggest there is in terms of more DEA agents working closer with local law enforcement. This afternoon there will be an announcement of how we are trying to begin to get federal agents to the field. We are going to do everything we can to get support to the field in places that it can count. We will work with local prosecutors to make sure that we handle the cases we're supposed to be handling, they handle the cases best suited for State court, and we do it the right way.

Your third point is restructuring the criminal justice system. You have a man probably more experienced than anybody in this room, and that's Judge Si Gelber who is now Mayor Gelber of Miami Beach, and he and I have worked long and hard in the area of juvenile justice. Both of us have seen the concept of juvenile justice change, and your remarks and this plan go to the heart of what he and I feel; that for too long now too many police officers have come to us and said, "Look, these kids come in at 13 and 14 having committed violent crime and they just laugh at us saying, 'hey, man, nothing's going to happen to me, nothing ever happens to anybody in the juvenile justice system.'"

We have got to join together, and I pledge to you to work with your law enforcement agencies through our Office of Juvenile Justice and Delinquency Prevention to establish appropriate responses to youth violence, to let young people know that if they commit a crime by putting a gun up beside somebody's head and hurting them they are going to be punished. But it will be a fair, humane, certain, firm punishment that lets them know there is a consequence for their act.

You all know, far better than anybody else, how important it is if you punish them and then you put them back out on the streets without jobs, without job training, without addressing their substance abuse problem, without addressing their family situation, it is going to recur and you're going to waste money. Community police are joining with others in developing after-care programs. We've got to make sure that boot camp provision in the crime bill has after-care provisions and followup. And we have all got to make clear to everybody who might disagree with us that we will never begin to solve the problem of youth violence unless we provide real job opportunity and the job training and the child development to go with it to give people the skills to fill the jobs.

You, more than any other single group of public servants I know, understand how we've got to balance punishment and prevention. And it's not an either/or choice. It's both and doing it the right way, and I thank you for your leadership in this effort.

You've asked that we do much through the Office of Juvenile Justice and Delinquency Prevention in your plan, and I have already given it a high profile. I have met with them. They say it's the first time they've seen an Attorney General in years, it's the first time they've been asked to submit a budget, and it is a unit and a bureau that I care deeply about. But the challenges are new, for a new problem that we've never seen in the juvenile justice area before, and we're going to join with you in trying to address that problem.

Your last two points go to the issue of long-term strategies and partnerships to prevent violent crime, and I blend those two together. I think you all wrote my speeches over the last 8 years. I have never seen anything like it in terms of an understanding of public officials, public officials Republican and Democrat who have to run for office, who know what it's like to go to the people, to tell people the real facts, to explain to them that it can't be done with 30-second sound bytes, that you need long-term strategies that can make a difference.

I have been to your cities—to Ft. Worth, to Salt Lake City, to Wichita—and I've watched what you're doing in your communities as you build neighborhood coalitions, as you reach out to the federal government through weed and seed initiatives, as you do your own weed and seed initiatives. As the mayor of Ft. Worth has said, "Weed and seed is not just a program, it is a concept and a philosophy." And so many of you around this nation are evidencing that philosophy of bringing disciplines together, of going to the people, of involving the people in what you do, and you are setting an example for the nation. And, Mr. Mayor, I'd like to do everything I can to continue to work with the conference to support you in every way possible.

It is a difficult process, because I had enough problems dealing with my 26 cities in Dade County plus Miami. Now, I've got all of you plus many others around the nation, and how we design a federal structure where the federal government can truly be responsive to the people and to mayors and to local communities is one of the most difficult tasks we face. I've often likened it, however—my dream would be that we could have a Ft. Worth desk in Washington, and that instead of going from HUD to Labor to Justice with hat in hand, the city of Ft. Worth could come up with its plan of its needs and resources, what it needs to do the job.

There could be one Ft. Worth expert in Washington who represented the different agencies that could touch on the situation in Ft. Worth. We would try to figure out how federal resources, limited, too, could go together to fill the cracks and how we could support each other. We could challenge Ft. Worth to leverage dollars by providing matches. We could do so much if we learn from high technology how we can communicate and say that this Nation hasn't become too big that this government can't work with cities throughout the nation on an individual basis, recognizing the strength and wonder and beauty of the small and large cities throughout the nation.

This past week we had a meeting of United States Attorneys. They all came to Washington and the snow helped keep everybody in and we had a wonderful 3-day discussion. What we talked about primarily was a violence initiative, and I would like to share with you a concept that many of you are undertaking now. The Center for Disease Control and Prevention is undertaking some remarkable work in violence. Dr. Mark Rosenberg is leading this effort, and I commend to you all contact with the Center for developing further information that might be useful to you.

Sometimes, we think the problem of violence is overwhelming us. But if we take it and look at the hard facts and if we approach it from the point of view of good public servants that are also interested in the scientific background of it, I think we can make a significant difference in utilizing our shrinking resources far more wisely than we have.

Each community can oftentimes identify the core of career criminals that are causing the problem, and through proactive initiatives with the Alcohol, Tobacco, and Firearms Bureau, with the FBI, we want to join with you in focusing on those people. And whether it be state or federal court, whatever is best for the case, we want to make sure those people are put away for the longest possible time we can get them away. Those 10 percent of the criminals are committing as much as 40 percent of your crime. Too many of your police officers engage in a revolving door effort. As they pick them up and put them in they come right back. Let's get them put away.

There are many cities that are focusing on violent traffickers where the federal agencies have come together working with local law enforcement to look at violent drug gangs. Getting those people put away has seen a reduction in the violent crime in that community. But it becomes a more effective reduction when you move in after you've gotten a drug organization off that street corner, move in with something positive so that the organization down the street doesn't start filling the vacuum. The balanced punishment and prevention approach that you call for in this plan can make a significant difference.

Let us look and realize that organized crime hasn't gone away. It's coming on in new and different forms, and we've got to be prepared and we will be prepared to work with you and share information.

The same with gangs. It was amazing to me because my jurisdiction was 365 miles south of the nearest state border, to visit Salt Lake City and see the impact of youth gangs sweeping up from California and then across to Wichita and across to Omaha. We can share information with you that can forecast, and we can work with you in using limited resources to focus on this type of violence.

What impressed me so much about this plan is you all don't forget anything. You understand that domestic violence is critical to all these issues because I'll bet every one of your police chiefs have told you how many of their calls involve response to family violence and that these are oftentimes the most dangerous and difficult calls they make. We can't ignore that any more. We have got to develop domestic intervention programs, domestic courts, prosecutors trained in these efforts. Most of these cases can be handled better by local government. But in any way I can support you in that effort, I want to do so.

Some of your jurisdictions—I was in one recently—has [sic] an incredible incidence of child abuse. We can focus on that, provide followup, work with you, and do everything possible.

But here are the statistics that stagger my imagination, that I think we all have to understand. Because there are many of your cities that have experienced a reduction in violence. But what you haven't seen is a reduction in youth violence. Instead, you have seen an escalation. And people wonder why the American people are so concerned about violence if it is on the decline. The reason they are concerned is because they are seeing youngsters do things that we could never, ever dream that youngsters did. Youngsters who have never developed the conscience and the concept of reward and punishment. And we're all grappling with what to do.

But I would urge you again to work with the Center for Disease Control to understand what the situation is in your community. This is the report that has been furnished to me: Taking young American males age 15 to 24 in 1986, there were 22 deaths—homicides—of young American males between the ages of 15 to 24. By 1991, that number had grown to 37 per 100,000 for all young American males. It was only 17 per 100,000 for young white American males between the ages of 15 and 24. It was 159 per 100,000 for young black males between the ages of 15 and 24, and you have the strategy to deal with this terrible tragedy more than anybody else that I have seen. You understand the problem.

What the Center for Disease Control found was that the victim and the assailant were acquainted, for the most part, it was the same race, predominantly male, that it started from arguments, that it was usually not felony related; that alcohol was usually involved, and that firearms were usually present. Of the 159 total, 139 per 100,000 involved firearms.

Those are figures that we can understand, and we can begin to devise strategies that do something about it. But for the first time firearm deaths for young teenagers, both white and black, now exceeds the deaths in those age groups for all natural causes. And it won't be long before firearms deaths exceed motor vehicle deaths for that category. If we focus on this in terms of doing it right, of getting rid of the partisanship in crime, in getting rid of the 30 second sound bytes, and in saying for youngsters when they first get in trouble, if we design a fair, firm, understandable punishment, if we follow through with after-care and followup and alternate housing in certain situations and jobs and case managers and make an investment in our future, we can make a difference.

Now, there are going to be your constituents that suggest, "But, wait a minute, we don't want to do that." We're not going to have a work force, much less reduce violence, unless we make an investment in our children. But you understand better than anybody else that we have also got to make an investment in prevention.

In all that you do in your national policy for children, from strong parents to prenatal care to Head Start to programs, afternoon and the evening, you understand it.

I look forward to working with you. You have given me such encouragement, in these 10 months that I have been in office, that I was on the right track. I am deeply grateful to you all, and I look forward to working with you in every way possible.

# Fear and Terror[8]

## F. Forrester Church IV

*Born September 23, 1948, Boise, ID; B.A., Stanford University, 1970; M.Div., 1974, Ph.D., 1978, Harvard University; minister, Unitarian Church of All Souls, New York, 1978–; visiting professor, Dartmouth College, 1989; author,* Father and Son: A Personal Biography of Senator Frank Church of Idaho by His Son *(1985),* The Devil and Dr. Church *(1986),* Entertaining Angels *(1986),* The Essential Tillich *(1987),* The Seven Deadly Virtures *(1989),* God and Other Famous Liberals: Reclaiming the Politics of America *(1992).*

### Editor's introduction

In a sermon to his congregation, Reverend F. Forrester Church spoke about the April 19, 1995, bombing of the Alfred P. Murrah Federal Building in Oklahoma City. While subsequent investigations revealed that the bombing was committed by an American, it was initially assumed that Middle Eastern terrorist groups were responsible. Church declared this to be an unfair accusation. As Church noted, "no people, no faith, have anything like a corner on hatred." It follows that in immediately assuming someone from the Mideast to be responsible for the bombing, we are guilty of the same prejudice and hatred that motivated the real bombers.

---

How very long ago Easter seems. Only a week ago we gathered in this peaceful sanctuary to trumpet the victory of love over death. One week later we are left to sort through the rubble and carnage that litter the once quiet streets of Oklahoma City, our hearts possessed with grief, anger, and fear. It's as if Easter this year has been turned on its head, the holy calendar reversed, resurrection first and then, three days later, the crucifixion.

Obviously whatever I had planned to speak about this morning is of no consequence in light of the week's events. In a single blast, the world we live in is unalterably changed.

There is little we can do about this. In fact, apart from the perilous, if completely understandable, urge for retribution, our grief, anger, and fear are accompanied by a hollow sense of powerlessness. I did send, on your behalf, the following overnight letter to our fellow unitarian Universalists at the First Unitarian Church in Oklahoma City. It's only a gesture, but at times like this, watching at a distance, we are sometimes forced to rely on mere gestures. At least they connect us to those whose pain is more immediate than our own.

*Dear Unitarian Universalist Friends in Oklahoma City:*

*Please know how deeply we feel for you and your neighbors in the wake of the terrible tragedy that has befallen you, and indeed, our entire country. Having struggled with our own fears following the World Trade Center bombing two years ago, we in New York have at least a sense of the bewilderment you must surely be experiencing. Our prayers this Sunday are with you and the loved ones of those members of your congregation whose lives have been affected or swept away by this senseless, evil act. If we can be of any assistance whatsoever, please do not hesitate to call.*

*In faith and with profound sorrow,*

*Forrest Church (on behalf of the congregation of All Souls in New York City)*

First Unitarian Church is near the Federal Building in Oklahoma City. The impact of the bomb caused some structural damage. Two members of the church are among the missing, and therefore presumed dead. Carolyn and I will send a check directly to the church for their relief fund. I invite you to join us. Give it or send it to me and I'll pass it along. This too is a small thing, a gesture, but it connects us with

[8]Delivered to the congregation of the All Souls Unitarian Church, in New York, New York, on April 23, 1995. 

our religious family. It permits us to do something, however small, at a time when so little we can say or do seems to matter all that much.

The question remains, how do we sort through the rubble and carnage? How can we extricate some meaning or guidance from this terrible tragedy? I am as off balance as you are. Having been transfixed by the television reports, I now want to run from them, from the images of horror, from the tears and the anger. I am looking for a good movie, even a bad movie, anything to take me away. And I will find one. I found one yesterday. I will find one today. But I also know that I must look deeper and further, both into myself and into the life we share as citizens of this country, even of the world.

I must look deeper into myself, in part because my initial response to the Oklahoma City bombing was to fix my attention and fear on a composite, stereotypical image of Muslim terrorist: bearded, wiry, dark-eyed, alien, inscrutable, fanatical, terrifying. Even after I saw the composite drawings of the two suspects, I thought to myself, "Well, the one could be Arab. Perhaps the other is a bad rendering. After all, they caught that man on his way from Oklahoma City to Jordan, his bags filled with bomb-making material and photographs of American miliary sites."

His name was Amad Abrahim. They held him for sixteen hours. He was very cooperative. His bags were not filled with bomb-making material and photographs of American military sites. Nor did the other suspects I read about, Asad and Anis Siddiqy, have anything to do with the bombing. They were Queens taxi drivers working on an immigration problem. They lived with Mohammed Chaff. He too was grilled for fifteen hours. I understand that. All leads had to be scrupulously followed. But I also know that if I were given a multiple choice terrorist quiz two days ago, and asked to guess between Asad Siddiqy, Mohammed Chaff, Amad Abrahim, Timothy McVeigh, and Terry Nichols, I would have failed the test.

The threat of internationally sponsored murder and mayhem by such groups as the Hamas and Hesbollah is very real. An old friend of mine, Steve Emerson, author of the now-famous documentary "Jihad in America," presents the evidence in convincing detail. But I also know, or should know, that no people, no faith, have anything like a corner on hatred. Take the woman who said of our Muslim neighbors on a talk show this week, "No wonder this happened. These countries, their culture, have no respect for human life." Or the caller who threatened to blow up a discount variety store on Fifth Avenue owned by Syrian-born Albert Cabal. "We're going to get you and we're going to get your family." "This is not a question of anybody's country of origin," President Clinton reminds us. "This is not a question of anybody's religion. This was murder, this was evil, this was wrong. Human beings everywhere, all over the world, will condemn this out of their own religious convictions."

So I am troubled, deeply troubled, by my knee-jerk reaction. All of us are prejudiced. But when thoughtful people do not work hard to temper their prejudices, bigots—those who celebrate prejudice—will only be vested with more power. Bigots like Timothy McVeigh and Terry Nichols.

I've noticed that a favorite question posed by reporters to people on the street is some variation of, "Does it bother you that Americans are responsible for this?" "It devastates me," one woman replied. "I just can't believe that an American, that a human being, could do this." There are millions of Arab Americans, millions of Muslim Americans—Muslim American human beings. They are only as likely to buy the hatred spewed by the Hamas or Hesbollah as are white-bread Mid-Western Christian Americans likely to feed on the equally bigoted and dangerous paranoia fostered by groups like the Michigan Militia, led by Norman Olson, self-styled "pistol-packin' preacher," and gun store owner. Or the Arizona Patriots, whose members believe that the United States is being run by the Protocol of Zion or about to be conquered by the United Nations.

Friday's *New York Post* [Apr. 23, 1995] ran a cartoon of three Muslims laughing and burning an American flag at the base of the Statue of Liberty, which read "Give us your tired, your poor, your huddled masses, your terrorists, your murderers, your slime, your evil cowards, your religious fanatics, your welfare cheats." I can think of at least two flag-waving Christians wedded to their own perverse reading of the Bill of Rights, who would have laughed knowingly at that cartoon. Believing that our government has fallen prey to foreigners, welfare cheats, and slime, among whom they numbered Blacks and Jews, and obsessed with their guns, these two unimaginably sick Americans are responsible for the death of some two hundred innocent people, victims of the same kind of hate that such a cartoon unwittingly fosters.

Timothy McVeigh, a "quiet, shy churchgoing youth from upstate New York, who liked computers, basketball, and cars." Terry Nichols, a "good neighbor," with a bumper-sticker on his car that boasted the words, "American and Proud." The former, arrested carrying a licensed Glock semi-automatic pistol, loaded with hollow point bullets, known as cop-killers, slept with his guns. The latter was known to have experimented with making fertilizer bombs in his barn.

Tom Metzger, head of something called the White Aryan Resistance, said yesterday: "I have told people for years, at least since 1984, when The Order declared war on the central government of the United States that the government of this country—what we call the criminals—had better start listening to the dispossessed white people, the dispossessed majority. There was a hot war in the 1980's, and since then there's been a cold war, and now things are heating up again."

We don't need to look outside our borders or to another faith to discover our common enemy. He also lurks within, inspired not by the Koran but by the Book of Revelation, his hatred of the government fed by the incendiary, divisive anti-government rhetoric employed so successfully by certain of our political leaders, his fears fomented into paranoia and then violence by the American gun lobby.

We don't have to look any further than *The Turner Diaries*, a hateful, frightening book deemed the Bible of the survivalist movement. Positing the secret take-over of the government by Jews seeking to strip good Americans of their guns in an attempt to establish a new world order, the book begins with these words: "Today, it finally began. After all those years of talking—and nothing but talking—we have finally taken our first action. We are at war with the system, and it is no longer a war of words." Extremists blow up a federal office building at 9:15 in the morning. "Our worries about the relatively small size of the bomb were unfounded; the damage is immense. The scene in the courtyard was one of utter devastation. Overturned trucks and automobiles, smashed office furniture and building rubble were strewn wildly about—and so were the bodies of a shockingly large number of victims. They have clearly made the decision to portray the bombing of the FBI building as the atrocity of the century. All the bombings, arsons and assassinations carried out by the Left in this country have been rather small time in comparison."

And so we come to April 19th. The day that American patriots defended Lexington and Concord against the Redcoats in 1775. The day that survivalist Randy Weaver, holed up in Ruby Ridge, Idaho, was informed by compatriots of a government plot against him in 1992. The day that the Branch Davidians immolated themselves in 1993. And the day that white-supremacist Richard Snell, who murdered a black police officer and a Jewish business man was to be executed in Arkansas in 1995. That was last Wednesday. With this date as a mantra, one right-wing newsletter, *The Montana Militia*, warned that Snell would die, "unless we act now!!!" Snell, a murderer, did die. So did 200 innocents. Two centuries after the first minutemen bravely fought at the Lexington bridge, two centuries after our founders, mindful of events leading up to the shot heard round the world, passed the second amendment to our nation's constitution establishing our right to a citizens' militia, a far deadlier blast in Oklahoma City has been heard round the world, and history itself, our own nation's history, lies twisted in the wreckage.

There will be great pressure in the days ahead to enact an Omnibus Counter-terrorism Act to protect us from Muslim fanatics. I wish only that certain of the most vociferous proponents of this legislation would examine their own consciences to ponder how their support for lifting a ban on semi-automatic weapons actually enhances the opportunity for terrorism to occur in this country. I hope they will hear their own words about protecting our sacred right to buy and keep arms echo back from the writings and voices of the hate mongers actually responsible for the tragedy in Oklahoma City. I hope they will think, at least a little, about how the seeds of division grow, how rhetoric that plays on our fears of one another, on our differences, the rhetoric that scapegoats, that pits neighbor against neighbor, can so easily blossom into full-blown bigotry, and with such devastating consequence.

One final thought. When we try to fight hatred with hate and fire with fire, we do not lessen but only compound the object of our enmity.

We do not destroy the Randy Weavers of this world by sending federal agents to storm their Idaho shack, killing his wife and child in the crossfire. We do not extirpate the power expressed in David Koresh's paranoia and fascination with violence by killing four of his followers and then embargoing his compound until he and his sect immolate themselves. We do nothing to diminish the white-supremacism and anti-Semitism spewed by Richard Snell when we execute him for his heinous crimes. As the tragedy in Oklahoma City reminds us, violence only begets more violence. Even the most just violence, whether institutional or accidental, only contributes to the climate of fear and hatred which spawns yet more violence in an endless spiral.

If we have learned anything, we should have learned this from the endless succession of terrorist activity in the Middle East. Now we can study it on our own soil. If I were asked yesterday whether the perpetrators of this unimaginably evil act should receive the death penalty, I would have said yes. Today, I say no. I couldn't bear for them to become martyrs for the next wave of Timothy McVeighs and Terry Nichols. Let the blood be on their hands, not ours.

I expect that we will execute them. When we do, even as I have wrestled this week with my own prejudice against Arab Americans, I will again, I am sure, wrestle against, and perhaps unsuccessfully, my own primitive, human desire for vengeance. Not my finest part, but part of me will cheer when these brutal men die. I am ashamed of that, but it is so.

What I will be far more ashamed of is this. I will be far more ashamed if I do not dedicate a greater part of my energy to combating—and that is not too strong a word—the climate of violence that is poisoning this country. Begin with guns. Ban more. Restrict others. Enforce and enhance licensing procedures. Make them difficult to buy. Enact severe penalties for illegal sale or possession. And drive every lackey of the American gun lobby from office, however high-minded and perversely patriotic his or her rhetoric.

I will also be ashamed if I do not do everything in my small power to reclaim the history and symbols of this great nation from the anti-American, anti-Christian white supremacist and survivalist zealots who have turned the courageous minutemen of Concord and the American Bill of Rights into fertilizer for their bombs. So far as it is in our power, and while admitting some necessary abridgment forced by prudence, we must not permit ourselves to be held hostage by our fears, driven to compromise precious American rights far more essential to the survival of this republic than the right to bear arms. The only way to do this is to answer fear, the fear these zealots and their unwitting political champions foment so successfully, with greater faith, the faith of our founders, a faith in one nation, indivisible, with liberty and justice for all. We must answer in the spirit of the people of Oklahoma City, whose courage, bravery, self-sacrifice, and neighborly love remind us once again of what it really means to be a true American. We must answer according to the best that is within the human heart, not imitate the worst.

Perhaps the best way to counter fear with faith is to begin with our own prejudices. These we can do something about, something more than a gesture. Tomorrow I shall call a Muslim cleric, Shaykh Abd'Allah Ali, Leader of the Admiral Family Circle, and invite him to preach at All Souls as soon as possible. This afternoon, at the Adult Education Committee meeting, I will urge that we devote a month next fall to the study of Islam. Most of us are profoundly ignorant about the teachings of Islam, an ignorance that feeds our prejudice.

In the meantime, mindful of life's fragility, let us remember how fortunate we are. Please, treat one another with kindness. Be thankful for the days we are given. There is time for us, there is still time, time to love and also time to learn.

# Index to Speakers

# Index